Anatomical Kinesiology

SES 220

Abbie Ferris

Jeremy Smith

Gary Heise

UNIV OF NORTHERN COLORADO

EXERCISE & SPORT SCIENCES

create.mheducation.com

ISBN-13: 9781307758054

ISBN-10: 1307758053

Contents

ONLINE SUPPLEMENTS 621

Unit 1

PART ONE: ORGANIZATION OF THE BODY

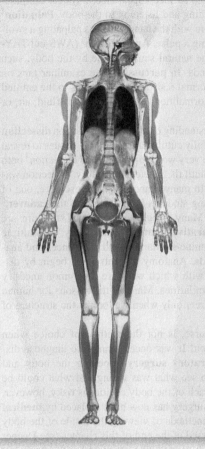

A colorized MRI scan of the human body
©Science Photo Library/Getty Images

CHAPTER 1

MAJOR THEMES OF ANATOMY AND PHYSIOLOGY

Anatomy & Physiology
Revealed®4.0

Module 1: Body Orientation

No branch of science hits as close to home as the science of our own bodies. We're grateful for the dependability of our hearts; we're awed by the capabilities of muscles and joints displayed by Olympic athletes; and we ponder with philosophers the ancient mysteries of mind and emotion. We want to know how our body works, and when it malfunctions, we want to know what's happening and what we can do about it. Even the most ancient writings of civilization include medical documents that attest to humanity's timeless drive to know itself. You are embarking on a subject that is as old as civilization, yet one that grows by thousands of scientific publications every week.

This book is an introduction to human structure and function, the biology of the human body. It is meant primarily to give you a foundation for advanced study in health care, exercise physiology, pathology, and other fields related to health and fitness. Beyond that purpose, however, it can also provide you with a deeply satisfying sense of self-understanding.

As rewarding and engrossing as this subject is, the human body is highly complex, and understanding it requires us to comprehend a great deal of detail. The details will be more manageable if we relate them to a few broad, unifying concepts. The aim of this chapter, therefore, is to introduce such concepts and put the rest of the book into perspective. We consider the historical development of anatomy and physiology, the thought processes that led to the knowledge in this book, the meaning of human life, some central concepts of physiology, and how to better understand medical terminology.

1.1   The Scope of Anatomy and Physiology

Expected Learning Outcomes

When you have completed this section, you should be able to

a. define *anatomy* and *physiology* and relate them to each other;

b. describe several ways of studying human anatomy; and

c. define a few subdisciplines of human physiology.

Anatomy is the study of structure, and **physiology** is the study of function. These approaches are complementary and never entirely separable. Together, they form the bedrock of the health sciences. When we study a structure, we want to know, What does it do? Physiology thus lends meaning to anatomy; conversely, anatomy is what makes physiology possible. This *unity of form and function* is an important point to bear in mind as you study the body. Many examples of it will be apparent throughout the book—some of them pointed out for you, and others you will notice for yourself.

1.1a   Anatomy—The Study of Form

There are several ways to examine the structure of the human body. The simplest is **inspection**—simply looking at the body's appearance, as in performing a physical examination or making a clinical diagnosis from surface appearance. Physical examinations also involve touching and listening to the body. **Palpation**[1] means feeling a structure with the hands, such as palpating a swollen lymph node or taking a pulse. **Auscultation**[2] (AWS-cul-TAY-shun) is listening to the natural sounds made by the body, such as heart and lung sounds. In **percussion,** the examiner taps on the body, feels for abnormal resistance, and listens to the emitted sound for signs of abnormalities such as pockets of fluid, air, or scar tissue.

But a deeper understanding of the body depends on **dissection** (dis-SEC-shun)—carefully cutting and separating tissues to reveal their relationships. The very words *anatomy*[3] and *dissection*[4] both mean "cutting apart"; until the nineteenth century, dissection was called "anatomizing." In many schools of health science, one of the first steps in training students is dissection of the **cadaver,**[5] a dead human body. Many insights into human structure are obtained from **comparative anatomy**—the study of multiple species in order to examine similarities and differences and analyze evolutionary trends. Anatomy students often begin by dissecting other animals with which we share a common ancestry and many structural similarities. Many of the reasons for human structure become apparent only when we look at the structure of other animals.

Dissection, of course, is not the method of choice when studying a living person! It was once common to diagnose disorders through **exploratory surgery**—opening the body and taking a look inside to see what was wrong and what could be done about it. Any breach of the body cavities is risky, however, and most exploratory surgery has now been replaced by **medical imaging** techniques—methods of viewing the inside of the body without surgery, discussed at the end of this chapter (see Deeper Insight 1.5). The branch of medicine concerned with imaging is called **radiology.** Structure that can be seen with the naked eye—whether by surface observation, radiology, or dissection—is called **gross anatomy.**

Ultimately, the functions of the body result from its individual cells. To see those, we usually take tissue specimens, thinly slice and stain them, and observe them under the microscope. This approach is called **histology**[6] **(microscopic anatomy).** **Histopathology** is the microscopic examination of tissues for signs of disease. **Cytology**[7] is the study of the structure and function of individual cells. **Ultrastructure** refers to fine detail, down to the molecular level, revealed by the electron microscope.

1.1b   Physiology—The Study of Function

Physiology[8] uses the methods of experimental science discussed later. It has many subdisciplines such as *neurophysiology* (physiology of the nervous system), *endocrinology* (physiology of

---

[1]*palp* = touch, feel; *ation* = process
[2]*auscult* = listen; *ation* = process
[3]*ana* = apart; *tom* = cut
[4]*dis* = apart; *sect* = cut
[5]from *cadere* = to fall down or die
[6]*histo* = tissue; *logy* = study of
[7]*cyto* = cell; *logy* = study of
[8]*physio* = nature; *logy* = study of

hormones), and *pathophysiology* (mechanisms of disease). Partly because of limitations on experimentation with humans, much of what we know about bodily function has been gained through **comparative physiology,** the study of how different species have solved problems of life such as water balance, respiration, and reproduction. Comparative physiology is also the basis for the development of new drugs and medical procedures. For example, a cardiac surgeon may learn animal surgery before practicing on humans, and a vaccine cannot be used on human subjects until it has been demonstrated through animal research that it confers significant benefits without unacceptable risks.

BEFORE YOU GO ON

Answer the following questions to test your understanding of the preceding section:

1. What is the difference between anatomy and physiology? How do these two sciences support each other?

2. Name the method that would be used for each of the following: listening to a patient for a heart murmur; studying the microscopic structure of the liver; microscopically examining liver tissue for signs of hepatitis; learning the blood vessels of a cadaver; and performing a breast self-examination.

1.2 The Origins of Biomedical Science

Expected Learning Outcomes

When you have completed this section, you should be able to

a. give examples of how modern biomedical science emerged from an era of superstition and authoritarianism; and

b. describe the contributions of some key people who helped to bring about this transformation.

Any science is more enjoyable if we consider not just the current state of knowledge, but how it compares to past understandings of the subject and how our knowledge was gained. Of all sciences, medicine has one of the most fascinating histories. Medical science has progressed far more in the last 50 years than in the 2,500 years before that, but the field didn't spring up overnight. It is built upon centuries of thought and controversy, triumph and defeat. We cannot fully appreciate its present state without understanding its past—people who had the curiosity to try new things, the vision to look at human form and function in new ways, and the courage to question authority.

1.2a The Greek and Roman Legacy

As early as 3,000 years ago, physicians in Mesopotamia and Egypt treated patients with herbal drugs, salts, physical therapy, and faith healing. The "father of medicine," however, is usually considered to be the Greek physician **Hippocrates** (c. 460–c. 375 BCE). He and his followers established a code of ethics for physicians, the Hippocratic Oath, which is still recited in modern form by graduating physicians at some medical schools. Hippocrates urged physicians to stop attributing disease to the activities of gods and demons and to seek their natural causes, which could afford the only rational basis for therapy.

Aristotle (384–322 BCE) was one of the first philosophers to write about anatomy and physiology. He believed that diseases and other natural events could have either supernatural causes, which he called *theologi,* or natural ones, which he called *physici* or *physiologi.* We derive such terms as *physician* and *physiology* from the latter. Until the nineteenth century, physicians were called "doctors of physic." In his anatomy book, *On the Parts of Animals,* Aristotle tried to identify unifying themes in nature. Among other points, he argued that complex structures are built from a smaller variety of simple components—a perspective that we will find useful later in this chapter.

▶▶▶ APPLY WHAT YOU KNOW

When you have completed this chapter, discuss the relevance of Aristotle's philosophy to our current thinking about human structure.

Claudius Galen (129–c. 200), physician to the Roman gladiators, wrote the most influential medical textbook of the ancient era—a book worshipped to excess by medical professors for centuries to follow. Cadaver dissection was banned in Galen's time because of some horrid excesses that preceded him, including public dissection of living slaves and prisoners. Aside from what he could learn by treating gladiators' wounds, Galen was therefore limited to dissecting pigs, monkeys, and other animals. Because he was not permitted to dissect cadavers, he had to guess at much of human anatomy and made some incorrect deductions from animal dissections. He described the human liver, for example, as having five fingerlike lobes, somewhat like a baseball glove, because that's what he had seen in baboons. But Galen saw science as a method of discovery, not a body of fact to be taken on faith. He warned that even his own books could be wrong and advised his followers to trust their own observations more than any book. Unfortunately, his advice was not heeded. For nearly 1,500 years, medical professors dogmatically taught what they read in Aristotle and Galen, seldom daring to question the authority of these "ancient masters."

1.2b The Birth of Modern Medicine

In the Middle Ages, the state of medical science varied greatly from one religious culture to another. Science was severely repressed in the Christian culture of Europe until about the sixteenth century, although some of the most famous medical schools of Europe were founded during this era. Their professors, however, taught medicine primarily as a dogmatic commentary on Galen and Aristotle, not as a field of original research. Medieval medical illustrations were crude representations of the body intended more to decorate a page than to depict the body realistically **(fig. 1.1a).** Some were astrological charts that showed which sign of the zodiac was thought to influence each organ of the body. From such pseudoscience came the word *influenza,* Italian for "influence."

Free inquiry was less inhibited in Jewish and Muslim culture during this time. Jewish physicians were the most esteemed practitioners of their art—and none more famous than *Moses ben Maimon* (1135–1204), known in Christendom as **Maimonides.** Born in Spain, he fled to Egypt at age 24 to escape antisemitic persecution. There he served the rest of his life as physician to the court of the sultan, Saladin. A highly admired rabbi, Maimonides wrote voluminously on Jewish law and theology, but also wrote 10 influential medical books and numerous treatises on specific diseases.

Among Muslims, probably the most highly regarded medical scholar was *Ibn Sina* (980–1037), known in the West as **Avicenna** or "the Galen of Islam." He studied Galen and Aristotle, combined their findings with original discoveries, and questioned authority when the evidence demanded it. Medicine in the Mideast soon became superior to European medicine. Avicenna's textbook, *The Canon of Medicine,* was the leading authority in European medical schools for over 500 years.

Chinese medicine had little influence on Western thought and practice until relatively recently; the medical arts evolved in China quite independently of European medicine. Later chapters of this book describe some of the insights of ancient China and India.

Modern Western medicine began around the sixteenth century in the innovative minds of such people as the anatomist Andreas Vesalius and the physiologist William Harvey.

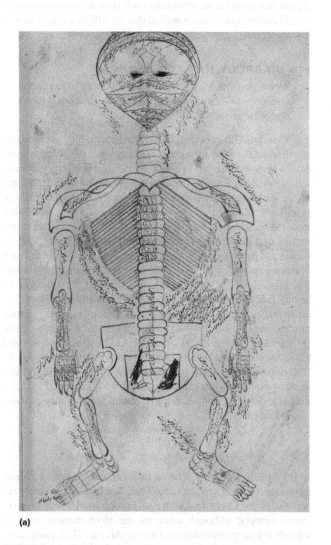

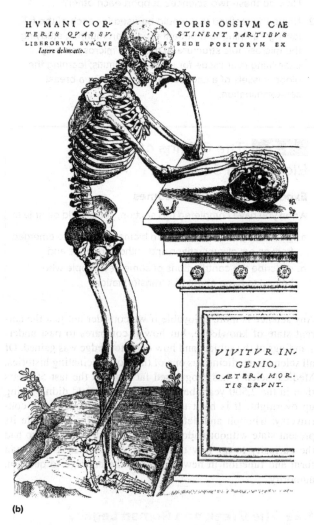

(a)   (b)

FIGURE 1.1 The Evolution of Medical Art. Two illustrations of the skeletal system made about 500 years apart. (a) From an eleventh-century work attributed to Persian physician Avicenna. (b) From *De Humani Corporis Fabrica* by Andreas Vesalius, 1543.

a: Source: Wellcome Library, London/CC BY 4.0; b: Suzan Oschmann/Shutterstock

Andreas Vesalius (1514–64) taught anatomy in Italy. In his time, the Catholic Church relaxed its prohibition against cadaver dissection, in part to allow autopsies in cases of suspicious death. Furthermore, the Italian Renaissance created an environment more friendly to innovative scholarship. Dissection gradually found its way into the training of medical students throughout Europe. It was an unpleasant business, however, and most professors considered it beneath their dignity. In those days before refrigeration or embalming, the odor from the decaying cadaver was unbearable. Dissections were a race against decay. Bleary medical students had to fight the urge to vomit, lest they incur the wrath of an overbearing professor. Professors typically sat in an elevated chair, the *cathedra,* reading dryly in Latin from Galen or Aristotle while a lower-ranking *barber–surgeon* removed putrefying organs from the cadaver and held them up for the students to see. Barbering and surgery were considered to be "kindred arts of the knife"; today's barber poles date from this era, their red and white stripes symbolizing blood and bandages.

Vesalius broke with tradition by coming down from the cathedra and doing the dissections himself. He was quick to point out that much of the anatomy in Galen's books was wrong, and he was the first to publish accurate illustrations for teaching anatomy **(fig. 1.1b).** When others began to plagiarize them, Vesalius published the first atlas of anatomy, *De Humani Corporis Fabrica (On the Structure of the Human Body),* in 1543. This book began a rich tradition of medical illustration that has been handed down to us through such milestones as *Gray's Anatomy* (1856) and the vividly illustrated atlases and textbooks of today.

Anatomy preceded physiology and was a necessary foundation for it. What Vesalius was to anatomy, the Englishman **William Harvey** (1578–1657) was to physiology. Harvey is remembered especially for his studies of blood circulation and a little book he published in 1628, known by its abbreviated title *De Motu Cordis (On the Motion of the Heart).* He and **Michael Servetus** (1511–53) were the first Western scientists to realize that blood must circulate continuously around the body, from the heart to the other organs and back to the heart again. This flew in the face of Galen's belief that the liver converted food to blood, the heart pumped blood through the veins to all other organs, and those organs consumed it. Harvey's colleagues, wedded to the ideas of Galen, ridiculed Harvey for his theory, though we now know he was correct (see chapter 20 prologue). Despite persecution and setbacks, Harvey lived to a ripe old age, served as physician to the kings of England, and later did important work in embryology. Most importantly, Harvey's contributions represent the birth of experimental physiology—the method that generated most of the information in this book.

Modern medicine also owes an enormous debt to two inventors from this era, Robert Hooke and Antony van Leeuwenhoek, who extended the vision of biologists to the cellular level. **Robert Hooke** (1635–1703), an Englishman, designed scientific instruments of various kinds, including the compound microscope. This is a tube with a lens at each end—an *objective lens* near the specimen, which produces an initial magnified image, and an *ocular lens (eyepiece)* near the observer's eye, which magnifies the first image still further. Although crude compound microscopes had existed since 1595, Hooke improved the optics and invented several of the helpful features found in microscopes today—a stage to hold the specimen, an illuminator, and coarse and fine focus controls. His microscopes magnified only about 30 times, but with them, he was the first to see and name cells. In 1663, he observed thin shavings of cork and observed that they "consisted of a great many little boxes," which he called *cellulae* (little cells) after the cubicles of a monastery **(fig. 1.2).** He later observed living cells "filled with juices." Hooke became particularly interested in microscopic examination of such material as insects, plant tissues, and animal parts. He published the first comprehensive book of microscopy, *Micrographia,* in 1665.

Antony van Leeuwenhoek (an-TOE-nee vahn LAY-wen-hook) (1632–1723), a Dutch textile merchant, invented a *simple* (single-lens) *microscope,* originally for the purpose of examining the weave of fabrics. His microscope was a beadlike lens mounted in a metal plate equipped with a movable specimen clip.

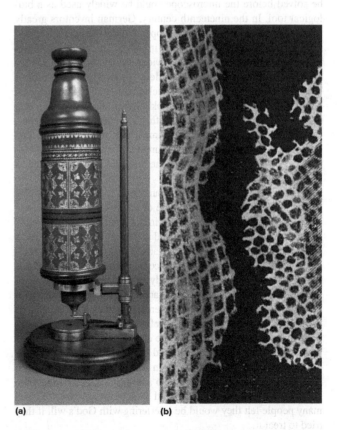

(a)   (b)

FIGURE 1.2 Hooke's Compound Microscope. (a) The compound microscope had a lens at each end of a tubular body. (b) Hooke's drawing of cork cells, showing the thick cell walls characteristic of plants.

a: Source: National Museum of Health and Medicine, Silver Spring, MD; b: Bettmann/Getty Images

Even though his microscopes were simpler than Hooke's, they achieved much greater useful magnification (up to 200×) owing to Leeuwenhoek's superior lens-making technique. Out of curiosity, he examined a drop of lake water and was astonished to find a variety of microorganisms—"little animalcules," he called them, "very prettily a-swimming." He went on to observe practically everything he could get his hands on, including blood cells, blood capillaries, sperm, muscular tissue, and bacteria from tooth scrapings. Leeuwenhoek began submitting his observations to the Royal Society of London in 1673. He was praised at first, and his observations were eagerly read by scientists, but enthusiasm for the microscope didn't last. By the end of the seventeenth century, it was treated as a mere toy for the upper classes, as amusing and meaningless as a kaleidoscope. Leeuwenhoek and Hooke had even become the brunt of satire. But probably no one in history had looked at nature in such a revolutionary way. By taking biology to the cellular level, the two men had laid an entirely new foundation for the modern medicine to follow centuries later.

The Hooke and Leeuwenhoek microscopes produced poor images with blurry edges *(spherical aberration)* and rainbow-like distortions *(chromatic aberration)*. These problems had to be solved before the microscope could be widely used as a biological tool. In the nineteenth century, German inventors greatly improved the compound microscope, adding the condenser and developing superior optics. With improved microscopes, biologists began eagerly examining a wider variety of specimens. By 1839, botanist **Matthias Schleiden** (1804–81) and zoologist **Theodor Schwann** (1810–82) concluded that all organisms were composed of cells. Although it took another century for this idea to be generally accepted, it became the first tenet of the **cell theory,** added to by later biologists and summarized in section 3.1a. The cell theory was perhaps the most important breakthrough in biomedical history; all functions of the body are now interpreted as the effects of cellular activity.

Although the philosophical foundation for modern medicine was largely established by the time of Leeuwenhoek, Hooke, and Harvey, clinical practice was still in a dismal state. Few doctors attended medical school or received any formal education in basic science or human anatomy. Physicians tended to be ignorant, ineffective, and pompous. Their practice was heavily based on expelling imaginary toxins from the body by bleeding their patients or inducing vomiting, sweating, or diarrhea. They performed operations with filthy hands and instruments, spreading lethal infections from one patient to another and refusing, in their vanity, to believe that they themselves were the carriers of disease. Countless women died of infections acquired during childbirth from their obstetricians. Fractured limbs often became gangrenous and had to be amputated, and there was no anesthesia to lessen the pain. Disease was still widely attributed to demons and witches, and many people felt they would be interfering with God's will if they tried to treat it.

1.2c Living in a Revolution

This short history brings us only to the threshold of modern biomedical science; it stops short of such momentous discoveries as the germ theory of disease, the mechanisms of heredity,

and the structure of DNA. In the twentieth century, basic biology and biochemistry yielded a much deeper understanding of how the body works. Advances in medical imaging enhanced our diagnostic ability and life-support strategies. We witnessed monumental developments in chemotherapy, immunization, anesthesia, surgery, organ transplants, and human genetics. By the close of the twentieth century, we had discovered the chemical "base sequence" of every human gene and begun attempting gene therapy to treat children born with diseases recently considered incurable. As future historians look back on the turn of this century, they may exult about the Genetic Revolution in which you are now living.

Several discoveries of the nineteenth and twentieth centuries, and the men and women behind them, are covered in short historical sketches in later chapters. Yet, the stories told in this chapter are different in a significant way. The people discussed here were pioneers in establishing the scientific way of thinking. They helped to replace superstition with an appreciation of natural law. They bridged the chasm between mystery and medication. Without this intellectual revolution, those who followed could not have conceived of the right questions to ask, much less a method for answering them.

BEFORE YOU GO ON

Answer the following questions to test your understanding of the preceding section:

3. In what way did the followers of Galen disregard his advice? How does Galen's advice apply to you and this book?

4. Describe two ways in which Vesalius improved medical education and set standards that remain relevant today.

5. How is our concept of human form and function today affected by inventors from the seventeenth to the nineteenth centuries?

1.3   Scientific Method

Expected Learning Outcomes

When you have completed this section, you should be able to

a. describe the inductive and hypothetico–deductive methods of obtaining scientific knowledge;

b. describe some aspects of experimental design that help to ensure objective and reliable results; and

c. explain what is meant by *hypothesis, fact, law,* and *theory* in science.

Prior to the seventeenth century, science was done in a haphazard way by a small number of isolated individuals. The philosophers **Francis Bacon** (1561–1626) in England and **René Descartes** (1596–1650) in France envisioned science as a far greater, systematic enterprise with enormous possibilities for human health and welfare. They detested those who endlessly debated ancient philosophy without creating anything new. Bacon argued against biased thinking and for more objectivity in science. He outlined a systematic way of seeking similarities, differences, and trends in nature and drawing useful generalizations from observable facts. You will see echoes of Bacon's philosophy in the discussion of scientific method that follows.

Though the followers of Bacon and Descartes argued bitterly with one another, both men wanted science to become a public, cooperative enterprise, supported by governments and conducted by an international community of scholars rather than a few isolated amateurs. Inspired by their vision, the French and English governments established academies of science that still flourish today. Bacon and Descartes are credited with putting science on the path to modernity, not by discovering anything new in nature or inventing any techniques—for neither man was a scientist—but by inventing new habits of scientific thought.

When we say "scientific," we mean that such thinking is based on assumptions and methods that yield reliable, objective, testable information about nature. The assumptions of science are ideas that have proven fruitful in the past—for example, the idea that natural phenomena have natural causes and nature is therefore predictable and understandable. The methods of science are highly variable. **Scientific method** refers less to observational procedures than to certain habits of disciplined creativity, careful observation, logical thinking, and honest analysis of one's observations and conclusions. It is especially important in health science to understand these habits. This field is littered with more fads and frauds than any other. We are called upon constantly to judge which claims are trustworthy and which are bogus. To make such judgments depends on an appreciation of how scientists think, how they set standards for truth, and why their claims are more reliable than others (**fig. 1.3**).

FIGURE 1.3 Biomedical Research. Research scientists employ habits of thought we call the scientific method to ensure the objectivity, reliability, and reproducibility of their results and conclusions.
AshTproductions/Shutterstock

1.3a The Inductive Method

The **inductive method,** first prescribed by Bacon, is a process of making numerous observations until one feels confident in drawing generalizations and predictions from them. What we know of anatomy is a product of the inductive method. We describe the normal structure of the body based on observations of many bodies.

This raises the issue of what is considered proof in science. We can never prove a claim beyond all possible refutation. We can, however, consider a statement as proven *beyond reasonable doubt* if it was arrived at by reliable methods of observation, tested and confirmed repeatedly, and not falsified by any credible observation. In science, all truth is tentative; there's no room for dogma. We must always be prepared to abandon yesterday's truth if tomorrow's facts disprove it.

1.3b The Hypothetico–Deductive Method

Most physiological knowledge was obtained by the **hypothetico–deductive method.** An investigator begins by asking a question and formulating a **hypothesis**—an educated speculation or possible answer to the question. A good hypothesis must be (1) consistent with what is already known and (2) capable of being tested and possibly falsified by evidence. **Falsifiability** means that if we claim something is scientifically true, we must be able to specify what evidence it would take to prove it wrong. If nothing could possibly prove it wrong, then it's not scientific.

▶▶▶ APPLY WHAT YOU KNOW

The ancients thought that gods or invisible demons caused epilepsy. Today, epileptic seizures are attributed to bursts of abnormal electrical activity in nerve cells of the brain. Explain why one of these claims is falsifiable (and thus scientific), whereas the other claim is not.

The purpose of a hypothesis is to suggest a method for answering a question. From the hypothesis, a researcher makes a deduction, typically in the form of an "if–then" prediction: *If* my hypothesis on epilepsy is correct and I record the brain waves of patients during seizures, *then* I should observe abnormal bursts of activity. A properly conducted experiment yields observations that either support a hypothesis or require the scientist to modify or abandon it, formulate a better hypothesis, and test that one. Hypothesis testing operates in cycles of conjecture and disproof until one is found that is supported by the evidence.

1.3c Experimental Design

Doing an experiment properly involves several important considerations. What shall I measure and how can I measure it? What effects should I watch for and which ones should I ignore? How can I be sure my results are due to the variables that I manipulate and not due to something else? When working on human subjects, how can I prevent the subject's expectations or state of mind from influencing the results? How can I eliminate my own biases and be sure that even the most skeptical critics will have as much confidence in my conclusions as I do? Several elements of experimental design address these issues:

- **Sample size.** The number of subjects (animals or people) used in a study is the sample size. An adequate sample size controls for chance events and individual variations in response and thus enables us to place more confidence in the outcome. For example, would you rather trust your health to a drug that was tested on 5 people or one tested on 5,000? Why?

- **Controls.** Biomedical experiments require comparison between treated and untreated individuals so that we can judge whether the treatment has any effect. A **control group** consists of subjects that are as much like the **treatment group** as possible except with respect to the variable being tested. For example, there is evidence that garlic lowers blood cholesterol levels. In one study, volunteers with high cholesterol were each given 800 mg of garlic powder daily for 4 months and exhibited an average 12% reduction in cholesterol. Was this a significant reduction, and was it due to the garlic? It's impossible to say without comparison to a control group of similar people who received no treatment. In this study, the control group averaged only a 3% reduction in cholesterol, so garlic *seems* to have made a difference.

- **Psychosomatic effects.** Psychosomatic effects (effects of the subject's state of mind on his or her physiology) can have an undesirable effect on experimental results if we do not control for them. In drug research, it is therefore customary to give the control group a **placebo** (pla-SEE-bo)—a substance with no significant physiological effect on the body. If we were testing a drug, for example, we could give the treatment group the drug and the control group identical-looking sugar tablets. Neither group must know which tablets it is receiving. If the two groups showed significantly different effects, we could feel confident that it did not result from a knowledge of what they were taking.

- **Experimenter bias.** In the competitive, high-stakes world of medical research, experimenters may want certain results so much that their biases, even subconscious ones, can affect their interpretation of the data. One way to control for this is the **double-blind method.** In this procedure, neither the subject to whom a treatment is given nor the person giving it and recording the results knows whether that subject is receiving the experimental treatment or the placebo. A researcher may prepare identical-looking tablets, some with the drug and some with placebo; label them with code numbers; and distribute them to participating physicians. The physicians themselves do not know whether they are administering drug or placebo, so they cannot give the subjects even accidental hints of which substance they are taking. When the data are collected, the researcher can correlate them with the composition of the tablets and determine whether the drug had more effect than the placebo.

- **Statistical testing.** If you tossed a coin 100 times, you would expect it to come up about 50 heads and 50 tails. If it actually came up 48:52, you would probably attribute this to random error rather than bias in the coin. But what if it came up 40:60? At what point would you begin to suspect bias? This type of problem is faced routinely in research—how great a difference must there be between control and experimental groups before we feel confident that it was due to the treatment and not merely random variation? What if a treatment group exhibited a 12% reduction in cholesterol level and the placebo group a 10% reduction? Would this be enough to conclude that the treatment was effective? Scientists are well grounded in **statistical tests** that can be applied to the data—the chi-square test, the *t* test, and analysis of variance, for example. A typical outcome of a statistical test may be expressed, "We can be 99.5% sure that the difference between group A and group B was due to the experimental treatment and not to random variation." Science is grounded not in statements of absolute truth, but in statements of probability.

1.3d Peer Review

When a scientist applies for funds to support a research project or submits results for publication, the application or manuscript is submitted to **peer review**—a critical evaluation by other experts in that field. Even after a report is published, if the results are important or unconventional, other scientists may attempt to reproduce them to see if the author was correct. At every stage from planning to postpublication, scientists are therefore subject to intense scrutiny by their colleagues. Peer review is one mechanism for ensuring honesty, objectivity, and quality in science.

1.3e Facts, Laws, and Theories

The most important product of scientific research is understanding how nature works—whether it be the nature of a pond to an ecologist or the nature of a liver cell to a physiologist. We express our understanding as *facts, laws,* and *theories* of nature. It is important to appreciate the differences among these.

A scientific **fact** is information that can be independently verified by any trained person—for example, the fact that an iron deficiency leads to anemia. A **law of nature** is a generalization about the predictable ways in which matter and energy behave. It is the result of inductive reasoning based on repeated, confirmed observations. Some laws are expressed as concise verbal statements, such as the *law of complementary base pairing:* In the double helix of DNA, a chemical base called adenine always pairs with one called thymine, and a base called guanine always pairs with cytosine (see section 4.1a). Other laws are expressed as mathematical formulae, such as *Boyle's law,* used in respiratory physiology: Under specified conditions, the volume of a gas *(V)* is inversely proportional to its pressure *(P)*—that is,

$$V \propto 1/P.$$

A **theory** is an explanatory statement or set of statements derived from facts, laws, and confirmed hypotheses. Some theories have names, such as the *cell theory,* the *fluid-mosaic theory* of cell membranes, and the *sliding filament theory* of muscle contraction. Most, however, remain unnamed. The purpose of a theory is not only to concisely summarize what we already know but, moreover, to suggest directions for further study and to help predict what the findings should be if the theory is correct.

Law and *theory* mean something different in science than they do to most people. In common usage, a law is a rule created and enforced by people; we must obey it or risk a penalty. A law of nature, however, is a description; laws do not *govern* the universe—they *describe* it. Laypeople tend to use the word *theory* for what a scientist would call a hypothesis—for example, "I have a theory why my car won't start." The difference in meaning causes significant confusion when it leads people to think that a scientific theory (such as the theory of evolution) is merely a guess or conjecture, instead of recognizing it as a summary of conclusions drawn from a large body of observed facts. The concepts of gravity and electrons are theories, too, but this does not mean they are merely speculations.

▶▶▶ APPLY WHAT YOU KNOW

Was the cell theory proposed by Schleiden and Schwann more a product of the hypothetico–deductive method or of the inductive method? Explain your answer.

BEFORE YOU GO ON

Answer the following questions to test your understanding of the preceding section:

6. Describe the general process involved in the inductive method.

7. Describe some sources of potential bias in biomedical research. What are some ways of minimizing such bias?

8. Is there more information in an individual scientific fact or in a theory? Explain.

1.4   Human Origins and Adaptations

Expected Learning Outcomes

When you have completed this section, you should be able to

a. explain why evolution is relevant to understanding human form and function;

b. define *evolution* and *natural selection;*

c. describe some human characteristics that can be attributed to the tree-dwelling habits of earlier primates; and

d. describe some human characteristics that evolved later in connection with upright walking.

If any two theories have the broadest implications for understanding the human body, they are probably the *cell theory* and the *theory of natural selection.* No understanding of human form and function is complete without an understanding of our evolutionary history, of how natural selection adapted the body to its ancestral habitat. As an explanation of how species originate and change through time, natural selection was the brainchild of **Charles Darwin** (1809–82)—certainly the most influential biologist who ever lived. His book, *On the Origin of Species by Means of Natural Selection* (1859), has been called "the book that shook the world." In presenting the first well-supported theory of how evolution works, it not only caused the restructuring of all of biology but also profoundly changed the prevailing view of our origin, nature, and place in the universe. In *The Descent of Man* (1871), Darwin directly addressed the issue of human evolution and emphasized features of anatomy and behavior that reveal our relationship to other animals. Here we will touch just briefly on how natural selection helps explain some of the distinctive characteristics seen in *Homo sapiens* today.

1.4a   Evolution, Selection, and Adaptation

Evolution simply means change in the genetic composition of a population of organisms. Examples include the evolution of bacterial resistance to antibiotics, the appearance of new strains of the AIDS virus, and the emergence of new species of organisms.

Evolution works largely through the principle of **natural selection,** which states essentially this: Some individuals within a species have hereditary advantages over their competitors—for example, better camouflage, disease resistance, or ability to attract mates—that enable them to produce more offspring. They pass these advantages on to their offspring, and such characteristics therefore become more and more common in successive generations. This brings about the genetic change in a population that constitutes evolution.

Natural forces that promote the reproductive success of some individuals more than others are called **selection pressures.** They include such things as climate, predators, disease, competition, and food. **Adaptations** are features of anatomy, physiology, and behavior that evolve in response to these selection pressures and enable an organism to cope with the challenges of its environment.

Darwin could scarcely have predicted the overwhelming mass of genetic, molecular, fossil, and other evidence of human evolution that would accumulate in the twentieth century and further substantiate his theory. A technique called DNA hybridization, for example, reveals a difference of only 1.6% in DNA structure between humans and chimpanzees. Chimpanzees and gorillas differ by 2.3%. DNA structure thus suggests that a chimpanzee's closest living relative is not the gorilla—it is us, *Homo sapiens.*

Several aspects of our anatomy make little sense without an awareness that the human body has a history (see Deeper Insight 1.1). Our evolutionary relationship to other species is also important in choosing animals for biomedical research. If there were no issues of cost, availability, or ethics, we might test drugs on our close living relatives, the chimpanzees, before approving them for human use. Their genetics, anatomy, and physiology are most similar to ours, and their reactions to drugs therefore afford the best prediction of how the human body would react. On the other hand, if we had no kinship with any other species, the selection of a test species would be arbitrary; we might as well use frogs or snails. In reality, we compromise.

DEEPER INSIGHT 1.1

EVOLUTIONARY MEDICINE

Vestiges of Human Evolution

One of the classic lines of evidence for evolution, debated even before Darwin was born, is *vestigial organs*. These structures are the remnants of organs that apparently were better developed and more functional in the ancestors of a species. They now serve little or no purpose or, in some cases, have been converted to new functions.

Our bodies, for example, are covered with millions of hairs, each equipped with a useless little *arrector muscle*. In other mammals, these muscles fluff the hair and conserve heat. In humans, they merely produce goose bumps. Above each ear, we have three *auricularis muscles*. In other mammals, they move the ears to receive sounds better or to flick off flies and other pests, but most people cannot contract them at all. As Darwin said, it makes no sense that humans would have such structures were it not for the fact that we came from ancestors in which they were functional.

Rats and mice are used extensively for research because they are fellow mammals with a physiology similar to ours, but they present fewer of the aforementioned issues than chimpanzees or other mammals do. An animal species or strain selected for research on a particular problem is called a **model**—for example, a mouse model for leukemia.

1.4b Our Basic Primate Adaptations

We belong to an order of mammals called the Primates, which also includes the monkeys and apes. Some of our anatomical and physiological features can be traced to the earliest primates, which descended from certain squirrel-size, insect-eating, African mammals that took up life in the trees 55 to 60 million years ago. This **arboreal**[9] (treetop) habitat probably afforded greater safety from predators, less competition, and a rich food supply of leaves, fruit, insects, and lizards. But the forest canopy is a challenging world, with dim and dappled sunlight, swaying branches, shifting shadows, and prey darting about in the dense foliage. Any new feature that enabled arboreal animals to move about more easily in the treetops would have been strongly favored by natural selection. Thus, the shoulder became more mobile and enabled primates to reach out in any direction (even overhead, which few other mammals can do). The thumbs became fully **opposable**—they could cross the palm to touch the fingertips—and enabled primates to hold small objects and manipulate them more precisely than other mammals could. Opposable thumbs made the hands **prehensile**[10]—able to grasp objects by encircling them with the thumb and fingers (**fig. 1.4**). The thumb is so important that it receives highest priority in the repair of hand injuries. If the thumb can be saved, the hand can be reasonably functional; if it is lost, hand functions are severely diminished.

FIGURE 1.4 Human Adaptations Shared with Other Primates. Some major aspects of primate evolution are the opposable thumb, prehensile hand, forward-facing eyes, and stereoscopic vision. In humans, the hand became refined for increasingly sophisticated manipulation of objects.
Chimpanzee: Tim Davis/Science Source

The eyes of primates moved to a more forward-facing position, which allowed for **stereoscopic**[11] vision (depth perception). This adaptation provided better hand–eye coordination in catching and manipulating prey, with the added advantage of making it easier to judge distances accurately in leaping from tree to tree. Color vision, rare among mammals, is also a primate hallmark. Primates eat mainly fruit and leaves. The ability to distinguish subtle shades of orange and red enables them to distinguish ripe, sugary fruits from unripe ones. Distinguishing subtle shades of green helps them to differentiate between tender young leaves and tough, more toxic older foliage.

Various fruits ripen at different times and in widely separated places in the tropical forest. This requires a good memory of what will be available, when, and how to get there. Larger brains might have evolved in response to the challenge of efficient food finding and, in turn, laid the foundation for more sophisticated social organization.

---

[9]*arbor* = tree; *eal* = pertaining to
[10]*prehens* = to seize

[11]*stereo* = solid; *scop* = vision

None of this is meant to imply that humans evolved from monkeys—a common misconception about evolution that no biologist believes. Monkeys, apes, and humans do, however, share common ancestors. Our relationship is not like parent and child, but more like cousins who have the same grandparents. Observations of monkeys and apes provide insight into how primates adapt to the arboreal habitat and therefore how certain human adaptations probably originated.

1.4c Walking Upright

About 4 to 5 million years ago, parts of Africa became hotter and drier, and much of the forest was replaced by savanna (grassland). Some primates adapted to living on the savanna, but this was a dangerous place with more predators and less protection. Just as squirrels and monkeys stand briefly on their hind legs to look around for danger, so would these early ground dwellers. Being able to stand up not only helps an animal stay alert, but also frees the forelimbs for purposes other than walking. Chimpanzees sometimes walk upright to carry food, infants, or weapons (sticks and rocks), and it is reasonable to suppose that our early ancestors did so too.

These advantages are so great that they favored skeletal modifications that made **bipedalism**[12]—standing and walking on two legs—easier. Fossil evidence indicates that bipedalism was firmly established more than 4 million years ago. The anatomy of the human pelvis, femur, knee, great toe, foot arches, spinal column, skull, arms, and many muscles became adapted for bipedal locomotion (see Deeper Insight 8.5), as did many aspects of human family life and society. As the skeleton and muscles became adapted for bipedalism, brain volume increased dramatically, from 400 mL around 4 million years ago to an average of 1,350 mL today. It must have become increasingly difficult for a fully developed, large-brained infant to pass through the mother's pelvic outlet at birth. This may explain why humans are born in a relatively immature, helpless state compared with other mammals, before their nervous systems have matured and the bones of the skull have fused. The helplessness of human young and their extended dependence on parental care may help to explain why humans have such exceptionally strong family ties.

Most of the oldest bipedal primates are classified in the genus *Australopithecus* (aus-TRAL-oh-PITH-eh-cus). About 2.5 million years ago, hominids appeared with taller stature, greater brain volumes, simple stone tools, and probably articulate speech. These are the earliest members of the genus *Homo*. By at least 1.8 million years ago, *Homo erectus* migrated from Africa to parts of Asia. Anatomically modern *Homo sapiens*, our own species, originated in Africa about 200,000 years ago and is the sole surviving hominid species.

This brief account barely begins to explain how human anatomy, physiology, and behavior have been shaped by ancient selection pressures. Later chapters further demonstrate that the evolutionary perspective provides a meaningful understanding of why humans are the way we are. Evolution is the basis for comparative anatomy and physiology, which have been so fruitful for the understanding of human biology. If we weren't related to any other species, those sciences would be pointless.

The emerging science of **evolutionary medicine** analyzes how human disease and dysfunctions can be traced to differences between the artificial environment in which we now live, and the prehistoric environment to which *Homo sapiens* was biologically adapted. For example, we can relate sleep and mood disorders to artificial lighting and night-shift work, and the rise of asthma to our modern obsession with sanitation. Other examples in this book will relate evolution to obesity, diabetes, low-back pain, skin cancer, and other health issues.

BEFORE YOU GO ON

Answer the following questions to test your understanding of the preceding section:

9. Define *adaptation* and *selection pressure*. Why are these concepts important in understanding human anatomy and physiology?

10. Select any two human characteristics and explain how they might have originated in primate adaptations to an arboreal habitat.

11. Select two other human characteristics and explain how they might have resulted from later adaptation to a grassland habitat.

1.5 Human Structure

Expected Learning Outcomes
When you have completed this section, you should be able to

a. list the levels of human structure from the most complex to the simplest;

b. discuss the value of both reductionistic and holistic viewpoints to understanding human form and function; and

c. discuss the clinical significance of anatomical variation among humans.

Earlier in this chapter, we observed that human anatomy is studied by a variety of techniques—dissection, palpation, and so forth. In addition, anatomy is studied at several levels of detail, from the whole body down to the molecular level.

1.5a The Hierarchy of Complexity

Consider for the moment an analogy to human structure: The English language, like the human body, is very complex, yet an infinite variety of ideas can be conveyed with a limited number of words. All words in English are, in turn, composed of various combinations of just 26 letters. Between an essay and an alphabet are successively simpler levels of organization: paragraphs, sentences, words, and syllables. We can say that language exhibits a

---

[12]*bi* = two; *ped* = foot

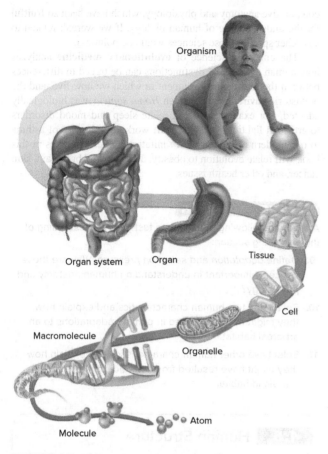

FIGURE 1.5 The Body's Structural Hierarchy.

hierarchy of complexity, with letters, syllables, words, and so forth being successive levels of the hierarchy. Humans have an analogous hierarchy of complexity, as follows (**fig. 1.5**):

The organism is composed of organ systems,
    organ systems are composed of organs,
       organs are composed of tissues,
         tissues are composed of cells,
           cells are composed partly of organelles,
             organelles are composed of molecules, and
               molecules are composed of atoms.

The **organism** is a single, complete individual.

An **organ system** is a group of organs with a unique collective function, such as circulation, respiration, or digestion. The human body has 11 organ systems, illustrated in atlas A immediately following this chapter: the integumentary, skeletal, muscular, nervous, endocrine, circulatory, lymphatic, respiratory, urinary, digestive, and reproductive systems. Usually, the organs of one system are physically interconnected, such as the kidneys, ureters, urinary bladder, and urethra, which compose the urinary system. Beginning with chapter 6, this book is organized around the organ systems.

An **organ** is a structure composed of two or more tissue types that work together to carry out a particular function. Organs have definite anatomical boundaries and are visibly distinguishable from adjacent structures. Most organs and higher levels of structure are within the domain of gross anatomy. However, there are organs within organs—the large organs visible to the naked eye often contain smaller organs visible only with the microscope. The skin, for example, is the body's largest organ. Included within it are thousands of smaller organs: Each hair, nail, gland, nerve, and blood vessel of the skin is an organ in itself. A single organ can belong to two organ systems. For example, the pancreas belongs to both the endocrine and digestive systems.

A **tissue** is a mass of similar cells and cell products that forms a discrete region of an organ and performs a specific function. The body is composed of only four primary classes of tissue: epithelial, connective, nervous, and muscular tissue. Histology, the study of tissues, is the subject of chapter 5.

Cells are the smallest units of an organism that carry out all the basic functions of life; nothing simpler than a cell is considered alive. A cell is enclosed in a *plasma membrane* composed of lipids and proteins. Most cells have one nucleus, an organelle that contains its DNA. *Cytology,* the study of cells and organelles, is the subject of chapters 3 and 4.

Organelles[13] are microscopic structures in a cell that carry out its individual functions. Examples include mitochondria, centrioles, and lysosomes.

Organelles and other cellular components are composed of **molecules.** The largest molecules, such as proteins, fats, and DNA, are called *macromolecules* (see chapter 2). A molecule is a particle composed of at least two **atoms,** the smallest particles with unique chemical identities.

The theory that a large, complex system such as the human body can be understood by studying its simpler components is called **reductionism.** First espoused by Aristotle, this has proved to be a highly productive approach; indeed, it is essential to scientific thinking. Yet the reductionistic view is not the only way of understanding human life. Just as it would be very difficult to predict the workings of an automobile transmission merely by looking at a pile of its disassembled gears and levers, one could never predict the human personality from a complete knowledge of the circuitry of the brain or the genetic sequence of DNA. **Holism**[14] is the complementary theory that there are "emergent properties" of the whole organism that cannot be predicted from the properties of its separate parts—human beings are more than the sum of their parts. To be most effective, a health-care provider treats not merely a disease or an organ system, but a whole person. A patient's perceptions, emotional responses to life, and confidence in the nurse, therapist, or physician profoundly affect the outcome of treatment. In fact, these psychological factors often play a greater role in a patient's recovery than the physical treatments administered.

[13]*elle* = little
[14]*holo* = whole, entire

1.5b Anatomical Variation

A quick look around any classroom is enough to show that no two humans are exactly alike; on close inspection, even identical twins exhibit differences. Yet anatomy atlases and textbooks can easily give the impression that everyone's internal anatomy is the same. This simply is not true. Books such as this one can teach you only the most common structure—the anatomy seen in about 70% or more of people. Someone who thinks that all human bodies are the same internally would make a very confused medical student or an incompetent surgeon.

Some people lack certain organs. For example, most of us have a *palmaris longus* muscle in the forearm and a *plantaris* muscle in the leg, but these are absent from others. Most of us have five lumbar vertebrae (bones of the lower spine), but some people have six and some have four. Most of us have one spleen and two kidneys, but some have two spleens or only one kidney. Most kidneys are supplied by a single *renal artery* and are drained by one *ureter,* but some have two renal arteries or ureters. **Figure 1.6** shows some common variations in human anatomy, and Deeper Insight 1.2 describes a particularly dramatic and clinically important variation.

▶▶▶**APPLY WHAT YOU KNOW**

People who are allergic to aspirin or penicillin often wear MedicAlert bracelets or necklaces that note this fact in case they need emergency medical treatment and are unable to communicate. Why would it be important for a person with situs inversus (see Deeper Insight 1.2) to have this noted on a MedicAlert bracelet?

 DEEPER INSIGHT 1.2

CLINICAL APPLICATION

Situs Inversus and Other Unusual Anatomy

In most people, the spleen, pancreas, sigmoid colon, and most of the heart are on the left, while the appendix, gallbladder, and most of the liver are on the right. The normal arrangement of these and other internal organs is called *situs solitus* (SITE-us). About 1 in 8,000 people, however, is born with an abnormality called *situs inversus*—the organs of the thoracic and abdominal cavities are reversed between right and left. A selective right–left reversal of the heart is called *dextrocardia.* In *situs perversus,* a single organ occupies an atypical position—for example, a kidney located low in the pelvic cavity instead of high in the abdominal cavity.

Conditions such as dextrocardia in the absence of complete situs inversus can cause serious medical problems. Complete situs inversus, however, usually causes no functional problems because all of the viscera, though reversed, maintain their normal relationships to one another. Situs inversus is often discovered in the fetus by sonography, but many people remain unaware of their condition for decades until it is discovered by medical imaging, on physical examination, or in surgery. You can easily imagine the importance of such conditions in diagnosing appendicitis, performing gallbladder surgery, interpreting an X-ray, auscultating the heart valves, or recording an electrocardiogram.

BEFORE YOU GO ON

Answer the following questions to test your understanding of the preceding section:

12. In the hierarchy of human structure, what is the level between organ system and tissue? Between cell and molecule?

13. How are tissues relevant to the definition of an organ?

14. Why is reductionism a necessary but not sufficient point of view for fully understanding a patient's illness?

15. Why should medical students observe multiple cadavers and not be satisfied to dissect only one?

1.6   Human Function

Expected Learning Outcomes

When you have completed this section, you should be able to

a. state the characteristics that distinguish living organisms from nonliving objects;

b. explain the importance of physiological variation among persons;

c. define *homeostasis* and explain why this concept is central to physiology;

d. define *negative feedback,* give an example of it, and explain its importance to homeostasis;

e. define *positive feedback* and give examples of its beneficial and harmful effects; and

f. define *gradient,* describe the variety of gradients in human physiology, and identify some forms of matter and energy that flow down gradients.

1.6a Characteristics of Life

Why do we consider a growing child to be alive, but not a growing crystal? Is abortion the taking of a human life? If so, what about a contraceptive foam that kills only sperm? As a patient is dying, at what point does it become ethical to disconnect life-support equipment and remove organs for donation? If these organs are alive, as they must be to serve someone else, then why isn't the donor considered alive? Such questions have no easy answers, but they demand a concept of what life is—a concept that may differ with one's biological, medical, legal, or religious perspective.

From a biological viewpoint, life is not a single property. It is a collection of properties that help to distinguish living from nonliving things:

· **Organization.** Living things exhibit a far higher level of organization than the nonliving world around them. They expend a great deal of energy to maintain order, and a breakdown in this order is accompanied by disease and often death.

· **Cellular composition.** Living matter is always compartmentalized into one or more cells.

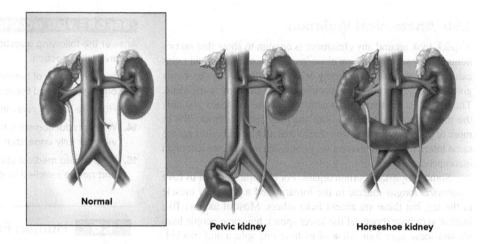

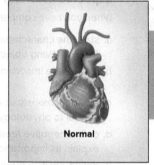

Normal   **Pelvic kidney**   **Horseshoe kidney**

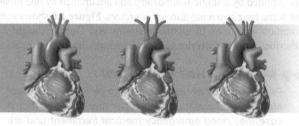

Normal   **Variations in branches of the aorta**

FIGURE 1.6 Variation in Anatomy of the Kidneys and the Major Arteries Near the Heart.

- **Metabolism.** Living things take in molecules from the environment and chemically change them into molecules that form their own structures, control their physiology, or provide them with energy. **Metabolism**[15] is the sum of all this internal chemical change. It inevitably produces chemical wastes, some of which are toxic if they accumulate. There is a constant turnover of molecules in the body. Although you sense a continuity of personality and experience from your childhood to the present, nearly every molecule of your body has been replaced within the past year.

- **Responsiveness** and **movement.** The ability to sense and react to **stimuli** (changes in the environment) is called *responsiveness* or *excitability*. It occurs at all levels from the single cell to the entire body, and it characterizes all living things from bacteria to you. Responsiveness is especially obvious in animals because of nerve and muscle cells that exhibit high sensitivity to environmental stimuli, rapid transmission of information, and quick reactions. Most living organisms are capable of self-propelled movement from

place to place, and all organisms and cells are at least capable of moving substances internally, such as moving food along the digestive tract or moving molecules and organelles from place to place within a cell.

- **Homeostasis.** Although the environment around an organism changes, the organism maintains relatively stable internal conditions—for example, a stable temperature, blood pressure, and body weight. This ability to maintain internal stability, called *homeostasis,* is explored in section 1.6c.

- **Development.** Development is any change in form or function over the lifetime of the organism. In most organisms, it involves two major processes: (1) **differentiation,** the transformation of cells with no specialized function into cells that are committed to a particular task; and (2) **growth,** an increase in size. Some nonliving things grow, but not in the way your body does. If you let a saturated sugar solution evaporate, crystals will grow from it, but not through a change in the composition of the sugar. They merely add more sugar molecules from the solution to the crystal surface. The growth of the body, by contrast, occurs through chemical change (metabolism); for the most part, your body is not composed of the

---

[15]*metabol* = change; *ism* = process

molecules you ate but of molecules made by chemically altering your food.

- **Reproduction.** All living organisms can produce copies of themselves, thus passing their genes on to new, younger containers—their offspring.

- **Evolution.** All living species exhibit genetic change from generation to generation and therefore evolve. This occurs because *mutations* (changes in DNA structure) are inevitable and because environmental selection pressures favor the transmission of some genes more than others. Unlike the other characteristics of life, evolution is a characteristic seen only in the population as a whole. No single individual evolves over the course of its life.

Clinical and legal criteria of life differ from these biological criteria. A person who has shown no brain waves for 24 hours, and has no reflexes, respiration, or heartbeat other than what is provided by artificial life support, can be declared legally dead. At such time, however, most of the body is still biologically alive and its organs may be useful for transplant.

1.6b Physiological Variation

Earlier we considered the clinical importance of variations in human anatomy, but physiology is even more variable. Physiological variables differ with sex, age, weight, diet, degree of physical activity, genetics, and environment, among other things. Failure to consider such variation leads to medical mistakes such as over-medication of the elderly or medicating women on the basis of research done on young men. If a textbook states a typical human heart rate, blood pressure, red blood cell count, or body temperature, it is generally assumed, unless otherwise stated, that such values refer to a healthy 22-year-old weighing 58 kg (128 lb) for a female and 70 kg (154 lb) for a male, and a lifestyle of light physical activity and moderate caloric intake (2,000 and 2,800 kcal/day, respectively).

1.6c Negative Feedback and Homeostasis

The human body has a remarkable capacity for self-restoration. Hippocrates commented that it usually returns to a state of equilibrium by itself, and people recover from most illnesses even without the help of a physician. This tendency results from homeostasis[16] (HO-me-oh-STAY-sis), the body's ability to detect change, activate mechanisms that oppose it, and thereby maintain relatively stable internal conditions.

French physiologist **Claude Bernard** (1813–78) observed that the internal conditions of the body remain quite constant even when external conditions vary greatly. For example, whether it is freezing cold or swelteringly hot outdoors, the internal temperature of the body stays within a range of about 36° to 37°C (97°–99°F). American physiologist **Walter Cannon** (1871–1945) coined the term *homeostasis* for this tendency to maintain internal stability. This has been one of the most enlightening theories in physiology. We now see physiology as largely a group of mechanisms for maintaining homeostasis, and the loss of homeostatic control as the cause of illness and death. Pathophysiology is essentially the study of unstable conditions that result when our homeostatic controls go awry.

Do not, however, overestimate the degree of internal stability. Internal conditions aren't absolutely constant but fluctuate within a limited range, such as the range of body temperatures noted earlier. The internal state of the body is best described as a **dynamic equilibrium** (balanced change), in which there is a certain **set point** or average value for a given variable (such as 37°C for body temperature) and conditions fluctuate slightly around this point.

The fundamental mechanism that keeps a variable close to its set point is **negative feedback**—a process in which the body senses a change and activates mechanisms that negate or reverse it. By maintaining stability, negative feedback is the key mechanism for maintaining health.

These principles can be understood by comparison to a home heating system **(fig. 1.7a)**. Suppose it is a cold winter day and you have set your thermostat for 20°C (68°F)—the set point. If the room becomes too cold, a temperature-sensitive switch in the thermostat turns on the furnace. The temperature rises until it is slightly above the set point, and then the switch breaks the circuit and turns off the furnace. This is a negative feedback process that reverses the falling temperature and restores it to the set point. When the furnace turns off, the temperature slowly drops again until the switch is reactivated—thus, the furnace cycles on and off all day. The room temperature doesn't stay at exactly 20°C but fluctuates slightly—the system maintains a state of dynamic equilibrium in which the temperature averages 20°C and deviates only slightly from the set point. Because feedback mechanisms alter the original changes that triggered them (temperature, for example), they are often called **feedback loops.**

Body temperature is similarly regulated by a "thermostat"—a group of nerve cells in the base of the brain that monitor the temperature of the blood. If you become overheated, the thermostat triggers heat-losing mechanisms **(fig. 1.7b)**. One of these is **vasodilation** (VAY-zo-dy-LAY-shun), the widening of blood vessels. When blood vessels of the skin dilate, warm blood flows closer to the body surface and loses heat to the surrounding air. If this isn't enough to return your temperature to normal, sweating occurs; the evaporation of water from the skin has a powerful cooling effect (see Deeper Insight 1.3). Conversely, if it is cold outside and your body temperature drops much below 37°C, these nerve cells activate heat-conserving mechanisms. The first to be activated is **vasoconstriction,** a narrowing of the blood vessels in the skin, which serves to retain warm blood deeper in your body and reduce heat loss. If this isn't enough, the brain activates shivering—muscle tremors that generate heat.

Let's consider one more example—a case of homeostatic control of blood pressure. When you first rise from bed in the morning, gravity causes some of your blood to drain away from

---

[16]*homeo* = the same; *stas* = to place, stand, stay

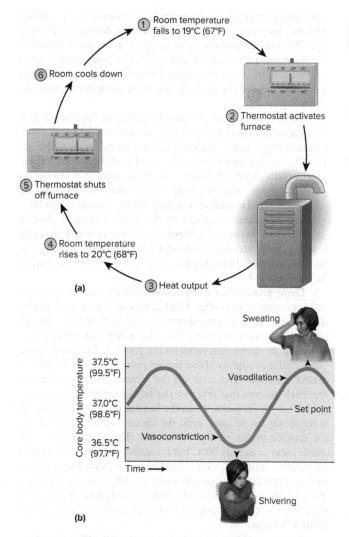

FIGURE 1.7 Negative Feedback in Thermoregulation.
(a) The negative feedback loop that maintains room temperature.
(b) Negative feedback usually keeps the human body temperature within about 0.5°C of a 37°C set point. Cutaneous vasoconstriction and shivering set in when the body temperature falls too low, and soon raise it. Cutaneous vasodilation and sweating set in when body temperature rises too high, and soon lower it.

? *How does vasodilation reduce the body temperature?*

your head and upper torso, resulting in falling blood pressure in this region—a local imbalance in your homeostasis (**fig. 1.8**). This is detected by sensory nerve endings called *baroreceptors* in large arteries near the heart. They transmit nerve signals to the brainstem, where we have a *cardiac center* that regulates the heart rate. The cardiac center responds by transmitting nerve signals to the heart, which speed it up. The faster heart rate quickly raises the blood pressure and restores normal homeostasis. In elderly people, this feedback loop is sometimes insufficiently responsive, and they may feel dizzy as they rise from a reclining

DEEPER INSIGHT 1.3

MEDICAL HISTORY

Men in the Oven

English physician Charles Blagden (1748–1820) staged a rather theatrical demonstration of homeostasis long before Cannon coined the word. In 1775, Blagden spent 45 minutes in a chamber heated to 127°C (260°F)—along with a dog, a beefsteak, and some research associates. Being dead and unable to maintain homeostasis, the steak was cooked. But being alive and capable of evaporative cooling, the dog panted, the men sweated, and all of them survived. History does not record whether the men ate the steak in celebration or shared it with the dog.

position and their cerebral blood pressure falls. This sometimes causes fainting.

This reflexive correction of blood pressure *(baroreflex)* illustrates three common, although not universal, components of a feedback loop: a receptor, an integrating center, and an effector. The **receptor** is a structure that senses a change in the body, such as the stretch receptors that monitor blood pressure. The **integrating (control) center,** such as the cardiac center of the

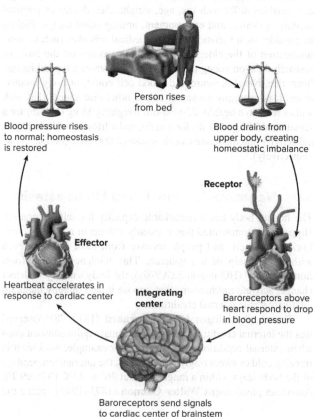

FIGURE 1.8 Homeostatic Compensation for a Postural Change in Blood Pressure.

brain, is a mechanism that processes this information, relates it to other available information (for example, comparing what the blood pressure is with what it should be), and makes a decision about what the appropriate response should be. The **effector** is the cell or organ that carries out the final corrective action. In the foregoing example, it is the heart. The response, such as the restoration of normal blood pressure, is then sensed by the receptor, and the feedback loop is complete.

1.6d Positive Feedback and Rapid Change

Positive feedback is a self-amplifying cycle in which a physiological change leads to even greater change in the same direction, rather than producing the corrective effects of negative feedback. Positive feedback is often a normal way of producing rapid change. When a woman is giving birth, for example, the head of the fetus pushes against her cervix (the neck of the uterus) and stimulates its nerve endings **(fig. 1.9).** Nerve signals travel to the brain, which, in turn, stimulates the pituitary gland to secrete the hormone oxytocin. Oxytocin travels in the blood and stimulates the uterus to contract. This pushes the fetus downward, stimulating the cervix

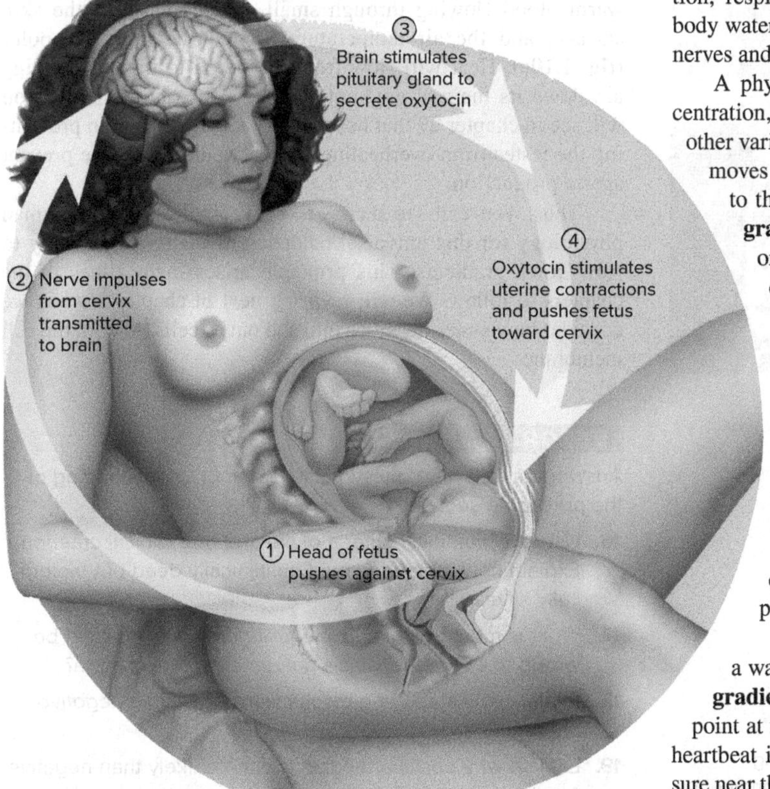

FIGURE 1.9 Positive Feedback in Childbirth.

❓ *Could childbirth as a whole be considered a negative feedback event? Discuss.*

still more and causing the positive feedback loop to be repeated. Labor contractions therefore become more and more intense until the fetus is expelled. Other cases of beneficial positive feedback are seen later in the book in, for example, blood clotting, protein digestion, and the generation of nerve signals.

Frequently, however, positive feedback is a harmful or even life-threatening process. This is because its self-amplifying nature can quickly change the internal state of the body to something far from its homeostatic set point. Consider a high fever, for example. A fever triggered by infection is beneficial up to a point, but if the body temperature rises much above 40°C (104°F), it may create a dangerous positive feedback loop. This high temperature raises the metabolic rate, which makes the body produce heat faster than it can get rid of it. Thus, temperature rises still further, increasing the metabolic rate and heat production still more. This "vicious circle" becomes fatal at approximately 45°C (113°F). Thus, positive feedback loops often create dangerously out-of-control situations that require emergency medical treatment.

1.6e Gradients and Flow

Another fundamental concept that will arise repeatedly in this book is that matter and energy tend to *flow down gradients*. This simple principle underlies processes as diverse as blood circulation, respiratory airflow, urine formation, nutrient absorption, body water distribution, temperature regulation, and the action of nerves and muscles.

A physiological **gradient** is a difference in chemical concentration, electrical charge, physical pressure, temperature, or other variable between one point and another. If matter or energy moves from the point where this variable has a higher value to the point with a lower value, we say it flows **down the gradient**—for example, from a warmer to a cooler point, or a place of high chemical concentration to one of lower concentration. Movement in the opposite direction is **up the gradient.**

Outside of biology, *gradient* can mean a hill or slope, and this affords us a useful analogy to biological processes **(fig. 1.10a).** A wagon released at the top of a hill will roll down it ("flow") spontaneously, without need for anyone to exert energy to move it. Similarly, matter and energy in the body spontaneously flow down gradients, without the expenditure of metabolic energy. Movement up a gradient does require an energy expenditure, just as we would have to push or pull a wagon to move it uphill.

Consider some examples and analogies. If you open a water tap with a garden hose on it, you create a **pressure gradient;** water flows down the hose from the high-pressure point at the tap to the low-pressure point at the open end. Each heartbeat is like that, creating a gradient from high blood pressure near the heart to low pressure farther away; blood flows down this gradient away from the heart **(fig. 1.10b).** When we inhale, air flows down a pressure gradient from the surrounding atmosphere to pulmonary air passages where the pressure is lower. A pressure gradient also drives the process in which the kidneys filter water and waste products from the blood.

The figure labels within the illustration:

③ Brain stimulates pituitary gland to secrete oxytocin

② Nerve impulses from cervix transmitted to brain

④ Oxytocin stimulates uterine contractions and pushes fetus toward cervix

① Head of fetus pushes against cervix

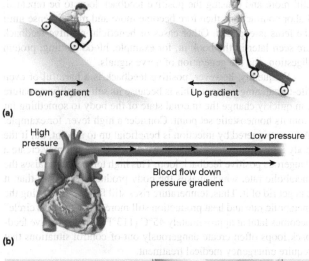

(a) Down gradient   Up gradient

(b) High pressure   Low pressure

Blood flow down pressure gradient

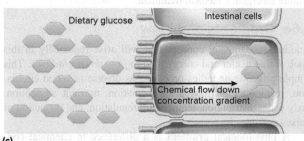

(c)

Dietary glucose   Intestinal cells

Chemical flow down concentration gradient

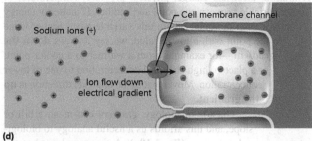

(d)

Cell membrane channel

Sodium ions (+)

Ion flow down electrical gradient

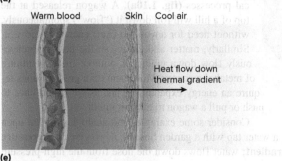

(e)

Warm blood   Skin   Cool air

Heat flow down thermal gradient

FIGURE 1.10 Flow Down Gradients. (a) A wagon rolling downhill (down a gradient) (left) is a useful analogy to spontaneous, gradient-driven physiological processes. Moving up a gradient (right) requires an energy input. (b) Blood flowing down a pressure gradient. (c) Dietary sugars flowing down a concentration gradient into an intestinal cell. (d) Sodium ions flowing down an electrical gradient into a cell. (e) Heat flowing down a thermal gradient to leave the body through the skin.

Chemicals flow down **concentration gradients.** When we digest starch, a high concentration of sugars accumulates in the small intestine. The cells lining the intestine contain only a low concentration of sugars, so sugars flow from the intestinal space into these cells, thus becoming absorbed into the body's tissues (**fig. 1.10c**). Water flows through cell membranes and epithelia by *osmosis,* from the side where it is more concentrated to the side where it is less so.

Charged particles flow down **electrical gradients.** Suppose there is a high concentration of sodium ions (Na^+) just outside a cell and much lower concentration inside, so the outer surface of the cell membrane has a relatively positive charge and the inner surface is relatively negative (**fig. 1.10d**). If we open channels in the membrane that will let sodium pass, sodium ions rush into the cell, flowing down their electrical gradient. Because each Na^+ carries a positive charge, this flow constitutes an electrical current through the membrane. We tap this current to make our nerves fire, our heart beat, and our muscles contract. In many cases, the flow of ions is governed by a combination of concentration and electrical charge differences between two points, and we say that ions flow down **electrochemical gradients.** These will be studied especially in connection with muscle and nerve action in chapters 11 and 12.

Heat flows down a **thermal gradient.** Suppose there is warm blood flowing through small arteries close to the skin surface, and the air temperature around the body is cooler (**fig. 1.10e**). Heat will flow from the blood to the surrounding air, down its thermal gradient, and be lost from the body. You will see in chapter 27 that heat flow is also important in preventing the testes from overheating, which would otherwise prevent sperm production.

Thus, you can see there are many applications in human physiology for this universal tendency of matter and energy to flow down gradients. This principle arises many times in the chapters to follow. We will revisit it next in chapter 3 when we consider how materials move into and out of cells through the cell membrane.

BEFORE YOU GO ON

Answer the following questions to test your understanding of the preceding section:

16. List four biological criteria of life and one clinical criterion. Explain how a person could be clinically dead but biologically alive.

17. What is meant by *dynamic equilibrium*? Why would it be wrong to say homeostasis prevents internal change?

18. Explain why stabilizing mechanisms are called *negative feedback.*

19. Explain why positive feedback is more likely than negative feedback to disturb homeostasis.

20. Active tissues generate carbon dioxide, which diffuses out of the tissue into the bloodstream, to be carried away. Is this diffusion into the blood a case of flow up a gradient, or down? Explain.

1.7 The Language of Medicine

Expected Learning Outcomes

When you have completed this section, you should be able to

a. explain why modern anatomical terminology is so heavily based on Greek and Latin;

b. recognize eponyms when you see them;

c. describe the efforts to achieve an internationally uniform anatomical terminology;

d. break medical terms down into their basic word elements;

e. state some reasons why the literal meaning of a word may not lend insight into its definition;

f. relate singular noun forms to their plural and adjective forms; and

g. discuss why precise spelling is important in anatomy and physiology.

One of the greatest challenges faced by students of anatomy and physiology is the vocabulary. In this book, you will encounter such Latin terms as *corpus callosum* (a brain structure), *ligamentum arteriosum* (a small fibrous band near the heart), and *extensor carpi radialis longus* (a forearm muscle). You may wonder why structures aren't named in "just plain English," and how you will ever remember such formidable names. This section will give you some answers to these questions and some useful tips on mastering anatomical terminology.

1.7a The History of Anatomical Terminology

The major features of human gross anatomy have standard international names prescribed by a book titled the *Terminologia Anatomica (TA)*. The *TA* was codified in 1998 by an international committee of anatomists and approved by professional associations of anatomists in more than 50 countries.

About 90% of today's medical terms are formed from just 1,200 Greek and Latin roots. Why those two languages? Scientific investigation began in ancient Greece and soon spread to Rome. The Greeks and Romans coined many of the words still used in human anatomy today: *duodenum, uterus, prostate, cerebellum, diaphragm, sacrum, amnion,* and others. In the Renaissance, the fast pace of discovery required a profusion of new terms to describe things. Anatomists in different countries began giving different names to the same structures. Adding to the confusion, they often named new structures and diseases in honor of their esteemed teachers and predecessors, giving us such nondescriptive terms as *fallopian tube* and *duct of Santorini*. Terms coined from the names of people, called **eponyms,**[17] afford little clue as to what a structure or condition is.

In hopes of resolving this growing confusion, anatomists began meeting as early as 1895 to devise a uniform international

terminology. After several false starts, they agreed on a list of terms that rejected all eponyms and gave each structure a unique Latin name to be used worldwide. Even if you were to look at an anatomy atlas in Korean or Arabic, the illustrations may be labeled with the same Latin terms as in an English-language atlas. That list served for many decades until recently replaced by the *TA,* which prescribes both Latin names and accepted English equivalents. The terminology in this book conforms to the *TA* except where undue confusion would result from abandoning widely used, yet unofficial, terms.

1.7b Analyzing Medical Terms

The task of learning medical terminology seems overwhelming at first, but it is a simple skill to become more comfortable with the technical language of medicine. People who find scientific terms confusing and difficult to pronounce, spell, and remember often feel more confident once they realize the logic of how terms are composed. A term such as *hyponatremia* is less forbidding once we recognize that it is composed of three common word elements: *hypo-* (below normal), *natr-* (sodium), and *-emia* (blood condition). Thus, hyponatremia is a deficiency of sodium in the blood. Those word elements appear over and over in many other medical terms: *hypothermia, natriuretic, anemia,* and so on. Once you learn the meanings of *hypo-, natri-,* and *-emia,* you already have the tools to at least partially understand hundreds of other biomedical terms. In appendix E, you will find a lexicon of word elements commonly footnoted in this book.

Scientific terms are typically composed of one or more of the following elements:

- At least one *root (stem)* that bears the core meaning of the word. In *cardiology,* for example, the root is *cardi-* (heart). Many words have two or more roots. In *cardiomyopathy,* for example, the roots are *cardi-* (heart), *my-* (muscle), and *path-* (disease).

- *Combining vowels* that are often inserted to join roots and make the word easier to pronounce. In *cardiomyopathy,* each *o* is a combining vowel. Although *o* is the most common combining vowel, all vowels of the alphabet are used in this way, such as *a* in *ligament, e* in *vitreous, i* in *fusiform, u* in *ovulation,* and *y* in *tachycardia.* Some words, such as *intervertebral,* have no combining vowels. A combination of a root and combining vowel is called a *combining form;* for example, *chrom-* (color) + *o* (a combining vowel) make the combining form *chromo-,* as in *chromosome.*

- A *prefix* may be present to modify the core meaning of the word. For example, *gastric* (pertaining to the stomach or to the belly of a muscle) takes on a variety of new meanings when prefixes are added to it: *epigastric* (above the stomach), *hypogastric* (below the stomach), *endogastric* (within the stomach), and *digastric* (a muscle with two bellies).

- A *suffix* may be added to the end of a word to modify its core meaning. For example, *microscope, microscopy, microscopic,* and *microscopist* have different meanings because of their suffixes alone. Often two or more suffixes, or a

---

[17]*epo = epi* = upon, based upon; *nym* = name

root and suffix, occur together so often that they are treated jointly as a *compound suffix;* for example, *log* (study) + *y* (process) form the compound suffix *-logy* (the study of). Prefixes and suffixes are collectively called *affixes.*

To summarize these basic principles, consider the word *gastroenterology,* a branch of medicine dealing with the stomach and small intestine. It breaks down into *gastro/entero/logy:*

gastro	=	a combining form meaning "stomach"
entero	=	a combining form meaning "small intestine"
logy	=	a compound suffix meaning "the study of"

"Dissecting" words in this way and paying attention to the word-origin footnotes throughout this book will help you become more comfortable with the language of anatomy. Knowing how a word breaks down and knowing the meaning of its elements make it far easier to pronounce a word, spell it, and remember its definition.

There are a few unfortunate exceptions, however. The path from original meaning to current usage has often become obscured by history (see Deeper Insight 1.4). The foregoing approach also is no help with eponyms or **acronyms**[18]—words composed of the first letter, or first few letters, of a series of words. For example, a common medical imaging method is the PET scan, an acronym for *positron emission tomography.* Note that PET is a pronounceable word, hence a true acronym. Acronyms are not to be confused with simple abbreviations such as DNA and MRI, in which each letter must be pronounced separately.

1.7c Plurals, Adjectives, and Possessive Forms

A point of confusion for many beginning students is how to recognize the plural forms of medical terms. Few people would fail to recognize that *ovaries* is the plural of *ovary,* but the connection is harder to make in other cases: For example, the plural of *cortex* is *cortices* (COR-ti-sees), the plural of *corpus* is *corpora,* and the plural of *ganglion* is *ganglia.* **Table 1.1** will help you make the connection between common singular and plural noun terminals.

In some cases, what appears to the beginner to be two completely different words may be only the noun and adjective forms of the same word. For example, *brachium* denotes the arm, and *brachii* (as in the muscle name *biceps brachii*) means "of the arm." *Carpus* denotes the wrist, and *carpi,* a word used in several muscle names, means "of the wrist." Adjectives can also take different forms for the singular and plural and for different degrees of comparison. The *digits* are the fingers and toes. The word *digiti* in a muscle name means "of a single finger (or toe)," whereas *digitorum* is the plural, meaning "of multiple fingers (or toes)." Thus, the *extensor digiti minimi muscle* extends only the little finger, whereas the *extensor digitorum muscle* extends all fingers except the thumb.

[18]*acro* = beginning; *nym* = name

DEEPER INSIGHT 1.4
MEDICAL HISTORY

Obscure Medical Word Origins

The literal translation of a word doesn't always provide great insight into its modern meaning. The history of language is full of twists and turns that are fascinating in their own right and say much about the history of human culture, but they can create confusion for students.

For example, the *amnion* is a transparent sac that forms around the developing fetus. The word is derived from *amnos,* from the Greek for "lamb." From this origin, *amnos* came to mean a bowl for catching the blood of sacrificial lambs, and from there the word found its way into biomedical usage for the membrane that emerges (quite bloody) as part of the afterbirth. The *acetabulum,* the socket of the hip joint, literally means "vinegar cup." Apparently the hip socket reminded an anatomist of the little cups used to serve vinegar as a condiment on dining tables in ancient Rome. The word *testicles* can be translated "little pots" or "little witnesses." The history of medical language has several amusing conjectures as to why this word was chosen to name the male gonads.

TABLE 1.1	Singular and Plural Forms of Some Noun Terminals	
Singular Ending	**Plural Ending**	**Examples**
-a	-ae	axilla, axillae
-en	-ina	lumen, lumina
-ex	-ices	cortex, cortices
-is	-es	diagnosis, diagnoses
-is	-ides	epididymis, epididymides
-ix	-ices	appendix, appendices
-ma	-mata	carcinoma, carcinomata
-on	-a	ganglion, ganglia
-um	-a	septum, septa
-us	-era	viscus, viscera
-us	-i	villus, villi
-us	-ora	corpus, corpora
-x	-ges	phalanx, phalanges
-y	-ies	ovary, ovaries
-yx	-yces	calyx, calyces

The English words *large, larger,* and *largest* are examples of the positive, comparative, and superlative degrees of comparison. In Latin, these are *magnus, major* (from *maior*), and *maximus.* We find these in the muscle names *adductor magnus* (a *large* muscle of the thigh), the *pectoralis major* (the *larger* of two pectoral muscles of the chest), and *gluteus maximus* (the *largest* of the three gluteal muscles of the buttock).

Some noun variations indicate the possessive, such as the *rectus abdominis,* a straight (*rectus*) muscle of the abdomen (*abdominis,* "of the abdomen"), and the *erector spinae,* a muscle that straightens (*erector*) the spinal column (*spinae,* "of the spine").

Anatomical terminology also frequently follows the Greek and Latin practice of placing the adjective after the noun. Thus, we have such names as the *stratum lucidum* for a clear *(lucidum)* layer *(stratum)* of the epidermis, the *foramen magnum* for a large *(magnum)* hole *(foramen)* in the skull, and the aforementioned *pectoralis major* muscle of the chest.

This is not to say that you must be conversant in Latin or Greek grammar to proceed with your study of anatomy. These few examples, however, may alert you to some patterns to watch for in the terminology you study and, ideally, will make your encounters with anatomical terminology less confusing.

1.7d Pronunciation

Pronunciation is another stumbling block for many beginning anatomy and physiology students. This book gives simple pro-NUN-see-AY-shun guides for many terms when they are first introduced. Read the syllables of these guides phonetically and accent the syllables in capital letters. You can also hear pronunciations of most of the anatomical terms within Anatomy & Physiology REVEALED®.

1.7e The Importance of Spelling

A final word of advice for your study of anatomy and physiology: Be accurate in your spelling and use of terms. It may seem trivial if you misspell *trapezius* as *trapezium,* but in doing so, you would be changing the name of a back muscle to the name of a wrist bone. Similarly, changing *occipitalis* to *occipital* or *zygomaticus* to *zygomatic* changes other muscle names to bone names. Changing *malleus* to *malleolus* changes the name of a middle-ear bone to the name of a bony protuberance of the ankle. And there is only a one-letter difference between *ileum* (the final portion of the small intestine) and *ilium* (part of the hip bone), and between *gustation* (the sense of taste) and *gestation* (pregnancy).

The health professions demand the utmost attention to detail and accuracy—people's lives may one day be in your hands. The habit of carefulness must extend to your use of language as well. Many patients have died simply because of tragic written and oral miscommunication in the hospital. Compared to this, it is hardly tragic if your instructor deducts a point or two for an error in spelling. It should be considered a lesson learned about the importance of accuracy.

BEFORE YOU GO ON

Answer the following questions to test your understanding of the preceding section:

21. Explain why modern anatomical terminology is so heavily based on Greek and Latin.

22. Distinguish between an eponym and an acronym, and explain why both of these present difficulties for interpreting anatomical terms.

23. Break each of the following words down into its roots, prefixes, and suffixes, and state their meanings, following the example of *gastroenterology* analyzed earlier: *pericardium, appendectomy, subcutaneous, phonocardiogram, otorhinolaryngology.* Consult the list of word elements in appendix E for help.

24. Write the singular form of each of the following words: *pleurae, gyri, ganglia, fissures.* Write the plural form of each of the following: *villus, tibia, encephalitis, cervix, stoma.*

1.8   Review of Major Themes

To close this chapter, let's distill a few major points from it. These themes can provide you with a sense of perspective that will make the rest of the book more meaningful and not just a collection of disconnected facts. These are some key unifying principles behind all study of human anatomy and physiology:

- **Unity of form and function.** *Form and function complement each other; physiology cannot be divorced from anatomy.* This unity holds true even down to the molecular level. Our very molecules, such as DNA and proteins, are structured in ways that enable them to carry out their functions. Slight changes in molecular structure can destroy their activity and threaten life.

- **Cell theory.** *All structure and function result from the activity of cells.* Every physiological concept in this book ultimately must be understood from the standpoint of how cells function. Even anatomy is a result of cellular function. If cells are damaged or destroyed, we see the results in disease symptoms of the whole person.

- **Evolution.** *The human body is a product of evolution.* Like every other living species, we have been molded by millions of years of natural selection to function in a changing environment. Many aspects of human anatomy and physiology reflect our ancestors' adaptations to their environment. Human form and function cannot be fully understood except in light of our evolutionary history.

- **Hierarchy of complexity.** *Human structure can be viewed as a series of levels of complexity.* Each level is composed of a smaller number of simpler subunits than the level above it. These subunits are arranged in different ways to form diverse structures of higher complexity. Understanding the simpler components is the key to understanding higher levels of structure.

- **Homeostasis.** *The purpose of most normal physiology is to maintain stable conditions within the body.* Human physiology is essentially a group of homeostatic mechanisms that produce stable internal conditions favorable to cellular function. Any serious departure from these conditions can be harmful or fatal to cells and thus to the whole body.

- **Gradients and flow.** Matter and energy tend to flow down gradients such as differences in chemical concentration, pressure, temperature, and electrical charge. This accounts for much of their movement in human physiology.

▶▶▶ **APPLY WHAT YOU KNOW**

Architect Louis Henri Sullivan coined the phrase, "Form ever follows function." What do you think he meant by this? Discuss how this idea could be applied to the human body and cite a specific example of human anatomy to support it.

DEEPER INSIGHT 1.5
CLINICAL APPLICATION

Medical Imaging

The development of techniques for looking into the body without having to do exploratory surgery has greatly accelerated progress in medicine. A few of these techniques are described here.

Radiography

Radiography, first performed in 1895, is the process of photographing internal structures with X-rays **(fig. 1.11a).** Until the 1960s, this was the only widely available imaging method; even today, it accounts for more than 50% of all clinical imaging. X-rays pass through the soft tissues of the body to a photographic film or detector on the other side, where they produce relatively dark images. They are absorbed, however, by dense matter such as bones,

teeth, tumors, and tuberculosis nodules, which leave the image lighter in these areas. The term *X-ray* also applies to an image *(radiograph)* made by this method. Radiography is commonly used in dentistry, mammography, diagnosis of fractures, and examination of the chest. Hollow organs can be visualized by filling them with a contrast medium that absorbs X-rays. Barium sulfate, for example, is given orally for examination of the esophagus, stomach, and small intestine or by enema for examination of the large intestine. Some disadvantages of radiography are that images of overlapping organs can be confusing and slight differences in tissue density are not easily detected. In addition, X-rays can cause mutations leading to cancer and birth defects. Radiography therefore cannot be used indiscriminately.

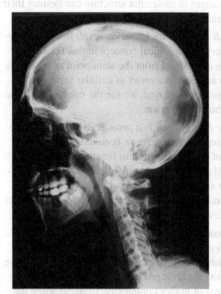

(a) X-ray (radiograph)

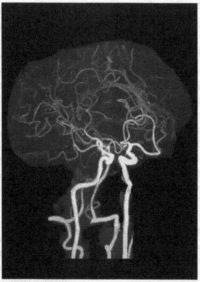

(b) Cerebral angiogram

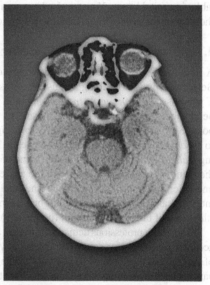

(c) Computed tomographic (CT) scan

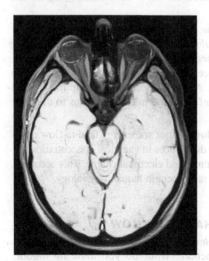

(d) Magnetic resonance image (MRI)

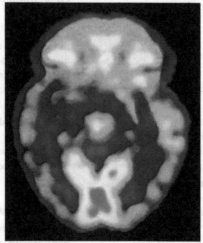

(e) Positron emission tomographic (PET) scan

FIGURE 1.11 Radiologic Images of the Head. (a) X-ray (radiograph) of the skull. (b) Digital subtraction angiogram (DSA) of the cerebral blood vessels. (c) CT scan at the level of the eyes. (d) MRI scan at the level of the eyes. The optic nerves appear in red and the muscles that move the eyes appear in green. (e) A PET scan of the brain of an unmedicated schizophrenic patient. Red areas indicate regions of high metabolic rate. In this patient, the visual center of the brain at the rear of the head (bottom of photo) was especially active during the scan.

❓ *What structures are seen better by MRI than by X-ray? What structures are seen better by X-ray than by PET?*

a: U.H.B. Trust/The Image Bank/Getty Images;
b: pang_oasis/Shutterstock; c: Miriam Maslo/Science Source; d: UHB Trust/Getty Images;
e: ISM/Sovereign/Medical Images

Blood vessels can be seen especially clearly with a radiographic method called *digital subtraction angiography (DSA)* **(fig. 1.11b).** This entails taking X-rays before and after injecting a contrast medium into a vessel. A computer then "erases" the first image from the second, leaving a clear, dark image of just the injected vessels without the overlying and surrounding tissues. This is useful for showing vascular blockages and anatomical malformations, abnormalities of cerebral blood flow, and narrowing (stenosis) of renal arteries, and as an aid in threading catheters into blood vessels. DSA is already being replaced in many clinics, however, by yet newer methods that are less invasive and avoid contrast medium and radiation exposure.

Computed Tomography

Computed tomography[19] (a *CT scan*) **(fig. 1.11c)** is a more sophisticated application of X-rays. The patient is moved through a ring-shaped machine that emits low-intensity X-rays on one side and receives them with a detector on the opposite side. A computer analyzes signals from the detector and produces an image of a "slice" of the body about as thin as a coin. The advantage of such thin planes of view is that there is little overlap of organs, so the image is much sharper than a conventional X-ray. It requires extensive knowledge of cross-sectional anatomy to interpret the images. CT scanning is useful for identifying tumors, aneurysms, cerebral hemorrhages, kidney stones, and other abnormalities.

Magnetic Resonance Imaging

Magnetic resonance imaging (MRI) **(fig. 1.11d)** is better than CT for visualizing some soft tissues. The patient lies in either a tube or an open-sided scanner surrounded by a powerful electromagnet. Hydrogen atoms in the patient's tissues alternately align themselves with this magnetic field and with a radio-frequency field turned on and off by the technologist. These changes in hydrogen alignment generate signals that are analyzed by computer to produce an anatomical image. MRI can "see" clearly through the skull and spine to produce images of the nervous tissue within, and it is better than CT for distinguishing between soft tissues such as the white and gray matter of the brain. MRI also avoids X-ray exposure and its risks.

MRI has disadvantages, however, such as the claustrophobic feeling some patients experience in the scanner, loud noises generated by the machine, and long exposure times that prevent sharp images being made of the constantly moving stomach and intestines. It requires a patient to lie still in the enclosed space for up to 45 minutes to scan one region of the body and may entail 90 minutes to scan multiple regions such as the abdominal and pelvic cavities. Some patients find they cannot tolerate this. Open-sided MRI machines are favored by some claustrophobic or obese patients, but have weaker magnetic fields, produce poorer images, and may miss important tissue abnormalities.

Functional MRI (fMRI) is a variation that visualizes moment-to-moment changes in tissue function. fMRI scans of the brain, for example, show shifting patterns of activity as the brain applies itself to a specific sensory, mental, or motor task. fMRI has lately replaced the PET scan as the most important method for visualizing brain function. The use of fMRI in brain imaging is further discussed in Deeper Insight 14.5.

Positron Emission Tomography

Positron emission tomography (the *PET scan*) **(fig. 1.11e)** is used to assess the metabolic state of a tissue and distinguish which tissues are most active at a given moment. The procedure begins with an injection of radioactively labeled glucose, which emits positrons (electron-like particles with a positive charge). When a positron and electron meet, they annihilate each other and give off a pair of gamma rays that can be detected by sensors and analyzed by computer. The computer displays a color image that shows which tissues were using the most glucose at the moment. PET scans are generally low-resolution, as in this photo, but nevertheless provide valuable diagnostic information. In cardiology, PET scans can show the extent of tissue death from a heart attack. Since it consumes little or no glucose, the damaged tissue appears dark. PET scans are also widely used to diagnose cancer and evaluate tumor status. The PET scan is an example of *nuclear medicine*—the use of radioactive isotopes to treat disease or to form diagnostic images of the body.

Sonography

Sonography[20] **(fig. 1.12)** is the second oldest and second most widely used method of imaging. A handheld device pressed against the skin produces high-frequency ultrasound waves and receives the signals that echo back from internal organs. Sonography isn't very useful for examining bones or lungs, but it is the method of choice in obstetrics, where the image *(sonogram)* can be used to locate the placenta and evaluate fetal age, position, and development. Sonography is also used to view tissues in motion, such as fetal movements, actions of the heart wall and valves, and blood ejection from the heart and flow through arteries and veins. Sonographic imaging of the beating heart is called *echocardiography.* Sonography avoids the harmful effects of X-rays, and the equipment is inexpensive and portable. Some disadvantages are that sonography can't penetrate bone and it usually doesn't produce a very sharp image.

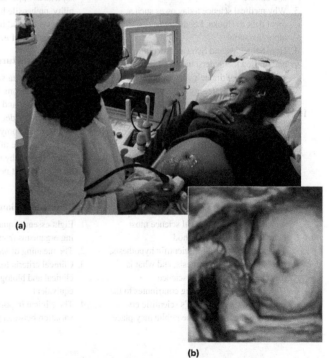

(a)

(b)

FIGURE 1.12 Fetal Sonography. (a) Producing a sonogram. (b) Three-dimensional fetal sonogram at 32 weeks of gestation.

a: Kevin Brofsky/Getty Images; b: Ken Saladin

---

[19]*tomo* = section, cut, slice; *graphy* = recording process
[20]*sono* = sound; *graphy* = recording process

STUDY GUIDE

▶ Assess Your Learning Outcomes

To test your knowledge, discuss the following topics with a study partner or in writing, ideally from memory.

1.1 The Scope of Anatomy and Physiology

1. The meanings of *anatomy* and *physiology* and what it means to say these two sciences are complementary and inseparable
2. Methods of study in anatomy and clinical examination
3. Branches of anatomy that study the body at different levels of detail
4. How comparative physiology advances the understanding of human function

1.2 The Origins of Biomedical Science

1. Greek and Roman scholars who first gave medicine a scientific basis
2. Ways in which the work of Maimonides, Avicenna, Vesalius, and Harvey were groundbreaking in the context of their time and culture
3. Why medical science today owes such a great debt to Hooke, Leeuwenhoek, and other inventors
4. How Schleiden and Schwann revolutionized and unified the understanding of biological structure, ultimately including human anatomy and physiology

1.3 Scientific Method

1. How philosophers Bacon and Descartes revolutionized society's view of science, even though neither of them was a scientist
2. The essential qualities of the scientific method
3. The nature of the inductive and hypothetico–deductive methods, how they differ, and which areas of biomedical science most heavily employ each method
4. The qualities of a valid scientific hypothesis, the function of a hypothesis, and what is meant by *falsifiability* in science
5. How each of the following contributes to the reliability of a researcher's scientific conclusions and the trust that the public may place

in science: sample size, control groups, the double-blind method, statistical testing, and peer review
6. The distinctions between scientific facts, laws, and theories; the purpose of a theory; and how the scientific meanings of *law* and *theory* differ from the common lay meanings

1.4 Human Origins and Adaptations

1. The meanings of *evolution, natural selection, selection pressure,* and *adaptation,* with examples of each
2. The historical origin of the theory of natural selection and how this theory is relevant to a complete understanding of human anatomy and physiology
3. How the kinship among all species is relevant to the choice of model animals for biomedical research
4. Ecological conditions thought to have selected for such key characteristics of *Homo sapiens* as opposable thumbs, shoulder mobility, prehensile hands, stereoscopic vision, color vision, and bipedal locomotion
5. The meaning of *evolutionary medicine*

1.5 Human Structure

1. Levels of human structural complexity from organism to atom
2. Reductionism and holism; how they differ and why both ideas are relevant to the study of human anatomy and physiology and to the clinical care of patients
3. Examples of why the anatomy presented in textbooks is not necessarily true of every individual

1.6 Human Function

1. Eight essential qualities that distinguish living organisms from nonliving things
2. The meaning of *metabolism*
3. Clinical criteria for life and death, and why clinical and biological death are not exactly equivalent
4. The clinical importance of physiological variation between people, and the

assumptions that underlie typical values given in textbooks
5. The meaning of *homeostasis;* its importance for survival; and the historical origin of this concept
6. How negative feedback contributes to homeostasis; the meaning of *negative feedback loop;* how a receptor, integrating center, and effector are involved in many negative feedback loops; and at least one example of such a loop
7. How positive feedback differs from negative feedback; examples of beneficial and harmful cases of positive feedback
8. The concept of matter and energy flowing down gradients and how this applies to various areas of human physiology

1.7 The Language of Medicine

1. The origin and purpose of the *Terminologia Anatomica (TA)* and its relevance for anatomy students
2. How to break biomedical terms into familiar roots, prefixes, and suffixes, and why the habit of doing so aids in learning
3. Acronyms and eponyms, and why they cannot be understood by trying to analyze their roots
4. How to recognize when two or more words are singular and plural versions of one another; when one word is the possessive form of another; and when medical terms built on the same root represent different degrees of comparison (such as terms denoting *large, larger,* and *largest*)
5. Why accuracy in spelling and usage of medical terms can be a matter of life or death in a hospital or clinic, and how seemingly trivial spelling errors can radically alter meaning

1.8 Review of Major Themes

1. A description of six core themes of this book: unity of form and function, cell theory, evolution, hierarchy of complexity, homeostasis, and gradients and flow

STUDY GUIDE

▶ Testing Your Recall

Answers in Appendix A

1. Structure that can be observed with the naked eye is called
   a. gross anatomy.
   b. ultrastructure.
   c. microscopic anatomy.
   d. histology.
   e. cytology.

2. The word prefix *homeo-* means
   a. tissue.
   b. metabolism.
   c. change.
   d. human.
   e. same.

3. The simplest structures considered to be alive are
   a. organisms.
   b. organs.
   c. tissues.
   d. cells.
   e. organelles.

4. Which of the following people revolutionized the teaching of gross anatomy?
   a. Vesalius
   b. Aristotle
   c. Hippocrates
   d. Leeuwenhoek
   e. Cannon

5. Which of the following embodies the greatest amount of scientific information?
   a. a fact
   b. a law of nature
   c. a theory
   d. a deduction
   e. a hypothesis

6. An informed, uncertain, but testable conjecture is
   a. a natural law.
   b. a scientific theory.
   c. a hypothesis.
   d. a deduction.
   e. a scientific fact.

7. A self-amplifying chain of physiological events is called
   a. positive feedback.
   b. negative feedback.
   c. dynamic constancy.
   d. homeostasis.
   e. metabolism.

8. Which of the following is *not* a human organ system?
   a. integumentary
   b. muscular
   c. epithelial
   d. nervous
   e. endocrine

9. _____ means studying anatomy by touch.
   a. Gross anatomy
   b. Auscultation
   c. Osculation
   d. Palpation
   e. Percussion

10. The prefix *hetero-* means
    a. same.
    b. different.
    c. both.
    d. solid.
    e. below.

11. Cutting and separating tissues to reveal structural relationships is called _____.

12. A difference in chemical concentration between one point and another is called a concentration _____.

13. By the process of _____, a medical researcher predicts what the result of a certain experiment will be if his or her hypothesis is correct.

14. Physiological effects of a person's mental state are called _____ effects.

15. The tendency of the body to maintain stable internal conditions is called _____.

16. Blood pH averages 7.4 but fluctuates from 7.35 to 7.45. A pH of 7.4 can therefore be considered the _____ for this variable.

17. Self-corrective mechanisms in physiology are called _____ loops.

18. A/an _____ is the simplest body structure to be composed of two or more types of tissue.

19. Depth perception, or the ability to form three-dimensional images, is also called _____ vision.

20. Our hands are said to be _____ because they can encircle an object such as a branch or tool. The presence of an _____ thumb is important to this ability.

▶ Building Your Medical Vocabulary

Answers in Appendix A

State a meaning of each word element, and give a medical term from this chapter that uses it or a slight variation of it.

1. auscult-
2. dis-
3. homeo-
4. metabolo-
5. palp-
6. physio-
7. -sect
8. -stasis
9. stereo-
10. tomo-

STUDY GUIDE

▶ What's Wrong with These Statements?

Answers in Appendix A

Briefly explain why each of the following statements is false, or reword it to make it true.

1. The technique for taking a patient's pulse at the wrist is auscultation.

2. For a pregnant woman to have an MRI scan would expose her fetus to radiation that can potentially cause mutation and birth defects.

3. We usually depend on positive feedback to restore homeostatic balance and have a beneficial effect on the body.

4. There are far more cells than organelles in the body.

5. Matter doesn't generally move down a gradient in the body unless the body expends metabolic energy to move it.

6. Leeuwenhoek was a biologist who invented the simple microscope in order to examine organisms in lake water.

7. A scientific theory is just a speculation until someone finds the evidence to prove it.

8. In a typical clinical research study, volunteer patients are in the treatment group and the physicians and scientists who run the study constitute the control group.

9. Human evolution is basically a theory that humans came from monkeys.

10. Negative feedback usually has a negative (harmful) effect on the body.

▶ Testing Your Comprehension

1. Ellen is pregnant and tells Janet, one of her coworkers, that she is scheduled to get a fetal sonogram. Janet expresses alarm and warns Ellen about the danger of exposing a fetus to X-rays. Discuss why you think Janet's concern is warranted or unwarranted.

2. Which of the characteristics of living things are possessed by an automobile? What bearing does this have on our definition of life?

3. About 1 out of every 120 live-born infants has a structural defect in the heart such as a hole between two heart chambers. Such infants often suffer pulmonary congestion and heart failure, and about one-third of them die as a result. Which of the major themes in this chapter does this illustrate? Explain your answer.

4. How might human anatomy be different today if the forerunners of humans had never inhabited the forest canopy?

5. Suppose you have been doing heavy yard work on a hot day and sweating profusely. You become very thirsty, so you drink a tall glass of lemonade. Explain how your thirst relates to the concept of homeostasis. Which type of feedback—positive or negative—does this illustrate?

ATLAS

A

GENERAL ORIENTATION TO HUMAN ANATOMY

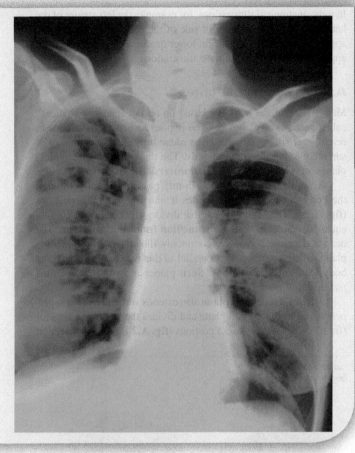

Colorized chest X-ray showing lung damage from tuberculosis
SPL/Science Source

ATLAS OUTLINE

DEEPER INSIGHTS

Anatomy & Physiology
Revealed 4.0

Module 1: Body Orientation

A.1 General Anatomical Terminology

A.1a Anatomical Position

In describing the human body, anatomists assume that it is in **anatomical position (fig. A.1)**—that of a person standing upright with the feet flat on the floor, arms at the sides, and the palms and face directed forward. Without such a frame of reference, to say that a structure such as the sternum, thyroid gland, or aorta is "above the heart" would be vague, since it would depend on whether the subject was standing, lying face down *(prone),* or lying face up *(supine).* From the perspective of anatomical position, however, we can describe the thyroid as *superior* to the heart, the sternum as *anterior* to it, and the aorta as *posterior* to it. These descriptions remain valid regardless of the subject's position. Even if the body is lying down, such as a cadaver on the medical student's dissection table, to say the sternum is anterior to the heart invites the viewer to imagine the body is standing in anatomical position and not to call it "above the heart" simply because that is the way the body happens to be lying.

Unless stated otherwise, assume that all anatomical descriptions refer to anatomical position. Bear in mind that if a subject is facing you, the subject's left will be on your right and vice versa.

In most anatomical illustrations, for example, the left atrium of the heart appears toward the right side of the page, and although the appendix is located in the right lower quadrant of the abdomen, it appears on the left side of most illustrations.

A.1b Anatomical Planes

Many views of the body are based on real or imaginary "slices" called sections or planes. *Section* implies an actual cut or slice to reveal internal anatomy, whereas *plane* implies an imaginary flat surface passing through the body. The three primary anatomical planes are *sagittal, frontal,* and *transverse* (fig. A.1).

A **sagittal**[1] **plane** (SADJ-ih-tul) passes vertically through the body or an organ and divides it into right and left portions **(fig. A.2a).** The sagittal plane that divides the body or organ into equal halves is also called the **median (midsagittal) plane.** The head and pelvic organs are commonly illustrated on the median plane. Other sagittal planes parallel to this (off center) divide the body into unequal portions. Such planes are sometimes called *parasagittal*[2] planes.

A **frontal (coronal) plane** also extends vertically, but it is perpendicular to the sagittal plane and divides the body into anterior (front) and posterior (back) portions **(fig. A.2b).** A frontal section

---

[1] *sagitta* = arrow
[2] *para* = next to

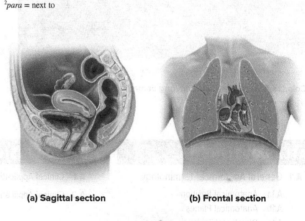

(a) Sagittal section   (b) Frontal section

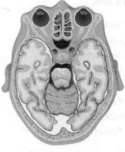

(c) Transverse section

FIGURE A.2 Body Sections Cut Along the Three Primary Anatomical Planes. (a) Sagittal section of the pelvic region. (b) Frontal section of the thoracic region. (c) Transverse section of the head at the level of the eyes.

FIGURE A.1 Anatomical Position and the Three Primary Anatomical Planes.

Joe DeGrandis/McGraw-Hill Education

TABLE A.1	Directional Terms in Human Anatomy A&PR	
Term	**Meaning**	**Examples of Usage**
Ventral	Toward the front* or belly	The aorta is ventral to the vertebral column.
Dorsal	Toward the back or spine	The vertebral column is dorsal to the aorta.
Anterior	Toward the ventral side*	The sternum is anterior to the heart.
Posterior	Toward the dorsal side*	The esophagus is posterior to the trachea.
Cephalic	Toward the head or superior end	The brain develops from the cephalic end of the neural tube.
Rostral	Toward the forehead or nose	The forebrain is rostral to the brainstem.
Caudal	Toward the tail or inferior end	The spinal cord is caudal to the brain.
Superior	Above	The heart is superior to the diaphragm.
Inferior	Below	The liver is inferior to the diaphragm.
Medial	Toward the median plane	The heart is medial to the lungs.
Lateral	Away from the median plane	The eyes are lateral to the nose.
Proximal	Closer to the point of attachment or origin	The elbow is proximal to the wrist.
Distal	Farther from the point of attachment or origin	The fingernails are at the distal ends of the fingers.
Ipsilateral	On the same side of the body (right or left)	The liver is ipsilateral to the appendix.
Contralateral	On opposite sides of the body (right and left)	The spleen is contralateral to the liver.
Superficial	Closer to the body surface	The skin is superficial to the muscles.
Deep	Farther from the body surface	The bones are deep to the muscles.

*In humans only; definition differs for other animals.

of the head, for example, would divide it into one portion bearing the face and another bearing the back of the head. Contents of the thoracic and abdominal cavities are most commonly shown as frontal sections.

A **transverse (horizontal) plane** passes across the body or an organ perpendicular to its long axis; it divides the body or organ into superior (upper) and inferior (lower) portions (**fig. A.2c**). CT scans are typically transverse sections (see fig. 1.11c).

A.1c Directional Terms

Words that describe the location of one structure relative to another are called the **directional terms** of anatomy. **Table A.1** summarizes those most frequently used. Most of these terms exist in pairs with opposite meanings: *anterior* versus *posterior, rostral* versus *caudal, superior* versus *inferior, medial* versus *lateral, proximal* versus *distal, ipsilateral* versus *contralateral,* and *superficial* versus *deep.* Intermediate directions are often indicated by combinations of these terms. For example, one's cheeks may be described as *inferolateral* to the eyes (below and to the side).

The terms *proximal* and *distal* are used especially in the anatomy of the limbs, with **proximal** used to denote something relatively close to the limb's point of attachment (the shoulder or hip) and **distal** to denote something farther away. These terms do have some applications to anatomy of the trunk, however—for example, in referring to certain aspects of the intestines and microscopic anatomy of the kidneys. But when describing the trunk and referring to a structure that lies above or below another, **superior** and **inferior** are the preferred terms. These terms are not usually used for the limbs. Although it may be technically correct, one would not generally say that the elbow is superior to the wrist, but proximal to it.

Because of the bipedal, upright stance of humans, some directional terms have different meanings for humans than they do for other animals. ***Anterior,*** for example, denotes the region of the body that leads the way in normal locomotion. For a four-legged animal such as a cat, this is the head end of the body; for a human, however, it is the front of the chest and abdomen. Thus, *anterior* has the same meaning as *ventral* for a human but not for a cat. ***Posterior*** denotes the region of the body that comes last in normal locomotion—the tail end of a cat but the dorsal side (back) of a human. In the anatomy of most other animals, *ventral* denotes the surface of the body closest to the ground and *dorsal* denotes the surface farthest away from the ground. These two words are too entrenched in human anatomy to completely ignore them, but we will minimize their use in this book to avoid confusion. You must keep such differences in mind, however, when dissecting other animals for comparison to human anatomy.

One vestige of the term *dorsal* is ***dorsum,*** used to denote the upper surface of the foot and the back of the hand. If you consider how a cat stands, the corresponding surfaces of its paws are uppermost, facing the same direction as the dorsal side of its trunk. Although these surfaces of the human hand and foot face entirely different directions in anatomical position, the term *dorsum* is still used.

A.2 Major Body Regions

Knowledge of the external anatomy and landmarks of the body is important in performing a physical examination and many other clinical procedures. For purposes of study, the body is divided into two major regions called the *axial* and *appendicular* regions. Smaller areas within the major regions are described in the following paragraphs and illustrated in **figure A.3.**

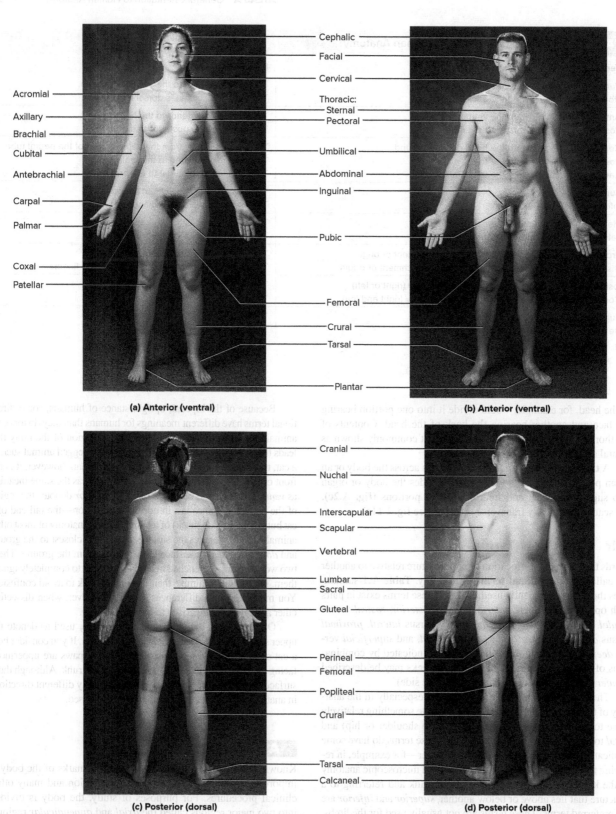

Cephalic
Facial
Cervical
Thoracic:
Sternal
Pectoral
Umbilical
Abdominal
Inguinal
Pubic
Femoral
Crural
Tarsal
Plantar

Acromial
Axillary
Brachial
Cubital
Antebrachial
Carpal
Palmar
Coxal
Patellar

(a) Anterior (ventral)

(b) Anterior (ventral)

Cranial
Nuchal
Interscapular
Scapular
Vertebral
Lumbar
Sacral
Gluteal
Perineal
Femoral
Popliteal
Crural
Tarsal
Calcaneal

(c) Posterior (dorsal)

(d) Posterior (dorsal)

FIGURE A.3   The Adult Female and Male Body Regions.   (a) Female, anterior. (b) Male, anterior. (c) Female, posterior. (d) Male, posterior.

a–d: Joe DeGrandis/McGraw-Hill Education

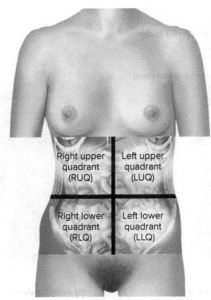

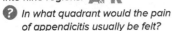

FIGURE A.4 The Four Quadrants and Nine Regions of the Abdomen. (a) External division into four quadrants. (b) External division into nine regions. **APR**

❓ *In what quadrant would the pain of appendicitis usually be felt?*

(a) Abdominopelvic quadrants

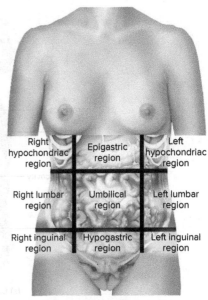

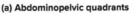

(b) Abdominopelvic regions

A.2a Axial Region

The **axial region** consists of the **head, neck (cervical**[3] **region),** and **trunk.** The trunk is further divided into the **thoracic region** above the diaphragm and the **abdominal region** below it.

One way of referring to the locations of abdominal structures is to divide the region into quadrants. Two perpendicular lines intersecting at the umbilicus (navel) divide the abdomen into a **right upper quadrant (RUQ), right lower quadrant (RLQ), left upper quadrant (LUQ),** and **left lower quadrant (LLQ) (fig. A.4a).** The quadrant scheme is often used to describe the site of an abdominal pain or abnormality.

The abdomen also can be divided into nine regions defined by four lines that intersect like a tic-tac-toe grid **(fig. A.4b).** Each vertical line is called a *midclavicular line* because it passes through the midpoint of the clavicle (collarbone). The superior horizontal line is called the *subcostal*[4] *line* because it connects the inferior borders of the lowest costal cartilages (cartilage connecting the tenth rib on each side to the inferior end of the sternum). The inferior horizontal line is called the *intertubercular*[5] *line* because it passes from left to right between the tubercles *(anterior superior spines)* of the pelvis—two points of bone located about where the front pockets open on most pants. The three lateral regions of this grid, from upper to lower, are the **hypochondriac,**[6] **lumbar,** and **inguinal**[7] **(iliac) regions.** The three medial regions from upper to lower are the **epigastric,**[8] **umbilical,** and **hypogastric (pubic) regions.**

A.2b Appendicular Region

The **appendicular region** (AP-en-DIC-you-lur) of the body consists of the **upper** and **lower limbs** (also called *appendages* or *extremities*). The upper limb includes the **arm (brachial region)** (BRAY-kee-ul), **forearm (antebrachial**[9] **region)** (AN-teh-BRAY-kee-ul), **wrist (carpal region), hand,** and **fingers (digits).** The lower limb includes the **thigh (femoral region), leg (crural region)** (CROO-rul), **ankle (tarsal region), foot,** and **toes (digits).** In strict anatomical terms, *arm* refers only to that part of the upper limb between the shoulder and elbow. *Leg* refers only to that part of the lower limb between the knee and ankle.

A **segment** of a limb is a region between one joint and the next. The arm, for example, is the segment between the shoulder and elbow joints, and the forearm is the segment between the elbow and wrist joints. Flexing your fingers, you can easily see that your thumb has two segments (proximal and distal), whereas the other four digits have three segments (proximal, middle, and distal). The segment concept is especially useful in describing the locations of bones and muscles and the movements of the joints.

A.3 Body Cavities and Membranes

The body wall encloses multiple **body cavities (fig. A.5, table A.2),** each lined with a membrane and containing internal organs called **viscera** (VISS-er-uh) (singular, *viscus*[10]). Some of these membranes are two-layered, having one layer against the organ surface (such as the heart or lung) and one layer against a surrounding structure (forming, for example, the inner lining of the rib cage); there

---

[3]*cervic* = neck
[4]*sub* = below; *cost* = rib
[5]*inter* = between; *tubercul* = little swelling
[6]*hypo* = below; *chondr* = cartilage
[7]*inguin* = groin
[8]*epi* = above, over; *gastr* = stomach

[9]*ante* = fore, before; *brachi* = arm
[10]*viscus* = body organ

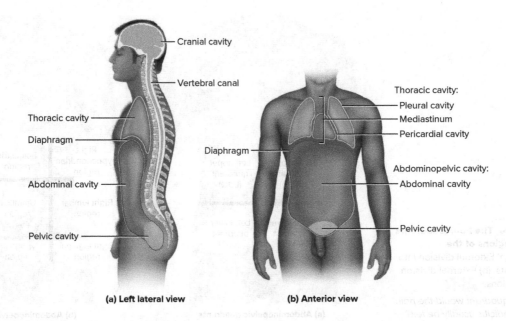

FIGURE A.5 **The Major Body Cavities.** (a) Left lateral view. (b) Anterior view.

TABLE A.2	Body Cavities and Membranes	APR
Name of Cavity	**Associated Viscera**	**Membranous Lining**
Cranial cavity	Brain	Meninges
Vertebral canal	Spinal cord	Meninges
Thoracic cavity		
Pleural cavities (2)	Lungs	Pleurae
Pericardial cavity	Heart	Pericardium
Abdominopelvic cavity		
Abdominal cavity	Digestive organs, spleen, kidneys	Peritoneum
Pelvic cavity	Bladder, rectum, reproductive organs	Peritoneum

is only a thin film of liquid between them. In such cases, the inner layer, against the organ, is called the **visceral layer** (VISS-er-ul) of the membrane, and the more superficial or outer one, the **parietal**[11] **layer** (pa-RY-eh-tul).

A.3a Cranial Cavity and Vertebral Canal

The **cranial cavity** is enclosed by the cranium (braincase) and contains the brain. The **vertebral canal** is enclosed by the vertebral column (spine) and contains the spinal cord. The two are continuous with each other and are lined by three membrane layers

called the **meninges** (meh-NIN-jeez). Among other functions, the meninges protect the delicate nervous tissue from the hard protective bone that encloses it.

A.3b Thoracic Cavity

The trunk of your body contains two major spaces, the thoracic cavity and abdominopelvic cavity, separated by a transverse muscular sheet, the **diaphragm.** Superior to the diaphragm, in your chest, is the **thoracic cavity,** and inferior to it, in your abdomen, is the **abdominopelvic cavity.** Both cavities are lined with thin **serous membranes,** which secrete a lubricating film of moisture similar to blood serum (hence their name).

The thoracic cavity is divided by a thick median wall called the **mediastinum**[12] (ME-dee-ah-STY-num) **(fig. A.5b).** This is the region between the lungs, extending from the base of the neck to the diaphragm. It is occupied by the heart, the major blood vessels connected to it, the esophagus, the trachea and bronchi, and a gland called the thymus.

The heart is enfolded in a two-layered membrane called the **pericardium.**[13] The inner layer of the pericardium forms the surface of the heart itself and is called the **visceral layer.** The outer layer is called the **parietal layer.** These layers are separated by a space called the **pericardial cavity (fig. A.6a),** which is lubricated by **pericardial fluid.** This space allows the heart freedom of movement during its contraction and relaxation, but can pose a life-threatening problem if it fills with serous fluid or blood (see Deeper Insight A.1).

[11]*pariet* = wall

[12]*mediastinum* = in the middle
[13]*peri* = around; *cardi* = heart

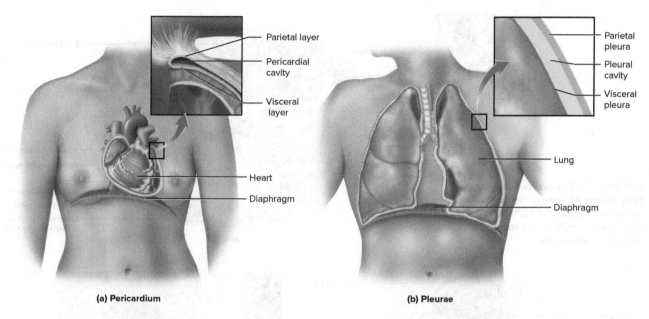

(a) Pericardium

(b) Pleurae

FIGURE A.6 Parietal and Visceral Layers of Double-Walled Membranes. (a) Relationship of the pericardium to the heart. (b) Relationship of the pleurae to the lungs.

 DEEPER INSIGHT A.1

CLINICAL APPLICATION

Cardiac Tamponade

Being confined by the pericardium can cause a problem for the heart under some circumstances. If a heart wall weakened by disease should rupture, or if it suffers a penetrating injury such as a knife or gunshot wound, blood spurts from the heart into the pericardial cavity, filling the cavity more and more with each heartbeat. Diseased hearts also sometimes seep serous fluid into the pericardial sac. Either way, the effect is the same: The pericardial sac has little room to expand, so the accumulating fluid puts pressure on the heart, squeezing it and preventing it from refilling between beats. This condition is called *cardiac tamponade*. If the heart chambers cannot refill, then cardiac output declines and a person may die of catastrophic circulatory failure. A similar situation occurs if serous fluid or air accumulates in the pleural cavity, causing collapse of a lung.

The right and left sides of the thoracic cavity contain the lungs. Each lung is enfolded by a serous membrane called the **pleura**[14] (PLOOR-uh) **(fig. A.6b).** Like the pericardium, the pleura has visceral (inner) and parietal (outer) layers. The **visceral pleura** forms the external surface of the lung, and the **parietal pleura** lines the inside of the rib cage. The narrow space between them is called the **pleural cavity** (see fig. B.11 in atlas B, following chapter 10). It is lubricated by slippery **pleural fluid.**

Note that in both the pericardium and the pleura, the visceral layer of the membrane *covers* an organ surface and the parietal layer *lines* the inside of a body cavity. We will see this pattern elsewhere, including the abdominopelvic cavity.

A.3c Abdominopelvic Cavity

The abdominopelvic cavity consists of the **abdominal cavity** superiorly and the **pelvic cavity** inferiorly. The abdominal cavity contains most of the digestive organs as well as the spleen, kidneys, and ureters. It extends inferiorly to the level of a bony landmark called the *brim* of the pelvis (see figs. B.7 and 8.36). The pelvic cavity, below the brim, is continuous with the abdominal cavity (no wall separates them), but it is markedly narrower and tilts posteriorly (see fig. A.5a). It contains the rectum, urinary bladder, urethra, and reproductive organs.

The abdominopelvic cavity contains a two-layered serous membrane called the **peritoneum**[15] (PERR-ih-toe-NEE-um). Its outer layer, the **parietal peritoneum,** lines the cavity wall. Along the posterior midline, it turns inward and becomes another layer, the **visceral peritoneum,** suspending certain abdominal viscera from the body wall, covering their outer surfaces, and holding them in place. The **peritoneal cavity** is the space between the parietal and visceral layers. It is lubricated by **peritoneal fluid.**

Some organs of the abdominal cavity lie against the posterior body wall and are covered by peritoneum only on the side facing the peritoneal cavity. They are said to have a **retroperitoneal**[16] position **(fig. A.7).** These include the kidneys, ureters, adrenal glands, most of the pancreas, and abdominal portions of two major blood vessels—the aorta and inferior vena cava (see fig. B.6). Organs that are encircled by peritoneum and connected to the posterior body wall by peritoneal sheets are described as **intraperitoneal.**[17]

The visceral peritoneum is also called a **mesentery**[18] (MESS-en-tare-ee) at points where it forms a translucent, membranous

[14]*pleur* = rib, side

[15]*peri* = around; *tone* = stretched
[16]*retro* = behind
[17]*intra* = within
[18]*mes* = in the middle; *enter* = intestine

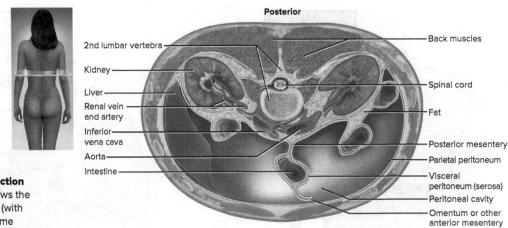

FIGURE A.7 Transverse Section Through the Abdomen. Shows the peritoneum, peritoneal cavity (with most viscera omitted), and some retroperitoneal organs.

Posterior

2nd lumbar vertebra
Kidney
Liver
Renal vein and artery
Inferior vena cava
Aorta
Intestine

Back muscles
Spinal cord
Fat
Posterior mesentery
Parietal peritoneum
Visceral peritoneum (serosa)
Peritoneal cavity
Omentum or other anterior mesentery

Anterior

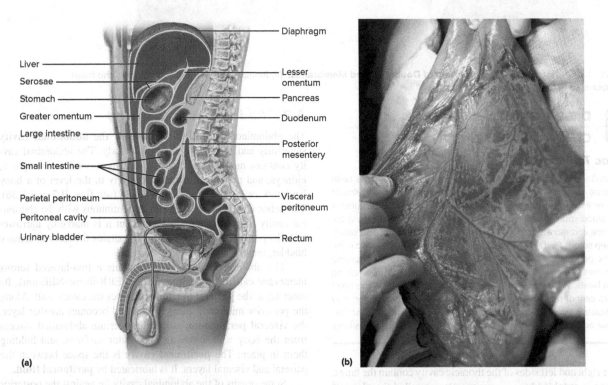

Diaphragm

Liver
Serosae
Stomach
Greater omentum
Large intestine
Small intestine
Parietal peritoneum
Peritoneal cavity
Urinary bladder

Lesser omentum
Pancreas
Duodenum
Posterior mesentery
Visceral peritoneum
Rectum

(a)   (b)

FIGURE A.8 Serous Membranes of the Abdominal Cavity. (a) Sagittal section, left lateral view. (b) Photo of the mesentery of the small intestine. Mesenteries contain blood vessels, lymphatic vessels, and nerves supplying the viscera. **APR**

❓ *Is the urinary bladder in the peritoneal cavity?*

b: MedicImage/Universal Images Group/Getty Images

curtain suspending and anchoring the viscera **(fig. A.8),** and a **serosa** (seer-OH-sa) at points where it enfolds and covers the outer surfaces of organs such as the stomach and small intestine. The intestines are suspended from the posterior (dorsal) abdominal wall by the **posterior mesentery.** The posterior mesentery of the large intestine is called the **mesocolon.** In some places, after wrapping around the intestines or other viscera, the mesentery continues toward the anterior body wall as the **anterior mesentery.** The most

significant example of this is a fatty membrane called the **greater omentum,**[19] which hangs like an apron from the inferolateral margin of the stomach and overlies the intestines (figs. A.8a and B.4). The greater omentum is unattached at its inferior border and can be lifted to reveal the intestines. A smaller **lesser omentum** extends from the superomedial margin of the stomach to the liver.

[19]*omentum* = covering

DEEPER INSIGHT A.2
CLINICAL APPLICATION

Peritonitis

Peritonitis is inflammation of the peritoneum. It is a critical, life-threatening condition necessitating prompt treatment. The most serious cause of peritonitis is a perforation in the digestive tract, such as a ruptured appendix or a gunshot wound. Digestive juices cause immediate chemical inflammation of the peritoneum, followed by microbial inflammation as intestinal bacteria invade the body cavity. Anything that perforates the abdominal wall can also lead to peritonitis, such as abdominal trauma or surgery. So, too, can free blood in the abdominal cavity, as from a ruptured aneurysm (a weak point in a blood vessel) or ectopic pregnancy (implantation of an embryo anywhere other than the uterus); blood itself is a chemical irritant to the peritoneum. Peritonitis tends to shift fluid from the circulation into the abdominal cavity. Death can follow within a few days from severe electrolyte imbalance, respiratory distress, kidney failure, and widespread blood clotting called *disseminated intravascular coagulation*.

A.3d Potential Spaces

Some of the spaces between body membranes are considered to be **potential spaces,** so named because under normal conditions, the membranes are pressed firmly together and there is no actual space between them. The membranes are not physically attached, however, and under unusual conditions, they may separate and create a space filled with fluid or other matter. Thus there is normally no actual space, but only a potential for membranes to separate and create one.

The pleural cavity is one example. Normally the parietal and visceral pleurae are pressed together without a gap between them, but under pathological conditions, air or serous fluid can accumulate between the membranes and open up a space. The internal cavity (**lumen**) of the uterus is another. In a nonpregnant uterus, the mucous membranes of opposite walls are pressed together so that there is no open space in the organ. In pregnancy, of course, a growing fetus occupies this space and pushes the mucous membranes apart.

A.4   Organ Systems

The human body has 11 **organ systems (fig. A.9)** and an immune system, which is better described as a population of cells that inhabit multiple organs rather than as an organ system. The organ systems are classified in the following list by their principal functions, but this is an unavoidably flawed classification. Some organs belong to two or more systems—for example, the male urethra is part of both the urinary and reproductive systems; the pharynx is part of the respiratory and digestive systems; and the mammary glands can be considered part of the integumentary and female reproductive systems. The organ systems are as follows:

Systems of protection, support, and movement
Integumentary system
Skeletal system
Muscular system

Systems of internal communication and control
Nervous system
Endocrine system

Systems of fluid transport
Circulatory system
Lymphatic system

Systems of intake and output
Respiratory system
Urinary system
Digestive system

Systems of reproduction
Male reproductive system
Female reproductive system

Some medical terms combine the names of two systems—for example, the *musculoskeletal system, cardiopulmonary system,* and *urogenital (genitourinary) system.* These terms serve to call attention to the close anatomical or physiological relationships between two systems, but these are not literally individual organ systems.

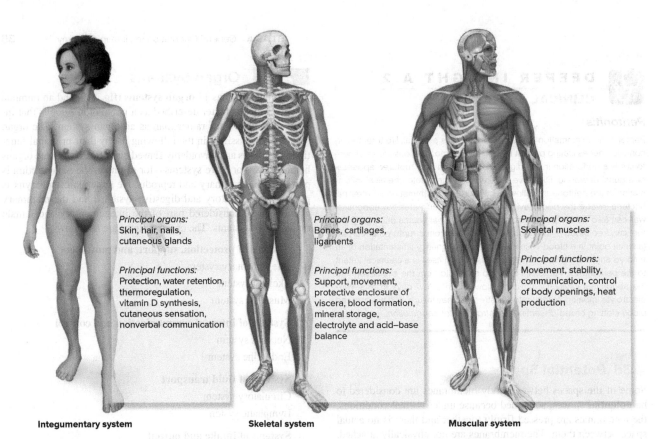

Integumentary system

Principal organs:
Skin, hair, nails,
cutaneous glands

Principal functions:
Protection, water retention,
thermoregulation,
vitamin D synthesis,
cutaneous sensation,
nonverbal communication

Skeletal system

Principal organs:
Bones, cartilages,
ligaments

Principal functions:
Support, movement,
protective enclosure of
viscera, blood formation,
mineral storage,
electrolyte and acid–base
balance

Muscular system

Principal organs:
Skeletal muscles

Principal functions:
Movement, stability,
communication, control
of body openings, heat
production

Lymphatic system

Principal organs:
Lymph nodes,
lymphatic vessels,
thymus, spleen, tonsils

Principal functions:
Recovery of excess
tissue fluid, detection of
pathogens, production
of immune cells, defense
against disease

Respiratory system

Principal organs:
Nose, pharynx, larynx,
trachea, bronchi, lungs

Principal functions:
Absorption of oxygen,
discharge of carbon
dioxide, acid–base
balance, speech

Urinary system

Principal organs:
Kidneys, ureters, urinary
bladder, urethra

Principal functions:
Elimination of wastes;
regulation of blood
volume and pressure;
stimulation of red blood
cell formation; control
of fluid, electrolyte,
and acid–base balance;
detoxification

FIGURE A.9 The Human Organ Systems.

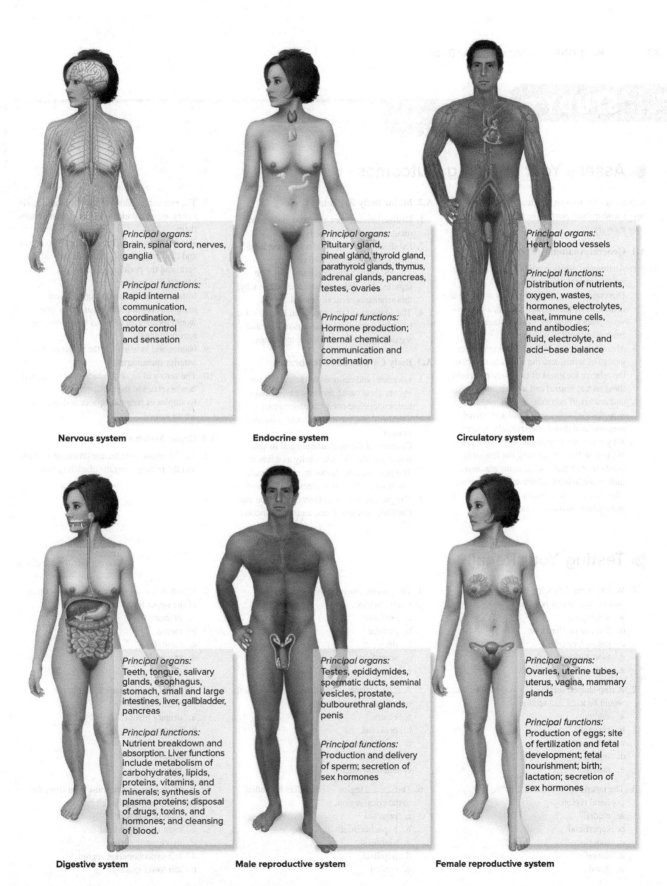

Nervous system

Principal organs:
Brain, spinal cord, nerves, ganglia

Principal functions:
Rapid internal communication, coordination, motor control and sensation

Endocrine system

Principal organs:
Pituitary gland, pineal gland, thyroid gland, parathyroid glands, thymus, adrenal glands, pancreas, testes, ovaries

Principal functions:
Hormone production; internal chemical communication and coordination

Circulatory system

Principal organs:
Heart, blood vessels

Principal functions:
Distribution of nutrients, oxygen, wastes, hormones, electrolytes, heat, immune cells, and antibodies; fluid, electrolyte, and acid–base balance

Digestive system

Principal organs:
Teeth, tongue, salivary glands, esophagus, stomach, small and large intestines, liver, gallbladder, pancreas

Principal functions:
Nutrient breakdown and absorption. Liver functions include metabolism of carbohydrates, lipids, proteins, vitamins, and minerals; synthesis of plasma proteins; disposal of drugs, toxins, and hormones; and cleansing of blood.

Male reproductive system

Principal organs:
Testes, epididymides, spermatic ducts, seminal vesicles, prostate, bulbourethral glands, penis

Principal functions:
Production and delivery of sperm; secretion of sex hormones

Female reproductive system

Principal organs:
Ovaries, uterine tubes, uterus, vagina, mammary glands

Principal functions:
Production of eggs; site of fertilization and fetal development; fetal nourishment; birth; lactation; secretion of sex hormones

FIGURE A.9 The Human Organ Systems (continued).

STUDY GUIDE

▶ Assess Your Learning Outcomes

To test your knowledge, discuss the following topics with a study partner or in writing, ideally from memory.

A.1 General Anatomical Terminology

1. Anatomical position and why it is important for anatomical description
2. Directions along which the body or an organ is divided by the sagittal, frontal, and transverse planes; how the median plane differs from other sagittal planes
3. Meanings of each of the following pairs or groups of terms, and the ability to describe the relative locations of two body parts using these terms: *ventral* and *dorsal; anterior* and *posterior; cephalic, rostral,* and *caudal; superior* and *inferior; medial* and *lateral; proximal* and *distal; superficial* and *deep*
4. Why the terms *ventral* and *dorsal* are ambiguous in human anatomy but less so in most other animals; what terms are used in their place in human anatomy; and reasons why they are occasionally appropriate or unavoidable in human anatomy

A.2 Major Body Regions

1. Distinctions between the axial and appendicular regions of the body
2. Subdivisions of the axial region and landmarks that divide and define them
3. The abdomen's four quadrants and nine regions; their defining landmarks; and why this scheme is clinically useful
4. The segments of the upper and lower limbs; how the anatomical meanings of *arm* and *leg* differ from the colloquial meanings

A.3 Body Cavities and Membranes

1. Locations and contents of the cranial cavity, vertebral canal, thoracic cavity, and abdominopelvic cavity; the membranes that line them; and the main viscera contained in each
2. Contents of the mediastinum and its relationship to the thoracic cavity as a whole
3. The pericardium, its two layers, the space and fluid between the layers, and its function
4. The pleurae, their two layers, the space and fluid between the layers, and their function

5. The two subdivisions of the abdominopelvic cavity and the skeletal landmark that divides them
6. The peritoneum; its functions; its two layers and their relationship to the abdominal viscera; and the peritoneal fluid
7. Mesenteries and serosae
8. Intraperitoneal versus retroperitoneal organs, examples of both, and how one would identify an organ as being intra- or retroperitoneal
9. Names and locations of the posterior and anterior mesenteries
10. The serosa of an abdominopelvic organ and how it relates to the peritoneum
11. Examples of potential spaces and why they are so named

A.4 Organ Systems

1. The 11 organ systems, the functions of each, and the principal organs of each system

▶ Testing Your Recall

Answers in Appendix A

1. Which of the following is *not* an essential part of anatomical position?
   a. feet together
   b. feet flat on the floor
   c. palms forward
   d. mouth closed
   e. arms down to the sides

2. A ring-shaped section of the small intestine would be a _____ section.
   a. sagittal
   b. coronal
   c. transverse
   d. frontal
   e. median

3. The tarsal region is _____ to the popliteal region.
   a. medial
   b. superficial
   c. superior
   d. dorsal
   e. distal

4. The greater omentum is _____ to the small intestine.
   a. posterior
   b. parietal
   c. deep
   d. superficial
   e. proximal

5. A _____ plane passes through the sternum, umbilicus, and mons pubis.
   a. central
   b. proximal
   c. midclavicular
   d. midsagittal
   e. intertubercular

6. The _____ region is immediately medial to the coxal region.
   a. inguinal
   b. hypochondriac
   c. umbilical
   d. popliteal
   e. cubital

7. Which of the following regions is not part of the upper limb?
   a. plantar
   b. carpal
   c. cubital
   d. brachial
   e. palmar

8. Which of these organs is within the peritoneal cavity?
   a. urinary bladder
   b. kidneys
   c. heart
   d. liver
   e. brain

9. In which area do you think pain from the gallbladder would be felt?
   a. umbilical region
   b. right upper quadrant
   c. hypogastric region
   d. left hypochondriac region
   e. left lower quadrant

STUDY GUIDE

10. Which organ system regulates blood volume, controls acid–base balance, and stimulates red blood cell production?
    a. digestive system
    b. lymphatic system
    c. nervous system
    d. urinary system
    e. circulatory system

11. The translucent membranes that suspend the intestines and hold them in place are called _____.

12. The superficial layer of the pleura is called the _____ pleura.

13. The right and left pleural cavities are separated by a thick wall called the _____.

14. The back of the neck is the _____ region.

15. If two organs are on opposite sides of the body (right and left), we say they are _____ to each other.

16. The cranial cavity is lined by membranes called the _____.

17. Organs that lie within the abdominal cavity but not within the peritoneal cavity are said to have a _____ position.

18. The sternal region is _____ to the pectoral region.

19. The pelvic cavity can be described as _____ to the abdominal cavity in position.

20. The anterior pit of the elbow is the _____ region, and the corresponding (but posterior) pit of the knee is the _____ region.

▶ Building Your Medical Vocabulary

Answers in Appendix A

State a meaning of each word element, and give a medical term from this atlas that uses it or a slight variation of it.

1. ante-

2. cervico-

3. epi-

4. hypo-

5. inguino-

6. intra-

7. parieto-

8. peri-

9. retro-

10. sagitto-

▶ What's Wrong with These Statements?

Answers in Appendix A

Briefly explain why each of the following statements is false, or reword it to make it true.

1. Both lungs could be shown in one sagittal section of the body.

2. A single frontal section of the head cannot include both eyes.

3. The knee is distal to the tarsal region.

4. The diaphragm is posterior to the lungs.

5. The esophagus is inferior to the stomach.

6. The liver is in the lumbar region.

7. The heart is in the space between the parietal and visceral pericardium, called the pericardial cavity.

8. The kidneys are in the peritoneal cavity of the abdomen.

9. The peritoneum lines the inside of the stomach and intestines.

10. The sigmoid colon is in the lower right quadrant of the abdomen.

▶ Testing Your Comprehension

1. Identify which anatomical plane—sagittal, frontal, or transverse—is the only one that could *not* show (a) both the brain and tongue, (b) both eyes, (c) both the hypogastric and gluteal regions, (d) both kidneys, (e) both the sternum and vertebral column, and (f) both the heart and uterus.

2. Laypeople often misunderstand anatomical terminology. What do you think people

really mean when they say they have "planter's warts"?

3. Name one structure or anatomical feature that could be found in each of the following locations relative to the ribs: medial, lateral, superior, inferior, deep, superficial, posterior, and anterior. Try not to use the same example twice.

4. Based on the illustrations in this atlas, identify an internal organ that is (a) in the upper left quadrant and retroperitoneal, (b) in the lower right quadrant of the peritoneal cavity, (c) in the hypogastric region, (d) in the right hypochondriac region, and (e) in the pectoral region.

5. Why do you think people with imaginary illnesses came to be called hypochondriacs?

CHAPTER

3

CELLULAR FORM AND FUNCTION

Dividing cancer cells from an adenocarcinoma. Adenocarcinoma is a tumor arising from glands in the mucous membrane of an organ such as the lung.
Eye of Science/Science Source

Anatomy & Physiology
Revealed 4.0

Module 2: Cells and Chemistry

BRUSHING UP

BRUSHING UP

- The transport of matter through cell membranes follows the principles of flow down gradients (see section 1.6e).

- To adequately understand the structure of the cell surface, it is essential that you understand glycolipids and glycoproteins, as well as phospholipids and their amphipathic nature (see sections 2.4c and 2.4d).

- The proteins of cell membranes have a great variety of functions. To understand those depends on an acquaintance with the functions of proteins in general and how protein function depends on tertiary structure (see "Protein Structure" and "Protein Functions" in section 2.4e).

All organisms, from the simplest to the most complex, are composed of cells—whether the single cell of a bacterium or the trillions of cells that constitute the human body. These cells are responsible for all structural and functional properties of a living organism. A knowledge of cells is therefore indispensable to any true understanding of the workings of the human body, the mechanisms of disease, and the rationale of therapy. Thus, this chapter and the next one introduce the basic cell biology of the human body, and subsequent chapters expand upon this information as we examine the specialized cellular structure and function of specific organs.

3.1 Concepts of Cellular Structure

Expected Learning Outcomes

When you have completed this section, you should be able to

a. discuss the development and modern tenets of the cell theory;

b. describe cell shapes from their descriptive terms;

c. state the size range of human cells and discuss factors that limit their size;

d. discuss the way that developments in microscopy have changed our view of cell structure; and

e. outline the major components of a cell.

3.1a Development of the Cell Theory

Cytology,[1] the scientific study of cells, was born in 1663 when Robert Hooke observed the empty cell walls of cork and coined the word *cellulae* ("little cells") to describe them (see section 1.2). Soon he studied thin slices of fresh wood and saw living cells "filled with juices"—a fluid later named *cytoplasm*. Two centuries later, Theodor Schwann studied a wide range of animal tissues and concluded that all animals are made of cells.

Schwann and other biologists originally believed that cells came from nonliving body fluid that somehow congealed and acquired a membrane and nucleus. This idea of *spontaneous generation*—that living things arise from nonliving matter—was rooted in the scientific thought of the times. For centuries, it seemed to be simple common sense that decaying meat turned into maggots, stored grain into rodents, and mud into frogs. Schwann and his contemporaries merely extended this idea to cells. The idea of spontaneous generation wasn't discredited until some classic experiments by French microbiologist Louis Pasteur in 1859.

By the end of the nineteenth century, it was established beyond all reasonable doubt that cells arise only from other cells and every living organism is composed of cells and cell products. The cell came to be regarded, and still is, as the simplest structural and functional unit of life. There are no smaller subdivisions of a cell or organism that, in themselves, have all or most of the fundamental characteristics of life described in section 1.6a. Enzymes and organelles, for example, are not alive, although the life of a cell depends on their activity.

The development of biochemistry from the late nineteenth to the twentieth century made it further apparent that all physiological processes of the body are based on cellular activity and that the cells of all species exhibit remarkable biochemical unity. The various generalizations of these last two paragraphs now constitute the modern **cell theory.**

3.1b Cell Shapes and Sizes

We will shortly examine the structure of a generic cell, but the generalizations we draw shouldn't blind you to the diversity of cellular form and function in humans. There are about 200 kinds of cells in the human body, with a variety of shapes, sizes, and functions.

Descriptions of organ and tissue structure often refer to the shapes of cells by the following terms **(fig. 3.1):**

- **Squamous**[2] (SKWAY-mus)—a thin, flat, scaly shape, often with a bulge where the nucleus is, much like the shape of a fried egg "sunny side up." Squamous cells line the esophagus and form the surface layer (epidermis) of the skin.

- **Cuboidal**[3] (cue-BOY-dul)—squarish-looking in frontal sections and about equal in height and width; liver cells are a good example.

- **Columnar**—distinctly taller than wide, such as the inner lining cells of the stomach and intestines.

- **Polygonal**[4]—having irregularly angular shapes with four, five, or more sides.

- **Stellate**[5]—having multiple pointed processes projecting from the body of a cell, giving it a somewhat starlike shape. The cell bodies of many nerve cells are stellate.

---

[1]*cyto* = cell; *logy* = study of

[2]*squam* = scale; *ous* = characterized by
[3]*cub* = cube; *oidal* = like, resembling
[4]*poly* = many; *gon* = angles
[5]*stell* = star; *ate* = resembling, characterized by

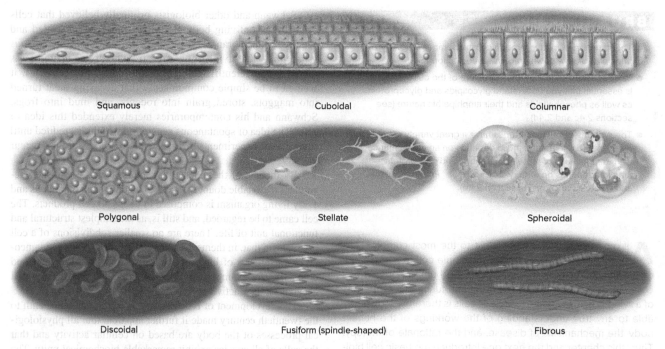

Squamous

Cuboidal

Columnar

Polygonal

Stellate

Spheroidal

Discoidal

Fusiform (spindle-shaped)

Fibrous

FIGURE 3.1 Common Cell Shapes. APR

- **Spheroidal** to **ovoid**—round to oval, as in egg cells and white blood cells.
- **Discoidal**—disc-shaped, as in red blood cells.
- **Fusiform**[6] (FEW-zih-form)—spindle-shaped; elongated, with a thick middle and tapered ends, as in smooth muscle cells.
- **Fibrous**—long, slender, and threadlike, as in skeletal muscle cells and the axons (nerve fibers) of nerve cells.

Some of these shapes refer to the way a cell looks in typical tissue sections, not to the complete three-dimensional shape of the cell. A cell that looks squamous, cuboidal, or columnar in a tissue section, for example, usually looks polygonal if viewed from its upper surface.

The most useful unit of measure for designating cell sizes is the **micrometer (μm)**, formerly called the micron—one-millionth (10^{-6}) of a meter, one-thousandth (10^{-3}) of a millimeter. (See appendix B for units of measurement.) The smallest objects most people can see with the naked eye are about 100 μm, which is about one-quarter the size of the period at the end of a typical sentence of print. A few human cells fall within this range, such as the egg cell and some fat cells, but most human cells are about 10 to 15 μm wide. The longest human cells are nerve cells (sometimes over a meter long) and muscle cells

(up to 30 cm long), but both are usually too slender to be seen with the naked eye.

There are several factors that limit the size of cells. If a cell swelled to excessive size, it could rupture like an overfilled water balloon. In addition, cell size is limited by the relationship between its volume and surface area. The surface area of a cell is proportional to the square of its diameter, while volume is proportional to the cube of its diameter. Thus, for a given increase in diameter, volume increases much more than surface area. Picture a cuboidal cell 10 μm on each side **(fig. 3.2).** It would have a surface area of 600 μm^2 (10 μm × 10 μm × 6 sides) and a volume of 1,000 μm^3 (10 × 10 × 10 μm). Now, suppose it grew by another 10 μm on each side. Its new surface area would be 2,400 μm^2 (20 μm × 20 μm × 6) and its volume would be 8,000 μm^3 (20 × 20 × 20 μm). The 20 μm cell has eight times as much cytoplasm needing nourishment and waste removal, but only four times as much membrane surface through which wastes and nutrients can be exchanged. A cell that is too big cannot support itself.

Further, if a cell were too large, molecules couldn't diffuse from place to place fast enough to support its metabolism. The time required for diffusion is proportional to the square of distance, so if a cell diameter doubled, the travel time for molecules within the cell would increase fourfold. For example, if it took 10 seconds for a molecule to diffuse from the surface to the center of a cell with a 10 μm radius, then we increased the cell radius to 1 mm, it would take 278 hours to reach the center—far too slow to support the cell's life activities.

---

[6]*fusi* = spindle; *form* = shape

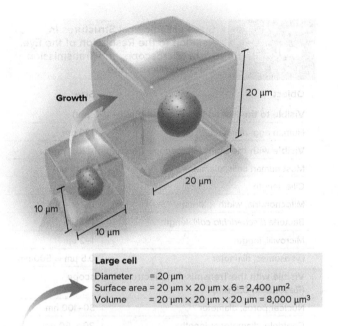

Large cell

Diameter   = 20 μm
Surface area = 20 μm × 20 μm × 6 = 2,400 μm^2
Volume   = 20 μm × 20 μm × 20 μm = 8,000 μm^3

Small cell

Diameter   = 10 μm
Surface area = 10 μm × 10 μm × 6 = 600 μm^2
Volume   = 10 μm × 10 μm × 10 μm = 1,000 μm^3

Effect of cell growth:

Diameter (*D*) increased by a factor of 2
Surface area increased by a factor of 4 (= *D*^{2})
Volume increased by a factor of 8 (= *D*^{3})

FIGURE 3.2 The Relationship Between Cell Surface Area and Volume. As a cell doubles in diameter, its volume increases eightfold, but its surface area increases only fourfold. A cell that is too large may have too little plasma membrane to serve the metabolic needs of the increased volume of cytoplasm.

Having organs composed of many small cells instead of fewer large ones has another advantage. The death of one or a few cells has less effect on the structure and function of the whole organ.

3.1c Basic Components of a Cell

In Schwann's time, little was known about cells except that they were enclosed in a membrane and contained a nucleus. The fluid between the nucleus and surface membrane, its **cytoplasm,**[7] was thought to be little more than a gelatinous mixture of chemicals and vaguely defined particles. The **transmission electron microscope (TEM),** invented in the mid-twentieth century, radically changed this concept. Using a beam of electrons in place of light, the TEM enabled biologists to see a cell's *ultrastructure,* a fine degree of detail extending even to the molecular level. The most important thing about a good microscope is not magnification but

[7]*cyto* = cell; *plasm* = formed, molded

resolution—the ability to reveal detail. Any image can be photographed and enlarged as much as we wish, but if enlargement fails to reveal any more useful detail, it is *empty magnification.* A big blurry image is not nearly as informative as one that is small and sharp. The TEM reveals far more detail than the light microscope (LM) **(fig. 3.3).** A later invention, the **scanning electron microscope (SEM),** produces dramatic three-dimensional images at high magnification and resolution (see fig. 3.10a), but can view only surface features.

A stunning application of SEM, often seen in this book, is the *vascular corrosion cast* technique for visualizing the blood vessels of an organ. The vessels are drained and flushed with saline, then carefully filled with a resin. After the resin solidifies, the actual tissue is dissolved with a corrosive agent such as potassium hydroxide. This leaves only a resin cast of the vessels, which is then photographed with the SEM. The resulting images are not only strikingly beautiful, but also give great insights into the blood supply to an organ from macro- to microscopic levels (see figs. 19.10c, 23.10a, and the opening page of chapter 17).

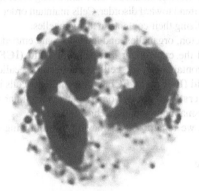

(a) Light microscope (LM)

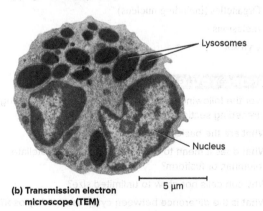

Lysosomes

Nucleus

5 μm

(b) Transmission electron microscope (TEM)

FIGURE 3.3 Magnification Versus Resolution. Two white blood cells (neutrophils) shown at the same magnification. (a) Photographed with the light microscope (LM). (b) Photographed with the transmission electron microscope (TEM). Note the finer detail (resolution) obtained with the TEM.

a: Alvin Telser/McGraw-Hill Education; b: Biophoto Associates/Science Source

Table 3.1 gives the sizes of some cells and subcellular objects relative to the resolution of the naked eye, light microscope, and TEM. You can see why the very existence of cells was unsuspected until the light microscope was invented, and why little was known about their internal components until the TEM became available.

Figure 3.4 shows some major constituents of a typical cell. The cell is surrounded by a **plasma (cell) membrane** made of proteins and lipids. The composition and functions of this membrane can differ significantly from one region of a cell to another, especially between the basal, lateral, and apical (upper) surfaces of cells like the one pictured.

The cytoplasm is crowded with fibers, tubules, passages, and compartments. It contains the *cytoskeleton,* a supportive framework of protein filaments and tubules; an abundance of *organelles,* diverse structures that perform various metabolic tasks for the cell; and *inclusions,* which are foreign matter or stored cell products. A cell may have 10 billion protein molecules, including potent enzymes with the potential to destroy the cell if they're not contained and isolated from other cellular components. You can imagine the enormous problem of keeping track of all this material, directing molecules to the correct destinations, and maintaining order against nature's incessant trend toward disorder. Cells maintain order partly by compartmentalizing their contents in the organelles.

The cytoskeleton, organelles, and inclusions are embedded in a clear gel called the **cytosol**[8] or **intracellular fluid (ICF).** All body fluids not contained in the cells are collectively called the **extracellular fluid (ECF).** The ECF located amid the cells is also called **tissue (interstitial) fluid.** Some other extracellular fluids include blood plasma, lymph, and cerebrospinal fluid.

In summary, we regard cells as having the following major components:

Plasma membrane

Cytoplasm

    Cytoskeleton

    Organelles (including nucleus)

    Inclusions

    Cytosol

BEFORE YOU GO ON

Answer the following questions to test your understanding of the preceding section:

1. What are the basic principles of the cell theory?
2. What does it mean to say a cell is squamous, stellate, columnar, or fusiform?
3. Why can cells not grow to unlimited size?
4. What is the difference between cytoplasm and cytosol?
5. Define *intracellular fluid (ICF)* and *extracellular fluid (ECF).*

---

[8]*cyto* = cell; *sol* = dissolved matter

TABLE 3.1	Sizes of Biological Structures in Relation to the Resolution of the Eye, Light Microscope, and Transmission Electron Microscope
Object	**Size**
Visible to the Naked Eye (Resolution 70–100 µm)	
Human egg, diameter	100 µm
Visible with the Light Microscope (Resolution 200 nm)	
Most human cells, diameter	10–15 µm
Cilia, length	7–10 µm
Mitochondria, width × length	0.2 × 4 µm
Bacteria *(Escherichia coli),* length	1–3 µm
Microvilli, length	1–2 µm
Lysosomes, diameter	0.5 µm = 500 nm
Visible with the Transmission Electron Microscope (Resolution 0.5 nm)	
Nuclear pores, diameter	30–100 nm
Centriole, diameter × length	20 × 50 nm
Poliovirus, diameter	30 nm
Ribosomes, diameter	15 nm
Globular proteins, diameter	5–10 nm
Plasma membrane, thickness	7.5 nm
DNA molecule, diameter	2.0 nm
Plasma membrane channels, diameter	0.8 nm

3.2   **The Cell Surface**

Expected Learning Outcomes

When you have completed this section, you should be able to

a. describe the structure of the plasma membrane;
b. explain the functions of the lipid, protein, and carbohydrate components of the plasma membrane;
c. describe a second-messenger system and discuss its importance in human physiology;
d. explain the composition and functions of the glycocalyx that coats cell surfaces; and
e. describe the structure and functions of microvilli, cilia, flagella, and pseudopods.

Many physiologically important processes occur at the surface of a cell—immune responses, the binding of egg and sperm, cell-to-cell signaling by hormones, and the detection of tastes and smells, for example. A substantial part of this chapter is therefore

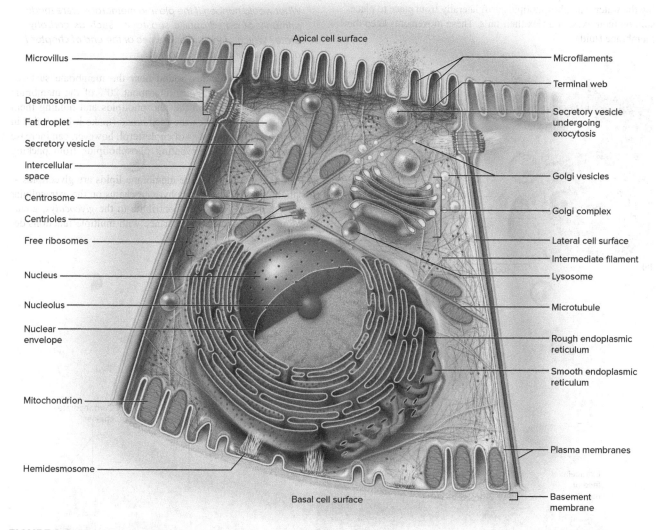

Apical cell surface

Microvillus

Desmosome

Fat droplet

Secretory vesicle

Intercellular space

Centrosome

Centrioles

Free ribosomes

Nucleus

Nucleolus

Nuclear envelope

Mitochondrion

Hemidesmosome

Basal cell surface

Microfilaments

Terminal web

Secretory vesicle undergoing exocytosis

Golgi vesicles

Golgi complex

Lateral cell surface

Intermediate filament

Lysosome

Microtubule

Rough endoplasmic reticulum

Smooth endoplasmic reticulum

Plasma membranes

Basement membrane

FIGURE 3.4 Structure of a Representative Cell.

concerned with the cell surface. Like explorers of a new continent, we will examine the interior only after we've investigated its coastline. In this section, we examine the structure of the plasma membrane, surface features such as cilia and microvilli, and methods of transport through the membrane.

3.2a The Plasma Membrane

The plasma membrane defines the boundaries of the cell, governs its interactions with other cells, and controls the passage of materials into and out of the cell. It appears to the electron microscope as a pair of dark parallel lines with a total thickness of about

7.5 nm (**fig. 3.5a**). The side that faces the cytoplasm is the *intracellular face* of the membrane, and the side that faces outward is the *extracellular face*. Similar membranes enclose most of a cell's organelles and control their uptake and release of chemicals.

Membrane Lipids

Figure 3.5b shows our current concept of the molecular structure of the plasma membrane—an oily film of lipids with proteins embedded in it. Typically about 98% of the membrane molecules are lipids, and about 75% of those are phospholipids. These amphipathic molecules arrange themselves into a bilayer, with their hydrophilic phosphate-containing heads facing the water on each side and their hydrophobic tails directed toward the center, avoiding the water. The phospholipids drift laterally from place to place, spin on their axes, and flex their tails. These movements keep the membrane fluid.

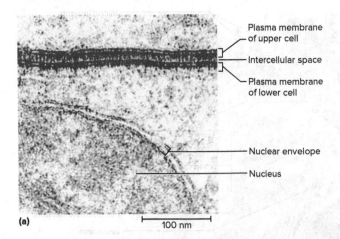

(a)

|← 100 nm →|

▶▶▶**APPLY WHAT YOU KNOW**

What would happen if the plasma membrane were made primarily of a hydrophilic substance such as carbohydrate? Which of the major themes at the end of chapter 1 does this point best exemplify?

Cholesterol molecules, found near the membrane surfaces amid the phospholipids, constitute about 20% of the membrane lipids. By interacting with the phospholipids and holding them still, cholesterol can stiffen the membrane (make it less fluid) in spots. Higher concentrations of cholesterol, however, can increase membrane fluidity by preventing phospholipids from packing closely together.

The remaining 5% of the membrane lipids are glycolipids—phospholipids with short carbohydrate chains on the extracellular face of the membrane. They contribute to the *glycocalyx*, a carbohydrate coating on the cell surface with multiple functions described shortly.

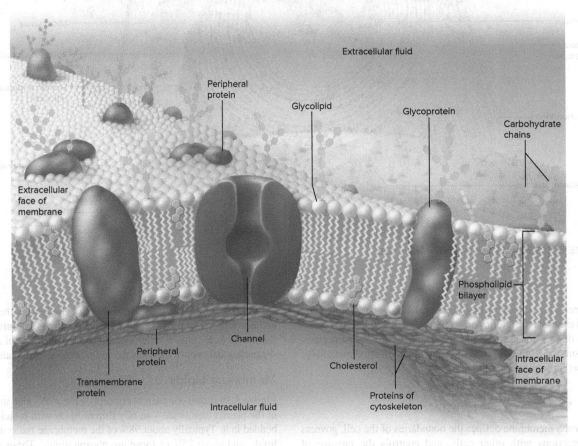

(b)

FIGURE 3.5 The Plasma Membrane. (a) Plasma membranes of two adjacent cells (TEM). (b) Molecular structure of the plasma membrane.

Membrane Proteins

Although proteins are only about 2% of the molecules of the plasma membrane, they are larger than lipids and average about 50% of the membrane weight. There are two broad classes of membrane proteins: transmembrane and peripheral. **Transmembrane proteins** pass completely through the phospholipid bilayer. They have hydrophilic regions in contact with the water on both sides of the membrane, and hydrophobic regions that pass back and forth through the lipid **(fig. 3.6).** Most transmembrane proteins are glycoproteins, bound to oligosaccharides on the extracellular side of the membrane. Many of these proteins drift about freely in the phospholipid film, like ice cubes floating in a bowl of water. Others are anchored to the *cytoskeleton*—an intracellular system of tubules and filaments discussed later. **Peripheral proteins** do not protrude into the phospholipid layer but adhere to either the inner or outer face of the membrane. Those on the inner face are typically anchored to a transmembrane protein as well as to the cytoskeleton.

The functions of membrane proteins include:

- **Receptors (fig. 3.7a).** Many of the chemical signals by which cells communicate (epinephrine, for example) cannot enter the target cell but bind to surface proteins called receptors. Receptors are usually specific for one particular messenger, much like an enzyme that is specific for one substrate. Plasma membranes also have receptor proteins that bind chemicals and transport them into the cell, as discussed later in this chapter.

- **Second-messenger systems.** When a messenger binds to a surface receptor, it may trigger changes within the cell that produce a second messenger in the cytoplasm. This process involves both transmembrane proteins (the receptors) and peripheral proteins. Second-messenger systems are also discussed later in more detail.

- **Enzymes (fig. 3.7b).** Enzymes in the plasma membrane carry out the final stages of starch and protein digestion in the small intestine, help produce second messengers, and break down hormones and other signaling molecules whose job is done, thus stopping them from excessively stimulating a cell.

- **Channel proteins (fig. 3.7c).** Channels are passages that allow water and hydrophilic solutes to move through the membrane. A channel is a tunnel that passes through a complex of multiple proteins or between subunits of an individual protein. Some of them, called **leak channels,** are always open and allow materials to pass through continually. Others, called **gates (gated channels),** open and close under different circumstances and allow solutes through at some times, but not others **(fig. 3.7d).** These gates respond to three types of stimuli: **ligand-gated channels** respond to chemical messengers, **voltage-gated channels** to changes in electrical potential (voltage) across the plasma membrane, and **mechanically gated channels** to physical stress on a cell, such as stretch and pressure. By controlling the movement of electrolytes through the plasma membrane, gated channels play an important role in the timing of nerve signals and muscle contraction (see Deeper Insight 3.1). Some receptors double in function as gated channels. When a nerve stimulates a muscle, for example, a chemical from the nerve fiber binds to a receptor on the muscle fiber and the receptor opens to allow sodium and potassium ions to flow through and excite the muscle. Defects in channel proteins are responsible for a family of diseases called *channelopathies.*

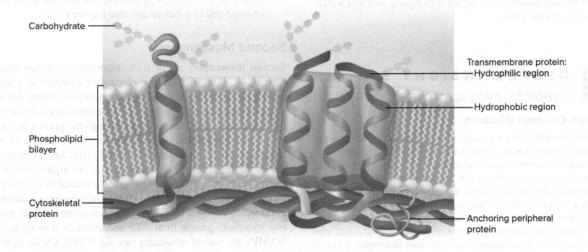

Carbohydrate

Phospholipid bilayer

Cytoskeletal protein

Transmembrane protein:
Hydrophilic region

Hydrophobic region

Anchoring peripheral protein

FIGURE 3.6 Transmembrane Proteins. A transmembrane protein has hydrophobic regions embedded in the phospholipid bilayer and hydrophilic regions projecting into the intracellular and extracellular fluids. The protein may cross the membrane once (left) or multiple times (right). The intracellular regions are often anchored to the cytoskeleton by peripheral proteins.

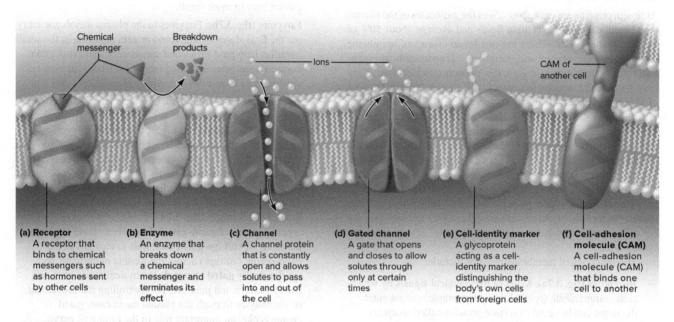

FIGURE 3.7 Some Functions of Membrane Proteins.

(a) Receptor A receptor that binds to chemical messengers such as hormones sent by other cells	**(b) Enzyme** An enzyme that breaks down a chemical messenger and terminates its effect

(c) Channel A channel protein that is constantly open and allows solutes to pass into and out of the cell

(d) Gated channel A gate that opens and closes to allow solutes through only at certain times

(e) Cell-identity marker A glycoprotein acting as a cell-identity marker distinguishing the body's own cells from foreign cells

(f) Cell-adhesion molecule (CAM) A cell-adhesion molecule (CAM) that binds one cell to another

- **Carriers** (see fig. 3.17). Carriers are transmembrane proteins that bind to glucose, electrolytes, and other solutes and transfer them to the other side of the membrane. Some carriers, called **pumps,** consume ATP in the process.
- **Cell-identity markers** (fig. 3.7e). Glycoproteins contribute to the glycocalyx, which acts like an "identification tag" that enables our bodies to tell which cells belong to it and which are foreign invaders.

- **Cell-adhesion molecules (fig. 3.7f).** Cells adhere to one another and to extracellular material through membrane proteins called cell-adhesion molecules (CAMs). With few exceptions (such as blood cells and metastasizing cancer cells), cells don't grow or survive normally unless they're mechanically linked to the extracellular material. Special events such as sperm–egg binding and the binding of an immune cell to a cancer cell also require CAMs.

Second Messengers

Second messengers are of such importance that they require a closer look. You will find this information essential for your later understanding of hormone and neurotransmitter action. Let's consider how the hormone epinephrine stimulates a cell. Epinephrine, the "first messenger," cannot pass through the plasma membrane, so it binds to a surface receptor. The receptor is linked on the intracellular side to a peripheral **G protein (fig. 3.8).** G proteins are named for the ATP-like chemical, guanosine triphosphate (GTP), from which they get their energy. When activated by the receptor, a G protein relays the signal to another membrane protein, **adenylate cyclase** (ah-DEN-ih-late SY-clase). Adenylate cyclase removes two phosphate groups from ATP and converts it to **cyclic AMP (cAMP),** the second messenger (see fig. 2.29b). Cyclic AMP then activates cytoplasmic enzymes called **kinases** (KY-nace-es), which add phosphate groups to other cellular enzymes. This activates some enzymes and deactivates others, but either way, it triggers a great variety of physiological changes within the cell. Up to 60% of drugs work by altering the activity of G proteins.

DEEPER INSIGHT 3.1
CLINICAL APPLICATION

Calcium Channel Blockers

Calcium channel blockers are a class of drugs that show the therapeutic relevance of understanding gated membrane channels. The walls of the arteries contain smooth muscle that contracts or relaxes to change their diameter. These changes modify the blood flow and strongly influence blood pressure. Blood pressure rises when the arteries constrict and falls when they relax and dilate. Excessive, widespread vasoconstriction can cause hypertension (high blood pressure), and vasoconstriction in the coronary blood vessels of the heart can cause pain (angina) due to inadequate blood flow to the cardiac muscle. In order to contract, a smooth muscle cell must open calcium channels in its plasma membrane and allow calcium to enter from the extracellular fluid. Calcium channel blockers prevent these channels from opening and thereby relax the arteries, increase blood flow, relieve angina, and lower the blood pressure.

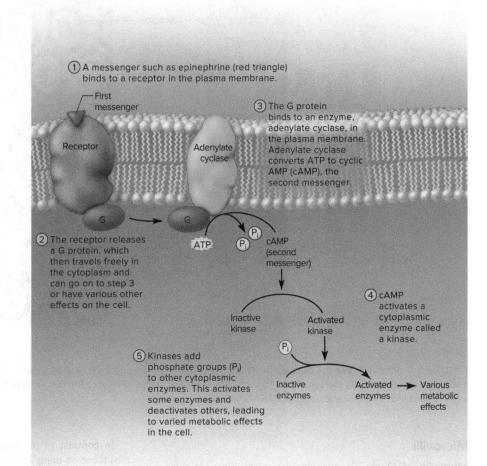

FIGURE 3.8 A Second-Messenger System.

 Is adenylate cyclase a transmembrane protein or a peripheral protein? What about the G protein?

3.2b The Glycocalyx

External to the plasma membrane, all animal cells have a fuzzy coat called the **glycocalyx**[9] (GLY-co-CAY-licks) **(fig. 3.9),** composed of the carbohydrate moieties of membrane glycolipids and glycoproteins. It is chemically unique in everyone but identical twins, and acts like an identification tag that enables the body to distinguish its own healthy cells from transplanted tissues, invading organisms, and diseased cells. Human blood types and transfusion compatibility are determined by glycolipids. Functions of the glycocalyx are summarized in **table 3.2.**

3.2c Extensions of the Cell Surface

Many cells have surface extensions called *microvilli, cilia, flagella,* and *pseudopods.* These aid in absorption, movement, and sensory processes.

TABLE 3.2	Functions of the Glycocalyx
Protection	Cushions the plasma membrane and protects it from physical and chemical injury
Immunity to infection	Enables the immune system to recognize and selectively attack foreign organisms
Defense against cancer	Changes in the glycocalyx of cancerous cells enable the immune system to recognize and destroy them
Transplant compatibility	Forms the basis for compatibility of blood transfusions, tissue grafts, and organ transplants
Cell adhesion	Binds cells together so tissues do not fall apart
Fertilization	Enables sperm to recognize and bind to eggs
Embryonic development	Guides embryonic cells to their destinations in the body

[9]*glyco* = sugar; *calyx* = cup, vessel

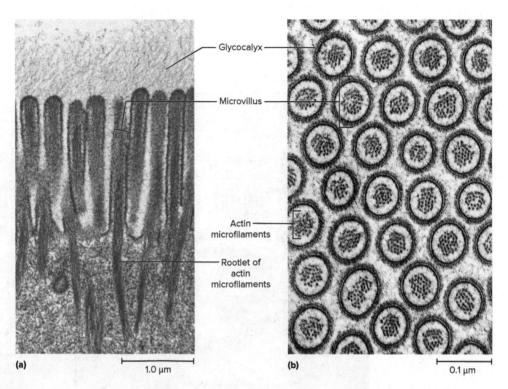

FIGURE 3.9 Microvilli and the Glycocalyx (TEM). The microvilli are anchored by microfilaments of actin, which occupy the core of each microvillus and project into the cytoplasm. (a) Longitudinal section, perpendicular to the cell surface. (b) Cross section.

a: Don W. Fawcett/Science Source; b: Biophoto Associates/Science Source

Microvilli

Microvilli[10] (MY-cro-VIL-eye; singular, *microvillus*) are extensions of the plasma membrane that serve primarily to increase a cell's surface area (figs. 3.9 and 3.10a, c). They are best developed in cells specialized for absorption, such as the epithelial cells of the intestines and kidneys. They give such cells 15 to 40 times as much absorptive surface area as they would have if their apical surfaces were flat.

Individual microvilli cannot be distinguished very well with the light microscope because they are only 1 to 2 μm long. On some cells, they are very dense and appear as a fringe called the **brush border** at the apical cell surface. With the scanning electron microscope, they resemble a deep-pile carpet. With the transmission electron microscope, microvilli typically look like finger-shaped projections of the cell surface. They show little internal structure, but some have a bundle of stiff filaments of a protein called *actin*. Actin filaments attach to the inside of the plasma membrane at the tip of the microvillus, and at its base they extend a little way into the cell and anchor the microvillus to a protein mesh called the *terminal web*. When tugged by another protein in the cytoplasm, actin can shorten a microvillus to milk its absorbed contents downward into the cell.

In contrast to the long, shaggy microvilli of absorptive cells, those on many other cells are little more than tiny bumps on the surface. On cells of the taste buds and inner ear, they are well developed but serve sensory rather than absorptive functions.

Cilia and Flagella

Cilia (SIL-ee-uh; singular, *cilium*[11]) **(fig. 3.10)** are hairlike processes about 7 to 10 μm long. Nearly every human cell has a single, nonmotile *primary cilium* a few micrometers long. Its function in some cases is still a mystery, but many of them are sensory, serving as the cell's "antenna" for monitoring nearby conditions. In the inner ear, they play a role in the sense of balance; in the retina of the eye, they are highly elaborate and form the light-absorbing part of the receptor cells; and in the kidney, they're thought to monitor the flow of fluid as it is processed into urine. In some cases, they open calcium gates in the plasma membrane, activating an informative signal in the cell. Sensory cells in the nose have multiple nonmotile cilia that bind odor molecules. Defects in the development, structure, or function of cilia—especially these nonmotile primary cilia—are sometimes responsible for birth defects and hereditary diseases called

---

[10]*micro* = small; *villi* = hairs

[11]*cilium* = eyelash

FIGURE 3.10 Cilia. (a) Epithelium of the uterine (fallopian) tube (SEM). The short, mucus-secreting cells between the ciliated cells show bumpy microvilli on their surfaces. (b) Three-dimensional structure of a cilium. (c) Cross section of a few cilia and microvilli (TEM). (d) Cross-sectional structure of a cilium. Note the relative sizes of cilia and microvilli in parts (a) and (c).

a: Steve Gschmeissner/Science Photo Library/Getty Images; c: Don Fawcett/Science Source

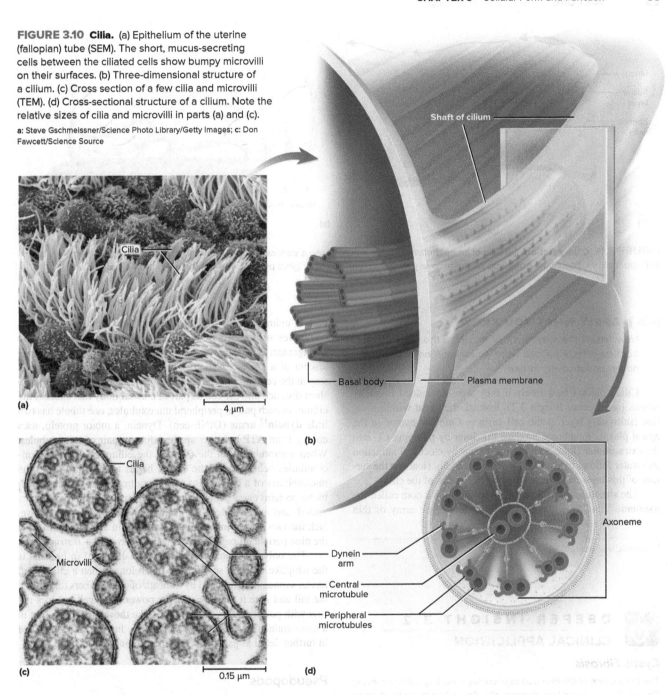

Cilia

4 μm

(a)

Shaft of cilium

Basal body

Plasma membrane

(b)

Cilia

Microvilli

(c)

0.15 μm

Dynein arm

Central microtubule

Peripheral microtubules

Axoneme

(d)

ciliopathies. (See Testing Your Comprehension question 5 at the end of this chapter.)

Motile cilia are less widespread, but more numerous on the cells that do have them. They occur in the respiratory tract, uterine (fallopian) tubes, internal cavities *(ventricles)* of the brain, and short ducts *(efferent ductules)* associated with the testes. There may be 50 to 200 cilia on the surface of one cell. They beat in waves that sweep across the surface of an epithelium, always in the same direction **(fig. 3.11)**, propelling such materials as mucus, an egg cell, or cerebrospinal fluid. Each cilium bends stiffly forward and produces a *power stroke* that pushes along the mucus or other matter. Shortly after a cilium begins its power stroke, the one just ahead of it begins, and the next and the next—collectively producing a wavelike motion. After a cilium completes its power stroke, it is pulled limply back by a *recovery stroke* that restores it to the upright position, ready to flex again.

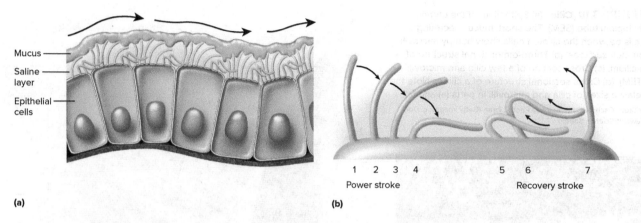

(a)

(b)

1 2 3 4   5 6   7
Power stroke   Recovery stroke

FIGURE 3.11 Ciliary Action. (a) Cilia of an epithelium moving mucus along a surface layer of saline. (b) Power and recovery strokes of an individual cilium. The cilium goes limp on the recovery stroke to return to its original position without touching the mucus above.

▶▶▶**APPLY WHAT YOU KNOW**

How would the movement of mucus in the respiratory tract be affected if cilia were equally stiff on both their power and recovery strokes?

Cilia couldn't beat freely if they were embedded in sticky mucus (see Deeper Insight 3.2). Instead, they beat within a saline (saltwater) layer at the cell surface. *Chloride pumps* in the apical plasma membrane produce this layer by pumping Cl^- into the extracellular fluid. Sodium ions follow by electrical attraction and water follows by osmosis. Mucus essentially floats on the surface of this layer and is pushed along by the tips of the cilia.

The structural basis for ciliary movement is a core called the **axoneme**[12] (ACK-so-neem), which consists of an array of thin

---

[12]*axo* = axis; *neme* = thread

DEEPER INSIGHT 3.2

CLINICAL APPLICATION

Cystic Fibrosis

The significance of chloride pumps becomes especially evident in *cystic fibrosis (CF)*, a hereditary disease affecting primarily white children of European descent. CF is usually caused by a defect in which cells make chloride pumps but fail to install them in the plasma membrane. Consequently, there is an inadequate saline layer on the cell surface and the mucus is dehydrated and overly sticky. This thick mucus plugs the ducts of the pancreas and prevents it from secreting digestive enzymes into the small intestine, so digestion and nutrition are compromised. In the respiratory tract, the mucus clogs the cilia and prevents them from beating freely. The respiratory tract becomes congested with thick mucus, often leading to chronic infection and pulmonary collapse. The mean life expectancy of people with CF is about 30 years.

protein cylinders called *microtubules*. There are two central microtubules surrounded by a ring of nine microtubule pairs—an arrangement called the *9 + 2 structure*. In cross section, it is reminiscent of a Ferris wheel (fig. 3.10d). The central microtubules stop at the cell surface, but the peripheral microtubules continue a short distance into the cell as part of a **basal body** that anchors the cilium. In each pair of peripheral microtubules, one tubule has two little **dynein**[13] **arms** (DINE-een). Dynein, a motor protein, uses energy from ATP to crawl up the adjacent pair of microtubules. When microtubules on the front of the cilium crawl up the microtubules behind them, the cilium bends toward the front. The microtubules of a cilium also act like railroad tracks along which motor proteins carry materials up and down the cilium for use in its growth and maintenance. The primary cilia, which cannot move, lack the two central microtubules and dynein arms, but still have the nine peripheral pairs; they are said to have a *9 + 0 structure*.

The only functional **flagellum**[14] (fla-JEL-um) in humans is the whiplike tail of a sperm. It is much longer than a cilium and has an axoneme surrounded by a sheath of coarse fibers that stiffen the tail and give it more propulsive power. A flagellum does not beat with power and recovery strokes like those of a cilium, but in a more undulating, snakelike or corkscrew fashion. It is described in further detail as part of sperm structure in section 27.4c.

Pseudopods

Pseudopods[15] (SOO-do-pods) are cytoplasm-filled extensions of the cell varying in shape from fine, filamentous processes to blunt fingerlike ones **(fig. 3.12).** Unlike the other three kinds of surface extensions, they change continually. Some form anew as the cell surface bubbles outward and cytoplasm flows into a lengthening

---

[13]*dyn* = power, energy; *in* = protein
[14]*flagellum* = whip
[15]*pseudo* = false; *pod* = foot

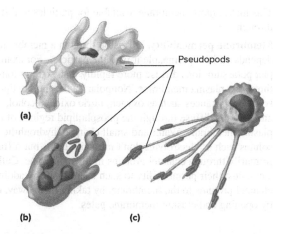

Pseudopods

(a)

(b)   (c)

FIGURE 3.12 Pseudopods. (a) *Amoeba*, a freshwater organism that crawls and captures food by means of pseudopods. (b) A neutrophil (white blood cell) that similarly uses pseudopods for locomotion and capturing bacteria. (c) A macrophage extending filamentous pseudopods to snare and "reel in" bacteria (the red rods).

pseudopod, while others are retracted into the cell by disassembling protein filaments that supported them like a scaffold.

The freshwater organism *Amoeba* furnishes a familiar example of pseudopods, which it uses for locomotion and food capture. White blood cells called *neutrophils* crawl about like amebae by means of fingerlike pseudopods, and when they encounter a bacterium or other foreign particle, they reach out with their pseudopods to surround and engulf it. *Macrophages*—tissue cells derived from certain white blood cells—reach out with thin filamentous pseudopods to snare bacteria and cell debris and "reel them in" to be digested by the cell. Like little janitors, macrophages thereby keep our tissues cleaned up. Blood platelets reach out with thin pseudopods to adhere to each other and to the walls of damaged blood vessels, forming plugs that temporarily halt bleeding (see fig. 18.20).

BEFORE YOU GO ON

Answer the following questions to test your understanding of the preceding section:

6. How does the structure of a plasma membrane depend on the amphipathic nature of phospholipids?

7. Define *peripheral* versus transmembrane *proteins*.

8. Explain the differences between a receptor, pump, and cell-adhesion molecule.

9. How does a gate differ from other channel proteins? What three factors open and close membrane gates?

10. What related roles do cAMP, adenylate cyclase, and kinases play in cellular function?

11. Identify several reasons why the glycocalyx is important to human survival.

12. How do microvilli and cilia differ in structure and function?

3.3 Membrane Transport

Expected Learning Outcomes

When you have completed this section, you should be able to

a. explain what is meant by a *selectively permeable membrane;*

b. describe the various mechanisms for transporting material through cellular membranes; and

c. define *osmolarity* and *tonicity* and explain their importance.

One of the most important functions of cellular membranes is to control the passage of materials into and out of the organelles and the cell as a whole. The plasma membrane is both a barrier and gateway between the cytoplasm and ECF. It is **selectively permeable**—it allows some things through, such as nutrients and wastes, but usually prevents other things, such as proteins and phosphates, from entering or leaving the cell.

The methods of moving substances through the membrane can be classified in two overlapping ways: as passive or active mechanisms and as carrier-mediated or not. *Passive* mechanisms require no energy (ATP) expenditure by the cell. In most cases, the random molecular motion of the particles themselves provides the necessary energy. Passive mechanisms include filtration, diffusion, and osmosis. *Active* mechanisms, however, consume ATP. These include active transport and vesicular transport. *Carrier-mediated* mechanisms use a membrane protein to transport substances from one side of the membrane to the other, but some transport processes, such as osmosis, do not involve carriers.

3.3a Filtration

Filtration is a process in which a physical pressure forces fluid through a selectively permeable membrane. A coffee filter is an everyday example. The weight of the water drives water and dissolved matter through the filter, while the filter holds back larger particles (the coffee grounds). In physiology, the most important case of filtration is seen in the blood capillaries, where blood pressure forces fluid through gaps in the capillary wall **(fig. 3.13)**. This is how water, salts, nutrients, and other solutes are transferred from the bloodstream to the tissue fluid and how the kidneys filter wastes from the blood. Capillaries hold back larger particles such as blood cells and proteins. In most cases, water and solutes filter through narrow gaps between the capillary cells. In some capillaries, however, the cells have large *filtration pores* through them, like the holes in a slice of Swiss cheese, allowing for more rapid filtration of large solutes such as protein hormones.

3.3b Simple Diffusion

Simple diffusion is the net movement of particles from a place of high concentration to a place of lower concentration as a result of their constant, spontaneous motion. In other words, substances diffuse *down their concentration gradients* (see "Gradients and Flow," section 1.6e). Molecules move at astonishing speeds.

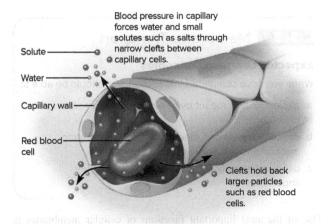

Blood pressure in capillary forces water and small solutes such as salts through narrow clefts between capillary cells.

Solute

Water

Capillary wall

Red blood cell

Clefts hold back larger particles such as red blood cells.

FIGURE 3.13 Filtration Through the Wall of a Blood Capillary. Water and small solutes pass through gaps between cells, while blood cells and other large particles are held back.

At body temperature, the average water molecule moves about 2,500 km/h (1,500 mi./h)! However, a molecule can travel only a short distance before colliding with another and careening off in a new direction, like colliding billiard balls. The rate of diffusion, therefore, is much slower than the speed of molecular motion.

Diffusion occurs readily in air or water and doesn't necessarily need a membrane—for example, when an odor spreads from its source to your nose. However, if there is a membrane in the path of the diffusing molecules, and if it is permeable to that substance, the molecules will pass from one side of the membrane to the other. This is how oxygen passes from the air we inhale into the bloodstream. Dialysis treatment for kidney patients is based on diffusion of solutes through artificial *dialysis membranes.*

Diffusion rates are important to cell survival because they determine how quickly a cell can acquire nutrients or rid itself of wastes. Some factors that affect the rate of diffusion through a membrane are as follows:

- **Temperature.** Diffusion is driven by the kinetic energy of the particles, and temperature is a measure of that kinetic energy. The warmer a substance is, the more rapidly its particles diffuse. This is why sugar diffuses more quickly through hot tea than through iced tea.
- **Molecular weight.** Heavy molecules such as proteins move more sluggishly and diffuse more slowly than light particles such as electrolytes and gases. Small molecules also pass through membrane pores more easily than large ones.
- **"Steepness" of the concentration gradient.** The steepness of a gradient refers to the concentration difference between two points. Particles diffuse more rapidly if there is a greater concentration difference.
- **Membrane surface area.** As noted earlier, the apical surface of cells specialized for absorption (for example, in the small intestine) is often extensively folded into microvilli.

This makes more membrane available for particles to diffuse through.

- **Membrane permeability.** Diffusion through a membrane depends on how permeable it is to the particles. For example, potassium ions diffuse more rapidly than sodium ions through a plasma membrane. Nonpolar, hydrophobic, lipid-soluble substances such as oxygen, nitric oxide, alcohol, and steroids diffuse through the phospholipid regions of a plasma membrane. Water and small charged, hydrophilic solutes such as electrolytes don't mix with lipids but diffuse primarily through channel proteins in the membrane. Cells can adjust their permeability to such a substance by adding channel proteins to the membrane, by taking them away, or by opening and closing membrane gates.

3.3c Osmosis

Osmosis[16] is the net flow of water from one side of a selectively permeable membrane to the other. It is crucial to the body's water distribution (fluid balance). Imbalances in osmosis underlie such problems as diarrhea, constipation, hypertension, and edema (tissue swelling); osmosis also is a vital consideration in intravenous (I.V.) fluid therapy.

Osmosis occurs through nonliving membranes, such as cellophane and dialysis membranes, and through the plasma membranes of cells. The usual direction of net movement is from the more watery side, with a lower concentration of dissolved matter, to the less watery side, with a greater concentration of solute. The reason for the accumulation of water on the high-solute side is that when water molecules encounter a solute particle, they tend to associate with it to form a *hydration sphere* (see fig. 2.9). Even though this is a loose, reversible attraction, it does make those water molecules less available to diffuse back across the membrane to the side from which they came. In essence, solute particles on one side of the membrane draw water away from the other side. Thus, water accumulates on the side with the most solute. All of this assumes that the solute molecules in question can't pass through the membrane, but stay on one side. The rate and direction of osmosis depend on the relative concentration of these nonpermeating solutes on the two sides of the membrane.

Significant amounts of water pass even through the hydrophobic, phospholipid regions of a plasma membrane, but water passes more easily through channel proteins called **aquaporins,** specialized for water. Cells can increase the rate of osmosis by installing more aquaporins in the membrane or decrease the rate by removing them. Certain cells of the kidney, for example, regulate the rate of urinary water loss by adding or removing aquaporins.

A cell can exchange a tremendous amount of water by osmosis. In red blood cells, for example, the amount of water passing through the plasma membrane every second is 100 times the volume of the cell.

---

[16]*osm* = push, thrust; *osis* = condition, process

Figure 3.14 is a conceptual model of osmosis. Imagine a chamber divided by a selectively permeable membrane. Side A contains distilled water and side B contains large particles of a *nonpermeating* solute—that is, a solute such as protein that cannot pass through the membrane pores because of its size or other properties. Water passes from side A to B (fig. 3.14a) and associates with the solute molecules on side B, hindering water movement back to side A.

Under such conditions, the water level in side A would fall and the level in side B would rise. It may seem as if this would continue indefinitely until side A dried up. This would not happen, however, because as water accumulated in side B, it would become heavier and exert more force, called **hydrostatic pressure,** on that side of the membrane. This would cause some filtration of water from B back to A. At some point, the rate of filtration would equal the rate of "forward" osmosis, water would pass through the membrane equally in both directions, and net osmosis would slow down and stop. At this point, an equilibrium (balance between opposing forces) would exist. The hydrostatic pressure required on side B to halt osmosis is called **osmotic pressure.** The more nonpermeating solute there is in B, the greater the osmotic pressure.

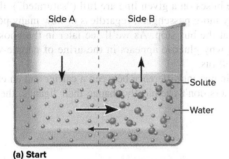

Side A   Side B

— Solute

— Water

(a) Start

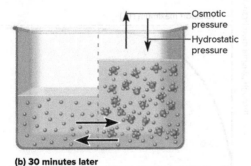

— Osmotic pressure

— Hydrostatic pressure

(b) 30 minutes later

FIGURE 3.14 Osmosis. The dashed line represents a selectively permeable membrane dividing the chamber in half. (a) Initial net flow of water from side A to side B. (b) Equilibrium between osmotic and hydrostatic pressure, hence between osmosis and filtration, with no net flow. Water molecules aggregate around solute molecules and thus accumulate on side B.

▶▶▶**APPLY WHAT YOU KNOW**

If the solute concentration on side B was half what it was in the original experiment, would the fluid on that side reach a higher or lower level than before? Explain.

Reverse osmosis is a process in which a mechanical pressure applied to one side of the system can override osmotic pressure and drive water through a membrane against its concentration gradient. This principle is used to create highly purified water for laboratory use and to desalinate seawater, converting it to drinkable freshwater—handy for arid countries and ships at sea. The body's principal pump, the heart, drives water out of the smallest blood vessels (the capillaries) by reverse osmosis—a process called *capillary filtration.* The equilibrium between osmosis and filtration will be an important consideration when we study fluid exchange by the capillaries in section 20.3. Blood plasma also contains albumin. In the preceding discussion, side B is analogous to the high-protein bloodstream and side A to the low-protein tissue fluid surrounding the capillaries. Water leaves the capillaries by filtration, but this is approximately balanced by water reentering the capillaries by osmosis.

3.3d Osmolarity and Tonicity

The **osmolarity,** or osmotic concentration, of body fluids has such a great effect on cellular function that it is important to understand the units in which it is measured. Physiologists and clinicians usually express this in terms of **milliosmoles per liter (mOsm/L),** a unit of measure that expresses the quantity of nonpermeating particles per liter of solution. The basis of this unit of concentration is explained in appendix B. Blood plasma, tissue fluid, and intracellular fluids measure about 300 mOsm/L.

Tonicity is the ability of a solution to affect the fluid volume and pressure in a cell. If a solute cannot pass through a plasma membrane but remains more concentrated on one side of the membrane than on the other, it causes osmosis. A **hypotonic**[17] solution has a lower concentration of nonpermeating solutes than the intracellular fluid (ICF). Cells in a hypotonic solution absorb water, swell, and may burst *(lyse)* **(fig. 3.15a).** Distilled water is the extreme example; a sufficient quantity given to a person intravenously would lyse the blood cells, with dire consequences. A **hypertonic**[18] solution is one with a higher concentration of nonpermeating solutes than the ICF. It causes cells to lose water and shrivel *(crenate)* **(fig. 3.15c).** Such cells may die of torn membranes and cytoplasmic loss. In **isotonic**[19] solutions, the total concentration of nonpermeating solutes is the same as in the ICF—hence, isotonic solutions cause no change in cell volume or shape **(fig. 3.15b).**

It is essential for cells to be in a state of osmotic equilibrium with the fluid around them, and this requires that the ECF have the same concentration of nonpermeating solutes as the ICF. Intravenous fluids given to patients are usually isotonic solutions, but

[17]*hypo* = less; *ton* = tension
[18]*hyper* = more; *ton* = tension
[19]*iso* = equal; *ton* = tension

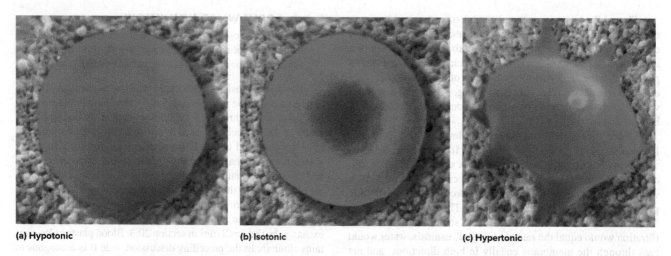

(a) Hypotonic

(b) Isotonic

(c) Hypertonic

FIGURE 3.15 Effects of Tonicity on Red Blood Cells (RBCs). (a) RBC swelling in a hypotonic medium such as distilled water. (b) Normal RBC size and shape in an isotonic medium such as 0.9% NaCl. (c) RBC shriveling in a hypertonic medium such as 2% NaCl.

a–c: David M. Phillips/Science Source

hypertonic or hypotonic fluids are given for special purposes. A 0.9% solution of NaCl, called *normal saline,* is isotonic to human blood cells.

It is important to note that osmolarity and tonicity are not the same. Urea, for example, is a small organic molecule that easily penetrates plasma membranes. If cells are placed in 300 mOsm/L urea, urea diffuses into them (down its concentration gradient), water follows by osmosis, and the cells swell and burst. Thus, 300 mOsm/L urea is not isotonic to the cells. Sodium chloride, by contrast, penetrates plasma membranes poorly. In 300 mOsm/L NaCl, there is little change in cell volume; this solution is isotonic to cells.

3.3e Carrier-Mediated Transport

The processes of membrane transport described up to this point don't necessarily require a cell membrane; they can occur as well through artificial membranes. Now, however, we come to processes for which a cell membrane is necessary, because they employ transport proteins, or carriers. Thus, the next three processes are classified as **carrier-mediated transport.** In these cases, a solute binds to a carrier in the plasma membrane, which then changes shape and releases the solute to the other side. Carriers can move substances into or out of a cell, and into or out of organelles within the cell. The process is very rapid; for example, one carrier can transport 1,000 glucose molecules per second across the membrane.

Carriers act like enzymes in some ways: The solute is a ligand that binds to a specific receptor site on the carrier, like a substrate binding to the active site of an enzyme. The carrier exhibits **specificity** for its ligand, just as an enzyme does for its substrate. A glucose carrier, for example, cannot transport fructose. Carriers also exhibit **saturation;** as the solute concentration rises, its rate of transport increases, but only up to a point. When every carrier is occupied, adding more solute can't

make the process go any faster. The carriers are saturated—no more are available to handle the increased demand, and transport levels off at a rate called the **transport maximum (T_m) (fig. 3.16).** You could think of carriers as analogous to buses. If all the buses on a given line are full ("saturated"), they can't carry any more passengers, regardless of how many people are waiting at the bus stop. As we'll see later in the book, the T_m explains why glucose appears in the urine of people with diabetes mellitus.

An important difference between a carrier and an enzyme is that carriers don't chemically change their ligands; they simply

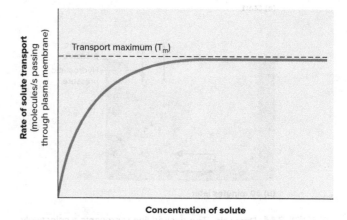

FIGURE 3.16 Carrier Saturation and Transport Maximum. Up to a point, increasing the solute concentration increases the rate of transport through a membrane. At the transport maximum (T_m), however, all carrier proteins are busy and cannot transport the solute any faster, even if more solute is added.

pick them up on one side of the membrane and release them, unchanged, on the other.

There are three kinds of carriers: uniports, symports, and antiports. A **uniport**[20] carries only one type of solute. For example, most cells pump out calcium by means of a uniport, maintaining a low intracellular concentration so calcium salts don't crystallize in the cytoplasm. Some carriers move two or more solutes through a membrane simultaneously in the same direction; this process is called **cotransport**[21] and the carrier protein that performs it is called a **symport.**[22] For example, absorptive cells of the small intestine and kidneys have a symport that takes up sodium and glucose simultaneously. Other carriers move two or more solutes in opposite directions; this process is called **countertransport** and the carrier protein is called an **antiport.**[23] For example, nearly all cells have an antiport called the *sodium–potassium pump* that continually removes Na^+ from the cell and brings in K^+.

There are three mechanisms of carrier-mediated transport: facilitated diffusion, primary active transport, and secondary active transport. **Facilitated**[24] **diffusion (fig. 3.17)** is the carrier-mediated transport of a solute through a membrane *down its concentration gradient.* It requires no expenditure of metabolic energy (ATP) by the cell. It transports solutes such as glucose

that cannot pass through the membrane unaided. The solute attaches to a binding site on the carrier, then the carrier changes conformation and releases the solute on the other side of the membrane.

Primary active transport is a process in which a carrier moves a substance through a cell membrane *up its concentration gradient* using energy provided by ATP. Just as rolling a ball up a ramp would require you to push it (an energy input), this mechanism requires energy to move material up its concentration gradient. ATP supplies this energy by transferring a phosphate group to the transport protein. The calcium pump mentioned previously uses this mechanism. Even though Ca^{2+} is already more concentrated in the ECF than within the cell, this carrier pumps still more of it out. Active transport also enables cells to absorb amino acids that are already more concentrated in the cytoplasm than in the ECF.

Secondary active transport also requires an energy input, but depends only indirectly on ATP. For example, certain kidney tubules have proteins called *sodium–glucose transporters (SGLTs)* that simultaneously bind sodium ions (Na^+) and glucose molecules and transport them into the tubule cells, saving glucose from being lost in the urine **(fig. 3.18).** An SGLT itself doesn't use ATP. However, it depends on the fact that the cell actively maintains a low internal Na^+ concentration, so Na^+ will diffuse down its gradient into the cell. Glucose "hitches a ride" with the incoming Na^+. But what keeps the intracellular Na^+ concentration low is that the basal membrane of the cell has an ATP-driven sodium–potassium pump that constantly removes Na^+ from the cell. If not for this, the Na^+ and glucose inflow via the SGLT would soon cease. Therefore, the SGLT doesn't use ATP directly, but depends on ATP to drive the

---

[20]*uni* = one; *port* = carry
[21]*co* = together; *trans* = across; *port* = carry
[22]*sym* = together; *port* = carry
[23]*anti* = opposite; *port* = carry
[24]*facil* = easy

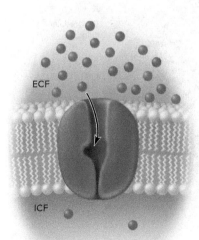 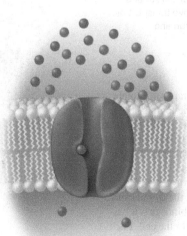 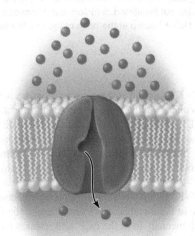

①A solute particle enters the channel of a membrane protein (carrier).

②The solute binds to a receptor site on the carrier and the carrier changes conformation.

③The carrier releases the solute on the other side of the membrane.

FIGURE 3.17 Facilitated Diffusion. Note that the solute moves down its concentration gradient.

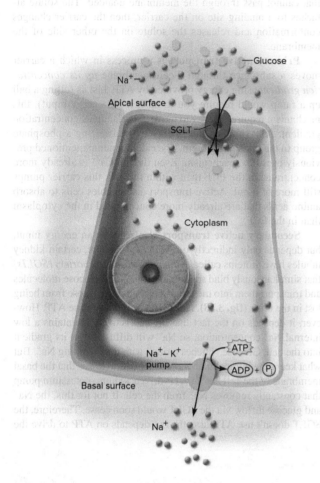

FIGURE 3.18 Secondary Active Transport. In this example, the sodium–glucose transporter (SGLT) at the apical cell surface carries out facilitated diffusion, but depends on active transport by the Na⁺–K⁺ pump at the base of the cell to keep it running.

Lest you question the importance of the Na⁺–K⁺ pump, consider that half of the calories you use each day go to this purpose alone. The pump typically operates at about 10 cycles/s, but under certain conditions it can achieve 100 cycles/s. Various types of cells have from just a few hundred Na⁺–K⁺ pumps (red blood cells) to millions of them (nerve cells), so an average cell may exchange 30 million Na⁺ ions and 20 million K⁺ ions and consume 10 million ATPs per second. Beyond compensating for a leaky plasma membrane, the Na⁺–K⁺ pump has at least four functions:

1. **Secondary active transport.** It maintains a steep Na⁺ concentration gradient across the membrane. Like water behind a dam, this gradient is a source of potential energy that can be tapped to do other work. The secondary active transport described previously is an example of this.

2. **Regulation of cell volume.** Certain anions are confined to the cell and cannot penetrate the plasma membrane. These "fixed anions," such as proteins and phosphates, attract and retain cations. If there were nothing to correct for it, the retention of these ions would cause osmotic swelling and possibly lysis of the cell. Cellular swelling, however, elevates activity of the Na⁺–K⁺ pumps. Since each cycle of the pump removes one ion more than it brings in, the pumps are part of a negative feedback loop that reduces intracellular ion concentration, controls osmolarity, and prevents cellular swelling.

Na⁺–K⁺ pump; it is therefore a secondary active transport protein. (*Secondary active transport* is an unfortunate name for this, as the SGLT is actually carrying out facilitated diffusion, but its dependence on a primary active transport pump has led to this name.)

The **sodium–potassium (Na⁺–K⁺) pump** itself **(fig. 3.19)** is a good example of primary active transport. It is also known as *Na⁺–K⁺ ATPase* because it is an enzyme that hydrolyzes ATP. The Na⁺–K⁺ pump binds three Na⁺ simultaneously on the cytoplasmic side of the membrane, releases these to the ECF, binds two K⁺ simultaneously from the ECF, and releases these into the cell. Each cycle of the pump consumes one ATP and exchanges three Na⁺ for two K⁺. This keeps the K⁺ concentration higher and the Na⁺ concentration lower within the cell than they are in the ECF. These ions continually leak through the membrane, and the Na⁺–K⁺ pump compensates like bailing out a leaky boat.

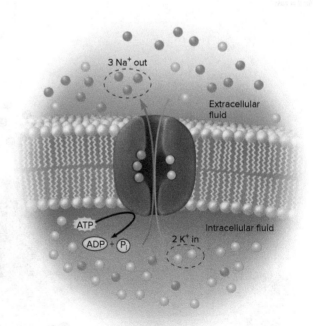

FIGURE 3.19 The Sodium–Potassium Pump (Na⁺–K⁺ ATPase).

❓ *Why would the Na⁺–K⁺ pump, but not osmosis, cease to function after a cell dies?*

3. **Maintenance of a membrane potential.** All living cells have an electrical charge difference called the *resting membrane potential* across the plasma membrane. Like the two poles of a battery, the inside of the membrane is negatively charged and the outside is positively charged. This difference stems from the unequal distribution of ions on the two sides of the membrane, maintained by the Na⁺–K⁺ pump. The membrane potential is essential to the excitability of nerve and muscle cells.

4. **Heat production.** When the weather turns chilly, we turn up not only the furnace in our home but also the "furnace" in our body. Thyroid hormone stimulates cells to produce more Na⁺–K⁺ pumps. As these pumps consume ATP, they release heat from it, compensating for the body heat we lose to the cold air around us.

▶▶▶**APPLY WHAT YOU KNOW**

An important characteristic of proteins is their ability to change conformation in response to the binding or dissociation of a ligand (see "Protein Structure" in section 2.4e). Explain how this characteristic is essential to carrier-mediated transport.

In summary, carrier-mediated transport is any process in which solute particles move through a membrane by means of a transport protein. The protein is a uniport if it transports only one solute, a symport if it carries two types of solutes at once in the same direction, and an antiport if it carries two or more solutes in opposite directions. If the carrier doesn't depend on ATP at all and it moves solutes down their concentration gradient, the process is called facilitated diffusion. If the carrier itself consumes ATP and moves solutes up their concentration gradient, the process is called primary active transport. If the carrier doesn't directly use ATP, but depends on a concentration gradient produced by ATP-consuming Na⁺–K⁺ pumps elsewhere in the plasma membrane, the process is called secondary active transport.

3.3f Vesicular Transport

So far, we have considered processes that move one or a few ions or molecules at a time through the plasma membrane. **Vesicular transport** processes, by contrast, move large particles, droplets of fluid, or numerous molecules at once through the membrane, contained in bubblelike **vesicles** of membrane. Vesicular processes that bring matter into a cell are called **endocytosis**[25] (EN-doe-sy-TOE-sis) and those that release material from a cell are called **exocytosis**[26] (EC-so-sy-TOE-sis). These processes employ motor proteins whose movements are energized by ATP.

There are three forms of endocytosis: phagocytosis, pinocytosis, and receptor-mediated endocytosis. **Phagocytosis**[27] (FAG-oh-sy-TOE-sis), or "cell eating," is the process of engulfing particles such as bacteria, dust, and cellular debris—particles large enough to be seen with a microscope. For example, neutrophils (a class of white blood cells) protect the body from infection by phagocytizing and killing bacteria. A neutrophil spends most of its life crawling about in the connective tissues by means of its pseudopods. When a neutrophil encounters a bacterium, it surrounds it with pseudopods and traps it in a vesicle called a **phagosome**[28]—a vesicle in the cytoplasm surrounded by a unit membrane (**fig. 3.20**). A lysosome merges with the phagosome, converting it to a *phagolysosome,* and contributes enzymes that destroy the invader. Some other kinds of phagocytic cells are described in section 21.1b. In general, phagocytosis is a way of keeping the tissues free of debris and infectious microbes. Some cells called *macrophages* (literally, "big eaters") phagocytize the equivalent of 25% of their own volume per hour.

Pinocytosis[29] (PIN-oh-sy-TOE-sis), or "cell drinking," is the process of taking in droplets of ECF containing molecules of some use to the cell. While phagocytosis occurs in only a few specialized cells, pinocytosis occurs in all human cells. The process begins as the plasma membrane becomes dimpled, or caved in, at points. These pits soon separate from the surface membrane and form small membrane-bounded **pinocytotic vesicles** in the cytoplasm. The vesicles contain droplets of the ECF with whatever molecules happen to be there.

Receptor-mediated endocytosis (fig. 3.21) is a more selective form of either phagocytosis or pinocytosis. It enables a cell to take in specific molecules from the ECF with a minimum of unnecessary matter. Particles in the ECF bind to specific receptors on the plasma membrane. The receptors then cluster together and the membrane sinks in at this point, creating a pit coated with a peripheral membrane protein called *clathrin.*[30] The pit soon pinches off to form a *clathrin-coated vesicle* in the cytoplasm. Clathrin may serve as an "address label" on the coated vesicle that directs it to an appropriate destination in the cell, or it may inform other structures in the cell what to do with the vesicle.

One example of receptor-mediated endocytosis is the uptake of *low-density lipoproteins (LDLs)*—protein-coated droplets of cholesterol and other lipids in the blood (described in section 26.1g). The thin endothelial cells that line our blood vessels have LDL receptors on their surfaces and absorb LDLs in clathrin-coated vesicles. Inside the cell, the LDL is freed from the vesicle and metabolized, and the membrane with its receptors is recycled to the cell surface.

Endothelial cells also imbibe insulin by receptor-mediated endocytosis. Insulin is too large to pass through channels in the plasma membrane, yet it must somehow get out of the blood and

---

[25]*endo* = into; *cyt* = cell; *osis* = process
[26]*exo* = out of; *cyt* = cell; *osis* = process

[27]*phago* = eating; *cyt* = cell; *osis* = process
[28]*phago* = eaten; *some* = body
[29]*pino* = drinking; *cyt* = cell; *osis* = process
[30]*clathr* = lattice; *in* = protein

94 **PART ONE** Organization of the Body

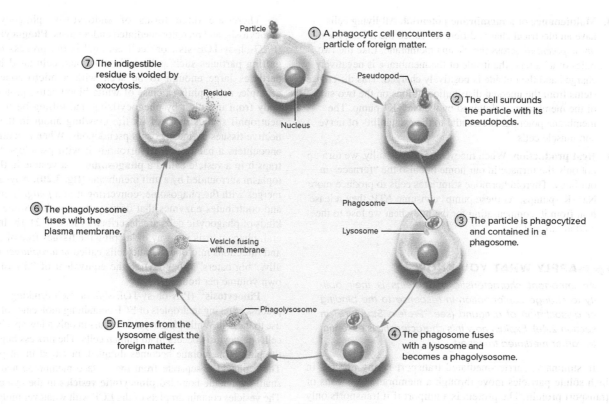

① A phagocytic cell encounters a particle of foreign matter.

Particle

Pseudopod

② The cell surrounds the particle with its pseudopods.

Nucleus

⑦ The indigestible residue is voided by exocytosis.

Residue

Phagosome

Lysosome

③ The particle is phagocytized and contained in a phagosome.

⑥ The phagolysosome fuses with the plasma membrane.

Vesicle fusing with membrane

Phagolysosome

④ The phagosome fuses with a lysosome and becomes a phagolysosome.

⑤ Enzymes from the lysosome digest the foreign matter.

FIGURE 3.20 **Phagocytosis, Intracellular Digestion, and Exocytosis.**

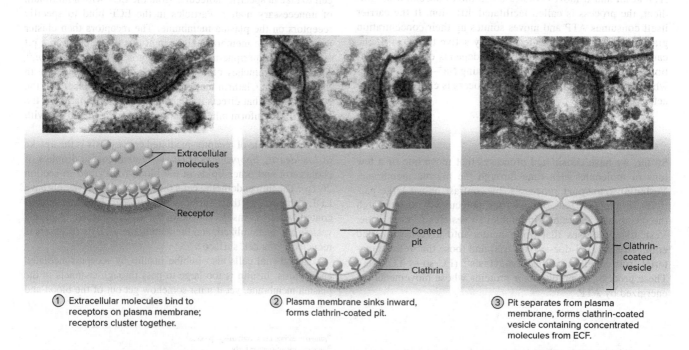

Extracellular molecules

Receptor

Coated pit

Clathrin

Clathrin-coated vesicle

① Extracellular molecules bind to receptors on plasma membrane; receptors cluster together.

② Plasma membrane sinks inward, forms clathrin-coated pit.

③ Pit separates from plasma membrane, forms clathrin-coated vesicle containing concentrated molecules from ECF.

FIGURE 3.21 **Receptor-Mediated Endocytosis.**

1–3: Courtesy of The Company of Biologists, Ltd.

reach the surrounding cells if it is to have any effect. Endothelial cells take up insulin by receptor-mediated endocytosis, transport the vesicles across the cell, and release the insulin on the other side, where tissue cells await it. Such transport of material across a cell (capture on one side and release on the other) is called **transcytosis**[31] (**fig. 3.22**). This process is especially active in muscle capillaries and transfers a significant amount of blood albumin into the tissue fluid.

Receptor-mediated endocytosis isn't always to our benefit; hepatitis, polio, and AIDS viruses trick our cells into engulfing them by receptor-mediated endocytosis, thus exploiting this mechanism to establish infection.

Exocytosis (fig. 3.23) is a process of discharging material from a cell. It occurs, for example, when endothelial cells release insulin to the tissue fluid, sperm cells release enzymes for penetrating an egg, mammary gland cells secrete milk sugar, and other gland cells release hormones. It bears a superficial resemblance to endocytosis in reverse. A secretory vesicle in the cell migrates to the surface and "docks" on peripheral proteins of the plasma membrane. These proteins pull the membrane inward and create a dimple that eventually fuses with the vesicle and allows it to release its contents.

The question might occur to you, If endocytosis continually takes away bits of plasma membrane to form intracellular vesicles, why doesn't the membrane grow smaller and smaller? Another purpose of exocytosis, however, is to replace plasma membrane that has been removed by endocytosis or that has become damaged or worn out. Plasma membrane is continually recycled from the cell surface into the cytoplasm and back to the surface.

Table 3.3 summarizes these mechanisms of transport.

---

[31]*trans* = across; *cyt* = cell; *osis* = process

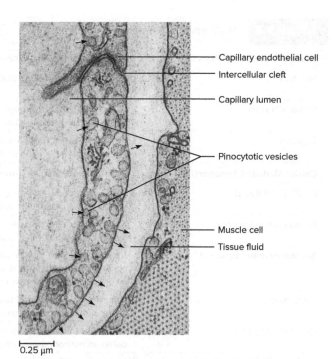

Capillary endothelial cell
Intercellular cleft
Capillary lumen

Pinocytotic vesicles

Muscle cell
Tissue fluid

0.25 µm

FIGURE 3.22 Transcytosis. An endothelial cell of a capillary imbibes droplets of blood plasma at sites indicated by arrows along the left. This forms pinocytotic vesicles, which the cell transports to the other side. Here, it releases the contents by exocytosis at sites indicated by arrows along the right side of the cell.

Don Fawcett/Science Source

? *Why isn't transcytosis listed as a separate means of membrane transport, in addition to pinocytosis and the others?*

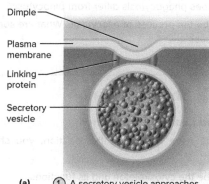
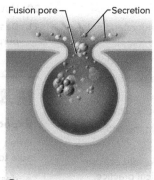
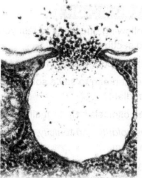

Dimple
Plasma membrane
Linking protein
Secretory vesicle

Fusion pore
Secretion

(a)

① A secretory vesicle approaches the plasma membrane and docks on it by means of linking proteins. The plasma membrane caves in at that point to meet the vesicle.

② The plasma membrane and vesicle unite to form a fusion pore through which the vesicle contents are released.

(b)

FIGURE 3.23 Exocytosis. (a) Stages of exocytosis. (b) Electron micrograph of exocytosis.

b: Courtesy Dr. Birgit Satir, Albert Einstein College of Medicine

TABLE 3.3	Methods of Membrane Transport
Transport Without Carriers	**Movement of Material Without the Aid of Carrier Proteins**
Filtration	Movement of water and solutes through a selectively permeable membrane as a result of hydrostatic pressure
Simple diffusion	Diffusion of particles through water or air or through a living or artificial membrane, down their concentration gradient, without the aid of membrane carriers
Osmosis	Net flow of water through a selectively permeable membrane, driven by either a difference in solute concentration or a mechanical force
Carrier-Mediated Transport	**Movement of Material Through a Cell Membrane by Carrier Proteins**
Facilitated diffusion	Transport of particles through a selectively permeable membrane, down their concentration gradient, by a carrier that does not directly consume ATP
Primary active transport	Transport of solute particles through a selectively permeable membrane, up their concentration gradient, by a carrier that consumes ATP
Secondary active transport	Transport of solute particles through a selectively permeable membrane, up their concentration gradient, by a carrier that doesn't use ATP itself but depends on concentration gradients produced by primary active transport elsewhere in the membrane
Cotransport	Simultaneous transport of two or more solutes in the same direction through a membrane by a carrier protein called a *symport*, using either facilitated diffusion or active transport
Countertransport	Transport of two or more solutes in opposite directions through a membrane by a carrier protein called an *antiport*, using either facilitated diffusion or active transport
Vesicular (Bulk) Transport	**Movement of Fluid and Particles Through a Plasma Membrane by Way of Membrane Vesicles; Consumes ATP**
Endocytosis	Vesicular transport of particles into a cell
Phagocytosis	Process of engulfing large particles by means of pseudopods; "cell eating"
Pinocytosis	Process of imbibing extracellular fluid in which the plasma membrane sinks in and pinches off small vesicles containing droplets of fluid; "cell drinking"
Receptor-mediated endocytosis	Phagocytosis or pinocytosis in which specific solute particles bind to receptors on the plasma membrane, and are then taken into the cell in clathrin-coated vesicles with a minimal amount of extraneous matter
Exocytosis	Process of eliminating material from a cell by means of a vesicle approaching the cell surface, fusing with the plasma membrane, and expelling its contents; used to release cell secretions, replace worn-out plasma membrane, and replace membrane that has been internalized by endocytosis

BEFORE YOU GO ON

Answer the following questions to test your understanding of the preceding section:

13. What is the importance of filtration to human physiology?

14. What does it mean to say a solute moves down its concentration gradient?

15. How does osmosis help to maintain blood volume?

16. Define *osmolarity* and *tonicity*, and explain the difference between them.

17. Define *hypotonic*, *isotonic*, and *hypertonic*, and explain why these concepts are important in clinical practice.

18. What do facilitated diffusion and active transport have in common? How are they different?

19. How does the Na⁺–K⁺ pump exchange sodium ions for potassium ions across the plasma membrane? What are some purposes served by this pump?

20. How does phagocytosis differ from pinocytosis?

21. Describe the process of exocytosis. What are some of its purposes?

3.4   The Cell Interior

Expected Learning Outcomes

When you have completed this section, you should be able to

a. describe the cytoskeleton and its functions;

b. list the main organelles of a cell, describe their structure, and explain their functions; and

c. give some examples of cell inclusions and explain how inclusions differ from organelles.

We now probe more deeply into the cell to study its internal structures. These are classified into three groups—*cytoskeleton, organelles,* and *inclusions*—all embedded in the clear, gelatinous cytosol.

3.4a The Cytoskeleton

The **cytoskeleton** is a network of protein filaments and cylinders that structurally support a cell, determine its shape, organize its contents, direct the movement of materials within the cell, and contribute to movements of the cell as a whole. It forms a dense supportive scaffold in the cytoplasm (**fig. 3.24**). It is connected to transmembrane proteins of the plasma membrane, and they in turn are connected to protein fibers external to the cell, creating a strong structural continuity from extracellular material to the cytoplasm. Cytoskeletal elements may even connect to chromosomes in the nucleus, enabling physical tension on a cell to move nuclear contents and mechanically stimulate genetic function.

The cytoskeleton is composed of *microfilaments, intermediate filaments,* and *microtubules.* If you think of intermediate filaments as being like the stiff rods of uncooked spaghetti, you could, by comparison, think of microfilaments as being like fine angel-hair pasta and microtubules as being like tubular penne pasta.

Microfilaments (thin filaments) are about 6 nm thick and are made of the protein *actin.* They are widespread throughout the cell but especially concentrated in a fibrous mat called the **terminal web (membrane skeleton)** on the cytoplasmic side of the plasma membrane. The phospholipids of the plasma membrane spread out over the terminal web like butter on a slice of bread. The web, like the bread, provides physical support, whereas the lipids, like butter, provide a permeability barrier. It is thought that without the support of the terminal web, the phospholipids would break up into little droplets and the plasma membrane would not hold together. As described earlier, actin microfilaments also form the supportive cores of the microvilli and play a role in cell movement. Through its role in cell motility, actin plays a crucial role in embryonic development, muscle contraction, immune function, wound healing, cancer metastasis, and other processes that involve cell migration.

Intermediate filaments (8–10 nm thick) are thicker and stiffer than microfilaments. They give the cell its shape, resist stress, and participate in junctions that attach cells to their neighbors. In epidermal cells, they are made of the tough protein *keratin* and occupy most of the cytoplasm. They are responsible for the strength of hair and fingernails.

Microtubules (25 nm in diameter) are cylinders made of 13 parallel strands called *protofilaments.* Each protofilament is a long chain of globular proteins called *tubulin* (**fig. 3.25**). Microtubules radiate from an area of the cell called the *centrosome.* They hold organelles in place, form bundles that maintain cell shape and rigidity, and act somewhat like monorail tracks. Motor proteins walk along these tracks carrying organelles and macromolecules to specific destinations in the cell. Microtubules form the axonemes of cilia and flagella and are responsible for their

beating movements, and form the mitotic spindle that guides chromosome movement during cell division. Microtubules are not permanent structures. They come and go moment by moment as tubulin molecules assemble into a tubule and then suddenly break apart again to be used somewhere else in the cell. The microtubules in cilia, flagella, basal bodies, and centrioles, however, are more stable.

3.4b Organelles

Organelles are internal structures of a cell that carry out specialized metabolic tasks. Some are surrounded by membranes and are therefore referred to as *membranous organelles.* These are the nucleus, mitochondria, lysosomes, peroxisomes, endoplasmic reticulum, and Golgi complex. Organelles without membranes include ribosomes, proteasomes, centrosomes, centrioles, and basal bodies.

The Nucleus

The **nucleus** (**fig. 3.26**) is usually the largest organelle and the only one clearly visible with the light microscope. It contains the cell's chromosomes and is therefore the genetic control center of cellular activity. It is typically spheroidal to elliptical in shape and about 5 μm in diameter. Most cells have a single nucleus, but there are exceptions. Mature red blood cells have none; they are **anuclear.** A few cell types are **multinuclear,** having 2 to 50 nuclei. Examples include skeletal muscle cells, some liver cells, and certain bone-dissolving cells.

Figure 3.27 shows the details of nuclear structure. The nucleus is enclosed in a double membrane, the **nuclear envelope.** The envelope is perforated with **nuclear pores** formed by a ring of proteins called the *nuclear pore complex.* These proteins regulate molecular traffic through the envelope and act like a rivet to hold the two membrane layers together. Hundreds of molecules pass through the nuclear pores every minute. Coming into the nucleus are raw materials for DNA and RNA synthesis, enzymes that are made in the cytoplasm but function in the nucleus, and hormones and other chemical messengers that activate certain genes. Going the other way, RNA is made in the nucleus but leaves to perform its job in the cytoplasm.

Immediately inside the nuclear envelope is a narrow but densely fibrous zone called the **nuclear lamina,** composed of a web of intermediate filaments. It supports the nuclear envelope and pores, provides points of attachment and organization for the chromosomes inside the nucleus, and plays a role in regulating DNA replication and the cell life cycle. Abnormalities of its structure or function are associated with certain genetic diseases and premature cell death.

The material in the nucleus is called **nucleoplasm.** This includes **chromatin**[32] (CRO-muh-tin)—fine threadlike matter composed of DNA and protein—and one or more dark-staining

---

[32]*chromat* = colored; *in* = substance

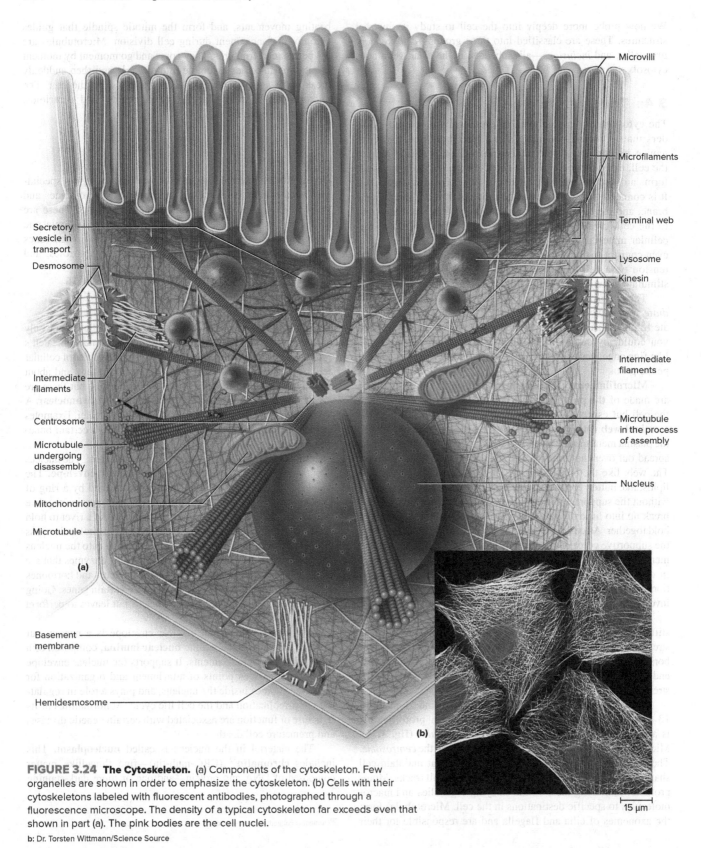

Microvilli

Microfilaments

Terminal web

Lysosome

Kinesin

Intermediate filaments

Microtubule in the process of assembly

Nucleus

Secretory vesicle in transport

Desmosome

Intermediate filaments

Centrosome

Microtubule undergoing disassembly

Mitochondrion

Microtubule

(a)

Basement membrane

Hemidesmosome

(b)

15 μm

FIGURE 3.24 The Cytoskeleton. (a) Components of the cytoskeleton. Few organelles are shown in order to emphasize the cytoskeleton. (b) Cells with their cytoskeletons labeled with fluorescent antibodies, photographed through a fluorescence microscope. The density of a typical cytoskeleton far exceeds even that shown in part (a). The pink bodies are the cell nuclei.

b: Dr. Torsten Wittmann/Science Source

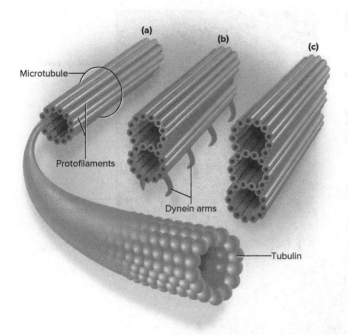

FIGURE 3.25 Microtubules. (a) A microtubule is composed of 13 protofilaments. Each protofilament is a helical array of globular proteins called tubulin. (b) One of the nine microtubule pairs that form the axonemes of cilia and flagella, with the motor protein dynein attached. (c) One of the nine microtubule triplets that form a centriole.

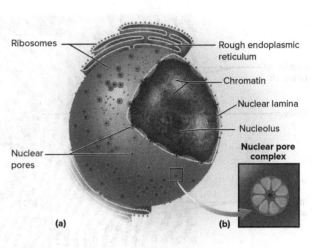

FIGURE 3.27 Structure of the Nucleus. (a) Cutaway view showing the nuclear surface and contents of the nucleoplasm. (b) Detail of a nuclear pore complex.

? *Why do these nuclear pores have to be larger in diameter than the channels in the cell's plasma membrane? (See table 3.1.)*

masses called **nucleoli** (singular, *nucleolus*), where ribosomes are produced. The genetic function of the nucleus is described in section 4.2.

Endoplasmic Reticulum

Endoplasmic reticulum (ER) literally means "little network within the cytoplasm." It is a system of interconnected channels

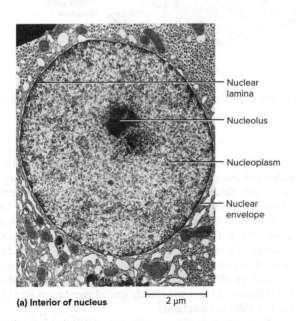

FIGURE 3.26 The Nucleus as Seen by Electron Microscopy. These photomicrographs were made by different TEM methods to show the internal structure of the nucleus and surface of the nuclear envelope. (a) Interior of the nucleus. (b) Surface of the nucleus, showing clusters of nuclear pores.

a: Richard Chao; b: ©E.G. Pollock

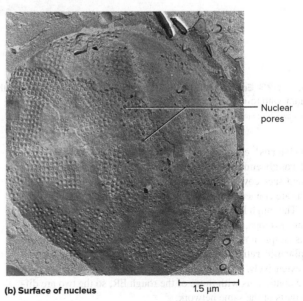

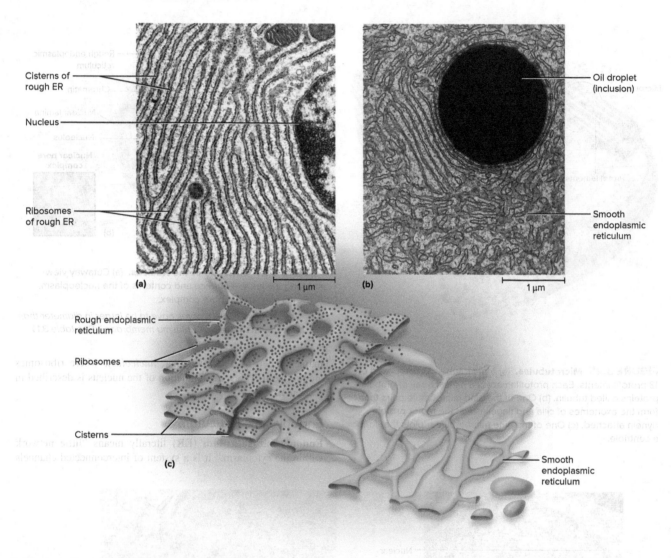

Cisterns of
rough ER

Nucleus

Ribosomes
of rough ER

(a)   1 μm

Oil droplet
(inclusion)

Smooth
endoplasmic
reticulum

(b)   1 μm

Rough endoplasmic
reticulum

Ribosomes

Cisterns

(c)

Smooth
endoplasmic
reticulum

FIGURE 3.28 Endoplasmic Reticulum (ER). (a) Rough ER. (b) Smooth ER and an inclusion (oil droplet). (c) Structure of the endoplasmic reticulum, with rough and smooth regions.

a-b: Don Fawcett/Science Source

called **cisterns**[33] enclosed by a unit membrane **(fig. 3.28).** In areas called **rough endoplasmic reticulum,** the cisterns are parallel, flattened sacs covered with granules called *ribosomes.* Adjacent cisterns are connected by bridges to create one continuous internal space. The rough ER is continuous with the outer membrane of the nuclear envelope, and some authorities regard the nuclear envelope as simply a modified extension of it. In areas called **smooth endoplasmic reticulum,** the cisterns are more tubular, branch more extensively, and lack ribosomes. The cisterns of the smooth ER are continuous with those of the rough ER, so the two are different parts of the same network.

The ER synthesizes steroids and other lipids, detoxifies alcohol and other drugs, and manufactures nearly all membranes of the cell. Rough ER produces the phospholipids and proteins of the plasma membrane and synthesizes proteins that are either secreted from the cell or packaged in organelles such as lysosomes. Rough ER is most abundant in cells that synthesize large amounts of protein, such as antibody-producing cells and cells of the digestive glands. In such cells, the ER is often the largest organelle of all, although it isn't visible to the light microscope (LM) because its thin and closely spaced membranes are beyond the LM's limit of resolution.

Most cells have only a scanty smooth ER, but it is relatively abundant in cells that engage extensively in detoxification, such as liver and kidney cells. Long-term abuse of alcohol, barbiturates, and other drugs leads to tolerance partly because the smooth ER

---

[33]*cistern* = reservoir

proliferates and detoxifies the drugs more quickly. Smooth ER is also abundant in cells of the testes and ovaries that synthesize steroid hormones. Skeletal and cardiac muscle contain extensive networks of smooth ER that store calcium and release it to trigger muscle contraction.

Ribosomes

Ribosomes are small granules of protein and RNA found in the nucleoli, in the cytosol, in mitochondria, and on the outer surfaces of the rough ER and nuclear envelope. They "read" coded genetic messages (messenger RNA) and assemble amino acids into proteins specified by the code. The unattached ribosomes scattered throughout the cytoplasm make enzymes and other proteins for use within the cell. Free ribosomes within the nucleus and mitochondria make proteins for use in those organelles. Ribosomes attach to the rough ER when they make proteins destined to be packaged in lysosomes or to be secreted from the cell, such as digestive enzymes, antibodies, and some hormones.

Golgi Complex

The **Golgi**[34] **complex** (GOAL-jee) is a small system of cisterns that synthesize carbohydrates and put the finishing touches on protein and glycoprotein synthesis. The complex resembles a stack of pita bread. It consists of only a few cisterns, slightly separated from each other; each cistern is a flattened, often curved sac with swollen edges (**fig. 3.29**). The Golgi complex receives newly synthesized proteins from the rough ER. It sorts

them, cuts and splices some of them, and adds carbohydrate moieties to some. Finally, the most mature cistern with the finished cell product breaks up into membrane-bounded **Golgi vesicles,** which are abundant in the neighborhood of the Golgi complex. Some vesicles become *lysosomes,* the organelle discussed next; some migrate to the plasma membrane and fuse with it, contributing fresh protein and phospholipid to the membrane; and some become **secretory vesicles** that store a cell product, such as breast milk or digestive enzymes, for later release. The roles of the endoplasmic reticulum, ribosomes, and Golgi complex in protein synthesis and secretion are detailed in sections 4.2c and 4.2d.

Lysosomes

A **lysosome**[35] (LY-so-some) (**fig. 3.30a**) is a package of enzymes bounded by a membrane. Although often round or oval, lysosomes are extremely variable in shape. When viewed with the TEM, they often exhibit dark gray contents devoid of structure, but sometimes show crystals or parallel layers of protein. At least 50 lysosomal enzymes have been identified. They hydrolyze proteins, nucleic acids, complex carbohydrates, phospholipids, and other substrates. In the liver, lysosomes break down glycogen to release glucose into the bloodstream. White blood cells use lysosomes to digest phagocytized bacteria. Lysosomes also digest and dispose of surplus or nonvital organelles and other cell components in order to recycle their nutrients to more important cell needs; this process is called **autophagy**[36] (aw-TOFF-uh-jee). Lysosomes also aid in a process of "cell suicide." Some cells are meant to do a certain job and then destroy themselves. The uterus, for example, weighs about 900 g at full-term pregnancy and shrinks to 60 g within 5 or 6 weeks after birth. This shrinkage is due to **autolysis,**[37] the digestion of surplus cells by their own lysosomal enzymes.

Peroxisomes

Peroxisomes (fig. 3.30b) resemble lysosomes but contain different enzymes. They are produced by collaboration between the endoplasmic reticulum and mitochondria and by fission of preexisting peroxisomes. Their general function is to use molecular oxygen (O_2) to oxidize organic molecules. These reactions produce hydrogen peroxide (H_2O_2)—hence, the name of the organelle. H_2O_2 is then used to oxidize other molecules, and the excess is broken down to water and oxygen by an enzyme called *catalase.*

Peroxisomes occur in nearly all cells but are especially abundant in liver and kidney cells. They neutralize free radicals and detoxify alcohol, other drugs, and a variety of blood-borne toxins. Peroxisomes also decompose fatty acids into two-carbon fragments that the mitochondria use as an energy source for ATP synthesis.

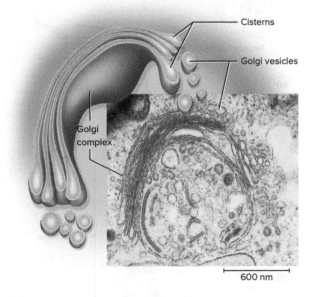

Cisterns

Golgi vesicles

Golgi complex

600 nm

FIGURE 3.29 The Golgi Complex.

David M. Phillips/Science Source

[34]Camillo Golgi (1843–1926), Italian histologist

[35]*lyso* = loosen, dissolve; *some* = body
[36]*auto* = self; *phagy* = eating
[37]*auto* = self; *lysis* = dissolving

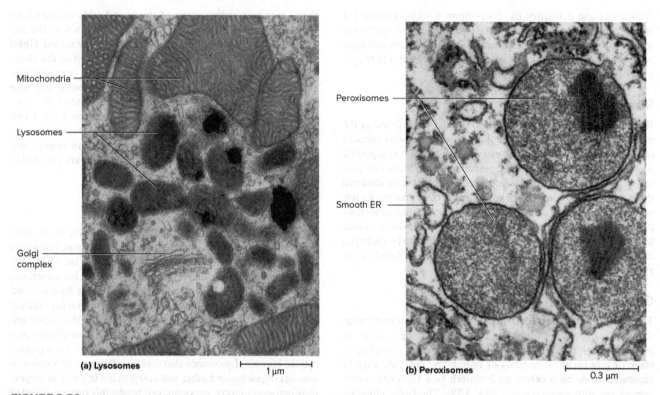

Mitochondria

Lysosomes

Golgi
complex

(a) Lysosomes   1 µm

Peroxisomes

Smooth ER

(b) Peroxisomes   0.3 µm

FIGURE 3.30 Lysosomes and Peroxisomes. (a) Lysosomes, produced from Golgi vesicles. (b) Peroxisomes, which look similar but are produced by mitochondria working with the endoplasmic reticulum, and by division of other peroxisomes.

a–b: Don Fawcett/Science Source

Proteasomes

Cells must tightly control the concentration of proteins in their cytoplasm. Therefore, they must not only synthesize new proteins, but also dispose of those that are no longer needed. Cells also need to rid themselves of damaged and nonfunctional proteins and foreign proteins introduced by such events as viral infection. Protein synthesis, we have seen, is the domain of the ribosomes; protein disposal is the function of another structurally simple organelle called a **proteasome.**

Proteasomes are hollow, cylindrical complexes of proteins located in both the cytoplasm and nucleus **(fig. 3.31).** A cell tags undesirable proteins for destruction and transports them to a proteasome. As the undesirable protein passes through the core of this organelle, the proteasome's enzymes unfold it and break it down into short peptides and free amino acids. These can be used to synthesize new proteins or be presented to the immune system for further degradation. Proteasomes degrade more than 80% of a cell's proteins.

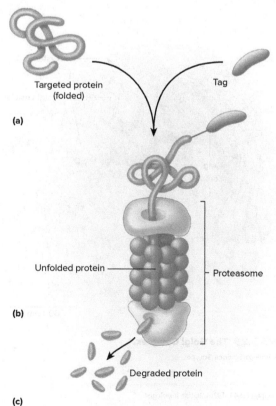

Targeted protein
(folded)

Tag

(a)

Unfolded protein

Proteasome

(b)

Degraded protein

(c)

FIGURE 3.31 Protein Degradation by a Proteasome.
(a) The unwanted protein targeted for destruction is tagged and transported to a proteasome. (b) As the protein passes down the core of the proteasome, it is unfolded and cleaved into small peptides and free amino acids. (c) The degraded protein fragments are released from the other end of the proteasome.

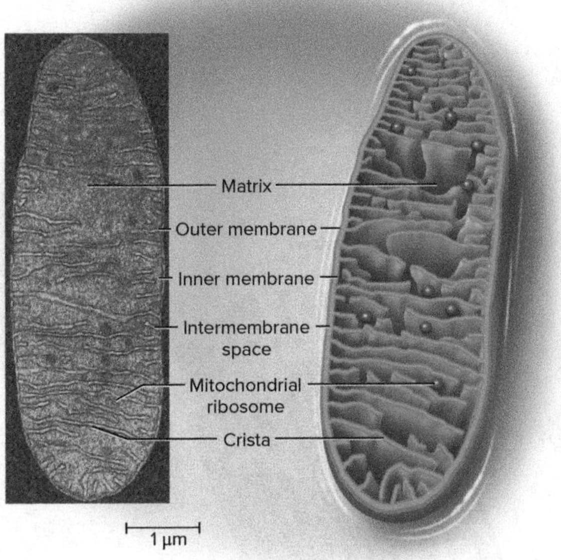

FIGURE 3.32 A Mitochondrion.

Keith R. Porter/Science Source

Mitochondria

Mitochondria[38] (MY-toe-CON-dree-uh) (singular, *mitochondrion*) are organelles specialized for synthesizing ATP. They have a variety of shapes—spheroidal, rod-shaped, kidney-shaped, or threadlike (**fig. 3.32**). They are quite mobile, squirming and changing shape continually. They sometimes undergo fusion (two mitochondria joining to become one) and fission (one mitochondrion dividing in two). Like the nucleus, a mitochondrion is surrounded by a double membrane. The inner membrane usually has folds called **cristae**[39] (CRIS-tee), which project like shelves across the organelle. The space between the cristae, called the **matrix,** contains ribosomes; enzymes used in ATP synthesis; and many small, circular DNA molecules called *mitochondrial DNA (mtDNA)*. Mitochondria are the "powerhouses" of the cell. Energy is not *made* here, but it is extracted from organic compounds and transferred to ATP, primarily by enzymes located on the cristae. The role of mitochondria in ATP synthesis is explained in detail in section 26.2d, and some evolutionary and clinical aspects of mitochondria are discussed in Deeper Insight 3.3.

---

[38]*mito* = thread; *chondr* = grain
[39]*crista* = crest

DEEPER INSIGHT 3.3

EVOLUTIONARY MEDICINE

Mitochondria—Evolution and Clinical Significance

It is virtually certain that mitochondria evolved from bacteria that invaded another primitive cell, survived in its cytoplasm, and became permanent residents. The double membranes around the mitochondrion suggest that the original bacterium provided the inner membrane, and the host cell's phagosome provided the outer membrane when the bacterium was phagocytized.

Several comparisons show the apparent relationship of mitochondria to bacteria. Their ribosomes are more like bacterial ribosomes than those of eukaryotic (nucleated) cells. Mitochondrial DNA (mtDNA) is a small, circular molecule that resembles the circular DNA of bacteria, not the linear DNA of the cell nucleus. It replicates independently of nuclear DNA. Mitochondrial DNA codes for some of the enzymes employed in ATP synthesis. It consists of 16,569 *base pairs* (explained in section 4.1), comprising 37 genes, compared with over 3 billion base pairs and about 20,000 genes in nuclear DNA.

When a sperm fertilizes an egg, any mitochondria introduced by the sperm are destroyed and only those provided by the egg are passed on to the developing embryo. Therefore, mtDNA is inherited exclusively through the mother. While nuclear DNA is reshuffled in every generation by sexual reproduction, mtDNA remains unchanged except by random mutation. Because of the known pace of such mutations, biologists and anthropologists can use mtDNA as a "molecular clock" to trace evolutionary lineages in humans and other species. The amount of difference between the mtDNAs of related species affords a record of how much time has passed since they diverged from their last common ancestor. Anthropologists have gained evidence from mtDNA that of all the women who lived in Africa 200,000 years ago, only one has any descendants still living today.

This "mitochondrial Eve" is ancestor to us all. Mitochondrial DNA has also been used as evidence in criminal law and to identify the remains of soldiers killed in combat. It was used in 2001 to identify the remains of the famed bandit Jesse James, who was killed in 1882.

Mutations in mtDNA are responsible for various rare hereditary diseases and death in early childhood. Tissues and organs with the highest energy demands are the most vulnerable to mitochondrial dysfunctions—nervous tissue, the heart, the kidneys, and skeletal muscles, for example.

Mitochondrial myopathy is a degenerative muscle disease in which the muscle displays "ragged red fibers," cells with abnormal mitochondria that stain red with a particular histological stain. Another mtDNA disease is *Leber hereditary optic neuropathy (LHON)*, a form of blindness that usually appears in young adulthood as a result of damage to the optic nerve. *Kearns–Sayre syndrome (KSS)* involves paralysis of the eye muscles, degeneration of the retina, heart disease, hearing loss, diabetes, and kidney failure. Damage to mtDNA has also been implicated as a possible factor in Alzheimer disease, Huntington disease, and other degenerative diseases of old age.

Some women known to carry mtDNA mutations can now avoid passing such diseases to their children through in vitro fertilization (IVF) with mitochondrial replacement therapy (MRT). The techniques of MRT are complex and diverse, but the essence of it is to provide an egg of the patient with healthy mitochondria from another woman, an egg donor; fertilize the recipient egg with the father's sperm; and implant this in the patient's uterus. The successful result is a "three-parent baby" who has the father's nuclear DNA, the birth mother's nuclear DNA, and the mitochondria donor's mtDNA.

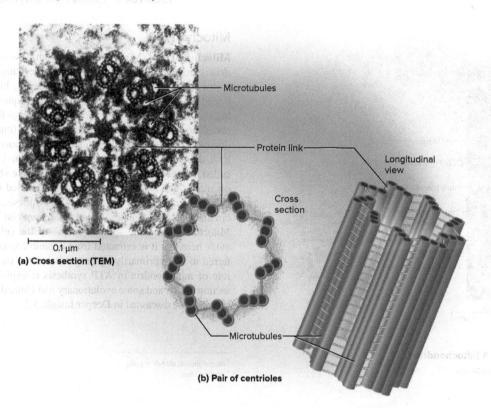

FIGURE 3.33 Centrioles. (a) Electron micrograph of a centriole as seen in cross section. (b) A pair of perpendicular centrioles.

a: Don W Fawcett/Getty Images

? *How does a centriole resemble the axoneme of a cilium? How does it differ?*

Centrioles

A **centriole** (SEN-tree-ole) is a short cylindrical assembly of microtubules, arranged in nine groups of three microtubules each **(fig. 3.33).** Near the nucleus, most cells have a small, clear patch of cytoplasm called the **centrosome**[40] containing a pair of mutually perpendicular centrioles **(see fig. 3.24).** Centrioles play a role in cell division described in section 4.3d. Each basal body of a flagellum or cilium is a single centriole oriented perpendicular to the plasma membrane. Basal bodies originate in a *centriolar organizing center* and migrate to the plasma membrane. Two microtubules of each triplet then elongate to form the nine pairs of peripheral microtubules of the axoneme. A cilium can grow to its full length in less than an hour.

3.4c Inclusions

Inclusions are of two kinds: accumulated cell products such as glycogen granules, pigments, and oil droplets (see fig. 3.28b); and

foreign bodies such as viruses, bacteria, and dust particles and other debris phagocytized by a cell. Inclusions are never enclosed in a membrane, and unlike the organelles and cytoskeleton, they are not essential to cell survival.

The major features of a cell are summarized in **table 3.4.**

> **BEFORE YOU GO ON**
>
> Answer the following questions to test your understanding of the preceding section:
>
> **22.** Distinguish between organelles and inclusions. State two examples of each.
>
> **23.** Briefly state how each of the following cell components can be recognized in electron micrographs: the nucleus, a mitochondrion, a lysosome, and a centriole. What is the primary function of each?
>
> **24.** What three organelles are involved in protein synthesis?
>
> **25.** In what ways do rough and smooth endoplasmic reticulum differ?
>
> **26.** Define *centriole, microtubule, cytoskeleton,* and *axoneme.* How are these structures related to one another?

---

[40]*centro* = central; *some* = body

TABLE 3.4	Summary of Organelles and Other Cellular Structures	
Structure	**Appearance to TEM**	**Function**
Plasma membrane (fig. 3.5)	Two dark lines at cell surface, separated by a narrow light space	Prevents escape of cell contents; regulates exchange of materials between cytoplasm and extracellular fluid; involved in intercellular communication
Microvilli (fig. 3.9)	Short, densely spaced, hairlike processes or scattered bumps on cell surface; interior featureless or with bundle of microfilaments	Increase absorptive surface area; widespread sensory roles (hearing, equilibrium, taste)
Cilia (fig. 3.10)	Long hairlike projections of apical cell surface; axoneme with usually a 9 + 2 array of microtubules	Move substances along cell surface; widespread sensory roles (equilibrium, smell, vision)
Flagellum	Long, single, whiplike process with axoneme	Sperm motility
Microfilaments (figs. 3.9 and 3.24)	Thin protein filaments (6 nm diameter), often in parallel bundles or dense networks in cytoplasm	Support microvilli and plasma membrane; involved in muscle contraction and other cell motility, endocytosis, and cell division
Intermediate filaments (fig. 3.24)	Thicker protein filaments (8–10 nm diameter) extending throughout cytoplasm or concentrated at cell-to-cell junctions	Give shape and physical support to cell; anchor cells to each other and to extracellular material; compartmentalize cell contents
Microtubules (figs. 3.24 and 3.25)	Hollow protein cylinders (25 nm diameter) radiating from centrosome	Form axonemes of cilia and flagella, centrioles, basal bodies, and mitotic spindles; enable motility of cell parts; form trackways that direct organelles and macromolecules to their destinations within a cell
Nucleus (figs. 3.4, 3.26, and 3.27)	Largest organelle in most cells, surrounded by double membrane with nuclear pores	Genetic control center of cell; directs protein synthesis; shelters the DNA
Rough ER (fig. 3.28a)	Extensive sheets of parallel membranes with ribosomes on outer surface	Protein synthesis and manufacture of cellular membranes
Smooth ER (fig. 3.28b)	Branching network of tubules with smooth surface (no ribosomes); usually broken into numerous small segments in TEM photos	Lipid synthesis, detoxification, calcium storage
Ribosomes (fig. 3.28c)	Small dark granules free in cytosol, on surface of rough ER and nuclear envelope, and inside nucleus and mitochondria	Interpret the genetic code and synthesize polypeptides
Golgi complex (fig. 3.29)	Several closely spaced, parallel cisterns with thick edges, usually near nucleus, often with many Golgi vesicles nearby	Receives and modifies newly synthesized polypeptides; synthesizes carbohydrates; adds carbohydrates to glycoproteins; packages cell products into Golgi vesicles
Golgi vesicles (fig. 3.29)	Round to irregular sacs near Golgi complex, usually with light, featureless contents	Become secretory vesicles and carry cell products to apical surface for exocytosis, or become lysosomes
Lysosomes (fig. 3.30a)	Round to oval sacs with single enclosing membrane, often a dark featureless interior but sometimes with protein layers or crystals	Contain enzymes for intracellular digestion, autophagy, programmed cell death, and glucose mobilization
Peroxisomes (fig. 3.30b)	Similar to lysosomes; often lighter in color	Contain enzymes for detoxification of free radicals, alcohol, and other drugs; oxidize fatty acids
Proteasomes (fig. 3.31)	Small cytoplasmic granules composed of a cylindrical array of proteins	Degrade proteins that are undesirable or no longer needed by a cell
Mitochondria (fig. 3.32)	Round, rod-shaped, bean-shaped, or threadlike structures with double enclosing membrane and shelflike infoldings called cristae	ATP synthesis
Centrioles (fig. 3.33)	Short cylindrical bodies, each composed of a circle of nine triplets of microtubules	Form mitotic spindle during cell division; unpaired centrioles form basal bodies of cilia and flagella
Centrosome (fig. 3.24)	Clear area near nucleus containing a pair of centrioles	Organizing center for formation of microtubules of cytoskeleton and mitotic spindle
Basal body (fig. 3.10b)	Unpaired centriole at the base of a cilium or flagellum	Point of origin, growth, and anchorage of a cilium or flagellum; produces axoneme
Inclusions (fig. 3.28b)	Highly variable—fat droplets, glycogen granules, protein crystals, dust, bacteria, viruses; never enclosed in membranes	Storage products or other products of cellular metabolism, or foreign matter retained in cytoplasm

STUDY GUIDE

▶ Assess Your Learning Outcomes

To test your knowledge, discuss the following topics with a study partner or in writing, ideally from memory.

3.1 Concepts of Cellular Structure

1. The scope of cytology
2. Basic tenets of the cell theory
3. The nine common cell shapes
4. The size range of most human cells; some extremes outside this range; and some factors that limit cells from growing indefinitely large
5. The two kinds of electron microscopes; why they have enhanced the modern understanding of cells; and the distinction between magnification and resolution in microscopy
6. Basic structural components of a cell
7. The distinction between intracellular fluid (ICF) and extracellular fluid (ECF)

3.2 The Cell Surface

1. The molecules of the plasma membrane and how they are organized
2. The distinctive roles of phospholipids, glycolipids, cholesterol, integral proteins, peripheral proteins, and glycoproteins in membrane structure
3. Seven roles played by membrane proteins
4. Distinctions between leak channels and gated channels, and between ligand-gated, voltage-gated, and mechanically gated channels
5. The function of second-messenger systems associated with the plasma membrane; the specific roles of membrane receptors, G proteins, adenylate cyclase, cyclic adenosine monophosphate, and kinases in the cAMP second-messenger system
6. Composition and functions of the glycocalyx
7. Structure and functions of microvilli, and where they are found
8. Structure and functions of cilia, and where they are found

3.3 Membrane Transport

1. What it means to say that a plasma membrane is selectively permeable, and why this property is important for human survival
2. Filtration, where it occurs in the body, and why it depends on hydrostatic pressure
3. Simple diffusion, factors that determine its speed, and examples of its physiological and clinical relevance
4. Osmosis, examples of its physiological and clinical relevance, factors that determine its speed and direction, and the role of aquaporins
5. Reverse osmosis, where it occurs in the body, and the purpose it serves
6. In relation to osmosis, the meaning of *osmotic pressure, osmolarity, tonicity,* and *milliosmoles per liter (mOsm/L)*
7. Distinctions between hypotonic, hypertonic, and isotonic solutions; their effects on cells; and how this relates to intravenous fluid therapy
8. How carrier-mediated transport differs from other types of transport, and the relevance of specificity to this process
9. How carrier-mediated transport is limited by carrier saturation and the transport maximum (T_m)
10. Distinctions between a uniport, symport, and antiport; the meanings of *cotransport* and *countertransport*; and examples of where each is relevant in human physiology
11. Similarities and differences between facilitated diffusion and active transport
12. The distinction between primary and secondary active transport
13. The mechanism and roles of the sodium–potassium (Na^+–K^+) pump
14. How vesicular transport differs from other modes of membrane transport; the difference between endocytosis and exocytosis; different forms of endocytosis; and examples of the physiological relevance of each kind of vesicular transport
15. Of the preceding mechanisms of transport, which ones require a membrane; which ones require a plasma membrane and which ones can also occur through artificial membranes; which ones require ATP and cease if ATP is unavailable, as upon death

3.4 The Cell Interior

1. Distinctions between cytoplasm, cytosol, cytoskeleton, organelles, and inclusions; and the respective, general roles of each in the internal organization of a cell
2. Overall functions of the cytoskeleton and the differences between microfilaments, intermediate filaments, and microtubules
3. Which organelles are considered membranous and why, and which of these are enclosed in single or double membranes
4. Structure and function of the nucleus, especially the nuclear envelope and nuclear lamina
5. General structure of the endoplasmic reticulum (ER); the two types of ER and the structural and functional differences between them
6. The composition, location, and function of ribosomes
7. The structure and functions of the Golgi complex; the origin and destiny of Golgi vesicles
8. The structures and functions of lysosomes and peroxisomes, and the similarities and differences between them
9. Structure and function of proteasomes
10. Structure and function of mitochondria
11. Structures and functions of centrioles, the centrosome, and basal bodies; and how these relate to each other
12. How inclusions differ from organelles; the origins and types of inclusions

▶ Testing Your Recall

Answers in Appendix A

1. The clear, structureless gel in a cell is its
   a. nucleoplasm.
   b. protoplasm.
   c. cytoplasm.
   d. neoplasm.
   e. cytosol.

2. The Na^+–K^+ pump is
   a. a peripheral protein.
   b. a transmembrane protein.
   c. a G protein.
   d. a glycolipid.
   e. a phospholipid.

3. Which of the following processes could occur *only* in the plasma membrane of a living cell?
   a. facilitated diffusion
   b. simple diffusion
   c. filtration
   d. active transport
   e. osmosis

STUDY GUIDE

4. Cells specialized for absorption of matter from the ECF are likely to show an abundance of
   a. lysosomes.
   b. microvilli.
   c. mitochondria.
   d. secretory vesicles.
   e. ribosomes.

5. Aquaporins are transmembrane proteins that promote
   a. pinocytosis.
   b. carrier-mediated transport.
   c. active transport.
   d. facilitated diffusion.
   e. osmosis.

6. Membrane carriers resemble enzymes except for the fact that carriers
   a. are not proteins.
   b. do not have binding sites.
   c. are not selective for particular ligands.
   d. change conformation when they bind a ligand.
   e. do not chemically change their ligands.

7. The cotransport of glucose derives energy from
   a. a Na^+ concentration gradient.
   b. the glucose being transported.
   c. a Ca^{2+} gradient.

d. the membrane voltage.
e. body heat.

8. The function of cAMP in a cell is
   a. to activate a G protein.
   b. to remove phosphate groups from ATP.
   c. to activate kinases.
   d. to bind to the first messenger.
   e. to add phosphate groups to enzymes.

9. Most cellular membranes are made by
   a. the nucleus.
   b. the cytoskeleton.
   c. enzymes in the peroxisomes.
   d. the endoplasmic reticulum.
   e. replication of existing membranes.

10. Matter can leave a cell by any of the following means *except*
    a. active transport.
    b. pinocytosis.
    c. an antiport.
    d. simple diffusion.
    e. exocytosis.

11. Most human cells are 10 to 15 _____ in diameter.

12. When a hormone cannot enter a cell, it activates the formation of a/an _____ inside the cell.

13. _____ channels in the plasma membrane open or close in response to changes in the electrical charge difference across the membrane.

14. The force exerted on a membrane by water is called _____.

15. A concentrated solution that causes a cell to shrink is _____ to the cell.

16. Fusion of a secretory vesicle with the plasma membrane and release of the vesicle's contents is a process called _____.

17. _____ and _____ are two granular organelles (enzyme complexes) that, respectively, synthesize and degrade proteins.

18. Liver cells can detoxify alcohol with two organelles, the _____ and _____.

19. An ion gate in the plasma membrane that opens or closes when a chemical binds to it is called a/an _____.

20. The space enclosed by the membranes of the Golgi complex and endoplasmic reticulum is called the _____.

▶ Building Your Medical Vocabulary

Answers in Appendix A

State a meaning of each word element, and give a medical term from this chapter that uses it or a slight variation of it.

1. anti-
2. chromato-
3. co-
4. cyto-
5. endo-
6. facil-
7. fusi-
8. -logy
9. -osis
10. phago-

▶ What's Wrong with These Statements?

Answers in Appendix A

Briefly explain why each of the following statements is false, or reword it to make it true.

1. If a cell were poisoned so it could not make ATP, osmosis through its membrane would cease.

2. Each cell of the human body has a single nucleus.

3. A cell's second messengers serve mainly to transport solutes through the membrane.

4. The Golgi complex makes all of a cell's lysosomes and peroxisomes.

5. Some membrane channels are peripheral proteins.

6. The plasma membrane consists primarily of protein molecules.

7. The brush border of a cell is composed of cilia.

8. Human cells placed in hypertonic saline will swell and burst.

9. The transport maximum (T_m) sets an upper limit on the rate of osmosis.

10. All of a cell's ribosomes are found on the nuclear envelope and the rough endoplasmic reticulum.

STUDY GUIDE

▶ Testing Your Comprehension

1. If someone bought a saltwater fish in a pet shop and put it in a freshwater aquarium at home, what would happen to the fish's cells? What would happen if someone put a freshwater fish in a saltwater aquarium? Explain.

2. A farmer's hand and forearm are badly crushed in a hay baler. When examined at the hospital, his blood potassium level is found to be abnormal. Would you expect it to be higher or lower than normal? Explain.

3. Many children worldwide suffer from a severe deficiency of dietary protein. As a result, they have very low levels of blood albumin. How do you think this affects the water content and volume of their blood? Explain.

4. It is often said, even in some textbooks, that mitochondria make energy for a cell. Why is this statement false?

5. Kartagener syndrome is a hereditary disease in which dynein arms are lacking from the axonemes of cilia and flagella. Predict the effect of Kartagener syndrome on a man's ability to father a child. Predict its effect on his respiratory health. Explain both answers.

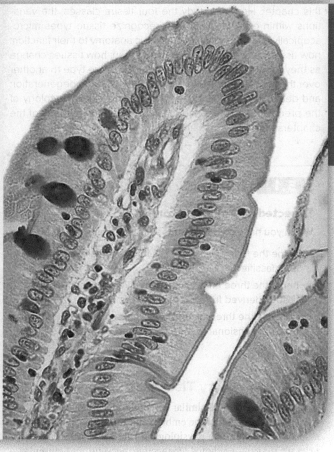

The lining of the small intestine, showing simple columnar epithelium with mucus-secreting goblet cells (magenta) (LM)

Victor P. Eroschenko

CHAPTER 5

THE HUMAN TISSUES

Anatomy & Physiology
Revealed® 4.0

Module 3: Tissues

BRUSHING UP

- This chapter details the structure of the body's serous and mucous membranes; refresh your memory of where such membranes are found in atlas A, section A.3.
- Connective tissues are characterized by a large amount of ground substance, two of the chief components of which are the glycoproteins and proteoglycans introduced in section 2.4c.
- The terminology of cell shapes introduced in figure 3.1 is used in the naming of epithelial tissue in this chapter.
- Secretory vesicles and exocytosis (see section 3.3f) are central to understanding the gland types to be introduced in this chapter.

W ith its 50 trillion cells and thousands of organs, the human body may seem to be a structure of forbidding complexity. Fortunately for our health, longevity, and self-understanding, biologists of the past were not discouraged by this complexity, but discovered patterns that made it more understandable. One such pattern is the fact that these trillions of cells belong to only 200 types or so, and they are organized into tissues that fall into just four primary categories—*epithelial, connective, nervous,* and *muscular tissue*—although there are at least 23 subtypes of these four.

Organs derive their function not from their cells alone but from how the cells are organized into tissues. Cells are specialized for certain tasks: muscle contraction, defense, enzyme secretion, and so forth. No one cell type can carry out all of the body's vital functions. Cells therefore work together at certain tasks and form tissues that carry out a particular function, such as nerve signaling or nutrient digestion. An organ is a structure with discrete boundaries that is composed of two or more tissue types.

The study of tissues and how they are arranged into organs is called **histology,**[1] or **microscopic anatomy**—the subject of

[1]*histo* = tissue; *logy* = study of

this chapter. Here we study the four tissue classes; the variations within each class; how to recognize tissue types microscopically and relate their microscopic anatomy to their function; how tissues are arranged to form an organ; how tissues change as they grow, shrink, or change from one tissue type to another over the life of the individual; and modes of tissue degeneration and death. Histology bridges the gap between the cytology of the preceding chapters and the organ system approach of the chapters that follow.

5.1   The Study of Tissues

Expected Learning Outcomes

When you have completed this section, you should be able to

a. name the four primary classes into which all adult tissues are classified;

b. name the three embryonic germ layers and some adult tissues derived from each; and

c. visualize the three-dimensional shape of a structure from a two-dimensional tissue section.

5.1a The Primary Tissue Classes

A **tissue** is a group of similar cells and cell products that arise from the same region of the embryo and work together to perform a specific structural or physiological role in an organ. The four *primary tissues*—epithelial, connective, nervous, and muscular— are summarized in **table 5.1.** They differ in the types and functions of their cells, the characteristics of the **matrix (extracellular material)** that surrounds the cells, and the relative amount of space occupied by the cells and matrix. In muscle and epithelium, the cells are so close together that the matrix is scarcely visible, but in most connective tissues, the matrix occupies much more space than the cells do.

TABLE 5.1	The Four Primary Tissue Classes		
Type	**Definition**		**Representative Locations**
Epithelial		Tissue composed of layers of closely spaced cells that cover organ surfaces, form glands, and serve for protection, secretion, and absorption	Epidermis Inner lining of digestive tract Liver and other glands
Connective		Tissue with usually more matrix than cell volume, often specialized to support and protect organs and to bind other tissues and organs to each other	Tendons and ligaments Cartilage and bone Blood
Nervous		Tissue containing excitable cells specialized for rapid transmission of coded information to other cells	Brain Spinal cord Nerves
Muscular		Tissue composed of elongated, excitable muscle cells specialized for contraction	Skeletal muscles Heart (cardiac muscle) Walls of viscera (smooth muscle)

Photos (Epithelial): ©Ed Reschke/Getty Images; (Connective): Dennis Strete/McGraw-Hill Education; (Nervous, Muscular): Ed Reschke

The matrix is composed of fibrous proteins and, usually, a clear gel variously known as **ground substance, tissue fluid, extracellular fluid (ECF),** or **interstitial[2] fluid.** In cartilage and bone, it can be rubbery or stony in consistency. The ground substance contains water, gases, minerals, nutrients, wastes, hormones, and other chemicals. This is the medium from which all cells obtain their oxygen, nutrients, and other needs, and into which cells release metabolic wastes, hormones, and other products.

In summary, a tissue is composed of cells and matrix, and the matrix is composed of fibers and ground substance.

5.1b Embryonic Tissues

Human development begins with a single cell, the fertilized egg, which soon divides to produce scores of identical, smaller cells. The first tissues appear when these cells start to organize themselves into layers—first two, and soon three strata called the **primary germ layers,** which give rise to all of the body's mature tissues. The three primary germ layers are called *ectoderm, mesoderm,* and *endoderm.* The **ectoderm**[3] is an outer layer that gives rise to the epidermis and nervous system. The innermost layer, the **endoderm,**[4] gives rise to the mucous membranes of the digestive and respiratory tracts and to the digestive glands, among other things. Between these two is the **mesoderm,**[5] a layer of more loosely organized cells. Mesoderm eventually turns to a gelatinous tissue called **mesenchyme,** composed of fine, wispy collagen (protein) fibers and branching *mesenchymal cells* embedded in a gelatinous ground substance. Mesenchyme gives rise to cardiac muscle, bone, and blood, among other tissues. (The development of the three primary tissues in the embryo is detailed at "Embryogenesis" in section 29.1f.) Most organs are composed of tissues derived from two or more primary germ layers. The rest of this chapter concerns the "mature" tissues that exist from infancy through adulthood.

5.1c Interpreting Tissue Sections

In your study of histology, you may be presented with various tissue preparations mounted on microscope slides. Most such preparations are thin slices called **histological sections.** The best anatomical insight depends on an ability to deduce the three-dimensional structure of an organ from these two-dimensional sections **(fig. 5.1).** This ability, in turn, depends on an awareness of how tissues are prepared for study.

---

[2]*inter* = between; *stit* = to stand
[3]*ecto* = outer; *derm* = skin

[4]*endo* = inner; *derm* = skin
[5]*meso* = middle; *derm* = skin

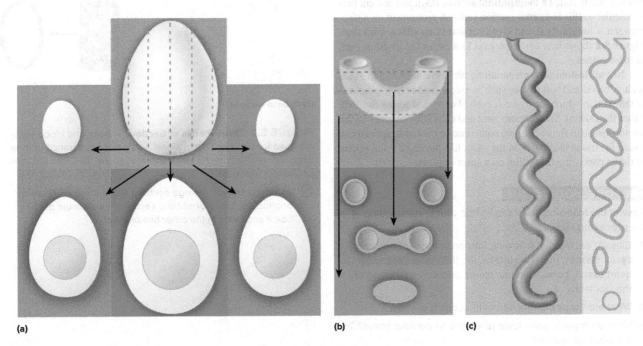

(a)   (b)   (c)

FIGURE 5.1 Three-Dimensional Interpretation of Two-Dimensional Images. (a) A boiled egg. Grazing sections (top left and right) would miss the yolk, just as a tissue section may miss a nucleus or other structure. (b) Elbow macaroni, which resembles many curved ducts and tubules. A section far from the bend would give the impression of two separate tubules; a section near the bend would show two interconnected lumina (cavities); and a section still farther down could miss the lumen completely. (c) A coiled gland in three dimensions and as it would look in a vertical tissue section of a tissue such as the lining of the uterus.

Histologists use a variety of techniques for preserving, sectioning (slicing), and staining tissues to show their structural details as clearly as possible. Tissue specimens are preserved in a **fixative**—a chemical such as formalin that prevents decay. After fixation, most tissues are cut into sections typically only one or two cells thick. Sectioning is necessary to allow the light of a microscope to pass through and so the image is not confused by too many layers of overlapping cells. The sections are then mounted on slides and artificially colored with histological **stains** to enhance detail. If they were not stained, most tissue sections would appear pale gray. With stains that bind to different components of a tissue, however, you may see pink cytoplasm; violet nuclei; and blue, green, or golden-brown protein fibers, depending on the stain used.

Sectioning a tissue reduces a three-dimensional structure to a series of two-dimensional slices. You must keep this in mind and try to translate the microscopic image into a mental image of the whole structure. Like the boiled egg and elbow macaroni in figure 5.1, an object may look quite different when it is cut at various levels, or *planes of section*. A coiled tube, such as a gland of the uterus (fig. 5.1c), is often broken up into multiple portions since it meanders in and out of the plane of section. An experienced viewer, however, recognizes that the separated pieces are parts of a single tube winding its way to the organ surface. Note that a grazing slice through a boiled egg might miss the yolk, just as a tissue section might miss the nucleus of a cell even though it was present.

Many anatomical structures are longer on one axis than another—the humerus and esophagus, for example. A tissue cut on its long axis is called a **longitudinal section (l.s.),** and one cut perpendicular to this is a **cross section (c.s.).** A section cut on a slant between a longitudinal and cross section is an **oblique section.** **Figure 5.2** shows how certain organs look when sectioned on each of these planes.

Not all histological preparations are sections. Liquid tissues such as blood and soft tissues such as spinal cord may be prepared as **smears,** in which the tissue is rubbed or spread across the slide rather than sliced. Some membranes and cobwebby tissues like the *areolar tissue* in figure 5.14 are sometimes mounted as **spreads,** in which the tissue is laid out on the slide, like placing a small square of tissue paper or a tuft of lint on a sheet of glass.

BEFORE YOU GO ON

Answer the following questions to test your understanding of the preceding section:

1. Classify each of the following into one of the four primary tissue classes: the skin surface, fat, the spinal cord, most heart tissue, bone, tendons, blood, and the inner lining of the stomach.

2. What are tissues composed of in addition to cells?

3. What embryonic germ layer gives rise to nervous tissue? To the liver? To muscle?

4. What is the term for a thin, stained slice of tissue mounted on a microscope slide?

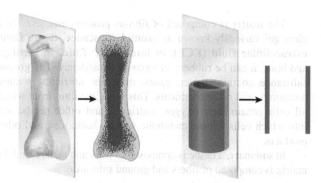

(a) Longitudinal sections

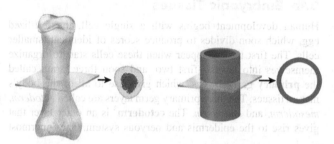

(b) Cross sections

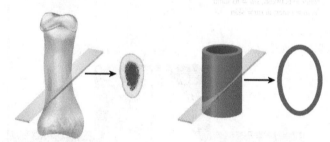

(c) Oblique sections

FIGURE 5.2 Three Planes of Section. A bone and blood vessel are used to relate two-dimensional sectioned appearance to three-dimensional structure. (a) Longitudinal sections. (b) Cross sections. (c) Oblique sections.

❓ *Would you classify the egg sections in the previous figure as longitudinal, cross, or oblique sections? How would the egg look if sectioned in the other two planes?*

5.2 Epithelial Tissue

Expected Learning Outcomes

When you have completed this section, you should be able to

a. describe the properties that distinguish epithelium from other tissue classes;

b. list and classify eight types of epithelium, distinguish them from each other, and state where each type can be found in the body;

c. explain how the structural differences between epithelia relate to their functional differences; and

d. visually recognize each epithelial type from specimens or photographs.

Epithelial[6] **tissue** consists of a sheet of closely adhering cells, one or more cells thick, with the upper surface usually exposed to the environment or to an internal space in the body. Epithelium covers the body surface, lines body cavities, forms the external and internal linings of many organs, and constitutes most gland tissue. The functions of epithelial tissue include

- **Protection.** Epithelia protect deeper tissues from invasion and injury. The epidermis of the skin, for example, is a barrier to infection, and the inner lining of the stomach protects its deeper tissues from stomach acid and enzymes.

- **Secretion.** Epithelia produce mucus, sweat, enzymes, hormones, and most of the body's other secretions; glands are composed largely of epithelial tissue.

- **Excretion.** Epithelia void wastes from the tissues, such as CO_2 across the pulmonary epithelium and bile from the epithelium of the liver.

- **Absorption.** Epithelia absorb chemicals from the adjacent medium; nutrients, for example, are absorbed through the epithelium of the small intestine.

- **Filtration.** All substances leaving the blood are selectively filtered through the epithelium that lines the blood vessels; all urinary waste is filtered through epithelia of the kidneys.

- **Sensation.** Epithelia are provided with nerve endings that sense stimulation ranging from a touch on the skin to irritation of the stomach.

The cells and extracellular material of an epithelium can be loosely compared to the bricks and mortar of a wall. The extracellular material ("mortar") is so thin, however, that it is barely visible with a light microscope, and the cells appear pressed very close together. Epithelia are *avascular*[7] (without blood vessels)—there is no room for them between the cells. Epithelia, however, usually lie on a vessel-rich layer of connective

tissue, which furnishes them with nutrients and waste removal. Epithelial cells closest to the connective tissue typically exhibit a high rate of mitosis. This allows epithelia to repair themselves quickly—an ability of special importance in protective epithelia that are highly vulnerable to such injuries as skin abrasions and erosion by stomach acid.

Between an epithelium and the underlying connective tissue is a layer called the **basement membrane.** It contains collagen, glycoproteins, and other protein–carbohydrate complexes, and blends into other proteins of the connective tissue. The basement membrane serves to anchor an epithelium to the connective tissue; it controls the exchange of materials between the epithelium and the underlying tissues; and it binds growth factors from below that regulate epithelial development. The surface of an epithelial cell that faces the basement membrane is its **basal surface,** the one that faces away from it toward the body surface or the internal cavity (lumen) of an organ is the **apical surface,** and between these two, the "sidewall" of a cell is called the **lateral surface.**

Epithelia are classified into two broad categories—*simple* and *stratified*—with four types in each category. In a simple epithelium, every cell is anchored to the basement membrane, whereas in a stratified epithelium, some cells rest on top of other cells and do not contact the basement membrane **(fig. 5.3).**

Table 5.2 (containing **figs. 5.4** to **5.7**) summarizes the structural and functional differences between the four simple epithelia. In this and subsequent tables, each photograph is accompanied by a labeled drawing of the same specimen. The drawings clarify cell boundaries and other relevant features that may otherwise be difficult to see or identify in photographs or through the microscope. Each figure indicates the approximate magnification at which the original photograph was made. Each is enlarged much more than this when printed in the book, but selecting the closest magnification on a microscope should enable you to see a comparable level of detail (resolution).

5.2a Simple Epithelia

Generally, a **simple epithelium** has only one layer of cells, although this is a somewhat debatable point in the *pseudostratified columnar* type. Three types of simple epithelia are named for the shapes of their cells: **simple squamous**[8] (thin scaly cells), **simple cuboidal** (squarish or round cells), and **simple columnar** (tall narrow cells). In the fourth type, **pseudostratified columnar,** not all cells reach the surface; the shorter cells are covered by the taller ones. This epithelium looks stratified in most tissue sections, but careful examination, especially with the electron microscope, shows that every cell reaches the basement membrane—like trees in a forest, where some grow taller than others but all are anchored in the soil below.

Simple columnar and pseudostratified columnar epithelia often have wineglass-shaped **goblet cells** that produce protective

---

[6] *epi* = upon; *theli* = nipple, female
[7] *a* = without; *vas* = blood vessels

[8] *squam* = scale

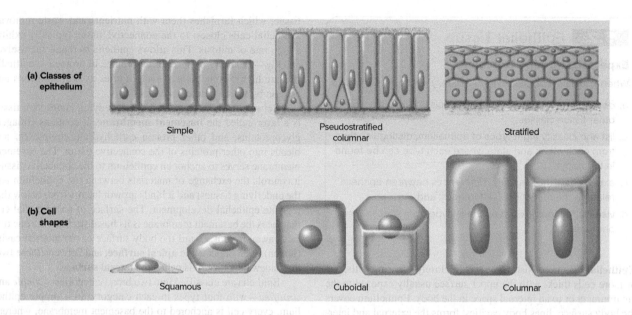

FIGURE 5.3 Cell Shapes and Epithelial Types. (a) Frontal sections of three classes of epithelium. Pseudostratified columnar epithelium is a special type of simple epithelium that gives a false appearance of multiple cell layers. (b) Frontal and oblique views of three cell shapes—squamous, cuboidal, and columnar. Note that these traditional terms describe the frontal appearance, but all three are polygonal when viewed from above.

mucous coatings over the mucous membranes. These cells have an expanded apical end filled with secretory vesicles; their product becomes mucus when it is secreted and absorbs water. The basal part of the cell is a narrow stem, like that of a wineglass, that reaches to the basement membrane.

5.2b Stratified Epithelia

Stratified epithelia range from 2 to 20 or more layers of cells, with some cells resting directly on others and only the deepest layer attached to the basement membrane **(table 5.3, containing figs. 5.8 to 5.11).** Three of the stratified epithelia are named for the shapes of their surface cells: **stratified squamous, stratified cuboidal,** and **stratified columnar epithelia.** The deeper cells, however, may be of a different shape than the surface cells. The fourth type, **urothelium,** is named for the fact that it's unique to the urinary tract. It is sometimes called by an older name, *transitional epithelium,* that arose from a misunderstanding that it represented a transitional stage between stratified squamous and stratified columnar epithelium.

Stratified columnar epithelium is rare and of relatively minor importance—seen only in places where two other epithelial types meet, as in limited regions of the pharynx, larynx, anal canal, and male urethra. We will not consider this type any further.

The most widespread epithelium in the body is stratified squamous epithelium, which deserves further discussion. Its deepest layer of cells are cuboidal to columnar, and include mitotically active stem cells. Their daughter cells push toward the surface and become flatter (more scaly) as they migrate farther upward, until they finally die and flake off. Their loss is called **exfoliation (desquamation) (fig. 5.12);** the study of exfoliated

cells is called *exfoliate cytology.* You can easily study exfoliated cells by scraping your gums with a toothpick, smearing this material on a slide, and staining it with iodine for microscopic examination. A similar procedure is used in the *Pap smear,* an examination of exfoliated cells from the cervix for signs of uterine cancer (see fig. 28.5).

Stratified squamous epithelia are of two kinds—keratinized and nonkeratinized. A **keratinized (cornified)** epithelium, found in the epidermis, is covered with a layer of dead compressed cells. These cells, called **keratinocytes,** are packed with the durable protein *keratin* and coated with a water-repellent glycolipid. The skin surface is therefore relatively dry; it retards water loss from the body; and it resists penetration by disease organisms. (Keratin is also the protein of which animal horns are made, hence its name.[9]) The tongue, esophagus, vagina, and a few other internal membranes are covered with the **nonkeratinized** type, which lacks the surface layer of dead cells. This type provides a surface that is, again, abrasion-resistant, but also moist and slippery. These characteristics are well suited to resist stress produced by chewing and swallowing food and by sexual intercourse and childbirth.

Urothelium is another particularly interesting type of stratified epithelium. Why is it limited to the urinary tract? The answer relates to the fact that urine is usually acidic and hypertonic to the intracellular fluid. It would tend to draw water out of the cells by osmosis and kill them if there were nothing to protect them. The

(text continued after table 5.3)

[9]*kerat* = horn

TABLE 5.2	Simple Epithelia
Simple Squamous Epithelium	**Simple Cuboidal Epithelium**

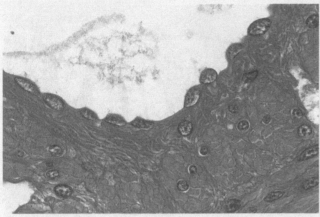

(a)

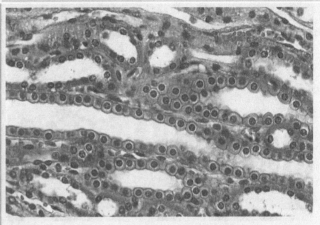

(a)

Squamous epithelial cells   Nuclei of smooth muscle

Basement membrane

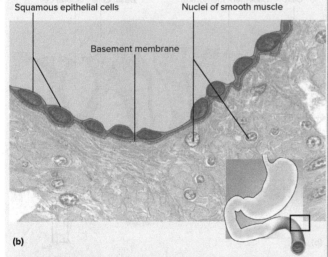

(b)

Lumen of kidney tubule   Cuboidal epithelial cells   Basement membrane

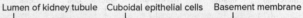
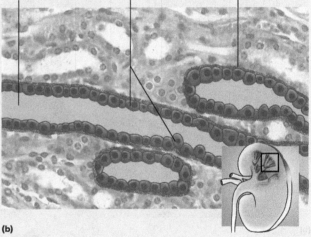

(b)

FIGURE 5.4 Simple Squamous Epithelium. Serosa of the small intestine (×400). (a) Light micrograph. (b) Labeled drawing. **APR**

a: Dennis Strete/McGraw-Hill Education

Microscopic appearance: Single layer of thin cells, shaped like fried eggs with bulge where nucleus is located; nucleus flattened in the plane of the cell, like an egg yolk; cytoplasm may be so thin it is hard to see in tissue sections; in surface view, cells have angular contours and nuclei appear round

Representative locations: Air sacs (alveoli) of lungs; glomerular capsules of kidneys; some kidney tubules; inner lining (endothelium) of heart and blood vessels; serous membranes of stomach, intestines, and some other viscera; surface mesothelium of pleura, pericardium, peritoneum, and mesenteries

Functions: Allows rapid diffusion or transport of substances through membrane; secretes lubricating serous fluid

FIGURE 5.5 Simple Cuboidal Epithelium. Kidney tubules (×400). (a) Light micrograph. (b) Labeled drawing. **APR**

a: Dennis Strete/McGraw-Hill Education

Microscopic appearance: Single layer of square or round cells; in glands, cells often pyramidal and arranged like segments of an orange around a central space; spherical, centrally placed nuclei; with a brush border of microvilli in some kidney tubules; ciliated in bronchioles of lung

Representative locations: Liver, thyroid, mammary, salivary, and other glands; most kidney tubules; bronchioles

Functions: Absorption and secretion; production of protective mucous coat; movement of respiratory mucus

TABLE 5.2	Simple Epithelia *(continued)*

Simple Columnar Epithelium	Pseudostratified Columnar Epithelium
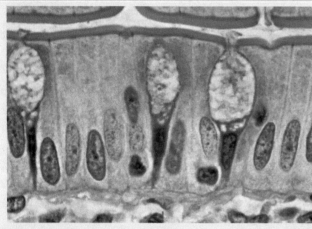 (a)	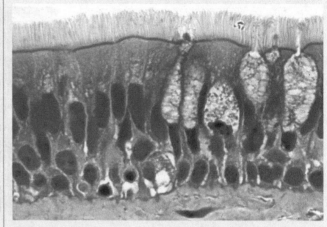 (a)
Brush border (microvilli) Connective tissue Basement membrane Nuclei Goblet cell Columnar cells 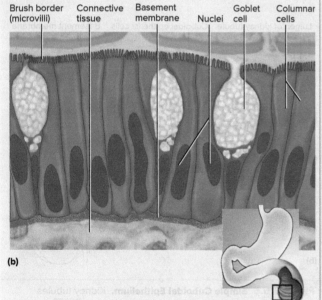 (b)	Cilia Basement membrane Basal cells Goblet cell 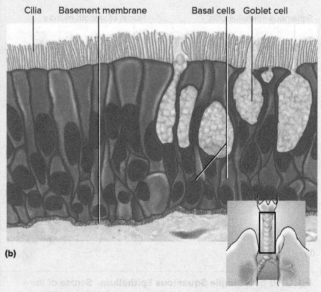 (b)

FIGURE 5.6 Simple Columnar Epithelium. Mucosa of the small intestine (×400). (a) Light micrograph. (b) Labeled drawing. **APR**

a: Ed Reschke/Getty Images

Microscopic appearance: Single layer of tall, narrow cells; oval or sausage-shaped nuclei, vertically oriented, usually in basal half of cell; apical portion of cell often shows secretory vesicles visible with TEM; often shows a brush border of microvilli; ciliated in some organs; may possess goblet cells

Representative locations: Inner lining of stomach, intestines, gallbladder, uterus, and uterine tubes; some kidney tubules

Functions: Absorption; secretion of mucus and other products; movement of egg and embryo in uterine tube

FIGURE 5.7 Ciliated Pseudostratified Columnar Epithelium. Mucosa of the trachea (×400). (a) Light micrograph. (b) Labeled drawing. **APR**

a: Dennis Strete/McGraw-Hill Education

Microscopic appearance: Looks multilayered; some cells do not reach free surface, but all cells reach basement membrane; nuclei at several levels in deeper half of epithelium; often with goblet cells; often ciliated

Representative locations: Respiratory tract from nasal cavity to bronchi; portions of male urethra

Functions: Secretes and propels mucus

TABLE 5.3	Stratified Epithelia

Stratified Squamous Epithelium—Keratinized	Stratified Squamous Epithelium—Nonkeratinized

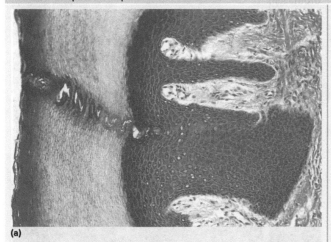

(a)

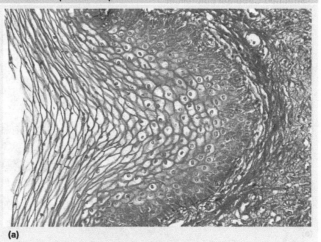

(a)

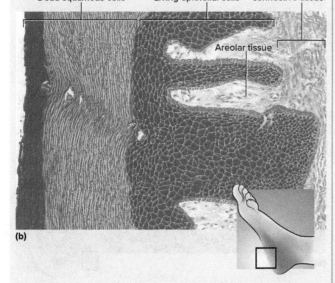

Dead squamous cells   Living epithelial cells   Dense irregular connective tissue

Areolar tissue

(b)

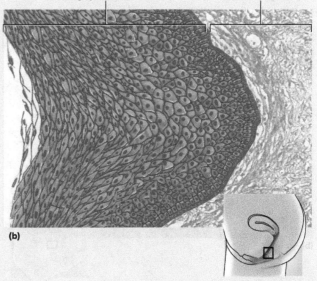

Living epithelial cells   Connective tissue

(b)

FIGURE 5.8 Keratinized Stratified Squamous Epithelium.
Epidermis of the sole of the foot (×400). (a) Light micrograph.
(b) Labeled drawing. **APR**
a: ©Ed Reschke

FIGURE 5.9 Nonkeratinized Stratified Squamous Epithelium.
Mucosa of the vagina (×400). (a) Light micrograph. (b) Labeled
drawing. **APR**
a: ©Ed Reschke

Microscopic appearance: Multiple cell layers with cells becoming
increasingly flat and scaly toward surface; surface covered with a
layer of compact dead cells without nuclei; basal cells may be cuboidal to columnar
Representative locations: Epidermis; palms and soles are especially
heavily keratinized
Functions: Resists abrasion and penetration by pathogenic organisms; retards water loss through skin

Microscopic appearance: Same as keratinized epithelium but without
the surface layer of dead cells
Representative locations: Tongue, oral mucosa, esophagus, anal
canal, vagina
Functions: Resists abrasion and penetration by pathogenic organisms

TABLE 5.3	**Stratified Epithelia** *(continued)*
Stratified Cuboidal Epithelium	**Urothelium**

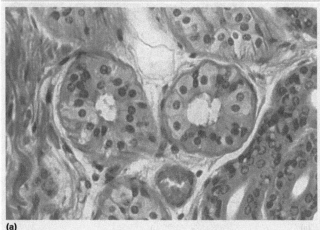

(a)

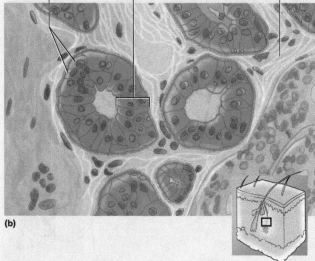

Cuboidal cells   Epithelium   Connective tissue

(b)

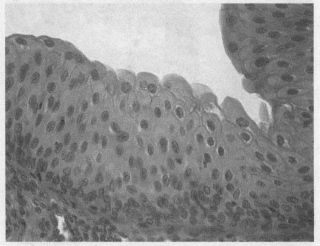

(a)

Basement   Connective   Binucleate
membrane   tissue   epithelial cell

(b)

FIGURE 5.10 Stratified Cuboidal Epithelium. Duct of a sweat gland (×400). (a) Light micrograph. (b) Labeled drawing. **APR**

a: Lester V. Bergman/Corbis NX/Getty Images

Microscopic appearance: Two or more layers of cells; surface cells square or round

Representative locations: Sweat gland ducts; egg-producing vesicles (follicles) of ovaries; sperm-producing ducts (seminiferous tubules) of testis

Functions: Contributes to sweat secretion; secretes ovarian hormones; produces sperm

FIGURE 5.11 Urothelium. Kidney (×400). (a) Light micrograph. (b) Labeled drawing. **APR**

a: Johnny R. Howze

Microscopic appearance: Somewhat resembles stratified squamous epithelium, but surface cells are rounded, not flattened, and often bulge at surface; typically five or six cells thick when relaxed and two or three cells thick when stretched; cells may be flatter and thinner when urothelium is stretched (as in a distended bladder); some cells have two nuclei

Representative locations: Urinary tract—part of kidney, ureter, bladder, part of urethra

Functions: Stretches to allow filling of urinary tract; protects underlying tissues from osmotic damage by urine

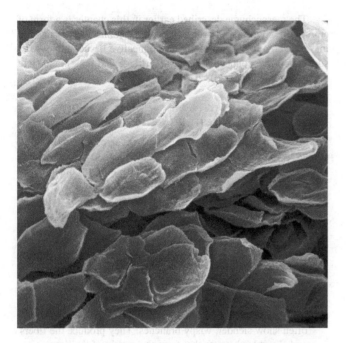

FIGURE 5.12 Exfoliation of Squamous Cells from the Mucosa of the Vagina.

David M. Phillips/Science Source

Aside from the gums and vagina, name another epithelium in the body that would look like this to the scanning electron microscope.

domed surface cells of urothelium, however, have a unique protective property. They are called **umbrella cells.** On the upper surface of an umbrella cell, the outer phospholipid layer of the plasma membrane is thicker than usual and has dense patches called *lipid rafts* with embedded proteins called *uroplakins.* Uroplakins are impermeable to urine and protect the urothelium, including the cytoplasm of the umbrella cell itself. Lipid rafts are connected to each other by hinges of ordinary plasma membrane. When the bladder is empty and relaxed, these plaques fold at the hinges (like folding a laptop computer) and drop into the cell interior for storage, and the cell bulges upward as seen in figure 5.11. As the bladder fills with urine, the hinges open (like opening the computer), the plaques spread out over the surface to protect the cell, and the umbrella cells become thinner and flatter. Not surprisingly, this type of epithelium is best developed in the bladder, where it is subject to prolonged contact with stored urine.

BEFORE YOU GO ON

Answer the following questions to test your understanding of the preceding section:

5. Distinguish between simple and stratified epithelia, and explain why pseudostratified columnar epithelium belongs in the former category despite its superficial appearance.

6. Explain how to distinguish a stratified squamous epithelium from a urothelium.

7. What function do keratinized and nonkeratinized stratified squamous epithelia have in common? What is the structural difference between these two? How is this structural difference related to a functional difference between them?

8. How do the epithelia of the esophagus and stomach differ? How does this relate to their respective functions?

 DEEPER INSIGHT 5.1

CLINICAL APPLICATION

Biopsy

Biopsy[10] means the removal and microscopic examination of a sample of living tissue. One purpose of a biopsy is diagnosis of diseases that can be identified only from the microscopic appearance of cells or tissues—for example, a malignancy such as colon cancer, an infection such as tuberculosis, or an inflammatory disease such as lupus. Diagnosis may include the *staging* of a cancer to express how advanced it is. (See Deeper Insight 28.1, Pap Smears and Cervical Cancer.) Another purpose is treatment planning. The appropriate drug for cancer chemotherapy, for example, may depend on the type of cancer revealed by the biopsy, and for cervical or breast cancer, it depends on the stage of the cancer. A third purpose is surgical guidance. A specimen from a patient undergoing lumpectomy for breast cancer, for example, may be examined for *clear margins* so the surgeon can know if all the malignant tissue has been removed or it is necessary to cut more widely.

Cutting out and examining an entire suspicious mass, such as a breast lump or lymph node, is called *excisional biopsy.* An *incisional*

(core) biopsy is removal of just a portion of the mass, such as a suspected skin melanoma, for diagnostic examination. A *needle biopsy* may be done to obtain a sample of cells when it isn't necessary to maintain the exact structure of the tissue, such as a sample of bone marrow for the diagnosis of leukemia. Sucking out such a specimen with a needle is called *needle aspiration biopsy.* Some needle biopsies employ an instrument with jaws, inserted through a needle, to take a "bite" of the suspicious tissue or remove an entire mass such as a colon polyp. In some procedures called *CT guided needle biopsy,* exact placement of the needle is guided by watching it on a CT monitor.

In some cases, the biopsy specimen will be examined by an in-house pathologist while the patient is still under anesthesia and the surgeon awaits the lab report in order to know how to proceed. In outpatient cases, a specimen such as a lymph node may be sent to a medical diagnostics laboratory elsewhere, which will report the result back to the physician.

---

[10]*bio* = living; *opsy* = viewing

5.3   Connective Tissue

Expected Learning Outcomes
When you have completed this section, you should be able to

a. describe the properties that most connective tissues have in common;

b. discuss the types of cells found in connective tissue;

c. explain what the matrix of a connective tissue is and describe its components;

d. name and classify 10 types of connective tissue, describe their cellular components and matrix, and explain what distinguishes them from each other; and

e. visually recognize each connective tissue type from specimens or photographs.

5.3a Overview

Connective tissues are the most abundant, widely distributed, and histologically variable of the primary tissues. They include fibrous tissue, adipose tissue, cartilage, bone, and blood. Such diverse tissues may seem to have little in common, but as a rule, their cells occupy less space than the extracellular matrix. Usually their cells are not in direct contact with each other, but are separated by expanses of matrix. Connective tissues vary greatly in vascularity, from rich networks of blood vessels in the loose connective tissues to few or no blood vessels in cartilage.

The functions of connective tissue include

- **Binding of organs.** Tendons bind muscle to bone, ligaments bind one bone to another, fat holds the kidneys and eyes in place, and fibrous tissue binds the skin to underlying muscle.

- **Support.** Bones support the body; cartilage supports the ears, nose, larynx, and trachea; fibrous tissues form the framework of organs such as the spleen.

- **Physical protection.** The cranium, ribs, and sternum protect delicate organs such as the brain, lungs, and heart; fatty cushions protect the kidneys and eyes.

- **Immune protection.** Connective tissue cells attack foreign invaders, and connective tissue fiber forms a "battlefield" under the skin and mucous membranes where immune cells can be quickly mobilized against disease agents.

- **Movement.** Bones provide the lever system for body movement, cartilages are involved in movement of the vocal cords, and cartilages on bone surfaces ease joint movements.

- **Storage.** Fat is the body's major energy reserve; bone is a reservoir of calcium and phosphorus that can be drawn upon when needed.

- **Heat production.** Metabolism of brown fat generates heat in infants and children.

- **Transport.** Blood transports gases, nutrients, wastes, hormones, and blood cells.

The mesenchyme described earlier in this chapter is a form of embryonic connective tissue. The mature connective tissues fall into four broad categories: fibrous connective tissue, adipose tissue, supportive connective tissues (cartilage and bone), and fluid connective tissue (blood).

5.3b Fibrous Connective Tissue

Fibrous connective tissue is the most diverse type. Nearly all connective tissues contain fibers, but the tissues considered here are classified together because the fibers are so conspicuous. Fibers are, of course, just one component of the tissue, which also includes cells and ground substance. Before examining specific types of fibrous connective tissue, let's examine these components.

Components of Fibrous Connective Tissue

Cells The cells of fibrous connective tissue include the following types:

- **Fibroblasts.**[11] These are large, fusiform or stellate cells that often show slender, wispy branches. They produce the fibers and ground substance that form the matrix of the tissue.

- **Macrophages.**[12] These are large phagocytic cells that wander through the connective tissues, where they engulf and destroy bacteria, other foreign particles, and dead or dying cells of our own body. They also activate the immune system when they sense foreign matter called *antigens*. They arise from white blood cells called *monocytes* or from the same stem cells as monocytes.

- **Leukocytes,**[13] or **white blood cells (WBCs).** WBCs travel briefly in the bloodstream, then crawl out through the walls of small blood vessels and spend most of their time in the connective tissues. The two most common types are *neutrophils,* which wander about attacking bacteria, and *lymphocytes,* which react against bacteria, toxins, and other foreign agents. Lymphocytes often form dense patches in the mucous membranes.

- **Plasma cells.** Certain lymphocytes turn into plasma cells when they detect foreign agents. The plasma cells then synthesize disease-fighting proteins called *antibodies.* Plasma cells are rarely seen except in the wall of the intestines and in inflamed tissue.

- **Mast cells.** These cells, found especially alongside blood vessels, secrete a chemical called *heparin* that inhibits blood clotting, and one called *histamine* that increases blood flow by dilating blood vessels.

- **Adipocytes** (AD-ih-po-sites), or **fat cells.** These appear in small clusters in some fibrous connective tissues. When they dominate an area, the tissue is called *adipose tissue.*

---

[11]*fibro* = fiber; *blast* = producing
[12]*macro* = big; *phage* = eater
[13]*leuko* = white; *cyte* = cell

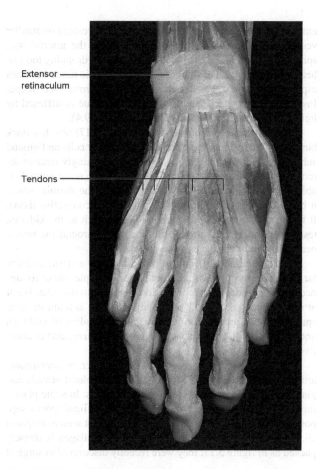

Extensor retinaculum

Tendons

FIGURE 5.13 Tendons and Ligament. The tendons of the hand and the ligamentous band (extensor retinaculum) of the wrist are composed of collagen, which has a white glistening appearance.
Rebecca Gray/McGraw-Hill Education

Fibers Three types of protein fibers are found in fibrous connective tissues:

- **Collagenous fibers** (col-LADJ-eh-nus). These fibers, made of collagen, are tough and flexible and resist stretching. Collagen is the body's most abundant protein, constituting about 25% of the total. It is the base of such animal products as gelatin, leather, and glue.[14] In fresh tissue, collagenous fibers have a glistening white appearance, as seen in tendons and some cuts of meat (**fig. 5.13**); thus, they are often called *white fibers*. In tissue sections, collagen forms coarse, wavy bundles, often dyed pink, blue, or green by the most common histological stains. Tendons, ligaments, and the dermis of the skin are made mainly of collagen. Less visibly, collagen pervades the matrix of cartilage and bone.
- **Reticular**[15] **fibers.** These are thin collagen fibers coated with glycoprotein. They form a spongelike framework for

such organs as the spleen and lymph nodes and constitute part of the basement membranes underlying epithelia.

- **Elastic fibers.** These are thinner than collagenous fibers, and they branch and rejoin each other along their course. They are made of a protein called **elastin** coated with a glycoprotein *(fibrillin)*. The coiled structure of elastin allows it to stretch and recoil like a rubber band. Elastic fibers account for the ability of the skin, lungs, and arteries to spring back after they are stretched. (Elasticity is not the ability to stretch, but the tendency to recoil when tension is released.)

Ground Substance Amid the cells and fibers in some tissue sections, there appears to be a lot of empty space. In life, this space is occupied by the featureless **ground substance.** Ground substance usually has a gelatinous to rubbery consistency resulting from three classes of large molecules: glycosaminoglycans, proteoglycans, and adhesive glycoproteins. It absorbs compressive forces and, like the styrofoam packing in a shipping carton, protects the more delicate cells from mechanical injury.

A **glycosaminoglycan (GAG)** (GLY-co-seh-ME-no-GLY-can) is a long polysaccharide composed of unusual disaccharides called *amino sugars* and *uronic acid.* GAGs are negatively charged and thus tend to attract sodium and potassium ions, which in turn cause them to absorb and retain water. Thus, GAGs play an important role in regulating the water and electrolyte balance of tissues. The most common GAG is **chondroitin sulfate** (con-DRO-ih-tin). It is abundant in blood vessels and bones and gives cartilage its relative stiffness. Other GAGs that you will read of in this book are *heparin* (an anticoagulant) and *hyaluronic acid* (HY-uh-loo-RON-ic). The latter is a gigantic molecule up to 20 μm long, as large as most cells. It is a viscous, slippery substance that forms a lubricant in the joints and constitutes much of the jellylike *vitreous body* of the eyeball.

A **proteoglycan** is another gigantic molecule. It is shaped somewhat like a bottle brush, with a central core of protein and bristlelike outgrowths composed of GAGs. The entire proteoglycan may be attached to hyaluronic acid, thus forming an enormous molecular complex. Proteoglycans form thick colloids similar to those of gravy, gelatin, and glue. This gel slows the spread of pathogenic organisms through the tissues. Some proteoglycans are embedded in the plasma membranes of cells, attached to the cytoskeleton on the inside and to other extracellular molecules in the matrix. They create a strong structural bond between cells and extracellular macromolecules and help to hold tissues together.

Adhesive glycoproteins are protein–carbohydrate complexes that bind plasma membrane proteins to extracellular collagen and proteoglycans. They bind the components of a tissue together and mark paths that guide migrating embryonic cells to their destinations in a tissue.

Types of Fibrous Connective Tissue

Fibrous connective tissue is divided into two broad categories according to the relative abundance of fiber: *loose* and *dense connective tissue.* In loose connective tissue, much of the space is

---

[14]*colla* = glue; *gen* = producing
[15]*ret* = network; *icul* = little

occupied by ground substance, which dissolves out of the tissue during histological fixation and leaves empty space in prepared tissue sections. The loose connective tissues we will discuss are *areolar* and *reticular tissue* (**table 5.4**). In **dense connective tissue,** fiber occupies more space than the cells and ground substance, and appears closely packed in tissue sections. We will discuss two types: *dense regular* and *dense irregular connective tissue* (**table 5.5**).

Areolar[16] **tissue** (AIR-ee-OH-lur) exhibits loosely organized fibers, abundant blood vessels, and a lot of seemingly empty space. It possesses all six of the aforementioned cell types. Its fibers run in random directions and are mostly collagenous, but elastic and reticular fibers are also present. Areolar tissue is highly variable in appearance. In many serous membranes, it looks like **figure 5.14,** but in the skin and mucous membranes, it is more compact (see fig. 5.8) and sometimes difficult to distinguish from dense irregular connective tissue. Some advice on how to tell them apart is given after the discussion of dense irregular connective tissue.

Areolar tissue is found in tissue sections from almost every part of the body. It surrounds blood vessels and nerves and penetrates with them even into the small spaces of muscle, tendon, and other tissues. Nearly every epithelium rests on a layer of areolar tissue, whose blood vessels provide the epithelium with nutrition, waste removal, and a ready supply of infection-fighting leukocytes in times of need. Because of the abundance of open, fluid-filled space, leukocytes can move about freely in areolar tissue and can easily find and destroy pathogens.

Reticular tissue (fig. 5.15) is a mesh of reticular fibers and fibroblasts. It forms the framework (stroma) of such organs as the lymph nodes, spleen, thymus, and bone marrow. The space amid the fibers is filled with blood cells. If you imagine a sponge soaked with blood, the sponge fibers are analogous to the reticular tissue stroma.

Dense regular connective tissue (fig. 5.16) is named for two properties: (1) The collagen fibers are closely packed (dense) and leave relatively little open space, and (2) the fibers are parallel to each other (regular). It is found especially in tendons and ligaments. The parallel arrangement of fibers is an adaptation to the fact that musculoskeletal stresses pull tendons and ligaments in predictable directions. With minor exceptions such as blood vessels and sensory nerve fibers, the only cells in this tissue are fibroblasts, visible by their slender, violet-staining nuclei squeezed between bundles of collagen. This type of tissue has few blood vessels, so injured tendons and ligaments are slow to heal.

The vocal cords and some spinal ligaments are made of a dense regular connective tissue called **elastic tissue.** In addition to the densely packed collagen fibers, it exhibits branching elastic fibers and more fibroblasts. The fibroblasts have larger, more conspicuous nuclei than seen in most dense regular connective tissue. Elastic tissue also forms wavy sheets in large and medium arteries. When the heart pumps blood into the arteries, these sheets

enable them to expand and relieve some of the pressure on smaller vessels downstream. When the heart relaxes, the arterial wall springs back and keeps the blood pressure from dropping too low between heartbeats. The importance of this elastic tissue becomes especially clear in diseases such as Marfan syndrome (see Deeper Insight 5.2) and arteriosclerosis, where the tissue is stiffened by lipid and calcium deposits (see Deeper Insight 19.4).

Dense irregular connective tissue (fig. 5.17) also has thick bundles of collagen and relatively little room for cells and ground substance, but the collagen bundles run in seemingly random directions. This arrangement enables the tissue to resist unpredictable stresses. This tissue constitutes most of the dermis, where it binds the skin to the underlying muscle and connective tissue. It forms a protective capsule around organs such as the kidneys, testes, and spleen and a tough fibrous sheath around the bones, nerves, and most cartilages.

It is sometimes difficult to judge whether a tissue is areolar or dense irregular. In the dermis, for example, these tissues occur side by side, and the transition from one to the other is not at all obvious (see fig. 5.8). A relatively large amount of clear space suggests areolar tissue, and thicker bundles of collagen and relatively little clear space suggest dense irregular connective tissue.

Fibrous connective tissue often forms a filler, or *interstitium,* around and between other structures such as blood vessels and gland ducts and within the walls of some organs. In some places, this interstitium is like a honeycomb of fluid-filled spaces supported by thick bundles of collagen. These are not seen in prepared slides, where the spaces are empty and the collagen is densely packed as in figure 5.17; they were recently discovered in surgical

DEEPER INSIGHT 5.2

CLINICAL APPLICATION

Marfan Syndrome—A Connective Tissue Disease

Marfan[17] *syndrome* is a hereditary defect in elastic fibers, usually resulting from a mutation in the gene for *fibrillin,* a glycoprotein that forms the structural scaffold for elastin. Clinical signs of Marfan syndrome include hyperextensible joints, hernias of the groin, and visual problems resulting from abnormally elongated eyes and deformed lenses. People with Marfan syndrome typically show unusually tall stature, long limbs, spidery fingers, abnormal spinal curvature, and a protruding "pigeon breast." More serious problems are weakened heart valves and arterial walls. The aorta, where blood pressure is highest, is sometimes enormously dilated close to the heart and may rupture. Marfan syndrome is present in about 1 out of 20,000 live births, and most victims die by their mid-30s. Abraham Lincoln's tall, gangly physique and spindly fingers led some authorities to suspect that he had Marfan syndrome, but the evidence is inconclusive. Some star athletes have died at a young age of Marfan syndrome, including Olympic volleyball champion Flo Hyman (1954–86), who died at the age of 31 of a ruptured aorta during a game in Japan.

---

[16]*areola* = little space

[17]Antoine Bernard-Jean Marfan (1858–1942), French physician

TABLE 5.4	Loose Connective Tissues
Areolar Tissue	**Reticular Tissue**

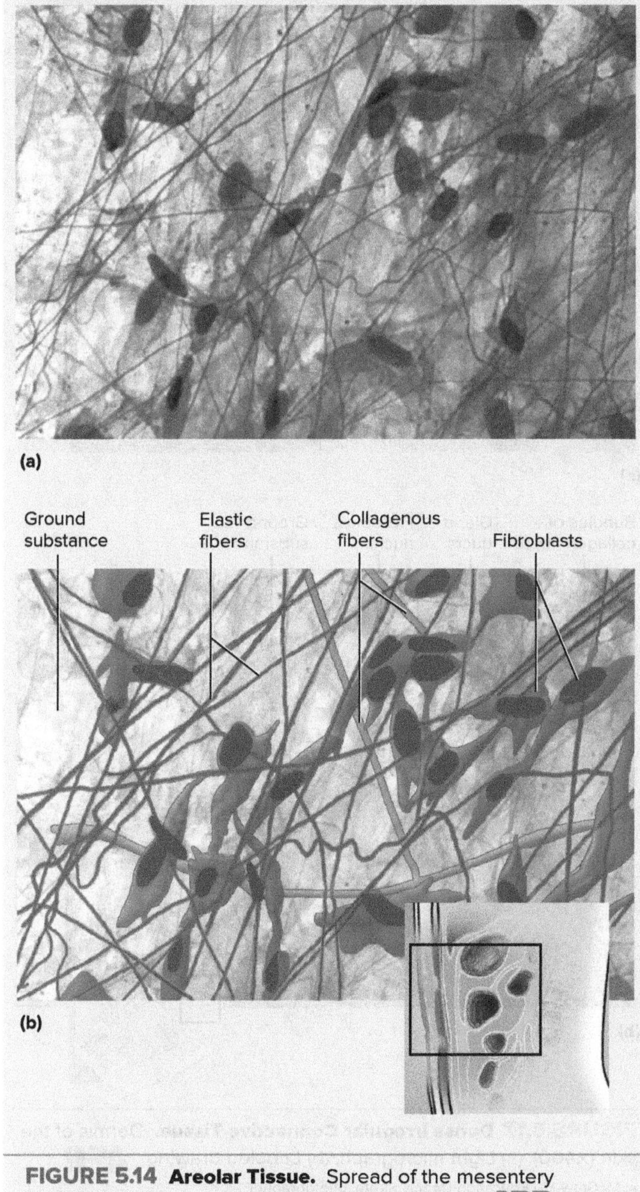

(a)

Ground substance   Elastic fibers   Collagenous fibers   Fibroblasts

(b)

Leukocytes   Reticular fibers

(a)

(b)

FIGURE 5.14 Areolar Tissue. Spread of the mesentery (×400). (a) Light micrograph. (b) Labeled drawing. **APR**

a: Dennis Strete/McGraw-Hill Education

Microscopic appearance: Loose arrangement of collagenous and elastic fibers; scattered cells of various types; abundant ground substance; numerous blood vessels
Representative locations: Underlying nearly all epithelia; surrounding blood vessels, nerves, esophagus, and trachea; fascia between muscles; mesenteries; visceral layers of pericardium and pleura
Functions: Loosely binds epithelia to deeper tissues; allows passage of nerves and blood vessels through other tissues; provides an arena for immune defense; blood vessels provide nutrients and waste removal for overlying epithelia

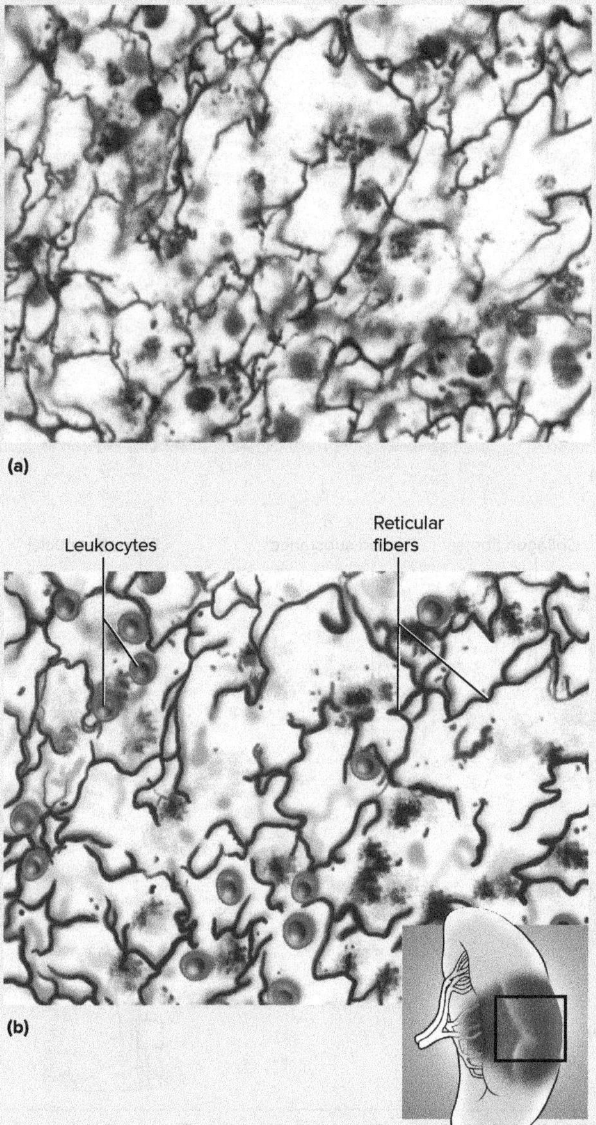

FIGURE 5.15 Reticular Tissue. Spleen (×400). (a) Light micrograph. (b) Labeled drawing. **APR**

a: McGraw-Hill Education/Al Telser, photographer

Microscopic appearance: Loose network of reticular fibers and cells, infiltrated with numerous leukocytes, especially lymphocytes
Representative locations: Lymph nodes, spleen, thymus, bone marrow
Function: Forms supportive stroma (framework) for lymphatic organs

TABLE 5.5	Dense Connective Tissues

Dense Regular Connective Tissue	Dense Irregular Connective Tissue
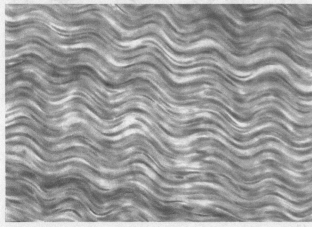 (a)	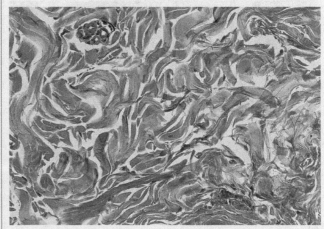 (a)
Collagen fibers Ground substance Fibroblast nuclei 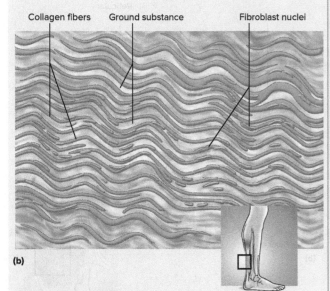 (b)	Bundles of Gland Fibroblast Ground collagen fibers ducts nuclei substance 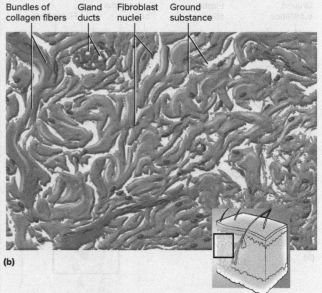 (b)

FIGURE 5.16 Dense Regular Connective Tissue. Tendon (×400). (a) Light micrograph. (b) Labeled drawing. **APR** a: Dennis Strete/McGraw-Hill Education	**FIGURE 5.17 Dense Irregular Connective Tissue.** Dermis of the skin (×400). (a) Light micrograph. (b) Labeled drawing. **APR** a: McGraw-Hill Education/Dennis Strete, photographer
Microscopic appearance: Densely packed, parallel, often wavy collagen fibers; slender fibroblast nuclei compressed between collagen bundles; scanty open space (ground substance); scarcity of blood vessels **Representative locations:** Tendons and ligaments **Functions:** Ligaments tightly bind bones together and resist stress; tendons attach muscle to bone and transfer muscular tension to bones	**Microscopic appearance:** Densely packed collagen fibers running in random directions; scanty open space (ground substance); few visible cells; scarcity of blood vessels **Representative locations:** Deeper portion of dermis of skin; capsules around viscera such as liver, kidney, spleen; fibrous sheaths around cartilages and bones **Functions:** Withstands stresses applied in unpredictable directions; imparts durability to tissues

patients by a new microscopic imaging technique. They are found especially in areas subject to frequent compression, such as the dermis of the skin, the bile duct, and walls of the digestive tract and urinary bladder. They drain into the lymph nodes and may be important as a route of cancer metastasis.

5.3c Adipose Tissue

Adipose tissue, or **fat,** is tissue in which adipocytes are the dominant cell type (**table 5.6** and **fig. 5.18**). Adipocytes may also occur singly or in small clusters in areolar tissue. The space between adipocytes is occupied by areolar tissue, reticular tissue, and blood capillaries.

Fat is the body's primary energy reservoir. The quantity of stored triglyceride and the number of adipocytes are quite stable in a person, but this doesn't mean stored fat is stagnant. New triglycerides are constantly synthesized and stored as others are hydrolyzed and released into circulation. Thus, there is a constant turnover of stored triglyceride, with an equilibrium between synthesis and hydrolysis, energy storage and energy use.

There are two kinds of fat in humans—white (or yellow) fat and brown fat. **White fat** is the more abundant and is the most significant adipose tissue of the adult body. Its adipocytes are usually 70 to 120 μm in diameter, but may be five times as large in obese people. They have a single large, central globule of triglyceride. Their cytoplasm is restricted to a thin layer immediately beneath the plasma membrane, and the nucleus is pushed against the edge of the cell. Since the triglyceride is dissolved out by most histological fixatives, fat cells in most specimens look empty and somewhat collapsed, with a resemblance to chicken wire.

White fat provides thermal insulation, anchors and cushions such organs as the eyeballs and kidneys, and contributes to body contours such as the female breasts and hips. On average, women have more fat relative to body weight than men do. It helps to meet the caloric needs of pregnancy and nursing an infant, and having too little fat reduces female fertility.

Brown fat is found mainly in fetuses, infants, and children, but adults also have small deposits of brown fat; it accounts for up to 6% of an infant's weight, and is concentrated especially in fat pads in the shoulders, upper back, and around the kidneys. It stores lipid in the form of multiple globules rather than one large one. It gets its color from an unusual abundance of blood vessels and certain enzymes in its mitochondria. Brown fat is a heat-generating tissue. It has numerous mitochondria, but their oxidative pathway is not linked to ATP synthesis. Therefore, when these cells oxidize fats, they release all of the energy as heat. Hibernating animals accumulate brown fat in preparation for winter.

▶▶▶ APPLY WHAT YOU KNOW

Why would infants and children have more need for brown fat than adults do? (Hint: *Smaller bodies have a higher ratio of surface area to volume than larger bodies do.*)

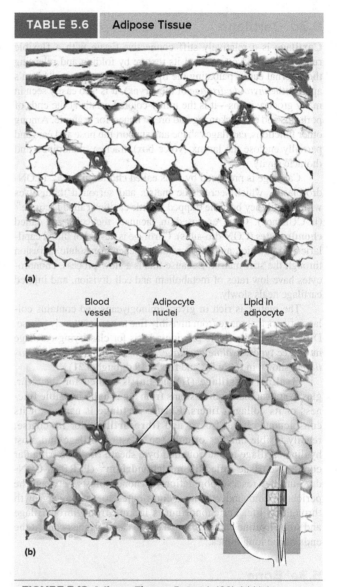

TABLE 5.6 | **Adipose Tissue**

(a)

Blood vessel   Adipocyte nuclei   Lipid in adipocyte

(b)

FIGURE 5.18 Adipose Tissue. Breast (×100). (a) Light micrograph. (b) Labeled drawing. **APR**

a: Dennis Strete/McGraw-Hill Education

Microscopic appearance: Dominated by adipocytes—large, empty-looking cells with thin margins; tissue sections often very pale because of scarcity of stained cytoplasm; adipocytes shrunken; nucleus pressed against plasma membrane; blood vessels present

Representative locations: Subcutaneous fat beneath skin; breast; heart surface; mesenteries; surrounding organs such as kidneys and eyes

Functions: Energy storage; thermal insulation; heat production by brown fat; protective cushion for some organs; filling space, shaping body

5.3d Cartilage

Cartilage is a relatively stiff connective tissue with a flexible rubbery matrix; you can feel its texture by folding and releasing the external ear or palpating the tip of your nose or your "Adam's apple" (the *thyroid cartilage* of the larynx). It is also easily seen in many grocery items—it is the milky-colored gristle at the ends of pork ribs and on chicken leg and breast bones, for example. Among other functions, cartilages shape and support the nose and ears and partially enclose the larynx (voice box), trachea (windpipe), and thoracic cavity.

Cartilage is produced by cells called **chondroblasts**[18] (CON-dro-blasts), which secrete the matrix and surround themselves with it until they become trapped in little cavities called **lacunae**[19] (la-CUE-nee). Once enclosed in lacunae, the cells are called **chondrocytes** (CON-dro-sites). Cartilage is devoid of blood capillaries, so nutrition and waste removal depend on solute diffusion through the stiff matrix. Because this is a slow process, chondrocytes have low rates of metabolism and cell division, and injured cartilage heals slowly.

The matrix is rich in glycosaminoglycans and contains collagen fibers that range from invisibly fine to conspicuously coarse. Differences in the fibers provide a basis for classifying cartilage into three types: *hyaline cartilage, elastic cartilage,* and *fibrocartilage* (shown in **table 5.7** and **figs. 5.19** through **5.21**).

Hyaline[20] **cartilage** (HY-uh-lin) is named for its clear, glassy appearance, which stems from the usually invisible fineness of its collagen fibers. **Elastic cartilage** is named for its conspicuous elastic fibers, and **fibrocartilage** for its coarse, readily visible bundles of collagen. Elastic cartilage and most hyaline cartilage are surrounded by a sheath of dense irregular connective tissue called the **perichondrium**[21] (PERR-ih-CON-dree-um). A reserve population of chondroblasts between the perichondrium and cartilage contributes to cartilage growth throughout life. Perichondrium is lacking from fibrocartilage and some hyaline cartilage, such as the cartilaginous caps at the ends of the long bones.

5.3e Bone

Bone, or **osseous tissue** (**table 5.8, fig. 5.22**), is a hard, calcified connective tissue that composes the skeleton. The term *bone* has two meanings in anatomy—an entire organ such as the femur and mandible, or just the osseous tissue. Bones are composed of not only **osseous tissue,** but also cartilage, bone marrow, dense irregular connective tissue, and other tissue types.

There are two forms of osseous tissue: (1) **Spongy bone** fills the heads of the long bones and forms the middle layer of flat bones such as the sternum and cranial bones. Although it is calcified and hard, its delicate slivers and plates give it a spongy appearance (see fig. 7.4a). (2) **Compact (dense) bone** is a denser calcified tissue with no spaces visible to the naked eye. It forms

the external surfaces of all bones, so spongy bone, when present, is always covered by a shell of compact bone.

Further differences between compact and spongy bone are described in sections 7.2c and 7.2d. Here, we examine only compact bone. Most specimens you study will probably be chips of dead, dried bone ground to microscopic thinness. In such preparations, the cells are absent but spaces reveal their former locations. Most compact bone is arranged in cylinders of tissue that surround **central (osteonic) canals,** which run longitudinally through the shafts of long bones such as the femur. Blood vessels and nerves travel through these canals. The bone matrix is deposited in **concentric lamellae**—onionlike layers around each canal. A central canal and its surrounding lamellae are called an **osteon.** Tiny lacunae between the lamellae are occupied by mature bone cells, or **osteocytes.**[22] Delicate channels called **canaliculi** radiate from each lacuna to its neighbors and allow the osteocytes to contact each other. The bone as a whole is covered with a tough fibrous **periosteum** (PERR-ee-OSS-tee-um) similar to the perichondrium of cartilage.

About one-third of the dry weight of bone is composed of collagen fibers and glycosaminoglycans, which enable a bone to bend slightly under stress. Two-thirds of its weight is minerals (mainly calcium and phosphate salts) that enable bones to withstand compression by the weight of the body.

5.3f Blood

Blood (table 5.9, fig. 5.23) is a fluid connective tissue that travels through tubular blood vessels. Its primary function is to transport cells and dissolved matter from place to place. It may seem odd that a tissue as fluid as blood and another as rock hard as bone are both considered connective tissues, but they have more in common than first meets the eye. Like other connective tissues, blood is composed of more ground substance than cells. Its ground substance is the **blood plasma** and its cellular components are collectively called the **formed elements.** Another factor placing blood in the connective tissue category is that it is produced by the connective tissues of the bone marrow and lymphatic organs. Unlike other connective tissues, blood doesn't exhibit fibers except when it clots.

The formed elements are of three kinds—erythrocytes, leukocytes, and platelets. **Erythrocytes**[23] (eh-RITH-ro-sites), or **red blood cells (RBCs),** are the most abundant. In stained blood films, they look like pink discs with thin, pale centers and no nuclei. Erythrocytes transport oxygen and carbon dioxide. **Leukocytes,** or **white blood cells (WBCs),** serve various roles in defense against infection and other diseases. They travel from one organ to another in the bloodstream and lymph but spend most of their lives in the connective tissues. Leukocytes are somewhat larger than erythrocytes and have conspicuous nuclei that usually appear violet in stained preparations. There are five kinds, distinguished partly by variations in nuclear shape: *neutrophils, eosinophils, basophils,*

---

[18]*chondro* = cartilage, gristle; *blast* = forming
[19]*lacuna* = lake, cavity
[20]*hyal* = glass
[21]*peri* = around; *chondri* = cartilage

[22]*osteo* = bone; *cyte* = cell
[23]*erythro* = red; *cyte* = cell

TABLE 5.7	Cartilage	
Hyaline Cartilage	**Elastic Cartilage**	**Fibrocartilage**

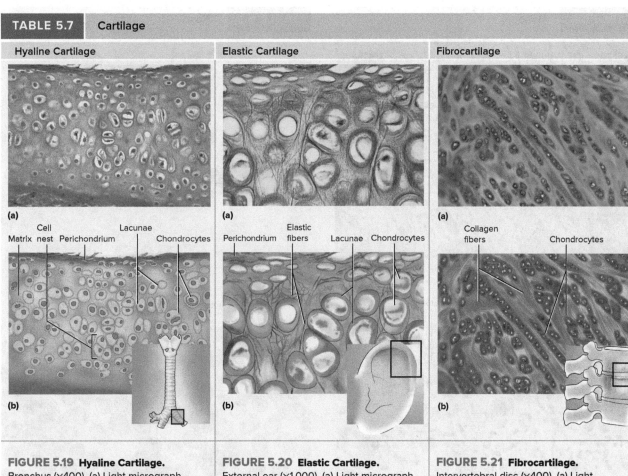

FIGURE 5.19 Hyaline Cartilage.
Bronchus (×400). (a) Light micrograph.
(b) Labeled drawing. **APR**
a: ©Ed Reschke

FIGURE 5.20 Elastic Cartilage.
External ear (×1,000). (a) Light micrograph.
(b) Labeled drawing. **APR**
a: ©Ed Reschke

FIGURE 5.21 Fibrocartilage.
Intervertebral disc (×400). (a) Light
micrograph. (b) Labeled drawing. **APR**
a: Dr. Alvin Telser

Microscopic appearance: Clear, glassy matrix, often stained light blue or pink in tissue sections; fine, dispersed collagen fibers, not usually visible; chondrocytes enclosed in lacunae, often in small clusters of three or four cells *(cell nests);* usually covered by perichondrium
Representative locations: A thin *articular cartilage*, lacking perichondrium, over the ends of bones at movable joints; supportive rings and plates around trachea and bronchi; a boxlike enclosure around the larynx; much of the fetal skeleton; and a *costal cartilage* attaches the end of a rib to the breastbone
Functions: Eases joint movements; holds airway open during respiration; moves vocal cords during speech; a precursor of bone in the fetal skeleton and the growth zones of long bones of children

Microscopic appearance: Elastic fibers form weblike mesh amid lacunae; always covered by perichondrium
Representative locations: External ear; epiglottis
Functions: Provides flexible, elastic support

Microscopic appearance: Parallel collagen fibers similar to those of tendon; rows of chondrocytes in lacunae between collagen fibers; never has a perichondrium
Representative locations: Pubic symphysis (anterior joint between two halves of pelvic girdle); intervertebral discs, which separate bones of vertebral column; menisci, or pads of shock-absorbing cartilage, in knee joint; at points where tendons insert on bones near articular hyaline cartilage
Functions: Resists compression and absorbs shock in some joints; often a transitional tissue between dense connective tissue and hyaline cartilage (for example, at some tendon–bone junctions)

TABLE 5.8	Bone

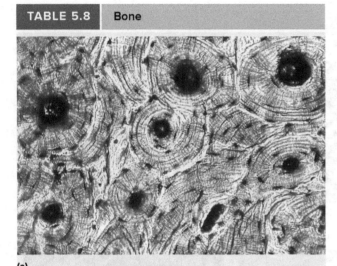

(a)

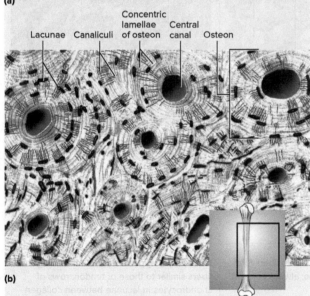

Lacunae   Canaliculi   Concentric lamellae of osteon   Central canal   Osteon

(b)

FIGURE 5.22 Compact Bone (×100). (a) Light micrograph. (b) Labeled drawing. **APR**

a: Dennis Strete/McGraw-Hill Education

Microscopic appearance (compact bone): Calcified matrix arranged in concentric lamellae around central canals; osteocytes in lacunae between adjacent lamellae; lacunae interconnected by delicate canaliculi

Representative location: Skeleton

Functions: Physical support of body; leverage for muscle action; protective enclosure of viscera; reservoir of calcium and phosphorus

TABLE 5.9	Blood

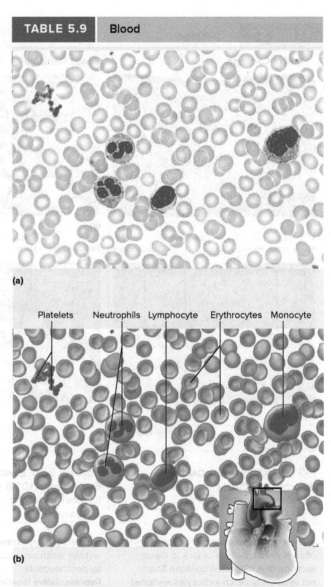

(a)

Platelets   Neutrophils   Lymphocyte   Erythrocytes   Monocyte

(b)

FIGURE 5.23 Blood Smear (×1,000). (a) Light micrograph. (b) Labeled drawing. **APR**

a: ©Ed Reschke

Microscopic appearance: Erythrocytes appear as pale pink discs with light centers and no nuclei; leukocytes are slightly larger, are much fewer, and have variously shaped nuclei, usually stained violet; platelets are cell fragments with no nuclei, about one-quarter the diameter of erythrocytes

Representative locations: Contained in heart and blood vessels

Functions: Transports gases, nutrients, wastes, chemical signals, and heat throughout body; provides defensive leukocytes; contains clotting agents to minimize bleeding; platelets secrete growth factors that promote tissue maintenance and repair

lymphocytes, and *monocytes.* Their individual characteristics are considered in detail in table 18.6. **Platelets** are small cell fragments scattered amid the blood cells. They are involved in clotting and other mechanisms for minimizing blood loss, and in secreting growth factors that promote blood vessel growth and maintenance.

BEFORE YOU GO ON

Answer the following questions to test your understanding of the preceding section:

9. What features do most or all connective tissues have in common to set this class apart from nervous, muscular, and epithelial tissue?

10. List the cell and fiber types found in fibrous connective tissues and state their functional differences.

11. What substances account for the gelatinous consistency of connective tissue ground substance?

12. What is areolar tissue? How can it be distinguished from any other kind of connective tissue?

13. Discuss the difference between dense regular and dense irregular connective tissue as an example of the relationship between form and function.

14. Describe some similarities, differences, and functional relationships between hyaline cartilage and bone.

15. What are the three basic kinds of formed elements in blood, and what are their respective functions?

5.4   Nervous and Muscular Tissues—Excitable Tissues

Expected Learning Outcomes

When you have completed this section, you should be able to

a. explain what distinguishes excitable tissues from other tissues;

b. name the cell types that compose nervous tissue;

c. identify the major parts of a nerve cell;

d. visually recognize nervous tissue from specimens or photographs;

e. name the three kinds of muscular tissue and describe the differences between them; and

f. visually identify any type of muscular tissue from specimens or photographs.

Excitability is a characteristic of all living cells, but it is developed to its highest degree in nervous and muscular tissues, which are therefore described as **excitable tissues.** The basis for their excitation is an electrical charge difference (voltage) called the *membrane potential,* which occurs across the plasma membranes of all cells. Nervous and muscular tissues respond quickly to outside stimuli by means of changes in membrane potential. In nerve cells, these changes result

in the rapid transmission of signals to other cells. In muscle cells, they result in contraction, or shortening of the cell.

5.4a   Nervous Tissue

Nervous tissue (table 5.10, fig. 5.24) is specialized for communication by means of electrical and chemical signals. It consists of **neurons** (NOOR-ons), or nerve cells, and a much greater number of **neuroglia** (noo-ROG-lee-uh), or **glial cells** (GLEE-ul), which protect and assist the neurons. Neurons detect stimuli, respond quickly, and transmit coded information rapidly to other cells. Each neuron has a prominent **neurosoma,** or cell body, that houses the nucleus and most other organelles. This is the cell's center of genetic control and protein synthesis. Neurosomas are usually round, ovoid, or stellate in shape. Extending from the neurosoma, there are usually multiple short, branched processes called **dendrites,**[24] which receive signals from other cells and conduct messages to the neurosoma; and a single, much longer **axon,** or **nerve fiber,** which sends outgoing signals to other cells. Some axons are more than a meter long and extend from the brainstem to the foot.

Glial cells constitute most of the volume of the nervous tissue. They are usually much smaller than neurons. There are six types of glial cells, described in section 12.3a, which provide a variety of supportive, protective, and "housekeeping" functions for the nervous system. Although they communicate with neurons and each other, they don't transmit long-distance signals.

Nervous tissue is found in the brain and spinal cord (central nervous system), nerves, and ganglia, which are knotlike swellings in nerves where the neurosomas outside the central nervous system are concentrated. Local variations in the structure of nervous tissue are described in chapters 12 to 16.

5.4b   Muscular Tissue

Muscular tissue is specialized to contract when stimulated, and thus to exert a physical force on other tissues, organs, or fluids—for example, a skeletal muscle pulls on a bone, the heart contracts and expels blood, and the bladder contracts and expels urine. Not only do movements of the body and its limbs depend on muscle, but so do such processes as digestion, waste elimination, breathing, speech, and blood circulation. The muscles are also an important source of body heat.

There are three types of muscular tissue—*skeletal, cardiac,* and *smooth*—which differ in appearance, physiology, and function (as shown in **table 5.11** and **figs. 5.25** through **5.27**). **Skeletal muscle** consists of long threadlike cells called **muscle fibers.** Most skeletal muscle is attached to bones, but there are exceptions in the tongue, upper esophagus, some facial muscles, and some **sphincter**[25] (SFINK-tur) muscles (muscular rings or cuffs that open and close body passages). Each cell contains multiple nuclei adjacent to the plasma membrane. Skeletal muscle is described as striated and voluntary. The first term refers to alternating light and

---

[24]*dendr* = tree; *ite* = little
[25]*sphinc* = squeeze, bind tightly

TABLE 5.10	Nervous Tissue

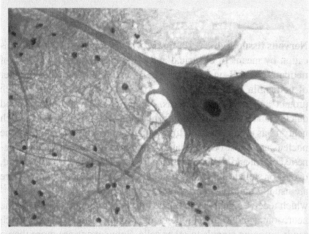

(a)

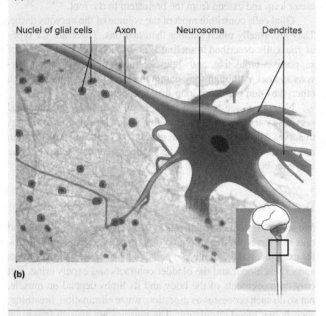

Nuclei of glial cells   Axon   Neurosoma   Dendrites

(b)

FIGURE 5.24 Neuron and Glial Cells. Spinal cord smear (×400). (a) Light micrograph. (b) Labeled drawing. **APR**

a: ©Ed Reschke

Microscopic appearance: Most sections show a few large neurons, usually with rounded or stellate cell bodies (neurosomas) and fibrous processes (axon and dendrites) extending from the neurosomas; neurons are surrounded by a greater number of much smaller glial cells, which lack dendrites and axons.
Representative locations: Brain, spinal cord, nerves, ganglia
Function: Internal communication

dark bands, or **striations** (stry-AY-shuns), created by the overlapping pattern of cytoplasmic protein filaments that cause muscle contraction. The second term, *voluntary,* refers to the fact that we usually have conscious control over skeletal muscle.

Cardiac muscle is limited to the heart. It too is striated, but it differs from skeletal muscle in its other features. Its cells are much shorter, so they are commonly called **cardiomyocytes**[26] rather than fibers. They are branched or notched at the ends. They contain only one nucleus, which is located near the center and often surrounded by a light-staining region of glycogen. Cardiomyocytes are joined end to end by junctions called **intercalated discs**[27] (in-TUR-kuh-LAY-ted). Mechanical connections in these discs keep the cells from pulling apart when the heart contracts. Electrical junctions in the discs allow a wave of electrical excitation to travel rapidly from cell to cell so that all the cardiomyocytes of a heart chamber are stimulated and contract almost simultaneously. Intercalated discs appear as dark transverse lines separating each cell from the next. They may be only faintly visible, however, unless the tissue has been specially stained for them. Cardiac muscle is considered *involuntary* because it is not usually under conscious control; it contracts even if all nerve connections to it are severed.

Smooth muscle lacks striations and is involuntary. Smooth muscle cells are fusiform and relatively short. They have only one, centrally placed nucleus. Small amounts of smooth muscle are found in the iris of the eye and in the skin, but most of it, called **visceral muscle,** forms layers in the walls of the digestive, respiratory, and urinary tracts; blood vessels; the uterus; and other viscera. In locations such as the esophagus and small intestine, smooth muscle forms adjacent layers, with the cells of one layer encircling the organ and the cells of the other layer running longitudinally. When the circular smooth muscle contracts, it may propel contents such as food through the organ. By regulating the diameter of blood vessels, smooth muscle is very important in controlling blood pressure and flow. Both smooth and skeletal muscle form sphincters that control the emptying of the bladder and rectum.

▶▶▶**APPLY WHAT YOU KNOW**

How does the meaning of the word fiber *differ in the following uses:* muscle fiber, nerve fiber, *and* connective tissue fiber?

BEFORE YOU GO ON

Answer the following questions to test your understanding of the preceding section:

16. What do nervous and muscular tissue have in common? What is the primary function of each?

17. What kinds of cells compose nervous tissue, and how can they be distinguished from each other?

18. Name the three kinds of muscular tissue, describe how to distinguish them from each other in microscopic appearance, and state a location and function for each.

---

[26]*cardio* = heart; *myo* = muscle; *cyte* = cell
[27]*inter* = between; *calated* = inserted

TABLE 5.11	Muscular Tissue	
Skeletal Muscle	**Cardiac Muscle**	**Smooth Muscle**

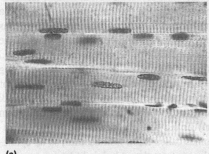

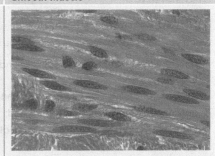

(a)

(a)

(a)

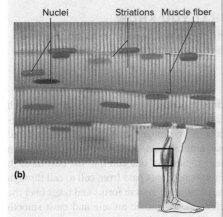

Nuclei   Striations   Muscle fiber

(b)

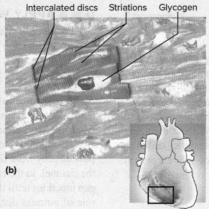

Intercalated discs   Striations   Glycogen

(b)

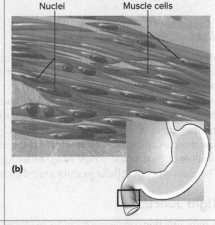

Nuclei   Muscle cells

(b)

FIGURE 5.25 Skeletal Muscle (×400).
(a) Light micrograph. (b) Labeled drawing.
APR
a: ©Ed Reschke

Microscopic appearance: Long, threadlike, unbranched cells (fibers), relatively parallel in longitudinal tissue sections; striations; multiple nuclei per cell, near plasma membrane

Representative locations: Skeletal muscles, mostly attached to bones but also in the tongue, esophagus, and encircling the lips, eyelids, urethra, and anus

Functions: Body movements, facial expression, posture, breathing, speech, swallowing, control of urination and defecation, and assistance in childbirth; under voluntary control

FIGURE 5.26 Cardiac Muscle (×400).
(a) Light micrograph. (b) Labeled drawing.
APR
a: ©Ed Reschke

Microscopic appearance: Short cells (cardiomyocytes) with notched or slightly branched ends; less parallel appearance in tissue sections; striations; intercalated discs; one nucleus per cell, centrally located and often surrounded by a light zone

Representative location: Heart

Functions: Pumping of blood; under involuntary control

FIGURE 5.27 Smooth Muscle. Intestinal wall (×1,000). (a) Light micrograph. (b) Labeled drawing. **APR**
a: McGraw-Hill Education/Dennis Strete, photographer

Microscopic appearance: Short fusiform cells overlapping each other; nonstriated; one nucleus per cell, centrally located

Representative locations: Usually found as sheets of tissue in walls of blood vessels and viscera such as the digestive tract; also in iris and associated with hair follicles; involuntary sphincters of urethra and anus

Functions: Swallowing; contractions of stomach and intestines; expulsion of feces and urine; labor contractions; control of blood pressure and flow; control of respiratory airflow; control of pupillary diameter; erection of hairs; under involuntary control

5.5 Cellular Junctions, Glands, and Membranes

Expected Learning Outcomes

When you have completed this section, you should be able to

a. describe the junctions that hold cells and tissues together;

b. describe or define different types of glands;

c. describe the typical anatomy of a gland;

d. name and compare different modes of glandular secretion; and

e. describe the types and composition of the body's membranes.

5.5a Cellular Junctions

Most cells—except for blood cells, macrophages, and metastatic cancer cells—must be anchored to each other and to the matrix if they are to grow and divide normally. The connections between one cell and another are called **cellular junctions.** They enable the cells to resist stress, communicate with each other, and control the movement of substances through tissues. Without them, cardiac muscle cells would pull apart when they contracted, and every swallow of food would scrape away the lining of your esophagus. The main types of cellular junctions are shown in **figure 5.28.**

Tight Junctions

A **tight junction** completely encircles an epithelial cell near its apical surface and joins it tightly to the neighboring cells, somewhat like the plastic harness on a six-pack of beverage cans. At a tight junction, the plasma membranes of two adjacent cells come very close together and are linked by transmembrane cell-adhesion proteins. These zipperlike interlocking proteins seal off the intercellular space and make it difficult or impossible for substances to pass between cells.

In the stomach and intestines, tight junctions prevent digestive juices from seeping between epithelial cells and digesting the underlying connective tissue. They also help to prevent bacteria from invading the tissues, and they ensure that most nutrients pass *through* the epithelial cells and not *between* them. In addition, some membrane proteins function in the apical domain of the cell, and others in the lateral or basal domains; tight junctions limit how far drifting proteins can travel and keep them segregated in the appropriate domains of the membrane where they are needed to perform their tasks.

Desmosomes

A **desmosome**[28] (DEZ-mo-some) is a patch that holds cells together somewhat like the snap on a pair of jeans. They are not continuous and cannot prevent substances from passing around them and going between the cells, but serve to keep cells from pulling apart and

enable a tissue to resist mechanical stress. Desmosomes are common in the epidermis, the epithelium of the uterine cervix, other epithelia, and cardiac muscle. Hooklike J-shaped proteins arise from the cytoskeleton, approach the cell surface from within, and penetrate into a thick protein plaque on the inner face of the plasma membrane; then the short arm of the J turns back into the cell—thus anchoring the cytoskeleton to the membrane plaque. Proteins of the plaque are linked to transmembrane proteins that, in turn, are linked to transmembrane proteins of the next cell, forming a zone of strong cell adhesion. Each cell mirrors the other and contributes half of the desmosome. Such connections create a strong structural network that binds cells together throughout the tissue. The basal cells of an epithelium are similarly linked to the underlying basement membrane by half-desmosomes called **hemidesmosomes,** so an epithelium cannot easily peel away from the underlying tissue.

▶▶▶ APPLY WHAT YOU KNOW

Why would desmosomes not be suitable as the sole type of cell junction between epithelial cells of the stomach?

Gap Junctions

A **gap (communicating) junction** is formed by a *connexon,* which consists of six transmembrane proteins arranged in a ring, somewhat like the segments of an orange, surrounding a water-filled channel. Ions, glucose, amino acids, and other small solutes can pass directly from the cytoplasm of one cell into the next through the channel. In the embryo, nutrients pass from cell to cell through gap junctions until the circulatory system forms and takes over the role of nutrient distribution. In cardiac muscle and most smooth muscle, gap junctions allow electrical excitation to pass directly from cell to cell so that the cells contract in near unison. (Gap junctions are absent from skeletal muscle.) In the lens and cornea of the eye, which lack blood vessels, gap junctions allow nutrients and other material to pass from cell to cell.

5.5b Glands

A **gland** is a cell or organ that secretes substances for use elsewhere in the body or for elimination as waste. The gland product may be something synthesized by its cells (such as digestive enzymes) or something removed from the tissues and modified by the gland (such as urine and bile pigments). The product is called a **secretion** if it is useful to the body (such as an enzyme or hormone) and an **excretion** if it is a waste product (such as urine and bile). Glands are composed mostly of epithelial tissue, but usually have a supportive connective tissue framework and capsule.

Endocrine and Exocrine Glands

Glands are classified as endocrine or exocrine. Both types originate as invaginations of a surface epithelium **(fig. 5.29).** **Exocrine**[29] **glands** (EC-so-crin) usually maintain their contact with the surface by way of a **duct,** an epithelial tube that conveys

---

[28]*desmo* = band, bond, ligament; *som* = body

[29]*exo* = out; *crin* = to separate, secrete

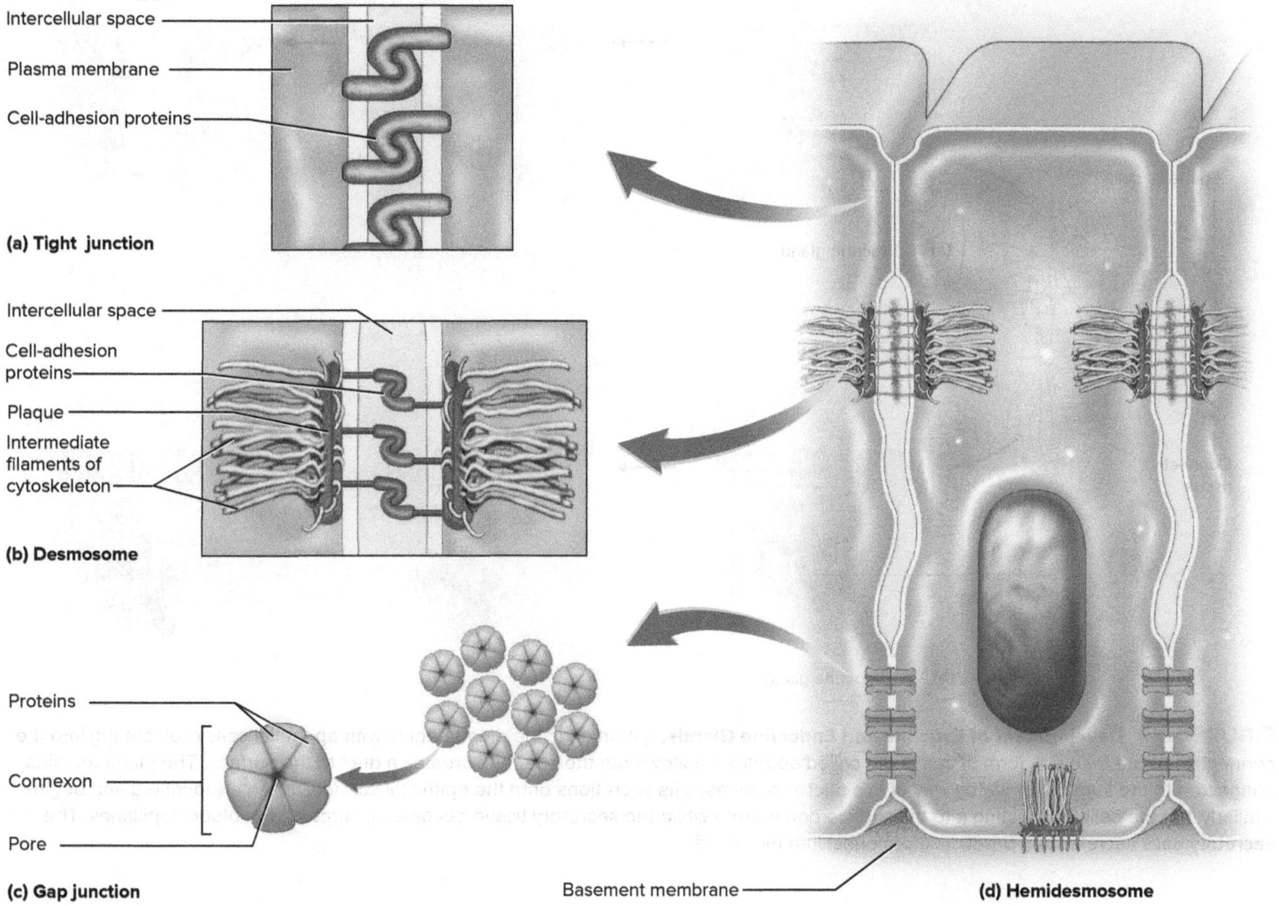

FIGURE 5.28 Structure of Four Kinds of Cellular Junctions. (a) Tight junction. (b) Desmosome. (c) Gap junction. (d) Hemidesmosome between cell and basement membrane.

❓ *Which of these junctions allows material to pass from one cell directly into the next?*

their secretion to the surface. The secretion may be released to the body surface, as in the case of sweat, mammary, and tear glands. More often, however, it is released into the cavity (lumen) of another organ such as the mouth or intestine; this is the case with salivary glands, the liver, and the pancreas.

Endocrine[30] **glands** lose contact with the surface and have no ducts. They do, however, have a high density of blood capillaries and secrete their products directly into the blood (**fig. 5.30a**). The secretions of endocrine glands, called *hormones,* function as chemical messengers to stimulate cells elsewhere in the body. Endocrine glands include the pituitary, thyroid, and adrenal glands.

The exocrine–endocrine distinction isn't always clear. The liver is an exocrine gland that secretes one of its products, bile, through a system of ducts, but secretes hormones, albumin, and other products directly into the blood. Several glands, such as the pancreas and kidney, have both exocrine and endocrine components. Nearly all of the viscera have at least some cells that secrete hormones, even though most of these organs are not usually thought of as glands (for example, the brain and heart).

Unicellular glands are secretory cells found in an epithelium that is predominantly nonsecretory. They can be endocrine or exocrine. For example, the respiratory tract, which is lined mainly by ciliated cells, also has a liberal scattering of exocrine goblet cells (see figs. 5.6 and 5.7). The stomach and small intestine have scattered endocrine cells, which secrete hormones that regulate digestion.

Endocrine glands are the subject of chapter 17 and are not further considered here.

Exocrine Gland Structure

Multicellular exocrine glands such as the pancreas and salivary glands are usually enclosed in a fibrous **capsule** (**fig. 5.30b**). The capsule often gives off extensions called **septa** (singular, *septum*),

---

[30]*endo* = in, into; *crin* = to separate, secrete

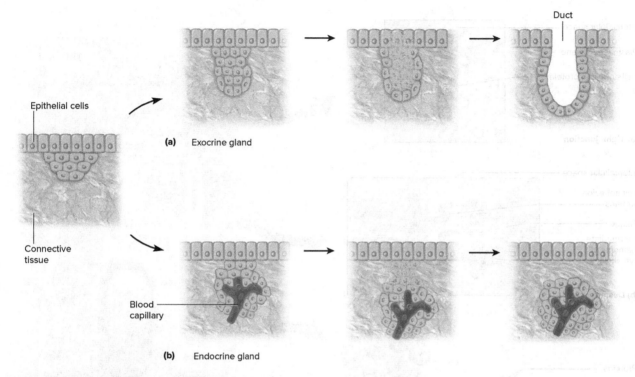

FIGURE 5.29 Development of Exocrine and Endocrine Glands. (a) An exocrine gland begins with epithelial cells proliferating into the connective tissue below. A form of cell death called *apoptosis* hollows out the core and creates a duct to the surface. The gland remains connected to the surface for life by way of this duct and releases its secretions onto the epithelial surface. (b) An endocrine gland begins similarly, but the cells connecting it to the surface degenerate while the secretory tissue becomes infiltrated with blood capillaries. The secretory cells secrete their products (hormones) into the blood.

or **trabeculae** (trah-BEC-you-lee), that divide the interior of the gland into compartments called **lobes,** which are visible to the naked eye. Finer connective tissue septa may further subdivide each lobe into microscopic **lobules.** Blood vessels, nerves, and the gland's own ducts generally travel through these septa. The connective tissue framework of the gland, called its **stroma,** supports and organizes the glandular tissue. The cells that perform the tasks of synthesis and secretion are collectively called the **parenchyma** (pa-REN-kih-muh). This is typically simple cuboidal or simple columnar epithelium.

Exocrine glands are classified according to their "architecture"—the branching of their ducts and the appearance and extent of their secretory portions (**fig. 5.31**). They are called **simple** if they have a single unbranched duct and **compound** if they have a branched duct. If the duct and secretory portion are of uniform diameter, the gland is called **tubular.** If the secretory cells form a dilated sac, the gland is called acinar and the sac is an **acinus**[31] (ASS-ih-nus), or **alveolus**[32] (AL-vee-OH-lus) (**fig. 5.30c**). A gland with secretory cells in both the tubular and acinar portions is called a **tubuloacinar (tubuloalveolar) gland.**

Types of Secretions

Glands are classified not only by their structure but also by the nature of their secretions. **Serous glands** (SEER-us) produce relatively thin, watery fluids such as perspiration, milk, tears, and digestive juices. **Mucous glands,** found in the oral and nasal cavities among other places, secrete a glycoprotein called *mucin* (MEW-sin). After it is secreted, mucin absorbs water and forms the sticky product *mucus.* Goblet cells are unicellular mucous glands. (Note that *mucus,* the secretion, is spelled differently from *mucous,* the adjective form of the word.) **Mixed glands,** such as the two pairs of salivary glands in the chin, contain both serous and mucous cells and produce a mixture of the two types of secretions.

Modes of Secretion

Exocrine glands are classified into *eccrine, apocrine,* and *holocrine* types according to how they release their secretions. **Eccrine**[33] **glands** (EC-rin), also called **merocrine**[34] **glands** (MERR-oh-crin), release their products by means of exocytosis. These include the tear glands, salivary glands, pancreas, and most others. Mammary glands

---

[31]*acinus* = berry
[32]*alveol* = cavity, pit

[33]*ec* = *ex* = out; *crin* = to separate, secrete
[34]*mero* = part; *crin* = to separate, secrete

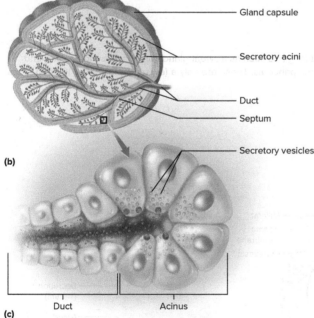

(a)

(b)

(c)

— Arterial blood supply

— Blood capillaries

— Hormone carried away in bloodstream

— Gland capsule

— Secretory acini

— Duct

— Septum

— Secretory vesicles

Duct   Acinus

FIGURE 5.30 General Structure of Endocrine and Exocrine Glands. (a) Endocrine glands have no ducts but have a high density of blood capillaries and secrete their products (hormones) directly into the bloodstream. (b) Exocrine glands usually have a system of ducts, which often follow connective tissue septa, until their finest divisions end in saccular acini of secretory cells. (c) Detail of an acinus and the beginning of a duct.

❓ *What membrane transport process are the cells of the acinus in (c) carrying out? (Review section 3.3.)*

secrete milk sugar (lactose) and proteins (casein, lactalbumin) by this method **(fig. 5.32a),** but secrete the milk fat by another method called **apocrine**[35] secretion **(fig. 5.32b).** Lipids coalesce from the cytosol into a droplet that buds from the cell surface, covered by a layer of plasma membrane and a very thin film of cytoplasm. Sweat

glands of the axillary (armpit) region were once thought to use the apocrine method as well. Closer study showed this to be untrue; they are eccrine, but they're nevertheless different from other merocrine glands in function and histological appearance (see figure 6.10) and are still referred to as apocrine sweat glands.

In **holocrine**[36] **glands,** cells accumulate a product and then the entire cell disintegrates, *becoming* the secretion instead of *releasing* one **(fig. 5.32c).** Holocrine secretions tend to be relatively thick and oily, composed of cell fragments and the substances the cells had synthesized before disintegrating. Only a few glands use this method, such as the oil-producing glands of the scalp and other areas of skin, and certain glands of the eyelid.

5.5c Membranes

Atlas A (section A.3) describes the major body cavities and the membranes that line them and cover their viscera. We now consider some histological aspects of these membranes. Membranes may be composed of epithelial tissue only; connective tissue only; or epithelial, connective, and muscular tissue.

The largest membrane of the body is the **cutaneous membrane**—or more simply, the skin (detailed in chapter 6). It consists of a stratified squamous epithelium (epidermis) resting on a layer of connective tissue (dermis). Unlike the other membranes to be considered, it is relatively dry. It resists dehydration of the body and provides an inhospitable environment for the growth of infectious organisms.

The two principal kinds of internal membranes are mucous and serous membranes. A **mucous membrane (mucosa) (fig. 5.33a)** lines passages that open to the exterior environment: the digestive, respiratory, urinary, and reproductive tracts. A mucous membrane consists of two to three layers: (1) an epithelium; (2) an areolar connective tissue layer called the **lamina propria**[37] (LAM-ih-nuh PRO-pree-uh); and (3) often a layer of smooth muscle called the **muscularis mucosae** (MUSK-you-LAIR-iss mew-CO-see). Mucous membranes have absorptive, secretory, and protective functions. They are often covered with mucus secreted by goblet cells, multicellular mucous glands, or both. The mucus traps bacteria and foreign particles, which keeps them from invading the tissues and aids in their removal from the body. The epithelium of a mucous membrane may also include absorptive, ciliated, and other types of cells.

A **serous membrane (serosa)** is composed of a simple squamous epithelium resting on a thin layer of areolar connective tissue **(fig. 5.33b).** Serous membranes produce watery **serous fluid,** which arises from the blood and derives its name from the fact that it is similar to blood serum in composition. Serous membranes line the insides of some body cavities and form a smooth outer surface on some of the viscera, such as the digestive tract. The pleurae, pericardium, and peritoneum described in atlas A are serous membranes. Their epithelial component is called **mesothelium.**

The circulatory system is lined with a simple squamous epithelium called **endothelium,** derived from mesoderm. The endothelium rests on a thin layer of areolar tissue, which often rests in turn on an elastic sheet. Collectively, these tissues make

---

[35]*apo* = from, off, away; *crin* = to separate, secrete

[36]*holo* = whole, entire; *crin* = to separate, secrete
[37]*lamina* = layer; *propria* = of one's own

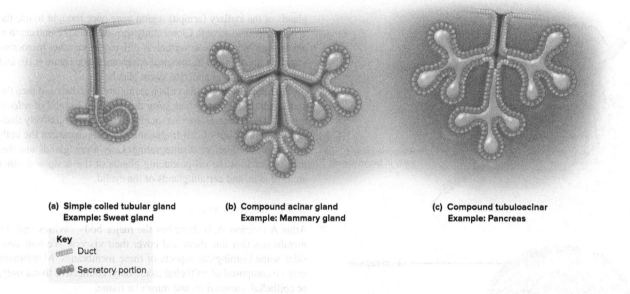

(a) **Simple coiled tubular gland**
Example: Sweat gland

(b) **Compound acinar gland**
Example: Mammary gland

(c) **Compound tubuloacinar**
Example: Pancreas

Key

  Duct

  Secretory portion

FIGURE 5.31 Some Types of Exocrine Glands. (a) A simple coiled tubular gland such as a sweat gland. (b) A compound acinar gland such as the mammary gland. (c) A compound tubuloacinar gland such as the pancreas. These are only a few examples of the 10 or so types of gland architecture.

Predict and sketch the appearance of a simple acinar gland.

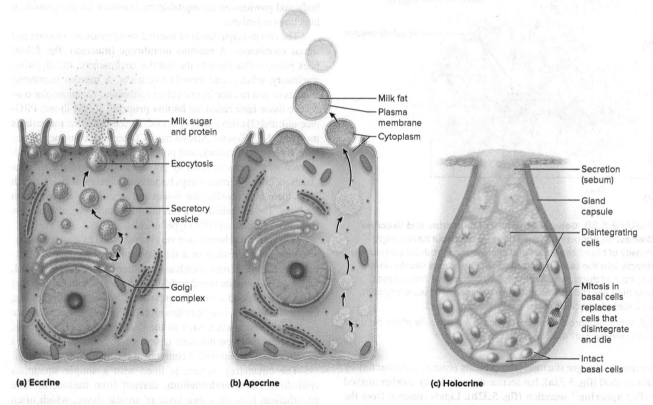

Milk fat
Plasma membrane
Cytoplasm

Milk sugar and protein
Exocytosis
Secretory vesicle
Golgi complex

(a) Eccrine

(b) Apocrine

Secretion (sebum)
Gland capsule
Disintegrating cells
Mitosis in basal cells replaces cells that disintegrate and die
Intact basal cells

(c) Holocrine

FIGURE 5.32 The Three Modes of Exocrine Secretion. (a) Eccrine secretion in a cell of the mammary gland, secreting milk sugar (lactose) and proteins (casein, lactalbumin) by exocytosis. (b) Apocrine secretion of fat by a cell of the mammary gland. Fat droplets coalesce in the cytosol, then bud from the cell surface with a thin coat of cytoplasm and plasma membrane. (c) Holocrine secretion by a sebaceous (oil) gland of the scalp. In this method, entire gland cells break down and become the secretion (sebum).

Which of these three glands would require the highest rate of mitosis? Why?

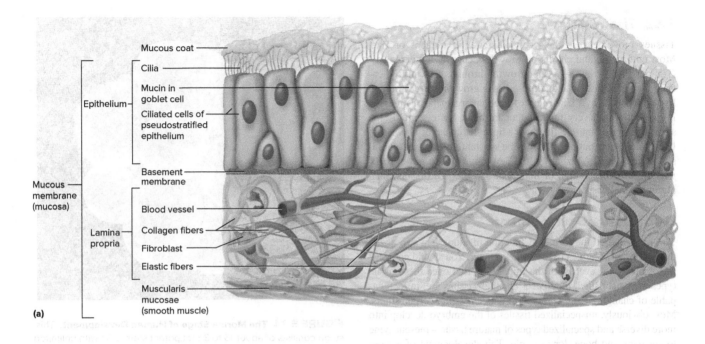

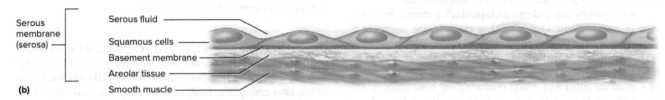

FIGURE 5.33 Histology of Mucous and Serous Membranes. (a) A mucous membrane such as the inner lining of the trachea. (b) A serous membrane such as the external surface of the small intestine.

up a membrane called the *tunica interna* of the blood vessels and *endocardium* of the heart.

The foregoing membranes are composed of two to three tissue types. By contrast, some membranes composed only of connective tissue include the *dura mater* around the brain, *synovial membranes* that enclose joints of the skeletal system, and the *periosteum* that covers each bone. Some membranes composed only of epithelium include the anterior surfaces of the lens and cornea of the eye. All of these are described in later chapters.

> **BEFORE YOU GO ON**

Answer the following questions to test your understanding of the preceding section:

19. Compare the structure of tight junctions and gap junctions. Relate their structural differences to their functional differences.

20. Distinguish between a simple gland and a compound gland, and give an example of each. Distinguish between a tubular gland and an acinar gland, and give an example of each.

21. Contrast the eccrine, apocrine, and holocrine methods of secretion, and name a gland product produced by each method.

22. Describe the differences between a mucous and a serous membrane.

23. Name the layers of a mucous membrane, and state which of the four primary tissue classes composes each layer.

5.6 Tissue Growth, Development, Repair, and Degeneration

Expected Learning Outcomes

When you have completed this section, you should be able to

a. name and describe the modes of tissue growth;

b. define *adult* and *embryonic stem cells* and their varied degrees of developmental plasticity;

c. name and describe the ways that a tissue can change from one type to another;

d. name and describe the modes and causes of tissue shrinkage and death; and

e. name and describe the ways the body repairs damaged tissues.

5.6a Tissue Growth

Tissues grow because their cells increase in number or size. Most embryonic and childhood growth occurs by **hyperplasia**[38] (HY-pur-PLAY-zhuh)—tissue growth through cell multiplication. Skeletal muscles and adipose tissue grow, however, through **hypertrophy**[39] (hy-PUR-truh-fee)—the enlargement of preexisting cells. Even a very muscular or fat adult has essentially the same number of muscle fibers or adipocytes as he or she had in late adolescence, but the cells may be substantially larger. **Neoplasia**[40] (NEE-oh-PLAY-zhuh) is the development of a tumor (*neoplasm*)—whether benign or malignant—composed of abnormal, nonfunctional tissue.

5.6b Tissue Development

You have studied the form and function of more than two dozen discrete types of human tissue in this chapter. You should not leave this subject, however, with the impression that once these tissue types are established, they never change. Tissues are, in fact, capable of changing from one type to another within certain limits. Most obviously, unspecialized tissues of the embryo develop into more diverse and specialized types of mature tissue—mesenchyme to cartilage and bone, for example. This development of a more specialized form and function is called **differentiation.**

Some tissues can undergo **metaplasia,**[41] a change from one type of mature tissue to another. For example, the vagina of a young girl is lined with a simple cuboidal epithelium. At puberty, it changes to a stratified squamous epithelium, better adapted to the future demands of intercourse and childbirth. The long bones of a child are filled with blood-producing red bone marrow, but by adulthood, most of this changes to adipose tissue. In smokers, the pseudostratified columnar epithelium of the bronchi may transform into a stratified squamous epithelium.

▶▶▶ APPLY WHAT YOU KNOW

What functions of a ciliated pseudostratified columnar epithelium could not be served by a stratified squamous epithelium? In light of this, what might be some consequences of bronchial metaplasia in heavy smokers?

5.6c Stem Cells

The growth and differentiation of tissues depend upon a supply of reserve **stem cells.** These are undifferentiated cells that are not yet performing any specialized function, but have the potential to differentiate into one or more types of mature functional cells, such as liver, brain, cartilage, or skin cells. Such cells have various degrees of **developmental plasticity,** or diversity of mature cell types to which they can give rise.

There are two types of stem cells: embryonic and adult. **Embryonic stem cells** compose the early human embryo

[38]*hyper* = excessive; *plas* = growth
[39]*hyper* = excessive; *trophy* = nourishment
[40]*neo* = new; *plas* = form, growth
[41]*meta* = change; *plas* = form, growth

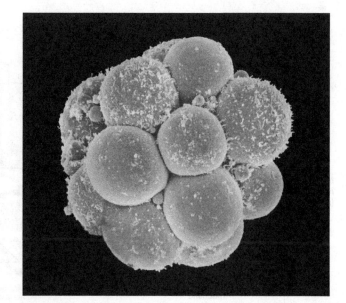

FIGURE 5.34 The Morula Stage of Human Development. This stage consists of about 16 to 32 totipotent stem cells with unlimited developmental plasticity.
Dr Yorgos Nikas/Science Photo Library/Getty Images

(fig. 5.34). In the early stages of development, these are called **totipotent stem cells,** because they have the potential to develop into any type of fully differentiated human cell—not only cells of the later embryonic, fetal, or adult body, but also cells of the temporary structures of pregnancy, such as the placenta and amniotic sac. Totipotency is unlimited developmental plasticity. About 4 days after fertilization, the developing embryo enters the *blastocyst* stage. The blastocyst is a hollow ball with an *outer cell mass* that helps form the placenta and other accessory organs of pregnancy, and an *inner cell mass (embryoblast)* that becomes the embryo itself (see fig. 29.4). Cells of the inner cell mass are called **pluripotent stem** cells; they can still develop into any cell type of the embryo, but not into the accessory organs of pregnancy. Thus their developmental plasticity is already somewhat limited.

Adult stem cells occur in small numbers in mature organs and tissues throughout a person's life. Typically an adult stem cell divides mitotically; one of its daughter cells remains a stem cell and the other one differentiates into a mature specialized cell. The latter cell may replace another that has grown old and died, contribute to the development of growing organs (as in a child), or help to repair damaged tissue. Some adult stem cells are **multipotent**—able to develop into two or more different cell lines, but not just any type of body cell. Certain multipotent bone marrow stem cells, for example, can give rise to red blood cells, five kinds of white blood cells, and platelet-producing cells. **Unipotent** stem cells have the most limited plasticity, as they can produce only one mature cell type. Examples include the cells that give rise to sperm, eggs, and keratinocytes (the majority cell type of the epidermis).

Both embryonic and adult stem cells have enormous potential for therapy, but advances in the field (see Deeper Insight 5.4) have

DEEPER INSIGHT 5.3

CLINICAL APPLICATION

Stem-Cell Therapy

Cell biologists, clinicians, and hopeful patients look to stem cells as a possible treatment for diseases arising from the loss of functional tissue. Conceivably, with the right biochemical coaxing, adult stem cells (AS cells) may be induced to differentiate into various kinds of mature, differentiated cells to replace cardiac muscle damaged by heart attack, restore an injured spinal cord, cure neurodegenerative diseases such as parkinsonism, or cure diabetes by replacing lost insulin-secreting cells. AS cells have limited developmental potential, however, and may be unable to make many of the cell types needed to treat a broad range of degenerative diseases. In addition, they are present in very small numbers and are difficult to harvest from a tissue and culture in the quantities needed for therapy.

Embryonic stem cells (ES cells) could overcome these shortcomings. They are obtained from surplus embryos of about 16 to 32 cells (fig. 5.34) produced by *in vitro fertilization (IVF)* clinics, putting them to good use instead of discarding them. Unfortunately, though, stem-cell research has yet to produce many safe and proven therapies. Questions remain as to whether implanted stem cells may lodge in the wrong place in the body or grow into tumors instead of healthy functional tissue. Stem

cells have proven their value as a "workhorse" of laboratory research in mechanisms of disease, toxicity screening, and drug testing; so far, however, the only therapies proven safe and effective, and approved by the U.S. Food and Drug Administration, are treatments using bone marrow and umbililcal cord blood for certain leukemias and other blood- and immune-related diseases (see Deeper Insight 18.3). Typically, the lag from a medical discovery to clinical use is about 20 years, and stem-cell therapy seems to be no exception. We may be in for a long wait to see if stem-cell technology will yield wider applications.

Meanwhile, unfortunately, fradulent stem-cell "clinics" have sprung up around the world charging vulnerable people tens of thousands of dollars (in nonrefundable cash, of course) for worthless and even life-threatening treatments. Such reports have emerged as a patient blinded by supposed stem-cell injections into the eyes and another in whom injected stem cells developed into a spinal tumor. The FDA is attempting to crack down on illegal treatments in the United States, but many vulnerable patients continue to be victimized by illicit providers in Mexico, South America, India, East Asia, and elsewhere.

---

been slowed both by technical difficulties and controversy over the use of embryonic cells.

5.6d Tissue Repair

Damaged tissues can be repaired in two ways: *regeneration* or *fibrosis*. **Regeneration** is the replacement of dead or damaged cells by the same type of cells as before; it restores normal function to the organ. Most skin injuries (cuts, scrapes, and minor burns) heal by regeneration. The liver also regenerates remarkably well. **Fibrosis** is the replacement of damaged tissue with scar tissue, composed mainly of collagen produced by fibroblasts. Scar tissue helps to hold an organ together, but it doesn't restore normal function. Examples include the healing of severe cuts and burns, the healing of muscle injuries, and scarring of the lungs in tuberculosis.

Figure 5.35 illustrates the following stages in the healing of a cut in the skin, where both regeneration and fibrosis are involved:

1. Severed blood vessels bleed into the cut. Mast cells and cells damaged by the cut release histamine, which dilates blood vessels, increases blood flow to the area, and makes blood capillaries more permeable. Blood plasma seeps into the wound, carrying antibodies and clotting proteins.

2. A blood clot forms in the tissue, loosely knitting the edges of the cut together and inhibiting the spread of pathogens from the site of injury into healthy tissues. The surface of the blood clot dries and hardens in the air, forming a scab that temporarily seals the wound and blocks infection. Beneath the scab, macrophages begin to phagocytize and digest tissue debris.

3. New blood capillaries sprout from nearby vessels and grow into the wound. The deeper portions of the clot become infiltrated by capillaries and fibroblasts and transform into

a soft mass called **granulation tissue.** Macrophages remove the blood clot while fibroblasts deposit new collagen to replace it. This *fibroblastic (reconstructive) phase* of repair begins 3 to 4 days after the injury and lasts up to 2 weeks.

4. Surface epithelial cells around the wound multiply and migrate into the wounded area, beneath the scab. The scab loosens and eventually falls off, and the epithelium grows thicker. Thus, the epithelium *regenerates* while the underlying connective tissue undergoes *fibrosis,* or scarring. Capillaries withdraw from the area as fibrosis progresses. The scar tissue may or may not show through the epithelium, depending on the severity of the wound. The wound may exhibit a depressed area at first, but this is often filled in by continued fibrosis and remodeling from below, until the scar becomes unnoticeable. This *remodeling (maturation) phase* of tissue repair begins several weeks after injury and may last as long as 2 years.

5.6e Tissue Degeneration and Death

Atrophy[42] (AT-ro-fee) is the shrinkage of a tissue through a loss in cell size or number. It results from both normal aging *(senile atrophy)* and lack of use of an organ *(disuse atrophy)*. Muscles that are not exercised exhibit disuse atrophy as their cells become smaller. This was a serious problem for the first astronauts who participated in prolonged microgravity space flights. Upon return to normal gravity, they were sometimes too weak from muscular atrophy to walk. Space stations and shuttles now include exercise equipment to maintain the crew's muscular condition. Disuse atrophy also occurs when a limb is immobilized in a cast or by

---

[42]*a* = without; *trophy* = nourishment

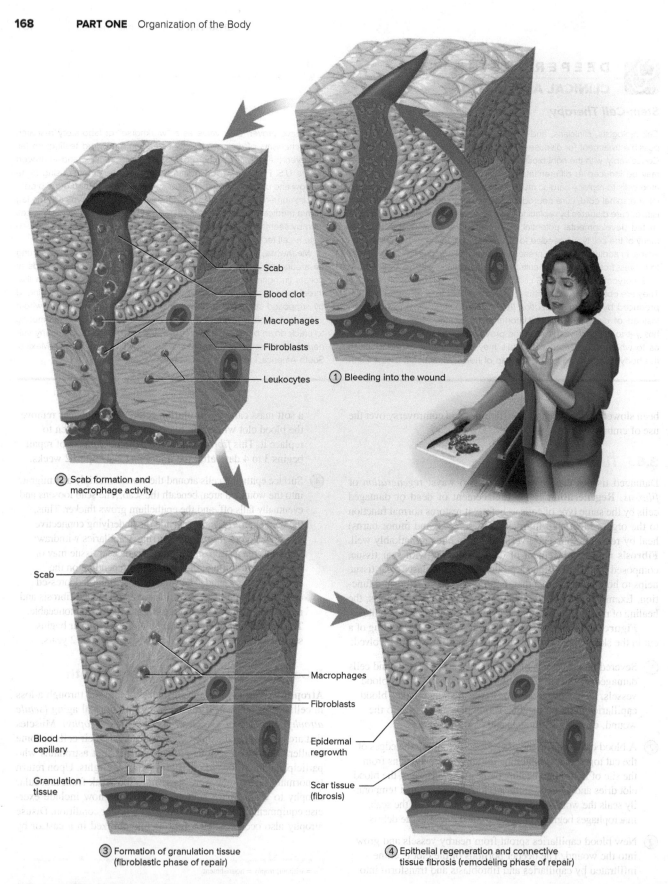

① Bleeding into the wound

- Scab
- Blood clot
- Macrophages
- Fibroblasts
- Leukocytes

② Scab formation and macrophage activity

- Scab
- Macrophages
- Fibroblasts
- Blood capillary
- Granulation tissue

③ Formation of granulation tissue (fibroblastic phase of repair)

- Epidermal regrowth
- Scar tissue (fibrosis)

④ Epithelial regeneration and connective tissue fibrosis (remodeling phase of repair)

FIGURE 5.35 Stages in the Healing of a Skin Wound.

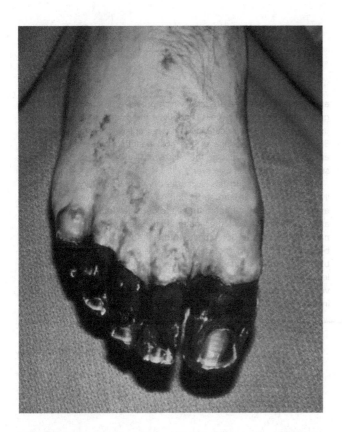

FIGURE 5.36 Dry Gangrene of the Foot Caused by Diabetes Mellitus.
Source: William Archibald/CDC

paralysis, or a person is confined to bed or a wheelchair by an illness or disability.

Necrosis[43] (neh-CRO-sis) is premature, pathological tissue death due to trauma, toxins, infection, and so forth; infarction and gangrene are two types of necrosis. **Infarction** is the sudden death of tissue, such as cardiac muscle *(myocardial infarction)* or brain tissue *(cerebral infarction),* that occurs when its blood supply is cut off. **Gangrene** is tissue necrosis resulting from infection or an obstructed blood supply. *Dry gangrene* often occurs in diabetics, especially in the feet. It is characterized by dry, shrunken skin with bluish-purple, brown, or black discoloration **(fig. 5.36).** A lack of sensation due to diabetic nerve damage can make a person oblivious to injury and infection, and poor blood circulation due to diabetic arterial damage results in slow healing and rapid spread of infection. This often necessitates the amputation of toes, feet, or legs. A **decubitus ulcer (bed sore** or **pressure sore)** is a form of dry gangrene that occurs when immobilized persons, such as those confined to a hospital bed or wheelchair, are unable to move, and continual pressure on the skin cuts off blood flow to an area. Pressure sores occur most often in places where a bone comes close to the body surface, such as the hips, sacral region, and ankles. Here,

the thin layer of skin and connective tissue is especially prone to compression between the bone and a bed or wheelchair.

Wet gangrene typically occurs in internal organs and involves neutrophil invasion, liquefaction of the tissue, pus, and a foul odor. It can result from appendicitis or an obstructed colon, for example. *Gas gangrene* is necrosis of a wound resulting from infection with certain bacteria of the genus *Clostridium,* usually introduced when a wound is contaminated with soil. The disorder is named for bubbles of gas (mainly hydrogen) that accumulate in the tissues. This is a deadly condition that requires immediate intervention, often including amputation.

Cells dying by necrosis usually swell, exhibit *blebbing* (bubbling) of their plasma membranes, and then rupture. The cell contents released into the tissues trigger an inflammatory response in which macrophages phagocytize the cellular debris.

Apoptosis[44] (AP-op-TOE-sis), or **programmed cell death,** is often the normal death of cells that have completed their function and best serve the body by dying and getting out of the way. Cells can be induced to undergo apoptosis in some pathological conditions, however. Cells undergoing apoptosis shrink and are quickly phagocytized by macrophages and other cells. The cell contents never escape, so there is no inflammatory response. Although billions of cells die every hour by apoptosis, they are engulfed so quickly that they are almost never seen except within macrophages.

Apparently, nearly every cell has a built-in "suicide program" that enables the body to dispose of it when necessary. In some cases, an extracellular suicide signal binds to a receptor protein in the plasma membrane, which then activates enzymes that degrade the cell's DNA and proteins. In other cases, cells seem to undergo apoptosis automatically if they stop receiving growth factors from other cells. For example, in embryonic development we produce about twice as many neurons as we need. Those that make connections with target cells survive, while the excess neurons die for lack of *nerve growth factor.* Apoptosis also dissolves the webbing between the fingers and toes during embryonic development; it frees the earlobe from the side of the head in people with the genotype for detached earlobes; and it causes shrinkage of the breasts after lactation ceases.

BEFORE YOU GO ON

Answer the following questions to test your understanding of the preceding section:

24. Distinguish between differentiation and metaplasia.

25. Tissues can grow through an increase in cell size or cell number. What are the respective terms for these two kinds of growth?

26. Distinguish between atrophy, necrosis, and apoptosis, and describe a circumstance under which each of these forms of tissue loss may occur.

27. Distinguish between regeneration and fibrosis. Which process restores normal cellular function? What good is the other process if it does not restore function?

---

[43]*necr* = death; *osis* = process

[44]*apo* = away; *ptosis* = falling

DEEPER INSIGHT 5.4

CLINICAL APPLICATION

Regenerative Medicine

As the population ages while science progresses in knowledge and technical skill, people look to the medical community with hopes of repairing or replacing body parts that are damaged, lost, defective from birth, or worn-out by age. Is it possible to repair brain or heart tissue; or a nose, ear, or finger; or even larger body parts lost to injury? The science of **regenerative medicine,** still in its infancy, seeks to do just that.

One of its approaches is **tissue engineering**—growing tissues and organs in the laboratory, ideally from the patient's own cells, and implanting them into the body. To produce something like a blood vessel or bronchus, tissue engineers start with an organ from a donor body and *decellularize* it—strip it of all living cells, leaving only its collagenous connective tissue framework, or scaffold. While preserving the shape and mechanical properties of the organ to be replaced, this cell-free scaffold eliminates the likelihood of immune rejection by the patient to receive it. It is then seeded with cells from the patient's body, such as chrondrocytes, fibroblasts, or keratinocytes. The product is maintained in

an incubator called a *bioreactor,* which provides nutrients, oxygen, and growth factors while the cells repopulate the scaffold. Some treatments use synthetic polymer scaffolds and even artificial organs produced by 3D inkjet bioprinters. One of the most daunting problems in growing artificial organs is producing the microvascular blood supply needed to sustain an organ such as a liver.

Tissue engineering has succeeded in the laboratory in producing liver, bone, cartilage, ureter, tendon, intestine, and breast tissue, and even a beating rodent heart. "Bench to bedside" translation to the clinic and real patients is another matter. Early successes, however, include nasofacial reconstruction, engineered skin for covering burns and diabetic foot ulcers, repair of damaged knee cartilages, and even urinary bladders grown from patients' own cells and transplanted into their bodies. Preclinical trials are underway on producing bioengineered blood vessels for coronary bypass surgery, and hopes for future development include heart valves and patches of cardiac muscle.

STUDY GUIDE

▶ Assess Your Learning Outcomes

To test your knowledge, discuss the following topics with a study partner or in writing, ideally from memory.

5.1   The Study of Tissues

1. Two names for the branch of biology concerned with tissue structure
2. The four primary tissue classes that constitute the body
3. The roles of cells, matrix, fibers, and ground substance in tissue composition, and how these terms relate to each other
4. Primary germ layers of the embryo and their relationship to mature tissues
5. How and why tissues are prepared as stained histological sections; the three common planes of section; and some ways that tissues are prepared other than sectioning

5.2   Epithelial Tissue

1. Characteristics that distinguish epithelium from the other three primary tissue classes
2. Functions of the basement membrane and its relationship to an epithelium
3. Defining characteristics of a simple epithelium
4. Four types of simple epithelium and the appearance, functions, and representative locations of each
5. Defining characteristics of a stratified epithelium
6. Four types of stratified epithelium and the appearance, functions, and representative locations of each
7. Distinctions between keratinized and nonkeratinized stratified squamous epithelium, including differences in histology, locations, and functions
8. The special protective property and mechanism of urothelium
9. Epithelial exfoliation and its clinical relevance

5.3   Connective Tissue

1. Characteristics that distinguish connective tissue from the other three primary tissue classes
2. Functions of connective tissues

3. Cell types found in fibrous connective tissue, and the functions of each
4. Fiber types found in fibrous connective tissue, their composition, and the functions of each
5. The composition and variations in the ground substance of fibrous connective tissue
6. The appearance, functions, and locations of areolar, reticular, dense irregular, and dense regular connective tissue
7. The appearance, functions, and locations of adipose tissue, including the differences between white fat and brown fat
8. Defining characteristics of cartilage as a class; the three types of cartilage and how they differ in histology, function, and location; the relationship of the perichondrium to cartilage; and where perichondrium is absent
9. Defining characteristics of osseous tissue as a class; the distinction between spongy and compact bone; and the relationship of the periosteum to bone
10. The appearance of cross sections of compact bone
11. Why blood is classified as connective tissue; the term for its matrix; and the major categories of formed elements in blood

5.4   Nervous and Muscular Tissues—Excitable Tissues

1. Why nervous and muscular tissues are called *excitable tissues* even though excitability is a property of all living cells
2. The two basic types of cells in nervous tissue and their functional differences
3. The general structure of neurons
4. Defining characteristics of muscular tissue as a class
5. Three types of muscle and how they differ in histology, function, and location

5.5   Cellular Junctions, Glands, and Membranes

1. The general function of cellular junctions
2. Differences in the structure and function of tight junctions, desmosomes, hemidesmosomes, and gap junctions

3. The definition of a *gland* and the two basic functions of glands
4. The developmental, structural, and functional distinctions between exocrine and endocrine glands; examples of each; and why some glands cannot be strictly classified into one category or the other
5. Examples of unicellular glands in both the exocrine and endocrine categories
6. General histology of a typical exocrine gland
7. The scheme for classifying exocrine glands according to the anatomy of their duct systems and their distribution of secretory cells
8. Differences between serous, mucous, and mixed glands, and examples of each
9. Comparison of the mode of secretion of eccrine, apocrine, and holocrine glands
10. The variety of serous, mucous, and other membranes in the body, and names of some specialized membranes of the skin, blood vessels, and joints

5.6   Tissue Growth, Development, Repair, and Degeneration

1. Differences between hyperplasia, hypertrophy, and neoplasia as normal and pathological modes of tissue growth
2. Differences between differentiation and metaplasia as modes of transformation from one tissue type to another
3. What stem cells are and how they relate to developmental plasticity; differences between embryonic and adult stem cells; and differences between totipotent, pluripotent, multipotent, and unipotent stem cells
4. Differences between regeneration and fibrosis as modes of tissue repair
5. Steps in the healing of a wound such as a cut in the skin
6. The general meaning of tissue *atrophy* and two forms or causes of atrophy
7. Differences between necrosis and apoptosis as modes of cell death and tissue shrinkage; some normal functions of apoptosis
8. Varieties of necrosis including infarction, dry gangrene, and gas gangrene

STUDY GUIDE

▶ Testing Your Recall

Answers in Appendix A

1. Urothelium is found in
   a. the urinary system.
   b. the respiratory system.
   c. the digestive system.
   d. the reproductive system.
   e. all of the above.

2. The external surface of the stomach is covered by
   a. a mucosa.
   b. a serosa.
   c. the parietal peritoneum.
   d. a lamina propria.
   e. a basement membrane.

3. Which of these is a primary germ layer?
   a. epidermis
   b. mucosa
   c. ectoderm
   d. endothelium
   e. epithelium

4. A seminiferous tubule of the testis is lined with _____ epithelium.
   a. simple cuboidal
   b. pseudostratified columnar ciliated
   c. stratified squamous
   d. transitional
   e. stratified cuboidal

5. _____ prevent fluids from seeping between epithelial cells.
   a. Glycosaminoglycans
   b. Hemidesmosomes
   c. Tight junctions
   d. Communicating junctions
   e. Basement membranes

6. A fixative serves to
   a. stop tissue decay.
   b. improve contrast.
   c. repair a damaged tissue.
   d. bind epithelial cells together.
   e. bind cardiac myocytes together.

7. The collagen of areolar tissue is produced by
   a. macrophages.
   b. fibroblasts.
   c. mast cells.
   d. leukocytes.
   e. chondrocytes.

8. Tendons are composed of _____ connective tissue.
   a. skeletal
   b. areolar
   c. dense irregular
   d. yellow elastic
   e. dense regular

9. The shape of the external ear is due to
   a. skeletal muscle.
   b. elastic cartilage.
   c. fibrocartilage.
   d. articular cartilage.
   e. hyaline cartilage.

10. The most abundant formed element(s) of blood is/are
    a. plasma.
    b. erythrocytes.
    c. platelets.
    d. leukocytes.
    e. proteins.

11. Any form of pathological tissue death is called _____.

12. The simple squamous epithelium that lines the peritoneal cavity is called _____.

13. Osteocytes and chondrocytes occupy little cavities called _____.

14. Muscle cells and axons are often called _____ because of their shape.

15. Tendons and ligaments are made mainly of the protein _____.

16. Of the three major categories of muscle, the only one that never has gap junctions is _____.

17. An epithelium rests on a layer called the _____ between its deepest cells and the underlying connective tissue.

18. Fibers and ground substance make up the _____ of a connective tissue.

19. A/An _____ adult stem cell can differentiate into two or more mature cell types.

20. Any epithelium in which every cell touches the basement membrane is called a/an _____ epithelium.

▶ Building Your Medical Vocabulary

Answers in Appendix A

State a meaning of each word element, and give a medical term from this chapter that uses it or a slight variation of it.

1. apo-
2. chondro-
3. ecto-
4. -gen
5. histo-
6. holo-
7. hyalo-
8. necro-
9. plas-
10. squamo-

STUDY GUIDE

▶ What's Wrong with These Statements?

Answers in Appendix A

Briefly explain why each of the following statements is false, or reword it to make it true.

1. The esophagus is protected from abrasion by a keratinized stratified squamous epithelium.

2. Only the basal cells of a pseudostratified columnar epithelium contact the basement membrane.

3. Skeletal muscle is defined by the fact that it is always attached to bones.

4. The secretions of a gland are produced by the cells of its stroma.

5. In all connective tissues, the matrix occupies more space than the cells do.

6. Adipocytes are limited to adipose tissue.

7. Tight junctions function primarily to prevent cells from pulling apart.

8. The development of mature tissue types from the immature tissues of a neonate (newborn) is called neoplasia.

9. Nerve and muscle cells are the body's only electrically excitable cells.

10. Cartilage is always covered by a fibrous perichondrium.

▶ Testing Your Comprehension

1. A woman in labor is often told to push. In doing so, is she consciously contracting her uterus to expel the baby? Justify your answer based on the muscular composition of the uterus.

2. A major tenet of the cell theory is that all bodily structure and function are based on cells. The structural properties of bone, cartilage, and tendons, however, are due more to their extracellular material than to their cells. Is this an exception to the cell theory? Why or why not?

3. When cartilage is compressed, water is squeezed out of it, and when pressure is taken off, water flows back into the matrix. This being the case, why do you think cartilage at weight-bearing joints such as the knees can degenerate from lack of exercise?

4. The epithelium of the respiratory tract is mostly of the pseudostratified columnar ciliated type, but in the alveoli—the tiny air sacs where oxygen and carbon dioxide are exchanged between the blood and inhaled air—the epithelium is simple squamous.

Explain the functional significance of this histological difference. That is, why don't the alveoli have the same kind of epithelium as the rest of the respiratory tract?

5. Which do you think would heal faster, cartilage or bone? Stratified squamous or simple columnar epithelium? Why?

7

BONE TISSUE

A bone cell (osteocyte) surrounded by calcified bone matrix
Eye of Science/Science Source

CHAPTER OUTLINE

DEEPER INSIGHTS

Anatomy & Physiology
Revealed® 4.0

Module 5: Skeletal System

BRUSHING UP

- Bones develop from an embryonic connective tissue called mesenchyme, described in section 5.1b.
- Hyaline cartilage histology (see table 5.7) is important for understanding bone development and certain features of the mature skeleton.
- Review stem cells (section 5.6c) to best understand bone cells and their origins.

In art and history, nothing has so often symbolized death as a skull or skeleton.[1] Bones and teeth are the most durable remains of a once-living body and the most vivid reminder of the impermanence of life.

The dry bones presented for laboratory study may wrongly suggest that the skeleton is a nonliving scaffold for the body, like the steel girders of a building. Seeing it in such a sanitized form makes it easy to forget that the living skeleton is made of dynamic tissues, full of cells—that it continually remodels itself and interacts physiologically with all of the other organ systems of the body. The skeleton is permeated with nerves and blood vessels, which attests to its sensitivity and metabolic activity.

Osteology,[2] the study of bone, is the subject of these next three chapters. In this chapter, we study bone as a tissue—its composition, its functions, how it develops and grows, how its metabolism is regulated, and some of its disorders. This will provide a basis for understanding the skeleton, joints, and muscles in the chapters that follow.

7.1 Tissues and Organs of the Skeletal System

Expected Learning Outcomes
When you have completed this section, you should be able to

a. name the tissues and organs that compose the skeletal system;

b. state several functions of the skeletal system;

c. distinguish between bone as a tissue and as an organ; and

d. describe the general features of a long bone and a flat bone.

The **skeletal system** is composed of bones, cartilages, and ligaments joined tightly to form a strong, flexible framework for the body. Cartilage, the forerunner of most bones in embryonic and childhood development, covers many joint surfaces in the mature skeleton. Ligaments hold bones together at the joints and are

discussed in chapter 9. Tendons are structurally similar to ligaments but attach muscle to bone; they are discussed with the muscular system in chapter 10. Here, we focus on the bones.

7.1a Functions of the Skeleton

The skeleton plays at least six roles:

1. **Support.** Bones of the limbs and vertebral column support the body; the mandible and maxilla support the teeth; and some viscera are supported by nearby bones.

2. **Protection.** Bones enclose and protect the brain, spinal cord, heart, lungs, pelvic viscera, and bone marrow.

3. **Movement.** Limb movements, breathing, and other movements are produced by the action of muscles on the bones.

4. **Electrolyte balance.** The skeleton stores calcium and phosphate ions and releases them into the tissue fluid and blood according to the body's physiological needs.

5. **Acid–base balance.** Bone tissue buffers the blood against excessive pH changes by absorbing or releasing alkaline phosphate and carbonate salts.

6. **Blood formation.** Red bone marrow is the major producer of blood cells, including cells of the immune system.

7.1b Bones and Osseous Tissue

Bone, or **osseous**[3] **tissue,** is a connective tissue in which the matrix is hardened by the deposition of calcium phosphate and other minerals. The hardening process is called **mineralization** or **calcification.** (Bone is not the hardest substance in the body; that distinction goes to tooth enamel.) Osseous tissue is only one of the tissues that make up a bone. Also present are blood, bone marrow, cartilage, adipose tissue, nervous tissue, and fibrous connective tissue. The word *bone* can denote an organ composed of all these tissues, or it can denote just the osseous tissue.

7.1c General Features of Bones

Bones have a wide variety of shapes correlated with their varied protective and locomotor functions. Most of the cranial bones are in the form of thin curved plates called **flat bones,** such as the paired parietal bones that form the dome of the top of the head. The sternum (breastbone), scapula (shoulder blade), ribs, and hip bones are also flat bones. The most important bones in movement are the **long bones** of the limbs—the humerus, radius, and ulna of the arm and forearm; the femur, tibia, and fibula of the thigh and leg; and the metacarpals, metatarsals, and phalanges of the hands and feet. Like crowbars, long bones serve as rigid levers that are acted upon by skeletal muscles to produce the major body movements. Various bones that don't fit the flat or long

---

[1]*skelet* = dried up
[2]*osteo* = bone; *logy* = study of

[3]*os, osse, oste* = bone

bone groups are sometimes called *short bones* (such as those of the wrist and ankle) or *irregular bones* (such as the vertebrae and some skull bones).

Figure 7.1 shows the general anatomy of a long bone. Much of it is composed of an outer shell of dense white osseous tissue called **compact (dense) bone** or **cortical bone.** The shell encloses a space called the **marrow cavity,** or **medullary cavity** (MED-you-lerr-ee), which contains bone marrow. At the ends of the bone, the central space is occupied by a more loosely organized form of osseous tissue called **spongy (cancellous) bone.** A narrow zone of spongy bone also occurs just inside the cortical bone of the shaft and in the middle of most flat, irregular, and short bones. The skeleton is about three-quarters compact bone and one-quarter spongy bone in dry weight. Spongy bone is always enclosed by a shell of more durable compact bone.

The principal features of a long bone are its shaft, called the **diaphysis**[4] (dy-AF-ih-sis), and an expanded head at each end called the **epiphysis**[5] (eh-PIF-ih-sis). The diaphysis provides leverage, and the epiphysis is enlarged to strengthen the joint and provide added surface area for the attachment of tendons and ligaments. Mature bones often exhibit an *epiphysial line* of slightly denser spongy bone between the epiphysis and diaphysis. This is a remnant of a childhood growth zone called an *epiphysial plate,* detailed later. The joint surface where one bone meets another is covered with a layer of hyaline cartilage called the **articular cartilage.** Together with a lubricating fluid secreted between the bones, this cartilage enables a joint to move far more easily than it would if one bone rubbed directly against the other. Blood vessels penetrate into the bone through minute holes called **nutrient foramina** (for-AM-ih-nuh); we will trace where they go when we consider the histology of bone.

Externally, a bone is covered with a sheath called the **periosteum.**[6] This has a tough, outer *fibrous layer* of collagen and an inner *osteogenic layer* of bone-forming cells described in the next section. Some collagen fibers of the outer layer are continuous with the tendons that bind muscle to bone, and some penetrate into the bone matrix as **perforating fibers.** The periosteum thus provides strong attachment and continuity from muscle to tendon to bone. The osteogenic layer is important to the growth of bone and healing of fractures. There is no periosteum over the articular cartilage.

A thin layer of reticular connective tissue called the **endosteum**[7] lines the internal marrow cavity, covers all the honeycombed surfaces of spongy bone, and lines a canal system found throughout the compact bone.

Flat bones have a sandwichlike construction with two layers of compact bone, called the *inner* and *outer tables,* enclosing a middle layer of spongy bone **(fig. 7.2).** The spongy layer in

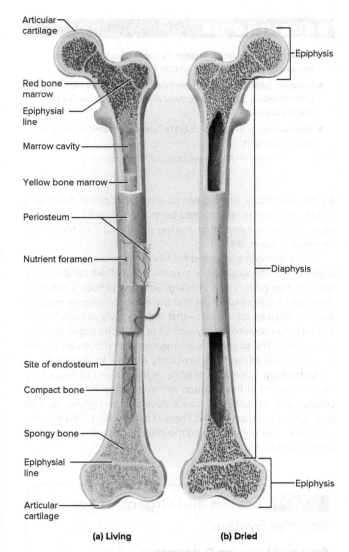

(a) Living **(b) Dried**

FIGURE 7.1 Anatomy of a Long Bone. (a) The femur, with its soft tissues including bone marrow, articular cartilage, blood vessels, and periosteum. (b) A dried femur in longitudinal section.

❓ *What is the functional significance of a long bone being wider at the epiphyses than at the diaphysis?*

Labels: Articular cartilage; Red bone marrow; Epiphysial line; Marrow cavity; Yellow bone marrow; Periosteum; Nutrient foramen; Site of endosteum; Compact bone; Spongy bone; Epiphysial line; Articular cartilage; Epiphysis; Diaphysis; Epiphysis

the cranium is called **diploe**[8] (DIP-lo-ee). A moderate blow to the skull can fracture the outer table of compact bone, but the diploe may absorb the impact and leave the inner table and brain unharmed. Both surfaces of a flat bone are covered with periosteum, and the marrow spaces amid the spongy bone are lined with endosteum.

---

[4]*dia* = across; *physis* = growth; originally named for a ridge on the shaft of the tibia
[5]*epi* = upon, above; *physis* = growth
[6]*peri* = around; *oste* = bone
[7]*endo* = within; *oste* = bone

[8]*diplo* = double

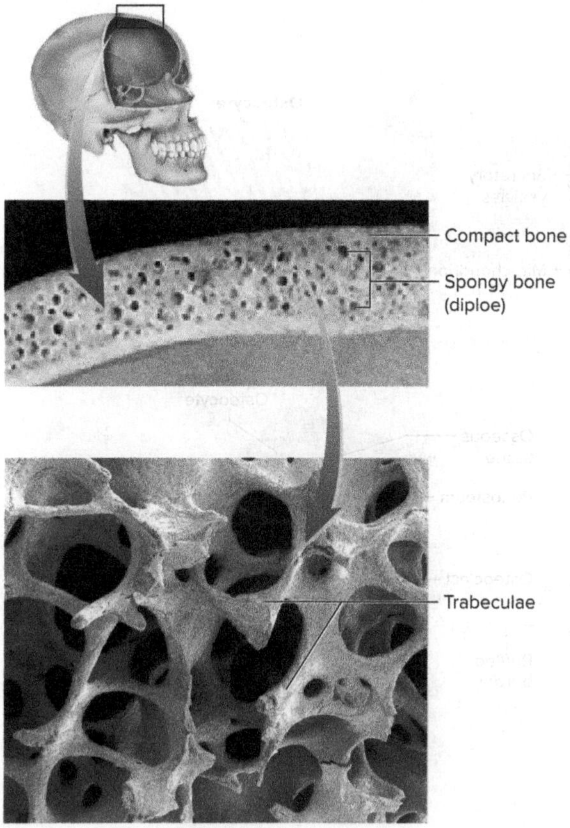

- Compact bone
- Spongy bone (diploe)
- Trabeculae

FIGURE 7.2 Anatomy of a Flat Bone.
Middle: Christine Eckel/McGraw-Hill Education; **Lower:** Steve Gschmeissner/Science Photo Library/Alamy Stock Photo

> **BEFORE YOU GO ON**

Answer the following questions to test your understanding of the preceding section:

1. Name at least five tissues found in a bone.

2. List three or more functions of the skeletal system other than supporting the body and protecting some of the internal organs.

3. Describe the anatomical differences between compact and spongy bone, and their spatial relationship to each other in a long bone and a flat bone.

4. State the anatomical terms for the shaft, head, growth zone, and fibrous covering of a long bone.

7.2   Histology of Osseous Tissue

Expected Learning Outcomes

When you have completed this section, you should be able to

a. list and describe the cells, fibers, and ground substance of bone tissue;

b. state the importance of each constituent of bone tissue;

c. compare the histology of the two types of bone tissue; and

d. distinguish between the two types of bone marrow.

7.2a Bone Cells

Like any other connective tissue, bone consists of cells, fibers, and ground substance. There are four principal types of bone cells (**fig. 7.3**):

1. **Osteogenic**[9] **cells** are stem cells that develop from embryonic mesenchyme and then give rise to most other bone cell types. They occur in the endosteum and inner layer of the periosteum. They multiply continually, and some go on to become the *osteoblasts* described next.

2. **Osteoblasts**[10] are bone-forming cells that synthesize the organic matter of the bone and then promote its mineralization. This bone-building activity is called **osteogenesis.** Osteoblasts form rows in the endosteum and inner layer of the periosteum and resemble a cuboidal epithelium on the bone surface (see fig. 7.8). They are nonmitotic, so the only source of new osteoblasts is the osteogenic cells. Stress and fractures stimulate accelerated mitosis of those cells and therefore a rapid rise in the number of osteoblasts, which then reinforce or rebuild the bone. Osteoblasts also have an endocrine function: They secrete the hormone *osteocalcin,* which stimulates insulin secretion by the pancreas, increases insulin sensitivity in adipocytes, and limits the growth of adipose tissue.

3. **Osteocytes** are former osteoblasts that have become trapped in the matrix they deposited (see this chapter's opening photo). They reside in tiny cavities called **lacunae,**[11] which are interconnected by slender channels called **canaliculi**[12] (CAN-uh-LIC-you-lye). Each osteocyte has delicate cytoplasmic processes that reach into the canaliculi to contact the processes from neighboring osteocytes. Some of them also contact osteoblasts on the bone surface. Neighboring osteocytes are connected by gap junctions where their processes meet, so they can pass nutrients and chemical signals to one another and pass their metabolic wastes to the nearest blood vessel for disposal.

    Osteocytes have multiple functions. Some resorb bone matrix and others deposit it, so they contribute to the homeostatic maintenance of bone density and blood concentrations of calcium and phosphate ions. Perhaps even more importantly, they are strain sensors. When a load is applied to a bone, it produces a flow in the extracellular fluid of the lacunae and canaliculi. This stimulates sensory cilia on the osteocytes and induces the cells to secrete signals that regulate bone remodeling—adjustments in bone shape and density to adapt to stress.

---

[9]*osteo* = bone; *genic* = producing
[10]*osteo* = bone; *blast* = form, produce
[11]*lac* = lake, hollow; *una* = little
[12]*canal* = canal, channel; *icul* = little

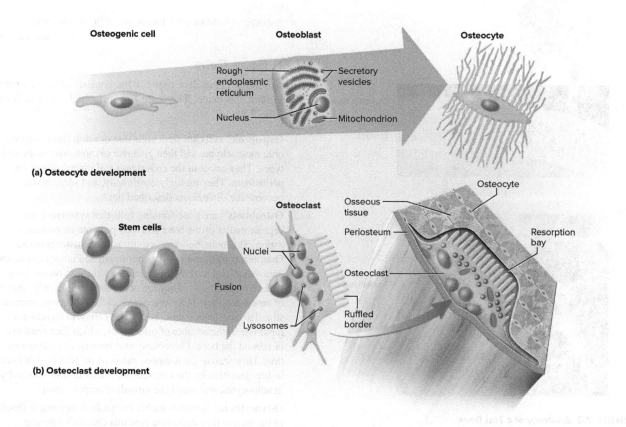

FIGURE 7.3 Bone Cells and Their Development. (a) Osteogenic cells give rise to osteoblasts, which deposit matrix around themselves and transform into osteocytes. (b) Bone marrow stem cells fuse to form osteoclasts.

4. **Osteoclasts**[13] are bone-dissolving cells on the bone surfaces. Their action is called **osteolysis,** the opposite of osteogenesis. They develop from the same bone marrow stem cells as blood cells. Thus, osteogenic cells, osteoblasts, and osteocytes all belong to one cell lineage, but osteoclasts have an independent origin (fig. 7.3). Several stem cells fuse to form each osteoclast, so osteoclasts are unusually large (up to 150 μm) and typically have 3 or 4 nuclei, but sometimes up to 50. The side of the osteoclast facing the bone surface has a *ruffled border* with many deep infoldings of the plasma membrane that increase surface area and the efficiency of bone resorption. Osteoclasts often reside in pits called *resorption bays* that they etch into the bone surface. Bone remodeling results from the combination of osteogenesis by osteoblasts and osteolysis by osteoclasts.

7.2b The Matrix

The matrix of osseous tissue averages, by dry weight, about one-third organic and two-thirds inorganic matter. The organic matter, synthesized by the osteoblasts, includes collagen and various protein–carbohydrate complexes such as glycosaminoglycans, proteoglycans, and glycoproteins (all described in section 2.4c). The inorganic matter is about 85% **hydroxyapatite,** a crystallized calcium phosphate salt [$Ca_{10}(PO_4)_6(OH)_2$]; 10% calcium carbonate ($CaCO_3$); and lesser amounts of magnesium, sodium, potassium, fluoride, sulfate, carbonate, and hydroxide ions. Several foreign elements behave chemically like bone minerals and become incorporated into osseous tissue as contaminants, sometimes with deadly results (see Deeper Insight 7.1).

▶▶▶ **APPLY WHAT YOU KNOW**

What two organelles do you think are especially prominent in osteoblasts? (Hint: *Consider the major substances that osteoblasts synthesize.*)

---

[13]*osteo* = bone; *clast* = destroy, break down

Bone is in a class of materials that engineers call a **composite,** a combination of two basic structural materials—in this case, a ceramic and a polymer. A composite can combine the optimal mechanical properties of each component. Consider a fiberglass fishing rod, for example, made of a ceramic (glass fibers) embedded in a polymer (resin). The resin alone would be too brittle and the fibers alone too flexible and limp to serve the purpose of a fishing rod, but together they produce a material of great strength and flexibility.

In bone, the polymer is collagen and the ceramic is hydroxyapatite and other minerals. The ceramic component enables a bone to support the weight of the body without sagging. When the bones are deficient in calcium salts, they are soft and bend easily. One way to demonstrate this is to soak a clean dry bone, such as a chicken bone, in vinegar for a few days. As the mild acid of the vinegar dissolves the minerals, the bone becomes flexible and rubbery. Such mineral deficiency and flexibility are the central problems in the childhood disease *rickets,* in which the soft bones of the lower limbs bend under the body's weight and become permanently deformed (see Deeper Insight 7.3).

The protein component gives bone a degree of flexibility. Without protein, a bone is excessively brittle, as in *osteogenesis imperfecta,* or *brittle bone disease* (see table 7.2). Without collagen, a jogger's bones would shatter under the impact of running. But normally, when a bone bends slightly toward one side, the tensile strength of the collagen fibers on the opposite side holds the bone together and prevents it from snapping like a stick of chalk. Collagen molecules have *sacrificial bonds* that break under stress, protecting a bone from fracture by dissipating some of the shock. The bonds re-form when the collagen is relieved of stress.

DEEPER INSIGHT 7.1

MEDICAL HISTORY

Bone Contamination

When Marie and Pierre Curie and Henri Becquerel received their 1903 Nobel Prize for the discovery of radioactivity (see Deeper Insight 2.1), radiation captured the public imagination. Not for several decades did anyone realize its dangers. For example, factories employed women to paint luminous numbers on watch and clock dials with radium paint. The women moistened their paint brushes with their tongues to keep them finely pointed and ingested radium in the process. The radium accumulated in their bones and caused many of them to develop a bone cancer called osteosarcoma. History remembers these women as the tragic "radium girls."

Even more horrific, in the wisdom of hindsight, was a deadly health fad in which people drank "tonics" made of radium-enriched water. One famous enthusiast was the millionaire playboy and championship golfer Eben Byers (1880–1932), who drank several bottles of radium tonic each day and praised its virtues as a wonder drug and aphrodisiac. Like the factory women, Byers contracted osteosarcoma. By the time of his death, holes had formed in his skull and doctors had removed his entire upper jaw and most of his mandible in an effort to halt the spreading cancer. Byers' bones and teeth were so radioactive they could expose photographic film in the dark. Brain damage left him unable to speak, but he remained mentally alert to the bitter end. His tragic decline and death shocked the world and helped put an end to the radium tonic fad.

Unlike fiberglass, bone varies from place to place in its ratio of minerals to collagen. The middle-ear bones, for example, are about 90% mineral, giving them the necessary stiffness to efficiently conduct sound vibrations to the inner ear. The limb bones, by contrast, have a higher percentage of collagen so they can bend slightly under the body's weight. Osseous tissue is thus adapted to different amounts of tension and compression exerted on different parts of the skeleton.

7.2c Compact Bone

The histological study of compact bone usually uses slices that have been dried, cut with a saw, and ground to translucent thinness. This procedure destroys the cells but reveals fine details of the matrix **(fig. 7.4)**. Such sections show onionlike **concentric lamellae**—layers of matrix concentrically arranged around a **central (haversian[14]) canal** and connected with each other by canaliculi. A central canal and its lamellae constitute an **osteon (haversian system)**—the basic structural unit of compact bone. In longitudinal views and three-dimensional reconstructions, we can see that an osteon is actually a cylinder of tissue surrounding a central canal. Along their length, central canals are joined by transverse or diagonal passages called **perforating canals.** The central and perforating canals are lined with endosteum. Each osteon is separated from its neighbors by a thin *cement line,* which blocks microfractures of the bone from spreading and minimizes the chance of them causing a large-scale fracture.

Collagen fibers "corkscrew" down the matrix of a given lamella in a helical arrangement like the threads of a screw. The helices coil in one direction in one lamella and in the opposite direction in the next lamella (fig. 7.4b). This enhances the strength of bone on the same principle as plywood, made of thin layers of wood with the grain running in different directions from one layer to the next. In areas where the bone must resist tension (bending), the helix is loosely coiled like the threads on a wood screw and the fibers are more stretched out on the longitudinal axis of the bone. In weight-bearing areas where resistance to compression is more important, the helix is tightly coiled like the closely spaced threads on a bolt, and the fibers are more nearly transverse.

The skeleton receives about half a liter of blood per minute. Blood vessels, along with nerves, enter the bone tissue through nutrient foramina on the surface. These foramina open into the perforating canals that cross the matrix and feed into the central canals. The innermost osteocytes around each central canal receive nutrients from these blood vessels and pass them along through their gap junctions to neighboring osteocytes. They also receive wastes from their neighbors and convey them to the central canal for removal by the bloodstream. Thus, the cytoplasmic processes of the osteocytes maintain a two-way flow of nutrients and wastes between the central canal and the outermost cells of the osteon.

Not all of the matrix is organized into osteons. The inner and outer boundaries of dense bone are arranged in *circumferential lamellae* that run parallel to the bone surface. Between osteons, we can find irregular regions called *interstitial lamellae,* the remains of old osteons that broke down as the bone grew and remodeled itself.

[14]Clopton Havers (1650–1702), English anatomist

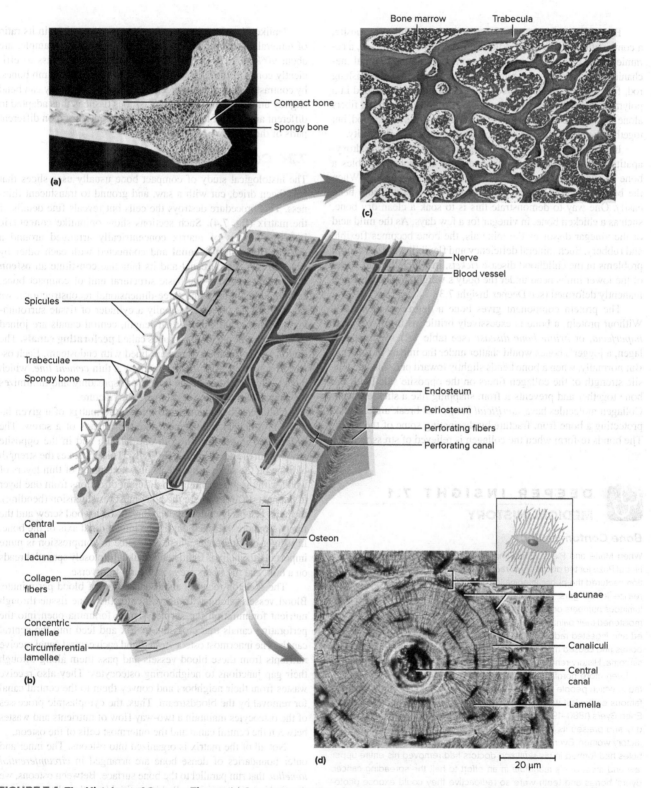

(a)

(c)

Bone marrow   Trabecula

Compact bone

Spongy bone

Nerve

Blood vessel

Spicules

Trabeculae

Spongy bone

Endosteum

Periosteum

Perforating fibers

Perforating canal

Central
canal

Lacuna

Collagen
fibers

Concentric
lamellae

Circumferential
lamellae

(b)

Osteon

Lacunae

Canaliculi

Central
canal

Lamella

(d)

20 μm

FIGURE 7.4 The Histology of Osseous Tissue. (a) Compact and spongy bone in a longitudinal section of the femur. (b) The three-dimensional structure of compact bone. Lamellae of one osteon are telescoped to show their alternating arrangement of collagen fibers. (c) Histology of decalcified spongy bone and red bone marrow. (d) Microscopic appearance of a cross section of an osteon of dried compact bone. The art inset relates osteocyte structure to the shapes of the lacunae and canaliculi of the bone. **A&PR**

a: B Christopher/Alamy Stock Photo; c: Biophoto Associates/Science Source; d: Ed Reschke/Getty Images

7.2d Spongy Bone

Spongy bone (fig. 7.4a–c) consists of a lattice of delicate slivers called **spicules**[15] (rods or spines) and **trabeculae**[16] (thin plates or beams). Although calcified and hard, it is named for its sponge-like appearance. It is covered with endosteum and permeated by spaces filled with bone marrow. The matrix is arranged in lamellae like those of compact bone, but there are few osteons. Central canals are not needed here because no osteocyte is very far from the marrow. Spongy bone is well designed to impart strength to a bone while adding a minimum of weight. Its trabeculae aren't randomly arranged as they may seem at a glance, but develop along the bone's lines of stress **(fig. 7.5).** Spongy bone has much more surface area exposed to osteoclast action than compact bone does. Therefore, when osteoclasts resorb bone tissue, it comes largely from the spongy bone, as we see in osteoporosis (see Deeper Insight 7.4 at the end of this chapter).

7.2e Bone Marrow

Bone marrow is a general term for soft tissue that occupies the marrow cavity of a long bone, the spaces amid the trabeculae of spongy bone, and the larger central canals. There are two kinds of marrow—red and yellow. We can best appreciate their differences by considering how marrow changes over a person's lifetime.

In a child, the marrow cavity of nearly every bone is filled with **red bone marrow (myeloid tissue).** This is often described as *hematopoietic*[17] *tissue* (he-MAT-o-poy-ET-ic)—tissue that produces blood cells—but it is actually composed of multiple tissues in a delicate but intricate arrangement, and is properly considered an organ unto itself. Its structure is further described in section 21.1d.

In adults, most of the red marrow is replaced by fatty **yellow bone marrow,** like the fat at the center of a ham bone. Red marrow is then limited to the skull, vertebrae, ribs, sternum, part of the pelvic (hip) girdle, and the proximal heads of the humerus and femur **(fig. 7.6).** Yellow bone marrow no longer produces blood, although in the event of severe or chronic anemia, it can transform back into red marrow and resume its hematopoietic function.

BEFORE YOU GO ON

Answer the following questions to test your understanding of the preceding section:

5. Suppose you had unlabeled electron micrographs of the four kinds of bone cells and their neighboring tissues. Name the four cells and explain how you could visually distinguish each one from the other three.

6. Name three organic components of the bone matrix.

7. What are the mineral crystals of bone called, and what are they made of?

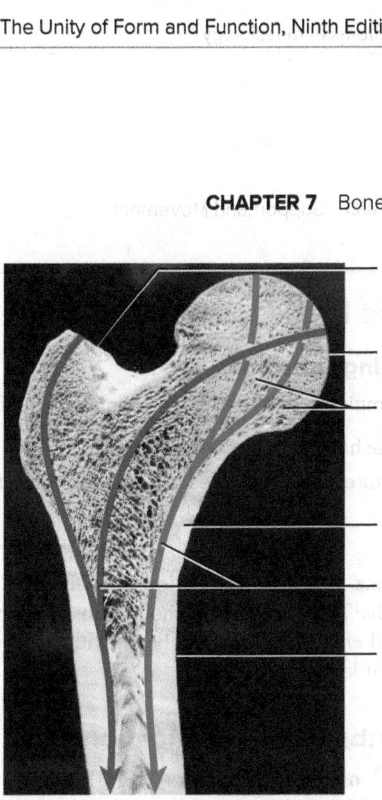

FIGURE 7.5 Spongy Bone Structure in Relation to Mechanical Stress. In this frontal section of the femur, the trabeculae of spongy bone can be seen oriented along lines of mechanical stress applied by the weight of the body or the pull of a muscle.
B Christopher/Alamy Stock Photo

Labels on figure: Greater trochanter; Head; Trabeculae of spongy bone; Compact bone; Lines of stress; Shaft (diaphysis)

8. Sketch a cross section of an osteon and label its major parts.

9. What are the two kinds of bone marrow? What does *hematopoietic tissue* mean? Which type of bone marrow fits this description?

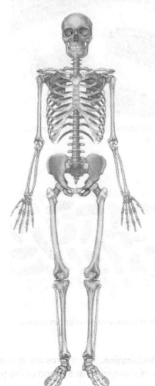

FIGURE 7.6 Adult Distribution of Red and Yellow Bone Marrow.

❓ *What would be the most accessible places to draw red bone marrow from an adult?*

---

[15]*spic* = dart, point; *ule* = little
[16]*trabe* = beam; *cul* = little
[17]*hemato* = blood; *poietic* = forming

7.3   Bone Development

Expected Learning Outcomes

When you have completed this section, you should be able to

a. describe two mechanisms of bone formation; and
b. explain how mature bone continues to grow and remodel itself.

The formation of bone is called **ossification** (OSS-ih-fih-CAY-shun) or **osteogenesis.** There are two methods of ossification—*intramembranous* and *endochondral*. Both begin with embryonic *mesenchyme* (MEZ-en-kime).

7.3a   Intramembranous Ossification

Intramembranous[18] **ossification** (IN-tra-MEM-bra-nus) produces the flat bones of the skull, most of the clavicle (collarbone), and part of the mandible. Follow its stages in **figure 7.7** as you read the correspondingly numbered descriptions here.

(1) Mesenchyme first condenses into a soft sheet of tissue permeated with blood vessels—the *membrane* to which

intramembranous refers. Mesenchymal cells line up along the blood vessels, become osteoblasts, and secrete a soft collagenous *osteoid*[19] *tissue (prebone)* (**fig. 7.8**) in the direction away from the vessel. Osteoid tissue resembles bone but is not yet calcified.

(2) Calcium phosphate and other minerals crystallize on the collagen fibers of the osteoid tissue and harden the matrix. Continued osteoid deposition and mineralization squeeze the blood vessels and future bone marrow into narrower and narrower spaces. As osteoblasts become trapped in their own hardening matrix, they become osteocytes.

(3) While the foregoing processes are occurring, more mesenchyme adjacent to the developing bone condenses and forms a fibrous periosteum on each surface. The spongy bone becomes a honeycomb of slender calcified trabeculae.

(4) At the surfaces, osteoblasts beneath the periosteum deposit layers of bone, fill in the spaces between trabeculae, and create a zone of compact bone on each side as well as thicken the bone overall. This process gives rise to the sandwichlike structure typical of a flat cranial bone—a layer of spongy bone between two layers of compact bone.

---

[18]*intra* = within; *membran* = membrane

[19]*oste* = bone; *oid* = like, resembling

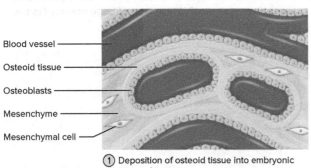

- Blood vessel
- Osteoid tissue
- Osteoblasts
- Mesenchyme
- Mesenchymal cell

(1) Deposition of osteoid tissue into embryonic mesenchyme

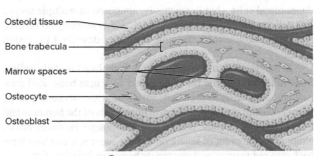

- Osteoid tissue
- Bone trabecula
- Marrow spaces
- Osteocyte
- Osteoblast

(2) Calcification of osteoid tissue and entrapment of osteocytes

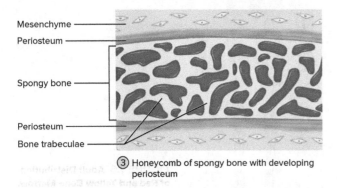

- Mesenchyme
- Periosteum
- Spongy bone
- Periosteum
- Bone trabeculae

(3) Honeycomb of spongy bone with developing periosteum

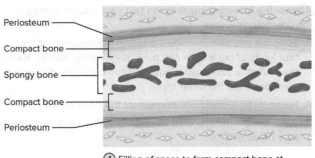

- Periosteum
- Compact bone
- Spongy bone
- Compact bone
- Periosteum

(4) Filling of space to form compact bone at surfaces, leaving spongy bone in middle

FIGURE 7.7   Intramembranous Ossification. The figures are drawn to different scales, with the highest magnification and detail at the beginning and backing off for a broader overview at the end of the process.

? *With the aid of chapter 8, name at least two specific bones other than the clavicle that would form by this process.*

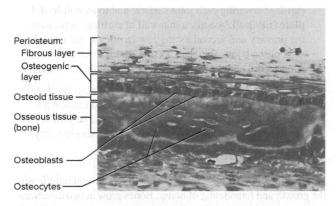

FIGURE 7.8 Intramembranous Ossification in the Fetal Cranium. Note the layers of osteoid tissue, osteoblasts, and fibrous periosteum on both sides of the bone.
Ken Saladin

Intramembranous ossification also plays an important role in the lifelong thickening, strengthening, and remodeling of the long bones discussed next. Throughout the skeleton, it is the method of depositing new tissue on the bone surface even past the age where the bones can no longer grow in length.

7.3b Endochondral Ossification

Endochondral[20] **ossification** (EN-doe-CON-drul) is a process in which a bone develops from a preexisting model composed of hyaline cartilage. It begins around the sixth week of fetal development and continues into a person's 20s. Most bones of the body develop in this way, including the vertebrae, ribs, sternum, scapula, pelvic girdle, and bones of the limbs.

Figure 7.9 shows the following steps in endochondral ossification. This figure uses a metacarpal bone from the palmar region of the hand as an example because of its relative simplicity, having only one *epiphysial plate* (growth center). Many other bones develop in more complex ways, having an epiphysial plate at both ends or multiple plates at each end, but the basic process is the same.

① Mesenchyme develops into a body of hyaline cartilage, covered with a fibrous perichondrium, in the location of a future bone. For a time, the perichondrium produces chondrocytes and the cartilage model grows in thickness.

② In a **primary ossification center** near the middle of this cartilage, chondrocytes begin to inflate and die, while the thin walls between them calcify. The perichondrium stops producing chondrocytes and begins producing osteoblasts. These deposit a thin collar of bone around the middle of the cartilage model,

[20]*endo* = within; *chondr* = cartilage

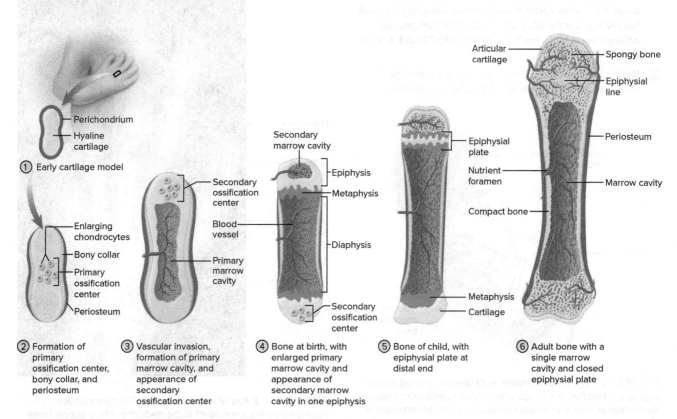

FIGURE 7.9 Stages of Endochondral Ossification. A metacarpal bone of the hand.

❓ *With the aid of chapter 8, name at least two specific bones that would have two epiphysial plates (proximal and distal) at stage 5.*

reinforcing it like a napkin ring. The former perichondrium is now considered to be a periosteum. As chondrocytes in the middle of the model die, their lacunae merge into a single cavity.

③ Blood vessels invade the primary ossification center, delivering blood-borne osteoclasts that digest the calcified tissue. This creates a hollowed-out center called the **primary marrow cavity.** Osteoblasts also arrive and deposit layers of bone lining the cavity, thickening the shaft. As the bony collar under the periosteum thickens and elongates, a wave of cartilage death progresses toward each end of the bone. Osteoclasts in the marrow cavity follow this wave, dissolving calcified cartilage remnants and enlarging the marrow cavity of the diaphysis. The region of transition from cartilage to bone at each end of the primary marrow cavity is called a **metaphysis** (meh-TAFF-ih-sis). Soon, chondrocyte enlargement and death and vascular invasion occur in the epiphysis of the model as well, creating a **secondary ossification center.** In the metacarpal bones, as illustrated in the figure, this occurs in only one epiphysis. In longer bones of the arms, forearms, legs, and thighs, it occurs at both ends.

④ The secondary ossification center hollows out by the same process as the diaphysis, generating a **secondary marrow cavity** in the epiphysis. This cavity expands outward from the center in all directions. At the time of birth, the bone typically looks like step 4 in the figure. In bones with two secondary ossification centers, one center lags behind the other, so at birth there is a secondary marrow cavity at one end while chondrocyte growth has just begun at the other. The joints of the limbs are still cartilaginous at birth, much as they are in the 12-week fetus in **figure 7.10.**

⑤ During infancy and childhood, the epiphyses fill with spongy bone. Cartilage is then limited to the articular

cartilage covering each joint surface, and to an **epiphysial plate** (EP-ih-FIZ-ee-ul), a thin wall of cartilage separating the primary and secondary marrow cavities at one or both ends of the bone. The plate persists through childhood and adolescence and serves as a growth zone for bone elongation.

⑥ By the late teens to early twenties, all remaining cartilage in the epiphysial plate is generally consumed and the gap between the epiphysis and diaphysis closes. The primary and secondary marrow cavities then unite into a single cavity.

7.3c Bone Growth and Remodeling

Ossification doesn't end at birth, but continues throughout life with the growth and remodeling of bones. Bones grow in two directions: length and width.

Bone Elongation

To understand growth in length, we must return to the epiphysial plates mentioned earlier (see fig. 7.9, step 5). From infancy through adolescence, an epiphysial plate is present at one or both ends of a long bone, at the junction between the diaphysis and epiphysis. On X-rays, it appears as a translucent line across the end of a bone, since it is not yet ossified (**fig. 7.11;** compare the X-ray of an adult hand in fig. 8.35). The epiphysial plate is a region of

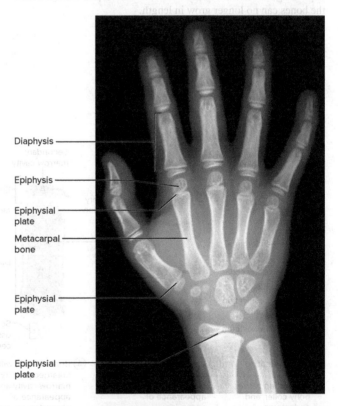

Diaphysis
Epiphysis
Epiphysial plate
Metacarpal bone
Epiphysial plate
Epiphysial plate

FIGURE 7.11 X-Ray of a Child's Hand. The cartilaginous epiphysial plates are evident at the ends of the long bones. Long bones of the hand and fingers develop only one epiphysial plate. Notice that the wrist is still largely cartilaginous (X-ray translucent).
Puwadol Jaturawutthichai/Shutterstock

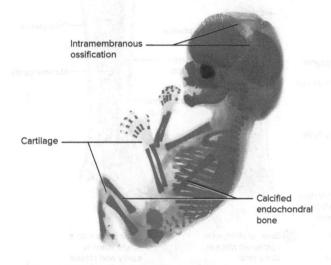

Intramembranous ossification

Cartilage

Calcified endochondral bone

FIGURE 7.10 The Fetal Skeleton at 12 Weeks. The red-stained regions are calcified at this age, whereas the elbow, wrist, knee, and ankle joints appear translucent because they are still cartilaginous.

❓ *Why are the joints of an infant weaker than those of an older child?*

Biophoto Associates/Science Source

transition from cartilage to bone, and functions as a growth zone where the bones elongate. Growth here is responsible for a person's increase in height.

The epiphysial plate consists of typical hyaline cartilage in the middle, with a transitional zone on each side where cartilage is being replaced by bone. The transitional zone, facing the marrow cavity, is called the **metaphysis** (meh-TAF-ih-sis). In figure 7.9, step 4, the cartilage is the blue region and each metaphysis is violet. **Figure 7.12** shows the histological structure of the metaphysis and the following steps in the replacement of cartilage by bone.

① **Zone of reserve cartilage.** This region, farthest from the marrow cavity, consists of typical hyaline cartilage with resting chondrocytes, not yet showing any sign of transformation into bone.

② **Zone of cell proliferation.** A little closer to the marrow cavity, chondrocytes multiply and arrange themselves into longitudinal columns of flattened lacunae.

③ **Zone of cell hypertrophy.** Next, the chondrocytes cease to multiply and begin to hypertrophy (enlarge), much like they

do in the primary ossification center of the fetus. The walls of matrix between lacunae become very thin.

④ **Zone of calcification.** Minerals are deposited in the matrix between the columns of lacunae and calcify the cartilage. These are not the permanent mineral deposits of bone, but only a temporary support for the cartilage that would otherwise soon be weakened by the breakdown of the enlarged lacunae.

⑤ **Zone of bone deposition.** Within each column, the walls between the lacunae break down and the chondrocytes die. This converts each column into a longitudinal channel (clear spaces in the figure), which is immediately invaded by blood vessels and marrow from the marrow cavity. Osteoblasts line up along the walls of these channels and begin depositing concentric lamellae of matrix, while osteoclasts dissolve the temporarily calcified cartilage.

The process of bone deposition in zone 5 creates a region of spongy bone at the end of the marrow cavity facing the metaphysis. This spongy bone remains for life, although with extensive lifelong

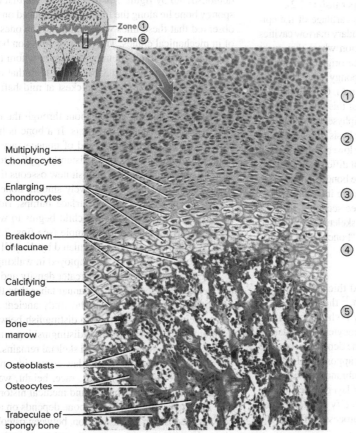

Zone ①
Zone ⑤

Multiplying chondrocytes

Enlarging chondrocytes

Breakdown of lacunae

Calcifying cartilage

Bone marrow

Osteoblasts

Osteocytes

Trabeculae of spongy bone

① Zone of reserve cartilage
Typical histology of resting hyaline cartilage

② Zone of cell proliferation
Chondrocytes multiplying and lining up in rows of small flattened lacunae

③ Zone of cell hypertrophy
Cessation of mitosis; enlargement of chondrocytes and thinning of lacuna walls

④ Zone of calcification
Temporary calcification of cartilage matrix between columns of lacunae

⑤ Zone of bone deposition
Breakdown of lacuna walls, leaving open channels; death of chondrocytes; bone deposition by osteoblasts, forming trabeculae of spongy bone

FIGURE 7.12 Zones of the Metaphysis. This micrograph shows the transition from cartilage to bone in the growth zone of a long bone.

❓ *Which two zones in this figure account for a child's growth in height?*

Victor Eroschenko

remodeling. But around the perimeter of the marrow cavity, continuing ossification converts this spongy bone to compact bone. Osteoblasts lining the aforementioned channels deposit layer after layer of bone matrix, so the channel grows narrower and narrower. These layers become the concentric lamellae of an osteon. Finally only a slender channel persists, the central canal of a new osteon. Osteoblasts trapped in the matrix become osteocytes.

▶▶▶**APPLY WHAT YOU KNOW**

In a given osteon, which lamellae are the oldest—those immediately adjacent to the central canal or those around the perimeter of the osteon? Explain your answer.

How does a child or adolescent grow in height? Chondrocyte multiplication in zone 2 and hypertrophy in zone 3 continually push the zone of reserve cartilage (1) toward the ends of the bone, so the bone elongates. In the lower limbs, this process causes a person to grow in height, while bones of the upper limbs grow proportionately.

Thus, bone elongation is really a result of cartilage growth. Cartilage growth from within, by the multiplication of chondrocytes and deposition of new matrix in the interior, is called **interstitial**[21] **growth.** The most common form of dwarfism results from a failure of cartilage growth in the long bones (see Deeper Insight 7.2).

In the late teens to early twenties, all the cartilage of the epiphysial plate is depleted. The primary and secondary marrow cavities now unite into one cavity. The junctional region where they meet is filled with spongy bone, and the site of the original epiphysial plate is marked with a line of slightly denser spongy bone called the **epiphysial line** (see figs. 7.1; 7.5; and 7.9, step 6). Often a delicate ridge on the bone surface marks the location of this line. When the epiphysial plate is depleted, we say that the epiphyses have "closed" because no gap between the epiphysis and diaphysis is visible on an X-ray. Once the epiphyses have all closed in the lower limbs, a person can grow no taller. The epiphysial plates close at different ages in different bones and in different regions of the same bone. The processes and rates of elongation and epiphysial closure are influenced especially by growth hormone and sex steroids (see section 7.4d). The state of closure in various bones of a subadult skeleton is often used in forensic science to estimate the individual's "bone age" at death.

Bone Widening and Thickening

Bones also continually grow in diameter and thickness. This involves a process called **appositional growth,**[22] the deposition of new tissue at the surface. Cartilages grow by both interstitial and appositional growth. In bone, however, osteocytes embedded in calcified matrix have little room to spare for the deposition of more matrix internally. Bone is therefore limited to appositional growth.

Appositional growth occurs by intramembranous ossification at the bone surface. Osteoblasts in the inner layer of periosteum deposit osteoid tissue on the bone surface, calcify it, and become trapped in it as osteocytes—much like the process in figure 7.8.

They lay down matrix in layers parallel to the surface, not in cylindrical osteons like those deeper in the bone. This process produces the surface layers of bone called *circumferential lamellae,* described earlier. As a bone increases in diameter, its marrow cavity also widens. This is achieved by osteoclasts of the endosteum dissolving tissue on the inner bone surface. Thus, flat bones develop by intramembranous ossificaton alone, whereas long bones develop by a combination of the intramembranous and endochondral methods.

Bone Remodeling

In addition to their growth, bones are continually remodeled throughout life by the absorption of old bone and deposition of new. This process replaces about 10% of the skeletal tissue per year. It releases minerals into the blood for uses elsewhere; reshapes bones in response to use and disuse; and repairs microfractures, preventing them from developing into catastrophic bone failure similar to metal fatigue.

Wolff's[23] **law of bone** states that the architecture of a bone is determined by the mechanical stresses placed upon it, and the bone thereby adapts to withstand them. Wolff's law is a fine example of the complementarity of form and function, showing that the form of a bone is shaped by its functional experience. It is admirably demonstrated by figure 7.5, in which we see that the trabeculae of spongy bone lie along the lines of stress placed on the femur. Wolff observed that these lines were similar to the ones engineers knew of in mechanical cranes. The effect of stress on bone development is quite evident in elite tennis players, in whom the cortical bone of the racket arm is up to 35% thicker than that of the other arm. Long bones of the limbs are thickest at midshaft, where they are subjected to the greatest stress.

Bone remodeling comes about through the collaborative action of osteoblasts and osteoclasts. If a bone is little used, osteoclasts remove matrix and get rid of unnecessary mass. If a bone is heavily used or stress is consistently applied to a particular region of a bone, osteoblasts deposit new osseous tissue and thicken it. Consequently, the comparatively smooth bones of an infant or toddler develop a variety of surface bumps, ridges, and spines (described in chapter 8) as the child begins to walk. The greater trochanter of the femur, for example (see figs. 7.5 and 8.39), is a massive outgrowth of bone stimulated by the pull of tendons from several powerful hip muscles employed in walking.

On average, bones have a greater density and mass in athletes and people engaged in heavy manual labor than they do in sedentary people. Anthropologists who study ancient skeletal remains use evidence of this sort to help distinguish between members of different social classes, such as distinguishing aristocrats from laborers. Even in studying modern skeletal remains, as in investigating a suspicious death, Wolff's law comes into play as the bones give evidence of a person's sex, race, height, weight, nutritional status, work or exercise habits, and medical history.

The orderly remodeling of bone depends on a precise balance between deposition and resorption, between osteoblasts and osteoclasts. If one process outpaces the other, or both processes occur

---

[21]*inter* = between; *stit* = to place, stand
[22]*ap* = *ad* = to, near; *posit* = to place

[23]Julius Wolff (1836–1902), German anatomist and surgeon

DEEPER INSIGHT 7.2

CLINICAL APPLICATION

Achondroplastic Dwarfism

Achondroplastic[24] *dwarfism* (a-con-dro-PLAS-tic) is a condition in which the long bones of the limbs stop growing in childhood, while the growth of other bones is unaffected. As a result, a person has a short stature but a normal-size head and trunk **(fig. 7.13).** As its name implies, achondroplastic dwarfism results from a failure of cartilage growth—specifically, failure of the chondrocytes in zones 2 and 3 of the metaphysis to multiply and enlarge. This is different from *pituitary dwarfism,* in which a deficiency of growth hormone stunts the growth of all of the bones, and a person has short stature but normal proportions throughout the skeletal system.

Achondroplastic dwarfism results from a spontaneous mutation that can arise any time DNA is replicated. Two people of normal height with no family history of dwarfism can therefore have a child with achondroplastic dwarfism. The mutant allele is dominant, so the offspring of a heterozygous achondroplastic dwarf have at least a 50% chance of exhibiting dwarfism, depending on the genotype of the other parent. Persons homozygous for the trait (those who inherit it from both parents) are usually stillborn or die soon after birth.

FIGURE 7.13 Achondroplastic Dwarfism. The student on the right, pictured with her roommate of normal height, is an achondroplastic dwarf with a height of about 122 cm (48 in.). Her parents were of normal height. Note the normal proportion of head to trunk but shortening of the limbs.

Joe DeGrandis/McGraw-Hill Education

[24]*a* = without; *chondr* = cartilage; *plast* = growth

too rapidly, various bone deformities, developmental abnormalities, and other disorders occur, such as *osteitis deformans* (Paget disease), *osteogenesis imperfecta* (brittle bone disease), and *osteoporosis* (see table 7.2 and Deeper Insight 7.4).

BEFORE YOU GO ON

Answer the following questions to test your understanding of the preceding section:

10. Describe the stages of intramembranous ossification. Name a bone that forms in this way.

11. Describe how a cartilage model transforms into a long bone in endochondral ossification.

12. Describe the five zones of a metaphysis and the major distinctions between them.

13. How does Wolff's law explain some of the structural differences between the bones of a young child and the bones of a young adult?

7.4 Physiology of Osseous Tissue

Expected Learning Outcomes

When you have completed this section, you should be able to

a. describe the processes by which minerals are added to and removed from bone tissue;

b. discuss the role of the bones in regulating blood calcium and phosphate levels; and

c. name the main hormones that regulate bone physiology, and describe their effects.

Even after a bone is fully formed, it remains a metabolically active organ with many roles to play. Not only is it involved in its own maintenance, growth, and remodeling, but it also exerts a profound influence on the rest of the body by exchanging minerals with the tissue fluid. Disturbances of calcium homeostasis in the skeleton can disrupt the functioning of other organ systems, especially the nervous and muscular systems. For reasons explained later, such disturbances can even cause death by suffocation.

7.4a Mineral Deposition and Resorption

Mineral deposition (mineralization) is a crystallization process in which calcium, phosphate, and other ions are taken from the blood plasma and deposited in bone tissue, mainly as needlelike crystals of hydroxyapatite. Deposition begins in fetal ossification and continues throughout life.

Osteoblasts begin the process by laying down collagen fibers in a helical pattern along the length of the osteon. These fibers then become encrusted with minerals that harden the matrix. The first few hydroxyapatite crystals to form act as "seed crystals" that attract more calcium and phosphate from solution. The more hydroxyapatite that forms, the more it attracts additional minerals from the tissue fluid, until the matrix is thoroughly calcified.

▶▶▶APPLY WHAT YOU KNOW

What positive feedback process can you recognize in bone deposition?

Abnormal calcification of tissues, called **ectopic**[25] **ossification,** sometimes occurs in the lungs, brain, eyes, muscles, tendons, arteries, and other organs. One example of this is arteriosclerosis, or "hardening of the arteries," which results from calcification of the arterial walls. A calcified mass in an otherwise soft organ such as the lungs is called a **calculus.**[26]

Mineral resorption is the process of dissolving bone. It releases minerals into the blood and makes them available for other uses. Resorption is carried out by osteoclasts. They have surface receptors for calcium and respond to falling levels of calcium in the tissue fluid. Hydrogen pumps in the ruffled border of the osteoclast secrete hydrogen ions into the tissue fluid, and chloride ions follow by electrical attraction. The space between the osteoclast and the bone thus becomes filled with concentrated hydrochloric acid with a pH of about 4. The acid dissolves the bone minerals. The osteoclast also secretes an acid-tolerant enzyme (protease) that digests the collagen of the bone matrix.

When orthodontic appliances (braces) are used to reposition teeth, a tooth moves because osteoclasts dissolve bone ahead of the tooth (where the appliance creates greater pressure of the tooth against the bone) and osteoblasts deposit bone in the low-pressure zone behind it.

[25]*ec* = out of; *top* = place
[26]*calc* = stone; *ulus* = little

7.4b Calcium Homeostasis

The adult body contains about 1,100 g of calcium, with 99% of it in the bones. Calcium is needed for much more than bone structure. It also plays roles in communication among neurons and in muscle contraction, blood clotting, and exocytosis. Calcium is deposited in the skeleton when the supply is ample and withdrawn when needed for these other purposes. The skeleton exchanges about 18% of its calcium with the blood each year.

This exchange is tightly regulated by hormones to maintain a blood calcium concentration of 9.2 to 10.4 mg/dL. This is a narrow margin of safety. A calcium deficiency, called **hypocalcemia**[27] (HY-po-cal-SEE-me-uh), causes excessive excitability of the nervous system and can lead to muscle tremors, spasms, or tetany—inability of the muscles to relax. Tetany of the muscles of the larynx can cause death by suffocation. A calcium excess, called **hypercalcemia,**[28] makes nerve and muscle cells less excitable than normal. This can be manifested in nervous system depression, emotional disturbances, muscle weakness, sluggish reflexes, and sometimes cardiac arrest.

Hypercalcemia is rare, but hypocalcemia can result from a wide variety of causes including vitamin D deficiency, diarrhea, thyroid tumors, or underactive parathyroid glands. Pregnancy and lactation put women at risk of hypocalcemia because of the calcium demanded by ossification of the fetal skeleton and synthesis of milk.

You can see how critical blood calcium level is, but what causes it to deviate from the norm, and how does the body correct such imbalances? Calcium homeostasis depends on a balance between dietary intake, urinary and fecal losses, and exchanges with the osseous tissue **(fig. 7.14).** It is regulated by three hormones: *calcitriol, calcitonin,* and *parathyroid hormone.*

[27]*hypo* = below normal; *calc* = calcium; *emia* = blood condition
[28]*hyper* = above normal; *calc* = calcium; *emia* = blood condition

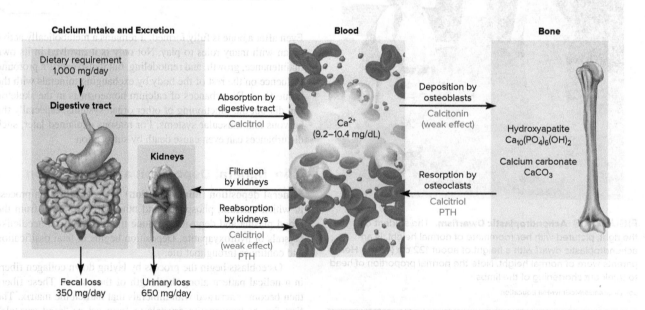

FIGURE 7.14 Hormonal Control of Calcium Balance. The central panel represents the blood reservoir of calcium and shows its normal (safe) range. Calcitriol and PTH regulate calcium exchanges between the blood and the small intestine and kidneys (left). Calcitonin, calcitriol, and PTH regulate calcium exchanges between blood and bone (right).

DEEPER INSIGHT 7.3

CLINICAL APPLICATION

Rickets and Osteomalacia

Rickets is a childhood disease in which the bones are soft and deformed as a result of vitamin D and calcium deficiency. It is characterized by fragile bones, bone pain, and frequent fractures; deformity of the chest, pelvis, and spine; and bowed legs **(fig. 7.15).** It is one of the most common childhood diseases of developing countries, but usually preventable by exposure to sunlight. Even 15 minutes per day is usually enough for adequate vitamin D synthesis. Vitamin D can also be obtained from fortified milk and dairy products, eggs, oily fish, and some mushrooms.

Rickets is common in areas wracked with warfare and famine. It also develops in infants who are breast-fed and kept from the sun without receiving supplemental vitamin D. In London during the early 1800s, it occurred in 80% to 90% of children who were kept indoors because of the heavy smog in the air and who were often exploited for long hours of factory work. The United States mandated the addition of vitamin D to milk in 1930 and outlawed child labor in 1937, greatly reducing rickets and other health problems. Yet rickets is increasing again as children spend more time indoors and even because of the increased use of sunscreen. The highest incidence today is in the Mideast, owing to covering of most or all of the body for religious or other cultural reasons.

Osteomalacia is a similar bone-softening, vitamin D deficiency disease of adults. It is especially common in nursing home residents and the homebound elderly. It often begins with lumbar aches and pains and

FIGURE 7.15 Rickets in a Boy of Eastern Kenya.
Jeff Rotman / Alamy Stock Photo

progresses to bone and joint pain, muscle weakness, difficulty walking and stair climbing, loss of height because of vertebral compression, a waddling gait due to spinal deformity, and pathological bone fractures.

Calcitriol

Calcitriol (CAL-sih-TRY-ol) is a form of vitamin D produced by the sequential action of the skin, liver, and kidneys **(fig. 7.16):**

1. Epidermal keratinocytes use ultraviolet radiation from sunlight to convert a steroid, 7-dehydrocholesterol, to previtamin D_3. Over another 3 days, the warmth of sunlight on the skin further converts this to vitamin D_3 *(cholecalciferol),* and a transport protein carries this to the bloodstream.

2. The liver adds a hydroxyl group, converting it to *calcidiol.*

3. The kidneys then add another hydroxyl group, converting calcidiol to calcitriol, the most active form of vitamin D.

Calcitriol behaves as a hormone—a blood-borne chemical messenger from one organ to another. It is called a vitamin only because it is added to the diet, mainly in fortified milk, as a safeguard for people who don't get enough sunlight to initiate adequate synthesis in the skin.

The principal function of calcitriol is to raise the blood calcium concentration. It does this in three ways (fig. 7.14), especially the first of these:

1. It increases calcium absorption by the small intestine, using mechanisms detailed in chapter 25 (see section 25.6f).

2. It increases calcium resorption from the skeleton. Calcitriol binds to osteoblasts, which then stimulate stem cells to differentiate into osteoclasts. The new osteoclasts liberate calcium and phosphate ions from bone.

3. It weakly promotes the reabsorption of calcium ions by the kidneys, so less calcium is lost in the urine.

Although calcitriol promotes bone resorption, it is also necessary for bone deposition. Without it, calcium and phosphate levels in the blood are too low for normal deposition. The result is a softness of the bones called **rickets** in children and **osteomalacia**[29] in adults (see Deeper Insight 7.3).

Calcitonin

Calcitonin is produced by *parafollicular (clear) cells* of the thyroid gland (see fig. 17.9). It is secreted when the blood calcium concentration rises too high, and it lowers the concentration by two principal mechanisms (figs. 7.14 and **7.17a):**

1. **Osteoclast inhibition.** Within 15 minutes after it is secreted, calcitonin reduces osteoclast activity by as much as 70%, so osteoclasts liberate less calcium from the skeleton.

2. **Osteoblast stimulation.** Within an hour, calcitonin increases the number and activity of osteoblasts, which deposit calcium into the skeleton.

Calcitonin plays an important role in children but has only a weak effect in most adults. The osteoclasts of children are highly active in skeletal remodeling and release 5 g or more of calcium into the blood each day. By inhibiting this, calcitonin

---

[29]*osteo* = bone; *malacia* = softening

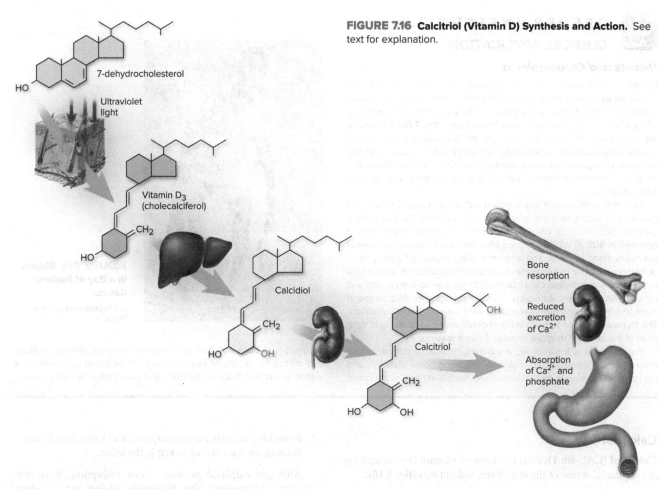

7-dehydrocholesterol

HO

Ultraviolet light

Vitamin D₃ (cholecalciferol)

CH₂

HO

Calcidiol

CH₂

HO   OH

Calcitriol

CH₂

HO   OH

Bone resorption

Reduced excretion of Ca²⁺

Absorption of Ca²⁺ and phosphate

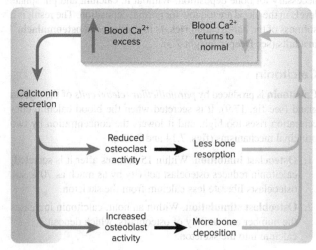

Blood Ca²⁺ excess

Blood Ca²⁺ returns to normal

Calcitonin secretion

Reduced osteoclast activity → Less bone resorption

Increased osteoblast activity → More bone deposition

(a) Correction for hypercalcemia

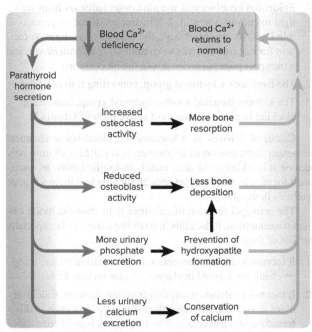

Blood Ca²⁺ deficiency

Blood Ca²⁺ returns to normal

Parathyroid hormone secretion

Increased osteoclast activity → More bone resorption

Reduced osteoblast activity → Less bone deposition

More urinary phosphate excretion → Prevention of hydroxyapatite formation

Less urinary calcium excretion → Conservation of calcium

(b) Correction for hypocalcemia

FIGURE 7.17 Negative Feedback Loops in Calcium Homeostasis. (a) The correction of hypercalcemia by calcitonin. (b) The correction of hypocalcemia by parathyroid hormone.

can significantly lower the blood calcium level in children. In adults, however, the osteoclasts release only about 0.8 g of calcium per day. Calcitonin cannot change adult blood calcium very much by suppressing this lesser contribution. Calcitonin deficiency isn't known to cause any adult disease. Calcitonin may, however, help to maintain bone density in pregnant and lactating women.

Parathyroid Hormone

Parathyroid hormone (PTH) is secreted by the parathyroid glands, which adhere to the posterior surface of the thyroid gland. These glands release PTH when blood calcium is low. A mere 1% drop in the calcium level doubles PTH secretion. PTH raises the calcium level by four mechanisms (figs. 7.14 and **7.17b**):

1. It binds to receptors on the osteoblasts, which in turn stimulate the osteoclast population and promote bone resorption.
2. It promotes calcium reabsorption by the kidneys, so less calcium is lost in the urine.
3. It promotes the final step of calcitriol synthesis in the kidneys, thus enhancing the calcium-raising effect of calcitriol.
4. It inhibits collagen synthesis by osteoblasts, thus inhibiting bone deposition.

7.4c Phosphate Homeostasis

The average adult has 500 to 800 g of phosphorus, of which 85% to 90% is in the bones. Phosphate is required not only for bone strength but also as a component of DNA, RNA, ATP, phospholipids, and other compounds. Plasma phosphorus concentration ranges from 3.5 to 4.0 mg/dL. Its level is not as tightly regulated as calcium. Nor, apparently, does it need to be; changes in plasma phosphate level are not associated with any immediate functional disorder. Calcitriol raises the phosphate level by promoting its absorption from the diet by the small intestine. This makes sense, because one effect of calcitriol is to promote bone deposition, and that requires both calcium and phosphate. Parathyroid hormone, on the other hand, lowers the blood phosphate level by promoting its urinary excretion.

▶▶▶ APPLY WHAT YOU KNOW

While raising the blood calcium level, PTH lowers the phosphate level. Explain why this is important for achieving the purpose of PTH.

7.4d Other Factors Affecting Bone

At least 20 more hormones, growth factors, and vitamins affect osseous tissue in complex ways that are still not well understood **(table 7.1)**. Bone growth is especially rapid in

TABLE 7.1	Agents Affecting Calcium and Bone Metabolism
Name	**Effect**
Hormones	
Calcitonin	Promotes mineralization and lowers blood Ca^{2+} concentration in children, but usually has little effect in adults; may prevent bone loss in pregnant and lactating women
Calcitriol (vitamin D)	Promotes intestinal absorption of Ca^{2+} and phosphate; reduces urinary excretion of both; promotes both resorption and mineralization; stimulates osteoclast activity
Cortisol	Inhibits osteoclast activity, but if secreted in excess (Cushing disease), can cause osteoporosis by reducing bone deposition (inhibiting cell division and protein synthesis), inhibiting growth hormone secretion, and stimulating osteoclasts to resorb bone
Estrogen	Stimulates osteoblasts and adolescent growth; prevents osteoporosis
Growth hormone	Stimulates bone elongation and cartilage proliferation at epiphysial plate; increases urinary excretion of Ca^{2+} but also increases intestinal Ca^{2+} absorption, which compensates for the loss
Insulin	Stimulates bone formation; significant bone loss occurs in untreated diabetes mellitus
Parathyroid hormone	Indirectly activates osteoclasts, which resorb bone and raise blood Ca^{2+} concentration; inhibits urinary Ca^{2+} excretion; promotes calcitriol synthesis
Testosterone	Stimulates osteoblasts and promotes protein synthesis, thus promoting adolescent growth and epiphysial closure
Thyroid hormone	Essential to bone growth; enhances synthesis and effects of growth hormone, but excesses can cause hypercalcemia, increased Ca^{2+} excretion in urine, and osteoporosis
Growth Factors	At least 12 hormonelike substances produced in bone itself that stimulate neighboring bone cells, promote collagen synthesis, stimulate epiphysial growth, and produce many other effects
Vitamins	
Vitamin A	Promotes glycosaminoglycan (chondroitin sulfate) synthesis
Vitamin C (ascorbic acid)	Required for collagen synthesis, bone growth, and fracture repair
Vitamin D	Normally functions as a hormone (see calcitriol)

puberty and adolescence, when surges of growth hormone, estrogen, and testosterone promote ossification. These hormones stimulate rapid multiplication of osteogenic cells, matrix deposition by osteoblasts, and multiplication and hypertrophy of the chondrocytes in the metaphyses. Adolescent girls grow faster than boys and attain their full height earlier, not only because they begin puberty earlier but also because estrogen has a stronger effect than testosterone. Since males grow for a longer time, however, they usually grow taller. Sex steroids eventually deplete the cartilage of the epiphysial plates, bring about closure of the epiphyses, and put an end to one's growth in height. A deficiency or excess of these steroids can therefore cause abnormalities ranging from stunted growth to very tall stature. The use of anabolic steroids by adolescent athletes can cause premature closure and result in abnormally short adult stature (see Deeper Insight 2.6). The excessive consumption of cola (more than three 12-ounce servings per day) is associated with loss of bone density in women, but not in men. The effect is thought to be due to the phosphoric acid in cola, which binds intestinal calcium and interferes with its absorption. Other soft drinks don't contain phosphoric acid or affect bone density.

BEFORE YOU GO ON

Answer the following questions to test your understanding of the preceding section:

14. Describe the role of collagen and seed crystals in bone mineralization.

15. Why is it important to regulate blood calcium concentration within such a narrow range?

16. What effect does calcitonin have on blood calcium concentration, and how does it produce this effect? Answer the same questions for parathyroid hormone.

17. How is vitamin D synthesized, and what effect does it have on blood calcium concentration?

7.5   Bone Disorders

Expected Learning Outcomes

When you have completed this section, you should be able to

a. name and describe several bone diseases;

b. name and describe the types of fractures;

c. explain how a fracture is repaired; and

d. discuss some clinical treatments for fractures and other skeletal disorders.

Most people probably give little thought to their skeletal systems unless they break a bone. This section describes bone fractures, their healing, and their treatment, followed by a summary of other bone diseases. Bone disorders are among the concerns of

orthopedics,[30] a branch of medicine that originated as the treatment of skeletal deformities in children. It is now much more extensive and deals with the prevention and correction of injuries and disorders of the bones, joints, and muscles. It includes the design of artificial joints and limbs and the treatment of athletic injuries.

7.5a Fractures and Their Repair

There are multiple ways of classifying bone fractures. A **stress fracture** is a break caused by abnormal trauma to a bone, such as fractures incurred in falls, athletics, auto accidents, and military combat. A **pathological fracture** is a break in a bone weakened by some other disease, such as bone cancer or osteoporosis, usually caused by a stress that would not normally fracture a bone. Fractures are also classified according to the direction of the fracture line, whether the skin is broken, and whether a bone is merely cracked or broken into separate pieces. For example, a *nondisplaced* fracture is one in which the bone pieces remain in proper anatomical alignment, whereas a *displaced* fracture is one in which at least one piece is shifted out of alignment with the other **(fig. 7.18a, b)**. A *comminuted* fracture is one in which a bone is broken into three or more pieces **(fig. 7.18c)**. A *greenstick* fracture is one in which the bone is incompletely broken on one side but merely bent on the opposite side **(fig. 7.18d)**, the way a green twig breaks only partially and not into separate pieces. Several other types of fractures are routinely taught in clinical and first aid courses.

The Healing of Fractures

An uncomplicated fracture heals in about 8 to 12 weeks, but complex fractures take longer and all fractures heal more slowly in older people. The healing process occurs in the following stages **(fig. 7.19)**:

1. **Formation of hematoma and granulation tissue.** A bone fracture severs blood vessels of the bone and periosteum, causing bleeding and the formation of a blood clot (*fracture hematoma*). Blood capillaries soon grow into the clot, while fibroblasts, macrophages, osteoclasts, and osteogenic cells invade the tissue from both the periosteal and medullary sides of the fracture. Osteogenic cells become very abundant within 48 hours of the injury. All of this capillary and cellular invasion converts the blood clot to a soft fibrous mass called **granulation tissue.**

2. **Formation of a soft callus.**[31] Fibroblasts deposit collagen in the granulation tissue, while some osteogenic cells become chondroblasts and produce patches of fibrocartilage called the **soft callus.**

---

[30]*ortho* = straight; *ped* = child, foot
[31]*call* = hard, tough

③ **Conversion to hard callus.** Other osteogenic cells differentiate into osteoblasts, which produce a bony collar called the **hard callus** around the fracture. The hard callus is cemented to dead bone around the injury site and acts as a temporary splint to join the broken ends or bone fragments together. It takes about 4 to 6 weeks for a hard callus to form. During this period, it is important that a broken bone be immobilized by traction or a cast to prevent reinjury.

④ **Remodeling.** The hard callus persists for 3 to 4 months. Meanwhile, osteoclasts dissolve small fragments of broken bone, and osteoblasts deposit spongy bone to bridge the gap between the broken ends. This spongy bone gradually fills in to become compact bone, in a manner similar to intramembranous ossification. Usually the fracture leaves a slight thickening of the bone visible by X-ray; such thickenings may serve as forensic evidence of child abuse. In some cases, however, healing is so complete that no trace of the fracture can be found.

The Treatment of Fractures

Most fractures are set by **closed reduction,** a procedure in which the bone fragments are manipulated into their normal positions without surgery. **Open reduction** involves the surgical exposure of the bone and the use of plates, screws, or pins to realign the fragments **(fig. 7.20).** To stabilize the bone during healing, fractures are often set in casts. Traction is used to treat fractures of the femur in children. It aids in the alignment of the bone fragments by overriding the force of the strong thigh muscles. Traction is rarely used for elderly patients, however, because the risks from long-term confinement to bed outweigh the benefits. Hip fractures are usually pinned, and early ambulation (walking) is encouraged because it promotes blood circulation and healing. Fractures that take longer than 2 months to heal may be treated with electrical stimulation, which accelerates repair by suppressing the effects of parathyroid hormone.

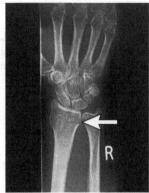
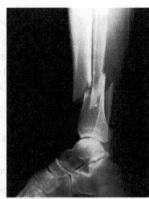
(a) Nondisplaced **(b) Displaced**

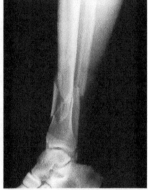
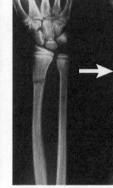
(c) Comminuted **(d) Greenstick**

FIGURE 7.18 X-Rays of Representative Fracture Types.
(a) Nondisplaced fracture of the distal humerus in a 3-year-old.
(b) Displaced fracture of the tibia and fibula. (c) Comminuted fracture of the tibia and fibula. (d) Greenstick fracture of the ulna.

a: Watney Collection/Medical Images; b: Howard Kingsnorth/The Image Bank/Getty Images; c: Lester V. Bergman/Corbis NX/Getty Images; d: Biophoto Associates/Science Source

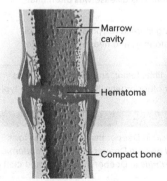
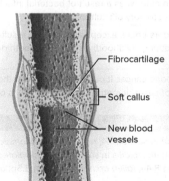
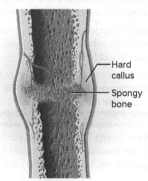

Marrow cavity

Hematoma

Compact bone

Fibrocartilage

Soft callus

New blood vessels

Hard callus

Spongy bone

① **Hematoma formation**
The hematoma is converted to granulation tissue by invasion of cells and blood capillaries.

② **Soft callus formation**
Deposition of collagen and fibrocartilage converts granulation tissue to a soft callus.

③ **Hard callus formation**
Osteoblasts deposit a temporary bony collar around the fracture to unite the broken pieces while ossification occurs.

④ **Bone remodeling**
Small bone fragments are removed by osteoclasts, while osteoblasts deposit spongy bone and then convert it to compact bone.

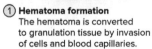
FIGURE 7.19 The Healing of a Bone Fracture.

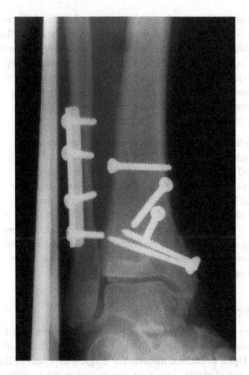

FIGURE 7.20 Open Reduction of an Ankle Fracture.
Southern Illinois University/Science Source

7.5b Other Bone Disorders

Several additional bone disorders are summarized in **table 7.2.** The most common bone disease, **osteoporosis,**[32] receives special consideration in Deeper Insight 7.4. The effects of aging on the skeletal system are described in section 29.4a.

BEFORE YOU GO ON

Answer the following questions to test your understanding of the preceding section:

18. Name and describe four types of bone fractures.

19. Why would osteomyelitis be more likely to occur in an open fracture than in a closed fracture?

20. What is a callus? How does it contribute to fracture repair?

TABLE 7.2	Bone Diseases
Osteitis deformans (Paget[33] disease)	Excessive proliferation of osteoclasts and resorption of excess bone, with osteoblasts attempting to compensate by depositing extra bone. This results in rapid, disorderly bone remodeling and weak, deformed bones. Osteitis deformans usually passes unnoticed, but in some cases it causes pain, disfiguration, and fractures. It is most common in males over the age of 50.
Osteomyelitis[34]	Inflammation of osseous tissue and bone marrow as a result of bacterial infection. This disease was often fatal before the discovery of antibiotics and is still very difficult to treat.
Osteogenesis imperfecta (brittle bone disease)	A defect in collagen deposition that renders bones exceptionally brittle, resulting in fractures present at birth or occurring with extraordinary frequency during childhood; also causing tooth deformity, and hearing loss due to deformity of middle-ear bones.
Osteosarcoma[35] (osteogenic sarcoma)	The most common and deadly form of bone cancer. It occurs most often in the tibia, femur, and humerus of males between the ages of 10 and 25. In 10% of cases, it metastasizes to the lungs or other organs; if untreated, death typically occurs within 1 year.
You can find other skeletal system disorders described in the following places:	
Achondroplastic dwarfism in Deeper Insight 7.2; *ectopic ossification* in section 7.4; *rickets* and *osteomalacia* in Deeper Insight 7.3; *bone fractures* (in general) in section 7.5a; *osteoporosis* in Deeper Insight 7.4; *mastoiditis* in section 8.2a; *herniated discs* in Deeper Insight 8.4; *abnormal spinal curvatures* in Deeper Insight 8.3; *fractured clavicle* in section 8.4a; *fallen arches* in section 8.5b; *arthritis* in Deeper Insight 9.5; and cleft palate in Deeper Insight 29.4.	

[32]*osteo* = bone; *por* = porous; *osis* = condition
[33]Sir James Paget (1814–99), English surgeon
[34]*osteo* = bone; *myel* = marrow; *itis* = inflammation
[35]*osteo* = bone; *sarc* = flesh; *oma* = tumor

DEEPER INSIGHT 7.4

CLINICAL APPLICATION

Osteoporosis

Osteoporosis is the most common of all bone diseases. It can be defined as a disorder in which bone density declines to the extent that the bones become brittle and subject to pathological fractures. Starting around age 40, bone resorption outpaces deposition, so we lose overall bone density. The loss comes especially from spongy bone, because it has the greatest surface area exposed to osteoclast action **(fig. 7.21a)**. Proportionate amounts of organic matrix and minerals are lost, so the bone that remains is normal in composition. By old age, however, it may be insufficient in quantity to support the body's weight and withstand normal stresses.

People with osteoporosis are especially vulnerable to fractures of the hip, wrist, and spine. Their bones may break under stresses as slight as sitting down too quickly. Among the elderly, slowly healing hip fractures can impose prolonged immobility and lead to fatal complications such as pneumonia. Those who survive often face a long, costly recovery. Spinal deformity is also a common consequence of osteoporosis. As the bodies of the vertebrae lose spongy bone, they become compressed by body weight **(fig. 7.21b)** and the spine can develop an exaggerated thoracic curvature called hyperkyphosis **(fig. 7.21c)**.

Postmenopausal women of European and Asian ancestry are at the greatest risk for osteoporosis. About 30% of U.S. women suffer a fracture due to osteoporosis at some point in their lives. Compared to men, they have less initial bone mass and begin to lose it at an earlier age. Since estrogen supports bone mass, the risk of osteoporosis rises sharply after menopause, when the ovaries cease to produce it. By age 70, the average white woman has lost 30% of her bone mass, and some as much as 50%. Osteoporosis is less common among women of African ancestry because of their greater initial bone density.

Other risk factors include family history; a light body build; dietary deficiencies of calcium, vitamin D, and protein; inadequate exercise; smoking; and overuse of alcohol. Osteoporosis is surprisingly common in young female runners, dancers, and gymnasts in spite of their vigorous exercise. They sometimes have such a low percentage of body fat that they stop ovulating, and without developing follicles, their ovaries secrete low levels of estrogen. About 20% of osteoporosis sufferers are men. In early long-term space missions, astronauts developed osteoporosis because in a microgravity environment, their bones were subjected to too little of the stress that normally stimulates bone deposition. This and the prevention of muscle atrophy are reasons why exercise equipment is now standard on space stations.

Osteoporosis is now diagnosed by *bone mineral density (BMD)* tests using low-dose X-rays. This has enabled earlier diagnosis and more effective treatment. However, the severity of osteoporosis depends not on bone density alone, but also on the degree of connectivity between the spongy bone trabeculae, which is lost as trabeculae deteriorate. Neither BMD testing nor any other diagnostic method yet available can detect this.

Treatment is aimed at promoting bone deposition with drugs that either stimulate osteoblasts or slow the rate of bone resorption. Osteoblasts can be stimulated to build bone by pulsed treatment with a synthetic parathyroid hormone (PTH) or by selective estrogen–receptor modulators (SERMs), which mimic the effects of estrogen without producing undesirable estrogen side effects such as the risk of stroke or breast cancer. Resorption can be inhibited with a family of drugs called bisphosphanates. This is an intensive area of clinical research and new drugs are brought to market often.

As with so many other disorders, prevention is far preferable to treatment. Prevention is best begun in the young, bone-forming years of one's 20s and 30s, but continued even into old age. It includes weight-bearing exercise; ample dietary intake of calcium, vitamin D, and protein; and of course avoiding such risk factors as smoking and a sedentary lifestyle. For the elderly, such weight-bearing exercises as dancing, stair climbing, walking, and running can be pleasurable ways of minimizing the risk of osteoporosis.

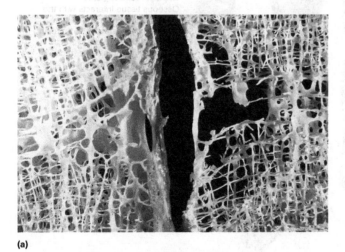

(a)

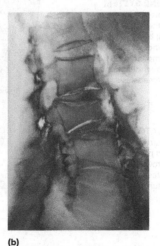

(b)

(c)

FIGURE 7.21 Spinal Osteoporosis. (a) Spongy bone in the body of a vertebra in good health (left) and with osteoporosis (right). (b) X-ray of lumbar vertebrae severely damaged by osteoporosis. (c) Woman with severe hyperkyphosis due to compression of thoracic vertebrae.

a: Michael Klein/Photolibrary/Getty Images; b: Dr. P. Marazzi/Science Source; c: Phanie/Alamy

CONNECTIVE ISSUES

Effects of the **SKELETAL SYSTEM** on Other Organ Systems

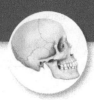

INTEGUMENTARY SYSTEM
Bones lying close to the body surface support and shape the skin.

MUSCULAR SYSTEM
Bones are the attachment sites for most skeletal muscles and provide leverage for muscle action; calcium homeostasis, important for muscle contraction, is achieved partly through a balance between bone deposition and resorption.

NERVOUS SYSTEM
The cranium and vertebral column protect the brain and spinal cord; osseous tissue provides the calcium homeostasis needed for nerve function.

ENDOCRINE SYSTEM
Bones protect endocrine glands in the head, thorax, and pelvis; bones secrete the hormone osteocalcin, which promotes insulin action; hormone secretion depends on calcium homeostasis.

CIRCULATORY SYSTEM
Bone marrow forms blood cells and platelets; osseous tissue provides the calcium homeostasis needed for cardiac function and blood clotting.

LYMPHATIC AND IMMUNE SYSTEMS
White blood cells produced in the bone marrow carry out the body's immune functions.

RESPIRATORY SYSTEM
Ventilation of the lungs is achieved by musculoskeletal actions of the thoracic cage; the thoracic cage protects the delicate lungs from trauma; bones support and shape the nasal cavity.

URINARY SYSTEM
The thoracic cage partially protects the kidneys, and the pelvic girdle protects the lower urinary tract.

DIGESTIVE SYSTEM
Osseous tissue interacts with the digestive system in maintaining calcium homeostasis; the thoracic cage and pelvic girdle protect portions of the digestive tract; musculoskeletal movements are necessary for chewing.

REPRODUCTIVE SYSTEM
The pelvic girdle protects the internal reproductive organs; childbirth is adapted to the anatomy of the female pelvic girdle; ligaments anchor the penis, clitoris, uterus, and ovaries to the pelvic girdle.

STUDY GUIDE

▶ Assess Your Learning Outcomes

To test your knowledge, discuss the following topics with a study partner or in writing, ideally from memory.

7.1 Tissues and Organs of the Skeletal System

1. The branch of medicine and biology that deals with the skeleton and bone tissue
2. Organs and tissues that constitute the skeletal system
3. Functions of the skeletal system
4. Which primary tissue category includes bone, and how bone differs from other tissues in that category
5. The relationship of compact bone, spongy bone, and the marrow cavity in the anatomy of a long bone
6. Other anatomical features of a long bone including the diaphysis, epiphysis, epiphysial plate, articular cartilage, periosteum, and endosteum
7. Structure of a typical flat bone

7.2 Histology of Osseous Tissue

1. The four cell types in bone tissue; their functions, origins, and locations in the tissue
2. Organic and inorganic components of the bone matrix; their respective contributions to bone strength; and the significance of the helical arrangement of collagen fibers in bone
3. Osteon structure and the relationship of osteonic bone to interstitial and circumferential lamellae

4. The route by which nerves and blood vessels penetrate throughout a bone
5. Comparisons of the histology of spongy bone with that of compact bone; where spongy bone is found; and why bones are not composed solely of compact bone
6. Location and functions of the bone marrow; the composition and childhood versus adult distribution of the two types of marrow

7.3 Bone Development

1. Stages of intramembranous ossification; some bones that form in this way; and how far this process has progressed by birth
2. The same points concerning endochondral ossification
3. Histology, cell transformations, and tissue zones of the metaphysis; which zones and processes account for a child's or adolescent's growth in height
4. How stresses on bones remodel them throughout life; the difference between interstitial and appositional growth

7.4 Physiology of Osseous Tissue

1. The purpose and process of mineralization of osseous tissue, and the identity of the cells that carry it out
2. The purpose and process of bone resorption, and the identity of the cells and cell secretions that carry it out
3. Functions of calcium in the body; the normal range of blood calcium concentration;

and causes and consequences of hypocalcemia and hypercalcemia
4. The role of the skeleton as a calcium reservoir in regulating blood calcium levels
5. How calcitriol is synthesized and the mechanisms by which it supports or raises blood calcium level
6. The source of calcitonin and how it corrects hypercalcemia
7. The source of parathyroid hormone and multiple mechanisms by which it corrects hypocalcemia
8. Two forms of phosphate ions in the blood; the bodily functions of phosphate; and how calcitriol and parathyroid hormone affect blood phosphate levels
9. Effects of dietary vitamins A, C, and D on bone metabolism
10. Effects of cortisol, estrogen, testosterone, growth hormone, insulin, and thyroid hormone on bone metabolism

7.5 Bone Disorders

1. The difference between a stress fracture and a pathological fracture; stages in the healing of a fractured bone; and approaches to the clinical treatment of fractures
2. Causes of osteoporosis; its risk factors, pathological effects, diagnosis, treatment, and prevention

▶ Testing Your Recall

Answers in Appendix A

1. Which cells have a ruffled border and secrete hydrochloric acid?
   a. C cells
   b. osteocytes
   c. osteogenic cells
   d. osteoblasts
   e. osteoclasts

2. The marrow cavity of an adult bone may contain
   a. myeloid tissue.
   b. hyaline cartilage.
   c. periosteum.
   d. osteocytes.
   e. articular cartilages.

3. The spurt of growth in puberty results from cell proliferation and hypertrophy in
   a. the epiphysis.
   b. the epiphysial line.
   c. compact bone.
   d. the epiphysial plate.
   e. spongy bone.

4. Osteoclasts are most closely related, by common descent, to
   a. osteoprogenitor cells.
   b. osteogenic cells.
   c. blood cells.
   d. fibroblasts.
   e. osteoblasts.

5. The walls between cartilage lacunae break down in the zone of
   a. cell proliferation.
   b. calcification.
   c. reserve cartilage.
   d. bone deposition.
   e. cell hypertrophy.

6. Which of these is *not* an effect of PTH?
   a. rise in blood phosphate level
   b. reduction of calcium excretion
   c. increased intestinal calcium absorption
   d. increased number of osteoclasts
   e. increased calcitriol synthesis

STUDY GUIDE

7. A child jumps to the ground from the top of a playground "jungle gym." His leg bones do not shatter mainly because they contain
   a. an abundance of glycosaminoglycans.
   b. young, resilient osteocytes.
   c. an abundance of calcium phosphate.
   d. collagen fibers.
   e. hydroxyapatite crystals.

8. One long bone meets another at its
   a. diaphysis.
   b. epiphysial plate.
   c. periosteum.
   d. metaphysis.
   e. epiphysis.

9. Calcitriol is made from
   a. calcitonin.
   b. 7-dehydrocholesterol.

c. hydroxyapatite.
d. estrogen.
e. PTH.

10. One sign of osteoporosis is
    a. osteosarcoma.
    b. osteomalacia.
    c. osteomyelitis.
    d. a spontaneous wrist fracture.
    e. hypocalcemia.

11. Calcium phosphate crystallizes in bone as a mineral called _____.

12. Osteocytes contact each other through channels called _____ in the bone matrix.

13. A bone increases in diameter only by _____ growth, the addition of new surface lamellae.

14. Seed crystals of hydroxyapatite form only when the levels of calcium and phosphate in the tissue fluid exceed the _____.

15. A calcium deficiency called _____ can cause death by suffocation.

16. _____ are cells that secrete collagen and stimulate calcium phosphate deposition.

17. The most active form of vitamin D, produced mainly by the kidneys, is _____.

18. The most common bone disease is _____.

19. The transitional region between epiphysial cartilage and the primary marrow cavity of a young bone is called the _____.

20. A pregnant, poorly nourished woman may suffer a softening of the bones called _____.

▶ Building Your Medical Vocabulary

Answers in Appendix A

State a meaning of each word element, and give a medical term from this chapter that uses it or a slight variation of it.

1. calc-
2. -clast

3. -malacia
4. myelo-
5. ortho-
6. osse-

7. osteo-
8. -physis
9. spic-
10. topo-

▶ What's Wrong with These Statements?

Answers in Appendix A

Briefly explain why each of the following statements is false, or reword it to make it true.

1. The flat cranial bones are composed of compact bone only, with no spongy bone.

2. In endochondral ossification, bone tissue is formed by the calcification of preexisting cartilage.

3. Fractures are the most common bone disorder.

4. The growth zone of the long bones of adolescents is the articular cartilage.

5. Osteoclasts develop from osteoblasts.

6. Osteoblasts are multipotent stem cells.

7. The protein of the bone matrix is called hydroxyapatite.

8. Osteocytes are nourished by blood capillaries in the canaliculi of the osteons.

9. Vitamin D promotes bone deposition, not resorption.

10. Parathyroid hormone stimulates bone deposition by osteoblasts.

▶ Testing Your Comprehension

1. Most osteocytes of an osteon are far removed from blood vessels, but still receive blood-borne nutrients. Explain how this is possible.

2. A 50-year-old business executive decides he has not been getting enough exercise for the last several years. He takes up hiking and finds that he really loves it. Within 2 years,

he is spending many of his weekends hiking with a heavy backpack and camping in the mountains. Explain what changes in his anatomy could be predicted from Wolff's law of bone.

3. How does the regulation of blood calcium concentration exemplify negative feedback and homeostasis?

4. Describe how the arrangement of trabeculae in spongy bone demonstrates the unity of form and function.

5. Identify two bone diseases you would expect to see if the epidermis were a completely effective barrier to UV radiation and a person took no dietary supplements to compensate for this. Explain your answer.

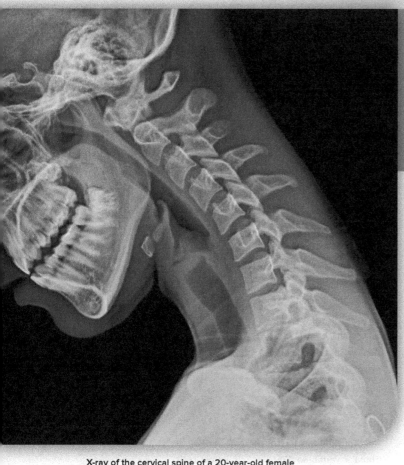

X-ray of the cervical spine of a 20-year-old female
Science Photo Library - Zephyr/Getty Images

THE SKELETAL SYSTEM

CHAPTER OUTLINE

DEEPER INSIGHTS

Anatomy & Physiology
Revealed 4.0

Module 5: Skeletal System

BRUSHING UP

- Anatomical descriptions of the skeletal system depend heavily on the directional terminology introduced in atlas A, table A.1.
- Understanding skeletal anatomy also depends on knowledge of the terms for body regions and cavities described in atlas A.

Knowledge of skeletal anatomy will be useful as you study later chapters. It provides a point of reference for studying the gross anatomy of other organ systems because many organs are named for their relationships to nearby bones. The subclavian artery and vein, for example, lie adjacent to the clavicle; the temporalis muscle is attached to the temporal bone; the ulnar nerve and radial artery travel beside the ulna and radius of the forearm; and the frontal, parietal, temporal, and occipital lobes of the brain are named for adjacent bones of the cranium. Understanding how the muscles produce body movements also depends on knowledge of skeletal anatomy. Additionally, the positions, shapes, and processes of bones can serve as landmarks for clinicians in determining where to give an injection or record a pulse, what to look for in an X-ray, and how to perform physical therapy and other clinical procedures.

8.1   Overview of the Skeleton

Expected Learning Outcomes

When you have completed this section, you should be able to

a. define the two subdivisions of the skeleton;
b. state the approximate number of bones in the adult body;
c. explain why this number varies with age and from one person to another; and
d. define several terms that denote surface features of bones.

The skeleton (**fig. 8.1**) is divided into two regions: the axial skeleton and appendicular skeleton. The **axial skeleton,** which forms the central supporting axis of the body, includes the skull, auditory ossicles (middle-ear bones), hyoid bone, vertebral column, and thoracic cage (ribs and sternum). The **appendicular skeleton** includes the bones of the upper limb and pectoral girdle and the bones of the lower limb and pelvic girdle.

8.1a Bones of the Skeletal System

It is often stated that there are 206 bones in the skeleton, but this is only a typical adult count, not an invariable number. At birth there are about 270, and even more bones form during childhood. With age, however, the number decreases as separate bones gradually fuse. For example, each side of a child's pelvic girdle has three bones—the *ilium, ischium,* and *pubis*—but in adults, these are fused into a single *hip bone* on each side. The

fusion of several bones, completed by late adolescence to the mid-20s, brings about the average adult number of 206. These bones are listed in **table 8.1.**

This number varies even among adults. One reason is the development of **sesamoid**[1] **bones**—bones that form within

[1]*sesam* = sesame seed; *oid* = resembling

TABLE 8.1	Bones of the Adult Skeletal System
Axial Skeleton	
Skull (22 bones)	
Cranial bones	
Frontal bone (1)	Temporal bones (2)
Parietal bones (2)	Sphenoid bone (1)
Occipital bone (1)	Ethmoid bone (1)
Facial bones	
Maxillae (2)	Nasal bones (2)
Palatine bones (2)	Vomer (1)
Zygomatic bones (2)	Inferior nasal conchae (2)
Lacrimal bones (2)	Mandible (1)
Auditory ossicles (6 bones)	
Malleus (2)	Stapes (2)
Incus (2)	
Hyoid bone (1 bone)	
Vertebral column (26 bones)	
Cervical vertebrae (7)	Sacrum (1)
Thoracic vertebrae (12)	Coccyx (1)
Lumbar vertebrae (5)	
Thoracic cage (25 bones plus thoracic vertebrae)	
Ribs (24)	
Sternum (1)	
Appendicular Skeleton	
Pectoral girdle (4 bones)	
Scapulae (2)	Clavicles (2)
Upper limbs (60 bones)	
Humerus (2)	Carpal bones (16)
Radius (2)	Metacarpal bones (10)
Ulna (2)	Phalanges (28)
Pelvic girdle (2 bones)	
Hip bones (2)	
Lower limbs (60 bones)	
Femurs (2)	Tarsal bones (14)
Patellae (2)	Metatarsal bones (10)
Tibiae (2)	Phalanges (28)
Fibulae (2)	
Grand Total: 206 Bones	

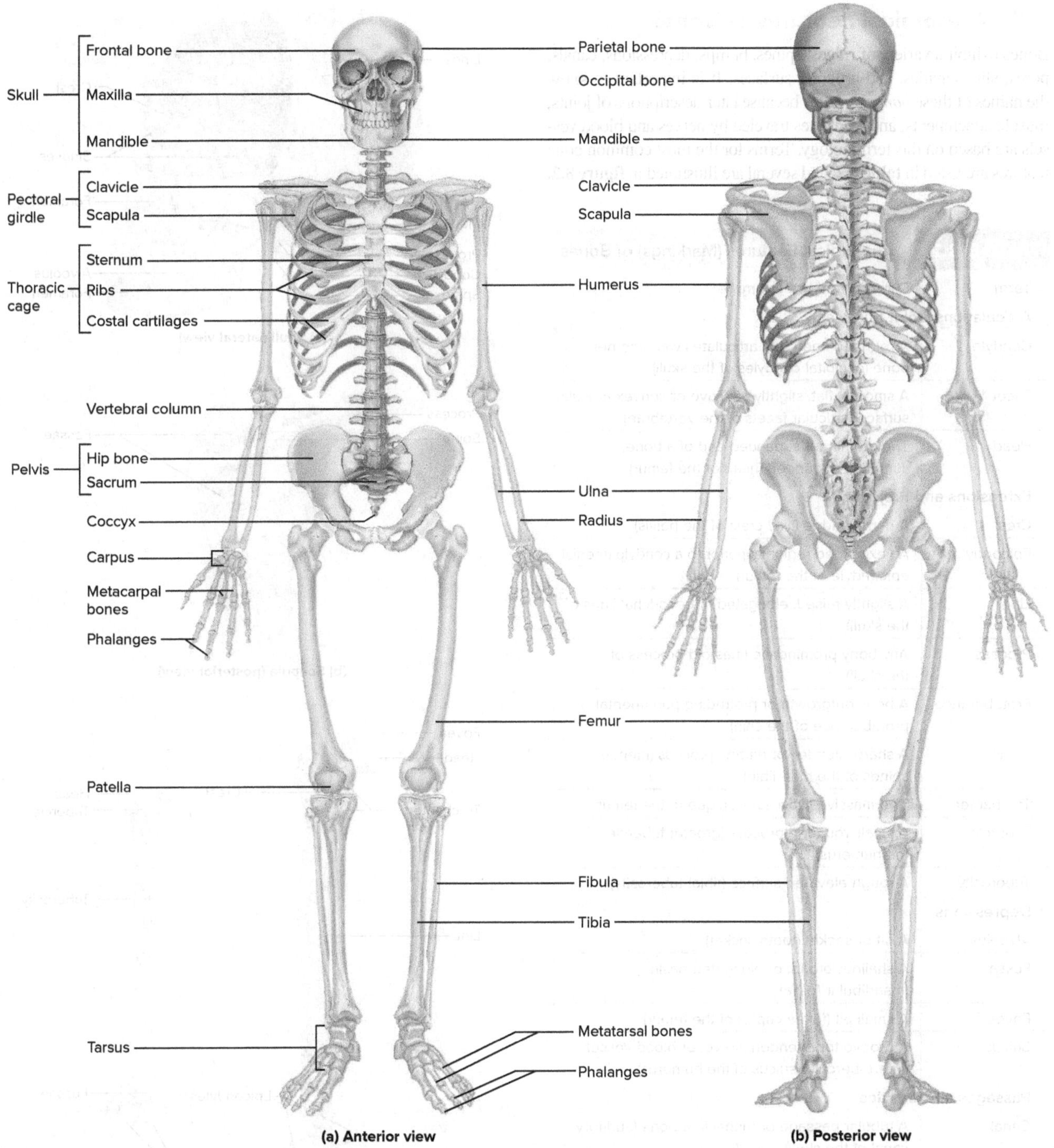

FIGURE 8.1 The Adult Skeleton. (a) Anterior view. (b) Posterior view. The appendicular skeleton is colored green, and the rest is axial skeleton. **APR**

some tendons in response to strain. The patella (kneecap) is the largest of these; most of the others are small, rounded bones in such locations as the hands and feet (see fig. 8.35c).

Another reason for adult variation is that some people have extra bones in the skull called **sutural bones** (SOO-chur-ul) (see fig. 8.6).

8.1b Anatomical Features of Bones

Bones exhibit a variety of ridges, spines, bumps, depressions, canals, pores, slits, cavities, and articular surfaces. It is important to know the names of these *bone markings* because later descriptions of joints, muscle attachments, and the routes traveled by nerves and blood vessels are based on this terminology. Terms for the most common bone features are listed in **table 8.2,** and several are illustrated in **figure 8.2.**

TABLE 8.2	Anatomical Features (Markings) of Bones
Term	**Description and Example**
Articulations (Joint Surfaces)	
Condyle	A rounded knob that articulates with another bone (occipital condyles of the skull)
Facet	A smooth, flat, slightly concave or convex articular surface (articular facets of the vertebrae)
Head	The prominent expanded end of a bone, sometimes rounded (head of the femur)
Extensions and Projections	
Crest	A narrow ridge (iliac crest of the pelvis)
Epicondyle	An expanded region superior to a condyle (medial epicondyle of the femur)
Line	A slightly raised, elongated ridge (nuchal lines of the skull)
Process	Any bony prominence (mastoid process of the skull)
Protuberance	A bony outgrowth or protruding part (mental protuberance of the chin)
Spine	A sharp, slender, or narrow process (mental spines of the mandible)
Trochanter	Two massive processes unique to the femur
Tubercle	A small, rounded process (greater tubercle of the humerus)
Tuberosity	A rough elevated surface (tibial tuberosity)
Depressions	
Alveolus	A pit or socket (tooth socket)
Fossa	A shallow, broad, or elongated basin (mandibular fossa)
Fovea	A small pit (fovea capitis of the femur)
Sulcus	A groove for a tendon, nerve, or blood vessel (intertubercular sulcus of the humerus)
Passages and Cavities	
Canal	A tubular passage or tunnel in a bone (auditory canal of the skull)
Fissure	A slit through a bone (orbital fissures behind the eye)
Foramen	A hole through a bone, usually round (foramen magnum of the skull)
Meatus	A canal (external acoustic meatus of the ear)
Sinus	An air-filled space in a bone (frontal sinus of the forehead)

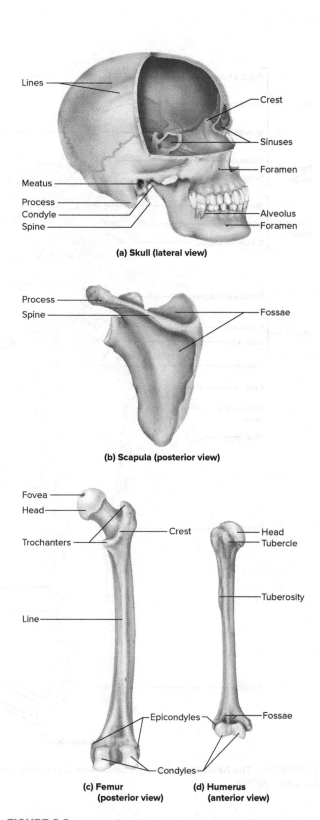

(a) Skull (lateral view)

(b) Scapula (posterior view)

(c) Femur (posterior view)

(d) Humerus (anterior view)

FIGURE 8.2 Anatomical Features of Bones. (a) Skull, lateral view. (b) Scapula, posterior view. (c) Femur, posterior view. (d) Humerus, anterior view. Most of these features also occur on many other bones of the body.

You will probably study both **articulated** skeletons (dried bones held together by wires and rods to show their spatial relationships to each other) and **disarticulated** bones (bones taken apart so their surface features can be studied in more detail). As you study this chapter, also use yourself as a model. You can easily palpate (feel) many of the bones and some of their details through the skin. Rotate your forearm, cross your legs, palpate your skull and wrist, and think about what is happening beneath the surface or what you can feel through the skin. You will gain the most from this chapter (and indeed, the entire book) if you are conscious of your own body in relation to what you are studying.

BEFORE YOU GO ON

Answer the following questions to test your understanding of the preceding section:

1. Name the major components of the axial skeleton. Name those of the appendicular skeleton.

2. Explain why an adult does not have as many bones as a child does. Explain why one adult may have more bones than another.

3. Briefly describe each of the following bone features: a condyle, crest, tubercle, fossa, sulcus, and foramen.

8.2 The Skull

Expected Learning Outcomes

When you have completed this section, you should be able to

a. distinguish between cranial and facial bones;

b. name the bones of the skull and their anatomical features;

c. identify the cavities in the skull and in some of its individual bones;

d. name the principal sutures that join the bones of the skull;

e. describe some bones that are closely associated with the skull; and

f. describe the development of the skull from infancy through childhood.

The skull is the most complex part of the skeleton. **Figures 8.3** through **8.6** present an overview of the skull's general anatomy. Although it may seem to consist only of the mandible (lower jaw) and "the rest," it is composed of 22 bones and sometimes more. Most of these are connected by immovable joints called **sutures** (SOO-chures), which are visible as seams on the surface (fig. 8.4). These are important landmarks in the descriptions that follow.

The skull contains several prominent cavities **(fig. 8.7).** The largest, with an adult volume of about 1,350 mL, is the **cranial cavity,** which encloses the brain. Other cavities include the **orbits** (eye sockets), **nasal cavity, oral (buccal) cavity, middle-** and **inner-ear cavities,** and **paranasal sinuses.** The sinuses are named for the bones in which they occur (fig. 8.8)—the **frontal, sphenoidal, ethmoidal,** and **maxillary sinuses.** They are connected with the nasal cavity, lined by mucous membranes, and filled with air. They lighten the anterior portion of the skull and act as chambers that add resonance to the voice. The latter effect can be sensed in the way your voice changes when you have a cold and mucus obstructs the travel of sound into the sinuses and back.

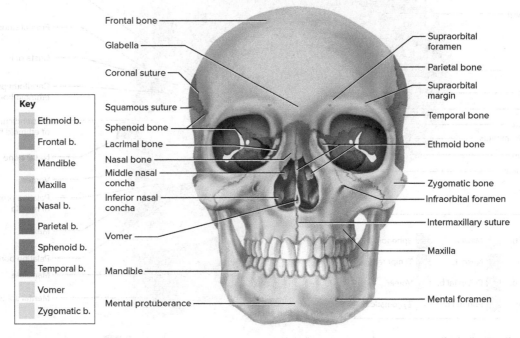

Key

- Ethmoid b.
- Frontal b.
- Mandible
- Maxilla
- Nasal b.
- Parietal b.
- Sphenoid b.
- Temporal b.
- Vomer
- Zygomatic b.

Labels (left): Frontal bone, Glabella, Coronal suture, Squamous suture, Sphenoid bone, Lacrimal bone, Nasal bone, Middle nasal concha, Inferior nasal concha, Vomer, Mandible, Mental protuberance

Labels (right): Supraorbital foramen, Parietal bone, Supraorbital margin, Temporal bone, Ethmoid bone, Zygomatic bone, Infraorbital foramen, Intermaxillary suture, Maxilla, Mental foramen

FIGURE 8.3 The Skull (Anterior View). A&PR

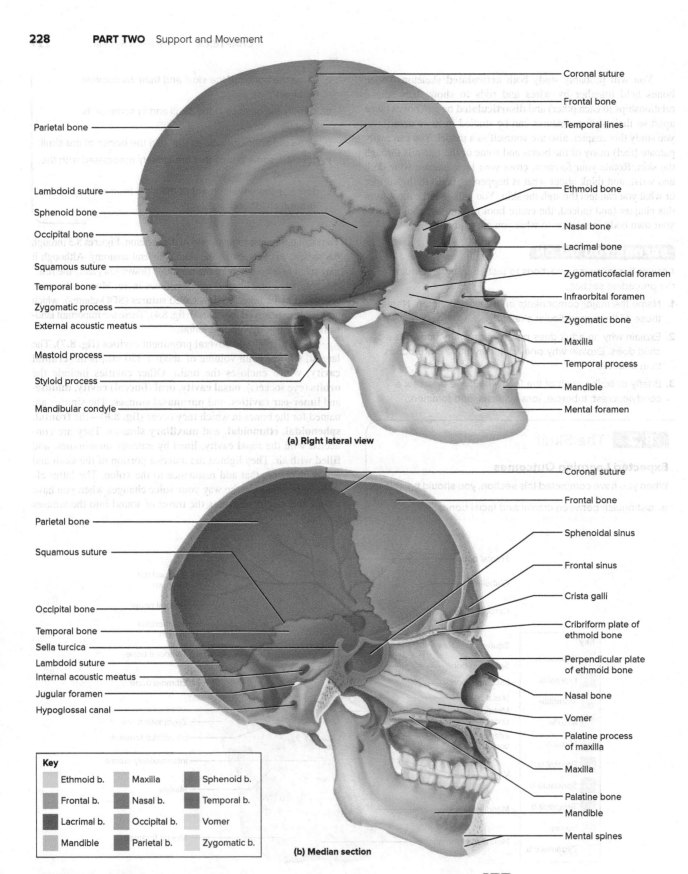

(a) Right lateral view

Coronal suture
Frontal bone
Temporal lines
Parietal bone
Ethmoid bone
Lambdoid suture
Sphenoid bone
Nasal bone
Occipital bone
Lacrimal bone
Squamous suture
Zygomaticofacial foramen
Temporal bone
Infraorbital foramen
Zygomatic process
Zygomatic bone
External acoustic meatus
Maxilla
Mastoid process
Temporal process
Styloid process
Mandible
Mandibular condyle
Mental foramen

(b) Median section

Coronal suture
Frontal bone
Parietal bone
Sphenoidal sinus
Squamous suture
Frontal sinus
Crista galli
Occipital bone
Cribriform plate of ethmoid bone
Temporal bone
Sella turcica
Perpendicular plate of ethmoid bone
Lambdoid suture
Nasal bone
Internal acoustic meatus
Vomer
Jugular foramen
Palatine process of maxilla
Hypoglossal canal
Maxilla
Palatine bone
Mandible
Mental spines

Key

Ethmoid b.	Maxilla	Sphenoid b.
Frontal b.	Nasal b.	Temporal b.
Lacrimal b.	Occipital b.	Vomer
Mandible	Parietal b.	Zygomatic b.

FIGURE 8.4 The Skull. (a) Right lateral surface anatomy. (b) Internal anatomy, median section. **APR**

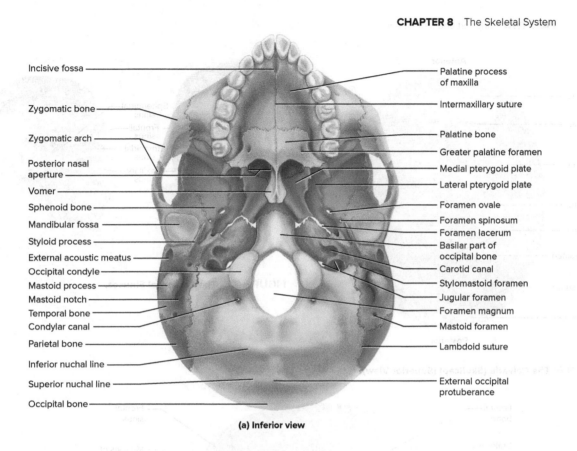

Incisive fossa

Zygomatic bone

Zygomatic arch

Posterior nasal aperture

Vomer

Sphenoid bone

Mandibular fossa

Styloid process

External acoustic meatus

Occipital condyle

Mastoid process

Mastoid notch

Temporal bone

Condylar canal

Parietal bone

Inferior nuchal line

Superior nuchal line

Occipital bone

Palatine process of maxilla

Intermaxillary suture

Palatine bone

Greater palatine foramen

Medial pterygoid plate

Lateral pterygoid plate

Foramen ovale

Foramen spinosum

Foramen lacerum

Basilar part of occipital bone

Carotid canal

Stylomastoid foramen

Jugular foramen

Foramen magnum

Mastoid foramen

Lambdoid suture

External occipital protuberance

(a) Inferior view

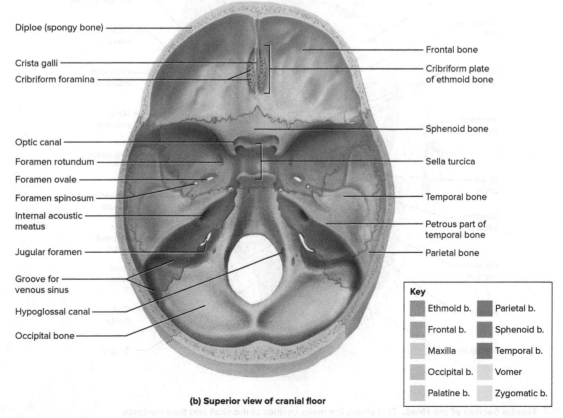

Diploe (spongy bone)

Crista galli

Cribriform foramina

Optic canal

Foramen rotundum

Foramen ovale

Foramen spinosum

Internal acoustic meatus

Jugular foramen

Groove for venous sinus

Hypoglossal canal

Occipital bone

Frontal bone

Cribriform plate of ethmoid bone

Sphenoid bone

Sella turcica

Temporal bone

Petrous part of temporal bone

Parietal bone

Key

Ethmoid b.	Parietal b.
Frontal b.	Sphenoid b.
Maxilla	Temporal b.
Occipital b.	Vomer
Palatine b.	Zygomatic b.

(b) Superior view of cranial floor

FIGURE 8.5 The Base of the Skull. (a) Inferior view. (b) Superior view of the cranial floor. **APR**

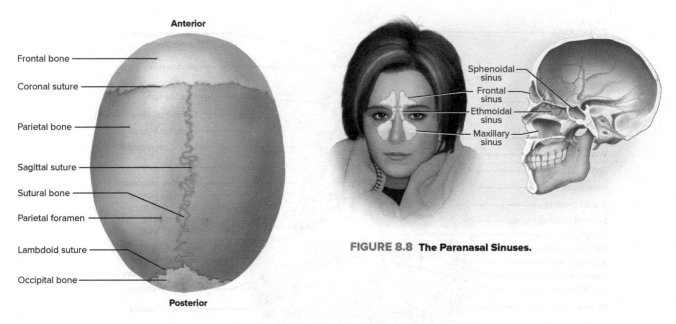

FIGURE 8.8 The Paranasal Sinuses.

FIGURE 8.6 The Calvaria (Skullcap) (Superior View). APR

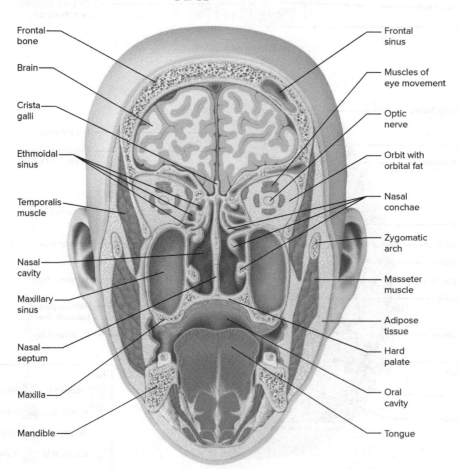

FIGURE 8.7 Frontal Section of the Head. This shows the major cavities of the skull and their contents.

Bones of the skull have especially conspicuous **foramina**—singular, *foramen* (fo-RAY-men)—holes that allow passage for nerves and blood vessels. Some major foramina are summarized in **table 8.3.** Some of the details will mean more after you study cranial nerves and blood vessels in later chapters.

8.2a Cranial Bones

Cranial bones are those that enclose the brain; collectively, they compose the **cranium**[2] (braincase). The delicate brain tissue doesn't come directly into contact with the bones, but is separated from them by three membranes called the *meninges* (meh-NIN-jeez) (see section 14.2a). The thickest and toughest of these, the *dura mater*[3] (DUE-rah MAH-tur), is pressed against the inside of the cranium in most places and firmly attached to it at a few points.

The cranium is a rigid structure with an opening, the *foramen magnum* (literally "large hole"), where the spinal cord meets the brain. The cranium consists of two major parts—the calvaria and the base. The **calvaria**[4] (skullcap) isn't a single bone but simply the dome of the top of the skull; it is composed of parts of multiple bones that form the roof and walls (see fig. 8.6). In skulls prepared

---

[2]*crani* = helmet
[3]*dura* = tough, strong; *mater* = mother
[4]*calvar* = bald, skull

for study, the calvaria is often sawed so that part of it can be lifted off for examination of the interior. This reveals the **base** (floor) of the cranial cavity (see fig. 8.5b), which exhibits three paired depressions called cranial fossae. These correspond to the contour of the inferior surface of the brain **(fig. 8.9).** The relatively shallow **anterior cranial fossa** is crescent-shaped and accommodates the frontal lobes of the brain. The **middle cranial fossa,** which drops abruptly deeper, is shaped like a pair of outstretched bird's wings and accommodates the temporal lobes. The **posterior cranial fossa** is deepest and houses a large posterior division of the brain called the cerebellum.

There are eight cranial bones:

1 frontal bone	1 occipital bone
2 parietal bones	1 sphenoid bone
2 temporal bones	1 ethmoid bone

The Frontal Bone

The **frontal bone** extends from the forehead back to a prominent *coronal suture,* which crosses the crown of the head from right to left and joins the frontal bone to the parietal bones (see figs. 8.3 and 8.4). The frontal bone forms the anterior wall and about one-third of the roof of the cranial cavity, and it turns inward to form nearly all of the anterior cranial fossa and the roof of the orbit.

TABLE 8.3	Foramina of the Skull and the Nerves and Blood Vessels Transmitted Through Them
Bones and Their Foramina	**Structures Transmitted**
Frontal Bone	
Supraorbital foramen or notch	Supraorbital nerve, artery, and vein; ophthalmic nerve
Temporal Bone	
Carotid canal	Internal carotid artery
External acoustic meatus	Sound waves to eardrum
Jugular foramen	Internal jugular vein; glossopharyngeal, vagus, and accessory nerves
Occipital Bone	
Foramen magnum	Spinal cord; accessory nerve; vertebral arteries
Hypoglossal canal	Hypoglossal nerve to muscles of tongue
Sphenoid Bone	
Foramen ovale	Mandibular division of trigeminal nerve; accessory meningeal artery
Foramen rotundum	Maxillary division of trigeminal nerve
Optic canal	Optic nerve; ophthalmic artery
Superior orbital fissure	Oculomotor, trochlear, and abducens nerves; ophthalmic division of trigeminal nerve; ophthalmic veins
Maxilla	
Inferior orbital fissure	Infraorbital nerve; zygomatic nerve; infraorbital vessels
Infraorbital foramen	Infraorbital nerve and vessels
Mandible	
Mental foramen	Mental nerve and vessels
Mandibular foramen	Inferior alveolar nerves and vessels to the lower teeth

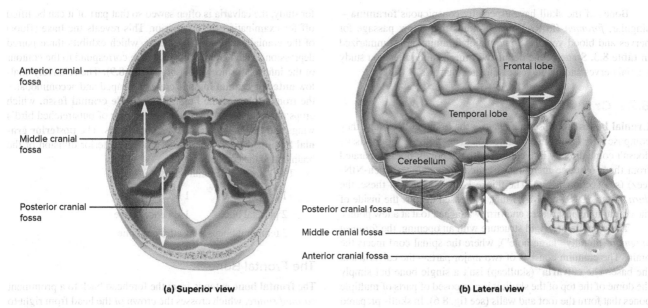

FIGURE 8.9 Cranial Fossae. (a) Superior view. (b) Lateral view showing how the three fossae conform to the contours of the base of the brain.

Deep to the eyebrows it has a ridge called the **supraorbital margin.** Each margin is perforated by a single **supraorbital foramen** (see figs. 8.3 and 8.14), which provides passage for a nerve, artery, and veins. In some people, the edge of this foramen breaks through the margin of the orbit and forms a *supraorbital notch.* A person may have a foramen on one supraorbital margin and a notch on the other. The smooth area of the frontal bone just above the root of the nose is called the **glabella.**[5] The frontal bone also contains the frontal sinus. You may not see this sinus on all skulls. On some, the calvaria is cut too high to show it, and some people simply don't have one. Along the cut edge of the calvaria, you can also see the diploe (DIP-lo-ee)—the layer of spongy bone in the middle of the cranial bones (see fig. 8.5b).

The Parietal Bones

The right and left **parietal bones** (pa-RY-eh-tul) form most of the cranial roof and part of its walls (see figs. 8.4 and 8.6). Each is bordered by four sutures that join it to the neighboring bones: (1) a **sagittal suture** between the parietal bones; (2) the **coronal**[6] **suture** at the anterior margin; (3) the **lambdoid**[7] **suture** (LAM-doyd) at the posterior margin; and (4) the **squamous suture** laterally. Small sutural bones are often seen along the sagittal and lambdoid sutures, like little islands of bone with the suture lines passing around them. Internally, the parietal and frontal bones have markings that look a bit like aerial photographs of river tributaries (see fig. 8.4b). These represent places where the bone molded itself around blood vessels of the meninges.

Externally, the parietal bones have few features. A **parietal foramen** sometimes occurs near the corner of the lambdoid and sagittal sutures (see fig. 8.6). It is an exit for a small vein from a blood sinus atop the brain. A pair of slight lateral thickenings, the superior and inferior **temporal lines,** form an arc across the parietal and frontal bones (see fig. 8.4a). They mark the attachment of the large, fan-shaped *temporalis muscle,* a chewing muscle that converges on the mandible.

The Temporal Bones

If you palpate your skull just above and anterior to the ear—that is, the temporal region—you can feel the **temporal bone,** which forms the lower wall and part of the floor of the cranial cavity **(fig. 8.10).** The temporal bone derives its name from the fact that people often develop their first gray hairs on the temples with the passage of time.[8] The relatively complex shape of the temporal bone is best understood by dividing it into four parts:

1. The **squamous**[9] **part** (which you just palpated) is relatively flat and vertical. It is encircled by the squamous suture. It bears two prominent features: (a) the **zygomatic process,** which extends anteriorly to form part of the *zygomatic arch,* described later; and (b) the **mandibular fossa,** a depression where the mandible articulates with the cranium.

2. The **tympanic**[10] **part** is a small ring of bone that borders the opening of the **external acoustic meatus** (me-AY-tus), or ear canal. It has a pointed spine on its inferior surface,

[5]*glab* = smooth
[6]*corona* = crown
[7]Shaped like the Greek letter lambda (λ)

[8]*tempor* = time
[9]*squam* = flat; *ous* = characterized by
[10]*tympan* = drum (eardrum); *ic* = pertaining to

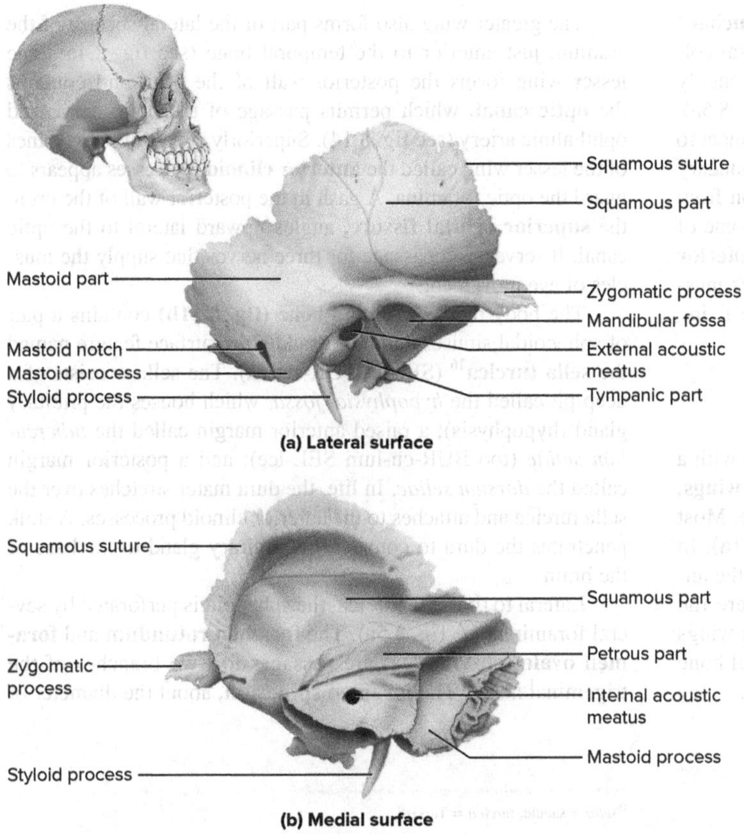

Squamous suture
Squamous part
Mastoid part
Zygomatic process
Mandibular fossa
Mastoid notch
External acoustic meatus
Mastoid process
Styloid process
Tympanic part

(a) Lateral surface

Squamous suture
Squamous part
Petrous part
Zygomatic process
Internal acoustic meatus
Styloid process
Mastoid process

(b) Medial surface

FIGURE 8.10 The Right Temporal Bone. (a) The lateral surface, facing the scalp and external ear. (b) The medial surface, facing the brain. **APR**

List five bones that articulate with the temporal bone.

the **styloid process,** named for its resemblance to the stylus used by ancient Greeks and Romans to write on wax tablets. The styloid process provides attachment for muscles of the tongue, pharynx, and hyoid bone.

3. The **mastoid**[11] **part** lies posterior to the tympanic part. It bears a heavy **mastoid process,** which you can palpate as a prominent lump behind the earlobe. It is filled with small air sinuses that communicate with the middle-ear cavity. These sinuses are subject to infection and inflammation *(mastoiditis),* which can erode the bone and spread to the brain. A groove called the **mastoid notch** lies medial to the mastoid process (see fig. 8.5a). It is the origin of the *digastric muscle,* which opens the mouth. The notch is perforated at its anterior end by the **stylomastoid foramen,** which is a passage for the facial nerve, and at its posterior end by the **mastoid foramen,** which passes a small artery and vein from the brain.

4. The **petrous**[12] **part** can be seen in the cranial floor, where it resembles a little mountain range separating the middle cranial fossa from the posterior fossa (fig. 8.10b). It houses the middle- and inner-ear cavities. The **internal acoustic meatus,** an opening on its posteromedial surface, allows passage of a nerve that carries signals for hearing and balance from the inner ear to the brain. On the inferior surface of the petrous part are two prominent foramina named for the major blood vessels that pass through them (see fig. 8.5a): (a) The **carotid canal** is a passage for the internal carotid artery, a major blood supply to the brain. This artery is so close to the inner ear that one can sometimes hear the pulsing of its blood when the ear is resting on a pillow or the heart is beating hard. (b) The **jugular foramen** is a large, irregular opening just medial to the styloid process, between the temporal and occipital bones. Blood from the brain drains through this foramen into the internal jugular vein of the neck. Three cranial nerves also pass through this foramen (see table 8.3).

The Occipital Bone

The **occipital bone** (oc-SIP-ih-tul) forms the rear of the skull *(occiput)* and much of its base (see fig. 8.5). Its most conspicuous feature, the **foramen magnum,** admits the spinal cord to the cranial cavity; the dura mater is attached to the rim of this foramen. An important consideration in head injuries is swelling of the brain. Since the cranium cannot expand, swelling puts pressure on the brain and results in even more tissue damage. Severe swelling can force the brainstem out through the foramen magnum, usually with fatal consequences.

The occipital bone continues anterior to this as a thick median plate, the **basilar part.** On either side of the foramen magnum is a smooth knob called the **occipital condyle** (CON-dile), where the skull rests on the vertebral column. Passing like a tunnel beneath each condyle is a **hypoglossal**[13] **canal,** named for the *hypoglossal nerve* that passes through it to innervate the muscles of the tongue. In some people, a **condylar canal** (CON-dih-lur) is found posterior to each occipital condyle. A small vein from a blood sinus of the brain passes through here.

Internally, the occipital bone displays impressions left by large venous sinuses that drain blood from the brain (see fig. 8.5b). One of these grooves travels along the midsagittal line. Just before reaching the foramen magnum, it branches into right and left grooves that wrap around the occipital bone like outstretched arms before terminating at the jugular foramina. The venous sinuses that occupy these grooves are described in table 20.4.

Other features of the occipital bone can be palpated on the back of your head. One is a prominent medial bump called the

---

[11]*mast* = breast; *oid* = shaped like

[12]*petr* = stone, rock; *ous* = like
[13]*hypo* = below; *gloss* = tongue

external occipital protuberance—the attachment for the **nuchal**[14] **ligament** (NEW-kul), which binds the skull to the vertebral column. A ridge, the **superior nuchal line,** can be traced horizontally from this protuberance toward the mastoid process (see fig. 8.5a). It defines the superior limit of the neck and provides attachment to the skull for several neck and back muscles. It forms the boundary where, in palpating the upper neck, you feel the transition from muscle to bone. By pulling down on the occipital bone, some of these muscles help to keep the head erect. The deeper **inferior nuchal line** provides attachment for some of the deep neck muscles. This inconspicuous ridge cannot be palpated on the living body but is visible on an isolated skull.

The Sphenoid Bone

The **sphenoid**[15] **bone** (SFEE-noyd) has a complex shape with a thick median **body** and outstretched **greater** and **lesser wings,** which give the bone as a whole a ragged mothlike shape. Most of it is best seen from the superior perspective **(fig. 8.11a).** In this view, the lesser wings form the posterior margin of the anterior cranial fossa and end at a sharp bony crest, where the sphenoid drops abruptly to the greater wings. The greater wings form about half of the middle cranial fossa (the temporal bone forming the rest) and are perforated by several foramina.

The greater wing also forms part of the lateral surface of the cranium just anterior to the temporal bone (see fig. 8.4a). The lesser wing forms the posterior wall of the orbit and contains the **optic canal,** which permits passage of the optic nerve and ophthalmic artery (see fig. 8.14). Superiorly, a pair of bony spines of the lesser wing called the **anterior clinoid processes** appears to guard the optic foramina. A gash in the posterior wall of the orbit, the **superior orbital fissure,** angles upward lateral to the optic canal. It serves as a passage for three nerves that supply the muscles of eye movement.

The body of the sphenoid bone **(fig. 8.11b)** contains a pair of sphenoidal sinuses and has a saddlelike surface feature named the **sella turcica**[16] (SEL-la TUR-sih-ca). The sella consists of a deep pit called the *hypophysial fossa,* which houses the pituitary gland (hypophysis); a raised anterior margin called the *tuberculum sellae* (too-BUR-cu-lum SEL-lee); and a posterior margin called the *dorsum sellae.* In life, the dura mater stretches over the sella turcica and attaches to the anterior clinoid processes. A stalk penetrates the dura to connect the pituitary gland to the base of the brain.

Lateral to the sella turcica, the sphenoid is perforated by several foramina (see fig. 8.5a). The **foramen rotundum** and **foramen ovale** (oh-VAY-lee) are passages for two branches of the trigeminal nerve. The **foramen spinosum,** about the diameter of

---

[14]*nucha* = back of the neck
[15]*sphen* = wedge; *oid* = resembling

[16]*sella* = saddle; *turcica* = Turkish

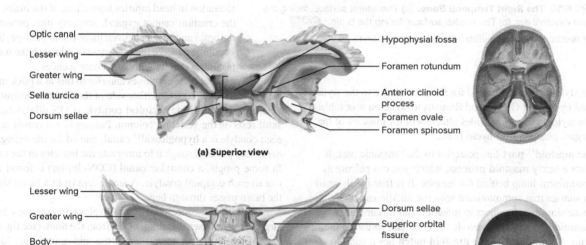

Optic canal —
Lesser wing —
Greater wing —
Sella turcica —
Dorsum sellae —

— Hypophysial fossa
— Foramen rotundum
— Anterior clinoid process
— Foramen ovale
— Foramen spinosum

(a) Superior view

Lesser wing —
Greater wing —
Body —
Foramen ovale —
Lateral pterygoid plate —
Medial pterygoid plate —

— Dorsum sellae
— Superior orbital fissure
— Foramen rotundum
— Pterygoid processes

(b) Posterior view

FIGURE 8.11 The Sphenoid Bone. (a) Superior view. (b) Posterior view, as if looking from the back of the head into the opened skull.

APR

a pencil lead, provides passage for an artery of the meninges. An irregular gash called the **foramen lacerum**[17] (LASS-eh-rum) occurs at the junction of the sphenoid, temporal, and occipital bones. It is filled with cartilage in life and transmits no major vessels or nerves.

In an inferior view of the skull, the sphenoid can be seen just anterior to the basilar part of the occipital bone. The internal openings of the nasal cavity seen here are called the **posterior nasal apertures,** or **choanae**[18] (co-AH-nee). Lateral to each aperture, the sphenoid bone exhibits a pair of parallel plates—the **medial** and **lateral pterygoid**[19] **plates** (TERR-ih-goyd) (see fig. 8.5a). Each plate has a narrower inferior extension called the **pterygoid process.** These plates and processes provide attachment for some of the jaw muscles.

The Ethmoid Bone

The **ethmoid**[20] **bone** (ETH-moyd) is an anterior cranial bone located between the eyes (figs. 8.7 and **8.12**). It contributes to the medial wall of the orbit, the roof and walls of the nasal cavity, and the nasal septum. It is a very porous and delicate bone, with three major portions:

1. The vertical **perpendicular plate,** a thin median plate of bone that forms the superior two-thirds of the nasal septum (see fig. 8.4b). (The lower part is formed by the *vomer,*

---

[17]*lacerum* = torn, lacerated
[18]*choana* = funnel
[19]*pteryg* = wing; *oid* = resembling
[20]*ethmo* = sieve, strainer; *oid* = resembling

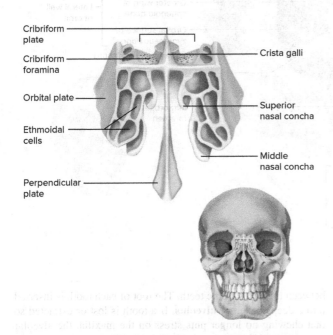

Cribriform plate

Cribriform foramina

Orbital plate

Ethmoidal cells

Perpendicular plate

Crista galli

Superior nasal concha

Middle nasal concha

FIGURE 8.12 The Ethmoid Bone (Anterior View). APR

? *List five bones that articulate with the ethmoid bone.*

---

discussed later.) The septum divides the nasal cavity into right and left air spaces called the **nasal fossae** (FOSS-ee). The septum is often curved, or deviated, toward one nasal fossa or the other.

2. A horizontal **cribriform**[21] **plate** (CRIB-rih-form), which forms the roof of the nasal cavity. This plate has a median blade called the **crista galli**[22] (GAL-eye), an attachment point for the dura mater. On each side of the crista is an elongated depressed area perforated with numerous holes, the **cribriform (olfactory) foramina.** A pair of *olfactory bulbs* of the brain, concerned with the sense of smell, rests in these depressions, and the foramina allow passage for olfactory nerves from the nasal cavity to the bulbs.

3. The **ethmoidal labyrinth,** a large mass on each side of the perpendicular plate. The labyrinth is named for the fact that internally, it has a maze of air spaces called the **ethmoidal cells.** Collectively, these constitute the *ethmoidal sinus* discussed earlier. The lateral surface of the labyrinth is a smooth, slightly concave **orbital plate** seen on the medial wall of the orbit (see fig. 8.14). The medial surface of the labyrinth gives rise to two curled, scroll-like plates of bone called the **superior** and **middle nasal conchae**[23] (CON-kee). These project into the nasal fossa from its lateral wall toward the septum (see figs. 8.7 and **8.13**). There is also a separate bone, the *inferior nasal concha,* discussed later. The three conchae occupy most of the nasal cavity, leaving little open space. By filling space and creating turbulence in the flow of inhaled air, they ensure that the air contacts the mucous membranes that cover these bones, which cleanse, humidify, and warm the inhaled air before it reaches the lungs. The superior concha and adjacent part of the nasal septum also bear the sensory cells of smell.

Usually, all that can be seen of the ethmoid is the perpendicular plate, by looking into the nasal cavity (see fig. 8.3); the orbital plate, by looking at the medial wall of the orbit (**fig. 8.14**); and the crista galli and cribriform plate, seen from within the cranial cavity (see fig. 8.5b).

8.2b Facial Bones

Facial bones do not enclose the brain but lie anterior to the cranial cavity. They support the orbital, nasal, and oral cavities, shape the face, and provide attachment for the muscles of facial expression and mastication. There are 14 facial bones:

2 maxillae	2 nasal bones
2 palatine bones	2 inferior nasal conchae
2 zygomatic bones	1 vomer
2 lacrimal bones	1 mandible

---

[21]*cribri* = sieve; *form* = in the shape of
[22]*crista* = crest; *galli* = of a rooster
[23]*concha* = conch (large marine snail)

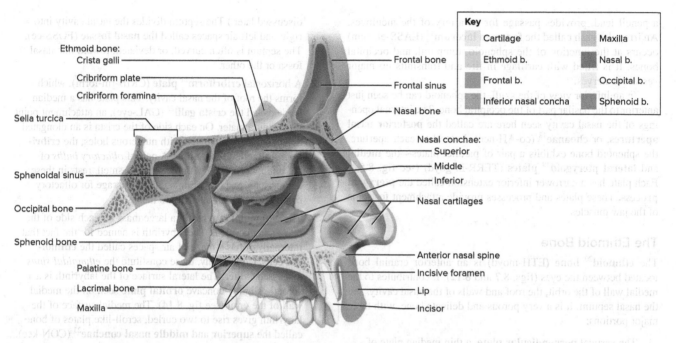

Ethmoid bone:
Crista galli
Cribriform plate
Cribriform foramina
Sella turcica
Sphenoidal sinus
Occipital bone
Sphenoid bone
Palatine bone
Lacrimal bone
Maxilla

Frontal bone
Frontal sinus
Nasal bone

Nasal conchae:
Superior
Middle
Inferior
Nasal cartilages

Anterior nasal spine
Incisive foramen
Lip
Incisor

Key
Cartilage
Ethmoid b.
Frontal b.
Inferior nasal concha
Maxilla
Nasal b.
Occipital b.
Sphenoid b.

FIGURE 8.13 The Left Nasal Cavity, Sagittal Section with Nasal Septum Removed. APR

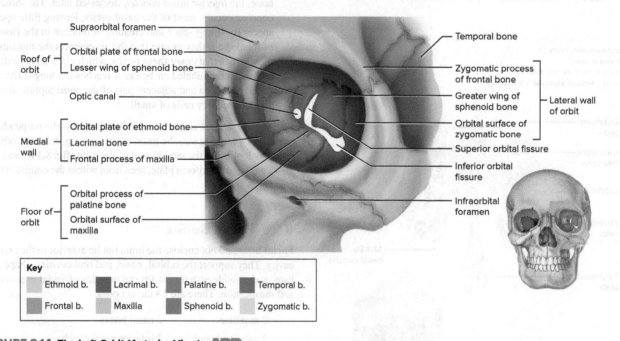

Supraorbital foramen

Roof of orbit
Orbital plate of frontal bone
Lesser wing of sphenoid bone
Optic canal

Medial wall
Orbital plate of ethmoid bone
Lacrimal bone
Frontal process of maxilla

Floor of orbit
Orbital process of palatine bone
Orbital surface of maxilla

Temporal bone
Zygomatic process of frontal bone
Greater wing of sphenoid bone
Orbital surface of zygomatic bone
Superior orbital fissure
Inferior orbital fissure
Infraorbital foramen

Lateral wall of orbit

Key
Ethmoid b.
Frontal b.
Lacrimal b.
Maxilla
Palatine b.
Sphenoid b.
Temporal b.
Zygomatic b.

FIGURE 8.14 The Left Orbit (Anterior View). A&PR

The Maxillae

The **maxillae** (mac-SILL-ee) are the largest facial bones. They form the upper jaw and meet each other at a median *intermaxillary suture* (see figs. 8.3, 8.4a, and 8.5a). Small points of maxillary bone called **alveolar processes** grow into the spaces between the bases of the teeth. The root of each tooth is inserted into a deep socket, or **alveolus.** If a tooth is lost or extracted so that chewing no longer puts stress on the maxilla, the alveolar processes are resorbed and the alveolus fills in with new bone, leaving a smooth area on the maxilla.

Although they are preserved with the skull, the teeth are not bones. They are discussed in detail in section 25.2a.

▶▶▶**APPLY WHAT YOU KNOW**

Suppose you were studying a skull with some teeth missing. How could you tell whether the teeth had been lost after the person's death or years before it?

Each maxilla extends from the teeth to the inferomedial wall of the orbit. Just below the orbit, it exhibits an **infraorbital foramen,** which provides passage for a blood vessel to the face and a nerve that receives sensations from the nasal region and cheek. This nerve emerges through the foramen rotundum into the cranial cavity. The maxilla forms part of the floor of the orbit, where it exhibits a gash called the **inferior orbital fissure** that angles downward and medially (fig. 8.14). The inferior and superior orbital fissures form a sideways V whose apex lies near the optic canal. The inferior orbital fissure is a passage for blood vessels and sensory nerves from the face.

The **palate** forms the roof of the mouth and floor of the nasal cavity. Its function is to separate the nasal cavity from the oral cavity, enabling us (and other mammals) to continue breathing while chewing. The high metabolic rate of humans requires rapid digestion of food, which in turn is aided by prolonged and thorough mastication into small, easily digested particles. This would be difficult if such prolonged mastication required an interruption of airflow.

The palate consists of a bony **hard palate** anteriorly and a fleshy **soft palate** posteriorly. Most of the hard palate is formed by horizontal extensions of the maxilla called **palatine processes** (PAL-uh-tine) (see fig. 8.5a). Just behind the incisors (front teeth) is a median pit, the **incisive fossa,** which is a passage for an artery to the palate and a nerve to the lower part of the nasal septum and the six front teeth of the maxilla. One or two pairs of *incisive foramina* open into this fossa (fig. 8.13) but are difficult to see. The palatine processes normally meet at the intermaxillary suture at about 12 weeks of gestation. Failure to join results in a *cleft palate* (see Deeper Insight 8.1).

DEEPER INSIGHT 8.1

CLINICAL APPLICATION

Cleft Palate and Lip

Failure of the fetal maxillae to join results in a cleft palate—a median fissure between the oral and nasal cavities, often accompanied by an upper lip cleft on one or both sides. A cleft palate makes it difficult for an infant to generate the suction needed for nursing, and may be accompanied by frequent ear infections and difficulties in hearing and speech. Cleft palate and lip can be surgically corrected with good cosmetic results, but may require follow-up speech therapy. Correction by 18 months of age can improve language acquisition and avoid the psychosocial problems often faced by school-age children with the condition.

The Palatine Bones

The **palatine bones** divide the oral and nasal cavities from each other posteriorly (fig. 8.13). Each has an L shape formed by a *horizontal plate* and a *perpendicular plate.* The horizontal plates form the posterior one-third of the bony palate. Each is marked by a large **greater palatine foramen,** a nerve passage to the palate. The perpendicular plate is a thin, delicate, irregularly shaped plate that forms part of the wall between the nasal cavity and the orbit (see figs. 8.5a and 8.13).

The Zygomatic Bones

The **zygomatic**[24] **bones,** colloquially called the cheekbones, form the angles of the cheeks at the inferolateral margins of the orbits and part of the lateral wall of each orbit; they extend about halfway to the ear (see figs. 8.4a and 8.5a). Each zygomatic bone has an inverted T shape and usually a small **zygomaticofacial foramen** (ZY-go-MAT-ih-co-FAY-shul) near the intersection of the stem and crossbar of the T. A nerve passes through here to supply the skin on the prominence of the cheek. The prominent zygomatic arch that flares from each side of the skull is formed mainly by the union of the zygomatic bone, temporal bone, and maxilla (see fig. 8.4a).

The Lacrimal Bones

The **lacrimal**[25] **bones** (LACK-rih-mul) form part of the medial wall of each orbit (fig. 8.14). They are the smallest bones of the skull, about the size of the little fingernail. A depression called the **lacrimal fossa** houses a membranous *lacrimal sac* in life. Tears from the eye collect in this sac and drain into the nasal cavity.

The Nasal Bones

Two small rectangular **nasal bones** form the bridge of the nose (see fig. 8.3) and support cartilages that shape its lower portion. If you palpate the bridge, you can easily feel where the nasal bones end and the cartilages begin. The nasal bones are often fractured by blows to the nose.

The Inferior Nasal Conchae

There are three conchae in the nasal cavity. The superior and middle conchae, as discussed earlier, are parts of the ethmoid bone. The **inferior nasal concha**—the largest of the three—is a separate bone (fig. 8.13).

The Vomer

The **vomer** forms the inferior half of the nasal septum (see figs. 8.3 and 8.4b). Its name literally means "plowshare," which refers to its resemblance to the blade of a plow. The superior half of the nasal septum is formed by the perpendicular plate of the ethmoid bone, as mentioned earlier. The vomer and perpendicular plate support a wall of *septal cartilage* that forms most of the anterior part of the septum.

---

[24]*zygo* = to join, unite
[25]*lacrim* = tear, to cry

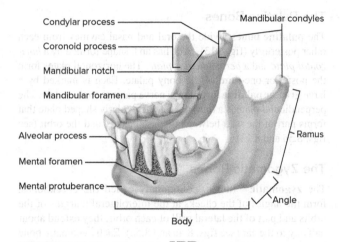

FIGURE 8.15 The Mandible. APR

The Mandible

The **mandible (fig. 8.15)** is the strongest bone of the skull and the only one that can move significantly. It supports the lower teeth and provides attachment for muscles of mastication and facial expression. The horizontal portion, bearing the teeth, is called the **body;** the vertical to oblique posterior portion is the **ramus** (RAY-mus) (plural, *rami*); and these two portions meet at a corner called the **angle.** The mandible develops as separate right and left bones in the fetus, joined by a median cartilaginous joint called the **mental symphysis** (SIM-fih-sis) at the point of the chin. This joint ossifies in early childhood, uniting the two halves into a single bone. The point of the chin itself is called the **mental protuberance.** The inner (posterior) surface of the mandible in this region has a pair of small points, the **mental spines,** which serve for attachment of certain chin muscles (see fig. 8.4b).

On the anterolateral surface of the body, the **mental foramen** permits the passage of nerves and blood vessels of the chin. The inner surface of the body has a number of shallow depressions and ridges to accommodate muscles and salivary glands. The angle of the mandible has a rough lateral surface for insertion of the *masseter,* a muscle of mastication. Like the maxilla, the mandible has pointed alveolar processes between the teeth.

The ramus is somewhat Y-shaped. Its posterior branch, called the **condylar process** (CON-dih-lur), bears the **mandibular condyle**—an oval knob that articulates with the mandibular fossa of the temporal bone. The meeting of this condyle with the temporal bone forms a hinge, the **temporomandibular joint (TMJ).** The anterior branch of the ramus is a blade called the **coronoid process.** It is the point of insertion for the temporalis muscle, which pulls the mandible upward when you bite. The U-shaped arch between the two processes is the **mandibular notch.** Just below the notch, on the medial surface of the ramus, is the **mandibular foramen.** The nerve and blood vessels that supply the lower teeth enter this foramen and then travel through the bone of the mandibular body, giving off branches to each tooth along the way. Dentists commonly inject lidocaine near the mandibular foramen to deaden sensation from the lower teeth.

8.2c Bones Associated with the Skull

Seven bones are closely associated with the skull but not considered part of it. These are the three auditory ossicles in each middle-ear cavity and the hyoid bone beneath the chin. The **auditory ossicles**[26]—named the **malleus** (hammer), **incus** (anvil), and **stapes** (STAY-peez) (stirrup)—are discussed in connection with hearing in "Anatomy of the Ear" in section 16.4.

The **hyoid**[27] **bone** is a slender U-shaped bone between the chin and larynx **(fig. 8.16).** It is one of the few bones that doesn't articulate with any other. It is suspended from the styloid processes of the skull, somewhat like a hammock, by the small *stylohyoid muscles* and *stylohyoid ligaments.* The median **body** of the hyoid is flanked on either side by hornlike projections called the **greater** and **lesser horns (cornua).** The larynx (voice box) is suspended from the hyoid bone by a broad ligament (see fig. 22.4a), and the hyoid serves for attachment of several muscles that control the mandible, tongue, and larynx. Forensic pathologists look for a fractured hyoid as evidence of strangulation.

8.2d The Skull in Infancy and Childhood

The head of an infant couldn't fit through the mother's pelvic outlet at birth if not for the fact that the bones of its skull are not yet fused. The shifting of the cranial bones during birth may cause the infant's head to appear deformed, but it soon assumes a more normal shape. Spaces between the unfused cranial bones are called **fontanelles,**[28] after the fact that pulsation of the infant's blood can be felt there. The bones are joined at these points only by fibrous membranes, in which intramembranous ossification is completed later (see fig. 7.10). Four of these sites are especially prominent and regular in location: the **anterior, posterior, sphenoid (anterolateral),**

---

[26]*os* = bone; *icle* = little
[27]*hy* = the letter U; *oid* = resembling
[28]*fontan* = fountain; *elle* = little

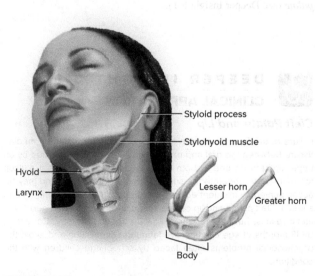

FIGURE 8.16 The Hyoid Bone.

DEEPER INSIGHT 8.2

CLINICAL APPLICATION

Cranial Assessment of the Newborn

Obstetric nurses routinely assess the fontanelles of newborns by palpation. In a difficult delivery, one cranial bone may override another along a suture line, which calls for close monitoring of the infant. Abnormally wide sutures may indicate hydrocephalus, the accumulation of excessive amounts of cerebrospinal fluid, which causes the cranium to swell. Bulging fontanelles suggest abnormally high intracranial pressure, while depressed fontanelles indicate dehydration.

and **mastoid (posterolateral) fontanelles (fig. 8.17).** Most fontanelles ossify by the time the infant is a year old, but the largest one—the anterior fontanelle—can still be palpated 18 to 24 months after birth.

The frontal bone and mandible are separate right and left bones at birth, but fuse medially in early childhood. The frontal

bones usually fuse by age 5 or 6, but in some children a *metopic*[29] *suture* persists between them. Traces of this suture are evident in some adult skulls.

The face of a newborn is flat and the cranium relatively large. To accommodate the growing brain, the skull grows more rapidly than the rest of the skeleton during childhood. It reaches about half its adult size by 9 months of age, three-quarters by age 2, and nearly final size by 8 or 9 years. The heads of babies and children are therefore much larger in proportion to the trunk than the heads of adults—an attribute thoroughly exploited by cartoonists and advertisers who draw big-headed characters to give them a more endearing or immature appearance. In humans and other animals, the large, rounded heads of the young are thought to promote survival by stimulating parental caregiving instincts.

BEFORE YOU GO ON

Answer the following questions to test your understanding of the preceding section:

4. Name the paranasal sinuses and state their locations. Name any four other cavities in the skull.

5. Explain the difference between a cranial bone and a facial bone. Give four examples of each.

6. Draw an oval representing a superior view of the calvaria. Draw lines representing the coronal, lambdoid, and sagittal sutures. Label the four bones separated by these sutures.

7. State which bone has each of these features: a squamous part, hypoglossal canal, greater horn, greater wing, condylar process, and cribriform plate.

8. Determine which of the following structures cannot normally be palpated on a living person: the mastoid process, crista galli, superior orbital fissure, palatine processes, zygomatic bone, mental protuberance, and stapes. You may find it useful to palpate some of these on your own skull as you try to answer.

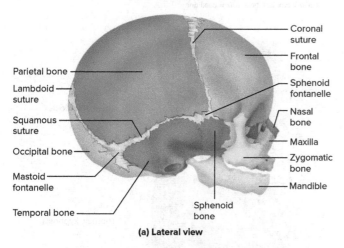

Parietal bone

Lambdoid suture

Squamous suture

Occipital bone

Mastoid fontanelle

Temporal bone

Coronal suture

Frontal bone

Sphenoid fontanelle

Nasal bone

Maxilla

Zygomatic bone

Mandible

Sphenoid bone

(a) Lateral view

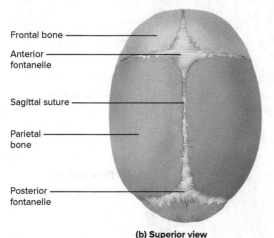

Frontal bone

Anterior fontanelle

Sagittal suture

Parietal bone

Posterior fontanelle

(b) Superior view

8.3   The Vertebral Column and Thoracic Cage

Expected Learning Outcomes

When you have completed this section, you should be able to

a. describe the general features of the vertebral column and those of a typical vertebra;

b. describe the structure of the intervertebral discs and their relationship to the vertebrae;

c. describe the special features of vertebrae in different regions of the vertebral column, and discuss the functional significance of the regional differences; and

d. describe the anatomy of the sternum and ribs and how the ribs articulate with the thoracic vertebrae.

FIGURE 8.17   The Fetal Skull Near the Time of Birth. (a) Lateral view. (b) Superior view of the calvaria.

[29]*met* = beyond; *op* = the eyes

8.3a General Features of the Vertebral Column

The **vertebral column,** or **spine,** physically supports the skull and trunk, allows for their movement, protects the spinal cord, and absorbs stresses produced by walking, running, and lifting. It also provides attachment for the limbs, thoracic cage, and postural muscles. Although commonly called the backbone, it consists of not a single bone but a flexible chain of 33 **vertebrae** with **intervertebral discs** of fibrocartilage between most of them.

The adult vertebral column averages about 71 cm (28 in.) long, with the intervertebral discs accounting for about one-quarter of the length. Most people are about 1% shorter when they go to bed at night than when they first rise in the morning. This is because during the day, the weight of the body compresses the intervertebral discs and squeezes water out of them. When one is sleeping, with the weight off the spine, the discs reabsorb water and swell.

As shown in **figure 8.18,** the vertebrae are divided into five groups, usually numbering 7 *cervical vertebrae* (SUR-vih-cul)

in the neck, 12 *thoracic vertebrae* in the chest, 5 *lumbar vertebrae* in the lower back, 5 *sacral vertebrae* at the base of the spine, and 4 tiny *coccygeal vertebrae* (coc-SIDJ-ee-ul). To help remember the numbers of cervical, thoracic, and lumbar vertebrae—7, 12, and 5—think of a typical workday: Go to work at 7, have lunch at 12, and go home at 5. All mammals have 7 cervical vertebrae, even in the famously long necks of giraffes.

Variations in this arrangement occur in about 1 person in 20. For example, the last lumbar vertebra is sometimes incorporated into the sacrum, producing four lumbar and six sacral vertebrae. In other cases, the first sacral vertebra fails to fuse with the second, producing six lumbar and four sacral vertebrae. The coccyx usually has four but sometimes five vertebrae. The cervical and thoracic vertebrae are more constant in number.

Beyond the age of 3 years, the vertebral column has four bends that give it an undulating S shape **(fig. 8.19).** A bend that is concave in the anterior direction (curved outward toward the back) is called a **kyphosis.**[30] There are two of these, the *thoracic kyphosis* and *pelvic kyphosis.* A bend toward the front,

---

[30]*kypho* = crooked, bent; *osis* = condition

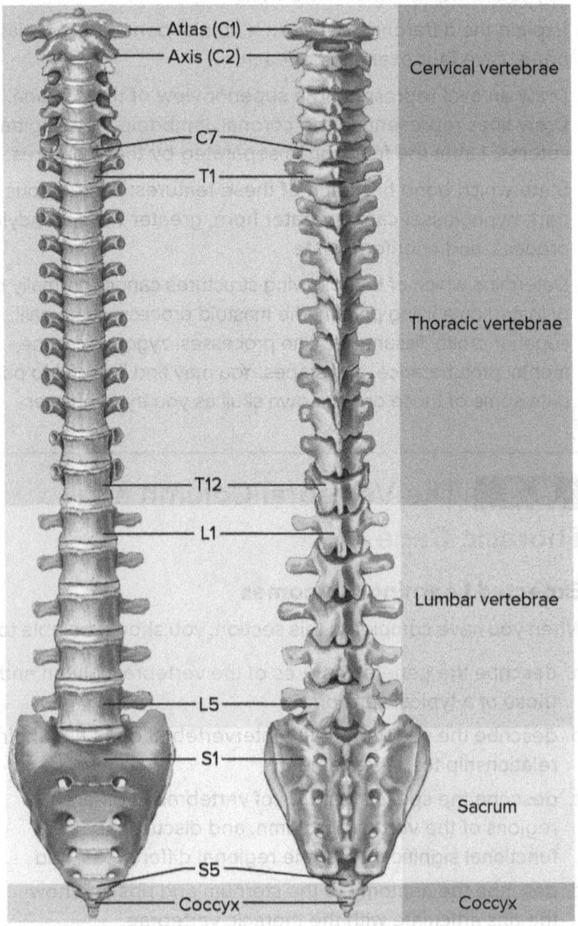

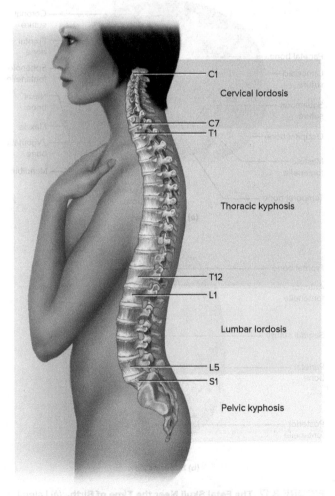

Atlas (C1)
Axis (C2)
Cervical vertebrae
C7
T1
Thoracic vertebrae
T12
L1
Lumbar vertebrae
L5
S1
Sacrum
S5
Coccyx   Coccyx

(a) Anterior view   (b) Posterior view

FIGURE 8.18 The Vertebral Column. (a) Anterior view. (b) Posterior view. **APR**

C1
Cervical lordosis
C7
T1
Thoracic kyphosis
T12
L1
Lumbar lordosis
L5
S1
Pelvic kyphosis

FIGURE 8.19 Curvatures of the Adult Vertebral Column.

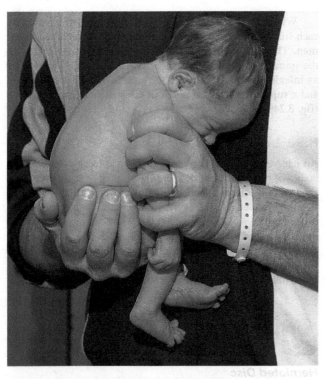

FIGURE 8.20 Spinal Curvature of the Newborn Infant. At this age, the spine forms a single C-shaped curve.

Bob Coyle/McGraw-Hill Education

concave posteriorly, is called a **lordosis,**[31] and there are also two of these—the *cervical lordosis* and *lumbar lordosis.* These are not present in the newborn, whose spine exhibits one continuous C-shaped curve, as it does in monkeys, apes, and most other four-legged animals **(fig. 8.20).** As an infant begins to crawl and lift its head, the cervical region becomes curved toward the posterior side, enabling an infant on its belly to look up. As a toddler begins walking, another curve develops in the same direction in the lumbar region. The resulting S shape makes sustained bipedal walking possible (see Deeper Insight 8.5). The thoracic and pelvic kyphoses are called *primary curvatures* because they exist from birth. The cervical and lumbar lordoses are called *secondary curvatures* because they develop later, in the child's first few years of crawling and walking. Abnormal lateral and anteroposterior curvatures are among the most common disorders of the spine (see Deeper Insight 8.3).

8.3b General Structure of a Vertebra

A representative vertebra and intervertebral disc are shown in **figure 8.22.** The most obvious feature of a vertebra is the **body (centrum)**—a mass of spongy bone and red bone marrow covered with a thin shell of compact, cortical bone. This is the weight-bearing portion of the vertebra. Its rough superior and inferior surfaces provide firm attachment to the intervertebral discs.

---

[31]*lordo* = backward; *osis* = condition

 DEEPER INSIGHT 8.3

CLINICAL APPLICATION

Abnormal Spinal Curvatures

Abnormal spinal curvatures **(fig. 8.21)** can result from disease, weakness or paralysis of the trunk muscles, poor posture, pregnancy, or congenital defects in vertebral anatomy. The most common deformity is an abnormal lateral curvature called *scoliosis.* It occurs most often in the thoracic region, particularly among adolescent girls. It sometimes results from a developmental abnormality in which the body and arch fail to develop on one side of a vertebra. If the person's skeletal growth is not yet complete, scoliosis can be corrected with a back brace.

An exaggerated thoracic curvature is called *hyperkyphosis.* It is usually a result of osteoporosis (see fig. 7.21), but it also occurs in people with osteomalacia or spinal tuberculosis and in adolescents who engage heavily in such spine-loading sports as wrestling and weight lifting. An exaggerated lumbar curvature is called *hyperlordosis.* It may have the same causes as hyperkyphosis, or it may result from added abdominal weight in pregnancy or obesity.

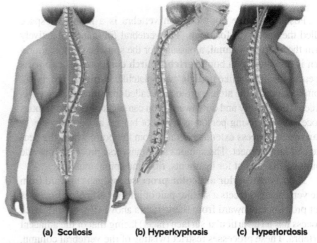

(a) Scoliosis   **(b) Hyperkyphosis**   **(c) Hyperlordosis**

Key
— Normal
— Pathological

FIGURE 8.21 Abnormal Spinal Curvatures. (a) Scoliosis. (b) Hyperkyphosis. (c) Hyperlordosis.

Posterior

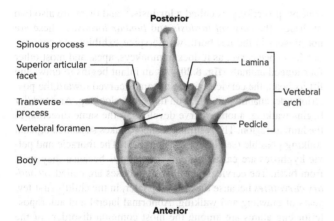

Spinous process

Superior articular
facet

Lamina

Transverse
process

Vertebral
arch

Vertebral foramen

Pedicle

Body

Anterior

(a) 2nd lumbar vertebra (L2)

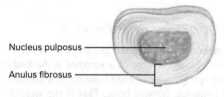

Nucleus pulposus

Anulus fibrosus

(b) Intervertebral disc

FIGURE 8.22 A Representative Vertebra and Intervertebral Disc (Superior Views). (a) A typical vertebra. (b) An intervertebral disc, oriented the same way as the vertebral body in part (a) for comparison.

▶▶▶**APPLY WHAT YOU KNOW**

The vertebral bodies and intervertebral discs get progressively larger as we look lower and lower on the vertebral column. What is the functional significance of this trend?

Posterior to the body of each vertebra is a triangular space called the **vertebral foramen.** The vertebral foramina collectively form the **vertebral canal,** a passage for the spinal cord. Each foramen is bordered by a bony **vertebral arch** composed of two parts on each side: a pillarlike **pedicle**[32] and platelike **lamina.**[33] Extending from the apex of the arch, a projection called the **spinous process** is directed posteriorly and downward. You can see and feel the spinous processes on a living person as a row of bumps along the spine. A **transverse process** extends laterally from the point where the pedicle and lamina meet. The spinous and transverse processes provide points of attachment for ligaments, ribs, and spinal muscles.

A pair of **superior articular processes** projects upward from one vertebra and meets a similar pair of inferior articular processes that projects downward from the vertebra above **(fig. 8.24a).** Each process has a flat articular surface (facet) facing that of the adjacent vertebra. These processes restrict twisting of the vertebral column, which could otherwise severely damage the spinal cord.

[32]*ped* = foot; *icle* = little
[33]*lamina* = plate

When two vertebrae are joined, they exhibit an opening on each side between their pedicles called the **intervertebral foramen.** These allow passage for spinal nerves that connect with the spinal cord at regular intervals. Each foramen is formed by an **inferior vertebral notch** in the pedicle of the upper vertebra and a **superior vertebral notch** in the pedicle of the lower one **(fig. 8.24b).**

8.3c Intervertebral Discs

An intervertebral disc is a cartilaginous pad located between the bodies of two adjacent vertebrae. It consists of an inner gelatinous **nucleus pulposus** surrounded by a ring of fibrocartilage, the **anulus fibrosus** (see fig. 8.22b). There are 23 discs—the first one between cervical vertebrae 2 and 3 (C2–C3) and the last one between the last lumbar vertebra and the sacrum (L5–S1). They help to bind adjacent vertebrae together, support the weight of the body, allow spinal mobility, and absorb shock. Discs can rupture painfully when subjected to excessive stress (see Deeper Insight 8.4).

DEEPER INSIGHT 8.4
CLINICAL APPLICATION

Herniated Disc

Stress on the vertebral column, as in lifting a heavy weight, compresses the intervertebral discs and makes them bulge laterally. Excessive stress can crack the anulus fibrosus, allowing the gelatinous nucleus pulposus to ooze out **(fig. 8.23).** This is called a *herniated disc* (colloquially, a "ruptured disc," or more inaccurately, "slipped disc"). Herniation usually occurs at the posterolateral corners of the discs because the anulus fibrosus is thinnest on the posterior side and corners are least supported by nearby spinal ligaments. About 95% of herniations are at the L4–L5 or L5–S1 level because these bear the most weight. Disc herniation rarely occurs in young people because of their well-hydrated, thick, resilient discs. Herniated discs are one of the most common causes of lower back pain, stemming from inflammation stimulated by the nucleus and pressure of the oozing nucleus on spinal nerve roots passing through this tight space. Over 80% of patients recover from the pain with only oral analgesics, requiring no surgery; up to 76% of cases resolve partially or completely within 1 year.

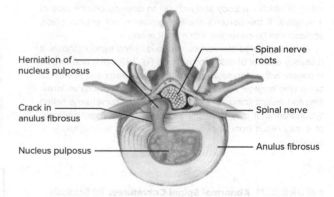

Herniation of
nucleus pulposus

Spinal nerve
roots

Crack in
anulus fibrosus

Spinal nerve

Nucleus pulposus

Anulus fibrosus

FIGURE 8.23 Herniated Disc.

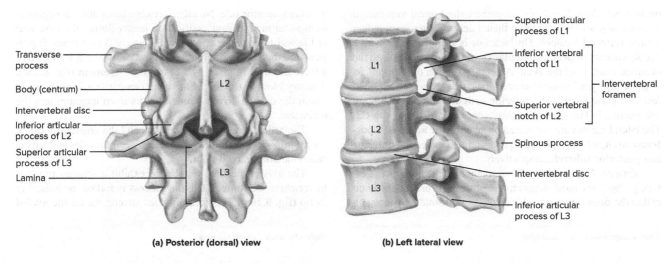

(a) Posterior (dorsal) view

Transverse process

Body (centrum)

Intervertebral disc

Inferior articular process of L2

Superior articular process of L3

Lamina

L2

L3

(b) Left lateral view

Superior articular process of L1

Inferior vertebral notch of L1

Intervertebral foramen

Superior vertebral notch of L2

Spinous process

Intervertebral disc

Inferior articular process of L3

L1

L2

L3

FIGURE 8.24 Articulated Vertebrae. (a) Posterior view. (b) Left lateral view.

8.3d Regional Characteristics of Vertebrae

We are now prepared to consider how vertebrae differ from one region of the vertebral column to another and from the generalized anatomy just described. Knowing these variations will enable you to identify the region of the spine from which an isolated vertebra was taken. More importantly, these modifications in form reflect functional differences among the vertebrae.

The Cervical Vertebrae

The cervical vertebrae (C1–C7) are relatively small. Their function is to support the head and allow for its movements. The first two (C1 and C2) have unique structures for this purpose **(fig. 8.25).** Vertebra C1 is called the **atlas** because it supports the head in a manner reminiscent of Atlas, the giant of Greek mythology who was condemned by Zeus to carry the heavens

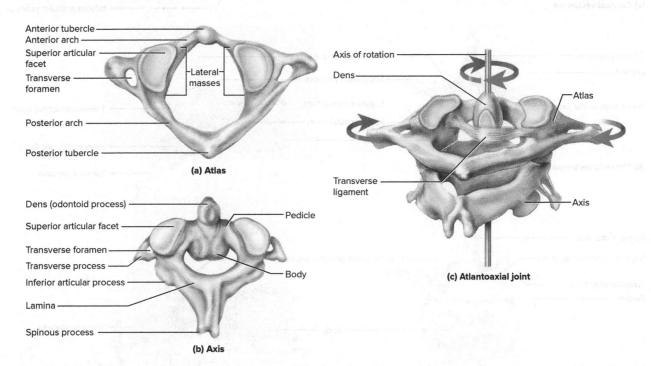

Anterior tubercle

Anterior arch

Superior articular facet

Transverse foramen

Lateral masses

Posterior arch

Posterior tubercle

(a) Atlas

Dens (odontoid process)

Superior articular facet

Transverse foramen

Transverse process

Inferior articular process

Lamina

Spinous process

Pedicle

Body

(b) Axis

Axis of rotation

Dens

Atlas

Transverse ligament

Axis

(c) Atlantoaxial joint

FIGURE 8.25 The Atlas and Axis, Cervical Vertebrae C1 and C2. (a) The atlas, superior view. (b) The axis, posterosuperior view. (c) Articulation of the atlas and axis and rotation of the atlas. This movement turns the head from side to side, as in gesturing "no." Note the transverse ligament holding the dens of the axis in place. **APR**

❓ *What serious consequence could result from a rupture of the transverse ligament?*

Anatomical Kinesiology

on his shoulders. It scarcely resembles the typical vertebra; it has no body, and is little more than a delicate ring surrounding a large vertebral foramen. On each side is a **lateral mass** with a deeply concave **superior articular facet** that articulates with the occipital condyle of the skull. A nodding motion of the skull, as in gesturing "yes," causes the occipital condyles to rock back and forth on these facets. The **inferior articular facets,** which are comparatively flat or only slightly concave, articulate with C2. The lateral masses are connected by an **anterior arch** and a **posterior arch,** which bear slight protuberances called the **anterior** and **posterior tubercle,** respectively.

Vertebra C2, the **axis,** allows rotation of the head as in gesturing "no." Its most distinctive feature is a prominent knob called the **dens** (pronounced "denz"), or **odontoid**[34] **process,** on its anterosuperior side. No other vertebra has a dens. It begins to form as an independent ossification center during the first year of life and fuses with the axis by the age of 3 to 6 years. It projects into the vertebral foramen of the atlas, where it is nestled in a facet and held in place by a **transverse ligament** (fig. 8.25c). A heavy blow to the top of the head can cause a fatal injury in which the dens is driven through the foramen magnum into the brainstem.

The articulation between the atlas and the cranium is called the **atlanto–occipital joint;** the one between the atlas and axis is called the **atlantoaxial joint.**

The axis is the first vertebra to exhibit a spinous process. In vertebrae C2 through C6, the process is forked, or *bifid,*[35] at its tip **(fig. 8.26a).** This fork provides attachment for the *nuchal*

---

[34]*dens* = *odont* = tooth; *oid* = resembling

[35]*bifid* = branched, cleft into two parts

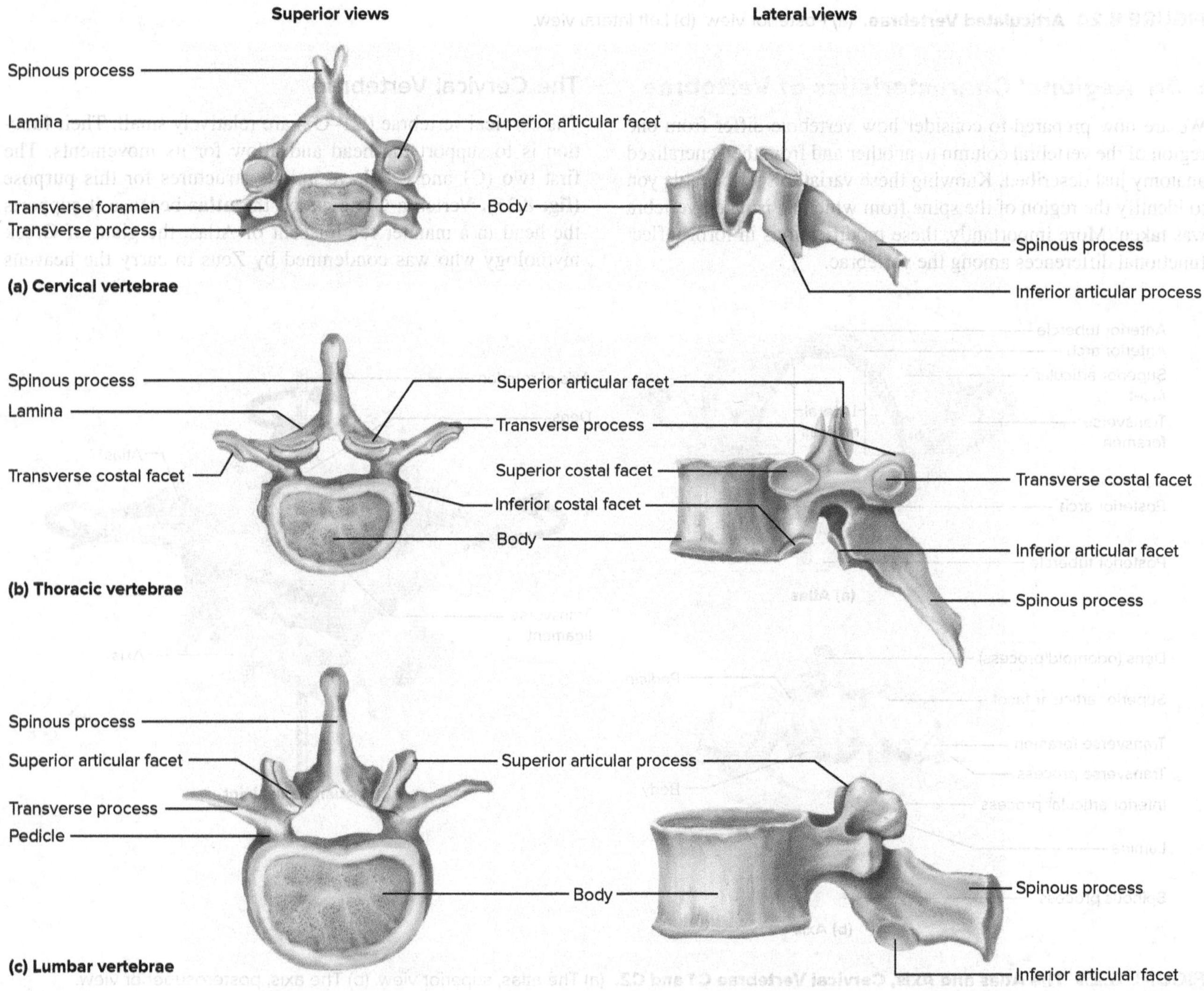

(a) Cervical vertebrae

(b) Thoracic vertebrae

(c) Lumbar vertebrae

FIGURE 8.26 Regional Differences in Vertebrae. (a) Cervical vertebrae. (b) Thoracic vertebrae. (c) Lumbar vertebrae. The left-hand figures are superior views and the right-hand figures are left lateral views. **APR**

ligament of the back of the neck. All seven cervical vertebrae have a prominent round **transverse foramen** in each transverse process. These foramina provide passage and protection for the *vertebral arteries,* which supply blood to the brain, and *vertebral veins,* which drain blood from various neck structures (but not from the brain). Transverse foramina occur in no other vertebrae and thus provide an easy means of recognizing a cervical vertebra.

Cervical vertebrae C3 through C6 are similar to the typical vertebra depicted in figure 8.22a, with the addition of the transverse foramina and bifid spinous processes. Vertebra C7 is a little different—its spinous process is not bifid, but is especially long and forms a prominent bump on the lower back of the neck. C7 is sometimes called the *vertebra prominens* because of this conspicuous spinous process. This feature is a convenient landmark for counting vertebrae by palpation. One can easily identify the largest bump on the neck as C7, then count up or down from there to identify others.

The Thoracic Vertebrae

There are 12 **thoracic vertebrae** (T1–T12), corresponding to the 12 pairs of ribs attached to them; no other vertebrae have ribs. One function of the thoracic vertebrae is to support the thoracic cage enclosing the heart and lungs. They lack the transverse foramina and bifid processes that distinguish the cervical vertebrae, but possess the following distinctive features of their own **(fig. 8.26b):**

• The spinous processes are relatively pointed and angle sharply downward.

• The body is somewhat heart-shaped, more massive than in the cervical vertebrae but less than in the lumbar vertebrae.

• The body has small, smooth, slightly concave spots called *costal facets* for attachment of the ribs.

• Vertebrae T1 through T10 have a shallow, cuplike **transverse costal**[36] **facet** at the end of each transverse process. These provide a second point of articulation for ribs 1 to 10. There are no transverse costal facets on T11 and T12 because ribs 11 and 12 attach only to the bodies of those two vertebrae.

Thoracic vertebrae vary among themselves mainly in the mode of articulation with the ribs (see fig. 8.30). In most cases, a rib inserts between two vertebrae, so each vertebra contributes one-half of the articular surface. A rib articulates with the **inferior costal facet** of the upper vertebra and the **superior costal facet** of the vertebra below that. This terminology may be a little confusing, but note that the superior and inferior facets are named for their position on the vertebral body, not for which part of the rib's articulation they provide. Vertebrae T1 and T10 through T12, however, have complete costal facets on the bodies for ribs 1 and 10 through 12, which articulate on the vertebral bodies instead of between vertebrae. Vertebrae T11 and T12, as noted, have no transverse costal facets. These variations will

be more functionally understandable after you have studied the anatomy of the ribs, so we will return then to the details of these articular surfaces.

Each thoracic vertebra has a pair of superior articular facets that face posteriorly and a pair of inferior articular facets that face anteriorly (except in vertebra T12). Thus, the superior facets of one vertebra articulate with the inferior facets of the next one above it. In vertebra T12, however, the inferior articular facets face somewhat laterally instead of anteriorly. This positions them to articulate with the medially facing superior articular facets of the first lumbar vertebra. T12 thus shows an anatomical transition between the thoracic and lumbar pattern, described next.

The Lumbar Vertebrae

There are five **lumbar vertebrae** (L1–L5). Their most distinctive features are a thick, stout body and a blunt, squarish spinous process for attachment of the strong lumbar muscles **(fig. 8.26c).** In addition, their articular processes are oriented differently than on other vertebrae. The superior processes face medially (like the palms of your hands about to clap), and the inferior processes face laterally, toward the superior processes of the next vertebra. This arrangement resists twisting of the lower spine. These differences are best observed on an articulated skeleton.

The Sacrum

The **sacrum** (SACK-rum, SAY-krum) is a bony plate that forms the posterior wall of the pelvic girdle **(fig. 8.27).** It was named *sacrum* for its prominence as the largest and most durable bone of the vertebral column.[37] There are five separate **sacral vertebrae** (S1–S5) in children, but they begin to fuse around age 16 and are fully fused by age 26.

The anterior surface of the sacrum is relatively smooth and concave and has four transverse lines that indicate where the five vertebrae have fused. This surface exhibits four pairs of large **anterior sacral foramina,** which allow for passage of nerves and arteries to the pelvic organs. The posterior surface is very rough. The spinous processes of the vertebrae fuse into a ridge called the **median sacral crest.** The transverse processes fuse into a less prominent **lateral sacral crest** on each side of the median crest. Again on the posterior side of the sacrum, there are four pairs of openings for spinal nerves, the **posterior sacral foramina.** The nerves that emerge here supply the gluteal region and lower limbs.

A **sacral canal** runs through the sacrum and ends in an inferior opening called the **sacral hiatus** (hy-AY-tus). This canal contains spinal nerve roots. On each side of the sacrum is an ear-shaped region called the **auricular**[38] **surface** (aw-RIC-you-lur). This articulates with a similarly shaped surface on the hip bone (see fig. 8.37b) and forms the strong, nearly immovable **sacroiliac**

---

[36]*costa* = rib; *al* = pertaining to

[37]*sacr* = great, prominent

[38]*auri* = ear; *cul* = little; *ar* = pertaining to

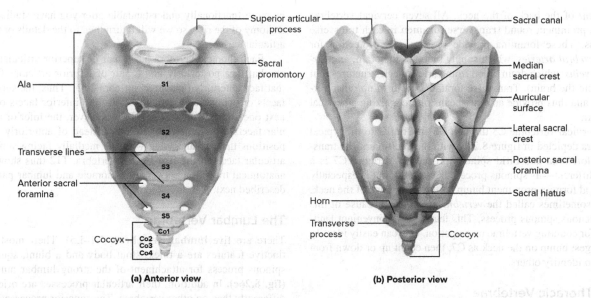

FIGURE 8.27 The Sacrum and Coccyx. (a) The anterior surface, which faces the viscera of the pelvic cavity. (b) The posterior surface. The processes of this surface can be palpated in the sacral region. **APR**

(SI) joint (SACK-ro-ILL-ee-ac). The body of vertebra S1 juts anteriorly to form a **sacral promontory,** which supports the body of vertebra L5. Lateral to the median sacral crest, S1 also has a pair of **superior articular processes** that articulate with vertebra L5. Lateral to these is a pair of large, rough, winglike extensions called the **alae**[39] (AIL-ee).

The Coccyx

Four (sometimes five) tiny **coccygeal vertebrae** (Co1 to Co4 or Co5) fuse by the age of 20 to 30 years to form the **coccyx**[40] (COC-six) (fig. 8.27), colloquially called the tailbone. Although it is indeed the vestige of an ancestral tail, it is not entirely useless; it provides attachment for the muscles of the pelvic floor. Vertebra Co1 has a pair of **horns (cornua)** that serve as attachment points for ligaments that bind the coccyx to the sacrum. The coccyx can be fractured by a difficult childbirth or a hard fall on the buttocks.

8.3e The Thoracic Cage

The **thoracic cage (fig. 8.28)** consists of the thoracic vertebrae, sternum, and ribs. It forms a roughly conical enclosure for the lungs and heart and provides attachment for the pectoral girdle and upper limb. It has a broad base and a somewhat narrower superior apex. Its inferior border is the arc of the lower ribs, called the **costal margin.** The cage protects not only the

thoracic organs but also the spleen, most of the liver, and to some extent the kidneys. Most important is its role in breathing; it is rhythmically expanded by the respiratory muscles to create a vacuum that draws air into the lungs, and then compressed to expel air.

The Sternum

The **sternum** (breastbone) is a bony plate anterior to the heart. It is subdivided into three regions: the manubrium, body, and xiphoid process. The **manubrium**[41] (ma-NOO-bree-um) is the broad superior portion, shaped like the knot of a necktie. It lies at the level of vertebrae T3 to T4. It has a median **suprasternal (jugular) notch,** which you can easily palpate between your clavicles (collarbones), and right and left **clavicular notches** where it articulates with the clavicles. The dagger-shaped **body,** or **gladiolus,**[42] is the longest part of the sternum, lying at the level of vertebrae T5 through T9. It joins the manubrium at the **sternal angle,** which can be palpated as a transverse ridge at the point where the sternum projects farthest forward. In some people, however, the angle is rounded or concave. The second rib attaches here, making the sternal angle a useful landmark for counting ribs by palpation. The manubrium and body have scalloped lateral margins where cartilages of the ribs are attached. At the inferior end (vertebral level T10 to T11) is a small, pointed **xiphoid**[43] **process** (ZIF-oyd) that provides attachment for some of the abdominal muscles. In cardiopulmonary resuscitation,

---

[39]*alae* = wings
[40]*coccyx* = cuckoo (named for resemblance to a cuckoo's beak)

[41]*manubrium* = handle
[42]*gladiolus* = sword
[43]*xipho* = sword; *oid* = resembling

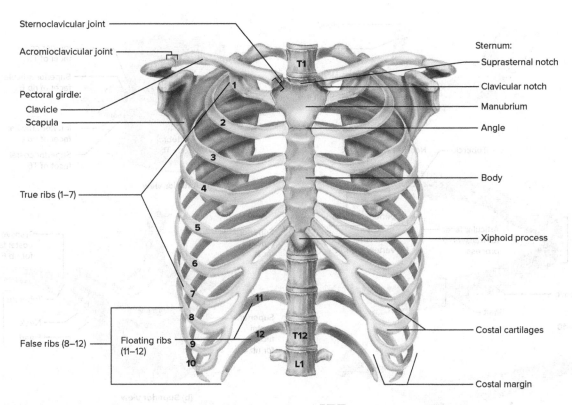

Sternoclavicular joint

Acromioclavicular joint

Pectoral girdle:
  Clavicle
  Scapula

True ribs (1–7)

False ribs (8–12)

Floating ribs
(11–12)

Sternum:
  Suprasternal notch
  Clavicular notch
  Manubrium
  Angle

Body

Xiphoid process

Costal cartilages

Costal margin

FIGURE 8.28 The Thoracic Cage and Pectoral Girdle (Anterior View). **A&PR**

improperly performed chest compressions can drive the xiphoid process into the liver and cause a fatal hemorrhage.

The Ribs

There are 12 pairs of **ribs,** with no difference in number between the sexes (despite popular religious belief). Each is attached at its posterior (proximal) end to the vertebral column, and most of them are also attached at the anterior (distal) end to the sternum. The anterior attachment is by way of a long strip of hyaline cartilage called the **costal cartilage** (COSS-tul).

As a rule, the ribs increase in length from 1 through 7 and become progressively smaller again through rib 12. They are increasingly oblique (slanted) in orientation from 1 through 9, then less so from 10 through 12. They also differ in their individual structure and attachments at different levels of the thoracic cage, so we will examine them in order as we descend the chest, taking note of their universal characteristics as well as their individual variations.

Rib 1 is peculiar. On an articulated skeleton, you must look for its vertebral attachment just below the base of the neck; much of this rib lies above the level of the clavicle (fig. 8.28). It is a short, flat, C-shaped plate of bone **(fig. 8.29a).** At the vertebral end, it exhibits a knobby **head** that articulates with the body of vertebra T1. On an isolated vertebra, you can find a smooth costal

facet for this attachment on the middle of the body. Immediately distal to the head, the rib narrows to a **neck** and then widens again to form a rough area called the **tubercle.** This is its point of attachment to the transverse costal facet of the same vertebra. Beyond the tubercle, the rib flattens and widens into a gently sloping bladelike **shaft.** The shaft ends distally in a squared-off, rough area. In the living individual, the costal cartilage begins here and spans the rest of the distance to the upper sternum. The superior surface of rib 1 has a pair of shallow grooves that serve as platforms for the subclavian artery and subclavian vein.

Ribs 2 through 7 present a more typical appearance **(fig. 8.29b).** At the proximal end, each exhibits a head, neck, and tubercle. The head is wedge-shaped and inserts between two vertebrae. Each margin of the wedge has a smooth surface called an *articular facet.* The **superior articular facet** joins the inferior costal facet of the vertebra above; the **inferior articular facet** joins the superior costal facet of vertebra below. The tubercle of the rib articulates with the transverse costal facet of each same-numbered vertebra. **Figure 8.30** details the rib–vertebra attachments typical of this region of the rib cage.

Beyond the tubercle, each rib makes a sharp curve around the side of the chest and then progresses anteriorly to approach the sternum (see fig. 8.28). The curve is called the **angle** of the rib and the rest of the bony blade distal to it is the **shaft.** The inferior margin of the shaft has a **costal groove** that marks the path of the

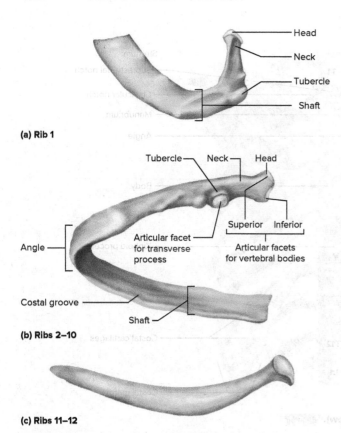

(a) Rib 1

(b) Ribs 2–10

(c) Ribs 11–12

FIGURE 8.29 Anatomy of the Ribs. (a) Rib 1 (superior view) is an atypical flat plate. (b) Typical features of ribs 2 to 10. (c) Appearance of the floating ribs, 11 and 12.

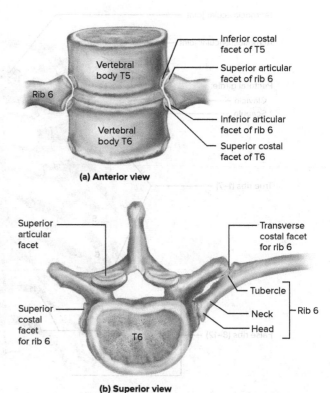

(a) Anterior view

(b) Superior view

FIGURE 8.30 Articulation of Rib 6 with Vertebrae T5 and T6. (a) Anterior view. Note the relationship of the articular facets of the rib with the costal facets of the two vertebrae. (b) Superior view. Note that the rib articulates with a vertebra at two points: the costal facet on the vertebral body and the transverse costal facet on the transverse process.

intercostal blood vessels and nerve. Each of these ribs, like rib 1, ends in a blunt, rough area where the costal cartilage begins. Each has its own costal cartilage connecting it to the sternum; because of this feature, ribs 1 through 7 are called **true ribs.**

Ribs 8 through 12 are called **false ribs** because they lack independent cartilaginous connections to the sternum. In 8 through 10, the costal cartilages sweep upward and end on the costal cartilage of rib 7 (see fig. 8.28). Rib 10 also differs from 2 through 9 in that it attaches to the body of a single vertebra (T10) rather than between vertebrae. Thus, vertebra T10 has a complete costal facet on its body for rib 10.

Ribs 11 and 12 are again unusual **(fig. 8.29c).** Posteriorly, they articulate with the bodies of vertebrae T11 and T12, but they do not have tubercles and do not attach to the transverse processes of the vertebrae. Those two vertebrae therefore have no transverse costal facets. At the distal end, these two relatively small, delicate ribs taper to a point and are capped by a small cartilaginous tip, but there is no cartilaginous connection to the sternum or to any of the higher costal cartilages. The ribs are merely embedded in lumbar muscle at this end. Consequently, 11 and 12 are also called **floating ribs.** In people of Japanese and some other ancestries, rib 10 is also usually

floating. **Table 8.4** summarizes these variations in rib anatomy and their vertebral and sternal attachments.

BEFORE YOU GO ON

Answer the following questions to test your understanding of the preceding section:

9. Discuss the contribution of the intervertebral discs to the length and flexibility of the spine.

10. Construct a three-column table headed C4, T4, and L4. In each column, list all anatomical features that would distinguish that vertebra from the other two.

11. Name the three parts of the sternum. How many ribs attach (directly or indirectly) to each part?

12. Describe how rib 5 articulates with the spine. How do ribs 1 and 12 differ from this and from each other in their modes of articulation?

13. Distinguish between true, false, and floating ribs. Which ribs fall into each category?

14. Name the three divisions of the sternum and list the sternal features that can be palpated on a living person.

TABLE 8.4	Articulations of the Ribs				
Rib	Type	Costal Cartilage	Articulating Vertebral Bodies	Articulating with a Transverse Costal Facet?	Rib Tubercle
1	True	Individual	T1	Yes	Present
2	True	Individual	T1 and T2	Yes	Present
3	True	Individual	T2 and T3	Yes	Present
4	True	Individual	T3 and T4	Yes	Present
5	True	Individual	T4 and T5	Yes	Present
6	True	Individual	T5 and T6	Yes	Present
7	True	Individual	T6 and T7	Yes	Present
8	False	Shared with rib 7	T7 and T8	Yes	Present
9	False	Shared with rib 7	T8 and T9	Yes	Present
10	False	Shared with rib 7	T10	Yes	Present
11	False, floating	None	T11	No	Absent
12	False, floating	None	T12	No	Absent

8.4 The Pectoral Girdle and Upper Limb

Expected Learning Outcome

When you have completed this section, you should be able to

a. identify and describe the features of the clavicle, scapula, humerus, radius, ulna, and bones of the wrist and hand.

8.4a The Pectoral Girdle

The **pectoral girdle** (shoulder girdle) supports the arm and links it to the axial skeleton. It consists of two bones on each side of the body: the *clavicle* (collarbone) and *scapula* (shoulder blade). The medial end of the clavicle articulates with the sternum at the **sternoclavicular joint,** and its lateral end articulates with the scapula at the **acromioclavicular joint** (see fig. 8.28). The scapula also articulates with the humerus at the **glenohumeral joint.** These are loose attachments that result in a shoulder far more flexible than that of most other mammals, but they also make the shoulder joint easy to dislocate.

▶▶▶APPLY WHAT YOU KNOW

How is the unusual flexibility of the human shoulder joint related to the habitat of our primate ancestors?

The Clavicle

The **clavicle**[44] **(fig. 8.31)** is slightly S-shaped, somewhat flattened from the upper to lower surface, and easily seen and palpated on

---

[44]*clav* = hammer, club, key; *icle* = little

the upper thorax (see atlas B, fig. B.1b). The superior surface is relatively smooth and rounded, whereas the inferior surface is flatter and marked by grooves and ridges for muscle attachment. The medial **sternal end** has a rounded, hammerlike head, and the lateral **acromial end** is markedly flattened. Near the acromial end is a rough tuberosity called the **conoid tubercle**—a ligament attachment that faces toward the rear and slightly downward.

The clavicle braces the shoulder, keeping the upper limb away from the midline of the body, and is an attachment for some of the muscles of head movement (sternocleidomastoid and trapezius). It also transfers force from the arm to the axial region of the body, as when doing pushups. It is thickened in people who do heavy manual labor, and in right-handed people, the right clavicle is usually stronger and shorter than the left because of the workload placed on it. Without the clavicles, the pectoralis major muscles would pull the shoulders forward and medially—which indeed happens when a clavicle is fractured. The clavicle is one of the

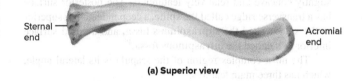

Sternal end · Acromial end

(a) Superior view

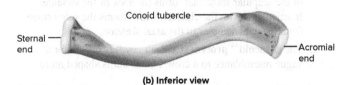

Conoid tubercle

Sternal end · Acromial end

(b) Inferior view

FIGURE 8.31 The Right Clavicle. (a) Superior view. (b) Inferior view. **APR**

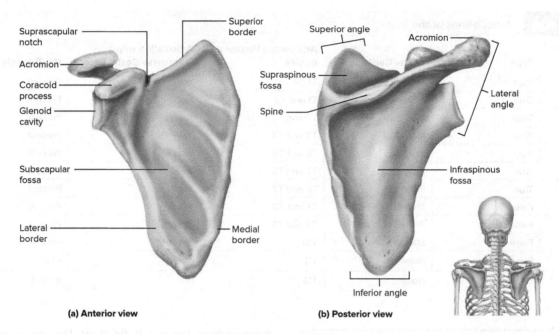

(a) Anterior view

(b) Posterior view

FIGURE 8.32   The Right Scapula. (a) Anterior view. (b) Posterior view. **APR**

most commonly fractured bones in the body because it is so close to the surface and because people often reach out with their arms to break a fall.

The Scapula

The **scapula**[45] **(fig. 8.32),** named for its resemblance to a spade or shovel, is a triangular plate that posteriorly overlies ribs 2 through 7. Its only direct attachment to the thorax is by muscles; it glides across the rib cage as the arm and shoulder move. The three sides of the triangle are called the **superior, medial (vertebral),** and **lateral (axillary) borders,** and its three angles are the **superior, inferior,** and **lateral angles.** A conspicuous **suprascapular notch** in the superior border provides passage for a nerve. The broad anterior surface of the scapula, called the **subscapular fossa,** is slightly concave and relatively featureless. The posterior surface has a transverse ridge called the **spine,** a deep indentation superior to the spine called the **supraspinous fossa,** and a broad surface inferior to it called the **infraspinous fossa.**[46]

The most complex region of the scapula is its lateral angle, which has three main features:

1. The **acromion**[47] (ah-CRO-me-on) is a platelike extension of the scapular spine that forms the apex of the shoulder. It articulates with the clavicle, which forms the sole bridge from the appendicular to the axial skeleton.

2. The **coracoid**[48] **process** (COR-uh-coyd) is named for a vague resemblance to a crow's beak, but is shaped more

like a bent finger; it provides attachment for tendons of the *biceps brachii* and other muscles of the arm.

3. The **glenoid**[49] **cavity** (GLEN-oyd) is a shallow socket that articulates with the head of the humerus, forming the glenohumeral joint. The anatomy of this joint is detailed in section 9.3b and figure 9.24.

8.4b The Upper Limb

Each upper limb contains 30 bones distributed in the following three limb segments:

1. The arm proper (**brachial region** or **brachium**[50] [BRAY-kee-um]) extends from shoulder to elbow. It contains only one bone, the *humerus.*

2. The forearm (**antebrachial region** or **antebrachium**[51]) extends from elbow to wrist and contains two bones: the *radius* and *ulna.* In anatomical position, these bones are parallel and the radius is lateral to the ulna.

3. The hand consists of the **carpal**[52] **region,** with 8 small carpal bones arranged in two rows in the base of the hand; the **metacarpal region** in the palm, with 5 bones; and the fingers (**digits**), with 14 bones. The two hands together contain 54 of the 206 bones in the body—over one-quarter of the total.

Note that what we colloquially call the wrist—the narrow region where one may wear a bracelet or wristwatch—is not what

---

[45]*scap* = spade, shovel; *ula* = little
[46]*supra* = above; *infra* = below
[47]*acr* = extremity, point, apex; *omi* = shoulder
[48]*corac* = crow; *oid* = resembling

[49]*glen* = pit, socket; *oid* = resembling
[50]*brachi* = arm
[51]*ante* = before
[52]*carp* = wrist

anatomists call the wrist (carpal region): the thick, fleshy base of the hand proximal to the hollow of the palm.

The Humerus

The **humerus** has a hemispherical **head** that articulates with the glenoid cavity of the scapula (**fig. 8.33**). The smooth surface of the head (covered with articular cartilage in the living state) is bordered by a groove called the **anatomical neck.** Other prominent features of the proximal end are muscle attachments called the **greater** and **lesser tubercles** and an **intertubercular sulcus** between them that accommodates a tendon of the biceps muscle. The **surgical neck,** a common fracture site, is a narrowing of the bone just distal to the tubercles, at the transition from the head to the shaft. The shaft has a rough area called the **deltoid tuberosity** on its lateral surface. This is an insertion for the *deltoid muscle* of the shoulder.

The distal end of the humerus has two smooth condyles. The lateral one, called the **capitulum**[53] (ca-PIT-you-lum), is shaped like a wide tire and articulates with the radius. The medial one, called the **trochlea**[54] (TROCK-lee-uh), is pulleylike and articulates with

[53]*capit* = head; *ulum* = little
[54]*troch* = wheel, pulley

the ulna. Immediately proximal to these condyles, the humerus flares out to form two bony processes, the **lateral** and **medial epicondyles,** which are the bumps you can palpate at the widest point of your elbow. The medial epicondyle protects the *ulnar nerve,* which passes close to the surface across the back of the elbow. This epicondyle is popularly known as the "funny bone" because striking the elbow on the edge of a table stimulates the ulnar nerve and produces a sharp tingling sensation. Immediately proximal to the epicondyles, the margins of the humerus are called the **lateral** and **medial supracondylar ridges.** These are attachments for certain forearm muscles described in chapter 10.

The distal end of the humerus also shows three deep pits: two anterior and one posterior. The posterior pit, called the **olecranon fossa** (oh-LEC-ruh-non), accommodates a process of the ulna called the *olecranon* when the elbow is extended. On the anterior surface, a medial pit called the **coronoid fossa** accommodates the *coronoid process* of the ulna when the forearm is flexed. The lateral pit is the **radial fossa,** named for the nearby head of the radius.

The Radius

The **radius** has a distinctive discoidal **head** at its proximal end (**fig. 8.34**). When the forearm is rotated so the palm turns forward

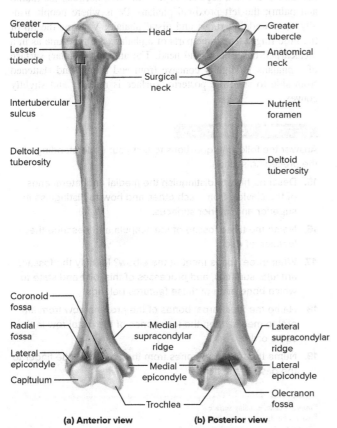

Greater tubercle
Lesser tubercle
Intertubercular sulcus
Deltoid tuberosity
Coronoid fossa
Radial fossa
Lateral epicondyle
Capitulum

Head
Surgical neck
Trochlea

Greater tubercle
Anatomical neck
Surgical neck
Nutrient foramen
Deltoid tuberosity
Medial supracondylar ridge
Medial epicondyle

Lateral supracondylar ridge
Lateral epicondyle
Olecranon fossa

(a) Anterior view   **(b) Posterior view**

FIGURE 8.33 The Right Humerus. (a) Anterior view. (b) Posterior view. **APR**

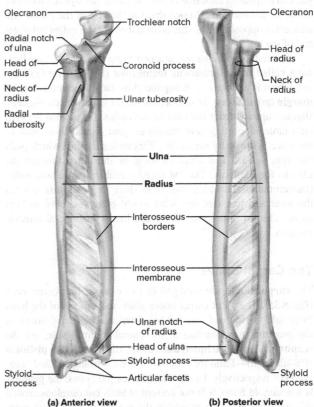

Olecranon
Radial notch of ulna
Head of radius
Neck of radius
Radial tuberosity

Trochlear notch
Coronoid process
Ulnar tuberosity

Olecranon
Head of radius
Neck of radius

Ulna
Radius
Interosseous borders
Interosseous membrane

Styloid process

Ulnar notch of radius
Head of ulna
Styloid process
Articular facets

Styloid process

(a) Anterior view   **(b) Posterior view**

FIGURE 8.34 The Right Radius and Ulna. (a) Anterior view. (b) Posterior view. **APR**

and back, the circular superior surface of this disc spins on the capitulum of the humerus, and the edge of the disc spins on the radial notch of the ulna. Immediately distal to the head, the radius has a narrower **neck** and then widens to a rough prominence, the **radial tuberosity,** on its medial surface. The distal tendon of the biceps muscle terminates on this tuberosity.

The distal end of the radius has the following features, from lateral to medial:

1. a bony point, the **styloid process,** which can be palpated proximal to the thumb;

2. two shallow depressions (articular facets) that articulate with the scaphoid and lunate bones of the wrist; and

3. the **ulnar notch,** which articulates with the end of the ulna.

The Ulna

At the proximal end of the **ulna** (fig. 8.34) is a deep, C-shaped **trochlear notch** that wraps around the trochlea of the humerus. The posterior side of this notch is formed by a prominent **olecranon**— the bony point where you rest your elbow on a table. The anterior side is formed by a less prominent **coronoid process.** Laterally, the head of the ulna has a less conspicuous **radial notch,** which accommodates the edge of the head of the radius. At the distal end **(head)** of the ulna is a medial **styloid process.** The bony lumps you can palpate on each side of your wrist are the styloid processes of the radius and ulna. Notice that the "heads" of the radius and ulna are at opposite ends—the proximal end of the radius but distal end of the ulna.

The radius and ulna are attached along their shafts by a ligament called the **interosseous membrane (IM)** (IN-tur-OSS-ee-us), which is attached to an angular ridge called the **interosseous margin** on each bone. Most fibers of the IM are oriented obliquely, slanting upward from the ulna to the radius. If you lean forward on a table supporting your weight on your hands, about 80% of the force is borne by the radius. This tenses the IM, which pulls the ulna upward and transfers some of this force through the ulna to the humerus. The IM thereby enables two elbow joints (humeroradial and humeroulnar) to share the load; this reduces the wear and tear that one joint would otherwise have to bear alone. The IM also serves as an attachment for several forearm muscles.

The Carpal Bones

The **carpal bones** are arranged in two rows of four bones each **(fig. 8.35).** The short carpal bones allow movements of the hand from side to side and anterior to posterior. The carpal bones of the proximal row, starting at the lateral (thumb) side, are the **scaphoid, lunate, triquetrum** (tri-QUEE-trum), and **pisiform** (PY-sih-form)—Latin for "boat-," "moon-," "triangle-," and "pea-shaped," respectively. Unlike the other carpal bones, the pisiform is a sesamoid bone; it is not present at birth but develops around the age of 9 to 12 years within the tendon of the *flexor carpi ulnaris muscle.*

The bones of the distal row, again starting on the lateral side, are the **trapezium,**[55] **trapezoid, capitate,**[56] and **hamate.**[57] The hamate can be recognized by a prominent hook called the **hamulus** on the palmar side (fig. 8.35b). The hamulus is an attachment for the *flexor retinaculum,* a fibrous sheet in the wrist that covers the carpal tunnel (see fig. 10.31).

The Metacarpal Bones

The **metacarpal**[58] bones span the palmar region of the hand. Metacarpal I is located proximal to the base of the thumb and metacarpal V proximal to the base of the little finger. On a skeleton, the metacarpal bones look like extensions of the fingers, making the fingers seem much longer than they really are. The proximal end of a metacarpal bone is called the **base,** the shaft is called the **body,** and the distal end is called the **head.** The heads of the metacarpal bones form the knuckles when you clench your fist.

The Phalanges

The bones of the fingers are called **phalanges** (fah-LAN-jeez), in the singular, *phalanx* (FAY-lanks). There are two phalanges in the thumb and three in each of the other digits. Phalanges are identified by roman numerals preceded by *proximal, middle,* and *distal.* For example, proximal phalanx I is in the basal segment of the thumb (the first segment beyond the web between the thumb and palm); the left proximal phalanx IV is where people usually wear wedding rings; and distal phalanx V forms the tip of the little finger. The three parts of a phalanx are the same as in a metacarpal: base, body, and head. The anterior (palmar) surface of a phalanx is slightly concave from end to end and flattened from side to side; the posterior surface is rounder and slightly convex.

> **BEFORE YOU GO ON**

Answer the following questions to test your understanding of the preceding section:

15. Describe how to distinguish the medial and lateral ends of the clavicle from each other, and how to distinguish its superior and inferior surfaces.

16. Name the three fossae of the scapula and describe the location of each.

17. What three bones meet at the elbow? Identify the fossae, articular surfaces, and processes of this joint and state to which bone each of these features belongs.

18. Name the four carpal bones of the proximal row from lateral to medial, then the four bones of the distal row in the same order.

19. Name the four long bones from the tip of the little finger to the base of the hand.

[55]*trapez* = table, grinding surface
[56]*capit* = head; *ate* = possessing
[57]*ham* = hook; *ate* = possessing
[58]*meta* = beyond; *carp* = wrist

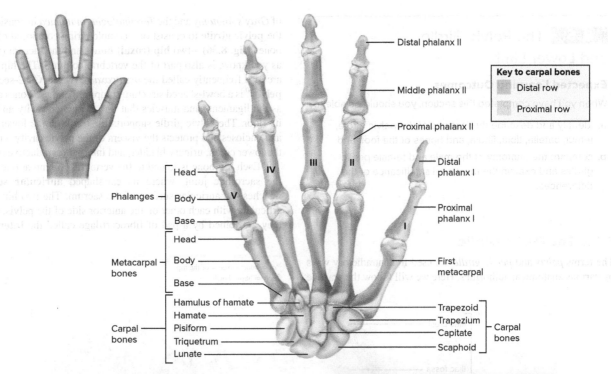

(a) Anterior view

Key to carpal bones
- Distal row
- Proximal row

Distal phalanx II

Middle phalanx II

Proximal phalanx II

Distal phalanx I

Proximal phalanx I

First metacarpal

Trapezoid
Trapezium
Capitate
Scaphoid

Carpal bones

Phalanges
- Head
- Body
- Base

Metacarpal bones
- Head
- Body
- Base

Carpal bones
- Hamulus of hamate
- Hamate
- Pisiform
- Triquetrum
- Lunate

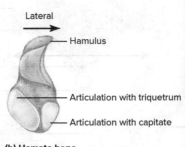

Lateral

Hamulus

Articulation with triquetrum

Articulation with capitate

(b) Hamate bone

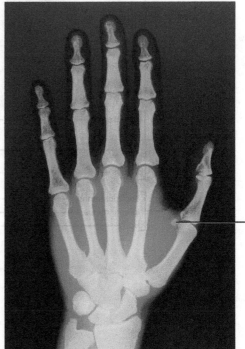

Sesamoid bone

(c) X-ray of adult hand

FIGURE 8.35 The Right Hand. (a) Carpal bones color-coded to distinguish the proximal and distal rows. (b) The right hamate bone, viewed from the palmar side to show its distinctive hook. This unique bone is a useful landmark for locating the others when studying the skeleton. (c) X-ray of an adult hand. Identify the unlabeled bones in the X-ray by comparing it with the drawing in part (a). A small sesamoid bone is visible at the base of the thumb. The pisiform bone in part (a) is also a sesamoid bone. **APR**

❓ *How does part (c) differ from the X-ray of a child's hand in figure 7.11?*

c: RNHRD NHS Trust/The Image Bank/Getty Images

8.5 The Pelvic Girdle and Lower Limb

Expected Learning Outcomes

When you have completed this section, you should be able to

a. identify and describe the features of the pelvic girdle, femur, patella, tibia, fibula, and bones of the foot; and

b. compare the anatomy of the male and female pelvic girdles and explain the functional significance of the differences.

8.5a The Pelvic Girdle

The terms *pelvis* and *pelvic girdle* are used in contradictory ways by various anatomical authorities. Here we will follow the practice of *Gray's Anatomy* and the *Terminologia Anatomica* in considering the **pelvic girdle** to consist of a complete ring composed of three bones (**fig. 8.36**)—two **hip (coxal) bones** and the sacrum (which, as you know, is also part of the vertebral column). The hip bones are also frequently called the *ossa coxae*[59] (OS-sa COC-see). The **pelvis**[60] is a bowl-shaped structure composed of these bones as well as the ligaments and muscles that line the pelvic cavity and form its floor. The pelvic girdle supports the trunk on the lower limbs and encloses and protects the viscera of the pelvic cavity—mainly the lower colon, urinary bladder, and internal reproductive organs.

Each hip bone is joined to the vertebral column at one point, the sacroiliac joint, where its ear-shaped **auricular surface** matches the auricular surface of the sacrum. The two hip bones articulate with each other on the anterior side of the pelvis, where they are joined by a pad of fibrocartilage called the **interpubic**

[59]*os* = bone; *coxae* = of the hip
[60]*pelv* = basin, bowl

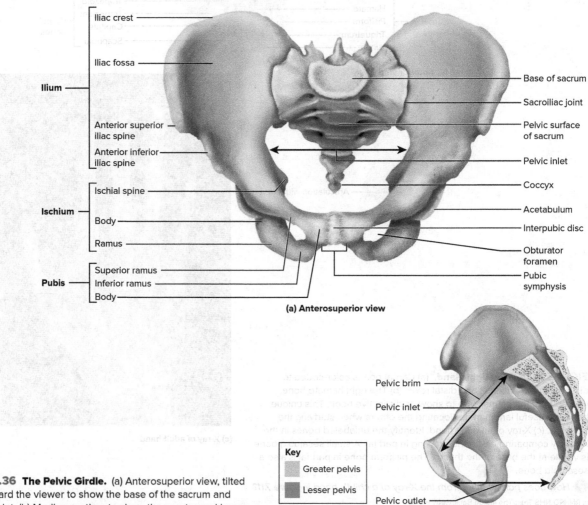

(a) Anterosuperior view

Key
Greater pelvis
Lesser pelvis

Pelvic brim
Pelvic inlet
Pelvic outlet

(b) Median section

FIGURE 8.36 The Pelvic Girdle. (a) Anterosuperior view, tilted slightly toward the viewer to show the base of the sacrum and the pelvic inlet. (b) Median section, to show the greater and lesser pelvis and the pelvic inlet and outlet. **APR**

disc. The disc and the adjacent region of each pubic bone constitute the **pubic symphysis,**[61] which can be palpated as a hard prominence immediately above the genitalia.

The pelvis is divided into the broad **greater (false) pelvis** between the flare of the hips and the narrower **lesser (true) pelvis** below. The two are separated by a round margin called the **pelvic brim.** The opening circumscribed by the brim is called the **pelvic inlet**—an entry into the lesser pelvis through which an infant's head passes during birth. The lower margin of the lesser pelvis is called the **pelvic outlet.**

The hip bones have three distinctive features that will serve as landmarks for further description. These are the **iliac**[62] **crest** (superior crest of the hip); **acetabulum**[63] (ASS-eh-TAB-you-lum) (the hip socket—named for its resemblance to vinegar cups used on ancient Roman dining tables); and **obturator**[64] **foramen** (a large round-to-triangular hole below the acetabulum, closed by a ligament called the *obturator membrane* in living persons).

The adult hip bone forms by the fusion of three childhood bones called the *ilium* (ILL-ee-um), *ischium* (ISS-kee-um), and *pubis* (PEW-biss), identified by color in **figure 8.37.** The largest of these is the **ilium,** which extends from the iliac crest to the center of the acetabulum. The iliac crest extends from an anterior point or angle called the **anterior superior iliac spine** to a sharp posterior angle called the **posterior superior iliac spine.** In a lean person, the anterior superior spines form visible anterior protrusions at a point where the front pockets usually open on a pair of pants, and the posterior superior spines are sometimes marked by dimples above the buttocks where connective tissue attached to the spines pulls inward on the skin (see atlas B, fig. B.15). The latter is a genetic trait like cheek dimples.

Below the superior spines are the **anterior** and **posterior inferior iliac spines.** Below the latter is a deep **greater sciatic notch** (sy-AT-ic), named for the thick sciatic nerve that passes through it and continues down the posterior side of the thigh.

The posterolateral surface of the ilium is relatively rough-textured because it serves for attachment of several muscles of the buttocks and thighs. The anteromedial surface, by contrast, is the smooth, slightly concave **iliac fossa,** covered in life by the broad *iliacus muscle.* Medially, the ilium exhibits an auricular surface that matches the one on the sacrum, so that the two bones form the sacroiliac (SI) joint.

(a) Lateral view

(b) Medial view

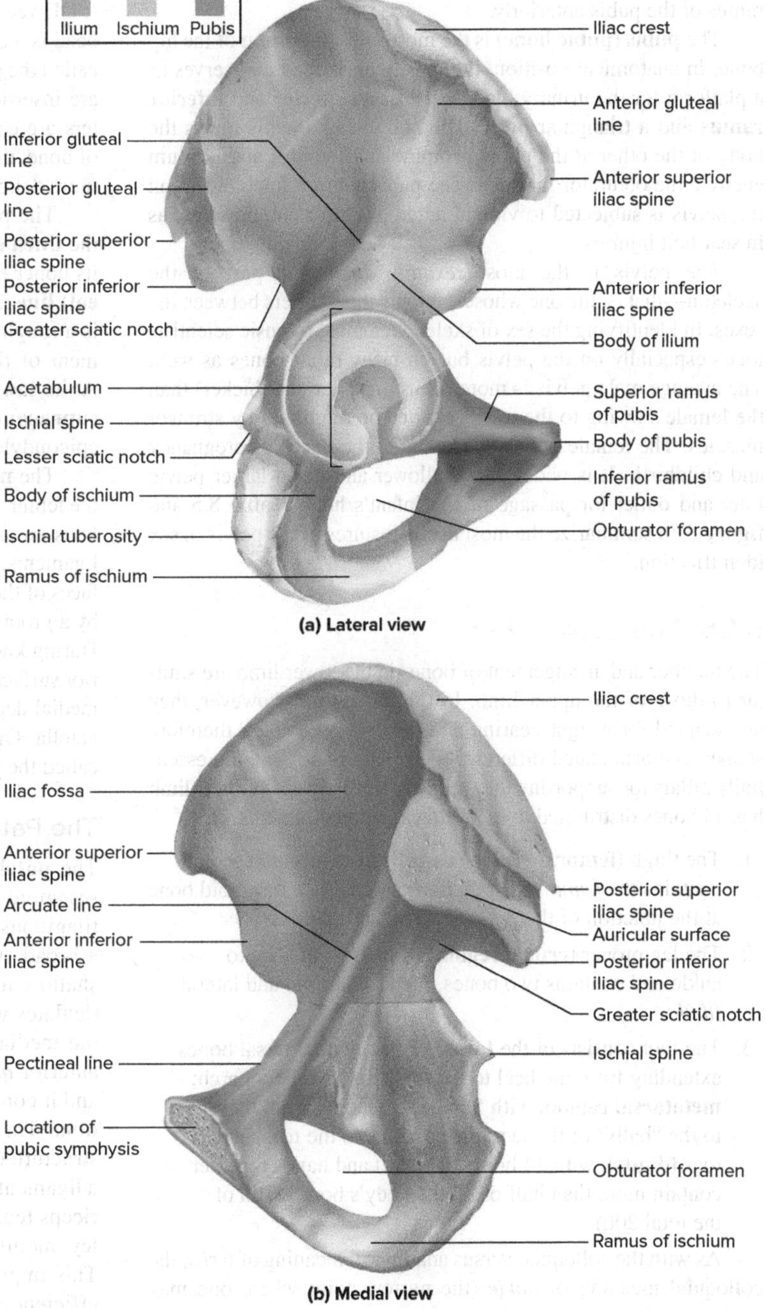

FIGURE 8.37 The Right Hip Bone. (a) Lateral view. (b) Medial view. The three childhood bones that fuse to form the adult hip bone are identified by color according to the key. **APR**

The **ischium** is the inferoposterior portion of the hip bone. Its heavy **body** is marked with a prominent **ischial spine.** Inferior to the spine is a slight indentation, the **lesser sciatic notch,** and then the thick, rough-surfaced **ischial tuberosity,** which supports your body when you are sitting. The tuberosity can be palpated by

[61]*sym* = together; *physis* = growth
[62]*ili* = flank, loin; *ac* = pertaining to
[63]*acetabulum* = vinegar cup
[64]*obtur* = to close, stop up; *ator* = that which

sitting on your fingers. The **ramus** of the ischium joins the inferior ramus of the pubis anteriorly.

The **pubis (pubic bone)** is the most anterior portion of the hip bone. In anatomical position, it is nearly horizontal and serves as a platform for the urinary bladder. It has a **superior** and **inferior ramus** and a triangular **body.** The body of one pubis meets the body of the other at the pubic symphysis. The pubis and ischium encircle the obturator foramen. The pubis is often fractured when the pelvis is subjected to violent anteroposterior compression, as in seat-belt injuries.

The pelvis is the most *sexually dimorphic* part of the skeleton—that is, the one whose anatomy most differs between the sexes. In identifying the sex of skeletal remains, forensic scientists focus especially on the pelvis but on many other bones as well. The average male pelvis is more robust (heavier and thicker) than the female's owing to the forces exerted on the bones by stronger muscles. The female pelvis is adapted to the needs of pregnancy and childbirth. It is wider and shallower and has a larger pelvic inlet and outlet for passage of the infant's head. **Table 8.5** and **figure 8.38** summarize the most useful features of the pelvis in sex identification.

8.5b The Lower Limb

The number and arrangement of bones in the lower limb are similar to those of the upper limb. In the lower limb, however, they are adapted for weight bearing and locomotion and are therefore shaped and articulated differently. The femur and tibia are essentially pillars for supporting the weight of the body. Each lower limb has 30 bones distributed in the following three segments.

1. The thigh (**femoral region**) extends from hip to knee and contains the *femur.* The *patella* (kneecap) is a sesamoid bone at the junction of the femoral and crural regions.

2. The leg proper (**crural region**) extends from knee to ankle and contains two bones, the medial *tibia* and lateral *fibula.*

3. The foot consists of the **tarsal region,** with 7 tarsal bones extending from the heel to the midpoint of the foot arch; **metatarsal region,** with 5 bones extending from there to the "balls" of the feet just proximal to the toes; and toes (**digits**), with 14 bones. The feet and hands together contain more than half of all the body's bones (106 of the total 206).

As with the colloquial versus anatomical meaning of *wrist,* the colloquial meaning of *ankle* (the narrow point where one may wear an ankle bracelet) is different from the anatomical meaning: the posterior half of the foot containing the seven tarsal (ankle) bones. In anatomical terms, the wrist is part of the hand and the ankle is part (indeed, about half) of the foot.

The Femur

The **femur** (FEE-mur) is the longest and strongest bone of the body, measuring about one-quarter of one's height (**fig. 8.39**). It has a hemispherical head that articulates with the acetabulum of the pelvis, forming a quintessential *ball-and-socket joint.* A

ligament extends from the acetabulum to a pit, the **fovea capitis**[65] (FOE-vee-uh CAP-ih-tiss), in the head of the femur. Distal to the head is a constricted **neck** and then two massive, rough processes called the **greater** and **lesser trochanters**[66] (tro-CAN-turs), which are insertions for the powerful muscles of the hip. The trochanters are connected on the posterior side by a thick oblique ridge of bone, the **intertrochanteric crest,** and on the anterior side by a more delicate **intertrochanteric line.**

The primary feature of the shaft is a posterior ridge called the **linea aspera**[67] (LIN-ee-uh ASS-peh-ruh) at its midpoint. At its upper end, the linea aspera forks into a medial **spiral (pectineal) line** and a lateral **gluteal tuberosity.** The gluteal tuberosity is a rough ridge (sometimes a depression) that serves for attachment of the powerful *gluteus maximus* muscle of the buttock. At its lower end, the linea aspera forks into **medial** and **lateral supracondylar lines,** which continue down to the respective epicondyles.

The **medial** and **lateral epicondyles** are the widest points of the femur, easily palpated at the knee. These and the supracondylar lines are attachments for certain thigh and leg muscles and knee ligaments. At the distal end of the femur are two smooth round surfaces of the knee joint, the **medial** and **lateral condyles,** separated by a groove called the **intercondylar fossa** (IN-tur-CON-dih-lur). During knee flexion and extension, the condyles rock on the superior surface of the tibia. On the anterior side of the femur, a smooth medial depression called the **patellar surface** articulates with the patella. On the posterior side is a flat or slightly depressed area called the **popliteal surface.**

The Patella

The **patella,**[68] or kneecap (fig. 8.39), is a roughly triangular sesamoid bone embedded in the tendon of the knee. It is cartilaginous at birth and ossifies at 3 to 6 years of age. It has a broad superior **base,** a pointed inferior **apex,** and a pair of shallow **articular facets** on its posterior surface where it articulates with the femur. The lateral facet is usually larger than the medial. The *quadriceps femoris tendon* extends from the anterior *quadriceps femoris muscle* of the thigh to the patella, and it continues as the *patellar ligament* from the patella to the tibia. This is a change in terminology more than a change in structure or function, as a tendon connects muscle to bone and a ligament connects bone to bone. Because of the way the quadriceps tendon loops over the patella, the patella acts like a pulley, modifying the direction of pull by the quadriceps muscle. This improves its efficiency in extending the knee, hence the efficiency of walking and running.

The Tibia

The leg has two bones: a thick strong tibia (TIB-ee-uh) on the medial side and a slender fibula (FIB-you-luh) on the lateral side

---

[65]*fovea* = pit; *capitis* = of the head
[66]*trochanter* = to run
[67]*linea* = line; *asper* = rough
[68]*pat* = pan; *ella* = little

TABLE 8.5	Comparison of the Male and Female Pelvic Girdles	
Feature	**Male**	**Female**
General appearance	More massive; rougher; heavier processes	Less massive; smoother; more delicate processes
Tilt	Upper end of pelvis relatively vertical	Upper end of pelvis tilted forward
Depth of greater pelvis	Deeper; ilium projects farther above sacroiliac joint	Shallower; ilium does not project as far above sacroiliac joint
Width of greater pelvis	Hips less flared; anterior superior spines closer together	Hips more flared; anterior superior spines farther apart
Pelvic inlet	Heart-shaped	Round or oval
Pelvic outlet	Smaller	Larger
Subpubic angle	Narrower, usually 90° or less	Wider, usually 100° or more
Pubic symphysis	Taller	Shorter
Body of pubis	More triangular	More rectangular
Greater sciatic notch	Narrower	Wider
Obturator foramen	Rounder	More oval to triangular
Acetabulum	Larger, faces more laterally	Smaller, faces slightly anteriorly
Sacrum	Narrower and deeper	Wider and shallower
Coccyx	Less movable; more vertical	More movable; tilted posteriorly

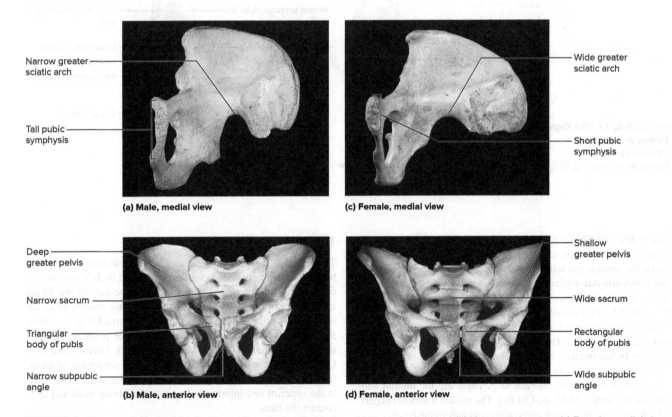

Narrow greater sciatic arch

Tall pubic symphysis

(a) Male, medial view

Wide greater sciatic arch

Short pubic symphysis

(c) Female, medial view

Deep greater pelvis

Narrow sacrum

Triangular body of pubis

Narrow subpubic angle

(b) Male, anterior view

Shallow greater pelvis

Wide sacrum

Rectangular body of pubis

Wide subpubic angle

(d) Female, anterior view

FIGURE 8.38 Comparison of the Male and Female Pelvic Girdles. (a) Male, medial view. (b) Male, anterior view. (c) Female, medial view. (d) Female, anterior view. Compare with table 8.5.

(top, both): David Hunt/specimens from the National Museum of Natural History, Smithsonian Institution; **(bottom, both):** VideoSurgery/Science Source

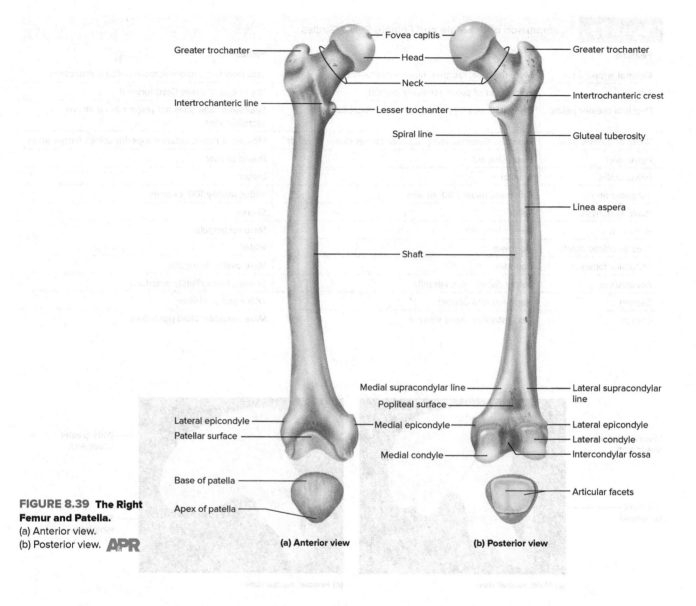

Greater trochanter
Fovea capitis
Head
Neck
Intertrochanteric line
Lesser trochanter
Spiral line
Greater trochanter
Intertrochanteric crest
Gluteal tuberosity
Linea aspera
Shaft
Medial supracondylar line
Popliteal surface
Lateral supracondylar line
Lateral epicondyle
Patellar surface
Medial epicondyle
Lateral epicondyle
Lateral condyle
Intercondylar fossa
Medial condyle
Base of patella
Apex of patella
Articular facets

FIGURE 8.39 The Right Femur and Patella.
(a) Anterior view.
(b) Posterior view. **APR**

(a) Anterior view   **(b) Posterior view**

(fig. 8.40). The **tibia** is the only weight-bearing bone of the crural region. Its broad superior head has two fairly flat articular surfaces, the **medial** and **lateral condyles,** separated by a ridge called the **intercondylar eminence.** The condyles of the tibia articulate with those of the femur. The rough anterior surface of the upper tibia, the **tibial tuberosity,** can be palpated just below the patella. This is an attachment for the powerful thigh muscles that extend (straighten) the knee. Distal to this, the shaft has a sharply angular **anterior border,** which can be palpated in the shin. At the ankle, just above the rim of a standard dress shoe, you can palpate a prominent bony knob on each side. These are the **medial** and **lateral malleoli**[69] (MAL-ee-OH-lie). The medial malleolus is part of the tibia, and the lateral malleolus is the part of the fibula.

The Fibula

The **fibula**[70] (fig. 8.40) is a slender lateral strut that helps to stabilize the ankle. It does not bear any of the body's weight; indeed, orthopedic surgeons sometimes remove part of the fibula and use it to replace damaged or missing bone elsewhere in the body. The fibula is somewhat thicker and broader at its proximal end, the **head,** than at the distal end. The point of the head is called the **apex.** The distal expansion is the lateral malleolus. Like the radius and ulna, the tibia and fibula are joined by an interosseous membrane along their shafts, and by shorter ligaments at the superior and inferior ends where the fibular head and apex contact the tibia.

[69]*malle* = hammer; *olus* = little

[70]*fibula* = little pin or clasp; from a garment pin in ancient Greece and Rome

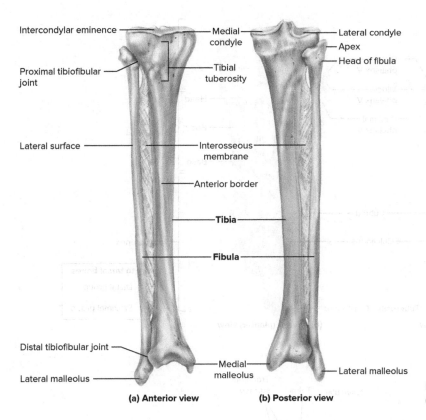

Intercondylar eminence
Proximal tibiofibular joint
Lateral surface
Medial condyle
Tibial tuberosity
Interosseous membrane
Anterior border
Tibia
Fibula
Lateral condyle
Apex
Head of fibula
Distal tibiofibular joint
Lateral malleolus
Medial malleolus
Lateral malleolus

(a) Anterior view   **(b) Posterior view**

FIGURE 8.40 The Right Tibia and Fibula.
(a) Anterior view. (b) Posterior view. **APR**

The Ankle and Foot

The **tarsal bones** of the ankle are arranged in proximal and distal groups somewhat like the carpal bones of the wrist **(fig. 8.41).** Because of the load-bearing role of the ankle, however, their shapes and arrangement are conspicuously different from those of the carpal bones, and they are fully integrated into the structure of the foot. The largest tarsal bone is the **calcaneus**[71] (cal-CAY-nee-us), which forms the heel. Its posterior end is the point of attachment for the **calcaneal (Achilles) tendon** from the calf muscles. The second-largest tarsal bone, and the most superior, is the **talus.** It has three articular surfaces: an inferoposterior one that articulates with the calcaneus, a superior **trochlear surface** that articulates with the tibia, and an anterior surface that articulates with a short, wide tarsal bone called the **navicular.**[72] The talus, calcaneus, and navicular are considered the proximal row of tarsal bones.

The distal group forms a row of four bones. Proceeding from the medial to lateral, these are the **medial, intermediate,** and **lateral cuneiforms**[73] (cue-NEE-ih-forms) and the **cuboid.** The cuboid is the largest.

▶▶▶**APPLY WHAT YOU KNOW**

The upper and lower limbs each contain 30 bones, yet we have 8 carpal bones in the upper limb and only 7 tarsal bones in the lower limb. What makes up the difference in the lower limb?

The remaining bones of the foot are similar in arrangement and name to those of the hand. The proximal **metatarsal**[74] **bones** are similar to the metacarpals. They are **metatarsals I** through **V** from medial to lateral, metatarsal I being proximal to the great toe. Metatarsals I to III articulate with the first through third cuneiforms; metatarsals IV and V both articulate with the cuboid.

Bones of the toes, like those of the fingers, are called phalanges. The great toe contains only two bones, the proximal and distal phalanx I. The other toes each contain a proximal, middle, and distal phalanx, and are numbered II through V from medial to lateral. Thus middle phalanx V, for example, would be the middle bone of the smallest toe. The metatarsal and phalangeal bones each have a base, body, and head, like the bones of the hand. All of them, especially the phalanges, are slightly concave on the inferior (plantar) side.

Note that roman numeral I represents the *medial* group of bones in the foot but the *lateral* group in the hand. In both cases,

---

[71]*calc* = stone, chalk
[72]*navi* = boat; *cul* = little; *ar* = like
[73]*cunei* = wedge; *form* = in the shape of

[74]*meta* = beyond; *tars* = ankle

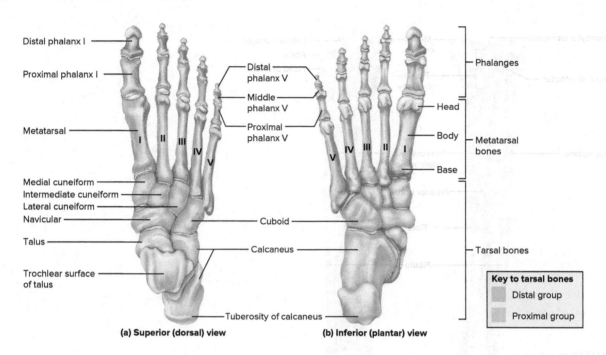

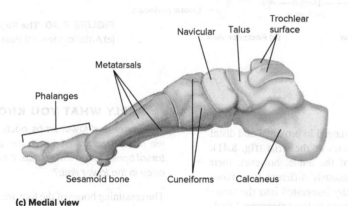

FIGURE 8.41 The Right Foot. (a) Superior (dorsal) view.
(b) Inferior (plantar) view. (c) Medial view. **APR**

❓ *Contrast the tarsal bones with the carpal bones. Which ones
are similar in location? Which ones are different?*

however, it refers to the largest digit of the limb. The reason for the
difference between the hand and foot lies in a rotation of the limbs
that occurs in the seventh week of embryonic development. Early
in the seventh week, the limbs extend anteriorly from the body,
the foot is a paddlelike *foot plate,* and the *hand plate* is also more
or less paddlelike with the finger buds showing early separation
(fig. 8.42a). The future thumb and great toe are both directed superiorly, and the future palms and soles face each other medially.
But then each limb rotates about 90° in opposite directions. The
upper limb rotates laterally. To visualize this, hold your hands
straight out in front of you with the palms facing each other as if

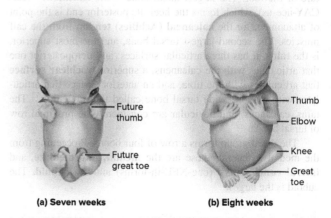

FIGURE 8.42 Embryonic Limb Rotation. (a) Rotation of the
hands and feet in opposite directions in week 7. (b) Resulting
orientation of hands and feet establilshed by week 8.

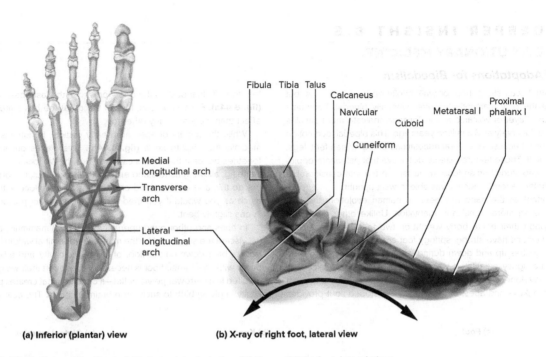

(a) Inferior (plantar) view

(b) X-ray of right foot, lateral view

FIGURE 8.43 Arches of the Foot. (a) Inferior (plantar) view. (b) X-ray of right foot, lateral view.

b: stockdevil/123RF

you were about to clap. Then rotate your forearms so the thumbs face away from each other (laterally) and the palms face upward. The lower limbs rotate in the opposite direction, medially, so that the soles face downward and the great toes become medial. So even though the thumb and great toe (digit I of the hand and foot) start out facing in the same direction, these opposite rotations result in their being on opposite sides of the hand and foot **(fig. 8.42b).** This rotation also explains why the elbow flexes posteriorly and the knee flexes anteriorly, and why (as you will see in chapter 10) the muscles that flex the elbow are on the anterior side of the arm, whereas those that flex the knee are on the posterior side of the thigh.

The foot normally doesn't rest flat on the ground, but has three springy arches that distribute the body's weight between the heel and the heads of the metatarsal bones and absorb the stress of walking **(fig. 8.43).** The **medial longitudinal arch,** which essentially extends from heel to great toe, is formed from the calcaneus, talus, navicular, cuneiforms, and metatarsals I to III. It is normally well above the ground, as evidenced by the shape of a wet footprint. The **lateral longitudinal arch** extends from heel to little toe and includes the calcaneus, cuboid, and metatarsals IV and V. The **transverse arch** includes the cuboid, cuneiforms, and proximal heads of the metatarsal bones. These arches are held together by short, strong ligaments. Excessive weight, repetitive stress, or congenital weakness of these ligaments can stretch them, resulting in *pes planus* (commonly called flat feet or fallen arches). This condition makes a person less tolerant of prolonged standing and walking. A comparison of the flat-footed apes with humans underscores the significance of the human foot arches (see Deeper Insight 8.5).

BEFORE YOU GO ON

Answer the following questions to test your understanding of the preceding section:

20. Name the bones of the adult pelvic girdle. What three bones of a child fuse to form the hip bone of an adult?

21. Name any four structures of the pelvis that you can palpate and describe where to palpate them.

22. Describe several ways in which the male and female pelvic girdles differ.

23. What parts of the femur are involved in the hip joint? What parts are involved in the knee joint?

24. Name the prominent knobs on each side of your ankle. What bones contribute to these structures?

25. Name all the bones that articulate with the talus and describe the location of each.

DEEPER INSIGHT 8.5

EVOLUTIONARY MEDICINE

Skeletal Adaptations for Bipedalism

Some mammals can stand, hop, or walk briefly on their hind legs, but humans are the only mammals that are habitually bipedal. Footprints preserved in a layer of volcanic ash in Tanzania indicate that hominids walked upright as early as 3.6 million years ago. This bipedal locomotion is possible only because of several adaptations of the human feet, legs, spine, and skull. These features are so distinctive that paleoanthropologists (those who study human fossil remains) can tell with considerable certainty whether a fossil species was able to walk upright.

As important as the hand has been to human evolution, the foot may be an even more significant adaptation. Unlike other mammals, humans support their entire body weight on two feet. While apes are flat-footed, humans have strong, springy foot arches that absorb shock as the body jostles up and down during walking and running. The tarsal bones are tightly articulated with one another, and the calcaneus is strongly developed. The great toe is not opposable as it is in most Old World monkeys and apes, but it is highly developed so it provides

the "toe-off" that pushes the body forward in the last phase of the stride **(fig. 8.44a).** For this reason, loss of the great toe has a more crippling effect than the loss of any other toe.

While the femurs of apes are nearly vertical, in humans they angle medially from hip to knee **(fig. 8.44b).** This places our knees closer together, beneath the body's center of gravity. We lock our knees when standing, allowing us to stand erect with little muscular effort. Apes cannot do this and cannot stand on two legs for very long without tiring—much as you would if you tried to maintain an erect posture with your knees slightly bent.

In apes and other quadrupedal (four-legged) mammals, the abdominal viscera are supported by the muscular abdominal wall. In humans, the viscera bear down on the floor of the pelvic cavity, and a bowl-shaped pelvis with an inturned floor is necessary to support their weight. This has resulted in a narrower pelvic outlet—a condition that creates pain and difficulty in giving birth to such large-brained infants. The pain of childbirth

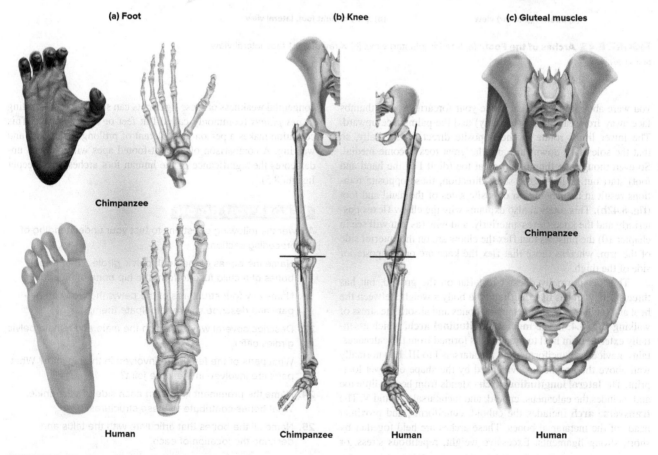

(a) Foot   **(b) Knee**   **(c) Gluteal muscles**

Chimpanzee

Human   Chimpanzee   Human

Chimpanzee

Human

FIGURE 8.44 Skeletal Adaptations for Bipedalism. Human adaptations for bipedalism are best understood by comparison to our close living relative, the chimpanzee, which is not adapted for a comfortable or sustained erect stance. See the text for the relevance of each comparison. (a) Foot. (b) Knee. (c) Gluteal muscles. (d) Pelvis. (e) Vertebral column. (f) Skull.

(figure continues)

seems unique to humans and, one could say, is a price we must pay for having both a large brain and a bipedal stance.

The largest muscle of the buttock, the *gluteus maximus,* serves in apes primarily as an abductor of the thigh—that is, it moves the leg laterally. In humans, however, the ilium has expanded posteriorly, so the gluteus maximus originates behind the hip joint. This changes the function of the muscle—instead of abducting the thigh, it pulls the thigh back in the second half of a stride (pulling back on your right thigh, for example, when your left foot is off the ground and swinging forward). Two other buttock muscles, the *gluteus medius* and *gluteus minimus,* extend laterally in humans from the surface of the ilium to the greater trochanter of the femur **(fig. 8.44c).** In walking, when one foot is lifted from the ground, these muscles shift the body weight over the other foot so we don't fall over. The actions of all three gluteal muscles, and the corresponding evolutionary remodeling of the pelvis, account for the smooth, efficient stride of a human as compared with the awkward, shuffling gait of a chimpanzee or gorilla when walking upright. The posterior growth of the ilium **(fig. 8.44d)** is the reason the greater sciatic notch is so deeply concave.

The lumbar lordosis of the human spine allows for efficient bipedalism by shifting the body's center of gravity to the rear, above and slightly behind the hip joint **(fig. 8.44e).** Because of their C-shaped spines, chimpanzees cannot stand as easily. Their center of gravity is anterior to the hip joint when they stand; they must make a constant muscular effort to keep from falling forward, and they fatigue quickly. Humans, by contrast, require little effort to keep their balance. Our australopithecine ancestors probably could travel all day with relatively little fatigue.

The human head is balanced on the vertebral column with the gaze directed forward. The cervical curvature of the spine and remodeling of the skull have made this possible. The foramen magnum has moved to a more inferior and anterior location, and the face is much flatter than an ape's face **(fig. 8.44f),** so there is less weight anterior to the occipital condyles. Being balanced on the spine, the head doesn't require strong muscular attachments to hold it erect.

The forelimbs of apes are longer than the hindlimbs; indeed, some species such as the orangutan and gibbons hold their long forelimbs over their heads when they walk on their hind legs. By contrast, our forelimbs are shorter than our hindlimbs and far less muscular than the forelimbs of apes. No longer needed for locomotion, our forelimbs have become better adapted for carrying objects, holding things closer to the eyes, and manipulating them more precisely.

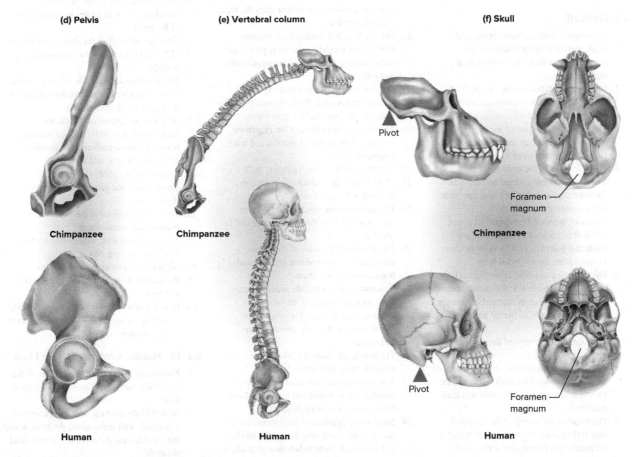

(d) Pelvis **(e) Vertebral column** **(f) Skull**

Chimpanzee Chimpanzee Pivot Foramen magnum Chimpanzee

Human Human Pivot Foramen magnum Human

FIGURE 8.44 Skeletal Adaptations for Bipedalism *(continued).*

STUDY GUIDE

▶ Assess Your Learning Outcomes

To test your knowledge, discuss the following topics with a study partner or in writing, ideally from memory.

8.1 Overview of the Skeleton

1. The difference between the axial and appendicular skeletons, and the bones in each category
2. The typical number of named bones in an adult; why this number differs in newborns and children; and why the number varies among adults
3. Sutural and sesamoid bones, and examples of the latter
4. Names of the various outgrowths, depressions, articular surfaces, cavities, and passages in bones

8.2 The Skull

1. The usual number of bones in the adult skull, and the collective name of the seams or joints that bind most of them together
2. Names and locations of the cavities that enclose the brain, nose, ears, and eyes, and of the paranasal sinuses
3. The collective function of the skull foramina; the location and function of the largest one, the foramen magnum
4. Major features of the cranium; the difference between its base and calvaria; the three cranial fossae and how they relate to brain anatomy
5. Names of the six different cranial bones; which ones are solitary and which are bilaterally paired; and what distinguishes a cranial bone from a facial bone
6. The location and extent of the frontal bone; the suture that binds it to the parietal bones; and the locations of its supraorbital margin and foramen, glabella, frontal sinus, and diploe
7. The location and extent of the parietal bones; the suture formed where they meet the occipital bone and the one that separates the parietal bones from each other; and the locations of the parietal foramen and temporal lines
8. The location and extent of the temporal bones; the suture that borders them; and the names and boundaries of their four major parts

9. The location and extent of the occipital bone, its basilar part, and the names and locations of its foramina, canals, and surface protrusions
10. The location and extent of the sphenoid bone; its wings, body, pterygoid plates, clinoid processes, and foramina; its relationships with the pituitary gland and nasal apertures
11. The location and extent of the ethmoid bone; its part in defining the nasal fossae; and the locations of its plates, foramina, air cells, and nasal conchae
12. Names of the eight different facial bones; which ones are solitary and which are bilaterally paired
13. The location and extent of the maxilla; its foramina, alveoli, and alveolar and palatine processes; and the suture that joins the right and left maxillae
14. The location and extent of the palatine bones; their foramina; and their part in partially defining the walls of the nasal cavity and orbit
15. Structure of the palate, including the hard and soft regions and the contributions of the palatine processes and palatine bones
16. The location and extent of the zygomatic bones, and the temporal process and main foramen of each
17. The three parts of the zygomatic arch
18. The locations and structures of the tiny lacrimal and nasal bones
19. The inferior nasal concha and why it is distinguished from the superior and middle conchae
20. The location and extent of the vomer; contributions of the vomer and ethmoid bone to the nasal septum
21. Structure of the mandible, including the body, ramus, and angle; its two main processes and the notch between them; its foramina, symphysis, protuberance, and spines
22. The bones, and their specific features, that form the temporomandibular joint
23. The locations and names of the auditory ossicles; location and features of the hyoid bone; and functions of these bones
24. Names and locations of the fontanelles of the neonatal skull; why they exist; and how a child's skull changes between birth and 9 years of age

8.3 The Vertebral Column and Thoracic Cage

1. The number of vertebrae and intervertebral discs in the vertebral column (spine)
2. Four curvatures of the adult spine; which ones are present at birth; and when and how the others develop
3. Features of a typical vertebra
4. The five classes of vertebrae and the number of vertebrae in each class; the system of numbering them; and why the number of vertebrae in a child differs from the number at 30 years of age and beyond
5. Features that identify an isolated vertebra as cervical, thoracic, or lumbar
6. How the anatomy of the first two vertebrae (C1–C2) relates to movements of the head
7. How the anatomy of the thoracic vertebrae (T1–T12) relates to the articulations of the ribs
8. The structure and function of intervertebral discs; which vertebrae have discs between them and which ones do not
9. Anatomical features of the sacrum, including its foramina, crests, canal and hiatus, auricular surface and sacroiliac joint, promontory, and alae
10. Features of the coccyx
11. Components and general shape of the thoracic cage
12. Three main regions of the sternum; its notches and sternal angle
13. The number of ribs; which ones are true, false, and floating ribs
14. All features seen in most of the ribs
15. Which ribs differ from that typical anatomy, and how
16. How the ribs articulate with the vertebrae, including variations from the top to bottom of the rib cage

8.4 The Pectoral Girdle and Upper Limb

1. Names and locations of the 4 bones of the pectoral girdle and 30 bones of each upper limb
2. Names of the joints at which the humerus articulates with the scapula, the scapula with the clavicle, and the clavicle with the axial skeleton

STUDY GUIDE

3. Features of the clavicle, including the sternal and acromial ends and conoid tubercle; function of the clavicles
4. Features of the scapula, including its borders and angles, fossae, suprascapular notch, acromion, coracoid process, and glenoid cavity
5. Names of the four regions of the upper limb and the bones contained in each
6. Features of the humerus, including the head, necks, tubercles, intertubercular sulcus, deltoid tuberosity, capitulum, trochlea, epicondyles, supracondylar ridges, and three fossae
7. Features of the radius, including the head, neck, radial tuberosity, styloid process, and ulnar notch
8. Features of the ulna, including the trochlear and radial notches, coronoid and styloid processes, and olecranon; and the relationship of the radius and ulna to the interosseous membrane
9. Names of the carpal bones, in order, from lateral to medial in the proximal row and lateral to medial in the distal row; the unusual structure of the hamate bone
10. The system of naming and numbering the 5 metacarpal bones of the palmar region and 5 sets of phalanges in the digits; why there

are 5 digits but only 14 phalanges; the base, body, and head of all 19 metacarpals and phalanges

8.5 The Pelvic Girdle and Lower Limb

1. Names and locations of the 3 bones of the pelvic girdle and 30 bones of each lower limb
2. Names of the joints at which the lower limb articulates with the pelvic girdle and the pelvic girdle articulates with the axial skeleton
3. The distinction between the pelvic girdle and pelvis
4. Three childhood bones that fuse to form each adult hip (coxal) bone, and the boundaries of each on the hip bone
5. Features of the hip (coxal) bones and pelvic girdle including the auricular surfaces; interpubic disc and pubic symphysis; greater and lesser pelves; pelvic brim, inlet, and outlet; iliac crest; acetabulum; obturator foramen; four ischial spines; two sciatic notches; iliac fossa; and parts of the ischium and pubis
6. Differences between the male and female pelvic girdles and the essential reason for these differences
7. Names of the four regions of the lower limb and the bones contained in each

8. Features of the femur, including the head, neck, fovea capitis, trochanters, intertrochanteric crest, gluteal tuberosity, condyles, intercondylar fossa, epicondyles, lines, and patellar and popliteal surfaces
9. Features of the patella, including the base, apex, and articular facets
10. Features of the tibia, including the lateral and medial condyles and intercondylar eminence; tibial tuberosity; anterior crest; and medial malleolus
11. Features of the fibula, including the head, apex, and lateral malleolus
12. Names of the tarsal bones from posterior to anterior, and from lateral to medial in the distal row; why they are more fully integrated into the foot than the carpal bones are into the hand
13. The system of naming and numbering the 5 metatarsal bones of the foot and 5 sets of phalanges in the digits; why there are 5 digits but only 14 phalanges; the base, body, and head of all 19 metatarsals and phalanges
14. Why the elbows and knees flex in opposite directions, and why the largest digit is lateral in the hand but medial in the foot
15. Names and locations of the three foot arches

▶ Testing Your Recall

Answers in Appendix A

1. Which of these is *not* a paranasal sinus?
   a. frontal
   b. temporal
   c. sphenoidal
   d. ethmoidal
   e. maxillary

2. Which of these is a facial bone?
   a. frontal
   b. ethmoid
   c. occipital
   d. temporal
   e. lacrimal

3. Which of these *cannot* be palpated on a living person?
   a. the crista galli
   b. the mastoid process
   c. the zygomatic arch
   d. the superior nuchal line
   e. the hyoid bone

4. All of the following are groups of vertebrae *except* for _____, which is a spinal kyphosis.
   a. thoracic   d. pelvic
   b. cervical   e. sacral
   c. lumbar

5. Thoracic vertebrae do *not* have
   a. transverse foramina.
   b. costal facets.
   c. spinous processes.
   d. transverse processes.
   e. pedicles.

6. The tubercle of a rib articulates with
   a. the sternal notch.
   b. the margin of the gladiolus.
   c. the costal facets of two vertebrae.
   d. the body of a vertebra.
   e. the transverse process of a vertebra.

7. The disc-shaped head of the radius articulates with the _____ of the humerus.
   a. radial tuberosity
   b. trochlea
   c. capitulum
   d. olecranon
   e. glenoid cavity

8. All of the following are carpal bones, *except* the _____, which is a tarsal bone.
   a. trapezium   d. triquetrum
   b. cuboid   e. pisiform
   c. trapezoid

9. The bone that supports your body weight when you are sitting down is
   a. the acetabulum.
   b. the pubis.
   c. the ilium.
   d. the coccyx.
   e. the ischium.

STUDY GUIDE

10. Which of these is the bone of the heel?
    a. cuboid   d. trochlear
    b. calcaneus   e. talus
    c. navicular

11. Gaps between the cranial bones of an infant are called _____.

12. The external auditory canal is a passage in the _____ bone.

13. Bones of the skull are joined along lines called _____.

14. The _____ bone has greater and lesser wings and protects the pituitary gland.

15. A herniated disc occurs when a ring called the _____ cracks.

16. The transverse ligament of the atlas holds the _____ of the axis in place.

17. The sacroiliac joint is formed where the _____ surface of the sacrum articulates with that of the ilium.

18. The _____ processes of the radius and ulna form bony protuberances on each side of the wrist.

19. Nerves and blood vessels pass through small holes in the skull called _____. The singular form of this word is _____.

20. The _____ arch of the foot extends from the heel to the great toe.

▶ Building Your Medical Vocabulary

Answers in Appendix A

State a meaning of each word element, and give a medical term from this chapter that uses it or a slight variation of it.

1. costo-

2. cranio-

3. dura

4. glosso-

5. -icle

6. masto-

7. pedo-

8. pterygo-

9. supra-

10. tarso-

▶ What's Wrong with These Statements?

Answers in Appendix A

Briefly explain why each of the following statements is false, or reword it to make it true.

1. The internal jugular vein passes out the foramen magnum of the skull and down the neck.

2. The hands have more phalanges than the feet.

3. As an adaptation to pregnancy, the female's pelvis is deeper than the male's.

4. A wristwatch or bracelet normally encircles the area of the carpal (wrist) bones.

5. On a living person, it would be possible to palpate the acromion and spine of the scapula but not the muscles of the infraspinous fossa.

6. If you rest your chin on your hands and your elbows on a table, the coronoid process of the ulna rests on the table.

7. The lumbar vertebrae do not articulate with any ribs and therefore do not have transverse processes.

8. The most frequently broken bone is the humerus.

9. In strict anatomical terminology, the words *arm* and *leg* both refer to regions with only one bone.

10. Sesamoid bones are found along the sutures between cranial bones in some people.

▶ Testing Your Comprehension

1. Most bones form joints with at least two others. For example, there are 12 joints between vertebra T6 and other, adjacent bones. Identify at least 10 of them.

2. By palpating the hind leg of a cat or dog or by examining a laboratory skeleton, you can see that cats and dogs stand on the heads of their metatarsal bones; the calcaneus does not touch the ground. How is this similar to the stance of a woman wearing high-heeled shoes? How is it different?

3. Between any two of the unfused vertebrae (cervical through lumbar), there is an intervertebral disc—except between C1 and C2. Give some reasons for the unique absence of a disc at that location.

4. In adolescents, trauma sometimes separates the head of the femur from the neck. Why do you think this is more common in adolescents than in adults?

5. Discuss all the ways you can in which the differences between vertebrae C5 and L3 exemplify this book's theme of the unity of form and function.

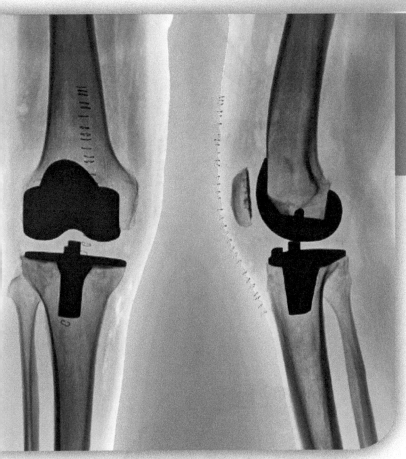

X-ray of knee replacement prosthesis, frontal and lateral views
Zephyr/Getty Images

CHAPTER

9

JOINTS

CHAPTER OUTLINE

DEEPER INSIGHTS

**Anatomy &
Physiology**
Revealed 4.0

Module 5: Skeletal System

BRUSHING UP

- Understanding the anatomy and function of the joints requires familiarity with the names of all the major bones (see table 8.1 and fig. 8.1).

- Understanding joint action also requires knowledge of the surface features of bones, especially at the articular surfaces of the limb bones, described throughout chapter 8 and itemized in general terms in table 8.2.

- Movements of the joints are described with reference to the basic anatomical planes defined in atlas A, figure A.1.

Joints, or articulations, link the bones of the skeletal system into a functional whole—a system that supports the body, permits effective movement, and protects the softer organs. Joints such as the shoulder, elbow, and knee are remarkable specimens of biological design—self-lubricating, almost friction-less, and able to bear heavy loads and withstand compression while executing smooth and precise movements **(fig. 9.1).** Yet it is equally important that other joints be less movable or even immobile. Such joints are better able to support the body and protect delicate organs. The vertebral column, for example, is only moderately mobile, for it must allow for flexibility of the torso and yet protect the delicate spinal cord and support much of the body's weight. Bones of the cranium must protect the brain and sense organs, but need not allow for movement (except during birth); thus, they are locked together by immobile joints, the sutures studied in chapter 8.

In everyday life, we take the greatest notice of the most freely mobile joints of the limbs, and it is here that people feel most severely compromised by such disabling diseases as ar-thritis. Much of the work of physical therapists focuses on limb mobility. In this chapter, we will survey all types of joints, from the utterly immobile to the most mobile, but with an emphasis on the latter. This survey of joint anatomy and movements will provide a foundation for the study of muscle actions in chapter 10.

FIGURE 9.1 Joint Flexibility.

Rubberball/Erik Isakson/Getty Images

9.1   Joints and Their Classification

Expected Learning Outcomes

When you have completed this section, you should be able to

a. explain what joints are, how they are named, and what functions they serve;

b. name and describe the four major categories of joints;

c. describe the three types of fibrous joints and give an example of each;

d. distinguish between the three types of sutures;

e. describe the two types of cartilaginous joints and give an example of each; and

f. explain, with examples, why some joints change categories as a person ages.

Any point where two bones meet is called a **joint (articulation),** whether or not the bones are mobile at that interface. The science of joint structure, function, and dysfunction is called **arthrol-ogy.**[1] The study of musculoskeletal movement is **kinesiology**[2] (kih-NEE-see-OL-oh-jee).

The name of a joint is typically derived from the names of the bones involved. For example, the *atlanto–occipital joint* is where the atlas meets the occipital condyles; the *glenohumeral joint* is where the glenoid cavity of the scapula meets the humerus; and the *radioulnar joint* is where the radius meets the ulna.

Joints can be classified according to the manner in which the adjacent bones are bound to each other, with corresponding differences in how freely the bones can move. Authorities differ in their classification schemes, but one common view places the

---

[1]*arthro* = joint; *logy* = study of
[2]*kinesio* = movement; *logy* = study of

joints in four major categories: *bony, fibrous, cartilaginous,* and *synovial joints*. This section describes the first three of these and the subclasses of each. The remainder of the chapter will then be concerned primarily with synovial joints.

9.1a Bony Joints

A **bony joint,** or **synostosis**[3] (SIN-oss-TOE-sis), is an immobile joint formed when the gap between two bones ossifies and they become, in effect, a single bone. Bony joints can form by ossification of either fibrous or cartilaginous joints. An infant is born with right and left frontal and mandibular bones, for example, but these soon fuse seamlessly into a single frontal bone and mandible. Three childhood bones—the ilium, ischium, and pubis—fuse to form a single hip bone on each side of an adult. The epiphyses and

---

[3]*syn* = together; *ost* = bone; *osis* = condition

diaphyses of the long bones are joined by cartilaginous joints in childhood and adolescence, and these become bony joints in early adulthood. In old age, the first rib often fuses with the sternum and the two parietal bones sometimes fuse along the sagittal suture.

9.1b Fibrous Joints

A **fibrous joint** is also called a **synarthrosis**[4] (SIN-ar-THRO-sis). It is a point at which adjacent bones are bound by collagen fibers that emerge from one bone, cross the space between them, and penetrate into the other **(fig. 9.2).** There are three kinds of fibrous joints: *sutures, gomphoses,* and *syndesmoses.* In sutures and gomphoses, the fibers are very short and allow for little or no movement. In syndesmoses, the fibers are longer and the attached bones are more mobile.

---

[4]*syn* = together; *arthr* = joined; *osis* = condition

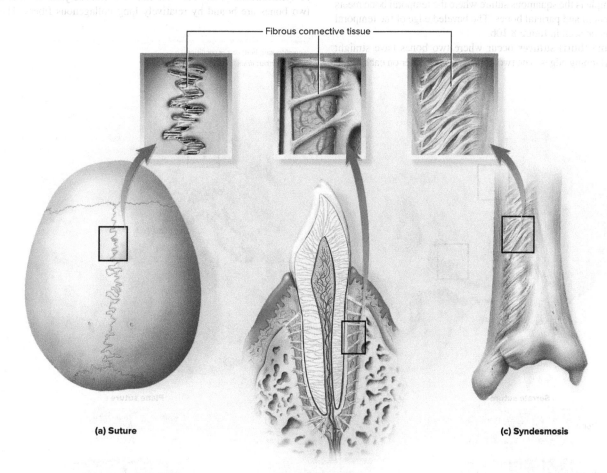

Fibrous connective tissue

(a) Suture

(b) Gomphosis

(c) Syndesmosis

FIGURE 9.2 Fibrous Joints. (a) A suture between the parietal bones. (b) A gomphosis between a tooth and the jaw. (c) A syndesmosis between the tibia and fibula.

❓ *If we narrowly define a joint as an attachment of one bone to another, one of these three would not qualify. Which one and why?*

Sutures

Sutures are immobile or only slightly mobile fibrous joints that closely bind the bones of the skull to each other; they occur nowhere else. In chapter 8, we didn't take much notice of the differences between one suture and another, but some differences may have caught your attention as you studied the diagrams in that chapter or examined laboratory specimens. Sutures can be classified as *serrate, lap,* and *plane sutures*. Readers with some knowledge of woodworking may recognize that the structures and functional properties of these sutures have something in common with basic types of carpentry joints **(fig. 9.3).**

Serrate sutures appear as wavy lines along which the adjoining bones firmly interlock with each other by their serrated margins, like pieces of a jigsaw puzzle. Serrate sutures are analogous to a dovetail wood joint. Examples include the coronal, sagittal, and lambdoid sutures that border the parietal bones.

Lap (squamous) sutures occur where two bones have overlapping beveled edges, like a miter joint in carpentry. On the surface, a lap suture appears as a relatively smooth (nonserrated) line. An example is the squamous suture where the temporal bone meets the sphenoid and parietal bones. The beveled edge of the temporal bone can be seen in figure 8.10b.

Plane (butt) sutures occur where two bones have straight nonoverlapping edges. The two bones merely border on each other,

like two boards glued together in a butt joint. This type of joint is represented by the intermaxillary suture in the roof of the mouth (see fig. 8.5a).

Gomphoses

Even though the teeth are not bones, the attachment of a tooth to its socket is classified as a joint called a **gomphosis** (gom-FOE-sis). The term refers to its similarity to a nail hammered into wood.[5] The tooth is held firmly in place by a fibrous **periodontal ligament,** which consists of collagen fibers that extend from the bone matrix of the jaw into the dental tissue (see fig. 9.2b). The periodontal ligament allows the tooth to move or give a little under the stress of chewing. Along with associated nerve endings, this slight tooth movement allows us to sense how hard we're biting and to sense a particle of food stuck between the teeth.

Syndesmoses

A **syndesmosis**[6] (SIN-dez-MO-sis) is a fibrous joint at which two bones are bound by relatively long collagenous fibers. The

[5]*gomph* = nail, bolt; *osis* = condition
[6]*syn* = together; *desm* = band; *osis* = condition

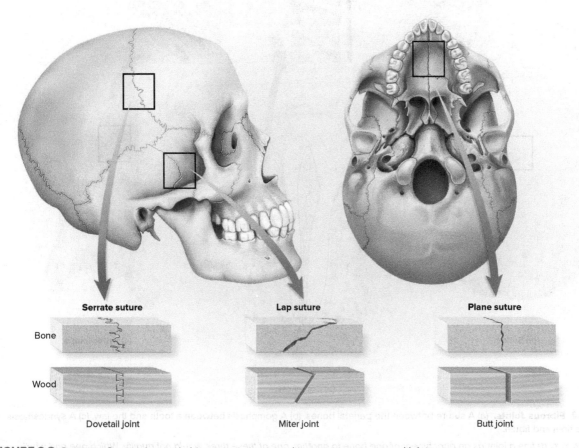

Serrate suture   **Lap suture**   **Plane suture**

Bone

Wood

Dovetail joint   Miter joint   Butt joint

FIGURE 9.3 Sutures. Serrate, lap, and plane sutures compared to some common wood joints.

separation between the bones and length of the fibers give these joints more mobility than a suture or gomphosis has. An especially mobile syndesmosis exists between the shafts of the radius and ulna, which are joined by a broad fibrous *interosseous membrane.* This permits such movements as pronation and supination of the forearm. A less mobile syndesmosis is the one that binds the distal ends of the tibia and fibula together, side by side (see fig. 9.2c).

9.1c Cartilaginous Joints

A **cartilaginous joint** is also called an **amphiarthrosis**[7] (AM-fee-ar-THRO-sis). In these joints, two bones are linked by cartilage **(fig. 9.4).** The two types of cartilaginous joints are *synchondroses* and *symphyses.*

Synchondroses

A **synchondrosis**[8] (SIN-con-DRO-sis) is a joint in which the bones are bound by hyaline cartilage. An example is the temporary joint between the epiphysis and diaphysis of a long bone in a child, formed by the cartilage of the epiphysial plate. Another is the attachment of the first rib to the sternum by a hyaline costal cartilage

---

[7]*amphi* = on all sides; *arthr* = joined; *osis* = condition
[8]*syn* = together; *chondr* = cartilage; *osis* = condition

(fig. 9.4a). (The other costal cartilages are joined to the sternum by synovial joints.)

Symphyses

In a **symphysis**[9] (SIM-fih-sis), two bones are joined by fibrocartilage (fig. 9.4b, c). One example is the pubic symphysis, in which the right and left pubic bones are joined anteriorly by the cartilaginous interpubic disc. Another is the joint between the bodies of two vertebrae, united by an intervertebral disc. The surface of each vertebral body is covered with hyaline cartilage. Between the vertebrae, this cartilage becomes infiltrated with collagen bundles to form fibrocartilage. Each intervertebral disc permits only slight movement between adjacent vertebrae, but the collective effect of all 23 discs gives the spine considerable flexibility.

▶▶▶ APPLY WHAT YOU KNOW

The intervertebral joints are symphyses only in the cervical through the lumbar region. How would you classify the intervertebral joints of the sacrum and coccyx in a middle-aged adult?

---

[9]*sym* = together; *physis* = growth

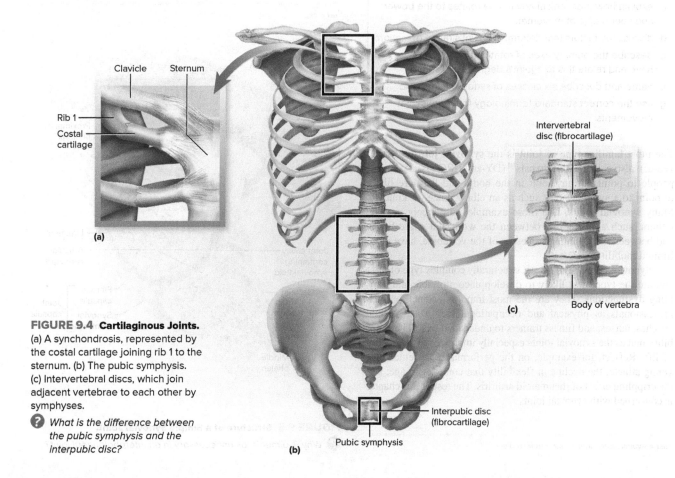

FIGURE 9.4 Cartilaginous Joints.
(a) A synchondrosis, represented by the costal cartilage joining rib 1 to the sternum. (b) The pubic symphysis. (c) Intervertebral discs, which join adjacent vertebrae to each other by symphyses.

❓ *What is the difference between the pubic symphysis and the interpubic disc?*

Clavicle   Sternum
Rib 1
Costal cartilage
(a)
Intervertebral disc (fibrocartilage)
Body of vertebra
(c)
Interpubic disc (fibrocartilage)
Pubic symphysis
(b)

Answer the following questions to test your understanding of the preceding section:

1. What is the difference between arthrology and kinesiology?

2. Distinguish between a synostosis, synarthrosis, and amphiarthrosis.

3. Define *suture*, *gomphosis*, and *syndesmosis,* and explain what these three joints have in common.

4. Name the three types of sutures and describe how they differ.

5. Name two synchondroses and two symphyses.

6. Give some examples of joints that become synostoses with age.

9.2 Synovial Joints

Expected Learning Outcomes

When you have completed this section, you should be able to

a. identify the anatomical components of a typical synovial joint;

b. classify any given joint action as a first-, second-, or third-class lever;

c. explain how mechanical advantage relates to the power and speed of joint movement;

d. discuss the factors that determine a joint's range of motion;

e. describe the primary axes of rotation that a bone can have and relate this to a joint's degrees of freedom;

f. name and describe six classes of synovial joints; and

g. use the correct standard terminology for various joint movements.

The most familiar type of joint is the **synovial joint** (sih-NO-vee-ul), also called a **diarthrosis**[10] (DY-ar-THRO-sis). Ask most people to point out any joint in the body, and they are likely to point to a synovial joint such as an elbow, knee, or knuckle. Many synovial joints, like these examples, are freely mobile. Others, such as the joints between the wrist and ankle bones and between the articular processes of the vertebrae, have more limited mobility.

Synovial joints are the most structurally complex type of joint and are the type most likely to develop uncomfortable and crippling dysfunctions. They are the most important joints for such professionals as physical and occupational therapists, athletic coaches, nurses, and fitness trainers to understand well. Their mobility makes the synovial joints especially important to the quality of life. Reflect, for example, on the performance extremes of a young athlete, the decline in flexibility that comes with age, and the crippling effect of rheumatoid arthritis. The rest of this chapter is concerned with synovial joints.

9.2a General Anatomy

In synovial joints, the facing surfaces of the two bones are covered with **articular cartilage,** a layer of hyaline cartilage up to 2 or 3 mm thick. These surfaces are separated by a narrow space, the **joint (articular) cavity,** containing a slippery lubricant called **synovial fluid (fig. 9.5).** This fluid, for which the joint is named, is rich in albumin and hyaluronic acid, which give it a viscous, slippery texture similar to raw egg white.[11] It nourishes the articular cartilages, removes their wastes, and makes movements at synovial joints almost friction-free. A connective tissue **joint (articular) capsule** encloses the cavity and retains the fluid. It has an outer **fibrous capsule** continuous with the periosteum of the adjoining bones, and an inner, cellular **synovial membrane.** The synovial membrane is composed mainly of fibroblast-like cells that secrete the fluid, and is populated by macrophages that remove debris from the joint cavity. Joint capsules and ligaments are well supplied with *lamellar corpuscles* (see section 16.2b) and other sensory nerve endings that enable the brain to monitor limb positions and joint movements.

In a few synovial joints, fibrocartilage grows inward from the joint capsule and forms a pad between the articulating bones. In the jaw (temporomandibular) joint, at both ends of the clavicle (sternoclavicular and acromioclavicular joints), and between the ulna and carpal bones, the pad crosses the entire joint capsule and

[11]*ovi* = egg

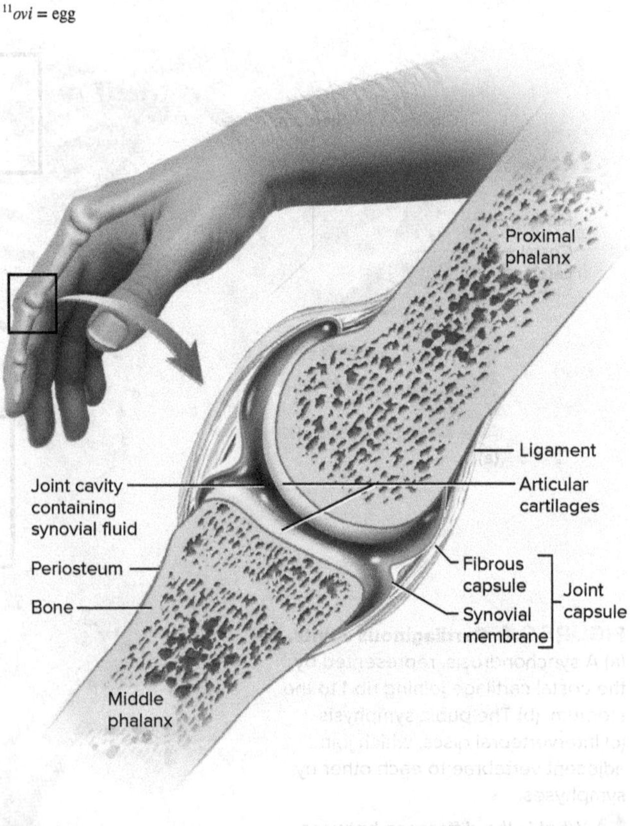

FIGURE 9.5 Structure of a Simple Synovial Joint.

❓ *Why is a meniscus unnecessary in an interphalangeal joint?*

Proximal phalanx

Joint cavity containing synovial fluid

Periosteum

Bone

Ligament

Articular cartilages

Fibrous capsule

Synovial membrane

Joint capsule

Middle phalanx

[10]*dia* = separate, apart; *arthr* = joint; *osis* = condition

is called an **articular disc** (see fig. 9.23c). In the knee, two cartilages extend inward from the left and right but don't entirely cross the joint (see fig. 9.28d). Each is called a **meniscus**[12] because of its crescent-moon shape. These cartilages absorb shock and pressure, guide the bones across each other, improve the fit between the bones, and stabilize the joint, reducing the chance of dislocation.

Accessory structures associated with a synovial joint include tendons, ligaments, and bursae. A **tendon** is a strip or sheet of tough collagenous connective tissue that attaches a muscle to a bone. Tendons are often the most important structures in stabilizing a joint. A **ligament** is a similar tissue that attaches one bone to another. Several ligaments are named and illustrated in our discussion of individual joints later in this chapter, and tendons are more fully considered in chapter 10 along with the gross anatomy of muscles.

A **bursa**[13] is a fibrous sac of synovial fluid located between adjacent muscles, where a tendon passes over a bone, or between bone and skin (see fig. 9.24). Bursae cushion muscles, help tendons slide more easily over the joints, and sometimes enhance the mechanical effect of a muscle by modifying the direction in which its tendon pulls. **Tendon (synovial) sheaths** are elongated cylindrical bursae wrapped around a tendon, seen especially in the hand and foot **(fig. 9.6).** They enable tendons to move back and forth more freely in such tight spaces as the wrist and ankle.

---

[12]*men* = moon, crescent; *isc* = little
[13]*bursa* = purse

DEEPER INSIGHT 9.1

CLINICAL APPLICATION

Exercise and Articular Cartilage

When synovial fluid is warmed by exercise, it becomes thinner (less viscous), like warm oil, and more easily absorbed by the articular cartilage. The cartilage then swells and provides a more effective cushion against compression. For this reason, a warm-up period before vigorous exercise helps protect the articular cartilage from undue wear and tear.

Because cartilage is nonvascular, repetitive compression during exercise is important to its nutrition and waste removal. Each time a cartilage is compressed, fluid and metabolic wastes are squeezed out of it. When weight is taken off the joint, the cartilage absorbs synovial fluid like an expanding sponge, and the fluid carries oxygen and nutrients to the chondrocytes. Without exercise, articular cartilages deteriorate more rapidly from inadequate nutrition, oxygenation, and waste removal.

Weight-bearing exercise builds bone mass and strengthens the muscles that stabilize many of the joints, thus reducing the risk of joint dislocations. Excessive joint stress, however, can hasten the progression of osteoarthritis by damaging the articular cartilage (see Deeper Insight 9.5). Swimming and bicycling are good ways of exercising the joints with minimal damage.

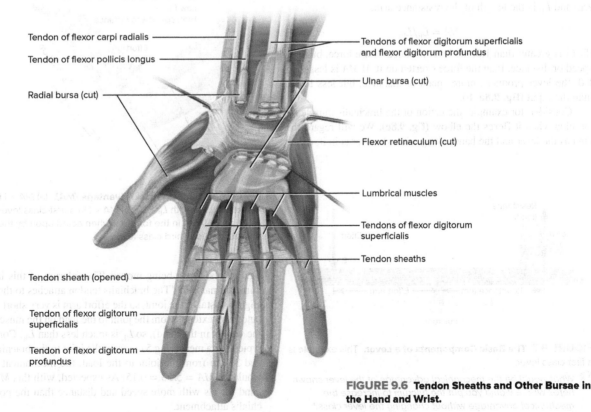

Tendon of flexor carpi radialis

Tendon of flexor pollicis longus

Radial bursa (cut)

Tendons of flexor digitorum superficialis and flexor digitorum profundus

Ulnar bursa (cut)

Flexor retinaculum (cut)

Lumbrical muscles

Tendons of flexor digitorum superficialis

Tendon sheaths

Tendon sheath (opened)

Tendon of flexor digitorum superficialis

Tendon of flexor digitorum profundus

FIGURE 9.6 Tendon Sheaths and Other Bursae in the Hand and Wrist.

9.2b Joints and Lever Systems

Many bones, especially the long bones, act as levers to enhance the speed or power of limb movements. A lever is any elongated, rigid object that rotates around a fixed point called the **fulcrum** **(fig. 9.7)**. Rotation occurs when an effort applied to one point on the lever overcomes a resistance (load) at some other point. The portion of a lever from the fulcrum to the point of effort is called the **effort arm,** and the part from the fulcrum to the point of resistance is called the **resistance arm.** In skeletal anatomy, the fulcrum is a joint; the effort is applied by a muscle; and the resistance can be an object against which the body is working (as in weight lifting), the weight of the limb itself, or the tension in an opposing muscle.

Levers, Speed, and Force

The function of a lever is to produce a gain in the speed, distance, or force of a motion—either to exert more force against a resisting object than the force applied to the lever (for example, in moving a heavy object with a crowbar), or to move the resisting object farther or faster than the effort arm is moved (as in rowing a boat, where the blade of the oar moves much farther and faster than the handle). A single lever cannot confer both advantages. There is a trade-off between force on one hand and speed or distance on the other—as one increases, the other decreases.

The **mechanical advantage (MA)** of a lever is the ratio of its output force to its input force. If L_E is the length of the effort arm and L_R is the length of the resistance arm,

$$MA = L_E/L_R.$$

If MA is greater than 1.0, the lever produces more force, but less speed or distance, than the force exerted on it. If MA is less than 1.0, the lever produces more speed or distance, but less force, than the input **(fig. 9.8a, b)**.

Consider, for example, the action of the brachialis muscle on the ulna when it flexes the elbow **(fig. 9.8c)**. We will regard the ulna as the lever and the hand, along with whatever is in it, as the

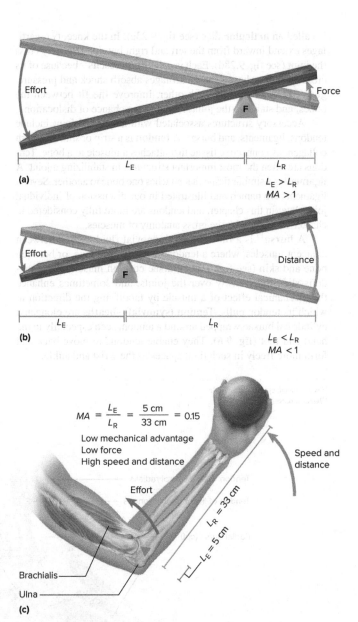

$$MA = \frac{L_E}{L_R} = \frac{5 \text{ cm}}{33 \text{ cm}} = 0.15$$

Low mechanical advantage
Low force
High speed and distance

Speed and distance

Effort

L_R = 33 cm

L_E = 5 cm

Brachialis

Ulna

(c)

FIGURE 9.8 Mechanical Advantage (MA). (a) MA > 1 in a first-class lever with $L_E > L_R$. (b) MA < 1 in a first-class lever with $L_E < L_R$. (c) MA < 1 in the forearm; when acted upon by the brachialis muscle, this is a third-class lever.

load or resistance being moved. The fulcrum of this lever is the humeroulnar joint. The brachialis tendon attaches to the ulna only slightly distal to the joint, so the effort arm is very short. The resistance arm extends from the joint to the load on the muscle (such as the weight in the hand), so L_E is much less than L_R. Considering a typical ulna measuring 5 cm from the joint to the brachialis tendon and 33 cm from the joint to the load, the mechanical advantage would be $MA = 5/33 = 0.15$. As expected, with this MA < 1, the hand travels with more speed and distance than the point of brachialis attachment.

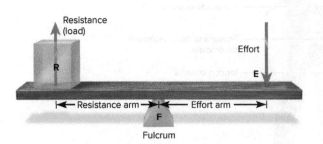

FIGURE 9.7 The Basic Components of a Lever. This example is a first-class lever.

? *What would be the mechanical advantage of the lever shown here? Where would you put the fulcrum to increase the mechanical advantage without changing the lever class?*

In chapter 10, you will often find that two or more muscles act on the same joint, seemingly producing the same effect. This may seem redundant, but it makes sense if the tendinous attachments of the muscles are at different points on a bone and produce different mechanical advantages. A sprinter taking off from the starting line, for example, uses "low-gear" (high-*MA*) muscles that don't generate much speed, but have the power to overcome the inertia of the body. The runner then "shifts into high gear" by using muscles with different attachments that confer a lower mechanical advantage but produce more speed at the feet. This is analogous to the way an automobile transmission uses one gear to get a car moving and other gears to cruise at higher speeds.

Types of Levers

There are three classes of levers that differ with respect to which component is in the middle—the fulcrum (F), effort (E), or resistance (R) **(fig. 9.9).**

1. A **first-class lever** is one with the fulcrum in the middle (EFR), such as a seesaw. An anatomical example is the atlanto–occipital joint of the neck, where the muscles of the back of the neck pull down on the occipital bone of the skull and oppose the tendency of the head to tip forward. Loss of muscle tone here can be embarrassing if you nod off in class. Rocking of the foot on the tibia as the toes are raised and lowered also exemplifies a first-class lever. (It is often misinterpreted as a second-class lever because of a superficial resemblance between standing on tiptoes and the wheelbarrow example that follows.)

2. A **second-class lever** has the resistance in the middle (FRE). Lifting the handles of a wheelbarrow, for example, causes it to pivot on the axle of the wheel at the opposite end and lift a load in the middle. If you sit in a chair and raise one thigh, like bouncing a small child on your knee, the femur pivots on the hip joint (the fulcrum), the quadriceps femoris muscle of the anterior thigh elevates the tibia like the wheelbarrow handles, and the resistance is the weight of the child or the thigh itself.

3. In a **third-class lever,** the effort is applied between the fulcrum and resistance (REF). For example, in paddling a canoe, the relatively stationary grip at the upper end of the paddle is the fulcrum, the effort is applied to the middle of the shaft, and the resistance is produced by the water against the blade. Most musculoskeletal levers are third class. The forearm acts as a third-class lever when you flex your elbow. The fulcrum is the joint between the ulna and humerus, the effort is applied partly by the biceps brachii muscle, and the resistance can be any weight in the hand or the weight of the forearm itself.

The classification of a lever changes as it performs different actions. We use the forearm as a third-class lever when we flex the elbow, as in weight lifting, but we use it as a first-class lever when we extend it, as in hammering nails. The mandible is a second-class lever when we open the mouth and a third-class lever when we close it to bite off a piece of food.

Range of Motion

One aspect of joint performance and physical assessment of a patient is a joint's flexibility, or **range of motion (*ROM*)**—the degrees through which a joint can move. The knee, for example, can flex through an arc of 130° to 140°, the metacarpophalangeal joint of the index finger about 90°, and the ankle about 74°. *ROM* obviously affects a person's functional independence and quality of life. It is also an important consideration in training for athletics or dance, in clinical diagnosis, and in monitoring the progress of rehabilitation. The *ROM* of a joint is normally determined by the following factors:

- **Structure of the articular surfaces of the bones.** In many cases, joint movement is limited by the shapes of the bone surfaces. For example, you cannot straighten your elbow beyond 180° or so because, as it straightens, the olecranon of the ulna swings into the olecranon fossa of the humerus and the fossa prevents it from moving any farther.

- **Strength and tautness of ligaments and joint capsules.** Some bone surfaces impose little if any limitation on joint movement. The articulations of the phalanges are an example; as one can see by examining a dry skeleton, an interphalangeal joint can bend through a broad arc. In the living body, however, these bones are joined by ligaments that limit their movement. As you flex one of your knuckles, ligaments on the anterior (palmar) side of the joint go slack, but ligaments on the posterior (dorsal) side tighten and prevent the joint from flexing beyond 90° or so. The knee is another case in point. In kicking a football, the knee rapidly extends to about 180°, but it can go no farther. Its motion is limited in part by a *cruciate ligament* and other knee ligaments described later. Gymnasts, dancers, and acrobats increase the *ROM* of their synovial joints by gradually stretching their ligaments during training. "Double-jointed" people have unusually large *ROM*s at some joints, not because the joint is actually double or fundamentally different from normal in its anatomy, but because the ligaments are unusually long or slack.

- **Action of the muscles and tendons.** Extension of the knee is also limited by the *hamstring muscles* on the posterior side of the thigh. In many other joints, too, pairs of muscles oppose each other and moderate the speed and range of joint motion. Even a resting muscle maintains a state of tension called *muscle tone,* which serves in many cases to stabilize a joint. One of the major factors preventing dislocation of the shoulder joint, for example, is tension in the *biceps brachii* muscle, whose tendons cross the joint, insert on the scapula, and hold the head of the humerus against the glenoid cavity. The nervous system continually monitors and adjusts joint angles and muscle tone to maintain joint stability and limit unwanted movements.

Axes of Rotation

In solid geometry, we recognize three mutually perpendicular axes, *x, y,* and *z.* In anatomy, these correspond to the transverse, frontal, and sagittal planes of the body. Just as we can describe any point

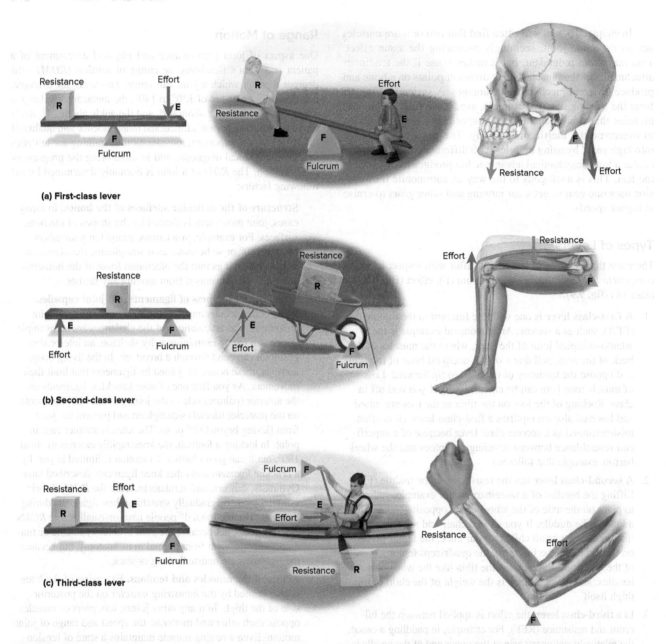

Resistance   Effort

R

E

F

Fulcrum

(a) First-class lever

Resistance

R

E

F

Effort   Fulcrum

(b) Second-class lever

Resistance   Effort

R   E

F

Fulcrum

(c) Third-class lever

FIGURE 9.9 The Three Classes of Levers. Left: The lever classes defined by the relative positions of the resistance (load), fulcrum, and effort. Center: Mechanical examples. Right: Anatomical examples. (a) Muscles of the back of the neck pull down on the occipital bone to oppose the tendency of the head to drop forward. The fulcrum is the occipital condyles. (b) The quadriceps muscle of the anterior thigh elevates the knee. The fulcrum is the hip joint. (c) In flexing the elbow, the biceps brachii muscle exerts an effort on the radius. Resistance is provided by the weight of the forearm or anything held in the hand. The fulcrum is the elbow joint.

in space by its *x*, *y*, and *z* coordinates, we can describe any joint movement by reference to the transverse, frontal, or sagittal anatomical planes.

A moving bone has a relatively stationary **axis of rotation** that passes through the bone in a direction perpendicular to the plane of movement. Think of a door for comparison; it moves horizontally as it opens and closes, and it rotates on hinges that are oriented on the vertical axis. Now consider the shoulder joint **(fig. 9.10)**, where

the convex head of the humerus inserts into the concave glenoid cavity of the scapula. If you raise your arm to one side of your body, the head of the humerus rotates on an axis that passes from anterior to posterior; the arm rises in the frontal plane whereas its axis of rotation is in the sagittal plane. If you lift your arm to point at something straight in front of you, it moves through the sagittal plane whereas its axis of rotation is on the frontal plane, passing through the shoulder from lateral to medial. And if you swing your

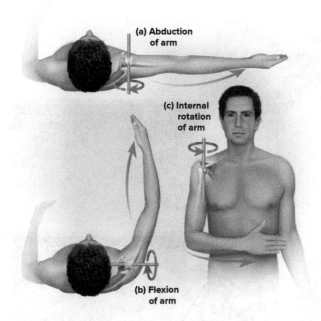

FIGURE 9.10 Axes of Joint Rotation. (a) Abduction of the arm in the frontal plane. (b) Flexion of the arm in the sagittal plane. (c) Internal rotation of the arm. All three axes are represented in movements of the multiaxial ball-and-socket joint of the shoulder.

arm in a horizontal arc, for example to grasp the opposite shoulder, the humeral head rotates in the transverse plane and its axis of rotation passes vertically through the joint.

Because the arm can move in all three anatomical planes, the shoulder joint is said to have three **degrees of freedom,** or to be a **multiaxial** joint. Other joints move through only one or two planes; they have one or two degrees of freedom and are called **monaxial** and **biaxial** joints, respectively. Degrees of freedom are a factor used in classifying the synovial joints.

Classes of Synovial Joints

There are six fundamental types of synovial joints, distinguished by the shapes of their articular surfaces and their degrees of freedom. We will begin by looking at these six types in simple terms, but then see that this is an imperfect classification for reasons discussed at the end. All six types can be found in the upper limb **(fig. 9.11).** They are listed here in descending order of mobility: one multiaxial type (ball-and-socket), three biaxial types (condylar, saddle, and plane), and two monaxial types (hinge and pivot).

1. **Ball-and-socket joints.** These are the shoulder and hip joints—the only multiaxial joints in the body. In both cases, one bone (the humerus or femur) has a smooth hemispherical head that fits into a cuplike socket on the other (the glenoid cavity of the scapula or the acetabulum of the hip bone).

2. **Condylar (ellipsoid) joints.** These joints exhibit an oval convex surface on one bone that fits into a complementary-shaped depression on the other. The radiocarpal joint of the wrist and metacarpophalangeal (MET-uh-CAR-po-fah-LAN-jee-ul)

joints at the bases of the fingers are examples. They are biaxial joints, capable of movement in two planes. To demonstrate this, hold your hand with the palm facing you. Make a fist, and these joints flex in the sagittal plane. Fan your fingers apart, and they move in the frontal plane.

3. **Saddle joints.** Here, both bones have a saddle-shaped surface—concave in one direction (like the front-to-rear curvature of a horse's saddle) and convex in the other (like the left-to-right curvature of a saddle). The clearest example of this is the trapeziometacarpal joint between the trapezium of the wrist and metacarpal I at the base of the thumb. Saddle joints are biaxial. The thumb, for example, moves in a frontal plane when you spread the fingers apart, and in a sagittal plane when you move it as if to grasp a tool such as a hammer. This range of motion gives us and other primates that invaluable anatomical hallmark, the opposable thumb. Another saddle joint is the sternoclavicular joint, where the clavicle articulates with the sternum. The clavicle moves vertically in the frontal plane at this joint when you lift a suitcase, and moves horizontally in the transverse plane when you reach forward to push open a door.

4. **Plane (gliding) joints.** Here the bone surfaces are flat or only slightly concave and convex. The adjacent bones slide over each other and have relatively limited movement. Plane joints are found between the carpal bones of the wrist, the tarsal bones of the ankle, and the articular processes of the vertebrae. Their movements, although slight, are complex. They are usually biaxial. For example, when the head is tilted forward and back, the articular facets of the vertebrae slide anteriorly and posteriorly; when the head is tilted from side to side, the facets slide laterally. Although any one joint moves only slightly, the combined action of the many joints in the wrist, ankle, and vertebral column allows for a significant amount of overall movement.

5. **Hinge joints.** These are essentially monaxial joints, moving freely in one plane with very little movement in any other, like a door hinge. Some examples are the elbow, knee, and interphalangeal (finger and toe) joints. In these cases, one bone has a convex (but not hemispherical) surface, such as the trochlea of the humerus and the condyles of the femur. This fits into a concave depression on the other bone, such as the trochlear notch of the ulna and the condyles of the tibia.

6. **Pivot joints.** These are monaxial joints in which a bone spins on its longitudinal axis like the axle of a bicycle wheel. There are two principal examples: the atlantoaxial joint between the first two vertebrae, and the radioulnar joint at the elbow. At the atlantoaxial joint, the dens of the axis projects into the vertebral foramen of the atlas and is held against the anterior arch of the atlas by the transverse ligament (see fig. 8.25c). As the head rotates left and right, the skull and atlas pivot around the dens. At the radioulnar joint, the anular ligament of the ulna wraps around the neck of the radius. During pronation and supination of the forearm, the disclike radial head pivots like a wheel turning on its axle. The edge of the wheel spins against the radial notch of the ulna like a car tire spinning in snow.

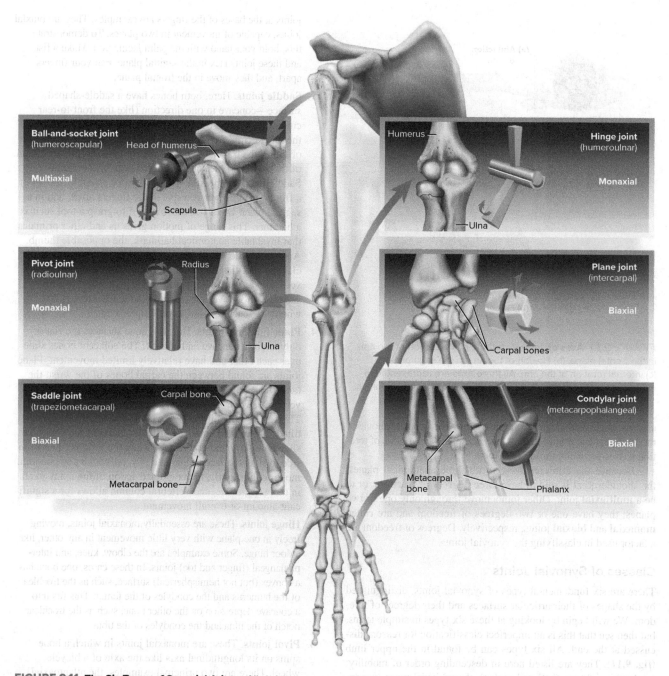

FIGURE 9.11 The Six Types of Synovial Joints. All six have representatives in the forelimb. Mechanical models show the types of motion possible at each joint.

Some joints cannot be easily classified into any one of these six categories. The jaw joint, for example, has some aspects of condylar, hinge, and plane joints. It clearly has an elongated condyle where it meets the temporal bone of the cranium, but it moves in a hingelike fashion when the mandible moves up and down in speaking, biting, and chewing; it glides slightly forward when the jaw juts forward to take a bite; and it glides from side to side to grind food between the molars. To observe the importance of the forward glide, try to open

your mouth while pushing the jaw posteriorly with the heel of your hand; it is difficult to open the mouth more than 1 or 2 cm when there is resistance to protraction of the mandible.

The knee is a classic hinge joint, but has an element of the pivot type; when we lock our knees to stand more effortlessly, the femur pivots slightly on the tibia. The humeroradial joint acts as a hinge joint when the elbow flexes and a pivot joint when the forearm pronates.

9.2c Movements of Synovial Joints

Kinesiology, physical therapy, and other medical and scientific fields have a specific vocabulary for the movements of synovial joints. The following terms form a basis for describing the muscle actions in chapter 10 and may also be indispensable to your advanced coursework or intended career. This section introduces the terms for joint movements, many of which are presented in pairs or groups with opposite or contrasting meanings. This section relies on familiarity with the three cardinal anatomical planes and the directional terms in atlas A, table A.1. All directional terms used here refer to a person in standard anatomical position. When one is standing in anatomical position, each joint is said to be in its **zero position.** Joint movements can be described as deviating from the zero position or returning to it.

Flexion and Extension

Flexion (fig. 9.12) is a movement that decreases a joint angle, usually in the sagittal plane. This is particularly common at hinge joints—for example, bending the elbow so that the arm and forearm go from a 180° angle to 90° or less. It occurs in other types of joints as well. For example, if you hold out your hands with the palms up, flexion of the wrist tips your palms toward you. The meaning of *flexion* is perhaps least obvious in the ball-and-socket joints of the shoulder and hip. At the shoulder, it means to raise your arm as if pointing at something directly in front of you or to continue in that arc and point toward the sky. At the hip, it means to raise the thigh, for example to place your foot on the next higher step when ascending a flight of stairs.

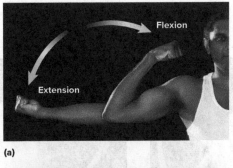

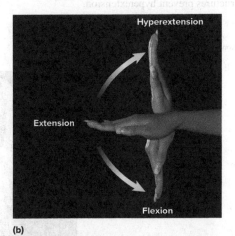

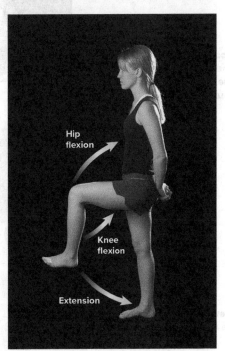

FIGURE 9.12 Flexion and Extension. (a) Flexion and extension of the elbow. (b) Flexion, extension, and hyperextension of the wrist. (c) Flexion and hyperextension of the shoulder. (d) Flexion and extension of the hip and knee.

a–d: Timothy L. Vacula/McGraw-Hill Education

Extension (fig. 9.12) is a movement that straightens a joint and generally returns a body part to the zero position—for example, straightening the elbow, wrist, or knee, or returning the arm or thigh back to zero position. In stair climbing, both the hip and knee extend when lifting the body to the next higher step.

Further extension of a joint beyond the zero position is called **hyperextension.**[14] For example, if you hold your hand in front of you with the palm down, then raise the back of your hand as if you were admiring a new ring, you hyperextend the wrist. Hyperextension of the upper or lower limb means to move the limb to a position behind the frontal plane of the trunk, as if reaching around with your arm to scratch your back. Each backswing of the lower limb when you walk hyperextends the hip.

Flexion and extension occur at nearly all diarthroses, but hyperextension is limited to only a few. At most diarthroses, ligaments or bone structures prevent hyperextension.

Abduction and Adduction

Abduction[15] (ab-DUC-shun) **(fig. 9.13a)** is the movement of a body part in the frontal plane away from the midline of the body—for example, moving the feet apart to stand spread-legged, or raising an arm to one side of the body. **Adduction**[16] **(fig. 9.13b)** is movement in the frontal plane back toward the midline. Some joints can be **hyperadducted,** as when you stand with your ankles crossed, cross your fingers, or hyperadduct the shoulder to stand with your elbows straight and your hands clasped below your waist. You **hyperabduct** the arm if you raise it high enough to cross slightly over the front or back of your head.

Elevation and Depression

Elevation (fig. 9.14a) is a movement that raises a body part vertically in the frontal plane. **Depression (fig. 9.14b)** lowers a

---

[14]*hyper* = excessive, beyond normal

[15]*ab* = away; *duc* = to lead or carry
[16]*ad* = toward; *duc* = to lead or carry

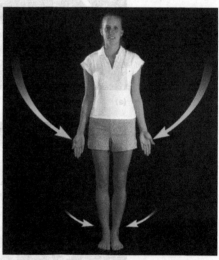

(a) Abduction   (b) Adduction

FIGURE 9.13 Abduction and Adduction.
(a) Abduction of the limbs. (b) Adduction of the limbs, returning them to zero position.
a, b: Timothy L. Vacula/McGraw-Hill Education

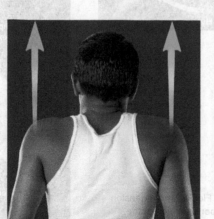

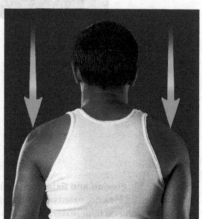

(a) Elevation   (b) Depression

FIGURE 9.14 Elevation and Depression.
(a) Elevation of the shoulders. (b) Depression of the shoulders.
a, b: Timothy L. Vacula/McGraw-Hill Education

(a) Protraction

(b) Retraction

FIGURE 9.15 Protraction and Retraction. (a) Protraction of the shoulder, as in pushing open a door. (b) Retraction of the shoulder.

a, b: Timothy L. Vacula/McGraw-Hill Education

body part in the same plane. For example, to lift a suitcase from the floor, you elevate your scapula; in setting it down again, you depress the scapula. These are also important jaw movements in biting.

Protraction and Retraction

Protraction[17] **(fig. 9.15a)** is the anterior movement of a body part in the transverse (horizontal) plane, and **retraction**[18] **(fig. 9.15b)** is posterior movement. Your shoulder protracts, for example, when you reach in front of you to push a door open. It retracts when you return it to the resting (zero) position or pull the shoulders back to stand at military attention. Such exercises as rowing a boat, bench presses, and push-ups involve repeated protraction and retraction of the shoulders.

Circumduction

In **circumduction**[19] **(fig. 9.16),** one end of an appendage remains fairly stationary while the other end makes a circular motion. If an artist standing at an easel reaches forward and draws a circle on a canvas, she circumducts the upper limb; the shoulder remains stationary while the hand moves in a circle. A baseball player winding up for the pitch circumducts the upper limb in a more extreme "windmill" fashion. One can also circumduct an individual finger, the hand, the thigh, the foot, the trunk, and the head.

---

[17]*pro* = forward; *trac* = to pull or draw
[18]*re* = back; *trac* = to pull or draw
[19]*circum* = around; *duc* = to carry, lead

**FIGURE 9.16
Circumduction.**

Timothy L. Vacula/McGraw-Hill Education

▶▶▶ **APPLY WHAT YOU KNOW**

Choose any example of circumduction and explain why this motion is actually a sequence of flexion, abduction, extension, and adduction.

Rotation

Rotation (fig. 9.17) is a movement in which a bone spins on its longitudinal axis, like the axle of a bicycle wheel. For example, if you stand with bent elbow and move your forearm to grasp your opposite arm, your humerus spins in a motion called **medial (internal) rotation.** If you make the opposite action, so the forearm points away from your trunk, your humerus undergoes **lateral**

(a) Medial (internal) rotation

(b) Lateral (external) rotation

FIGURE 9.17 Medial (Internal) and Lateral (External) Rotation. (a) Medial (internal) rotation of the humerus and femur. (b) Lateral (external) rotation of both.

a, b: Timothy L. Vacula/McGraw-Hill Education

(external) rotation. Good examples of lateral and medial rotation of the humerus are its movements in the forehand and backhand strokes of tennis. The femur can also rotate. If you stand and turn your right foot so your toes point toward your left foot, then turn it so your toes point away from the left foot, your femur undergoes medial and lateral rotation, respectively. Powerful left and right rotation at the waist is important in such actions as baseball pitching and golf. Other examples are given in the coming discussions of forearm and head movements.

Supination and Pronation

Supination and pronation are known primarily as forearm movements, but see also the later discussion of foot movements. **Supination**[20] (SOO-pih-NAY-shun) **(fig. 9.18a)** of the forearm is a movement that turns the palm to face anteriorly or upward; in anatomical position, the forearm is supinated and the radius is parallel to the ulna. **Pronation**[21] **(fig. 9.18b)** is the opposite movement, causing the palm to face posteriorly or downward, and the radius to cross the ulna like an X. During these movements, the concave end of the disc-shaped head of the radius spins on the capitulum of the humerus, and the edge of the disc spins in the radial notch of the ulna. The ulna remains relatively stationary.

As an aid to remembering these terms, think of it this way: You are *prone* to stand in the most comfortable position, which is with the forearm *pronated*. But if you were holding a bowl of *soup* in your palm, you would need to *supinate* the forearm to keep from spilling it.

Chapter 10 describes the muscles that perform these actions (see table 10.10). Of these, the *supinator* is the most powerful. Supination is the type of movement you would usually make with your right hand to turn a doorknob clockwise or to drive a screw into a piece of wood. The threads of screws and bolts are designed with the relative strength of the supinator in mind, so the greatest power can be applied when driving them with a screwdriver in the right hand.

We will now consider a few body regions that combine the foregoing motions, or that have unique movements and terminology.

Special Movements of the Head and Trunk

Flexion of the spine produces forward-bending movements, as in tilting the head forward or bending at the waist in a toe-touching exercise **(fig. 9.19a)**. *Extension* of the vertebral column straightens the trunk or the neck, as in standing up or returning the head to a forward-looking zero position. *Hyperextension* is employed in looking up toward the sky or bending over backward **(fig. 9.19b)**.

Lateral flexion is tilting the head or trunk to the right or left of the midline **(fig. 9.19c)**. Twisting at the waist or turning of the head is called **right rotation** or **left rotation** when the chest or the face turns to the right or left of the forward-facing

zero position **(fig. 9.19d, e)**. Powerful right and left rotation at the waist is important in baseball pitching, golf, discus throwing, and other sports.

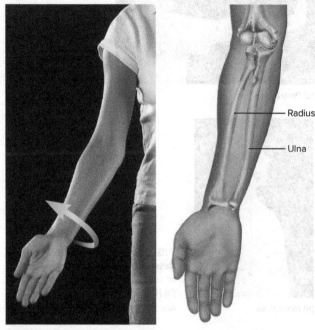

(a) Supination

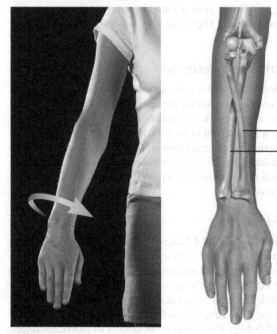

(b) Pronation

FIGURE 9.18 Supination and Pronation of the Forearm.
(a) Supination. (b) Pronation. Note the way these forearm rotations affect the relationship of the radius and ulna. Relative positions of muscles, nerves, and blood vessels are similarly affected.

[20]*supin* = to lay back
[21]*pron* = to bend forward

(a) Flexion

(b) Hyperextension

(c) Lateral flexion

(d) Right rotation

(e) Rotation

FIGURE 9.19 Movements of the Head and Trunk. (a) Anterior flexion of the spine. (b) Hyperextension of the spine. (c) Lateral flexion of the spine. (d) Right rotation at the waist. (e) Right and left rotation of the head.

❓ *In rotation of the head (e), what bone spins on its axis?*

a–e: Timothy L. Vacula/McGraw-Hill Education

Special Movements of the Mandible

Movements of the mandible are concerned especially with biting and chewing. Imagine taking a bite of raw carrot. Most people have some degree of overbite; at rest, the upper incisors (front teeth) overhang the lower ones. For effective biting, however, the chisel-like edges of the incisors must meet. In preparation to bite, we therefore *protract* the mandible to bring the lower incisors forward. After the bite is taken, we *retract* it **(fig. 9.20a, b).** To actually take the bite, we must *depress* the mandible to open the mouth, then *elevate* it so the incisors cut off the piece of food.

Next, to chew the food, we don't simply raise and lower the mandible as if hammering away at the food between the teeth; rather, we exercise a grinding action that shreds the food between the broad, bumpy surfaces of the premolars and molars. This entails a side-to-side movement of the mandible called **lateral excursion** (movement to the left or right of the zero position) and **medial excursion** (movement back to the median, zero position) **(fig. 9.20c, d).**

Special Movements of the Hand and Digits

The hand moves anteriorly and posteriorly by flexion and extension of the wrist. It can also move in the frontal plane. **Ulnar flexion**

tilts the hand toward the little finger, and **radial flexion** tilts it toward the thumb **(fig. 9.21a, b).** We often use such motions when waving hello to someone with a side-to-side wave of the hand, or when washing windows, polishing furniture, or keyboarding.

Movements of the digits are more varied, especially those of the thumb. *Flexion* of the fingers is curling them; *extension* is straightening them. Most people cannot hyperextend their fingers. Spreading the fingers apart is *abduction* **(fig. 9.21c),** and bringing them together again so they touch along their surfaces is *adduction* (as in fig. 9.21a, b).

The thumb is different, however, because in embryonic development it rotates nearly 90° from the rest of the hand. If you hold your hand in a completely relaxed position (but not resting on a table), you will probably see that the plane that contains your thumb and index finger is about 90° to the plane that contains the index through little fingers. Much of the terminology of thumb movement therefore differs from that of the other four fingers. *Flexion* of the thumb is bending the joints so the tip of the thumb is directed toward the palm, and *extension* is straightening it. If you now place the palm of your hand on a tabletop with all five digits parallel and touching, the thumb is extended. Keeping your hand there, if you move your thumb away from the index finger so they

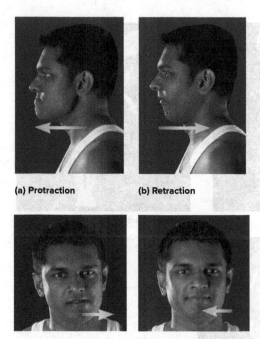

(a) Protraction   (b) Retraction

(c) Lateral excursion   (d) Medial excursion

FIGURE 9.20 Movements of the Mandible. (a) Protraction and (b) retraction. (c) Lateral and (d) medial excursion, as in chewing food.

a–d: Timothy L. Vacula/McGraw-Hill Education

form a 90° angle (but both are on the plane of the table), the thumb movement is called **radial abduction** (as in fig. 9.21c). Another movement, **palmar abduction,** moves the thumb away from the plane of the hand so it points anteriorly, as you would do if you were about to wrap your hand around a tool handle **(fig. 9.21d).** From either position—radial or palmar abduction—*adduction* of the thumb means to bring it back to zero position, touching the base of the index finger.

Two terms are unique to the thumb: **Opposition**[22] means to move the thumb to approach or touch the tip of any of the other four fingers **(fig. 9.21e). Reposition**[23] is the return to zero position.

Special Movements of the Foot

A few additional movement terms are unique to the foot. **Dorsiflexion** is a movement in which the toes are elevated, as you might do to trim your toenails **(fig. 9.22a).** In each step you take, the foot dorsiflexes as it comes forward. This prevents you from scraping your toes on the ground and results in the characteristic *heel strike* of human locomotion when the foot touches down in front of you. **Plantar flexion** is movement of the foot so the toes point downward, as in pressing the gas pedal of a car or standing on tiptoes. This motion also produces the *toe-off* in each step you take, as the heel of the foot behind you lifts off the ground. Plantar flexion can be a very powerful motion, epitomized by high jumpers and the jump shots of basketball players.

[22]*op* = against; *posit* = to place
[23]*re* = back; *posit* = to place

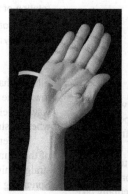   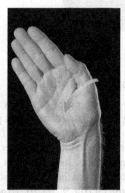   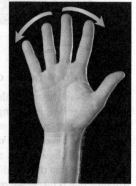

(a) Radial flexion   (b) Ulnar flexion   (c) Abduction of fingers

FIGURE 9.21 Movements of the Hand and Digits. (a) Radial flexion of the wrist. (b) Ulnar flexion of the wrist. (c) Abduction of the fingers. The thumb position in this figure is called *radial abduction*. Parts (a) and (b) show adduction of the fingers. (d) Palmar abduction of the thumb. (e) Opposition of the thumb; reposition is shown in parts (a) and (b).

a–e: Timothy L. Vacula/McGraw-Hill Education

(d) Palmar abduction of thumb   (e) Opposition of thumb

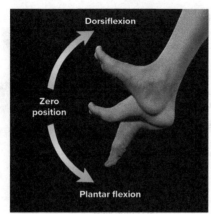

(b) Inversion

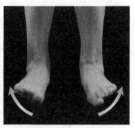

(c) Eversion

(a) Flexion of ankle

FIGURE 9.22 Movements of the Foot. (a) Plantar flexion and dorsiflexion of the ankle. (b) Inversion of the feet. (c) Eversion of the feet.

a–c: Timothy L. Vacula/McGraw-Hill Education

Inversion[24] is a foot movement that tips the soles medially, somewhat facing each other, and **eversion**[25] is a movement that tips the soles laterally, away from each other **(fig. 9.22b, c).** These movements are important in walking on uneven surfaces such as a rocky trail. They are common in fast sports such as tennis and football, and sometimes cause ankle sprains. These terms also refer to congenital deformities of the feet, which are often corrected by orthopedic shoes or braces.

Pronation and *supination,* referring mainly to forearm movements, also apply to the feet but refer here to a more complex combination of movements. Pronation of the foot is a combination of dorsiflexion, eversion, and abduction—that is, the toes are elevated and turned away from the other foot and the sole is tilted away from the other foot. Supination of the foot is a combination of plantar flexion, inversion, and adduction—the toes are lowered and turned toward the other foot and the sole is tilted toward it. These may seem a little difficult to visualize and consciously perform, but they are common motions in walking, running, ballet, and crossing uneven surfaces.

You can perhaps understand why these terms apply to the feet if you place the palms of your hands on a table and pretend they are your soles. Tilt your hands so the inner edge (thumb side) of each is raised from the table. This is like raising the medial edge of your foot from the ground, and as you can see, it involves a slight supination of your forearms. Resting your hands palms down on a table, your forearms are already pronated; but if you raise the outer edges of your hands (the little finger side), like pronating the feet, you will see that it involves a continuation of the pronation movement of the forearm.

> **BEFORE YOU GO ON**

Answer the following questions to test your understanding of the preceding section:

7. Describe the roles of articular cartilage and synovial fluid in joint mobility.

8. Give an anatomical example of each class of levers and explain why each example belongs in that class.

9. Give an example of each of the six classes of synovial joints and state how many axes of rotation each example has.

10. Suppose you reach overhead and screw a lightbulb into a ceiling fixture. Name each joint that would be involved and the joint actions that would occur.

11. Where are the effort, fulcrum, and resistance in the act of dorsiflexion? What class of lever does the foot act as during dorsiflexion? Would you expect it to have a mechanical advantage greater or less than 1.0? Why?

9.3 Anatomy of Selected Diarthroses

Expected Learning Outcomes

When you have completed this section, you should be able to

a. identify the major anatomical features of the jaw, shoulder, elbow, hip, knee, and ankle joints; and

b. explain how the anatomical differences between these joints are related to differences in function.

We now examine the gross anatomy of certain diarthroses. It is beyond the scope of this book to discuss all of them, but the ones selected here most often require medical attention and many of them have a strong bearing on athletic performance and everyday mobility.

9.3a The Jaw Joint

The **temporomandibular (jaw) joint (TMJ)** is the articulation of the condyle of the mandible with the mandibular fossa of the temporal bone **(fig. 9.23).** You can feel its action by pressing your fingertips against the jaw immediately anterior to the ear while opening and closing your mouth.

The synovial cavity of the TMJ is divided into superior and inferior chambers by an articular disc, which permits lateral and

---

[24]*in* = inward; *version* = turning
[25]*e* = outward; *version* = turning

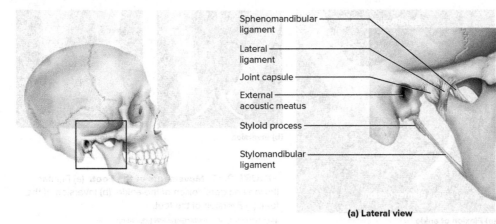

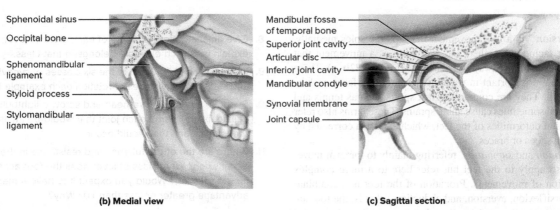

FIGURE 9.23 The Temporomandibular (Jaw) Joint (TMJ). (a) Lateral view. (b) Medial view of bisected skull. (c) Sagittal section of joint. **APR**

medial excursion of the mandible. Two ligaments support the joint. The **lateral ligament** prevents posterior displacement of the mandible. If the jaw receives a hard blow, this ligament normally prevents the condylar process from being driven upward and fracturing the base of the skull. The **sphenomandibular ligament** on

DEEPER INSIGHT 9.2

CLINICAL APPLICATION

TMJ Dysfunction

Temporomandibular joint dysfunction (TMD) afflicts 20% to 30% of the adult population worldwide, and ranks second only to toothache among the most common causes of orofacial pain. It seems to be a cluster of disorders with symptoms that include clicking, popping, or grating noises; restricted jaw movements that may cause problems eating or speaking; and aching pain in the TMJ and associated chewing muscles that intensifies in chewing and yawning. The causes of TMD are so poorly understood that there is no agreement on the best treatment and there are, indeed, more than a dozen different names for it. Pain medication (analgesics) can be helpful. Since TMD is often associated with anxiety, depression, or stress, some patients and physicians report success with behavioral therapies as diverse as meditation, biofeedback, and yoga.

the medial side of the joint extends from the sphenoid bone to the ramus of the mandible. A *stylomandibular ligament* extends from the styloid process to the angle of the mandible but is not part of the TMJ proper.

A deep yawn or other strenuous depression of the mandible can dislocate the TMJ by making the condyle pop out of the fossa and slip forward. The joint is relocated by pressing down on the molars while pushing the jaw posteriorly.

9.3b The Shoulder Joint

The **glenohumeral (humeroscapular) joint,** or shoulder joint, is where the hemispherical head of the humerus articulates with the glenoid cavity of the scapula (**fig. 9.24**). Together, the shoulder and elbow joints serve to position the hand for the performance of a task; without a hand, shoulder and elbow movements are almost useless. The relatively loose shoulder joint capsule and shallow glenoid cavity sacrifice joint stability for freedom of movement (see Deeper Insight 9.3). The cavity, however, has a ring of fibrocartilage called the **glenoid labrum**[26] around its margin, making it somewhat deeper than it looks on a dried skeleton.

---

[26]*glen* = socket; *oid* = resembling; *labrum* = lip

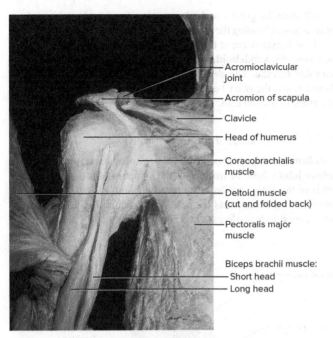

(a) Anterior dissection

Acromioclavicular joint
Acromion of scapula
Clavicle
Head of humerus
Coracobrachialis muscle
Deltoid muscle (cut and folded back)
Pectoralis major muscle
Biceps brachii muscle:
Short head
Long head

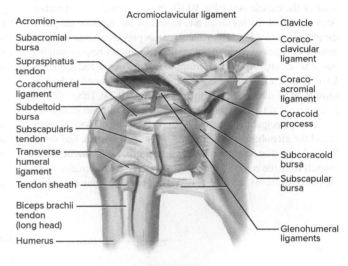

(b) Anterior view

Acromion
Subacromial bursa
Supraspinatus tendon
Coracohumeral ligament
Subdeltoid bursa
Subscapularis tendon
Transverse humeral ligament
Tendon sheath
Biceps brachii tendon (long head)
Humerus

Acromioclavicular ligament
Clavicle
Coraco-clavicular ligament
Coraco-acromial ligament
Coracoid process
Subcoracoid bursa
Subscapular bursa
Glenohumeral ligaments

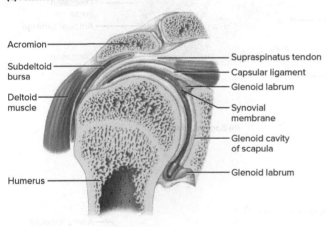

(c) Frontal section

Acromion
Subdeltoid bursa
Deltoid muscle
Humerus

Supraspinatus tendon
Capsular ligament
Glenoid labrum
Synovial membrane
Glenoid cavity of scapula
Glenoid labrum

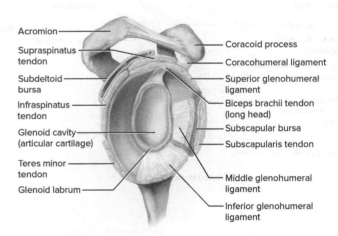

(d) Lateral view, humerus removed

Acromion
Supraspinatus tendon
Subdeltoid bursa
Infraspinatus tendon
Glenoid cavity (articular cartilage)
Teres minor tendon
Glenoid labrum

Coracoid process
Coracohumeral ligament
Superior glenohumeral ligament
Biceps brachii tendon (long head)
Subscapular bursa
Subscapularis tendon
Middle glenohumeral ligament
Inferior glenohumeral ligament

FIGURE 9.24 The Glenohumeral (Shoulder) Joint. (a) Anterior view of dissected cadaver shoulder. (b) Anterior view of shoulder ligaments and bursae. (c) Frontal section, showing joint cavity. (d) Lateral view of the shoulder socket (glenoid cavity of the scapula) with the humerus removed. **APR**

a: Rebecca Gray/McGraw-Hill Education

 DEEPER INSIGHT 9.3

CLINICAL APPLICATION

Shoulder Dislocation

The anatomy and mobility of the shoulder joint make it especially susceptible to dislocation. Over 95% of cases are classified as *anterior dislocation* (displacement of the humeral head in the anterior direction). Such dislocations are usually caused when the arm is abducted and receives a blow from above—for example, by heavy objects falling from a shelf. A complex of nerves and blood vessels traverses the axillary region, and shoulder dislocation can easily damage the axillary nerve or artery (see figs. 13.17 and 20.39). Left untreated, this can lead to muscle atrophy, weakness, or paralysis. Greek physician Hippocrates taught students to treat shoulder dislocation by placing a heel in the patient's axilla and pulling on the arm, but this can cause even worse nerve damage and is never done anymore by professionals. Because the shoulder is so easily dislocated, one also should never attempt to move an unconscious or immobilized person by pulling on his or her arm.

The shoulder is stabilized mainly by the biceps brachii muscle on the anterior side of the arm. One of its tendons arises from the *long head* of the muscle (see table 10.10), passes through the intertubercular groove of the humerus, and inserts on the superior margin of the glenoid cavity. It acts as a taut strap that presses the humeral head against the glenoid cavity. Four additional muscles help to stabilize this joint: the *supraspinatus, infraspinatus, teres minor,* and *subscapularis*. Their tendons form the **rotator cuff,** which is fused to the joint capsule on all sides except the inferior (see fig. 10.24). Table 10.9 and Deeper Insight 10.4 further describe the rotator cuff and its injuries.

Five principal ligaments also support this joint. Three of them, called the **glenohumeral ligaments,** are relatively weak and sometimes absent. The other two are the **coracohumeral ligament,** which extends from the coracoid process of the scapula to the greater tubercle of the humerus, and the **transverse humeral ligament,** which

extends from the greater to the lesser tubercle of the humerus and forms a tunnel housing the tendon from the long head of the biceps.

Four bursae occur at the shoulder. Their names describe their locations: the **subdeltoid, subacromial, subcoracoid,** and **subscapular bursae.** The *deltoid* is the large muscle that caps the shoulder, and the other bursae are named for parts of the scapula described in section 8.4a.

9.3c The Elbow Joint

The elbow is a hinge joint composed of two articulations: the **humeroulnar joint** where the trochlea of the humerus joins the trochlear notch of the ulna, and the **humeroradial joint** where the capitulum of the humerus meets the head of the radius (**fig. 9.25**). Both are enclosed in a single joint capsule. On the posterior side of the

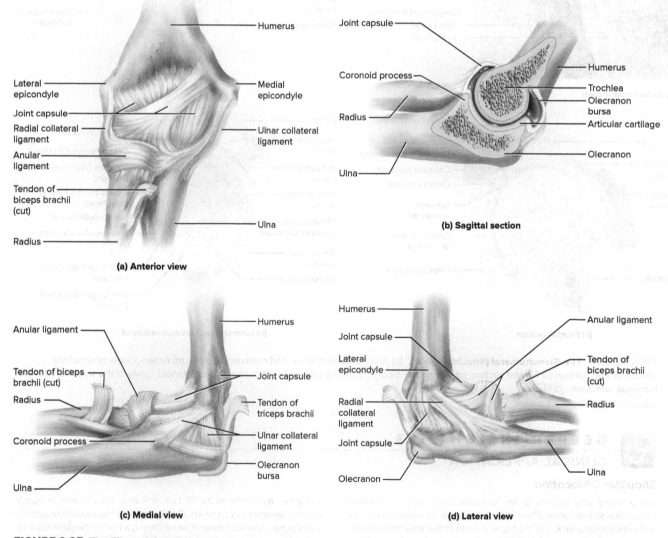

FIGURE 9.25 The Elbow Joint. This region includes two joints that form the elbow hinge—the humeroulnar and humeroradial—and one joint, the radioulnar, not involved in the hinge. (a) Anterior elbow ligaments. (b) Sagittal section, showing joint cavity. (c) Medial elbow ligaments. (d) Lateral elbow ligaments. **APR** A&P

elbow, there is a prominent **olecranon bursa** to ease the movement of tendons over the joint. Side-to-side motions of the elbow joint are restricted by a pair of ligaments: the **radial (lateral) collateral ligament** and **ulnar (medial) collateral ligament.**

Another joint occurs in the elbow region, the **proximal radioulnar joint,** but it is not involved in the hinge. At this joint, the edge of the disclike head of the radius fits into the radial notch of the ulna. It is held in place by the **anular ligament,** which encircles the radial head

and is attached at each end to the ulna. The radial head rotates like a wheel against the ulna as the forearm is pronated or supinated.

9.3d The Hip Joint

The **coxal (hip) joint** is the point where the head of the femur inserts into the acetabulum of the hip bone **(fig. 9.26).** Because the coxal joints bear much of the body's weight, they have deep sockets

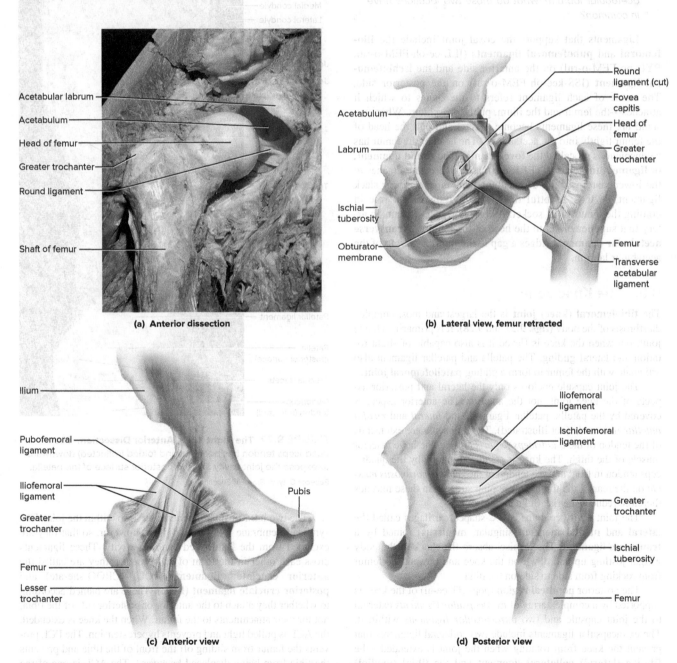

(a) **Anterior dissection**

(b) **Lateral view, femur retracted**

(c) **Anterior view**

(d) **Posterior view**

FIGURE 9.26 The Coxal (Hip) Joint. (a) Anterior view of dissected cadaver hip. (b) Lateral view of hip joint with femur retracted from acetabulum. (c) Anterior hip ligaments. (d) Posterior hip ligaments.

a: Rebecca Gray/McGraw-Hill Education

and are much more stable than the shoulder joint. The depth of the socket is somewhat greater than you see on dried bones because of a horseshoe-shaped ring of fibrocartilage, the **acetabular labrum,** attached to its rim. Dislocations of the hip are therefore rare.

▶▶▶**APPLY WHAT YOU KNOW**

Where else in the body is there a structure similar to the acetabular labrum? What do those two locations have in common?

Ligaments that support the coxal joint include the **ilio-femoral** and **pubofemoral ligaments** (ILL-ee-oh-FEM-o-rul, PYU-bo-FEM-o-rul) on the anterior side and the **ischiofemo-ral ligament** (ISS-kee-oh-FEM-o-rul) on the posterior side. The name of each ligament refers to the bones to which it attaches—the femur and the ilium, pubis, or ischium. When you stand up, these ligaments become twisted and pull the head of the femur tightly into the acetabulum. The head of the femur has a conspicuous pit called the **fovea capitis.** The **round ligament,** or **ligamentum teres**[27] (TERR-eez), arises here and attaches to the lower margin of the acetabulum. This is a relatively slack ligament, so it is doubtful that it plays a significant role in holding the femur in its socket. It does, however, contain an artery that supplies blood to the head of the femur. A **transverse acetabular ligament** bridges a gap in the inferior margin of the acetabular labrum.

9.3e The Knee Joint

The **tibiofemoral (knee) joint** is the largest and most complex diarthrosis of the body **(figs. 9.27** and **9.28).** It is primarily a hinge joint, but when the knee is flexed it is also capable of slight rotation and lateral gliding. The patella and patellar ligament also articulate with the femur to form a gliding **patellofemoral joint.**

The joint capsule encloses only the lateral and posterior aspects of the knee joint, not the anterior. The anterior aspect is covered by the patella, patellar ligament, and *lateral* and *medial patellar retinacula* (not illustrated). The retinacula are extensions of the tendon of the *quadriceps femoris muscle,* the large anterior muscle of the thigh. The knee is stabilized mainly by the quadriceps tendon in front and the tendon of the *semimembranosus muscle* on the rear of the thigh. Developing strength in these muscles therefore reduces the risk of knee injury.

The joint cavity contains two C-shaped cartilages called the **lateral** and **medial menisci** (singular, **meniscus**) joined by a **transverse ligament.** The menisci absorb the shock of the body weight jostling up and down on the knee and prevent the femur from rocking from side to side on the tibia.

The posterior **popliteal region** (pop-LIT-ee-ul) of the knee is supported by a complex array of *extracapsular ligaments* external to the joint capsule and two *intracapsular ligaments* within it. The extracapsular ligaments include two collateral ligaments that prevent the knee from rotating when the joint is extended—the **fibular (lateral) collateral ligament** and the **tibial (medial) collateral ligament**—and other ligaments not illustrated.

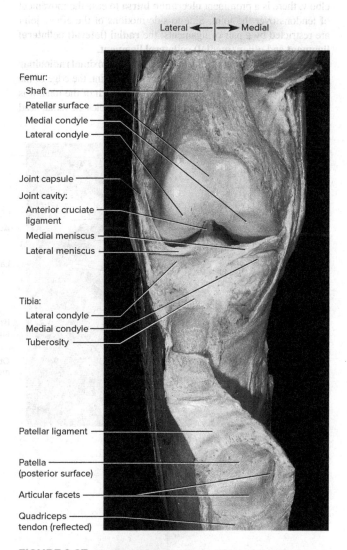

Lateral ◀——|——▶ Medial

Femur:
Shaft
Patellar surface
Medial condyle
Lateral condyle
Joint capsule
Joint cavity:
Anterior cruciate ligament
Medial meniscus
Lateral meniscus
Tibia:
Lateral condyle
Medial condyle
Tuberosity
Patellar ligament
Patella (posterior surface)
Articular facets
Quadriceps tendon (reflected)

FIGURE 9.27 The Right Knee, Anterior Dissection. The quadriceps tendon has been cut and folded (reflected) downward to expose the joint cavity and the posterior surface of the patella.
Rebecca Gray/McGraw-Hill Education

The two intracapsular ligaments lie deep within the joint. The synovial membrane folds around them, however, so that they are excluded from the fluid-filled synovial cavity. These ligaments cross each other in the form of an X; hence, they are called the **anterior cruciate**[28] **ligament (ACL)** (CROO-she-ate) and **posterior cruciate ligament (PCL).** These are named according to whether they attach to the anterior or posterior side of the tibia, not for their attachments to the femur. When the knee is extended, the ACL is pulled tight and prevents hyperextension. The PCL prevents the femur from sliding off the front of the tibia and prevents the tibia from being displaced backward. The ACL is one of the most common sites of knee injury (see Deeper Insight 9.4).

[27]*teres* = round

[28]*cruci* = cross; *ate* = characterized by

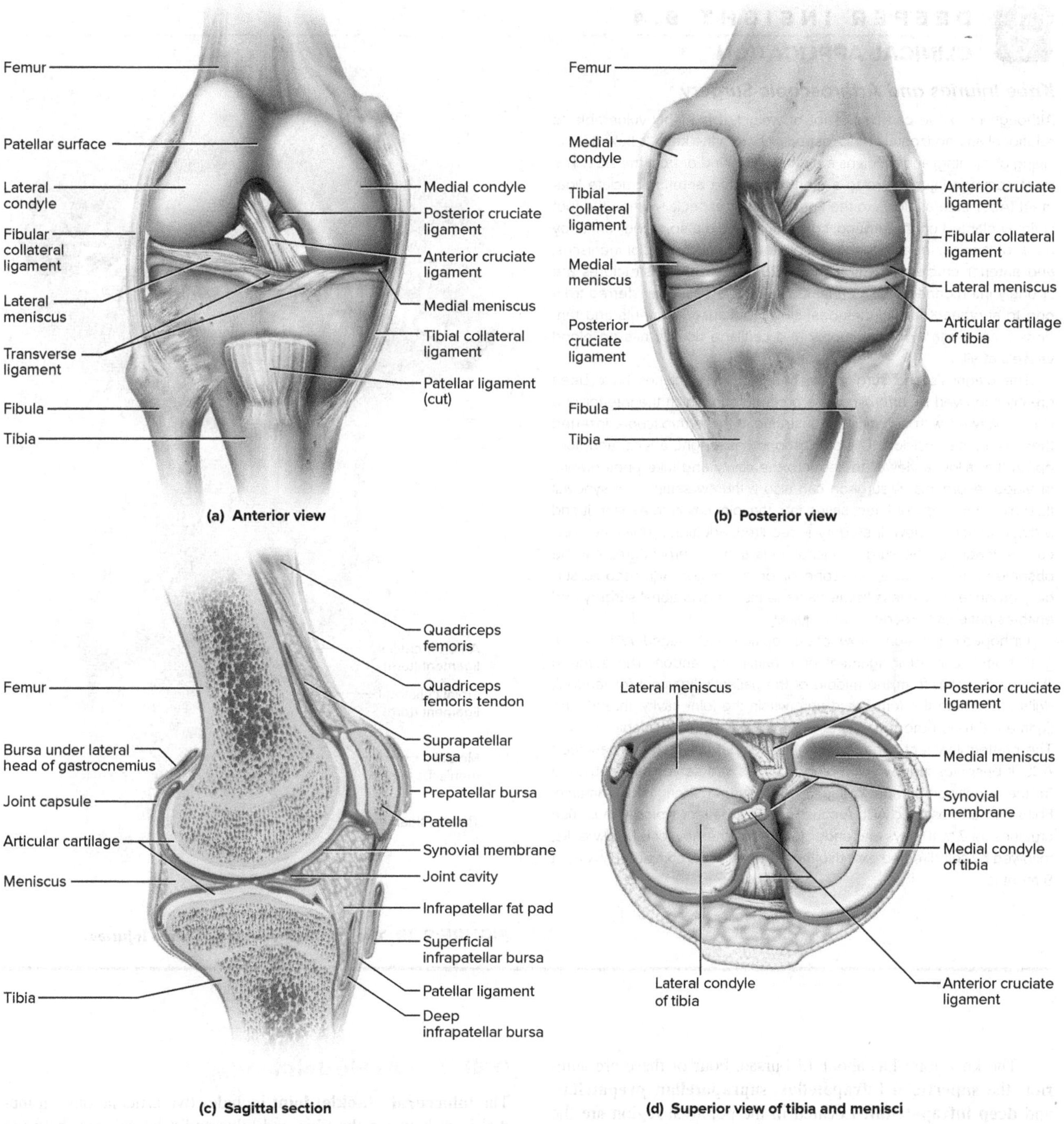

(a) Anterior view

(b) Posterior view

(c) Sagittal section

(d) Superior view of tibia and menisci

FIGURE 9.28 **The Right Tibiofemoral (Knee) Joint.** (a) Anterior view of knee joint with patella removed. (b) Posterior view. (c) Sagittal section of knee showing joint cavity and bursae. (d) Superior view of tibia showing the menisci. **APR**

▶▶▶ **APPLY WHAT YOU KNOW**

What structure in the elbow joint serves the same function as the ACL of the knee?

An important aspect of human bipedalism is the ability to lock the knees and stand erect without tiring the extensor muscles of the leg. When the knee is extended to the fullest degree allowed by the ACL, the femur rotates medially on the tibia. This action locks the knee, and in this state, all the major knee ligaments are twisted and taut. To unlock the knee, the *popliteus* muscle rotates the femur laterally and untwists the ligaments.

DEEPER INSIGHT 9.4

CLINICAL APPLICATION

Knee Injuries and Arthroscopic Surgery

Although the knee can bear a lot of weight, it is highly vulnerable to rotational and horizontal stress, especially when the knee is flexed (as in skiing or running) and receives a blow from behind or from the side. The most common injuries are to a meniscus or the anterior cruciate ligament (ACL). Lateral blows to the knee or body, especially when the foot is firmly planted on the ground, sometimes cause a so-called "unhappy triad" of injuries: tears in the tibial collateral ligament, medial meniscus, and anterior cruciate ligament **(fig. 9.29).** These three structures are strongly interconnected, so an injurious force is easily transferred from one to another. Knee injuries heal slowly because ligaments and tendons have a scanty blood supply and cartilage usually has no blood vessels at all.

The diagnosis and surgical treatment of knee injuries have been greatly improved by *arthroscopy*, a procedure in which the interior of a joint is viewed with a pencil-thin instrument, the *arthroscope*, inserted through a small incision. The arthroscope has a light, a lens, and fiber optics that allow a viewer to see into the cavity and take photographs or video recordings. A surgeon can also withdraw samples of synovial fluid by arthroscopy or inject saline into the joint cavity to expand it and provide a clearer view. If surgery is required, additional small incisions can be made for the surgical instruments and the procedures can be observed through the arthroscope or on a monitor. Arthroscopic surgery produces much less tissue damage than conventional surgery and enables patients to recover more quickly.

Orthopedic surgeons now often replace a damaged ACL with a graft from the patellar ligament or a hamstring tendon. The surgeon "harvests" a strip from the middle of the patient's ligament (or tendon), drills a hole into the femur and tibia within the joint cavity, threads the ligament through the holes, and fastens it with biodegradable screws. The grafted ligament is more taut and "competent" than the damaged ACL. It becomes ingrown with blood vessels and serves as a substrate for the deposition of more collagen, which further strengthens it in time. Following arthroscopic ACL reconstruction, a patient typically must use crutches for 7 to 10 days and undergo physical therapy for 6 to 10 weeks, followed by self-directed exercise therapy. Healing is completed in about 9 months.

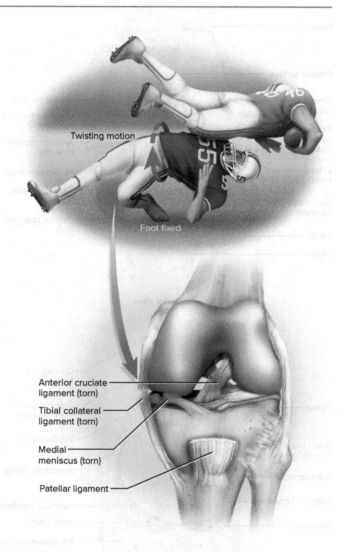

FIGURE 9.29 The "Unhappy Triad" of Knee Injuries.

The knee joint has about 13 bursae. Four of these are anterior: the **superficial infrapatellar, suprapatellar, prepatellar,** and **deep infrapatellar.** Located in the popliteal region are the *popliteal bursa* and *semimembranosus bursa* (not illustrated). At least seven more bursae are found on the lateral and medial sides of the knee joint. From figure 9.28c, your knowledge of the relevant word elements (*infra-, supra-, pre-*), and the terms *superficial* and *deep*, you should be able to work out the reasoning behind most of these names and develop a system for remembering the locations of these bursae.

9.3f The Ankle Joint

The **talocrural**[29] **(ankle) joint** includes two articulations—a medial joint between the tibia and talus and a lateral joint between the fibula and talus, both enclosed in one joint capsule **(fig. 9.30).** The malleoli of the tibia and fibula overhang the talus on each side like a cap and prevent most side-to-side motion. The ankle therefore has a more restricted range of motion than the wrist.

---

[29]*talo* = ankle; *crural* = pertaining to the leg

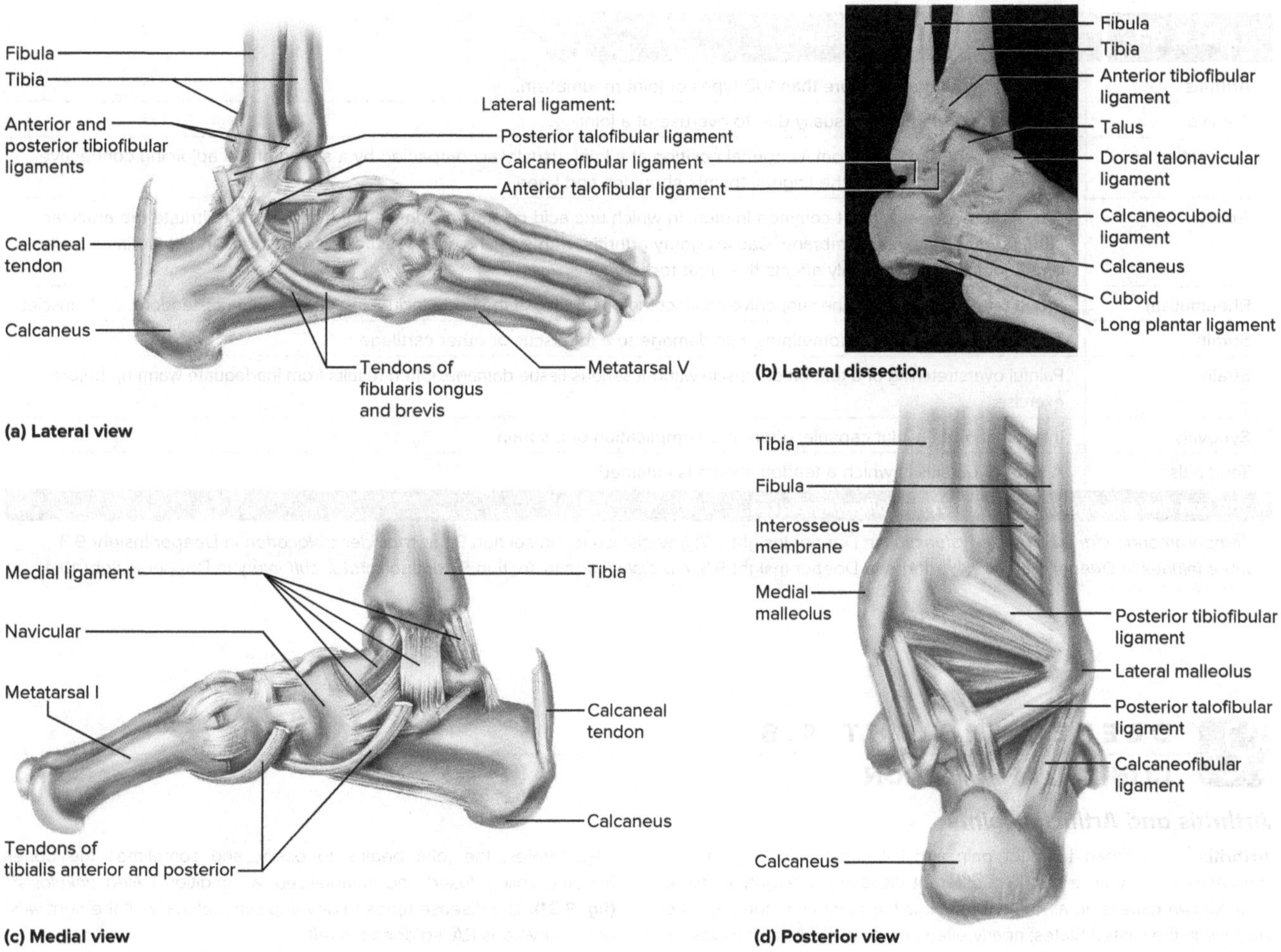

(a) Lateral view

Fibula
Tibia
Anterior and posterior tibiofibular ligaments
Calcaneal tendon
Calcaneus

Lateral ligament:
Posterior talofibular ligament
Calcaneofibular ligament
Anterior talofibular ligament

Tendons of fibularis longus and brevis
Metatarsal V

(b) Lateral dissection

Fibula
Tibia
Anterior tibiofibular ligament
Talus
Dorsal talonavicular ligament
Calcaneocuboid ligament
Calcaneus
Cuboid
Long plantar ligament

(c) Medial view

Medial ligament
Navicular
Metatarsal I
Tendons of tibialis anterior and posterior

Tibia
Calcaneal tendon
Calcaneus

(d) Posterior view

Tibia
Fibula
Interosseous membrane
Medial malleolus
Calcaneus

Posterior tibiofibular ligament
Lateral malleolus
Posterior talofibular ligament
Calcaneofibular ligament

FIGURE 9.30 The Talocrural (Ankle) Joint and Ligaments of the Right Foot. (a) Lateral view. (b) Lateral ligaments in dissected cadaver ankle. (c) Medial view. (d) Posterior view. **APR**

b: Christine Eckel/McGraw-Hill Education

The ligaments of the ankle include (1) **anterior** and **posterior tibiofibular ligaments,** which bind the tibia to the fibula; (2) a multipart **medial (deltoid**[30]**) ligament,** which binds the tibia to the foot on the medial side; and (3) a multipart **lateral (collateral) ligament,** which binds the fibula to the foot on the lateral side. The **calcaneal (Achilles) tendon** extends from the calf muscles to the calcaneus. It plantarflexes the foot and limits dorsiflexion. Plantar flexion is limited by extensor tendons on the anterior side of the ankle and by the anterior part of the joint capsule.

Sprains (torn ligaments and tendons) are common at the ankle, especially when the foot is suddenly inverted or everted to excess. They are painful and usually accompanied by immediate swelling. They are best treated by immobilizing the joint and reducing swelling with an ice pack, but in extreme cases may require a cast or surgery. Sprains and other joint disorders are briefly described in **table 9.1.**

BEFORE YOU GO ON

Answer the following questions to test your understanding of the preceding section:

12. What keeps the mandibular condyle from slipping out of its fossa in a posterior direction?

13. Explain how the biceps brachii tendon braces the shoulder joint.

14. Identify the three joints found at the elbow and name the movements in which each joint is involved.

15. What keeps the femur from slipping backward off the tibia?

16. What keeps the tibia from slipping sideways off the talus?

[30]*delt* = triangular, Greek letter delta (Δ); *oid* = resembling

TABLE 9.1	**Some Common Joint Disorders**
Arthritis	Broad term embracing more than 100 types of joint rheumatism.
Bursitis	Inflammation of a bursa, usually due to overuse of a joint.
Dislocation	Displacement of a bone from its normal position at a joint, usually accompanied by a sprain of the adjoining connective tissues. Most common at the fingers, thumb, shoulder, and knee.
Gout	A hereditary disease, most common in men, in which uric acid crystals accumulate in the joints and irritate the articular cartilage and synovial membrane. Causes gouty arthritis, with swelling, pain, tissue degeneration, and sometimes fusion of the joint. Most commonly affects the great toe.
Rheumatism	Broad term for any pain in the supportive and locomotory organs of the body, including bones, ligaments, tendons, and muscles.
Sprain	Torn ligament or tendon, sometimes with damage to a meniscus or other cartilage.
Strain	Painful overstretching of a tendon or muscle without serious tissue damage. Often results from inadequate warm-up before exercise.
Synovitis	Inflammation of a joint capsule, often as a complication of a sprain.
Tendinitis	A form of bursitis in which a tendon sheath is inflamed.

You can find other joint disorders in the following places:

Temporomandibular joint (TMJ) dysfunction in Deeper Insight 9.2; *jaw dislocation* in section 9.3a; *shoulder dislocation* in Deeper Insight 9.3; *knee injuries* in Deeper Insight 9.4; *arthritis* in Deeper Insight 9.5; *hip dislocation* in section 9.3d; and *rotator cuff injury* in Deeper Insight 10.4.

DEEPER INSIGHT 9.5

CLINICAL APPLICATION

Arthritis and Artificial Joints

Arthritis[31] is a broad term for pain and inflammation of a joint and embraces more than a hundred different diseases of largely obscure or unknown causes. In all of its forms, it is the most common crippling disease in the United States; nearly everyone past middle age develops arthritis to some degree. Physicians who treat arthritis and other joint disorders are called *rheumatologists.*

The most common form of arthritis is *osteoarthritis (OA),* also called "wear-and-tear arthritis" because it is apparently a normal consequence of years of wear on the joints. As joints age, the articular cartilages soften and degenerate. As the cartilage becomes roughened by wear, joint movement may be accompanied by crunching or crackling sounds called *crepitus.* OA affects especially the fingers, intervertebral joints, hips, and knees. As the articular cartilage wears away, exposed bone tissue often develops spurs that grow into the joint cavity, restrict movement, and cause pain. OA rarely occurs before age 40, but it affects about 85% of people older than 70, especially those who are overweight. It usually doesn't cripple, but in severe cases it can immobilize the hip.

Rheumatoid arthritis (RA), which is far more severe than osteoarthritis, results from an autoimmune attack against the joint tissues. It begins when the body produces antibodies to fight an infection. Failing to recognize the body's own tissues, a misguided antibody known as *rheumatoid factor* also attacks the synovial membranes. Inflammatory cells accumulate in the synovial fluid and produce enzymes that degrade the articular cartilage. The synovial membrane thickens and adheres to the articular cartilage, fluid accumulates in the joint capsule, and the capsule is invaded by fibrous connective tissue. As articular cartilage

degenerates, the joint begins to ossify, and sometimes the bones become solidly fused and immobilized, a condition called *ankylosis*[32] **(fig. 9.31).** The disease tends to develop symmetrically—if the right wrist or hip develops RA, so does the left.

Rheumatoid arthritis is named for the fact that symptoms tend to flare up and subside (go into remission) periodically.[33] It affects women far more often than men, and because RA typically begins as early as age 30 to 40, it can cause decades of pain and disability. There is no cure, but joint damage can be slowed with hydrocortisone or other steroids. Because long-term use of steroids weakens the bone, however, aspirin is the treatment of first choice to control the inflammation. Physical therapy is also used to preserve the joint's range of motion and the patient's functional ability.

Arthroplasty,[34] a treatment of last resort, is the replacement of a diseased joint with an artificial device called a *joint prosthesis.*[35] Joint prostheses were first developed to treat injuries in World War II and the Korean War. Total hip replacement (THR), first performed in 1963 by English orthopedic surgeon Sir John Charnley, is now the most common orthopedic procedure for the elderly. The first knee replacements were performed in the 1970s. Joint prostheses are now available for finger, shoulder, and elbow joints, as well as the hip and knee. Arthroplasty is performed on over 250,000 patients per year in the United States, primarily to relieve pain and restore function in elderly people with OA or RA.

---

[31]*arthr* = joint; *itis* = inflammation

[32]*ankyl* = bent, crooked; *osis* = condition
[33]*rheumat* = tending to change
[34]*arthro* = joint; *plasty* = surgical repair
[35]*prosthe* = something added

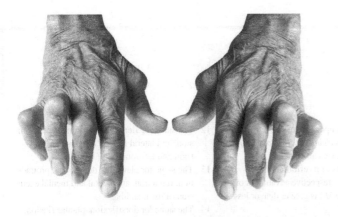

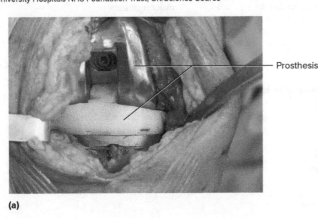

(a)

(b)

FIGURE 9.31 Rheumatoid Arthritis (RA). (a) A severe case with ankylosis of the joints. (b) X-ray of severe RA of the hands.

a: chaowalit407/iStock/Getty Images; b: Clinical Photography, Central Manchester University Hospitals NHS Foundation Trust, UK/Science Source

Arthroplasty presents ongoing challenges for biomedical engineering. An effective prosthesis must be strong, nontoxic, and corrosion-resistant. In addition, it must bond firmly to the patient's bones and enable a normal range of motion with a minimum of friction. The heads of long bones are usually replaced with prostheses made of very hard ceramics such as titanium carbide, cobalt–chromium, or other metal alloys. Joint sockets are made of polyethylene **(fig. 9.32)**. Prostheses are bonded to the patient's bone with screws or bone cement.

Improvements in technology have resulted in long-lasting prostheses. Over 75% of artificial knees last 20 years, nearly 85% last 15 years, and over 90% last 10 years. The most common form of failure is detachment of the prosthesis from the bone. This problem has been reduced by using *porous-coated prostheses,* which become infiltrated by the patient's own bone and create a firmer bond. A prosthesis isn't as strong as a natural joint, however, and is not an option for many young, active patients.

Arthroplasty has been greatly improved by *computer-assisted design and manufacture (CAD/CAM).* A computer scans X-rays from the patient and presents several design possibilities for review. Once a design is selected, the computer generates a program to operate the machinery that produces the prosthesis. CAD/CAM has reduced the waiting period for a prosthesis from 12 weeks to about 2 weeks and has lowered the cost dramatically.

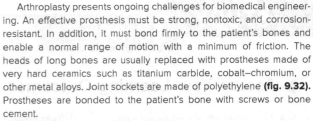

Prosthesis

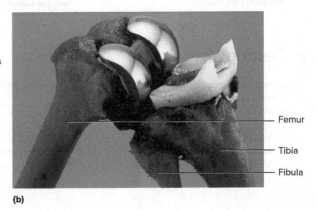

Femur

Tibia

Fibula

(a)

(b)

FIGURE 9.32 Joint Prostheses. (a) Knee replacement surgery. (b) Knee prostheses bonded to natural bone of the femur and tibia. Compare to the X-ray on the opening page of this chapter.

a: Samrith Na Lumpoon/Shutterstock; b: Ron Mensching/Medical Images RM

STUDY GUIDE

▶ Assess Your Learning Outcomes

To test your knowledge, discuss the following topics with a study partner or in writing, ideally from memory.

9.1 Joints and Their Classification

1. The fundamental definition of *joint (articulation)* and why it cannot be defined as a point at which one bone moves relative to an adjacent bone
2. Relationships and differences between the sciences of arthrology, kinesiology, and biomechanics
3. The typical system for naming most joints after the bones they involve; examples of this
4. Basic criteria for classifying joints
5. Characteristics and examples of bony joints (synostoses)
6. Characteristics of fibrous joints (synarthroses) and each of their subclasses, with examples
7. Characteristics of cartilaginous joints (amphiarthroses) and each of their subclasses, with examples

9.2 Synovial Joints

1. The definition and anatomical features of a *synovial joint (diarthrosis)*, examples of this type, and why this type is of greatest interest for kinesiology
2. General anatomy of tendons, ligaments, bursae, and tendon sheaths, and their contributions to joint function

3. Three essential components of a lever
4. The meaning of *mechanical advantage* (MA); how the *MA* of a lever can be determined from measurements of its effort and resistance arms; and the respective advantages of levers in which the *MA* is greater than or less than 1.0
5. Comparison of first-, second-, and third-class levers, and anatomical examples of each
6. Variables that determine a joint's range of motion *(ROM)*, and the clinical relevance of *ROM*
7. Axes of rotation and degrees of freedom in joint movement, and how this relates to the classification of joints as monaxial, biaxial, or multiaxial
8. Six kinds of synovial joints; how each is classified as monaxial, biaxial, or multiaxial; imperfections in this classification; and examples of each type in the body
9. The concept of *zero position* and how it relates to the description of joint function
10. Examples of each of the following limb movements, including an ability to describe or demonstrate them: flexion, extension, hyperextension, abduction, adduction, hyperabduction, hyperadduction, circumduction, medial rotation, and lateral rotation
11. The same for supination, pronation, ulnar flexion, and radial flexion of the forearm and hand, and opposition, reposition, abduction, and adduction of the thumb

12. The same for flexion, extension, hyperextension, and lateral flexion of the spine, and right and left rotation of the trunk
13. The same for elevation, depression, protraction, retraction, and lateral and medial excursion of the mandible
14. The same for dorsiflexion, plantar flexion, inversion, eversion, pronation, and supination of the foot

9.3 Anatomy of Selected Diarthroses

1. Features of the jaw (temporomandibular) joint including the mandibular condyle, mandibular fossa, synovial cavity, articular disc, and principal ligaments
2. Features of the shoulder (glenohumeral) joint including the humeral head, glenoid cavity and labrum, five major ligaments and four bursae, and tendons of the biceps brachii and four rotator cuff muscles
3. Features of the elbow; the three joints that occur here; the olecranon bursa and four major ligaments
4. Features of the hip (coxal) joint including the femoral head, fovea capitis, acetabulum and labrum, and five principal ligaments
5. Features of the knee (tibiofemoral and patellofemoral joints), including the menisci, cruciate and other ligaments, and four major bursae around the patella
6. Features of the ankle (talocrural) joint, including the malleoli, calcaneal tendon, and major ligaments

▶ Testing Your Recall

Answers in Appendix A

1. Internal and external rotation of the humerus is made possible by a _____ joint.
   a. pivot
   b. condylar
   c. ball-and-socket
   d. saddle
   e. hinge

2. Which of the following is the least movable?
   a. a diarthrosis
   b. a synostosis
   c. a symphysis
   d. a synovial joint
   e. a condylar joint

3. Which of the following movements are unique to the foot?
   a. dorsiflexion and inversion
   b. elevation and depression
   c. circumduction and rotation
   d. abduction and adduction
   e. opposition and reposition

STUDY GUIDE

4. Which of the following joints cannot be circumducted?
   a. carpometacarpal
   b. metacarpophalangeal
   c. glenohumeral
   d. coxal
   e. interphalangeal

5. Which of the following terms denotes a general condition that includes the other four?
   a. gout
   b. arthritis
   c. rheumatism
   d. osteoarthritis
   e. rheumatoid arthritis

6. In the adult, the ischium and pubis are united by
   a. a synchondrosis.
   b. a diarthrosis.
   c. a synostosis.
   d. an amphiarthrosis.
   e. a symphysis.

7. In a second-class lever, the effort
   a. is applied to the end opposite the fulcrum.
   b. is applied to the fulcrum itself.
   c. is applied between the fulcrum and resistance.

   d. always produces an *MA* less than 1.0.
   e. is applied on one side of the fulcrum to move a resistance on the other side.

8. Which of the following joints has anterior and posterior cruciate ligaments?
   a. the shoulder
   b. the elbow
   c. the hip
   d. the knee
   e. the ankle

9. To bend backward at the waist involves _____ of the vertebral column.
   a. rotation
   b. hyperextension
   c. dorsiflexion
   d. abduction
   e. flexion

10. The rotator cuff includes the tendons of all of the following muscles *except*
    a. the subscapularis.
    b. the supraspinatus.
    c. the infraspinatus.
    d. the biceps brachii.
    e. the teres minor.

11. The lubricant of a diarthrosis is called _____.

12. A fluid-filled sac that eases the movement of a tendon over a bone is called a/an _____.

13. A _____ joint allows one bone to swivel on another.

14. _____ is the science of movement.

15. The joint between a tooth and the mandible is called a/an _____.

16. In a _____ suture, the articulating bones have interlocking wavy margins, somewhat like a dovetail joint in carpentry.

17. In kicking a football, what type of action does the knee joint exhibit?

18. The angle through which a joint can move is called its _____.

19. The menisci of the knee are functionally similar to the _____ of the temporomandibular joint.

20. At the ankle, both the tibia and fibula articulate with what tarsal bone?

▶ Building Your Medical Vocabulary

Answers in Appendix A

State a meaning of each word element, and give a medical term from this chapter that uses it or a slight variation of it.

1. ab-
2. arthro-
3. -ate
4. cruci-
5. cruro-
6. -duc
7. kinesio-
8. men-
9. supin-
10. -trac

▶ What's Wrong with These Statements?

Answers in Appendix A

Briefly explain why each of the following statements is false, or reword it to make it true.

1. More people get rheumatoid arthritis than osteoarthritis.

2. A doctor who treats arthritis is called a kinesiologist.

3. Synovial joints are also known as synarthroses.

4. Menisci occur in the elbow and knee joints.

5. Reaching behind you to take something out of your hip pocket involves flexion of the shoulder.

6. The cruciate ligaments are in the feet.

7. The femur is held tightly in the acetabulum mainly by the round ligament.

8. The knuckles are amphiarthroses.

9. Synovial fluid is secreted by the bursae.

10. Like most ligaments, the periodontal ligaments attach one bone (the tooth) to another (the mandible or maxilla).

STUDY GUIDE

▶ Testing Your Comprehension

1. All second-class levers produce a mechanical advantage greater than 1.0 and all third-class levers produce a mechanical advantage less than 1.0. Explain why.

2. For each of the following joint movements, state what bone the axis of rotation passes through and which of the three anatomical planes contains the axis of rotation. You may find it helpful to produce some of these actions on an articulated laboratory skeleton so you can more easily visualize the axis of rotation. (a) Plantar flexion; (b) flexion of the hip; (c) adduction of the thigh; (d) flexion of the knee; (e) flexion of the first interphalangeal joint of the index finger. (Do not bend the fingers of a wired laboratory skeletal hand, because they can break off.)

3. In order of occurrence, list the joint actions (flexion, pronation, etc.) and the joints where they would occur as you (a) sit down at a table, (b) reach out and pick up an apple, (c) take a bite, and (d) chew it. Assume that you start in anatomical position.

4. The deltoid muscle inserts on the deltoid tuberosity of the humerus and abducts the arm. Imagine a person holding a weight in the hand and abducting the arm. On a laboratory skeleton, identify the fulcrum; measure the effort arm and resistance arm; determine the mechanical advantage of this movement; and determine which of the three lever types the upper limb acts as when performing this movement.

5. List the six types of synovial joints, and for each one, if possible, identify a joint in the upper limb and a joint in the lower limb that fall into each category. Which of these six joints has/have no examples in the lower limb?

CHAPTER

11

MUSCULAR TISSUE

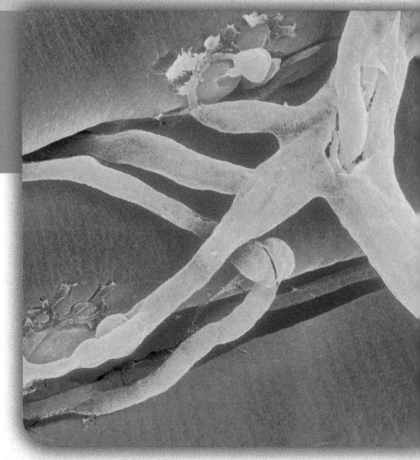

Neuromuscular junctions (SEM)
Dr. Donald Fawcett/Science Source

Anatomy & Physiology
Revealed 4.0

Module 6: Muscular System

BRUSHING UP

● You should be familiar with the organization of a typical skeletal muscle and its associated connective tissues (see section 10.1 b).

● You should know the basic neuron structure introduced in table 5.10 to understand the nerve–muscle relationship in this chapter.

● The stimulation of a muscle fiber by a neuron is based on principles of plasma membrane proteins as receptors and as ligand- and voltage-gated ion channels (see "Membrane Proteins" in section 3.2a).

● Section 1.6e, "Gradients and Flow," provides a core concept (especially electrochemical gradients) for understanding muscle excitation and the activation of contraction.

● The differences between aerobic respiration and anaerobic fermentation (see fig. 2.31) are central to understanding exercise physiology and the energy metabolism of muscle.

● Familiarity with desmosomes and gap junctions (see section 5.5a) will enhance your appreciation of the fundamental properties of cardiac and smooth muscle.

11.1 Types and Characteristics of Muscular Tissue

Expected Learning Outcomes

When you have completed this section, you should be able to

a. describe the physiological properties that all muscle types have in common;

b. list the defining characteristics of skeletal muscle; and

c. discuss the elastic functions of the connective tissue components of a muscle.

11.1a Universal Characteristics of Muscle

The functions of the muscular system were detailed in the preceding chapter: movement, stability, communication, control of body openings and passages, heat production, and glycemic control. To carry out those functions, all muscle cells have the following characteristics.

- **Excitability (responsiveness).** Excitability is a property of all living cells, but muscle and nerve cells have developed this property to the highest degree. When stimulated by chemical signals, stretch, and other stimuli, muscle cells respond with electrical changes across the plasma membrane.

- **Conductivity.** Stimulation of a muscle cell produces more than a local effect. Local electrical excitation sets off a wave of excitation that travels rapidly along the cell and initiates processes leading to contraction.

- **Contractility.** Muscle cells are unique in their ability to shorten substantially when stimulated. This enables them to pull on bones and other organs to create movement.

- **Extensibility.** In order to contract, a muscle cell must also be extensible—able to stretch again between contractions. Most cells rupture if they are stretched even a little, but skeletal muscle cells can stretch to as much as three times their contracted length.

- **Elasticity.** When a muscle cell is stretched and then released, it recoils to a shorter length. If it were not for this elastic recoil, resting muscles would be too slack or flabby. Owing to a *length–tension relationship* to be described in this chapter, they wouldn't contract very strongly when stimulated.

Movement is a fundamental characteristic of all living organisms, from bacteria to humans. Even plants and other seemingly immobile organisms move cellular components from place to place. Across the entire spectrum of life, the molecular mechanisms of movement are very similar, involving motor proteins such as myosin and dynein. But in animals, movement has developed to the highest degree, with the evolution of **muscle cells** specialized for this function. A muscle cell is essentially a device for converting the chemical energy of ATP into the mechanical energy of movement.

The three types of muscular tissue—skeletal, cardiac, and smooth—are described and compared in table 5.11. Cardiac and smooth muscle are further described in this chapter, and cardiac muscle is discussed most extensively in chapter 19. Most of the present chapter, however, concerns skeletal muscle, the type that holds the body erect against the pull of gravity and produces its outwardly visible movements.

This chapter treats the structure, contraction, and metabolism of skeletal muscle at the molecular, cellular, and tissue levels of organization. Understanding muscle at these levels provides an indispensable basis for understanding such aspects of motor performance as quickness, strength, endurance, and fatigue. Such factors have obvious relevance to athletic performance, and they become very important when a lack of physical conditioning, old age, or injury interferes with a person's ability to carry out everyday tasks or meet the extra demands for speed or strength that we all occasionally encounter.

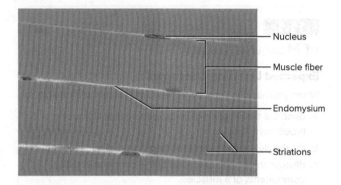

FIGURE 11.1 Skeletal Muscle Fibers. APR

Ed Reschke

? *What tissue characteristics evident in this photo distinguish this from cardiac and smooth muscle?*

11.1b Skeletal Muscle

Skeletal muscle may be defined as voluntary striated muscle that is usually attached to one or more bones. A skeletal muscle exhibits alternating light and dark transverse bands, or **striations** **(fig. 11.1),** that reflect an overlapping arrangement of their internal contractile proteins. Skeletal muscle is called **voluntary** because it is usually subject to conscious control. The other types of muscle are **involuntary** (not usually under conscious control), and they are never attached to bones.

A typical skeletal muscle cell is about 100 μm in diameter and 3 cm (30,000 μm) long; some are as thick as 500 μm and as long as 30 cm. Because of their extraordinary length, skeletal muscle cells are usually called **muscle fibers** or **myofibers.**

Recall that a skeletal muscle is composed not only of muscular tissue, but also of fibrous connective tissue: the *endomysium* that surrounds each muscle fiber, the *perimysium* that bundles muscle fibers together into fascicles, and the *epimysium* that encloses the entire muscle (see fig. 10.1). These connective tissues are continuous with the collagen fibers of tendons and those, in turn, with the collagen of the bone matrix. Thus, when a muscle fiber contracts, it pulls on these collagen fibers and typically moves a bone.

Collagen is neither excitable nor contractile, but it is somewhat extensible and elastic. When a muscle lengthens, for example during extension of a joint, its collagenous components resist excessive stretching and protect the muscle from injury. When a muscle relaxes, elastic recoil of the collagen may help to return the muscle to its resting length and keep it from becoming too flaccid. Some authorities contend that recoil of the tendons and other collagenous tissues contributes significantly to the power output and efficiency of a muscle. When you are running, for example, recoil of the calcaneal tendon may help to lift the heel and produce some of the thrust as your toes push off from the ground. (Such recoil contributes significantly to the long, efficient leaps of a kangaroo.) Others feel that the elasticity of these components is negligible in humans and that the recoil is

produced entirely by certain intracellular proteins of the muscle fibers themselves.

BEFORE YOU GO ON

Answer the following questions to test your understanding of the preceding section:

1. Define *responsiveness, conductivity, contractility, extensibility,* and *elasticity.* State why each of these properties is necessary for muscle function.
2. How is skeletal muscle different from the other types of muscle?
3. Name and define the three layers of collagenous connective tissue in a skeletal muscle.

11.2   Skeletal Muscle Cells

Expected Learning Outcomes
When you have completed this section, you should be able to

a. describe the structural components of a muscle fiber;
b. relate the striations of a muscle fiber to the overlapping arrangement of its protein filaments; and
c. name the major proteins of a muscle fiber and state the function of each.

11.2a The Muscle Fiber

In order to understand muscle function, you must know how the organelles and macromolecules of a muscle fiber are arranged. Perhaps more than any other cell, a muscle fiber exemplifies the adage, Form follows function. It has a complex, tightly organized internal structure in which even the spatial arrangement of protein molecules is closely tied to its contractile function.

The plasma membrane of a muscle fiber is called the **sarcolemma,**[1] and its cytoplasm is called the **sarcoplasm.** The sarcoplasm is occupied mainly by long protein cords called **myofibrils** about 1 μm in diameter **(fig. 11.2).** It also contains an abundance of **glycogen,** a starchlike carbohydrate that provides energy for the cell during heightened levels of exercise, and the red oxygen-binding pigment **myoglobin,** which provides some of the oxygen needed for muscular activity.

Muscle fibers have multiple flattened or sausage-shaped nuclei pressed against the inside of the sarcolemma. This unusual multinuclear condition results from the embryonic development of a muscle fiber—several stem cells called **myoblasts**[2] fuse to produce each fiber, with each myoblast contributing one nucleus. Some myoblasts remain as unspecialized **satellite cells** between the muscle fiber and endomysium. These play an important role in the regeneration of damaged skeletal muscle.

---

[1]*sarco* = flesh, muscle; *lemma* = husk
[2]*myo* = muscle; *blast* = precursor

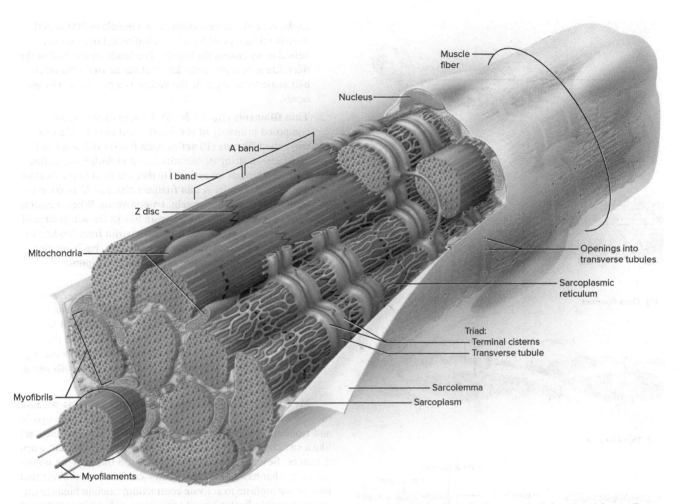

FIGURE 11.2 **Structure of a Skeletal Muscle Fiber.** This is a single cell containing 11 myofibrils (9 shown at the left end and 2 cut off at midfiber). A few myofilaments are shown projecting from the myofibril at the left. Most muscle fibers have from several dozen to a thousand or more myofibrils. Myofibril fine structure is shown in figure 11.3.

? *After reading a little farther in this chapter, explain why it is important for the transverse tubule to be so closely associated with the terminal cisterns.*

Most other organelles of the cell, such as mitochondria, are packed into the spaces between the myofibrils. The smooth endoplasmic reticulum, here called the **sarcoplasmic reticulum (SR),** forms a network around each myofibril (the blue web in fig. 11.2). It periodically exhibits dilated end sacs called **terminal cisterns,** which cross the muscle fiber from one side to the other. The sarcolemma has tubular infoldings called **transverse (T) tubules,** which penetrate through the cell and emerge on the other side. Each T tubule is closely associated with two terminal cisterns running alongside it, one on each side. The T tubule and the two cisterns associated with it constitute a *triad.*

Muscle has a high demand for ATP and therefore possesses an exceptionally large number of mitochondria wedged in between the myofibils. Muscle contraction also requires a lot of calcium ions (Ca^{2+}), as you will see, but this presents a problem. A high concentration of Ca^{2+} in the cytosol is lethal—it can react with phosphate ions to precipitate as calcium phosphate crystals, and can trigger cell death by apoptosis. Therefore, at rest, a muscle cell stores its Ca^{2+} in the sarcoplasmic reticulum, safely bound to

a protein called **calsequestrin.**[3] In a resting muscle fiber, Ca^{2+} is about 10,000 times as concentrated in the SR as it is in the cytosol. When the cell is stimulated, ion gates in the SR membrane open and Ca^{2+} floods into the cytosol to activate contraction. The T tubule signals the SR when to release these calcium bursts.

11.2b Myofilaments

Let's return to the myofibrils just mentioned—the long protein cords that fill most of the muscle cell—and look at their structure at a finer, molecular level. It is here that the key to muscle contraction lies. Each myofibril is a bundle of parallel proteins called **muscle filaments** or **myofilaments** (see the left end of fig. 11.2). There are three kinds of myofilaments:

1. **Thick filaments (fig. 11.3a, b)** are about 15 nm in diameter. Each is made of several hundred molecules of a motor

---

[3]*cal* = calcium; *sequestr* = to set apart or separate; *in* = protein

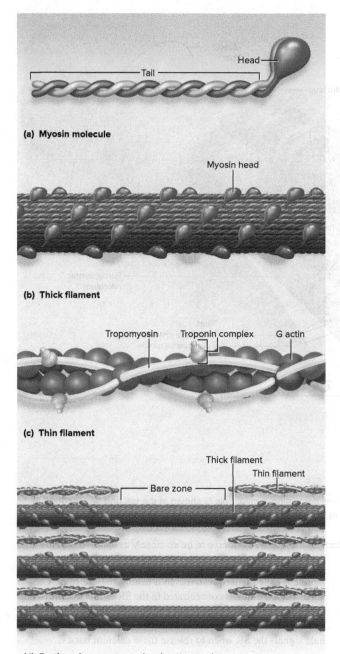

(a) Myosin molecule

(b) Thick filament

(c) Thin filament

(d) Portion of a sarcomere showing the overlap of thick and thin filaments

FIGURE 11.3 Molecular Structure of Thick and Thin Filaments. (a) A single myosin molecule composed of two intertwined proteins. (b) A thick filament composed of a bundle of myosin molecules. (c) A thin filament composed of actin, tropomyosin, and troponin. (d) A region of overlap between the thick and thin filaments.

protein called **myosin.** A myosin molecule is shaped like a golf club, with two chains intertwined to form a shaft-like *tail* and a double globular *head* projecting from it at an

angle. A thick filament consists of a bundle of 200 to 500 myosin molecules with their heads directed outward in a helical array around the bundle. The heads on one half of the thick filament angle to the left, and the heads on the other half angle to the right; in the middle is a *bare zone* with no heads.

2. **Thin filaments (fig. 11.3c, d),** 7 nm in diameter, are composed primarily of two intertwined strands of a protein called **fibrous (F) actin.** Each F actin is like a bead necklace—a string of subunits called **globular (G) actin.** Each G actin has an **active site** that can bind to the head of a myosin molecule. A thin filament also has 40 to 60 molecules of yet another protein, **tropomyosin.** When a muscle fiber is relaxed, each tropomyosin blocks the active sites of six or seven G actins and prevents myosin from binding to them. Each tropomyosin molecule, in turn, has a smaller, three-part calcium-binding protein called **troponin** bound to it.

3. **Elastic filaments** (see fig. 11.5b), 1 nm in diameter, are made of a huge springy protein called **titin.**[4] They run through the core of each thick filament and anchor it to structures called the *Z disc* at one end and *M line* at the other. Titin stabilizes the thick filament, centers it between the thin filaments, prevents overstretching, and recoils like a spring after a muscle is stretched.

Myosin and actin are called **contractile proteins** because they do the work of shortening the muscle fiber. Tropomyosin and troponin are called **regulatory proteins** because they act like a switch to determine when the fiber can contract and when it cannot. Several clues as to how they do this may be apparent from what has already been said—calcium ions are released into the sarcoplasm to activate contraction; calcium binds to troponin; troponin is also bound to tropomyosin; and tropomyosin blocks the active sites of actin, so that myosin cannot bind to it when the muscle is not stimulated. Perhaps you are already forming some idea of the contraction mechanism to be explained shortly.

At least seven other accessory proteins occur in the thick and thin filaments or are associated with them. Among other functions, they anchor the myofilaments, regulate their length, and keep them aligned with each other for optimal contractile effectiveness. The most clinically important of these is **dystrophin,** an enormous protein located between the sarcolemma and the outermost myofilaments. It links actin filaments to a peripheral protein on the inner face of the sarcolemma. Through a series of linking proteins **(fig. 11.4),** this leads ultimately to the fibrous endomysium surrounding the muscle fiber. Therefore, when the thin filaments move, dystrophin transfers the force to the basal lamina, endomysium, and ultimately to the tendon. Genetic defects in dystrophin are responsible for the disabling disease *muscular dystrophy* (see Deeper Insight 11.4).

[4]*tit* = giant; *in* = protein

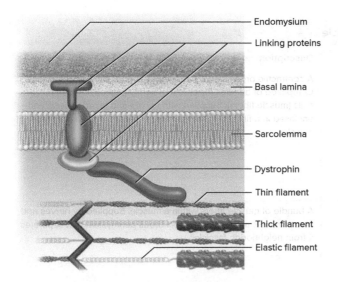

FIGURE 11.4 Dystrophin. Dystrophin ultimately transfers the force of moving actin filaments to tissues leading to the tendon of a muscle.

11.2c Striations

Myosin and actin are not unique to muscle; they occur in nearly all cells, where they function in cellular motility, mitosis, and transport of intracellular materials. In skeletal and cardiac muscle they are especially abundant, however, and are organized in a precise array that accounts for the striations of these muscle types (**figs. 11.5,** 11.3d).

Striated muscle has dark **A bands** alternating with lighter **I bands.** (*A* stands for *anisotropic* and *I* for *isotropic,* which refer to the way these bands affect polarized light. To help remember which band is which, think "d**A**rk" and "l**I**ght.") Each A band consists of thick filaments lying side by side. Part of the A band, where thick and thin filaments overlap, is especially dark. In this region, each thick filament is surrounded by a hexagonal array of thin filaments. In the middle of the A band, there is a lighter region called the **H band,**[5] into which the thin filaments do not reach. In the middle of the H band, the thick filaments are linked to each other through a dark, transverse protein complex called the **M line.**[6]

Each light I band is bisected by a dark narrow **Z disc**[7] (**Z line**), which provides anchorage for the thin and elastic filaments. Each segment of a myofibril from one Z disc to the next is called a **sarcomere**[8] (SAR-co-meer), the functional contractile unit of the muscle

[5]*H* = *helle* = bright (German)
[6]*M* = *Mittel* = middle (German)
[7]*Z* = *Zwichenscheibe* = between disc (German)
[8]*sarco* = muscle; *mere* = part, segment

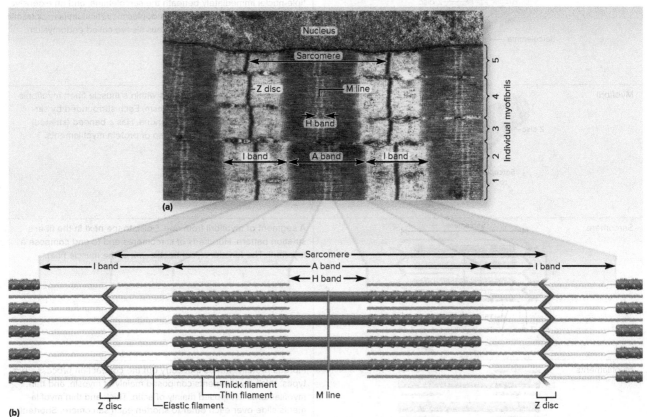

FIGURE 11.5 Muscle Striations and Their Molecular Basis. (a) Five myofibrils of a single muscle fiber, showing the striations in the relaxed state (TEM). (b) The overlapping pattern of thick and thin filaments that accounts for the striations seen in part (a). **APR**

a: Don W. Fawcett/Science Source

TABLE 11.1	The Structural Hierarchy of a Skeletal Muscle

Structural Level	Description
Muscle 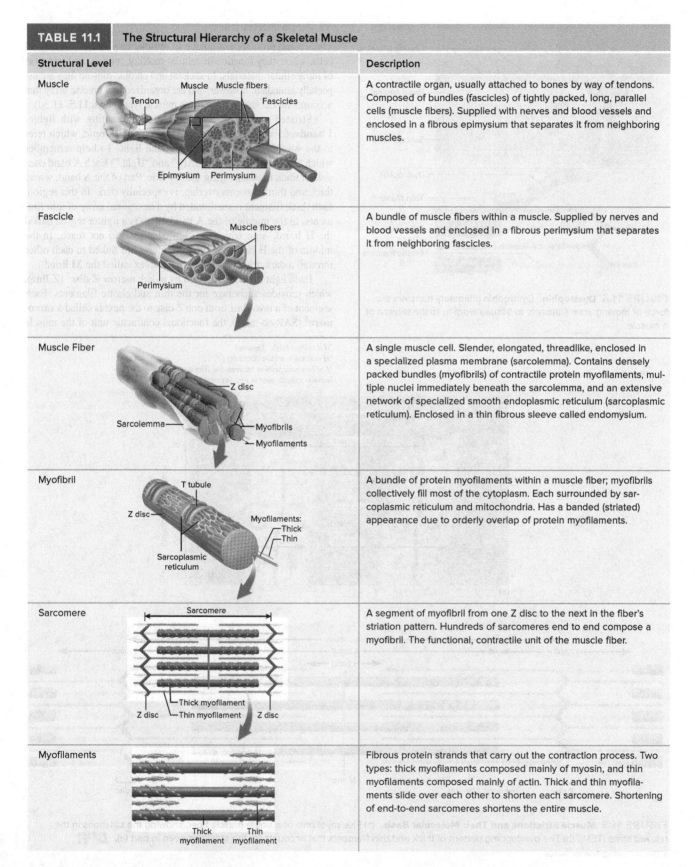	A contractile organ, usually attached to bones by way of tendons. Composed of bundles (fascicles) of tightly packed, long, parallel cells (muscle fibers). Supplied with nerves and blood vessels and enclosed in a fibrous epimysium that separates it from neighboring muscles.
Fascicle	A bundle of muscle fibers within a muscle. Supplied by nerves and blood vessels and enclosed in a fibrous perimysium that separates it from neighboring fascicles.
Muscle Fiber	A single muscle cell. Slender, elongated, threadlike, enclosed in a specialized plasma membrane (sarcolemma). Contains densely packed bundles (myofibrils) of contractile protein myofilaments, multiple nuclei immediately beneath the sarcolemma, and an extensive network of specialized smooth endoplasmic reticulum (sarcoplasmic reticulum). Enclosed in a thin fibrous sleeve called endomysium.
Myofibril	A bundle of protein myofilaments within a muscle fiber; myofibrils collectively fill most of the cytoplasm. Each surrounded by sarcoplasmic reticulum and mitochondria. Has a banded (striated) appearance due to orderly overlap of protein myofilaments.
Sarcomere	A segment of myofibril from one Z disc to the next in the fiber's striation pattern. Hundreds of sarcomeres end to end compose a myofibril. The functional, contractile unit of the muscle fiber.
Myofilaments	Fibrous protein strands that carry out the contraction process. Two types: thick myofilaments composed mainly of myosin, and thin myofilaments composed mainly of actin. Thick and thin myofilaments slide over each other to shorten each sarcomere. Shortening of end-to-end sarcomeres shortens the entire muscle.

fiber. A muscle shortens because its individual sarcomeres shorten and pull the Z discs closer to each other, and dystrophin and the linking proteins pull on the extracellular proteins of the muscle. As the Z discs are pulled closer together, they pull on the sarcolemma to achieve overall shortening of the cell.

Table 11.1 reviews the organization of skeletal muscle at successive structural levels from the whole muscle to the myofilaments.

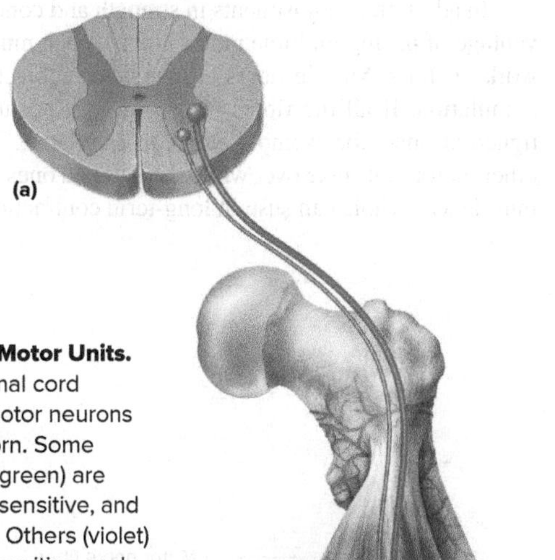

(a)

FIGURE 11.6 Motor Units.
(a) A slice of spinal cord depicting two motor neurons in its anterior horn. Some motor neurons (green) are small, relatively sensitive, and easily activated. Others (violet) are large, less sensitive, and activated only when greater muscular strength is needed. (b) In the muscle, the muscle fibers of small motor units are relatively small. Large motor units have larger and more numerous muscle fibers. Note that the muscle fibers of any given motor unit are distributed throughout the muscle and commingled with the fibers of other motor units (red), not clustered in one place.

(b)

BEFORE YOU GO ON

Answer the following questions to test your understanding of the preceding section:

4. What special terms are given to the plasma membrane, cytoplasm, and smooth ER of a muscle cell?

5. What is the difference between a myofilament and a myofibril?

6. List five proteins of the myofilaments and describe their physical arrangement.

7. Sketch the overlapping pattern of myofilaments to show how they account for the A bands, I bands, H bands, and Z discs.

11.3   The Nerve–Muscle Relationship

Expected Learning Outcomes
When you have completed this section, you should be able to

a. explain what a motor unit is and how it relates to muscle contraction;

b. describe the structure of the junction where a nerve fiber meets a muscle fiber; and

c. explain why a cell has an electrical charge difference across its plasma membrane and, in general terms, how this relates to muscle contraction.

Skeletal muscle cannot contract unless it is stimulated by a nerve (or with electrodes). If its nerve connections are severed or poisoned, a muscle is paralyzed. If the connection is not restored, the paralyzed muscle wastes away in a shrinkage called *denervation atrophy.* Thus, muscle contraction cannot be understood without first understanding the relationship between nerve and muscle cells.

11.3a Motor Neurons and Motor Units

Skeletal muscles are served by nerve cells called *somatic motor neurons,* whose cell bodies are in the brainstem and spinal cord. Their axons, called **somatic motor fibers,** lead to the muscles. Each nerve fiber branches out to multiple muscle fibers, but each muscle fiber is supplied by only one motor neuron.

When a nerve signal approaches the end of an axon, it spreads out over all of its terminal branches and stimulates all muscle fibers supplied by them. Thus, these muscle fibers contract in unison; there is no way to stimulate some but not all of them. Since they behave as a single functional unit, one nerve fiber and all the

muscle fibers innervated by it are called a **motor unit (fig. 11.6).** The muscle fibers of a motor unit are not clustered together but dispersed throughout a muscle. Therefore, when stimulated, they cause a weak contraction over a wide area—not just a local twitch in one small region. Effective muscle contraction usually requires the activation of many motor units at once.

On average, about 200 muscle fibers are innervated by each motor neuron, but motor units can be much smaller or larger than this to serve different purposes. Where fine control is needed, we have *small motor units.* These typically are supplied by small, relatively sensitive neurons. Where strength is more important than fine control, we have *large motor units.* These are innervated by less sensitive neurons with larger cell bodies, activated when strength is needed for a demanding task.

Consider a hand or eye muscle that requires fine motor control. Here, 1,000 muscle fibers may be innervated by 200 to 300 motor neurons with small motor units of only 3 to 5 muscle fibers each. Turning a few motor units on or off would produce small, subtle changes in muscle action. Then consider a powerful thigh or calf muscle such as the quadriceps femoris or gastrocnemius. Here, every 1,000 muscle fibers may be controlled by only 1 or 2 neurons with large motor units of 500 to 1,000 muscle fibers each. Turning a few motor units on or off would produce relatively large changes in muscle action, with large increments in strength but little fine control or subtlety.

In addition to adjustments in strength and control, another advantage of having multiple motor units in each muscle is that they work in shifts. Muscle fibers fatigue when subjected to continual stimulation. If all the fibers in one of your postural muscles fatigued at once, for example, you could collapse. To prevent this, other motor units take over while the fatigued ones recover, and the muscle as a whole can sustain long-term contraction.

11.3b The Neuromuscular Junction

The point where a nerve fiber meets any target cell is called a **synapse** (SIN-aps). When the target cell is a muscle fiber, the synapse is also called a **neuromuscular junction (NMJ)** or **motor end plate (fig. 11.7).** Each terminal branch of the nerve fiber within the NMJ forms a separate synapse with the muscle fiber. The sarcolemma of the NMJ is irregularly indented, a little like a handprint

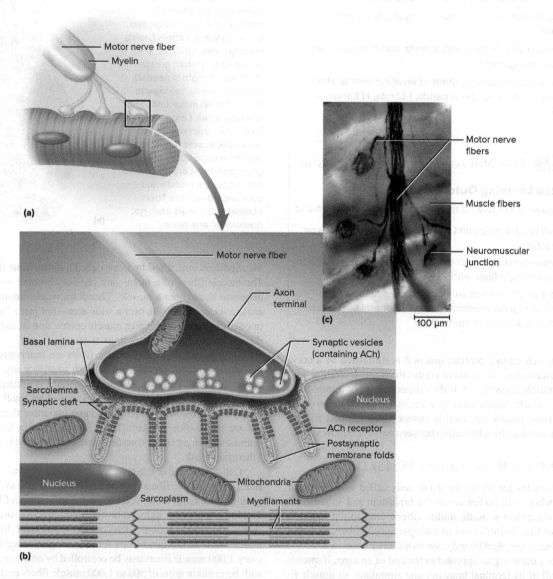

100 μm

FIGURE 11.7 Innervation of Skeletal Muscle. (a) Motor nerve ending on a muscle fiber. (b) Detail of the neuromuscular junction. (c) Light micrograph (LM) of neuromuscular junctions (compare the SEM photo on the opening page of this chapter). **APR**

c: Al Telser/McGraw-Hill Education

pressed into soft clay. If you imagine the nerve fiber to be like your forearm, branching out at the end like your fingers, the individual synapses would be like the dents where your fingertips press into the clay. Thus, one nerve fiber stimulates the muscle fiber at several nearby points within the NMJ.

At each synapse, the nerve fiber ends in a bulbous swelling called the **axon terminal.** The terminal doesn't directly touch the muscle fiber but is separated from it by a narrow space called the **synaptic cleft,** about 60 to 100 nm wide (scarcely wider than the thickness of one plasma membrane).

The axon terminal contains spheroidal organelles called **synaptic vesicles,** which are filled with a chemical, **acetylcholine (ACh)** (ASS-eh-till-CO-leen)—one of many *neurotransmitters* to be introduced in the next chapter. The electrical signal (nerve impulse) traveling down a nerve fiber cannot cross the synaptic cleft like a spark jumping between two electrodes—rather, it causes the synaptic vesicles to undergo exocytosis, releasing ACh into the cleft. ACh thus functions as a chemical messenger from the nerve cell to the muscle cell.

To respond to ACh, each synapse has about 50 million **ACh receptors**—proteins incorporated into the sarcolemma across from the axon terminals. To maximize the number of ACh receptors and thus its sensitivity to the neurotransmitter, the sarcolemma in this area has infoldings about 1 μm deep, called **postsynaptic membrane folds (junctional folds),** which increase the surface area of ACh-sensitive membrane. The muscle nuclei beneath the folds are specifically dedicated to the synthesis of ACh receptors and other proteins of the local sarcolemma. A deficiency of ACh receptors leads to muscle weakness in the disease *myasthenia gravis* (see Deeper Insight 11.4).

The entire NMJ is enclosed in a **basal lamina,** a mat of collagen and glycoprotein that separates the muscle fiber and nerve ending from the surrounding connective tissue. The basal lamina also passes through the synaptic cleft and virtually fills it. Both the sarcolemma and that part of the basal lamina in the cleft contain **acetylcholinesterase (AChE)** (ASS-eh-till-CO-lin-ESS-terase). This is an enzyme that breaks down ACh after the ACh has stimulated the muscle cell; thus, it is important in turning off muscle contraction and allowing the muscle to relax (see Deeper Insight 11.1).

11.3c Electrically Excitable Cells

Muscle and nerve cells are regarded as *electrically excitable cells* because their plasma membranes exhibit voltage changes in response to stimulation. The study of the electrical activity of cells, called **electrophysiology,** is a key to understanding nerve activity, muscle contraction, the heartbeat and electrocardiogram, and other physiological phenomena. The details of electrophysiology are presented in section 12.4, but a few fundamental principles must be introduced here so you can understand muscle excitation.

The electrical activity of cells hinges on differences in the concentration of ions in the intracellular fluid (ICF) and extracellular fluid (ECF) adjacent to the plasma membrane. The ICF contains a greater concentration of negative anions than the ECF does—especially negatively charged proteins, nucleic acids, and phosphates, which are trapped in the cell and give its interior a net negative charge. That is, the membrane is **polarized,** like a little battery. Also contained in the ICF is a great excess of potassium ions (K^+), whereas the ECF contains a great excess of sodium ions (Na^+). The electrical events that initiate muscle contraction are driven by the movements of these two cations through the membrane when a muscle or nerve cell is excited.

DEEPER INSIGHT 11.1

CLINICAL APPLICATION

Neuromuscular Toxins and Paralysis

Toxins that interfere with synaptic function can paralyze the muscles. Organophosphate pesticides such as malathion are *cholinesterase inhibitors* that bind to AChE and prevent it from degrading ACh. Depending on the dose, this can prolong the action of ACh and produce *spastic paralysis,* a state in which the muscles contract and cannot relax; clinically, this is called a *cholinergic crisis.* It poses a danger of suffocation if it affects the laryngeal and respiratory muscles. Another example of spastic paralysis is *tetanus (lockjaw),* caused by the toxin of a soil bacterium, *Clostridium tetani.* In the spinal cord, a neurotransmitter called glycine normally stops motor neurons from producing unwanted muscle contractions. The tetanus toxin blocks glycine release and thus causes overstimulation and spastic paralysis of the muscles.

Flaccid paralysis is a state in which the muscles are limp and cannot contract. This too can cause respiratory arrest if it affects the thoracic muscles. Among the causes of flaccid paralysis are poisons such as curare (cue-RAH-ree), which competes with ACh for receptor sites but doesn't stimulate the muscle. Curare is extracted from certain plants and used by some South American natives to poison blowgun darts. It has been used to treat muscle spasms in some neurological disorders and to relax abdominal muscles for surgery, but other muscle relaxants have now replaced curare for most purposes.

Another cause of flaccid paralysis is *botulism,* a type of food poisoning caused by a neuromuscular toxin secreted by the bacterium *Clostridium botulinum.* Botulinum toxin blocks ACh release. Purified botulinum toxin is marketed as Botox Cosmetic. It is injected in small doses into specific facial muscles. Wrinkles gradually disappear as muscle paralysis sets in over the next few hours. The effect lasts about 4 months until the muscles retighten and the wrinkles return. Botox treatment has become the fastest-growing cosmetic medical procedure in the United States, as its usage has expanded to other conditions and many people go for cosmetic treatment every few months. It has had some undesirable consequences, however, as it is sometimes administered by unqualified practitioners. Even some qualified physicians use it for treatments not yet approved by the FDA, and some host festive "Botox parties" for treatment of patients in assembly-line fashion.

A difference in electrical charge from one point to another is called an *electrical potential,* or *voltage.* It typically measures 12 volts (V) for a car battery and 1.5 V for a flashlight battery, for example. On the sarcolemma of a muscle cell, the voltage is much smaller, about −90 millivolts (mV), but critically important to life. (The negative sign refers to the relatively negative charge on the intracellular side of the membrane.) This voltage is called the **resting membrane potential (RMP).** It is maintained by the sodium–potassium pump, as explained in section 12.4b.

When a nerve or muscle cell is stimulated, dramatic things happen electrically, as we shall soon see in the excitation of muscle. Ion channels in the plasma membrane open and Na^+ instantly flows into the cell, driven both by its concentration difference across the membrane and by its attraction to the negative charge of the cell interior—that is, it flows down an **electrochemical gradient.** These Na^+ cations override the negative charge just inside the membrane, so the inside of the membrane briefly becomes positive. This is called **depolarization** of the membrane. Immediately, Na^+ channels close and K^+ channels open. K^+ rushes out of the cell, partly because it is repelled by the positive sodium charge and partly because it is more concentrated in the ICF than in the ECF—that is, it flows down its own electrochemical gradient in the direction opposite from the sodium movement. The loss of K^+ ions from the cell turns the inside of the membrane negative again **(repolarization).** This quick up-and-down voltage shift, from the negative RMP to a positive value and then back to the RMP again, is called an **action potential.** The RMP is a stable voltage seen in a "waiting" cell, whereas the action potential is a quickly fluctuating voltage seen in an active, stimulated cell.

Action potentials have a way of perpetuating themselves—an action potential at one point on a plasma membrane causes another one to happen immediately in front of it, which triggers another one a little farther along, and so forth. A wave of action potentials spreading along a nerve fiber like this is called a *nerve impulse* or *nerve signal.* Such signals also travel along the sarcolemma of a muscle fiber. Next we will see how this leads to muscle contraction.

BEFORE YOU GO ON

Answer the following questions to test your understanding of the preceding section:

8. What differences would you expect to see between a motor unit where muscular strength is more important than fine control and another motor unit where fine control is more important?

9. State the functions of the axon terminal and its synaptic vesicles.

10. Distinguish between acetylcholine, an acetylcholine receptor, and acetylcholinesterase. State where each is found and describe the function it serves.

11. What accounts for the resting membrane potential seen in unstimulated nerve and muscle cells?

12. What is the difference between a resting membrane potential and an action potential?

11.4 Behavior of Skeletal Muscle Fibers

Expected Learning Outcomes

When you have completed this section, you should be able to

a. explain how a nerve fiber stimulates a skeletal muscle fiber;

b. explain how stimulation of a muscle fiber activates its contractile mechanism;

c. explain the mechanism of muscle contraction;

d. explain how a muscle fiber relaxes; and

e. explain why the force of a muscle contraction depends on the muscle's length prior to stimulation.

The process of muscle contraction and relaxation has four major phases: (1) excitation, (2) excitation–contraction coupling, (3) contraction, and (4) relaxation. Each phase occurs in several smaller steps, which we now examine in detail.

11.4a Excitation

Excitation is the process in which action potentials in the nerve fiber lead to action potentials in the muscle fiber. The steps in excitation are shown in **figure 11.8.** Follow these carefully as you read the following description to ensure understanding of the process.

① A nerve signal arrives at the axon terminal and opens voltage-gated calcium channels. Calcium ions enter the terminal.

② Calcium stimulates the synaptic vesicles to release acetylcholine (ACh) into the synaptic cleft. One action potential causes exocytosis of about 60 vesicles, and each vesicle releases about 10,000 molecules of ACh.

③ ACh diffuses across the synaptic cleft and binds to receptors on the sarcolemma.

④ These receptors are ligand-gated ion channels. Two ACh molecules must bind to each receptor to open the channel. When it opens, Na^+ flows quickly into the cell and K^+ flows out. The voltage on the sarcolemma quickly rises to a less negative value as Na^+ enters the cell, then falls back to the RMP as K^+ exits. This rapid up-and-down fluctuation in voltage at the motor end plate is called the **end-plate potential (EPP).**

⑤ Areas of sarcolemma next to the end plate have voltage-gated ion channels that open in response to the EPP. Some of these are specific for Na^+ and admit it to the cell, while others are specific for K^+ and allow it to leave. These ion movements create an *action potential.* The muscle fiber is now excited.

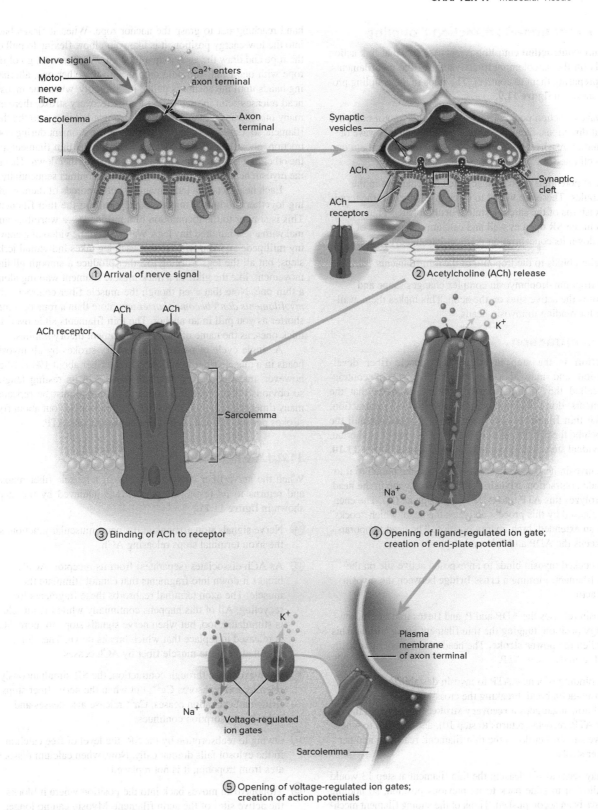

① Arrival of nerve signal

Nerve signal

Motor nerve fiber

Sarcolemma

Ca²⁺ enters axon terminal

Axon terminal

② Acetylcholine (ACh) release

Synaptic vesicles

ACh

ACh receptors

Synaptic cleft

③ Binding of ACh to receptor

ACh

ACh

ACh receptor

Sarcolemma

④ Opening of ligand-regulated ion gate; creation of end-plate potential

K⁺

Na⁺

⑤ Opening of voltage-regulated ion gates; creation of action potentials

K⁺

Na⁺

Voltage-regulated ion gates

Plasma membrane of axon terminal

Sarcolemma

FIGURE 11.8 Excitation of a Muscle Fiber. These events link action potentials in a nerve fiber to the generation of action potentials in the muscle fiber. See the corresponding numbered steps in the text for explanation.

11.4b Excitation–Contraction Coupling

Excitation–contraction coupling refers to events that link action potentials on the sarcolemma to activation of the myofilaments, thereby preparing them to contract. The steps in the coupling process are shown in **figure 11.9.**

6 A wave of action potentials spreads from the motor end plate in all directions, like ripples on a pond. When this wave of excitation reaches the T tubules, it continues down them into the cell interior.

7 Action potentials open voltage-gated ion channels in the T tubules. These are linked to calcium channels in the terminal cisterns of the sarcoplasmic reticulum (SR). Thus, channels in the SR open as well and calcium diffuses out of the SR, down its concentration gradient into the cytosol.

8 Calcium binds to the troponin of the thin filaments.

9 The troponin–tropomyosin complex changes shape and exposes the active sites on the actin. This makes them available for binding to myosin heads.

11.4c Contraction

Contraction is the step in which the muscle fiber develops tension and may shorten. The mechanism of contraction is called the **sliding filament theory.** It holds that the myofilaments don't become any shorter during contraction; rather, the thin filaments slide over the thick ones and pull the Z discs behind them, causing each sarcomere as a whole to shorten. The individual steps in this mechanism are shown in **figure 11.10.**

10 The myosin head must have an ATP molecule bound to it to initiate contraction. **Myosin ATPase,** an enzyme in the head, hydrolyzes this ATP into ADP and phosphate (P_i). The energy released by this process activates the head, which "cocks" into an extended, high-energy position. The head temporarily keeps the ADP and P_i bound to it.

11 The cocked myosin binds to an exposed active site on the thin filament, forming a **cross-bridge** between the myosin and actin.

12 Myosin releases the ADP and P_i and flexes into a bent, low-energy position, tugging the thin filament along with it. This is called the **power stroke.** The head remains bound to actin until it binds a new ATP.

13 The binding of a new ATP to myosin destabilizes the myosin–actin bond, breaking the cross-bridge. The myosin head now undergoes a **recovery stroke.** It hydrolyzes the new ATP, recocks (returns to step 10), and attaches to a new active site farther down the thin filament, ready for another power stroke.

It may seem as if releasing the thin filament at step 13 would simply allow it to slide back to its previous position, so nothing would have been accomplished. Think of the sliding filament mechanism, however, as being similar to the way you would pull in a boat anchor hand over hand. When the myosin head cocks, it is like your

hand reaching out to grasp the anchor rope. When it flexes back into the low-energy position, it is like your elbow flexing to pull on the rope and draw the anchor up a little bit. When you let go of the rope with one hand, you hold onto it with the other one, alternating hands until the anchor is pulled in. Similarly, when one myosin head releases actin in preparation for the recovery stroke, there are many other heads on the same thick filament holding onto the thin filament so it doesn't slide back. At any given moment during contraction, about half of the heads are bound to the thin filament and the other half are extending forward to grasp it farther down. That is, the myosin heads don't all stroke at once but contract sequentially.

Each head acts in a jerky manner, but hundreds of them working together produce a smooth, steady pull on the thin filament. This is similar to the locomotion of a millipede—a wormlike animal with a few hundred tiny legs. Watch an online video of a crawling millipede and you will see that each leg takes individual jerky steps, but all the legs working together produce a smooth gliding movement, like the glide of a thick muscle filament walking along a thin one. Note that even though the muscle fiber contracts, the *myofilaments don't become shorter* any more than a rope becomes shorter as you pull in an anchor. The thin filaments slide over the thick ones, as the name of the sliding filament theory implies.

A single cycle of power and recovery strokes by all myosin heads in a muscle fiber would shorten the fiber about 1%. A fiber, however, may shorten by as much as 40% of its resting length, so obviously the cycle of power and recovery must be repeated many times by each myosin head. Each head carries out about five strokes per second, and each stroke consumes one ATP.

11.4d Relaxation

When the nerve fiber stops stimulating it, a muscle fiber relaxes and returns to its resting length. This is achieved by the steps shown in **figure 11.11.**

14 Nerve signals stop arriving at the neuromuscular junction, so the axon terminal stops releasing ACh.

15 As ACh dissociates (separates) from its receptor, AChE breaks it down into fragments that cannot stimulate the muscle. The axon terminal reabsorbs these fragments for recycling. All of this happens continually while the muscle is stimulated, too, but when nerve signals stop, no more ACh is released to replace that which breaks down. Therefore, stimulation of the muscle fiber by ACh ceases.

16 From excitation through contraction, the SR simultaneously releases and reabsorbs Ca^{2+}; but when the nerve fiber stops firing and excitation ceases, Ca^{2+} release also ceases and only its reabsorption continues.

17 Owing to reabsorption by the SR, the level of free calcium in the cytosol falls dramatically. Now, when calcium dissociates from troponin, it is not replaced.

18 Tropomyosin moves back into the position where it blocks the active sites of the actin filament. Myosin can no longer bind to actin, and the muscle fiber ceases to produce or maintain tension.

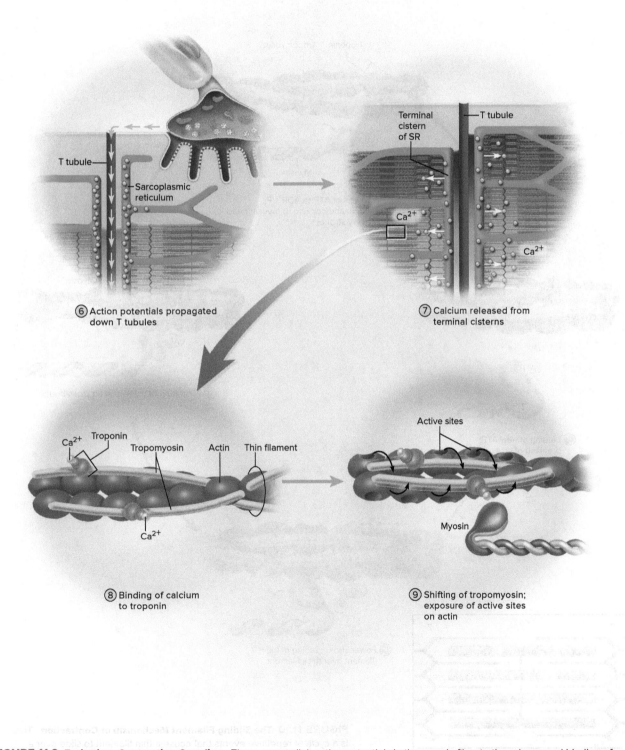

⑥ Action potentials propagated down T tubules

⑦ Calcium released from terminal cisterns

⑧ Binding of calcium to troponin

⑨ Shifting of tropomyosin; exposure of active sites on actin

FIGURE 11.9 Excitation–Contraction Coupling. These events link action potentials in the muscle fiber to the release and binding of calcium ions. See the corresponding numbered steps in the text for explanation. The numbers in this figure begin where figure 11.8 ended.

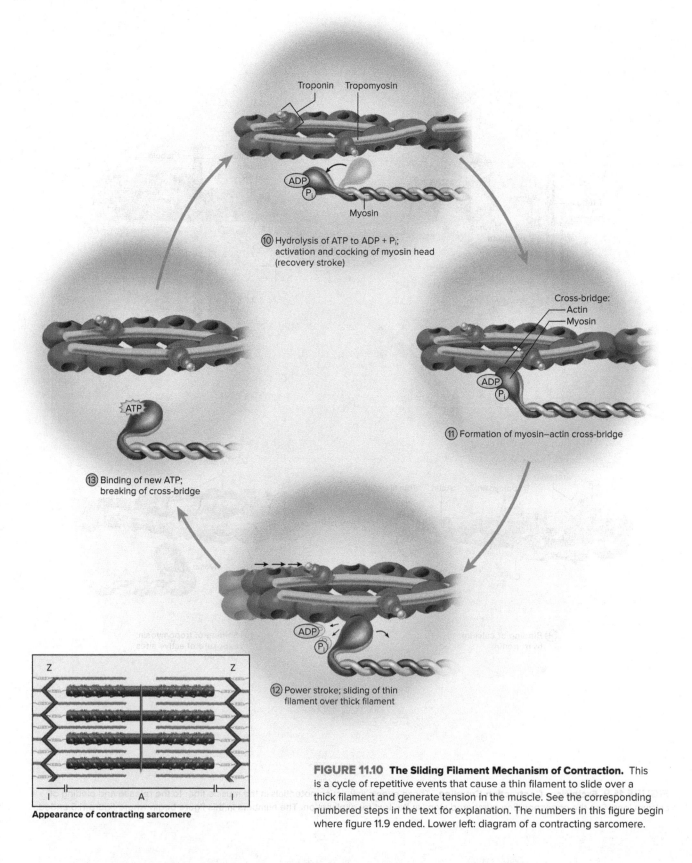

Troponin Tropomyosin

Myosin

⑩ Hydrolysis of ATP to ADP + Pᵢ;
activation and cocking of myosin head
(recovery stroke)

Cross-bridge:
Actin
Myosin

⑪ Formation of myosin–actin cross-bridge

ATP

⑬ Binding of new ATP;
breaking of cross-bridge

⑫ Power stroke; sliding of thin
filament over thick filament

Z   Z

I   A   I

Appearance of contracting sarcomere

FIGURE 11.10 The Sliding Filament Mechanism of Contraction. This
is a cycle of repetitive events that cause a thin filament to slide over a
thick filament and generate tension in the muscle. See the corresponding
numbered steps in the text for explanation. The numbers in this figure begin
where figure 11.9 ended. Lower left: diagram of a contracting sarcomere.

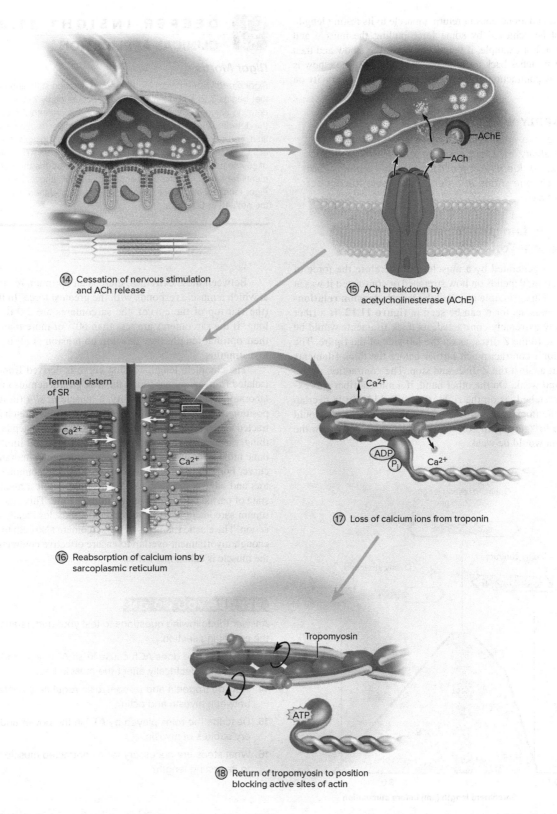

⑭ Cessation of nervous stimulation and ACh release

⑮ ACh breakdown by acetylcholinesterase (AChE)

Terminal cistern of SR

Ca²⁺

Ca²⁺

⑯ Reabsorption of calcium ions by sarcoplasmic reticulum

Ca²⁺

ADP P₁ Ca²⁺

⑰ Loss of calcium ions from troponin

Tropomyosin

ATP

⑱ Return of tropomyosin to position blocking active sites of actin

FIGURE 11.11 Relaxation of a Muscle Fiber. These events lead from the cessation of a nerve signal to the release of thin filaments by myosin. See the corresponding numbered steps in the text for explanation. The numbers in this figure begin where figure 11.10 ended.

Relaxation alone doesn't return a muscle to its resting length. That must be achieved by some force pulling the muscle and stretching it. For example, if the biceps flexes the elbow and then relaxes, it stretches back to its resting length only if the elbow is extended by contraction of the triceps or by the pull of gravity on the forearm.

▶▶▶**APPLY WHAT YOU KNOW**

One of the most important properties of proteins is their ability to change shape repeatedly (see section 2.4e). Identify at least two muscle proteins that must change shape in order for a muscle to contract and relax.

11.4e The Length–Tension Relationship and Muscle Tone

The tension generated by a muscle, and therefore the force of its contraction, depends on how stretched or contracted it was at the outset. This principle is called the **length–tension relationship.** The reasons for it can be seen in **figure 11.12.** If a fiber was already extremely contracted, its thick filaments would be rather close to the Z discs, as on the left side of the figure. The fiber couldn't contract much farther before the thick filaments would butt against the Z discs and stop. The contraction would be brief and weak. On the other hand, if a muscle fiber was extremely stretched, as on the right, there would be little overlap between the thick and thin filaments. The myosin heads would be unable to "get a grip" on the thin filaments, and again the contraction would be weak.

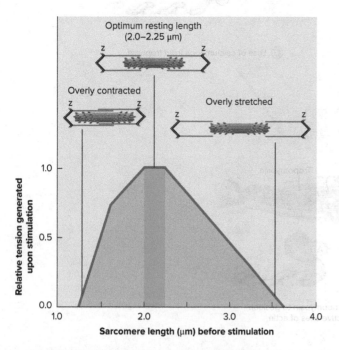

FIGURE 11.12 The Length–Tension Relationship.

DEEPER INSIGHT 11.2
CLINICAL APPLICATION
Rigor Mortis

Rigor mortis[9] is the hardening of the muscles and stiffening of the body that begins 3 to 4 hours after death. It occurs partly because the deteriorating sarcoplasmic reticulum releases calcium into the cytosol, and the deteriorating sarcolemma admits more calcium from the extracellular fluid. The calcium activates myosin–actin cross-bridging. Once bound to actin, myosin cannot release it without first binding an ATP molecule, and of course no ATP is available in a dead body. Thus, the thick and thin filaments remain rigidly cross-linked until the myofilaments begin to decay. Rigor mortis peaks about 12 hours after death and then diminishes over the next 48 to 60 hours.

Between these extremes, there is an optimum resting length at which a muscle responds with the greatest force. In this range (the flat top of the curve), the sarcomeres are 2.0 to 2.25 μm long. If the sarcomeres are less than 60% or more than 175% of their optimal length, they develop no tension at all in response to a stimulus.

The complete length–tension curve is derived from muscles isolated from an animal (often the frog gastrocnemius muscle) for laboratory stimulation. In reality, a muscle *in situ* (in its natural position in the living body) is never as extremely stretched or contracted as the far right and left sides of the figure depict. For one thing, the attachments of muscles to the bones and limitations on bone movement restrict muscle contraction to the midrange of the curve. For another, the central nervous system continually monitors and adjusts the length of the resting muscles, maintaining a state of partial contraction called **muscle tone.** This maintains optimum sarcomere length and makes the muscles ideally ready for action. The elastic filaments of the sarcomere also help to maintain enough myofilament overlap to ensure effective contraction when the muscle is called into action.

▸ **BEFORE YOU GO ON**

Answer the following questions to test your understanding of the preceding section:

13. What change does ACh cause in an ACh receptor? How does this electrically affect the muscle fiber?

14. How do troponin and tropomyosin regulate the interaction between myosin and actin?

15. Describe the roles played by ATP in the power and recovery strokes of myosin.

16. What steps are necessary for a contracted muscle to return to its resting length?

[9]*rigor* = rigidity; *mortis* = of death

11.5 Behavior of Whole Muscles

Expected Learning Outcomes

When you have completed this section, you should be able to

a. describe the stages of a muscle twitch;

b. explain how successive muscle twitches can add up to produce stronger muscle contractions;

c. distinguish between isometric and isotonic contraction; and

d. distinguish between concentric and eccentric contraction.

Now you know how an individual muscle cell shortens. Our next objective is to move up to the organ grade of structure and consider how this relates to the action of the muscle as a whole.

11.5a Threshold, Latent Period, and Twitch

The timing and strength of a muscle's contraction can be shown in a chart called a **myogram (fig. 11.13).** A weak (subthreshold) electrical stimulus to a muscle produces no reaction. By gradually increasing the voltage and stimulating the muscle again, one can determine the **threshold,** or minimum voltage necessary to generate an action potential in the muscle fiber. At threshold or higher, a single stimulus causes a quick cycle of contraction and relaxation called a **twitch.**

There is a delay, or **latent period,** of about 2 milliseconds (ms) between the onset of the stimulus and onset of the twitch. This is the time required for excitation, excitation–contraction coupling, and tensing of the elastic components of the muscle. The force generated during this time is called *internal tension.* It isn't visible on the myogram because it causes no shortening of the muscle. On the left side, the myogram is therefore flat.

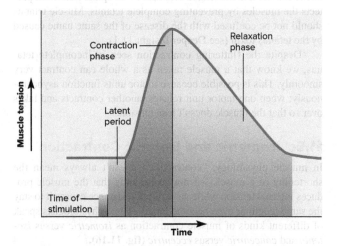

FIGURE 11.13 Idealized Myogram of a Muscle Twitch.

? *What role does ATP play during the relaxation phase?*

Labels in figure: Contraction phase; Relaxation phase; Latent period; Time of stimulation; Muscle tension; Time

Once the elastic components are taut, the muscle begins to produce *external tension* and move a resisting object, or load, such as a bone or body limb. This is called the **contraction phase** of the twitch. By analogy, imagine lifting a weight suspended from a rubber band. At first, internal tension would only stretch the rubber band. Then, as the rubber band became taut, external tension would lift the weight.

The contraction phase is short-lived, because the sarcoplasmic reticulum quickly reabsorbs Ca^{2+} before the muscle develops maximal force. As the Ca^{2+} level in the cytoplasm falls, myosin releases the thin filaments and muscle tension declines. This is seen in the myogram as the **relaxation phase.** As shown by the asymmetry of the myogram, the muscle contracts more quickly than it relaxes. The entire twitch lasts from about 7 to 100 ms, so a muscle could theoretically complete about 10 to 140 twitches per second (if only the math mattered).

11.5b Contraction Strength of Twitches

We have seen that a subthreshold stimulus induces no muscle contraction at all, but at threshold intensity, a twitch is produced. Increasing the stimulus voltage still more, however, produces twitches no stronger than those at threshold. Superficially, the muscle fiber seems to be giving its maximum response once the stimulus intensity is at threshold or higher. However, even for a constant voltage, twitches vary in strength. This is so for a variety of reasons:

- Twitch strength depends on how stretched the muscle was just before it was stimulated, as we have just seen in the length–tension relationship.

- Twitches become weaker as a muscle fatigues, as discussed later in this chapter.

- Twitches vary with the temperature of the muscle; a warmed-up muscle contracts more strongly because enzymes such as the myosin heads work more quickly.

- Twitch strength varies with the muscle's state of hydration, which affects the spacing between thick and thin filaments and therefore the ability to form myosin–actin cross-bridges.

- Twitch strength varies with stimulus frequency; stimuli arriving close together produce stronger twitches than stimuli arriving at longer time intervals, as we will see shortly.

It should not be surprising that twitches vary in strength. Indeed, an individual twitch isn't strong enough to do any useful work. Muscles must contract with variable strength for different tasks, such as lifting a glass of champagne compared with lifting barbells at the gym.

Let us examine more closely the contrasting effects of stimulus *intensity* versus stimulus *frequency* on contraction strength. Suppose we apply a stimulating electrode to a motor nerve that supplies a muscle, such as a laboratory preparation of a frog sciatic nerve connected to its gastrocnemius muscle. Subthreshold stimulus voltages produce no response (**fig. 11.14**). At threshold, we see a weak twitch (at *3* in the bottom row of the figure), and if we

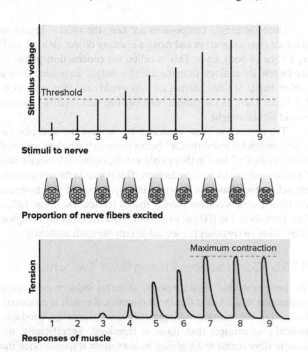

FIGURE 11.14   The Relationship Between Stimulus Intensity (Voltage) and Muscle Tension. Top row: Nine stimuli of increasing strengths. The first two are subthreshold stimuli. Middle row: Cross section of a motor nerve with seven nerve fibers. The colored nerve fibers are the excited ones; note that none are excited by the subthreshold stimuli above. Bottom row: Graph of muscle tension. Subthreshold stimuli (1–2) produce no muscle contraction. When stimuli reach or exceed threshold (3–7), they excite more and more nerve fibers and motor units; thus, they produce stronger and stronger contractions. This is multiple motor unit summation (recruitment). Once all of the nerve fibers are stimulated (7–9), further increases in stimulus strength produce no further increase in muscle tension.

continue to raise the voltage, we see stronger twitches. The reason for this is that higher voltages excite more and more nerve fibers in the motor nerve (middle row of the figure), and thus stimulate more and more motor units to contract. The process of bringing more motor units into play is called **recruitment,** or **multiple motor unit (MMU) summation.** This is seen not just in artificial stimulation, but is part of the way the nervous system behaves naturally to produce varying muscle contractions. The neuromuscular system behaves according to the **size principle**—smaller, less powerful motor units with smaller, slower nerve fibers are activated first. This is sufficient for delicate tasks and refined movements, but if more power is needed, then larger motor units with larger, faster nerve fibers are subsequently activated.

But even when stimulus intensity (voltage) remains constant, twitch strength can vary with stimulus frequency. High-frequency stimulation produces stronger twitches than low-frequency stimulation. In **figure 11.15a,** we see that when a muscle is stimulated at low frequency, say 5 to 10 stimuli/s, it produces an identical twitch for each stimulus and fully recovers between twitches.

At higher stimulus frequencies, say 20 to 40 stimuli/s, each new stimulus arrives before the previous twitch is over. Each new twitch "rides piggyback" on the previous one and generates higher tension (**fig. 11.15b**). This phenomenon goes by two names: **temporal**[10] **summation,** because it results from two stimuli arriving close together in time, or **wave summation,** because it results from one wave of contraction added to another. Wave upon wave, each twitch reaches a higher level of tension than the one before, and the muscle relaxes only partially between stimuli. This effect produces a state of sustained fluttering contraction called **incomplete tetanus.**

In the laboratory, an isolated muscle can be stimulated at such high frequency that the twitches fuse into a single, nonfluctuating contraction called **complete (fused) tetanus (fig. 11.15c).** This doesn't happen in the body, however, because motor neurons don't fire that fast. Indeed, there is an inhibitory mechanism in the spinal cord that prevents them from doing so. Complete tetanus is injurious to muscle and associated soft tissues, so spinal inhibition protects the muscles by preventing complete tetanus. Muscle tetanus should not be confused with the disease of the same name caused by the tetanus toxin (see Deeper Insight 11.1).

Despite the fluttering contraction seen in incomplete tetanus, we know that a muscle taken as a whole can contract very smoothly. This is possible because motor units function asynchronously; when one motor unit relaxes, another contracts and takes over so that the muscle doesn't lose tension.

11.5c Isometric and Isotonic Contraction

In muscle physiology, "contraction" doesn't always mean the shortening of a muscle—it may mean only that the muscle produces internal tension while an external resistance causes it to stay the same length or even become longer. Thus, physiologists speak of different kinds of muscle contraction as *isometric* versus *isotonic* and *concentric* versus *eccentric* (**fig. 11.16**).

[10]*tempor* = time; *al* = pertaining to

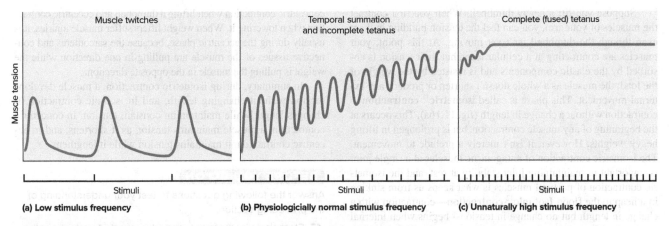

FIGURE 11.15 The Relationship Between Stimulus Frequency and Muscle Tension. (a) Twitch. At an unnaturally low stimulus frequency, as in laboratory preparations, the muscle relaxes completely between stimuli and shows twitches of uniform strength. (b) At a stimulus frequency within normal physiological range, the muscle doesn't have time to relax completely between twitches and the force of each twitch builds on the previous one, creating the state of incomplete tetanus. In this state, a muscle can attain three to four times as much tension, or force, as a single twitch produces. (c) At an unnaturally high stimulus frequency, attained only in laboratory preparations, the muscle can't relax at all between twitches, and twitches fuse into a state of complete tetanus.

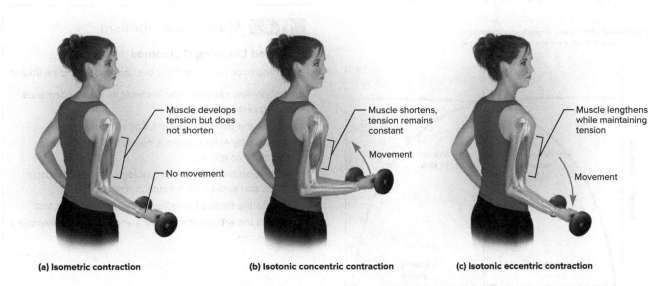

FIGURE 11.16 Isometric and Isotonic Contraction. (a) Isometric contraction, in which a muscle develops tension but doesn't shorten. (b) Isotonic concentric contraction, in which the muscle shortens while maintaining a constant degree of tension. (c) Isotonic eccentric contraction, in which the muscle maintains tension while it lengthens, allowing a muscle to relax without going suddenly limp.

❓ *Name a muscle that undergoes eccentric contraction as you sit down in a chair.*

Suppose you lift a heavy dumbbell. When you first contract the muscles of your arm, you can feel the tension building in them even though the dumbbell isn't yet moving. At this point, your muscles are contracting at a cellular level, but their tension is absorbed by the elastic components and is resisted by the weight of the load; the muscle as a whole doesn't shorten or produce any external movement. This phase is called **isometric**[11] **contraction**—contraction without a change in length (fig. 11.16a). This occurs at the beginning of any muscle contraction, but is prolonged in lifting heavy weights. However, it isn't merely a prelude to movement. The isometric contraction of antagonistic muscles at a single joint is important in maintaining joint stability at rest, and the isometric contraction of postural muscles is what keeps us from sinking in a heap to the floor. **Isotonic**[12] **contraction**—contraction with a change in length but no change in tension—begins when internal tension builds to the point that it overcomes the resistance. The muscle now shortens, moves the load, and maintains essentially the same tension from then on (fig. 11.16b). Isometric and isotonic contraction are both phases of normal muscular action (**fig. 11.17**).

There are two forms of isotonic contraction: concentric and eccentric. In **concentric contraction,** a muscle shortens as it maintains tension—for example, when the biceps contracts and flexes the elbow. In **eccentric contraction,** a muscle lengthens as it maintains tension. If you set that dumbbell down again (fig. 11.16c), your biceps lengthens as you extend your elbow, but it maintains tension to act as a brake and keep you from simply dropping the weight. A weight lifter uses concentric contraction when lifting a dumbbell and eccentric contraction when lowering it. When weight lifters suffer muscle injuries, it is usually during the eccentric phase, because the sarcomeres and connective tissues of the muscle are pulling in one direction while the weight is pulling the muscle in the opposite direction.

In summary, during isometric contraction, a muscle develops tension without changing length, and in isotonic contraction, it changes length while maintaining constant tension. In concentric contraction, a muscle maintains tension as it shortens, and in eccentric contraction, it maintains tension while it lengthens.

> ### BEFORE YOU GO ON
> Answer the following questions to test your understanding of the preceding section:
>
> **17.** State three or more reasons why muscle twitch strength can vary even when stimulus intensity remains constant.
>
> **18.** Explain the role of tetanus in normal muscle action.
>
> **19.** Describe an everyday activity not involving the arms in which your muscles would switch from isometric to isotonic contraction.
>
> **20.** Describe an everyday activity not involving the arms that would involve concentric contraction and one that would involve eccentric contraction.

[11]*iso* = same, uniform; *metr* = length; *ic* = pertaining to
[12]*iso* = same, uniform; *ton* = tension; *ic* = pertaining to

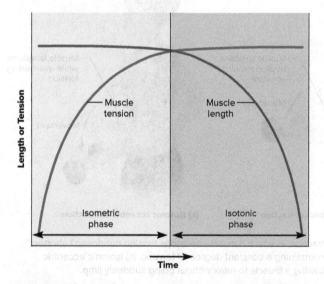

FIGURE 11.17 Isometric and Isotonic Phases of Contraction. At the beginning of a contraction (isometric phase), muscle tension rises but the length remains constant (the muscle does not shorten). When tension overcomes the resistance of the load, the tension levels off and the muscle begins to shorten and move the load (isotonic phase).

? *How would you extend this graph in order to show eccentric contraction?*

11.6 Muscle Metabolism

Expected Learning Outcomes
When you have completed this section, you should be able to

a. explain how skeletal muscle meets its energy demands during rest and exercise;

b. explain the basis of muscle fatigue and soreness;

c. discuss why extra oxygen is needed even after an exercise has ended;

d. distinguish between two physiological types of muscle fibers, and explain their functional roles;

e. discuss the factors that affect muscular strength; and

f. discuss the effects of resistance and endurance exercises on muscles.

11.6a ATP Sources

All muscle contraction depends on ATP; no other energy source can serve in its place. The supply of ATP depends, in turn, on the availability of oxygen and organic fuels such as glucose and fatty acids. To understand how muscle manages its ATP budget, you must be acquainted with the two main pathways of ATP synthesis: *anaerobic fermentation* and *aerobic respiration* (see fig. 2.31). Each of these has advantages and disadvantages. Anaerobic fermentation enables a cell to produce ATP without the need for oxygen, but the ATP yield is very limited and the process generates

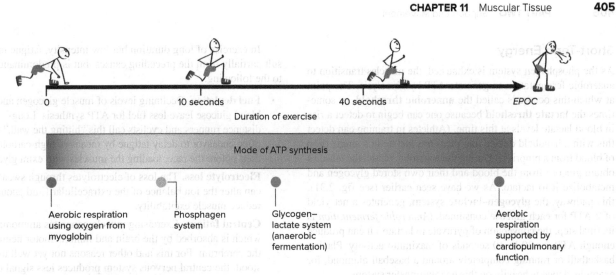

Duration of exercise

Mode of ATP synthesis

Aerobic respiration using oxygen from myoglobin

Phosphagen system

Glycogen–lactate system (anaerobic fermentation)

Aerobic respiration supported by cardiopulmonary function

FIGURE 11.18 Modes of ATP Synthesis During Exercise.

a toxic by-product, lactate (lactic acid), which must be removed from the muscle and disposed of by the liver. By contrast, aerobic respiration produces far more ATP and no lactate, but it requires a continual supply of oxygen. Although aerobic respiration is best known as a pathway for glucose oxidation, it is also used to extract energy from other organic compounds. In a resting muscle, most ATP is generated by the aerobic respiration of fatty acids.

During the course of exercise, different mechanisms of ATP synthesis are used depending on the exercise duration. We will view these from the standpoint of immediate, short-term, and long-term energy, but it must be stressed that muscle doesn't make sudden shifts from one mechanism to another like an automobile transmission shifting gears. Rather, these mechanisms blend and overlap as the exercise continues **(fig. 11.18)**.

Immediate Energy

In a short, intense exercise such as a 100 m dash, the myoglobin in a muscle fiber supplies oxygen for a limited amount of aerobic respiration at the outset, but this oxygen supply is quickly depleted. Until the respiratory and cardiovascular systems catch up with the heightened oxygen demand, the muscle meets most of its ATP needs by borrowing phosphate groups (P_i) from other molecules and transferring them to ADP. Two enzyme systems control these phosphate transfers **(fig. 11.19)**:

1. **Myokinase** (MY-oh-KY-nase) transfers P_i from one ADP to another, converting the latter to ATP that myosin can use.

2. **Creatine kinase** (CREE-uh-tin KY-nase) obtains P_i from a phosphate-storage molecule, **creatine phosphate (CP),** and donates it to ADP to make ATP. This is a fast-acting system that helps to maintain the ATP level while other ATP-generating mechanisms are being activated.

ATP and CP, collectively called the **phosphagen system,** provide nearly all the energy used for short bursts of intense activity. Muscle contains about 5 millimoles of ATP and 15 millimoles of CP per kilogram of tissue. Perhaps surprisingly, at the outset of an intense exercise, the amount of ATP in the muscle fibers changes

very little, but the amount of CP drops rapidly. The total supply of ATP + CP is enough to power about 1 minute of brisk walking or 6 seconds of sprinting or fast swimming. The phosphagen system is especially important in activities requiring short bursts of maximal effort, such as football, baseball, and weight lifting.

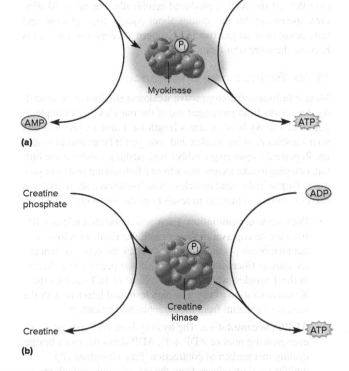

(a)

(b)

FIGURE 11.19 The Phosphagen System. (a) Myokinase, which obtains phosphates from ADP. (b) Creatine kinase, which obtains phosphates from creatine phosphate.

Short-Term Energy

As the phosphagen system is exhausted, the muscles transition to anaerobic fermentation to generate ATP by glycolysis. The point at which this occurs is called the **anaerobic threshold,** or sometimes the **lactate threshold** because one can begin to detect a rise in blood lactate levels at this time. (Athletes in training can detect this with a handheld device that measures lactate in a single drop of blood from a pinprick.) During the anaerobic phase, the muscles obtain glucose from the blood and their own stored glycogen and metabolize it to lactate. As we have seen earlier (see fig. 2.31), this pathway, the **glycogen–lactate system,** generates a net yield of 2 ATP for each glucose consumed. (*Anaerobic fermentation* is its final step, the conversion of pyruvate to lactate.) It can produce enough ATP for 30 to 40 seconds of maximum activity. Playing basketball or running completely around a baseball diamond, for example, depends heavily on this energy-transfer system.

Long-Term Energy

After 40 seconds or so, the respiratory and cardiovascular systems "catch up" and deliver oxygen to the muscles fast enough for aerobic respiration to once again meet most of the ATP demand. Aerobic respiration produces much more ATP than glycolysis does—typically another 30 ATP per glucose. Thus it is a very efficient means of meeting the ATP demands of prolonged exercise. One's rate of oxygen consumption rises for 3 to 4 minutes and then levels off at a *steady state* in which aerobic ATP production keeps pace with the demand. In exercises lasting more than 10 minutes, over 90% of the ATP is produced aerobically. For up to 30 minutes, the energy for this comes about equally from glucose and fatty acids; then, as glucose and glycogen are depleted, fatty acids become the more significant fuel.

11.6b Fatigue and Endurance

Muscle **fatigue** is the progressive weakness and loss of contractility that results from prolonged use of the muscles. For example, if you hold a heavy book at arm's length for a minute, you will feel your muscles growing weaker and soon you'll be unable to hold it up. Repeatedly squeezing a rubber ball, pushing a video game button, or trying to take lecture notes from a fast-talking professor produces fatigue in the hand muscles. In high-intensity, short-duration exercise, fatigue is thought to result from the following factors:

- **Potassium accumulation.** Each action potential releases K^+ from the sarcoplasm to the extracellular fluid. This lowers the membrane potential (hyperpolarizes the cell) and makes the muscle fiber less excitable. This is especially significant in the T tubules, where the low volume of ECF enables the K^+ concentration to rise to a high level and interfere with the release of calcium from the sarcoplasmic reticulum.
- **ADP/P_i accumulation.** The hydrolysis of ATP generates an ever-growing pool of ADP + P_i. ADP slows the cross-bridge cycling mechanism of contraction. Free phosphate (P_i) inhibits calcium release from the sarcoplasmic reticulum, calcium sensitivity of the contractile mechanism, and force production by the myofibrils. It is now thought to be a major contributor to muscle fatigue.

In exercise of long duration but low intensity, fatigue may result partially from the preceding causes, but is predominantly due to the following:

- **Fuel depletion.** Declining levels of muscle glycogen and blood glucose leave less fuel for ATP synthesis. Long-distance runners and cyclists call this "hitting the wall," and often endeavor to delay fatigue by means of high-carbohydrate diets before the race, loading the muscles with extra glycogen.
- **Electrolyte loss.** The loss of electrolytes through sweating can alter the ion balance of the extracellular fluid enough to reduce muscle excitability.
- **Central fatigue.** Exercising muscle generates ammonia, which is absorbed by the brain and inhibits motor neurons of the cerebrum. For this and other reasons not yet well understood, the central nervous system produces less signal output to the skeletal muscles. This is where psychological factors come into play, such as the will to complete a marathon.

Some former hypotheses on muscle fatigue have been discredited by more recent research. ATP depletion per se is no longer thought to cause fatigue; the ATP level in fatigued muscle is almost as great as in rested muscle. It was also long thought that the lactate from anaerobic fermentation contributed to fatigue by lowering the pH in the muscle fiber. Alterations in protein conformation by low pH could interfere with many processes required for contraction, such as Ca^{2+} binding by troponin, cross-bridge formation, and ATP hydrolysis by myosin, among others. Evidence has now shown, however, that lactate is removed to the liver about as fast as the muscles produce it, so it doesn't accumulate in the muscle tissue and probably has little or nothing to do with fatigue.

The ability to maintain high-intensity exercise for more than 4 or 5 minutes is determined in large part by one's **maximum oxygen uptake (Vo_2max)**—the point at which the rate of oxygen consumption reaches a plateau and increases no further with an added workload. Vo_2max is proportional to body size; it peaks around age 20; it is usually greater in males than in females; and it can be twice as great in a trained endurance athlete as in an untrained person. A typical sedentary adult uses a maximum of about 35 milliliters of oxygen per minute per kilogram of body weight. Such a person weighing 73 kg (160 lb) and exercising at maximum intensity could therefore "burn" oxygen at about 2.6 L/min., which sets a limit to his rate of ATP production. Elite endurance athletes can have a Vo_2max of about 70 mL/min./kg (5.2 L/min. for the same body weight).

11.6c Excess Postexercise Oxygen Consumption

You have probably noticed that you breathe heavily not only during strenuous exercise but also for several minutes afterward (fig. 11.18). This is to meet a metabolic demand called **excess postexercise oxygen consumption (EPOC),** also known by an older popularized term, **oxygen debt.** EPOC is the difference between the elevated rate of oxygen consumption at the end of an exercise and the normal rate at rest. It occurs in part because oxygen is needed to regenerate ATP aerobically, and that ATP goes in part to regenerate creatine phosphate. A small amount of oxygen serves to reoxygenate the muscle myoglobin, and the liver consumes oxygen in disposing of the lactate generated by exercise. In addition, exercise raises the body temperature and overall metabolic rate, which in itself consumes more oxygen.

ATP and CP are replenished in the early minutes of heaviest postexercise breathing, and oxygen consumption remains elevated for as much as an hour more as the liver uses it to oxidize lactate. EPOC can be as much as six times one's basal oxygen consumption, indicating that anaerobic mechanisms of ATP production during exercise allow six times as much physical exertion as would have been possible without those mechanisms.

11.6d Physiological Classes of Muscle Fibers

Not all muscle fibers are alike or adapted for the same tasks. For example, the weight-bearing and postural muscles of the back and lower limbs react slowly to stimulation and take up to 100 ms to reach peak tension. By contrast, muscles that control eye and hand movements react quickly to stimulation and reach peak tension in as little as 7.5 ms. The predominant fibers that compose these muscles are therefore called *slow-twitch* and *fast-twitch* fibers, respectively. We can find reasons for their differences in response time by looking at their cellular structure and biochemistry (**table 11.2**). The different fiber types can be identified in tissue sections with special histochemical staining (**fig. 11.20**).

Slow-twitch fibers are also called **slow oxidative (SO)** or **type I fibers.** They are well adapted for endurance and fatigue

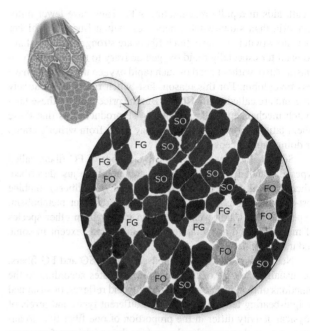

FIGURE 11.20 Skeletal Muscle Fiber Types. (FG, fast glycolytic fibers; SO, slow oxidative fibers; FO, fast oxidative fibers)
G W Willis/Getty Images

resistance, so they are particularly important in muscles that support the body and maintain posture, such as the erector spinae and quadratus lumborum of the back. Their fatigue resistance stems from their *oxidative* mode of ATP production—that is, aerobic respiration. Oxidative metabolism, of course, requires a liberal supply of oxygen and the means to use it efficiently. Therefore, these fibers are surrounded by a dense network of blood capillaries, they are rich in mitochondria, and they have a high concentration of myoglobin, the red pigment that facilitates diffusion of oxygen from the blood into the muscle fiber. Slow-twitch fibers are also relatively thin, which minimizes the distance that oxygen must diffuse to even the deepest mitochondria. The slowness of these muscles is due to a sarcoplasmic reticulum that is relatively slow to release and reabsorb calcium, and a form of myosin ATPase that is relatively slow in its ATP hydrolysis and cross-bridge cycling. The high myoglobin concentration of these fibers gives them a relatively bright red color, so they are also called **red fibers.**

Fast-twitch fibers are also called **fast glycolytic (FG)** or **type II fibers.** They are well adapted for quick responses, so they are particularly important in the aforesaid eye and hand muscles, and in large muscles such as the gastrocnemius and biceps brachii, which we employ in such actions as jumping and elbow flexion. Their quickness stems from an especially extensive sarcoplasmic reticulum with fast release and reabsorption of calcium, and a form of myosin with very quick ATP hydrolysis and cross-bridge cycling. For energy, they depend primarily on glycolysis and anaerobic fermentation, which produces ATP more quickly (yet less efficiently) than aerobic respiration. To support this, they contain a high concentration of glycogen. They also have a high concentration of creatine phosphate, which, you will

TABLE 11.2	Classification of Skeletal Muscle Fibers	
	Fiber Type	
Property	Slow-Twitch (Slow Oxidative)	Fast-Twitch (Fast Glycolytic)
Twitch duration	As long as 100 ms	As short as 7.5 ms
Motor unit size	Smaller	Larger
Motor neurons	Smaller, more excitable	Larger, less excitable
Motor unit strength	Weaker	Stronger
Relative diameter	Smaller	Larger
ATP synthesis	Aerobic	Anaerobic
Fatigue resistance	Good	Poor
ATP hydrolysis	Slow	Fast
Glycolysis	Moderate	Fast
Myoglobin content	Abundant	Low
Glycogen content	Low	Abundant
Mitochondria	Abundant and large	Fewer and smaller
Capillaries	Abundant	Fewer
Color	Red	White, pale
Representative muscles in which fiber type is predominant	Soleus Erector spinae Quadratus lumborum	Gastrocnemius Biceps brachii Muscles of eye movement

recall, aids in rapidly regenerating ATP. They have fewer mitochondria than slow-twitch fibers. Fast-twitch fibers are thicker than slow-twitch, because thick fibers are stronger and they have no need for especially rapid oxygen delivery to the deepest cytoplasm. Also, without need of such rapid oxygen uptake, they have less myoglobin. For this reason, fast-twitch fibers are relatively pale and are called **white fibers.** But the price paid for these fast-twitch mechanisms and anaerobic ATP production is that these fibers fatigue more easily, as you may know from writer's cramp or doing rapid biceps curls.

Some authorities recognize two subtypes of FG fibers called types IIA and IIB. Type IIB is the common type just described, whereas IIA (**intermediate** or **fast oxidative [FO] fibers**) combine fast-twitch responses with aerobic fatigue-resistant metabolism. Type IIA fibers, however, are known mainly from other species of mammals and are relatively rare in humans except in some endurance-trained athletes.

Nearly all muscles are composed of both SO and FG fibers, but usually one type or the other predominates according to the functions of that muscle—quick motility and reflexes, or sustained weight-bearing tension. People with different types and levels of physical activity differ in the proportion of one fiber type to another even in the same muscle, such as the *quadriceps femoris* of the anterior thigh (**table 11.3**). It is thought that people are born with a genetic predisposition for a certain ratio of fiber types. Those who go into competitive sports discover the sports at which they can excel and gravitate toward those for which heredity has best equipped them. One person might be a "born sprinter" and another a "born marathoner."

In humans, small motor units are composed of relatively small SO muscle fibers and supplied by small but easily excited motor neurons. These motor units are not as strong as large ones but produce more precise movements. Large motor units are composed of larger FG fibers; supplied by larger, less excitable neurons; and produce more power but less fine control. In the *size principle* discussed earlier (section 11.5b), the nervous system recruits small SO motor units first, then larger FG motor units only if more strength is needed for a particular task.

Muscles composed mainly of SO fibers are called *red muscles,* and those composed mainly of FG fibers are called *white muscles* because of the color difference stemming from their difference in myoglobin content. Anyone who eats chicken or turkey may be unwittingly

familiar with this distinction. The thighs are dark meat composed of SO fibers adapted to long periods of standing, and the breast is white meat composed of FG fibers adapted for short bursts of power when the birds take flight. Duck breast, however, is dark meat (red muscle) adapted for long-distance flight, because unlike chickens and turkeys, domestic ducks are descended from migratory ancestors.

We saw in chapter 10 that sometimes two or more muscles act across the same joint and seem to have the same function. We have already seen some reasons why such muscles are not as redundant as they seem. Another reason is that they may differ in the proportion of SO to FG fibers. For example, the gastrocnemius and soleus muscles of the calf both insert on the calcaneus, so they exert the same pull on the heel. The gastrocnemius, however, is a white, predominantly FG muscle adapted for quick, powerful movements such as jumping, whereas the soleus is a red, SO muscle that does most of the work in standing and in endurance exercises such as jogging and skiing.

11.6e Muscular Strength and Conditioning

We have far more muscular strength than we normally use. The gluteus maximus can generate 1,200 kg of tension, and all the muscles collectively can produce a total tension of 22,000 kg (nearly 25 tons). Indeed, the muscles can generate more tension than the bones and tendons can withstand—a fact that accounts for many injuries to the patellar and calcaneal tendons. Muscular strength depends on a variety of anatomical and physiological factors:

- **Muscle size.** The strength of a muscle depends primarily on its size; thicker muscles can form more myosin–actin cross-bridges and therefore generate more tension. A muscle can exert a tension of about 3 to 4 kg/cm^2 of cross-sectional area. This is why weight lifting increases both size and strength of a muscle.
- **Fascicle arrangement** (see fig. 10.2). Pennate muscles such as the rectus femoris are stronger than parallel muscles such as the sartorius, which in turn are stronger than circular muscles such as the orbicularis oculi.
- **Size of active motor units.** Large motor units produce stronger contractions than small ones.
- **Multiple motor unit summation.** When a stronger muscle contraction is desired, the nervous system activates more and larger motor units. Getting "psyched up" for athletic competition is partly a matter of multiple motor unit (MMU) summation.
- **Temporal summation.** Nerve impulses usually arrive at a muscle in a series of closely spaced action potentials. Because of the temporal summation described earlier, the greater the frequency of stimulation, the stronger the muscle contraction.
- **The length–tension relationship.** As noted earlier, a muscle resting at optimum length is prepared to contract more forcefully than a muscle that is excessively contracted or stretched. This is affected by one's posture, such as a runner's crouch, just before the onset of muscular effort.

TABLE 11.3	Proportion of Slow Oxidative (SO) and Fast Glycolytic (FG) Fibers in the Quadriceps Femoris Muscle of Male Athletes	
Sample Population	SO	FG
Marathon runners	82%	18%
Swimmers	74	26
Average males	45	55
Sprinters and jumpers	37	63

- **Fatigue.** Rested muscles contract more strongly than fatigued ones.

As fitness trainers and exercise enthusiasts know, there are two kinds of exercise with different effects on muscles—resistance and endurance exercise. **Resistance exercise,** such as weight lifting, is the contraction of muscles against a load that resists movement. A few minutes of resistance exercise at a time, a few times each week, is enough to stimulate muscle growth. Growth results primarily from cellular enlargement, not cellular division. The muscle fibers synthesize more myofilaments and the myofibrils grow thicker. Myofibrils split longitudinally when they reach a certain size, so a well-conditioned muscle has more myofibrils than a poorly conditioned one. Muscle fibers themselves are incapable of mitosis, but there is some evidence that as they enlarge, they too may split longitudinally. A small part of muscle growth may therefore result from an increase in the number of fibers, but most of it results from the enlargement of fibers that have existed since puberty.

Endurance (aerobic) exercise, such as jogging or swimming, improves the fatigue resistance of the muscles by enhancing the delivery and use of oxygen. Slow-twitch fibers, especially, produce more mitochondria and glycogen and acquire a greater density of blood capillaries as a result of conditioning. Endurance exercise also improves skeletal strength; increases the red blood cell count and the oxygen transport capacity of the blood; and enhances the function of the cardiovascular, respiratory, and nervous systems.

Endurance training doesn't significantly increase muscular strength, and resistance training doesn't improve endurance. Optimal performance and musculoskeletal health require **cross-training,** which incorporates elements of both types. If muscles aren't kept sufficiently active, they become *deconditioned*—weaker and more easily fatigued.

▶▶▶**APPLY WHAT YOU KNOW**

Is a weight lifter's muscle growth mainly the result of hypertrophy or hyperplasia?

BEFORE YOU GO ON

Answer the following questions to test your understanding of the preceding section:

21. From which two molecules can ADP borrow a phosphate group to become ATP? What is the enzyme that catalyzes each transfer?

22. In a long period of intense exercise, why does muscle generate ATP anaerobically at first and then switch to aerobic respiration?

23. List four causes of muscle fatigue.

24. List three causes of excess postexercise oxygen consumption.

25. What properties of fast glycolytic and slow oxidative fibers adapt them for different physiological purposes?

11.7 Cardiac and Smooth Muscle

Expected Learning Outcomes

When you have completed this section, you should be able to

a. describe the structural and physiological differences between cardiac muscle and skeletal muscle;

b. explain why these differences are important to cardiac function;

c. describe the structural and physiological differences between smooth muscle and skeletal muscle; and

d. relate the unique properties of smooth muscle to its locations and functions.

Cardiac and smooth muscle have special structural and physiological properties in common with each other, but different from those of skeletal muscle (**table 11.4**). These are related to their distinctive functions.

Any of the three types of muscle cells can be called **myocytes.** This term is preferable to *muscle fiber* for smooth and cardiac muscle because these two types of cells don't have the long fibrous shape of skeletal muscle cells. They are relatively short, and in further contrast to skeletal muscle fibers, they have only one or two nuclei. Cardiac muscle cells are also called **cardiomyocytes.**

Cardiac and smooth muscle are *involuntary* muscle tissues, not usually subject to our conscious control. They receive no innervation from somatic motor neurons, but cardiac muscle and some smooth muscle receive nerves from the sympathetic and parasympathetic divisions of the autonomic nervous system (see chapter 15).

11.7a Cardiac Muscle APR

Cardiac muscle is limited to the heart, where its function is to pump blood. Knowing that, we can predict the properties that it must have: (1) It must contract with a regular rhythm; (2) it must function in sleep and wakefulness, without fail or need of conscious attention; (3) it must be highly resistant to fatigue; (4) the cardiomyocytes of a given heart chamber must contract in unison so that the chamber can effectively expel blood; and (5) each contraction must last long enough to expel blood from the chamber. These functional necessities are the key to understanding how cardiac muscle differs structurally and physiologically from skeletal muscle (table 11.4).

Cardiac muscle is striated like skeletal muscle, but cardiomyocytes are shorter and thicker. They have one or two nuclei near the middle of the cell. Each cell is enclosed in an endomysium, but there is no perimysium or epimysium as in skeletal muscle. Cardiomyocytes branch slightly so each is joined end to end with several others. These intercellular connections, called **intercalated discs** (in-TUR-kuh-LAY-ted), appear as thick dark lines in stained tissue sections. An intercalated disc

TABLE 11.4	Comparison of Skeletal, Cardiac, and Smooth Muscle		
Feature	Skeletal Muscle	Cardiac Muscle	Smooth Muscle
Location	Associated with skeletal system	Heart	Walls of viscera and blood vessels, iris of eye, arrector muscle of hair follicles
Cell shape	Long threadlike fibers	Short, slightly branched cells	Short fusiform cells
Cell length	100 µm–30 cm	50–120 µm	30–200 µm
Cell width	10–500 µm	10–20 µm	5–10 µm
Striations	Present	Present	Absent
Nuclei	Multiple nuclei, adjacent to sarcolemma	Usually one nucleus, near middle of cell	One nucleus, near middle of cell
Connective tissues	Endomysium, perimysium, epimysium	Endomysium only	Endomysium only
Sarcoplasmic reticulum	Abundant	Present	Scanty
T tubules	Present, narrow	Present, wide	Absent
Gap junctions	Absent	Present in intercalated discs	Present in unitary smooth muscle
Autorhythmicity	Absent	Present	Present in unitary smooth muscle
Thin filament attachment	Z discs	Z discs	Dense bodies
Regulatory proteins	Tropomyosin, troponin	Tropomyosin, troponin	Calmodulin, myosin light-chain kinase
Ca^{2+} source	Sarcoplasmic reticulum	Sarcoplasmic reticulum and extracellular fluid	Mainly extracellular fluid
Ca^{2+} receptor	Troponin of thin filament	Troponin of thin filament	Calmodulin of thick filament
Innervation and control	Somatic motor fibers (voluntary)	Autonomic fibers (involuntary)	Autonomic fibers (involuntary)
Nervous stimulation required?	Yes	No	No
Effect of nervous stimulation	Excitatory only	Excitatory or inhibitory	Excitatory or inhibitory
Mode of tissue repair	Limited regeneration, mostly fibrosis	Limited regeneration, mostly fibrosis	Relatively good capacity for regeneration

has electrical *gap junctions* that allow each cardiomyocyte to directly stimulate its neighbors, and mechanical junctions that keep the cardiomyocytes from pulling apart when the heart contracts. The sarcoplasmic reticulum is less developed than in skeletal muscle, but the T tubules are larger and admit Ca^{2+} from the extracellular fluid. Damaged cardiac muscle is repaired by fibrosis. Cardiac muscle has no satellite cells, and even though mitosis has been detected in cardiomyocytes following heart attacks, it does not produce a significant amount of regenerated functional muscle.

Unlike skeletal muscle, cardiac muscle can contract without the need of nervous stimulation. The heart has a built-in **pacemaker** that rhythmically sets off a wave of electrical excitation, which travels through the muscle and triggers the contraction of the heart chambers. The heart is said to be **autorhythmic**[13]

because of this ability to contract rhythmically and independently. Stimulation by the autonomic nervous system, however, can increase or decrease the heart rate and contraction strength. Cardiac muscle does not exhibit quick twitches like skeletal muscle. Rather, it maintains tension for about 200 to 250 ms, giving the heart time to expel blood.

Cardiac muscle uses aerobic respiration almost exclusively. It is very rich in myoglobin and glycogen, and it has especially large mitochondria that fill about 25% of the cell, compared with smaller mitochondria occupying about 2% of a skeletal muscle fiber. Cardiac muscle is very adaptable with respect to the fuel used, but very vulnerable to interruptions in oxygen supply. Because it makes little use of anaerobic fermentation, cardiac muscle is highly resistant to fatigue.

11.7b Smooth Muscle APR

Smooth muscle is named for the fact that it has no striations, for a reason to be described shortly. Its myocytes are relatively small,

[13]*auto* = self

allowing for fine control of such tissues and organs as a single hair, the iris of the eye, and the tiniest arteries; yet, in the pregnant uterus, the myocytes become quite large and contribute to the powerful contractions of childbirth.

Smooth muscle isn't always innervated, but when it is, the nerve supply is autonomic, like that of the heart. Autonomic nerve fibers usually don't form precisely localized neuromuscular junctions with the myocytes. Rather, a nerve fiber has as many as 20,000 periodic swellings called **varicosities** along its length **(fig. 11.21).** Each varicosity contains synaptic vesicles from which it releases neurotransmitters—usually norepinephrine from the sympathetic fibers and acetylcholine from the parasympathetic fibers. The myocyte has no motor end plate, but instead has receptors for these neurotransmitters distributed over its surface. The varicosities simply release a flood of neurotransmitter into the tissue, and each myocyte may respond to more than one nerve fiber.

Whether innervated or not, smooth muscle responds to a wide variety of stimuli and often without any electrical excitation of the sarcolemma. It is much slower than skeletal and cardiac muscle to contract and relax, but it can remain contracted for a long time without fatigue and with minimal energy expenditure.

Smooth muscle doesn't usually form organs in itself, but forms layers in the walls of larger organs such as the stomach, intestines, uterus, and urinary bladder. In such cases, the muscle layer is quite variable in complexity. It can consist of as little as one cell in small arteries. The esophagus and intestines have an outer layer of longitudinal smooth muscle adjacent to a deeper, inner layer of circular muscle **(fig. 11.22).** When the longitudinal layer contracts, it shortens and dilates the organ; when the circular layer contracts, it constricts and lengthens the organ. In

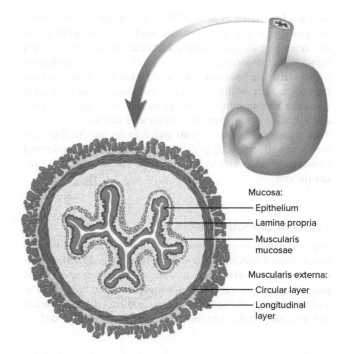

FIGURE 11.22 Layers of Visceral Muscle in a Cross Section of the Esophagus.

Mucosa:
- Epithelium
- Lamina propria
- Muscularis mucosae

Muscularis externa:
- Circular layer
- Longitudinal layer

the stomach, urinary bladder, and uterus, smooth muscle forms three or more layers with bundles of myocytes running in multiple directions.

Smooth muscle can propel the contents of an organ, such as driving food through the digestive tract, voiding urine and feces, and expelling the infant in childbirth. By dilating or constricting the blood vessels and airway, it can modify the speed of air and blood flow, maintain blood pressure, and reroute blood from one pathway to another.

Unlike skeletal and cardiac muscle, smooth muscle is capable of not only hypertrophy (cellular growth) but also mitosis and hyperplasia (cell division). Thus, an organ such as the pregnant uterus grows by the addition of new myocytes as well as enlargement of existing ones. Injured smooth muscle regenerates well by mitosis.

Myocyte Structure

Smooth muscle myocytes have a fusiform shape, typically about 5 to 10 μm wide at the middle, tapering to a point at each end, and usually ranging from 30 to 200 μm long—but up to 500 μm long in the pregnant uterus. They are enclosed in endomysium but have no perimysium, fascicles, or epimysium. There is only one nucleus, located near the middle of the cell. The sarcoplasmic reticulum is scanty and there are no T tubules. Thick and thin filaments are present, but there are no striations, sarcomeres, or myofibrils because the myofilaments are not bundled and aligned with each other the way

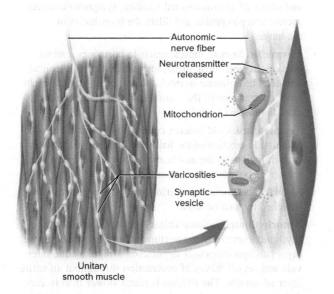

Autonomic nerve fiber

Neurotransmitter released

Mitochondrion

Varicosities

Synaptic vesicle

Unitary smooth muscle

FIGURE 11.21 Varicosities of an Autonomic Nerve Fiber in Unitary Smooth Muscle.

they are in striated muscle. Z discs are absent. In their place are protein plaques called **dense bodies,** some adhering to the inner face of the plasma membrane and others dispersed throughout the sarcoplasm (see fig. 11.24). The membrane-associated dense bodies of one cell are often directly across from those of another, with linkages between them so that contractile force can be transmitted from cell to cell. Associated with the dense bodies is an extensive cytoskeletal network of intermediate filaments. Actin filaments attach to the intermediate filaments as well as directly to the dense bodies, so their movement (powered by myosin) is transferred to the sarcolemma and shortens the cell.

Types of Smooth Muscle

Smooth muscle tissue shows a range of types between two extremes called *multiunit* and *unitary* types **(fig. 11.23). Multiunit smooth muscle** occurs in some of the largest arteries and pulmonary air passages, arrector muscles of the hair follicles, and eye muscles that control the iris and lens. Its innervation, although autonomic, is to some degree similar to that of skeletal

muscle—the terminal branches of a nerve fiber synapse with individual myocytes and form a motor unit. Each varicosity is associated with a particular myocyte, and each myocyte responds independently of all the others—hence the name *multiunit*. Multiunit smooth muscle does not, however, generate action potentials. It contracts in response to variable (graded) electrical changes in the sarcolemma or even in the absence of electrical excitation.

Unitary (single-unit) smooth muscle is more common. It occurs in most blood vessels and in the digestive, respiratory, urinary, and reproductive tracts—therefore, it is also called **visceral muscle.** This type forms the aforementioned layers in many of the hollow viscera. The names *unitary* and *single-unit* refer to the fact that the myocytes of this type of muscle are electrically coupled to each other by gap junctions. This allows them to directly stimulate each other, so numerous cells contract as a unit, almost as if they were a single cell. In this muscle type, the nerve varicosities are not associated with a specific myocyte, but stimulate several of them at once when they release neurotransmitter.

Excitation of Smooth Muscle

Whereas skeletal muscle contracts only in response to excitatory stimulation by a somatic motor fiber, smooth muscle can be stimulated in a multitude of ways. Some stimuli excite the myocyte and others inhibit it. Some produce action potentials in the sarcolemma, particularly in unitary smooth muscle, whereas others stimulate the myocyte by nonelectrical means. Some smooth muscle has no nerve supply at all. Modes of smooth muscle stimulation and some examples include

- **Autonomic nerve fibers and neurotransmitters.** For example, parasympathetic nerves secrete acetylcholine and stimulate gastrointestinal motility; sympathetic nerves secrete norepinephrine and dilate the bronchioles of the lungs.

- **Chemicals.** Smooth muscle reacts to hormones, carbon dioxide, oxygen, nitric oxide, low pH, and other chemical stimuli. The hormone oxytocin, for example, stimulates the labor contractions of the uterus, and histamine relaxes the smooth muscle of arteries.

- **Temperature.** Cold induces contraction of smooth muscle resulting in erection of the hairs and tautening of the skin in such regions as the areola and scrotum, whereas warmth relaxes smooth muscle in arteries of the skin.

- **Stretch.** The stomach and urinary bladder contract when stretched by food or urine.

- **Autorhythmicity.** Some unitary smooth muscle is autorhythmic, especially in the stomach and intestines. Some myocytes spontaneously depolarize at regular time intervals and set off waves of contraction throughout an entire layer of muscle. The rhythm is much slower than in cardiac muscle.

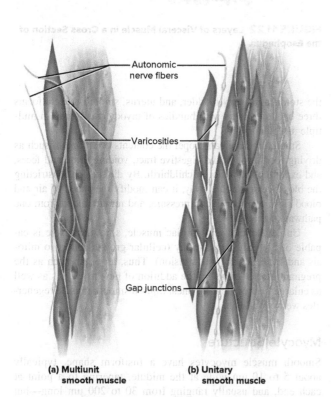

(a) Multiunit smooth muscle   **(b) Unitary smooth muscle**

FIGURE 11.23 Multiunit and Unitary Smooth Muscle.
(a) Multiunit smooth muscle, in which each muscle cell receives its own nerve supply and contracts independently. (b) Unitary smooth muscle, in which a nerve fiber passes through the tissue without synapsing with any specific muscle cell, and muscle cells are coupled by electrical gap junctions.

Autonomic nerve fibers — Varicosities — Gap junctions

Regardless of how a myocyte is stimulated, however, the immediate trigger for contraction is the same as in skeletal and cardiac muscle—calcium ions. In some cases, the Ca^{2+} comes from the sarcoplasmic reticulum (SR), as it does in skeletal muscle. With a relatively sparse SR, however, smooth muscle usually gets most of its Ca^{2+} from the extracellular fluid by way of gated calcium channels in the sarcolemma. Compensating for the paucity of SR, the sarcolemma has numerous little pockets called **caveolae** (CAV-ee-OH-lee) where its calcium channels are concentrated. Calcium is 10,000 times as concentrated in the ECF as in the cytosol, so if these channels are opened, it diffuses quickly into the cell. Because smooth muscle cells are relatively small, the incoming Ca^{2+} quickly reaches all of the myofilaments.

What opens these gated channels? Some are mechanically gated and open in response to physical distortion such as stretch. This is the case in organs that periodically fill and empty, such as the stomach and urinary bladder. Some are voltage-gated and open in response to electrical depolarization of the sarcolemma. Still others are ligand-gated and open in response to chemicals originating outside the cell or from the cytosol. Acetylcholine and norepinephrine, for example, bind to surface receptors and activate the formation of second messengers within the smooth muscle cell. This leads to a series of intracellular events that open the surface calcium channels from within.

▶▶▶APPLY WHAT YOU KNOW

How is smooth muscle contraction affected by the drugs called calcium channel blockers? (See Deeper Insight 3.1.)

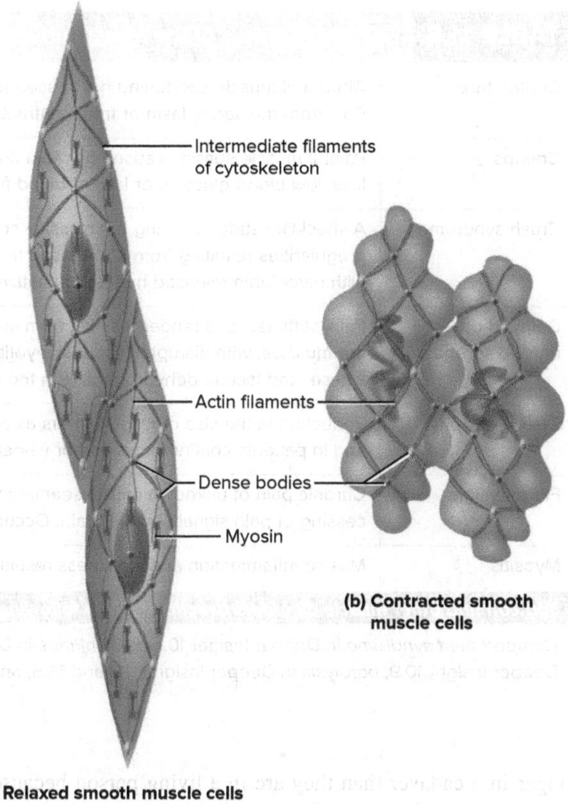

Contraction and Relaxation

Calcium ions are the immediate trigger for contraction, but unlike skeletal and cardiac muscle, smooth muscle has no troponin to bind it. Calcium binds instead to a similar protein called **calmodulin**[14] (cal-MOD-you-lin), associated with myosin. Calmodulin then activates an enzyme called **myosin light-chain kinase,** which adds a phosphate group to a small regulatory protein on the myosin head. This activates the myosin ATPase, enabling it to bind to actin and hydrolyze ATP. The myosin then produces repetitive power and recovery strokes like those of skeletal muscle.

As thick filaments pull on the thin ones, the thin filaments pull on the dense bodies and membrane plaques. Through the dense bodies and cytoskeleton, force is transferred to the plasma membrane and the entire cell shortens. When a smooth muscle cell contracts, it puckers and twists somewhat like wringing out a wet towel **(fig. 11.24).**

In skeletal muscle, there is typically a 2 ms latent period between stimulation and the onset of contraction. In smooth muscle, by contrast, the latent period is 50 to 100 ms long. Tension peaks about 500 ms (0.5 second) after the stimulus and then declines over

[14]acronym for *calcium modulating protein*

(b) Contracted smooth muscle cells

(a) Relaxed smooth muscle cells

FIGURE 11.24 Smooth Muscle Contraction. (a) Relaxed cells. (b) Contracted cells.

a period of 1 to 2 seconds. The effect of all this is that compared with skeletal muscle, smooth muscle is very slow to contract and relax. It is slow to contract because its myosin ATPase is a slow enzyme. It is slow to relax because the pumps that remove Ca^{2+} from the cytosol are also slow. As the Ca^{2+} level falls, myosin releases its phosphate group and is no longer able to hydrolyze ATP and execute power strokes. However, it doesn't necessarily detach from actin immediately. It has a **latch-bridge mechanism** that enables it to remain attached to actin for a prolonged time without consuming more ATP.

Smooth muscle often exhibits tetanus and is very resistant to fatigue. It makes most of its ATP aerobically, but its ATP requirement is small and it has relatively few mitochondria. Skeletal muscle requires 10 to 300 times as much ATP as smooth muscle to maintain the same amount of tension. The fatigue resistance and latch-bridge mechanism of smooth muscle are important in enabling it to maintain a state of continual tonic contraction called **smooth muscle tone.** Muscle tone keeps the arteries in a state of partial constriction called *vasomotor tone.* A widespread loss of muscle tone in the arteries can cause a dangerous drop in blood pressure. Smooth muscle tone also keeps the intestines partially contracted. The intestines are much

TABLE 11.5	Some Disorders of the Muscular System
Contracture	Abnormal muscle shortening not caused by nervous stimulation. Can result from failure of the calcium pump to remove Ca^{2+} from the sarcoplasm or from contraction of scar tissue, as in burn patients.
Cramps	Painful muscle spasms caused by rapid firing of motor neurons; triggered by heavy exercise, cold, dehydration, electrolyte loss, low blood glucose, or lack of blood flow.
Crush syndrome	A shocklike state following the massive crushing of muscles; associated with high and potentially fatal fever, cardiac irregularities resulting from K^+ released from the muscle, and kidney failure resulting from blockage of the renal tubules with myoglobin released by the traumatized muscle. Myoglobinuria (myoglobin in the urine) is a common sign.
Delayed-onset muscle soreness	Pain, stiffness, and tenderness felt from several hours to a day after strenuous exercise. Associated with microtrauma to the muscles; with disrupted Z discs, myofibrils, and plasma membranes; and with elevated levels of myoglobin, creatine kinase, and lactate dehydrogenase in the blood.
Disuse atrophy	Reduction in the size of muscle fibers as a result of nerve damage or muscular inactivity, for example in limbs in a cast and in patients confined to a bed or wheelchair. Muscle strength can be lost at a rate of 3% per day of bed rest.
Fibromyalgia	Chronic pain of unknown cause, seeming to come from the muscles and bones but actually arising from abnormal processing of pain signals by the brain. Occurring twice as often in women as in men, especially between ages 30 and 50.
Myositis	Muscle inflammation and weakness resulting from infection or autoimmune disease.

You can find other muscle disorders described in the following places:

Compartment syndrome in Deeper Insight 10.1; *back injuries* in Deeper Insight 10.2; *hernia* in Deeper Insight 10.3; *common athletic injuries* in Deeper Insight 10.9; *paralysis* in Deeper Insights 11.1 and 13.5; and *muscular dystrophy* and *myasthenia gravis* in Deeper Insight 11.4.

longer in a cadaver than they are in a living person because of the loss of muscle tone at death.

Response to Stretch

Stretch alone sometimes causes smooth muscle to contract by opening mechanically gated calcium channels in the sarcolemma. Distension of the esophagus with food or the colon with feces, for example, evokes a wave of contraction called **peristalsis** (PERR-ih-STAL-sis) that propels the contents along the organ.

Smooth muscle exhibits a reaction called the **stress–relaxation (or receptive-relaxation) response.** When stretched, it briefly contracts and resists, but then relaxes. The significance of this response is apparent in the urinary bladder. If the stretched bladder contracted and didn't soon relax, it would expel urine almost as soon as it began to fill, thus failing to store the urine until an opportune time.

Remember that skeletal muscle cannot contract very forcefully if it is overstretched. Smooth muscle, however, is less limited by the length–tension relationship. It contracts forcefully even when greatly stretched, so hollow organs such as the stomach and bladder can fill and then expel their contents efficiently. Skeletal muscle must be within 30% of optimum length in order to contract strongly when stimulated. Smooth muscle, by contrast, can be anywhere from half to twice its resting length and still contract powerfully. There are three reasons for this: (1) There are no Z discs, so thick filaments cannot butt against them and stop the contraction; (2) since the thick and thin filaments are not arranged in orderly sarcomeres, stretching of the muscle doesn't cause a situation in which there is too little overlap for cross-bridges to form; and (3) the thick filaments of smooth muscle have myosin heads along their entire length (there is no bare zone), so cross-bridges can form anywhere, not just at the ends. Smooth muscle also exhibits **plasticity**—the ability to adjust its tension to the degree of stretch. Thus, a hollow organ such as the bladder can be greatly stretched yet not become flabby when it is empty.

The muscular system suffers fewer diseases than any other organ system, but several of its more common dysfunctions are listed in **table 11.5.** The effects of aging on the muscular system are described in section 29.4a.

BEFORE YOU GO ON

Answer the following questions to test your understanding of the preceding section:

26. Explain why intercalated discs are important to cardiac muscle function.

27. Explain why it is important for cardiac muscle to have longer-lasting contractions than skeletal muscle.

28. How do unitary and multiunit smooth muscle differ in innervation and contractile behavior?

29. How does smooth muscle differ from skeletal muscle with respect to its source of calcium and its calcium receptor?

30. Explain why the stress–relaxation response is an important factor in smooth muscle function.

DEEPER INSIGHT 11.4

CLINICAL APPLICATION

Muscular Dystrophy and Myasthenia Gravis

Muscular dystrophy[15] is a collective term for several hereditary diseases in which the muscles degenerate, weaken, and are gradually replaced by fat and fibrous scar tissue. The most common form of the disease is *Duchenne*[16] *muscular dystrophy (DMD)*, a sex-linked recessive trait affecting about 1 out of every 3,500 live-born boys.

DMD is not evident at birth, but begins to exhibit its effects as a child shows difficulty keeping up with other children, falls frequently, and finds it hard to stand again. It is typically diagnosed between the ages of 2 and 10 years. It affects the muscles of the hips first; then the legs; and then progresses to the abdominal, spinal, and respiratory muscles as well as cardiac muscle. The muscles shorten as they atrophy, causing postural abnormalities such as scoliosis. Persons with DMD are usually wheelchair-dependent by the age of 10 or 12, and seldom live past the age of 20. For obscure reasons, they also frequently suffer a progressive decline in mental ability. Death usually results from respiratory insufficiency, pulmonary infection, or heart failure. DMD is incurable, but is treated with exercise to slow the atrophy of the muscles and with braces to reinforce the weakened hips and maintain posture.

The underlying cause of DMD is a mutation in the gene for the muscle protein dystrophin (see fig. 11.4)—a large gene highly vulnerable to mutation. Without dystrophin, there is no coupling between the thin myofilaments and the sarcolemma. The sarcomeres move independently of the sarcolemma, creating tears in the membrane. The torn membrane admits excess Ca^{2+} into the cell, which activates intracellular proteases (protein-digesting enzymes). These enzymes degrade the contractile proteins of the muscle, leading to weakness and cellular necrosis. Dying muscle fibers are replaced with scar tissue, which blocks blood circulation in the muscle and thereby contributes to still further necrosis. Muscle degeneration accelerates in a fatal spiral of positive feedback.

Genetic screening can identify heterozygous carriers of DMD, allowing for counseling of prospective parents on the risk of having a child with the disease. However, about one out of three cases arises by a new spontaneous mutation and therefore cannot be predicted by genetic testing.

Myasthenia gravis[17] *(MG)* (MY-ass-THEE-nee-uh GRAV-is) usually occurs in women between the ages of 20 and 40. It is an autoimmune disease in which antibodies attack the neuromuscular junctions and bind ACh receptors together in clusters. The muscle fiber then removes the clusters from the sarcolemma by endocytosis. As a result, the muscle fibers become less and less sensitive to ACh. The effects often appear first in the facial muscles and commonly include drooping eyelids (*ptosis,* **fig. 11.25**) and double vision (due to *strabismus,* inability to fixate on the same point with both eyes). The initial symptoms are often followed by difficulty in swallowing, weakness of the limbs, and poor physical endurance. Some people with MG die quickly as a result of respiratory failure, but others have normal life spans. One method of assessing the progress of the disease is to use *bungarotoxin,* a protein from cobra venom that binds to ACh receptors. The amount that binds is proportional to the number of receptors that are still functional. The muscle of an MG patient sometimes binds less than one-third as much bungarotoxin as normal muscle does.

Myasthenia gravis is often treated with cholinesterase inhibitors. These drugs retard the breakdown of ACh in the neuromuscular junction and enable it to stimulate the muscle longer. Immunosuppressive agents such as prednisone and azathioprine (Imuran) may be used to suppress the production of the antibodies that destroy ACh receptors. Since certain immune cells are stimulated by hormones from the thymus, removal of the thymus *(thymectomy)* helps to dampen the overactive immune response that causes myasthenia gravis. Also, a technique called *plasmapheresis* may be used to remove harmful antibodies from the blood plasma.

---

[15] *dys* = bad, abnormal; *trophy* = growth
[16] Guillaume B. A. Duchenne (1806–75), French physician

[17] *my* = muscle; *asthen* = weakness; *grav* = severe

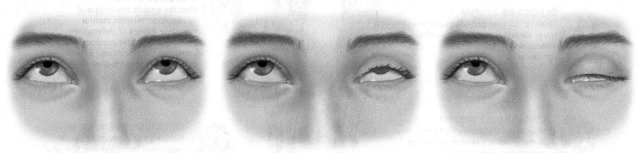

At start   At 60 seconds   At 90 seconds

FIGURE 11.25 Test of Myasthenia Gravis. The subject is told to gaze upward. Within 60 to 90 seconds, there is obvious sagging (ptosis) of one eyelid due to inability to sustain stimulation of the orbicularis oculi muscle.

CONNECTIVE ISSUES

Effects of the **MUSCULAR SYSTEM** on Other Organ Systems

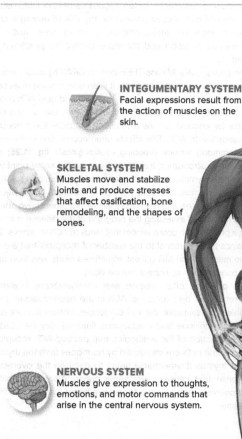

INTEGUMENTARY SYSTEM
Facial expressions result from the action of muscles on the skin.

SKELETAL SYSTEM
Muscles move and stabilize joints and produce stresses that affect ossification, bone remodeling, and the shapes of bones.

NERVOUS SYSTEM
Muscles give expression to thoughts, emotions, and motor commands that arise in the central nervous system.

ENDOCRINE SYSTEM

Skeletal muscles provide protective cover for some endocrine glands; muscle mass affects insulin sensitivity.

CIRCULATORY SYSTEM

Muscle contractions affect blood flow in many veins; exercise stimulates growth of new blood vessels.

LYMPHATIC AND IMMUNE SYSTEMS
Muscle contractions aid flow of lymph; exercise elevates levels of immune cells and antibodies in circulation; excessive exercise can inhibit immunity.

RESPIRATORY SYSTEM
Muscle contractions ventilate the lungs; muscles of the larynx and pharynx regulate airflow and speech; CO_2 generated by muscular activity stimulates respiration; abdominal muscles produce pressure bursts of coughing and sneezing and aid in deep breathing.

URINARY SYSTEM
A skeletal muscle sphincter retains urine in bladder until convenient for release; abdominal and pelvic muscles aid in compressing and emptying bladder; muscles of pelvic floor support bladder; bulbospongiosus muscle helps clear urine from male urethra.

DIGESTIVE SYSTEM
Muscles enable chewing and swallowing; muscles control voluntary aspect of defecation; abdominal muscles produce vomiting; abdominal and lumbar muscles protect digestive organs.

REPRODUCTIVE SYSTEM
Muscles are involved in sexual responses including erection and ejaculation; abdominal and pelvic muscles aid in childbirth.

STUDY GUIDE

▶ Assess Your Learning Outcomes

To test your knowledge, discuss the following topics with a study partner or in writing, ideally from memory.

11.1 Types and Characteristics of Muscular Tissue

1. Five physiological properties of all muscular tissue and their relevance to muscle function
2. Distinguishing characteristics of skeletal muscle
3. Dimensions of a typical skeletal muscle fiber and of the longest fibers
4. Connective tissues associated with a muscle fiber and their relationship to muscle–bone attachments

11.2 Skeletal Muscle Cells

1. The sarcolemma and sarcoplasm, and the roles of glycogen and myoglobin in the sarcoplasm
2. The role of myoblasts in the development of a muscle fiber, and how they give rise to the multinuclear condition of the muscle fiber and to the satellite cells external to the fiber
3. Structure and function of the sarcoplasmic reticulum and transverse tubules
4. Types of myofilaments that constitute a myofibril
5. Composition and molecular organization of a thick filament, and the structure of a myosin molecule
6. Composition of a thin filament; the organization of its actin, tropomyosin, and troponin; and the active sites of its actin monomers
7. Composition of elastic filaments and their relationship to the thick filaments and Z discs
8. The position and function of dystrophin in the muscle fiber
9. Names of the striations of skeletal and cardiac muscle and how they relate to the overlapping arrangement of thick and thin filaments
10. The definition of *sarcomere*

11.3 The Nerve–Muscle Relationship

1. Motor units; the meanings of *large* and *small motor units;* and the respective advantages of the two types
2. Structure of a neuromuscular junction and function of each of its components
3. The source, role, and fate of acetylcholine (ACh) in the neuromuscular junction

4. The role of acetylcholinesterase in neuromuscular function
5. How a nerve or muscle cell generates a resting membrane potential (RMP); the typical voltage of this potential in a skeletal muscle fiber
6. How an action potential differs from the RMP, and the effects of an action potential on a nerve or muscle cell

11.4 Behavior of Skeletal Muscle Fibers

1. Excitation of a muscle fiber; how a nerve signal leads to a traveling wave of electrical excitation in a muscle fiber
2. Excitation–contraction coupling; how electrical excitation of a muscle fiber leads to exposure of the active sites on the actin of a thin myofilament
3. The sliding filament mechanism of contraction; how exposure of the active sites leads to repetitive binding of myosin to actin and sliding of the thin filaments over the thick filaments
4. Muscle relaxation; how the cessation of the nerve signal leads to blockage of the active sites so myosin can no longer bind to them and maintain muscle tension
5. The roles of calcium, troponin, tropomyosin, and ATP in these processes
6. The length–tension relationship in muscle; why muscle would contract weakly if it was overcontracted or overstretched just prior to stimulation; and how this principle relates to the function of muscle tone

11.5 Behavior of Whole Muscles

1. Terms for the minimum stimulus intensity needed to make a muscle contract, and for the delay between stimulation and contraction
2. The phases of a muscle twitch
3. Reasons why muscle twitches vary in strength (tension)
4. How recruitment and tetanus are produced and how they affect muscle tension
5. Differences between isometric and isotonic contraction, and between the concentric and eccentric forms of isotonic contraction

11.6 Muscle Metabolism

1. Why a muscle cannot contract without ATP
2. Differences between aerobic respiration and anaerobic fermentation with respect to muscle function

3. The use of myoglobin and aerobic respiration to generate ATP at the outset of exercise
4. Two ways in which the phosphagen system generates ATP for continued exercise
5. How anaerobic fermentation generates ATP after the phosphagen system is depleted
6. Why a muscle is able to switch back to aerobic respiration to generate ATP after 40 seconds or so of exercise
7. Causes of muscle fatigue
8. Vo_2max, why it partially determines one's ability to maintain high-intensity exercise, and why it differs from one person to another
9. Why exercise is followed by a prolonged state of elevated oxygen consumption, and the name of that state
10. Differences between slow oxidative and fast glycolytic muscle fibers; the respective advantages of each; how they relate to the power and recruitment of motor units; and examples of muscles in which each type predominates
11. Factors that determine the strength of a muscle
12. Examples of resistance exercise and endurance exercise, and the effects of each on muscle performance

11.7 Cardiac and Smooth Muscle

1. Reasons why cardiac muscle must differ physiologically from skeletal muscle
2. Structural differences between cardiomyocytes and skeletal muscle fibers
3. The autorhythmicity of the heart and its ability to contract without nervous stimulation
4. The unusual fatigue resistance of cardiac muscle; structural and biochemical properties that account for it
5. Functional differences between smooth muscle and the two forms of striated muscle
6. How the innervation of smooth muscle differs from that of skeletal muscle
7. Variations in the complexity and anatomical organization of smooth muscle
8. Various functions of smooth muscle
9. Two modes of growth of smooth muscle tissue
10. The structure of smooth muscle cells and what takes the place of the absent Z discs and T tubules
11. Differences between multiunit and unitary smooth muscle, and the nerve–muscle relationship of each

STUDY GUIDE

12. Various modes of stimulation of smooth muscle
13. How excitation–contraction coupling in smooth muscle differs from that in skeletal muscle; the roles of calmodulin and myosin light-chain kinase in smooth muscle contraction
14. The nature and effect of the latch-bridge mechanism in smooth muscle
15. The role of smooth muscle in peristalsis
16. Benefits of the stress–relaxation response of smooth muscle, and of its absence of a length–tension relationship

▶ Testing Your Recall

Answers in Appendix A

1. To make a muscle contract more strongly, the nervous system can activate more motor units. This process is called
   a. recruitment.
   b. summation.
   c. incomplete tetanus.
   d. twitch.
   e. concentric contraction.

2. The functional unit of a muscle fiber is the _____, a segment from one Z disc to the next.
   a. myofibril
   b. I band
   c. sarcomere
   d. neuromuscular junction
   e. striation

3. Before a skeletal muscle fiber can contract, ATP must bind to
   a. a Z disc.
   b. the myosin head.
   c. tropomyosin.
   d. troponin.
   e. actin.

4. Before a skeletal muscle fiber can contract, Ca^{2+} must bind to
   a. calsequestrin.
   b. calmodulin.
   c. the myosin head.
   d. troponin.
   e. actin.

5. Which of the following muscle proteins is *not* intracellular?
   a. actin
   b. myosin
   c. collagen
   d. troponin
   e. dystrophin

6. Smooth muscle cells have _____, whereas skeletal muscle fibers do not.
   a. sarcoplasmic reticulum
   b. tropomyosin
   c. calmodulin
   d. Z discs
   e. myosin ATPase

7. ACh receptors are found mainly in
   a. synaptic vesicles.
   b. terminal cisterns.
   c. thick filaments.
   d. thin filaments.
   e. junctional folds.

8. Unitary smooth muscle cells can stimulate each other because they have
   a. a latch-bridge.
   b. diffuse junctions.
   c. gap junctions.
   d. tight junctions.
   e. cross-bridges.

9. A person with a high Vo_2max
   a. needs less oxygen than someone with a low Vo_2max.
   b. has stronger muscles than someone with a low Vo_2max.
   c. is less likely to show muscle tetanus than someone with a low Vo_2max.
   d. has fewer muscle mitochondria than someone with a low Vo_2max.
   e. experiences less muscle fatigue during exercise than someone with a low Vo_2max.

10. Slow oxidative fibers have all of the following *except*
    a. an abundance of myoglobin.
    b. an abundance of glycogen.
    c. high fatigue resistance.
    d. a red color.
    e. a high capacity to synthesize ATP aerobically.

11. The minimum stimulus intensity that will make a muscle contract is called _____.

12. Red muscles consist mainly of slow _____, or type I, muscle fibers.

13. Parts of the sarcoplasmic reticulum called _____ lie on each side of a T tubule.

14. Thick filaments consist mainly of the protein _____.

15. The neurotransmitter that stimulates skeletal muscle is _____.

16. Muscle contains an oxygen-binding pigment called _____.

17. The _____ of skeletal muscle play the same role as dense bodies in smooth muscle.

18. In autonomic nerve fibers that stimulate unitary smooth muscle, the neurotransmitter is contained in swellings called _____.

19. A state of continual partial muscle contraction is called _____.

20. _____ is an increase in muscle tension without a change in length.

▶ Building Your Medical Vocabulary

Answers in Appendix A

State a meaning of each word element, and give a medical term from this chapter that uses it or a slight variation of it.

1. astheno-
2. auto-
3. dys-
4. iso-
5. metri-
6. myo-
7. sarco-
8. temporo-
9. tono-
10. -trophy

STUDY GUIDE

▶ What's Wrong with These Statements?

Answers in Appendix A

Briefly explain why each of the following statements is false, or reword it to make it true.

1. Each motor neuron supplies one muscle fiber.

2. Somatic motor neurons excite skeletal muscle but inhibit cardiac muscle.

3. Fast glycolytic muscle fibers are relatively resistant to fatigue.

4. Thin myofilaments are found only in the I bands of striated muscle.

5. Thin myofilaments shorten when a muscle contracts.

6. Smooth muscle lacks striations because it does not have thick and thin myofilaments.

7. A muscle must contract to the point of complete tetanus if it is to move a load.

8. If no ATP were available to a muscle fiber, it could still be excited but it could not contract.

9. For the first 30 seconds of an intense exercise, muscle gets most of its energy from lactate.

10. Like cardiac muscle, all smooth muscle is autorhythmic.

▶ Testing Your Comprehension

1. Without ATP, relaxed muscle cannot contract and a contracted muscle cannot relax. Explain why.

2. Smooth muscle controls the curvature of the lens of the eye and the diameter of the pupil, but it would serve poorly for controlling eye movements as in tracking a flying bird or reading a page of print. Explain why.

3. Why would skeletal muscle be unsuitable for the wall of the urinary bladder? Explain how this illustrates the complementarity of form and function at a cellular and molecular level.

4. As skeletal muscle contracts, one or more bands of the sarcomere become narrower and disappear, and one or more of them remain the same width. Which bands will change—A, H, or I—and why?

5. Polio is a muscle-paralyzing disease caused by infection with poliovirus. This virus, however, never infects muscular tissue. (a) Explain how it could paralyze the muscles without invading them. (b) Explain why it does not paralyze cardiac muscle and stop the heart.

PART THREE: INTERNAL COORDINATION AND CONTROL

CHAPTER

12

NERVOUS TISSUE

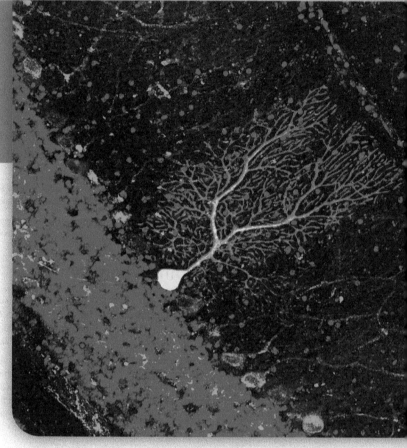

A Purkinje cell, a neuron from the cerebellum of the brain
SPL/Science Source

Anatomy & Physiology Revealed 4.0

Module 7: Nervous System

BRUSHING UP

- This chapter explains the electrophysiology of neurons, and must assume you are familiar with concentration and electrochemical gradients (see section 1.6e).

- This topic also assumes familiarity with "Membrane Proteins" in section 3.2a—especially receptors, enzymes, ligand- and voltage-gated ion channels, leak channels, and the sodium–potassium pump.

The nervous system is one of great complexity and mystery, and will absorb our attention for the next five chapters. It is the foundation of all our conscious experience, personality, and behavior. It profoundly intrigues biologists, physicians, psychologists, and even philosophers. Its scientific study, called **neurobiology,** is regarded by many as the ultimate challenge facing the behavioral and life sciences. We will begin at the simplest organizational level—the nerve cells *(neurons)* and cells called *neuroglia* that support their function in various ways. We will then progress to the organ level to examine the spinal cord (chapter 13), brain (chapter 14), autonomic nervous system (chapter 15), and sense organs (chapter 16).

12.1 Overview of the Nervous System

Expected Learning Outcomes
When you have completed this section, you should be able to

a. describe the overall function of the nervous system; and
b. describe its major anatomical and functional subdivisions.

If the body is to maintain homeostasis and function effectively, its trillions of cells must work together in a coordinated fashion. If each cell behaved without regard to what others were doing, the result would be physiological chaos and death. We have two organ systems dedicated to maintaining internal coordination—the **endocrine system** (see chapter 17), which communicates by means of chemical messengers (hormones) secreted into the blood, and the **nervous system (fig. 12.1),** which employs electrical and chemical means to send messages very quickly from cell to cell.

The nervous system carries out its coordinating task in three basic steps: (1) It receives information about changes in the body and external environment and transmits messages to the *central nervous system (CNS).* (2) The CNS processes this information and determines what response, if any, is appropriate to the circumstances. (3) The CNS issues commands primarily to muscle and gland cells to carry out such responses.

The nervous system has two major anatomical subdivisions **(fig. 12.2):**

- The **central nervous system (CNS)** consists of the brain and spinal cord, which are enclosed and protected by the cranium and vertebral column.

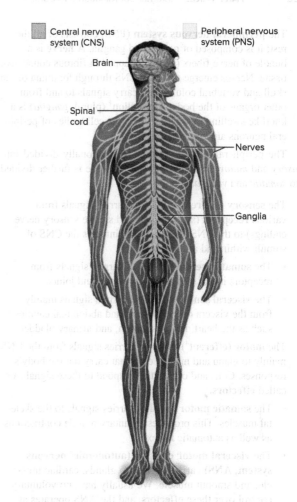

FIGURE 12.1 **The Nervous System.**

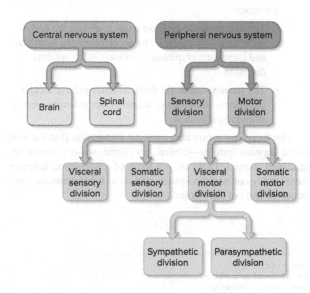

FIGURE 12.2 **Subdivisions of the Nervous System.**

- The **peripheral nervous system (PNS)** consists of all the rest; it is composed of nerves and ganglia. A **nerve** is a bundle of nerve fibers (axons) wrapped in fibrous connective tissue. Nerves emerge from the CNS through foramina of the skull and vertebral column and carry signals to and from other organs of the body. A **ganglion**[1] (plural, *ganglia*) is a knotlike swelling in a nerve where the cell bodies of peripheral neurons are concentrated.

The peripheral nervous system is functionally divided into *sensory* and *motor* divisions, and each of these is further divided into *somatic* and *visceral* subdivisions.

- The **sensory (afferent**[2]**) division** carries signals from various **receptors** (sense organs and simple sensory nerve endings) to the CNS. This pathway informs the CNS of stimuli within and around the body.

  - The **somatic**[3] **sensory division** carries signals from receptors in the skin, muscles, bones, and joints.

  - The **visceral sensory division** carries signals mainly from the viscera of the thoracic and abdominal cavities, such as the heart, lungs, stomach, and urinary bladder.

- The **motor (efferent**[4]**) division** carries signals from the CNS mainly to gland and muscle cells that carry out the body's responses. Cells and organs that respond to these signals are called **effectors.**

  - The **somatic motor division** carries signals to the skeletal muscles. This produces voluntary muscle contractions as well as automatic reflexes.

  - The **visceral motor division (autonomic**[5] **nervous system, ANS)** carries signals to glands, cardiac muscle, and smooth muscle. We usually have no voluntary control over these effectors, and the ANS operates at an unconscious level. The responses of the ANS and its effectors are *visceral reflexes*. The ANS has two further divisions:

    - The **sympathetic division** tends to arouse the body for action—for example, by accelerating the heartbeat and increasing respiratory airflow—but it inhibits digestion.

    - The **parasympathetic division** tends to have a calming effect—slowing the heartbeat, for example—but it stimulates digestion.

The foregoing terms may give the impression that we have several nervous systems—central, peripheral, sensory, motor, somatic, and visceral. These are just terms of convenience, however. There is only one nervous system, and these subsystems are interconnected parts of the whole.

---

[1] *gangli* = knot
[2] *af* = *ad* = toward; *fer* = to carry
[3] *somat* = body; *ic* = pertaining to
[4] *ef* = *ex* = out, away; *fer* = to carry
[5] *auto* = self; *nom* = law, governance

BEFORE YOU GO ON

Answer the following questions to test your understanding of the preceding section:

1. What is a receptor? Give two examples of effectors.
2. Distinguish between the central and peripheral nervous systems, and between visceral and somatic divisions of the sensory and motor systems.
3. What is another name for the visceral motor nervous system? What are its two subdivisions? What are their functions?

12.2   Properties of Neurons

Expected Learning Outcomes

When you have completed this section, you should be able to

a. describe three functional properties found in all neurons;
b. define the three most basic functional categories of neurons;
c. identify the parts of a neuron; and
d. explain how neurons transport materials between the cell body and tips of the axon.

12.2a Universal Properties

The communicative role of the nervous system is carried out by **nerve cells,** or **neurons.** These cells have three fundamental physiological properties that enable them to communicate with other cells:

1. **Excitability.** All cells are excitable—that is, they respond to environmental changes (**stimuli**). Neurons exhibit this property to the highest degree.
2. **Conductivity.** Neurons respond to stimuli by producing electrical signals that are quickly conducted to other cells at distant locations.
3. **Secretion.** When the signal reaches the end of a nerve fiber, the neuron secretes a *neurotransmitter* that crosses the gap and stimulates the next cell.

▶▶▶ **APPLY WHAT YOU KNOW**

What basic physiological properties do a nerve cell and a muscle cell have in common? Name a physiological property of each that the other one lacks.

12.2b Functional Classes

There are three general classes of neurons (**fig. 12.3**) corresponding to the three major aspects of nervous system function listed earlier:

① **Sensory (afferent) neurons** are specialized to detect stimuli such as light, heat, pressure, and chemicals, and transmit information about them to the CNS. Such neurons begin in almost

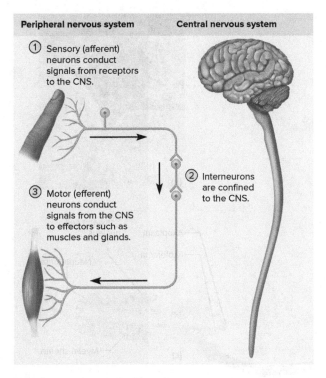

FIGURE 12.3 The Three Functional Classes of Neurons. All neurons can be classified as sensory, motor, or interneurons depending on their location and the direction of signal conduction.

every organ of the body and end in the CNS; the word *afferent* refers to signal conduction *toward* the CNS. Some receptors, such as those for pain and smell, are themselves neurons. In other cases, such as taste and hearing, the receptor is a separate cell that communicates directly with a sensory neuron.

② **Interneurons** lie entirely within the CNS. They receive signals from many other neurons and carry out the integrative function of the nervous system—that is, they process, store, and retrieve information and "make decisions" that determine how the body responds to stimuli. About 90% of our neurons are interneurons. The word *interneuron* refers to the fact that they lie *between,* and interconnect, the incoming sensory pathways and the outgoing motor pathways of the CNS.

③ **Motor (efferent) neurons** send signals predominantly to muscle and gland cells, the effectors. They are called *motor* neurons because most of them lead to muscle cells, and *efferent* neurons to signify signal conduction *away from* the CNS.

12.2c Structure of a Neuron

There are several varieties of neurons, but a good starting point for discussion is a motor neuron of the spinal cord **(fig. 12.4).** The control center of the neuron is the **neurosoma,**[6] also called the

soma, cell body, or **perikaryon.**[7] It has a centrally located nucleus with a large nucleolus. The cytoplasm contains mitochondria, lysosomes, a Golgi complex, numerous inclusions, and an extensive rough endoplasmic reticulum and cytoskeleton. The cytoskeleton consists of a dense mesh of microtubules and **neurofibrils** (bundles of actin filaments), which compartmentalize the rough ER into dark-staining regions called **chromatophilic**[8] **substance** (fig. 12.4e). This is unique to neurons and a helpful clue to identifying them in tissue sections with mixed cell types. Mature neurons have no centrioles and cannot undergo any further mitosis after adolescence. Consequently, neurons that die are usually irreplaceable; surviving neurons cannot multiply to replace those lost. However, neurons are unusually long-lived cells, capable of functioning for over a hundred years.

The major inclusions in the neurosoma are glycogen granules, lipid droplets, melanin, and a golden brown pigment called *lipofuscin*[9] (LIP-oh-FEW-sin), produced when lysosomes degrade worn-out organelles and other products. Lipofuscin accumulates with age and pushes the nucleus to one side of the cell. Lipofuscin granules are also called "wear-and-tear granules" because they are most abundant in old neurons. They are also associated with certain degenerative diseases such as macular degeneration of the eye and amyotrophic lateral sclerosis (ALS).

The somas of most neurons give rise to a few thick processes that branch into a vast number of **dendrites**[10]—named for their striking resemblance to the bare branches of a tree in winter. Dendrites are the primary site for receiving signals from other neurons. Some neurons have only one dendrite and some have thousands. The more dendrites a neuron has, the more information it can receive and incorporate into its decision making. As tangled as the dendrites may seem, they provide exquisitely precise pathways for the reception and processing of neural information.

On one side of the neurosoma is a mound called the **axon hillock,** from which the **axon (nerve fiber)** originates. The axon is cylindrical and relatively unbranched for most of its length, although it may give rise to a few branches called *axon collaterals* near the soma, and most axons branch extensively at their distal end. An axon is specialized for rapid conduction of nerve signals to points remote from the soma. Its cytoplasm is called the **axoplasm** and its membrane the **axolemma.**[11] A neuron never has more than one axon, and some neurons have none.

Somas range from 5 to 135 μm in diameter, and axons from 1 to 20 μm in diameter and from a few millimeters to more than a meter long. (In the great blue whale, one nerve cell can be more than 30 m, or 100 ft, long.) The dimensions of a human neuron are more impressive when we scale them up to the size of familiar objects. If the soma of a spinal motor neuron were the size of a tennis ball, its dendrites would form a dense bushy mass that could

---

[6]*soma* = body

[7]*peri* = around, surrounding; *karyo* = nucleus
[8]*chromato* = color; *philic* = loving, attracting
[9]*lipo* = fat, lipid; *fusc* = dusky, brown
[10]*dendr* = tree, branch; *ite* = little
[11]*axo* = axis, axon; *lemma* = husk, peel, sheath

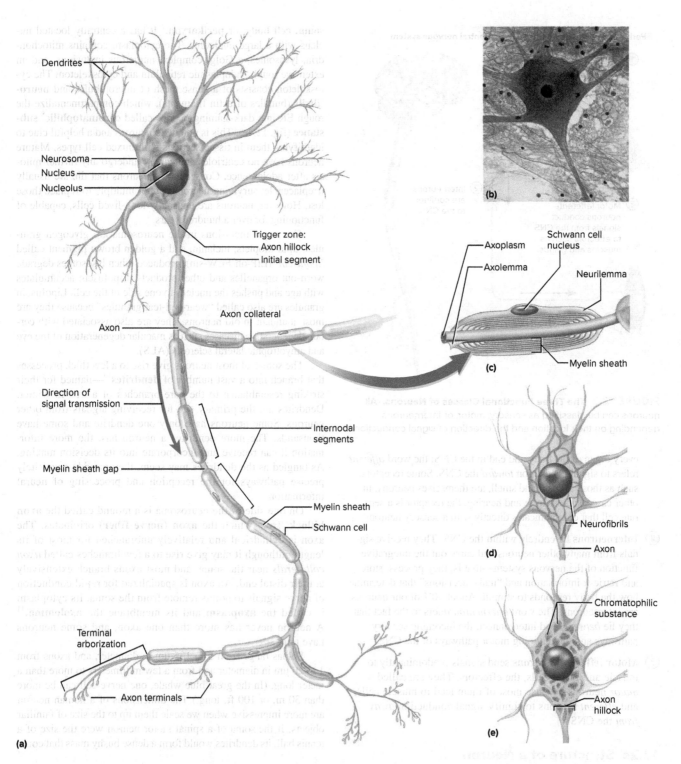

FIGURE 12.4 General Structure of a Neuron. (a) Structure of a multipolar neuron such as a spinal motor neuron. (b) Photograph of this neuron type. (c) Detail of the myelin sheath. (d) Neurofibrils of the neurosoma. (e) Chromatophilic substance, stained masses of rough ER separated by the bundles of neurofibrils shown in part (d). See section 12.3b for description of the myelin sheath.

b: Ed Reschke

fill a 30-seat classroom from floor to ceiling. Its axon would be up to a mile long but a little narrower than a garden hose. This is quite a point to ponder. The neuron must assemble molecules and organelles in its "tennis ball" soma and deliver them through its "mile-long garden hose" to the end of the axon. How it achieves this remarkable feat is explained shortly.

At the distal end, an axon usually has a **terminal arborization**[12]—an extensive complex of fine branches. Each branch ends in a bulbous **axon terminal (terminal button),** which forms a junction (**synapse**[13]) with the next cell. It contains **synaptic vesicles** full of neurotransmitter. In most autonomic neurons, however, the axon has numerous beads called **varicosities** along its length (see fig. 11.21). Each varicosity contains synaptic vesicles and secretes neurotransmitter.

Not all neurons fit the preceding description. Neurons are classified structurally according to the number of processes extending from the soma **(fig. 12.5):**

- **Multipolar neurons** are those, like the preceding, that have one axon and multiple dendrites. This is the most common type and includes most neurons of the brain and spinal cord.

- **Bipolar neurons** have one axon and one dendrite. Examples include olfactory cells of the nose, certain neurons of the retina, and sensory neurons of the ear.

- **Unipolar neurons** have only a single process leading away from the soma. They are represented by the neurons that carry signals to the spinal cord for such senses as touch and pain. They are also called *pseudounipolar* because they start out as bipolar neurons in the embryo, but their two processes fuse into one as the neuron matures. A short distance away from the soma, the process branches like a T into a *peripheral fiber* and a *central fiber*. The peripheral fiber begins with a sensory ending often far away from the soma—in the skin, for example. Its signals travel toward the soma, but bypass it and continue along the central fiber for a short remaining distance to the spinal cord. The dendrites are considered to be only the short receptive endings. The rest of the process, both peripheral and central, is the axon, defined by the presence of myelin and the ability to generate action potentials.

- **Anaxonic neurons** have multiple dendrites but no axon. They communicate locally through their dendrites and do not produce action potentials. Some anaxonic neurons are found in the brain, retina, and adrenal medulla. In the retina, they help in visual processes such as the perception of contrast.

12.2d Axonal Transport

All of the proteins needed by a neuron must be made in the soma, where the protein-synthesizing organelles such as the nucleus,

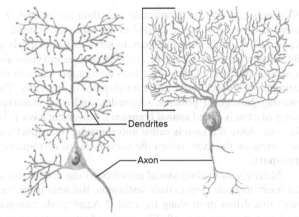

(a) Multipolar neurons

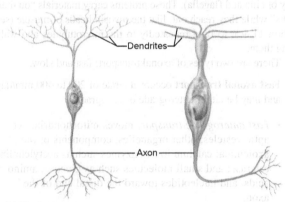

(b) Bipolar neurons

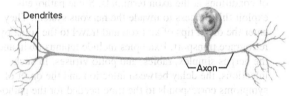

(c) Unipolar neuron

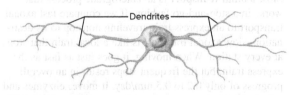

(d) Anaxonic neuron

FIGURE 12.5 Variation in Neuron Structure. (a) Two multipolar neurons of the brain—a pyramidal cell *(left)* and a Purkinje cell. (b) Two bipolar neurons—a bipolar cell of the retina *(left)* and an olfactory neuron. (c) A unipolar neuron of the type involved in the senses of touch and pain. (d) An anaxonic neuron—an amacrine cell of the retina.

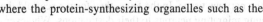

[12]*arbor* = tree
[13]*syn* = together; *aps* = to touch, join

ribosomes, and rough endoplasmic reticulum are located. Yet many of these proteins are needed in the axon, for example to repair and maintain the axolemma, to serve as ion channels in the membrane, or to act in the axon terminal as enzymes and signaling molecules. Other substances are transported from the axon terminals back to the soma for disposal or recycling. The two-way passage of proteins, organelles, and other materials along an axon is called **axonal transport.** Movement away from the soma down the axon is called **anterograde**[14] **transport** and movement up the axon toward the soma is called **retrograde**[15] **transport.**

Materials travel along axonal microtubules that act like monorail tracks to guide them to their destination. But what is the "engine" that drives them along the tracks? Anterograde transport employs a motor protein called *kinesin*[16] and retrograde transport uses one called *dynein*[17] (the same protein responsible for the motility of cilia and flagella). These proteins carry materials "on their backs" while they reach out, like the myosin heads of muscle (see section 11.4c), to bind repeatedly to the microtubules and walk along them.

There are two types of axonal transport: fast and slow.

1. **Fast axonal transport** occurs at a rate of 200 to 400 mm/day and may be either anterograde or retrograde:

   • *Fast anterograde transport* moves mitochondria; synaptic vesicles; other organelles; components of the axolemma; calcium ions; enzymes such as acetylcholinesterase; and small molecules such as glucose, amino acids, and nucleotides toward the distal end of the axon.

   • *Fast retrograde transport* returns used synaptic vesicles and other materials to the soma and informs the soma of conditions at the axon terminals. Some pathogens exploit this process to invade the nervous system. They enter the distal tips of an axon and travel to the soma by retrograde transport. Examples include tetanus toxin and the herpes simplex, rabies, and polio viruses. In such infections, the delay between infection and the onset of symptoms corresponds to the time needed for the pathogens to reach the somas.

2. **Slow axonal transport** is an anterograde process that works in a stop-and-go fashion. If we compare fast axonal transport to an express train traveling nonstop to its destination, slow axonal transport is like a local train that stops at every station. When moving, it goes just as fast as the express train, but the frequent stops result in an overall progress of only 0.2 to 0.5 mm/day. It moves enzymes and cytoskeletal components down the axon, renews worn-out axoplasmic components in mature neurons, and supplies

new axoplasm for developing or regenerating neurons. Damaged nerves regenerate at a speed governed by slow axonal transport.

▶▶▶ **APPLY WHAT YOU KNOW**

The axon of a neuron has a dense cytoskeleton. Considering the functions of the cytoskeleton discussed in section 3.4a, give two reasons why this is so important to neuron structure and function.

BEFORE YOU GO ON

Answer the following questions to test your understanding of the preceding section:

4. Sketch a multipolar neuron and label its neurosoma, dendrites, axon, terminal arborization, axon terminals, and myelin sheath.

5. Explain the differences between a sensory neuron, motor neuron, and interneuron.

6. What is the functional difference between a dendrite and an axon?

7. How do proteins and other chemicals synthesized in the soma get to the axon terminals? By what process can a virus that invades a peripheral nerve fiber get to the soma of that neuron?

12.3   Supportive Cells

Expected Learning Outcomes

When you have completed this section, you should be able to

a. name the six types of cells that aid neurons, and state their respective functions;

b. describe the myelin sheath that is found around certain nerve fibers, and explain its importance;

c. describe the relationship of unmyelinated nerve fibers to their supportive cells; and

d. explain how damaged nerve fibers regenerate.

There are about a trillion (10^{12}) neurons in the nervous system—10 times as many neurons in your body as there are stars in our galaxy! Because they branch so extensively, they make up about 50% of the volume of the nervous tissue. Yet they are outnumbered at least 10 to 1 by cells called **neuroglia** (noo-ROG-lee-uh), or **glial cells** (GLEE-ul). Glial cells protect the neurons and help them function. The word *glia,* which means "glue," implies one of their roles—to bind neurons together and provide a supportive framework for the nervous tissue. In the fetus, they form a scaffold that guides young migrating neurons to their destinations. Wherever a mature neuron is not in synaptic contact with another cell, it is covered with glial cells. This prevents neurons from contacting each other except at points specialized for signal transmission, thus giving precision to their conduction pathways.

---

[14]*antero* = forward; *grad* = to walk, to step
[15]*retro* = back; *grad* = to walk, to step
[16]*kines* = motion; *in* = protein
[17]*dyne* = force; *in* = protein

12.3a Types of Neuroglia

There are six kinds of neuroglia, each with a unique function (**table 12.1**). The first four types occur only in the central nervous system (**fig. 12.6**):

1. **Oligodendrocytes**[18] (OL-ih-go-DEN-dro-sites) somewhat resemble an octopus; they have a bulbous body with as many as 15 arms. Each arm reaches out to a nerve fiber and spirals around it like electrical tape wrapped repeatedly around a wire. This wrapping, called the *myelin sheath,* insulates the nerve fiber from the extracellular fluid and speeds up signal conduction in the nerve fiber.

2. **Ependymal**[19] **cells** (ep-EN-dih-mul) resemble a cuboidal epithelium lining the internal cavities of the brain and spinal cord. Unlike true epithelial cells, however, they have no basement membrane and they exhibit rootlike processes that penetrate into the underlying tissue. Ependymal cells produce *cerebrospinal fluid (CSF),* a liquid that bathes the CNS and fills its internal cavities. They have patches of cilia on their apical surfaces that help to circulate the CSF. Ependymal cells and CSF are considered in more detail in section 14.2b.

3. **Microglia** are small macrophages that develop from white blood cells called monocytes. They wander through the CNS, putting out fingerlike extensions to constantly probe the tissue for cellular debris or other problems. They are thought to perform a complete checkup on the brain tissue

---

[18]*oligo* = few; *dendro* = branches; *cyte* = cell
[19]*ependyma* = upper garment

TABLE 12.1	Types of Glial Cells
Types	**Functions**
Neuroglia of CNS	
Oligodendrocytes	Form myelin in brain and spinal cord
Ependymal cells	Line cavities of brain and spinal cord; secrete and circulate cerebrospinal fluid
Microglia	Phagocytize and destroy microorganisms, foreign matter, and dead nervous tissue
Astrocytes	Cover brain surface and nonsynaptic regions of neurons; form supportive framework in CNS; induce formation of blood–brain barrier; nourish neurons; produce growth factors that stimulate neurons; promote the formation of synapses and neural circuitry; communicate electrically with neurons and may influence synaptic signaling; remove K^+ and some neurotransmitters from ECF of brain and spinal cord; help to regulate composition of ECF; form scar tissue to replace damaged nervous tissue
Neuroglia of PNS	
Schwann cells	Form neurilemma around all PNS nerve fibers and myelin around most of them; aid in regeneration of damaged nerve fibers
Satellite cells	Surround somas of neurons in the ganglia; provide electrical insulation and regulate chemical environment of neurons

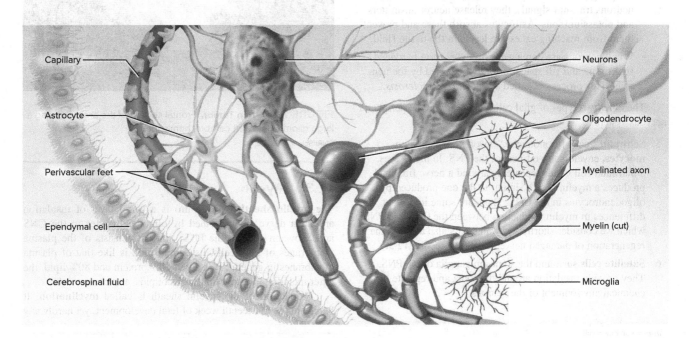

Capillary
Neurons
Astrocyte
Oligodendrocyte
Perivascular feet
Myelinated axon
Ependymal cell
Myelin (cut)
Cerebrospinal fluid
Microglia

FIGURE 12.6 Neuroglia of the Central Nervous System.

several times a day, phagocytizing dead tissue, microorganisms, and other foreign matter. They become concentrated in areas damaged by infection, trauma, or stroke. Pathologists look for clusters of microglia in brain tissue as a clue to sites of injury. Microglia also aid in synaptic remodeling, changing the connections between neurons.

4. **Astrocytes**[20] are the most abundant glial cells in the CNS and constitute over 90% of the tissue in some areas of the brain. They cover the entire brain surface and most nonsynaptic regions of the neurons in the gray matter. They are named for their many-branched, somewhat starlike shape. They have the most diverse functions of any glia:

- They form a supportive framework for the nervous tissue.
- They have extensions called *perivascular feet,* which contact the blood capillaries and stimulate them to form a tight, protective seal called the blood–brain barrier (see section 14.2c).
- They monitor neuron activity, stimulate dilation and constriction of blood vessels, and thus regulate blood flow in the brain tissue to meet changing needs for oxygen and nutrients.
- They convert blood glucose to lactate and supply this to the neurons for nourishment.
- They secrete *nerve growth factors* that regulate nerve development (see Deeper Insight 12.3).
- They promote synapse formation and fine-tune neural circuitry.
- They communicate electrically with neurons and influence synaptic signaling between them.
- They regulate the composition of the tissue fluid. When neurons transmit signals, they release neurotransmitters and potassium ions. Astrocytes absorb these and prevent them from reaching excessive levels in the tissue fluid.
- When neurons are damaged, astrocytes form hardened scar tissue and fill space formerly occupied by the neurons. This process is called *astrocytosis* or *sclerosis.*

The other two types of glial cells occur only in the peripheral nervous system:

5. **Schwann**[21] **cells** (pronounced "shwon"), or **neurilemmocytes,** envelop nerve fibers of the PNS. In most cases, a Schwann cell winds repeatedly around a nerve fiber and produces a myelin sheath similar to the one produced by oligodendrocytes in the CNS. There are some important differences in myelin production between the CNS and PNS, which we consider shortly. Schwann cells also assist in the regeneration of damaged nerve fibers (see section 12.3e).

6. **Satellite cells** surround the somas in ganglia of the PNS. They provide insulation around the soma and regulate the chemical environment of the neurons.

DEEPER INSIGHT 12.1

CLINICAL APPLICATION

Glial Cells and Brain Tumors

A tumor consists of a mass of rapidly dividing cells. Mature neurons, however, have little or no capacity for mitosis and seldom form tumors. Some brain tumors arise from the meninges (protective membranes of the CNS) or arise by metastasis from tumors elsewhere, such as malignant melanoma and colon cancer. Most adult brain tumors, however, are composed of glial cells, which are mitotically active throughout life. Such tumors are called *gliomas*[22] **(fig. 12.7).** Gliomas usually grow rapidly and are highly malignant. Because of the blood–brain barrier, brain tumors usually do not yield to chemotherapy and must be treated with radiation or surgery.

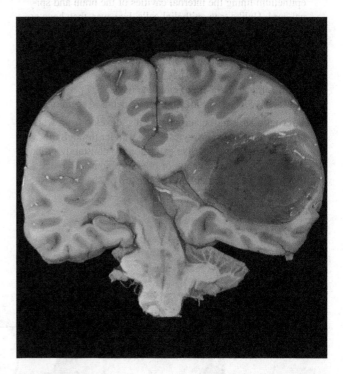

FIGURE 12.7 Brain Tumor. Frontal section of the brain showing a large glioma in the left cerebral hemisphere.
CNRI/Science Source

12.3b Myelin

The **myelin sheath** (MY-eh-lin) is a spiral layer of insulation around a nerve fiber, formed by oligodendrocytes in the CNS and Schwann cells in the PNS. Since it consists of the plasma membranes of glial cells, its composition is like that of plasma membranes in general. It is about 20% protein and 80% lipid, the latter including phospholipids, glycolipids, and cholesterol.

Production of the myelin sheath is called **myelination.** It begins in the fourteenth week of fetal development, yet hardly any

[20]*astro* = star; *cyte* = cell
[21]Theodor Schwann (1810–82), German histologist

[22]*glia* = glial cells; *oma* = tumor

myelin exists in the brain at the time of birth. Myelination proceeds rapidly in infancy and isn't completed until late adolescence. Since myelin has such a high lipid content, dietary fat is important to early nervous system development. It is best not to give children under 2 years old the sort of low-fat diets (skimmed milk, etc.) that may be beneficial to an adult.

In the PNS, a Schwann cell spirals repeatedly around a single nerve fiber, laying down up to 100 compact layers of its own membrane with almost no cytoplasm between the membranes **(fig. 12.8a).** These layers constitute the myelin sheath. The Schwann cell spirals outward as it wraps the nerve fiber, finally ending with a thick outermost coil called the **neurilemma**[23] (noor-ih-LEM-ah). Here, the bulging body of the Schwann cell contains its nucleus and most of its cytoplasm. External to the neurilemma is a basal lamina and then a thin sleeve of fibrous connective tissue called the *endoneurium.* To visualize this myelination process, imagine that you wrap an almost-empty tube of toothpaste tightly around a pencil. The pencil represents the axon, and the spiral layers of toothpaste tube represent the myelin. The toothpaste, like the cytoplasm of the cell, would be forced to one end of the tube and form a bulge on the external surface of the wrapping, like the body of the Schwann cell.

In the CNS, each oligodendrocyte reaches out to myelinate several nerve fibers in its immediate vicinity **(fig. 12.8b).** Since it is anchored to multiple nerve fibers, it can't migrate around any one of them like a Schwann cell does. It must push newer layers of myelin under the older ones, so myelination spirals inward toward the nerve fiber. Nerve fibers of the CNS have no neurilemma or endoneurium. The contrasting modes of myelination are called *centrifugal myelination* ("away from the center") in the PNS and *centripetal myelination* ("toward the center") in the CNS.

In both the PNS and CNS, a nerve fiber is much longer than the reach of a single glial cell, so it requires many Schwann cells or oligodendrocytes to cover one nerve fiber. Consequently, the myelin sheath is segmented. Each gap between segments is called a **myelin sheath gap** or **node of Ranvier**[24] (RON-vee-AY) (*node* for short); the myelin-covered segments from each node to the next are called **internodal segments** (see fig. 12.4a). These segments are about 0.2 to 1.0 mm long. The short section of nerve fiber between the axon hillock and the first glial cell is called the **initial segment.** Since the axon hillock and initial segment play an important role in initiating a nerve signal, they are collectively called the **trigger zone.**

12.3c Unmyelinated Nerve Fibers

Many nerve fibers in the CNS and PNS are unmyelinated. In the PNS, however, even the unmyelinated fibers are enveloped in Schwann cells. In this case, one Schwann cell harbors from 1 to 12 small nerve fibers in grooves in its surface **(fig. 12.9).** The Schwann cell's plasma membrane doesn't spiral repeatedly around the fiber as it does in a myelin sheath, but folds once around each fiber and may somewhat overlap itself along the edges. This wrapping is the neurilemma. Most nerve fibers travel through individual channels in

the Schwann cell, but small fibers are sometimes bundled together within a single channel, as on the right side of this figure. A basal lamina surrounds the entire Schwann cell along with its nerve fibers.

12.3d Conduction Speed of Nerve Fibers

The speed at which a nerve signal travels along a nerve fiber depends on two factors: the diameter of the fiber and the presence or absence of myelin. Signal conduction occurs along the surface of a fiber, not deep within its axoplasm. Large fibers have more surface area and conduct signals more rapidly than small fibers. Myelin further speeds signal conduction by a mechanism to be explained in section 12.4f. Nerve signals travel about 0.5 to 2.0 m/s in small unmyelinated fibers (2–4 μm in diameter); 3 to 15 m/s in myelinated fibers of the same size; and as fast as 120 m/s in large myelinated fibers (up to 20 μm in diameter). One may wonder why all of our nerve fibers aren't large, myelinated, and fast; but if this were so, our nervous system would be impossibly bulky or limited to far fewer fibers. Large nerve fibers require large somas and a large expenditure of energy to maintain them. The evolution of myelin allowed for the subsequent evolution of more complex and responsive nervous systems with smaller, more energy-efficient neurons. Slow unmyelinated fibers are quite sufficient for processes in which quick responses aren't

DEEPER INSIGHT 12.2

CLINICAL APPLICATION

Diseases of the Myelin Sheath

Multiple sclerosis and Tay–Sachs disease are degenerative disorders of the myelin sheath. In *multiple sclerosis*[25] *(MS)*, the oligodendrocytes and myelin sheaths of the CNS deteriorate and are replaced by hardened scar tissue, especially between the ages of 20 and 40. Nerve conduction is disrupted, with effects that depend on what part of the CNS is involved—double vision, blindness, speech defects, neurosis, tremors, or numbness, for example. Patients experience variable cycles of milder and worse symptoms until they eventually become bedridden. The cause of MS remains uncertain; most hypotheses suggest that it is an autoimmune disorder triggered by a virus in genetically susceptible individuals. There is no cure. There is conflicting evidence of how much it shortens a person's life expectancy, if at all. A few die within 1 year of diagnosis, but many people live with MS for 25 or 30 years.

Tay–Sachs[26] disease is a hereditary disorder seen mainly in infants of Eastern European Jewish ancestry. It results from the abnormal accumulation of a glycolipid called GM_2 (ganglioside) in the myelin sheath. GM_2 is normally decomposed by a lysosomal enzyme, but this enzyme is lacking from people who are homozygous recessive for the Tay–Sachs allele. As GM_2 accumulates, it disrupts the conduction of nerve signals and the victim typically suffers blindness, loss of coordination, and dementia. Signs begin to appear before the child is a year old, and most victims die by the age of 3 or 4 years. Asymptomatic adult carriers can be identified by a blood test and advised by genetic counselors on the risk of their children having the disease.

---

[23]*neuri* = nerve; *lemma* = husk, peel, sheath
[24]L. A. Ranvier (1835–1922), French histologist and pathologist

[25]*scler* = hard, tough; *osis* = condition
[26]Warren Tay (1843–1927), English physician; Bernard Sachs (1858–1944), American neurologist

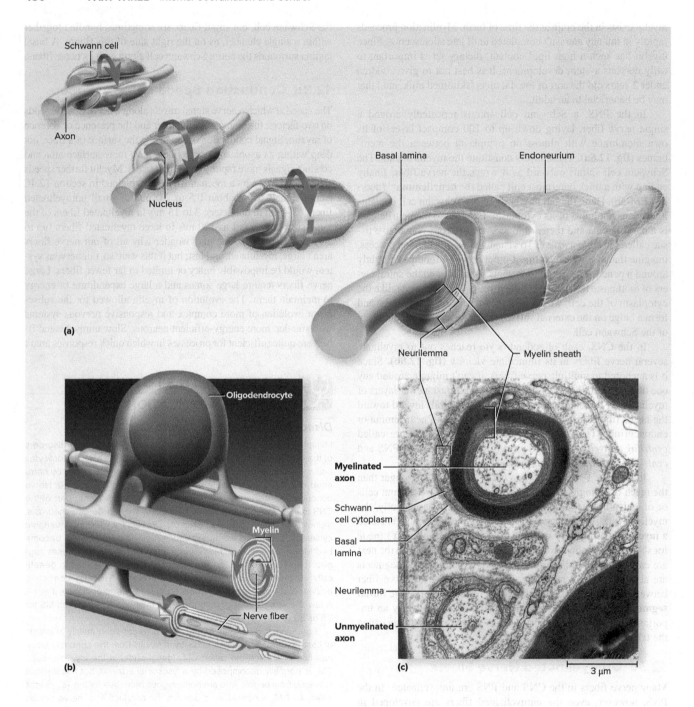

FIGURE 12.8 Myelination. (a) A Schwann cell of the PNS, wrapping repeatedly around an axon to form the multilayered myelin sheath. The myelin spirals outward away from the axon as it is laid down. (b) An oligodendrocyte of the CNS wrapping around the axons of multiple neurons. Here, the myelin spirals inward toward the axon as it is laid down. (c) A myelinated axon (top) and unmyelinated axon (bottom) (TEM).

c: Dr. Dennis Emery, Iowa State University/McGraw-Hill Education

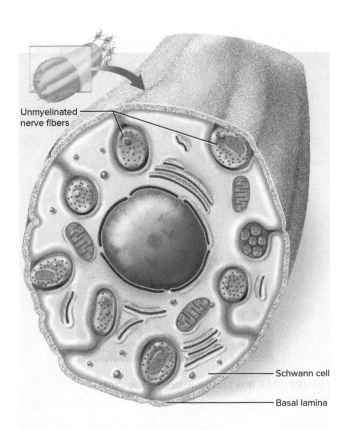

Unmyelinated nerve fibers

Schwann cell

Basal lamina

FIGURE 12.9 Unmyelinated Nerve Fibers.

❓ *What is the functional disadvantage of an unmyelinated nerve fiber? What is its anatomical advantage?*

particularly important, such as secreting stomach acid or dilating the pupil. Fast myelinated fibers are employed where speed is more important, as in motor commands to the skeletal muscles and sensory signals for vision and balance.

12.3e Nerve Regeneration

Nerve fibers of the PNS are vulnerable to cuts, crushing injuries, and other trauma. A damaged peripheral nerve fiber may regenerate, however, if its soma is intact and at least some neurilemma remains. **Figure 12.10** shows the process of regeneration, taking as its example a somatic motor neuron:

① In the normal nerve fiber, note the size of the soma and the size of the muscle fibers for comparison to later stages.

② When a nerve fiber is cut, the fiber distal to the injury can't survive because it is incapable of protein synthesis. Protein-synthesizing organelles are mostly in the soma. As the distal fiber degenerates, so do its Schwann cells, which depend on it for their maintenance. Macrophages clean up tissue debris at the point of injury and beyond.

③ The soma exhibits a number of abnormalities of its own, probably because it is cut off from the supply of nerve growth factors from the neuron's target cells (see

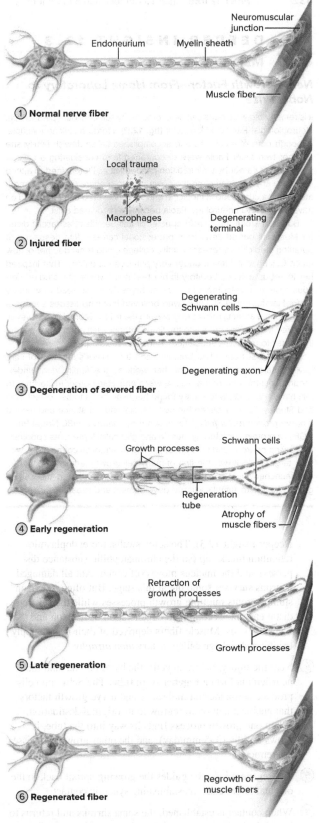

① **Normal nerve fiber**
Endoneurium   Myelin sheath   Neuromuscular junction   Muscle fiber

② **Injured fiber**
Local trauma   Macrophages   Degenerating terminal

③ **Degeneration of severed fiber**
Degenerating Schwann cells   Degenerating axon

④ **Early regeneration**
Growth processes   Schwann cells   Regeneration tube   Atrophy of muscle fibers

⑤ **Late regeneration**
Retraction of growth processes   Growth processes

⑥ **Regenerated fiber**
Regrowth of muscle fibers

FIGURE 12.10 Regeneration of a Damaged Nerve Fiber. See numbered steps in text for explanation. Nerve fibers of the PNS can regenerate if the neurosoma is intact.

DEEPER INSIGHT 12.3
MEDICAL HISTORY

Nerve Growth Factor—From Home Laboratory to Nobel Prize

It is remarkable what odds can be overcome by self-confident persistence. Neurobiologist Rita Levi-Montalcini **(fig. 12.11)** affords a striking example. Although born of a cultured and accomplished Italian Jewish family, she and her twin sister Paola were discouraged from considering a college education or career by their tradition-minded father. Determined to attend university anyway, they hired their own tutor to prepare them. Rita graduated summa cum laude in medicine and surgery in 1930 and embarked on advanced study in neurology. Paola became a renowned artist.

But then arose the sinister specter of anti-Semitism, as fascist dictator Mussolini barred Jews from professional careers. Rita despaired of pursuing medicine or research until a college friend reminded her of how much Cajal had achieved under very primitive conditions. That inspired her to set up a little laboratory in her bedroom, where she studied nervous system development in chick embryos. She had read of work by Viktor Hamburger in St. Louis, who believed that limb tissues secrete a chemical that attracts nerves to grow into them. Levi-Montalcini, however, believed that nerves grow into the limbs without such attractants, but die if they fail to receive a substance needed to sustain them.

Fleeing first from Allied bombing and then Hitler's invasion of Italy, Levi-Montalcini had to abandon her work as the family went underground until the end of the war. At war's end, Hamburger invited her to join him in America, where they found her hypothesis to be correct. She and Stanley Cohen isolated the nerve-sustaining substance and named it *nerve growth factor (NGF),* for which they shared a 1986 Nobel Prize. NGF is a protein secreted by muscle and glial cells. It prevents apoptosis in growing neurons and thus enables them to establish connections with their target cells. It was the first of many cell growth factors discovered, and launched what is today a vibrant field of research in the use of growth factors to stimulate tissue development and repair.

FIGURE 12.11 Rita Levi-Montalcini (1909–2012).
Olycom/SIPA/Newscom

Rita and Paola created the Levi-Montalcini Foundation to support the career development of young people and especially the scientific education of women in Africa. Rita also served as an honored member of the Italian Senate from 2001 until 2012, when she died at the age of 103.

Deeper Insight 12.3). The soma swells, the endoplasmic reticulum breaks up (so the chromatophilic substance disperses), and the nucleus moves off center. Not all damaged neurons survive; some die at this stage. But often, the axon stump sprouts multiple growth processes while the severed distal end shows continued degeneration of its axon and Schwann cells. Muscle fibers deprived of their nerve supply exhibit a shrinkage called *denervation atrophy.*

④ Near the injury, Schwann cells, the basal lamina, and the neurilemma form a **regeneration tube.** The Schwann cells produce cell-adhesion molecules and nerve growth factors that enable a neuron to regrow to its original destination. When one growth process finds its way into the tube, it grows rapidly (3–5 mm/day), and the other growth processes are retracted.

⑤ The regeneration tube guides the growing sprout back to the original target cells, reestablishing synaptic contact.

⑥ When contact is established, the soma shrinks and returns to its original appearance, and the reinnervated muscle fibers regrow.

Regeneration isn't perfect. Some nerve fibers connect to the wrong muscle fibers or never find a muscle fiber at all, and some damaged neurons simply die. Nerve injury is therefore often followed by some degree of functional deficit. Even when regeneration is achieved, the slow rate of axon regrowth means that some nerve function may take as long as 2 years to recover.

Schwann cells and endoneurium are required for nerve fiber regeneration. Both of these are lacking from the CNS, so damaged CNS nerve fibers cannot regenerate at all. However, since the CNS is encased in bone, it suffers less trauma than the peripheral nerves.

> **BEFORE YOU GO ON**
>
> Answer the following questions to test your understanding of the preceding section:
>
> 8. How is a glial cell different from a neuron? List the six types of glial cells and discuss their functions.
>
> 9. How is myelin produced? How does myelin production in the CNS differ from that in the PNS?
>
> 10. How can a severed peripheral nerve fiber find its way back to the cells it originally innervated?

12.4 Electrophysiology of Neurons

Expected Learning Outcomes

When you have completed this section, you should be able to

a. explain why a cell has an electrical charge difference (voltage) across its membrane;

b. explain how stimulation of a neuron causes a local electrical response in its membrane;

c. explain how local responses generate a nerve signal; and

d. explain how the nerve signal is conducted down an axon.

The nervous system has intrigued scientists and philosophers since ancient times. Galen, the preeminent physician of ancient Rome, thought that the brain pumped a vapor called *psychic pneuma* through hollow nerves and squirted it into the muscles to make them contract. The French philosopher René Descartes still argued for this theory in the seventeenth century. It finally fell out of favor in the eighteenth century, when Luigi Galvani discovered the role of electricity in muscle contraction (see Deeper Insight 11.3). Further progress had to await improvements in microscope technology and histological staining methods. Italian histologist Camillo Golgi (1843–1926) developed an important method for staining neurons with silver. This enabled Spanish histologist Santiago Ramón y Cajal (1852–1934), with tremendous skill and patience, to trace the course of nerve fibers over long distances through serial tissue sections. He demonstrated that the nervous pathway was not a continuous "wire" or tube, but a series of cells separated by the gaps we now call synapses. Golgi and Cajal, even though they intensely disliked each other, shared the 1906 Nobel Prize for Physiology or Medicine for these important discoveries.

Cajal's theory suggested another direction for research: How do neurons communicate? Two key issues in neurophysiology are (1) How does a neuron generate an electrical signal? and (2) How does it transmit a meaningful message to the next cell? These are the questions to which this section and the next are addressed.

12.4a Electrical Potentials and Currents

Neural communication, like muscle excitation, is based on electrophysiology—cellular mechanisms for producing electrical potentials and currents. An **electrical potential** is a difference in the concentration of charged particles between one point and another. It is a form of potential energy that, under the right circumstances, can produce a current. An electrical **current** is a flow of charged particles from one point to another. A new flashlight battery, for example, typically has a potential, or charge, of 1.5 volts (V). If a lightbulb and the two poles of the battery are connected by a wire, electrons flow through the wire from one pole to the other, creating a current that lights the bulb. As long as the battery has a potential (voltage), we say it is **polarized.**

Living cells are also polarized. The charge difference across the plasma membrane is called the **resting membrane potential (RMP).** It is much less than the potential of a flashlight battery—typically about –70 millivolts (mV) in an unstimulated, "resting"

neuron. The negative value means there are more negatively charged particles on the inside of the membrane than on the outside.

We don't have free electrons in the body as we do in an electrical circuit. Electrical currents in the body are created, instead, by the flow of ions such as Na^+ and K^+ through gated channels in the plasma membrane. Gated channels can be opened and closed by various stimuli, as we have seen earlier (see "Membrane Proteins" in section 3.2a and "Electrically Excitable Cells," section 11.3c). This enables cells to turn electrical currents on and off.

12.4b The Resting Membrane Potential

The reason a cell has a resting membrane potential is that electrolytes are unequally distributed between the extracellular fluid (ECF) on the outside of the plasma membrane and the intracellular fluid (ICF) on the inside. The RMP results from the combined effect of three factors: (1) the diffusion of ions down their concentration gradients through the membrane; (2) selective permeability of the membrane, allowing some ions to pass more easily than others; and (3) the electrical attraction of cations and anions to each other.

Potassium ions (K^+) have the greatest influence on the RMP because the plasma membrane is more permeable to K^+ than to any other ion. Imagine a hypothetical cell in which all the K^+ starts out in the ICF, with none in the ECF. Also in the ICF are a number of cytoplasmic anions that cannot escape from the cell because of their size or charge—phosphates, sulfates, small organic acids, proteins, ATP, and RNA. Potassium ions diffuse freely through leak channels in the plasma membrane, down their concentration gradient and out of the cell, leaving these cytoplasmic anions behind **(fig. 12.12).** As a result, the ICF grows more and more negatively charged. But as the ICF becomes more negative, it

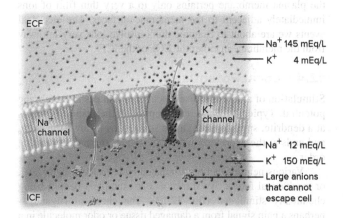

FIGURE 12.12 Ionic Basis of the Resting Membrane Potential. Note that sodium ions are much more concentrated in the extracellular fluid (ECF) than in the intracellular fluid (ICF), while potassium ions are more concentrated in the ICF. Large anions unable to penetrate the plasma membrane give the cytoplasm a negative charge relative to the ECF.

exerts a stronger attraction for the positive potassium ions and attracts some of them back into the cell. Eventually an *equilibrium* is reached in which K⁺ is moving out of the cell (down its concentration gradient) and into the cell (by electrical attraction) at equal rates. There is no further *net* diffusion of K⁺. At the point of equilibrium, K⁺ is about 40 times as concentrated in the ICF as in the ECF.

If K⁺ were the only ion affecting the RMP, it would give the membrane a potential of about –90 mV. However, sodium ions (Na⁺) also enter the picture. Sodium is about 12 times as concentrated in the ECF as in the ICF. The resting plasma membrane is much less permeable to Na⁺ than to K⁺, but Na⁺ does diffuse down its concentration gradient into the cell, attracted by the negative charge in the ICF. This sodium leak is only a trickle, but it is enough to cancel some of the negative charge and reduce the voltage across the membrane.

Sodium leaks into the cell and potassium leaks out, but the sodium–potassium (Na⁺–K⁺) pump continually compensates for this leakage. It pumps 3 Na⁺ out of the cell for every 2 K⁺ it brings in, consuming 1 ATP for each exchange cycle (see fig. 3.19). By removing more cations from the cell than it brings in, it contributes about –3 mV to the RMP. The resting membrane potential of –70 mV is the net effect of all these ion movements—K⁺ diffusion out of the cell, Na⁺ diffusion inward, and the Na⁺–K⁺ pump continually offsetting this ion leakage.

The Na⁺–K⁺ pump accounts for about 70% of the energy (ATP) requirement of the nervous system. Every signal generated by a neuron slightly upsets the distribution of Na⁺ and K⁺, so the pump must work continually to restore equilibrium. This is why nervous tissue has one of the highest rates of ATP consumption of any tissue in the body, and why it demands so much glucose and oxygen. Although a neuron is said to be resting when it is not producing signals, it is highly active maintaining its RMP and "waiting," as it were, for something to happen.

The uneven distribution of Na⁺ and K⁺ on the two sides of the plasma membrane pertains only to a very thin film of ions immediately adjacent to the membrane surfaces. The electrical events we are about to examine don't involve ions very far away from the membrane in either the ECF or the ICF.

12.4c Local Potentials

Stimulation of a neuron causes local disturbances in membrane potential. Typically (but with exceptions), the response begins at a dendrite, spreads through the soma, travels down the axon, and ends at the axon terminal. We consider the process in that order.

Various neurons can be stimulated by chemicals, light, heat, or mechanical forces. We'll take as our example a neuron being chemically stimulated (**fig. 12.13**). The chemical (ligand)—perhaps a pain signal from a damaged tissue or odor molecule in a breath of air—binds to receptors on the neuron. This opens ligand-gated sodium channels that allow Na⁺ to flow into the cell. The Na⁺ inflow cancels some of the internal negative charge, so the voltage across the membrane at that point drifts toward zero. Any such case in which the voltage shifts to a less negative value is called **depolarization.**

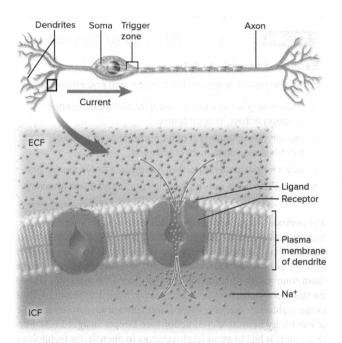

FIGURE 12.13 Excitation of a Neuron by a Chemical Stimulus.

The incoming Na⁺ diffuses for short distances along the inside of the plasma membrane, creating a wave of excitation that spreads out from the point of stimulation, like ripples spreading across a pond when you drop a stone into it. This short-range change in voltage is called a **local potential.** There are four characteristics that distinguish local potentials from the action potentials we will study in the next section (**table 12.2**). You will appreciate these distinctions more fully after you have studied action potentials.

1. Local potentials are **graded,** meaning they vary in magnitude (voltage) according to the strength of the stimulus. An intense or prolonged stimulus opens more gated ion channels than a weaker stimulus, and they stay open longer. Thus, more Na⁺ enters the cell and the voltage changes more than it does with a weaker stimulus.

2. Local potentials are **decremental,** meaning they get weaker as they spread from the point of origin. They decline in strength partly because the Na⁺ leaks back out of the cell through channels along its path, and partly because as Na⁺ spreads out under the plasma membrane and depolarizes it, K⁺ flows out and reverses the effect of the Na⁺ inflow. Therefore, the voltage shift caused by Na⁺ diminishes rapidly with distance. This prevents local potentials from having long-distance effects.

3. Local potentials are **reversible,** meaning that if stimulation ceases, cation diffusion out of the cell quickly returns the membrane voltage to its resting potential.

4. Local potentials can be either **excitatory** or **inhibitory.** So far, we have considered only excitatory local potentials, which depolarize a cell and make a neuron more likely to

TABLE 12.2	Comparison of Local Potentials and Action Potentials
Local Potential	**Action Potential**
Produced by gated channels on the dendrites and soma	Produced by voltage-gated channels on the trigger zone and axon
May be a positive (depolarizing) or negative (hyperpolarizing) voltage change	Always begins with depolarization
Graded; proportional to stimulus strength	All or none; either does not occur at all or exhibits the same peak voltage regardless of stimulus strength
Reversible; returns to RMP if stimulation ceases before threshold is reached	Irreversible; goes to completion once it begins
Local; has effects for only a short distance from point of origin	Self-propagating; has effects a great distance from point of origin
Decremental; signal grows weaker with distance	Nondecremental; signal maintains same strength regardless of distance

produce an action potential. Acetylcholine usually has this effect. Other neurotransmitters, such as glycine, cause an opposite effect—they **hyperpolarize** a cell, or make the membrane more negative. This inhibits a neuron, making it less sensitive and less likely to produce an action potential. A balance between excitatory and inhibitory potentials is very important to information processing in the nervous system (see section 12.6b).

12.4d Action Potentials

An **action potential** is a more dramatic change produced by voltage-gated ion channels in the plasma membrane. Action potentials occur only where there is a high enough density of voltage-gated channels. Most of the soma has only 50 to

75 channels per square micrometer (μm^2), not dense enough to generate action potentials. The trigger zone, however, has 350 to 500 channels/μm^2. If an excitatory local potential spreads all the way to the trigger zone and is still strong enough when it arrives, it can open these channels and generate an action potential.

The action potential is a rapid up-and-down shift in voltage. **Figure 12.14a** shows an action potential numbered to correspond to the following description.

① When the local current arrives at the axon hillock, it depolarizes the membrane at that point. This appears as a steadily rising local potential.

② For anything more to happen, this local potential must rise to a critical voltage called the **threshold** (typically about –55 mV), the minimum needed to open voltage-gated channels.

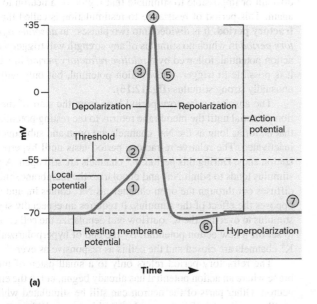

(a)

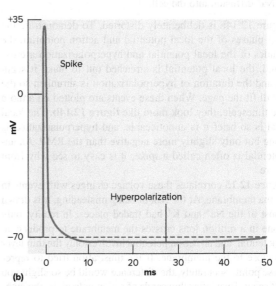

(b)

FIGURE 12.14 An Action Potential. (a) Diagrammed with a distorted timescale to make details of the action potential visible. Numbers correspond to stages discussed in the text. (b) On a more accurate timescale, the local potential is so brief it is imperceptible, the action potential appears as a spike, and the hyperpolarization is very prolonged.

(3) The neuron now "fires," or produces an action potential. At threshold, voltage-gated Na^+ channels open quickly, while gated K^+ channels open more slowly. The initial effect on membrane potential is therefore due to Na^+. Initially, only a few Na^+ channels open, but as Na^+ enters the cell, it further depolarizes the membrane. This stimulates still more voltage-gated Na^+ channels to open and admit even more Na^+, a positive feedback loop that causes the membrane voltage to rise even more rapidly.

(4) As the rising potential passes 0 mV, Na^+ channels are *inactivated* and begin closing. By the time they all close and Na^+ inflow ceases, the voltage peaks at approximately +35 mV. (The peak is as low as 0 mV in some neurons and as high as 50 mV in others.) The membrane is now positive on the inside and negative on the outside—its polarity is reversed compared to the RMP.

(5) By the time the voltage peaks, the slow K^+ channels are fully open. Potassium ions, repelled by the positive ICF, now exit the cell. Their outflow **repolarizes** the membrane—that is, it shifts the voltage back into the negative numbers. The action potential consists of the up-and-down voltage shifts that occur from the time the threshold is reached to the time the voltage returns to the RMP.

(6) Potassium channels stay open longer than Na^+ channels, so slightly more K^+ leaves the cell than the amount of Na^+ that entered. Therefore, the membrane voltage drops to 1 or 2 mV more negative than the original RMP, producing a negative overshoot called *hyperpolarization*.

(7) As you can see, Na^+ and K^+ switch places across the membrane during an action potential. During hyperpolarization, the membrane voltage gradually returns to the RMP because of Na^+ diffusion into the cell.

Figure 12.14a is deliberately distorted. To demonstrate the different phases of the local potential and action potential, the magnitudes of the local potential and hyperpolarization are exaggerated, the local potential is stretched out to make it seem longer, and the duration of hyperpolarization is shrunken so the graph will fit the page. When these events are plotted on a more realistic timescale, they look more like **figure 12.14b**. The local potential is so brief it is unnoticeable, and hyperpolarization is very long but only slightly more negative than the RMP. An action potential is often called a *spike;* it is easy to see why from this figure.

Figure 12.15 correlates these voltage changes with events in the plasma membrane. At the risk of being misleading, it is drawn as if most of the Na^+ and K^+ had traded places. In reality, only about one in a million ions crosses the membrane to produce an action potential, and an action potential involves only the thin layer of ions close to the membrane. If the illustration tried to represent these points accurately, the difference would be so slight you couldn't see it. Even after thousands of action potentials, the cytosol still has a higher concentration of K^+ and a lower concentration of Na^+ than the ECF does.

Earlier we saw that local potentials are graded, decremental, and reversible. We can now contrast this with action potentials.

- Action potentials follow an **all-or-none law.** If a stimulus depolarizes the neuron to threshold, the neuron fires at its maximum voltage (such as +35 mV); if threshold is not reached, the neuron doesn't fire at all. Above threshold, stronger stimuli don't produce stronger action potentials. Thus, action potentials are not graded (proportional to stimulus strength) like local potentials are.

- Action potentials are **nondecremental.** They don't get weaker with distance. The last action potential at the end of a nerve fiber is just as strong as the first one in the trigger zone, no matter how far away—even in a pain fiber that extends from your toes to your brainstem.

- Action potentials are **irreversible.** If a neuron reaches threshold, the action potential goes to completion; it can't be stopped once it begins.

In some respects, we can compare the firing of a neuron to the firing of a gun. As the trigger is squeezed, a gun either fires with maximum force or doesn't fire at all (analogous to the all-or-none law). You can't fire a fast bullet by squeezing the trigger hard or a slow bullet by squeezing it gently—once the trigger is pulled to its "threshold," the bullet always leaves the muzzle at the same velocity. And, like an action potential, the firing of a gun is irreversible once the threshold is reached; neither a bullet nor an action potential can be called back. Table 12.2 further contrasts a local potential with an action potential, including some characteristics of action potentials explained in the following sections.

12.4e The Refractory Period

During an action potential and for a few milliseconds after, it is difficult or impossible to stimulate that region of a neuron to fire again. This period of resistance to restimulation is called the **refractory period.** It is divided into two phases: an *absolute refractory period* in which no stimulus of any strength will trigger a new action potential, followed by a *relative refractory period* in which it is possible to trigger a new action potential, but only with an unusually strong stimulus (**fig. 12.16**).

The absolute refractory period lasts from the start of the action potential until the membrane returns to the resting potential—that is, for as long as the Na^+ channels are open and subsequently inactivated. The relative refractory period lasts until hyperpolarization ends. During this period, K^+ channels are still open. A new stimulus tends to admit Na^+ and depolarize the membrane, but K^+ diffuses out through the open channels as Na^+ comes in, and thus opposes the effect of the stimulus. It requires an especially strong stimulus to override the K^+ outflow and depolarize the cell enough to set off a new action potential. By the end of hyperpolarization, K^+ channels are closed and the cell is as responsive as ever.

The refractory period refers only to a small patch of membrane where an action potential has already begun, not to the entire neuron. Other parts of the neuron can still be stimulated while a small area of it is refractory, and even this area quickly recovers once the nerve signal has passed.

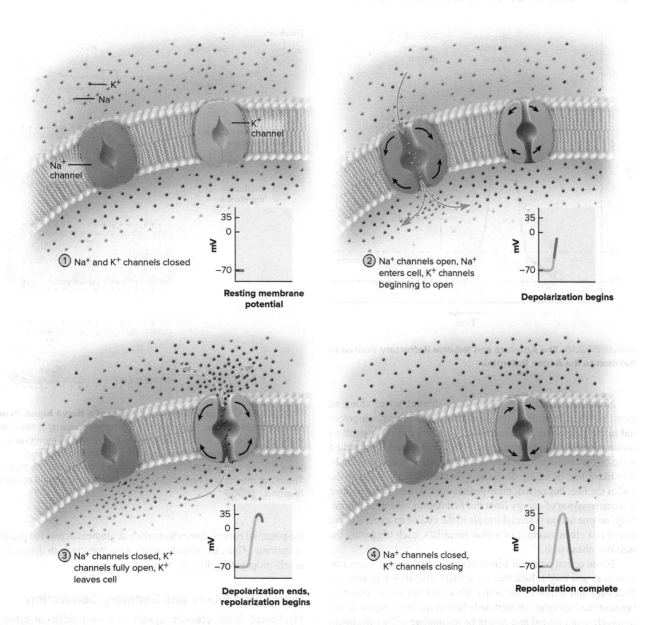

FIGURE 12.15 Actions of the Sodium and Potassium Channels During an Action Potential. The red part of each graph shows the point in the action potential where the events of steps 1 through 4 occur. APR

12.4f Signal Conduction in Nerve Fibers

If a neuron is to communicate with another cell, a signal has to travel to the end of the axon. We now examine how this is achieved.

Unmyelinated Fibers and Continuous Conduction

Unmyelinated fibers present a relatively simple case of signal conduction, easy to understand based on what we have already covered **(fig. 12.17)**. An unmyelinated fiber has voltage-gated channels along its entire length. When an action potential occurs at the trigger zone, Na^+ enters the axon and diffuses for a short distance just beneath the plasma membrane. The resulting depolarization excites voltage-gated channels immediately distal to the action potential. Sodium and potassium channels open and close just as they did at the trigger zone, and a new action potential is produced. By repetition, this excites the membrane immediately distal to that. This chain reaction continues until the traveling signal reaches the end of the axon. Because this produces an uninterrupted wave of electrical excitation all along the fiber, this mechanism is called **continuous conduction.**

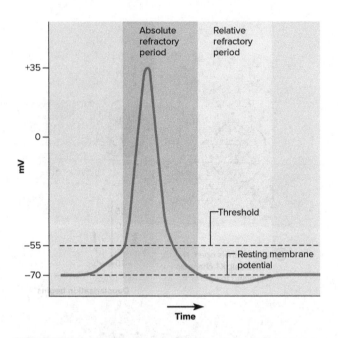

FIGURE 12.16 The Absolute and Relative Refractory Periods in Relation to the Action Potential.

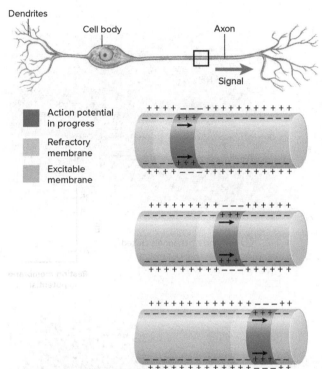

FIGURE 12.17 Continuous Conduction of a Nerve Signal in an Unmyelinated Fiber. Note that the membrane polarity is reversed in the region of the action potential (red). A region of membrane in its refractory period (yellow) trails the action potential and prevents the nerve signal from going backward toward the soma. The other membrane areas (green) are fully polarized and ready to respond. **APR**

Note that an action potential itself doesn't travel along an axon; rather, it stimulates the production of a new action potential in the membrane just ahead of it. Thus, we can distinguish an action potential from a nerve signal. The **nerve signal** is a traveling wave of excitation produced by self-propagating action potentials. It is like a line of falling dominoes. No one domino travels to the end of the line, but each domino pushes over the next one and there is a transmission of energy from the first domino to the last. Similarly, no one action potential travels to the end of an axon; a nerve signal is a chain reaction of action potentials, each triggering the next one ahead of it.

If one action potential stimulates the production of a new one next to it, you might think that the signal could also start traveling backward and return to the soma. This does not occur, however, because the membrane immediately behind the nerve signal is still in its refractory period and cannot be restimulated. Only the membrane ahead is sensitive to stimulation. The refractory period thus ensures that nerve signals are conducted in the proper direction, from the soma to the axon terminals.

A traveling nerve signal is an electrical current, but it isn't the same as a current traveling through a wire. A current in a wire travels millions of meters per second and is decremental—it gets weaker with distance. A nerve signal is much slower (not more than 2 m/s in unmyelinated fibers), but as already noted, it is nondecremental. To clarify this concept, we can compare the nerve signal to a burning fuse on a firecracker. When a fuse is lit, the heat ignites powder immediately in front of this point, and this repeats itself in a self-propagating fashion until the end of the fuse is reached. At the end, the fuse burns just as hotly as it did at the beginning. In a fuse, the combustible powder is the source of potential energy that keeps the process going in a nondecremental fashion. In an axon,

the potential energy comes from the ion gradient across the plasma membrane. Thus, the signal doesn't grow weaker with distance; it is self-propagating, like the burning of a fuse.

Myelinated Fibers and Saltatory Conduction

Myelinated fibers conduct signals in a very different manner called **saltatory**[27] **conduction**—meaning "leaping" or "jumping." These fibers cannot conduct a signal in continuous mode, like a burning fuse, because voltage-gated ion channels are too scarce in the myelin-covered internodal segments—fewer than $25/\mu m^2$ in these regions compared with 2,000 to $12,000/\mu m^2$ at the myelin sheath gaps (nodes of Ranvier). There would be little point in having ion channels in the internodal segments anyway—myelin insulates the fiber from the ECF in these segments, and Na^+ from the ECF couldn't flow into the cell even if more channels were present. Therefore, no action potentials can occur in the internodal segments, and the nerve signal requires some other way of traversing the distance from one node to the next.

---

[27]from *saltare* = to leap, to dance

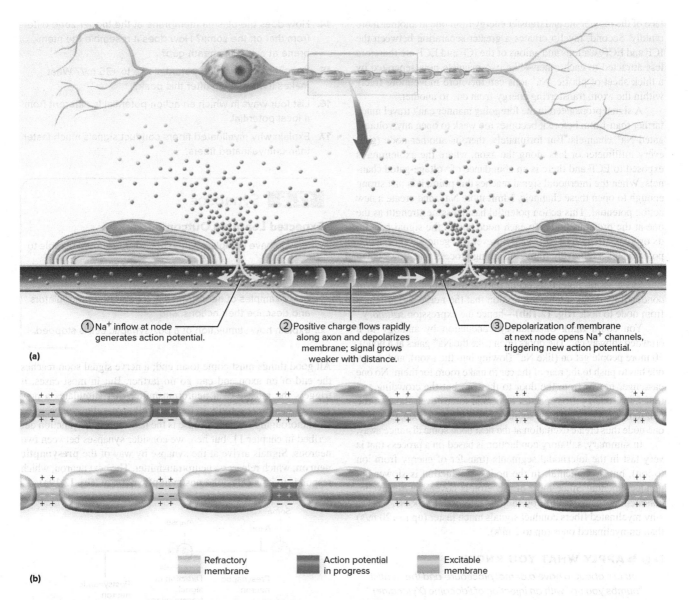

①Na⁺ inflow at node generates action potential.

②Positive charge flows rapidly along axon and depolarizes membrane; signal grows weaker with distance.

③Depolarization of membrane at next node opens Na⁺ channels, triggering new action potential.

(a)

(b)

Refractory membrane

Action potential in progress

Excitable membrane

FIGURE 12.18 Saltatory Conduction of a Nerve Signal in a Myelinated Fiber. (a) Sodium inflow at myelin sheath gaps, regenerating the flow of positive charges at each gap. (b) Action potentials can occur only at myelin sheath gaps, so the nerve signal appears as if it were jumping from gap to gap. The membrane (yellow) behind each action potential is temporarily in the refractive state, whereas the membrane (green) ahead of it is fully excitable and ready for action.

When Na⁺ enters the axon at a node, it diffuses for a short distance along the inner face of the membrane **(fig. 12.18a).** Each sodium ion has an electrical field around it. When one Na⁺ moves toward another, its field repels the other ion, which moves slightly and repels another, and so forth—like two magnets that repel each other if you try to push their north poles together. No one ion moves very far, but this energy transfer travels down the axon much faster and farther than any of the individual ions. The signal grows weaker with distance, however, partly because the axoplasm resists the movement of the ions and partly because Na⁺ leaks back out of the axon along the way. Therefore, with distance, there is a lower and

lower concentration of Na⁺ to relay the charge. Furthermore, with a surplus of positive charges on the inner face of the axolemma and a surplus of negative charges on the outer face, these cations and anions are attracted to each other through the membrane—like the opposite poles of two magnets attracting each other through a sheet of paper. This results in a "storage" (called *capacitance*) of unmoving or sluggishly moving charges on the membrane.

Myelin speeds up signal conduction in two ways. First of all, by wrapping tightly around the axon, it seals the nerve fiber and greatly increases its resistance to the leakage of Na⁺ out of the axon. Sodium ions therefore maintain a higher density on the inner face of the membrane and transfer energy from one to another more rapidly. Second, myelin creates a greater separation between the ICF and ECF. Cations and anions of the ICF and ECF are therefore less attracted to each other—like two magnets now separated by a thick sheet of plastic. Na^+ ions can therefore move more freely within the axon, transferring energy from one to another.

A signal propagated in the foregoing manner can't travel much farther than 1 mm before it becomes too weak to open any voltage-gated Na^+ channels. But fortunately, there is another node (gap) every millimeter or less along the axon, where the axolemma is exposed to ECF and there is an abundance of voltage-gated channels. When the internodal signal reaches this point, it is just strong enough to open these channels, admit more Na^+, and create a new action potential. This action potential has the same strength as the one at the previous node, so each node boosts the signal back to its original strength (+35 mV). However, the generation of action potentials is a relatively time-consuming process that slows down the nerve signal at the nodes.

Since action potentials occur only at the nodes, this mode of conduction creates a false impression that the nerve signal jumps from node to node (**fig. 12.18b**)—hence the expression *saltatory*.

You could think of saltatory conduction by analogy to a crowded subway car. The doors open (like the Na^+ gates at a node), 20 more people get on (like Na^+ flowing into the axon), and everyone has to push to the rear of the car to make room for them. No one passenger moves from the door to the rear, but the crowding and transfer of energy from person to person forces even those at the rear to move a little, like the sodium ions at the next node. Events at one node thus create excitation at the next node some distance away.

In summary, saltatory conduction is based on a process that is very fast in the internodal segments (transfer of energy from ion to ion), but decremental. In the nodes, conduction is slower but nondecremental. Since most of the axon is covered with myelin, conduction occurs mainly by the fast internodal process. This is why myelinated fibers conduct signals much faster (up to 120 m/s) than unmyelinated ones (up to 2 m/s).

▶▶▶**APPLY WHAT YOU KNOW**

You are about to have a dental procedure and the dentist "numbs you up" with an injection of lidocaine (Xylocaine). This is a local anesthetic that prevents voltage-gated Na^+ channels from opening. Explain why this mechanism would block the conduction of pain signals from your teeth to your brain.

BEFORE YOU GO ON

Answer the following questions to test your understanding of the preceding section:

11. What causes K^+ to diffuse out of a resting cell? What attracts it into the cell?

12. What happens to Na^+ when a neuron is stimulated on its dendrite? Why does the movement of Na^+ raise the voltage on the plasma membrane?

13. What does it mean to say a local potential is graded, decremental, and reversible?

14. How does the plasma membrane at the trigger zone differ from that on the soma? How does it resemble the membrane at a myelin sheath gap?

15. What makes an action potential rise to +35 mV? What makes it drop again after this peak?

16. List four ways in which an action potential is different from a local potential.

17. Explain why myelinated fibers conduct signals much faster than unmyelinated fibers.

12.5   Synapses

Expected Learning Outcomes

When you have completed this section, you should be able to

a. explain how messages are transmitted from one neuron to another;

b. give examples of neurotransmitters and neuromodulators and describe their actions; and

c. explain how stimulation of a postsynaptic cell is stopped.

All good things must come to an end; a nerve signal soon reaches the end of an axon and can go no farther. But in most cases, it triggers the release of a neurotransmitter that stimulates a new wave of electrical activity in the next cell across the synapse. The most thoroughly studied synapse is the neuromuscular junction described in chapter 11, but here we consider synapses between two neurons. Signals arrive at the synapse by way of the **presynaptic neuron,** which releases a neurotransmitter. The next neuron, which responds to it, is called the **postsynaptic neuron (fig. 12.19a).**

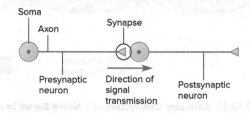

(a)

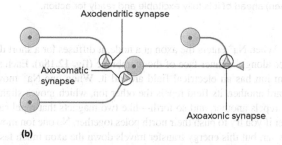

(b)

FIGURE 12.19 Synaptic Relationships Between Neurons.
(a) Pre- and postsynaptic neurons. (b) Types of synapses defined by the site of contact on the postsynaptic neuron.

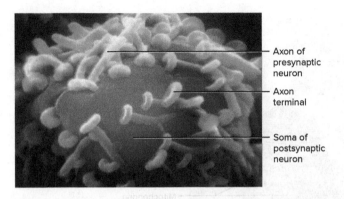

FIGURE 12.20 Axon Terminals Synapsing with the Soma of a Neuron in a Marine Slug, *Aplysia* (SEM).
Omikron/Science Source/Getty Images

The presynaptic neuron may synapse with a dendrite, the soma, or the axon of a postsynaptic neuron, forming an *axodendritic, axosomatic,* or *axoaxonic synapse,* respectively (**fig. 12.19b**). A neuron can have an enormous number of synapses (**fig. 12.20**). For example, a spinal motor neuron is covered with about 10,000 axon terminals from other neurons—8,000 ending on its dendrites and another 2,000 on the soma. In a part of the brain called the cerebellum, one neuron can have as many as 100,000 synapses.

12.5a The Discovery of Neurotransmitters

In the early twentieth century, biologists assumed that synaptic communication was electrical—a logical hypothesis given that neurons seemed to touch each other and signals were transmitted so quickly from one to the next. Cajal's careful histological examinations, however, revealed a 20 to 40 nm gap between neurons—the **synaptic cleft**—casting doubt on the possibility of electrical transmission. Cajal was rudely criticized for such a "preposterous" idea, but he was eventually proved correct.

In 1921, German pharmacologist Otto Loewi conclusively demonstrated that neurons communicate by releasing chemicals. The *vagus nerves* supply the heart, among other organs, and slow it down. Loewi opened two frogs and flooded the hearts with saline to keep them moist. He stimulated the vagus nerve of one frog, and its heart rate dropped as expected. He then removed saline from that heart and squirted it onto the heart of the second frog. The solution alone reduced that frog's heart rate. Evidently it contained something released by the vagus nerve of the first frog. Loewi had discovered what we now call acetylcholine—the first known neurotransmitter.

▶▶▶ APPLY WHAT YOU KNOW

As described, does the previous experiment conclusively prove that the second frog's heart slowed as a result of something released by the vagus nerves? If you were Loewi, what control experiment would you do to rule out alternative hypotheses?

Following Loewi's work, the idea of electrical communication between cells fell into disrepute. Now, however, we realize that some neurons, neuroglia, and cardiac and unitary smooth muscle do indeed have **electrical synapses,** where adjacent cells are joined by gap junctions and ions diffuse directly from one cell into the next. These junctions have the advantage of quick transmission because there is no delay for the release and binding of neurotransmitter. They are important in synchronizing the activity of local suites of neurons in certain regions of the brain. Their disadvantage, however, is that they cannot integrate information and make decisions. The ability to do that is a property of **chemical synapses,** in which neurons communicate by neurotransmitters. Chemical synapses are also the site of learning and memory, the target of many prescription drugs, and the site of action of drugs of addiction, among other things.

12.5b Structure of a Chemical Synapse

The axon terminal (**fig. 12.21**) contains synaptic vesicles, many of which are "docked" at release sites on the plasma membrane, ready to release neurotransmitter on demand. A reserve pool of synaptic vesicles is located a little farther away from the membrane, tethered to the cytoskeleton.

The postsynaptic neuron lacks these conspicuous specializations. At this end, the neuron has no synaptic vesicles and cannot release neurotransmitter. Its membrane does, however, have neurotransmitter receptors and ligand-gated ion channels.

12.5c Neurotransmitters and Related Messengers

More than 100 neurotransmitters have been identified since Loewi's time. Neurotransmitters can be defined as molecules that are synthesized by a neuron, released when a nerve signal reaches an axon terminal or varicosity of the nerve fiber, and have a specific effect on a receiving cell's physiology. Most of them are small organic molecules that are released by exocytosis and bind to specific receptors on the receiving cell, but there are exceptions. Some of the best-known neurotransmitters are listed in **table 12.3.** Parts of the brain referred to in this table will become familiar as you study chapter 14, and you may wish to refer back to this table then to enhance your understanding of brain function. Most neurotransmitters fall into the following categories (**fig. 12.22**).

1. **Acetylcholine** is in a class by itself. It is formed from acetic acid (acetate) and choline.

2. **Amino acid** neurotransmitters include glycine, glutamate, aspartate, and γ-aminobutyric acid (GABA).

3. **Monoamines (biogenic amines)** are synthesized from amino acids by removal of the —COOH group. They retain the —NH_2 (amino group), hence their name. Some monoamine neurotransmitters are epinephrine, norepinephrine, dopamine, serotonin (5-hydroxytryptamine, or 5-HT), and histamine. The first three of these are in a subclass called **catecholamines** (CAT-eh-COAL-uh-meens).

4. **Purines** serving as neurotransmitters include adenosine and ATP (adenosine triphosphate).

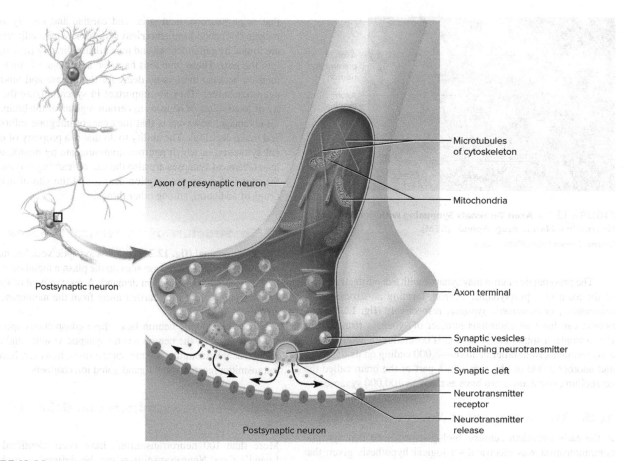

FIGURE 12.21 Structure of a Chemical Synapse.

Axon of presynaptic neuron

Postsynaptic neuron

Postsynaptic neuron

Microtubules of cytoskeleton

Mitochondria

Axon terminal

Synaptic vesicles containing neurotransmitter

Synaptic cleft

Neurotransmitter receptor

Neurotransmitter release

5. **Gases,** specifically nitric oxide (NO) and carbon monoxide (CO), are inorganic exceptions to the usual definition of neurotransmitters. They are synthesized as needed rather than stored in synaptic vesicles; they simply diffuse out of the axon terminal rather than being released by exocytosis; and they diffuse into the postsynaptic neuron rather than bind to a surface receptor.

6. **Neuropeptides** are chains of 2 to 40 amino acids. Some examples are cholecystokinin (CCK) and the endorphins. Neuropeptides are stored in *secretory granules (dense-core vesicles)* that are about 100 nm in diameter, twice as large as typical synaptic vesicles. Some neuropeptides also function as hormones or as *neuromodulators* (see section 12.5f). Some are produced not only by neurons but also by the digestive tract; thus, they are known as *gut–brain peptides.* Some of these cause cravings for specific nutrients such as fat, protein, or carbohydrates (see section 26.1b) and may be associated with certain eating disorders.

▶▶▶ **APPLY WHAT YOU KNOW**

Unlike other neurotransmitters, neuropeptides can be synthesized only in the soma and must be transported to the axon terminals. Why is their synthesis limited to the soma?

We will see, especially in chapter 15, that a given neurotransmitter does not have the same effect everywhere in the body. There are multiple receptor types in the body for a particular neurotransmitter—over 14 receptor types for serotonin, for example—and it is the receptor that governs what effect a neurotransmitter has on its target cell. Most human and other mammalian neurons can secrete two or more neurotransmitters and can switch from one to another under different circumstances.

12.5d Synaptic Transmission

Some neurotransmitters are excitatory, some are inhibitory, and for some the effect depends on what kind of receptor the postsynaptic cell has. Some open ligand-gated ion channels and others act through second messengers. Bearing this diversity in mind, we will examine three kinds of synapses with different modes of action.

An Excitatory Cholinergic Synapse

A **cholinergic**[28] (CO-lin-UR-jic) synapse employs acetylcholine (ACh) as its neurotransmitter. ACh excites some postsynaptic cells (such as skeletal muscle) and inhibits others (such as

[28]*cholin* = acetylcholine; *erg* = work, action

TABLE 12.3	Neurotransmitters (Selected Examples)
Name	**Locations and Actions**
Acetylcholine (ACh)	Neuromuscular junctions, most synapses of autonomic nervous system, retina, and many parts of the brain; excites skeletal muscle, inhibits cardiac muscle, and has excitatory or inhibitory effects on smooth muscle and glands depending on location
Amino Acids	
Glutamate	Cerebral cortex and brainstem; accounts for about 75% of all excitatory synaptic transmission in the brain; involved in learning and memory
Aspartate	Spinal cord; effects similar to those of glutamate
Glycine	Inhibitory neurons of the brain, spinal cord, and retina; most common inhibitory neurotransmitter in the spinal cord
GABA	Thalamus, hypothalamus, cerebellum, occipital lobes of cerebrum, and retina; the most common inhibitory neurotransmitter in the brain
Monoamines	
Norepinephrine	Sympathetic nervous system, cerebral cortex, hypothalamus, brainstem, cerebellum, and spinal cord; involved in dreaming, waking, and mood; excites cardiac muscle; can excite or inhibit smooth muscle and glands depending on location
Epinephrine	Hypothalamus, thalamus, spinal cord, and adrenal medulla; effects similar to those of norepinephrine
Dopamine	Hypothalamus, limbic system, cerebral cortex, and retina; highly concentrated in substantia nigra of midbrain; involved in elevation of mood and control of skeletal muscles
Serotonin	Hypothalamus, limbic system, cerebellum, retina, and spinal cord; also secreted by blood platelets and intestinal cells; involved in sleepiness, alertness, thermoregulation, and mood
Histamine	Hypothalamus; also a potent vasodilator released by mast cells of connective tissue and basophils of the blood
Neuropeptides	
Substance P	Basal nuclei, midbrain, hypothalamus, cerebral cortex, small intestine, and pain-receptor neurons; mediates pain transmission
Enkephalins	Hypothalamus, limbic system, pituitary, pain pathways of spinal cord, and nerve endings of digestive tract; act as analgesics (pain relievers) by inhibiting substance P; inhibit intestinal motility; modulate immune responses
β-endorphin	Digestive tract, spinal cord, and many parts of the brain; also secreted as a hormone by the pituitary; suppresses pain; secretion rises sharply during labor and delivery and in response to other pain situations
Cholecystokinin	Cerebral cortex and small intestine; suppresses appetite

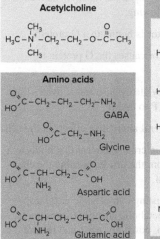

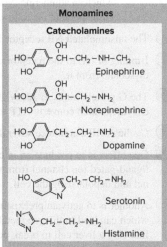

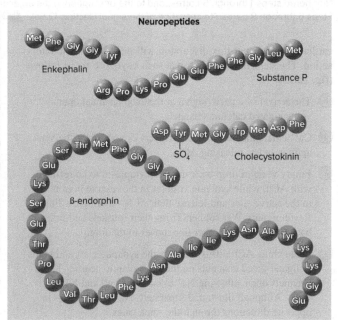

FIGURE 12.22 Classification of Some Neurotransmitters. The neuropeptides are chains of amino acids, each identified by its three-letter code. Appendix D explains the codes.

⑤ As Na⁺ enters, it spreads out along the inside of the plasma membrane and depolarizes it, producing a local voltage shift called the **postsynaptic potential**. Like other local potentials, if this is strong and persistent enough (that is, if enough current makes it to the axon hillock), it opens voltage-gated ion channels in the trigger zone and causes the postsynaptic neuron to fire.

Steps 6 through 8 in figure 12.23 concern the mechanism for halting transmission and are explained shortly (see section 12.5e).

An Inhibitory GABA-ergic Synapse

Synapses that employ γ-aminobutyric acid (GABA) as their neurotransmitter are called **GABA-ergic synapses**. Amino acid neurotransmitters such as GABA work by the same mechanism as ACh; they bind to ion channels and cause immediate changes in membrane potential. The release of GABA and binding to its receptor are similar to the preceding case. The GABA receptor, however, is a chloride channel. When it opens, Cl⁻ enters the cell and makes the inside even more negative than the resting membrane potential. The neuron is therefore inhibited, or less likely to fire.

An Excitatory Adrenergic Synapse

An **adrenergic synapse** employs the neurotransmitter norepinephrine (NE), also called noradrenaline. NE, other monoamines, and neuropeptides act through second-messenger systems such as cyclic AMP (cAMP). The receptor is not an ion channel but a transmembrane protein associated with a G protein on the inner face of the membrane. **Figure 12.24** shows some ways in which an adrenergic synapse can function, numbered to correspond to the following:

① The unstimulated NE receptor is bound to a G protein.

② Binding of NE to the receptor causes the G protein to dissociate from it.

③ The G protein binds to adenylate cyclase and activates this enzyme, which converts ATP to cAMP.

④ Cyclic AMP can induce several alternative effects in the cell.

⑤ One effect is to produce an internal chemical that binds to a ligand-gated ion channel from the inside, opening the channel and depolarizing the cell.

⑥ Another is to activate preexisting cytoplasmic enzymes, which can lead to diverse metabolic changes (for example, inducing a liver cell to break down glycogen and release glucose into the blood).

⑦ Yet another is for cAMP to induce genetic transcription, so that the cell produces new enzymes leading to diverse metabolic effects.

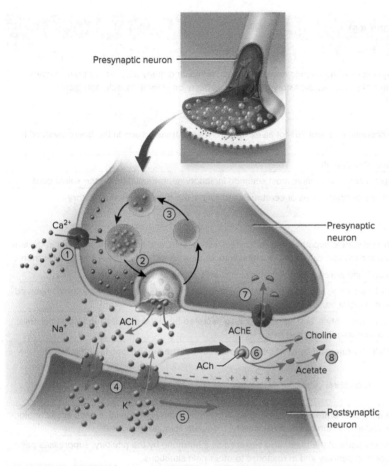

FIGURE 12.23 Transmission at a Cholinergic Synapse. Acetylcholine directly opens ion channels in the plasma membrane of the postsynaptic neuron. Numbered steps 1 through 5 correspond to the description in the adjacent text. Steps 6 through 8 pertain to cessation of the signal (section 12.5e). **APR**

cardiac muscle), but this discussion will describe an excitatory action. The steps in transmission at such a synapse are as follows **(fig. 12.23):**

① The arrival of a nerve signal at the axon terminal opens voltage-gated calcium channels.

② Ca²⁺ enters the terminal and triggers exocytosis of the synaptic vesicles, releasing ACh.

③ Empty vesicles drop back into the cytoplasm to be refilled with ACh, while synaptic vesicles in the reserve pool move to the active sites and release their ACh—a bit like a line of Revolutionary War soldiers firing their muskets and falling back to reload as another line moves to the fore.

④ Meanwhile, ACh diffuses across the synaptic cleft and binds to ligand-gated channels on the postsynaptic neuron. These channels open, allowing Na⁺ to enter the cell and K⁺ to leave. Although illustrated separately, Na⁺ and K⁺ pass in opposite directions through the same gates.

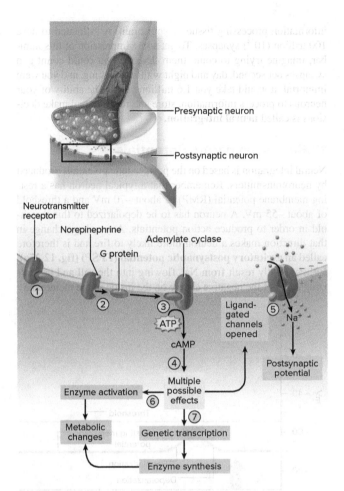

FIGURE 12.24 Transmission at an Adrenergic Synapse.
Numbered steps correspond to the description in nearby text.

Although slower to respond than cholinergic and GABA-ergic synapses, adrenergic synapses do have an advantage—**signal amplification.** A single NE molecule binding to a receptor can induce the formation of many cAMPs, each of those can activate many enzyme molecules or induce the transcription of a gene to generate numerous mRNA molecules, and each of those can result in the production of a vast number of enzyme molecules and metabolic products such as glucose molecules.

As complex as synaptic events may seem, they typically require only 0.5 ms or so—an interval called **synaptic delay.** This is the time from the arrival of a signal at the axon terminal of a presynaptic cell to the beginning of an action potential in the postsynaptic cell.

12.5e Cessation of the Signal

It is important not only to stimulate a postsynaptic cell but also to turn off the stimulus in due time. Otherwise the postsynaptic neuron could continue firing indefinitely, causing a breakdown in physiological coordination. But a neurotransmitter molecule binds to its receptor for only 1 ms or so, then dissociates from it. If the presynaptic

cell continues to release neurotransmitter, one molecule is quickly replaced by another and the postsynaptic cell is restimulated. This immediately suggests a way of stopping synaptic transmission—stop adding new neurotransmitter and get rid of that which is already there. The first step is achieved simply by the cessation of signals in the presynaptic nerve fiber. The second can be achieved in the following ways, pictured as steps 6 to 8 in figure 12.23:

6. **Neurotransmitter degradation.** An enzyme in the synaptic cleft breaks the neurotransmitter down into fragments that have no stimulatory effect on the postsynaptic cell. Depicted here is acetylcholinesterase (AChE) breaking ACh down into choline and acetate.

7. **Reuptake.** A neurotransmitter or its breakdown products are reabsorbed by transport proteins in the axon terminal, removing them from the synapse and ending their stimulatory effect. Choline from ACh is recycled to make new ACh. Amino acid and monoamine neurotransmitters are similarly reabsorbed, then broken down within the axon terminal by an enzyme called **monoamine oxidase (MAO).** Some antidepressant drugs work by inhibiting MAO (see Deeper Insight 15.2). Some cases of autism, attention-deficit/hyperactivity disorder (ADHD), parkinsonism, and depression stem from mutations that render some of these transport proteins nonfunctional.

8. **Diffusion.** Neurotransmitters or their breakdown products simply diffuse away from the synapse into the nearby extracellular fluid. As shown in figure 12.23, this is what happens to the acetate component of ACh, but in other cases, the neurotransmitter escapes the synapse intact. In the CNS, astrocytes absorb stray neurotransmitters and return them to the presynaptic neurons. In ganglia of the PNS, it seems that the satellite cells that surround neurons perform this role; this is an area of current scientific investigation.

12.5f Neuromodulators

Neurons sometimes secrete chemical signals that have long-term effects on entire groups of neurons instead of brief, quick effects at an individual synapse. Some call these **neuromodulators** to distinguish them from neurotransmitters; others use the term *neurotransmitter* broadly to include these. Neuromodulators adjust, or *modulate,* the activity of neuron groups in various ways: increasing the release of neurotransmitters by presynaptic neurons; adjusting the sensitivity of postsynaptic neurons to neurotransmitters; or altering the rate of neurotransmitter reuptake or breakdown to prolong their effects.

The simplest neuromodulator is the gas **nitric oxide (NO).** NO diffuses readily into a postsynaptic cell and activates second-messenger pathways with such effects as relaxing smooth muscle. This has the effect of dilating small arteries and increasing blood flow to a tissue; this is the basis for the action of drugs for erectile dysfunction (see Deeper Insight 27.4). The neuropeptides are neuromodulators; among these are the **enkephalins** and **endorphins,** which inhibit spinal neurons from transmitting pain signals to the brain (see section 16.2d). Other neuromodulators include hormones and some neurotransmitters such as dopamine, serotonin, and histamine. The last point may seem confusing, but the terms *neurotransmitter, hormone,* and *neuromodulator* define not so much the chemical itself, but the role it plays in a given context. One chemical can play two or more of these roles in different places and circumstances.

BEFORE YOU GO ON

Answer the following questions to test your understanding of the preceding section:

18. Concisely describe five steps that occur between the arrival of an action potential at the axon terminal and the beginning of a new action potential in the postsynaptic neuron.

19. Contrast the actions of acetylcholine, GABA, and norepinephrine at their respective synapses.

20. Describe three mechanisms that stop synaptic transmission.

21. What is the function of neuromodulators? Compare and contrast neuromodulators and neurotransmitters.

12.6   Neural Integration

Expected Learning Outcomes

When you have completed this section, you should be able to

a. explain how a neuron "decides" whether or not to generate action potentials;

b. explain how the nervous system translates complex information into a simple code;

c. explain how neurons work together in groups to process information and produce effective output; and

d. describe how memory works at the cellular and molecular levels.

Synaptic delay slows the transmission of nerve signals; the more synapses there are in a neural pathway, the longer it takes information to get from its origin to its destination. You may wonder, therefore, why we have synapses—why a nervous pathway is not, indeed, a continuous "wire" as biologists believed before Cajal. The presence of synapses is not due to limitations on axon length—after all, one nerve fiber can reach from your toes to your brainstem. (In the neck of the giraffe, the *recurrent laryngeal nerve* has nerve fibers 4.6 m, or 15 ft, long. Nerve fibers from the hind foot to the brainstem are even longer by far.) We also have seen that cells communicate much more quickly through gap junctions than through chemical synapses. So why have chemical synapses at all?

What we value most about our nervous system is its ability to process information, store it, and make decisions—and chemical synapses are the decision-making devices of the system. The more synapses a neuron has, the greater its information-processing capability. At this moment, you are using certain *pyramidal cells* of the cerebral cortex (see fig. 12.5a) to read and comprehend this passage. Each pyramidal cell has about 40,000 synaptic contacts with other neurons. The cerebral cortex alone (the main

information-processing tissue of your brain) is estimated to have 100 trillion (10^{14}) synapses. To get some impression of this number, imagine trying to count them. Even if you could count two synapses per second, day and night without stopping, and you were immortal, it would take you 1.6 million years. The ability of your neurons to process information, store and recall it, and make decisions is called **neural integration.**

12.6a   Postsynaptic Potentials

Neural integration is based on the postsynaptic potentials produced by neurotransmitters. Remember that a typical neuron has a resting membrane potential (RMP) of about –70 mV and a threshold of about –55 mV. A neuron has to be depolarized to this threshold in order to produce action potentials. Any voltage change in that direction makes a neuron more likely to fire and is therefore called an **excitatory postsynaptic potential (EPSP) (fig. 12.25a).** EPSPs usually result from Na^+ flowing into the cell and neutralizing some of the negative charge on the inside of the membrane.

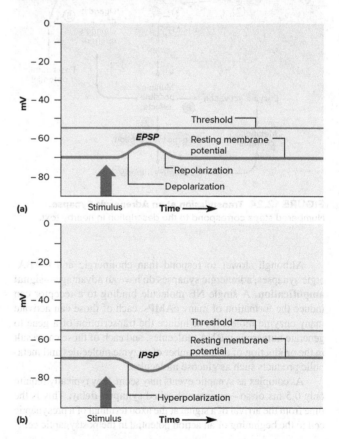

FIGURE 12.25 Postsynaptic Potentials. (a) An excitatory postsynaptic potential (EPSP), which shifts the membrane voltage closer to threshold and makes the cell more likely to fire. (b) An inhibitory postsynaptic potential (IPSP), which shifts the membrane voltage farther away from threshold and makes the cell less likely to fire. The sizes of these postsynaptic potentials are greatly exaggerated here for clarity; compare figure 12.27.

? *Why is a single EPSP insufficient to make a neuron fire?*

In other cases, a neurotransmitter hyperpolarizes the postsynaptic cell and makes it more negative than the RMP. Since this makes the postsynaptic cell less likely to fire, it is called an **inhibitory postsynaptic potential (IPSP) (fig. 12.25b).** Some IPSPs are produced by a neurotransmitter opening ligand-gated chloride channels, causing Cl⁻ to flow into the cell and make the cytosol more negative. A less common way is to open selective K⁺ channels, increasing K⁺ diffusion out of the cell.

We must recognize that because of ion leakage through their membranes, all neurons fire at a certain background rate even when they are not being stimulated. EPSPs and IPSPs don't determine whether or not a neuron fires, but only change the rate of firing by stimulating or inhibiting the production of more action potentials.

Glutamate and aspartate are excitatory brain neurotransmitters that produce EPSPs. Glycine and GABA produce IPSPs and are therefore inhibitory. Acetylcholine (ACh) and norepinephrine are excitatory to some cells and inhibitory to others, depending on the type of receptors present. For example, ACh excites skeletal muscle but inhibits cardiac muscle because of different types of ACh receptors.

12.6b Summation, Facilitation, and Inhibition

One neuron may receive input from thousands of other neurons. Some incoming nerve fibers may produce EPSPs while others produce IPSPs. The neuron's response depends on whether the *net* input is excitatory or inhibitory. If EPSPs override the IPSPs, threshold may be reached and set off an action potential; if IPSPs prevail, they inhibit the neuron from firing. **Summation** is the process of adding up postsynaptic potentials and responding to their net effect. It occurs in the trigger zone.

Suppose, for example, you're working in the kitchen and accidentally touch a hot pot. EPSPs in your motor neurons might cause you to jerk your hand back quickly and avoid being burned. Yet a moment later, you might nonchalantly sip a cup of hot tea. Since you are expecting it to be hot, you don't jerk it away from your lips. You have learned that it won't injure you, so at some level of the nervous system, IPSPs prevail and inhibit the motor response.

It is fundamentally a balance between EPSPs and IPSPs that enables the nervous system to make decisions. A postsynaptic neuron is like a little cellular democracy acting on the "majority vote" of hundreds or thousands of presynaptic cells. In the tea example, some presynaptic neurons send messages that signify "Hot! Danger!" in the form of EPSPs that may activate a hand-withdrawal reflex, while at the same time, others produce IPSPs that signify "Safe" and suppress the reflex. Whether you jerk your hand away depends on whether the EPSPs override the IPSPs or vice versa.

Weak stimulation of a postsynaptic neuron may generate an EPSP, but it fades before reaching threshold. A typical EPSP is a voltage change of only 0.5 mV and lasts only 15 to 20 ms. If a neuron has an RMP of −70 mV and a threshold of −55 mV, it needs at least 30 EPSPs to reach threshold and fire. There are two ways in which EPSPs can add up to do this, and both may occur simultaneously.

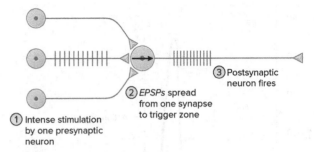

(a) Temporal summation

① Intense stimulation by one presynaptic neuron

② *EPSPs* spread from one synapse to trigger zone

③ Postsynaptic neuron fires

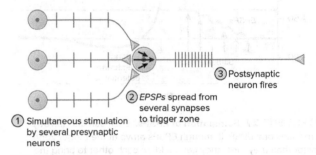

(b) Spatial summation

① Simultaneous stimulation by several presynaptic neurons

② *EPSPs* spread from several synapses to trigger zone

③ Postsynaptic neuron fires

FIGURE 12.26 Temporal and Spatial Summation. Vertical lines on the nerve fibers indicate relative firing frequency. Arrows within the postsynaptic neuron indicate the path of local graded potentials. (a) Temporal summation resulting from rapid firing of a single presynaptic neuron. (b) Spatial summation as an additive effect of multiple presynaptic neurons firing at moderate rates.

1. **Temporal summation (fig. 12.26a).** This occurs when a single synapse generates EPSPs so quickly that each is generated before the previous one fades. This allows the EPSPs to add up over time to a threshold voltage that triggers an action potential **(fig. 12.27).** Temporal summation can occur if even one presynaptic neuron stimulates the postsynaptic neuron at a fast enough rate.

2. **Spatial summation (fig. 12.26b).** This occurs when EPSPs from several synapses add up to threshold at the axon hillock. Any one synapse may generate only a weak signal, but several synapses acting together can bring the hillock to threshold. The presynaptic neurons collaborate to induce the postsynaptic neuron to fire.

Neurons routinely work in groups to modify each other's actions. **Presynaptic facilitation** is a process in which one neuron enhances the effect of another. **Figure 12.28** depicts such an interaction between three neurons we will call neuron F for a facilitating neuron, S for a stimulating neuron, and R for a responding neuron. Neuron F forms an axoaxonic synapse with the axon terminal of neuron S. When neuron F is quiescent, neuron S shows only a low level of activity, releasing some neurotransmitter but not necessarily enough to excite neuron R to threshold. But if circumstances call for enhancing information transmission across synapse S–R, neuron F can release a neurotransmitter

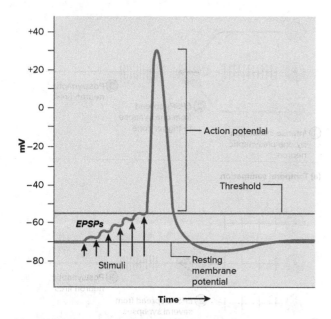

FIGURE 12.27 Summation of EPSPs. Each stimulus (arrow) produces one EPSP. If enough EPSPs arrive at the trigger zone faster than they fade, they can build on each other to bring the neuron to threshold and trigger an action potential.

such as serotonin. Serotonin makes voltage-gated calcium channels in the axon terminal of S remain open longer. Increased calcium inflow increases neurotransmitter release by S, which now excites neuron R. The facilitating neuron F thus accentuates synaptic transmission.

The spatial summation seen in figure 12.26b is another way of facilitating the firing of a postsynaptic neuron. One neuron acting

alone may be unable to induce a postsynaptic neuron to fire, but when they collaborate, their combined "effort" does induce firing in the postsynaptic cell.

Presynaptic inhibition is the opposite of facilitation, a mechanism in which one presynaptic neuron suppresses another one. This mechanism is used to reduce or halt unwanted synaptic transmission. In **figure 12.29**, we see another three neurons in which the facilitating neuron is replaced by an inhibitory neuron, I. When neuron I is silent, neuron S releases its neurotransmitter and triggers a response in R. But when there is a need to block transmission across this pathway, neuron I releases the inhibitory neurotransmitter GABA. GABA prevents the voltage-gated calcium channels of neuron S from opening. Consequently, neuron S releases less neurotransmitter or none, and fails to stimulate neuron R.

12.6c Neural Coding

The nervous system must interpret and pass along both quantitative and qualitative information about its environment—whether a light is dim or bright, red or green; whether a taste is mild or intense, salty or sour; whether a sound is loud or soft, high-pitched or low. Considering the complexity of information to be communicated about conditions in and around the body, it seems a marvel that it can be done in the form of something as simple as action potentials—particularly since all the action potentials of a given neuron are identical. Yet when we considered the genetic code in chapter 4, we saw that complex messages can indeed be expressed in simple codes. The way in which the nervous system converts information to a meaningful pattern of action potentials is called **neural coding** (or *sensory coding* when it occurs in the sense organs).

The most important mechanism for transmitting qualitative information is the **labeled line code.** This code is based on the

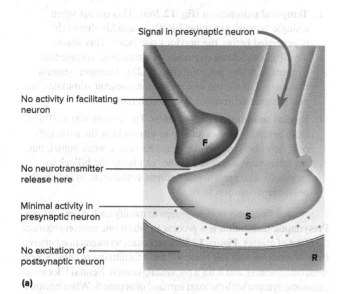

No activity in facilitating neuron

No neurotransmitter release here

Minimal activity in presynaptic neuron

No excitation of postsynaptic neuron

(a)

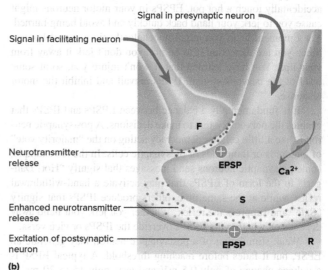

Signal in facilitating neuron

Signal in presynaptic neuron

Neurotransmitter release

Enhanced neurotransmitter release

Excitation of postsynaptic neuron

(b)

FIGURE 12.28 Presynaptic Facilitation. F, facilitating neuron; S, stimulating neuron; R, responding postsynaptic neuron; +, excitation (EPSP). (a) Inactivity of neuron R owing to absence of stimulation by neuron F. (b) Activity in neuron R owing to stimulation (facilitation) of the S–R synapse by neuron F.

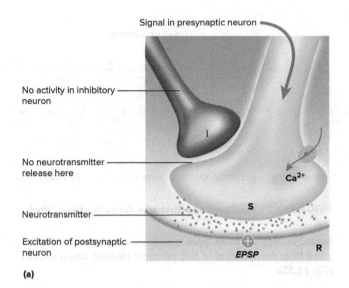

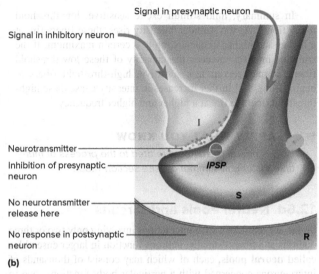

FIGURE 12.29 Presynaptic Inhibition. S, stimulating neuron; I, inhibitory neuron; R, responding postsynaptic neuron; +, excitation (EPSP); –, inhibition (IPSP). (a) Activity in the S-R synapse in the absence of inhibition by neuron I. (b) Activity of neuron I inhibiting synaptic transmission between S and R.

fact that each nerve fiber to the brain leads from a receptor that specifically recognizes a particular stimulus type. Nerve fibers in the optic nerve, for example, carry signals only from light receptors in the eye; these fibers never carry information about taste or sound. The brain therefore interprets any signals in those fibers in terms of light—even if the signals result from artificial stimulation of the nerve. This effect is seen when you rub your eyelids and see flashes of light as the pressure on the eyeball mechanically stimulates optic nerve fibers. Electrical stimulation of the auditory nerve can enable deaf people to hear sounds of different frequencies, even when receptors in the inner ear are nonfunctional. Thus, each nerve fiber to the brain is a line of communication "labeled," or recognized by the brain, as representing a particular stimulus quality—the color of a light, the pitch of a sound, or the salty or sour quality of a taste, for example.

Quantitative information—information about the intensity of a stimulus—is encoded in two ways. One depends on the fact that different neurons have different thresholds of excitation. A weak stimulus excites sensitive neurons with the lowest thresholds, while a strong stimulus excites less sensitive high-threshold neurons. Bringing additional neurons into play as the stimulus becomes stronger is called **recruitment.** It enables the nervous system to judge stimulus strength by which neurons, and how many of them, are firing.

Another way of encoding stimulus strength depends on the fact that the more strongly a neuron is stimulated, the more frequently it fires. A weak stimulus may cause a neuron to generate 6 action potentials per second, and a strong stimulus, 600 per second. Thus, the central nervous system can judge stimulus strength from the firing frequency of afferent neurons **(fig. 12.30).**

There is a limit to how often a neuron can fire, set by its absolute refractory period. Think of an electronic camera flash by analogy. If you take a photograph and your flash unit takes 10 seconds to recharge, then you can't take more than six photos per minute.

Similarly, if a nerve fiber takes 1 ms to repolarize after it has fired, then it can't fire more than 1,000 times per second. Refractory periods may be as short as 0.5 ms, which sets a theoretical limit to firing frequency of 2,000 action potentials per second. The highest frequencies actually observed, however, are 500 to 1,000 per second.

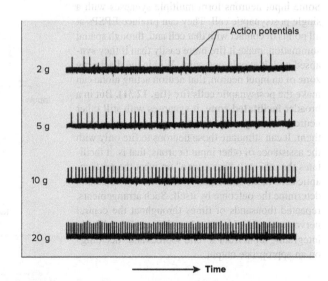

FIGURE 12.30 An Example of Neural Coding. This figure is based on recordings made from a sensory fiber of the frog sciatic nerve as the gastrocnemius muscle was stretched by suspending weights from it. As the stimulus strength (weight) and stretch increase, the firing frequency of the neuron increases. Firing frequency is a coded message that informs the CNS of stimulus intensity.

❓ *In what other way is the CNS informed of stimulus intensity?*

In summary, mild stimuli excite sensitive, low-threshold nerve fibers. As the stimulus intensity rises, these fibers fire at a higher and higher frequency, up to a certain maximum. If the stimulus intensity exceeds the capacity of these low-threshold fibers, it may recruit less sensitive, high-threshold fibers to begin firing. Still further increases in intensity cause these high-threshold fibers to fire at a higher and higher frequency.

▶▶▶**APPLY WHAT YOU KNOW**

How is neural recruitment related to the process of multiple motor unit summation (see section 11.5b)?

12.6d Neural Pools and Circuits

So far, we have dealt with interactions involving only two or three neurons at a time. Actually, neurons function in larger ensembles called **neural pools,** each of which may consist of thousands of interneurons concerned with a particular body function—one to control the rhythm of your breathing, one to move your limbs rhythmically as you walk, one to regulate your sense of hunger, and another to interpret smells, for example. At this point, we explore a few ways in which neural pools collectively process information.

Discharge and Facilitated Zones

Information arrives at a neural pool through one or more input neurons, which branch repeatedly and synapse with numerous interneurons in the pool. Some input neurons form multiple synapses with a single postsynaptic cell. They can produce EPSPs at all points of contact with that cell and, through spatial summation, make it fire more easily than if they synapsed with it at only one point. Within the **discharge zone** of an input neuron, that neuron acting alone can make the postsynaptic cells fire (**fig. 12.31**). But in a broader **facilitated zone,** it synapses with still other neurons in the pool, with fewer synapses on each of them. It can stimulate those neurons to fire only with the assistance of other input neurons; that is, it facilitates the others. It "has a vote" on what the postsynaptic cells in the facilitated zone will do, but it cannot determine the outcome by itself. Such arrangements, repeated thousands of times throughout the central nervous system, give neural pools great flexibility in integrating input from several sources and "deciding" on an appropriate output.

Types of Neural Circuits

The functioning of a radio can be understood from a circuit diagram showing its components and their connections. Similarly, the functions of a neural pool are partly determined by its **neural circuit**—the pathways among its neurons. Just as a wide variety of electronic devices are constructed from a relatively

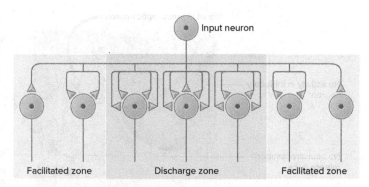

FIGURE 12.31 Facilitated and Discharge Zones in a Neural Pool.

limited number of circuit types, a wide variety of neural functions result from the operation of four principal kinds of neural circuits (**fig. 12.32**):

1. In a **diverging circuit,** an individual neuron sends signals to multiple downstream neurons, or one neural pool may send output to multiple downstream neural pools. Each of those neurons or neural pools may communicate with several more, so input from just one pathway may produce output through hundreds of others. Such a circuit allows signals from one motor neuron of the brain, for example, to ultimately stimulate thousands of muscle fibers.

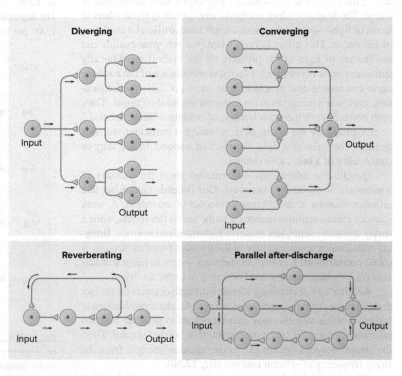

FIGURE 12.32 Four Types of Neural Circuits. Arrows indicate the direction of the nerve signal.

❓ *Which of these four circuits is likely to fire the longest after a stimulus ceases? Why?*

2. A **converging circuit** is the opposite of a diverging circuit—input from many nerve fibers or neural pools is funneled to fewer and fewer intermediate or output pathways. For example, you have a brainstem respiratory center that receives converging information from other parts of your brain, blood chemistry sensors in your arteries, and stretch receptors in your lungs. The respiratory center can then produce an output that takes all of these factors into account and sets an appropriate pattern of breathing.

3. In a **reverberating circuit,** neurons stimulate each other in a linear sequence from input to output neurons, but some of the neurons late in the path send axon collaterals back to neurons earlier in the path and restimulate them. As an exceedingly simplified model of such a circuit, consider a path such as A $\longrightarrow$ B $\longrightarrow$ C $\longrightarrow$ D, in which neuron C sends an axon collateral back to A. As a result, every time C fires it not only stimulates output neuron D, but also restimulates A and starts the process over. Such a circuit produces a prolonged or repetitive effect that lasts until one or more neurons in the circuit fail to fire, or an inhibitory signal from another source stops one of them from firing. A reverberating circuit sends repetitious signals to your diaphragm and intercostal muscles, for example, to make you inhale. Sustained output from the circuit ensures that the respiratory muscles contract for the 2 seconds or so that it normally takes to fill the lungs. When the circuit stops firing, you exhale; the next time it fires, you inhale again. Reverberating circuits may also be involved in short-term memory, as discussed in the next section, and they may play a role in the uncontrolled "storms" of neural activity that occur in epilepsy.

4. In a **parallel after-discharge** circuit, an input neuron diverges to stimulate several chains of neurons. Each chain has a different number of synapses, but eventually they all reconverge on one or a few output neurons. Since the chains differ in total synaptic delay, their signals arrive at the output neurons at different times, and the output neurons may go on firing for some time after input has ceased. Unlike a reverberating circuit, this type has no feedback loop. Once all the neurons in the circuit have fired, the output ceases. Continued firing after the stimulus stops is called *after-discharge.* It explains why you can stare at a lamp, then close your eyes and continue to see an image of it for a while. Such a circuit is also important in withdrawal reflexes, in which a brief pain produces a longer-lasting output to the limb muscles and causes you to draw back your hand or foot from danger.

Serial and Parallel Processing

In relation to these circuit types, the nervous system handles information in two modes called serial and parallel processing. In **serial processing,** neurons and neural pools relay information along a pathway in a relatively simple linear fashion and can process only one flow of information at a time. For example, you can read your e-mail or listen to a class lecture, and the language recognition centers of your brain can process one linguistic input or the other; however, you can't do both simultaneously. To understand the e-mail, you have to stop paying attention to the lecture; to understand the lecture, you have to stop checking your e-mail. You may jump back and forth between one and the other, only half understanding each, but you can't simultaneously process the written message in an e-mail and the spoken language of the lecture. Each must be processed separately and serially.

In **parallel processing,** information is transmitted along diverging circuits through different pathways that act on it simultaneously, to different purposes. For example, when you're driving your car, your visual system (eye and brain) must simultaneously process information about color, shape, depth of field, and motion in the scene before your eyes. This requires complex parallel processing circuits from the retinas of your eyes through the visual centers at the rear of your brain. At the same time, you must process traffic sounds and signals from your body's own joint and motion sensors to know, for example, how hard you are pressing the gas or brake pedal. Efficient simultaneous processing of such information is crucial to your own ability to drive safely.

Serial and parallel processing certainly occur as well in innumerable unconscious processes much simpler than the foregoing examples. In chapter 13, you should be able to see how they apply to certain spinal reflexes.

12.6e Memory and Synaptic Plasticity

You may have wondered as you studied this chapter, How am I going to remember all of this? It seems fitting that we end this chapter with the subject of how memory works, for you now have the information necessary to understand its cellular and chemical basis.

The things we learn and remember aren't stored in individual "memory cells" in the brain. You don't have a neuron assigned to remember your phone number and another to remember your grandmother's face, for example. Instead, the physical basis of memory is a *pathway* through the brain called a **memory trace (engram**[29]**),** in which new synapses have formed or existing synapses have been modified to make transmission easier. In other words, synapses aren't fixed for life; in response to experience, they can be added, taken away, or modified to make transmission easier or harder. Indeed, synapses can be created or deleted in as little as 1 or 2 hours. The ability of synapses to change is called **synaptic plasticity.**

Think about when you learned as a child to tie your shoes. The procedure was very slow, confusing, and laborious at first, but eventually it became so easy you could do it with little thought—like a motor program playing out in your brain without requiring your conscious attention. It became easier to do because the synapses in a certain pathway were modified to allow signals to travel more easily across them than across "untrained" synapses thus creating your *motor memory* for the task. The process of making transmission easier is called **synaptic potentiation** (one form of synaptic plasticity).

Neuroscientists still argue about how to classify the various forms of memory, but three kinds often recognized are *immediate*

---

[29]*en* = inner; *gram* = mark, trace, record

memory, short-term memory, and *long-term memory.* We also know of different modes of synaptic potentiation that last from just a few seconds to a lifetime, and we can correlate these at least tentatively with different forms of memory.

Immediate Memory

Immediate memory is the ability to hold something in mind for just a few seconds. By remembering what just happened, we get a feeling for the flow of events and a sense of the present. Immediate memory is indispensable to the ability to read; you must remember the earliest words of a sentence until you get to its end in order to extract any meaning from it. You couldn't make any sense of what you read if you forgot each word as soon as you moved on to the next one. Immediate memory may be based on reverberating circuits. Our impression of what just happened can thus echo in our minds for a few seconds as we experience the present moment and anticipate the next one.

Short-Term Memory

Short-term memory (STM) lasts from a few seconds to a few hours. Information stored in STM may be quickly forgotten if you stop mentally reciting it, you are distracted, or you have to remember something new. **Working memory** is a form of STM that allows you to hold an idea in mind long enough to carry out an action such as calling a telephone number you just looked up, working out the steps of a mathematics problem, or searching for a lost set of keys while remembering where you've already looked. It is limited to a few bits of information such as the digits of a telephone number. Evidence suggests that working memory resides in a circuit of facilitated synapses that remain quiescent (consuming little energy) most of the time, but are reactivated by new stimulation.

Making it easier to transmit signals across a synapse is called **synaptic facilitation** (different from the facilitation of one neuron by another that we studied earlier in the chapter). Synaptic facilitation can be produced by *tetanic stimulation,* the rapid arrival of repetitive signals at a synapse. Each signal causes a certain amount of Ca^{2+} to enter the axon terminal. If signals arrive rapidly, the neuron cannot pump out all the Ca^{2+} admitted by one action potential before the next action potential occurs. More and more Ca^{2+} accumulates in the terminal. Since Ca^{2+} is what triggers the release of neurotransmitter, each new signal releases more neurotransmitter than the one before. With more neurotransmitter, the EPSPs in the postsynaptic cell become stronger and stronger, and that cell is more likely to fire.

Memories lasting for a few hours, such as remembering what someone said to you earlier in the day or remembering an upcoming appointment, may involve **posttetanic potentiation.** In this process, the Ca^{2+} level in the axon terminal stays elevated for so long that another signal, coming well after the tetanic stimulation has ceased, releases an exceptionally large burst of neurotransmitter. That is, if a synapse has been heavily used in the recent past, a new stimulus can excite the postsynaptic cell more easily. Thus, your memory may need only a slight jog to recall something from several hours earlier.

Long-Term Memory

Long-term memory (LTM) lasts up to a lifetime and is less limited than STM in the amount of information it can store. LTM allows you to memorize the lines of a play, the words of a favorite song, or (one hopes!) textbook information for an exam. On a still longer timescale, it enables you to remember your name, the route to your home, and your childhood experiences.

There are two forms of long-term memory: explicit and implicit. **Explicit** or **declarative memory** is the retention of events and facts that you can put into words—numbers, names, dates, and so forth. You must think to remember these things. **Implicit memory** is the memory of things that come reflexively or unconsciously, including *emotional memories* (such as the fear of being stung if a wasp lands on you) and *procedural memory,* the retention of motor skills—how to tie your shoes, play a musical instrument, or type on a keyboard. These forms of memory involve different regions of the brain but are probably similar at the cellular level.

Some LTM involves the physical remodeling of synapses or the formation of new ones through the growth and branching of axon terminals and dendrites. In the pyramidal cells of the brain, the dendrites are studded with knoblike *dendritic spines* that increase the area of synaptic contact (see fig. 12.5a). Studies on fish and other experimental animals have shown that social and sensory deprivation causes these spines to decline in number, while a richly stimulatory environment causes them to proliferate—an intriguing clue to the importance of a stimulating environment to infant and child development. In some cases of LTM, a new synapse grows beside the original one, giving the presynaptic cell twice as much input into the postsynaptic cell.

LTM can also be grounded in molecular changes called **long-term potentiation (LTP).** This involves *NMDA*[30] *receptors,* which are glutamate-binding receptors found on the dendritic spines of pyramidal cells. NMDA receptors are usually blocked by magnesium ions (Mg^{2+}), but when they bind glutamate *and* are simultaneously subjected to high-frequency stimulation, they expel the Mg^{2+} and open to admit Ca^{2+} into the dendrite. When Ca^{2+} enters, it acts as a second messenger with multiple effects. A high Ca^{2+} level activates enzymes called *protein kinases,* which phosphorylate (add phosphate to) proteins employed in building and strengthening synapses. The neuron also produces even more NMDA receptors, making it more sensitive to glutamate, and it may send signals such as nitric oxide (NO) back to the presynaptic cell to enhance its release of neurotransmitter.

You can see that in all of these ways, long-term potentiation can increase transmission across "experienced" synapses. Remodeling a synapse or installing more neurotransmitter receptors has longer-lasting effects than facilitation or posttetanic potentiation.

---

[30]*N-methyl-D-aspartate,* a chemical similar to glutamate

How We Forget

Forgetting is arguably as important as remembering; we would likely be driven mad if we couldn't forget the myriad trivial things we encounter every day. People with a pathological inability to forget trivial information have great difficulty in reading comprehension and other functions that require us to distinguish what is important from what is not.

Immediate and short-term memories vanish simply as neural circuits cease to fire. Long-term memories can be erased by a process of **long-term depression (LTD).** Low-frequency stimulation of a synapse results in low levels of intracellular Ca^{2+}. This activates *protein phosphatases,* which dephosphorylate synaptic proteins such as actin microfilaments that support dendritic spines. These proteins are then degraded by *proteasomes* (see section 3.4b, fig. 3.31), which tear down dendritic spines and remove little-used synapses from the neural circuits.

The anatomical sites of memory in the brain are discussed in section 14.5d. Regardless of the sites, however, the cellular mechanisms are as described here.

DEEPER INSIGHT 12.4

CLINICAL APPLICATION

Alzheimer and Parkinson Diseases

Alzheimer and Parkinson diseases are the two most common degenerative disorders of the brain. Both are associated with neurotransmitter deficiencies.

Alzheimer[31] *disease (AD)* may begin before the age of 50 with signs so slight and ambiguous that early diagnosis is difficult. One of its first signs is memory loss, especially for recent events. A person with AD may ask the same questions repeatedly, show a reduced attention span, and become disoriented and lost in previously familiar places. Family members often feel helpless and confused as they watch their loved one's personality gradually deteriorate beyond recognition. The AD patient may become moody, confused, paranoid, combative, or hallucinatory. The patient may eventually lose even the ability to read, write, talk, walk, and eat. Death typically ensues from pneumonia or other complications of confinement and immobility.

AD affects about 11% of the U.S. population over the age of 65; the incidence rises to 47% by age 85. It accounts for nearly half of all nursing home admissions and is a leading cause of death among the elderly. AD claims about 100,000 lives per year in the United States.

Diagnosis of AD can be confirmed by autopsy. There is atrophy of some of the gyri (folds) of the cerebral cortex and the hippocampus, an important center of memory. Nerve cells exhibit *neurofibrillary tangles*—dense masses of broken and twisted cytoskeleton **(fig. 12.33).** Alois Alzheimer first observed these in 1907 in the brain of a patient who had died of senile dementia. The more severe the signs of disease, the more neurofibrillary tangles are seen at autopsy. In the intercellular spaces, there are *senile plaques* consisting of aggregations of cells, altered nerve fibers, and a core of *β-amyloid protein*—the breakdown product of a glycoprotein of plasma membranes. Amyloid protein is rarely seen in elderly people without AD. Oxidative stress (free radical injury) is now widely believed to underlie the formation of amyloid protein and neurofibrillary tangles, and all the other aspects of AD pathology. This has led to interest in whether dietary antioxidants or antioxidant therapy can reduce the incidence or progression of AD.

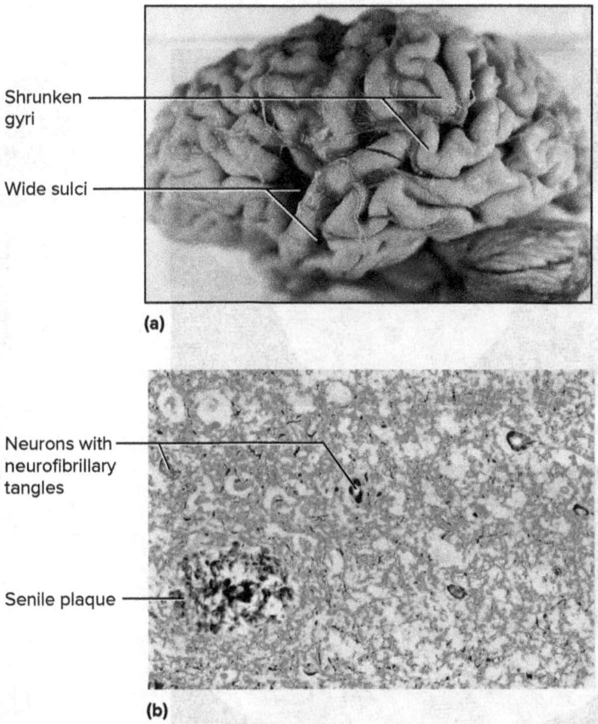

[31]Alois Alzheimer (1864–1915), German neurologist

BEFORE YOU GO ON

Answer the following questions to test your understanding of the preceding section:

22. Contrast the two types of summation at a synapse and explain how they function in synaptic decision making.

23. Describe how the nervous system communicates quantitative and qualitative information about stimuli.

24. List the four types of neural circuits and describe their similarities and differences. Discuss the unity of form and function in these four types—that is, explain why each type would not perform as it does if its neurons were connected differently.

25. Contrast serial and parallel processing and describe how each can be involved in your everyday mental experiences.

26. State the essence of how immediate, short-term, and long-term memory work.

27. Explain how long-term potentiation and long-term depression influence what you remember and forget.

Shrunken gyri

Wide sulci

(a)

Neurons with neurofibrillary tangles

Senile plaque

(b)

FIGURE 12.33 Alzheimer Disease. (a) Brain of a person who died of AD. Note the shrunken folds of cerebral tissue (gyri) and wide gaps (sulci) between them. (b) Cerebral tissue from a person with AD. Neurofibrillary tangles are present within the neurons, and a senile plaque is evident in the extracellular matrix.

a: ©Science Source; **b:** Simon Fraser/Science Source

454   **PART THREE**   Internal Coordination and Control

Intense biomedical research efforts are currently geared toward identifying the causes of AD and developing treatment strategies. Three genes on chromosomes 1, 14, and 21 have been implicated in various forms of early- and late-onset AD. Interestingly, persons with Down syndrome (trisomy-21), who have three copies of chromosome 21 instead of the usual two, tend to show early-onset Alzheimer disease. Nongenetic (environmental) factors also seem to be involved.

As for treatment, considerable attention now focuses on trying to halt β-amyloid formation or stimulate the immune system to clear β-amyloid from the brain tissue, but clinical trials in both of these approaches have been suspended until certain serious side effects can be resolved. AD patients show deficiencies of acetylcholine (ACh) and nerve growth factor (NGF). Some patients show improvement when treated with NGF or cholinesterase inhibitors, but results so far have been modest.

Parkinson[32] *disease (PD)*, also called *paralysis agitans* or *parkinsonism*, is a progressive loss of motor function beginning in a person's 50s or 60s. It is due to degeneration of dopamine-releasing neurons in a portion of the brainstem called the *substantia nigra* (**fig. 12.34**). A gene has recently been identified for a hereditary form of PD, but most cases are nonhereditary and of little-known cause; some authorities suspect environmental neurotoxins.

Dopamine (DA) is an inhibitory neurotransmitter that normally prevents excessive activity in motor centers of the brain called the *basal nuclei*. Degeneration of dopamine-releasing neurons leads to an excessive ratio of ACh to DA, causing hyperactivity of the basal nuclei. As a result, a person with PD suffers involuntary muscle contractions. These take such forms as shaking of the hands (tremor) and compulsive "pill-rolling" motions of the thumb and fingers. In addition, the facial muscles may become rigid and produce a staring, expressionless face with a slightly open mouth. The patient's range of motion diminishes. He or she takes smaller steps and develops a slow, shuffling gait with a forward-bent posture and a tendency to fall forward. Speech becomes slurred and handwriting becomes cramped and eventually illegible. Tasks such as buttoning clothes and preparing food become increasingly laborious.

Patients cannot be expected to recover from PD, but its effects can be alleviated with drugs and physical therapy. Treatment with dopamine is ineffective because it can't cross the blood–brain barrier, but its precursor, levodopa (L-dopa), does cross the barrier and has been used to treat PD since the 1960s. L-dopa affords some relief, but it doesn't slow progression of the disease and it has undesirable side effects on the liver and heart. It is effective for only 5 to 10 years of treatment. A newer drug, deprenyl, is a monoamine oxidase (MAO) inhibitor that retards neural degeneration and slows the development of PD.

A surgical technique called *pallidotomy* has been used since the 1940s to quell severe tremors. It involves the destruction of a small portion of cerebral tissue in an area called the *globus pallidus*. Pallidotomy fell out of favor in the late 1960s when L-dopa came into common use. By the early 1990s, however, the limitations of L-dopa had become apparent, while MRI- and CT-guided methods had improved surgical precision and reduced the risks of brain surgery. Pallidotomy has thus made a comeback. Other surgical treatments for parkinsonism target brain areas called the *subthalamic nucleus* and the *ventral intermediate nucleus* of the thalamus, and involve either the destruction of tiny areas of tissue or the implantation of a stimulating electrode. Such procedures are generally used only in severe cases that are unresponsive to medication.

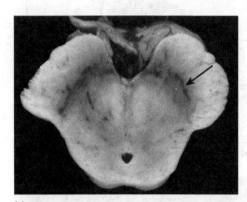

(a)

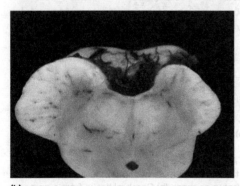

(b)

(c)

FIGURE 12.34 Parkinson Disease (PD).
(a) Cross section of midbrain of a healthy person showing normal, dark band of substantia nigra at arrow. (b) Midbrain section of a PD patient showing absence of substantia nigra. (c) Dyskinesia, a difficulty in walking and forward-tilted stance characteristic of persons with PD.

a–b: ISM/Pr J.J. Hauw/Medical Images

[32]James Parkinson (1755–1824), British physician

CONNECTIVE ISSUES

Effects of the NERVOUS SYSTEM on Other Organ Systems

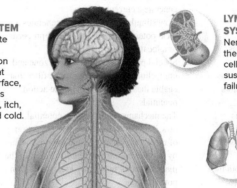

INTEGUMENTARY SYSTEM

Cutaneous nerves regulate piloerection, sweating, cutaneous vasoconstriction and vasodilation, and heat loss through the body surface, and provide for cutaneous sensations such as touch, itch, tickle, pressure, heat, and cold.

SKELETAL SYSTEM

Nervous stimulation maintains the muscle tension that stimulates bone growth and remodeling; nerves in the bones respond to strains and fractures.

MUSCULAR SYSTEM

Skeletal muscles cannot contract without nervous stimulation; the nervous system controls all body movements and muscle tone.

ENDOCRINE SYSTEM

The hypothalamus controls the pituitary gland; the sympathetic nervous system controls the adrenal medulla; neuroendocrine cells are neurons that secrete hormones such as oxytocin; sensory and other nervous input influences the secretion of numerous other hormones.

CIRCULATORY SYSTEM

The nervous system regulates the rate and force of the heartbeat, regulates blood vessel diameters, monitors and controls blood pressure and blood gas concentrations, routes blood to organs where needed, and influences blood clotting.

LYMPHATIC AND IMMUNE SYSTEMS

Nerves to lymphatic organs influence the development and activity of immune cells; emotional states influence susceptibility to infection and other failures of immunity.

RESPIRATORY SYSTEM

The brainstem regulates the rhythm of breathing, monitors blood pH and blood gases, and adjusts the respiratory rate and depth to control these within normal ranges.

URINARY SYSTEM

Sympathetic nerves modify the rate of urine production by the kidneys; nervous stimulation of urinary sphincters aids in urine retention in the bladder, and nervous reflexes control its emptying.

DIGESTIVE SYSTEM

The nervous system regulates appetite, feeding behavior, digestive secretion and motility, and defecation.

REPRODUCTIVE SYSTEM

The nervous system regulates sex drive, arousal, and orgasm; the brain regulates the secretion of pituitary hormones that control spermatogenesis in males and the ovarian cycle in females; the nervous system controls various aspects of pregnancy and childbirth; the brain produces oxytocin, which is involved in labor contractions and lactation.

STUDY GUIDE

▶ Assess Your Learning Outcomes

To test your knowledge, discuss the following topics with a study partner or in writing, ideally from memory.

12.1 Overview of the Nervous System

1. What the nervous and endocrine systems have in common
2. Three fundamental functions of the nervous system; the roles of receptors and effectors in carrying out these functions
3. Differences between the central nervous system (CNS) and peripheral nervous system (PNS); between the sensory and motor divisions of the PNS; and between the somatic and visceral subdivisions of both the sensory and motor divisions
4. The autonomic nervous system and its two divisions

12.2 Properties of Neurons

1. Three fundamental physiological properties of neurons
2. Differences between sensory (afferent) neurons, interneurons (association neurons), and motor (efferent) neurons
3. The parts of a generalized multipolar neuron, and their functions
4. Differences between multipolar, bipolar, unipolar, and anaxonic neurons; an example of each
5. Ways in which neurons transport substances between the neurosoma and the distal ends of the axon

12.3 Supportive Cells

1. Six kinds of neuroglia; the structure and functions of each; and which kinds are found in the CNS and which ones in the PNS
2. Structure of the myelin sheath, and how CNS and PNS glial cells produce it
3. How fiber diameter and the presence or absence of myelin affect the conduction speed of a nerve fiber
4. The regeneration of a damaged nerve fiber; the roles of Schwann cells, the basal lamina, and neurilemma in regeneration; and why CNS neurons cannot regenerate

12.4 Electrophysiology of Neurons

1. The meanings of *electrical potential* and *resting membrane potential* (RMP); the typical voltage of an RMP

2. What an electrical current is, and how sodium ions and gated membrane channels generate a current
3. How stimulation of a neuron generates a local potential; the physiological properties of a local potential
4. Special properties of the trigger zone and unmyelinated regions of a nerve fiber that enable these regions to generate action potentials
5. The mechanism of an action potential; how it relates to ion flows and the action of membrane channels; and what is meant by *depolarization* and *repolarization* of the plasma membrane during local and action potentials
6. The all-or-none law and how it applies to an action potential; other properties of action potentials in contrast to local potentials
7. The basis and significance of the refractory period that follows an action potential
8. How one action potential triggers another; how the continuous conduction seen in unmyelinated nerve fibers result from a chain reaction of action potentials; and what normally prevents the signal from traveling backward to the neurosoma
9. Saltatory conduction in a myelinated nerve fiber; differences in conduction mechanisms of the myelin sheath gaps and internodal segments; and why signals travel faster in myelinated fibers than in unmyelinated fibers of comparable size

12.5 Synapses

1. The structure and locations of synapses
2. The role of neurotransmitters in synaptic transmission
3. Categories of neurotransmitters and common examples of each
4. Why the same neurotransmitter can have different effects on different cells
5. Excitatory synapses; how acetylcholine and norepinephrine excite a postsynaptic neuron
6. Inhibitory synapses; how γ-aminobutyric acid (GABA) inhibits a postsynaptic neuron
7. How second-messenger systems function at synapses
8. Three ways in which synaptic transmission is ended
9. Neuromodulators, their chemical nature, and how they affect synaptic transmission

12.6 Neural Integration

1. Why synapses slow down nervous communication; the overriding benefit of synapses
2. The meaning of *excitatory* and *inhibitory postsynaptic potentials* (EPSPs and IPSPs)
3. Why the production of an EPSP or IPSP may depend on both the neurotransmitter released by the presynaptic neuron and the type of receptor on the postsynaptic neuron
4. How a postsynaptic neuron's decision to fire depends on the ratio of EPSPs to IPSPs
5. Temporal and spatial summation, where they occur, and how they determine whether a neuron fires
6. Mechanisms of presynaptic facilitation and inhibition, and how communication between two neurons can be strengthened or weakened by a third neuron employing one of these mechanisms
7. Mechanisms of neural coding; how a neuron communicates qualitative and quantitative information
8. Why the refractory period sets a limit to how frequently a neuron can fire
9. The meanings of *neural pool* and *neural circuit*
10. The difference between a neuron's discharge zone and facilitated zone, and how this relates to neurons working in groups
11. Diverging, converging, reverberating, and parallel after-discharge circuits of neurons; examples of their relevance to familiar body functions
12. The difference between serial and parallel processing of information and how they influence everyday body functions
13. The cellular basis of memory; what memory consists of in terms of neural pathways, and how it relates to synaptic plasticity and potentiation
14. Types of things remembered in immediate memory, short-term memory (STM), and long-term memory (LTM), and in the explicit and implicit forms of LTM
15. Neural mechanisms thought to be involved in these different forms of memory and in forgetting

STUDY GUIDE

▶ Testing Your Recall

Answers in Appendix A

1. The integrative functions of the nervous system are performed mainly by
   a. afferent neurons.
   b. efferent neurons.
   c. neuroglia.
   d. sensory neurons.
   e. interneurons.

2. The highest density of voltage-gated ion channels is found in the _____ of a neuron.
   a. dendrites
   b. neurosoma
   c. myelin sheath gaps
   d. internodal segments
   e. axon terminals

3. The neurosoma of a mature neuron lacks
   a. a nucleus.
   b. endoplasmic reticulum.
   c. lipofuscin.
   d. centrioles.
   e. ribosomes.

4. The glial cells that fight infections in the CNS are
   a. microglia.
   b. satellite cells.
   c. ependymal cells.
   d. oligodendrocytes.
   e. astrocytes.

5. Posttetanic potentiation of a synapse increases the amount of _____ in the axon terminal.
   a. neurotransmitter
   b. neurotransmitter receptors
   c. calcium
   d. sodium
   e. NMDA

6. An IPSP is _____ of the postsynaptic neuron.
   a. a refractory period
   b. an action potential
   c. a depolarization
   d. a repolarization
   e. a hyperpolarization

7. Saltatory conduction occurs only
   a. at chemical synapses.
   b. in the initial segment of an axon.
   c. in both the initial segment and axon hillock.
   d. in myelinated nerve fibers.
   e. in unmyelinated nerve fibers.

8. Some neurotransmitters can have either excitatory or inhibitory effects depending on the type of
   a. receptors on the postsynaptic cell.
   b. synaptic vesicles in the axon.
   c. synaptic potentiation that occurs.
   d. postsynaptic potentials on the axon terminal.
   e. neuromodulator involved.

9. Differences in the volume of a sound are likely to be encoded by differences in _____ in nerve fibers from the inner ear.
   a. neurotransmitters
   b. signal conduction velocity
   c. types of postsynaptic potentials
   d. firing frequency
   e. voltage of the action potentials

10. Motor effects that depend on repetitive output from a neural pool are most likely to use
    a. parallel after-discharge circuits.
    b. reverberating circuits.
    c. facilitated circuits.
    d. diverging circuits.
    e. converging circuits.

11. Neurons that convey information to the CNS are called sensory, or _____, neurons.

12. To perform their role, neurons must have the properties of excitability, secretion, and _____.

13. The _____ is a period of time in which a neuron is producing an action potential and cannot respond to another stimulus of any strength.

14. Neurons receive incoming signals by way of specialized extensions of the cell called _____.

15. In the CNS, myelin is produced by glial cells called _____.

16. A myelinated nerve fiber can produce action potentials only in specialized regions called _____.

17. The trigger zone of a neuron consists of its _____ and _____.

18. The neurotransmitter secreted at an adrenergic synapse is _____.

19. A presynaptic nerve fiber cannot cause other neurons in its _____ to fire, but it can make them more sensitive to stimulation from other presynaptic fibers.

20. _____ are substances released along with a neurotransmitter that modify the neurotransmitter's effect.

▶ Building Your Medical Vocabulary

Answers in Appendix A

State a meaning of each word element, and give a medical term from this chapter that uses it or a slight variation of it.

1. antero-

2. -aps

3. astro-

4. dendro-

5. -fer

6. gangli-

7. -grad

8. neuro-

9. sclero-

10. somato-

STUDY GUIDE

▶ What's Wrong with These Statements?

Answers in Appendix A

Briefly explain why each of the following statements is false, or reword it to make it true.

1. A neuron may have anywhere from one to several axons.

2. Astrocytes perform the same function in the brain as Schwann cells do in the peripheral nerves.

3. A resting neuron has a higher concentration of Na^+ in its cytoplasm than in the extracellular fluid surrounding it.

4. During an action potential, most of the Na^+ and K^+ exchange places across the plasma membrane.

5. Excitatory postsynaptic potentials lower the threshold of a neuron and thus make it easier to stimulate.

6. In theory, there is no upper limit to how often a neuron can fire if it is stimulated strongly enough.

7. A given neurotransmitter has the same effect no matter where in the body it is secreted.

8. Myelinated nerve fibers conduct signals more rapidly than unmyelinated ones because they have gaps in the myelin sheath.

9. Learning occurs by increasing the number of neurons in the brain tissue.

10. Dead neurons in the brain are quickly replaced by mitosis of surviving neurons.

▶ Testing Your Comprehension

1. Schizophrenia is sometimes treated with drugs such as chlorpromazine that inhibit dopamine receptors. A side effect is that patients begin to develop muscle tremors, speech impairment, and other disorders similar to Parkinson disease. Explain.

2. Hyperkalemia is an excess of potassium in the extracellular fluid. What effect would this have on the resting membrane potentials of the nervous system and on neural excitability?

3. Suppose a poison were to slow down the Na^+–K^+ pumps of nerve cells. How would this affect the resting membrane potentials of neurons? Would it make neurons more excitable than normal, or make them more difficult to stimulate? Explain.

4. The unity of form and function is an important concept in understanding synapses. Give two structural reasons why nerve signals cannot travel backward across a chemical synapse. What could be the consequences if signals did travel freely in both directions?

5. Positive feedback is usually harmful to the body, or even life-threatening, but there are a few cases where it is beneficial and necessary. Identify such a case in neuron electrophysiology. If necessary, review the defining characteristics of positive feedback in section 1.6d.

Unit 2

Unit 2

PART FOUR: CIRCULATION AND DEFENSE

CHAPTER

18

THE CIRCULATORY SYSTEM: BLOOD

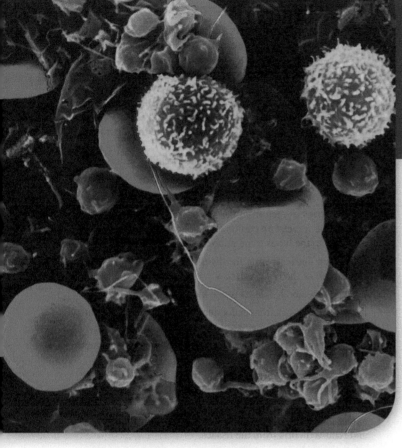

Red blood cells (red concave discs), white blood cells (blue), platelets (green), and filaments of the clotting protein fibrin (gray) (SEM)

Science Photo Library/Alamy Stock Photo

Anatomy & Physiology Revealed® 4.0

Module 9: Cardiovascular System

BRUSHING UP

- Conjugated proteins and prosthetic groups are important for understanding the structure of hemoglobin and its oxygen-binding property (see section 2.4e).

- One of the most important physical properties of blood is its osmolarity. Review osmotic pressure and osmolarity in section 3.3c and in appendix B.

- A good understanding of blood types, sickle-cell disease, and hemophilia depends on a knowledge of dominant and recessive alleles, homozygous and heterozygous genotypes, multiple alleles, and sex linkage (see sections 4.4b–4.4e).

Blood has always had a special mystique. From time immemorial, people have seen blood flow from the body and, with it, the life of the individual. It is no wonder that blood was thought to carry a mysterious "vital force." Ancient Romans drank the blood of fallen gladiators in a belief that they could acquire a gladiator's vitality or that it could cure epilepsy. Even today, we become especially alarmed when we find ourselves bleeding, and the emotional impact of blood makes many people faint at the sight of it. From ancient Egypt to nineteenth-century America, physicians drained "bad blood" from their patients to treat everything from gout to headaches, from menstrual cramps to mental illness. It was long thought that hereditary traits were transmitted through the blood, and people still use such unfounded or metaphorical expressions as "I have one-quarter Cherokee blood."

Scarcely anything meaningful was known about blood until its cells were seen with the first microscopes. Even though blood is a uniquely accessible tissue, most of what we know about it dates only to the mid-twentieth century. Recent developments in this field have empowered us to save and improve the lives of countless people who would otherwise have suffered or died.

18.1   Introduction

Expected Learning Outcomes

When you have completed this section, you should be able to

a. describe the functions and major components of the circulatory system;

b. describe the components and physical properties of blood;

c. describe the composition of blood plasma;

d. explain the significance of blood viscosity and osmolarity; and

e. describe in general terms how blood is produced.

18.1a Functions of the Circulatory System

The **circulatory system** consists of the heart, blood vessels, and blood. The term **cardiovascular**[1] **system** refers only to the heart and vessels, which are the subject of the next two chapters. The study of blood, treated in this chapter, is called **hematology.**[2]

The fundamental purpose of the circulatory system is to transport substances from place to place in the body. Blood is the liquid medium in which these materials travel, blood vessels ensure the proper routing of blood to its destinations, and the heart is the pump that keeps the blood flowing.

More specifically, the functions of the circulatory system are as follows:

Transport

- Blood carries oxygen from the lungs to all of the body's tissues, while it picks up carbon dioxide from those tissues and carries it to the lungs to be removed from the body.

- It picks up nutrients from the digestive tract and delivers them to all of the body's tissues.

- It carries metabolic wastes to the kidneys for removal.

- It carries hormones from endocrine cells to their target organs.

- It transports a variety of stem cells from the bone marrow and other origins to the tissues where they lodge and mature.

Protection

- Blood plays several roles in inflammation, a mechanism for limiting the spread of infection.

- White blood cells destroy microorganisms and cancer cells and remove debris from the tissues.

- Antibodies and other blood proteins neutralize toxins and help to destroy pathogens.

- Platelets secrete factors that initiate blood clotting and other processes for minimizing blood loss, and contribute to tissue growth and blood vessel maintenance.

Regulation

- By absorbing or giving off fluid under different conditions, the blood capillaries stabilize fluid distribution in the body.

- By buffering acids and bases, blood proteins stabilize the pH of the extracellular fluids.

- Cutaneous blood flow is extremely important in dissipating metabolic heat from the body. Shifts in blood flow regulate body temperature by routing blood to the skin for heat loss or retaining it deeper in the body to conserve heat.

Considering the importance of efficiently transporting nutrients, wastes, hormones, and especially oxygen from place to place, it is easy to understand why an excessive loss of blood is quickly fatal, and why the circulatory system needs mechanisms for minimizing such losses.

---

[1]*cardio* = heart; *vas* = vessel
[2]*hem, hemato* = blood; *logy* = study of

18.1b Components and General Properties of Blood

Adults generally have about 4 to 6 liters of blood. It is a liquid connective tissue, like other connective tissues, of cells and an extracellular matrix. Its matrix is the blood **plasma,** a clear, light yellow fluid constituting a little over half of the blood volume. Suspended in the plasma are the **formed elements**—cells and cell fragments including the red blood cells, white blood cells, and platelets **(fig. 18.1).** The term *formed element* alludes to the fact that these are membrane-enclosed bodies with a definite structure visible with the microscope. Strictly speaking, they can't all be called *cells* because the platelets, as explained later, are merely fragments torn from certain bone marrow cells.

The formed elements are classified as follows:

    Erythrocytes[3] (red blood cells, RBCs)

    Platelets

    Leukocytes[4] (white blood cells, WBCs)

        Granulocytes

            Neutrophils

            Eosinophils

            Basophils

        Agranulocytes

            Lymphocytes

            Monocytes

Thus, there are seven kinds of formed elements: the erythrocytes, platelets, and five kinds of leukocytes. The five leukocyte types are divided into two categories, the *granulocytes* and *agranulocytes,* on grounds explained later.

    Blood fractionation, the separation of blood into its basic components, is based on centrifugation and coagulation **(fig. 18.2).** First, a sample of blood in a tube is spun in a centrifuge for a few minutes. RBCs, the densest elements, settle to the bottom of the tube and typically constitute 37% to 52% of the total volume—a value called the **hematocrit** or **packed cell volume.** WBCs and platelets settle into a narrow cream- or buff-colored zone called the *buffy coat* just above the RBCs; they total 1% or less of the blood volume. At the top of the tube is the plasma, which is about 47% to 63% of the blood volume. If plasma is separated, allowed to coagulate (clot), and centrifuged again, the clotting proteins (mainly fibrin) settle to the bottom of the tube and the overlying fluid is then called **blood serum.** Serum is clinically valuable as a vehicle for vaccines, antivenins, and other therapies; for certain blood tests,

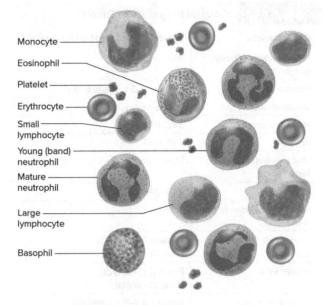

FIGURE 18.1   The Formed Elements of Blood.

Monocyte
Eosinophil
Platelet
Erythrocyte
Small lymphocyte
Young (band) neutrophil
Mature neutrophil
Large lymphocyte
Basophil

❓ *Identify all the unlabeled formed elements by comparison to the labeled ones.*

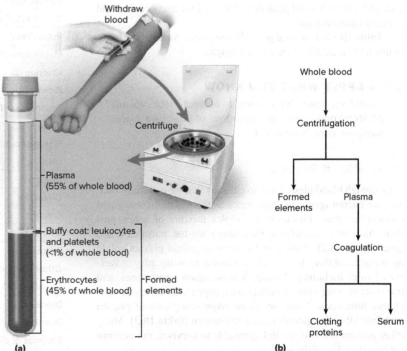

Withdraw blood

Centrifuge

Plasma (55% of whole blood)

Buffy coat: leukocytes and platelets (<1% of whole blood)

Erythrocytes (45% of whole blood)   Formed elements

(a)

Whole blood

Centrifugation

Formed elements   Plasma

Coagulation

Clotting proteins   Serum

(b)

FIGURE 18.2   The Components of Blood. (a) Centrifuging a sample of blood to separate formed elements from plasma and determine the hematocrit. (b) Fractionation of blood into formed elements, plasma, and serum.

---

[3]*erythro* = red; *cyte* = cell
[4]*leuko* = white; *cyte* = cell

TABLE 18.1	General Properties of Blood
Characteristic	Typical Values for Healthy Adults*
Mean fraction of body weight	8%
Volume in adult body	Female: 4–5 L; male: 5–6 L
Volume/body weight	80–85 mL/kg
Mean temperature	38°C (100.4°F)
pH	7.35–7.45
Viscosity (relative to water)	Whole blood: 4.5–5.5; plasma: 2.0
Osmolarity	280–296 mOsm/L
Mean salinity (mainly NaCl)	0.9%
Hematocrit (packed cell volume)	Female: 37% to 48% Male: 45% to 52%
Hemoglobin	Female: 12–16 g/dL Male: 13–18 g/dL
Mean RBC count	Female: 4.2–5.4 million/μL Male: 4.6–6.2 million/μL
Platelet count	130,000–360,000/μL
Total WBC count	5,000–10,000/μL

*Values vary slightly depending on the testing methods used.

such as for hepatitis and prostate cancer; and for many clinical and research laboratory uses.

Table 18.1 lists several properties of blood. Some of the terms in that table are defined later in the chapter.

▶▶▶**APPLY WHAT YOU KNOW**

Based on your body weight, estimate the volume (in liters) and weight (in kilograms) of your own blood, using the data in table 18.1.

18.1c Blood Plasma

Even though blood plasma has no anatomy that we can study visually, we cannot ignore its importance as the matrix of this liquid connective tissue. Plasma is a complex mixture of water, proteins, nutrients, electrolytes, nitrogenous wastes, hormones, and gases (**table 18.2**). Protein is the most abundant plasma solute by weight, totaling 6 to 9 g/dL. Plasma proteins play a variety of roles including clotting, defense against pathogens, and transport of other solutes such as iron, copper, lipids, and hydrophobic hormones. There are three major categories of plasma proteins: albumin, globulins, and fibrinogen (**table 18.3**). Many other plasma proteins are indispensable to survival, but account for less than 1% of the total.

Albumin is the smallest and most abundant plasma protein. It serves to transport various solutes and buffer the pH of blood plasma. It also makes a major contribution to two physical

TABLE 18.2	Composition of Blood Plasma
Blood Component*	Typical Values for Healthy Adults
Water	92% by weight
Proteins	Total 6–9 g/dL
Albumin	60% of total protein, 3.2–5.5 g/dL
Globulins	36% of total protein, 2.3–3.5 g/dL
Fibrinogen	4% of total protein, 0.2–0.3 g/dL
Nutrients	
Glucose (dextrose)	70–110 mg/dL
Amino acids	33–51 mg/dL
Lactate	6–16 mg/dL
Total lipid	450–850 mg/dL
Cholesterol	120–220 mg/dL
Fatty acids	190–420 mg/dL
High-density lipoprotein (HDL)	30–80 mg/dL
Low-density lipoprotein (LDL)	62–185 mg/dL
Triglycerides (neutral fats)	40–150 mg/dL
Phospholipids	6–12 mg/dL
Iron	50–150 μg/dL
Trace elements	Traces
Vitamins	Traces
Electrolytes	
Sodium (Na^+)	135–145 mEq/L
Calcium (Ca^{2+})	9.2–10.4 mEq/L
Potassium (K^+)	3.5–5.0 mEq/L
Magnesium (Mg^{2+})	1.3–2.1 mEq/L
Chloride (Cl^-)	100–106 mEq/L
Bicarbonate (HCO_3^-)	23.1–26.7 mEq/L
Phosphate (HPO_4^{2-})	1.4–2.7 mEq/L
Sulfate (SO_4^{2-})	0.6–1.2 mEq/L
Nitrogenous Wastes	
Urea	10–20 mg/dL
Uric acid	1.5–8.0 mg/dL
Creatinine	0.6–1.5 mg/dL
Creatine	0.2–0.8 mg/dL
Ammonia	0.02–0.09 mg/dL
Bilirubin	0–1.0 mg/dL
Other Components	
Dissolved CO_2	2.62 mL/dL
Dissolved O_2	0.29 mL/dL
Dissolved N_2	0.98 mL/dL
Enzymes of diagnostic value	—
Hormones	—

*This table is limited to substances of greatest relevance to this and later chapters. Concentrations refer to plasma only, not to whole blood.

TABLE 18.3	Major Proteins of the Blood Plasma
Proteins	**Functions**
Albumin (60%)*	Responsible for colloid osmotic pressure; major contributor to blood viscosity; transports lipids, hormones, calcium, and other solutes; buffers blood pH
Globulins (36%)*	Transport and defense functions as itemized below
Alpha (α) Globulins	
Haptoglobulin	Transports hemoglobin released by dead erythrocytes
Ceruloplasmin	Transports copper
Prothrombin	Promotes blood clotting
Others	Transport lipids, fat-soluble vitamins, and hormones
Beta (β) Globulins	
Transferrin	Transports iron
Complement proteins	Aid in destruction of toxins and microorganisms
Others	Transport lipids
Gamma (γ) Globulins	Antibodies; combat pathogens
Fibrinogen (4%)*	Becomes fibrin, the major component of blood clots

*Mean percentage of the total plasma protein by weight

properties of blood: its *viscosity* and *osmolarity,* discussed shortly. Through its effects on these two variables, changes in albumin concentration can significantly affect blood volume, pressure, and flow. **Globulins** are divided into three subclasses; from smallest to largest in molecular weight, they are the alpha (α), beta (β), and gamma (γ) globulins. Globulins play various roles in solute transport, clotting, and immunity. **Fibrinogen** is a soluble precursor of *fibrin,* a sticky protein that forms the framework of a blood clot. Some of the other plasma proteins are enzymes involved in the clotting process.

The liver produces as much as 4 g of plasma protein per hour, contributing all of the major proteins except gamma globulins. The gamma globulins come from *plasma cells*—connective tissue cells that are descended from white blood cells called *B lymphocytes.*

▶▶▶**APPLY WHAT YOU KNOW**

How could a disease such as liver cancer or hepatitis result in impaired blood clotting?

In addition to protein, the blood plasma contains such nitrogen-containing compounds as free amino acids and nitrogenous wastes. **Nitrogenous wastes** are toxic end products of catabolism. The most abundant is *urea,* a product of amino acid

catabolism. These wastes are normally excreted by the kidneys at a rate that balances their production.

The plasma also transports nutrients absorbed by the digestive tract, including glucose, amino acids, fats, cholesterol, phospholipids, vitamins, and minerals. It transports dissolved oxygen, carbon dioxide, and nitrogen (see table 18.2). The dissolved nitrogen normally has no physiological role in the body (but see Deeper Insight 22.5).

Electrolytes are another important component of the blood plasma. Sodium ions constitute about 90% of the plasma cations. Sodium is more important than any other solute to the osmolarity of the blood. As such, it has a major influence on blood volume and pressure; people with high blood pressure are often advised to limit their sodium intake. Electrolyte concentrations are carefully regulated by the body and have rather stable concentrations in the plasma.

18.1d Blood Viscosity and Osmolarity

Two important properties of blood—viscosity and osmolarity—arise from the formed elements and plasma composition. **Viscosity** is the resistance of a fluid to flow, resulting from the cohesion of its particles. Loosely speaking, it is the thickness or stickiness of a fluid. At a given temperature, mineral oil is more viscous than water, for example, and honey is more viscous than mineral oil. Whole blood is 4.5 to 5.5 times as viscous as water, mainly because of the RBCs; plasma alone is 2.0 times as viscous as water, mainly because of its protein. Viscosity is important in circulatory function because it partially governs the flow of blood through the vessels. An RBC or protein deficiency reduces viscosity and causes blood to flow too easily, whereas an excess causes blood to flow too sluggishly. Either of these conditions puts a strain on the heart that may lead to serious cardiovascular problems if not corrected.

The **osmolarity** of blood, another important factor in cardiovascular function, is the total molarity of dissolved particles that cannot pass through the blood vessel wall. In order to nourish surrounding cells and remove their wastes, substances must pass between the bloodstream and tissue fluid through the capillary walls. This transfer of fluids depends on a balance between the filtration of fluid from the capillary and its reabsorption by osmosis (see section 20.3c). The rate of reabsorption is governed by the relative osmolarity of the blood versus the tissue fluid. If the blood osmolarity is too high, the bloodstream absorbs too much water. This raises the blood volume, resulting in high blood pressure and a potentially dangerous strain on the heart and arteries. If its osmolarity drops too low, too much water remains in the tissues. They become edematous (swollen) and the blood pressure may drop to dangerously low levels because of the water lost from the bloodstream.

It is therefore important that the blood maintain an optimal osmolarity. The osmolarity of the blood is a product mainly of its sodium ions, protein, and erythrocytes. The contribution of protein to blood osmotic pressure—called the **colloid osmotic pressure (COP)**—is especially important, as we see from the effects of extremely low-protein diets (see Deeper Insight 18.1).

DEEPER INSIGHT 18.1

CLINICAL APPLICATION

Starvation and Plasma Protein Deficiency

Several conditions can lead to *hypoproteinemia*, a deficiency of plasma protein: extreme starvation or dietary protein deficiency, liver diseases that interfere with protein synthesis, and protein loss through the urine or body surface in the cases of kidney disease and severe burns, respectively. As the protein content of the blood plasma drops, so does its osmolarity. The bloodstream loses more fluid to the tissues than it reabsorbs by osmosis. Thus, the tissues become edematous and a pool of fluid may accumulate in the abdominal cavity—a condition called *ascites* (ah-SY-teez) (see Deeper Insight 20.4).

Children who suffer severe dietary protein deficiencies often exhibit a condition called *kwashiorkor* (KWASH-ee-OR-cor) **(fig. 18.3)**. The arms and legs are emaciated for lack of muscle, the skin is shiny and tight with edema, and the abdomen is swollen by ascites. *Kwashiorkor* is a Ghanian word for a "deposed" or "displaced" child who is no longer breast-fed. Symptoms appear when a child is weaned and placed on a diet consisting mainly of rice or other cereals. Children with kwashiorkor often die of diarrhea and dehydration.

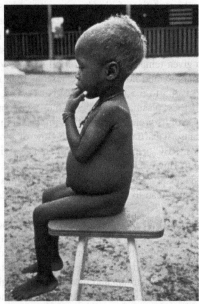

FIGURE 18.3 Child with Kwashiorkor. Note the thin limbs and fluid-distended abdomen.
IMTSSA/CNRI/Science Source

18.1e How Blood Is Produced APR

We lose blood continually, not only from bleeding but also as blood cells grow old and die and plasma components are consumed or excreted from the body. Therefore, we must continually replace it. Every day, an adult typically produces 400 billion platelets, 200 billion RBCs, and 10 billion WBCs. The production of blood, especially its formed elements, is called **hematopoiesis**[5] (he-MAT-oh-poy-EE-sis). A knowledge of this process provides an indispensable foundation for understanding leukemia, anemia, and other blood disorders.

The tissues that produce blood cells are called **hematopoietic tissues.** The first hematopoietic tissues of the human embryo form in the *yolk sac*, a membrane associated with all vertebrate embryos. In most vertebrates (fish, amphibians, reptiles, and birds), this sac encloses the egg yolk, transfers its nutrients to the growing embryo, and produces the forerunners of the first blood cells. Even animals that don't lay eggs, however, have a yolk sac that retains its hematopoietic function. (It is also the source of cells that later produce eggs and sperm.) Cell clusters called *blood islands* form here by the third week of human development. They produce primitive stem cells that migrate into the embryo proper and colonize the bone marrow, liver, spleen, and thymus. Here, the stem cells multiply and give rise to blood cells throughout fetal development. The liver stops producing blood cells around the time of birth. The spleen stops producing RBCs soon after, but it continues to produce lymphocytes for life.

From infancy onward, the red bone marrow produces all seven kinds of formed elements, while lymphocytes are also produced in the lymphatic tissues and organs—especially the thymus, tonsils, lymph nodes, spleen, and mucous membranes. Blood formation in the bone marrow and lymphatic organs is called, respectively, **myeloid**[6] and **lymphoid hematopoiesis.**

All formed elements trace their origins to a common type of **hematopoietic stem cell (HSC)** in the bone marrow. In the stem-cell terminology of section 5.6c, HSCs would be classified as multipotent stem cells, destined to develop into multiple mature cell types. Hematologists, however, often call them *pluripotent stem cells (PPSCs)*. (Stem-cell biology is a young science and specialists in different fields sometimes use different terminology.) HSCs multiply to maintain a small but persistent population in the bone marrow, but some of them go on to become a variety of more specialized cells called **colony-forming units (CFUs).** Each CFU is destined to produce one or another class of formed elements. The specific processes leading from an HSC to RBCs, WBCs, and platelets are described at later points in this chapter.

Blood plasma also requires continual replacement. It is composed mainly of water, which it obtains primarily by absorption from the digestive tract. Its electrolytes and organic nutrients are also acquired there, and its gamma globulins come from connective tissue plasma cells and its other proteins mainly from the liver.

BEFORE YOU GO ON

Answer the following questions to test your understanding of the preceding section:

1. Identify at least two each of the transport, protective, and regulatory functions of the circulatory system.

2. What are the two principal components of the blood?

3. List the three major classes of plasma proteins. Which one is absent from blood serum?

4. Define the *viscosity* and *osmolarity* of blood. Explain why each of these is important for human survival.

5. What does *hematopoiesis* mean? After birth, what one cell type is the starting point for all hematopoiesis?

---

[5]*hemato* = blood; *poiesis* = formation

[6]*myel* = bone marrow

18.2 Erythrocytes

Expected Learning Outcomes

When you have completed this section, you should be able to

a. discuss the structure and function of erythrocytes (RBCs);

b. describe the structure and function of hemoglobin;

c. state and define some clinical measurements of RBC and hemoglobin quantities;

d. describe the life history of erythrocytes; and

e. name and describe the types, causes, and effects of RBC excesses and deficiencies.

Erythrocytes, or **red blood cells (RBCs),** have two principal functions: (1) to pick up oxygen from the lungs and deliver it to tissues elsewhere, and (2) to pick up carbon dioxide from the tissues and unload it in the lungs. RBCs are the most abundant formed elements of the blood and therefore the most obvious things one sees upon its microscopic examination. They are also the most critical to survival; a severe deficiency of leukocytes or platelets can be fatal within a few days, but a severe deficiency of RBCs can be fatal within mere minutes. It is the lack of life-giving oxygen, carried by erythrocytes, that leads rapidly to death in cases of major trauma or hemorrhage.

18.2a Erythrocyte Form and Function

An erythrocyte is a discoidal cell with a biconcave shape—a thick rim and a thin sunken center. It is about 7.5 μm in diameter and 2.0 μm thick at the rim **(fig. 18.4).** Although most cells, including white blood cells, have an abundance of organelles, RBCs lose their nucleus and other organelles during maturation and are thus remarkably devoid of internal structure. When viewed with the transmission electron microscope, the interior of an RBC appears uniformly gray. Lacking mitochondria, RBCs rely exclusively on anaerobic fermentation to produce ATP. The lack of aerobic respiration prevents them from consuming the oxygen that they must transport to other tissues. If they were aerobic and consumed oxygen, they would be like a pizza delivery driver who ate a slice of your pizza on the way to your house. RBCs are made to deliver oxygen, not consume it. They are the only human cells that carry on anaerobic fermentation indefinitely.

The cytoplasm of an RBC consists mainly of a 33% solution of **hemoglobin** (about 280 million molecules per cell). This is the red pigment that gives an RBC its color and name. It is known especially for its role in oxygen transport, but it also aids in the transport of carbon dioxide and the buffering of blood pH. The cytoplasm also contains an enzyme, *carbonic anhydrase (CAH),* that catalyzes the reaction $CO_2 + H_2O \rightleftharpoons H_2CO_3$. The role of CAH in gas transport and pH balance is discussed in later chapters.

The plasma membrane of a mature RBC has glycolipids on the outer surface that determine a person's blood type. On its

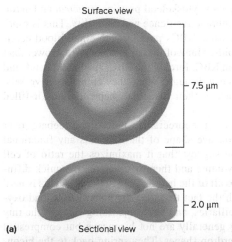

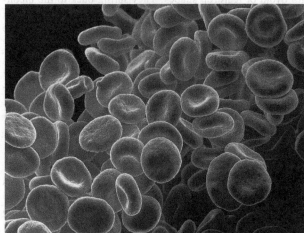

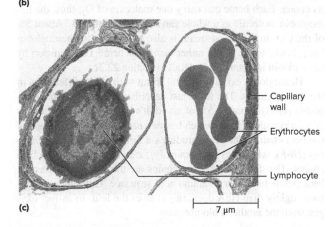

FIGURE 18.4 The Structure of Erythrocytes. (a) Dimensions and shape of an erythrocyte. (b) SEM photo showing the biconcave shape of RBCs. (c) TEM photo of a lymphocyte (left) and two erythrocytes (right) in blood capillaries of the lung. Note how thin the RBCs are at the center, and their lack of organelles or other internal structure. **APR**

b: Susumu Nishinaga/Getty Images; c: Thomas Deernick, NCMIR/Science Source

❓ *Why are erythrocytes caved in at the center?*

inner surface are two cytoskeletal proteins, *spectrin* and *actin,* that give the membrane resilience and durability. This is especially important when RBCs pass through small blood capillaries and sinusoids. Many of these passages are narrower than the diameter of an RBC, forcing the RBCs to stretch, bend, and fold as they squeeze through. When they enter larger vessels, RBCs spring back to their discoidal shape like an air-filled inner tube.

There has been appreciable, unresolved debate over whether the biconcave shape of the RBC has any functional advantage. Some suggest that it maximizes the ratio of cell surface area to volume and thereby promotes the quick diffusion of oxygen to all of the hemoglobin in the cell. This is hard to reconcile with the fact that the only place RBCs load oxygen is in the capillaries, and while squeezing through the tiny capillaries, they generally are not biconcave but compressed into ovoid or teardrop shapes. They spring back to the biconcave shape when reentering larger blood vessels, but no oxygen pickup occurs here. Another hypothesis is that the biconcave shape minimizes RBC spin (like a spinning ice-skater with her arms extended) and turbulence, enabling the dense slurry of RBCs to flow through the larger blood vessels with a smooth *laminar flow.* It has also been argued that it is simply the easiest, most stable shape for the cell and its cytoskeleton to relax into when the nucleus is removed, and it may have no physiological function at all.

18.2b Hemoglobin

Hemoglobin consists of four protein chains called **globins (fig. 18.5).** Two of these, the *alpha* (α) *chains,* are 141 amino acids long, and the other two, the *beta* (β) *chains,* are 146 amino acids long. Each chain is conjugated with a nonprotein moiety called the **heme** group, which binds oxygen to an iron atom (Fe) at its center. Each heme can carry one molecule of O_2; thus, the hemoglobin molecule as a whole can transport up to 4 O_2. About 5% of the CO_2 in the bloodstream is also transported by hemoglobin but is bound to the globin rather than to the heme. Gas transport by hemoglobin is discussed in detail in section 22.3c.

Hemoglobin exists in several forms with slight differences in the globin chains. The form just described is called *adult hemoglobin (HbA).* About 2.5% of an adult's hemoglobin, however, is of a form called HbA_2, which has two *delta* (δ) *chains* in place of the beta chains. The fetus produces a form called *fetal hemoglobin (HbF),* which has two *gamma* (γ) *chains* in place of the beta chains. The delta and gamma chains are the same length as the beta chains but differ in amino acid sequence. HbF binds oxygen more tightly than HbA does; this enables the fetus to extract oxygen from the mother's bloodstream.

18.2c Quantities of Erythrocytes and Hemoglobin

The RBC count and hemoglobin concentration are important clinical data because they determine the amount of oxygen the blood can carry. Three of the most common measurements are hematocrit, hemoglobin concentration, and RBC count. The

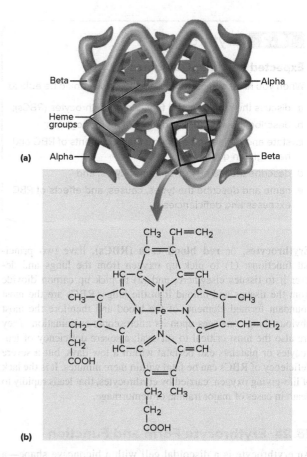

FIGURE 18.5 The Structure of Hemoglobin. (a) The hemoglobin molecule consists of two alpha proteins and two beta proteins, each conjugated to a nonprotein heme group. (b) Structure of the heme group. Oxygen binds to iron (Fe) at the center of the heme.

? *In what way does this exemplify a quaternary protein structure? What is the prosthetic group of hemoglobin?* (Hint: See "Protein Structure" in section 2.4e.)

hematocrit[7] **(packed cell volume, PCV)** is the percentage of whole blood volume composed of RBCs (see fig. 18.2). In men, it normally ranges between 42% and 52%; in women, between 37% and 48%. The **hemoglobin concentration** of whole blood is normally 13 to 18 g/dL in men and 12 to 16 g/dL in women. The RBC count is normally 4.6 to 6.2 million RBCs/μL in men and 4.2 to 5.4 million/μL in women. This is often expressed as cells per cubic millimeter (mm^3); 1 μL = 1 mm^3.

Notice that these values tend to be lower in women than in men. There are three physiological reasons for this: (1) Androgens stimulate RBC production, and men have higher androgen levels than women; (2) women of reproductive age have periodic menstrual losses; and (3) the hematocrit is inversely

[7]*hemato* = blood; *crit* = to separate

proportional to percentage body fat, which averages higher in women than in men. In men, the blood also clots faster and the skin has fewer blood vessels than in women. Such differences are not limited to humans. From the evolutionary standpoint, their adaptive value may lie in the fact that male animals fight more than females and suffer more injuries. These traits may serve to minimize or compensate for their blood loss.

▶▶▶**APPLY WHAT YOU KNOW**

Explain why the hemoglobin concentration could appear deceptively high in a patient who is dehydrated, when in fact the patient does not have a hemoglobin or RBC excess.

18.2d The Erythrocyte Life History

An erythrocyte lives for an average of 120 days from the time it is produced in the red bone marrow until it dies and breaks up. In a state of balance and stable RBC count, the birth and death of RBCs amount to nearly 100 billion cells per day (1 million per second), or a packed cell volume of 20 mL/day.

Erythrocyte Production

Erythrocyte production is called **erythropoiesis** (eh-RITH-ro-poy-EE-sis). The process normally takes 3 to 5 days and involves four major developments: a reduction in cell size, an increase in cell number, the synthesis of hemoglobin, and the loss of the nucleus and other organelles.

Erythropoiesis begins when a hematopoietic stem cell (HSC) becomes an *erythrocyte colony-forming unit (ECFU)* **(fig. 18.6),** which has receptors for **erythropoietin (EPO),** a hormone secreted by the kidneys. EPO stimulates the ECFU to transform into an *erythroblast (normoblast).* Erythroblasts multiply, build up a large cell population, and synthesize hemoglobin. When this task is completed, the nucleus shrivels and is discharged from the cell. The cell is now called a *reticulocyte,* named for a temporary network (reticulum) of ribosome clusters transcribing the cell's remaining mRNA (polyribosomes; see the photo on the opening page of chapter 4).

Reticulocytes leave the bone marrow and enter the circulating blood. In a day or two, the last of the polyribosomes disintegrate

and disappear, and the cell is a mature erythrocyte. Normally, about 0.5% to 1.5% of the circulating RBCs are reticulocytes, but this percentage rises under certain circumstances. Blood loss, for example, stimulates accelerated erythropoiesis and leads to an increasing number of reticulocytes in circulation—as if the bone marrow is in such a hurry to replenish the lost RBCs that it rushes many developing RBCs into circulation a little early.

Iron Metabolism

Iron is a critical part of the hemoglobin molecule and therefore one of the key nutritional requirements for erythropoiesis. Men lose about 0.9 mg of iron per day through the urine, feces, and bleeding, and women of reproductive age lose an average of 1.7 mg/day through these routes and the added factor of menstruation. Since we absorb only a fraction of the iron in our food, we must consume 5 to 20 mg/day to replace our losses. A pregnant woman needs 20 to 48 mg/day, especially in the last 3 months, to meet not only her own need but also that of the fetus.

Dietary iron exists in two forms: ferric (Fe^{3+}) and ferrous (Fe^{2+}) ions. Stomach acid converts most Fe^{3+} to Fe^{2+}, the only form that the small intestine can absorb **(fig. 18.7).** A protein called **gastroferritin,**[8] produced by the stomach, then binds Fe^{2+} and transports it to the small intestine. Here, it is absorbed into the blood, binds to a plasma protein called **transferrin,** and travels to the bone marrow, liver, and other tissues. Bone marrow uses iron for hemoglobin synthesis; muscle uses it to make the oxygen-binding protein myoglobin; and nearly all cells use iron to make electron-transport molecules called cytochromes in their mitochondria. The liver binds surplus iron to a protein called *apoferritin,*[9] forming an iron-storage complex called **ferritin.** It releases Fe^{2+} into circulation when needed.

Some other nutritional requirements for erythropoiesis are vitamin B_{12} and folic acid, required for the rapid cell division and DNA synthesis that occurs in erythropoiesis, and vitamin C and copper, which are cofactors for some of the enzymes that synthesize hemoglobin.

---

[8]*gastro* = stomach; *ferrit* = iron; *in* = protein
[9]*apo* = separated from; *ferrit* = iron; *in* = protein

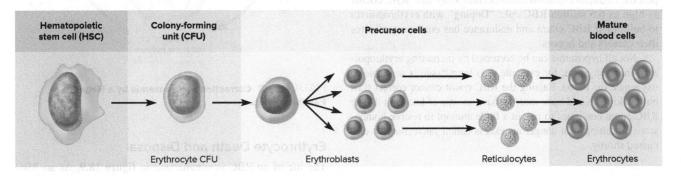

Hematopoietic stem cell (HSC)	Colony-forming unit (CFU)	Precursor cells		Mature blood cells
	Erythrocyte CFU	Erythroblasts	Reticulocytes	Erythrocytes

FIGURE 18.6 Erythropoiesis. Stages in the development of a red blood cell.

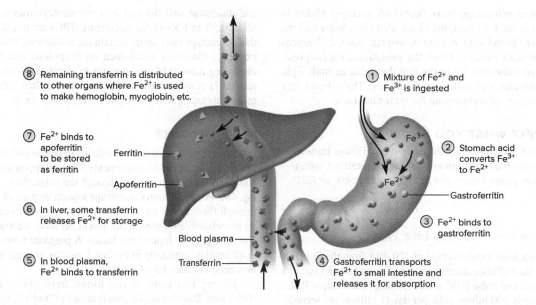

⑧ Remaining transferrin is distributed to other organs where Fe^{2+} is used to make hemoglobin, myoglobin, etc.

① Mixture of Fe^{2+} and Fe^{3+} is ingested

② Stomach acid converts Fe^{3+} to Fe^{2+}

⑦ Fe^{2+} binds to apoferritin to be stored as ferritin

Ferritin

Apoferritin

Gastroferritin

③ Fe^{2+} binds to gastroferritin

⑥ In liver, some transferrin releases Fe^{2+} for storage

Blood plasma

⑤ In blood plasma, Fe^{2+} binds to transferrin

Transferrin

④ Gastroferritin transports Fe^{2+} to small intestine and releases it for absorption

FIGURE 18.7 Iron Metabolism. Read clockwise from the upper right.

Erythrocyte Homeostasis

RBC count is maintained in a classic negative feedback manner **(fig. 18.8).** If the count should drop (for example, because of hemorrhaging), it may result in a state of **hypoxemia**[10] (oxygen deficiency in the blood). The kidneys detect this and increase their EPO output. Three or four days later, the RBC count begins to rise and reverses the hypoxemia that started the process.

Hypoxemia has many causes other than blood loss. Another is a low level of oxygen in the atmosphere. If you were to move from Miami to Denver, for example, the lower O_2 level at the high elevation of Denver would produce temporary hypoxemia and stimulate EPO secretion and erythropoiesis. The blood of an average adult has about 5 million RBCs/μL, but people who live at high elevations may have counts of 7 to 8 million RBCs/μL. Another cause of hypoxemia is an abrupt increase in the body's oxygen consumption. If a formerly lethargic person takes up tennis or aerobics, for example, the muscles consume oxygen more rapidly and create a state of hypoxemia that stimulates erythropoiesis. Endurance-trained athletes commonly have RBC counts as high as 6.5 million RBCs/μL. "Doping" with erythropoietin to build their RBC count and endurance has cost many athletes their careers and honors.

Not all hypoxemia can be corrected by increasing erythropoiesis. In emphysema, for example, less lung tissue is available to oxygenate the blood. Raising the RBC count cannot correct this, but the kidneys and bone marrow have no way of knowing it. The RBC count continues to rise in a futile attempt to restore homeostasis, resulting in a dangerous excess called *polycythemia,* discussed shortly.

Hypoxemia (inadequate O_2 transport)

Sensed by liver and kidneys

Increased O_2 transport

Secretion of erythropoietin

Increased RBC count

Accelerated erythropoiesis

Stimulation of red bone marrow

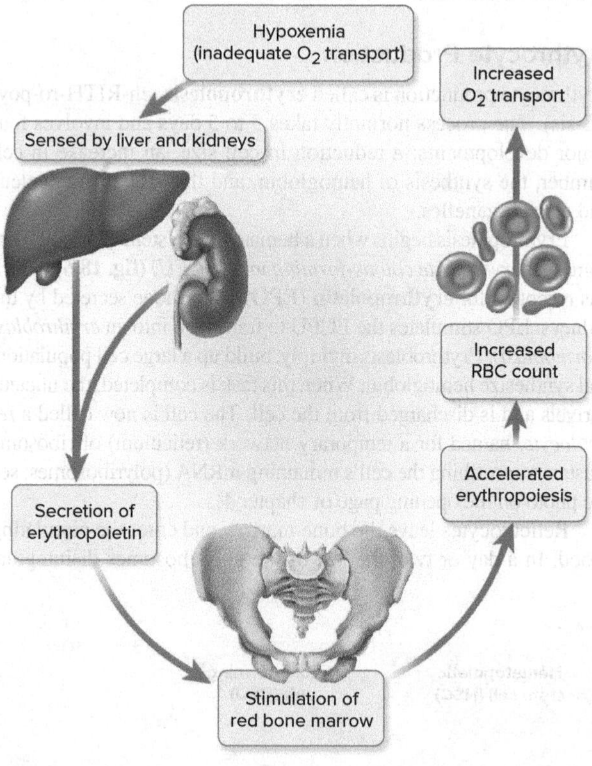

FIGURE 18.8 Correction of Hypoxemia by a Negative Feedback Loop.

Erythrocyte Death and Disposal

The life of an RBC is summarized in **figure 18.9.** As an RBC ages and its membrane proteins (especially spectrin) deteriorate, the membrane grows increasingly fragile. Without a nucleus or

[10]*hyp* = below normal; *ox* = oxygen; *emia* = blood condition

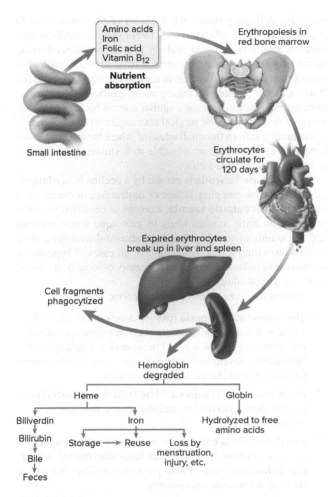

Small intestine

Amino acids
Iron
Folic acid
Vitamin B_{12}

Nutrient absorption

Erythropoiesis in red bone marrow

Erythrocytes circulate for 120 days

Expired erythrocytes break up in liver and spleen

Cell fragments phagocytized

Hemoglobin degraded

Heme | Globin

Biliverdin | Iron | Hydrolyzed to free amino acids

Bilirubin | Storage ⟶ Reuse | Loss by menstruation, injury, etc.

Bile

Feces

FIGURE 18.9 The Life and Death of Erythrocytes. Note especially the stages of hemoglobin breakdown and disposal.

ribosomes, an RBC cannot synthesize new spectrin. Many RBCs die in the spleen, which has been called the "erythrocyte grave-yard." The spleen has channels as narrow as 3 μm that severely test the ability of old, fragile RBCs to squeeze through the organ. Old cells become trapped, broken up, and destroyed. An enlarged and tender spleen sometimes indicates diseases in which RBCs are rapidly breaking down.

Hemolysis[11] (he-MOLL-ih-sis), the rupture of RBCs, releases hemoglobin and leaves empty plasma membranes. The membrane fragments are easily digested by macrophages in the liver and spleen, but hemoglobin disposal is a bit more complicated. It must be disposed of efficiently, however, or it can block kidney tubules and cause renal failure. Macrophages begin the disposal process by separating the heme from the globin. They hydrolyze the globin into free amino acids, which can be used for energy-releasing ca-tabolism or recycled for protein synthesis.

Disposing of the heme is another matter. First, the macro-phage removes the iron and releases it into the blood, where it

combines with transferrin and is used or stored in the same way as dietary iron. The macrophage converts the rest of the heme into a greenish pigment called **biliverdin**[12] (BIL-ih-VUR-din), then further converts most of this to a yellow-green pigment called **bilirubin.**[13] Bilirubin is released by the macrophages and binds to albumin in the blood plasma. The liver removes it from the albumin and secretes it into the bile, to which it imparts a dark green color as the bile becomes concentrated in the gallbladder. Biliverdin and bilirubin are collectively known as **bile pigments.** The gallbladder discharges the bile into the small intestine, where bacteria convert bilirubin to *urobilinogen,* responsible for the brown color of the feces. Another hemoglobin breakdown pig-ment, *urochrome,* produces the yellow color of urine. A high level of bilirubin in the blood causes *jaundice,* a yellowish cast in the skin and whites of eyes. Jaundice may be a sign of rapid hemoly-sis or a liver disease or bile duct obstruction that interferes with bilirubin disposal.

18.2e Erythrocyte Disorders

Any imbalance between the rates of erythropoiesis and RBC destruction may produce an excess or deficiency of red cells. An RBC excess is called *polycythemia*[14] (POL-ee-sy-THEE-me-uh), and a deficiency of either RBCs or hemoglobin is called *anemia.*[15]

Polycythemia

Primary polycythemia (polycythemia vera) is due to cancer of the erythropoietic line of the red bone marrow. It can result in an RBC count as high as 11 million RBCs/μL and a hematocrit as high as 80%. Polycythemia from all other causes, called **second-ary polycythemia,** is characterized by RBC counts as high as 6 to 8 million RBCs/μL. It can result from dehydration because water is lost from the bloodstream while erythrocytes remain and become abnormally concentrated. More often, it is caused by smoking, air pollution, emphysema, high altitude, excessive aerobic exercise, or other factors that create a state of hypoxemia and stimulate eryth-ropoietin secretion.

The principal dangers of polycythemia are increased blood volume, pressure, and viscosity. Blood volume can double in pri-mary polycythemia and cause the circulatory system to become tremendously engorged. Blood viscosity may rise to three times normal. Circulation is poor, the capillaries are congested with vis-cous blood, and the heart is dangerously strained. Chronic (long-term) polycythemia can lead to embolism, stroke, or heart failure. The deadly consequences of emphysema and some other lung dis-eases are due in part to polycythemia.

Anemia

The causes of **anemia** fall into three categories: (1) inadequate erythropoiesis or hemoglobin synthesis, (2) **hemorrhagic**

---

[11]*hemo* = blood; *lysis* = splitting, breakdown

[12]*bili* = bile; *verd* = green; *in* = substance
[13]*bili* = bile; *rub* = red; *in* = substance
[14]*poly* = many; *cyt* = cell; *hem* = blood; *ia* = condition
[15]*an* = without; *em* = blood; *ia* = condition

TABLE 18.4	Causes of Anemia
Categories of Anemia	**Causes or Examples**
Inadequate Erythropoiesis	
Iron-deficiency anemia	Dietary iron deficiency
Other nutritional anemias	Dietary folic acid, vitamin B_{12}, or vitamin C deficiency
Anemia due to renal insufficiency	Deficiency of EPO secretion
Pernicious anemia	Deficiency of intrinsic factor leading to inadequate vitamin B_{12} absorption
Hypoplastic and aplastic anemia	Destruction of myeloid tissue by radiation, viruses, some drugs and poisons (arsenic, benzene, mustard gas), or autoimmune disease
Anemia of old age	Declining erythropoiesis due to nutritional deficiencies, reduced physical activity, gastric atrophy (reduced intrinsic factor secretion), or renal atrophy (depressed EPO secretion)
Blood Loss (Hemorrhagic Anemia)	
From hereditary clotting deficiencies	Hemophilia
From nonhereditary causes	Trauma, aneurysm, menstruation, ulcer, etc.
RBC Destruction (Hemolytic Anemia)	
Drug reactions	Penicillin allergy
Poisoning	Mushroom toxins, snake and spider venoms
Parasitic infection	RBC destruction by malaria parasites
Hereditary hemoglobin defects	Sickle-cell disease, thalassemia
Blood type incompatabilities	Hemolytic disease of the newborn, transfusion reactions

anemia from bleeding, and (3) **hemolytic anemia** from RBC destruction. **Table 18.4** gives specific examples and causes for each category.

Anemia often results from kidney failure, because RBC production depends on erythropoietin, which is produced mainly by the kidneys. Erythropoiesis also declines with age, simply because the kidneys atrophy and produce less and less EPO as we get older. Compounding this problem, elderly people tend to get less exercise and eat less well, and both of these factors reduce erythropoiesis.

Nutritional anemia results from a dietary deficiency of any of the requirements for erythropoiesis discussed earlier. Its most common form is **iron-deficiency anemia,** characterized by small pale erythrocytes. Iron-deficiency anemia is usually caused by blood loss without getting enough dietary iron to compensate for it. A deficiency of vitamin B_{12} also causes anemia, but B_{12} is so abundant in meat that a deficiency is rare except in strict vegetarians. More

often, B_{12} deficiency occurs when glands of the stomach fail to produce a substance called **intrinsic factor** that the small intestine needs to absorb the vitamin. Elderly people sometimes develop **pernicious anemia,** an autoimmune disease in which antibodies destroy stomach tissue. Pernicious anemia can also be hereditary. Without proper postsurgical management, gastric-bypass and gastrectomy patients can develop a similar anemia because of the removal of stomach tissue or surgical rearrangement of the stomach, disconnecting it from the small intestine where the intrinsic factor is needed. Such anemias are treatable with vitamin B_{12} injections or oral B_{12} and intrinsic factor.

Hypoplastic[16] **anemia** is caused by a decline in erythropoiesis, whereas the complete failure or destruction of the myeloid tissue produces **aplastic anemia,** a complete cessation of erythropoiesis. Aplastic anemia leads to grotesque tissue necrosis and blackening of the skin. Barring successful treatment, most victims die within a year. About half of all cases of hypoplastic anemia are of unknown or hereditary cause, especially in adolescents and young adults.

Anemia has three potential consequences:

1. The tissues suffer **hypoxia** (oxygen deprivation). The individual is lethargic and becomes short of breath upon physical exertion. The skin is pallid because of the deficiency of hemoglobin. Severe anemic hypoxia can cause life-threatening necrosis of brain, heart, and kidney tissues.

2. Blood osmolarity is reduced. More fluid thus transfers from the bloodstream to the intercellular spaces, resulting in edema.

3. Blood viscosity is reduced. Because the blood puts up less resistance to flow, the heart beats faster than normal and cardiac failure may ensue. Blood pressure also drops because of the reduced volume and viscosity.

Sickle-Cell Disease

Sickle-cell disease and thalassemia (see table 18.8) are hereditary hemoglobin defects that occur mostly among people of African and Mediterranean descent, respectively. **Sickle-cell disease** afflicts about 1.3% of people of African-American heritage. It is caused by a recessive allele that modifies the hemoglobin. Sickle-cell hemoglobin (HbS) differs from normal HbA only in the sixth amino acid of the beta chain, where HbA has glutamic acid and HbS has valine. People who are homozygous for HbS exhibit sickle-cell disease. People who are heterozygous for it—about 7.7% of African-Americans—have *sickle-cell trait* but rarely have severe symptoms. However, if two carriers reproduce, each of their children has a 25% chance of being homozygous and having the disease.

HbS doesn't bind oxygen very well. At low oxygen concentrations, it becomes deoxygenated, polymerizes, and forms a gel that makes erythrocytes become elongated and pointed at the ends **(fig. 18.10),** hence the name of the disease. Sickled

[16]*hypo* = below normal; *plas* = formation; *tic* = pertaining to

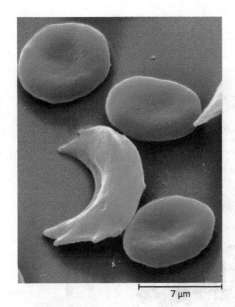

7 μm

FIGURE 18.10 Sickle-Cell Disease. Shows one deformed, pointed erythrocyte and three normal erythrocytes.

Eye of Science/Science Source

erythrocytes are sticky; they **agglutinate**[17] (clump) and block small blood vessels, causing intense pain in oxygen-starved tissues. Blockage of the circulation can also lead to kidney or heart failure, stroke, severe joint pain, or paralysis. Hemolysis of the fragile cells causes anemia, which results in a hypoxemia that triggers further sickling in a deadly positive feedback loop. Chronic hypoxemia also causes fatigue, weakness, poor mental development, and deterioration of the heart and other organs. In a futile effort to counteract the hypoxemia, the hematopoietic tissues become so active that bones of the cranium and elsewhere become enlarged and misshapen. The spleen reverts to a hematopoietic role, while also disposing of dead RBCs, and becomes enlarged and fibrous. Sickle-cell disease is a prime example of *pleiotropy*—the occurrence of multiple phenotypic effects arising from a change in a single gene.

Without treatment, a child with sickle-cell disease has little chance of living to age 2. Advances in treatment, however, have steadily raised life expectancy to a little beyond age 50.

Why does sickle-cell disease exist? In Africa, where it originated, vast numbers of people die of malaria. Malaria is caused by a parasite that invades the RBCs and feeds on hemoglobin. Sickle-cell hemoglobin is detrimental to the parasites, and people heterozygous for sickle-cell disease are resistant to malaria. The lives saved by this gene far outnumber the deaths of homozygous individuals, so the gene persists in the population. The sickle-cell gene is less common in the United States and other essentially nonmalarious regions than it is in Africa.

[17]*ag* = together; *glutin* = glue

BEFORE YOU GO ON

Answer the following questions to test your understanding of the preceding section:

6. Describe the size, shape, and contents of an erythrocyte, and explain how it acquires its unusual shape.

7. What is the function of hemoglobin? What are its protein and nonprotein moieties called?

8. Define *hematocrit, hemoglobin concentration,* and *RBC count* and give the units of measurement in which each is expressed.

9. List the stages in the production of an RBC and describe how each stage differs from the previous one.

10. What is the role of erythropoietin in the regulation of RBC count? What is the role of gastroferritin?

11. What happens to each component of an RBC and its hemoglobin when it dies and disintegrates?

12. What are the three primary causes or categories of anemia? What are its three primary consequences?

18.3   Blood Types

Expected Learning Outcomes

When you have completed this section, you should be able to

a. explain what determines a person's ABO and Rh blood types and how this relates to transfusion compatibility;

b. list some blood groups other than ABO and Rh and explain how they may be useful; and

c. describe the effects of a blood type incompatibility between mother and fetus.

Blood types and transfusion compatibility are a matter of interactions between the plasma and erythrocytes. Ancient Greek physicians attempted to transfuse blood from one person to another by squeezing it from a pig's bladder through a porcupine quill into the recipient's vein. Although some patients benefited from the procedure, it was fatal to others. The reason some people have compatible blood and some don't remained obscure until 1900, when Karl Landsteiner discovered blood types A, B, and O—a discovery that won him a Nobel Prize in 1930; type AB was discovered later. World War II stimulated great improvements in transfusions, blood banking, and blood substitutes (see Deeper Insight 18.2).

Blood types are based on large molecules called *antigens* and *antibodies.* Explained more fully in chapter 21, these will be introduced only briefly here. **Antigens** are complex molecules such as proteins, glycoproteins, and glycolipids that are genetically unique to each individual (except identical twins). They occur on the surfaces of all cells and enable the body to distinguish its own cells from foreign matter. When the body detects an antigen of foreign origin, it activates an immune response. This response consists partly of the *plasma cells,* mentioned earlier, secreting proteins called **antibodies.**

DEEPER INSIGHT 18.2

MEDICAL HISTORY

Charles Drew—Blood-Banking Pioneer

Charles Drew **(fig. 18.11)** was a scientist remembered for his seminal contributions in hematology and civil rights, and for a sadly ironic end to his life. After receiving his M.D. from McGill University of Montreal in 1933, Drew became the first black person to pursue the advanced degree of Doctor of Science in Medicine, for which he studied transfusion and blood banking at Columbia University. He became the director of a new blood bank at Columbia Presbyterian Hospital in 1939 and organized numerous blood banks during World War II.

Drew saved countless lives by convincing physicians to use plasma rather than whole blood for battlefield and other emergency transfusions. Whole blood could be stored for only a week and given only to recipients with compatible blood types. Plasma could be stored longer and was less likely to cause transfusion reactions.

When the U.S. War Department issued a directive forbidding the storage of "Caucasian and Negro blood" in the same military blood banks, Drew denounced the order and resigned his position. He became a professor of surgery at Howard University in Washington, D.C., and later chief of staff at Freedmen's Hospital. He was a mentor for numerous young black physicians and campaigned to get them accepted into the medical community. The American Medical Association, however, refused to admit black members until the 1960s, excluding even Drew himself.

Late one night in 1950, Drew and three colleagues set out to volunteer their medical services to an annual free clinic in Tuskegee, Alabama. Drew fell asleep at the wheel and was critically injured in the resulting accident. Contrary to a myth that Drew was refused emergency treatment because of his race, doctors at the nearest hospital administered blood and attempted to revive him. Yet, for all the lives he saved through his pioneering work in transfusion, Drew himself bled to death at the age of 45.

FIGURE 18.11   Charles Drew (1904–50).
Alfred Eisenstaedt/The LIFE Picture Collection/Getty Images

Antibodies bind to antigens and mark them, or the cells bearing them, for destruction. One method of antibody action is **agglutination,** in which each antibody molecule binds to two or more foreign cells and sticks them together. Repetition of this process produces large clumps of cells that can cause the complications of the transfusion reaction discussed shortly. The RBC surface antigens that trigger agglutination are called **agglutinogens** (ah-glue-TIN-oh-jens) and the plasma antibodies that bind to them are called **agglutinins** (ah-GLUE-tih-nins).

18.3a The ABO Group

Blood types A, B, AB, and O form the **ABO blood group** **(table 18.5).** One's ABO blood type is determined by the hereditary presence or absence of antigens A and B on the RBCs. The genetic determination of blood types is explained in section 4.4c. The antigens are glycolipids—membrane phospholipids with short carbohydrate chains bonded to them. **Figure 18.12** shows how the carbohydrate moieties of RBC surface antigens determine the ABO blood types.

Antibodies of the ABO group begin to appear in the plasma 2 to 8 months after birth. They reach their maximum concentrations between 8 and 10 years of age and then slowly decline for the rest of one's life. They are produced mainly in response to bacteria that inhabit the intestines, but they cross-react with RBC antigens and are therefore best known for their significance in transfusions.

Antibodies of the ABO group react against any A or B antigen except one's own. The antibody that reacts against antigen A is called *alpha agglutinin,* or *anti-A;* it is present in the plasma of people with type O or type B blood—that is, anyone who does *not* possess antigen A. The antibody that reacts against antigen B is *beta agglutinin,* or *anti-B,* and is present in type O and type A individuals—those who do not possess antigen B. Each antibody molecule has 10 binding sites where it can attach to either an A or B antigen. An antibody can therefore attach to several RBCs at once and agglutinate them **(fig. 18.13).**

A person's ABO blood type can be determined by placing one drop of blood in a pool of anti-A serum and another drop in a pool of anti-B. Blood type AB exhibits conspicuous agglutination in

TABLE 18.5	The ABO Blood Group			
	ABO Blood Type			
Characteristics	Type O	Type A	Type B	Type AB
Possible genotypes*	*ii*	$I^A I^A$ or $I^A i$	$I^B I^B$ or $I^B i$	$I^A I^B$
RBC antigen	Neither A nor B	A	B	Both A and B
Plasma antibody	Anti-A, anti-B	Anti-B	Anti-A	Neither
May safely receive RBCs of	Type O	Type O or A	Type O or B	Type O, A, B, or AB
May safely donate RBCs to	Type O, A, B, or AB	Type A or AB	Type B or AB	Type AB
Frequency in U.S. Population				
White	45%	40%	11%	4%
Black	49%	27%	20%	4%
Hispanic	63%	14%	20%	3%
Japanese	31%	38%	22%	9%
Native American	79%	16%	4%	<1%

*I^A is the dominant allele for agglutinogen A; I^B is the dominant allele for agglutinogen B; and allele *i* is recessive to both of these.

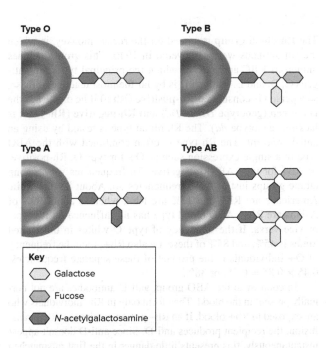

FIGURE 18.12 Chemical Basis of the ABO Blood Types. The terminal carbohydrates of the antigenic glycolipids are shown. All of them end with galactose and fucose (not to be confused with fructose). In type A, the galactose also has *N*-acetylgalactosamine added to it; in type B, it has another galactose; and in type AB, both of these chain types are present.

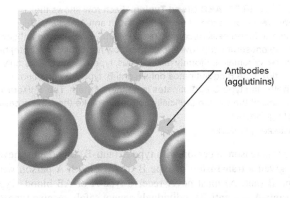

FIGURE 18.13 Agglutination of RBCs by an Antibody. Anti-A and anti-B have 10 binding sites, located at the 2 tips of each of the 5 Ys, and can therefore bind multiple RBCs to each other.

both antisera; type A or B agglutinates only in the corresponding antiserum; and type O doesn't agglutinate in either one (**fig. 18.14**).

Type O blood is the most common and AB is the rarest in the United States. Percentages differ from one region of the world to another and among ethnic groups. People tend to marry within their locality and ethnic group, thus perpetuating statistical variations particular to that group (table 18.5).

In giving transfusions, it is imperative that the donor's RBCs not agglutinate as they enter the recipient's bloodstream. For example, if type B blood were transfused into a type A recipient, the recipient's anti-B would immediately agglutinate the donor's RBCs (**fig. 18.15**). A mismatch causes a **transfusion reaction**—the agglutinated RBCs block small blood vessels, hemolyze, and release their hemoglobin over the next few hours to days. Free hemoglobin can block the kidney tubules and cause death from acute renal failure within a week or so.

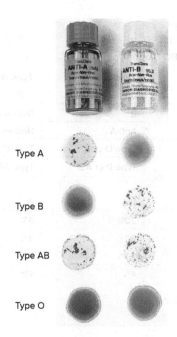

FIGURE 18.14 ABO Blood Typing. Each row shows the appearance of a drop of blood mixed with anti-A and anti-B antisera. Blood cells become clumped if they possess the antigens for the antiserum (top row left, second row right, third row both) but otherwise remain uniformly mixed. Thus, type A agglutinates only in anti-A; type B agglutinates only in anti-B; type AB agglutinates in both; and type O agglutinates in neither of them. The antisera in the vials at the top are artificially colored to make them more easily distinguishable.

Claude Revey/Phototake

For this reason, a person with type A (anti-B) blood must never be given a transfusion of type B or AB blood. A person with type B (anti-A) must never receive type A or AB blood. Type O (anti-A and anti-B) individuals cannot safely receive type A, B, or AB blood.

Type AB is sometimes called the *universal recipient* because this blood type lacks both anti-A and anti-B antibodies; thus, it will not agglutinate donor RBCs of any ABO type. However, this overlooks the fact that the *donor's* plasma can agglutinate the *recipient's* RBCs if it contains anti-A, anti-B, or both. For similar reasons, type O is sometimes called the *universal donor*. The plasma of a type O donor, however, can agglutinate the RBCs of a type A, B, or AB recipient. There are procedures for reducing the risk of a transfusion reaction in certain mismatches, however, such as giving packed RBCs with a minimum of plasma.

Contrary to some people's belief, blood type is not changed by transfusion. It is fixed at conception and remains the same for life.

▶▶▶**APPLY WHAT YOU KNOW**

Scientists have developed a method of enzymatically splitting N-acetylgalactosamine off the glycolipid of type A blood cells (see fig. 18.12). What clinical benefit do you think they saw as justifying their research effort?

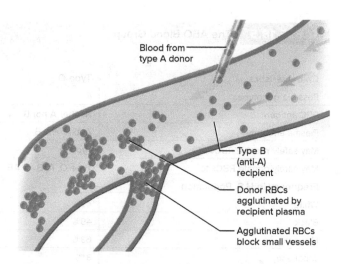

FIGURE 18.15 Effects of a Mismatched Transfusion. Donor RBCs become agglutinated in the recipient's blood plasma. The agglutinated RBCs lodge in smaller blood vessels downstream from this point and cut off the blood flow to vital tissues.

18.3b The Rh Group

The **Rh blood group** is named for the rhesus monkey, in which the Rh antigens were discovered in 1940. This group includes numerous RBC antigens, of which the principal types are antigens C, D, and E. Antigen D is by far the most reactive of these, so a person is considered **Rh-positive (Rh+)** if he or she has the D antigen (genotype *DD* or *Dd*) and **Rh-negative (Rh–)** if it is lacking (genotype *dd*). The Rh blood type is tested by using an anti-D reagent. The Rh type is often combined with the ABO type in a single expression such as O+ for type O, Rh-positive; or AB– for type AB, Rh-negative. Rh frequencies vary among ethnic groups just as ABO frequencies do. About 85% of white Americans are Rh+ and 15% are Rh–, whereas about 99% of Asians are Rh+. ABO blood type has no influence on Rh type, or vice versa. If the frequency of type O whites in the United States is 45%, and 85% of these are also Rh+, then the frequency of O+ individuals is the product of these separate frequencies: $0.45 \times 0.85 = 0.38$, or 38%.

In contrast to the ABO group, anti-D antibodies are not normally present in the blood. They form only in Rh– individuals who are exposed to Rh+ blood. If an Rh– person receives an Rh+ transfusion, the recipient produces anti-D. Since anti-D doesn't appear instantaneously, this presents little danger in the first mismatched transfusion. But if that person should later receive another Rh+ transfusion, his or her anti-D could agglutinate the donor's RBCs.

18.3c Other Blood Groups

ABO and Rh are not the only known blood groups. There are 33 groups in all, with more than 300 RBC antigens in addition to A, B, and D. Other groups include the Duffy, Kell, Kidd, Lewis, and MNS groups. These rarely cause transfusion reactions, but they are useful for such legal purposes as paternity and criminal cases and for research in anthropology and population genetics.

Now that DNA sequencing is more economical, however, it has replaced blood typing in many such applications.

18.3d Maternal–Fetal Mismatches

A condition called **hemolytic disease of the newborn (HDN),** or **erythroblastosis fetalis,** can occur when a woman has a baby with a mismatched blood type—most famously, but by no means all cases, when she is Rh– and carries an Rh+ fetus. The first pregnancy is likely to be uneventful because the placenta normally prevents maternal and fetal blood from mixing. However, if there is placental leakage during pregnancy, or at the time of birth, or if a miscarriage occurs, the mother is exposed to Rh+ fetal blood. She then begins to produce anti-D antibodies (**fig. 18.16**). If she becomes pregnant again with an Rh+ fetus, her anti-D antibodies may pass through the placenta and agglutinate the fetal erythrocytes. Agglutinated RBCs hemolyze, and the baby is born with hemolytic anemia, HDN.

If an Rh– woman has had one or more previous Rh+ pregnancies, her subsequent Rh+ children have about a 17% probability of being born with HDN. Such infants are often severely anemic. As the fetal hematopoietic tissues respond to the need for more RBCs, erythroblasts (immature RBCs) enter the circulation prematurely—hence the name *erythroblastosis fetalis.* Hemolyzed RBCs release

hemoglobin, which is converted to bilirubin. High bilirubin levels can cause *kernicterus,* a syndrome of toxic brain damage that can be lethal or leave the child with motor, sensory, and mental deficiencies. HDN can be treated with *phototherapy*—exposing the infant to ultraviolet radiation, which degrades bilirubin as blood passes through capillaries of the skin. In more severe cases, an *exchange transfusion* may be given to completely replace the infant's Rh+ blood with Rh–. In time, the infant's hematopoietic tissues will replace the donor's RBCs with Rh+ cells, and by then the mother's antibody will have disappeared from the infant's blood.

Rh-based HDN, like so many other disorders, is easier to prevent than to treat. If an Rh– woman gives birth to (or miscarries) an Rh+ child, she can be given an *Rh immune globulin* (sold under such trade names as RhoGAM and Gamulin Rh). The immune globulin binds fetal RBC antigens so they cannot stimulate her immune system to produce anti-D. It is now common to give immune globulin at 28 to 32 weeks' gestation and at birth in any pregnancy in which the mother is Rh–.

Although an Rh mismatch produces the most severe HDN, it isn't the most common cause. Two out of three cases are due to ABO mismatches. In about 15% of U.S. pregnancies, the mother is type O and her fetus is type A, B, or AB. About 3% of these

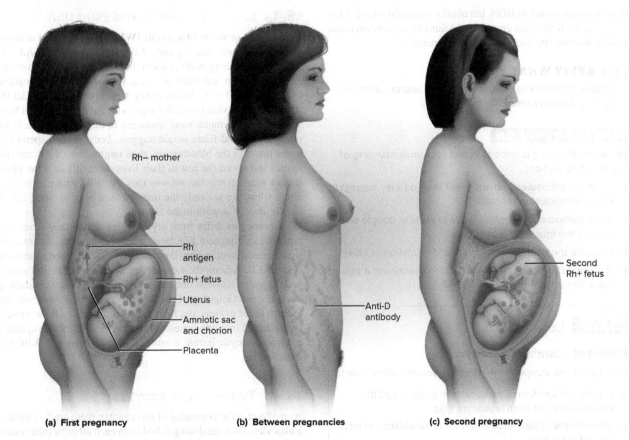

(a) First pregnancy   **(b) Between pregnancies**   **(c) Second pregnancy**

- Rh– mother
- Rh antigen
- Rh+ fetus
- Uterus
- Amniotic sac and chorion
- Placenta
- Anti-D antibody
- Second Rh+ fetus

FIGURE 18.16 Hemolytic Disease of the Newborn (HDN). (a) When an Rh– woman is pregnant with an Rh+ fetus, she is exposed to D (Rh) antigens, especially during childbirth. (b) Following that pregnancy, her immune system produces anti-D antibodies. (c) If she later becomes pregnant with another Rh+ fetus, her anti-D antibodies can cross the placenta and agglutinate the blood of that fetus, causing that child to be born with HDN.

DEEPER INSIGHT 18.3

CLINICAL APPLICATION

Bone Marrow and Cord Blood Transplants

A bone marrow transplant is one treatment option for leukemia, sickle-cell disease, and some other disorders. The principle is to eradicate the patient's original bone marrow with radiation or chemotherapy, including immune T cells that would attack transplanted marrow, and then replace with donor stem cells in hopes that they will rebuild a population of normal marrow and blood cells. Marrow is drawn from the donor's sternum or hip bone and injected into the recipient's circulation. Donor stem cells colonize the patient's marrow cavities and, ideally, build healthy marrow.

There are, however, drawbacks to this procedure. It is difficult to find compatible donors; surviving T cells in the patient may attack the donor marrow; and donor T cells may attack the patient's tissues (the graft-versus-host response). To inhibit graft rejection, the patient must take immunosuppressant drugs for life. These leave a person vulnerable to infection and have other adverse side effects. Infections are sometimes contracted from the donated marrow itself. In short, marrow transplant is a high-risk procedure; up to one-third of patients die from complications of treatment (see the David Vetter case in fig 21.29).

An alternative is to use blood from placentas, which are normally discarded at every childbirth. Placental blood contains more stem cells than adult bone marrow, and is less likely to carry infectious microbes. With the parents' consent, it can be harvested from the umbilical cord with a syringe and stored almost indefinitely at cord blood banks. The immature immune cells in cord blood have less tendency to attack the recipient's tissues; thus, cord blood transplants have lower rejection rates and don't require as close a match between donor and recipient, meaning that more donors are available to a patient in need. Pioneered in the 1980s, cord blood transplants have successfully treated leukemia and a wide range of other blood diseases.

The use of cord blood may soon be overshadowed, however, by stem cell harvesting from peripheral blood (drawn from the blood vessels). Peripheral blood is more accessible than bone marrow, and with improvements in technique, it yields faster replacement of hematopoietic stem cells in the recipient.

---

pregnancies also result in HDN, but usually with mild effects. Mismatches in the Kell blood group are the third most common cause of HDN, followed by Kidd and Duffy mismatches.

▶▶▶ APPLY WHAT YOU KNOW

A baby with HDN typically has jaundice and an enlarged spleen. Explain these effects.

BEFORE YOU GO ON

Answer the following questions to test your understanding of the preceding section:

13. What are antibodies and antigens? How do they interact to cause a transfusion reaction?

14. What antibodies and antigens are present in people with each of the four ABO blood types?

15. Describe the causes, prevention, and treatment of HDN.

16. Why might someone be interested in determining a person's blood type other than ABO/Rh?

18.4   Leukocytes

Expected Learning Outcomes

When you have completed this section, you should be able to

a. explain the function of leukocytes in general and the individual role of each leukocyte type;

b. describe the appearance and relative abundance of each type of leukocyte;

c. describe the formation and life history of leukocytes; and

d. discuss the types, causes, and effects of leukocyte excesses and deficiencies.

18.4a Leukocyte Form and Function

Leukocytes, or **white blood cells (WBCs),** are the least abundant formed elements, totaling only 5,000 to 10,000 WBCs/μL. Yet we cannot live long without them, because they afford protection against infection and other diseases. WBCs are easily recognized in stained blood films because they have conspicuous nuclei that stain from light violet to dark purple with the most common blood stains. They are much more abundant in the body than their low number in blood films would suggest, because they spend only a few hours in the bloodstream, then migrate into the connective tissues and spend the rest of their lives there. It's as if the bloodstream were merely the subway that the WBCs take to work; in blood films, we see only the ones on their way to work, not the WBCs already at work in the tissues.

Leukocytes differ from erythrocytes in that they retain their organelles throughout life; thus, when viewed with the transmission electron microscope, they show a complex internal structure **(fig. 18.17).** Among their organelles are the usual instruments of protein synthesis—the nucleus, rough endoplasmic reticulum, ribosomes, and Golgi complex—for leukocytes must synthesize proteins in order to carry out their functions. Some of these proteins are packaged into lysosomes and other organelles, which appear as conspicuous cytoplasmic granules that distinguish one WBC type from another.

18.4b Types of Leukocytes

As outlined at the beginning of this chapter, there are five kinds of leukocytes. They are distinguished from each other by their relative size and abundance, the size and shape of their nuclei, the presence or absence of certain cytoplasmic granules, the coarseness and staining properties of those granules, and most importantly by their functions. Individual WBC types rise or fall in number in various disease conditions and physiological states.

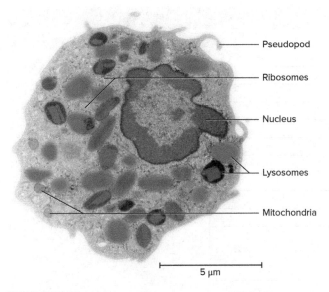

Pseudopod

Ribosomes

Nucleus

Lysosomes

Mitochondria

5 µm

FIGURE 18.17 The Structure of a Leukocyte (TEM). This example is an eosinophil. The lysosomes seen here in orange are the coarse pink granules seen in the eosinophil in table 18.6.

Scott Camazine/Alamy

All WBCs have lysosomes called **nonspecific granules** in the cytoplasm, also called *azurophilic*[18] *granules* because they absorb the blue or violet dyes of blood stains. Three of the five types—neutrophils, eosinophils, and basophils—are called **granulocytes** because they also have various kinds of **specific granules** that stain conspicuously and distinguish each cell type from the others. Basophils are named for the fact that their specific granules stain with methylene blue, a basic dye in a common blood-staining mixture called Wright's stain. Eosinophils are so named because they stain with eosin, an acidic dye in Wright's stain. The specific granules of neutrophils don't stain intensely with either basic or acidic stains. The colors in the following descriptions and table are those typically seen with Wright's stain, but may differ on slides you examine because of the use of other stains. Specific granules contain enzymes and other chemicals employed in defense against pathogens. The two remaining WBC types—monocytes and lymphocytes—are called **agranulocytes** because they lack specific granules. Nonspecific granules are inconspicuous to the light microscope, and these cells therefore have relatively clear-looking cytoplasm. **Table 18.6** shows the appearance and summarizes the characteristics and functions of each of the following WBC types.

Granulocytes

- **Neutrophils** (NEW-tro-fills) are the most abundant WBCs—generally about 4,150 cells/µL and constituting 60% to 70% of the circulating leukocytes. The nucleus is clearly visible and, in a mature neutrophil, typically consists of three to five lobes connected by slender nuclear strands. These strands are sometimes so delicate that they are scarcely visible, and

the neutrophil may seem as if it had multiple nuclei. Young neutrophils have an undivided band-shaped nucleus and are called *band cells.* Neutrophils are also called *polymorphonuclear leukocytes (PMNs)* because of their varied nuclear shapes. The cytoplasm contains fine reddish to violet specific granules, which contain lysozyme and other antimicrobial agents. The individual granules are barely visible with the light microscope, but their combined effect gives the cytoplasm a pale lilac color. Neutrophils are aggressively antibacterial cells. Their numbers rise—a condition called *neutrophilia*—in response to bacterial infections. They destroy bacteria in ways detailed in section 21.2b.

- **Eosinophils** (EE-oh-SIN-oh-fills) are harder to find in a blood film because they are only 2% to 4% of the WBC total, typically averaging about 170 cells/µL. Although relatively scanty in the blood, eosinophils are abundant in the mucous membranes of the respiratory, digestive, and lower urinary tracts. The eosinophil nucleus usually has two large lobes connected by a thin strand, and the cytoplasm has an abundance of coarse rosy to orange-colored specific granules. Eosinophils secrete chemicals that weaken or destroy relatively large parasites such as hookworms and tapeworms, too big for any one WBC to phagocytize. They also phagocytize and dispose of inflammatory chemicals, antigen–antibody complexes, and allergens (foreign antigens that trigger allergies). Allergies, parasitic infections, collagen diseases, and diseases of the spleen and central nervous system can cause an elevated eosinophil count called *eosinophilia.* The eosinophil count also fluctuates greatly from day to night, seasonally, and with the phase of the menstrual cycle.

- **Basophils** are the rarest of all formed elements. They average about 40 cells/µL and usually constitute less than 0.5% of the WBC count. They can be recognized mainly by an abundance of very coarse, dark violet specific granules. The nucleus is largely hidden from view by these granules, but is large, pale, and typically S- or U-shaped. Basophils secrete two chemicals that aid in the body's defense processes: (1) **histamine,** a vasodilator that widens the blood vessels, speeds the flow of blood to an injured tissue, and makes the blood vessels more permeable so that blood components such as neutrophils and clotting proteins can get into the connective tissues more quickly; and (2) **heparin,** an anticoagulant that inhibits blood clotting and thus promotes the mobility of other WBCs in the area. They also release chemical signals that attract eosinophils and neutrophils to a site of infection.

Agranulocytes

- **Lymphocytes** (LIM-fo-sites) are second to neutrophils in abundance and are thus quickly spotted when you examine a blood film. They average about 2,200 cells/µL and are 25% to 33% of the WBC count. They include the smallest WBCs; at 5 to 17 µm in diameter, they range from smaller than RBCs to two and a half times as large. They are sometimes classified into three size classes (table 18.6), but there are gradations between them. Medium and large lymphocytes are usually seen in fibrous connective tissues and only occasionally in the

---

[18]*azuro* = blue; *philic* = loving

TABLE 18.6	The White Blood Cells (Leukocytes)	
Neutrophils		
Differential count (% of WBCs)	60% to 70%	
Mean absolute count	4,150 cells/μL	
Diameter	9–12 μm	
Appearance		
Nucleus usually with 3–5 lobes in S- or C-shaped array		
Fine reddish to violet specific granules in cytoplasm		
Variations in Number		
Increase in bacterial infections		
Functions		
Phagocytize bacteria		
Release antimicrobial chemicals		Neutrophil 10 μm
Eosinophils		
Differential count (% of WBCs)	2% to 4%	
Mean absolute count	165 cells/μL	
Diameter	10–14 μm	
Appearance		
Nucleus usually has two large lobes connected by thin strand		
Large orange-pink specific granules in cytoplasm		
Variations in Number		
Fluctuate greatly from day to night, seasonally, and with phase of menstrual cycle		
Increases in parasitic infections, allergies, collagen diseases, and diseases of spleen and central nervous system		
Functions		Eosinophil 10 μm
Phagocytize antigen–antibody complexes, allergens, and inflammatory chemicals		
Release enzymes that weaken or destroy parasites such as worms		
Basophils		
Differential count (% of WBCs)	< 0.5%	
Mean absolute count	44 cells/μL	
Diameter	8–10 μm	
Appearance		
Nucleus large and U- to S-shaped, but typically pale and obscured from view		
Coarse, abundant, dark violet specific granules in cytoplasm		
Variations in Number		
Relatively stable		
Increase in chickenpox, sinusitis, diabetes mellitus, myxedema, and polycythemia		
Functions		Basophils 10 μm
Secrete histamine (a vasodilator), which increases blood flow to a tissue		
Secrete heparin (an anticoagulant), which promotes mobility of other WBCs by preventing clotting		

circulating blood (see fig. 18.1). The lymphocytes seen in blood films are mostly in the small size class. These are sometimes difficult to distinguish from basophils, but most basophils are conspicuously grainy, whereas

the lymphocyte nucleus is uniform or merely mottled. Basophils also lack the rim of clear cytoplasm seen in most lymphocytes. Large lymphocytes are sometimes difficult to distinguish from monocytes. The lymphocyte

TABLE 18.6	The White Blood Cells (Leukocytes) *(continued)*

Lymphocytes

Differential count (% of WBCs)	25% to 33%
Mean absolute count	2,185 cells/μL
Diameter	
Small class	5–8 μm
Medium class	10–12 μm
Large class	14–17 μm

Appearance

Nucleus round, ovoid, or slightly dimpled on one side, of uniform or mottled dark violet color

In small lymphocytes, nucleus fills nearly all of the cell and leaves only a scanty rim of clear, light blue cytoplasm.

In larger lymphocytes, cytoplasm is more abundant; large lymphocytes may be hard to differentiate from monocytes.

Variations in Number

Increase in diverse infections and immune responses

Functions

Several functional classes usually indistinguishable by light microscopy

Destroy cancer cells, cells infected with viruses, and foreign cells

Present antigens to activate other cells of immune system

Coordinate actions of other immune cells

Secrete antibodies

Serve in immune memory

Lymphocyte — 10 μm

Monocytes

Differential count (% of WBCs)	3% to 8%
Mean absolute count	456 cells/μL
Diameter	12–15 μm

Appearance

Nucleus ovoid, kidney-shaped, or horseshoe-shaped; violet

Abundant cytoplasm with sparse, fine nonspecific granules

Sometimes very large with stellate or polygonal shapes

Variations in Number

Increase in viral infections and inflammation

Functions

Differentiate into macrophages (large phagocytic cells of the tissues)

Phagocytize pathogens, dead neutrophils, and debris of dead cells

Present antigens to activate other cells of immune system

Monocyte — 10 μm

Photos: (Neutrophil, Eosinophil, Lymphocyte): Alvin Telser/McGraw-Hill Education; **(Basophils):** LindseyRN/Shutterstock; **(Monocyte):** Victor P. Eroschenko

nucleus is round, ovoid, or slightly dimpled on one side, and usually stains dark violet. In small lymphocytes, it fills nearly the entire cell and leaves only a narrow rim of light blue cytoplasm, often barely detectable, around the cell perimeter. The cytoplasm is more abundant in medium and large lymphocytes. There are several subclasses of lympho-

cytes with different immune functions (see section 21.1b), but they cannot be distinguished by microscopic examination of blood films. Collectively, they destroy cells that have been infected with viruses or turned malignant, and foreign cells (including parasites) that have been introduced into the body; they secrete chemicals that communicate with other

WBCs and coordinate their actions; they present antigens to activate immune responses; they give rise to the cells that secrete antibodies; and they provide long-term immunity to pathogens.

- **Monocytes** (MON-oh-sites) are usually the largest WBCs seen on a blood slide, often two or three times the diameter of an RBC. They average about 460 cells/μL and about 3% to 8% of the WBC count. The nucleus is large and clearly visible, often a relatively light violet, and typically ovoid, kidney-shaped, or horseshoe-shaped. The cytoplasm is abundant and contains sparse, fine granules. In prepared blood films, monocytes often assume sharply angular to spiky shapes (see fig. 18.1). The monocyte count rises in inflammation and viral infections. Monocytes go to work only after leaving the bloodstream and transforming into large tissue cells called **macrophages** (MAC-ro-fay-jez). Macrophages are highly phagocytic cells that consume dead or dying host and foreign cells, pathogenic chemicals and microorganisms, and other foreign matter equivalent to as much as 25% of their own volume per hour. They also chop up or process foreign antigens and display fragments of them on the cell surface to alert the immune system to the presence of a pathogen. Thus, they and a few other cells are called *antigen-presenting cells (APCs)*. The functions of macrophages are further detailed in chapter 21.

18.4c The Leukocyte Life History

Leukopoiesis (LOO-co-poy-EE-sis), the production of white blood cells, begins with the same hematopoietic stem cells (HSCs) as erythropoiesis. Some HSCs differentiate into distinct types of colony-forming units (CFUs) and then go on to produce the following cell lines (yellow zone in **fig. 18.18**), each of them now irreversibly committed to a certain outcome.

1. *Myeloblasts,* which ultimately differentiate into the three types of granulocytes (neutrophils, eosinophils, and basophils)
2. *Monoblasts,* which look identical to myeloblasts but lead ultimately to monocytes
3. *Lymphoblasts,* which produce all lymphocyte types

CFUs have receptors for *colony-stimulating factors (CSFs).* Mature lymphocytes and macrophages secrete several types of CSFs in response to infections and other immune challenges. Each CSF stimulates a different WBC type to develop in response to specific needs. Thus, a bacterial infection may trigger the production of neutrophils, whereas an allergy stimulates eosinophil production, each process working through its own CSF.

The red bone marrow stores granulocytes and monocytes until they are needed and contains 10 to 20 times more of these cells than the circulating blood does. Lymphocytes begin developing in the bone marrow but don't stay there. Some types mature there and others migrate to the thymus to complete their development. Mature lymphocytes from both locations then colonize the spleen, lymph nodes, and other lymphatic organs and tissues.

Circulating leukocytes don't stay in the blood for very long. Granulocytes circulate for 4 to 8 hours and then migrate into the tissues, where they live another 4 or 5 days. Monocytes travel in the blood for 10 to 20 hours, then migrate into the tissues and transform into a variety of macrophages, which can live as long as a few years. Lymphocytes, responsible for long-term immunity, survive from a few weeks to decades; they leave the bloodstream for the tissues and eventually enter the lymphatic system, which empties them back into the bloodstream. Thus, they are continually recycled from blood to tissue fluid to lymph and back to the blood.

When leukocytes die, they are generally phagocytized and digested by macrophages. Dead neutrophils, however, are responsible for the creamy color of pus, and are sometimes disposed of by the rupture of a blister onto the skin surface.

▶▶▶ APPLY WHAT YOU KNOW

It is sometimes written that RBCs do not live as long as WBCs because RBCs do not have a nucleus and therefore cannot repair and maintain themselves. Explain the flaw in this argument.

18.4d Leukocyte Disorders

The total WBC count is normally 5,000 to 10,000 WBCs/μL. A count below this range, called **leukopenia**[19] (LOO-co-PEE-nee-uh), is seen in lead, arsenic, and mercury poisoning; radiation sickness; and such infectious diseases as measles, mumps, chickenpox, polio, influenza, typhoid fever, and AIDS. It can also be produced by glucocorticoids, anticancer drugs, and immunosuppressant drugs given to organ-transplant patients. Since WBCs are protective cells, leukopenia presents an elevated risk of infection and cancer. A count above 10,000 WBCs/μL, called **leukocytosis,**[20] usually indicates infection, allergy, or other diseases but can also occur in response to dehydration or emotional disturbances. More useful than a total WBC count is a *differential WBC count,* which identifies what percentage of the total WBC count consists of each type of leukocyte (see Deeper Insight 18.4).

Leukemia is a cancer of the hematopoietic tissues that usually produces an extraordinarily high number of circulating leukocytes and their precursors **(fig. 18.19)**. Leukemia is classified as myeloid or lymphoid, acute or chronic. **Myeloid leukemia** is marked by uncontrolled granulocyte production, whereas **lymphoid leukemia** involves uncontrolled lymphocyte or monocyte production. **Acute leukemia** appears suddenly, progresses rapidly, and causes death within a few months if it is not treated. **Chronic leukemia** develops more slowly and may go undetected for many months; if untreated, the typical survival time is about 3 years. Both myeloid and lymphoid leukemia occur in acute and chronic forms. The greatest success in treatment and cure has been with acute lymphoblastic leukemia, the most common type of childhood cancer. Treatment employs chemotherapy and marrow transplants along with the control of side effects such as anemia, hemorrhaging, and infection.

As leukemic cells proliferate, they replace normal bone marrow and a person suffers from a deficiency of normal granulocytes,

---

[19]*leuko* = white; *penia* = deficiency
[20]*leuko* = white; *cyt* = cell; *osis* = condition

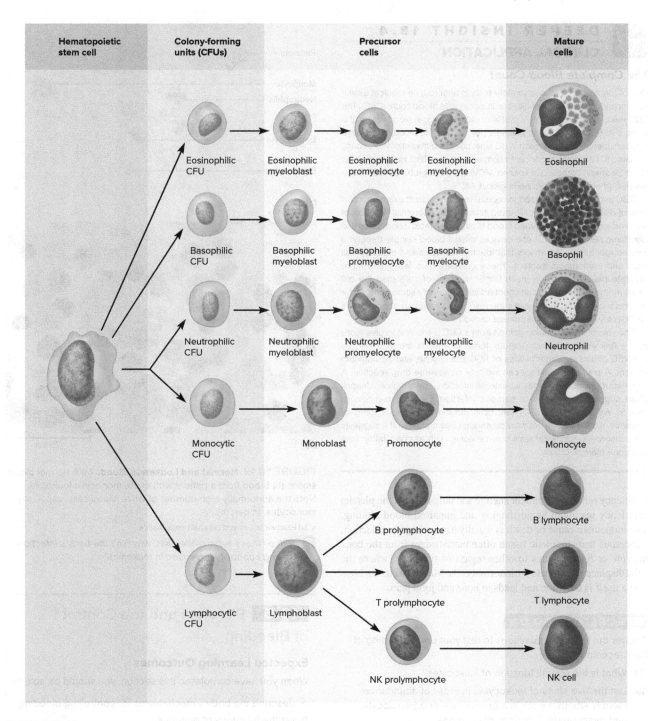

Hematopoietic stem cell	Colony-forming units (CFUs)	Precursor cells			Mature cells
	Eosinophilic CFU	Eosinophilic myeloblast	Eosinophilic promyelocyte	Eosinophilic myelocyte	Eosinophil
	Basophilic CFU	Basophilic myeloblast	Basophilic promyelocyte	Basophilic myelocyte	Basophil
	Neutrophilic CFU	Neutrophilic myeloblast	Neutrophilic promyelocyte	Neutrophilic myelocyte	Neutrophil
	Monocytic CFU	Monoblast	Promonocyte		Monocyte
	Lymphocytic CFU	Lymphoblast	B prolymphocyte		B lymphocyte
			T prolymphocyte		T lymphocyte
			NK prolymphocyte		NK cell

FIGURE 18.18 Leukopoiesis. Stages in the development of white blood cells. The hematopoietic stem cell at the left also is the ultimate source of red blood cells (see fig. 18.6) and platelet-producing cells.

Explain the meaning and relevance of the combining form myelo- *seen in so many of these cell names.*

erythrocytes, and platelets. Although enormous numbers of leukocytes are produced and spill over into the bloodstream, they don't provide the usual protective functions of WBCs. They are like an army of children, present in vast numbers but too immature to perform a useful defensive role. The deficiency of competent WBCs leaves the patient vulnerable to **opportunistic infection**— the establishment of pathogenic organisms that usually cannot get a foothold in people with healthy immune systems. The RBC

DEEPER INSIGHT 18.4

CLINICAL APPLICATION

The Complete Blood Count

One of the most common laboratory tests in both routine medical examinations and the diagnosis of disease is a *complete blood count (CBC)*. The CBC yields a highly informative profile of data on multiple blood values: the number of RBCs, WBCs, and platelets per microliter of blood; the relative numbers (percentages) of each WBC type, called a *differential WBC count;* hematocrit; hemoglobin concentration; and various *RBC indices* such as RBC size *(mean corpuscular volume, MCV)* and hemoglobin concentration per RBC *(mean corpuscular hemoglobin, MCH)*.

RBC and WBC counts used to require the microscopic examination of films of diluted blood on a calibrated slide, and a differential WBC count required examination of stained blood films. Today, most laboratories use *electronic cell counters*. These devices draw a blood sample through a very narrow tube with sensors that identify cell types and measure cell sizes and hemoglobin content. These counters give faster and more accurate results based on much larger numbers of cells than the old visual methods. However, cell counters still misidentify some cells, and a medical technologist must review the results for suspicious abnormalities and identify cells that the instrument cannot.

The wealth of information gained from a CBC is too vast to give more than a few examples here. Various forms of anemia are indicated by low RBC counts or abnormalities of RBC size, shape, and hemoglobin content. A platelet deficiency can indicate an adverse drug reaction. A high neutrophil count suggests bacterial infection, and a high eosinophil count suggests an allergy or parasitic infection. Elevated numbers of specific WBC types or WBC stem cells can indicate various forms of leukemia. If a CBC does not provide enough information or if it suggests other disorders, additional tests may be done, such as coagulation time and bone marrow biopsy.

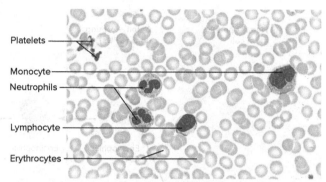

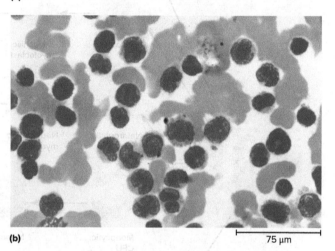

FIGURE 18.19 Normal and Leukemic Blood. (a) A normal blood smear. (b) Blood from a patient with acute monocytic leukemia. Note the abnormally high number of white blood cells, especially monocytes, in part (b).

a: Ed Reschke; **b:** Leonard Lessin/Science Source

? *With all these extra white cells, why isn't the body's infection-fighting capability increased in leukemia?*

---

deficiency renders the patient anemic and fatigued, and the platelet deficiency results in hemorrhaging and impaired blood clotting. The immediate cause of death is usually hemorrhage or infection. Cancerous hematopoietic tissue often metastasizes from the bone marrow or lymph nodes to other organs of the body, where the cells displace or compete with normal cells. Metastasis to the bone tissue itself is common and leads to bone and joint pain.

BEFORE YOU GO ON

Answer the following questions to test your understanding of the preceding section:

17. What is the overall function of leukocytes?

18. List the five kinds of leukocytes in order of abundance, identify whether each is a granulocyte or agranulocyte, and describe the functions of each one.

19. What does leukopoiesis have in common with erythropoiesis? How does it differ?

20. What can cause an abnormally high or low WBC count?

21. Suppose myeloblasts began multiplying out of control, but their subsequent development remained normal. What types of mature WBCs would be produced in excess? What types would not?

18.5 Platelets and the Control of Bleeding

Expected Learning Outcomes

When you have completed this section, you should be able to

a. describe the body's mechanisms for controlling bleeding;

b. list the functions of platelets;

c. describe two reaction pathways that produce blood clots;

d. explain what happens to blood clots when they are no longer needed;

e. explain what keeps blood from clotting in the absence of injury; and

f. describe some disorders of blood clotting.

Circulatory systems developed very early in animal evolution, and with them evolved mechanisms for stopping leaks, which are potentially fatal. **Hemostasis**[21] is the cessation of bleeding. Although hemostatic mechanisms may not stop a hemorrhage from a large blood vessel, they are quite effective at closing breaks in small ones. Platelets play multiple roles in hemostasis, so we begin with a consideration of their form and function.

18.5a Platelet Form and Function

Platelets are not cells but small fragments of marrow cells called *megakaryocytes*. They are the second most abundant formed elements, after erythrocytes; a normal platelet count in blood from a fingerstick ranges from 130,000 to 400,000 platelets/μL (averaging about 250,000). The platelet count can vary greatly, however, under different physiological conditions and in blood samples taken from various places in the body. In spite of their numbers, platelets are so small (2 to 4 μm in diameter) that they contribute even less than WBCs to the blood volume.

Platelets have a complex internal structure that includes lysosomes, mitochondria, microtubules, and microfilaments; **granules** filled with platelet secretions; and a system of channels called the **open canalicular system,** which opens onto the platelet surface **(fig. 18.20a).** They have no nucleus. When activated, they form pseudopods and are capable of ameboid movement.

Despite their small size, platelets have a greater variety of functions than any of the true blood cells:

- They secrete *vasoconstrictors,* chemicals that stimulate spasmodic constriction of broken vessels and thereby help to reduce blood loss.

- They stick together to form temporary *platelet plugs* that seal small breaks in injured blood vessels.

- They secrete *procoagulants,* or clotting factors, which promote blood clotting.

- They initiate the formation of a clot-dissolving enzyme that dissolves blood clots that have outlasted their usefulness.

- They secrete chemicals that attract neutrophils and monocytes to sites of inflammation.

- They internalize and destroy bacteria.

- They secrete *growth factors* that stimulate mitosis in fibroblasts and smooth muscle and thereby help to maintain and repair blood vessels.

18.5b Platelet Production

The production of platelets is a division of hematopoiesis called **thrombopoiesis** (THROM-bo-poy-EE-sis). (Platelets are occasionally called *thrombocytes.*[22]) Thrombopoiesis is stimulated by a hormone from the liver and kidneys called *thrombopoietin* (THROM-bo-POY-eh-tin). Some hematopoietic stem cells develop receptors for thrombopoietin and, under its influence, become *megakaryoblasts*—cells committed to the platelet-producing line.

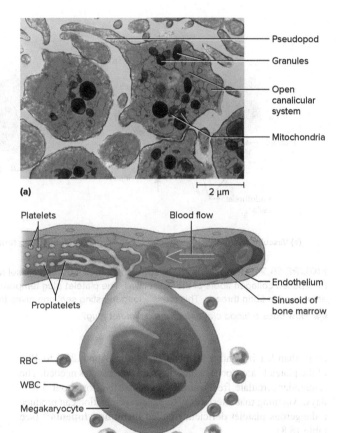

FIGURE 18.20 Platelets. (a) Structure of blood platelets (TEM). (b) Platelets being produced by the shearing of proplatelets from a megakaryocyte. Note the sizes of the megakaryocyte and platelets relative to RBCs and WBCs. **APR**

a: NIBSC/Science Photo Library/Science Source

The megakaryoblast duplicates its DNA repeatedly without undergoing nuclear or cytoplasmic division. The result is a **megakaryocyte**[23] (MEG-ah-CAR-ee-oh-site), a gigantic cell up to 150 μm in diameter, visible to the naked eye, with a huge multilobed nucleus and multiple sets of chromosomes **(fig. 18.20b).** Most megakaryocytes live in the red bone marrow adjacent to blood-filled spaces called *sinusoids,* lined with a thin simple squamous epithelium called the *endothelium* (see fig. 21.8). Recent animal research has discovered, however, that megakaryocytes migrate freely between the lungs and bone marrow and produce most platelets while in the lungs. Whether this is also true in humans awaits confirmation.

A megakaryocyte sprouts long tendrils called *proplatelets* that protrude through the endothelium into the blood of the sinusoid. The blood flow shears off the proplatelets, which break up into platelets as they travel in the bloodstream. Much of this breakup is thought to occur when they pass through the small vessels of the lungs, because blood counts show more proplatelets entering the

---

[21]*hemo* = blood; *stasis* = stability
[22]*thrombo* = clotting; *cyte* = cell

[23]*mega* = giant; *karyo* = nucleus; *cyte* = cell

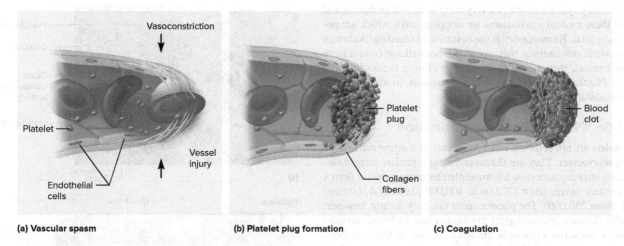

| (a) Vascular spasm | (b) Platelet plug formation | (c) Coagulation |

FIGURE 18.21 Hemostasis. (a) Vasoconstriction of a broken vessel reduces bleeding. (b) A platelet plug forms as platelets adhere to exposed collagen fibers of the vessel wall. The platelet plug temporarily seals the break. (c) A blood clot forms as platelets become enmeshed in fibrin threads. This forms a longer-lasting seal and gives the vessel a chance to repair itself.

❓ *How does a blood clot differ from a platelet plug?*

lungs than leaving and more platelets exiting. About 25% to 40% of the platelets are stored in the spleen and released as needed. The remainder circulate freely in the blood and live for about 5 to 6 days. Anything that interferes with platelet production can produce a dangerous platelet deficiency called **thrombocytopenia**[24] (see table 18.8).

18.5c Hemostasis

There are three hemostatic mechanisms—*vascular spasm, platelet plug formation,* and *blood clotting (coagulation)* (**fig. 18.21**). Platelets play an important role in all three.

Vascular Spasm

The most immediate protection against blood loss is **vascular spasm,** a prompt constriction of the broken vessel. Several things trigger this reaction. An injury stimulates pain receptors, some of which directly innervate nearby blood vessels and cause them to constrict. This effect lasts only a few minutes, but other mechanisms take over by the time it subsides. Injury to the smooth muscle of the blood vessel itself causes a longer-lasting vasoconstriction, and platelets release serotonin, a chemical vasoconstrictor. Thus, the vascular spasm is maintained long enough for the other two hemostatic mechanisms to come into play.

Platelet Plug Formation

Platelets don't adhere to the endothelium that lines healthy blood vessels and the heart. The endothelium is normally very smooth and coated with **prostacyclin,** a platelet repellent. When a vessel is broken, however, collagen fibers of its wall are exposed to the blood. Upon contact with collagen or other rough surfaces, platelets grow long spiny pseudopods that adhere to the vessel and to other platelets; the pseudopods then contract and draw the walls of the vessel together. The mass of platelets thus formed, called a **platelet plug,** may reduce or stop minor bleeding. The platelet plug is looser and more delicate than the blood clot to follow; for this reason, a bleeding injury should be blotted with absorbent paper rather than wiped.

As platelets aggregate, they undergo **degranulation**—the exocytosis of their cytoplasmic granules and release of factors that promote hemostasis. Among these are serotonin, a vasoconstrictor; adenosine diphosphate (ADP), which attracts more platelets to the area and stimulates their degranulation; and **thromboxane A$_2$,** an eicosanoid that promotes platelet aggregation, degranulation, and vasoconstriction. Thus, a positive feedback cycle is activated that can quickly seal a small break in a blood vessel.

Coagulation

Coagulation (clotting) of the blood is the last but most effective defense against bleeding. It is important for the blood to clot quickly when a vessel has broken, but equally important for it not to clot in the absence of vessel damage. Because of this delicate balance, coagulation is one of the most complex processes in the body, involving over 30 chemical reactions. It is presented here in a very simplified form.

Perhaps clotting is best understood if we first consider its goal. The objective is to convert the plasma protein fibrinogen into **fibrin,** a sticky protein that adheres to the walls of a vessel. As blood cells and platelets arrive, they stick to the fibrin like insects in a spider web (**fig. 18.22,** inset). The resulting mass of fibrin, blood cells, and platelets ideally seals the break in the blood vessel. The complexity of clotting lies in how the fibrin is formed.

[24]*thrombo* = clotting; *cyto* = cell; *penia* = deficiency

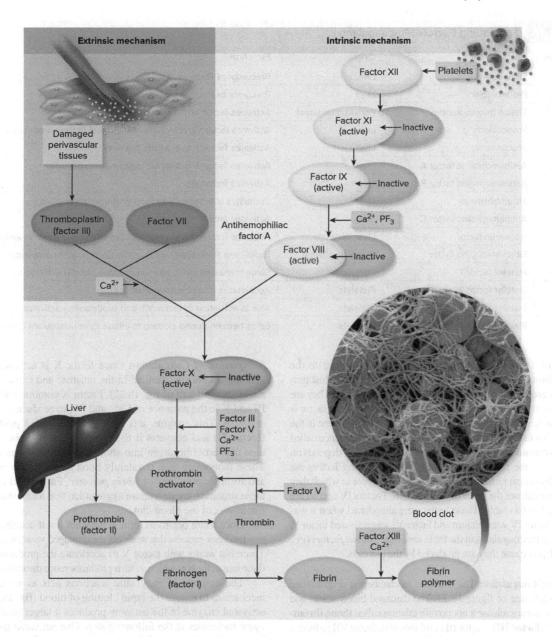

FIGURE 18.22 The Pathways of Coagulation. Most clotting factors act as enzymes that convert the next factor from an inactive form to an active form. One enzyme molecule at any given level activates many enzyme molecules at the next level down, so the overall effect becomes amplified at each step. Inset: Erythrocytes trapped in a mesh of sticky fibrin polymer.

(inset): Steve Gschmeissner/Science Photo Library/Getty Images

❓ *After you read about hemophilia C later in section 18.5f, explain whether it would affect the extrinsic mechanism, the intrinsic mechanism, or both.*

There are two reaction pathways to coagulation. One of them, the **extrinsic mechanism** (left side of fig. 18.22), is initiated by clotting factors released by the damaged blood vessel and perivascular[25] tissues. The word *extrinsic* refers to the fact that these factors come from sources external to the blood itself. Blood may

also clot, however, without these tissue factors—for example, when platelets adhere to a fatty plaque of atherosclerosis or to a test tube. The reaction pathway in this case is called the **intrinsic mechanism** (right side of the figure) because it uses only clotting factors found in the blood itself. In most cases of bleeding, both the extrinsic and intrinsic mechanisms work simultaneously and interact with each other to achieve hemostasis.

[25]*peri* = around; *vas* = vessel; *cular* = pertaining to

TABLE 18.7	Clotting Factors (Procoagulants)		
Number	Name	Origin	Function
I	Fibrinogen	Liver	Precursor of fibrin
II	Prothrombin	Liver	Precursor of thrombin
III	Tissue thromboplastin	Perivascular tissue	Activates factor VII
V	Proaccelerin	Liver	Activates factor VII; combines with factor X to form prothrombin activator
VII	Proconvertin	Liver	Activates factor X in extrinsic pathway
VIII	Antihemophiliac factor A	Liver	Activates factor X in intrinsic pathway
IX	Antihemophiliac factor B	Liver	Activates factor VIII
X	Thrombokinase	Liver	Combines with factor V to form prothrombin activator
XI	Antihemophiliac factor C	Liver	Activates factor IX
XII	Hageman factor	Liver, platelets	Activates factor XI and plasmin; converts prekallikrein to kallikrein
XIII	Fibrin-stabilizing factor	Platelets, plasma	Cross-links fibrin filaments to make fibrin polymer and stabilize clot
PF_1	Platelet factor 1	Platelets	Same role as factor V; also accelerates platelet activation
PF_2	Platelet factor 2	Platelets	Accelerates thrombin formation
PF_3	Platelet factor 3	Platelets	Aids in activation of factor VIII and prothrombin activator
PF_4	Platelet factor 4	Platelets	Binds heparin during clotting to inhibit its anticoagulant effect

Clotting factors are called **procoagulants,** in contrast to the **anticoagulants** discussed later (see Deeper Insight 18.6). Most procoagulants are proteins produced by the liver (**table 18.7).** They are always present in the plasma in inactive form, but when one factor is activated, it functions as an enzyme that activates the next one in the pathway. That factor activates the next, and so on, in a sequence called a **reaction cascade**—a series of reactions, each of which depends on the product of the preceding one. Many of the clotting factors are identified by roman numerals, which indicate the order in which they were discovered, not the order of the reactions. Factors IV and VI are not included in this table. These terms were abandoned when it was found that factor IV was calcium and factor VI was activated factor V. The last four procoagulants in the table are called *platelet factors* (PF_1 through PF_4) because they are produced by the platelets.

Initiation of Coagulation The extrinsic mechanism is diagrammed on the top left side of figure 18.22. The damaged blood vessel and perivascular tissues release a lipoprotein mixture called **tissue thromboplastin**[26] **(factor III).** Factor III combines with factor VII to form a complex that, in the presence of Ca^{2+}, activates factor X. The extrinsic and intrinsic pathways differ only in how they arrive at active factor X. Therefore, before examining their common pathway from factor X to the end, let's consider how the intrinsic pathway reaches this step.

The intrinsic mechanism is diagrammed on the top right side of figure 18.22. Everything needed to initiate it is present in the plasma or platelets. When platelets degranulate, they release factor XII (Hageman factor, named for the patient in whom it was discovered). Through a cascade of reactions, this leads to activated factors XI, IX, and VIII, in that order—each serving as an enzyme that catalyzes the next step—and finally to factor X. This pathway also requires Ca^{2+} and PF_3.

Completion of Coagulation Once factor X is activated, the remaining events are identical in the intrinsic and extrinsic mechanisms (bottom half of fig. 18.22). Factor X combines with factors III and V in the presence of Ca^{2+} and PF_3 to produce *prothrombin activator*. This enzyme acts on a globulin called **prothrombin (factor II)** and converts it to the enzyme **thrombin.** Thrombin then converts fibrinogen into shorter strands of *fibrin monomer*. These monomers then covalently bond to each other end to end and form longer fibers of *fibrin polymer*. Factor XIII cross-links these strands to create a dense aggregation that forms the structural framework of the blood clot.

Once a clot begins to form, it launches a self-accelerating positive feedback process that seals off the damaged vessel more quickly. Thrombin works with factor V to accelerate the production of prothrombin activator, which in turn produces more thrombin.

The cascade of enzymatic reactions acts as an amplifying mechanism to ensure the rapid clotting of blood (**fig. 18.23).** Each activated enzyme in the pathway produces a larger number of enzyme molecules at the following step. One activated molecule of factor XII at the start of the intrinsic pathway, for example, very quickly produces thousands if not millions of fibrin molecules. Note the similarity of this process to the *signal amplification* that occurs in hormone action (see fig. 17.21).

Notice that the extrinsic mechanism requires fewer steps to activate factor X than the intrinsic mechanism does; it is a "shortcut" to coagulation. It takes 3 to 6 minutes for a clot to form by the intrinsic pathway but only 15 seconds or so by the extrinsic pathway. For this reason, when a small wound bleeds, you can stop the bleeding sooner by massaging the site. This releases thromboplastin from the perivascular tissues and activates or speeds up the extrinsic pathway.

After a clot has formed, spinous pseudopods of the platelets adhere to strands of fibrin and contract. This pulls on the fibrin

[26]*thrombo* = clot; *plast* = forming; *in* = substance

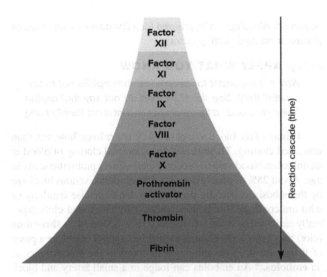

FIGURE 18.23 The Reaction Cascade in Blood Clotting. Each clotting factor produces many molecules of the next one, so the number of active clotting factors increases rapidly and a large amount of fibrin is quickly formed. The example shown here is for the intrinsic mechanism.

❓ *How does this compare with signal amplification in hormone action (compare fig. 17.21)?*

threads and draws the edges of the broken vessel together, like a drawstring closing a purse. Through this process of **clot retraction,** the clot becomes more compact within about 30 minutes.

A number of laboratory tests are used to evaluate the efficiency of coagulation. Normally, the bleeding of a fingerstick should stop within 2 to 3 minutes, and a sample of blood in a clean test tube should clot within 15 minutes. **Bleeding time** is most precisely measured by the *Ivy method*—inflating a blood pressure cuff on the arm to 40 mm Hg, making a 1 mm deep incision in the forearm, and measuring the time for it to stop bleeding. Normally it should stop in 1 to 9 minutes. Other techniques are available that can separately assess the effectiveness of the intrinsic and extrinsic mechanisms.

18.5d The Fate of Blood Clots

Once a clot has formed, a process of local tissue repair begins. Platelets and endothelial cells secrete a mitotic stimulant named **platelet-derived growth factor (PDGF).** PDGF stimulates fibroblasts and smooth muscle cells to multiply and repair the damaged blood vessel. Fibroblasts also invade the clot and produce fibrous connective tissue, which helps to strengthen and seal the vessel while the repairs take place.

Eventually, tissue repair is completed and the clot must be disposed of. **Fibrinolysis,** the dissolution of a clot, is achieved by a small cascade of reactions with a positive feedback component **(fig. 18.24).** In addition to promoting clotting, factor XII catalyzes the formation of a plasma enzyme called **kallikrein** (KAL-ih-KREE-in). Kallikrein, in turn, converts the inactive protein *plasminogen* into **plasmin,** a fibrin-dissolving enzyme that breaks up the clot. Thrombin also activates plasmin, and plasmin indirectly promotes the formation of more kallikrein, thus completing a positive feedback loop.

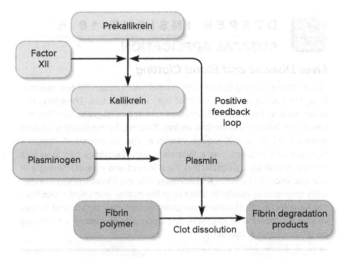

FIGURE 18.24 The Mechanism for Dissolving Blood Clots. Prekallikrein is converted to kallikrein. Kallikrein is an enzyme that catalyzes the formation of plasmin. Plasmin is an enzyme that dissolves the blood clot.

18.5e Prevention of Inappropriate Clotting

Precise controls are required to prevent coagulation when it isn't needed. These include the following:

- **Platelet repulsion.** As noted earlier, platelets don't adhere to the smooth prostacyclin-coated endothelium of healthy blood vessels.

- **Dilution.** Small amounts of thrombin form spontaneously in the plasma, but at normal rates of blood flow, the thrombin is diluted so quickly that a clot has little chance to form. If flow decreases, however, enough thrombin can accumulate to cause clotting. This can happen in circulatory shock, for example. When output from the heart is diminished and circulation slows down, widespread clotting throughout the circulatory system may occur.

- **Anticoagulants.** Thrombin formation is suppressed by anticoagulants in the plasma. **Antithrombin,** secreted by the liver, deactivates thrombin before it can act on fibrinogen. **Heparin,** secreted by basophils and mast cells, interferes with the formation of prothrombin activator, blocks the action of thrombin on fibrinogen, and promotes the action of antithrombin. Heparin is given by injection to patients with abnormal clotting tendencies.

18.5f Clotting Disorders

In a process as complex as coagulation, it's not surprising that things can go wrong. Clotting deficiencies can result from causes as diverse as malnutrition, leukemia, and gallstones (see Deeper Insight 18.5).

A deficiency of any clotting factor can shut down the coagulation cascade. This happens in **hemophilia,** a family of hereditary diseases characterized by deficiencies of one factor or another. Because of the sex-linked recessive mechanism of heredity, hemophilia occurs predominantly in males. They can inherit it only from their mothers, however, as happened with the descendants of Queen Victoria.

DEEPER INSIGHT 18.5

CLINICAL APPLICATION

Liver Disease and Blood Clotting

Proper blood clotting depends on normal liver function for two reasons. First, the liver synthesizes most of the clotting factors. Therefore, diseases such as hepatitis, cirrhosis, and cancer that degrade liver function result in a deficiency of clotting factors. Second, the synthesis of clotting factors II, VII, IX, and X require vitamin K. The absorption of vitamin K from the diet requires bile, a liver secretion. Gallstones can lead to a clotting deficiency by obstructing the bile duct and thus interfering with bile secretion and vitamin K absorption. Efficient blood clotting is especially important in childbirth, since both the mother and infant bleed from the trauma of birth. Therefore, pregnant women may be advised to take vitamin K supplements to ensure fast clotting, and newborn infants may be given vitamin K injections.

The lack of factor VIII causes *classical hemophilia (hemophilia A),* which accounts for about 83% of cases and afflicts 1 in 5,000 males worldwide. Lack of factor IX causes *hemophilia B,* which accounts for 15% of cases and occurs in about 1 out of 30,000 males. Factors VIII and IX are therefore known as *antihemophilic factors A* and *B.* A rarer form called *hemophilia C* (factor XI deficiency) is autosomal and not sex-linked, so it occurs equally in both sexes.

Before purified factor VIII became available in the 1960s, more than half of those with hemophilia died before age 5 and only 10% lived to age 21. Physical exertion causes bleeding into the muscles and joints. Excruciating pain and eventual joint immobility can result from intramuscular and joint **hematomas**[27] (masses of clotted blood in the tissues). Hemophilia varies in severity, however. Half of the normal level of clotting factor is enough to prevent the symptoms, and the symptoms are mild even in individuals with as little as 30% of the normal amount. Such cases may go undetected even into

[27] *hemato* = blood; *oma* = mass

adulthood. Bleeding can be relieved for a few days by transfusion of plasma or purified clotting factors.

▶▶▶ APPLY WHAT YOU KNOW

Why is it important for people with hemophilia not to use aspirin? (Hint: See fig. 17.24, and do not say that aspirin "thins the blood," a figure of speech that is not literally true.)

Failure of the blood to clot takes far fewer lives, however, than unwanted clotting. **Thrombosis,** the abnormal clotting of blood in an unbroken blood vessel, becomes increasingly problematic in old age. About 25% of people over age 50 experience venous blockage by thrombosis, especially people who don't exercise regularly or who are confined to a bed or wheelchair. The blood clots especially easily in the veins, where blood flow is slowest. A **thrombus** (clot) may grow large enough to obstruct a small vessel, or a piece of it may break loose and begin to travel in the bloodstream as an **embolus.**[28] An embolus can lodge in a small artery and block blood flow from that point on. If that vessel supplies vital tissue of the heart, brain, lung, or kidney, *infarction* (tissue death) may result. About 650,000 Americans die annually of *thromboembolism* (traveling blood clots) in the cerebral, coronary, and pulmonary arteries. Most strokes and heart attacks are due to thrombosis, and pulmonary failure often results from thromboembolism.

Thrombosis is more likely to occur in veins than in arteries because blood flows more slowly in the veins and doesn't dilute thrombin and fibrin as rapidly. Most venous blood flows directly to the heart and then to the lungs. Therefore, blood clots arising in the limbs commonly lodge in the lungs and cause *pulmonary embolism.* When blood cannot circulate freely through the lungs, it cannot receive oxygen and a person may die of hypoxia.

Table 18.8 describes some additional disorders of the blood. The effects of aging on the blood are described in section 29.4a.

[28] *em* = in, within; *bolus* = ball, mass

TABLE 18.8	Some Disorders of the Blood
Disseminated intravascular coagulation (DIC)	Widespread clotting within unbroken vessels, limited to one organ or occurring throughout the body. Usually triggered by septicemia but also occurs when blood circulation slows markedly (as in cardiac arrest). Marked by widespread hemorrhaging, congestion of the vessels with clotted blood, and tissue necrosis in blood-deprived organs.
Infectious mononucleosis	Infection of B lymphocytes with Epstein–Barr virus, most commonly in adolescents and young adults. Usually transmitted by exchange of saliva, as in kissing. Causes fever, fatigue, sore throat, inflamed lymph nodes, and leukocytosis. Usually self-limiting and resolves within a few weeks.
Septicemia	Bacteremia (bacteria in the bloodstream) accompanying infection elsewhere in the body. Often causes fever, chills, and nausea, and may cause DIC or septic shock.
Thalassemia	A group of hereditary anemias most common in Greeks, Italians, and others of Mediterranean descent; shows a deficiency or absence of alpha or beta hemoglobin and RBC counts that may be less than 2 million/µL.
Thrombocytopenia	A platelet count below 100,000/mL. Causes include bone marrow destruction by radiation, drugs, poisons, or leukemia. Signs include small hemorrhagic spots in the skin or hematomas in response to minor trauma.

You can find other hematologic disorders described in the following places:

Hypoproteinemia in Deeper Insight 18.1; *anemia, polycythemia, hypoxemia,* and *sickle-cell disease* in section 18.2e; *transfusion reactions* and *hemolytic disease of the newborn* in sections 18.3b and 18.3d; *leukemia, leukocytosis,* and *leukopenia* in section 18.4d; and *hematoma, hemophilia, thrombosis,* and *thromboembolism* in section 18.5f.

BEFORE YOU GO ON

Answer the following questions to test your understanding of the preceding section:

22. What are the three basic mechanisms of hemostasis?

23. How do the extrinsic and intrinsic mechanisms of coagulation differ? What do they have in common?

24. In what respect does blood clotting represent a negative feedback loop? What part of it is a positive feedback loop?

25. Describe some of the mechanisms that prevent clotting in undamaged vessels.

26. Describe a common source and effect of pulmonary embolism.

DEEPER INSIGHT 18.6

CLINICAL APPLICATION

Clinical Management of Blood Clotting

For many cardiovascular patients, the goal of treatment is to prevent clotting or to dissolve clots that have already formed. Several strategies employ inorganic salts and products of bacteria, plants, and animals with anticoagulant and clot-dissolving effects.

Preventing Clots from Forming

Since calcium is an essential requirement for blood clotting, blood samples can be kept from clotting by adding a few crystals of sodium oxalate, sodium citrate, or EDTA[29]—salts that bind calcium ions and prevent them from participating in the coagulation reactions. Blood-collection equipment such as hematocrit tubes may also be coated with heparin, a natural anticoagulant whose action was explained earlier.

Since vitamin K is required for the synthesis of clotting factors, anything that antagonizes vitamin K usage makes the blood clot less readily. One vitamin K antagonist is *coumarin*[30] (COO-muh-rin), a sweet-smelling extract of tonka beans, sweet clover, and other plants, used in perfume. Taken orally by patients at risk for thrombosis, coumarin takes up to 2 days to act, but it has longer-lasting effects than heparin. A similar vitamin K antagonist is the pharmaceutical preparation *warfarin*[31] *(Coumadin)*, which was originally developed as a pesticide—it makes rats bleed to death. Obviously, such anticoagulants must be used in humans with great care.

Many parasites feed on the blood of vertebrates and secrete anticoagulants to keep the blood flowing. Among these are aquatic worms known as leeches. Leeches secrete a local anesthetic that makes their bites painless; therefore, as early as 1567 BCE, physicians used them for bloodletting. This method was less painful and repugnant to their patients than *phlebotomy*[32]—cutting a vein—and indeed, leeching became very popular. In seventeenth-century France, it was quite the rage; tremendous numbers of leeches were used in ill-informed attempts to treat headaches, insomnia, whooping cough, obesity, tumors, menstrual cramps, mental illness, and almost anything else doctors or their patients imagined to be caused by "bad blood."

The first known anticoagulant was discovered in the saliva of the medicinal leech, *Hirudo medicinalis*, in 1884. Named *hirudin*, it is a polypeptide that prevents clotting by inhibiting thrombin. It causes the blood to flow freely while the leech feeds and for as long as an hour thereafter. While the doctrine of bad blood is now long discredited, leeches have lately reentered medical usage for other reasons **(fig. 18.25)**. A major problem in reattaching a severed body part such as a finger or ear is that the tiny veins draining these organs are too small to reattach surgically. Since arterial blood flows into the reattached organ and can't flow out as easily, it pools and clots there. This inhibits the regrowth of veins and the flow of fresh blood through the organ, and often leads to necrosis. Some vascular

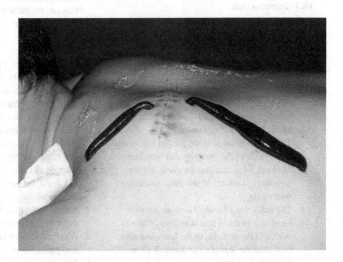

FIGURE 18.25 A Modern Use of Leeching. Two medicinal leeches are being used to remove clotted blood from a postsurgical hematoma. Despite their formidable size, the leeches secrete a natural anesthetic and produce a painless bite.
SPL/Science Source

❓ *How does the modern theory behind leeching differ from the theory of leeching that was popular a few centuries ago?*

surgeons now place leeches on the reattached part. Their anticoagulant keeps the blood flowing freely and allows new veins to grow. After 5 to 7 days, venous drainage is restored and leeching can be stopped.

Dissolving Clots That Have Already Formed

When a clot has already formed, it can be treated with clot-dissolving drugs such as *streptokinase*, an enzyme made by certain bacteria (streptococci). Intravenous streptokinase is used to dissolve blood clots in coronary vessels, for example. It is nonspecific, however, and digests almost any protein. *Tissue plasminogen activator (TPA)* works faster, is more specific, and is now made by transgenic bacteria. TPA converts plasminogen into the clot-dissolving enzyme plasmin. Some anticoagulants of animal origin also work by dissolving fibrin. A giant Amazon leech, *Haementeria*, produces one such anticoagulant named *hementin*. This, too, has been successfully produced by genetically engineered bacteria and used in cardiac patients to dissolve blood clots that do not yield to streptokinase or other drugs.

---

[29]ethylenediaminetetraacetic acid
[30]*coumaru* = tonka bean tree

[31]acronym from Wisconsin Alumni Research Foundation
[32]*phlebo* = vein; *tomy* = cutting

STUDY GUIDE

▶ Assess Your Learning Outcomes

To test your knowledge, discuss the following topics with a study partner or in writing, ideally from memory.

18.1 Introduction

1. Components of the circulatory system; the difference between the terms *circulatory system* and *cardiovascular system*
2. The diverse functions of blood; contributions of the blood to homeostasis
3. The two main components of whole blood; relative amounts of plasma and formed elements in the blood; and the three main categories of formed elements
4. The composition of blood plasma and serum
5. Importance of the viscosity and osmolarity of blood, what accounts for each, and the pathological effects of abnormal viscosity or osmolarity
6. The definition of *colloid osmotic pressure*
7. General aspects of hematopoiesis; where it occurs in the embryo, in the fetus, and after birth; and the stem cell with which all hematopoietic pathways begin

18.2 Erythrocytes

1. Erythrocyte (RBC) structure and function
2. The functions of hemoglobin and carbonic anhydrase
3. Hemoglobin structure and what parts of it bind O_2 and CO_2
4. Three ways of quantifying the RBCs and hemoglobin level of the blood; the definition and units of measurement of each; and reasons for the differences between male and female values
5. Stages of erythropoiesis and major transformations in each
6. Why iron is essential; how the stomach converts dietary iron to a usable form; and the roles of gastroferritin, transferrin, and ferritin in iron metabolism
7. Homeostatic regulation of erythropoiesis, including the origins and role of erythropoietin (EPO)
8. The life span of an RBC and how the body disposes of old RBCs
9. How the body disposes of the hemoglobin from expired RBCs and how this relates to the pigments of bile, feces, and urine

10. Excesses and deficiencies in RBC count and the forms, causes, and pathological consequences of each
11. Causes and effects of hemoglobin deficiencies and the pathology of sickle-cell disease and thalassemia

18.3 Blood Types

1. What determines a person's blood type; blood types of the ABO group and how they differ in genetics and RBC antigens
2. Why an individual does not have plasma antibodies against the ABO types at birth, but develops them during infancy; how these antibodies limit transfusion compatibility
3. The cause and mechanism of a transfusion reaction and why it can lead to renal failure and death; the meanings of *agglutination* and *hemolysis*
4. Blood types of the Rh group and how they differ in their genetics and RBC antigens
5. What can cause a person to develop antibodies against Rh-positive RBCs
6. Blood groups other than ABO and Rh, and their usefulness for certain purposes
7. Hemolytic disease of the newborn; why it seldom occurs in a woman's first susceptible child, but is more common in later pregnancies; and how it is treated and prevented

18.4 Leukocytes

1. The general function of all leukocytes (WBCs)
2. Three kinds of granulocytes, two kinds of agranulocytes, and what distinguishes granulocytes from agranulocytes as a class
3. The appearance, relative size and number, and functions of each WBC type, and the conditions under which each type increases in a differential WBC count
4. Three principal cell lines, the stages, and the anatomical sites of leukopoiesis
5. The relative length of time that WBCs travel in the bloodstream and spend in other tissues; which type recirculates into the blood and which types do not; and the relative life spans of WBCs
6. Causes and effects of leukopenia and leukocytosis

7. The naming and classification of various kinds of leukemia; why leukemia is typically accompanied by RBC and platelet deficiencies and elevated risk of opportunistic infection

18.5 Platelets and the Control of Bleeding

1. Platelet structure and functions, a typical platelet count, and why platelets are not considered to be cells
2. The sites and process of platelet production, and the hormone that stimulates it
3. Three mechanisms of hemostasis and their relative quickness and effectiveness
4. The general objective of coagulation; the end product of the coagulation reactions, and basic differences between the extrinsic and intrinsic mechanisms
5. Essentials of the extrinsic mechanism including the chemical that initiates it, other procoagulants involved, and the point at which it converges with the intrinsic mechanism at a common intermediate
6. Essentials of the intrinsic mechanism including the chemical that initiates it, other procoagulants involved, and the aforesaid point of convergence with the extrinsic mechanism
7. Steps in the continuation of coagulation from factor X to fibrin, including the procoagulants involved
8. The roles of positive feedback and enzyme amplification in coagulation
9. The processes of clot retraction, vessel repair, and fibrinolysis
10. Three mechanisms of preventing inappropriate coagulation in undamaged vessels
11. Causes of clotting deficiencies including the types, genetics, and pathology of hemophilia
12. Terms for unwanted or inappropriate clotting in a vessel, the clot itself, and a clot that breaks free and travels in the bloodstream
13. Why spontaneous clotting more often occurs in the veins than in the arteries; the danger presented by traveling blood clots; and why traveling clots so often lodge in the lungs even if they originate as far away as the lower limbs

STUDY GUIDE

▶ Testing Your Recall

Answers in Appendix A

1. Antibodies belong to a class of plasma proteins called
   a. albumins.
   b. gamma globulins.
   c. alpha globulins.
   d. procoagulants.
   e. agglutinins.

2. Serum is blood plasma minus its
   a. sodium ions.
   b. calcium ions.
   c. clotting proteins.
   d. globulins.
   e. albumin.

3. Which of the following conditions is most likely to cause hemolytic anemia?
   a. folic acid deficiency
   b. iron deficiency
   c. mushroom poisoning
   d. alcoholism
   e. hypoxemia

4. It is impossible for a type O+ baby to have a type _____ mother.
   a. AB–
   b. O–
   c. O+
   d. A+
   e. B+

5. Which of the following is *not* a component of hemostasis?
   a. platelet plug formation
   b. agglutination
   c. clot retraction
   d. vascular spasm
   e. degranulation

6. Which of the following contributes most to the viscosity of blood?
   a. albumin
   b. sodium
   c. globulins
   d. erythrocytes
   e. fibrin

7. Which of these is a granulocyte?
   a. a monocyte
   b. a lymphocyte
   c. a macrophage
   d. an eosinophil
   e. an erythrocyte

8. Excess iron is stored in the liver as a complex called
   a. gastroferritin.
   b. transferrin.
   c. ferritin.
   d. hepatoferritin.
   e. erythropoietin.

9. Pernicious anemia is a result of
   a. hypoxemia.
   b. iron deficiency.
   c. malaria.
   d. lack of intrinsic factor.
   e. Rh incompatibility.

10. The first clotting factor that the intrinsic and extrinsic pathways have in common is
    a. thromboplastin.
    b. Hageman factor.
    c. factor X.
    d. prothrombin activator.
    e. factor VIII.

11. Production of all the formed elements of blood is called _____.

12. The percentage of blood volume composed of RBCs is called the _____.

13. The extrinsic pathway of coagulation is activated by _____ from damaged perivascular tissues.

14. The RBC antigens that determine transfusion compatibility are called _____.

15. The hereditary lack of factor VIII causes a disease called _____.

16. The overall cessation of bleeding, involving several mechanisms, is called _____.

17. _____ results from a mutation that changes one amino acid in the hemoglobin molecule.

18. An excessively high RBC count is called _____.

19. Intrinsic factor enables the small intestine to absorb _____.

20. The kidney hormone _____ stimulates RBC production.

▶ Building Your Medical Vocabulary

Answers in Appendix A

State a meaning of each word element, and give a medical term from this chapter that uses it or a slight variation of it.

1. an-

2. -blast

3. erythro-

4. glutino-

5. hemo-

6. leuko-

7. -penia

8. phlebo-

9. -poiesis

10. thrombo-

STUDY GUIDE

▶ What's Wrong with These Statements?

Answers in Appendix A

Briefly explain why each of the following statements is false, or reword it to make it true.

1. Erythrocytes normally constitute most of the volume of the blood.

2. An abnormal increase in blood albumin concentration causes the blood to flow more sluggishly and therefore reduces blood pressure.

3. Anemia is caused by a low oxygen concentration in the blood.

4. *Hemostasis, coagulation,* and *clotting* are three terms for the same process.

5. If a type B+ woman has a baby with type O– blood, then her husband, who is type A+, cannot be the biological father.

6. Lymphocytes are the most abundant WBCs in the blood.

7. Potassium ions are a necessary cofactor at several steps in the blood-clotting process.

8. All formed elements of the blood except platelets come ultimately from the same pluripotent stem cells.

9. When RBCs die and break down, the globin moiety of hemoglobin is excreted and the heme is recycled to new RBCs.

10. Leukemia is a severe deficiency of white blood cells.

▶ Testing Your Comprehension

1. Why would erythropoiesis not correct the hypoxemia resulting from lung cancer?

2. People with chronic kidney disease often have hematocrits of less than half the normal value. Explain why.

3. An elderly white woman is hit by a bus and severely injured. Accident investigators are informed that she lives in an abandoned warehouse, where her few personal effects include several empty wine bottles and an expired driver's license indicating she is 72 years old. At the hospital, she is found to be severely anemic. List all the factors you can think of that may contribute to her anemia.

4. How is coagulation different from agglutination?

5. Although fibrinogen and prothrombin are equally necessary for blood clotting, fibrinogen is about 4% of the plasma protein whereas prothrombin is present only in small traces. In light of the roles of these clotting factors and your knowledge of enzymes, explain this difference in abundance.

CHAPTER 19

THE CIRCULATORY SYSTEM: HEART

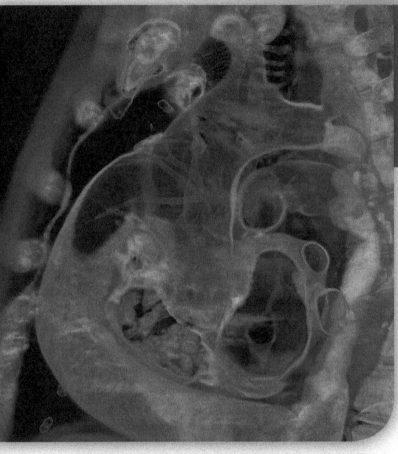

A three-dimensional CT scan of the heart; lateral view of a person facing left

Gondelon/Science Source

Anatomy & Physiology Revealed 4.0

Module 9: Cardiovascular System

BRUSHING UP

- For the best understanding of cardiac muscle, be sure you are familiar with desmosomes and gap junctions (see section 5.5a) and with the structure of striated muscle cells (see section 11.2, which describes skeletal muscle fibers but also applies to cardiac muscle).

- You must be familiar with membrane resting potentials and action potentials (see sections 12.4b–12.4c) to understand cardiac pacemaker physiology and the excitation of cardiac muscle.

- Review excitation–contraction coupling in skeletal muscle (see fig. 11.9 and the associated text) for comparison with the process in cardiac muscle.

- The length–tension relationship of striated muscle (see fig. 11.12 and the associated text) helps to explain variation in the ejection of blood by the heart.

- Adjustment of cardiac output to states of rest and physical exertion hinges on understanding the anatomy and action of the sympathetic and parasympathetic nervous systems (see section 15.3a).

We are more conscious of our heart than we are of most organs, and more wary of its failure. Speculation about the heart is at least as old as written history. Some ancient Chinese, Egyptian, Greek, and Roman scholars correctly surmised that the heart is a pump for filling the vessels with blood. Aristotle's views, however, were a step backward. Perhaps because the heart quickens its pace when we're emotionally aroused, and because grief causes "heartache," he regarded it primarily as the seat of emotion, as well as a source of heat to aid digestion. During the Middle Ages, Western medical schools clung dogmatically to the ideas of Aristotle. Perhaps the only significant advance came from Arabic medicine, when thirteenth-century physician Ibn an-Nafis described the role of the coronary blood vessels in nourishing the heart. The sixteenth-century dissections and anatomical charts of Vesalius, however, greatly improved knowledge of cardiovascular anatomy and set the stage for a more scientific study of the heart and treatment of its disorders—the science we now call **cardiology.**[1]

In the early decades of the twentieth century, little could be recommended for heart disease other than bed rest. Then nitroglycerin was found to improve coronary circulation and relieve the pain resulting from physical exertion, digitalis proved helpful for treating abnormal heart rhythms, and diuretics were first used to reduce hypertension. Coronary bypass surgery; replacement of diseased valves; clot-dissolving enzymes; heart transplants; and artificial pacemakers, valves, and hearts have made cardiology one of today's most dramatic and attention-getting fields of medicine.

19.1 Overview of the Cardiovascular System

Expected Learning Outcomes
When you have completed this section, you should be able to

a. define and distinguish between the *pulmonary circuit* and *systemic circuit;*

b. describe the general location, size, and shape of the heart; and

c. describe the pericardium that encloses the heart.

The **cardiovascular**[2] **system** consists of the heart and blood vessels. The heart is a muscular pump that keeps blood flowing through the vessels. The vessels deliver the blood to all the body's organs and then return it to the heart. The broader term *circulatory system* also includes the blood, and some authorities use it to include the lymphatic system as well (described in section 21.1).

19.1a The Pulmonary and Systemic Circuits

The cardiovascular system has two major divisions: a **pulmonary circuit,** which carries blood to the lungs for gas exchange and returns it to the heart, and a **systemic circuit,** which supplies blood to every organ of the body, including other parts of the lungs and the wall of the heart itself **(fig. 19.1).**

The right half of the heart supplies the pulmonary circuit. It receives blood that has circulated through the body, unloaded its oxygen and nutrients, and picked up a load of carbon dioxide and other wastes. It pumps this oxygen-poor blood into a large artery, the *pulmonary trunk,* which immediately divides into right and left *pulmonary arteries.* These transport blood to the air sacs *(alveoli)* of the lungs, where carbon dioxide is unloaded and oxygen is picked up. The oxygen-rich blood then flows by way of the *pulmonary veins* to the left side of the heart.

The left side supplies the systemic circuit. Blood leaves it by way of another large artery, the *aorta.* The aorta turns like an inverted U, the *aortic arch,* and passes downward posterior to the heart. The arch gives off arteries that supply the head, neck, and upper limbs. The aorta then travels through the thoracic and abdominal cavities and issues smaller arteries to the other organs before branching into the lower limbs. After circulating through the body, the now deoxygenated systemic blood returns to the right side of the heart mainly by way of two large veins: the *superior vena cava* (draining the upper body) and *inferior vena cava* (draining everything below the diaphragm). The major arteries and veins entering and leaving the heart are called the *great vessels (great arteries* and *veins)* because of their relatively large diameters. These circulatory routes are detailed in the next chapter.

---

[1]*cardio* = heart; *logy* = study

[2]*cardio* = heart; *vas* = vessel

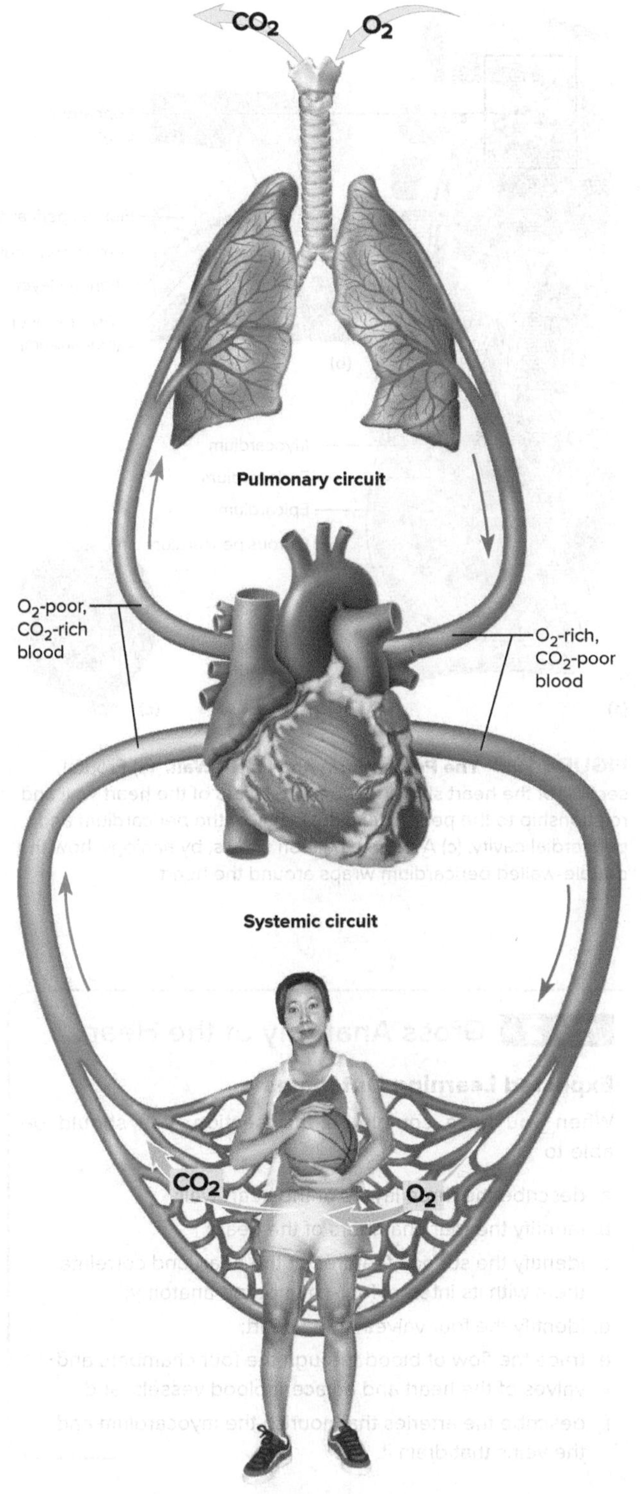

FIGURE 19.1 General Schematic of the Cardiovascular System.

 Are the lungs supplied by the pulmonary circuit, the systemic circuit, or both? Explain. **APR**

19.1b Position, Size, and Shape of the Heart

The heart lies within a thick partition called the **mediastinum** between the two lungs. It extends from a broad **base** at its uppermost end, where the great vessels are attached, to a bluntly pointed **apex** at the lower end, just above the diaphragm. It tilts toward the left from base to apex, so somewhat more than half the heart is to the left of the body's median plane. We can see this especially in a cross (horizontal) section through the thorax (**fig. 19.2;** see also figs. B.10, B.11 in atlas B).

The adult heart is about 9 cm (3.5 in.) wide at the base, 13 cm (5 in.) from base to apex, and 6 cm (2.5 in.) from anterior to posterior at its thickest point. Whatever one's body size, from child to adult, the heart is roughly the same size as the fist. It weighs about 300 g (10 ounces) in adults.

19.1c The Pericardium

The heart is enclosed in a double-walled sac called the **pericardium.**[3] The outer wall of the pericardium is a tough fibrous sac called the **fibrous pericardium.** It surrounds the heart but isn't attached to it. Deep to this is a thin membrane called the **serous pericardium.** This has two layers—a *parietal layer* that lines the inside of the fibrous pericardium, and a *visceral layer* that adheres to the heart surface and forms the outermost layer of the heart itself, the *epicardium* (**fig. 19.3).** The fibrous pericardium is anchored by ligaments to the diaphragm below and the sternum anterior to it, and more loosely anchored by fibrous connective tissue to mediastinal tissue posterior to the heart.

The space between the parietal and visceral layers of the serous pericardium is called the **pericardial cavity** (figs. 19.2b, 19.3). The heart isn't inside the pericardial cavity but enfolded by it. The relationship of the heart to the pericardium is often described by comparison to a fist pushed into an underinflated balloon (fig. 19.3c). The balloon surface in contact with the fist is like the epicardium; the outer balloon surface is like the parietal layer, and the air space between them is like the pericardial cavity.

The pericardial cavity contains 5 to 30 mL of **pericardial fluid,** exuded by the serous pericardium. The fluid lubricates the membranes and allows the heart to beat with minimal friction. In *pericarditis*—inflammation of the pericardium—the membranes may become roughened and produce a painful *friction rub* with each heartbeat. In addition to reducing friction, the pericardium isolates the heart from other thoracic organs and anchors it within the thorax. It allows the heart room to expand, yet resists excessive expansion (see *cardiac tamponade* in Deeper Insight A.1 in atlas A).

BEFORE YOU GO ON

Answer the following questions to test your understanding of the preceding section:

1. Distinguish between the pulmonary and systemic circuits and state which part of the heart supplies each one.

2. Predict the effect of a fibrous pericardium that fits too tightly around the heart. Predict the effect of a failure of the serous pericardium to secrete pericardial fluid.

---

[3]*peri* = around; *cardi* = heart

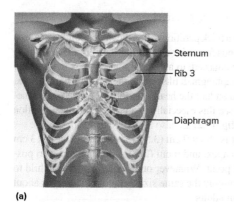

(a)

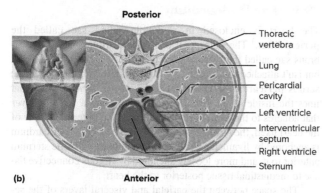

(b)

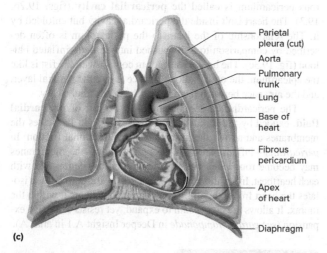

(c)

FIGURE 19.2 Position of the Heart in the Thoracic Cavity.
(a) Relationship to the thoracic cage. (b) Cross section of the thorax at the level of the heart. (c) Frontal view with the lungs slightly retracted and the fibrous pericardium opened. **APR**

? *Does most of the heart lie to the right or left of the median plane?*

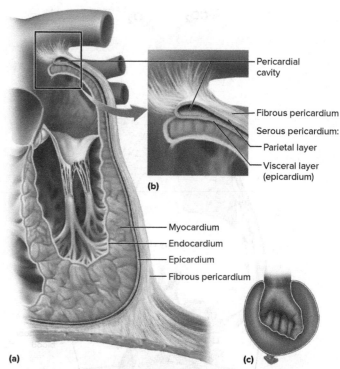

FIGURE 19.3 The Pericardium and Heart Wall. (a) Frontal section of the heart showing the three layers of the heart wall and relationship to the pericardium. (b) Detail of the pericardium and pericardial cavity. (c) A fist in a balloon shows, by analogy, how the double-walled pericardium wraps around the heart.

19.2   Gross Anatomy of the Heart

Expected Learning Outcomes

When you have completed this section, you should be able to

a. describe the three layers of the heart wall;

b. identify the four chambers of the heart;

c. identify the surface features of the heart and correlate them with its internal four-chambered anatomy;

d. identify the four valves of the heart;

e. trace the flow of blood through the four chambers and valves of the heart and adjacent blood vessels; and

f. describe the arteries that nourish the myocardium and the veins that drain it.

19.2a The Heart Wall

The heart wall consists of three layers: *epicardium, myocardium,* and *endocardium.*

The **epicardium**[4] (visceral layer of the serous pericardium) is a serous membrane of the external heart surface. It consists mainly of a simple squamous epithelium overlying a thin layer of areolar tissue. In some places, it also includes a thick layer of adipose tissue, whereas in other areas it is fat-free and translucent, so the muscle of the underlying myocardium shows through (**figs. 19.4a, 19.5**). The largest branches of the coronary blood vessels travel through the epicardium.

[4]*epi* = upon; *cardi* = heart

The **endocardium,**[5] a similar layer, lines the interior of the heart chambers (figs. 19.3, **19.4b**). Like the epicardium, this is a simple squamous epithelium overlying a thin areolar tissue layer; however, it has no adipose tissue. The endocardium covers the valve surfaces and is continuous with the endothelium of the blood vessels.

The **myocardium**[6] between these two is composed of cardiac muscle. This is by far the thickest layer and performs the work of the heart. Its thickness is proportional to the workload on the individual chambers. Its muscle is organized into bundles that spiral around the heart, forming the **vortex of the heart** (**fig. 19.6**). Consequently, when the ventricles contract, they exhibit a twisting or wringing motion that enhances the ejection of blood. Later we will examine the microscopic structure of the cardiac muscle cells, or *cardiomyocytes,* more closely.

The heart also has a framework of collagenous and elastic fibers that make up the **fibrous skeleton.** This tissue is especially concentrated in the walls between the heart chambers, in *fibrous rings (anuli fibrosi)* around the valves, and in sheets of tissue that interconnect these rings (fig. 19.8). The fibrous skeleton

[5]*endo* = internal, within; *cardi* = heart
[6]*myo* = muscle; *cardi* = heart

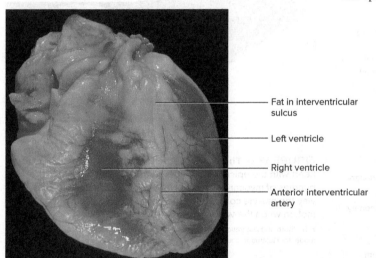

Fat in interventricular sulcus

Left ventricle

Right ventricle

Anterior interventricular artery

(a) Anterior view, external anatomy

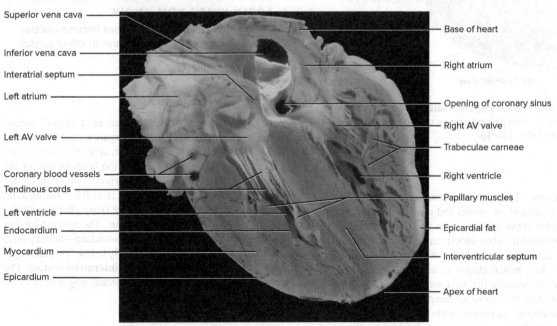

Superior vena cava

Inferior vena cava

Interatrial septum

Left atrium

Left AV valve

Coronary blood vessels

Tendinous cords

Left ventricle

Endocardium

Myocardium

Epicardium

Base of heart

Right atrium

Opening of coronary sinus

Right AV valve

Trabeculae carneae

Right ventricle

Papillary muscles

Epicardial fat

Interventricular septum

Apex of heart

(b) Posterior view, internal anatomy

FIGURE 19.4 The Heart of a Human Cadaver. (a) Anterior view, external anatomy. (b) Posterior view, internal anatomy. **APR**

a, b: McGraw-Hill Education

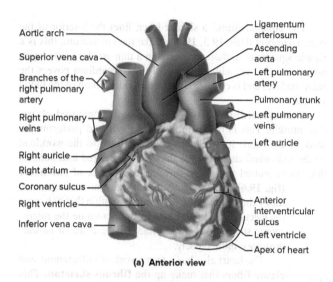

(a) **Anterior view**

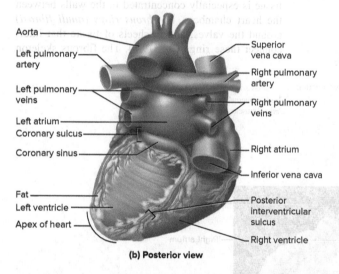

(b) **Posterior view**

FIGURE 19.5 Surface Anatomy of the Heart. (a) Anterior view. (b) Posterior view. The coronary blood vessels on the heart surface are identified in figure 19.10. **APR**

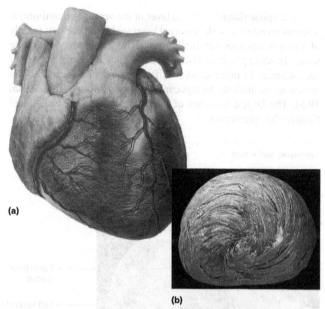

FIGURE 19.6 The Vortex of the Heart. (a) Anterior view of the heart with the epicardium rendered transparent to expose the bundles of myocardial muscle. (b) View from the apex to show the way the muscle coils around the heart. This results in a twisting motion when the ventricles contract.

a, b: Photo and illustration by Roy Schneider, University of Toledo. Plastinated heart model for illustration courtesy of Dr. Carlos Baptista, University of Toledo

▶▶▶**APPLY WHAT YOU KNOW**

Parts of the fibrous skeleton sometimes become calcified in old age. How would you expect this to affect cardiac function?

19.2b The Chambers

The heart has four chambers, best seen in a frontal section (**fig. 19.7;** also see fig. 19.4b). The two superior chambers are the **right** and **left atria** (AY-tree-uh; singular, *atrium*[7]). They are receiving chambers for blood returning to the heart by way of the great veins. Most of the mass of each atrium is on the posterior side of the heart, so only a small portion is visible from an anterior view. Here, each atrium has an earlike flap called an **auricle**[8] that slightly increases its volume (fig. 19.5a). The atria exhibit thin flaccid walls corresponding to their light workload—all they do is pump blood into the ventricles immediately below. They are separated from each other by a wall called the **interatrial septum.** The right atrium and both auricles exhibit internal ridges of myocardium called **pectinate**[9] **muscles.**

has multiple functions: (1) It provides structural support for the heart, especially around the valves and the openings of the great vessels; it holds these orifices open and prevents them from excessively stretching when blood surges through them. (2) It anchors the cardiomyocytes and gives them something to pull against. (3) As a nonconductor of electricity, it serves as electrical insulation between the atria and the ventricles, so the atria cannot stimulate the ventricles directly. This insulation is important to the timing and coordination of electrical and contractile activity. (4) Some authorities think (though others disagree) that elastic recoil of the fibrous skeleton may aid in refilling the heart with blood after each beat in a manner described later.

---

[7]*atrium* = entryway
[8]*auricle* = little ear
[9]*pectin* = comb; *ate* = like

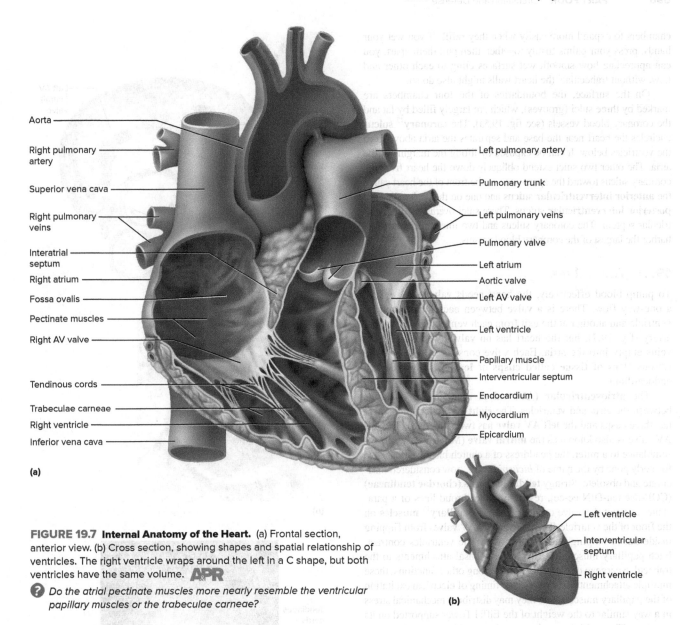

Aorta

Right pulmonary artery

Superior vena cava

Right pulmonary veins

Interatrial septum

Right atrium

Fossa ovalis

Pectinate muscles

Right AV valve

Tendinous cords

Trabeculae carneae

Right ventricle

Inferior vena cava

(a)

Left pulmonary artery

Pulmonary trunk

Left pulmonary veins

Pulmonary valve

Left atrium

Aortic valve

Left AV valve

Left ventricle

Papillary muscle

Interventricular septum

Endocardium

Myocardium

Epicardium

Left ventricle

Interventricular septum

Right ventricle

(b)

FIGURE 19.7 Internal Anatomy of the Heart. (a) Frontal section, anterior view. (b) Cross section, showing shapes and spatial relationship of ventricles. The right ventricle wraps around the left in a C shape, but both ventricles have the same volume. **APR**

❓ *Do the atrial pectinate muscles more nearly resemble the ventricular papillary muscles or the trabeculae carneae?*

The two inferior chambers, the **right** and **left ventricles,**[10] are the pumps that eject blood into the arteries and keep it flowing around the body. The right ventricle constitutes most of the anterior aspect of the heart, whereas the left ventricle forms the apex and inferoposterior aspect. Internally, the ventricles are separated by a thick muscular wall, the **interventricular septum.** The right ventricle pumps blood only to the lungs and back to the left atrium, so its wall is only moderately muscular. The wall of the left ventricle, including the septum, is two to four times as thick because it bears the greatest workload of all four chambers, pumping blood

through the entire body. The left ventricle is roughly circular in cross section, whereas the right ventricle wraps around the left and has a C shape (fig. 19.7b). To help visualize this, make a fist of your left hand and enfold it in your right hand; your left and right hands then approximate the shapes and spatial relationship of the left and right ventricles.

Both ventricles exhibit internal ridges called **trabeculae carneae**[11] (trah-BEC-you-lee CAR-nee-ee). It is thought that these ridges may serve to keep the ventricular walls from clinging to each other like suction cups when the heart contracts, and thus allow the

---

[10]*ventr* = belly, lower part; *icle* = little

[11]*trabecula* = little beam; *carne* = flesh, meat

chambers to expand more easily when they refill. If you wet your hands, press your palms firmly together, then pull them apart, you can appreciate how smooth wet surfaces cling to each other and how, without trabeculae, the heart walls might also do so.

On the surface, the boundaries of the four chambers are marked by three sulci (grooves), which are largely filled by fat and the coronary blood vessels (see fig. 19.5a). The **coronary**[12] **sulcus** encircles the heart near the base and separates the atria above from the ventricles below. It can be exposed by lifting the margins of the atria. The other two sulci extend obliquely down the heart from the coronary sulcus toward the apex—one on the front of the heart called the **anterior interventricular sulcus** and one on the back called the **posterior interventricular sulcus.** These sulci overlie the interventricular septum. The coronary sulcus and two interventricular sulci harbor the largest of the coronary blood vessels.

19.2c The Valves

To pump blood effectively, the heart needs valves that ensure a one-way flow. There is a valve between each atrium and its ventricle and another at the exit from each ventricle into its great artery (fig. 19.7), but the heart has no valves where the great veins empty into the atria. Each valve consists of two or three fibrous flaps of tissue called **cusps** or **leaflets,** covered with endocardium.

The **atrioventricular (AV) valves** regulate the openings between the atria and ventricles. The **right AV (tricuspid) valve** has three cusps and the **left AV valve** has two **(fig. 19.8).** The left AV valve is also known as the **mitral valve** (MY-trul) after its resemblance to a miter, the headdress of a church bishop; it has also formerly gone by the name of *bicuspid valve,* now considered inaccurate and obsolete. Stringy **tendinous cords (chordae tendineae)** (COR-dee ten-DIN-ee-ee), resembling the shroud lines of a parachute, connect the valve cusps to conical **papillary**[13] **muscles** on the floor of the ventricle. They prevent the AV valves from flipping inside out or bulging into the atria when the ventricles contract. Each papillary muscle has two or three basal attachments to the trabeculae carneae of the heart wall. Among other functions, these multiple attachments may govern the timing of electrical excitation of the papillary muscles, and they may distribute mechanical stress in a way similar to the weight of the Eiffel Tower supported on its four legs. The multiple attachments also provide some redundancy that protects an AV valve from complete mechanical failure should one attachment fail.

The **semilunar**[14] **valves** (pulmonary and aortic valves) regulate the flow of blood from the ventricles into the great arteries. The **pulmonary valve** controls the opening from the right ventricle into the pulmonary trunk, and the **aortic valve** controls the opening from the left ventricle into the aorta. Each has three cusps shaped like shirt pockets (fig. 19.8b). When blood is ejected from the ventricles, it pushes through these valves from below and

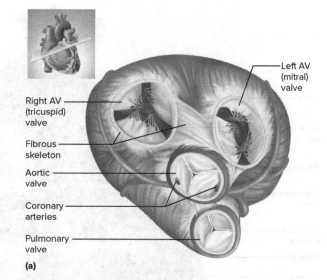

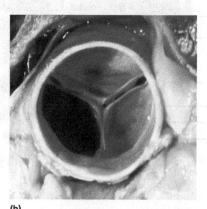

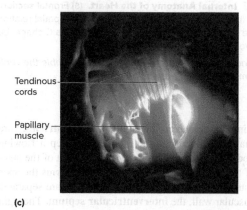

FIGURE 19.8 The Heart Valves. (a) Superior view of the heart with the atria removed. (b) The aortic valve, superior view, showing the three cusps meeting like a Y. One cusp is darkened by a blood clot. (c) Papillary muscle and tendinous cords seen from within the right ventricle. The upper ends of the cords are attached to the cusps of the right AV valve.

b: Biophoto Associates/Science Source; c: McGraw-Hill Education

---

[12]*coron* = crown; *ary* = pertaining to
[13]*papill* = nipple; *ary* = like, shaped
[14]*semi* = half; *lun* = moon

presses their cusps against the arterial walls. When the ventricles relax, arterial blood flows backward toward the ventricles, but quickly fills the cusps. The inflated pockets meet at the center and quickly seal the opening, so little blood flows back into the ventricles. Because of the way these valves are attached to the arterial wall, they cannot prolapse any more than a shirt pocket turns inside out if you jam your hand into it. Thus, they don't require or possess tendinous cords.

The valves don't open and close by any muscular effort of their own. The cusps are simply pushed open and closed by changes in blood pressure that occur as the heart chambers contract and relax. Later in this chapter, we will take a closer look at these pressure changes and their effect on the valves.

19.2d Blood Flow Through the Chambers

Until the sixteenth century, blood was thought to flow directly from the right ventricle into the left through invisible pores in the septum. This of course is not true. Blood is kept entirely separate on the right and left sides of the heart. **Figure 19.9** shows the pathway of the blood as it travels from the right atrium through the body and back to the starting point.

Blood that has been through the systemic circuit returns by way of the superior and inferior venae cavae to the right atrium. It flows directly from the right atrium, through the right AV (tricuspid) valve, into the right ventricle. When the right ventricle contracts, it ejects blood through the pulmonary valve into the pulmonary trunk, on its way to the lungs to exchange carbon dioxide for oxygen.

Blood returns from the lungs by way of two pulmonary veins on the left and two on the right; all four of these empty into the left atrium. Blood flows through the left AV (mitral) valve into the left ventricle. Contraction of the left ventricle ejects this blood through the aortic valve into the ascending aorta, on its way to another trip around the systemic circuit.

19.2e The Coronary Circulation

If your heart lasts for 80 years and beats an average of 75 times a minute, it will beat more than 3 billion times and each ventricle will pump more than 200 million liters of blood. It is, in short, a remarkably hardworking organ, and understandably, it needs an abundant supply of oxygen and nutrients. These needs aren't met to any appreciable extent by the blood in the heart chambers, because the diffusion of substances from there through the myocardium

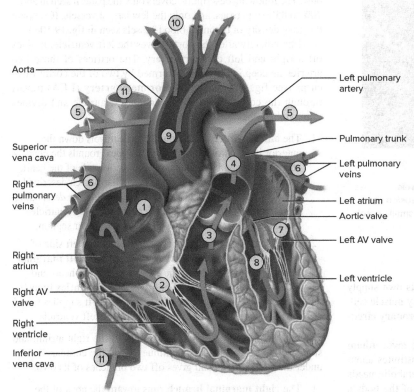

① Blood enters right atrium from superior and inferior venae cavae.

② Blood in right atrium flows through right AV valve into right ventricle.

③ Contraction of right ventricle forces pulmonary valve open.

④ Blood flows through pulmonary valve into pulmonary trunk.

⑤ Blood is distributed by right and left pulmonary arteries to the lungs, where it unloads CO_2 and loads O_2.

⑥ Blood returns from lungs via pulmonary veins to left atrium.

⑦ Blood in left atrium flows through left AV valve into left ventricle.

⑧ Contraction of left ventricle (simultaneous with step 3) forces aortic valve open.

⑨ Blood flows through aortic valve into ascending aorta.

⑩ Blood in aorta is distributed to every organ in the body, where it unloads O_2 and loads CO_2.

⑪ Blood returns to right atrium via venae cavae.

Aorta
Left pulmonary artery
Superior vena cava
Pulmonary trunk
Right pulmonary veins
Left pulmonary veins
Left atrium
Aortic valve
Left AV valve
Right atrium
Left ventricle
Right AV valve
Right ventricle
Inferior vena cava

FIGURE 19.9 The Pathway of Blood Flow Through the Heart. The pathway from 4 through 6 is the pulmonary circuit, and the pathway from 9 through 11 is the systemic circuit. Violet arrows indicate oxygen-poor blood; orange arrows indicate oxygen-rich blood. **APR**

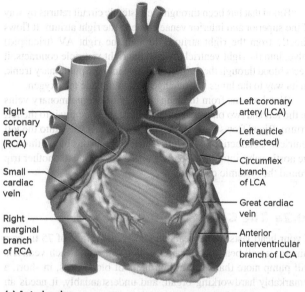

Right coronary artery (RCA)

Left coronary artery (LCA)

Left auricle (reflected)

Circumflex branch of LCA

Small cardiac vein

Great cardiac vein

Right marginal branch of RCA

Anterior interventricular branch of LCA

(a) Anterior view

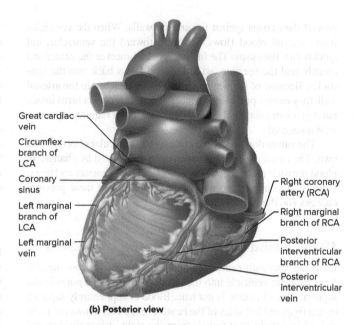

Great cardiac vein

Circumflex branch of LCA

Coronary sinus

Left marginal branch of LCA

Left marginal vein

Right coronary artery (RCA)

Right marginal branch of RCA

Posterior interventricular branch of RCA

Posterior interventricular vein

(b) Posterior view

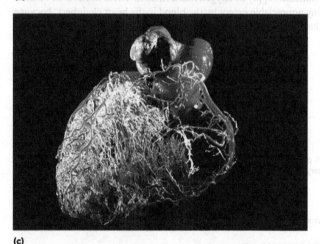

FIGURE 19.10 The Principal Coronary Blood Vessels.
(a) Anterior view. (b) Posterior view. (c) A vascular corrosion cast of the coronary circulation. Note the great density of small vessels that service the hardworking myocardium. **APR**

c: Science Photo Library/Science Source

would be too slow. Instead, the myocardium has its own supply of arteries and capillaries that deliver blood to every muscle cell. The blood vessels of the heart wall constitute the **coronary circulation (fig. 19.10).**

At rest, the coronary blood vessels supply the myocardium with about 250 mL of blood per minute. This constitutes about 5% of the circulating blood going to meet the metabolic needs of the heart, even though the heart is only 0.5% of the body's weight. It receives 10 times its "fair share" to sustain its strenuous workload.

Arterial Supply

The coronary circulation is the most variable aspect of cardiac anatomy. The following description covers only the pattern seen in about 70% to 85% of persons, and only the few largest vessels. (Compare the great density of coronary blood vessels seen in fig. 19.10c.)

Immediately after the aorta leaves the left ventricle, it gives off a right and left coronary artery. The orifices of these two arteries lie deep in the pockets formed by two of the aortic valve cusps (see fig. 19.8a). The **left coronary artery (LCA)** travels through the coronary sulcus under the left auricle and divides into two branches:

1. The **anterior interventricular branch** travels down the anterior interventricular sulcus to the apex, rounds the bend, and travels a short distance up the posterior side of the heart. There it joins the posterior interventricular branch described shortly. Clinically, it is also called the *left anterior descending (LAD) branch.* This artery supplies blood to both ventricles and the anterior two-thirds of the interventricular septum.

2. The **circumflex branch** continues around the left side of the heart in the coronary sulcus. It gives off a **left marginal branch** that passes down the left margin of the heart and furnishes blood to the left ventricle. The circumflex branch then ends on the posterior side of the heart. It supplies blood to the left atrium and posterior wall of the left ventricle.

The **right coronary artery (RCA)** supplies the right atrium and sinuatrial node (pacemaker), continues along the coronary sulcus under the right auricle, and gives off two branches of its own:

1. The **right marginal branch** runs toward the apex of the heart and supplies the lateral aspect of the right atrium and ventricle.

2. The RCA continues around the right margin of the heart to the posterior side, sends a small branch to the atrioventricular node, then gives off a large **posterior interventricular branch.** This branch travels down the corresponding sulcus and supplies the posterior walls of both ventricles as well as the posterior portion of the interventricular septum. It ends by joining the anterior interventricular branch of the LCA.

The energy demand of the cardiac muscle is so critical that an interruption of the blood supply to any part of the myocardium can cause necrosis within minutes. A fatty deposit or blood clot in a coronary artery can cause a **myocardial infarction**[15] **(MI),** or heart attack (see Deeper Insight 19.1). To protect against this, some coronary arteries converge at various points and combine their blood flow to points farther downstream. Points where two arteries come together are called *arterial anastomoses* (ah-NASS-tih-MO-seez). They provide alternative routes of blood flow (*collateral circulation)* that can supply the heart tissue with blood if the primary route becomes obstructed.

In organs other than the heart, blood flow usually peaks when the heart contracts and ejects blood into the systemic arteries, and diminishes when the ventricles relax and refill. The opposite is true in the coronary arteries: Flow peaks when the heart relaxes. There are three reasons for this. (1) Contraction of the myocardium squeezes the coronary arteries and obstructs blood flow. (2) When the ventricles contract, the aortic valve is forced open and its cusps cover the openings to the coronary arteries, blocking blood from flowing into them. (3) When they relax, blood in the aorta briefly surges back toward the heart. It fills the aortic valve cusps and some of it flows into the coronary arteries, like water pouring into a bucket and flowing out through a hole in the bottom. In the coronary blood vessels, therefore, blood flow increases during ventricular relaxation.

19.2f Venous Drainage

Venous drainage refers to the route by which blood leaves an organ. After flowing through capillaries of the heart wall, about 5% to 10% of the coronary blood empties from multiple tiny vessels called *small cardiac veins* directly into the heart chambers, especially the right ventricle. The rest returns to the right atrium by the following route:

- The **great cardiac vein** collects blood from the anterior aspect of the heart and travels alongside the anterior interventricular artery. It carries blood from the apex toward the coronary sulcus, then arcs around the left side of the heart and empties into the coronary sinus.

- The **posterior interventricular (middle cardiac) vein,** found in the posterior interventricular sulcus, collects blood from the posterior aspect of the heart. It, too, carries blood from the apex upward and drains into the same sinus.

- The **left marginal vein** travels from a point near the apex up the left margin, and also empties into the coronary sinus.

- The **coronary sinus,** a large transverse vein in the coronary sulcus on the posterior side of the heart, collects blood from all three of the aforementioned veins as well as some smaller ones. It empties blood into the right atrium.

DEEPER INSIGHT 19.1

CLINICAL APPLICATION

Angina and Heart Attack

An obstruction of coronary blood flow can cause a chest pain known as *angina pectoris*[16] (an-JY-na PEC-toe-riss) or, more seriously, *myocardial infarction* (heart attack). Angina is a sense of heaviness or pain in the chest resulting from temporary and reversible *ischemia*[17] (iss-KEE-me-ah), or deficiency of blood flow to the cardiac muscle. It typically occurs when a partially blocked coronary artery constricts. The oxygen-deprived myocardium shifts to anaerobic fermentation, producing lactate, which stimulates pain receptors in the heart. The pain abates when the artery relaxes and normal blood flow resumes.

Myocardial infarction (MI), on the other hand, is the sudden death of a patch of myocardium resulting from long-term obstruction of the coronary circulation. Coronary arteries often become obstructed by a blood clot or fatty deposit called an *atheroma* (see Deeper Insight 19.4). As cardiac muscle downstream from the obstruction dies, the individual commonly feels a sense of heavy pressure or squeezing pain in the chest, often "radiating" to the shoulder and left arm. Some MIs are painless, "silent" heart attacks, especially in elderly or diabetic individuals. Infarctions weaken the heart wall and disrupt electrical conduction pathways, potentially leading to fibrillation and cardiac arrest. MI causes about 27% of deaths in the United States.

BEFORE YOU GO ON

Answer the following questions to test your understanding of the preceding section:

3. Name the three layers of the heart and describe their structural differences.

4. What are the functions of the fibrous skeleton?

5. Trace the flow of blood through the heart, naming each chamber and valve in order.

6. What are the three principal branches of the left coronary artery? Where are they located on the heart surface? What are the branches of the right coronary artery, and where are they located?

7. What is the medical significance of anastomoses in the coronary arterial system?

8. Why do the coronary arteries carry a greater blood flow during ventricular relaxation than they do during ventricular contraction?

9. What are the three major veins that empty into the coronary sinus?

---

[15]*infarct* = to stuff
[16]*angina* = to choke, strangle; *pectoris* = of the chest
[17]*isch* = holding back; *em* = blood; *ia* = condition

19.3 Cardiac Muscle and the Cardiac Conduction System

Expected Learning Outcomes

When you have completed this section, you should be able to

a. describe the unique structural and metabolic characteristics of cardiac muscle;

b. explain the nature and functional significance of the intercellular junctions between cardiac muscle cells; and

c. describe the heart's pacemaker and internal electrical conduction system.

The most obvious physiological fact about the heart is its rhythmicity. It contracts at regular intervals, typically about 75 beats per minute (bpm) in a resting adult. Among invertebrates such as clams, crabs, and insects, each heartbeat is triggered by a pacemaker in the nervous system. But in vertebrates from fish to humans, the heartbeat is said to be *myogenic*[18] because the signal originates within the heart itself. The heart is described as **autorhythmic**[19] because it doesn't depend on the nervous system for its rhythm. It has its own built-in pacemaker and electrical system. We now turn our attention to the cardiac muscle, pacemaker, and internal electrical system—the foundations for its electrical activity and rhythmic beat.

19.3a Structure of Cardiac Muscle

The heart is mostly muscle. Cardiac muscle is striated like skeletal muscle, but quite different from it in other structural and functional respects—and it has to be if we want it to pump infallibly, more than once every second, for at least eight or nine decades.

Cardiomyocytes, the muscle cells of the heart, are relatively short, thick, branched cells, typically 50 to 100 μm long and 10 to 20 μm wide (**fig. 19.11**). The ends of the cell are slightly branched, like a log with deep notches in the end. Through these branches, each cardiomyocyte contacts several others, so collectively they form a network throughout each pair of heart chambers—one network in the atria and one in the ventricles.

Most cardiomyocytes have a single, centrally placed nucleus, but up to one-third of them have two or more nuclei. The nucleus is often surrounded by a light-staining mass of glycogen. The sarcoplasmic reticulum is less developed than in skeletal muscle; it lacks terminal cisterns, although it does have footlike sacs associated with the T tubules. The T tubules are much larger than in skeletal muscle. During excitation of the cell, they admit calcium ions from the extracellular fluid to activate muscle contraction.

Cardiomyocytes are joined end to end by thick connections called **intercalated discs** (in-TUR-ka-LAY-ted). With the right histological stain, these appear as dark lines thicker than the

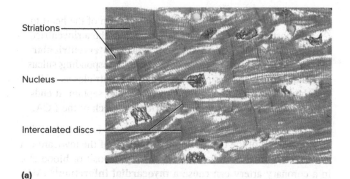

(a)

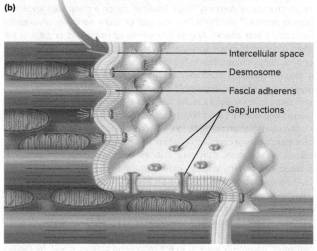

(b)

(c)

FIGURE 19.11 Cardiac Muscle. (a) Light micrograph. (b) Structure of a cardiomyocyte and its relationship to adjacent cardiomyocytes. All of the colored area is a single cell. Note that it is notched at the ends and typically linked to two or more neighboring cardiomyocytes by the mechanical and electrical junctions of the intercalated discs. (c) Structure of an intercalated disc.

a: Ed Reschke

---

[18]*myo* = muscle; *genic* = arising from
[19]*auto* = self

striations. An intercalated disc is a complex steplike structure with three distinctive features not found in skeletal muscle:

1. **Interdigitating folds.** The plasma membrane at the end of the cell is folded somewhat like the bottom of an egg carton. The folds of adjoining cells interlock with each other and increase the surface area of intercellular contact.

2. **Mechanical junctions.** The cells are tightly joined by two types of mechanical junctions: the fascia adherens and desmosomes. The *fascia adherens*[20] (FASH-ee-ah ad-HEER-enz) is the most extensive. It is a broad band, analogous to a strip of Velcro, in which the actin of the thin myofilaments is anchored to the plasma membrane and each cell is linked to the next via transmembrane proteins. The fascia adherens is interrupted here and there by *desmosomes*—patches of mechanical linkage that prevent the contracting cardiomyocytes from pulling apart. Both desmosomes and gap junctions (next) are described in greater detail in section 5.5a.

3. **Electrical junctions.** The intercalated discs also contain *gap junctions,* which form channels that allow ions to flow from the cytoplasm of one cardiomyocyte directly into the next. They enable each cardiomyocyte to electrically stimulate its neighbors. Thus, the entire myocardium of the two atria behaves almost like a single cell, as does the entire myocardium of the two ventricles. This unified action is essential for the effective pumping of a heart chamber.

Skeletal muscle contains satellite cells that can divide and replace dead muscle fibers to some extent. Cardiac muscle lacks these, however, so the repair of damaged cardiac muscle is almost

---

[20]*fascia* = band; *adherens* = adhering

entirely by fibrosis (scarring). Cardiac muscle has very limited capacity for mitosis and regeneration.

19.3b Metabolism of Cardiac Muscle

Cardiac muscle depends almost exclusively on aerobic respiration to make ATP. It is very rich in myoglobin (a short-term source of oxygen for aerobic respiration) and glycogen (for stored energy). Its huge mitochondria fill about 25% of the cell; skeletal muscle fibers, by comparison, have much smaller mitochondria that occupy only 2% of the fiber. Cardiac muscle is relatively adaptable with respect to the organic fuels used. At rest, the heart gets about 60% of its energy from fatty acids, 35% from glucose, and 5% from other fuels such as ketones, lactate, and amino acids. Cardiac muscle is more vulnerable to an oxygen deficiency than it is to the lack of any specific fuel. Because it makes little use of anaerobic fermentation or the oxygen debt mechanism, it is not prone to fatigue. You can easily appreciate this fact by squeezing a rubber ball in your fist once every second for a minute or two. You will soon feel weakness and fatigue in your hand muscles and perhaps feel all the more grateful that cardiac muscle can maintain a rhythm like this, without fatigue, for a lifetime.

19.3c The Conduction System

The heartbeat is coordinated by a **cardiac conduction system** composed of an internal pacemaker and nervelike conduction pathways through the myocardium. It generates and conducts rhythmic electrical signals in the following order **(fig. 19.12):**

① The **sinuatrial (SA) node** is a patch of modified cardiomyocytes in the right atrium, just under the epicardium near the superior vena cava. This is the **pacemaker** that initiates each heartbeat and determines the heart rate.

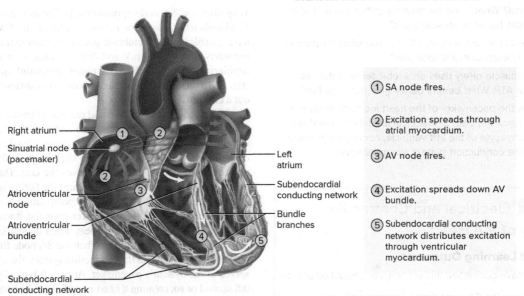

① SA node fires.

② Excitation spreads through atrial myocardium.

③ AV node fires.

④ Excitation spreads down AV bundle.

⑤ Subendocardial conducting network distributes excitation through ventricular myocardium.

Right atrium
Sinuatrial node (pacemaker)
Atrioventricular node
Atrioventricular bundle
Subendocardial conducting network
Left atrium
Subendocardial conducting network
Bundle branches

FIGURE 19.12 The Cardiac Conduction System. Electrical signals travel along the pathways indicated by the arrows.

❓ *Which atrium is first to receive the signal that induces atrial contraction?*

② Signals from the SA node spread throughout the atria, as shown by the red arrows in the figure.

③ The **atrioventricular (AV) node** is located at the lower end of the interatrial septum near the right AV valve. This node acts as an electrical gateway to the ventricles; the fibrous skeleton acts as an insulator to prevent currents from getting to the ventricles by any other route.

④ The **atrioventricular (AV) bundle** is the pathway by which signals leave the AV node. The bundle soon forks into **right** and **left bundle branches,** which enter the interventricular septum and descend toward the apex.

⑤ The **subendocardial conducting network** (formerly called *Purkinje fibers*) consists of processes that arise from the lower end of the bundle branches. Although nervelike in their action, they are composed of modified cardiomyocytes specialized for electrical conduction rather than contraction. At the apex of the heart, they turn upward and ramify throughout the ventricular myocardium, distributing electrical excitation to the cardiomyocytes of the ventricles. They form a more elaborate network in the left ventricle than in the right. Once they have delivered the electrical signal to their limits, the cardiomyocytes themselves perpetuate it by passing ions from cell to cell through their gap junctions.

BEFORE YOU GO ON

Answer the following questions to test your understanding of the preceding section:

10. What organelle(s) is/are less developed in cardiac muscle than in skeletal muscle? What one(s) is/are more developed? What is the functional significance of these differences between muscle types?

11. What exactly is an intercalated disc, and what function is served by each of its components?

12. Cardiac muscle rarely uses anaerobic fermentation to generate ATP. What benefit do we gain from this fact?

13. Where is the pacemaker of the heart located? What is it called? Trace the path of electrical excitation from there to a cardiomyocyte of the left ventricle, naming each component of the conduction system along the way.

19.4 Electrical and Contractile Activity of the Heart

Expected Learning Outcomes

When you have completed this section, you should be able to

a. explain why the SA node fires spontaneously and rhythmically;

b. explain how the SA node excites the myocardium;

c. describe the unusual action potentials of cardiac muscle and relate them to the contractile behavior of the heart; and

d. interpret a normal electrocardiogram.

In this section, we examine how the electrical events in the heart produce its cycle of contraction and relaxation. Contraction is called **systole** (SIS-toe-lee) and relaxation is **diastole** (dy-ASS-toe-lee). These terms can refer to a specific part of the heart (for example, atrial systole), but if no particular chamber is specified, they usually refer to the more conspicuous and important ventricular action, which ejects blood from the heart.

19.4a The Cardiac Rhythm

The normal heartbeat triggered by the SA node is called the **sinus rhythm.** At rest, the adult heart typically beats about 70 to 80 times per minute, although heart rates from 60 to 100 bpm are not unusual.

Any region of spontaneous firing other than the SA node is called an **ectopic**[21] **focus.** If the SA node is damaged, an ectopic focus may take over the governance of the heart rhythm. The most common ectopic focus is the AV node, which produces a slower heartbeat of 40 to 50 bpm called a **nodal (junctional) rhythm.** If neither the SA nor AV node is functioning, other ectopic foci fire at rates of 20 to 40 bpm. The nodal rhythm is sufficient to sustain life, but a rate of 20 to 40 bpm provides too little flow to the brain to be survivable. This is one of the conditions that can call for an artificial pacemaker.

19.4b Pacemaker Physiology

Why does the SA node spontaneously fire at regular intervals? Unlike skeletal muscle or neurons, cells of the SA node don't have a stable resting membrane potential. Their membrane potential starts at about –60 mV and drifts upward, showing a gradual depolarization called the **pacemaker potential (prepotential) (fig. 19.13).** This results primarily from a slow inflow of Na^+ without a compensating outflow of K^+.

When the pacemaker potential reaches a threshold of –40 mV, voltage-gated calcium channels open and Ca^{2+} flows in from the extracellular fluid. This produces the rising (depolarizing) phase of the action potential, which peaks slightly above 0 mV. At that point, K^+ channels open and K^+ leaves the cell. This makes the cytosol increasingly negative and creates the falling (repolarizing) phase of the action potential. When repolarization is complete, the K^+ channels close and the pacemaker potential starts over, on its way to producing the next heartbeat. Each depolarization of the SA node sets off one heartbeat. When the SA node fires, it excites the other components in the conduction system; thus, the SA node serves as the system's pacemaker. At rest, it typically fires every 0.8 second or so, creating a heart rate of about 75 bpm.

[21]*ec* = out of; *top* = place

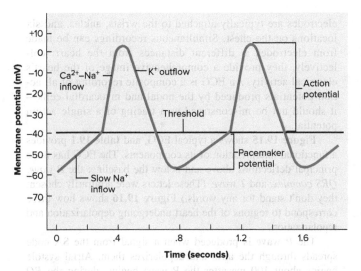

FIGURE 19.13 Pacemaker Potentials and Action Potentials of the SA Node.

19.4c Impulse Conduction to the Myocardium

Firing of the SA node excites atrial cardiomyocytes and stimulates the two atria to contract almost simultaneously. The signal travels at a speed of about 1 m/s through the atrial myocardium and reaches the AV node in about 50 ms. In the AV node, the signal slows down to about 0.05 m/s, partly because the cardiomyocytes here are thinner, but more importantly because they have fewer gap junctions over which the signal can be transmitted. This delays the signal at the AV node for about 100 ms—like

highway traffic slowing down at a small town. This delay is essential because it gives the ventricles time to fill with blood before they begin to contract.

The ventricular myocardium has a conduction speed of only 0.3 to 0.5 m/s. If this were the only route of travel for the excitatory signal, some cardiomyocytes would be stimulated much sooner than others. Ventricular contraction wouldn't be synchronized and the pumping effectiveness of the ventricles would be severely compromised. But signals travel through the AV bundle and subendocardial conducting network at a speed of 4 m/s, the fastest in the conduction system, owing to their very high density of gap junctions. Consequently, the entire ventricular myocardium depolarizes within 200 ms after the SA node fires, causing the ventricles to contract in near unison.

Ventricular systole begins at the apex of the heart, which is first to be stimulated, and progresses upward—pushing the blood upward toward the semilunar valves. Because of the spiral arrangement of the vortex of the heart, the ventricles twist slightly as they contract, like someone wringing out a towel.

▶▶▶ APPLY WHAT YOU KNOW

Some people have abnormal cords or bridges of myocardium that extend from atrium to ventricle, bypassing the AV node and other parts of the conduction system. How would you expect this to affect the cardiac rhythm?

19.4d Electrical Behavior of the Myocardium

The action potentials of cardiomyocytes are significantly different from those of neurons and skeletal muscle fibers **(fig. 19.14).**

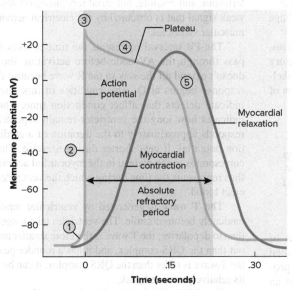

① Voltage-gated Na⁺ channels open.

② Na⁺ inflow depolarizes the membrane and triggers the opening of still more Na⁺ channels, creating a positive feedback cycle and a rapidly rising membrane voltage.

③ Na⁺ channels close when the cell depolarizes, and the voltage peaks at nearly +30 mV.

④ Ca²⁺ entering through slow Ca²⁺ channels prolongs depolarization of membrane, creating a plateau. Plateau falls slightly because of some K⁺ leakage, but most K⁺ channels remain closed until end of plateau.

⑤ Ca²⁺ channels close and Ca²⁺ is transported out of cell. K⁺ channels open, and rapid K⁺ outflow returns membrane to its resting potential.

FIGURE 19.14 Action Potential of a Ventricular Cardiomyocyte. The green curve is the action potential. The red curve represents rising and falling muscle tension as the myocardium contracts and relaxes.

❓ *What is the benefit of having such a long absolute refractory period in cardiac muscle?*

Cardiomyocytes have a stable resting potential of –90 mV and normally depolarize only when stimulated, unlike cells of the SA node. A stimulus opens voltage-gated sodium channels, causing a Na^+ inflow and depolarizing the cell to its threshold. The threshold voltage rapidly opens additional Na^+ channels and triggers a positive feedback cycle like the one seen in the firing of a neuron. The action potential peaks at nearly +30 mV. The Na^+ channels close quickly, and the rising phase of the action potential is very brief.

As action potentials spread over the plasma membrane, they open voltage-gated **slow calcium channels,** which admit a small amount of Ca^{2+} from the extracellular fluid into the cell. This Ca^{2+} binds to ligand-gated Ca^{2+} channels on the sarcoplasmic reticulum (SR), opening them and releasing a greater quantity of Ca^{2+} from the SR into the cytosol. This second wave of Ca^{2+} binds to troponin and triggers contraction in the same way as it does in skeletal muscle. The SR provides 90% to 98% of the Ca^{2+} needed for myocardial contraction.

In skeletal muscle and neurons, an action potential falls back to the resting potential within 2 ms. In cardiac muscle, however, the depolarization is prolonged for 200 to 250 ms (at a heart rate of 70–80 bpm), producing a long plateau in the action potential— perhaps because the Ca^{2+} channels of the SR are slow to close or because the SR is slow to remove Ca^{2+} from the cytosol. Cardiomyocytes remain contracted for as long as the action potential is in its plateau. Thus, in the figure, you can see the development of muscle tension (myocardial contraction) following closely behind the depolarization and plateau. Rather than showing a brief twitch like skeletal muscle, cardiac muscle has a more sustained contraction necessary to expel blood from the heart chambers. Both atrial and ventricular cardiomyocytes exhibit these plateaus, but they are more pronounced in the ventricles.

At the end of the plateau, Ca^{2+} channels close and K^+ channels open. Potassium diffuses rapidly out of the cell and Ca^{2+} is transported back into the extracellular fluid and SR. Membrane voltage drops rapidly, and muscle tension declines soon afterward.

Cardiac muscle has an *absolute refractory period* of 250 ms, compared with 1 to 2 ms in skeletal muscle. This long refractory period prevents wave summation and tetanus (in contrast to skeletal muscle, fig. 11.15), which would stop the pumping action of the heart if they occurred.

▶▶▶ APPLY WHAT YOU KNOW

With regard to the ions involved, how does the falling (repolarization) phase of a myocardial action potential differ from that of a neuron's action potential? (See fig. 12.14.)

19.4e The Electrocardiogram

We can detect electrical currents in the heart by means of electrodes *(leads)* applied to the skin. An instrument called the *electrocardiograph* amplifies these signals and produces a record, usually on a moving paper chart, called an **electrocardiogram**[22] **(ECG** or **EKG).** To record an ECG,

electrodes are typically attached to the wrists, ankles, and six locations on the chest. Simultaneous recordings can be made from electrodes at different distances from the heart; collectively, they provide a comprehensive image of the heart's electrical activity. An ECG is a composite recording of all action potentials produced by the nodal and myocardial cells— it should not be misconstrued as a tracing of a single action potential.

Figure 19.15 shows a typical ECG, and **table 19.1** provides a functional interpretation of its components. The ECG has three principal deflections above and below the baseline: the *P wave, QRS complex,* and *T wave.* (These letters were arbitrarily chosen; they don't stand for any words.) **Figure 19.16** shows how these correspond to regions of the heart undergoing depolarization and repolarization.

The **P wave** is produced when a signal from the SA node spreads through the atria and depolarizes them. Atrial systole begins about 100 ms after the P wave begins, during the *PQ segment.* This segment is about 160 ms long and represents the time required for impulses to travel from the SA node to the AV node.

The **QRS complex** consists of a small downward deflection (Q), a tall sharp peak (R), and a final downward deflection (S). It is produced when the signal from the AV node spreads through the ventricular myocardium and depolarizes the muscle. This is the most conspicuous part of the ECG because it is produced mainly by depolarization of the ventricles, which constitute the largest muscle mass of the heart and generate the greatest electrical current. Its complex shape is due to the different sizes of the two ventricles and the different times required for them to depolarize. Ventricular systole begins shortly after the QRS complex, in the *ST segment.* The QRS interval is also a time of atrial repolarization and diastole, but atrial repolarization sends a relatively weak signal that is obscured by the electrical activity of the more muscular ventricles.

The PR interval represents the time it takes for a signal to pass through the AV node before activating the ventricles. It doesn't extend all the way to the R wave because the ventricular response begins at Q. Abnormalities in this interval can thus indicate defects that affect conduction time. The QT interval indicates how long the ventricles remain depolarized, and corresponds approximately to the duration of a cardiomyocyte action potential. It gets shorter during exercise. The ST segment corresponds to the plateau in the myocardial action potential and thus represents the time during which the ventricles contract and eject blood.

The **T wave** is generated by ventricular repolarization immediately before diastole. The ventricles take longer to repolarize than to depolarize; the T wave is therefore smaller and more spread out than the QRS complex, and it has a rounder peak. Even when the T wave is taller than the QRS complex, it can be recognized by its relatively rounded peak.

The ECG affords a wealth of information about the normal electrical activity of the heart. Deviations from normal—such as enlarged, inverted, or misshapen waves and abnormal time intervals between waves—are invaluable for diagnosing abnormalities

---

[22]*electro* = electricity; *cardio* = heart; *gram* = record of; the common abbreviation *EKG* comes from the German spelling, *elektrokardiogramm*

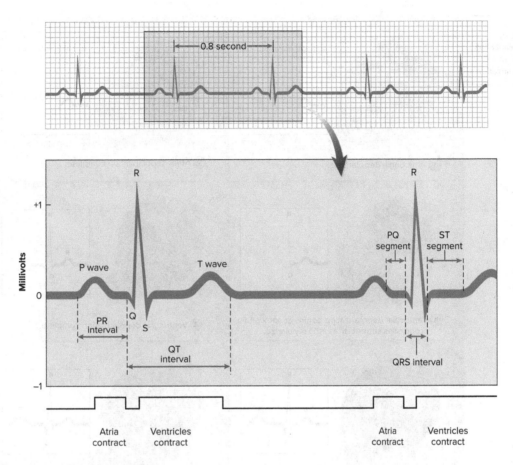

FIGURE 19.15 The Normal Electrocardiogram.

in the conduction pathways, myocardial infarction, enlargement of the heart, and electrolyte and hormone imbalances, among other disorders (see Deeper Insight 19.2).

TABLE 19.1	Interpretation of the Electrocardiogram
P wave	Atrial depolarization
QRS complex	Ventricular depolarization
T wave	Ventricular repolarization
PR interval	Signal conduction through AV node, before activating ventricles
QT interval	Duration of ventricular depolarization; shorter during exercise.
QRS interval	Atrial repolarization and diastole; repolarization concealed by QRS wave.
PQ segment	Signal conduction from SA node to AV node; atrial systole begins.
ST segment	Ventricular systole and ejection of blood; corresponds to plateau of cardiomyocyte action potential.

Any deviation from the regular, SA node–driven sinus rhythm of the heartbeat is called an **arrhythmia.** The most familiar and feared of these is **ventricular fibrillation (VF, VFib),**[23] the hallmark of a heart attack (myocardial infarction). Most cases occur in patients with a history of coronary artery disease. In striking contrast to the steady sinus rhythm, the ECG shows weak, chaotic ventricular depolarizations (compare **fig. 19.17a, b**) as electrical signals travel randomly about the myocardium and return to repeatedly restimulate the same area instead of dying out like a normal ventricular depolarization. To the surgeon's eye and hand, a fibrillating ventricle exhibits squirming, uncoordinated contractions often described as feeling "like a bag of worms." A fibrillating ventricle pumps no blood, so there is no coronary blood flow and myocardial tissue rapidly dies of ischemia, as does cerebral tissue. *Cardiac arrest* is the cessation of cardiac output, with the ventricles either motionless or in fibrillation.

Fibrillation kills quickly if it isn't stopped. *Defibrillation* is an emergency procedure in which the heart is given a strong electrical

[23]*fibril* = small fiber; *ation* = action, process

Key
- Wave of depolarization
- Wave of repolarization

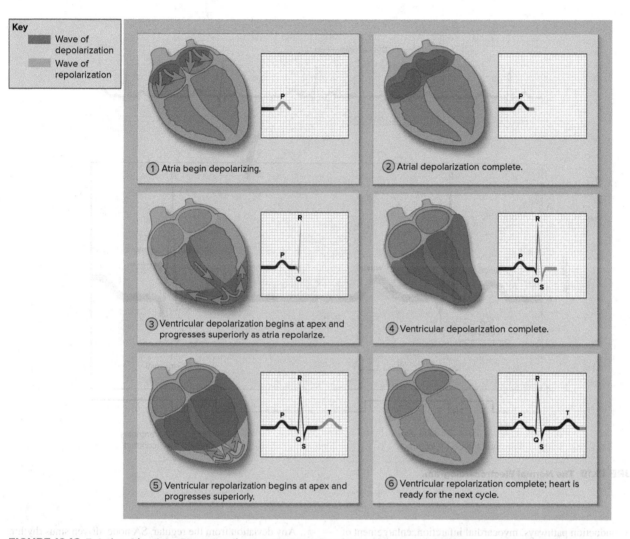

① Atria begin depolarizing.

② Atrial depolarization complete.

③ Ventricular depolarization begins at apex and progresses superiorly as atria repolarize.

④ Ventricular depolarization complete.

⑤ Ventricular repolarization begins at apex and progresses superiorly.

⑥ Ventricular repolarization complete; heart is ready for the next cycle.

FIGURE 19.16 Relationship of the Electrocardiogram (ECG) to Electrical Activity and Contraction of the Myocardium. Each heart diagram indicates the events occurring at the time of the colored segment of the ECG. Red indicates depolarizing or depolarized myocardium, and green indicates repolarizing or repolarized myocardium. Arrows indicate the direction in which a wave of depolarization or repolarization is traveling. **APR**

shock with a pair of paddle electrodes. The purpose is to depolarize the entire myocardium and stop the fibrillation, with the hope that the SA node will resume its sinus rhythm. This doesn't correct the underlying cause of the fibrillation, but it may sustain a patient's life long enough to allow for other corrective action.

BEFORE YOU GO ON

Answer the following questions to test your understanding of the preceding section:

14. Define *systole* and *diastole*.

15. How does the pacemaker potential of the SA node differ from the resting membrane potential of a neuron? Why is this important in creating the heart rhythm?

16. Why is it important that the AV node slow down signal conduction to the ventricles?

17. How does excitation–contraction coupling in cardiac muscle resemble that of skeletal muscle? How is it different?

18. What produces the plateau in the action potentials of cardiomyocytes? Why is this important to the pumping ability of the heart?

19. Identify the portion of the ECG that coincides with each of the following events: atrial depolarization, atrial systole, atrial repolarization, ventricular depolarization, ventricular systole, ventricular repolarization, ventricular diastole.

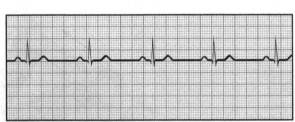

(a) Sinus rhythm (normal)

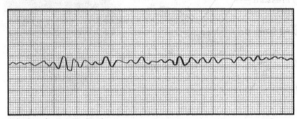

(b) Ventricular fibrillation

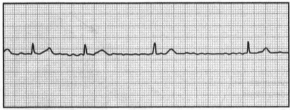

(c) Atrial fibrillation

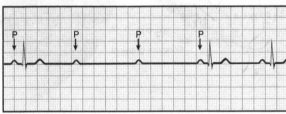

(d) Heart block

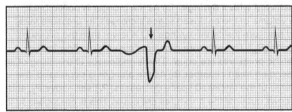

(e) Premature ventricular contraction

FIGURE 19.17 Normal and Pathological Electrocardiograms. (a) Normal sinus rhythm. (b) Ventricular fibrillation, with grossly irregular waves of depolarization, as seen in a heart attack (myocardial infarction). (c) Atrial fibrillation; between heartbeats, the atria exhibit weak, chaotic, high-frequency depolarizations instead of normal P waves. (d) Heart block, in which some atrial depolarizations (P waves) are not conducted to the ventricles and not followed by ventricular QRS waves. (e) Premature ventricular contraction, or extrasystole (at arrow); note the absence of a P wave, the inverted QRS complex, and the misshapen QRS and elevated T.

DEEPER INSIGHT 19.2

CLINICAL APPLICATION

Cardiac Arrhythmias

Ventricular fibrillation **(fig. 19.17b)** is the most widely known arrhythmia, but others are not uncommon. *Atrial fibrillation (AF, AFib)* **(fig. 19.17c)** is a weak rippling contraction in the atria, manifested in the ECG by chaotic, high-frequency depolarizations (400–650/min.). Fibrillating atria fail to stimulate the ventricles, so we see a dissociation between the random atrial depolarizations and the ventricular QRS and T waves of the ECG. This is the most common atrial arrhythmia in the elderly. It can result from such causes as valvular disease, thyroid hormone excess, or myocardial inflammation, and is often seen in alcoholism. Blood continues to flow through the atria into the ventricles even during AF, so AF isn't immediately life-threatening. Blood flow is more sluggish, however, and there is a higher risk of blood clots causing pulmonary embolism or stroke.

Heart block is a failure of any part of the cardiac conduction system to conduct signals, usually as the result of disease and degeneration of conduction system fibers. In the ECG, one sees rhythmic atrial P waves, but the ventricles fail to receive the signal and no QRS wave follows the P (as in the second and third P waves of **fig. 19.17d**). A *bundle branch block* is a heart block resulting from damage to one or both branches of the AV bundle. Damage to the AV node causes *total heart block,* in which signals from the atria fail to reach the ventricles at all, and the ventricles beat at their own intrinsic rhythm of 20 to 40 bpm.

Premature ventricular contraction (PVC) is the result of a ventricular ectopic focus firing and setting off an extra beat *(extrasystole)* before the normal signal from the SA node arrives. The P wave is missing and the QRS wave is inverted and misshapen (see arrow in **fig. 19.17e**). PVCs can occur singly or in bursts. An occasional extra beat isn't serious, and may result from emotional stress, lack of sleep, or irritation of the heart by stimulants (nicotine, caffeine). Persistent PVCs, however, can indicate more serious pathology and sometimes lead to ventricular fibrillation and sudden death.

19.5 Blood Flow, Heart Sounds, and the Cardiac Cycle

Expected Learning Outcomes

When you have completed this section, you should be able to

a. explain why blood pressure is expressed in millimeters of mercury;

b. describe how changes in blood pressure operate the heart valves;

c. explain what causes the sounds of the heartbeat;

d. describe in detail one complete cycle of heart contraction and relaxation; and

e. relate the events of the cardiac cycle to the volume of blood entering and leaving the heart.

A **cardiac cycle** consists of one complete contraction and relaxation of all four heart chambers. We will examine these events in detail to see how they relate to the entry and expulsion of blood, but first we consider two related issues: (1) some general principles of pressure changes and how they affect the flow of blood, and (2) the heart sounds produced during the cardiac cycle, which we can then relate to the stages of the cycle.

19.5a Principles of Pressure and Flow

A fluid is a state of matter that can flow in bulk from place to place. In the body, this includes both liquids and gases—blood, lymph, air, and urine, among others. Certain basic principles of fluid movement (*fluid dynamics*) apply to all of these. In particular, flow is governed by two main variables: **pressure,** which impels a fluid to move, and **resistance,** which opposes flow. In this chapter, we will focus on how pressure changes govern the operation of the heart valves, the entry of blood into the heart chambers, and its expulsion into the arteries. In the next chapter, we will examine the roles of pressure and resistance in the flow of blood through the blood vessels, and later in the book, we apply the same principles to respiratory airflow. The flow of blood and of air down their pressure gradients are two applications of the general principle of gradients and flow described in section 1.6e.

Measurement of Pressure

Pressure is commonly measured by a device called a *manometer.* In simplest form, this is typically a J-shaped glass tube partially filled with mercury. The sealed upper end, above the mercury, contains a vacuum, whereas the lower end is open. Pressure applied at the lower end is measured in terms of how high it can push the mercury column up the evacuated end of the tube. In principle, any liquid would do, but mercury is used because it's so dense; it enables us to measure pressure with shorter columns than we would need with a less dense liquid such as water. Pressures are therefore commonly expressed in millimeters of mercury (mm Hg). Blood pressure, specifically, has been traditionally measured with a **sphygmomanometer**[24] (SFIG-mo-ma-NOM-eh-tur)—a calibrated mercury manometer with its open lower end attached to an inflatable pressure cuff wrapped around the arm (although mercury sphygmomanometers have been increasingly replaced by dial and digital devices). Blood pressure and the method of measuring it are discussed in greater detail in section 20.2a.

Pressure Gradients and Flow

A fluid flows only if it is subjected to more pressure at one point than at another. The difference creates a **pressure gradient,** and fluids always flow down their pressure gradients, from the high-pressure point to the low-pressure point. Before we relate this to blood flow, it may be easier to begin with an analogy—an air-filled syringe **(fig. 19.18).**

At rest, the air pressures within the syringe barrel and in the atmosphere surrounding it are equal. But for a given quantity (mass) of air, and assuming a constant temperature, pressure is inversely proportional to the volume of the container—the greater

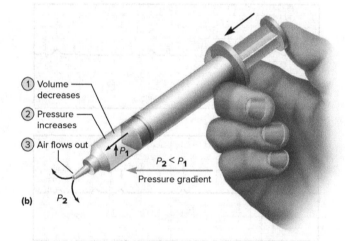

FIGURE 19.18 Principles of Volume, Pressure, and Flow Illustrated with a Syringe. (a) As the plunger is pulled back, the volume of the enclosed space increases, its pressure falls, and pressure inside the syringe (P_1) is lower than the pressure outside (P_2). The pressure gradient causes air to flow inward until the pressures are equal. This is analogous to the filling of an expanding heart chamber. (b) As the plunger is depressed, the volume of the enclosed space decreases, P_1 rises above P_2, and air flows out until the pressures are equal. This is analogous to the ejection of blood from a contracting heart chamber. In both cases, fluids flow down their pressure gradients.

the volume, the lower the pressure, and vice versa. Suppose you pull back the plunger of the syringe (fig. 19.18a). This increases the volume and thus lowers the air pressure within the barrel. Now you have a pressure gradient, with pressure outside the syringe being greater than the pressure inside. Air will flow down its gradient into the syringe until the two pressures are equal. If you then push the plunger in (fig. 19.18b), pressure inside the barrel will rise above the pressure outside, and air will flow out—again going down its pressure gradient but in the reverse direction.

[24]*sphygmo* = pulse; *mano* = rare, sparse, roomy

The syringe barrel is analogous to a heart chamber such as the left ventricle. When the ventricle expands, its internal pressure falls. If the AV valve is open, blood flows into the ventricle from the atrium above. When the ventricle contracts, its internal pressure rises. When the aortic valve opens, blood is ejected from the ventricle into the aorta.

The opening and closing of the heart valves are governed by these pressure changes. Remember that the valves are just soft flaps of connective tissue with no muscle. They don't exert any effort of their own, but are passively pushed open and closed by the changes in blood pressure on the upstream and downstream sides of the valve.

When the ventricles are relaxed and their pressure is low, the AV valve cusps hang down limply and both valves are open

(fig. 19.19a). Blood flows freely from the atria into the ventricles even before the atria contract. As the ventricles fill with blood, the cusps float upward toward the closed position. When the ventricles contract, their internal pressure rises sharply and blood surges against the AV valves from below. This pushes the cusps together, seals the openings, and prevents blood from flowing back into the atria. The papillary muscles contract slightly before the rest of the ventricular myocardium and tug on the tendinous cords, preventing the valves from bulging excessively (prolapsing) into the atria or turning inside out like windblown umbrellas. (See *mitral valve prolapse* in Deeper Insight 19.3.)

The rising pressure in the ventricles also acts on the aortic and pulmonary valves. Up to a point, pressure in the aorta and pulmonary trunk opposes their opening, but when the ventricular

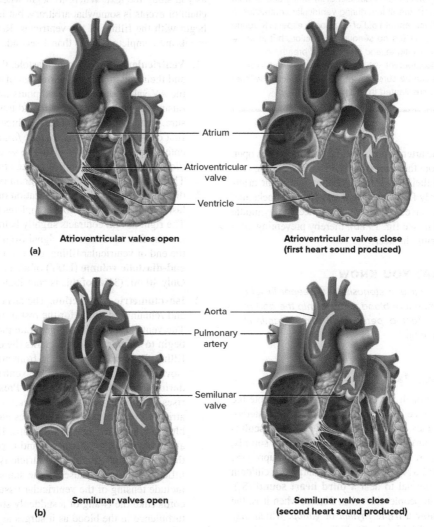

Atrium

Atrioventricular valve

Ventricle

Atrioventricular valves open
(a)

Atrioventricular valves close
(first heart sound produced)

Aorta

Pulmonary artery

Semilunar valve

Semilunar valves open
(b)

Semilunar valves close
(second heart sound produced)

FIGURE 19.19 Operation of the Heart Valves. These are correlated with the heart sounds described in section 19.5b. (a) The atrioventricular valves. When atrial pressure is greater than ventricular pressure, the valve opens and blood flows through (green arrows). When ventricular pressure rises above atrial pressure, the blood in the ventricle pushes the valve cusps closed. (b) The semilunar valves. When the pressure in the ventricles is greater than the pressure in the great arteries, the semilunar valves are forced open and blood is ejected. When ventricular pressure is lower than arterial pressure, arterial blood holds these valves closed.

❓ *What role do the tendinous cords play?*

DEEPER INSIGHT 19.3

CLINICAL APPLICATION

Valvular Insufficiency

Valvular insufficiency (incompetence) refers to any failure of a valve to prevent *reflux* (regurgitation)—the backward flow of blood. *Valvular stenosis*[25] is a form of insufficiency in which the cusps are stiffened and the opening is constricted by scar tissue. It frequently results from rheumatic fever, an autoimmune disease in which antibodies produced to fight a bacterial infection also attack the mitral and aortic valves. As the valves become scarred and constricted, the heart is overworked by the effort to force blood through the openings and may become enlarged. Regurgitation of blood through the incompetent valves creates turbulence that can be heard with a stethoscope as a *heart murmur.*

Mitral valve prolapse (MVP) is an insufficiency in which one or both mitral valve cusps bulge into the atrium during ventricular contraction. It is often hereditary and affects about 1 out of 40 people, especially young women. In many cases, it causes no serious dysfunction, but in some people it causes chest pain, fatigue, and shortness of breath.

In some cases, an incompetent valve can eventually lead to heart failure. A defective valve can be surgically repaired or replaced with an artificial valve or a valve transplanted from a pig heart.

---

pressure rises above the arterial pressure, it forces the valves open and blood is ejected from the heart (**fig. 19.19b**). Then as the ventricles relax again and their pressure falls below that in the arteries, arterial blood briefly flows backward and fills the pocketlike cusps of the semilunar valves. The three cusps meet in the middle of the orifice and seal it (see fig. 19.8b), thereby preventing arterial blood from reentering the heart.

▶▶▶ APPLY WHAT YOU KNOW

How would aortic valvular stenosis (see Deeper Insight 19.3) affect the amount of blood pumped into the aorta? How might this affect a person's physical stamina? Explain your reasoning.

19.5b Heart Sounds

As we follow events through the cardiac cycle, we will note the occurrence of two or three *heart sounds* audible with a stethoscope. Listening to sounds made by the body is called **auscultation** (AWS-cul-TAY-shun). The **first** and **second heart sounds,** symbolized S_1 and S_2, are often described as a "lubb-dupp"—S_1 is louder and longer and S_2 a little softer and sharper. In children and adolescents, it is normal to hear a **third heart sound** (S_3). This is rarely audible in people older than 30, but when it is, the heartbeat is said to show a *triple rhythm* or *gallop,* which may indicate an enlarged and failing heart. If the normal sounds are roughly simulated by drumming two fingers on a table, a triple rhythm sounds a little like drumming with three fingers. The heart

valves themselves operate silently, but S_1 and S_2 occur in conjunction with the closing of the valves as a result of turbulence in the bloodstream and movements of the heart wall.

19.5c Phases of the Cardiac Cycle

We now examine the phases of the cardiac cycle, the pressure changes that occur, and how the pressure changes and valves govern the flow of blood. Cardiovascular physiologist Carl J. Wiggers (1883–1963) devised an enormously informative chart, now known as the *Wiggers diagram* (**fig. 19.20**), for showing the major events that occur simultaneously at each moment throughout the cardiac cycle. Here, it is divided into colored and numbered bars to correspond to the following phases. Closely follow the figure as you study the text. Where to begin when describing a circular chain of events is somewhat arbitrary, but in this presentation, we begin with the filling of the ventricles. Remember that all these events are completed in less than 1 second.

1. **Ventricular filling.** During diastole, the ventricles expand and their pressure drops below that of the atria. As a result, the AV valves open and blood pours into the ventricles, raising the ventricular pressure and lowering atrial pressure. Ventricular filling occurs in three phases: (**1a**) The first one-third is *rapid ventricular filling,* when blood enters especially quickly. (**1b**) The second one-third, called *diastasis* (di-ASS-tuh-sis), is marked by slower filling. The P wave of the electrocardiogram occurs at the end of diastasis, marking the depolarization of the atria. (**1c**) In the last one-third, *atrial systole* completes the filling process. The right atrium contracts slightly before the left because it is the first to receive the signal from the SA node. At the end of ventricular filling, each ventricle contains an **end-diastolic volume (EDV)** of about 130 mL of blood. Only 40 mL (31%) of this is contributed by atrial systole.

2. **Isovolumetric contraction.** The atria repolarize, relax, and remain in diastole for the rest of the cardiac cycle. The ventricles depolarize, generate the QRS complex, and begin to contract. Wave Q marks the end of ventricular filling; R marks the transition from atrial systole to isovolumetric contraction of the ventricles; and S occurs during isovolumetric contraction. Pressure in the ventricles rises sharply and reverses the pressure gradient between atria and ventricles. The AV valves close as ventricular blood surges back against the cusps. Heart sound S_1 occurs at the beginning of this phase and is produced mainly by the left ventricle; the right ventricle is thought to make little contribution. Causes of the sound are thought to include tensing of the ventricular tissues and tendinous cords (like the twang of a suddenly stretched rubber band), turbulence in the blood as it surges against the closed AV valves, and impact of the heart against the chest wall. This phase is called *isovolumetric*[26] because even though the ventricles contract, they don't eject blood yet and

---

[25]*steno* = narrow; *osis* = condition

[26]*iso* = same; *volum* =volume; *metr* = measure

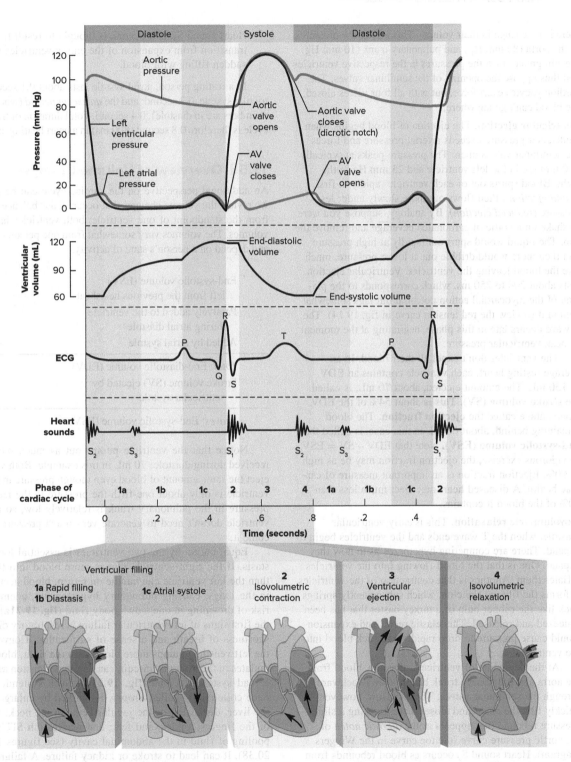

FIGURE 19.20 Modified Wiggers Diagram, Illustrating Events of the Cardiac Cycle. Two cycles are shown. The phases are numbered across the bottom to correspond to the text description.

? *Explain why the aortic pressure curve begins to rise abruptly at about 0.5 second.*

there is no change in their volume. This is because pressures in the aorta (80 mm Hg) and pulmonary trunk (10 mm Hg) are still greater than the pressures in the respective ventricles and thus oppose the opening of the semilunar valves. The cardiomyocytes exert force, but with all four valves closed, the blood can't go anywhere.

3. **Ventricular ejection.** The ejection of blood begins when ventricular pressure exceeds arterial pressure and forces the semilunar valves open. The pressure peaks at typically 120 mm Hg in the left ventricle and 25 mm Hg in the right. Blood spurts out of each ventricle rapidly at first *(rapid ejection),* then flows out more slowly under less pressure *(reduced ejection).* By analogy, suppose you were to shake up a bottle of carbonated beverage and remove the cap. The liquid would spurt out rapidly at high pressure and then more would dribble out at lower pressure, much like the blood leaving the ventricles. Ventricular ejection lasts about 200 to 250 ms, which corresponds to the plateau of the myocardial action potential but lags somewhat behind it (review the red tension curve in fig. 19.14). The T wave occurs late in this phase, beginning at the moment of peak ventricular pressure.

The ventricles don't expel all their blood. In an average resting heart, each ventricle contains an EDV of 130 mL. The amount ejected, about 70 mL, is called the **stroke volume (SV).** This is about 54% of the EDV, a percentage called the **ejection fraction.** The blood remaining behind, about 60 mL in this case, is called the **end-systolic volume (ESV).** Note that EDV – SV = ESV. In vigorous exercise, the ejection fraction may be as high as 90%. Ejection fraction is an important measure of cardiac health. A diseased heart may eject much less than 50% of the blood it contains.

4. **Isovolumetric relaxation.** This is early ventricular diastole, when the T wave ends and the ventricles begin to expand. There are competing hypotheses as to how they expand. One is that the blood flowing into the ventricles inflates them. Another is that contraction of the ventricles deforms the fibrous skeleton, which subsequently springs back like the rubber bulb of a turkey baster that has been squeezed and released. This elastic recoil and expansion would cause pressure to drop rapidly and suck blood into the ventricles.

At the beginning of ventricular diastole, blood from the aorta and pulmonary trunk briefly flows backward through the semilunar valves. The backflow, however, quickly fills the cusps and closes them, creating a slight pressure rebound that appears as the *dicrotic notch* of the aortic pressure curve (the top curve in the Wiggers diagram). Heart sound S_2 occurs as blood rebounds from the closed semilunar valves and the ventricles expand. This phase is called *isovolumetric* because the semilunar valves are closed, the AV valves haven't yet opened, and the ventricles are therefore taking in no blood. When the AV valves open, ventricular filling (phase 1) begins again.

Heart sound S_3, if it occurs, is thought to result from the transition from expansion of the empty ventricles to their sudden filling with blood.

In a resting person, atrial systole lasts about 0.1 second; ventricular systole, 0.3 second; and the *quiescent period* (when all four chambers are in diastole), 0.4 second. Total duration of the cardiac cycle is therefore 0.8 second (800 ms) in a heart beating at 75 bpm.

19.5d Overview of Volume Changes

An additional perspective on the cardiac cycle can be gained if we review the volume changes that occur. This "balance sheet" is from the standpoint of one ventricle; both ventricles have equal volumes. The volumes vary somewhat from one person to another and depend on a person's state of activity.

End-systolic volume (ESV) left from the previous heartbeat	60 mL
Passively added to the ventricle during atrial diastole	+ 30 mL
Added by atrial systole	+ 40 mL
Total: End-diastolic volume (EDV)	130 mL
Stroke volume (SV) ejected by ventricular systole	– 70 mL
Leaves: End-systolic volume (ESV)	60 mL

Notice that the ventricle pumps out as much blood as it received during diastole: 70 mL in this example. Both ventricles eject the same amount of blood even though pressure in the right ventricle is only about one-fifth the pressure in the left. Blood pressure in the pulmonary trunk is relatively low, so the right ventricle doesn't need to generate very much pressure to overcome it.

Equal output by the two ventricles is essential for homeostasis. If the right ventricle pumps more blood into the lungs than the left ventricle can handle on return, blood accumulates in the lungs, causing pulmonary hypertension, edema, and a risk of drowning in one's own body fluid **(fig. 19.21a).** One of the first signs of left ventricular failure is respiratory distress— shortness of breath and a sense of suffocation. Conversely, if the left ventricle pumps more blood than the right, blood accumulates in the systemic circuit, causing hypertension and widespread systemic edema **(fig. 19.21b).** Such systemic edema, once colloquially called *dropsy,* is marked by enlargement of the liver; distension of the jugular veins in the neck; swelling of the fingers, ankles, and feet; and **ascites** (ah-SITE-eez), a pooling of fluid in the abdominal cavity (see figures 18.3 and 20.38). It can lead to stroke or kidney failure. A failure of one ventricle increases the workload on the other, which stresses it and often leads to its eventual failure as well. In principle, if the output of the left ventricle were just 1% greater than output of the right, it would completely drain the lungs of blood in less than 10 minutes (although death would occur much sooner).

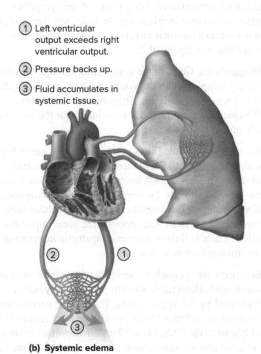

1. Right ventricular output exceeds left ventricular output.
2. Pressure backs up.
3. Fluid accumulates in pulmonary tissue.

(a) Pulmonary edema

1. Left ventricular output exceeds right ventricular output.
2. Pressure backs up.
3. Fluid accumulates in systemic tissue.

(b) Systemic edema

FIGURE 19.21 The Necessity of Balanced Ventricular Output. (a) If the left ventricle pumps less blood than the right, blood pressure backs up into the lungs and causes pulmonary edema. (b) If the right ventricle pumps less blood than the left, pressure backs up in the systemic circulation and causes systemic edema. To maintain homeostasis, both ventricles must pump the same average amount of blood.

Fluid accumulation in either circuit due to insufficiency of ventricular pumping is called **congestive heart failure (CHF).** Common causes of CHF are myocardial infarction, chronic hypertension, valvular defects, and congenital (birth) defects in cardiac anatomy.

BEFORE YOU GO ON

Answer the following questions to test your understanding of the preceding section:

20. Explain how a pressure gradient across a heart valve determines whether a ventricle ejects blood.

21. What factors are thought to cause the first and second heart sounds? When do these sounds occur?

22. What phases of the cardiac cycle are isovolumetric? Explain what this means.

23. Define *end-diastolic volume* and *end-systolic volume;* explain verbally why stroke volume is the difference between these two.

24. Why is it so important that neither the right nor left ventricle pump more blood than the other one for any prolonged time?

19.6 Regulation of Cardiac Output

Expected Learning Outcomes

When you have completed this section, you should be able to

a. trace the routes of sympathetic and parasympathetic nerves to their target cells in the heart;

b. define *cardiac output* and explain its importance;

c. identify the factors that govern cardiac output;

d. discuss some of the nervous and chemical factors that alter heart rate, stroke volume, and cardiac output;

e. explain how the right and left ventricles achieve balanced output; and

f. describe some effects of exercise on cardiac output.

The heart doesn't pump the same amount of blood every minute of every day, but varies its output according to states of rest, exercise, emotion, and other factors. We all know of circumstances that make our hearts beat faster or harder. In this section, we explore how the sympathetic and parasympathetic nervous systems, hormones and drugs, and other factors regulate the heart.

19.6a Autonomic Innervation of the Heart

Even though the heart has its own pacemaker, its rhythm and contraction strength are moderated by signals arising from two **cardiac centers** in the medulla oblongata of the brainstem. One of these, the **cardioacceleratory center,** communicates with the heart by way of right and left **cardiac nerves** carrying sympathetic postganglionic nerve fibers. The other is the nearby **cardioinhibitory center,** which communicates with the heart by way of the right and left **vagus nerves** carrying parasympathetic preganglionic nerve fibers.

The sympathetic pathway to the heart is shown on the left side of **figure 19.22,** numbered as follows:

1. Stimulatory signals from the cardioacceleratory center descend to the upper thoracic segments (T1–T4) of the spinal cord, ending on the sympathetic preganglionic neurons

in the lateral horn. Preganglionic fibers arise here and travel to the adjacent sympathetic chain ganglia.

2. Some of these fibers synapse with postganglionic neurons at the level of entry into the chain, and others ascend to the cervical ganglia and meet the postganglionic neurons there.

3. Postganglionic fibers emerging from the sympathetic chain form the cardiac nerves. These lead to the **cardiac plexus,** a web of mixed sympathetic and parasympathetic fibers tucked in between the aortic arch, pulmonary trunk, and lower trachea.

4. Postganglionic fibers continue through the plexus without synapsing and end on several targets in and near the heart: the SA node, AV node, atrial and ventricular myocardium, aorta, pulmonary trunk, and coronary arteries.

Sympathetic stimulation increases the heart rate and contraction strength and dilates the coronary arteries to increase blood supply to the exercising myocardium.

The parasympathetic pathway is shown on the right side of the same figure. Parasympathetic signals from the cardioinhibitory center exit the medulla oblongata through the two vagus nerves. These nerves travel down the right and left sides of the mediastinum, but both are shown on the right side of the figure just for diagrammatic convenience. For a photo of the sympathetic chain and right vagus nerve in relation to the heart, see figure 15.3. The vagus nerves travel to their targets in the heart by the route numbered as follows in figure 19.22:

5. Preganglionic fibers of the vagus travel through the cardiac plexus, mingling with the sympathetic fibers. They synapse with short postganglionic fibers here in the plexus or in the epicardium of the atria, especially near the SA and AV nodes.

6. Short postganglionic fibers of the right vagus nerve lead mainly to the SA node and those of the left vagus lead mainly to the AV node, but each has some fibers that cross over to the other target cells. Furthermore, some parasympathetic fibers terminate on sympathetic fibers and inhibit them from stimulating the heart and opposing the parasympathetic effect. There is little or no parasympathetic innervation of the myocardium or ventricles.

In general, the sympathetic nerves dominate the control of contraction strength. Heart rate is strongly influenced by both divisions, but dominated by the vagus nerves. The cardiac nerves carry not only sympathetic efferent fibers, but also sensory (afferent) fibers from the heart to the CNS. These fibers are important in cardiovascular reflexes and the transmission of pain signals from the heart.

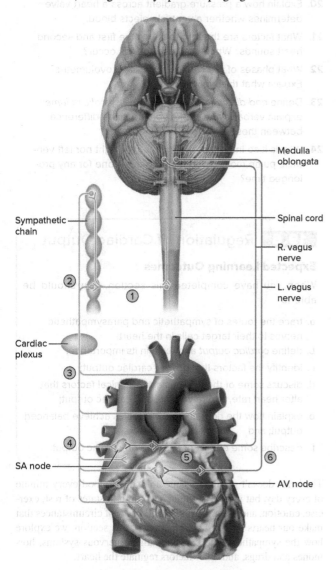

FIGURE 19.22 Autonomic Innervation of the Heart.
For schematic purposes, the cardiac plexus is shown offset from the heart, not in its natural location. The sympathetic and parasympathetic pathways both occur on the right and left, even though the sympathetic chain and nerves are illustrated only on the left and both vagus nerves are illustrated on the right.

Labels in figure: Medulla oblongata; Spinal cord; R. vagus nerve; L. vagus nerve; Sympathetic chain; Cardiac plexus; SA node; AV node

19.6b Cardiac Output

The entire point of all the cardiac physiology we have considered is to eject blood from the heart. The amount ejected by each ventricle in 1 minute is called the **cardiac output (CO).** If HR is heart rate (beats/min.) and SV is stroke volume (mL/beat),

$$CO = HR \times SV$$

At typical resting values,

CO = 75 beats/min. × 70 mL/beat = 5,250 mL/min.

Thus, the body's total volume of blood (4–6 L) passes through the heart every minute; or to look at it another way, an RBC leaving the left ventricle will, on average, arrive back at the left ventricle in about 1 minute.

Cardiac output varies with the body's state of activity. Vigorous exercise increases CO to as much as 21 L/min. in a person in good condition, and more than 40 L/min. in world-class athletes. The difference between the maximum and resting cardiac output is called **cardiac reserve.** People with severe heart disease may have little or no cardiac reserve and little tolerance of physical exertion.

Given that cardiac output equals HR × SV, you can see that there are only two ways to change it: Change the heart rate or change the stroke volume. We will consider factors that influence each of these variables, but bear in mind that heart rate and stroke volume are somewhat interdependent. They usually change together and in opposite directions. As heart rate goes up, stroke volume goes down, and vice versa.

19.6c Heart Rate and Chronotropic Agents

Heart rate is most easily measured by taking a person's **pulse** at some point where an artery runs close to the body surface, such as the *radial artery* in the wrist or *common carotid artery* in the neck. Each beat of the heart produces a surge of pressure that can be felt by palpating a superficial artery with the fingertips. Heart rate can be obtained by counting the number of pulses in 15 seconds and multiplying by 4 to get beats per minute. In newborn infants, the resting heart rate is commonly 120 bpm or greater. It declines steadily with age, averaging 72 to 80 bpm in young adult females and 64 to 72 bpm in young adult males. It rises again in the elderly.

Tachycardia[27] is a persistent, resting adult heart rate above 100 bpm. It can be caused by stress, anxiety, stimulants, heart disease, or fever. Heart rate also rises to compensate to some extent for a drop in stroke volume. Thus, the heart races when the body has lost a significant quantity of blood or when there is damage to the myocardium.

Bradycardia[28] is a persistent, resting adult heart rate below 60 bpm. It is common during sleep and in endurance-trained athletes. Endurance training enlarges the heart and increases its stroke volume, enabling it to maintain the same output with fewer beats. Hypothermia (low body temperature) also slows the heart and may be deliberately induced in preparation for cardiac surgery. Diving mammals such as whales and seals exhibit bradycardia during the dive, as do humans to some extent when the face is immersed in cool water.

Factors outside of the heart itself that raise the heart rate are called **positive chronotropic**[29] **agents,** and factors that lower it are **negative chronotropic agents.** We next consider some

chronotropic effects of the autonomic nervous system, hormones, electrolytes, and blood gases.

The Autonomic Nervous System

Although the nervous system doesn't initiate the heartbeat, it does modulate its rhythm and force through the aforementioned autonomic nerves. The sympathetic nervous system exerts its effects directly through the cardiac nerves and indirectly by stimulating the adrenal medulla. The nerve fibers secrete norepinephrine (NE) and the adrenal medulla secretes a mixture of about 85% epinephrine (Epi) and 15% NE—known collectively as *catecholamines.* Both of these have positive chronotropic *and* inotropic effects on the heart, but for the moment, we will focus on the chronotropic effect.

Epi and NE bind to β-adrenergic receptors in the heart and activate the cyclic adenosine monophosphate (cAMP) second-messenger system (see fig. 3.8). Cyclic AMP activates an enzyme that opens Ca^{2+} channels in the plasma membrane, admitting calcium from the extracellular fluid into the SA node and cardiomyocytes. This accelerates depolarization of the SA node and speeds up signal conduction through the AV node. Both of these quicken the contractions of the ventricular myocardium and speed up the heartbeat. In addition, cAMP accelerates the reuptake of Ca^{2+} by the sarcoplasmic reticulum of the cardiomyocytes. Quick Ca^{2+} reuptake shortens ventricular systole and the QT interval (see table 19.1), enabling the ventricles to relax and refill sooner than they do at rest. By accelerating *both* the contraction and relaxation of the heart, cAMP increases the heart rate.

Adrenergic stimulation can, in fact, raise the heart rate to as high as 230 bpm. This limit is set mainly by the refractory period of the SA node, which prevents it from firing any more frequently. Cardiac output peaks, however, at a rate of 160 to 180 bpm. At rates any higher than this, the ventricles have too little time to fill between beats. At a resting rate of 65 bpm, ventricular diastole lasts about 0.62 second, but at 200 bpm, it lasts only 0.14 second. Thus you can see that at excessively high heart rates, diastole is too brief to allow complete filling of the ventricles, and therefore stroke volume and cardiac output are reduced.

The parasympathetic vagus nerves, by contrast, have a negative chronotropic effect. Left to itself, the SA node and the heart as a whole have a resting rhythm of about 100 bpm; this is seen if all nerves to the heart are severed or if all sympathetic and parasympathetic action is pharmacologically blocked. But with intact, functional innervation, the vagus nerves have a steady background firing rate called **vagal tone** that holds the heart rate down to its usual 70 to 80 bpm at rest. The heart can be accelerated not only by sympathetic stimulation but also by reducing vagal tone and allowing the heart to "do its own thing." Extreme vagal stimulation can reduce the heart rate to as low as 20 bpm or even stop the heart briefly.

The postganglionic neurons of the vagus are cholinergic—they secrete acetylcholine (ACh) at the SA and AV nodes. ACh binds to muscarinic receptors and opens K^+ gates in the nodal cells. The resulting outflow of K^+ hyperpolarizes the cells, so the SA node fires less frequently and the heart slows down. ACh acts primarily on the SA node but also slows signal conduction through the AV

---

[27]*tachy* = speed, fast; *card* = heart; *ia* = condition
[28]*brady* = slow; *card* = heart; *ia* = condition
[29]*chrono* = time; *trop* = to change, to influence

node, thus delaying excitation of the ventricles. The vagus nerves have a faster-acting effect on the heart than the sympathetic nerves because ACh acts directly on membrane ion channels; sympathetic effects are slower because of the time taken for the cAMP system to open ion channels.

▶▶▶ APPLY WHAT YOU KNOW

Which of the intervals or segments of the electrocardiogram do you think is or are most affected by ACh? Explain your answer.

The Central Nervous System

There is a benefit to placing heart rate under the influence of cardiac centers in the medulla—these centers can receive input from many other sources and integrate it into a decision as to whether the heart should beat more quickly or slowly. Sensory and emotional stimuli can act on the cardiac centers by way of the cerebral cortex, limbic system, and hypothalamus; therefore, heart rate can climb even as you anticipate taking the first plunge on a roller coaster or competing in an athletic event, and it is influenced by emotions such as love and anger. The medulla also receives input from the following receptors in the muscles, joints, arteries, and brainstem:

- **Proprioceptors** in the muscles and joints provide information on changes in physical activity. Thus, the heart can increase its output even before the metabolic demands of the muscles rise.
- **Baroreceptors (pressoreceptors)** are pressure sensors in the aorta and internal carotid arteries (see figs. 15.1, 20.4). They send a continual stream of signals to the medulla. When the heart rate rises, cardiac output increases and raises the blood pressure at the baroreceptors. The baroreceptors increase their signaling to the medulla and, depending on circumstances, the medulla may issue vagal output to lower the heart rate. Conversely, the baroreceptors also inform the medulla of drops in blood pressure. The medulla can then issue sympathetic output to increase the heart rate, bringing cardiac output and blood pressure back up to normal (see fig. 1.8). Either way, a negative feedback loop usually prevents the blood pressure from deviating too far from normal.
- **Chemoreceptors** occur in the aortic arch, carotid arteries, and the medulla oblongata itself, and are sensitive to blood pH, CO_2, and O_2 levels. They are more important in respiratory control than in cardiovascular control, but they do influence the heart rate. If circulation to the tissues is too slow to remove CO_2 as fast as the tissues produce it, then CO_2 accumulates in the blood and cerebrospinal fluid (CSF) and produces a state of *hypercapnia* (CO_2 excess). Furthermore, CO_2 generates hydrogen ions by reacting with water: $CO_2 + H_2O \longrightarrow HCO_3^- + H^+$. The hydrogen ions lower the pH of the blood and CSF and may create a state of *acidosis* (pH < 7.35). Hypercapnia and acidosis stimulate the cardiac centers to increase the heart rate,

thus improving perfusion of the tissues and restoring homeostasis. The chemoreceptors also respond to extreme *hypoxemia* (oxygen deficiency), as in suffocation, but the effect is usually to slow down the heart, perhaps so the heart doesn't compete with the brain for the limited oxygen supply.

Such responses to fluctuations in blood chemistry and blood pressure, called **chemoreflexes** and **baroreflexes,** are good examples of negative feedback loops. They are discussed more fully in the next chapter.

Hormones, Drugs, and Other Chronotropic Chemicals

Heart rate is influenced by many other factors besides the autonomic nervous system. Thyroid hormone accelerates it by stimulating the up-regulation of β-adrenergic receptors, making the heart more sensitive to sympathetic stimulation; this is why tachycardia is one of the signs of hyperthyroidism. Glucagon, secreted by the alpha cells of the pancreatic islets, accelerates the heart by promoting cAMP production. Glucagon is sometimes given in cardiac emergencies to stimulate the heartbeat, and epinephrine is frequently given to support cardiac output and blood pressure in life-threatening allergic reactions.

Food-borne drugs and medications also have well-known chronotropic effects related to the catecholamine–cAMP mechanism. Nicotine accelerates the heart by stimulating catecholamine secretion. Caffeine and the related stimulants in tea and chocolate accelerate it by inhibiting cAMP breakdown, prolonging its adrenergic effect. Hypertension is often treated with drugs called *beta blockers,* which inhibit the binding of catecholamines to the β-adrenergic receptors and slow down the heart.

Electrolyte concentrations also strongly influence heart rate and contraction strength. The most powerful chronotropic effects are from potassium ions (K^+). In *hyperkalemia,*[30] a potassium excess, K^+ diffuses into the cardiomyocytes and keeps the membrane voltage elevated, inhibiting cardiomyocyte repolarization. The myocardium becomes less excitable, the heart rate becomes slow and irregular, and the heart may arrest in diastole. In *hypokalemia,* a potassium deficiency, K^+ diffuses out of the cardiomyocytes and they become hyperpolarized—the membrane potential is more negative than normal. This makes them harder to stimulate. These potassium imbalances are very dangerous and require emergency medical treatment.

Calcium also affects heart rate. A calcium excess *(hypercalcemia)* causes a slow heartbeat, whereas a calcium deficiency *(hypocalcemia)* elevates the heart rate. Such calcium imbalances are relatively rare, however, and when they do occur, their primary effect is on contraction strength, which is considered in the coming section on contractility. Section 24.2 further explores the causes and effects of imbalances in potassium, calcium, and other electrolytes.

---

[30]*hyper* = excess; *kal* = potassium (Latin, *kalium*); *emia* = blood condition

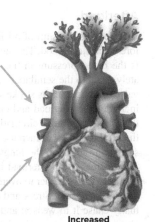

Increased   **Reduced**

Cardiac Output
(CO = HR × SV)

FIGURE 19.23 Summary of Factors Affecting Cardiac Output. Factors on the left (green boxes) increase cardiac output, whereas factors on the right (red boxes) reduce it. These include the intrinsic state of the heart and adjacent arteries at a given time (preload, contractility, and afterload), and extrinsic agents that act on the heart (chronotropic and inotropic agents).

Several positive and negative chronotropic agents are shown in the top half of **figure 19.23,** summarizing how they affect cardiac output by altering heart rate. We move on now to the bottom half of the figure and inotropic agents, which act on cardiac output through their effects on contraction strength and stroke volume.

19.6d Stroke Volume and Inotropic Agents

The other factor in cardiac output is stroke volume. This is governed by three variables called *preload, contractility,* and *afterload.* Increased preload or contractility increases stroke volume, whereas increased afterload opposes the emptying of the ventricles and reduces stroke volume.

Preload

Preload is the amount of tension (stretch) in the ventricular myocardium immediately before it begins to contract. To understand how this influences stroke volume, imagine yourself engaged in heavy exercise. As active muscles massage your veins, they drive more blood back to the heart, increasing *venous return.* As more blood enters the heart, it stretches the myocardium. Because of the length–tension relationship of striated muscle (see fig. 11.12), moderate stretch enables the cardiomyocytes to generate more tension when they contract—that is, stretch increases preload. When the ventricles contract more forcefully, they expel more blood, thus adjusting cardiac output to the increase in venous return.

This principle is summarized by the **Frank–Starling law of the heart.**[31] In a concise, symbolic way, it states that SV ∝ EDV;

that is, stroke volume is proportional to the end-diastolic volume. In other words, the ventricles tend to eject as much blood as they receive. Within limits, the more they are stretched, the harder they contract on the next beat.

Although relaxed skeletal muscle is normally at an optimum length for the most forceful contraction, relaxed cardiac muscle is at less than optimum length. Additional stretch therefore produces a significant increase in contraction force on the next beat. This helps balance the output of the two ventricles. For example, if the right ventricle begins to pump an increased amount of blood, this soon arrives at the left ventricle, stretches it more than before, and causes it to increase its stroke volume and match that of the right.

Contractility

Contractility refers to how hard the myocardium contracts *for a given preload.* It doesn't describe the increase in tension produced by stretching the muscle, but rather an increase caused by factors that make the cardiomyocytes more responsive to stimulation. Factors that increase contractility are called **positive inotropic**[32] **agents,** and those that reduce it are **negative inotropic agents.**

Calcium has a strong, positive inotropic effect—it increases the strength of each contraction of the heart. This is not surprising, because Ca^{2+} not only is essential to the excitation–contraction coupling of muscle, but also prolongs the plateau of the myocardial action potential. Calcium imbalances therefore affect not only heart rate, as we have already seen, but also contraction strength. In hypercalcemia, extra Ca^{2+} diffuses into the cardiomyocytes and produces strong, prolonged contractions.

[31]Otto Frank (1865–1944), German physiologist; Ernest Henry Starling (1866–1927), English physiologist

[32]*ino* = fiber; *trop* = to change, to influence

In extreme cases, it can cause cardiac arrest in systole. In hypocalcemia, the cardiomyocytes lose Ca^{2+} to the extracellular fluid, leading to a weak, irregular heartbeat and potentially to cardiac arrest in diastole. However, severe hypocalcemia is likely to kill through skeletal muscle paralysis and suffocation before the cardiac effects are felt (see section 7.4b).

Agents that affect calcium availability have not only the chronotropic effects already examined, but also inotropic effects. We have already seen that norepinephrine increases calcium levels in the sarcoplasm; consequently, it increases not only heart rate but also contraction strength (as does epinephrine, for the same reason). The pancreatic hormone glucagon exerts an inotropic effect by stimulating cAMP production; a solution of glucagon and calcium chloride is sometimes used for the emergency treatment of heart attacks. Digitalis, a cardiac stimulant from the foxglove plant, also raises the intracellular calcium level and contraction strength; it is used to treat congestive heart failure.

Hyperkalemia has a negative inotropic effect because it reduces the strength of myocardial action potentials and thus reduces the release of Ca^{2+} into the sarcoplasm. The heart becomes dilated and flaccid. Hypokalemia, however, has little effect on contractility.

The vagus nerves have a negative inotropic effect on the atria, but they provide so little innervation to the ventricles that they have no significant effect on them.

▶▶▶**APPLY WHAT YOU KNOW**

Suppose a person has a heart rate of 70 bpm and a stroke volume of 70 mL. A negative inotropic agent then reduces the stroke volume to 50 mL. What would the new heart rate have to be to maintain the same cardiac output?

Afterload

Afterload is the sum of all forces a ventricle must overcome before it can eject blood. The most significant contribution to afterload is the blood pressure in the aorta and pulmonary trunk immediately distal to the semilunar valves; it opposes the opening of these valves and thus limits stroke volume. For this reason, hypertension increases the afterload and opposes ventricular ejection. Anything that impedes arterial circulation, such as atherosclerotic plaque in the arteries, can also increase the afterload. In some lung diseases, scar tissue forms in the lungs and restricts pulmonary circulation. This increases the afterload in the pulmonary trunk. As the right ventricle works harder to overcome this resistance, it gets larger like any other muscle. Stress and hypertrophy of a ventricle can eventually cause it to weaken and fail. Right ventricular failure due to obstructed pulmonary circulation is called *cor pulmonale*[33] (CORE PUL-mo-NAY-lee). It is a common complication of emphysema, chronic bronchitis, and black lung disease (see section 22.4b).

19.6e Exercise and Cardiac Output

It is no secret that exercise makes the heart work harder, and it should come as no surprise that this increases cardiac output. The main reason the heart rate increases at the beginning of exercise is that proprioceptors in the muscles and joints transmit signals to the cardiac centers, signifying that the muscles are active and will quickly need an increased blood flow. Sympathetic output from the cardiac centers then increases cardiac output to meet the expected demand. As the exercise progresses, muscular activity increases venous return. This increases the preload on the right ventricle and is soon reflected in the left ventricle as more blood

[33]*cor* = heart; *pulmo* = lung

TABLE 19.2	Some Disorders of the Heart
Acute pericarditis	Inflammation of the pericardium, sometimes due to infection, radiation therapy, or connective tissue disease, causing pain and friction rub
Cardiomyopathy	Any disease of the myocardium not resulting from coronary artery disease, valvular dysfunction, or other cardiovascular disorders; can cause dilation and failure of the heart, thinning of the heart wall, or thickening of the interventricular septum
Infective endocarditis	Inflammation of the endocardium, usually due to bacterial infection, especially *Streptococcus* and *Staphylococcus*
Myocardial ischemia	Inadequate blood flow to the myocardium, usually because of coronary atherosclerosis; can lead to myocardial infarction
Pericardial effusion	Seepage of fluid from the pericardium into the pericardial cavity, often resulting from pericarditis and sometimes causing cardiac tamponade
Septal defects	Abnormal openings in the interatrial or interventricular septum, resulting in blood from the right atrium flowing directly into the left atrium, or blood from the left ventricle returning to the right ventricle; results in pulmonary hypertension, difficulty breathing, and fatigue; often fatal in childhood if uncorrected

You can find other cardiac disorders described in the following places:

Cardiac tamponade in Deeper Insight A.1; *friction rub* in section 19.1c; *angina pectoris* and *myocardial infarction* in Deeper Insight 19.1; *ventricular fibrillation, atrial fibrillation, premature ventricular contraction, bundle branch block, total heart block,* and *cardiac arrest* in Deeper Insight 19.2; *valvular stenosis, mitral valve prolapse,* and *heart murmur* in Deeper Insight 19.3; *congestive heart failure* in section 19.5d; *bradycardia* and *tachycardia* in section 19.6c; *cor pulmonale* in section 19.6d; and *atherosclerosis, arteriosclerosis,* and *coronary artery disease* in Deeper Insight 19.4.

flows through the pulmonary circuit and reaches the left heart. As the heart rate and stroke volume rise, cardiac output rises, which compensates for the increased venous return.

A sustained program of exercise causes hypertrophy of the ventricles, which increases their stroke volume. As explained earlier, this allows the heart to beat more slowly and still maintain a normal resting cardiac output. Some world-class, endurance-trained athletes have resting heart rates as low as 30 to 40 bpm, but because of the higher stroke volume, their resting cardiac output is about the same as that of an untrained person. Such athletes have greater cardiac reserve, so they can tolerate more exertion than a sedentary person can.

The effects of aging on the heart are discussed in section 29.4a, and some common heart diseases are listed in **table 19.2.** Disorders of the blood and blood vessels are described in chapters 18 and 20.

DEEPER INSIGHT 19.4

CLINICAL APPLICATION

Coronary Artery Disease

Coronary artery disease (CAD) is a constriction of the coronary arteries usually resulting from *atherosclerosis*[34]—an accumulation of lipid deposits that degrade the arterial wall and obstruct the lumen. The most dangerous consequence of CAD is myocardial infarction (heart attack).

Pathogenesis

CAD begins when hypertension, diabetes, or other factors damage the arterial lining. Monocytes adhere to the lining, penetrate into the tissue, and become macrophages. Macrophages and smooth muscle cells absorb cholesterol and fat from the blood, which gives them a frothy appearance. They are then called *foam cells* and form visible *fatty streaks* on the arterial wall. Seen even in infants and children, these are harmless in themselves but have the potential to grow into atherosclerotic *plaques (atheromas*[35]*)*.

Platelets adhere to these plaques and secrete a growth factor that stimulates local proliferation of smooth muscle and fibroblasts and deposition of collagen. The plaque grows into a bulging mass of lipid, fiber, and smooth muscle and other cells. When it obstructs 75% or more of the arterial lumen, it begins to cause symptoms such as angina pectoris. More seriously, inflammation of the plaque roughens its surface and creates a focal point for thrombosis. A blood clot can block what remains of the lumen, or break free and lodge in a smaller artery downstream. Sometimes a piece of plaque breaks free and travels as a *fatty embolus*. Furthermore, the plaque can contribute to spasms of the coronary artery, cutting off blood flow to the myocardium. If the lumen is already partially obstructed by a plaque and perhaps a blood clot, such a spasm can temporarily shut off the remaining flow and precipitate an attack of angina.

Over time, the resilient muscular and elastic tissue of an inflamed artery becomes increasingly replaced with scar tissue and calcium deposits, transforming an atheroma into a hard *complicated plaque* **(fig. 19.24).** Hardening of the arteries by calcified plaques is one cause of *arteriosclerosis*.[36] For reasons explained in the next chapter, this results in excessive surges of blood pressure that may weaken and rupture smaller arteries, leading to stroke and kidney failure.

Answer the following questions to test your understanding of the preceding section:

25. Explain why the vagus nerves have no significant inotropic effect on the ventricular myocardium.

26. Define *cardiac output* in words and with a simple mathematical formula.

27. Describe the cardiac center and innervation of the heart.

28. Explain what is meant by positive and negative chronotropic and inotropic agents. Give two examples of each.

29. How do preload, contractility, and afterload influence stroke volume and cardiac output?

30. Explain the principle behind the Frank–Starling law of the heart. How does this mechanism normally prevent pulmonary or systemic congestion?

Risk, Prevention, and Treatment

A paramount risk factor for CAD is excess *low-density lipoproteins (LDLs)* in the blood combined with defective LDL receptors in the arterial walls. LDLs are protein-coated droplets of cholesterol, fats, free fatty acids, and phospholipids (see "Cholesterol and Serum Lipoproteins" in section 26.1g). Most cells have LDL receptors that enable them to absorb these droplets from the blood so they can metabolize the cholesterol and other lipids. CAD can occur when the arterial cells have dysfunctional LDL receptors that "don't know when to quit," so the cells absorb and accumulate excess cholesterol.

Some risk factors for CAD are unavoidable—for example, heredity and aging. Most risk factors, however, are preventable—obesity, smoking, lack of exercise, and a personality fraught with anxiety, stress, and aggression, all conducive to the hypertension that initiates arterial damage. Diet, of course, is very significant. Eating animal fat raises one's LDL level and reduces the number of LDL receptors. Foods high in soluble fiber (such as beans, apples, and oat bran) lower blood cholesterol by an interesting mechanism: The liver normally converts cholesterol to bile acids and secretes them into the small intestine to aid fat digestion. The bile acids are reabsorbed farther down the intestine and recycled to the liver for reuse. Soluble fiber, however, binds bile acids and carries them out in the feces. To replace them, the liver synthesizes more, thus consuming more cholesterol.

CAD is often treated with a *coronary artery bypass graft (CABG)*. Sections of the great saphenous vein of the leg or small thoracic arteries are used to construct a detour around the obstruction in the coronary artery. In *balloon angioplasty*,[37] a slender catheter is threaded into the coronary artery and then a balloon at its tip is inflated to press the atheroma against the arterial wall, widening the lumen. In *laser angioplasty*, the surgeon views the interior of the diseased artery with an illuminated catheter and vaporizes the atheroma with a laser. Angioplasty is less risky and expensive than bypass surgery, but is often followed by *restenosis*—atheromas grow back and reobstruct the artery months later. Insertion of a tube called a *stent* into the artery can prevent restenosis.

---

[34] *athero* = fat, fatty; *sclerosis* = hardening
[35] *athero* = fat, fatty; *oma* = mass, tumor
[36] *arterio* = artery; *sclerosis* = hardening

---

[37] *angio* = vessel; *plasty* = surgical repair

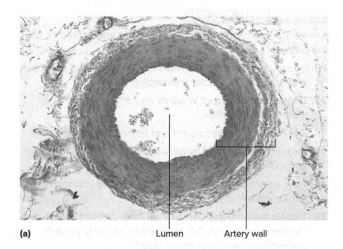

(a)   Lumen   Artery wall

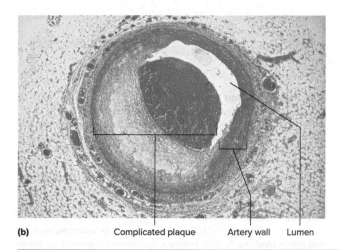

(b)   Complicated plaque   Artery wall   Lumen

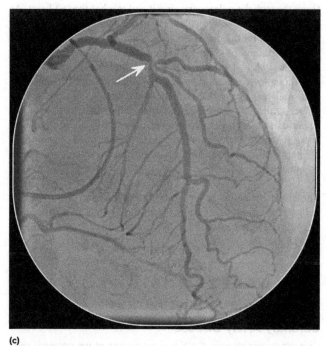

(c)

FIGURE 19.24 Coronary Artery Disease. (a) Cross section
of a healthy coronary artery. (b) Cross section of an artery with
advanced coronary atherosclerosis. Most of the original lumen
is obstructed by a *complicated plaque* composed of calcified
scar tissue. The lumen is reduced to a small space that can easily
be blocked by a stationary or traveling blood clot (thrombosis
or thromboembolism, respectively) or by vasoconstriction.
(c) Coronary angiogram showing 60% obstruction, at arrow, of the
anterior interventricular (left anterior descending, LAD) artery.

a: Ed Reschke/Getty Images; b: Image Source/Getty Images; c: kalewa/Shutterstock

STUDY GUIDE

▶ Assess Your Learning Outcomes

To test your knowledge, discuss the following topics with a study partner or in writing, ideally from memory.

19.1 Overview of the Cardiovascular System

1. Two subdivisions of the cardiovascular system and their respective functions
2. Names of the great vessels directly connected to the heart, and their relations to the heart chambers
3. The exact location of the heart, its size, and its base and apex
4. Anatomy and function of the pericardium and pericardial fluid

19.2 Gross Anatomy of the Heart

1. Three layers of the heart wall and their histological differences
2. Relative thickness of the myocardium in different chambers; the functional significance of those differences; and significance of the vortex of the heart
3. Structure and function of the fibrous skeleton of the heart
4. Anatomy and functions of the atria and ventricles; the internal septa that separate the four chambers and the external sulci that mark the chamber boundaries
5. Names and synonyms for all four valves of the heart
6. Structural differences between the valves; anatomy and function of the papillary muscles and tendinous cords
7. The path of blood flow through the heart chambers and valves
8. Anatomy of the coronary arteries and their main branches
9. Causes of myocardial infarction (MI) and how the collateral circulation in the coronary arteries reduces the risk of MI
10. Why coronary artery blood flow is greater when the heart relaxes than when it contracts, in contrast to the arterial system almost everywhere else in the body
11. Anatomy of the major veins that drain the myocardium, where this blood goes, and how the major veins are supplemented by the small cardiac veins

19.3 Cardiac Muscle and the Cardiac Conduction System

1. Structural properties of cardiomyocytes, how they differ from skeletal muscle, and how they relate to the unique function of cardiac muscle
2. Properties of cardiac muscle related to its nearly exclusive reliance on aerobic respiration
3. Components of the cardiac conduction system and the path traveled by electrical signals through the heart

19.4 Electrical and Contractile Activity of the Heart

1. The meanings of *systole* and *diastole*
2. Characteristics of the sinus rhythm of the heart; some causes of premature ventricular contraction; why an ectopic focus may take over control of the rhythm; how a nodal rhythm differs from the sinus rhythm; and the general term for any abnormal cardiac rhythm
3. The mechanism that causes cells of the SA node to depolarize rhythmically; a graph of the time course and voltages of the pacemaker potentials; how often this repeats itself in a normal resting heart; and the role of gated ion channels and specific ion inflows and outflows in creating the nodal rhythm
4. The spread of excitation through the atria, AV node, AV bundle and bundle branches, and subendocardial conducting network; changing conduction speeds at different points along this path, and why these changes are important; and the correlation of atrial and ventricular systole with the traveling wave of excitation
5. The twisting mode of ventricular contraction and the importance of the tendinous cords in preventing valvular prolapse
6. The cardiomyocyte resting potential; the actions of gated sodium, calcium, and potassium channels, and movements of these ions, in producing myocardial action potentials; how and why the shape of a myocardial action potential differs from that of a neuron; and how the plateau and unusually long refractory period of myocardial action potentials support the pumping effectiveness of the heart

7. Electrocardiograms and what happens in the heart during each ECG wave

19.5 Blood Flow, Heart Sounds, and the Cardiac Cycle

1. The principle on which a sphygmomanometer works, and why BP is expressed in millimeters of mercury (mm Hg)
2. The relationship of fluid volume, pressure, and flow, and how this relates to blood flow during the expansion and contraction of the heart chambers
3. Mechanisms that open and close the heart valves
4. The definition of *cardiac cycle,* and the names of its four phases
5. In each phase of the cardiac cycle, which chambers depolarize or repolarize, contract or relax; what each pair of valves does; what appears in the ECG; what accounts for the heart sounds; whether blood moves into or out of the atria or ventricles and where it is going when ejected; and blood volume and pressure changes in the left atrium, left ventricle, and aorta
6. The typical duration, in seconds, of atrial systole, ventricular systole, and the quiescent period, and how heart rate can be calculated from these values
7. The volume of blood typically found in each ventricle when it has finished filling; the volume ejected when a ventricle contracts; the percentage of ventricular blood that is ejected; the amount that remains behind when contraction is finished; and names of these four variables
8. Why it is necessary that each ventricle eject the same average amount of blood; what happens if either ventricle ejects more than the other over an extended period of time

19.6 Regulation of Cardiac Output

1. Pathways of sympathetic and parasympathetic innervation of the heart
2. The meaning of *cardiac output* and how to calculate it from heart rate and stroke volume
3. The typical resting heart rate and how it changes with age

4. Causes and terms for abnormally fast and slow resting heart rates
5. The definitions and cardiac effects of *positive* and *negative chronotropic agents*
6. Effects of the sympathetic and parasympathetic nervous systems on heart rate
7. The heart rate range associated with maximum cardiac output, and why cardiac output doesn't rise any farther at still faster heart rates
8. The intrinsic firing rate of the SA node and how vagal tone normally holds the resting heart rate below this

9. Control centers of the brainstem that regulate heart rate, and their mode of action
10. How proprioceptors, baroreceptors, and chemoreceptors influence heart rate
11. Effects of norepinephrine and acetylcholine on heart rate, and their mechanisms of action
12. Hormones and drugs that affect heart rate, and their mechanisms of action
13. Effects of potassium and calcium levels on heart rate, and their mechanisms of action
14. The meanings of *preload, contractility,* and *afterload,* and how each one affects stroke volume

15. How the Frank–Starling law of the heart matches stroke volume to venous return
16. The definitions and cardiac effects of *positive* and *negative inotropic agents*
17. How calcium and potassium affect myocardial contractility
18. How norepinephrine, glucagon, and digitalis affect contractility
19. How certain diseases reduce cardiac output by increasing afterload
20. The mechanisms by which exercise increases cardiac output
21. Why well-conditioned athletes may have unusually low resting heart rates

▶ Testing Your Recall

Answers in Appendix A

1. The cardiac conduction system includes all of the following *except*
   a. the SA node.
   b. the AV node.
   c. the bundle branches.
   d. the tendinous cords.
   e. the subendocardial conducting network.

2. To get from the right atrium to the right ventricle, blood flows through
   a. the pulmonary valve.
   b. the tricuspid valve.
   c. the bicuspid valve.
   d. the aortic valve.
   e. the mitral valve.

3. Assume that one ventricle of a child's heart has an EDV of 90 mL, an ESV of 60 mL, and a cardiac output of 2.55 L/min. What are the child's stroke volume (SV), ejection fraction (EF), and heart rate (HR)?
   a. SV = 60 mL; EF = 33%; HR = 85 bpm
   b. SV = 30 mL; EF = 60%; HR = 75 bpm
   c. SV = 150 mL; EF = 67%; HR = 42 bpm
   d. SV = 30 mL; EF = 33%; HR = 85 bpm
   e. Not enough information is given to calculate these.

4. A heart rate of 45 bpm and an absence of P waves suggest
   a. damage to the SA node.
   b. ventricular fibrillation.
   c. cor pulmonale.
   d. extrasystole.
   e. heart block.

5. There is/are _____ pulmonary vein(s) emptying into the right atrium of the heart.
   a. no
   b. one
   c. two
   d. four
   e. more than four

6. All of the following are positive chronotropic agents *except*
   a. caffeine.
   b. thyroid hormone.
   c. norepinephrine.
   d. acetylcholine.
   e. hypocalcemia.

7. The atria contract during
   a. the first heart sound.
   b. the second heart sound.
   c. the QRS complex.
   d. the PQ segment.
   e. the ST segment.

8. Cardiac muscle does not exhibit tetanus because it has
   a. fast Ca^{2+} channels.
   b. scanty sarcoplasmic reticulum.
   c. a long absolute refractory period.
   d. electrical synapses.
   e. exclusively aerobic respiration.

9. The blood contained in a ventricle during isovolumetric relaxation is
   a. the end-systolic volume.
   b. the end-diastolic volume.
   c. the stroke volume.
   d. the ejection fraction.
   e. none of these; the ventricle is empty then.

10. Drugs that increase myocardial contractility have a _____ effect.
    a. myogenic
    b. negative inotropic
    c. positive inotropic
    d. negative chronotropic
    e. positive chronotropic

11. The contraction of any heart chamber is called _____ and its relaxation is called _____.

12. The circulatory route from aorta to the venae cavae is the _____ circuit.

13. The circumflex artery travels in a groove called the _____.

14. The pacemaker potential of the SA node cells results from the slow inflow of _____.

15. Electrical signals pass quickly from one cardiomyocyte to another through the _____ of the intercalated discs.

16. Repolarization of the ventricles produces the _____ of the electrocardiogram.

17. The _____ nerves innervate the heart and tend to reduce the heart rate.

18. The death of cardiac tissue from lack of blood flow is commonly known as a heart attack, but clinically called _____.

19. Blood in the heart chambers is separated from the myocardium by a thin membrane called the _____.

20. The Frank–Starling law of the heart explains why the _____ of the left ventricle is the same as that of the right ventricle.

STUDY GUIDE

▶ Building Your Medical Vocabulary

Answers in Appendix A

State a meaning of each word element, and give a medical term from this chapter that uses it or a slight variation of it.

1. atrio-
2. brady-
3. cardio-
4. corono-
5. lun-
6. papillo-
7. semi-
8. tachy-
9. vaso-
10. ventro-

▶ What's Wrong with These Statements?

Answers in Appendix A

Briefly explain why each of the following statements is false, or reword it to make it true.

1. The blood supply to the myocardium is the coronary circulation; everything else is called the systemic circuit.

2. One-way valves prevent atrial systole from driving blood back into the venae cavae and pulmonary veins.

3. No blood can enter the ventricles until the atria contract.

4. The vagus nerves reduce the heart rate and the strength of ventricular contraction.

5. A high blood CO_2 level and low pH slow the heart rate.

6. The first heart sound occurs at the time of the P wave of the electrocardiogram.

7. If all nerves to the heart were severed, the heart would instantly stop beating.

8. If the two pulmonary arteries were clamped shut, pulmonary edema would soon follow.

9. Unlike skeletal muscle, cardiac muscle cells do not have a stable resting membrane potential.

10. An electrocardiogram is a tracing of the action potential of a cardiomyocyte.

▶ Testing Your Comprehension

1. Verapamil is a calcium channel blocker used to treat hypertension. It selectively blocks slow calcium channels. Would you expect it to have a positive or negative inotropic effect? Explain. (See Deeper Insight 3.1 to review calcium channel blockers.)

2. To temporarily treat tachycardia and restore the normal resting sinus rhythm, a physician may massage a patient's carotid artery near the angle of the mandible. Propose a mechanism by which this treatment would have the desired effect.

3. Becky, age 2, was born with a hole in her interventricular septum *(ventricular septal defect,* or *VSD).* Considering that the blood pressure in the left ventricle is significantly higher than blood pressure in the right ventricle, predict the effect of the VSD on Becky's pulmonary blood pressure, systemic blood pressure, and long-term changes in the ventricular walls.

4. In ventricular systole, the left ventricle is the first to begin contracting, but the right ventricle is the first to expel blood. Aside from the obvious fact that the pulmonary valve opens before the aortic valve, how can you explain this difference?

5. In dilated cardiomyopathy of the left ventricle, the ventricle can become enormously enlarged. Explain why this might lead to regurgitation of blood through the mitral valve (blood flowing from the ventricle back into the left atrium) during ventricular systole.

20

THE CIRCULATORY SYSTEM: BLOOD VESSELS AND CIRCULATION

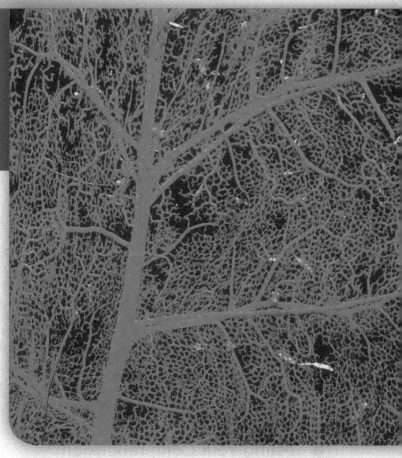

Blood capillary beds
Biophoto Associates/Science Source

CHAPTER OUTLINE

DEEPER INSIGHTS

Anatomy & Physiology
Revealed®4.0

Module 9: Cardiovascular System

BRUSHING UP

- The concepts of homeostatic set point and dynamic equilibrium should be reviewed (see section 1.6c) as background for understanding the control of blood pressure.

- Blood circulation is governed by the principle of flow down pressure gradients (see section 1.6e).

- The principles of blood volume, pressure, and flow discussed in this chapter hinge on the reasons explained in section 18.1d for the osmolarity and viscosity of blood.

- Familiarity with cardiac systole and diastole (see section 19.4) is necessary for understanding blood pressure in this chapter.

- The exchange of materials between the blood capillaries and surrounding tissues is based on the principles of filtration, osmosis and osmotic pressure, diffusion, and transcytosis introduced in section 3.3.

- Blood vessels of the limbs are described in this chapter with reference to muscle compartments (see section 10.1b, fig. 10.3) and interosseous membranes (see sections 8.4b, 8.5b; figs. 8.34, 8.40).

The route taken by the blood after it leaves the heart was a point of much confusion for many centuries. In Chinese medicine as early as 2650 BCE, blood was believed to flow in a complete circuit around the body and back to the heart, just as we know today. The Roman physician Claudius Galen (129–c. 199), however, argued that it flowed back and forth in the veins, like air in the bronchial tubes. He believed that the liver received food directly from the esophagus and converted it to blood, the heart pumped the blood through the veins to all other organs, and those organs consumed it. The arteries were thought to contain only a mysterious "vital spirit."

The Chinese view was right, but the first experimental demonstration of this didn't come for another 4,000 years. English physician William Harvey (1578–1657) studied the filling and emptying of the heart in snakes, tied off the vessels above and below the heart to observe the effects on cardiac filling and output, and measured cardiac output in a variety of living animals and estimated it in humans. He concluded that (1) the heart pumps more blood in half an hour than there is in the entire body, (2) not enough food is consumed to account for the continual production of so much blood, and therefore (3) the blood returns to the heart rather than being consumed by the peripheral organs. He couldn't explain how, since the microscope had yet to be developed to the point that enabled Antony van Leeuwenhoek (1632–1723) and Marcello Malpighi (1628–94) to discover the blood capillaries.

Harvey's work was the first experimental study of animal physiology and a milestone in the history of biology and medicine. But so entrenched were the ideas of Aristotle and Galen in the medical community, and so strange was the idea of doing experiments on living animals, that Harvey's contemporaries rejected his ideas. Indeed, some of them regarded him as a crackpot because his conclusion flew in the face of common sense—if the blood was continually recirculated and not consumed by the

tissues, they reasoned, then what purpose could it serve? We now know, of course, that he was right. Harvey's case is one of the most interesting in biomedical history, for it shows how empirical science overthrows old theories and spawns better ones, and how common sense and blind allegiance to authority can interfere with the acceptance of truth. But most importantly, Harvey's contributions represent the birth of experimental physiology.

20.1 General Anatomy of the Blood Vessels

Expected Learning Outcomes

When you have completed this section, you should be able to

a. describe the structure of a blood vessel;

b. describe the types of arteries, capillaries, and veins;

c. trace the general route usually taken by the blood from the heart and back again; and

d. describe some variations on this route.

There are three principal categories of blood vessels: arteries, veins, and capillaries **(fig. 20.1)**. **Arteries** are defined as the efferent vessels of the cardiovascular system—that is, vessels that carry blood away from the heart. **Veins** are defined as the afferent vessels that carry blood back to the heart. (They are not defined by whether the blood in them is high or low in oxygen; see later discussion.) **Capillaries** are microscopic, thin-walled vessels that connect the smallest arteries to the smallest veins.

20.1a The Vessel Wall

Aside from their general location and direction of blood flow, the three categories of blood vessels also differ in the histological structure of their walls. The walls of arteries and veins are composed of three layers called *tunics* **(fig. 20.2)**:

1. The **tunica interna (tunica intima)** lines the inside of the vessel and is exposed to the blood. It consists of a simple squamous epithelium called the **endothelium** overlying a basement membrane and a sparse layer of loose connective tissue; it is continuous with the endocardium of the heart. The endothelium acts as a selectively permeable barrier to materials entering or leaving the bloodstream; it secretes chemicals that stimulate dilation or constriction of the vessel; and it normally repels blood cells and platelets so that they flow freely without sticking to the vessel wall. When the endothelium is damaged, however, platelets may adhere to it and form a blood clot; and when the tissue around a vessel is inflamed, the endothelial cells produce *cell-adhesion molecules* that induce leukocytes to adhere to the surface. This causes leukocytes to congregate in tissues where their defensive actions are needed.

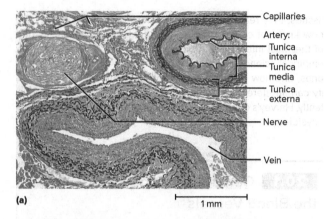

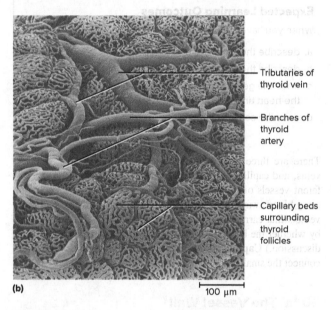

Capillaries

Artery:
Tunica interna
Tunica media
Tunica externa

Nerve

Vein

(a)

1 mm

Tributaries of thyroid vein

Branches of thyroid artery

Capillary beds surrounding thyroid follicles

(b)

100 μm

FIGURE 20.1 Micrographs of Blood Vessels. (a) A neurovascular bundle, composed of a small artery, vein, and nerve traveling together in a common sheath of connective tissue (LM). (b) A vascular cast of blood vessels of the thyroid gland (SEM). Each round mass of capillaries corresponds to one of the thyroid follicles seen in figure 17.9. These vessels pick up thyroid hormone for distribution throughout the body. a: Dennis Strete/McGraw-Hill Education; b: Susumu Nishinaga/Science Source

2. The **tunica media,** the middle layer, is usually the thickest. It consists of smooth muscle, collagen, and in some cases, elastic tissue. The relative amounts of smooth muscle and elastic tissue vary greatly from one vessel to another and form a basis for classifying vessels as described in the next section. The tunica media strengthens the vessels and prevents blood pressure from rupturing them, and it regulates the diameter of a blood vessel.

3. The **tunica externa (tunica adventitia**[1]**)** is the outermost layer. It consists of loose connective tissue that often merges with that of neighboring blood vessels, nerves, or other organs (fig. 20.1a). It anchors the vessel to adjacent tissues and provides passage for small nerves, lymphatic vessels, and smaller blood vessels that supply the tissues of the larger ones.

All blood vessels require nutrition, oxygenation, and waste-removal services for their own tissues, and the medium to large arteries and veins cannot have these needs fully met by the blood flowing through them. That blood flows too rapidly and the vessel wall is too thick for adequate exchange of chemicals between the blood and tissue fluid. Therefore, smaller vessels penetrate into the external surface of the large ones, gaining access through the tunica externa, and branch into capillaries that supply the deeper tissues of the larger vessel. The network of smaller vessels serving the larger one is called the **vasa vasorum**[2] (VAY-za vay-SO-rum). They are most conspicuous in the tunica externa because the loose organization of the tissue here doesn't hide them from view as much as tissue of the tunica media does. They supply blood to at least the outer half of the vessel wall. Tissues of the inner half are thought to be nourished by diffusion from blood in the lumen.

20.1b Arteries

Arteries are sometimes called the *resistance vessels* of the cardiovascular system because they have a relatively strong, resilient tissue structure. Each beat of the heart creates a surge of pressure in the arteries as blood is ejected into them, and arteries are built to withstand this. Being more muscular than veins, they retain their round shape even when empty, so they appear relatively circular or elliptical in tissue sections. They are divided into three classes by size, but of course there is a gradual transition from one class to the next.

1. **Conducting (elastic** or **large) arteries** are the biggest. Examples include the aorta, common carotid and subclavian arteries, pulmonary trunk, and common iliac arteries. They have a layer of elastic tissue called the *internal elastic lamina* at the border between the tunica interna and media, but microscopically, it is incomplete and difficult to distinguish from the elastic tissue of the media. The tunica media consists of 40 to 70 layers of elastic sheets, perforated like slices of Swiss cheese rolled into a tube, alternating with thin layers of smooth muscle, collagen, and elastic fibers. In histological sections, the view is dominated by this elastic tissue. The perforations allow for vasa vasorum and nerves to penetrate through all layers of the vessel and for smooth muscle cells to communicate with each other through gap junctions. There is an *external elastic lamina* at the border between the media and externa, but it, too, is difficult to distinguish from the elastic sheets of the tunica media. The tunica externa is quite

[1] *advent* = added to
[2] *vasa* = vessels; *vasorum* = of the vessels

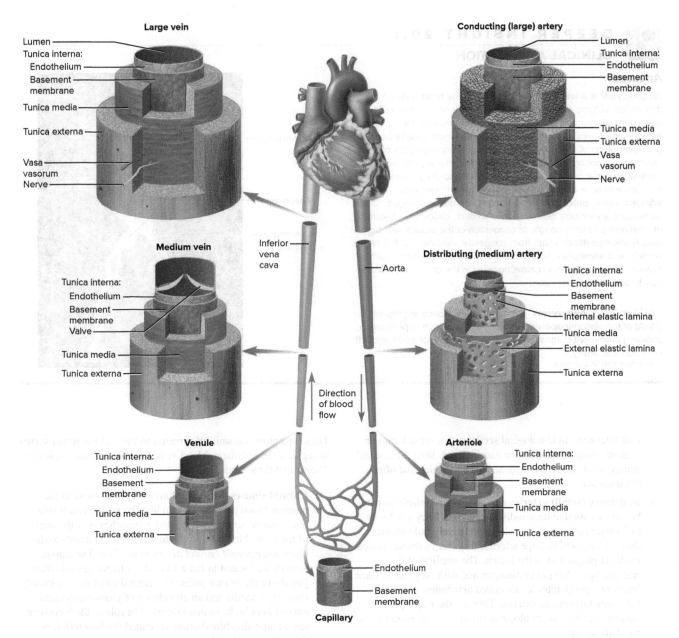

FIGURE 20.2 Histology of the Blood Vessels.

❓ *Why do the arteries have so much more elastic tissue than the veins do?*

sparse in the largest arteries but is well supplied with vasa vasorum. Conducting arteries expand as they receive blood during ventricular systole, and recoil during diastole. As explained in the next section, this relieves smaller arteries downstream of excessive and harmful pressure surges. As arteries stiffen with age *(arteriosclerosis),* this protective effect declines, downstream vessels are subjected to greater stress, and the risks of aneurysm and hemorrhage rise (see Deeper Insight 20.1).

2. **Distributing (muscular** or **medium) arteries** are smaller branches that distribute blood to specific organs. You could compare a conducting artery to an interstate highway and distributing arteries to the exit ramps and state highways that serve individual towns. Most arteries that have specific anatomical names are in these first two size classes. Distributing arteries include the brachial, femoral, renal, and splenic arteries. Distributing arteries typically have up to 40 layers of smooth muscle constituting about three-quarters of the

DEEPER INSIGHT 20.1

CLINICAL APPLICATION

Aneurysm

An *aneurysm*[3] is a weak point in an artery or the heart wall. It forms a thin-walled, bulging sac that pulsates with each beat of the heart and may eventually rupture. In a *dissecting aneurysm,* blood accumulates between the tunics of an artery and separates them, usually because of degeneration of the tunica media. The most common sites of aneurysms are the abdominal aorta **(fig. 20.3)**, renal arteries, and the arterial circle at the base of the brain. Even without hemorrhaging, aneurysms can cause pain or death by putting pressure on brain tissue, nerves, adjacent veins, pulmonary air passages, or the esophagus. Other consequences include neurological disorders, difficulty in breathing or swallowing, chronic cough, or congestion of the tissues with blood. Aneurysms sometimes result from congenital weakness of the blood vessels and sometimes from trauma or bacterial infections such as syphilis. The most common cause, however, is the combination of arteriosclerosis and hypertension.

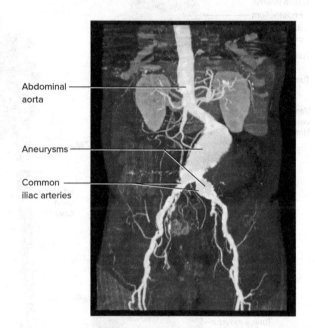

FIGURE 20.3 Aneurysms. A magnetic resonance angiogram (MRA) of the abdominopelvic region of a patient with hypertension, showing prominent bulges (aneurysms) of the inferior aorta and left common iliac artery.
Suttha Burawonk/Shutterstock

---

wall thickness. In histological sections, this smooth muscle is more conspicuous than the elastic tissue. Both the internal and external elastic laminae, however, are thick and often conspicuous.

3. **Resistance (small) arteries** are usually too variable in number and location to have individual names. They exhibit up to 25 layers of smooth muscle and relatively little elastic tissue. Compared to large arteries, they have a thicker tunica media in proportion to the lumen. The smallest of these arteries, up to 200 μm in diameter and with only one to three layers of smooth muscle, are called **arterioles.** Arterioles have very little tunica externa. They are the major point of control over how much blood an organ or tissue receives, as we shall see later.

In some places, such as the mesenteries, short vessels called **metarterioles**[4] **(thoroughfare channels)** link arterioles directly to venules and provide shortcuts through which blood can bypass the capillaries. They will be further discussed with capillary beds.

Arterial Sense Organs

Certain major arteries above the heart have sensory structures in their walls that monitor blood pressure and composition **(fig. 20.4).**

These receptors transmit information to the brainstem that serves to regulate the heartbeat, blood vessel diameters, and respiration. They are of three kinds:

1. **Carotid sinuses.** These are **baroreceptors**—sensors that monitor blood pressure. Ascending the neck on each side is a *common carotid artery,* which branches near the angle of the mandible, forming the *internal carotid artery* to the brain and *external carotid artery* to the face. The carotid sinuses are located in the wall of the internal carotid artery just above the branch point. The carotid sinus has a relatively thin tunica media and an abundance of glossopharyngeal nerve fibers in the tunica externa. The role of the baroreceptors in adjusting blood pressure, called the *baroreflex,* is described later in this chapter.

2. **Carotid bodies.** Also located near the branch of the common carotid arteries, these are oval receptors about 3×5 mm in size, innervated by sensory fibers of the glossopharyngeal nerves. They are **chemoreceptors**—sensors that monitor changes in blood composition. They primarily transmit signals to the brainstem respiratory centers, which adjust breathing to stabilize the blood pH and its CO_2 and O_2 levels.

3. **Aortic bodies.** These are one to three chemoreceptors located in the aortic arch near the arteries to the head and arms. They are structurally similar to the carotid bodies and have the same function, but transmit their signals to the brainstem via the vagus nerves.

---

[3]*aneurysm* = widening
[4]*meta* = beyond, next in a series

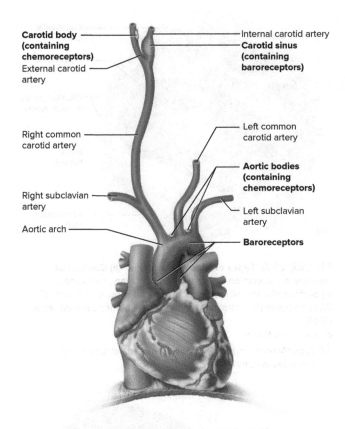

Carotid body (containing chemoreceptors)

External carotid artery

Right common carotid artery

Right subclavian artery

Aortic arch

Internal carotid artery

Carotid sinus (containing baroreceptors)

Left common carotid artery

Aortic bodies (containing chemoreceptors)

Left subclavian artery

Baroreceptors

FIGURE 20.4 Baroreceptors and Chemoreceptors in the Arteries Superior to the Heart. The structures shown here in the right carotid arteries are repeated in the left carotids. **APR**

20.1c Capillaries

For the blood to serve any purpose, materials such as nutrients, wastes, hormones, and leukocytes must pass between the blood and tissue fluids, through the walls of the vessels. There are only two places in the circulation where this occurs—the capillaries and some venules. We can think of these as the "business end" of the cardiovascular system, because all the rest of the system exists to serve the exchange processes that occur here. Since capillaries greatly outnumber venules, they are the more important of the two. Capillaries are sometimes called the *exchange vessels* of the cardiovascular system; the arterioles, capillaries, and venules are also called the **microvasculature (microcirculation).**

Capillaries (see figs. 20.1, 20.2) consist of only an endothelium and basal lamina. Their walls are as thin as 0.2 μm. They average about 5 μm in diameter at the proximal end (where they receive arterial blood), widen to about 9 μm at the distal end (where they empty into a small vein), and often branch along the way. Since erythrocytes are about 7.5 μm in diameter, they have

to stretch into elongated shapes to squeeze through the smallest capillaries.

Scarcely any cell in the body is more than 60 to 80 μm (about four to six cell widths) away from the nearest capillary. There are a few exceptions: Capillaries are scarce in tendons and ligaments and absent from epithelia, cartilage, and the cornea and lens of the eye.

Types of Capillaries

There are three types of capillaries, distinguished by the ease with which they allow substances to pass through their walls and by structural differences that account for their greater or lesser permeability.

1. **Continuous capillaries** (fig. 20.5a) occur in most tissues and organs, such as the skeletal muscles, lungs, and brain. Their endothelial cells, held together by tight junctions, form a continuous tube. A thin protein–carbohydrate layer, the **basal lamina,** surrounds the endothelium and separates it from the adjacent connective tissues. The endothelial cells are separated by narrow **intercellular clefts** about 4 nm wide. Small solutes such as glucose can pass through these clefts, but most plasma protein, other large molecules, and platelets and blood cells are held back. The continuous capillaries of the brain lack intercellular clefts and have more complete tight junctions that form the blood–brain barrier discussed in section 14.2c.

   Some continuous capillaries exhibit cells called **pericytes** that lie external to the endothelium. Pericytes have elongated tendrils that wrap around the capillary. They contain the same contractile proteins as muscle, and it is thought that they can contract and regulate blood flow through the capillaries. They also can differentiate into endothelial and smooth muscle cells and thus contribute to vessel growth and repair.

2. **Fenestrated capillaries** have endothelial cells riddled with patches of **filtration pores (fenestrations[5]) (fig. 20.5b, c).** These pores are about 20 to 100 nm in diameter, and are often spanned by a glycoprotein membrane that is much thinner than the cell's plasma membrane. They allow for the rapid passage of small molecules, but still retain most proteins and larger particles in the bloodstream. Fenestrated capillaries are important in organs that engage in rapid absorption or filtration—the kidneys, endocrine glands, small intestine, and choroid plexuses of the brain, for example.

3. **Sinusoids** are irregular blood-filled spaces in the liver, bone marrow, spleen, and some other organs **(fig. 20.6).** They are twisted, tortuous passageways, typically 30 to 40 μm wide, that conform to the shape of the surrounding tissue. The endothelial cells are separated by wide gaps

[5]*fenestra* = window

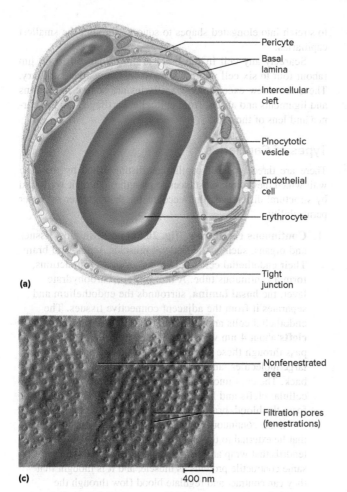

(a)

(c)

400 nm

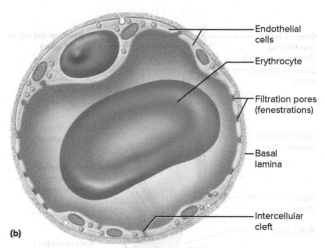

(b)

FIGURE 20.5 Types of Blood Capillaries. (a) Continuous capillary, cross section. (b) Fenestrated capillary, cross section. (c) Surface of a fenestrated endothelial cell showing patches of filtration pores (fenestrations) separated by nonfenestrated areas (SEM).

c: Courtesy of S. McNutt

❓ *Identify some organs that have fenestrated rather than continuous capillaries.*

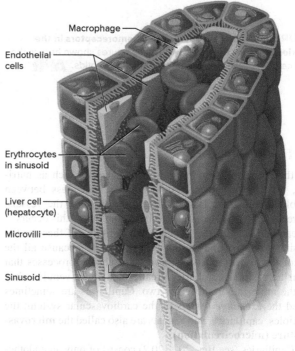

FIGURE 20.6 A Sinusoid of the Liver. Large gaps between the endothelial cells allow blood plasma to directly contact the liver cells but retain blood cells in the lumen of the sinusoid.

with no basal lamina, and the cells also frequently have especially large fenestrations through them. Even proteins and blood cells can pass through these pores; this is how albumin, clotting factors, and other proteins synthesized by the liver enter the blood, and how newly formed blood cells enter the circulation from the bone marrow and lymphatic organs. Some sinusoids contain macrophages or other specialized cells.

Capillary Beds

Capillaries are organized into webs called **capillary beds**—typically 10 to 100 capillaries supplied by a single arteriole or metarteriole (**fig. 20.7**; see also this chapter's opening photo). At their

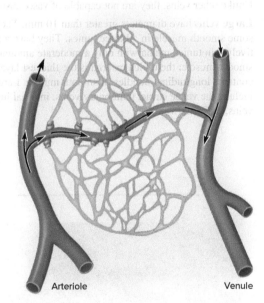

Precapillary sphincters
Metarteriole
Capillaries
Arteriole
Venule

(a) Sphincters open

Arteriole
Venule

(b) Sphincters closed

FIGURE 20.7 Perfusion of a Capillary Bed. (a) Precapillary sphincters dilated and capillaries well perfused. (b) Precapillary sphincters closed, with most blood bypassing the capillaries.

all of them at once. In the skeletal muscles, for example, about 90% of the capillaries have little or no blood flow during periods of rest. During exercise, they receive an abundant flow while capillaries elsewhere—for example, in the skin and intestines—shut down to compensate. Capillary flow (perfusion) is usually regulated by the dilation or constriction of arterioles upstream from the capillary beds. In capillary beds supplied with metarterioles, there is often a single smooth muscle cell that wraps like a cuff around the opening to each capillary; it acts as a **precapillary sphincter** regulating blood flow. If the sphincters are relaxed, the capillaries are well perfused (fig. 20.7a). If many of the sphincters constrict, blood bypasses the capillaries, leaving them less perfused or even bloodless, and the blood takes a shortcut through the metarteriole directly to a nearby venule (fig. 20.7b).

20.1d Veins

Veins are regarded as the *capacitance vessels* of the cardiovascular system because they are relatively thin-walled and flaccid, and expand easily to accommodate an increased volume of blood; that is, they have a greater *capacity* for blood containment than arteries do. At rest, about 64% of the blood is found in the systemic veins as compared with only 13% in the systemic arteries **(fig. 20.8).** The reason veins are so thin-walled and accommodating is that, being distant from the ventricles of the heart, they are subjected to relatively low blood pressure. In large arteries, blood pressure averages 90 to 100 mm Hg and surges to 120 mm Hg during systole, whereas in veins it averages about 10 mm Hg. Furthermore, the blood flow in the veins is steady, rather than pulsating with the heartbeat like the flow in the arteries. Veins therefore don't require thick, pressure-resistant walls. They collapse when empty and thus have relatively flattened, irregular shapes in histological sections (see fig. 20.1a).

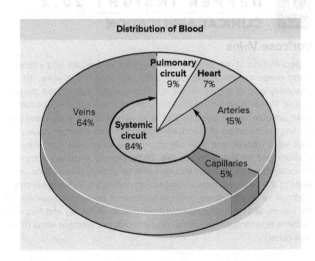

FIGURE 20.8 Typical Blood Distribution in a Resting Adult.

❓ *What anatomical fact allows the veins to contain so much more blood than the arteries do?*

distal end, capillaries transition to venules, gradually adding a thin tunica media. They may also drain into the distal end of a metarteriole, which then leads to a venule.

At any given time, about three-quarters of the body's capillaries are shut down because there isn't enough blood to supply

As we trace blood flow in the arteries, we find it splitting off repeatedly into smaller and smaller *branches* of the arterial system. In the venous system, conversely, we find small veins merging to form larger and larger ones as they approach the heart. We refer to the smaller veins as *tributaries,* by analogy to the streams that converge and act as tributaries to rivers. In examining the types of veins, we will follow the direction of blood flow, working up from the smallest to the largest vessels.

1. **Postcapillary venules** are the smallest of the veins, beginning with diameters of about 10 to 20 μm. They receive blood from capillaries directly or by way of the distal ends of the metarterioles. They have a tunica interna with only a few fibroblasts around it and no muscle. Like capillaries, they are often surrounded by pericytes. Postcapillary venules are even more porous than capillaries; therefore, venules also exchange fluid with the surrounding tissues. Most leukocytes emigrate from the bloodstream through the venule walls.

2. **Muscular venules** receive blood from the postcapillary venules. They are up to 1 mm in diameter. They have a tunica media of one or two layers of smooth muscle, and a thin tunica externa.

3. **Medium veins** range up to 10 mm in diameter. Most veins with individual names are in this category, such as the radial and ulnar veins of the forearm and the small and great saphenous veins of the leg. Medium veins have a tunica interna with an endothelium, basement membrane, loose connective tissue, and sometimes a thin internal elastic lamina. The tunica media is much thinner than it is in medium arteries; it exhibits bundles of

smooth muscle, but not a continuous muscular layer as seen in arteries. The muscle is interrupted by regions of collagenous, reticular, and elastic tissue. The tunica externa is relatively thick.

Many medium veins, especially in the limbs, exhibit infoldings of the tunica interna that meet in the middle of the lumen, forming **venous valves** directed toward the heart (see fig. 20.21). The pressure in the veins isn't high enough to push all of the blood upward against the pull of gravity in a standing or sitting person. The upward flow of blood in these vessels depends partly on the massaging action of skeletal muscles and the ability of these valves to keep the blood from dropping down again when the muscles relax. When the muscles surrounding a vein contract, they force blood through these valves. The propulsion of venous blood by muscular massaging, aided by the venous valves, is a mechanism of blood flow called the *skeletal muscle pump*. Varicose veins result in part from the failure of the valves (see Deeper Insight 20.2).

4. **Venous sinuses** are veins with especially thin walls, large lumens, and no smooth muscle. Examples include the coronary sinus of the heart and the dural sinuses of the brain. Unlike other veins, they are not capable of vasoconstriction.

5. **Large veins** have diameters greater than 10 mm. They have some smooth muscle in all three tunics. They have a relatively thin tunica media with only a moderate amount of smooth muscle; the tunica externa is the thickest layer and contains longitudinal bundles of smooth muscle. Large veins include the venae cavae, pulmonary veins, internal jugular veins, and renal veins.

DEEPER INSIGHT 20.2

CLINICAL APPLICATION

Varicose Veins

In people who stand for long periods, such as barbers and cashiers, blood tends to pool in the lower limbs and stretch the veins. This is especially true of superficial veins, which are not surrounded by supportive tissue. Stretching pulls the cusps of the venous valves farther apart until the valves become incapable of sealing the vessel and preventing the backflow of blood. As the veins become further distended, their walls weaken and they develop into *varicose veins* with irregular dilations and twisted pathways **(fig. 20.9)**. Obesity and pregnancy also promote development of varicose veins by putting pressure on large veins of the pelvic region and obstructing drainage from the lower limbs. Varicose veins sometimes develop because of hereditary weakness of the valves. With less drainage of blood, tissues of the leg and foot may become edematous and painful. *Hemorrhoids* are varicose veins of the anal canal.

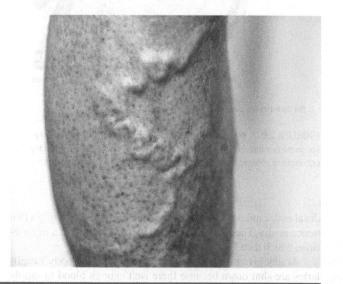

FIGURE 20.9 Varicose Veins.
Jaroslav Moravcik/Shutterstock

20.1e Circulatory Routes

The simplest and most common route of blood flow is heart → arteries → capillaries → veins → heart. Blood usually passes through only one network of capillaries from the time it leaves the heart until the time it returns **(fig. 20.10a),** but there are exceptions, notably portal systems and anastomoses.

In a **portal system (fig. 20.10b),** blood flows through two consecutive capillary networks before returning to the heart. Portal systems occur in the kidneys, connect the hypothalamus to the anterior pituitary gland, and connect the intestines to the liver (see section 20.7g).

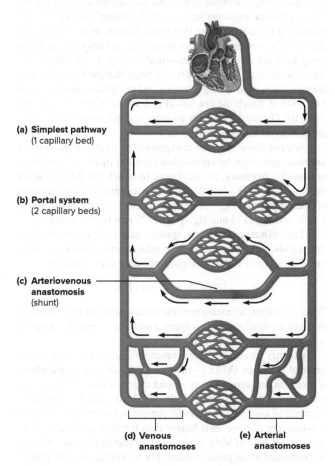

(a) Simplest pathway
(1 capillary bed)

(b) Portal system
(2 capillary beds)

(c) Arteriovenous anastomosis
(shunt)

(d) Venous anastomoses   **(e) Arterial anastomoses**

FIGURE 20.10 Variations in Circulatory Pathways. (a) The simplest and most common pathway, with one capillary bed. (b) Portal systems, with two capillary beds in series. (c) Arteriovenous anastomoses, bypassing capillaries. (d) Venous anastomoses, with one vein feeding into another. (e) Arterial anastomoses, with one artery feeding into another.

❓ *After studying the blood vessels in sections 20.7 and 20.8, identify specific sites in the body where one can find arterial anastomoses, venous anastomoses, and portal systems.*

An **anastomosis** is a point of convergence between two blood vessels other than capillaries. In an **arteriovenous anastomosis (shunt),** blood flows from an artery directly into a vein and bypasses the capillaries **(fig. 20.10c).** Shunts occur in the fingers, palms, toes, and ears, where they reduce heat loss in cold weather by allowing warm blood to bypass these exposed surfaces. Unfortunately, this makes these poorly perfused areas more susceptible to frostbite. The most common anastomoses are **venous anastomoses,** in which one vein empties directly into another **(fig. 20.10d).** These provide several alternative routes of drainage from an organ, so blockage of a vein is rarely as life-threatening as blockage of an artery. **Arterial anastomoses,** in which two arteries merge **(fig. 20.10e),** provide *collateral* (alternative) routes of blood supply to a tissue. Those of the coronary circulation were mentioned in section 19.2e. They are also common around joints where limb movement may temporarily compress an artery and obstruct one pathway. Several arterial and venous anastomoses are described later in this chapter.

BEFORE YOU GO ON

Answer the following questions to test your understanding of the preceding section:

1. Name the three tunics of a typical blood vessel and explain how they differ from each other.

2. Contrast the tunica media of a conducting artery, arteriole, and venule and explain how the histological differences are related to the functional differences between these vessels.

3. Describe the differences between a continuous capillary, a fenestrated capillary, and a sinusoid.

4. Describe two routes by which substances can escape the bloodstream and pass through a capillary wall into the tissue fluid.

5. Describe the differences between a medium vein and a medium (muscular) artery. State the functional reasons for these differences.

6. Contrast an anastomosis and a portal system with the more typical pathway of blood flow.

20.2 Blood Pressure, Resistance, and Flow

Expected Learning Outcomes

When you have completed this section, you should be able to

a. explain the relationship between blood pressure, resistance, and flow;

b. describe how blood pressure is measured and expressed;

c. show how pulse pressure and mean arterial pressure are calculated;

d. describe three factors that determine resistance to blood flow;

e. explain how vessel diameter influences blood pressure and flow; and

f. describe some local, neural, and hormonal influences on vessel diameter.

To sustain life, the circulatory system must deliver oxygen and nutrients to the tissues, and remove their wastes, at a rate that keeps pace with tissue metabolism. Inadequate circulatory services to a tissue can lead within minutes to tissue necrosis and possibly death of the individual. Thus, it is crucial for the cardiovascular system to respond promptly to local needs and ensure that the tissues have an adequate blood supply at all times. This section of the chapter explores the mechanisms for achieving this.

The blood supply to a tissue can be expressed in terms of *flow* and *perfusion*. **Flow** is the amount of blood flowing through an organ, tissue, or blood vessel in a given time (such as mL/min.). **Perfusion** is the flow per given volume or mass of tissue, usually expressed in milliliters of blood per 100 grams of tissue per minute. Thus, a large organ such as the femur could have a *greater flow* but *less perfusion* than a small organ such as the ovary, because the ovary receives much more blood per gram of tissue.

In a resting individual, *total* flow is quite constant and is equal to cardiac output (typically 5.25 L/min.). Flow through individual organs, however, varies from minute to minute as blood is redirected from one organ to another. Digestion, for example, requires abundant flow to the intestines, and the cardiovascular system makes this available by reducing flow through other organs such as the kidneys. When digestion and nutrient absorption are over, blood flow to the intestines declines and a higher priority is given to the kidneys and other organs. Great variations in regional flow can occur with little or no change in total flow.

Hemodynamics, the physical principles of blood flow, are based mainly on pressure and resistance. These relationships can be concisely summarized by the formula

$$F \propto \Delta P/R.$$

In other words, the greater the pressure difference (ΔP) between two points, the greater the flow (F)*;* the greater the resistance (R), the less the flow. Therefore, to understand the flow of blood, we must consider the factors that affect pressure and resistance.

20.2a Blood Pressure

Blood pressure (BP) is the force exerted by blood on a vessel wall. Contraction of the heart initiates a wave of pressure that sharply decreases as the blood flows farther and farther away from the ventricle of origin. Blood pressure measurement is a familiar part of a routine physical examination. It is typically measured at the **brachial artery** of the arm with a **sphygmomanometer** (SFIG-mo-meh-NOM-eh-tur). This device consists of an inflatable cuff connected to a rubber bulb for pumping air into it, and an aneroid dial gauge, digital sensor, or calibrated mercury column for measuring air pressure in the cuff. Mercury sphygmomanometers are

the "gold standard" for accuracy, but other devices have advantages for convenience and home use.

To take a patient's blood pressure with a mercury sphygmomanometer, the examiner wraps the cuff snugly around the patient's arm and inflates it with the bulb until it exceeds the systolic blood pressure. By squeezing the brachial muscles, this procedure collapses the brachial artery deep within. Even during systole, the heart can't force blood through the artery, and there is no blood flow distal to that point. The examiner now listens with a stethoscope at the bend of the elbow (cubital fossa) while slowly releasing air from the cuff.

At first there is no sound, but as soon as the systolic BP slightly exceeds the cuff pressure, each heartbeat forces the brachial artery open and allows a brief jet of blood to pass through. The vessel collapses again at diastole. This jet of blood and the subsequent surge of blood against the recollapsed artery cause turbulence that the examiner hears as a faint "bump" sound. The cuff pressure at the instant of the first bump is noted as the systolic BP. As the cuff pressure continues to decline, a bump can be heard every time the artery collapses—that is, once in each heartbeat. But soon the cuff pressure falls to a point that the brachial artery remains open even during diastole, and no further sounds occur. The point at which the last sound is detected is noted as the diastolic BP. Digital devices rely on detecting pulsations in the artery rather than detecting sounds from it.

Arterial blood pressure is expressed as a ratio of the **systolic pressure** generated by contraction (systole) of the left ventricle, to **diastolic pressure,** the minimum to which the BP falls when the ventricle is in diastole. Both are expressed in millimeters of mercury (mm Hg). A representative, healthy adult BP is 120/75 mm Hg (120 mm Hg systolic, 75 mm Hg diastolic).

The difference between systolic and diastolic pressure is called **pulse pressure** (not to be confused with pulse *rate*). For a blood pressure of 120/75, the pulse pressure (PP) would be

$$120 - 75 = 45 \text{ mm Hg}.$$

This is an important measure of the force that drives blood circulation and the maximum stress exerted on small arteries by the pressure surges generated by the heart.

Another measure of stress on the blood vessels is the **mean arterial pressure (MAP)**—the mean pressure you would obtain if you took measurements at several intervals (say every 0.1 second) throughout the cardiac cycle. MAP isn't simply an arithmetic mean of systolic and diastolic pressures, however, because the low-pressure diastole lasts longer than the high-pressure systole. A close estimate of MAP is obtained by adding diastolic pressure and one-third of the pulse pressure. For a blood pressure of 120/75,

$$MAP \approx 75 + 45/3 = 90 \text{ mm Hg}.$$

This is typical for vessels at the level of the heart, but *MAP* varies with the influence of gravity. In a standing adult, it is about 62 mm Hg in the major arteries of the head and 180 mm Hg in major arteries of the ankle.

It is the mean arterial pressure that most influences the risk of disorders such as **syncope** (SIN-co-pee) (fainting), atherosclerosis, kidney failure, edema, and aneurysm. The importance of preventing excessive blood pressure is therefore clear. One of the body's chief means of doing so is the ability of the arteries to stretch and recoil during the cardiac cycle. If the arteries were rigid tubes, pressure would rise much higher in systole and drop to nearly zero in diastole. Blood throughout the circulatory system would flow and stop, flow and stop, and put great stress on the small vessels. But healthy conducting (elastic) arteries expand with each systole, absorb some of the force of the ejected blood, and store potential energy. Then, when the heart is in diastole, their elastic recoil releases that as kinetic energy, exerts pressure on the blood, and maintains blood flow throughout the cardiac cycle. The elastic arteries thus smooth out pressure fluctuations and reduce stress on the smaller arteries.

▶▶▶ **APPLY WHAT YOU KNOW**

Explain how the histological structure of large arteries relates to their ability to stretch during systole and recoil during diastole.

Nevertheless, blood flow in the arteries is *pulsatile.* In the aorta, blood rushes forward at 120 cm/s during systole and has an average speed of 40 cm/s over the cardiac cycle. When measured farther away from the heart, systolic and diastolic pressures are lower and there is less difference between them **(fig. 20.11).** In capillaries and veins, the blood flows at a steady speed with little if any pulsation because the pressure surges have been damped out by the distance traveled and the elasticity of the arteries. This

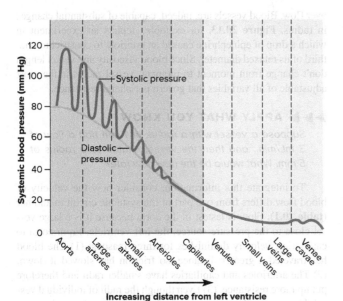

FIGURE 20.11 Changes in Blood Pressure Relative to Distance from the Heart. Because of arterial elasticity and the effect of friction against the vessel wall, all measures of blood pressure decline with distance—systolic pressure, diastolic pressure, pulse pressure, and mean arterial pressure. There is no pulse pressure beyond the arterioles, but there are slight pressure oscillations in the venae cavae caused by the respiratory pump described later in this chapter.

is why an injured vein exhibits relatively slow, steady bleeding, whereas blood jets intermittently from a severed artery. In the inferior vena cava near the heart, however, venous flow fluctuates with the respiratory cycle for reasons explained later, and there is some fluctuation in the jugular veins of the neck.

As we get older, our arteries become less distensible and absorb less systolic force. This increasing stiffness of the arteries is called **arteriosclerosis**[6] ("hardening of the arteries"). The primary cause of it is cumulative damage by free radicals, which cause gradual deterioration of the elastic and other tissues of the arterial walls—much like old rubber bands that become less stretchy. Another contributing factor is **atherosclerosis,** the growth of lipid deposits in the arterial walls (see Deeper Insight 19.4). These deposits can become calcified *complicated plaques,* giving the arteries a hard, crunchy or bonelike consistency. As a result of these degenerative changes, blood pressure rises with age. Common blood pressures at the age of 20 are about 123/76 for males and 116/72 for females. For healthy persons at age 70, typical blood pressures are around 145/82 and 159/85 for the two sexes, respectively.

Hypertension (high BP) is commonly considered to be a chronic resting blood pressure higher than 140/90. (*Temporary* high BP resulting from emotion or exercise is not hypertension.) Among other effects, hypertension can weaken arteries and cause aneurysms, and it promotes the development of atherosclerosis (see Deeper Insight 20.6). **Hypotension** is chronic low resting BP. It may be a consequence of blood loss, dehydration, anemia, or other factors and is normal in people approaching death. There is no particular numerical criterion for hypotension.

Blood pressure is physiologically determined by three principal variables: cardiac output, blood volume, and resistance to flow. Cardiac output was discussed in section 19.6. Blood volume is regulated mainly by the kidneys, which have a greater influence than any other organ on blood pressure (assuming there is a beating heart). Their influence on blood pressure is discussed in chapters 23 and 24. Resistance to flow is our next topic of consideration.

20.2b Peripheral Resistance

Peripheral resistance is the opposition to flow that the blood encounters in vessels away from the heart. Moving blood would exert no pressure against a vessel wall unless it encountered at least some downstream resistance. Thus, pressure and resistance are not independent variables in blood flow—rather, pressure is affected by resistance, and flow is affected by both. Resistance, in turn, hinges on three variables that we consider now: blood viscosity, vessel length, and vessel radius.

Blood Viscosity

The viscosity of blood stems mainly from its plasma proteins (albumin) and erythrocytes (see section 18.1d). A deficiency of erythrocytes (anemia) or albumin (hypoproteinemia) reduces viscosity and speeds up blood flow. On the other hand, viscosity increases and flow declines in such conditions as polycythemia and dehydration.

---

[6]*arterio* = artery; *sclerosis* = hardening

Vessel Length

The farther a liquid travels through a tube, the more cumulative friction it encounters; pressure and flow therefore decline with distance. Partly for this reason, if you were to measure mean arterial pressure in a reclining person, you would obtain a higher value in the arm, for example, than in the ankle. In a reclining person, a strong pulse in the dorsal artery of the foot is a good sign of adequate cardiac output. If perfusion is good at that distance from the heart, it is likely to be good elsewhere in the systemic circulation.

Vessel Radius

Blood viscosity and vessel lengths don't change in the short term, of course. In a healthy individual, the only significant ways of controlling peripheral resistance from moment to moment are **vasoconstriction,** the narrowing of a vessel, and **vasodilation,** the widening of a vessel. Vasoconstriction occurs when the smooth muscle of the tunica media contracts. Vasodilation, however, is brought about not by any muscular effort to widen a vessel, but rather by muscular passivity—relaxation of the smooth muscle, allowing blood pressure to expand the vessel. Vasoconstriction and vasodilation are collectively called **vasomotion.** Vasomotion is controlled in part by a nucleus in the medulla oblongata of the brain called the **vasomotor center.**

The effect of vessel radius on blood flow stems from the friction of the moving blood against the vessel walls. Blood normally exhibits smooth, silent **laminar[7] flow.** That is, it flows in layers—faster near the center of a vessel, where it encounters less friction, and slower near the walls, where it drags against the vessel. You can observe a similar effect from the vantage point of a riverbank. The current may be very swift in the middle of a river but quite sluggish near shore, where the water encounters more friction against the riverbank and bottom. When a blood vessel dilates, a greater portion of the blood is in the middle of the stream and the average flow may be quite swift. When the vessel constricts, more of the blood is close to the wall and the average flow is slower (**fig. 20.12**).

Thus, the radius of a vessel markedly affects blood flow. Indeed, flow (F) is proportional not merely to vessel radius (r) but to the *fourth power* of radius—that is, $F \propto r^4$. This makes radius a very potent factor in the control of flow. For the sake of simplicity, consider a hypothetical blood vessel with a 1 mm radius when maximally constricted and a 3 mm radius when completely dilated. At a 1 mm radius, suppose the flow rate is 1 mL/min. By the formula $F \propto r^4$, consider how the flow would change as radius changed:

if r = 1 mm, then $r^4 = 1^4 = 1$, and F = 1 mL/min. (given);

if r = 2 mm, then $r^4 = 2^4 = 16$, and F = 16 mL/min.; and

if r = 3 mm, then $r^4 = 3^4 = 81$, and F = 81 mL/min.

These actual numbers don't matter; what matters is that a mere 3-fold increase in radius has produced an 81-fold increase in flow—a demonstration that vessel radius exerts a very powerful influence

[7]*lamina* = layer

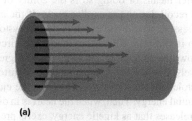

FIGURE 20.12 Laminar Flow and the Effect of Vessel Radius. Blood flows more slowly near the vessel wall, as indicated by shorter arrows, than it does near the center of the vessel. Each arrow can be construed as the distance that a hypothetical blood cell would travel in a given amount of time, varying with its distance from the vessel wall. (a) When the vessel radius is large, the average velocity of flow is high. (b) When the radius is less, the average velocity is lower because a larger portion of the blood is slowed down by friction against the vessel wall.

over flow. Blood vessels are, indeed, capable of substantial changes in radius. **Figure 20.13,** for example, depicts an experiment in which a drop of epinephrine caused an arteriole to constrict to one-third of its relaxed diameter. Since blood viscosity and vessel length don't change from moment to moment, vessel radius is the most adjustable of all variables that govern peripheral resistance.

▶▶▶ **APPLY WHAT YOU KNOW**

Suppose a vessel with a radius of 1 mm had a flow of 3 mL/min., and then the vessel dilated to a radius of 5 mm. What would be the new flow rate?

To integrate this information, consider how the velocity of blood flow differs from one part of the systemic circuit to another (**table 20.1**). Flow is fastest in the aorta because it is a large vessel close to the pressure source, the left ventricle. From aorta to capillaries, velocity diminishes for three reasons: (1) The blood has traveled a greater distance, so friction has slowed it down. (2) The arterioles and capillaries have smaller radii and therefore put up more resistance. (3) Even though the radii of individual vessels become smaller as we progress farther from the heart, the number of vessels and their *total* cross-sectional area become greater and greater. The aorta has a cross-sectional area of 3 to 5 cm^2, whereas the total cross-sectional area of all the capillaries is about 4,500 to 6,000 cm^2. Thus, a given volume of aortic blood is distributed over a greater total area in the capillaries, which *collectively* form a wider path in the bloodstream. Just as water slows down when a narrow mountain stream flows into a lake, blood slows down as it enters pathways with a greater total area or volume.

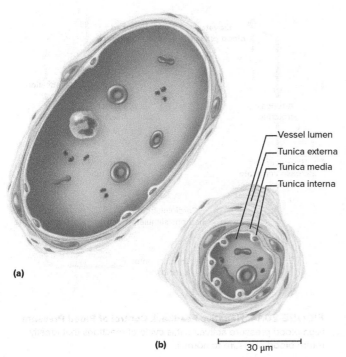

(a)

Vessel lumen
Tunica externa
Tunica media
Tunica interna

(b)   30 μm

FIGURE 20.13 The Capacity for Vasoconstriction in an Arteriole. (a) A dilated arteriole (cross section). (b) The same arteriole, at a point just 1 mm from the area shown in part (a). A single drop of epinephrine applied here caused the arteriole to constrict to about one-third of its dilated diameter. Drawn to scale from transmission electron micrographs.

TABLE 20.1	Blood Velocity in the Systemic Circuit	
Vessel	**Typical Lumen Diameter**	**Velocity***
Aorta	2.5 cm	1,200 mm/s
Arterioles	20–50 μm	15 mm/s
Capillaries	5–9 μm	0.4 mm/s
Venules	20 μm	5 mm/s
Inferior vena cava	3 cm	80 mm/s

*Peak systolic velocity in the aorta; mean or steady velocity in other vessels, assuming no upstream vasoconstriction adding to resistance

From capillaries to vena cava, velocity rises again. One reason for this is that the veins are larger than the capillaries, so they create less resistance. Furthermore, since many capillaries converge on one venule, and many venules on a larger vein, a large amount of blood is being forced into a progressively smaller channel—like water flowing from a lake into an outlet stream and thus flowing

faster again. Note, however, that blood in the veins never regains the velocity it had in the large arteries. This is because the veins are farther from the pressure head (the heart) and because they are more compliant than arteries—they stretch to accommodate more blood, and this reduces pressure and flow.

Arterioles are the most significant point of control over peripheral resistance and blood flow because (1) they are on the proximal sides of the capillary beds, so they are best positioned to regulate flow into the capillaries and thus regulate perfusion of the organs; (2) they greatly outnumber any other class of arteries and thus provide the most numerous control points; and (3) they are more muscular in proportion to their diameters than any other class of blood vessels and are highly capable of changing radius. Arterioles alone account for about half of the total peripheral resistance of the circulatory system. However, larger arteries and veins also influence peripheral resistance through their own constriction and dilation.

20.2c Regulation of Blood Pressure and Flow

Vasoreflexes, we have seen, are quick and powerful means of altering blood pressure and flow. There are three ways of controlling vasomotor activity: local, neural, and hormonal mechanisms. We now consider each of these influences in turn.

Local Control

Autoregulation is the ability of tissues to regulate their own blood supply. According to the *metabolic theory of autoregulation,* if a tissue is inadequately perfused, it becomes hypoxic and its metabolites (waste products) accumulate—CO_2, H^+, K^+, lactate, and adenosine, for example. These factors stimulate vasodilation, which increases blood flow. As the bloodstream delivers oxygen and carries away the metabolites, the vessels reconstrict. Thus, a homeostatic dynamic equilibrium is established that adjusts perfusion to the tissue's metabolic needs.

In addition, platelets, endothelial cells, and the perivascular tissues secrete a variety of **vasoactive chemicals** that stimulate vasodilation under such conditions as trauma, inflammation, and exercise. These include histamine, bradykinin, and prostaglandins. The drag of blood flowing against the endothelial cells creates a *shear stress* (like rubbing your palms together) that stimulates them to secrete prostacyclin and nitric oxide, which are vasodilators.

If a tissue's blood supply is cut off for a time and then restored, it often exhibits **reactive hyperemia**—an increase above the normal level of flow. This may be due to the accumulation of metabolites during the period of ischemia. Reactive hyperemia is seen when the skin flushes (reddens) after a person comes in from the cold. It also occurs in the forearm if a blood pressure cuff is inflated for too long and then loosened.

Over a longer time, a hypoxic tissue can increase its own perfusion by **angiogenesis**[8]—the growth of new blood vessels. (This

---

[8]*angio* = vessels; *genesis* = production of

term also refers to embryonic development of blood vessels.) Three situations in which this is important are the regrowth of the uterine lining after each menstrual period, the development of a higher density of blood capillaries in the muscles of well-conditioned athletes, and the growth of arterial bypasses around obstructions in the coronary circulation. There is great clinical importance in determining how growth factors and inhibitors control angiogenesis. Malignant tumors secrete growth factors that stimulate a dense network of vessels to grow into them and provide nourishment to the cancer cells. Oncologists are interested in finding a way to block *tumor angiogenesis,* thus to choke off a tumor's blood supply and perhaps shrink or kill it.

Neural Control

In addition to local control, the blood vessels are under remote control by the central and autonomic nervous systems. The vasomotor center of the medulla oblongata exerts sympathetic control over blood vessels throughout the body. (Precapillary sphincters have no innervation, however, and respond only to local and hormonal stimuli.) Sympathetic nerve fibers stimulate most blood vessels to constrict, and allow for vasodilation by reducing the nerve firing rate *(sympathetic tone).* The role of sympathetic and vasomotor tone in controlling vessel diameter is explained in section 15.3c.

The vasomotor center is an integrating center for three autonomic reflexes—*baroreflexes, chemoreflexes,* and the *medullary ischemic reflex.* A **baroreflex**[9] is a negative feedback response to changes in blood pressure (see fig. 15.1). The changes are detected by baroreceptors of the carotid sinuses (see fig. 20.4). Glossopharyngeal nerve fibers from these sinuses transmit signals continually to the brainstem. When blood pressure rises, their signaling rate rises. This *inhibits* the sympathetic cardiac and vasomotor neurons and reduces sympathetic tone, and it *excites* the vagal fibers to the heart. Thus, it reduces the heart rate and cardiac output, dilates the arteries and veins, and reduces blood pressure **(fig. 20.14).** When blood pressure drops below normal, on the other hand, the opposite reactions occur and BP rises back to normal.

Baroreflexes are important chiefly in short-term regulation of BP, for example in adapting to changes in posture. Perhaps you have jumped quickly out of bed and felt a little dizzy for a moment. This occurs because gravity draws the blood into the large veins of the abdomen and lower limbs when you stand, which reduces venous return to the heart and cardiac output to the brain. Normally, the baroreceptors respond quickly to this drop in pressure and restore cerebral perfusion (see fig. 1.8). Baroreflexes are not effective in correcting chronic hypertension, however. Within 2 days or less, they adjust their set point to the higher BP and maintain dynamic equilibrium at this new level.

A **chemoreflex** is an autonomic response to changes in blood chemistry, especially its pH and concentrations of O_2 and CO_2. It is initiated by the chemoreceptors called *aortic bodies* and *carotid bodies* described earlier. The primary role of chemoreflexes is to adjust respiration to changes in blood chemistry, but they have a secondary role in vasoreflexes. Hypoxemia (blood O_2 deficiency), hypercapnia

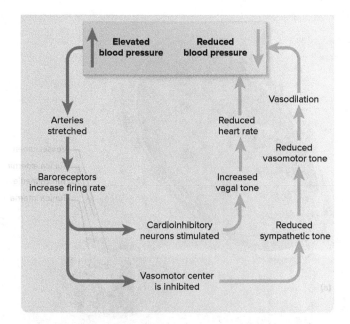

FIGURE 20.14 Negative Feedback Control of Blood Pressure. High blood pressure activates this cycle of reactions that ideally return blood pressure to normal.

(CO_2 excess), and acidosis (low blood pH) stimulate the chemoreceptors and act through the vasomotor center to induce widespread vasoconstriction. This increases overall BP, thus increasing perfusion of the lungs and the rate of gas exchange. Chemoreceptors also stimulate breathing, so increased ventilation of the lungs matches their increased perfusion. Increasing one without the other (airflow without blood flow, or vice versa) would be of little use.

The **medullary ischemic reflex** (iss-KEE-mic) is an autonomic response to reduced perfusion of the brain. The medulla oblongata monitors its own blood supply and activates corrective reflexes when it senses a state of ischemia (insufficient perfusion). Within seconds of a drop in perfusion, the cardiac and vasomotor centers of the medulla send sympathetic signals to the heart and blood vessels that accelerate the heart and constrict the vessels. These actions raise the blood pressure and ideally restore normal cerebral perfusion. The cardiac and vasomotor centers also receive input from other brain centers, so stress, anger, and arousal can raise the blood pressure. The hypothalamus acts through the vasomotor center to redirect blood flow in response to exercise or changes in body temperature.

Hormonal Control

Hormones are another means of remote control over perfusion. All of the following hormones influence blood pressure, some through their vasoactive effects and some through means such as regulating water balance:

- **Angiotensin II.** This is a potent vasoconstrictor that raises the blood pressure. Its synthesis and action are depicted in figure 23.15. Its synthesis requires *angiotensin-converting*

[9]*baro* = pressure

enzyme (ACE). Hypertension is often treated with drugs called *ACE inhibitors,* which block the action of this enzyme, thus lowering angiotensin II levels and blood pressure.

- **Aldosterone.** This "salt-retaining hormone" primarily promotes Na⁺ retention by the kidneys. Since water follows sodium osmotically, Na⁺ retention promotes water retention, thereby supporting blood pressure.

- **Natriuretic peptides.** These hormones, secreted by the heart, antagonize aldosterone. They increase Na⁺ excretion by the kidneys, thus reducing blood volume and pressure. They also have a generalized vasodilator effect that helps to lower blood pressure.

- **Antidiuretic hormone.** ADH primarily promotes water retention, but at pathologically high concentrations it is also a vasoconstrictor—hence its alternate name, *arginine vasopressin.* Both of these effects raise blood pressure.

- **Epinephrine and norepinephrine.** These adrenal and sympathetic catecholamines bind to α-adrenergic receptors on the smooth muscle of most blood vessels. This stimulates vasoconstriction and raises the blood pressure.

▶▶▶**APPLY WHAT YOU KNOW**

Renin inhibitors are drugs used to treat hypertension. Explain how you think they would produce the desired effect.

20.2d Two Purposes of Vasomotion

Vasomotion (vasoconstriction and vasodilation) serves two physiological purposes: a generalized raising or lowering of blood pressure throughout the body, and selectively modifying the perfusion

of a particular organ and rerouting blood from one region of the body to another.

A generalized increase in blood pressure requires centralized control—an action on the part of the medullary vasomotor center or by hormones that circulate throughout the system, such as angiotensin II or epinephrine. Widespread vasoconstriction raises the overall blood pressure because the whole "container" (the blood vessels) squeezes on a fixed amount of blood, like water pressure rising if you squeeze a plastic water bottle. This can be important in supporting cerebral perfusion in situations such as hemorrhaging or dehydration, in which blood volume has significantly fallen. Conversely, generalized vasodilation lowers BP throughout the system.

The rerouting of blood and changes in the perfusion of individual organs can be achieved by either central or local control. For example, during periods of exercise, the sympathetic nervous system can selectively reduce flow to the kidneys and digestive tract. Yet as we saw earlier, metabolite accumulation in a tissue can stimulate local vasodilation and increase perfusion of that tissue without affecting circulation elsewhere in the body.

If a specific artery constricts, pressure downstream from the constriction drops and pressure upstream from it rises. If blood can travel by either of two routes and one route puts up more resistance than the other, most blood follows the path of least resistance. This mechanism enables the body to redirect blood from one organ to another.

For example, if you are dozing in an armchair after a big meal **(fig. 20.15a)**, vasoconstriction shuts down blood flow to 90% or more of the capillaries in the muscles of your lower limbs (and muscles elsewhere). This raises the BP above the limbs, where the aorta gives off a branch, the superior mesenteric artery, supplying the small intestine. High resistance in the circulation of the limbs and low resistance in the superior mesenteric artery route blood to the small intestine, where it is needed to absorb the nutrients you are digesting.

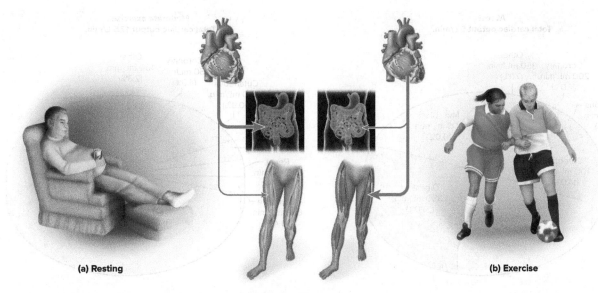

(a) Resting   **(b) Exercise**

FIGURE 20.15 Redirection of Blood Flow in Response to Changing Metabolic Needs. (a) After a meal, the intestines receive priority and the skeletal muscles receive relatively little flow. (b) During exercise, the muscles receive higher priority. The vasomotion that redirects such blood flow occurs mainly at the level of the arterioles in the respective organs.

On the other hand, during vigorous exercise, the arteries in your lungs, coronary circulation, and muscles dilate. To increase the circulation in these routes, vasoconstriction must occur elsewhere, such as the kidneys and digestive tract (**figs. 20.15b, 20.16**). That reduces their perfusion for the time being, making more blood available to the organs important in sustaining exercise. Thus, local changes in peripheral resistance can shift blood flow from one organ system to another to meet the changing metabolic priorities of the body.

BEFORE YOU GO ON

Answer the following questions to test your understanding of the preceding section:

7. Explain why a drop in diastolic pressure would raise one's pulse pressure even if systolic pressure remained unchanged. How could this rise in pulse pressure adversely affect the blood vessels?

8. Explain why arterial blood flow is pulsatile and venous flow is not.

9. What three variables affect peripheral resistance to blood flow? Which of these is most able to change from one minute to the next?

10. What are the three primary mechanisms for controlling vessel radius? Briefly explain each.

11. Explain how the baroreflex serves as an example of homeostasis and negative feedback.

12. Explain how the body can shift the flow of blood from one organ system to another.

20.3 Capillaries and Fluid Exchange

Expected Learning Outcomes

When you have completed this section, you should be able to

a. describe how materials get from the blood into the surrounding tissues;

b. describe and calculate the forces that enable capillaries to give off and reabsorb fluid; and

c. describe the causes and effects of edema.

Only 250 to 300 mL (5%) of the blood is in the capillaries at any given time. This, however, is the most important blood in the body, for it is mainly across capillary walls that exchanges occur between the blood and surrounding tissues. **Capillary exchange** refers to this two-way movement of fluid.

Chemicals given off by the capillary blood to the perivascular tissues include oxygen, glucose and other nutrients, antibodies, and hormones. Chemicals taken up by the capillaries include carbon dioxide and other wastes, and many of the same substances as they give off: glucose and fatty acids released from storage in the liver and adipose tissue; calcium and other minerals released from bone; antibodies secreted by immune cells; and hormones secreted by the endocrine glands. Thus, many chemicals have a two-way traffic between the blood and connective tissue, leaving the capillaries at one point and entering at another. Along with all these solutes, there is substantial movement of water into and out of the bloodstream across the capillary walls. Significant exchange also occurs across

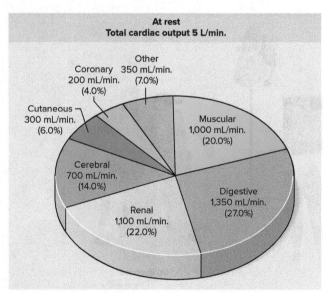

(a)

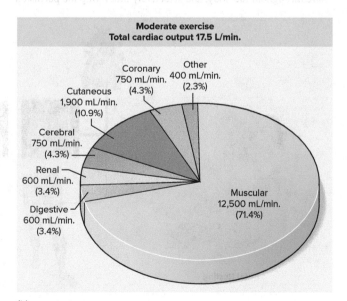

(b)

FIGURE 20.16 Differences in Systemic Blood Flow According to States of Physical Activity. (a) Relative blood flow at rest. (b) Relative blood flow during exercise.

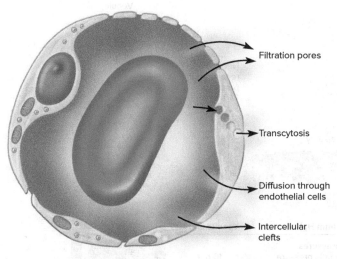

FIGURE 20.17 Routes of Fluid Exchange Across the Capillary Wall. Materials move through the capillary wall via filtration pores (in fenestrated capillaries only), by transcytosis, by diffusion through the endothelial cells, and via intercellular clefts.

Filtration pores

Transcytosis

Diffusion through endothelial cells

Intercellular clefts

the walls of the venules, but capillaries are the more important exchange site because they so greatly outnumber the venules.

The mechanisms of capillary exchange are difficult to study quantitatively because it is hard to measure pressure and flow in such small vessels. For some representative cutaneous capillaries, however, BP has been measured at 32 mm Hg at the arterial end and 15 mm Hg at the venous end, 1 mm away. Capillary BP drops rapidly because of the substantial friction the blood encounters in such narrow vessels. It takes 1 to 2 seconds for an RBC to pass through a typical capillary, traveling about 0.7 mm/s.

Chemicals pass through the capillary wall by three routes **(fig. 20.17):**

1. the endothelial cell cytoplasm;
2. intercellular clefts between the endothelial cells; and
3. filtration pores of the fenestrated capillaries.

The mechanisms of movement through the capillary wall are *diffusion, transcytosis, filtration,* and *reabsorption.*

20.3a Diffusion

The most important mechanism of exchange is diffusion. Glucose and oxygen, being more concentrated in the systemic blood than in the tissue fluid, diffuse out of the blood. Carbon dioxide and other wastes, being more concentrated in the tissue fluid, diffuse into the blood. (O_2 and CO_2 diffuse in the opposite directions in the lungs.) Such diffusion is possible only if the solute can either permeate the plasma membranes of the endothelial cells or find passages large enough to pass through—namely, the filtration pores and intercellular clefts. Such lipid-soluble substances as steroid hormones, O_2, and CO_2 diffuse easily through the plasma membranes. Substances insoluble in lipids, such as glucose and electrolytes, must pass through membrane channels, filtration pores, or intercellular clefts. Large molecules such as proteins are usually held back.

20.3b Transcytosis

Transcytosis is a process in which endothelial cells pick up material on one side of the plasma membrane by pinocytosis or receptor-mediated endocytosis, transport the vesicles across the cell, and discharge the material on the other side by exocytosis (see fig. 3.22). This probably accounts for only a small fraction of solute exchange across the capillary wall, but fatty acids, albumin, and some hormones such as insulin move across the endothelium by this mechanism.

20.3c Filtration and Reabsorption

Capillary fluid exchange is driven in large part by the equilibrium between filtration and osmosis discussed in section 3.3. Typically, fluid filters out of the arterial end of a capillary and osmotically reenters it at the venous end. This fluid delivers materials to the cells and rinses away their metabolic wastes. It may seem odd that a capillary could give off fluid at one point and reabsorb it at another. This comes about as the result of a shifting balance between osmosis and hydrostatic pressure **(fig. 20.18). Hydrostatic pressure** is the physical force exerted by a liquid against a surface such as a capillary wall. Blood pressure is one example.

A typical capillary has a blood pressure of about 30 mm Hg at the arterial end. The hydrostatic pressure of the interstitial space has been difficult to measure, but a typical value accepted by many authorities is –3 mm Hg. The negative value indicates that this is a slight suction, which helps draw fluid out of the capillary. (This force will be represented hereafter as 3_{out}.) In this case, the positive hydrostatic pressure within the capillary and the negative interstitial pressure work in the same direction, creating a total outward force of about 33 mm Hg.

These forces are opposed by **colloid osmotic pressure (COP),** the portion of the osmotic pressure due to protein. The blood has a COP of about 28 mm Hg, due mainly to albumin. Tissue fluid has less than one-third the protein concentration of blood plasma and has a COP of about 8 mm Hg. The difference between the COP of blood and tissue fluid is called **oncotic pressure:** $28_{in} - 8_{out} = 20_{in}$. Oncotic pressure tends to draw water into the capillary by osmosis, opposing hydrostatic pressure.

These opposing forces produce a **net filtration pressure (NFP)** of 13 mm Hg out, as follows:

Hydrostatic pressure		
Blood pressure		30_{out}
Interstitial pressure	+	3_{out}
Net hydrostatic pressure		33_{out}

Colloid osmotic pressure (COP)		
Blood COP		28_{in}
Tissue fluid COP	–	8_{out}
Net COP (oncotic pressure)		20_{in}

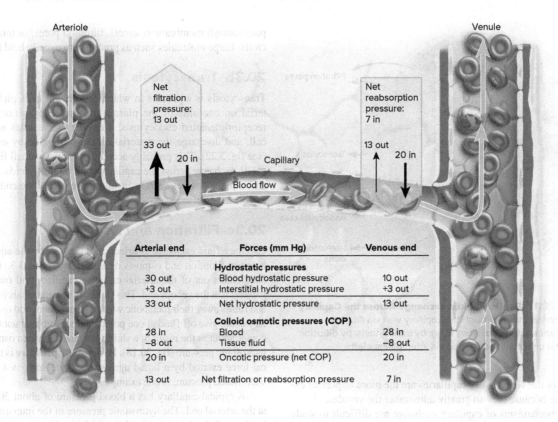

Arteriole

Venule

Net filtration pressure: 13 out

Net reabsorption pressure: 7 in

33 out   20 in

13 out   20 in

Capillary

Blood flow

Arterial end	Forces (mm Hg)	Venous end
	Hydrostatic pressures	
30 out	Blood hydrostatic pressure	10 out
+3 out	Interstitial hydrostatic pressure	+3 out
33 out	Net hydrostatic pressure	13 out
	Colloid osmotic pressures (COP)	
28 in	Blood	28 in
−8 out	Tissue fluid	−8 out
20 in	Oncotic pressure (net COP)	20 in
13 out	Net filtration or reabsorption pressure	7 in

FIGURE 20.18 **The Forces of Capillary Filtration and Reabsorption.** Note the shift from net filtration at the arterial end (left) to net reabsorption at the venous end (right). **APR**

Net filtration pressure (NFP)

Net hydrostatic pressure	33_{out}
Oncotic pressure	$-\ 20_{in}$
Net filtration pressure	13_{out}

The NFP of 13 mm Hg causes about 0.5% of the blood plasma to leave the capillaries at the arterial end.

At the venous end, however, capillary blood pressure is lower—about 10 mm Hg. All the other pressures are essentially unchanged. Thus, we get the following:

Hydrostatic pressure

Blood pressure	10_{out}
Interstitial pressure	$+\ 3_{out}$
Net hydrostatic pressure	13_{out}

Net reabsorption pressure

Oncotic pressure	20_{in}
Net hydrostatic pressure	$-\ 13_{out}$
Net reabsorption pressure	7_{in}

The prevailing force is inward at the venous end because osmotic pressure overrides filtration pressure. The **net reabsorption pressure** of 7 mm Hg inward causes the capillary to reabsorb fluid at this end.

Now you can see why a capillary gives off fluid at one end and reabsorbs it at the other. The only pressure that changes significantly from the arterial end to the venous end is the capillary blood pressure, and this change is responsible for the shift from filtration to reabsorption. With a reabsorption pressure of 7 mm Hg and a net filtration pressure of 13 mm Hg, it might appear that far more fluid would leave the capillaries than reenter them. However, since capillaries branch along their length, there are more of them at the venous end than at the arterial end, which partially compensates for the difference between filtration and reabsorption pressures. They also typically have nearly twice the diameter at the venous end than they have at the arterial end, so there is more capillary surface area available to reabsorb fluid than to give it off. Consequently, capillaries in most places reabsorb about 85% of the fluid they filter. The rest is absorbed and returned to the blood by way of the lymphatic system, as described in the next chapter.

Of course, water is not the only substance that crosses the capillary wall by filtration and reabsorption. Chemicals dissolved in the water are "dragged" along with it and pass through the capillary wall if they are not too large. This process, called **solvent drag,** will be important in our discussions of kidney function in chapter 23.

Variations in Capillary Filtration and Reabsorption

The figures in the preceding discussion are only examples; circumstances differ from place to place in the body and from time to time in the same capillaries. Capillaries usually reabsorb most of the fluid they filter, but not always. The kidneys have capillary networks called *glomeruli* in which there is little or no reabsorption; they are entirely devoted to filtration. Alveolar capillaries of the lungs, by contrast, are almost entirely dedicated to absorption so fluid doesn't fill the air spaces.

Capillary activity also varies from moment to moment. In a resting tissue, most precapillary sphincters are constricted and the capillaries are collapsed. Capillary BP is very low (if there is any flow at all), and reabsorption predominates. When a tissue becomes more metabolically active, its capillary flow increases. In active muscles, capillary pressure rises to the point that filtration overrides reabsorption along the entire length of the capillary. Fluid accumulates in the muscle and increases muscular bulk by as much as 25%. Capillary permeability is also subject to chemical influences. Traumatized tissue releases such chemicals as substance P, bradykinin, and histamine, which increase permeability and filtration.

20.3d Edema

Edema is the accumulation of excess fluid in a tissue. It often shows as swelling of the face, fingers, abdomen, or ankles **(fig. 20.19),** but also occurs in internal organs where its effects are hidden from view. Edema occurs when fluid filters into a tissue faster than it is reabsorbed. It has three fundamental causes:

1. **Increased capillary filtration.** Numerous conditions can increase the rate of capillary filtration and accumulation of fluid in the tissues. Kidney failure, for example, leads to water retention and hypertension, raising capillary blood pressure and filtration rate. Histamine dilates arterioles and raises

capillary pressure and makes the capillary wall more permeable. Capillaries generally become more permeable in old age as well, putting elderly people at increased risk of edema. Capillary blood pressure also rises in cases of poor venous return—the flow of blood from the capillaries back to the heart. As we will see in the next section, good venous return depends on muscular activity. Therefore, edema is a common problem among people confined to bed or a wheelchair.

Failure of the right ventricle of the heart tends to cause pressure to back up in the systemic veins and capillaries, thus resulting in systemic edema. Failure of the left ventricle causes pressure to back up in the lungs, causing pulmonary edema.

2. **Reduced capillary reabsorption.** Capillary reabsorption depends on oncotic pressure, which is proportional to the concentration of blood albumin. Therefore, a deficiency of albumin (hypoproteinemia) produces edema by reducing the reabsorption of tissue fluid. Since albumin is produced by the liver, liver diseases such as cirrhosis tend to lead to hypoproteinemia and edema. Edema is commonly seen in regions of famine due to dietary protein deficiency (see Deeper Insight 18.1). Hypoproteinemia and edema also commonly result from severe burns, owing to the loss of protein from body surfaces no longer covered with skin, and from kidney diseases that allow protein to escape in the urine.

3. **Obstructed lymphatic drainage.** The lymphatic system, described in detail in the next chapter, is a network of one-way vessels that collect fluid from the tissues and return it to the bloodstream. Obstruction of these vessels or the surgical removal of lymph nodes can interfere with fluid drainage and lead to the accumulation of tissue fluid distal to the obstruction.

Edema has multiple pathological consequences. As the tissues become congested with fluid, oxygen delivery and waste removal are impaired and the tissues may begin to die. Pulmonary edema presents a threat of suffocation as fluid replaces air in the lungs,

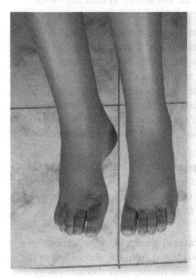
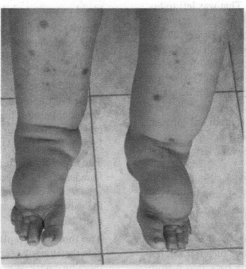

FIGURE 20.19 Lymphedema. On the right is a 52-year-old woman with severe lymphedema of the legs and feet; on the left, for comparison, is a 21-year-old woman without edema. Blockage of lymphatic vessels is one of several causes of edema.
MedicImage/Alamy

and cerebral edema can produce headaches, nausea, and sometimes delirium, seizures, and coma. In severe edema, so much fluid can transfer from the blood vessels to the tissue spaces that blood volume and pressure drop low enough to cause circulatory shock (described in the next section).

Answer the following questions to test your understanding of the preceding section:

13. List the three mechanisms of capillary exchange and relate each one to the structure of capillary walls.

14. What forces favor capillary filtration? What forces favor reabsorption?

15. How can a capillary shift from a predominantly filtering role at one time to a predominantly reabsorbing role at another?

16. State the three fundamental causes of edema and explain why edema can be dangerous.

20.4 Venous Return and Circulatory Shock

Expected Learning Outcomes

When you have completed this section, you should be able to

a. explain how blood in the veins is returned to the heart;

b. discuss the importance of physical activity in venous return;

c. discuss several causes of circulatory shock; and

d. name and describe the stages of shock.

Hieronymus Fabricius (1537–1619) discovered the valves of the veins but did not understand their function. That was left to his student, William Harvey, who performed simple experiments on the valves that you can easily reproduce. In **figure 20.20,** by Harvey, the experimenter has pressed on a vein at point H to block flow from the wrist toward the elbow. With another finger, he has milked the blood out of it up to point O, the first valve proximal to H. When he tries to force blood downward, it stops at that valve. It can go no farther, and it causes the vein to swell at that point. Blood can flow from right to left through that valve but not from left to right. So as Harvey correctly surmised, the valves serve to ensure a one-way flow of blood toward the heart.

You can easily demonstrate the action of these valves in your own hand. Hold your hand still, below waist level, until veins stand up on the back of it. (Do not apply a tourniquet!) Press on a vein close to your knuckles, and while holding it down, use another finger to milk that vein toward the wrist. It collapses as you force the blood out of it, and if you remove the second finger, it will not refill. The valves prevent blood from flowing back into it from

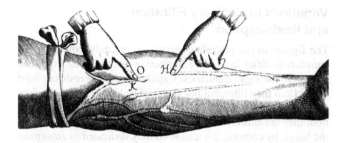

FIGURE 20.20 An Illustration from William Harvey's *De Motu Cordis* (1628). Such experiments demonstrated the existence of one-way valves in veins of the arms. See text for explanation.
UniversalImagesGroup/Getty Images

❓ *In the space between O and H, what (if anything) would happen if the experimenter lifted his finger from point O? What if he lifted his finger from point H? Why?*

above. When you remove the first finger, however, the vein fills from below.

20.4a Mechanisms of Venous Return

The flow of blood back to the heart, called **venous return,** is achieved by five mechanisms:

1. **The pressure gradient.** Pressure generated by the heart is the most important force in venous flow, even though it is substantially weaker in the veins than in the arteries. Pressure in the venules ranges from 12 to 18 mm Hg, and pressure at the point where the venae cavae enter the heart, called **central venous pressure,** averages 4.6 mm Hg. Thus, there is a venous pressure gradient (ΔP) of about 7 to 13 mm Hg favoring the flow of blood toward the heart. The pressure gradient and venous return increase when blood volume increases. Venous return also increases in the event of generalized, widespread vasoconstriction because this reduces the volume of the circulatory system and raises blood pressure and flow.

2. **Gravity.** When you are sitting or standing, blood from your head and neck returns to the heart simply by flowing downward through the large veins above the heart. Thus, the large veins of the neck are normally collapsed or nearly so, and their venous pressure is close to zero. The dural sinuses of the brain, however, have more rigid walls and cannot collapse. Their pressure is as low as −10 mm Hg, creating a risk of *air embolism* if they are punctured (see Deeper Insight 20.3).

3. **The skeletal muscle pump.** In the limbs, the veins are surrounded and massaged by the muscles. Contracting muscles squeeze the blood out of the compressed part of a vein, and the valves ensure that this blood can go only toward the heart **(fig. 20.21).**

4. **The thoracic (respiratory) pump.** This mechanism aids the flow of venous blood from the abdominal to the thoracic cavity. When you inhale, your thoracic cavity

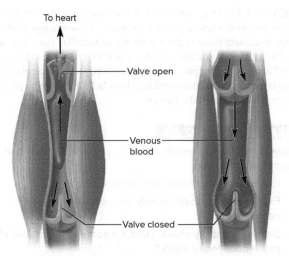

To heart

Valve open

Venous blood

Valve closed

(a) Contracted skeletal muscles   **(b) Relaxed skeletal muscles**

FIGURE 20.21 The Skeletal Muscle Pump. (a) Muscle contraction squeezes the deep veins and forces blood through the next valve in the direction of the heart. Valves below the point of compression prevent backflow. (b) When the muscles relax, blood flows back downward under the pull of gravity but can flow only as far as the nearest valve.

expands and its internal pressure drops, while downward movement of the diaphragm raises the pressure in your abdominal cavity. The *inferior vena cava (IVC)*, your largest vein, is a flexible tube passing through both of these cavities. If abdominal pressure on the IVC rises while thoracic pressure on it drops, then blood is squeezed upward toward the heart. It isn't forced back into the lower limbs because the valves there prevent this. Because of the thoracic pump, central venous pressure fluctuates from 2 mm Hg when you inhale to 6 mm Hg when you exhale, and blood flows faster when you inhale. This is what produces the slight fluctuations in blood pressure at the right end of the graph in figure 20.11.

5. **Cardiac suction.** During ventricular systole, the tendinous cords pull the AV valve cusps downward, slightly expanding the atrial space. This creates a slight suction that draws blood into the atria from the venae cavae and pulmonary veins.

20.4b Venous Return and Physical Activity

Exercise increases venous return for multiple reasons. The heart beats faster and harder, increasing cardiac output and blood pressure. Blood vessels of the skeletal muscles, lungs, and coronary circulation dilate, increasing flow. The increase in respiratory rate and depth enhances the action of the thoracic pump. Muscle contractions increase venous return by means of the skeletal muscle pump. Increased venous return then increases cardiac output, which is important in perfusion of the muscles just when they need it most.

Conversely, when a person is still, blood accumulates in the limbs because venous pressure isn't high enough to override the weight of the blood and drive it upward. Such accumulation of blood is called **venous pooling.** To demonstrate this effect, hold one hand below your waist and hold the other hand over your head. After about 1 minute, quickly bring your two hands together and compare the palms. The hand held overhead will likely appear pale because its blood has drained out of it; the hand held below the waist will likely be redder than normal because of venous pooling in its veins and capillaries. Venous pooling can be troublesome to people who must stand for prolonged periods—such as cashiers, barbers and hairdressers, members of a choir, and people in military service—and when sitting still for too long, as in a cramped seat on a long airline flight. If enough blood accumulates in the limbs, cardiac output may fall so low that the brain is inadequately perfused and a person may experience dizziness or syncope. This can usually be prevented by periodically tensing the calf and other muscles to keep the skeletal muscle pump active. Military jet pilots often perform maneuvers that could cause the blood to pool in the abdomen and lower limbs, causing loss of vision or consciousness. To prevent this, they wear pressurized *G suits* that inflate and tighten on the lower limbs during these maneuvers; in addition, they can tense their abdominal muscles to prevent venous pooling and blackout.

▶▶▶ APPLY WHAT YOU KNOW

Why is venous pooling not a problem when you are sleeping and the skeletal muscle pump is inactive?

20.4c Circulatory Shock

Circulatory shock (not to be confused with electrical or spinal shock) is any state in which cardiac output is insufficient to meet the body's metabolic needs. All forms of circulatory shock fall into two categories: (1) **cardiogenic shock,** caused by inadequate pumping by the heart, usually as a result of myocardial infarction; and (2) **low venous return (LVR) shock,** in which cardiac output is low because too little blood is returning to the heart.

There are three principal forms of LVR shock:

1. **Hypovolemic shock,** the most common form, is produced by a loss of blood volume as a result of hemorrhage, trauma, bleeding ulcers, burns, or dehydration. Dehydration is a major cause of death from heat exposure. In hot weather, the body excretes as much as 1.5 L of sweat per hour. Water transfers from the bloodstream to replace tissue fluid lost in the sweat, and blood volume may drop too low to maintain adequate circulation.

2. **Obstructed venous return shock** occurs when any object, such as a growing tumor or aneurysm, compresses a vein and impedes its blood flow.

3. **Venous pooling shock** occurs when the body has a normal total blood volume, but too much of it accumulates in the lower body. This can result from long periods of standing

FIGURE 20.22 Venous Pooling Shock. This is a common consequence of prolonged, rigid standing in ceremonial attention.
Carlo Allegri/AFP/Getty Images

or sitting (**fig. 20.22**) or from widespread vasodilation. **Neurogenic shock** is a form of venous pooling shock that results from a sudden loss of vasomotor tone, allowing the vessels to dilate. This can result from causes as severe as brainstem trauma or as slight as an emotional shock.

Elements of both venous pooling and hypovolemic shock are present in certain cases, such as septic shock and anaphylactic shock, which involve both vasodilation and a loss of fluid through abnormally permeable capillaries. **Septic shock** occurs when bacterial toxins trigger vasodilation and increased capillary permeability. **Anaphylactic shock,** discussed more fully in section 21.6, results from exposure to an antigen to which a person is allergic, such as bee venom. Antigen–antibody complexes trigger the release of histamine, which causes generalized vasodilation and increased capillary permeability.

Responses to Circulatory Shock

Shock is clinically described according to severity as compensated or decompensated. In **compensated shock,** several homeostatic mechanisms bring about spontaneous recovery. The hypotension resulting from low cardiac output triggers the sympathetic baroreflex and the production of angiotensin II, both of which counteract shock by stimulating vasoconstriction. Furthermore, if a person faints and falls to a horizontal position, gravity restores blood flow to the brain. Even quicker recovery is achieved if the person's feet are elevated to promote drainage of blood from the legs.

If these mechanisms prove inadequate, **decompensated shock** ensues and several life-threatening positive feedback loops occur. Poor cardiac output results in myocardial ischemia and infarction, which further weaken the heart and reduce output. Slow circulation of the blood can lead to disseminated intravascular coagulation

(DIC) (see table 18.8). As the vessels become congested with clotted blood, venous return grows even worse. Ischemia and acidosis of the brainstem depress the vasomotor and cardiac centers, causing loss of vasomotor tone, further vasodilation, and further drop in BP and cardiac output. Before long, damage to the cardiac and brain tissues may be unsurvivable. About half of those who go into decompensated shock die from it.

BEFORE YOU GO ON

Answer the following questions to test your understanding of the preceding section:

17. Explain how respiration aids venous return.

18. Explain how muscular activity and venous valves aid venous return.

19. Define *circulatory shock*. What are some of the causes of low venous return shock?

20.5 Special Circulatory Routes

Expected Learning Outcomes

When you have completed this section, you should be able to

a. explain how the brain maintains stable perfusion;

b. discuss the causes and effects of strokes and transient ischemic attacks;

c. explain the mechanisms that increase muscular perfusion during exercise; and

d. contrast the blood pressure of the pulmonary circuit with that of the systemic circuit, and explain why the difference is important in pulmonary function.

Certain circulatory pathways have special physiological properties adapted to the functions of their organs. Two of these are described in other chapters: the coronary circulation (see fig. 19.10) and fetal and placental circulation (see fig. 29.10). Here we take a closer look at the circulation to the brain, skeletal muscles, and lungs.

20.5a Brain

Total blood flow to the brain fluctuates less than that of any other organ (about 700 mL/min. at rest). Such constancy is important because even a few seconds of oxygen deprivation causes loss of consciousness, and 4 or 5 minutes of anoxia is time enough to cause irreversible damage. Although total cerebral perfusion is fairly stable, blood flow can be shifted from one part of the brain to another in a matter of seconds as different parts engage in motor, sensory, or cognitive functions (see fig. 14.41).

The brain regulates its own blood flow in response to changes in BP and chemistry. The cerebral arteries dilate when the systemic BP drops and constrict when it rises, thus minimizing fluctuations in cerebral BP. Cerebral blood flow therefore remains quite stable even when mean arterial pressure (MAP) fluctuates from 60 to 140 mm Hg. However, an MAP below 60 mm Hg produces syncope and an MAP above 160 mm Hg causes cerebral edema.

The main chemical stimulus for cerebral autoregulation is pH. Poor perfusion allows CO_2 to accumulate in the brain. This lowers the pH of the tissue fluid and triggers local vasodilation, which improves perfusion. Extreme hypercapnia, however, depresses neural activity. The opposite condition, hypocapnia, raises the pH and stimulates vasoconstriction, thus reducing perfusion and giving CO_2 a chance to rise to a normal level. Hyperventilation (exhaling CO_2 faster than the body produces it) induces hypocapnia, which leads to cerebral vasoconstriction, ischemia, dizziness, and sometimes syncope.

Brief episodes of cerebral ischemia produce **transient ischemic attacks (TIAs),** characterized by temporary dizziness, loss of vision or other senses, weakness, paralysis, headache, or aphasia. A TIA may result from spasms of diseased cerebral arteries. It lasts from just a moment to a few hours and is often an early warning of an impending stroke. People with TIAs should receive prompt medical attention to identify the cause using brain imaging and other diagnostic means. Immediate treatment should be initiated to prevent a stroke. **Stroke, or cerebrovascular accident (CVA),** is far more serious, entailing death (infarction) of brain tissue and often irreversible loss of bodily functions. Stroke is discussed more extensively in Deeper Insight 14.2.

20.5b Skeletal Muscles

In contrast to the brain, the skeletal muscles receive a highly variable blood flow depending on their state of exertion. At rest, the arterioles are constricted, most of the capillary beds are shut down, and total flow through the muscular system is about 1 L/min. During exercise, the arterioles dilate in response to muscle metabolites such as lactate, nitric oxide (NO), adenosine, CO_2, and H^+. Blood flow through the muscles can increase more than 20-fold during strenuous exercise, which requires that blood be diverted from other organs such as the digestive tract and kidneys to meet the needs of the working muscles.

Muscular contraction compresses the blood vessels and impedes flow. For this reason, isometric contraction causes fatigue more quickly than intermittent isotonic contraction. If you squeeze a rubber ball as hard as you can without relaxing your grip, you feel the muscles fatigue more quickly than if you intermittently squeeze and relax.

20.5c Lungs

After birth, the pulmonary circuit is the only route in which the arteries carry oxygen-poor blood and the veins carry oxygen-rich blood; the opposite situation prevails in the systemic circuit. The pulmonary arteries have thin distensible walls with less elastic tissue than the systemic arteries. Thus, they have a BP of only 25/10 mm Hg. Capillary hydrostatic pressure is about 10 mm Hg in the pulmonary circuit as compared with an average of 17 mm Hg in systemic capillaries. This lower pressure has two implications for pulmonary circulation: (1) Blood flows more slowly through the pulmonary capillaries, and therefore it has more time for gas exchange; and (2) oncotic pressure overrides hydrostatic pressure, so these capillaries are engaged almost entirely in absorption. This prevents fluid accumulation in the alveolar walls and lumens, which would compromise gas exchange. In a condition such as

mitral valve stenosis, however, blood may back up in the pulmonary circuit, raising the capillary hydrostatic pressure and causing pulmonary edema, congestion, and hypoxemia.

Another unique characteristic of the pulmonary arteries is their response to hypoxia. Systemic arteries dilate in response to local hypoxia and improve tissue perfusion. By contrast, pulmonary arteries constrict. Pulmonary hypoxia indicates that part of the lung is not being ventilated well, perhaps because of mucous congestion of the airway or a degenerative lung disease. Vasoconstriction in poorly ventilated regions of the lung redirects blood flow to better ventilated regions.

▶▶▶ **APPLY WHAT YOU KNOW**

What abnormal skin coloration would result from pulmonary edema?

BEFORE YOU GO ON

Answer the following questions to test your understanding of the preceding section:

20. In what conspicuous way does perfusion of the brain differ from perfusion of the skeletal muscles?

21. How does a stroke differ from a transient ischemic attack? Which of these bears closer resemblance to a myocardial infarction?

22. How does the low hydrostatic blood pressure in the pulmonary circuit affect the fluid dynamics of the capillaries there?

23. Contrast the vasomotor response of the lungs with that of skeletal muscles to hypoxia.

20.6 Anatomy of the Pulmonary Circuit

Expected Learning Outcome

When you have completed this section, you should be able to

a. trace the route of blood through the pulmonary circuit.

The next three sections of this chapter center on the names and pathways of the principal arteries and veins. The pulmonary circuit is described here, and the systemic arteries and veins are described in the two sections that follow.

The pulmonary circuit (**fig. 20.23**) begins with the **pulmonary trunk,** a large vessel that ascends diagonally from the right ventricle and branches into the right and left **pulmonary arteries.** As it approaches the lung, the right pulmonary artery branches in two, and both branches enter the lung at a medial indentation called the *hilum* (see fig. 22.9). The upper branch is the **superior lobar artery,** serving the superior lobe of the lung. The lower branch divides again within the lung to form the **middle lobar** and **inferior lobar arteries,** supplying the lower two lobes of that lung. The left pulmonary artery is much more variable. It gives off several superior lobar arteries to the superior lobe before entering

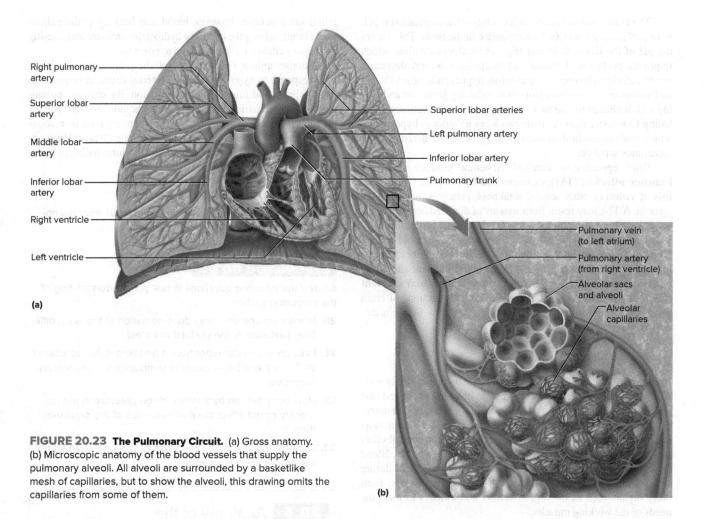

Right pulmonary artery

Superior lobar artery

Middle lobar artery

Inferior lobar artery

Right ventricle

Left ventricle

(a)

Superior lobar arteries

Left pulmonary artery

Inferior lobar artery

Pulmonary trunk

Pulmonary vein (to left atrium)

Pulmonary artery (from right ventricle)

Alveolar sacs and alveoli

Alveolar capillaries

(b)

FIGURE 20.23 The Pulmonary Circuit. (a) Gross anatomy. (b) Microscopic anatomy of the blood vessels that supply the pulmonary alveoli. All alveoli are surrounded by a basketlike mesh of capillaries, but to show the alveoli, this drawing omits the capillaries from some of them.

the hilum, then enters the lung and gives off a variable number of inferior lobar arteries to the inferior lobe.

In both lungs, these arteries lead ultimately to small basketlike capillary beds that surround the pulmonary alveoli (air sacs). This is where the blood unloads CO_2 and picks up O_2. After leaving the alveolar capillaries, the pulmonary blood flows into venules and veins, ultimately leading to the main **pulmonary veins** that exit the lung at the hilum. The left atrium of the heart receives two pulmonary veins on each side (see fig. 19.5b).

The purpose of the pulmonary circuit is primarily to exchange CO_2 for O_2. The lungs also receive a separate systemic blood supply by way of the *bronchial arteries* (see section 20.7d).

BEFORE YOU GO ON

Answer the following questions to test your understanding of the preceding section:

24. Trace the flow of an RBC from right ventricle to left atrium and name the vessels along the way.

25. The lungs have two separate arterial supplies. Explain their functions.

20.7 Systemic Vessels of the Axial Region

Expected Learning Outcomes

When you have completed this section, you should be able to

a. identify the principal systemic arteries and veins of the axial region; and

b. trace the flow of blood from the heart to any major organ of the axial region and back to the heart.

The systemic circuit (**figs. 20.24, 20.25**) supplies oxygen and nutrients to all organs and removes their metabolic wastes. The coronary circulation, already described, is part of this. This section surveys the remaining arteries and veins of the axial region—the head, neck, and trunk. The following sections, 20.7a through 20.7g, trace arterial outflow and venous return, region by region. They outline only the most common circulatory pathways; there is

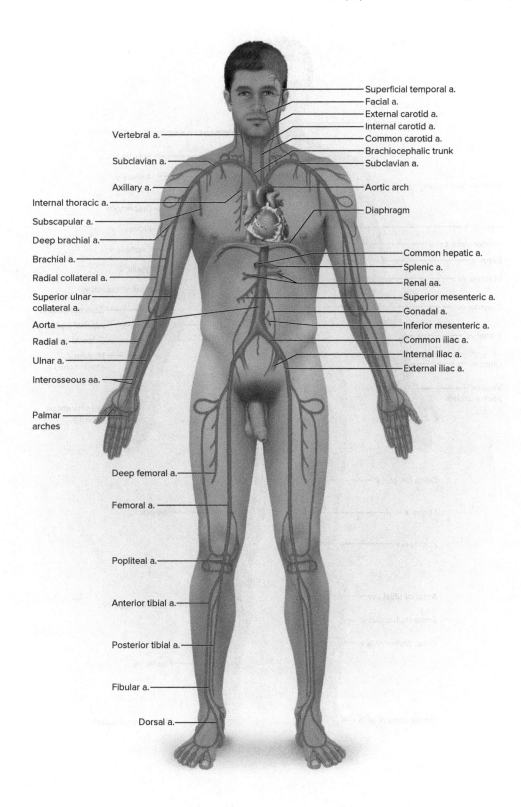

Superficial temporal a.
Facial a.
External carotid a.
Internal carotid a.
Common carotid a.
Brachiocephalic trunk
Subclavian a.

Vertebral a.
Subclavian a.
Axillary a.
Internal thoracic a.
Subscapular a.
Deep brachial a.
Brachial a.
Radial collateral a.
Superior ulnar collateral a.
Aorta
Radial a.
Ulnar a.
Interosseous aa.
Palmar arches

Aortic arch
Diaphragm
Common hepatic a.
Splenic a.
Renal aa.
Superior mesenteric a.
Gonadal a.
Inferior mesenteric a.
Common iliac a.
Internal iliac a.
External iliac a.

Deep femoral a.
Femoral a.
Popliteal a.
Anterior tibial a.
Posterior tibial a.
Fibular a.
Dorsal a.

FIGURE 20.24 The Major Systemic Arteries. Different arteries are illustrated on the left than on the right for clarity, but nearly all of those shown occur on both sides.

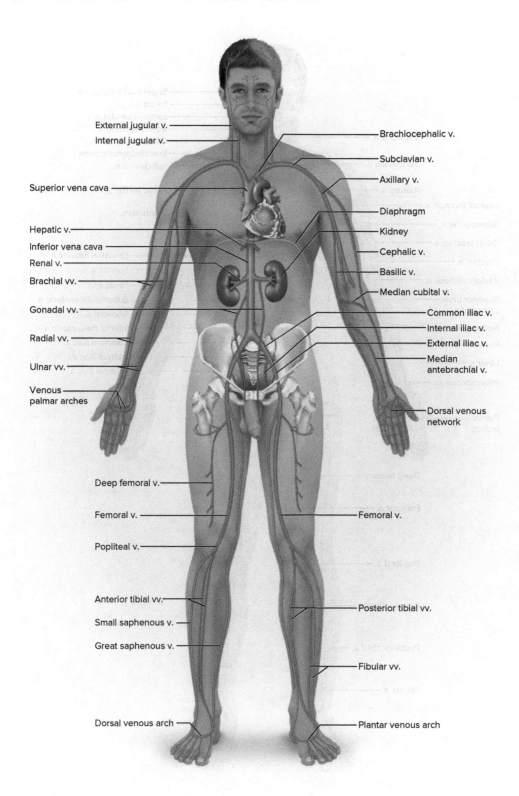

FIGURE 20.25 The Major Systemic Veins. Different veins are illustrated on the left than on the right for clarity, but nearly all of those shown occur on both sides.

a great deal of anatomical variation in the circulatory system from one person to another.

The names of the blood vessels often describe their location by indicating the body region traversed (as in the *axillary artery* and *brachial veins*), an adjacent bone (as in *temporal artery* and *ulnar vein*), or the organ supplied or drained by the vessel (as in *hepatic artery* and *renal vein*). In many cases, an artery and adjacent vein have similar names (*femoral artery* and *femoral vein,* for example).

As you trace blood flow in these sections, it is important to refer frequently to the illustrations. Verbal descriptions alone are likely to seem obscure if you don't make full use of the explanatory illustrations. Throughout the remaining figures, the abbreviations *a.* and *aa.* mean *artery* and *arteries,* and *v.* and *vv.* mean *vein* and *veins.*

20.7a The Aorta and Its Major Branches

All systemic arteries arise from the aorta, which has three principal regions, often compared to the shape of an umbrella handle (**fig. 20.26**).

1. The **ascending aorta** rises for about 5 cm above the left ventricle. Its only branches are the coronary arteries, which

arise behind two cusps of the aortic valve. They are the origins of the coronary circulation (see section 19.2e).

2. The **aortic arch** curves to the left like an inverted U superior to the heart. It gives off three major arteries in this order: the **brachiocephalic**[10] **trunk** (BRAY-kee-oh-seh-FAL-ic), **left common carotid artery** (cah-ROT-id), and **left subclavian**[11] **artery** (sub-CLAY-vee-un). These are further traced in sections 20.7b and 20.8a.

3. The **descending aorta** passes downward posterior to the heart, at first to the left of the vertebral column and then anterior to it, through the thoracic and abdominal cavities. It is called the **thoracic aorta** above the diaphragm and the **abdominal aorta** below it. It ends in the lower abdominal cavity by forking into the right and left *common iliac arteries.*

20.7b Arteries of the Head and Neck

All blood supply to the head, neck, and upper limbs comes from the aortic arch by way of the following arteries.

Origins of the Head–Neck Arteries

The head and neck (including the brain) receive blood from four pairs of arteries (**fig. 20.27**):

1. The **common carotid arteries,** probably the best-known avenues to the head, ascend the anterolateral region of the neck alongside the trachea. Shortly after leaving the aortic arch, the brachiocephalic trunk divides into the **right common carotid artery** to the head and the *right subclavian artery* leading to the right arm (further traced in section 20.7d). The **left common carotid artery** arises independently from the aortic arch a little distal to the brachiocephalic trunk.

2. The **vertebral arteries** arise from the right and left subclavian arteries, travel up the neck through the transverse foramina of vertebrae C1 through C6, and enter the cranial cavity through the foramen magnum.

3. The **thyrocervical**[12] **trunks** are tiny arteries arising from the subclavians lateral to the vertebral arteries. They supply the thyroid gland and some scapular muscles.

4. The **costocervical**[13] **trunks** arise from the subclavian arteries a little farther laterally. They supply the deep neck muscles and some of the intercostal muscles of the superior rib cage.

Continuation of the Common Carotid Arteries

The common carotid arteries have the most extensive distribution of all head–neck arteries. Near the laryngeal prominence ("Adam's apple"), each common carotid branches into an *external* and *internal carotid artery,* with further branches as follows:

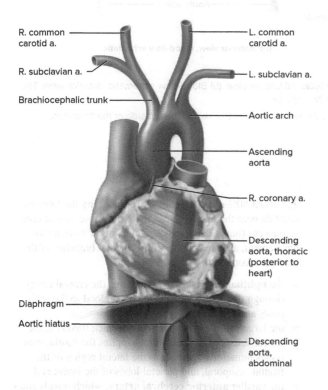

R. common carotid a.

R. subclavian a.

Brachiocephalic trunk

Diaphragm

Aortic hiatus

L. common carotid a.

L. subclavian a.

Aortic arch

Ascending aorta

R. coronary a.

Descending aorta, thoracic (posterior to heart)

Descending aorta, abdominal

FIGURE 20.26 The Thoracic Aorta. (L. = left; R. = right) **APR**

---

[10]*brachio* = arm; *cephal* = head
[11]*sub* = below; *clavi* = clavicle, collarbone
[12]*thyro* = thyroid gland; *cerv* = neck
[13]*costo* = rib; *cerv* = neck

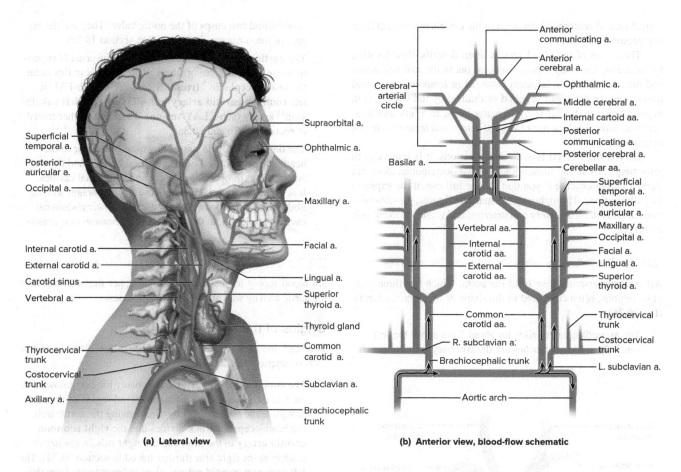

Anterior communicating a.
Anterior cerebral a.
Ophthalmic a.
Middle cerebral a.
Internal cartoid aa.
Posterior communicating a.
Posterior cerebral a.
Cerebellar aa.
Superficial temporal a.
Posterior auricular a.
Maxillary a.
Occipital a.
Facial a.
Lingual a.
Superior thyroid a.
Thyrocervical trunk
Costocervical trunk
L. subclavian a.

Cerebral arterial circle
Basilar a.
Vertebral aa.
Internal carotid aa.
External carotid aa.
Common carotid aa.
R. subclavian a:
Brachiocephalic trunk
Aortic arch

Supraorbital a.
Ophthalmic a.
Maxillary a.
Facial a.
Lingual a.
Superior thyroid a.
Thyroid gland
Common carotid a.
Subclavian a.
Brachiocephalic trunk

Superficial temporal a.
Posterior auricular a.
Occipital a.
Internal carotid a.
External carotid a.
Carotid sinus
Vertebral a.
Thyrocervical trunk
Costocervical trunk
Axillary a.

(a) Lateral view   **(b) Anterior view, blood-flow schematic**

FIGURE 20.27 Superficial (Extracranial) Arteries of the Head and Neck. (a) Lateral view. (b) Blood-flow schematic, anterior view. The upper part of the schematic depicts the cerebral circulation in figure 20.28. **APR**

? *List the arteries, in order, that an erythrocyte must travel to get from the left ventricle to the skin of the left side of the forehead.*

1. The **external carotid artery** ascends the side of the head external to the cranium and supplies most extracranial structures except the orbits. It gives rise to the following arteries in ascending order:
   a. the **superior thyroid artery** to the thyroid gland and larynx;
   b. the **lingual artery** to the tongue;
   c. the **facial artery** to the skin and muscles of the face;
   d. the **occipital artery** to the posterior scalp;
   e. the **maxillary artery** to the teeth, maxilla, oral cavity, and external ear; and
   f. the **superficial temporal artery** to the chewing muscles, nasal cavity, lateral aspect of the face, most of the scalp, and the dura mater.

2. The **internal carotid artery** passes medial to the angle of the mandible and passes through the carotid canal of the temporal bone into the cranial cavity. It supplies the orbits and about 80% of the cerebrum. Compressing the internal carotids near the mandible can therefore cause loss of consciousness (but is dangerous and must never be done for amusement, as some people do). Principal branches of the internal carotid artery (**fig. 20.28**) are

   a. the **ophthalmic artery,** which leaves the cranial cavity through the optic canal and supplies blood to the orbit, nose, and forehead;
   b. the large **middle cerebral artery,** which travels in the lateral sulcus of the cerebrum, supplies the insula, then issues numerous branches to the lateral region of the frontal, temporal, and parietal lobes of the brain; and
   c. the smaller **anterior cerebral artery,** which travels anteriorly, then turns back and arches posteriorly over the corpus callosum as far as the posterior limit of the parietal lobe; it gives off extensive branches to the frontal and parietal lobes.

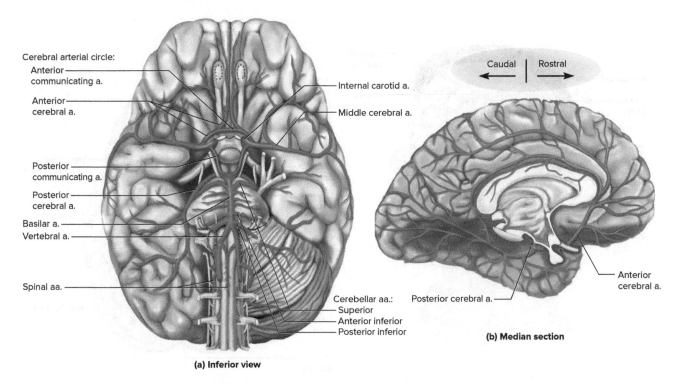

(a) Inferior view

(b) Median section

FIGURE 20.28 The Cerebral Blood Supply. (a) Inferior view of the brain showing the blood supply to the brainstem, cerebellum, and cerebral arterial circle. (b) Median section of the brain showing the more distal branches of the anterior and posterior cerebral arteries. Branches of the middle cerebral artery are distributed over the lateral surface of the cerebrum (not illustrated). **APR**

Continuation of the Vertebral Arteries

The vertebral arteries give rise to small branches that supply the spinal cord and its meninges, the cervical vertebrae, and deep muscles of the neck. They next enter the foramen magnum, supply the cranial bones and meninges, and continue as follows:

1. They converge to form a single median **basilar artery** at the junction of the medulla oblongata and pons. The basilar artery runs along the anterior aspect of the pons and gives off branches to the cerebellum, pons, and inner ear. At or near the pons–midbrain border, it divides into the following arteries.

2. Right and left **posterior cerebral arteries** arise from the basilar artery, sweep posteriorly to the rear of the brain, and serve the inferior and medial regions of the temporal and occipital lobes, the midbrain, and the thalamus.

The Cerebral Arterial Circle

In figure 20.28a and the upper part of 20.27b, you can see that a number of these arteries form a loop that encircles the pituitary gland and optic chiasm. This is called the **cerebral arterial circle** (*circle of Willis*[14]). Its components include the basilar artery;

internal carotid arteries; anterior, middle, and posterior cerebral arteries; and the following anastomoses that complete the loop:

1. one **anterior communicating artery** medially connecting the right and left anterior cerebral arteries; and

2. a slender, right and left **posterior communicating artery,** connecting the internal carotid and posterior cerebral arteries.

Only about 20% of people, however, have a complete cerebral arterial circle. Usually, one or more components are absent or so constricted as to provide no significant blood flow. Knowledge of the distribution of the arteries arising from the cerebral arterial circle is crucial for understanding the effects of blood clots, aneurysms, and strokes on brain function. Cerebral aneurysms occur most often in this complex of arteries or in the basilar artery proximal to the circle.

20.7c Veins of the Head and Neck

The head and neck are drained mainly by three pairs of veins—the *internal* and *external jugular veins* and *vertebral veins*. We will trace these from their origins to the *subclavian veins.*

Dural Venous Sinuses

After blood circulates through the brain, it collects in large, thin-walled, modified veins called **dural venous sinuses**—blood-filled spaces between the layers of the dura mater **(fig. 20.29).**

[14]Thomas Willis (1621–75), English anatomist

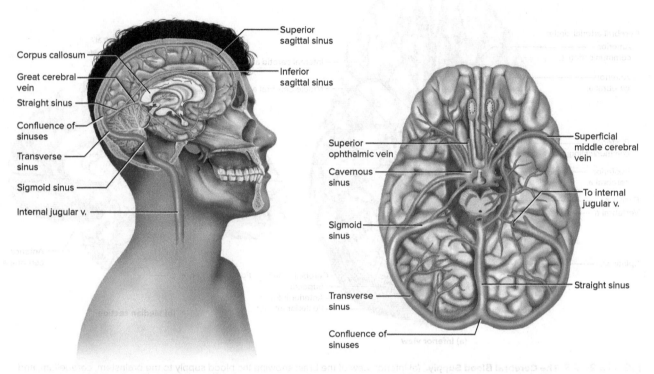

Corpus callosum

Great cerebral vein

Straight sinus

Confluence of sinuses

Transverse sinus

Sigmoid sinus

Internal jugular v.

Superior sagittal sinus

Inferior sagittal sinus

(a) Dural venous sinuses, medial view

Superior ophthalmic vein

Cavernous sinus

Sigmoid sinus

Transverse sinus

Confluence of sinuses

Superficial middle cerebral vein

To internal jugular v.

Straight sinus

(b) Dural venous sinuses, inferior view

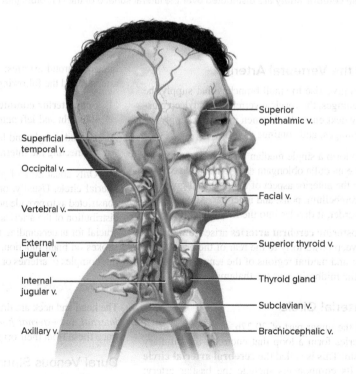

Superficial temporal v.

Occipital v.

Vertebral v.

External jugular v.

Internal jugular v.

Axillary v.

Superior ophthalmic v.

Facial v.

Superior thyroid v.

Thyroid gland

Subclavian v.

Brachiocephalic v.

FIGURE 20.29 Veins of the Head and Neck. (a) Dural venous sinuses seen in a median section of the cerebrum. (b) Dural venous sinuses seen in an inferior view of the cerebrum. (c) Superficial (extracranial) veins of the head and neck. **APR**

(c) Superficial veins of the head and neck

A reminder of the structure of the dura mater may be helpful in understanding these sinuses. This tough membrane between the brain and cranial bones has a *periosteal layer* against the bone and a *meningeal layer* against the brain. In a few places, a space exists between these layers to accommodate a blood-collecting sinus. Between the two cerebral hemispheres is a vertical, sickle-shaped wall of dura called the *falx cerebri,* which contains two of the sinuses. There are about 13 dural venous sinuses in all; we survey only the few most prominent ones here.

1. The **superior sagittal sinus** is contained in the superior margin of the falx cerebri and overlies the longitudinal cerebral fissure (fig. 20.29a; see also figs. 14.5, 14.7). It begins anteriorly near the crista galli of the skull and extends posteriorly to the level of the posterior occipital protuberance. Here it bends, usually to the right, and drains into a *transverse sinus.*

2. The **inferior sagittal sinus** is contained in the inferior margin of the falx cerebri and arches over the corpus callosum, deep in the longitudinal cerebral fissure. Posteriorly, it joins the *great cerebral vein* and their union forms the **straight sinus,** which continues to the rear of the head. There, the superior sagittal and straight sinuses meet in a space called the *confluence of the sinuses.*

3. Right and left **transverse sinuses** lead away from the confluence and encircle the inside of the occipital bone, leading toward the ears (fig. 20.29b); their path is marked by grooves on the inner surface of the occipital bone (see fig. 8.5b). The right transverse sinus receives blood mainly from the superior sagittal sinus, and the left one drains mainly the straight sinus. Laterally, each transverse sinus makes an S-shaped bend, the **sigmoid sinus,** then exits the cranium through the jugular foramen. From here, blood flows down the *internal jugular vein* of the neck.

4. The **cavernous sinuses** are honeycombs of blood-filled spaces on each side of the body of the sphenoid bone (fig. 20.29b). They receive blood from the *superior ophthalmic vein* of the orbit and the *superficial middle cerebral vein* of the brain, among other sources. They drain through several outlets including the transverse sinus, internal jugular vein, and facial vein. They are clinically important because infections can pass from the face and other superficial sites into the cranial cavity by this route. Also, inflammation of a cavernous sinus can injure important structures that pass through it, including the internal carotid artery and cranial nerves III to VI.

Major Veins of the Neck

Blood flows down the neck mainly through three veins on each side, all of which empty into the subclavian vein (fig. 20.29c).

1. The **internal jugular**[15] **vein** (JUG-you-lur) courses down the neck deep to the sternocleidomastoid muscle. It receives

---

[15]*jugul* = neck, throat

DEEPER INSIGHT 20.3
CLINICAL APPLICATION

Air Embolism

Injury to the dural sinuses or jugular veins presents less danger from loss of blood than from air sucked into the circulatory system. The presence of air in the bloodstream is called *air embolism* **(fig. 20.30).** This is an important concern to neurosurgeons, who sometimes operate with the patient in a sitting position. If a dural sinus is punctured, air can be sucked into the sinus and accumulate in the heart chambers, which blocks cardiac output and causes sudden death. Smaller air bubbles in the systemic circulation can cut off blood flow to the brain, lungs, myocardium, and other vital tissues. As little as 0.5 mL of air in a coronary artery can cause cardiac arrest.

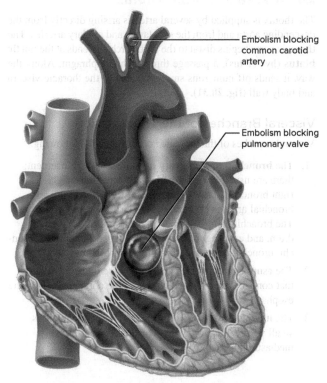

Embolism blocking common carotid artery

Embolism blocking pulmonary valve

FIGURE 20.30 Air Embolism.

most of the blood from the brain; picks up blood from the **facial vein, superficial temporal vein,** and **superior thyroid vein** along the way; passes behind the clavicle; and joins the subclavian vein (which is further traced in section 20.7e).

2. The **external jugular vein** courses down the side of the neck superficial to the sternocleidomastoid muscle and empties into the subclavian vein. It drains tributaries from

the parotid salivary gland, facial muscles, scalp, and other superficial structures. Some of this blood also follows venous anastomoses to the internal jugular vein.

3. The **vertebral vein** travels with the vertebral artery in the transverse foramina of the cervical vertebrae. Although the companion artery leads to the brain, the vertebral vein doesn't come from there. It drains the cervical vertebrae, spinal cord, and some of the small deep muscles of the neck, and empties into the subclavian vein.

Section 20.7e traces this blood flow the rest of the way to the superior vena cava and heart.

20.7d Arteries of the Thorax

The thorax is supplied by several arteries arising directly from the descending aorta and from the subclavian and axillary arteries. The thoracic aorta begins distal to the aortic arch and ends at the **aortic hiatus** (hy-AY-tus), a passage through the diaphragm. Along the way, it sends off numerous small branches to the thoracic viscera and body wall (**fig. 20.31**).

Visceral Branches of the Thoracic Aorta

Visceral branches of the thoracic aorta include the following:

1. The **bronchial arteries** vary in number and arrangement; there are usually two on the left and one on the right. The right bronchial artery usually arises from one of the left bronchial arteries or from a *posterior intercostal artery*. The bronchial arteries supply the visceral pleura, pericardium, and esophagus, and enter the lungs to supply the bronchi, bronchioles, and larger pulmonary blood vessels.

2. The **esophageal arteries** are four or five unpaired arteries that come off the anterior surface of the aorta and supply the esophagus.

3. The **mediastinal arteries** (not illustrated) are numerous small vessels that supply structures of the posterior mediastinum.

▶▶▶ APPLY WHAT YOU KNOW

Both the pulmonary arteries and bronchial arteries supply blood to the lungs, but when this blood emerges from the lungs, the pulmonary blood is richer in oxygen and the bronchial blood is poorer in oxygen. Explain why.

Parietal Branches of the Thoracic Aorta

The following branches supply chiefly the muscles, bones, and skin of the chest; only the first are illustrated.

1. The **posterior intercostal arteries** are nine pairs of vessels arising from the posterior side of the aorta. They course around the posterior side of the rib cage between ribs 3 through 12, then anastomose with the anterior intercostal arteries described in the next section. They supply the inter-

costal, pectoralis, serratus anterior, and some abdominal muscles, as well as the vertebrae, spinal cord, meninges, breasts, skin, and subcutaneous tissue.

2. One pair of **subcostal arteries** arises from the aorta inferior to rib 12. They supply the posterior intercostal tissues, vertebrae, spinal cord, and deep muscles of the back.

3. A variable number of **superior phrenic**[16] **arteries** (FREN-ic) arise at the aortic hiatus and supply the superior and posterior regions of the diaphragm.

▶▶▶ APPLY WHAT YOU KNOW

The posterior intercostal arteries are larger in lactating women than in men and nonlactating females. Explain why.

Branches of the Subclavian and Axillary Arteries

The thoracic wall is also supplied by branches of the subclavian arteries and their continuations, the *axillary arteries,* in the shoulder and axillary regions. Recall that the right subclavian artery arises from the brachiocephalic trunk and the left subclavian artery arises directly from the aortic arch (see fig. 20.26). On both the right and left, the subclavian artery gives off the internal thoracic artery, then continues as the axillary artery. Further divisions of these arteries are as follows:

1. The **internal thoracic (mammary) artery** supplies the breast and anterior thoracic wall. It issues the following branches:

   a. The **pericardiophrenic artery** supplies the pericardium and diaphragm.

   b. The **anterior intercostal arteries** arise from the internal thoracic artery as it descends alongside the sternum. They travel between the ribs; supply the ribs and the intercostal and pectoral muscles, breast, and skin; and, finally, anastomose with the posterior intercostal arteries. Each sends one branch along the lower margin of the rib above it and another, parallel branch along the upper margin of the rib below it.

2. The **thoracoacromial**[17] **trunk** (THOR-uh-co-uh-CRO-me-ul) provides branches to the superior shoulder and pectoral regions.

3. The **lateral thoracic artery** supplies the pectoral, serratus anterior, and subscapularis muscles. It also issues branches to the breast and is larger in females than in males.

4. The **subscapular artery** is the largest branch of the axillary artery. It supplies the scapula and the latissimus dorsi, serratus anterior, teres major, deltoid, triceps brachii, and intercostal muscles.

---

[16]*phren* = diaphragm
[17]*thoraco* = chest; *acr* = tip, apex; *om* = shoulder

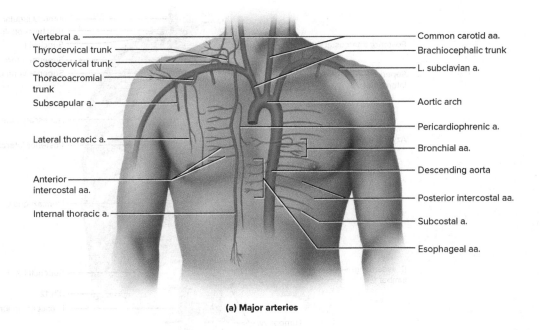

(a) Major arteries

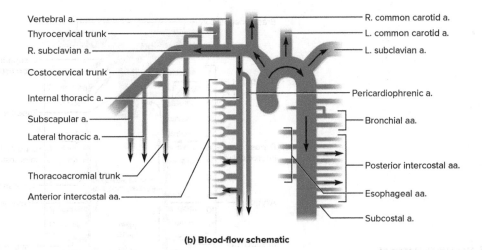

(b) Blood-flow schematic

FIGURE 20.31 Arteries of the Thorax. (a) Major thoracic arteries. (b) Blood-flow schematic of the thoracic arteries. **APR**

20.7e Veins of the Thorax

The superior vena cava receives all venous drainage not only from the head and neck as already described, but also from all thoracic organs and tissues.

Tributaries of the Superior Vena Cava

The most prominent veins of the upper thorax carry blood from the shoulder region to the heart (**fig. 20.32**); they are as follows:

1. The **subclavian vein** drains the upper limb (see "Deep Veins" in section 20.8b). It begins at the lateral margin of the first rib and travels posterior to the clavicle. It receives the external jugular and vertebral veins, then ends (changes names) where it receives the internal jugular vein.

2. The **brachiocephalic vein** forms by the union of the subclavian and internal jugular veins. The right brachiocephalic is only about 2.5 cm long and the left is about 6 cm long. They

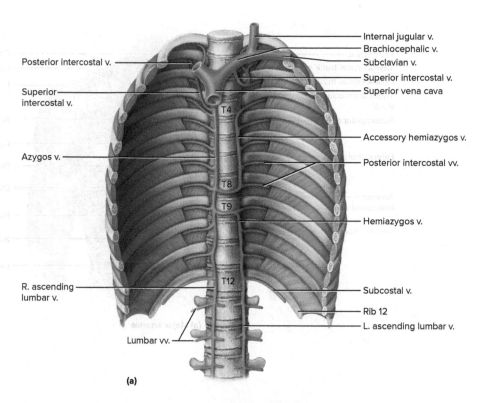

Posterior intercostal v.

Superior
intercostal v.

Azygos v.

R. ascending
lumbar v.

Lumbar vv.

Internal jugular v.
Brachiocephalic v.
Subclavian v.
Superior intercostal v.
Superior vena cava

Accessory hemiazygos v.

Posterior intercostal vv.

Hemiazygos v.

Subcostal v.
Rib 12
L. ascending lumbar v.

(a)

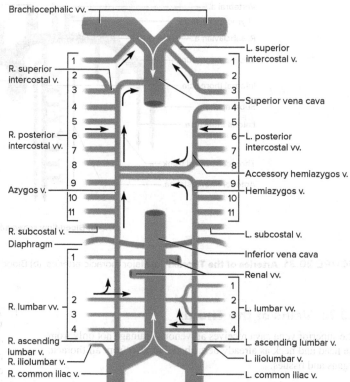

Brachiocephalic vv.

R. superior
intercostal v.

R. posterior
intercostal vv.

Azygos v.

R. subcostal v.
Diaphragm

R. lumbar vv.

R. ascending
lumbar v.
R. iliolumbar v.
R. common iliac v.

L. superior
intercostal v.

Superior vena cava

L. posterior
intercostal vv.

Accessory hemiazygos v.
Hemiazygos v.

L. subcostal v.

Inferior vena cava

Renal vv.

L. lumbar vv.

L. ascending lumbar v.
L. iliolumbar v.
L. common iliac v.

(b)

FIGURE 20.32 Venous Drainage of the Posterior Wall of the Thorax and Abdomen. (a) The azygos system of the thoracic wall. This system provides venous drainage from the wall and viscera of the thorax, but the visceral tributaries are not illustrated. (b) Blood-flow schematic of the thoracic and abdominal drainage. The components above the diaphragm constitute the azygos system. There is a great deal of individual variation in this anatomy.

receive tributaries from the vertebrae, thyroid gland, and upper thoracic wall and breast, then converge to form the next vein.

3. The **superior vena cava (SVC)** forms by the union of the right and left brachiocephalic veins. It travels inferiorly for about 7 cm and empties into the right atrium of the heart. Its main tributary is the *azygos vein*. It drains all structures superior to the diaphragm except the pulmonary circuit and coronary circulation. It also receives drainage from the abdominal cavity by way of the azygos system, described next.

The Azygos System

The principal venous drainage of the thoracic organs is by way of the *azygos system* (AZ-ih-goss) (fig. 20.32). The most prominent vein of this system is the **azygos**[18] **vein,** which ascends the right side of the posterior thoracic wall. It is named for the lack of a mate on the left. It receives the following tributaries, then empties into the superior vena cava at the level of vertebra T4.

1. The right **ascending lumbar vein** drains the right abdominal wall, then penetrates the diaphragm and enters the thoracic cavity. The azygos vein begins where the right ascending lumbar vein meets the right **subcostal vein** beneath rib 12.

2. The right **posterior intercostal veins** drain the intercostal spaces. The first (superior) one empties into the right brachiocephalic vein; intercostal veins 2 and 3 join to form the *right superior intercostal vein* before emptying into the azygos vein; and intercostal veins 4 through 11 each enter the azygos vein separately.

3. The right **esophageal, mediastinal, pericardial,** and **bronchial veins** (not illustrated) drain their respective organs into the azygos vein.

4. The **hemiazygos**[19] **vein** ascends the posterior thoracic wall on the left. It begins where the left ascending lumbar vein, having just penetrated the diaphragm, joins the subcostal vein below rib 12. The hemiazygos then receives the lower three posterior intercostal veins, esophageal veins, and mediastinal veins. At the left of vertebra T9, it crosses to the right and empties into the azygos vein.

5. The **accessory hemiazygos vein** descends the posterior thoracic wall on the left. It receives drainage from posterior intercostal veins 4 through 8 and sometimes the left bronchial veins. It crosses to the right at the level of vertebra T8 and empties into the azygos vein.

The left posterior intercostal veins 1 to 3 are the only ones on this side that do not ultimately drain into the azygos vein. The first one usually drains directly into the left brachiocephalic vein. The second and third unite to form the *left superior intercostal vein,* which empties into the left brachiocephalic vein.

20.7f Arteries of the Abdominal and Pelvic Regions

After passing through the aortic hiatus, the aorta descends through the abdominal cavity and ends at the level of vertebra L4, where it branches into the right and left common iliac arteries. The abdominal aorta is retroperitoneal.

Major Branches of the Abdominal Aorta

The abdominal aorta gives off arteries in the order listed here, from superior to inferior (**fig. 20.33**). Those named in the plural are paired left and right, whereas those named in the singular are solitary median arteries.

1. The **inferior phrenic arteries** supply the inferior surface of the diaphragm. They may arise from the aorta, celiac trunk, or renal artery. Each issues two or three small **superior suprarenal arteries** to the ipsilateral adrenal (suprarenal) gland.

2. The **celiac**[20] **trunk** (SEE-lee-ac) supplies the upper abdominal viscera (see next section).

3. The **superior mesenteric artery** supplies the intestines.

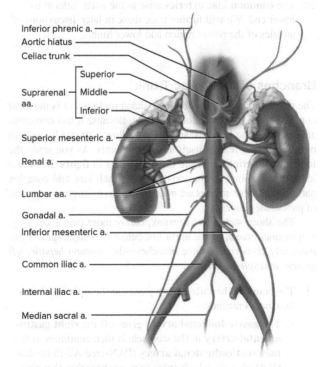

Inferior phrenic a.
Aortic hiatus
Celiac trunk

Superior
Suprarenal — Middle
aa.
Inferior

Superior mesenteric a.
Renal a.
Lumbar aa.
Gonadal a.
Inferior mesenteric a.
Common iliac a.
Internal iliac a.
Median sacral a.

FIGURE 20.33 The Abdominal Aorta and Its Major Branches. APR

---

[18]unpaired; from *a* = without; *zygo* = union, mate
[19]*hemi* = half

[20]*celi* = belly, abdomen

4. The **middle suprarenal arteries** arise laterally from the aorta, usually at the same level as the superior mesenteric artery. They supply the adrenal glands.

5. The **renal arteries** supply the kidneys and issue a small **inferior suprarenal artery** to each adrenal gland.

6. The **gonadal arteries—ovarian arteries** of the female and **testicular arteries** of the male—are long, slender arteries that arise from the midabdominal aorta and descend along the posterior body wall to the female pelvic cavity or male scrotum. They supply the gonads. The gonads begin their embryonic development near the kidneys, and the gonadal arteries are then quite short. As the gonads descend to the pelvic cavity, these arteries grow and acquire their peculiar length and course.

7. The **inferior mesenteric artery** supplies the distal end of the large intestine.

8. The **lumbar arteries** arise from the lower aorta in four pairs. They supply the posterior abdominal wall (muscles, joints, and skin) and the spinal cord and other tissues in the vertebral canal.

9. The **median sacral artery,** a tiny median artery at the inferior end of the aorta, supplies the sacrum and coccyx.

10. The **common iliac arteries** arise as the aorta forks at its lower end. We will further trace these in later discussions of arteries of the pelvic region and lower limb.

Branches of the Celiac Trunk

The celiac circulation to the upper abdominal viscera is the most complex route off the abdominal aorta. Because it has numerous anastomoses, the bloodstream doesn't follow a simple linear path but divides and rejoins itself at several points. As you study the following description, locate these branches in **figure 20.34** and identify the points of anastomosis. The small size and complex pathways of these arteries are major obstacles to surgical treatment of pancreatic cancer.

The short, stubby celiac trunk, barely more than 1 cm long, is a median branch of the aorta just below the diaphragm. It immediately gives rise to three branches—the *common hepatic, left gastric,* and *splenic arteries.*

1. The **common hepatic artery** passes to the right and issues two main branches:

   a. The **gastroduodenal artery** gives off the **right gastro-omental artery** to the stomach. It then continues as the **pancreaticoduodenal artery** (PAN-cree-AT-ih-co-dew-ODD-eh-nul), which splits into two branches that pass around the anterior and posterior sides of the head of the pancreas. These anastomose with the two branches of the *inferior pancreaticoduodenal artery,* discussed under "Mesenteric Blood Supply," following shortly.

   b. The **hepatic artery proper** ascends toward the liver. It gives off the **right gastric artery,** then branches into the

   right and **left hepatic arteries.** The right hepatic artery issues a **cystic artery** to the gallbladder, then the two hepatic arteries enter the liver from below.

2. The **left gastric artery** supplies the stomach and lower esophagus, arcs around the *lesser curvature* (superomedial margin) of the stomach, and anastomoses with the right gastric artery (fig. 20.34b). Thus, the right and left gastric arteries approach from opposite directions and supply this margin of the stomach. The left gastric also has branches to the lower esophagus, and the right gastric also supplies the duodenum.

3. The **splenic artery** supplies blood to the spleen, but gives off the following branches on the way there.

   a. Several small **pancreatic arteries** supply the pancreas.

   b. The **left gastro-omental artery** arcs around the *greater curvature* (inferolateral margin) of the stomach and anastomoses with the right gastro-omental artery. These two arteries stand off about 1 cm from the stomach itself and travel through the superior margin of the greater omentum, a fatty membrane suspended from the greater curvature (see figs. B.4 in atlas B, 25.3). They furnish blood to both the stomach and omentum.

   c. The **short gastric arteries** supply the upper portion (*fundus*) of the stomach.

Mesenteric Blood Supply

The mesentery is a translucent sheet that suspends the intestines and other abdominal viscera from the posterior body wall (see figs. A.8 in atlas A, 25.3). It contains numerous arteries, veins, and lymphatic vessels that supply and drain the intestines. The arterial supply arises from the *superior* and *inferior mesenteric arteries;* numerous anastomoses between these ensure adequate collateral circulation to the intestines even if one route is temporarily obstructed.

The **superior mesenteric artery (fig. 20.35a)** is the most significant intestinal blood supply, serving nearly all of the small intestine and the proximal half of the large intestine. It arises medially from the upper abdominal aorta and gives off the following branches:

1. The **inferior pancreaticoduodenal artery** branches to pass around the anterior and posterior sides of the pancreas and anastomose with the two branches of the superior pancreaticoduodenal artery.

2. Twelve to 15 **jejunal** and **ileal arteries** fan out through the mesentery to supply nearly all of the small intestine (portions called the *jejunum* and *ileum*).

3. The **ileocolic artery** (ILL-ee-oh-CO-lic) supplies the ileum, appendix, and parts of the large intestine (*cecum* and *ascending colon*).

4. The **right colic artery** also supplies the ascending colon.

5. The **middle colic artery** supplies most of the *transverse colon.*

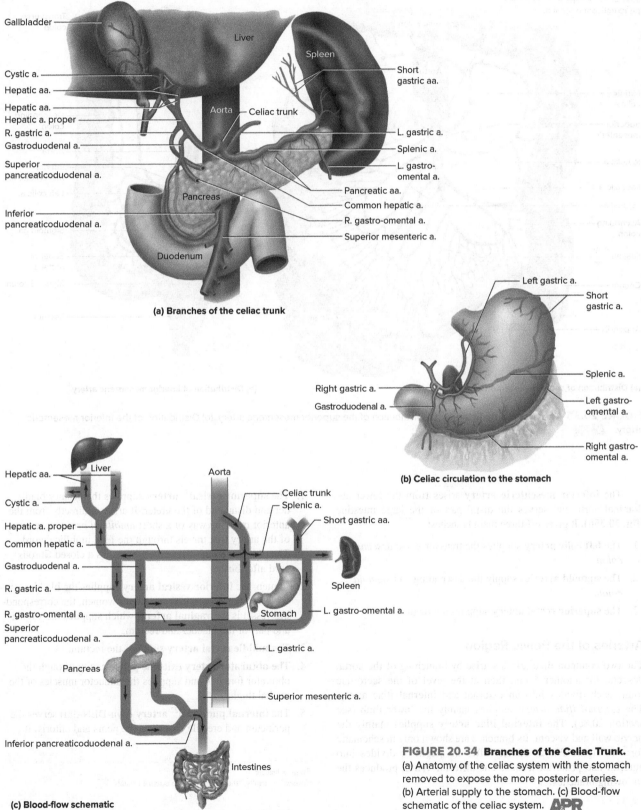

(a) Branches of the celiac trunk

(b) Celiac circulation to the stomach

(c) Blood-flow schematic

FIGURE 20.34 Branches of the Celiac Trunk.
(a) Anatomy of the celiac system with the stomach removed to expose the more posterior arteries.
(b) Arterial supply to the stomach. (c) Blood-flow schematic of the celiac system. **APR**

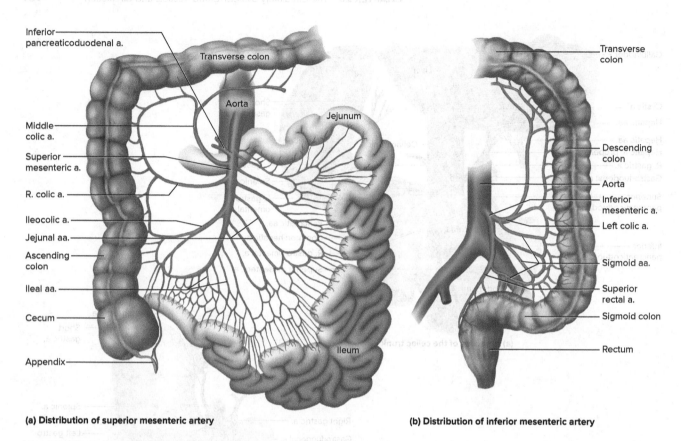

(a) Distribution of superior mesenteric artery

(b) Distribution of inferior mesenteric artery

FIGURE 20.35 **The Mesenteric Arteries.** (a) Distribution of the superior mesenteric artery. (b) Distribution of the inferior mesenteric artery. **APR**

The **inferior mesenteric artery** arises from the lower abdominal aorta and serves the distal part of the large intestine **(fig. 20.35b).** It gives off three main branches:

1. The **left colic artery** supplies the transverse and *descending colon.*

2. The **sigmoid arteries** supply the descending and *sigmoid colon.*

3. The **superior rectal artery** supplies the rectum.

Arteries of the Pelvic Region

The two common iliac arteries arise by branching of the aorta, descend for another 5 cm, then at the level of the sacroiliac joint, each divides into an external and internal iliac artery. The *external iliac artery* supplies mainly the lower limb (see section 20.8c). The **internal iliac artery** supplies mainly the pelvic wall and viscera. Its branches are shown only in schematic form in figure 20.42. Shortly after its origin, it divides into anterior and posterior trunks. The **anterior trunk** produces the following branches:

1. The **superior vesical**[21] **artery** supplies the urinary bladder and distal end of the ureter. It arises indirectly from the anterior trunk by way of a short *umbilical artery,* a remnant of the artery that travels through the fetal umbilical cord. The rest of the umbilical artery becomes a closed fibrous cord after birth.

2. In men, the **inferior vesical artery** supplies the bladder, ureter, prostate, and seminal vesicle. In women, the corresponding vessel is the **vaginal artery,** which supplies the vagina and part of the bladder and rectum.

3. The **middle rectal artery** supplies the rectum.

4. The **obturator artery** exits the pelvic cavity through the obturator foramen and supplies the adductor muscles of the medial thigh.

5. The **internal pudendal**[22] **artery** (pyu-DEN-dul) serves the perineum and erectile tissues of the penis and clitoris; it

---

[21]*vesic* = bladder

[22]*pudend* = literally, "shameful parts"; the external genitals

supplies blood for the vascular engorgement and erection of these organs during sexual arousal.

6. In women, the **uterine artery** is the main blood supply to the uterus and supplies some blood to the vagina. It enlarges substantially in pregnancy and is the chief source of blood to the placenta, and thus critically important to fetal development. It passes up the uterine margin, then turns laterally at the uterine tube and anastomoses with the ovarian artery, thus supplying blood to the ovary as well (see fig. 28.7).

7. The **inferior gluteal artery** supplies the gluteal muscles and hip joint.

The **posterior trunk** produces the following branches:

1. The **iliolumbar artery** supplies the lumbar body wall and pelvic bones.

2. The **lateral sacral arteries** lead to tissues of the sacral canal, skin, and muscles posterior to the sacrum. There are usually two of these, superior and inferior.

3. The **superior gluteal artery** supplies the skin and muscles of the gluteal region and the muscle and bone tissues of the pelvic wall.

20.7g Veins of the Abdominal and Pelvic Regions

The most significant route of venous drainage from all of the body below the diaphragm is the **inferior vena cava (IVC).** This is the body's largest blood vessel, having a diameter of about 3.5 cm. It forms by the union of the right and left common iliac veins at the level of vertebra L5 and drains many of the abdominal viscera as it ascends the posterior body wall. It is retroperitoneal and lies immediately to the right of the aorta.

Tributaries of the Inferior Vena Cava

The IVC picks up blood from numerous tributaries in the following ascending order (**fig. 20.36**):

1. The **internal iliac veins** drain the gluteal muscles, the medial aspect of the thigh, the urinary bladder, and rectum; the prostate and ductus deferens of the male; and the uterus and vagina of the female. They unite with the *external iliac veins,* which drain the lower limb and are described in section 20.8d. Their union forms the **common iliac veins,** which then converge to form the IVC.

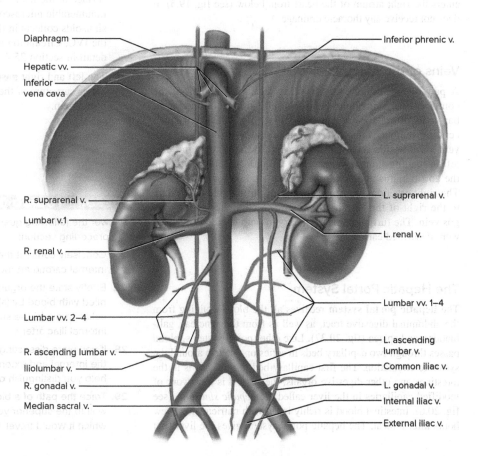

FIGURE 20.36 The Inferior Vena Cava and Its Tributaries. Compare the blood-flow schematic in figure 20.32b.

🔎 *Why do the veins that drain the ovaries and testes terminate so far away from the gonads?*

Diaphragm —
Hepatic vv. —
Inferior vena cava —
R. suprarenal v. —
Lumbar v.1 —
R. renal v. —
Lumbar vv. 2–4 —
R. ascending lumbar v. —
Iliolumbar v. —
R. gonadal v. —
Median sacral v. —

Inferior phrenic v.
L. suprarenal v.
L. renal v.
Lumbar vv. 1–4
L. ascending lumbar v.
Common iliac v.
L. gonadal v.
Internal iliac v.
External iliac v.

2. Four pairs of **lumbar veins** empty into the IVC as well as into the ascending lumbar veins described in the next section.

3. The **gonadal veins—ovarian veins** of the female and **testicular veins** of the male—drain the gonads. Like the gonadal arteries, and for the same reason, these are long slender vessels that end far from their origins. The left gonadal vein empties into the left renal vein, whereas the right gonadal vein empties directly into the IVC.

4. The **renal veins** drain the kidneys into the IVC. The left renal vein also receives blood from the left gonadal vein and left suprarenal veins. It is up to three times as long as the right renal vein, since the IVC lies to the right of the midline of the body.

5. The **suprarenal veins** drain the adrenal (suprarenal) glands. The right suprarenal empties directly into the IVC and the left suprarenal empties into the left renal vein.

6. The **inferior phrenic veins** drain the inferior aspect of the diaphragm.

7. Three **hepatic veins** drain the liver, extending a short distance from its superior surface to the IVC.

After receiving these inputs, the IVC penetrates the diaphragm and enters the right atrium of the heart from below (see fig. 19.5). It does not receive any thoracic drainage.

Veins of the Abdominal Wall

A pair of **ascending lumbar veins** receives blood from the common iliac veins below and from the aforementioned lumbar veins of the posterior body wall (see fig. 20.32b). The ascending lumbar veins give off anastomoses with the inferior vena cava beside them as they ascend to the diaphragm. The left ascending lumbar vein passes through the diaphragm via the aortic hiatus and continues as the hemiazygos vein above. The right ascending lumbar vein passes through the diaphragm to the right of the vertebral column and continues as the azygos vein. The further paths of the azygos and hemiazygos veins were described earlier.

The Hepatic Portal System

The **hepatic portal system** receives all the blood draining from the abdominal digestive tract, as well as from the pancreas, gallbladder, and spleen (**fig. 20.37**). Like other portal systems, blood passes through two capillary beds in series on one trip around the systemic circulation. The first capillary bed in this case is in the intestines and other digestive organs; the second is a network of modified capillaries in the liver called the *hepatic sinusoids* (see fig. 20.6). Intestinal blood is richly laden with nutrients for a few hours after a meal. The hepatic portal system gives the liver first

claim to these nutrients before they are distributed to the rest of the body. It also allows the liver to cleanse the blood of bacteria and toxins picked up from the intestines—an important function of the liver. The principal veins of the hepatic portal system are as follows:

1. The **inferior mesenteric vein** receives blood from the rectum and distal colon. It converges in a fanlike array in the mesentery and empties into the splenic vein.

2. The **superior mesenteric vein** receives blood from the entire small intestine, ascending colon, transverse colon, and stomach. It, too, exhibits a fanlike arrangement in the mesentery, then joins the splenic vein to form the hepatic portal vein.

3. The **splenic vein** drains the spleen and travels across the upper abdominal cavity toward the liver. Along the way, it picks up **pancreatic veins** from the pancreas, then picks up the inferior mesenteric vein, and ends where it meets the superior mesenteric vein.

4. The **hepatic portal vein** is the continuation beyond the convergence of the splenic and superior mesenteric veins. It travels about 8 cm upward and to the right, receives the **cystic vein** from the gallbladder, then enters the inferior surface of the liver. In the liver, it ultimately leads to the innumerable microscopic hepatic sinusoids. Blood from the sinusoids collects in the hepatic veins, and they empty into the IVC. Circulation within the liver is described in more detail in section 25.4.

5. The left and right **gastric veins** form an arc along the lesser curvature of the stomach and empty into the hepatic portal vein.

BEFORE YOU GO ON

Answer the following questions to test your understanding of the preceding section:

26. Concisely contrast the destinations of the external and internal carotid arteries.

27. Briefly state the organs or parts of organs that are supplied with blood by (a) the cerebral arterial circle, (b) the celiac trunk, (c) the superior mesenteric artery, and (d) the internal iliac artery.

28. If you were dissecting a cadaver, where would you look for the internal and external jugular veins? What muscle would help you distinguish one from the other?

29. Trace the path of a blood cell from the left lumbar body wall to the superior vena cava, naming the vessels through which it would travel.

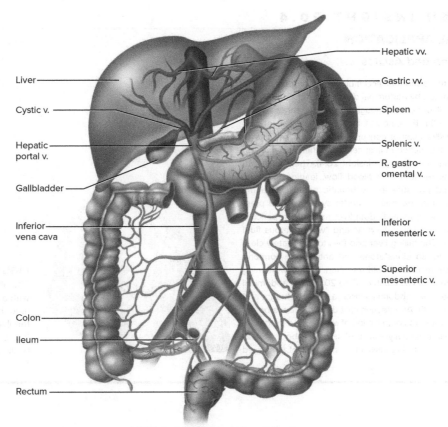

(a) Tributaries of the hepatic portal system

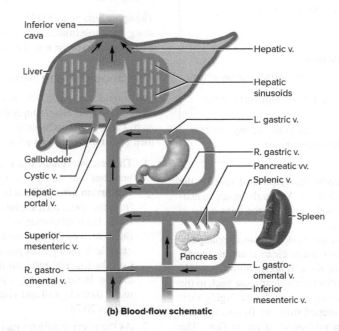

(b) Blood-flow schematic

FIGURE 20.37 The Hepatic Portal System. (a) Tributaries of the hepatic portal system. (b) Blood-flow schematic of the system.

DEEPER INSIGHT 20.4

CLINICAL APPLICATION

Portal Hypertension and Ascites

Ascites (ah-SY-teez) is the abnormal accumulation of serous fluid in the peritoneal cavity, marked by abdominal distension (**fig. 20.38**). It is usually associated with alcoholism, although it can have other causes such as malnutrition (see fig. 18.3), heart failure, infection, cancer, and chronic hepatitis. Excessive alcohol consumption causes *cirrhosis* of the liver—inflammation, destruction of liver cells, and their replacement by fatty and fibrous tissue (see Deeper Insight 26.4). The degenerating liver puts up excess resistance to blood flow, leading to *portal hypertension*—high blood pressure in the hepatic portal circulation. Since the spleen drains into the hepatic portal system, blood pressure backs up into the spleen as well. Both liver and spleen become enlarged (*hepatomegaly* and *splenomegaly*) and "weep" serous fluid into the peritoneal cavity. The failing liver also fails to adequately clear hormones from the blood, so aldosterone and antidiuretic hormone accumulate and stimulate increased fluid retention, further worsening the ascites. A person can retain as much as 10 to 20 liters of abdominal fluid, pressing up on the other abdominal viscera and diaphragm and producing shortness of breath. An infection called *spontaneous bacterial peritonitis (SBP)* is a frequent complication of ascites. The prognosis for recovery from ascites, especially with SBP, is poor; about 25% of patients die within one year of diagnosis, often because of continued heavy drinking.

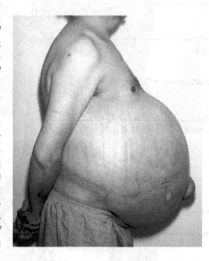

FIGURE 20.38 Ascites. The abdomen is distended with accumulated serous fluid that has filtered from the liver, spleen, and intestinal blood vessels.
Mediscan/Alamy

20.8 Systemic Vessels of the Appendicular Region

Expected Learning Outcomes

When you have completed this section, you should be able to

a. identify the principal systemic arteries and veins of the limbs; and

b. trace the flow of blood from the heart to any region of the upper or lower limb and back to the heart.

The principal vessels of the appendicular region are detailed in the following sections, 20.8a through 20.8d. Although the appendicular arteries are usually deep and well protected, the veins occur in both deep and superficial groups.

Venous pathways have more anastomoses than arterial pathways, so the route of flow is often not as clear. If all the anastomoses were illustrated, many of these venous pathways would look more like confusing networks than a clear route back to the heart. Therefore, most anastomoses—especially the highly variable and unnamed ones—are omitted from the figures to allow you to focus on the more general course of blood flow. The blood-flow schematics in several figures will also help, like road maps, to clarify these routes.

20.8a Arteries of the Upper Limb

The upper limb is supplied by a prominent artery that changes name along its course from *subclavian* to *axillary* to *brachial artery*, then issues branches to the arm, forearm, and hand (**fig. 20.39**).

The Shoulder and Arm

The shoulder and arm, like the head and most thoracic viscera, also receive their blood supply from arteries arising from the aortic arch. These pathways begin with the subclavian arteries, named for their proximity to the clavicles.

1. The brachiocephalic trunk arises from the aortic arch and branches into the right common carotid artery and **right subclavian artery.** The **left subclavian artery** arises directly from the aortic arch slightly distal to the brachiocephalic trunk. Each subclavian arches over the respective lung, rising as high as the base of the neck slightly superior to the clavicle. It then passes posterior to the clavicle, downward over the first rib, and ends in name only at the rib's lateral margin. In the shoulder, it gives off several small branches to the thoracic wall and viscera, which were described in section 20.7d.

2. As the artery continues past the first rib, it is named the **axillary artery.** It continues through the axillary region, gives off small thoracic branches, and ends, again in name

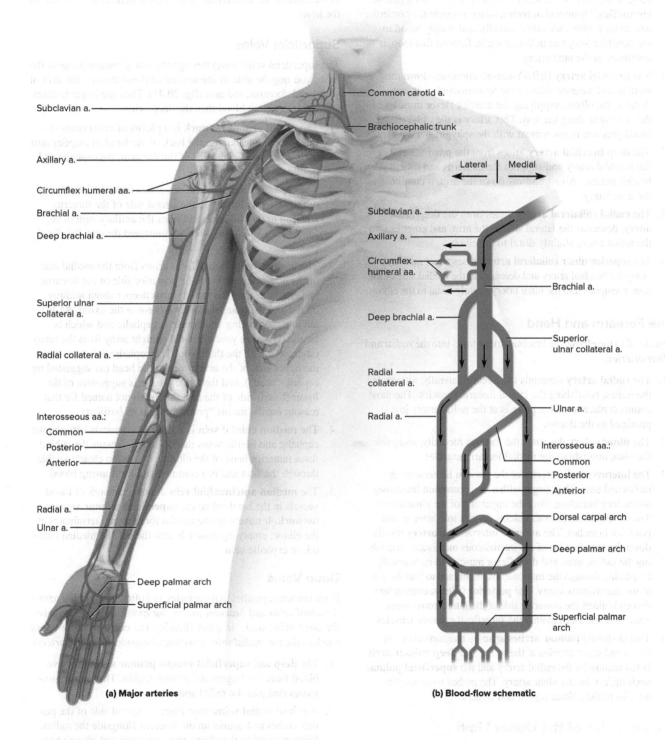

Common carotid a.

Brachiocephalic trunk

Subclavian a.

Axillary a.

Circumflex humeral aa.

Brachial a.

Deep brachial a.

Superior ulnar
collateral a.

Radial collateral a.

Interosseous aa.:
Common
Posterior
Anterior

Radial a.

Ulnar a.

Deep palmar arch

Superficial palmar arch

(a) Major arteries

Lateral | Medial

Subclavian a.

Axillary a.

Circumflex
humeral aa.

Brachial a.

Deep brachial a.

Superior
ulnar collateral a.

Radial
collateral a.

Radial a.

Ulnar a.

Interosseous aa.:
Common
Posterior
Anterior

Dorsal carpal arch

Deep palmar arch

Superficial palmar
arch

(b) Blood-flow schematic

FIGURE 20.39 Arteries of the Upper Limb. (a) The major arteries, anterior view. (b) Blood-flow schematic of the upper limb. **APR**

❓ *Why are arterial anastomoses especially common at joints such as the shoulder and elbow?*

only, at the neck of the humerus. Here, it gives off a pair of **circumflex**[23] **humeral arteries,** which encircle the humerus, anastomose with each other laterally, and supply blood to the shoulder joint and deltoid muscle. Beyond this loop, it continues as the next artery.

3. The **brachial artery** (BRAY-kee-ul) continues down the median and anterior sides of the humerus and ends just distal to the elbow, supplying the anterior flexor muscles of the brachium along the way. This artery is the usual site of blood pressure measurement with the sphygmomanometer.

4. The **deep brachial artery** arises from the proximal end of the brachial artery and supplies the humerus and triceps brachii muscle. About midway down the arm, it continues as the next artery.

5. The **radial collateral artery** arises from the deep brachial artery, descends the lateral side of the arm, and empties into the radial artery slightly distal to the elbow.

6. The **superior ulnar collateral artery** arises about midway along the brachial artery and descends in the medial side of the arm. It empties into the ulnar artery slightly distal to the elbow.

The Forearm and Hand

Just distal to the elbow, the brachial artery forks into the *radial* and *ulnar arteries.*

1. The **radial artery** descends the forearm laterally, alongside the radius, nourishing the lateral forearm muscles. The most common place to take a pulse is at the radial artery just proximal to the thumb.

2. The **ulnar artery** descends the forearm medially, alongside the ulna, nourishing the medial forearm muscles.

3. The **interosseous**[24] **arteries** of the forearm lie between the radius and ulna. They begin with a short **common interosseous artery** branching from the upper end of the ulnar artery. The common interosseous quickly divides into anterior and posterior branches. The **anterior interosseous artery** travels down the anterior side of the interosseous membrane, nourishing the radius, ulna, and deep flexor muscles. It ends distally by passing through the interosseous membrane to join the posterior interosseous artery. The **posterior interosseous artery** descends along the posterior side of the interosseous membrane and nourishes mainly the superficial extensor muscles.

4. Two U-shaped **palmar arches** arise by anastomosis of the radial and ulnar arteries at the wrist. The **deep palmar arch** is fed mainly by the radial artery and the **superficial palmar arch** mainly by the ulnar artery. The arches issue smaller arteries to the palmar region and fingers.

20.8b Veins of the Upper Limb

Both superficial and deep veins drain the upper limb **(fig. 20.40).** We will trace these veins in the order of blood flow, from the hand

to the axillary and subclavian veins, which, in turn, lead off toward the heart.

Superficial Veins

The superficial veins travel through the subcutaneous tissue of the limb; you may be able to see several of them through the skin of your hand, forearm, and arm **(fig. 20.41).** They are larger in diameter and carry more blood than the deep veins.

1. The **dorsal venous network** is a plexus of veins often visible through the skin on the back of the hand. It empties into the major superficial veins of the forearm, the cephalic and basilic veins.

2. The **cephalic**[25] **vein** (sef-AL-ic) arises from the lateral side of the network, travels up the lateral side of the forearm and arm to the shoulder, and joins the axillary vein there. Intravenous fluids are often administered through the distal end of this vein.

3. The **basilic**[26] **vein** (bah-SIL-ic) arises from the medial side of the network, travels up the posterior side of the forearm, and continues into the arm. It turns deeper about midway up the arm and joins the *brachial vein* at the axilla. As an aid to remembering which vein is cephalic and which is basilic, visualize your arm held straight away from the torso (abducted) with the thumb up. The cephalic vein runs along the upper side of the arm closer to the head (as suggested by *cephal,* "head"), and the name *basilic* is suggestive of the lower (basal) side of the arm (although not named for that reason; *basilic* means "prominent," as in *basilica*).

4. The **median cubital vein** is a short anastomosis between the cephalic and basilic veins that obliquely crosses the cubital fossa (anterior bend of the elbow). It is often clearly visible through the skin and is a common site for drawing blood.

5. The **median antebrachial vein** drains a network of blood vessels in the hand called the **superficial palmar venous network.** It travels up the medial forearm and terminates at the elbow, emptying variously into the basilic, median cubital, or cephalic vein.

Deep Veins

Deep veins run parallel to the arteries and often have similar names (*brachial veins* and *brachial artery,* for example). In some cases, the deep veins occur in pairs flanking the corresponding artery (such as the two *radial veins* traveling alongside the *radial artery*).

1. The **deep** and **superficial venous palmar arches** receive blood from the fingers and palmar region. They are anastomoses that join the radial and ulnar veins.

2. A pair of **radial veins** arise from the lateral side of the palmar arches and course up the forearm alongside the radius. Slightly distal to the elbow, they converge and give rise to one of the brachial veins.

---

[23]*circum* = around; *flex* = to bend
[24]*inter* = between; *osse* = bones

[25]*cephal* = head
[26]*basilic* = prominent, important

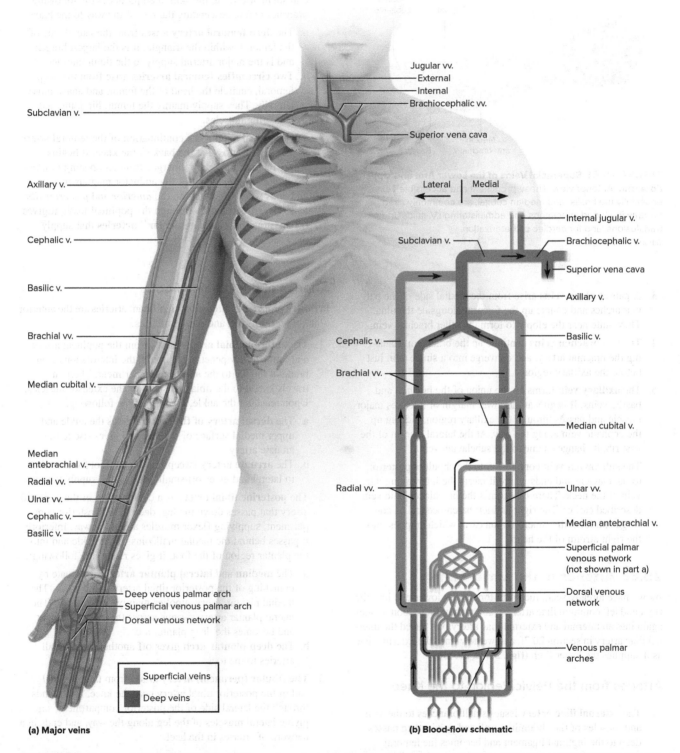

FIGURE 20.40 Veins of the Upper Limb. (a) The major veins, anterior view. (b) Blood-flow schematic of the upper limb. Variations on this pattern are highly common. Many venous anastomoses are omitted for clarity. **APR**

❓ *Name three veins that are often visible through the skin of the upper limb.*

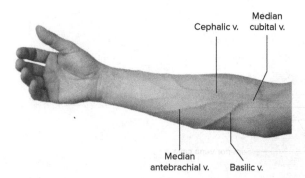

FIGURE 20.41 Superficial Veins of the Lower Arm and Upper Forearm. Anterior view. These prominent and accessible veins, especially the basilic and median cubital, are commonly used for drawing blood specimens and administering I.V. fluids and transfusions, and for cardiac catheterization.
Taborsk/Getty Images

3. A pair of **ulnar veins** arise from the medial side of the palmar arches and course up the forearm alongside the ulna. They unite near the elbow to form the other brachial vein.

4. The two **brachial veins** continue up the brachium, flanking the brachial artery, and converge into a single vein just before the axillary region.

5. The **axillary vein** forms by the union of the brachial and basilic veins. It begins at the lower margin of the teres major muscle and passes through the axillary region, picking up the cephalic vein along the way. At the lateral margin of the first rib, it changes name to the subclavian vein.

6. The **subclavian vein** continues into the shoulder posterior to the clavicle and ends where it meets the internal jugular vein of the neck. There it becomes the brachiocephalic vein described earlier. The right and left brachiocephalics converge and form the superior vena cava, which empties into the right atrium of the heart.

20.8c Arteries of the Lower Limb

As we have already seen, the aorta forks at its lower end into the right and left common iliac arteries, and each of these soon divides again into an internal and external iliac artery. We traced the internal iliac artery in section 20.7f, and we now trace the external iliac as it supplies the lower limb (**figs. 20.42, 20.43**).

Arteries from the Pelvic Region to the Knee

1. The **external iliac artery** issues small branches to the skin and muscles of the abdominal wall and pelvis, then passes deep to the inguinal ligament and becomes the femoral artery.

2. The **femoral artery** passes through the *femoral triangle* of the upper medial thigh, where its pulse can be palpated (see Deeper Insight 20.5). In the triangle, it gives off sev-

eral small arteries to the skin, then produces the following branches before descending the rest of the way to the knee.

   a. The **deep femoral artery** arises from the lateral side of the femoral, within the triangle. It is the largest branch and is the major arterial supply to the thigh muscles.

   b. Two **circumflex femoral arteries** arise from the deep femoral, encircle the head of the femur, and anastomose laterally. They supply mainly the femur, hip joint, and hamstring muscles.

3. The **popliteal artery** is a continuation of the femoral artery in the popliteal fossa at the back of the knee. It begins where the femoral artery emerges from an opening (*adductor hiatus*) in the tendon of the adductor magnus muscle and ends where it splits into the *anterior* and *posterior tibial arteries*. As it passes through the popliteal fossa, it gives off anastomoses called **genicular**[27] **arteries** that supply the knee joint.

Arteries of the Leg and Foot

In the leg proper, the three most significant arteries are the anterior tibial, posterior tibial, and fibular arteries.

1. The **anterior tibial artery** arises from the popliteal artery and immediately penetrates through the interosseous membrane of the leg to the anterior compartment. There, it travels lateral to the tibia and supplies the extensor muscles. Upon reaching the ankle, it gives off the following:

   a. The **dorsal artery of the foot** traverses the ankle and upper medial surface of the foot and gives rise to the arcuate artery.

   b. The **arcuate artery** sweeps across the foot from medial to lateral and gives off small arteries that supply the toes.

2. The **posterior tibial artery** is a continuation of the popliteal artery that passes down the leg, deep in the posterior compartment, supplying flexor muscles along the way. Inferiorly, it passes behind the medial malleolus of the ankle and into the plantar region of the foot. It gives rise to the following:

   a. The **median** and **lateral plantar arteries** originate by branching of the posterior tibial artery at the ankle. The medial plantar artery supplies mainly the great toe. The lateral plantar artery sweeps across the sole of the foot and becomes the deep plantar arch.

   b. The **deep plantar arch** gives off another set of small arteries to the toes.

3. The **fibular (peroneal) artery** arises from the proximal end of the posterior tibial artery near the knee. It descends through the lateral side of the posterior compartment, supplying lateral muscles of the leg along the way, and ends in a network of arteries in the heel.

---

[27]*genic* = of the knee

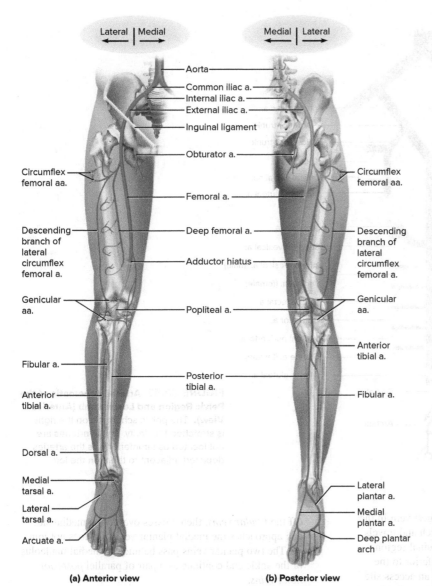

Lateral | Medial
Medial | Lateral

Aorta
Common iliac a.
Internal iliac a.
External iliac a.
Inguinal ligament
Obturator a.

Circumflex femoral aa.
Circumflex femoral aa.

Femoral a.

Descending branch of lateral circumflex femoral a.
Descending branch of lateral circumflex femoral a.

Deep femoral a.

Adductor hiatus

Genicular aa.
Genicular aa.

Popliteal a.

Anterior tibial a.

Fibular a.

Posterior tibial a.

Anterior tibial a.

Fibular a.

Dorsal a.

Medial tarsal a.

Lateral tarsal a.

Lateral plantar a.

Medial plantar a.

Arcuate a.

Deep plantar arch

(a) Anterior view   **(b) Posterior view**

FIGURE 20.42 Arteries of the Lower Limb. (a) The major arteries in anterior view, with the foot strongly plantar flexed so its upper (dorsal) surface faces the viewer. (b) The major arteries in posterior view, with the sole of the foot facing the viewer. **APR**

20.8d Veins of the Lower Limb

We will follow venous drainage of the lower limb from the toes to the inferior vena cava (**figs. 20.44, 20.45**). As in the upper limb, there are deep and superficial veins with anastomoses between them. Most of the anastomoses are omitted from the illustrations.

Superficial Veins

The superficial veins of the lower thigh and leg lie in the sub-cutaneous tissue; thus, they are often visible through the skin and accessible with relative ease for such purposes as I.V. fluid therapy. They are particularly prone to becoming varicose veins (see fig. 20.9).

1. The **dorsal venous arch** (fig. 20.44a) is often visible through the skin on the dorsum of the foot. It collects blood from the toes and more proximal part of the foot, and has numerous anastomoses similar to the dorsal venous network of the hand. It gives rise to the following:

2. The **small (short) saphenous**[28] **vein** (sah-FEE-nus) arises from the lateral side of the arch and passes up that side of the leg as far as the knee. There, it drains into the pop-liteal vein.

[28]*saphen* = standing

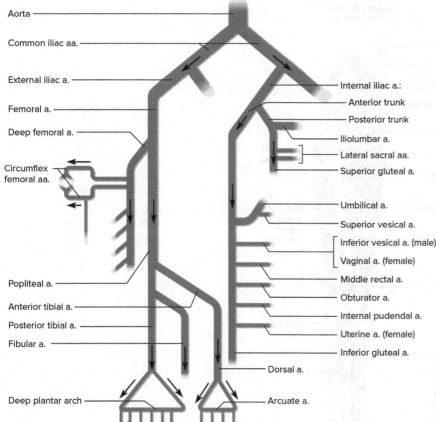

FIGURE 20.43 Arterial Schematic of the Pelvic Region and Lower Limb (Anterior View). The pelvic schematic on the right is stretched for clarity. These arteries are not located as far inferiorly as the arteries depicted adjacent to them on the left.

3. The **great (long) saphenous vein,** the longest vein in the body, arises from the medial side of the arch and travels all the way up the leg and thigh to the inguinal region. It empties into the femoral vein slightly inferior to the inguinal ligament. It is commonly used as an access site for the long-term administration of intravenous fluids and for cardiac catheterization. It is a relatively accessible vein in infants and in patients in shock whose veins have collapsed. Portions of this vein are commonly used as grafts in coronary artery bypass surgery. The great and small saphenous veins are among the most common sites of varicose veins.

Deep Veins

Deep veins of the lower limb accompany the deep arteries. Some of them mirror the arrangement seen in the forelimb, with paired veins flanking the corresponding artery (such as the two *posterior tibial veins* running alongside the *posterior tibial artery*).

1. The **deep plantar venous arch** receives blood from the toes and gives rise to **lateral** and **medial plantar veins** on the respective sides of the foot. The lateral plantar vein gives

off the *fibular veins,* then crosses over to the medial side and approaches the medial plantar vein (but does not join it). The two plantar veins pass behind the medial malleolus of the ankle and continue as a pair of parallel *posterior tibial veins.*

2. The two **posterior tibial veins** pass up the leg embedded deep in the calf muscles. They converge like an inverted Y into a single vein about two-thirds of the way up the tibia.

3. The two **fibular (peroneal) veins** ascend the back of the leg and similarly converge like an inverted Y.

4. The **popliteal** vein begins near the knee by convergence of these two Ys. It passes through the popliteal fossa at the back of the knee.

5. The two **anterior tibial veins** travel up the anterior compartment of the leg between the tibia and fibula (fig. 20.44a). They arise from the medial side of the dorsal venous arch, converge just distal to the knee, then flow into the popliteal vein.

6. The **femoral vein** is a continuation of the popliteal vein into the thigh. It drains blood from the deep thigh muscles and femur.

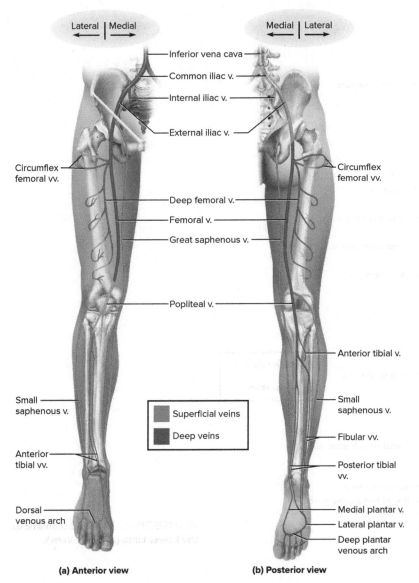

FIGURE 20.44 Veins of the Lower Limb. (a) The major veins in anterior view, with the foot strongly plantar flexed so its upper (dorsal) surface faces the viewer. (b) The major veins in posterior view, with the sole of the foot facing the viewer. **A&PR**

7. The **deep femoral vein** drains the femur and muscles of the thigh supplied by the deep femoral artery. It receives tributaries along the shaft of the femur, then a pair of *circumflex femoral veins* that encircle the upper femur. It finally drains into the upper femoral vein.

8. The **external iliac vein** forms by the union of the femoral and great saphenous veins near the inguinal ligament.

9. The **internal iliac vein** follows the course of the internal iliac artery and its distribution. Its tributaries drain the gluteal muscles; the medial aspect of the thigh; the urinary bladder, rectum, prostate, and ductus deferens of the male; and the uterus and vagina of the female.

10. The **common iliac vein** forms by the union of the external and internal iliac veins. The right and left

common iliacs then unite to form the inferior vena cava.

▶▶▶ **APPLY WHAT YOU KNOW**

There are certain similarities between the arteries of the hand and foot. What arteries of the wrist and hand are most comparable in arrangement and function to the arcuate artery and deep plantar arch of the foot?

Deeper Insight 20.5 exemplifies the relevance of vascular anatomy to emergency first aid. The most common cardiovascular diseases are atherosclerosis and hypertension. **Table 20.2** provides links to further information on these and several other vascular diseases. See "Circulatory System" in section 29.4a for the effects of aging on the blood vessels.

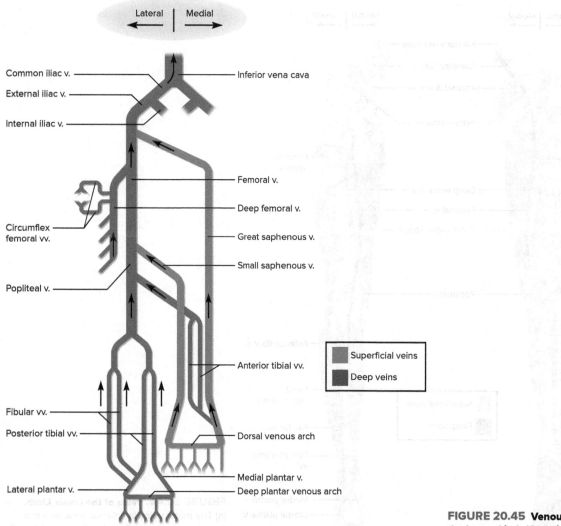

FIGURE 20.45 **Venous Schematic of the Lower Limb (Anterior View).**

TABLE 20.2	Some Vascular Disorders
Dissecting aneurysm	Splitting of the layers of an arterial wall from each other because of the accumulation of blood between layers. Results from either a tear in the tunica interna or rupture of the vasa vasorum.
Fat embolism	The presence of fat globules traveling in the bloodstream. Globules originate from bone fractures, fatty degeneration of the liver, and other causes and may block cerebral or pulmonary blood vessels.
Orthostatic hypotension	A decrease in blood pressure that occurs when one stands, often resulting in blurring of vision, dizziness, and syncope (fainting). Results from sluggish or inactive baroreflexes.

You can find other vascular disorders described in the following places:

Thrombosis and *thromboembolism* in section 18.5f; *air embolism* in Deeper Insight 20.3; *atherosclerosis* and *arteriosclerosis* in Deeper Insight 19.4 and section 20.2a; *aneurysm* in Deeper Insight 20.1; *hypertension* and *hypotension* in section 20.2a and Deeper Insight 20.6; *varicose veins* in Deeper Insight 20.2; *circulatory shock* in section 20.4c; *transient ischemic attack (TIA)* and *stroke* in section 20.5a; and *edema* in section 20.3d.

DEEPER INSIGHT 20.5

CLINICAL APPLICATION

Arterial Pressure Points

In some places, major arteries come close enough to the body surface to be palpated. These places can be used to take a pulse, and they can serve as emergency *pressure points*, where firm pressure can be applied to temporarily reduce arterial bleeding **(fig. 20.46a).** One of these points is the *femoral triangle* of the upper medial thigh

(fig. 20.46b, c). This is an important landmark for arterial supply, venous drainage, and innervation of the lower limb. Its boundaries are the sartorius muscle laterally, the inguinal ligament superiorly, and the adductor longus muscle medially. The femoral artery, vein, and nerve run close to the surface at this point.

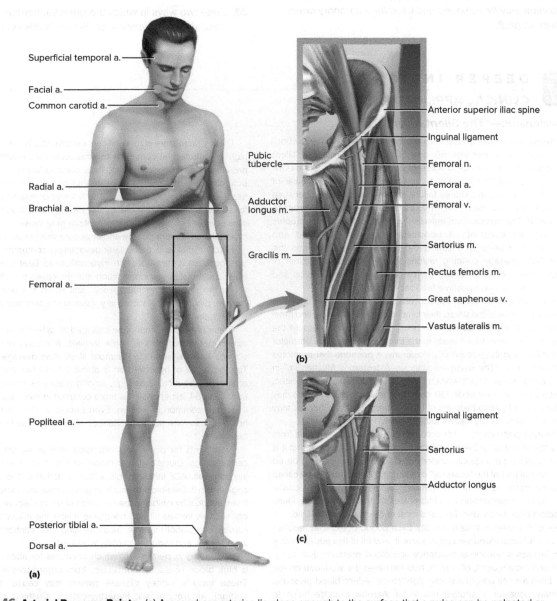

(a)

Superficial temporal a.

Facial a.

Common carotid a.

Radial a.

Brachial a.

Femoral a.

Popliteal a.

Posterior tibial a.

Dorsal a.

Pubic tubercle

Adductor longus m.

Gracilis m.

Anterior superior iliac spine

Inguinal ligament

Femoral n.

Femoral a.

Femoral v.

Sartorius m.

Rectus femoris m.

Great saphenous v.

Vastus lateralis m.

(b)

Inguinal ligament

Sartorius

Adductor longus

(c)

FIGURE 20.46 Arterial Pressure Points. (a) Areas where arteries lie close enough to the surface that a pulse can be palpated or pressure can be applied to reduce arterial bleeding. (b) Structures in the femoral triangle. (c) The three boundaries that define the femoral triangle.

▶▶▶ **APPLY WHAT YOU KNOW**

From the preceding discussion of arteries and veins of the limbs, identify an artery or vein with special relevance to each of the following clinical applications: (1) the artery from which blood pressure is usually measured; (2) the artery where a patient's pulse is most often taken; (3) a vessel where pressure should be applied to stop arterial bleeding from a laceration of the thigh; (4) upper and lower limb veins where intravenous fluid is often administered; (5) a vein where blood samples are commonly drawn; and (6) a vein from which a portion may be removed and used for a coronary artery bypass graft.

BEFORE YOU GO ON

Answer the following questions to test your understanding of the preceding section:

30. Trace one possible path of a red blood cell from the left ventricle to the toes.

31. Trace one possible path of a red blood cell from the fingers to the right atrium.

32. The subclavian, axillary, and brachial arteries are really one continuous artery. What is the reason for giving it three different names along its course?

33. State two ways in which the great saphenous vein has special clinical significance. Where is this vein located?

DEEPER INSIGHT 20.6

CLINICAL APPLICATION

Hypertension—"The Silent Killer"

Hypertension, the most common cardiovascular disease, affects about 30% of Americans over age 50, and 50% by age 74. It is a "silent killer" that can wreak its destructive effects for 10 to 20 years before the symptoms are first noticed. Hypertension is the major cause of heart failure, stroke, and kidney failure. It damages the heart because it increases the afterload, which makes the ventricles work harder to expel blood. The myocardium enlarges up to a point (the *hypertrophic response*), but eventually it becomes excessively stretched and less efficient. Hypertension strains the blood vessels and tears the endothelium, thereby creating lesions that become focal points of atherosclerosis. Atherosclerosis then worsens the hypertension and establishes an insidious positive feedback cycle.

Another positive feedback cycle involves the kidneys. Their arterioles thicken in response to the stress, their lumens become narrower, and renal blood flow declines. In response to the resulting drop in blood pressure, the kidneys release renin, which leads to the formation of the vasoconstrictor angiotensin II and the release of aldosterone, a hormone that promotes salt retention (see "The Renin–Angiotensin–Aldosterone Mechanism" in section 23.3d). These effects worsen the hypertension that already existed. If diastolic pressure exceeds 120 mm Hg, the kidneys and heart may deteriorate rapidly, blood vessels of the eye hemorrhage, blindness may ensue, and death usually follows within 2 years.

Primary hypertension, which accounts for 90% of cases, results from such a complex web of behavioral, hereditary, and other factors that it is difficult to sort out any specific underlying cause. It was once considered such a normal part of the "essence" of aging that it continues to be called by another name, *essential hypertension.* That term suggests a fatalistic resignation to hypertension as a fact of life, but this need not be. Many risk factors have been identified, and most of them are controllable.

One of the chief culprits is obesity. Each pound of extra fat requires miles of additional blood vessels to serve it, and all of this added vessel length increases peripheral resistance and blood pressure. Just carrying around extra weight, of course, also increases the workload on the heart. Even a small weight loss can significantly reduce blood pressure. Sedentary behavior is another risk factor. Aerobic exercise helps to reduce hypertension by controlling weight, reducing emotional tension, and stimulating vasodilation.

Dietary factors are also significant contributors to hypertension. Diets high in saturated fat contribute to atherosclerosis. Potassium and magnesium reduce blood pressure; thus, diets deficient in these minerals promote hypertension. The relationship of salt intake to hypertension has been a controversial subject. The kidneys compensate so effectively for excess salt intake that dietary salt has little effect on the blood pressure of most people. Reduced salt intake may, however, help to control hypertension in older people and in people with reduced renal function.

Nicotine makes a particularly devastating contribution to hypertension because it stimulates the myocardium to beat faster and harder, while it stimulates vasoconstriction and increases the afterload against which the myocardium must work. Just when the heart needs extra oxygen, nicotine causes coronary vasoconstriction and promotes myocardial ischemia.

Some risk factors cannot be changed at will—ancestry, heredity, and sex. Hypertension runs in some families. A person whose parents or siblings have hypertension is more likely than average to develop it. The incidence of hypertension is about 30% higher, and the incidence of strokes about twice as high, among blacks as among whites. From ages 18 to 54, hypertension is more common in men, but above age 65, it is more common in women. Even people at risk from these factors, however, can minimize their chances of hypertension by changing risky behaviors.

Treatments for primary hypertension include weight loss, diet, and certain drugs. Diuretics lower blood volume and pressure by promoting urination. ACE inhibitors block the formation of the vasoconstrictor angiotensin II. Beta-blockers such as propranolol also lower angiotensin II level, but do it by inhibiting the secretion of renin. Calcium channel blockers such as verapamil and nifedipine inhibit the inflow of calcium into cardiac and smooth muscle, thus inhibiting their contraction, promoting vasodilation, and reducing cardiac workload.

Secondary hypertension, which accounts for about 10% of cases, is high blood pressure that results from other identifiable disorders. These include kidney disease (which may cause renin hypersecretion), atherosclerosis, hyperthyroidism, Cushing syndrome, and polycythemia. Secondary hypertension is corrected by treating the underlying disease.

CONNECTIVE ISSUES

Effects of the CIRCULATORY SYSTEM on Other Organ Systems

ALL SYSTEMS
Blood delivers O_2 to all tissues and organs and removes CO_2 and other wastes from them, distributes nutrients and hormones throughout the body, and carries heat from deeper organs to the body surface for elimination.

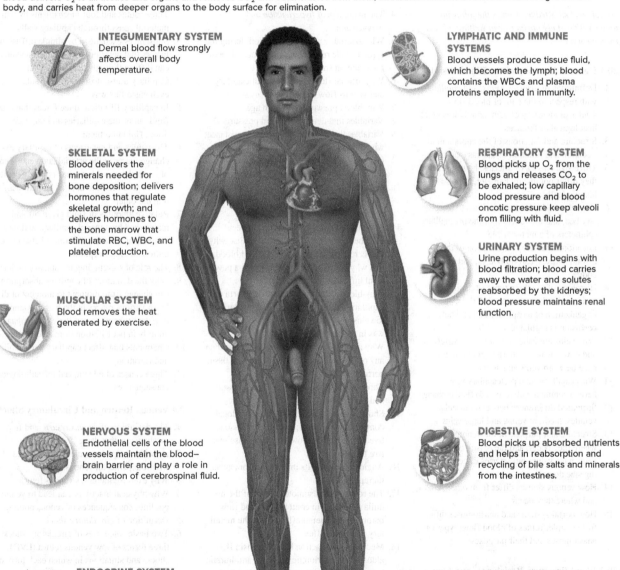

INTEGUMENTARY SYSTEM
Dermal blood flow strongly affects overall body temperature.

SKELETAL SYSTEM
Blood delivers the minerals needed for bone deposition; delivers hormones that regulate skeletal growth; and delivers hormones to the bone marrow that stimulate RBC, WBC, and platelet production.

MUSCULAR SYSTEM
Blood removes the heat generated by exercise.

NERVOUS SYSTEM
Endothelial cells of the blood vessels maintain the blood–brain barrier and play a role in production of cerebrospinal fluid.

ENDOCRINE SYSTEM
Blood is the medium in which all hormones travel to their target organs.

LYMPHATIC AND IMMUNE SYSTEMS
Blood vessels produce tissue fluid, which becomes the lymph; blood contains the WBCs and plasma proteins employed in immunity.

RESPIRATORY SYSTEM
Blood picks up O_2 from the lungs and releases CO_2 to be exhaled; low capillary blood pressure and blood oncotic pressure keep alveoli from filling with fluid.

URINARY SYSTEM
Urine production begins with blood filtration; blood carries away the water and solutes reabsorbed by the kidneys; blood pressure maintains renal function.

DIGESTIVE SYSTEM
Blood picks up absorbed nutrients and helps in reabsorption and recycling of bile salts and minerals from the intestines.

REPRODUCTIVE SYSTEM
Blood delivers the hormones that affect reproductive function; vasodilation produces erection in sexual response; blood provides nutrients, oxygen, and other metabolic needs to the fetus and removes its wastes.

STUDY GUIDE

▶ Assess Your Learning Outcomes

To test your knowledge, discuss the following topics with a study partner or in writing, ideally from memory.

20.1 General Anatomy of the Blood Vessels

1. Definitions of *arteries, veins,* and *capillaries* with respect to the path of blood flow
2. Tunics of an artery or vein, and their general histological differences
3. Structure and functions of the endothelium
4. Location and function of the vasa vasorum
5. Three size classes of arteries; how and why they differ not just in diameter, but also histologically
6. The relationship of metarterioles to a capillary bed, and the function of the precapillary sphincters of a metarteriole
7. Location, structure, and function of the carotid sinuses, carotid bodies, and aortic bodies
8. Histology of the three types of capillaries and how it relates to their functions
9. Organization of a capillary bed and how its perfusion is regulated
10. Why veins are called *capacitance vessels* and how this relates to the structural difference between veins and arteries
11. What capillaries and postcapillary venules have in common with respect to fluid exchange
12. Structural differences between muscular venules, medium veins, and large veins
13. Structure and purpose of the venous valves, where they occur, and the reason certain veins have valves but arteries of corresponding size do not
14. How venous sinuses differ from other veins, and where they occur
15. How portal systems and anastomoses differ from simpler routes of blood flow; types of anastomoses and their purposes

20.2 Blood Pressure, Resistance, and Flow

1. The difference between blood flow and perfusion
2. How blood flow is related to resistance and pressure differences; the mathematical expression of these relationships
3. How to determine systolic pressure, diastolic pressure, and pulse pressure; how to estimate mean arterial pressure (MAP), and why MAP differs from head to foot

4. The meanings of *hypertension* and *hypotension*
5. Why arterial expansion and recoil during the cardiac cycle reduce pulse pressure and ease the strain on small arteries
6. Why arterial flow is pulsatile but capillary and venous flow are not
7. Why blood pressure rises with age
8. Variables that determine blood pressure
9. Variables that determine peripheral resistance; whether each one is directly or inversely proportional to resistance; and which of them is most changeable from moment to moment
10. Terms for widening and narrowing of a blood vessel by muscular contraction and relaxation
11. The mathematical relationship between peripheral resistance and vessel radius; why this is related to the laminar flow of blood; and why it makes vasoreflexes such a powerful influence on blood flow
12. Why blood velocity declines from aorta to capillaries and rises again from capillaries to veins, but never rises as high in veins as it was in the aorta
13. Why arterioles exert a greater influence than any other category of blood vessels on tissue perfusion
14. Three levels of control over blood pressure and flow
15. Short- and long-term mechanisms of local control of blood flow; examples of vasoactive chemicals and how they can cause reactive hyperemia
16. Angiogenesis and its importance for cancer therapy
17. The role of the vasomotor center of the medulla oblongata in controlling blood flow; baroreflexes, chemoreflexes, and the medullary ischemic reflex
18. Mechanisms of action by angiotensin II, aldosterone, natriuretic peptides, antidiuretic hormone, epinephrine, and norepinephrine on blood pressure
19. How vasomotion can change systemwide blood pressure or redirect blood flow from one region to another; circumstances that call for redirection of blood flow

20.3 Capillaries and Fluid Exchange

1. The meaning of *capillary exchange,* and substances involved in the process

2. Three routes and four mechanisms by which materials pass through capillary walls
3. Substances exchanged by simple diffusion; factors that determine whether a substance can diffuse through a capillary wall
4. Capillary transcytosis and some substances exchanged this way
5. In capillary filtration, three forces that draw fluid out of the capillaries and one force that draws fluid into them
6. The values and net effects of capillary exchange forces at the arterial and venous ends of a capillary, and how they enable a capillary to give off fluid at one end and reabsorb it at the other
7. Relative amounts of fluid given off and reabsorbed by a model capillary, and what compensates for the difference between filtration and reabsorption
8. The role of solvent drag in capillary exchange
9. Why the dynamics of capillary absorption can change from moment to moment or differ in various places in the body; examples of places where the capillaries are engaged entirely in net filtration or reabsorption
10. Chemicals that affect capillary permeability and filtration
11. Three causes of edema, and its pathological consequences

20.4 Venous Return and Circulatory Shock

1. The definition of *venous return,* and five mechanisms that drive it
2. How the skeletal muscle pump works and why it depends on venous valves
3. Why exercise increases venous return
4. Why physical inactivity can lead to venous pooling; consequences of venous pooling
5. Definition of *circulatory shock*
6. Two basic categories of circulatory shock, three forms of low venous return (LVR) shock, and situations in which each form of shock may occur
7. Why septic and anaphylactic shock cannot be strictly classified into any single category of LVR shock
8. Differences between compensated and decompensated shock

20.5 Special Circulatory Routes

1. A typical value for cerebral blood flow and why its constancy is important

STUDY GUIDE

2. How the brain regulates its blood flow and what chemical stimulus is the most potent in activating its regulatory mechanisms

3. The causes, effects, and difference between a transient ischemic attack (TIA) and cerebral vascular accident (stroke)

4. Variability of skeletal muscle perfusion; what stimuli increase perfusion to meet the demands of exercise; and why isometric contraction causes fatigue more quickly than isotonic contraction does

5. How pulmonary circulation differs from systemic circulation with respect to blood pressure, capillary exchange, relative oxygenation of arterial and venous blood, and the vasomotor response to hypoxia

20.6 Anatomy of the Pulmonary Circuit

1. The route of blood flow in the pulmonary circuit

2. Where the capillaries of the pulmonary circuit are found and the function they serve

3. How the function of the pulmonary circuit differs from that of the bronchial arteries, which also supply the lungs

20.7 Systemic Vessels of the Axial Region

1. For all named blood vessels in this outline, their anatomical location; the vessel from which they arise; the course they follow; and the organs, body regions, or other blood vessels they supply

2. The ascending aorta, aortic arch, and descending aorta, and the thoracic and abdominal segments of the descending aorta (section 20.7a)

3. Branches that arise from the ascending aorta and aortic arch: the coronary arteries, brachiocephalic trunk, left common carotid artery, and left subclavian artery (section 20.7a)

4. Four principal arteries of the neck: the common carotid, vertebral artery, thyrocervical trunk, and costocervical trunk (section 20.7b)

5. The external and internal carotid arteries; branches of the external carotid (superior thyroid, lingual, facial, occipital, maxillary, and superficial temporal arteries); and branches of the internal carotid (ophthalmic, anterior cerebral, and middle cerebral arteries) (section 20.7b)

6. Convergence of the vertebral arteries to form the basilar artery; the posterior cerebral arteries and arteries to the cerebellum, pons, and inner ear arising from the basilar artery (section 20.7b)

7. The location and constituents of the cerebral arterial circle (section 20.7b)

8. Dural venous sinuses; the superior sagittal, inferior sagittal, transverse, and cavernous sinuses; outflow from the sinus system into the internal jugular veins (section 20.7c)

9. The internal jugular, external jugular, and vertebral veins of the neck (section 20.7c)

10. Visceral branches (bronchial, esophageal, and mediastinal arteries) and parietal branches (posterior intercostal, subcostal, and superior phrenic arteries) of the thoracic aorta (section 20.7d)

11. Arteries of the thorax and shoulder that arise from the subclavian artery and its continuation, the axillary artery: the internal thoracic artery, thoracoacromial trunk, lateral thoracic artery, and subscapular artery (section 20.7d)

12. The subclavian vein, brachiocephalic vein, and superior vena cava; landmarks that define the transition from one to another (section 20.7e)

13. The azygos system of thoracic veins, especially the azygos, hemiazygos, and accessory hemiazygos veins; their tributaries, including the posterior intercostal, subcostal, esophageal, mediastinal, pericardial, bronchial, and ascending lumbar veins (section 20.7e)

14. Branches of the abdominal aorta: inferior phrenic arteries; celiac trunk; and superior mesenteric, middle suprarenal, renal, gonadal (ovarian or testicular), inferior mesenteric, lumbar, median sacral, and common iliac arteries (section 20.7f)

15. The general group of organs supplied by the celiac trunk; its three primary branches—the common hepatic, left gastric, and splenic arteries—and smaller branches given off by each of these (section 20.7f)

16. Branches of the superior mesenteric artery: inferior pancreaticoduodenal, jejunal, ileal, and right and middle colic arteries (section 20.7f)

17. Branches of the inferior mesenteric artery: left colic, sigmoid, and superior rectal arteries (section 20.7f)

18. Two main branches of the common iliac artery, the posterior and anterior trunks of the internal iliac artery, and the organs supplied by those trunks (section 20.7f)

19. Convergence of the internal and external iliac veins to form the common iliac vein; convergence of the right and left common

iliac veins to form the inferior vena cava (IVC) (section 20.7g)

20. Abdominal tributaries of the IVC: lumbar, gonadal (ovarian or testicular), renal, suprarenal, hepatic, and inferior phrenic veins (section 20.7g)

21. The ascending lumbar veins, their drainage in the abdomen, and their continuation into the thorax (section 20.7g)

22. The hepatic portal system and its tributaries: the splenic vein; the pancreatic, inferior mesenteric, and superior mesenteric veins draining into it; continuation of the splenic vein as the hepatic portal vein; the cystic vein and gastric veins draining into the hepatic portal vein; hepatic sinusoids in the liver; and hepatic veins (section 20.7g)

20.8 Systemic Vessels of the Appendicular Region

1. The main artery to the upper limb, which changes name along its course from subclavian to axillary to brachial artery; branches of the brachial artery in the arm (deep brachial and superior ulnar collateral arteries); and the radial collateral artery (section 20.8a)

2. Brachial artery branches that supply the forearm: radial and ulnar arteries; anterior and posterior interosseous arteries; and deep and superficial palmar arches (section 20.8a)

3. The dorsal venous network of the hand; median antebrachial vein; and median cubital vein (section 20.8b)

4. The venous palmar arches, and brachial, basilic, axillary, and subclavian veins (section 20.8b)

5. Continuation of the external iliac artery as the femoral artery; deep femoral and circumflex femoral branches of the femoral artery; popliteal artery; and anterior and posterior tibial arteries (section 20.8c)

6. The dorsal pedal and arcuate arteries that arise from the anterior tibial artery; fibular, medial plantar, and lateral plantar arteries; and deep plantar arch (section 20.8c)

7. The superficial dorsal venous arch, small and great saphenous veins, and popliteal vein (section 20.8d)

8. The deep plantar venous arch; the lateral and medial plantar veins; fibular and posterior tibial veins; and anterior tibial veins (section 20.8d)

9. The femoral, deep femoral, and external iliac veins (section 20.8d)

STUDY GUIDE

▶ **Testing Your Recall**

Answers in Appendix A

1. Blood often flows into a capillary bed from
   a. the distributing arteries.
   b. the conducting arteries.
   c. a metarteriole.
   d. an arteriovenous anastomosis
   e. the venules.

2. Plasma solutes enter the tissue fluid most easily from
   a. continuous capillaries.
   b. fenestrated capillaries.
   c. arteriovenous anastomoses.
   d. collateral vessels.
   e. venous anastomoses.

3. A blood vessel adapted to withstand a high pulse pressure would be expected to have
   a. an elastic tunica media.
   b. a thick tunica interna.
   c. one-way valves.
   d. a flexible endothelium.
   e. a rigid tunica media.

4. The substance most likely to cause a rapid drop in blood pressure is
   a. epinephrine.
   b. norepinephrine.
   c. angiotensin II.
   d. serotonin.
   e. histamine.

5. A person with a systolic blood pressure of 130 mm Hg and a diastolic pressure of 85 mm Hg would have a mean arterial pressure of about
   a. 85 mm Hg.
   b. 100 mm Hg.
   c. 108 mm Hg.
   d. 115 mm Hg.
   e. 130 mm Hg.

6. The velocity of blood flow decreases if
   a. vessel radius increases.
   b. blood pressure increases.
   c. viscosity increases.
   d. viscosity decreases.
   e. afterload increases.

7. Blood flows faster in a venule than in a capillary because venules
   a. have one-way valves.
   b. are more muscular.
   c. are closer to the heart.
   d. have higher blood pressures.
   e. have larger diameters.

8. In a case where interstitial hydrostatic pressure is negative, the only force causing capillaries to reabsorb fluid is
   a. colloid osmotic pressure of the blood.
   b. colloid osmotic pressure of the tissue fluid.
   c. capillary hydrostatic pressure.
   d. interstitial hydrostatic pressure.
   e. net filtration pressure.

9. Intestinal blood flows to the liver by way of
   a. the superior mesenteric artery.
   b. the celiac trunk.
   c. the inferior vena cava.
   d. the azygos system.
   e. the hepatic portal system.

10. The brain receives blood from all of the following vessels *except* the _____ artery or vein.
    a. basilar
    b. vertebral
    c. internal carotid
    d. internal jugular
    e. anterior communicating

11. The highest arterial blood pressure attained during ventricular contraction is called _____ pressure. The lowest attained during ventricular relaxation is called _____ pressure.

12. The capillaries of skeletal muscles are of the structural type called _____.

13. _____ shock occurs as a result of exposure to an antigen to which one is hypersensitive.

14. The role of breathing in venous return is called the _____.

15. The difference between the colloid osmotic pressure of blood and that of the tissue fluid is called _____.

16. Movement across the capillary endothelium by the uptake and release of fluid droplets is called _____.

17. All efferent fibers of the vasomotor center belong to the _____ division of the autonomic nervous system.

18. The pressure sensors in the major arteries near the head are called _____.

19. Most of the blood supply to the brain comes from a ring of arterial anastomoses called the _____.

20. The major superficial veins of the arm are the _____ on the medial side and _____ on the lateral side.

▶ **Building Your Medical Vocabulary**

Answers in Appendix A

State a meaning of each word element, and give a medical term from this chapter that uses it or a slight variation of it.

1. angio-

2. brachio-

3. celi-

4. fenestra-

5. jugulo-

6. -orum

7. sapheno-

8. sub-

9. thoraco-

10. vesico-

STUDY GUIDE

▶ What's Wrong with These Statements?

Answers in Appendix A

Briefly explain why each of the following statements is false, or reword it to make it true.

1. Blood cannot get from an artery to a vein without first passing through some capillaries.

2. Blood returns from the brain to the heart by way of the external jugular veins.

3. The body's longest blood vessel is the inferior vena cava.

4. Arteries have a series of valves that ensure a one-way flow of blood.

5. If the radius of a blood vessel doubles and all other factors remain the same, blood flow through that vessel also doubles.

6. The femoral triangle is bordered by the inguinal ligament, sartorius muscle, and rectus femoris muscle.

7. The lungs receive blood exclusively from the pulmonary circuit of the circulatory system.

8. If blood capillaries fail to reabsorb all the fluid they emit, edema will occur.

9. An aneurysm is a ruptured blood vessel.

10. In the baroreflex, a drop in arterial blood pressure triggers a corrective vasodilation of the systemic blood vessels.

▶ Testing Your Comprehension

1. It is a common lay perception that systolic blood pressure should be 100 plus a person's age. Evaluate the validity of this statement.

2. Calculate the net filtration or reabsorption pressure at a point in a hypothetical capillary assuming a hydrostatic blood pressure of 28 mm Hg, an interstitial hydrostatic pressure of –2 mm Hg, a blood COP of 25 mm Hg, and an interstitial COP of 4 mm Hg. Give the magnitude (in mm Hg) and direction (in or out) of the net pressure.

3. Aldosterone secreted by the adrenal gland must be delivered to the kidney immediately below. Trace the route that an aldosterone molecule must take from the adrenal gland to the kidney, naming all major blood vessels in the order traveled.

4. People in shock commonly exhibit paleness, cool skin, tachycardia, and a weak pulse. Explain the physiological basis for each of these signs.

5. Discuss why it is advantageous to have baroreceptors in the aortic arch and carotid sinus rather than in some other location such as the common iliac arteries.

PART FIVE: INTAKE AND OUTPUT

CHAPTER

22

THE RESPIRATORY SYSTEM

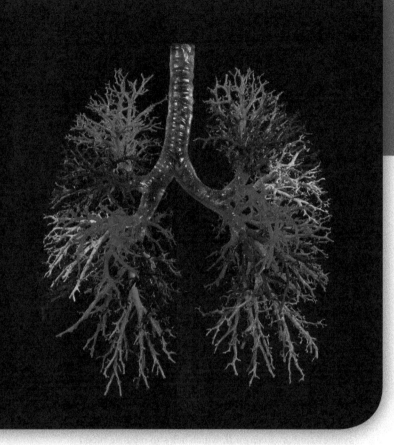

The bronchial trees with colors indicating bronchopulmonary segments
Mediscan/Alamy

Anatomy & Physiology
Revealed 4.0

Module 11: Respiratory System

BRUSHING UP

- The study of respiratory anatomy will draw on your knowledge of mucous and serous membranes (see section 5.5c); parietal and visceral layers of thoracic membranes (see atlas A, section A.3b); and simple squamous and ciliated pseudostratified columnar epithelia (see table 5.2).

- In reading on pulmonary ventilation, you may wish to refer back to the primary muscles of respiration (see table 10.4) and the accessory muscles that aid in breathing (see tables 10.5, 10.6, 10.7).

- Brushing up on the medulla oblongata and pons of the brainstem will help in understanding the respiratory control centers located there (see sections 14.3a, 14.3b).

- Respiratory airflow and gas exchange hinge on principles of flow down gradients (see section 1.6e) and effects of pressure and resistance on the flow of fluids (see section 19.5a).

- Diffusion and the factors that affect its rate are central to the exchange of gases in the lungs and peripheral tissues (see section 3.3b).

- Knowledge of hemoglobin structure is necessary for understanding oxygen transport in the blood (see section 18.2b).

B reath represents life. The first breath of a baby and the last gasp of a dying person are two of the most dramatic moments of human experience. But why do we breathe? It comes down to the fact that most of our metabolism directly or indirectly requires ATP. Most ATP synthesis requires oxygen and generates carbon dioxide—thus driving the need to breathe in order to supply the former and eliminate the latter. The respiratory system consists essentially of tubes that deliver air to the lungs, where oxygen diffuses into the blood and carbon dioxide diffuses out.

The respiratory and cardiovascular systems collaborate to deliver oxygen to tissues throughout the body and transport carbon dioxide to the lungs for elimination. Not only do these two systems have a close spatial relationship in the thoracic cavity, but they also have such a close functional relationship that they're often jointly called the *cardiopulmonary system.* A disorder that affects the lungs has direct and pronounced effects on the heart, and vice versa. As discussed in the next two chapters, the respiratory system also collaborates closely with the urinary system to regulate the body's acid–base balance, which is why we consider these systems consecutively in this group of chapters.

22.1   Anatomy of the Respiratory System

Expected Learning Outcomes

When you have completed this section, you should be able to

a. state the functions of the respiratory system;

b. name and describe the organs of this system;

c. trace the flow of air from the nose to the pulmonary alveoli; and

d. relate the function of any portion of the respiratory tract to its gross and microscopic anatomy.

The term *respiration* can mean ventilation of the lungs (breathing) or the use of oxygen in cellular metabolism. In this chapter, we are concerned with the first process. Cellular respiration was introduced in chapter 2 and is considered more fully in chapter 26.

The **respiratory system** is an organ system that rhythmically takes in air and expels it from the body, thereby supplying the body with oxygen and expelling the carbon dioxide that it generates. However, it has a broader range of functions than is commonly supposed:

1. **Gas exchange.** It provides for oxygen and carbon dioxide exchange between the blood and air.

2. **Communication.** It serves for speech and other vocalization (laughing, crying).

3. **Olfaction.** It provides the sense of smell, which is important in social interactions, food selection, and avoiding danger (such as a gas leak or spoiled food).

4. **Acid–base balance.** By eliminating CO_2, it helps to control the pH of the body fluids. Excess CO_2 reacts with water and generates carbonic acid; therefore, if respiration doesn't keep pace with CO_2 production, acid accumulates and the body fluids have an abnormally low pH *(acidosis).*

5. **Blood pressure regulation.** The lungs carry out a step in synthesizing *angiotensin II,* which helps to regulate blood pressure.

6. **Platelet production.** More than half of one's blood platelets are made by megakaryocytes in the lungs (not in the bone marrow).

7. **Blood and lymph flow.** Breathing creates pressure gradients between the thorax and abdomen that promote the flow of lymph and venous blood.

8. **Blood filtration.** The lungs filter small blood clots from the bloodstream and dissolve them, preventing clots from obstructing more vital pathways such as the coronary, cerebral, and renal circulation.

9. **Expulsion of abdominal contents.** Breath-holding and abdominal contraction help to expel abdominal contents during urination, defecation, and childbirth.

The principal organs of the respiratory system are the nose, pharynx, larynx, trachea, bronchi, and lungs **(fig. 22.1).** Within the lungs, air flows along a dead-end pathway consisting essentially of bronchi → bronchioles → alveoli (with some refinements to be introduced later). Incoming air stops in the *alveoli* (millions of tiny, thin-walled air sacs), exchanges gases with the bloodstream through the alveolar wall, and then flows back out.

The **conducting zone** of the respiratory system consists of those passages that serve only for airflow, essentially from the nostrils through the major bronchioles. The walls of these passages

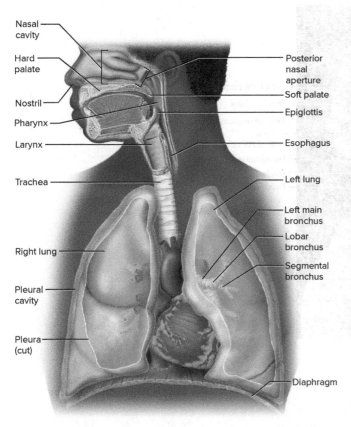

FIGURE 22.1 The Respiratory System. APR

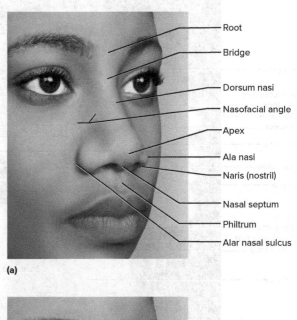

(a)

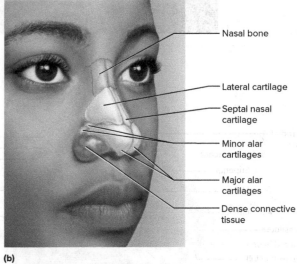

(b)

FIGURE 22.2 Anatomy of the Nasal Region. (a) Surface anatomy. (b) Connective tissues that shape the nose.
Joe DeGrandis/McGraw-Hill Education

are too thick for adequate diffusion of oxygen from the air into the blood. The **respiratory zone** consists of the alveoli and other gas-exchange regions of the distal airway. The airway from the nose through the larynx is often called the **upper respiratory tract** (that is, the respiratory organs in the head and neck), and the regions from the trachea through the lungs compose the **lower respiratory tract** (the respiratory organs of the thorax). However, these are inexact terms and various authorities place the dividing line between the upper and lower tracts at different points.

22.1a The Nose

The **nose** has several functions: It warms, cleanses, and humidifies inhaled air; it detects odors; and it serves as a resonating chamber that amplifies the voice. It extends from a pair of anterior openings called the **nostrils,** or **nares** (NAIR-eze) (singular, *naris*), to a pair of posterior openings called the **posterior nasal apertures,** or **choanae**[1] (co-AH-nee).

The facial part of the nose is shaped by bone and hyaline cartilage. Its superior half is supported by a pair of small nasal bones medially and the maxillae laterally. The inferior half is supported by the **lateral** and **alar cartilages (fig. 22.2).** By palpating your own nose, you can easily find the boundary between the bone above and

the more flexible cartilage below. The flared portion on each side of the lower end of the nose, called the **ala nasi**[2] (AIL-ah NAZE-eye), is shaped by the alar cartilages and dense connective tissue.

The internal chamber of the nose, called the **nasal cavity,** is divided into right and left halves called **nasal fossae** (FAW-see) **(fig. 22.3).** The dividing wall is a vertical plate, the **nasal septum,** composed of bone and hyaline cartilage. The vomer forms the inferior part of the septum, the perpendicular plate of the ethmoid bone forms its superior part, and the *septal cartilage* forms its anterior part. The ethmoid and sphenoid bones compose the roof of

---

[1]*choana* = funnel

[2]*ala* = wing; *nasi* = of the nose

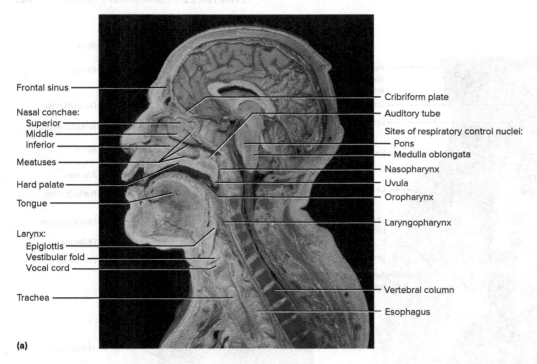

(a)

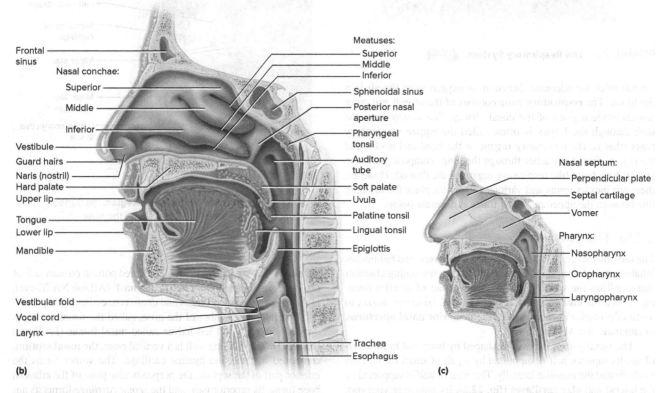

(b)   (c)

FIGURE 22.3 Anatomy of the Upper Respiratory Tract. (a) Median section of the head. (b) Internal anatomy. (c) The nasal septum and regions of the pharynx.

a: Rebecca Gray/McGraw-Hill Education

❓ *Draw a line across part (a) of this figure to indicate the boundary between the upper and lower respiratory tract.*

the nasal cavity, and the hard palate forms its floor. The palate separates the nasal cavity from the oral cavity and allows you to breathe while chewing food. The paranasal sinuses and the naso-lacrimal ducts of the orbits drain into the nasal cavity (see figs. 8.8, 16.24, respectively).

The nasal cavity begins with a small dilated chamber called the **vestibule** just inside the nostril, bordered by the ala nasi. This space is lined with stratified squamous epithelium like the facial skin, and has stiff **guard hairs,** or **vibrissae** (vy-BRISS-ee), that block debris from entering the nose. Posterior to the vestibule, the nasal cavity expands into a much larger chamber, but it doesn't have much open space. Most of it is occupied by three folds of tissue—the **superior, middle,** and **inferior nasal conchae**[3] (CON-kee), or **turbinates**—that project from the lateral walls toward the septum (fig. 22.3; see also fig. 8.7 for a frontal view). Beneath each concha is a narrow air passage called a **meatus** (me-AY-tus). The narrowness of these passages and the turbulence caused by the conchae ensure that most air contacts the mucous membrane on its way through. As it does, most dust in the air sticks to the mucus and the air picks up moisture and heat from the mucosa. The conchae thus enable the nose to cleanse, warm, and humidify the air more effectively than if the air had an unobstructed flow through a cavernous space.

Past the vestibule, the mucosa (mucous membrane) of the nasal cavity consists of a ciliated pseudostratified columnar epithelium overlying a loose connective tissue lamina propria (see figs. 5.7, 5.33). Over most of the mucosa, the epithelium is called the **respiratory epithelium.** Its **ciliated cells** are capped with a fringe of about 200 motile cilia per cell and coated with a layer of mucus. The second most abundant cells of the epithelium are the wine-glass-shaped **goblet cells,** which secrete most of the mucus. In lesser numbers, the respiratory epithelium also contains endocrine cells, chemosensory *brush cells*, and basal stem cells.

Inhaled dust, pollen, bacteria, and other foreign matter are trapped in the sticky blanket of mucus covering the epithelium. The cilia of the epithelium beat in waves that drive this debris-laden mucus posteriorly to the pharynx, where it is swallowed. The particulate debris is either digested or passes through the digestive tract rather than contaminating the lungs.

A small area of nasal mucosa has an **olfactory epithelium,** concerned with the sense of smell. It covers about 5 cm^2 in the roof of the nasal fossa and adjacent parts of the septum and superior concha. Its structure and function are detailed in section 16.3b (see fig. 16.7). A notable contrast with the respiratory epithelium is that the cilia of the olfactory epithelium are immobile. They lie flattened against the mucosal surface like a plate of spaghetti noodles and serve to bind odor molecules, not to propel mucus.

The lamina propria of the nasal cavity is loose (areolar) connective tissue. In the respiratory mucosa, it contains glands that supplement the mucus produced by the goblet cells. In the olfactory mucosa, the lamina propria has large serous **olfactory glands.** These secrete a watery serous fluid that bathes the olfactory cilia and facilitates the diffusion of odor molecules from inhaled air to their receptors on the cilia.

The lamina propria contains large blood vessels that help to warm the air. The inferior concha has an especially extensive venous plexus called the **erectile tissue (swell body).** Every 30 to 60 minutes, the erectile tissue on one side swells with blood and restricts airflow through that fossa. Most air is then directed through the other nostril, allowing the engorged side time to recover from drying. Thus, the preponderant flow of air shifts between the right and left nostrils once or twice each hour. If one nostril is blocked and the other nasal fossa is over-ventilated for several days, its pseudostratified columnar epithelium changes to stratified squamous, which better resists drying. This is an example of the *metaplasia* explained in section 5.6b.

22.1b The Pharynx

The **pharynx** (FAIR-inks, FAR-inks) is a muscular funnel extending about 13 cm (5 in.) from the posterior nasal apertures to the larynx. It has three regions: the *nasopharynx, oropharynx,* and *laryngopharynx* (fig. 22.3c).

The **nasopharynx** is distal to the posterior nasal apertures and superior to the soft palate. It receives the auditory (pharyngotympanic or eustachian) tubes from the middle ears and houses the pharyngeal tonsil. Inhaled air turns 90° downward as it passes through the nasopharynx. Relatively large particles (>10 µm) generally can't make the turn because of their inertia. They collide with the wall of the nasopharynx and stick to the mucosa near the tonsil, which is well positioned to respond to airborne pathogens.

The **oropharynx** is a space between the posterior margin of the soft palate and the epiglottis.

The **laryngopharynx** (la-RIN-go-FAIR-inks) lies mostly posterior to the larynx, extending from the superior margin of the epiglottis to the inferior margin of the cricoid cartilage. The esophagus begins at that point.

The nasopharynx passes only air and is lined by pseudostratified columnar epithelium, whereas the oropharynx and laryngopharynx pass air, food, and drink and are lined by more abrasion-resistant stratified squamous epithelium. Muscles of the pharynx play necessary roles in swallowing and speech.

22.1c The Larynx

The **larynx** (LAIR-inks) is a cartilaginous chamber about 4 cm (1.5 in.) long **(fig. 22.4).** Its primary function is to keep food and drink out of the airway, but it evolved the additional role of sound production *(phonation)* in many animals; hence, we colloquially think of it as the "voice box."

The superior opening of the larynx is guarded by a flap of tissue called the **epiglottis**[4] just posterior to the root of the tongue. At rest, the epiglottis stands almost vertically. During swallowing, however, *extrinsic muscles* of the larynx pull the larynx upward toward the epiglottis, the tongue pushes the epiglottis downward to meet it, and the epiglottis closes the airway and directs food and drink into the esophagus behind it. The *vestibular folds* of the larynx, discussed shortly, play a greater role in keeping food and drink out of the airway, however.

---

[3]*concha* = seashell

[4]*epi* = above, upon; *glottis* = back of the tongue

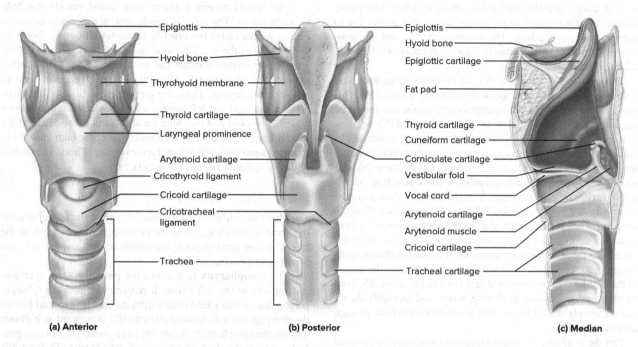

(a) Anterior

- Epiglottis
- Hyoid bone
- Thyrohyoid membrane
- Thyroid cartilage
- Laryngeal prominence
- Arytenoid cartilage
- Cricothyroid ligament
- Cricoid cartilage
- Cricotracheal ligament
- Trachea

(b) Posterior

(c) Median

- Epiglottis
- Hyoid bone
- Epiglottic cartilage
- Fat pad
- Thyroid cartilage
- Cuneiform cartilage
- Corniculate cartilage
- Vestibular fold
- Vocal cord
- Arytenoid cartilage
- Arytenoid muscle
- Cricoid cartilage
- Tracheal cartilage

FIGURE 22.4 Anatomy of the Larynx. (a) Anterior aspect. (b) Posterior aspect. (c) Median section with most muscles removed in order to show the cartilages. **APR**

❓ *Which three cartilages in this figure are more mobile than any of the others?*

In infants, the larynx is relatively high in the throat and the epiglottis touches the soft palate. This creates a more or less continuous airway from the nasal cavity to the larynx and allows an infant to breathe continually while swallowing. The epiglottis deflects milk away from the airstream, like rain running off a tent while it remains dry inside. By age 2, the root of the tongue becomes more muscular and forces the larynx to descend to a lower position. It then becomes impossible to breathe and swallow at the same time without choking.

The framework of the larynx consists of nine cartilages. The first three are solitary and relatively large. The most superior one, the **epiglottic cartilage,** is a spoon-shaped supportive plate of elastic cartilage in the epiglottis. The largest, the **thyroid**[5] **cartilage,** is named for its shieldlike shape. It broadly covers the anterior and lateral aspects of the larynx. The "Adam's apple" is an anterior peak of the thyroid cartilage called the *laryngeal prominence*. Testosterone stimulates the growth of this prominence, which is therefore larger in males than in females. Inferior to the thyroid cartilage is a ringlike **cricoid**[6] **cartilage** (CRY-coyd). The thyroid and cricoid cartilages essentially constitute the "box" of the voice box.

The remaining cartilages are smaller and occur in three pairs. Posterior to the thyroid cartilage are the two **arytenoid**[7] **cartilages** (AR-ih-TEE-noyd), and attached to their upper ends is a pair

of little horns, the **corniculate**[8] **cartilages** (cor-NICK-you-late). The arytenoid and corniculate cartilages function in speech, as explained shortly. A pair of **cuneiform**[9] **cartilages** (cue-NEE-ih-form) supports the soft tissues between the arytenoids and the epiglottis.

A group of fibrous ligaments binds the cartilages of the larynx together and forms a suspension system for the upper airway. A broad sheet called the **thyrohyoid membrane** suspends the larynx from the hyoid bone above it. Below, the **cricothyroid ligament** suspends the cricoid cartilage from the thyroid cartilage. This is the most clinically important of all these ligaments, as this is where emergency incisions are made in a *tracheotomy* to restore breathing when the airway above it is obstructed (see Deeper Insight 22.1). The **cricotracheal ligament** suspends the trachea from the cricoid cartilage. All of these are collectively called the *extrinsic ligaments* because they link the larynx to other organs. The *intrinsic ligaments* are contained entirely within the larynx and link its nine cartilages to each other; they include ligaments of the vocal cords and vestibular folds.

The interior wall of the larynx has two folds on each side that stretch from the thyroid cartilage in front to the arytenoid cartilages in back. The superior **vestibular folds** (fig. 22.4c) play no role in speech but close the larynx during swallowing. They are supported by the **vestibular ligaments.** The inferior **vocal cords** (**vocal folds**) produce sound when air passes between them. They

---

[5]*thyr* = shield; *oid* = resembling
[6]*crico* = ring; *oid* = resembling
[7]*aryten* = ladle; *oid* = resembling

[8]*corni* = horn; *cul* = little; *ate* = possessing
[9]*cune* = wedge; *form* = shape

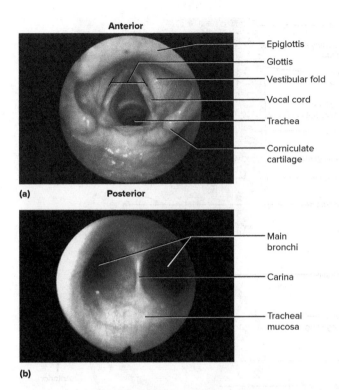

(a)

Anterior

- Epiglottis
- Glottis
- Vestibular fold
- Vocal cord
- Trachea
- Corniculate cartilage

Posterior

(b)

- Main bronchi
- Carina
- Tracheal mucosa

FIGURE 22.5 Endoscopic Views of the Respiratory Tract.
(a) Superior view of the larynx, seen with a laryngoscope. (b) Lower end of the trachea, where it forks into the two primary bronchi, seen with a bronchoscope.

a: CNRI/Science Photo Library; b: BSIP/Newscom

contain the **vocal ligaments** and are covered with stratified squamous epithelium, best suited to endure vibration and contact between the cords. The vocal cords and the opening between them are collectively called the **glottis (fig. 22.5a).**

The walls of the larynx are quite muscular. The superficial *extrinsic muscles* connect the larynx to the hyoid bone and elevate the larynx during swallowing. Also called the *infrahyoid group,* they are named and described in table 10.2.

The deeper *intrinsic muscles* control the vocal cords by pulling on the corniculate and arytenoid cartilages, causing the cartilages to pivot. Depending on their direction of rotation, the arytenoid cartilages abduct or adduct the vocal cords **(fig. 22.6).** Air forced between the adducted vocal cords vibrates them, producing a high-pitched sound when the cords are relatively taut and a lower-pitched sound when they are more slack. In adult males, the vocal cords are usually longer and thicker, vibrate more slowly, and produce lower-pitched sounds than in females. Loudness is determined by the force of the air passing between the vocal cords. Although the vocal cords alone produce sound, they don't produce intelligible speech; some anatomists have likened their sound to a hunter's duck call. The crude sounds from the larynx are formed into words by actions of the pharynx, oral cavity, tongue, and lips.

22.1d The Trachea

The **trachea** (TRAY-kee-uh), or "windpipe," is a tube about 12 cm (4.5 in.) long and 2.5 cm (1 in.) in diameter, anterior to the esophagus **(fig. 22.7a).** It is supported by 16 to 20 C-shaped rings of hyaline cartilage. The trachea is named for the corrugated texture imparted

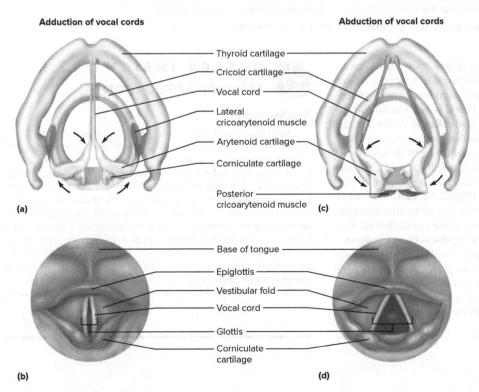

Adduction of vocal cords

Abduction of vocal cords

- Thyroid cartilage
- Cricoid cartilage
- Vocal cord
- Lateral cricoarytenoid muscle
- Arytenoid cartilage
- Corniculate cartilage
- Posterior cricoarytenoid muscle

Anterior

Posterior

(a)   **(c)**

- Base of tongue
- Epiglottis
- Vestibular fold
- Vocal cord
- Glottis
- Corniculate cartilage

(b)   **(d)**

FIGURE 22.6 Action of Some of the Intrinsic Laryngeal Muscles on the Vocal Cords.
(a) Adduction of the vocal cords by the *lateral cricoarytenoid muscles*. (b) Adducted vocal cords seen with the laryngoscope. (c) Abduction of the vocal cords by the *posterior cricoarytenoid muscles*. (d) Abducted vocal cords seen with the laryngoscope. The intrinsic muscles are much more numerous and complex than these two pairs isolated for illustration.

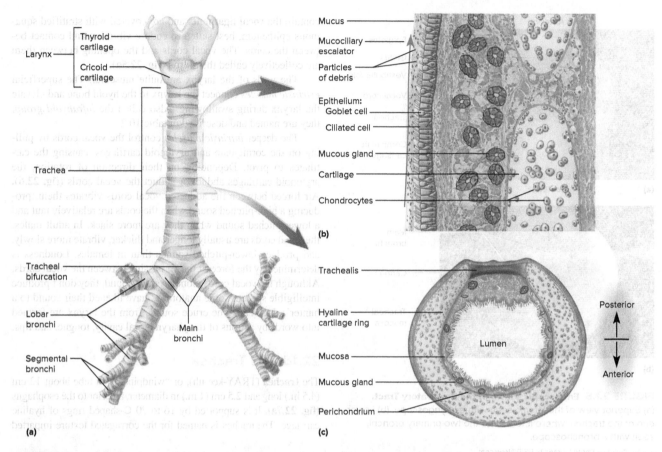

FIGURE 22.7 Anatomy of the Lower Respiratory Tract. (a) Anterior view. (b) Longitudinal section of the trachea showing the action of the mucociliary escalator. (c) Cross section of the trachea showing the C-shaped tracheal cartilage. **APR**

 Why do inhaled objects more often go into the right main bronchus than into the left?

by these rings;[10] you should be able to palpate a few of these between your larynx and sternum. Like the wire spiral in a vacuum cleaner hose, the cartilage rings reinforce the trachea and keep it from collapsing when you inhale. The open part of the C faces posteriorly, where it is spanned by a smooth muscle, the **trachealis (fig. 22.7c).** The gap in the C allows room for the esophagus to expand as swallowed food passes by. The trachealis contracts or relaxes to adjust airflow.

The inner lining of the trachea is a pseudostratified columnar epithelium composed mainly of mucus-secreting goblet cells, ciliated cells, and short basal stem cells **(figs. 22.7b, 22.8).** The mucus traps inhaled particles and the upward beating of the cilia drives the debris-laden mucus toward the pharynx, where it is swallowed. This mechanism of debris removal is called the **mucociliary escalator.**

The connective tissue beneath the tracheal epithelium contains lymphatic nodules, mucous and serous glands, and the tracheal cartilages. The outermost layer of the trachea, called the **adventitia,** is fibrous connective tissue that blends into the adventitia of other organs of the mediastinum, especially the esophagus.

---

[10]*trache* = rough

DEEPER INSIGHT 22.1

CLINICAL APPLICATION

Tracheotomy

The functional importance of the nasal cavity becomes especially obvious when it is bypassed. If the upper airway is obstructed, it may be necessary to make a temporary opening in the trachea inferior to the larynx and insert a tube to allow airflow—a procedure called *tracheotomy.* (A permanent opening is called a *tracheostomy.*) Lifesaving tracheotomies are performed hundreds of times per day in the United States alone. They prevent asphyxiation, but the inhaled air bypasses the nasal cavity and thus is not humidified. If the opening is left for long, the mucous membranes of the respiratory tract dry out and become encrusted, interfering with the clearance of mucus from the tract and promoting infection. When a patient is on a ventilator and air is introduced directly into the trachea *(intubation)*, the air must be filtered and humidified by the apparatus to prevent respiratory tract damage.

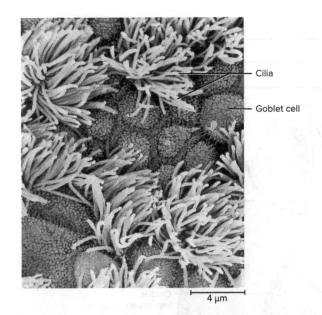

Cilia

Goblet cell

4 µm

FIGURE 22.8 The Tracheal Epithelium Showing Ciliated Cells and Nonciliated Goblet Cells (SEM). The small bumps on the goblet cells are microvilli.

Prof. P.M. Motta/Univ. "La Sapienza," Rome/Science Source

? *What is the function of the goblet cells?*

At the level of the sternal angle, the trachea ends at a fork called the *tracheal bifurcation,* where it gives off the right and left *main bronchi.* The lowermost tracheal cartilage has an internal median ridge called the **carina**[11] (ca-RY-na) that directs the airflow to the right and left **(fig. 22.5b).**

22.1e The Lungs and Bronchial Tree

Each **lung** is a somewhat conical organ with a broad, concave **base** resting on the diaphragm and a blunt peak called the **apex** projecting slightly above the clavicle **(fig. 22.9).** The broad **costal surface** is pressed against the rib cage, and the smaller concave **mediastinal surface** faces medially. The mediastinal surface exhibits a slit called the **hilum** through which the lung receives the main bronchus, blood vessels, lymphatics, and nerves. These structures constitute the **root** of the lung.

The lungs are crowded by adjacent organs and neither fill the entire rib cage, nor are they symmetrical **(fig. 22.10).** Inferior to the lungs and diaphragm, much of the space within the rib cage is occupied by the liver, spleen, and stomach (see fig. B.5 in atlas B). The right lung is shorter than the left because the liver rises higher on the right. The left lung, although taller, is narrower than the right because the heart tilts toward the left and occupies more space on this side of the mediastinum. On the medial surface, the left lung has an indentation called the **cardiac impression** where

the heart presses against it; part of this is visible anteriorly as a crescent-shaped **cardiac notch** in the margin of the lung. The right lung has three lobes—**superior, middle,** and **inferior.** A deep groove called the **horizontal fissure** separates the superior and middle lobes, and a similar **oblique fissure** separates the middle and inferior lobes. The left lung has only a **superior** and **inferior lobe** and a single oblique fissure.

The Bronchial Tree

Each lung has a branching system of air tubes called the **bronchial tree,** extending from the main bronchus to about 65,000 *terminal bronchioles.* Arising from the fork in the trachea, the **right main (primary) bronchus** (BRON-cus) is 2 to 3 cm long. It is slightly wider and more vertical than the left one; consequently, *aspirated* (inhaled) foreign objects lodge in the right bronchus more often than in the left. The right main bronchus gives off three branches—the **superior, middle,** and **inferior lobar (secondary) bronchi**—one to each lobe of the lung. The **left main bronchus** is about 5 cm long and slightly narrower and more horizontal than the right. It gives off superior and inferior lobar bronchi to the two lobes of the left lung.

In both lungs, the lobar bronchi branch into **segmental (tertiary) bronchi.** There are 10 of these in the right lung and 8 in the left. Each one ventilates a functionally independent unit of lung tissue called a **bronchopulmonary segment.** This chapter's opening photo shows a cast of the bronchial trees made by the corrosion cast technique described in chapter 3, with each bronchopulmonary segment injected with a different color of resin.

The main bronchi are supported, like the trachea, by rings of hyaline cartilage, whereas the cartilages transition to overlapping crescent-shaped plates by the time we reach the lobar and segmental bronchi. All of the bronchi are lined with ciliated pseudostratified columnar epithelium, but the cells grow shorter and the epithelium thinner as we progress distally. The lamina propria has an abundance of mucous glands and lymphatic nodules (*mucosa-associated lymphatic tissue, MALT),* favorably positioned to intercept inhaled pathogens. All divisions of the bronchial tree have a substantial amount of elastic connective tissue, which contributes to the recoil that expels air from the lungs in each respiratory cycle. The mucosa also has a well-developed layer of smooth muscle, the *muscularis mucosae,* which contracts or relaxes to constrict or dilate the airway, thus regulating airflow.

Bronchioles (BRON-kee-olz) are continuations of the airway that lack supportive cartilage and are 1 mm or less in diameter. The portion of the lung ventilated by one bronchiole is called a **pulmonary lobule.** Bronchioles have a ciliated cuboidal epithelium and a well-developed layer of smooth muscle in their walls. Spasmodic contractions of this muscle at death cause the bronchioles to exhibit a wavy lumen in most histological sections.

Each bronchiole divides into 50 to 80 **terminal bronchioles,** the final branches of the conducting zone **(fig. 22.11).** These measure 0.5 mm or less in diameter and have no mucous glands or goblet cells. They do have cilia, however, so that mucus draining into them from the more proximal air passages can be driven back by the mucociliary escalator, preventing congestion of the terminal bronchioles and alveoli.

[11]*carina* = keel

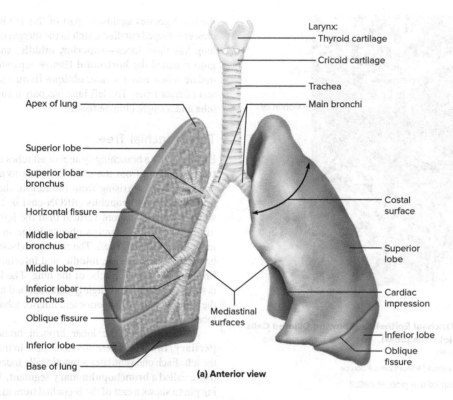

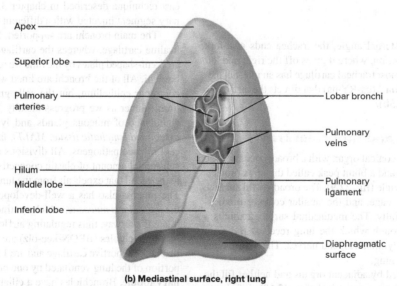

FIGURE 22.9 Gross Anatomy of the Lungs. (a) Anterior view, with frontal section through right lung. (b) Mediastinal surface of right lung, showing hilum. **APR**

Each terminal bronchiole gives off two or more smaller **respiratory bronchioles,** which have alveoli budding from their walls. They are considered the beginning of the respiratory zone because their alveoli participate in gas exchange. Their walls have scanty smooth muscle, and the smallest of them are nonciliated. Each respiratory bronchiole divides into 2 to 10 elongated, thin-walled passages called **alveolar ducts,** which also have alveoli along their walls. The alveolar ducts and smaller divisions have nonciliated simple squamous epithelia. The ducts end in **alveolar sacs,** which are clusters of alveoli arrayed around a central space called the **atrium.** The distinction between an alveolar duct and atrium is their shape—an elongated duct, or an atrium with about equal length and width. It is often a subjective judgment whether to regard a space as an alveolar duct or atrium.

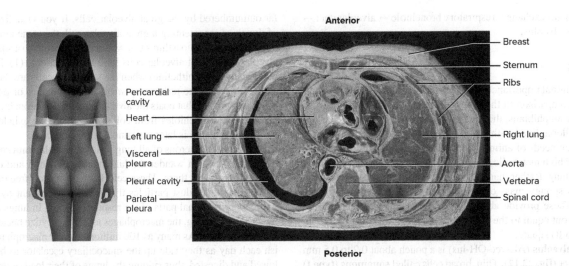

FIGURE 22.10 Cross Section Through the Thoracic Cavity. This photograph is oriented the same way as the reader's body. The pleural cavity is especially evident where the left lung has shrunken away from the thoracic wall, but in a living person the lung fully fills this space, the parietal and visceral pleurae are pressed together, and the pleural cavity is only a potential space between the membranes, as on the right side of this photograph.

Rebecca Gray/Don Kincaid/McGraw-Hill Education

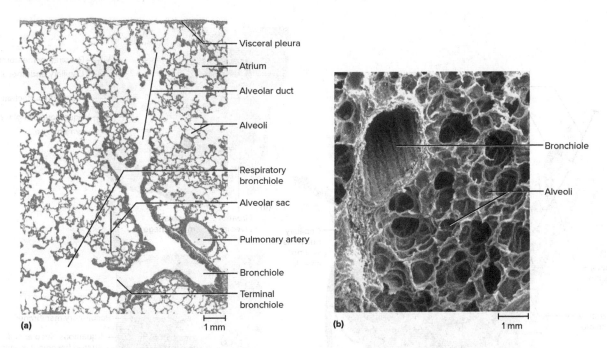

FIGURE 22.11 Histology of the Lung. (a) Light micrograph. (b) Scanning electron micrograph. Note the spongy texture of the lung.

a: MICROSCAPE/Science Source; **b:** Biophoto Associates/Science Source

Branches of the *pulmonary artery* closely follow the bronchial tree on their way to the alveoli. The *bronchial arteries* service the bronchi, bronchioles, and some other pulmonary and thoracic tissues (see section 20.7d); they don't extend to the alveoli.

In summary, the path of airflow is as follows. The first several passages belong to the conducting zone, where there are no alveoli and the tissue walls are too thick for any significant exchange of oxygen or carbon dioxide with the blood: nasal cavity → pharynx → trachea → main bronchus → lobar bronchus → segmental bronchus → bronchiole → terminal bronchiole. Then begins the respiratory zone, where all of the passages have alveoli along their walls (or are themselves alveoli) and thus engage in gas exchange: respiratory bronchiole → alveolar duct → atrium → alveolus.

Alveoli

The functional importance of human lung structure is best appreciated by comparison to the lungs of a few other animals. In frogs and other amphibians, the lung is a simple hollow sac, like an inflated balloon, lined with blood vessels. This is sufficient to meet the oxygen needs of animals with low metabolic rates. Mammals, with their high metabolic rates, could never have evolved with such a simple lung. Rather than consisting of one large sac, each human lung is a spongy mass composed of 150 million little sacs, the alveoli. These provide about 70 m² of gas-exchange surface per lung—about equal to the floor area of a handball court or a room 8.4 m (25 ft) square.

An **alveolus** (AL-vee-OH-lus) is a pouch about 0.2 to 0.5 mm in diameter **(fig. 22.12).** Thin, broad cells called **squamous (type I) alveolar cells** cover about 95% of the alveolar surface area. Their thinness allows for rapid gas diffusion between the air and blood. The other 5% is covered by round to cuboidal **great (type II) alveolar cells.** Squamous alveolar cells cover so much more surface area because they're so thin and spread out, even though they're far outnumbered by the great alveolar cells. If you visualize a ball of dough as representing a great alveolar cell, the same amount of dough rolled out into a thin sheet would be analogous to a squamous alveolar cell. Great alveolar cells have two functions: (1) They repair the alveolar epithelium when the squamous cells are damaged; and (2) they secrete *pulmonary surfactant,* a mixture of phospholipids and protein that coats the alveoli and smallest bronchioles and prevents the bronchioles from collapsing when one exhales. This surfactant function is later explained in greater detail.

The most numerous of all lung cells are **alveolar macrophages (dust cells),** which wander the lumens of the alveoli and connective tissue between them. These cells keep the alveoli free of debris by phagocytizing dust particles that escape entrapment by mucus in the more proximal parts of the respiratory tract. In lungs that are infected or bleeding, the macrophages also phagocytize bacteria and loose blood cells. As many as 100 million alveolar macrophages perish each day as they ride up the mucociliary escalator to be swallowed and digested, thus ridding the lungs of their load of debris.

Each alveolus is surrounded by a web of blood capillaries supplied by small branches of the pulmonary artery. The barrier between the alveolar air and blood, called the **respiratory membrane,** consists only of the squamous alveolar cell, the squamous endothelial cell of the capillary, and their shared basement

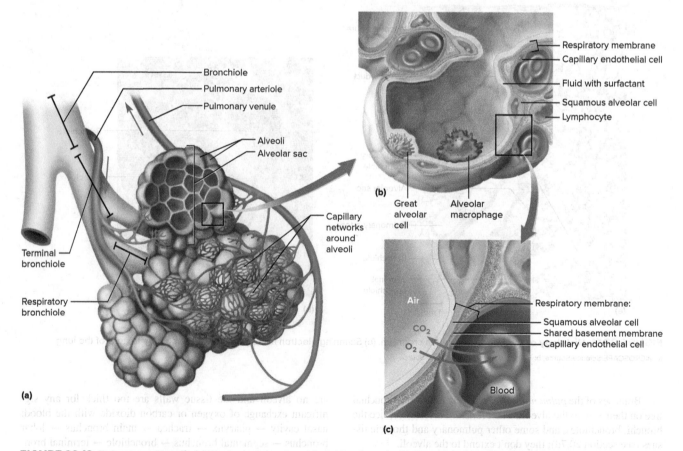

FIGURE 22.12 Pulmonary Alveoli. (a) Clusters of alveoli and their blood supply. (b) Structure of an alveolus. (c) Structure of the respiratory membrane.

membrane. These have a total thickness of only 0.5 μm, just 1/15 the diameter of a single erythrocyte.

It is crucial to prevent fluid from accumulating in the alveoli, because gases diffuse too slowly through liquid to sufficiently aerate the blood. Except for a thin film of moisture on the alveolar wall, the alveoli are kept dry by the absorption of excess water by the blood capillaries. The mean blood pressure in these capillaries is only 10 mm Hg compared to 30 mm Hg at the arterial end of the average capillary elsewhere. This low blood pressure is greatly over-ridden by the oncotic pressure that retains fluid in the capillaries (see the principles of capillary fluid exchange in section 20.3), so the osmotic uptake of water overrides filtration and keeps the alveoli free of excess fluid. The low capillary blood pressure also prevents rupture of the delicate respiratory membrane. The lungs also have a more extensive lymphatic drainage than any other organ in the body.

22.1f The Pleurae

A serous membrane, the **pleura** (PLOOR-uh), lines the thoracic wall and forms the surface of the lung. It has two layers, visceral and parietal. The **visceral pleura** forms the surface of the lung and extends even into the fissures between the lobes. At the hilum, it turns back on itself and forms the **parietal pleura,** which adheres to the mediastinum, inner surface of the rib cage, and superior sur-face of the diaphragm (see fig. 22.10). An extension of the parietal pleura, the *pulmonary ligament,* connects it to the diaphragm.

The space between the parietal and visceral pleurae is called the **pleural cavity.** The pleural cavity doesn't *contain* the lung; rather, it wraps around the lung, much like the pericardium wraps around the heart. The pleural cavity contains nothing but a thin film of lubricating **pleural fluid;** the cavity is only a *potential space,* meaning there is normally no room between the membranes. How-ever, under pathological conditions such as chest wounds or seep-age of fluid into the space *(pleural effusion)*, the pleural cavity can fill with air or liquid, as discussed later in this chapter.

The pleurae and pleural fluid have three functions:

1. **Reduction of friction.** Pleural fluid acts as a lubricant that enables the lungs to expand and contract with minimal fric-tion. Infection of the pleurae can produce a condition called *pleurisy,* in which the pleurae roughen and rub together, making each breath a painful experience.

2. **Creation of a pressure gradient.** The pleurae play a role, explained later, in the creation of a pressure gradient that expands the lungs when one inhales.

3. **Compartmentalization.** The pleurae, mediastinum, and pericardium compartmentalize the thoracic organs and prevent infections of one organ from spreading easily to neighboring organs.

BEFORE YOU GO ON

Answer the following questions to test your understanding of the preceding section:

1. A dust particle is inhaled and gets into an alveolus without being trapped along the way. Describe the path it takes,

naming all air passages from external naris to alveolus. What would happen to it after arrival in the alveolus?

2. Describe the histology of the epithelium and lamina propria of the nasal cavity and the functions of the cell types present.

3. Palpate two of your laryngeal cartilages and name them. Name the ones that cannot be palpated on a living person.

4. Describe the roles of the intrinsic muscles, corniculate cartilages, and arytenoid cartilages in speech.

5. Contrast the epithelium of the bronchioles with that of the alveoli and explain how the structural difference is related to their functional difference.

6. Explain why it is fallacious to say, as some sources do, that the lungs are contained in the pleural cavities.

22.2 Pulmonary Ventilation

Expected Learning Outcomes

When you have completed this section, you should be able to

a. name the muscles of respiration and describe their roles in breathing;

b. describe the brainstem centers that control breathing and the inputs they receive from other levels of the nervous system;

c. explain how pressure gradients account for the flow of air into and out of the lungs, and how those gradients are produced;

d. identify the sources of resistance to airflow and discuss their relevance to respiration;

e. explain the significance of anatomical dead space to alveolar ventilation;

f. define the clinical measurements of pulmonary volume and capacity; and

g. define terms for various deviations from the normal pattern of breathing.

With the foregoing anatomical background, our next objective is to understand how the lungs are ventilated. Breathing, or pulmonary ventilation, consists of a repetitive cycle of **inspiration** (inhaling) and **expiration** (exhaling). One complete breath, in and out, is called a **respiratory cycle.**

We must distinguish at times between quiet and forced respira-tion. **Quiet respiration** refers to relaxed, unconscious, automatic breathing, the way one would breathe when reading a book or lis-tening to a class lecture and not thinking about breathing. **Forced respiration** means unusually deep or rapid breathing, as in a state of exercise or when singing, playing a wind instrument, blowing up a balloon, coughing, or sneezing.

The lungs don't ventilate themselves. The only muscle they contain is smooth muscle in the walls of the bronchi and bronchi-oles. This muscle adjusts the diameter of the airway and affects the speed of airflow, but it doesn't create the airflow. That job belongs to the skeletal muscles of the trunk.

Air, like other fluids, flows down a pressure gradient from a point of higher pressure to one of lower pressure. Recall the syringe analogy (see fig. 19.18), in which we saw how an increase in the volume of a space reduces its pressure and results in an inflow of fluid. The action of the respiratory muscles is much like that of the syringe plunger—at one moment, to increase the volume and lower the pressure in the thoracic cavity, so air flows in; at the next moment, to reduce thoracic volume and raise pressure, so air flows out. We will next examine these muscular actions, how the nervous system controls them, and how the variables of pressure and resistance affect airflow and pulmonary ventilation.

22.2a The Respiratory Muscles

The principal muscles of respiration are the diaphragm and intercostal muscles **(fig. 22.13).** The diaphragm is the prime mover (see table 10.4); it alone produces about two-thirds of the pulmonary

airflow. When relaxed, it bulges upward to its farthest extent, pressing against the base of the lungs. The lungs are at their minimum volume. When the diaphragm contracts, it tenses and flattens somewhat, dropping about 1.5 cm in relaxed inspiration and as much as 12 cm in deep breathing. Not only does its descent enlarge the superior-to-inferior dimension of the thoracic cage, but its flattening also pushes outward on the sternum and ribs and enlarges the anterior-to-posterior dimension. Enlargement of the thoracic cavity lowers its internal pressure and produces an inflow of air. When the diaphragm relaxes, it bulges upward again, compresses the lungs, and expels air.

Several other muscles aid the diaphragm as synergists. Chief among these are the internal and external intercostal muscles between the ribs. Their primary function is to stiffen the thoracic cage during respiration and prevent it from collapsing when the diaphragm descends. However, they also contribute to enlargement and contraction of the thoracic cage and add about one-third of the air that ventilates the lungs. During quiet breathing, the scalene muscles of the neck fix ribs 1 and 2 (hold them stationary),

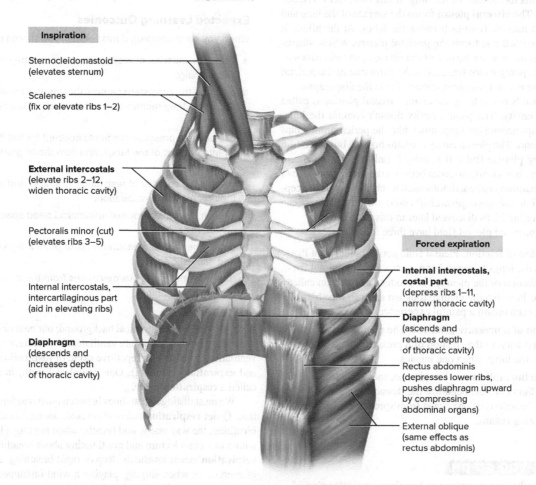

Inspiration

Sternocleidomastoid
(elevates sternum)

Scalenes
(fix or elevate ribs 1–2)

External intercostals
(elevate ribs 2–12,
widen thoracic cavity)

Pectoralis minor (cut)
(elevates ribs 3–5)

Internal intercostals,
intercartilaginous part
(aid in elevating ribs)

Diaphragm
(descends and
increases depth
of thoracic cavity)

Forced expiration

**Internal intercostals,
costal part**
(depress ribs 1–11,
narrow thoracic cavity)

Diaphragm
(ascends and
reduces depth
of thoracic cavity)

Rectus abdominis
(depresses lower ribs,
pushes diaphragm upward
by compressing
abdominal organs)

External oblique
(same effects as
rectus abdominis)

FIGURE 22.13 The Respiratory Muscles. Boldface indicates the principal respiratory muscles; the others are accessory. Arrows indicate the direction of muscle action. Muscles listed on the left are active during inspiration and those on the right are active during forced expiration. Note that the diaphragm is active in both phases, and different parts of the internal intercostal muscles serve for inspiration and expiration. Some other accessory muscles not shown here are discussed in the text.

while the external intercostal muscles pull the other ribs upward. Since most ribs are anchored at both ends—by their attachment to the vertebral column at the proximal (posterior) end and their attachment through the costal cartilage to the sternum at the distal (anterior) end—they swing upward like the handles on a bucket and thrust the sternum forward. These actions increase both the transverse (left to right) and anteroposterior diameters of the chest. In deep breathing, the anteroposterior dimension can increase as much as 20% as the chest swells.

Other muscles of the chest and abdomen also aid in breathing, especially during forced respiration; thus they are considered *accessory muscles* of respiration. Deep inspiration is aided by the erector spinae, which arches the back and increases chest diameter, and by several muscles that elevate the upper ribs: the sternocleidomastoids and scalenes of the neck; the pectoralis minor, pectoralis major, serratus anterior, and serratus posterior superior of the chest; and the *intercartilaginous part* of the internal intercostals (the anterior part between the costal cartilages). Although the scalenes merely fix the upper ribs during quiet respiration, they elevate them during forced inspiration.

Normal expiration is an energy-saving passive process achieved by the elasticity of the lungs and thoracic cage. The bronchial tree, the attachments of the ribs to the spine and sternum, and the tendons of the diaphragm and other respiratory muscles spring back when the muscles relax. As these structures recoil, the thoracic cage diminishes in size, the air pressure in the lungs rises above the atmospheric pressure outside, and the air flows out. The only muscular effort involved in normal expiration is a braking action—that is, the muscles relax gradually rather than abruptly, thus preventing the lungs from recoiling too suddenly. This makes the transition from inspiration to expiration smoother.

In forced expiration, the rectus abdominis pulls down on the sternum and lower ribs, while the *interosseous part* of the internal intercostals (the lateral part between the ribs proper) and the serratus posterior inferior pull the other ribs downward. These actions reduce the chest dimensions and expel air more rapidly and thoroughly than usual. Other lumbar, abdominal, and even pelvic muscles contribute to forced expiration by raising the pressure in the abdominal cavity and pushing some of the viscera, such as the stomach and liver, up against the diaphragm. This increases the pressure in the thoracic cavity and thus helps to expel air. Such "abdominal breathing" is particularly important in singing and public speaking.

Not only does abdominal pressure affect thoracic pressure, but the opposite is also true. Depression of the diaphragm raises abdominal pressure and helps to expel the contents of certain abdominal organs, thus aiding in childbirth, urination, defecation, and vomiting. During such actions, we often consciously or unconsciously employ the **Valsalva**[12] **maneuver.** This consists of taking a deep breath, holding it by closing the glottis, and then contracting the abdominal muscles to raise abdominal pressure and push the organ contents out.

---

[12]Antonio Maria Valsalva (1666–1723), Italian anatomist

22.2b Neural Control of Breathing

The heartbeat and breathing are the two most conspicuously rhythmic processes in the body. The heart, we have seen, has an internal pacemaker, but the lungs do not. No autorhythmic pacemaker cells for respiration have been found that are analogous to those of the heart, and the exact mechanism for setting the rhythm of respiration remains obscure. But we do know that breathing depends on repetitive stimuli from the brain. It ceases if the nerve connections to the thoracic muscles are severed or if the spinal cord is severed high on the neck. There are two reasons for this dependence on the brain: (1) Skeletal muscles, unlike cardiac muscle, can't contract without nervous stimulation. (2) Breathing involves the well-orchestrated action of multiple muscles and thus requires a central coordinating mechanism.

Breathing is controlled at two levels of the brain. One is cerebral and conscious, enabling us to inhale or exhale at will. The other is unconscious and automatic. Most of the time, we breathe without thinking about it—fortunately, for we otherwise couldn't go to sleep without fear of respiratory arrest (see Deeper Insight 22.2).

Brainstem Respiratory Centers

The automatic, unconscious cycle of breathing is controlled by three pairs of respiratory centers in the reticular formation of the medulla oblongata and pons **(fig. 22.14).** There is one of each on the right and left sides of the brainstem; the two sides communicate with each other so that the respiratory muscles contract symmetrically.

1. The **ventral respiratory group (VRG)** is the primary generator of the respiratory rhythm. It is an elongated neural network in the medulla with two commingled webs of neurons—**inspiratory (I) neurons** and **expiratory (E) neurons**—each forming a reverberating neural circuit (see fig. 12.32). In quiet breathing (called *eupnea*), the I neuron circuit fires for about 2 seconds at a time, issuing nerve signals to integrating centers in the spinal cord. The spinal centers relay signals by way of the phrenic nerves to the diaphragm and by way of intercostal nerves to the external intercostal muscles. Contraction of these muscles enlarges the thoracic cage and causes inspiration. As long as the I neurons are firing, they also inhibit the E neurons. Eventually, however, the I neurons stop firing, either because of fatigue or because they're inhibited by signals from an outside source. As their activity wanes, the E neurons begin firing. They further inhibit the I neurons, allowing the inspiratory muscles to relax. Elastic recoil of the thoracic cage expels air from the lungs. Relaxed expiration normally lasts about 3 seconds. Then the E neuron activity wanes, the I neurons resume firing, and the cycle repeats itself. In eupnea, this oscillating pattern of neural activity, alternating between the I neuron and E neuron circuits, produces a respiratory rhythm of about 12 breaths per minute.

2. The **dorsal respiratory group (DRG)** is one of the mechanisms that modifies this basic respiratory rhythm. It is a web of neurons that extends for much of the length of the medulla between the VRG and the central canal of the brainstem. Obviously, we don't always breathe at the same rate. Breathing can be faster or slower, shallower or deeper, as the DRG and other mechanisms modulate the VRG's activity. The DRG is an integrating center that receives input from several sources detailed in the coming discussion: a respiratory center in the pons (the PNG discussed next); a chemosensitive center of the anterior medulla oblongata; chemoreceptors in certain major arteries; stretch and irritant receptors in the airway; and higher brainstem centers that allow for emotional influences on breathing. The DRG issues output to the VRG that modifies the respiratory rhythm to adapt to varying conditions.

3. The **pontine respiratory group (PRG)** on each side of the pons receives input from higher brain centers including the hypothalamus, limbic system, and cerebral cortex, and issues output to both the DRG and VRG. By acting on those centers in the medulla, it hastens or delays the transition from inspiration to expiration, making each breath shorter and shallower, or longer and deeper. The PRG adapts breathing to special circumstances such as sleep, exercise, vocalization, and emotional responses (for example, in crying, gasping, or laughing).

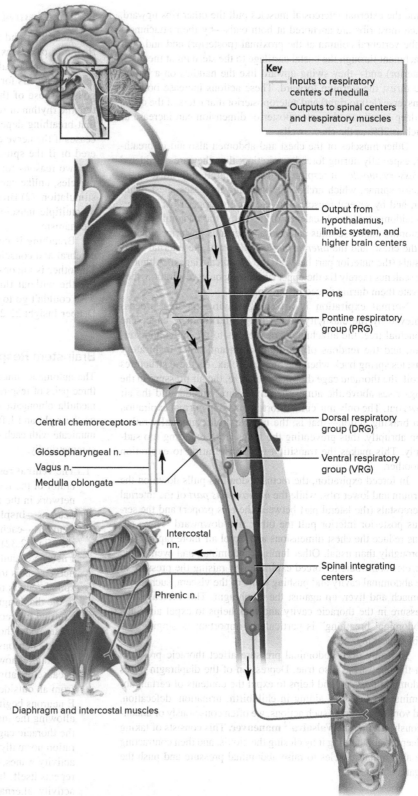

Key
— Inputs to respiratory centers of medulla
— Outputs to spinal centers and respiratory muscles

Output from hypothalamus, limbic system, and higher brain centers

Pons

Pontine respiratory group (PRG)

Central chemoreceptors

Glossopharyngeal n.

Vagus n.

Medulla oblongata

Dorsal respiratory group (DRG)

Ventral respiratory group (VRG)

Intercostal nn.

Spinal integrating centers

Phrenic n.

Diaphragm and intercostal muscles

Accessory muscles of respiration

FIGURE 22.14 Respiratory Control Centers in the Central Nervous System. See text for explanation of these centers and control pathways.

DEEPER INSIGHT 22.2

CLINICAL APPLICATION

Ondine's Curse

In German legend, there was a water nymph named Ondine who took a mortal lover. When her lover proved unfaithful, the king of the nymphs put a curse on him that took away his automatic physiological functions. Consequently, he had to remember to take each breath, and he couldn't go to sleep or he would die of suffocation—which, as exhaustion overtook him, was indeed his fate.

Some people suffer a disorder called *Ondine's curse,* in which the automatic respiratory functions are disabled. This can result from accidents of neurosurgery, brainstem damage from polio, or mutation of a gene that codes for chemoreceptors in the medulla oblongata and blunts the response to CO_2 accumulation. Victims of Ondine's curse must remember to take each breath and can't go to sleep without the aid of a mechanical ventilator.

▶▶▶ **APPLY WHAT YOU KNOW**

Some authorities refer to the respiratory rhythm as an autonomic function. Discuss whether you think this is an appropriate word for it. What are the effectors of the autonomic nervous system? (See chapter 15.) What are the effectors that ventilate the lungs? What bearing might this have on the question?

Central and Peripheral Input to the Respiratory Centers

Variations in the respiratory rhythm are possible because the respiratory centers of the medulla and pons receive input from several other levels of the nervous system and therefore respond to the body's varying physiological needs. For example, anxiety can trigger a bout of uncontrollable *hyperventilation* in some people, a state in which breathing is so rapid that it expels CO_2 from the body faster than it's produced. As blood CO_2 levels drop, the pH rises and causes the cerebral arteries to constrict. This reduces cerebral perfusion and may cause dizziness or fainting. Hyperventilation can be brought under control by having a person rebreathe the expired CO_2 from a paper bag held over the nose and mouth.

Multiple sensory receptors also provide information to the respiratory centers:

- **Central chemoreceptors** are brainstem neurons that respond especially to changes in the pH of the cerebrospinal fluid. They are concentrated on each side of the medulla oblongata at a point only 0.2 mm beneath its anterior surface. The pH of the CSF reflects the CO_2 level in the blood, so by regulating respiration to maintain a stable CSF pH, the respiratory centers also ensure a stable blood CO_2 level.

- **Peripheral chemoreceptors** are located in the carotid and aortic bodies of the large arteries above the heart **(fig. 22.15).** They respond to the O_2 and CO_2 content of the blood, but most of all to pH. The carotid bodies communicate with the

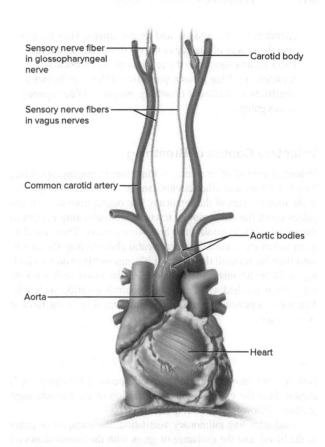

FIGURE 22.15 The Peripheral Chemoreceptors of Respiration. Peripheral chemoreceptors in the aortic arch and carotid bodies monitor blood gas concentrations and blood pH. They send signals about blood chemistry to the dorsal respiratory group of the medulla oblongata through sensory fibers in the vagus and glossopharyngeal nerves.

brainstem by way of the glossopharyngeal nerves, and the aortic bodies by way of the vagus nerves. Sensory fibers in these nerves enter the medulla and synapse with neurons of the DRG.

- **Stretch receptors** are found in the smooth muscle of the bronchi and bronchioles and in the visceral pleura. They respond to inflation of the lungs and signal the DRG by way of the vagus nerves. Excessive inflation triggers the **inflation (Hering–Breuer)[13] reflex,** a protective somatic reflex that strongly inhibits the I neurons and stops inspiration. In infants, this may be a normal mechanism of transition from inspiration to expiration, but after infancy it is activated only by extreme stretching of the lungs.

- **Irritant receptors** are nerve endings amid the epithelial cells of the airway. They respond to smoke, dust, pollen,

[13]Heinrich Ewald Hering (1866–1948), German physiologist; Josef Breuer (1842–1925), Austrian physician

chemical fumes, cold air, and excess mucus. They transmit signals by way of the vagus nerves to the DRG, and the DRG returns signals to the respiratory and bronchial muscles, resulting in such protective reflexes as broncho-constriction, shallower breathing, breath-holding *(apnea),* or coughing.

Voluntary Control of Breathing

Voluntary control of breathing is important in singing, speaking, breath-holding, and other circumstances. Such control originates in the motor cortex of the cerebrum. The output neurons send impulses down the corticospinal tracts to the integrating centers in the spinal cord, bypassing the brainstem centers. There are limits to voluntary control. Temperamental children may threaten to hold their breath until they die, but it's impossible to do so. Holding one's breath raises the CO_2 level of the blood until a *breaking point* is reached when automatic controls override one's will. This forces a person to resume breathing even if he or she has lost consciousness.

22.2c Pressure, Resistance, and Airflow

Now that we know the neuromuscular aspects of breathing, we'll explore how the expansion and contraction of the thoracic cage produce airflow into and out of the lungs.

Understanding pulmonary ventilation, the transport of gases in the blood, and the exchange of gases with the tissues draws on certain *gas laws* of physics. These are named after their discoverers and are not intuitively easy to remember by name. **Table 22.1** lists them for your convenience and may be a helpful reference as you progress through respiratory physiology.

TABLE 22.1	The Gas Laws of Respiratory Physiology
Boyle's law[14]	The pressure of a given quantity of gas is inversely proportional to its volume (assuming a constant temperature).
Charles's law[15]	The volume of a given quantity of gas is directly proportional to its absolute temperature (assuming a constant pressure).
Dalton's law[16]	The total pressure of a gas mixture is equal to the sum of the partial pressures of its individual gases.
Henry's law[17]	At the air–water interface, the amount of gas that dissolves in water is determined by its solubility in water and its partial pressure in the air (assuming a constant temperature).

[14]Robert Boyle (1627–91), Anglo–Irish physicist and chemist
[15]Jacques A. C. Charles (1746–1823), French physicist
[16]John Dalton (1766–1844), English physicist and chemist
[17]William Henry (1774–1836), English chemist

Pressure and Airflow

Respiratory airflow is governed by the same principles of flow, pressure, and resistance as blood flow. As we saw in section 20.2, the flow (F) of a fluid is directly proportional to the pressure difference between two points (ΔP) and inversely proportional to resistance (R):

$$F \propto \Delta P/R.$$

For the moment, we'll focus especially on ΔP, the pressure gradient that produces airflow. We'll deal with resistance later.

The pressure that drives inspiration is **atmospheric (barometric) pressure**—the weight of the air above us. At sea level, this averages 760 mm Hg, or by definition, *1 atmosphere (1 atm)*. It fluctuates with the weather from day to day and is lower at higher elevations, but we'll use the average sea-level value as a reference point for discussion.

One way to change the pressure of an enclosed gas is to change the volume of its container. This fact is summarized by **Boyle's law:** Assuming a constant temperature, *the pressure of a given quantity of gas is inversely proportional to its volume.* If the lungs contain a quantity of gas and lung volume increases, their internal pressure (**intrapulmonary pressure**) falls. Conversely, if lung volume decreases, intrapulmonary pressure rises. (Compare this to the syringe analogy.)

If the intrapulmonary pressure falls below the atmospheric pressure, then air tends to flow down its pressure gradient into the lungs. Conversely, if intrapulmonary pressure rises above atmospheric pressure, air flows out. Therefore, all we have to do to breathe is to cyclically raise and lower the intrapulmonary pressure, employing the neuromuscular mechanisms recently described.

When dealing with respiratory airflow and thoracic pressures generated by the foregoing muscle actions, we must use a new unit of measurement, different from what you're accustomed to. In recent chapters, we used *millimeters of mercury (mm Hg)* as a measure of blood pressure, and we'll use it again later in this chapter when we speak of atmospheric pressure and blood gases. Millimeters of mercury is a measure of how high up a vacuum tube a force such as blood pressure or the weight of the atmosphere can push a column of mercury. Mercury is a very heavy liquid, so we use it because pressures can be measured with a relatively short column of mercury, as in the sphygmomanometer of a doctor's office. But the pressures in respiratory airflow are so small that they couldn't move a mercury column much at all; mercury-based instruments aren't sensitive enough. Respiratory physiologists therefore traditionally used water columns, which are more sensitive, and we measure these pressures in *centimeters of water (cm H_2O).* (1 mm Hg $\approx$ 13.6 mm H_2O $\approx$ 1.4 cm H_2O.) Small pressure changes will move a column of water more than a column of mercury; one can see them and measure them more accurately (although now they're measured with electronic instruments rather than water-filled tubes).

Since respiratory airflow is driven by a *difference* between surrounding (ambient) atmospheric pressure and pressures in the chest, the following discussion is based on *relative* pressures. If we speak of pressure in the pulmonary alveoli reaching −2 cm H_2O during inspiration, we mean it falls 2 cm H_2O below the ambient atmospheric pressure; if it rises to +3 cm H_2O during expiration, it is 3 cm H_2O above ambient atmospheric pressure.

Inspiration

Now consider the flow of air into the lungs—inspiration. **Figure 22.16** traces the events and pressure changes that occur throughout a respiratory cycle.

At the beginning (step ① in the figure), there is no movement of the thoracic cage, no difference between the air pressure within the lungs and the ambient atmospheric pressure, and no airflow. What happens when the thoracic cage expands? Why don't the lungs remain the same size and simply occupy less space in the chest? Consider the two layers of the pleura: the parietal pleura lining the rib cage and the visceral pleura on the lung surface. They aren't anatomically attached to each other along their surfaces, but they're wet and cling together like sheets of wet paper. The space between them (*pleural cavity*) is only about 10 to 30 μm wide (about the width of one typical cell). At the end of a normal expiration, the chest wall (including the parietal pleura) tends to expand outward because of its elasticity while the lungs, because of their elasticity, tend to recoil inward. Thus, the lungs and chest wall are pulling in opposite directions. This creates a negative **intrapleural pressure,** averaging about –5 cm H_2O, between the parietal and visceral pleurae.

When the ribs swing up and out during inspiration (step ② in the figure), the parietal pleura follows. If not for the cohesion of water, this could pull the chest wall away from the lungs; but because the two wet membranes cling to each other, it only reduces the intrapleural pressure a little more, to about –8 cm H_2O. As the visceral pleura (lung surface) is pulled outward, it stretches the alveoli just below the surface of the lung. Those alveoli are mechanically linked to deeper ones by their walls, and stretch the deeper ones as well. Thus the entire lung expands along with the thoracic cage. As in the syringe analogy, the alveoli increase in volume and decrease in pressure. Pressure within the alveoli, the **intrapulmonary (alveolar) pressure,** drops to an average of –1 cm H_2O. So now there is a pressure gradient from the ambient pressure at the nostrils to the negative pressure in the alveoli. Air flows down its gradient and ventilates the lungs. In short, we inhale.

Yet this isn't the only force that expands the lungs. Another is warming of the inhaled air. As we see from **Charles's law** (see table 22.1), the volume of a given quantity of gas is directly proportional to its absolute temperature. Inhaled air is warmed to 37°C (99°F) by the time it reaches the alveoli. This means that on a cool North American day when the outdoor temperature is, say, 16°C (60°F), the air temperature would increase by 21°C (39°F) during inspiration, becoming comparable to air temperature in the tropics. An inhaled volume of 500 mL will expand to 536 mL and this thermal expansion will contribute to inflation of the lungs.

When the respiratory muscles stop contracting, the inflowing air quickly achieves an intrapulmonary pressure equal to atmospheric pressure, and flow stops. In quiet breathing, the dimensions of the thoracic cage increase by only a few millimeters in each direction, but this is enough to increase its total volume by about 500 mL. Typically, about 500 mL of air therefore flows into the respiratory tract.

▶▶▶ **APPLY WHAT YOU KNOW**

When you inhale, does your chest expand because your lungs inflate, or do your lungs inflate because your chest expands? Explain.

Expiration

Relaxed expiration is a passive process achieved, as we have seen, mainly by the elastic recoil of the thoracic cage. This recoil compresses the lungs and raises the intrapulmonary pressure to about +1 cm H_2O (step ③ in the figure). Air thus flows down its pressure gradient, out of the lungs. In forced breathing, the accessory muscles raise intrapulmonary pressure as high as +40 cm H_2O.

The effect of pulmonary elasticity is evident in a pathological state of pneumothorax and atelectasis. **Pneumothorax** is the presence of air in the pleural cavity. If the thoracic wall is punctured between the ribs, for example, inspiration sucks air through the wound into the pleural cavity and the visceral and parietal pleurae separate; what was a *potential space* between them becomes an air-filled cavity. Without the negative intrapleural pressure to keep the lungs inflated, the lungs recoil and collapse. The collapse of part or all of a lung is called **atelectasis**[18] (AT-eh-LEC-ta-sis). Atelectasis can also result from airway obstruction—for example, by a lung tumor, aneurysm, swollen lymph node, or aspirated object. Blood absorbs gases from the alveoli distal to the obstruction, and that part of the lung collapses because it can't be reinflated.

Resistance to Airflow

Pressure is one determinant of airflow; the other is resistance. The greater the resistance, the slower the flow. But what governs resistance? Two factors are of particular importance: diameter of the bronchioles and pulmonary compliance.

Like arterioles, the large number of bronchioles, their small diameter, and their ability to change diameter make them the primary means of controlling resistance. The trachea and bronchi can also change diameter to a degree, but are more constrained by the supporting cartilages in their walls. An increase in the diameter of a bronchus or bronchiole is called **bronchodilation** (BRON-co-dy-LAY-shun) and a reduction in diameter is called **bronchoconstriction.** Epinephrine and the sympathetic nerves (norepinephrine) stimulate bronchodilation and increase airflow. Histamine, parasympathetic nerves (acetylcholine), cold air, and chemical irritants are among the factors that stimulate bronchoconstriction. Many people have suffocated from the extreme bronchoconstriction brought on by anaphylactic shock or asthma (see Deeper Insight 21.3).

[18]*atel* = imperfect, incomplete; *ectasis* = expansion

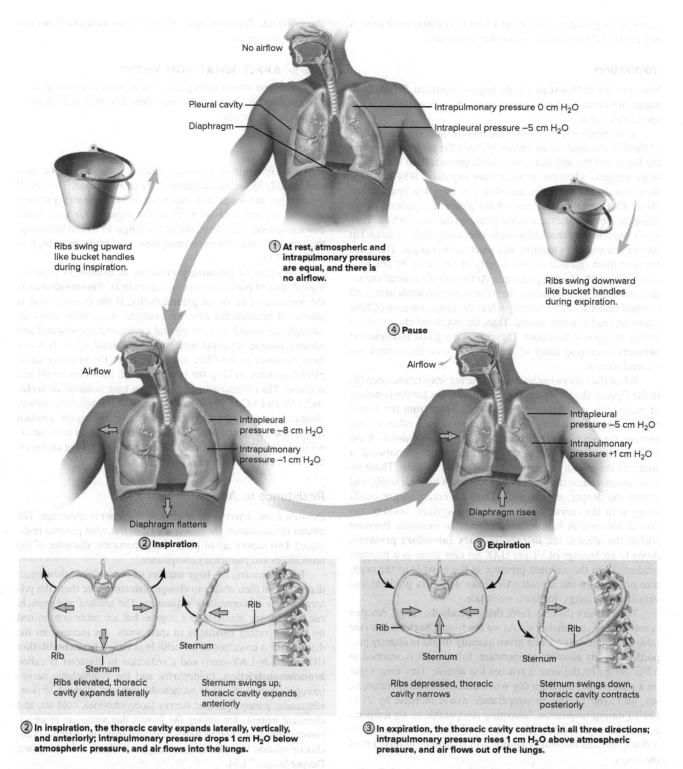

No airflow

Pleural cavity

Diaphragm

Intrapulmonary pressure 0 cm H$_2$O

Intrapleural pressure –5 cm H$_2$O

Ribs swing upward like bucket handles during inspiration.

① At rest, atmospheric and intrapulmonary pressures are equal, and there is no airflow.

Ribs swing downward like bucket handles during expiration.

④ Pause

Airflow

Airflow

Intrapleural pressure –8 cm H$_2$O

Intrapulmonary pressure –1 cm H$_2$O

Intrapleural pressure –5 cm H$_2$O

Intrapulmonary pressure +1 cm H$_2$O

Diaphragm flattens

② Inspiration

Diaphragm rises

③ Expiration

Rib

Sternum

Rib

Sternum

Ribs elevated, thoracic cavity expands laterally

Sternum swings up, thoracic cavity expands anteriorly

Rib

Sternum

Rib

Sternum

Ribs depressed, thoracic cavity narrows

Sternum swings down, thoracic cavity contracts posteriorly

② In inspiration, the thoracic cavity expands laterally, vertically, and anteriorly; intrapulmonary pressure drops 1 cm H$_2$O below atmospheric pressure, and air flows into the lungs.

③ In expiration, the thoracic cavity contracts in all three directions; intrapulmonary pressure rises 1 cm H$_2$O above atmospheric pressure, and air flows out of the lungs.

FIGURE 22.16 The Respiratory Cycle. All pressures given here are relative to atmospheric pressure external to the body, which is considered to be zero as a point of reference. Note that pressures governing respiratory airflow are measured in cm H$_2$O (centimeters of water), not mm Hg. Like bucket handles, each rib is attached at both ends (to the spine and sternum) and swings up and down during inspiration and expiration. **APR**

Pulmonary compliance means the ease with which the lungs expand, or more exactly, the change in lung volume relative to a given pressure change. Inspiratory effort may produce the same intrapleural pressure in two people, but the lungs will expand less in a person with poorer compliance (stiffer lungs), or at least that person must expend more effort to inflate the lungs to the same degree as the other. Think of the difference in effort it takes to blow up a brand-new party balloon (with low compliance) versus blowing up one that has been inflated before. Pulmonary compliance is reduced by degenerative lung diseases such as tuberculosis and black lung disease, in which the lungs are stiffened by scar tissue. In such conditions, the thoracic cage expands normally but the lungs expand relatively little.

A major limitation on pulmonary compliance is the thin film of water on the respiratory epithelium, especially from the respiratory bronchioles to the alveoli. This film is necessary for gas exchange, but creates a potential problem for pulmonary ventilation. Water molecules are attracted to each other by hydrogen bonds, creating surface tension, as we saw in section 2.2a. You can appreciate the strength of this attraction if you reflect on the difficulty of separating two sheets of wet paper compared with two sheets of dry paper. Surface tension draws the walls of the airway inward toward the lumen. If it went unchecked, parts of the airway would collapse with each expiration and would strongly resist reinflation. This is especially so in small airways such as the respiratory bronchioles and alveolar ducts leading to the alveoli.

The solution to this problem takes us back to the great alveolar cells and their surfactant. A surfactant is an agent that disrupts the hydrogen bonds of water and reduces surface tension; soaps and detergents are everyday examples. The pulmonary surfactant is composed of amphipathic proteins and phospholipids. These molecules are partially hydrophobic, so they spread out over the surface of the water film, partially embedded in it like ice cubes floating in a bowl of water. As the small airways deflate, the surfactants are squeezed closer together, like the ice cubes being pushed together into a smaller area. If the air spaces were covered with a film of water only, they could continue collapsing, because water molecules can pile up into a thicker film of moisture. The physical structure of the surfactants resists compression, however. They can't pile up into a thicker layer because their hydrophilic regions resist separation from the water below. As they become crowded into a small area and resist layering, they retard and then halt the collapse of the airway.

Deep breathing spreads pulmonary surfactant throughout the small airways. Patients recently out of surgery are encouraged to breathe deeply, even though it may hurt, in order to promote this spread of surfactant up the alveolar ducts and small bronchioles. Those who don't adhere to their breathing exercises can experience collapse of portions of the lung that are not adequately coated with surfactant.

The importance of this surfactant is especially apparent when it's lacking. Premature infants often have a surfactant deficiency and great difficulty breathing (see section 29.3b). The resulting *infant respiratory distress syndrome (IRDS)* can be treated by administering artificial surfactant.

22.2d Alveolar Ventilation

Air that actually enters the alveoli becomes available for gas exchange, but not all inhaled air gets that far. About 150 mL of it fills the conducting zone of the airway. Since this air cannot exchange gases with the blood, the conducting zone is called the **anatomical dead space.** The dead space is about 1 mL per pound of body weight in a healthy person. In some pulmonary diseases, however, it can be substantially greater. Some alveoli may be unable to exchange gases because they lack blood flow or because the pulmonary membrane is thickened by edema or fibrosis. **Physiological (total) dead space** is the sum of anatomical dead space and any pathological dead space that may exist.

The anatomical dead space varies with circumstances. In a state of relaxation, parasympathetic stimulation keeps the airway somewhat constricted. This minimizes the dead space so more of the inhaled air ventilates the alveoli. In a state of arousal or exercise, by contrast, the sympathetic nervous system dilates the airway, which increases airflow. The increased airflow outweighs the air that is wasted by filling the increased dead space.

If a person inhales 500 mL of air and 150 mL of it stays in the dead space, then 350 mL ventilates the alveoli. Multiplying this by the respiratory rate gives the **alveolar ventilation rate (AVR)**— for example,

$$350 \text{ mL/breath} \times 12 \text{ breaths/min.} = 4{,}200 \text{ mL/min.}$$

Of all measures of pulmonary ventilation, this one is most directly relevant to the body's ability to get oxygen to the tissues and dispose of carbon dioxide.

The air current taken in by inspiration never actually enters the alveoli. This *bulk flow* of air gets only as far as the terminal bronchioles. Beyond this point, the air passages are so narrow and their resistance to flow is so great that bulk flow ceases. Oxygen completes its journey to the alveoli, and carbon dioxide leaves them, by simple diffusion. Pulsation of the pulmonary arteries generated by the heartbeat probably compresses adjacent airways and accelerates this process, however.

The lungs never completely empty during expiration. There is always some leftover air called the *residual volume,* typically about 1,300 mL that one cannot exhale even with maximum effort. Residual air mixes with fresh air arriving on the next inspiration, so the same oxygen-depleted air doesn't remain in the lungs cycle after cycle. It takes about 90 seconds, or approximately 18 breaths at an average rate and depth of breathing, to completely replace all pulmonary air.

22.2e Measurement of Pulmonary Ventilation

Clinicians often measure a patient's pulmonary ventilation in order to assess the severity of a respiratory disease or monitor the patient's improvement or deterioration. The process of making such measurements is called **spirometry.**[19] It entails

---

[19]*spiro* = breath; *metry* = process of measuring

having the subject breathe into a device called a **spirometer** (**fig. 22.17a**), which recaptures the expired breath and records such variables as the rate and depth of breathing, speed of expiration, and rate of oxygen consumption. Representative measurements for a healthy adult male are given in **table 22.2** and explained in **figure 22.17b.** Female values are somewhat lower because of smaller average body size.

Four of these values are called *respiratory volumes:* tidal volume, inspiratory reserve volume, expiratory reserve volume, and residual volume. **Tidal volume (TV)** is the amount of air inhaled and exhaled in one cycle; in quiet breathing, it averages about 500 mL. Beyond the amount normally inhaled, it's typically possible to inhale another 3,000 mL with maximum effort; this is the **inspiratory reserve volume (IRV).** Similarly, with maximum

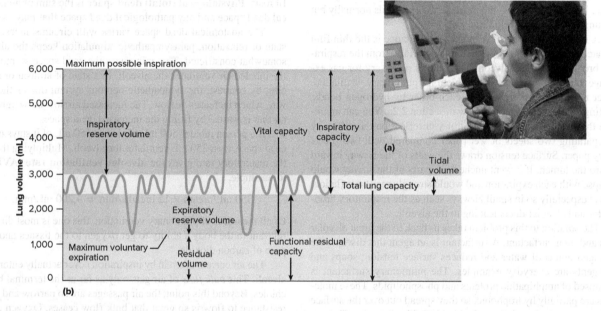

FIGURE 22.17 Respiratory Volumes and Capacities. (a) Subject breathing into a spirometer. (b) An idealized spirogram. The wavy line indicates inspiration when it rises and expiration when it falls. Compare with table 22.2.

a: BSIP/Science Source

? *Why is a nose clip necessary for obtaining a valid spirogram?*

TABLE 22.2	Respiratory Volumes and Capacities for an Average Young Adult Male	
Measurement	**Typical Value**	**Definition**
Respiratory Volumes		
Tidal volume (TV)	500 mL	Amount of air inhaled and exhaled in one cycle during quiet breathing
Inspiratory reserve volume (IRV)	3,000 mL	Amount of air in excess of tidal volume that can be inhaled with maximum effort
Expiratory reserve volume (ERV)	1,200 mL	Amount of air in excess of tidal volume that can be exhaled with maximum effort
Residual volume (RV)	1,300 mL	Amount of air remaining in the lungs after maximum expiration; the amount that can never be voluntarily exhaled
Respiratory Capacities		
Vital capacity (VC)	4,700 mL	The amount of air that can be inhaled and then exhaled with maximum effort; the deepest possible breath (VC = ERV + TV + IRV)
Inspiratory capacity (IC)	3,500 mL	Maximum amount of air that can be inhaled after a normal tidal expiration (IC = TV + IRV)
Functional residual capacity (FRC)	2,500 mL	Amount of air remaining in the lungs after a normal tidal expiration (FRC = RV + ERV)
Total lung capacity (TLC)	6,000 mL	Maximum amount of air the lungs can contain (TLC = RV + VC)

effort, one can normally exhale another 1,200 mL beyond the normal amount; this difference is the **expiratory reserve volume (ERV).** Even after a maximum voluntary expiration, there remains a **residual volume (RV)** of about 1,300 mL. This air allows gas exchange with the blood to continue even between the times one inhales fresh air.

Four other measurements, called *respiratory capacities,* are obtained by adding two or more of the respiratory volumes: **vital capacity (VC)** (ERV + TV + IRV), **inspiratory capacity** (TV + IRV), **functional residual capacity** (RV + ERV), and **total lung capacity** (RV + VC). Vital capacity, the maximum ability to ventilate the lungs in one breath, is an especially important measure of pulmonary health.

Spirometry helps to assess and distinguish between *restrictive* and *obstructive* lung disorders. **Restrictive disorders** are those that reduce pulmonary compliance, thus limiting the amount to which the lungs can be inflated. They show in spirometry as a reduced vital capacity. Any disease that produces pulmonary fibrosis has a restrictive effect: black lung disease and tuberculosis, for example. **Obstructive disorders** are those that interfere with airflow by narrowing or blocking the airway. They make it harder to inhale or exhale a given amount of air. Asthma and chronic bronchitis are the most common examples. Obstructive disorders can be measured by having the subject exhale as rapidly as possible into a spirometer and measuring **forced expiratory volume (FEV)**—the volume of air or the percentage of the vital capacity that can be exhaled in a given time interval. A healthy adult should be able to expel 75% to 85% of the vital capacity in 1.0 second (a value called the $FEV_{1.0}$). At home, asthma patients and others can monitor their respiratory function by blowing into a handheld meter that roughly measures **peak flow,** the maximum speed of expiration.

The amount of air inhaled per minute is the **minute respiratory volume (MRV).** MRV largely determines the alveolar ventilation rate. It can be measured directly with a spirometer or obtained by multiplying tidal volume by respiratory rate. For example, if a person has a tidal volume of 500 mL per breath and a rate of 12 breaths per minute, the MRV would be $500 \times 12 = 6,000$ mL/min. During heavy exercise, MRV may be as high as 125 to 170 L/min. This is called **maximum voluntary ventilation (MVV),** formerly called *maximum breathing capacity.*

22.2f Variations in the Respiratory Rhythm

Relaxed, quiet breathing is called **eupnea**[20] (YOOP-nee-uh). It is typically characterized by a tidal volume of about 500 mL and a respiratory rate of 12 to 15 breaths per minute. Conditions ranging from exercise or anxiety to various disease states can cause deviations such as abnormally fast, slow, or labored breathing. **Table 22.3** defines the clinical terms for several such variations. You should familiarize yourself with these before proceeding, because later discussions in this chapter assume a working knowledge of some of these terms.

TABLE 22.3	Variations in the Respiratory Rhythm
Apnea[21] (AP-nee-uh)	Temporary cessation of breathing (one or more skipped breaths)
Dyspnea[22] (DISP-nee-uh)	Labored, gasping breathing; shortness of breath
Hyperpnea[23] (HY-purp-NEE-uh)	Increased rate and depth of breathing in response to exercise, pain, or other conditions
Hyperventilation	Increased pulmonary ventilation in excess of metabolic demand, frequently associated with anxiety; expels CO_2 faster than it is produced, thus lowering the blood CO_2 concentration and raising the blood pH
Hypoventilation[24]	Reduced pulmonary ventilation; leads to an increase in blood CO_2 concentration if ventilation is insufficient to expel CO_2 as fast as it is produced
Kussmaul[25] respiration	Deep, rapid breathing often induced by acidosis; seen in diabetes mellitus
Orthopnea[26] (or-thop-NEE-uh)	Dyspnea that occurs when a person is lying down or in any position other than standing or sitting erect; seen in heart failure, asthma, emphysema, and other conditions
Respiratory arrest	Permanent cessation of breathing (unless there is medical intervention)
Tachypnea[27] (tack-ip-NEE-uh)	Accelerated respiration

Other variations in pulmonary ventilation serve the purposes of speaking, expressing emotion (laughing, crying), yawning, hiccuping, expelling noxious fumes, coughing, sneezing, and expelling abdominal contents. Coughing is induced by irritants in the lower respiratory tract. To cough, we close the glottis and contract the respiratory and abdominal muscles, producing high pressure in the lower respiratory tract. We then suddenly open the glottis and release an explosive burst of air at speeds over 900 km/h (600 mi./h). This drives mucus and foreign matter toward the pharynx and mouth. Sneezing is triggered by irritants in the nasal cavity. Its mechanism is similar to coughing except that the glottis is continually open, the soft palate and tongue block the flow of air while thoracic pressure builds, and then the soft palate is depressed to direct part of the airstream through the nose. These actions are coordinated by coughing and sneezing centers in the medulla oblongata.

---

[20]*eu* = easy, normal; *pnea* = breathing
[21]*a* = without; *pnea* = breathing
[22]*dys* = difficult, abnormal, painful; *pnea* = breathing
[23]*hyper* = above normal
[24]*hypo* = below normal
[25]Adolph Kussmaul (1822–1902), German physician
[26]*ortho* = straight, erect; *pnea* = breathing
[27]*tachy* = fast; *pnea* = breathing

BEFORE YOU GO ON

Answer the following questions to test your understanding of the preceding section:

7. Explain why contraction of the diaphragm causes inspiration but contraction of the transverse abdominal muscle causes expiration.

8. Which brainstem respiratory nucleus is indispensable to respiration? What do the other nuclei do?

9. Explain why Boyle's law is relevant to the action of the respiratory muscles.

10. Explain why eupnea requires little or no action by the muscles of expiration.

11. Identify a benefit and a disadvantage of normal (nonpathological) bronchoconstriction.

12. Suppose a healthy person has a tidal volume of 650 mL, an anatomical dead space of 160 mL, and a respiratory rate of 14 breaths per minute. Calculate her alveolar ventilation rate.

13. Suppose a person has a total lung capacity of 5,800 mL, a residual volume of 1,200 mL, an inspiratory reserve volume of 2,400 mL, and an expiratory reserve volume of 1,400 mL. Calculate his tidal volume.

22.3   Gas Exchange and Transport

Expected Learning Outcomes

When you have completed this section, you should be able to

a. define *partial pressure* and discuss its relationship to a gas mixture such as air;

b. contrast the composition of inspired and alveolar air;

c. discuss how partial pressure affects gas transport by the blood;

d. describe the mechanisms of transporting O_2 and CO_2;

e. describe the factors that govern gas exchange in the lungs and systemic capillaries;

f. explain how gas exchange is adjusted to the metabolic needs of different tissues; and

g. discuss the effect of blood gases and pH on the respiratory rhythm.

Ultimately, respiration is about gases, especially oxygen and carbon dioxide. We will turn our attention now to the behavior of these gases in the human body: how oxygen is obtained from inspired air and delivered to the tissues, and how carbon dioxide is removed from the tissues and released into the expired air. First, however, it is necessary to understand the composition of the air we inhale and how gases behave in contact with the water film that lines the alveoli.

22.3a   Composition of Air

Air consists of about 78.6% nitrogen; 20.9% oxygen; 0.04% carbon dioxide; several quantitatively minor gases such as argon, neon, helium, methane, and ozone; and a variable amount of water vapor. Water vapor constitutes from 0% to 4%, depending on temperature and humidity; we will use a value of 0.5%, typical of a cool clear day.

Total atmospheric pressure is a sum of the contributions of these individual gases—a principle known as **Dalton's law** (see table 22.1). The separate contribution of each gas in a mixture is called its **partial pressure** and is symbolized with a P followed by the formula of the gas, such as P_{O_2}. As we are now concerned with atmospheric pressures and how they influence the partial pressures of blood gases, we return to mm Hg as our unit of measurement (not cm H_2O as when we were considering pulmonary ventilation). If we assume the average sea-level atmospheric pressure of 760 mm Hg and oxygen is 20.9% of the atmosphere, then P_{O_2} is simply

$$0.209 \times 760 \text{ mm Hg} = 159 \text{ mm Hg}.$$

Applying Dalton's law to the aforementioned mixture of gases in the air gives us the following:

$$P_{N_2} + P_{O_2} + P_{H_2O} + P_{CO_2}$$
$$\approx 597 + 159 + 3.7 + 0.3$$
$$= 760.0 \text{ mm Hg}.$$

These values change dramatically at higher altitude (see Deeper Insight 22.3).

This is the composition of the air we inhale, but it's not the composition of air in the alveoli. Alveolar air can be sampled with an apparatus that collects the last 10 mL of expired air. As we see in **table 22.4,** its composition differs from that of the atmosphere because of three influences: (1) It is humidified by contact with the mucous membranes, so its P_{H_2O} is more than 10 times higher than that of the inhaled air. (2) Freshly inspired air mixes with residual air left from the previous respiratory cycle, so its oxygen is diluted and it is enriched with CO_2 from the residual air. (3) Alveolar air

TABLE 22.4	Composition of Inspired (Atmospheric) and Alveolar Air			
Gas	**Inspired Air***		**Alveolar Air**	
N_2	78.6%	597 mm Hg	74.9%	569 mm Hg
O_2	20.9%	159 mm Hg	13.7%	104 mm Hg
H_2O	0.5%	3.7 mm Hg	6.2%	47 mm Hg
CO_2	0.04%	0.3 mm Hg	5.3%	40 mm Hg
Total	100%	760 mm Hg	100%	760 mm Hg

* Typical values for a cool clear day; values vary with temperature and humidity. Other gases present in small amounts are disregarded.

DEEPER INSIGHT 22.3

MEDICAL HISTORY

The Flight of the Zenith

As any aviator or mountain hiker knows, the composition of air changes dramatically from sea level to high altitude. This was all too sadly realized by French physician Paul Bert (1833–86), who is commonly recognized as the founder of aerospace medicine. He invented the first pressure chamber capable of simulating the effects of high altitude, and undertook a variety of experiments on human and animal subjects to test the effects of variation in oxygen partial pressure. In 1875, balloonist Gaston Tissandier set out from Paris in a hot-air balloon named the *Zenith* with two of Bert's protégés in physiology. Their aim was to investigate the effects of the low oxygen pressures attainable only by ascending to a very high altitude. They ignored Bert's advice to breathe supplemental oxygen continually, rather than only when they felt the need for it. As they ascended, they observed each other and took notes. Seeing no ill effects, they continued to throw out ballast and go higher, eventually to 28,000 feet. But after passing 24,000 feet, they experienced stupefaction, muscular paralysis, euphoria, and finally unconsciousness. The balloon eventually descended on its own with two of the three men dead; only Tissandier lived to write about it.

exchanges O_2 and CO_2 with the blood. Thus, the P_{O_2} of alveolar air is about 65% that of inhaled air, and its P_{CO_2} is more than 130 times higher.

▶▶▶APPLY WHAT YOU KNOW

Expired air considered as a whole (not just the last 10 mL) is about 15.3% O_2 and 4.2% CO_2. Why would these values differ from the ones for alveolar air?

22.3b Alveolar Gas Exchange APR

Air in the alveolus is in contact with the film of water covering the alveolar epithelium. For oxygen to get into the blood, it must dissolve in this water and pass through the respiratory membrane separating the air from the bloodstream. For carbon dioxide to leave the blood, it must pass the other way and diffuse out of the water film into the alveolar air. This back-and-forth traffic of O_2 and CO_2 across the respiratory membrane is called **alveolar gas exchange.**

The reason O_2 diffuses in one direction and CO_2 in the other is that each gas diffuses down its own partial pressure gradient. Whenever air and water are in contact with each other, gases diffuse down their gradients until the partial pressure of each gas in the air is equal to its partial pressure in the water. If a gas has a greater partial pressure in the water than in the air, it diffuses into the air; the smell of chlorine near a swimming pool is evidence of

this. If the partial pressure of the gas is greater in the air, it diffuses into the water.

Henry's law states that *at the air–water interface, for a given temperature, the amount of gas that dissolves in the water is determined by its solubility in water and its partial pressure in the air* (**fig. 22.18**). Thus, the greater the P_{O_2} in the alveolar air, the more O_2 the blood picks up. And since blood arriving at an alveolus has a higher P_{CO_2} than air, it releases CO_2 into the alveolar air. At the alveolus, the blood is said to *unload* CO_2 and *load* O_2. Each gas in a mixture behaves independently; the diffusion of one gas doesn't influence the diffusion of another.

Both O_2 loading and CO_2 unloading involve erythrocytes (RBCs). The efficiency of these processes therefore depends on

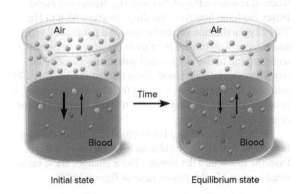

Initial state   Equilibrium state

(a) Oxygen

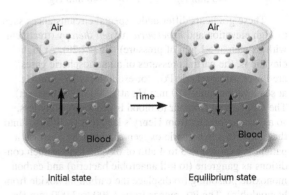

Initial state   Equilibrium state

(b) Carbon dioxide

FIGURE 22.18 Henry's Law and Its Relationship to Alveolar Gas Exchange. (a) The P_{O_2} of alveolar air is initially higher than the P_{O_2} of the blood arriving at an alveolus. Oxygen diffuses into the blood until the two are in equilibrium. (b) The P_{CO_2} of the arriving blood is initially higher than the P_{CO_2} of alveolar air. Carbon dioxide diffuses into the alveolus until the two are in equilibrium.

how long an RBC spends in an alveolar capillary compared with how long it takes for each gas to be fully loaded or unloaded—that is, for them to reach equilibrium concentrations in the capillary blood. It takes about 0.25 second to reach equilibrium. At rest, when blood circulates at its slowest speed, an RBC takes about 0.75 second to pass through an alveolar capillary—plenty of time to pick up a maximum load of oxygen. Even in vigorous exercise, when the blood flows faster, an erythrocyte is in the alveolar capillary for about 0.3 second, which is still adequate.

Several variables affect the efficiency of alveolar gas exchange, and under abnormal conditions, some of these can prevent the complete loading and unloading of gases:

- **Pressure gradients of the gases.** P_{O_2} is about 104 mm Hg in alveolar air and 40 mm Hg in blood arriving at an alveolus. Oxygen therefore diffuses from the air into the blood, where it reaches a P_{O_2} of 104 mm Hg. Before the blood leaves the lung, however, this drops to about 95 mm Hg. This oxygen dilution occurs because the pulmonary veins anastomose with bronchial veins in the lungs, so there is some mixing of the oxygen-rich pulmonary blood with oxygen-poor systemic blood. Even though the blood is 100% saturated with oxygen as it leaves the alveolar capillaries, it is nearly impossible for it to remain 100% saturated by the time it leaves the lungs.

  P_{CO_2} is about 46 mm Hg in blood arriving at the alveolus and 40 mm Hg in alveolar air. CO_2 therefore diffuses from the blood into the alveoli. These changes are summarized here and in the yellow zone of **figure 22.19.**

Blood entering lungs		*Blood leaving lungs*	
P_{O_2}	40 mm Hg	P_{O_2}	95 mm Hg
P_{CO_2}	46 mm Hg	P_{CO_2}	40 mm Hg

These gradients differ under special circumstances such as high elevation and *hyperbaric oxygen therapy* (treatment with oxygen at >1 atm of pressure) **(fig. 22.20).** At high elevations, the partial pressures of all atmospheric gases are lower. Atmospheric P_{O_2}, for example, is 159 mm Hg at sea level but only 110 mm Hg at 3,000 m (10,000 feet). The O_2 gradient from air to blood is proportionately less, so as we can predict from Henry's law, less O_2 diffuses into the blood. In a hyperbaric oxygen chamber, by contrast, a patient is exposed to 3 to 4 atm of oxygen to treat such conditions as gangrene (to kill anaerobic bacteria) and carbon monoxide poisoning (to displace the carbon monoxide from hemoglobin). The P_{O_2} ranges from 2,300 to 3,000 mm Hg. Thus, there is a very steep gradient of P_{O_2} from alveolus to blood and diffusion into the blood is accelerated.

- **Solubility of the gases.** Gases differ in their ability to dissolve in water. Carbon dioxide is about 20 times as soluble as oxygen, and oxygen is about twice as soluble as nitrogen. Even though the pressure gradient of O_2 is much greater than that of CO_2 across the respiratory membrane, equal amounts of the two gases are exchanged because CO_2 is so much more soluble and diffuses more rapidly.

- **Membrane thickness.** The respiratory membrane between the blood and alveolar air is only 0.5 μm thick in most places—much less than the 7 to 8 μm diameter of a single RBC. Thus, it presents little obstacle to diffusion **(fig. 22.21a).** In such heart conditions as left ventricular failure, however, blood pressure builds up in the lungs and promotes capillary filtration into the connective tissues, causing the respiratory membranes to become edematous and thickened (similar to their condition in pneumonia; **fig. 22.21b).** The gases have farther to travel between blood and air, so oxygen can't get to the RBCs quickly enough to fully load their hemoglobin. Under these circumstances, blood leaving the lungs has an unusually low P_{O_2} and high P_{CO_2}.

- **Membrane area.** In good health, each lung has about 70 m^2 of respiratory membrane available for gas exchange. Since the alveolar capillaries contain a total of only 100 mL of blood at any one time, this blood is spread very thinly. Several pulmonary diseases, however, decrease the alveolar surface area and thus lead to low blood P_{O_2}—for example, emphysema **(fig. 22.21c)** and lung cancer.

- **Ventilation–perfusion coupling.** Gas exchange requires not only good ventilation of the alveoli but also good perfusion of their capillaries. *Ventilation–perfusion coupling* refers to physiological responses that match airflow to blood flow and vice versa. For example, if part of a lung were poorly ventilated because of tissue destruction or an airway obstruction, it would be pointless to direct much blood to that tissue. Poor ventilation leads to a low P_{O_2} in that region of the lung. This stimulates local vasoconstriction, rerouting the blood to better-ventilated areas of the lung where it can pick up more oxygen (left side of **fig. 22.22a).** In contrast, increased ventilation raises the local blood P_{O_2} and this stimulates vasodilation, increasing blood flow to that region to take advantage of the oxygen availability (right side of same figure). These reactions of the pulmonary arteries are opposite from the reactions of systemic arteries, which dilate in response to hypoxia. Furthermore, changes in the blood flow to a region of a lung stimulate bronchoconstriction or dilation, adjusting ventilation so that air is directed to the best-perfused parts of the lung **(fig. 22.22b).**

22.3c Gas Transport

Gas transport is the process of carrying gases from the alveoli to the systemic tissues and vice versa. This section explains how the blood loads and transports O_2 and CO_2.

Oxygen

Arterial blood carries about 20 mL of oxygen per deciliter. About 98.5% of it is bound to hemoglobin in the RBCs and 1.5% is dissolved in the blood plasma. Hemoglobin is specialized for oxygen transport. It consists of four protein (globin) chains, each with one heme group (see fig. 18.5). Each heme can bind 1 O_2 to the iron atom at its center; thus, one

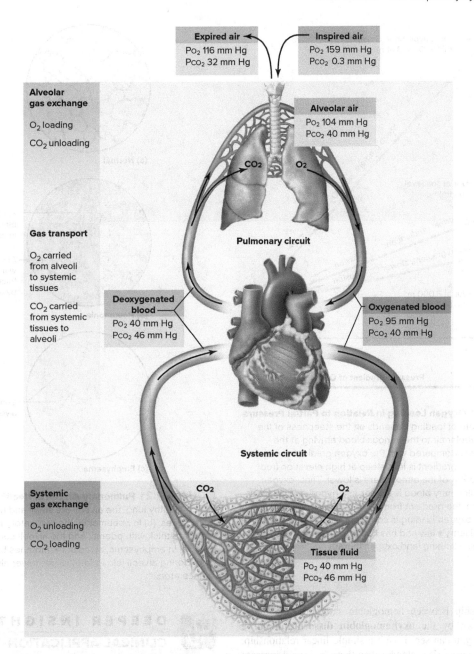

FIGURE 22.19 **Changes in PO₂ and PCO₂ Along the Circulatory Route.** **APR**

❓ *Trace the partial pressure of oxygen from inspired air to expired air and explain each change in PO₂ along the way. Do the same for PCO₂.*

hemoglobin molecule can carry up to 4 O_2. If one or more molecules of O_2 are bound to hemoglobin, the compound is called **oxyhemoglobin (HbO₂),** whereas hemoglobin with no oxygen bound to it is **deoxyhemoglobin (HHb).** When hemoglobin is 100% saturated, every molecule of it carries 4 O_2; if it is 75%

saturated, there is an average of 3 O_2 per hemoglobin molecule; if it is 50% saturated, there is an average of 2 O_2 per hemoglobin; and so forth. The poisonous effect of carbon monoxide stems from its competition for the O_2 binding site (see Deeper Insight 22.4).

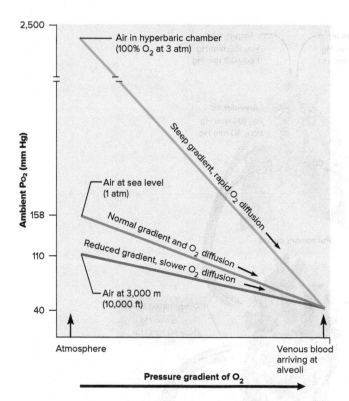

FIGURE 22.20 Oxygen Loading in Relation to Partial Pressure Gradient. The rate of loading depends on the steepness of the gradient from alveolar air to the venous blood arriving at the alveolar capillaries. Compared with the oxygen gradient at sea level (blue line), the gradient is less steep at high elevation (red line) because the Po_2 of the atmosphere is lower. Thus, oxygen loading of the pulmonary blood is slower. In a hyperbaric chamber with 100% oxygen, the gradient from air to blood is very steep (green line), and oxygen loading is correspondingly rapid. This is an illustration of Henry's law and has important effects in diving, aviation, mountain climbing, and oxygen therapy.

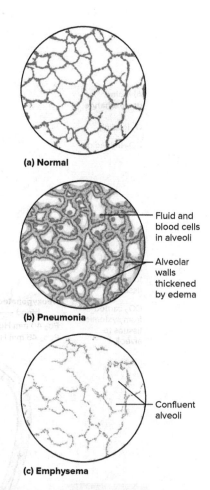

(a) Normal

(b) Pneumonia

Fluid and blood cells in alveoli

Alveolar walls thickened by edema

(c) Emphysema

Confluent alveoli

FIGURE 22.21 Pulmonary Alveoli in Health and Disease. (a) In a healthy lung, the alveoli are small and have thin respiratory membranes. (b) In pneumonia, the respiratory membranes (alveolar walls) are thick with edema, and the alveoli contain fluid and blood cells. (c) In emphysema, alveolar membranes break down and neighboring alveoli join to form larger, fewer alveoli with less total surface area.

The relationship between hemoglobin saturation and ambient Po_2 is shown by the **oxyhemoglobin dissociation curve** (**fig. 22.23**). As you can see, it isn't a simple linear relationship. At low Po_2, the curve rises slowly; then there is a rapid increase in oxygen loading as Po_2 rises farther. This reflects the way hemoglobin loads oxygen. When the first heme group binds O_2, hemoglobin changes shape in a way that facilitates uptake of the second O_2 by another heme group. This, in turn, promotes the uptake of the third and then the fourth O_2—hence the rapidly rising midportion of the curve. At high Po_2 levels, the curve levels off because the hemoglobin approaches 100% saturation and cannot load much more oxygen.

▶▶▶**APPLY WHAT YOU KNOW**

Is oxygen loading a positive or negative feedback process? Explain.

 DEEPER INSIGHT 22.4

CLINICAL APPLICATION

Carbon Monoxide Poisoning

The lethal effect of carbon monoxide (CO) is well known. This colorless, odorless gas occurs in cigarette smoke, engine exhaust, and fumes from gas furnaces and space heaters. It binds to the iron of hemoglobin to form *carboxyhemoglobin (HbCO)*. Thus, it competes with oxygen for the same binding site. Not only that, but it binds 210 times as tightly as oxygen. Thus, CO tends to tie up hemoglobin for a long time. Less than 1.5% of the hemoglobin is occupied by carbon monoxide in most nonsmokers, but this figure rises to as much as 3% in residents of heavily polluted cities and 10% in heavy smokers. An ambient concentration of 0.1% CO is enough to bind 50% of a person's hemoglobin, and a concentration of 0.2% is quickly lethal.

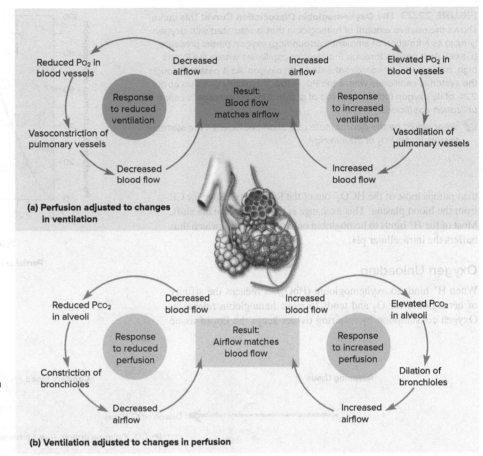

FIGURE 22.22 Ventilation–Perfusion Coupling. Negative feedback loops adjust airflow and blood flow to each other. (a) Blood circulation can be adjusted to match above- or below-normal ventilation of a part of the lung. (b) Ventilation can be adjusted to match above- or below-normal blood circulation to a part of the lung.

Carbon Dioxide

Carbon dioxide is transported in three forms: carbonic acid, carbamino compounds, and dissolved gas.

1. About 90% of the CO_2 is hydrated (reacts with water) to form **carbonic acid,** which then dissociates into bicarbonate and hydrogen ions:

$$CO_2 + H_2O \longrightarrow H_2CO_3 \longrightarrow HCO_3^- + H^+.$$

   More will be said about this reaction shortly.

2. About 5% binds to the amino groups of plasma proteins and hemoglobin to form **carbamino compounds**—chiefly **carbaminohemoglobin ($HbCO_2$).** The reaction with hemoglobin can be symbolized $Hb + CO_2 \longrightarrow HbCO_2$. Carbon dioxide doesn't compete with oxygen because CO_2 and O_2 bind to different sites on the hemoglobin molecule—oxygen to the heme moiety and CO_2 to the polypeptide chains. Hemoglobin can therefore transport both O_2 and CO_2 simultaneously. As we will see, however, each gas somewhat inhibits transport of the other.

3. The remaining 5% of the CO_2 is carried in the blood as dissolved gas, like the CO_2 in sparkling wines and carbonated beverages.

The relative amounts of CO_2 exchanged between the blood and alveolar air differ from the percentages just given. About 70% of the *exchanged* CO_2 comes from carbonic acid, 23% from carbamino compounds, and 7% from the dissolved gas. That is, blood gives up the dissolved CO_2 gas and CO_2 from the carbamino compounds more easily than it gives up the CO_2 in bicarbonate.

22.3d Systemic Gas Exchange

Systemic gas exchange is the unloading of O_2 and loading of CO_2 at the systemic capillaries (see fig. 22.19, bottom; **fig. 22.24**).

Carbon Dioxide Loading

Aerobic respiration produces a molecule of CO_2 for each O_2 it consumes. The tissue fluid therefore contains a relatively high P_{CO_2} and there is typically a CO_2 gradient of 46 → 40 mm Hg from tissue fluid to blood. Consequently, CO_2 diffuses into the bloodstream, where it is carried in the three forms already noted. Most of it reacts with water to produce bicarbonate ions (HCO_3^-) and hydrogen ions (H^+). This reaction occurs slowly in the blood plasma but much faster in the RBCs, where it is catalyzed by the enzyme *carbonic anhydrase*. An antiport called the *chloride–bicarbonate exchanger*

FIGURE 22.23 The Oxyhemoglobin Dissociation Curve. This curve shows the relative amount of hemoglobin that is saturated with oxygen (*y*-axis) as a function of ambient (surrounding) oxygen partial pressure (*x*-axis). As it passes through the alveolar capillaries where the P_{O_2} is high, hemoglobin becomes saturated with oxygen. As it passes through the systemic capillaries where the P_{O_2} is low, it typically gives up about 22% of its oxygen (color bar at top of graph). This percentage is called the *utilization coefficient.*

❓ *What would be the approximate utilization coefficient if the systemic tissues had a P_{O_2} of 30 mm Hg?*

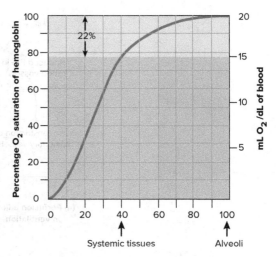

Partial pressure of O_2 (P_{O_2}) in mm Hg

then pumps most of the HCO_3^- out of the RBC in exchange for Cl^- from the blood plasma. This exchange is called the **chloride shift.** Most of the H^+ binds to hemoglobin or oxyhemoglobin, which thus buffers the intracellular pH.

Oxygen Unloading

When H^+ binds to oxyhemoglobin (HbO_2), it reduces the affinity of hemoglobin for O_2 and tends to make hemoglobin release it. Oxygen consumption by respiring tissues keeps the P_{O_2} of tissue

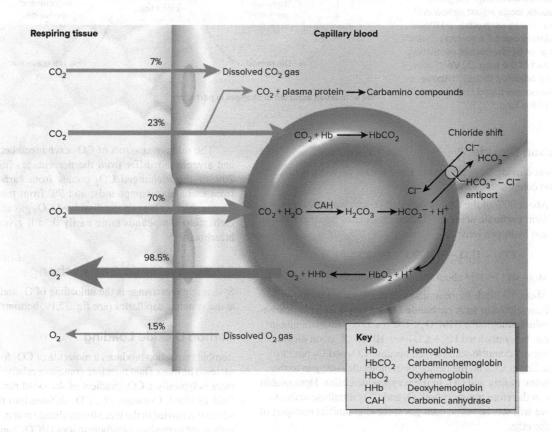

FIGURE 22.24 Systemic Gas Exchange. Blue arrows show the three mechanisms of CO_2 loading and transport; their thickness represents the relative amounts of CO_2 loaded in each of the three forms. Red arrows show the two mechanisms of O_2 unloading; their thickness indicates the relative amounts unloaded by each mechanism. Note that CO_2 loading releases hydrogen ions in the erythrocyte, and hydrogen ions promote O_2 unloading.

fluid relatively low, so there is typically a pressure gradient of about 95 → 40 mm Hg of oxygen from the arterial blood to the tissue fluid. Thus, the liberated oxygen—along with some that was carried as dissolved gas in the plasma—diffuses from the blood into the tissue fluid.

As blood arrives at the systemic capillaries, its oxygen concentration is about 20 mL/dL and the hemoglobin is about 97% saturated. As it leaves the capillaries of a typical resting tissue, its oxygen concentration is about 15.6 mL/dL and the hemoglobin is about 75% saturated. Thus, it has given up 4.4 mL/dL—about 22% of its oxygen load. This fraction is called the **utilization coefficient** (see fig. 22.23). The oxygen remaining in the blood after it passes through the capillary bed provides a **venous reserve** of oxygen, which can sustain life for 4 to 5 minutes even in the event of respiratory arrest. At rest, the circulatory system releases oxygen to the tissues at an overall rate of about 250 mL/min.

22.3e Alveolar Gas Exchange Revisited

The processes illustrated in figure 22.24 make it easier to understand alveolar gas exchange more fully. As shown in **figure 22.25**, the reactions that occur in the lungs are essentially the reverse of systemic gas exchange. As hemoglobin loads oxygen, its affinity for H^+ declines. Hydrogen ions dissociate from the hemoglobin and bind with bicarbonate ions (HCO_3^-) transported from the plasma into the RBCs. Chloride ions are transported back out of the RBC (a reverse chloride shift). The reaction of H^+ and HCO_3^- reverses the hydration reaction and generates free CO_2. This diffuses into the alveolus to be exhaled—as does the CO_2 released from carbaminohemoglobin and CO_2 gas that was dissolved in the plasma.

22.3f Adjustment to the Metabolic Needs of Tissues

Hemoglobin doesn't unload the same amount of oxygen to all tissues. Some tissues need more and some less, depending on their state of activity. Hemoglobin responds to such variations and unloads more oxygen to the tissues that need it most. In exercising skeletal muscles, for example, the utilization coefficient may be as high as 80%. Four factors adjust the rate of oxygen unloading to the metabolic rates of different tissues:

1. **Ambient P_{O_2}.** Since an active tissue consumes oxygen rapidly, the P_{O_2} of its tissue fluid remains low. From the

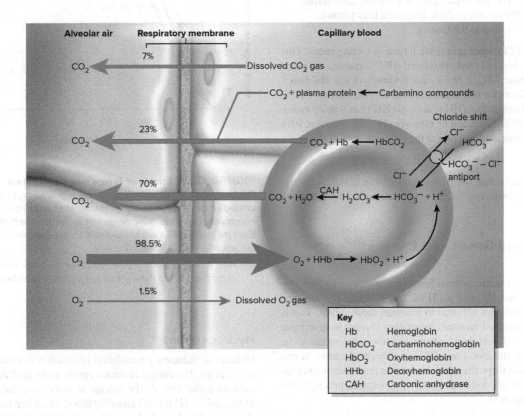

FIGURE 22.25 Alveolar Gas Exchange. Arrow colors and thicknesses represent the same variables as in the preceding figure. Note that O_2 loading promotes the decomposition of carbonic acid into H_2O and CO_2, and most exhaled CO_2 comes from the erythrocytes.

❓ *In what fundamental way does this differ from the preceding figure? Following alveolar gas exchange, will the blood contain a higher or lower concentration of bicarbonate ions than it did before?*

oxyhemoglobin dissociation curve (see fig. 22.23), you can see that at a low Po_2, HbO_2 releases more oxygen.

2. **Temperature.** When temperature rises, the oxyhemoglobin dissociation curve shifts to the right (**fig. 22.26a**); in other words, elevated temperature promotes oxygen unloading. Active tissues are warmer than less active ones and thus extract more oxygen from the blood passing through them.

3. **Ambient pH.** Active tissues also generate extra CO_2, which raises the H^+ concentration and lowers the pH of the blood. Hydrogen ions weaken the bond between hemoglobin and oxygen and thereby promote oxygen unloading—a phenomenon called the **Bohr[28] effect.** This can also be seen in the oxyhemoglobin dissociation curve, where a drop in pH shifts the curve to the right (**fig. 22.26b**). The effect is less pronounced at the high Po_2 present in the lungs, so pH has relatively little effect on pulmonary oxygen loading. In the systemic capillaries, however, Po_2 is lower and the Bohr effect is more pronounced.

4. **BPG.** Erythrocytes have no mitochondria and meet their energy needs solely by anaerobic fermentation. One of their metabolic intermediates is **bisphosphoglycerate (BPG),** which binds to hemoglobin and promotes oxygen unloading. An elevated body temperature (as in fever) stimulates BPG synthesis, as do thyroxine, growth hormone, testosterone, and epinephrine. All of these hormones thus promote oxygen unloading to the tissues.

The rate of CO_2 loading is also adjusted to varying needs of the tissues. A low level of oxyhemoglobin (HbO_2) enables the blood to transport more CO_2, a phenomenon known as the **Haldane[29] effect.** This occurs for two reasons: (1) HbO_2 doesn't bind CO_2 as well as deoxyhemoglobin (HHb) does. (2) HHb binds more hydrogen ions than HbO_2 does, and by removing H^+ from solution, HHb shifts the carbonic acid reaction to the right:

$$H_2O + CO_2 \longrightarrow HCO_3^- + H^+.$$

A high metabolic rate keeps oxyhemoglobin levels relatively low and thus allows more CO_2 to be transported by these two mechanisms.

22.3g Blood Gases and the Respiratory Rhythm

Normally the systemic arterial blood has a Po_2 of 95 mm Hg, a Pco_2 of 40 mm Hg, and a pH of 7.40 ± 0.05. The rate and depth of breathing are adjusted to maintain these values. This is possible because the brainstem respiratory centers receive input from central and peripheral chemoreceptors that monitor the composition of the blood and CSF, as described earlier in this chapter. Of these three chemical stimuli, the most potent stimulus for breathing is pH, followed by CO_2; perhaps surprisingly, the least significant is O_2.

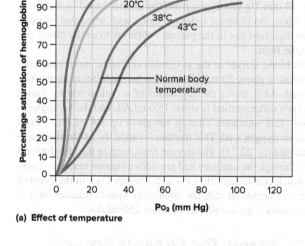

(a) **Effect of temperature**

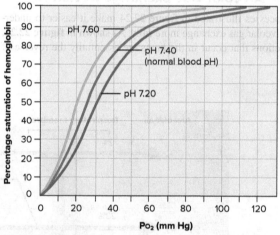

(b) **Effect of pH**

FIGURE 22.26 Effects of Temperature and pH on Oxyhemoglobin Dissociation. (a) For a given Po_2, hemoglobin unloads more oxygen at higher temperatures. (b) For a given Po_2, hemoglobin unloads more oxygen at lower pH (the Bohr effect). Both mechanisms cause hemoglobin to release more oxygen to tissues with higher metabolic rates.

? *Why is it physiologically beneficial to the body that the curves in part (a) shift to the right as temperature increases?*

Hydrogen Ions

Ultimately, pulmonary ventilation is adjusted to maintain the pH of the brain. The central chemoreceptors in the medulla oblongata mediate about 75% of the change in respiration induced by pH shifts, and yet H^+ doesn't cross the blood–brain barrier very easily. However, CO_2 does, and once it's in the CSF, it reacts with water to produce carbonic acid, and the carbonic acid dissociates into bicarbonate and hydrogen ions. The CSF contains relatively little protein to buffer the hydrogen ions, so most H^+ remains free, and

[28]Christian Bohr (1855–1911), Danish physiologist
[29]John Scott Haldane (1860–1936), Scottish physiologist

it strongly stimulates the central chemoreceptors. Hydrogen ions are also a potent stimulus to the peripheral chemoreceptors, which mediate about 25% of the respiratory response to pH changes.

How do we know it is the H^+ that stimulates the central chemoreceptors and not primarily the CO_2 that diffuses into the CSF? Experimentally, it is possible to vary the pH or the P_{CO_2} of the CSF while holding the other variable steady. When pH alone changes, there is a strong effect on respiration; when P_{CO_2} alone changes, the effect is weaker. Therefore, even though these two variables usually change together, we can see that the chemoreceptors react primarily to the H^+.

A blood pH lower than 7.35 is called **acidosis** and a pH greater than 7.45 is called **alkalosis.** The P_{CO_2} of arterial blood normally ranges from 37 to 43 mm Hg. A P_{CO_2} less than 37 mm Hg is called **hypocapnia,**[30] and is the most common cause of alkalosis. The most common cause of acidosis is **hypercapnia,** a P_{CO_2} greater than 43 mm Hg. When these pH imbalances occur because the rate of pulmonary ventilation doesn't match the rate of CO_2 production, they are called *respiratory acidosis* and *respiratory alkalosis* (further discussed under "Disorders of Acid–Base Balance" in section 24.3).

The corrective homeostatic response to acidosis is hyperventilation, "blowing off" CO_2 faster than the body produces it. As CO_2 is eliminated from the body, the carbonic acid reaction shifts to the left:

$$CO_2 + H_2O \longleftarrow H_2CO_3 \longleftarrow HCO_3^- + H^+.$$

Thus, the H^+ on the right is consumed, and as H^+ concentration declines, the pH rises and ideally returns the blood from the acidotic range to normal.

The corrective response to alkalosis is hypoventilation, which allows CO_2 to accumulate in the body fluids faster than we exhale it. Hypoventilation shifts the reaction to the right, raising the H^+ concentration and lowering the pH to normal:

$$CO_2 + H_2O \longrightarrow H_2CO_3 \longrightarrow HCO_3^- + H^+.$$

Although pH changes usually result from P_{CO_2} changes, they can have other causes. In diabetes mellitus, for example, rapid fat oxidation releases acidic ketone bodies, causing an abnormally low pH called *ketoacidosis.* Ketoacidosis tends to induce a form of dyspnea called *Kussmaul respiration* (see table 22.3). Hyperventilation cannot reduce the level of ketone bodies in the blood, but by blowing off CO_2, it reduces the concentration of CO_2-generated H^+ and compensates to some degree for the H^+ released by the ketone bodies.

Carbon Dioxide

Although the arterial P_{CO_2} has a strong influence on respiration, we have seen that it's mostly an indirect one, mediated through its effects on the pH of the CSF. Yet the experimental evidence described earlier shows that CO_2 has some effect even when pH remains stable. At the beginning of exercise, the rising blood CO_2

level may directly stimulate the peripheral chemoreceptors and trigger an increase in ventilation more quickly than the central chemoreceptors do.

Oxygen

The partial pressure of oxygen usually has little effect on respiration. Even in eupnea, the hemoglobin is at least 97% saturated with O_2, so little can be added by increasing pulmonary ventilation. Arterial P_{O_2} significantly affects respiration only if it drops below 60 mm Hg. At low elevations, such a low P_{O_2} seldom occurs even in prolonged holding of the breath. A moderate drop in P_{O_2} does stimulate the peripheral chemoreceptors, but another effect overrides this: As the level of HbO_2 falls, hemoglobin binds more H^+ (see fig. 22.24). This raises the blood pH, which inhibits respiration and counteracts the effect of low P_{O_2}.

At about 10,800 feet (3,300 m), arterial P_{O_2} falls to 60 mm Hg and the stimulatory effect of hypoxemia on the carotid bodies overrides the inhibitory effect of the pH increase. This produces heavy breathing in people who aren't acclimated to high elevation. Long-term hypoxemia can lead to a condition called **hypoxic drive,** in which respiration is driven more by the low P_{O_2} than by CO_2 or pH. This occurs in situations such as emphysema and pneumonia, which interfere with alveolar gas exchange, and in mountain climbing of at least 2 or 3 days' duration.

Respiration and Exercise

It is common knowledge that we breathe more heavily during exercise, and it's tempting to think this occurs because exercise raises CO_2 levels, lowers the blood pH, and lowers blood O_2 levels. However, this is not true; all these values remain essentially the same in exercise as they do at rest. It appears that the increased respiration has other causes: (1) When the brain sends motor commands to the muscles (via the lower motor neurons of the spinal cord), it also sends this information to the respiratory centers, so they increase pulmonary ventilation in anticipation of the needs of the exercising muscles. In contrast to homeostasis by negative feedback, this is considered a *feed-forward* mechanism, in which signals are transmitted to the effectors (brainstem respiratory centers) to produce a change *in anticipation* of need. (2) Exercise stimulates proprioceptors of the muscles and joints, and they transmit excitatory signals to the brainstem respiratory centers. Thus, the respiratory centers increase breathing because they're informed that the muscles have been told to move or are actually moving. The increase in pulmonary ventilation keeps blood gas values at their normal levels in spite of the elevated O_2 consumption and CO_2 generation by the muscles.

In summary, the main chemical stimulus to pulmonary ventilation is the H^+ in the CSF and tissue fluid of the brain. These hydrogen ions arise mainly from CO_2 diffusing into the CSF and brain and generating H^+ through the carbonic acid reaction. Therefore, the P_{CO_2} of the arterial blood is an important driving force in respiration, even though its action on the chemoreceptors is indirect. Ventilation is adjusted to maintain arterial pH at about 7.40 and arterial P_{CO_2} at about 40 mm Hg. This automatically ensures that the blood is at least 97% saturated with O_2 as well.

---

[30]*capn* = smoke

Under ordinary circumstances, arterial P_{O_2} has relatively little effect on respiration. When it drops below 60 mm Hg, however, it excites the peripheral chemoreceptors and stimulates an increase in ventilation. This can be significant at high elevations and in certain lung diseases. The increase in respiration during exercise results from the expected or actual activity of the muscles, not from any change in blood gas pressures or pH.

> **BEFORE YOU GO ON**
>
> Answer the following questions to test your understanding of the preceding section:
>
> 14. Why is the composition of alveolar air different from that of the atmosphere?
> 15. What four factors affect the efficiency of alveolar gas exchange?
> 16. Explain how perfusion of a pulmonary lobule changes if it is poorly ventilated.
> 17. How is most oxygen transported in the blood, and why does carbon monoxide interfere with this?
> 18. What are the three ways in which blood transports CO_2?
> 19. Give two reasons why highly active tissues can extract more oxygen from the blood than less active tissues do.
> 20. Define *hypocapnia* and *hypercapnia*. Name the pH imbalances that result from these conditions and explain the relationship between P_{CO_2} and pH.
> 21. What is the most potent chemical stimulus to respiration, and where are the most effective chemoreceptors for it located?
> 22. Explain how changes in pulmonary ventilation can correct pH imbalances.

22.4 Respiratory Disorders

Expected Learning Outcomes
When you have completed this section, you should be able to

a. describe the forms and effects of oxygen deficiency and oxygen excess;

b. describe the chronic obstructive pulmonary diseases and their consequences; and

c. explain how lung cancer begins, progresses, and exerts its lethal effects.

The delicate lungs are exposed to a wide variety of inhaled pathogens and debris, so it's not surprising that they're prone to a host of diseases. Several already have been mentioned in this chapter and some others are briefly described in **table 22.5**. The effects of aging on the respiratory system are discussed in section 29.4a.

22.4a Oxygen Imbalances
Hypoxia is a deficiency of oxygen in a tissue or the inability to use oxygen. It's not a respiratory disease in itself but is often a consequence of respiratory diseases. Hypoxia is classified according to cause:

- **Hypoxemic hypoxia,** a state of low arterial P_{O_2}, is usually due to inadequate pulmonary gas exchange. Some of its root causes include atmospheric deficiency of oxygen at high elevations; impaired ventilation, as in drowning or aspiration of foreign matter; respiratory arrest; and degenerative lung diseases. It also occurs in carbon monoxide poisoning, which prevents hemoglobin from transporting oxygen.
- **Ischemic hypoxia** results from inadequate blood circulation, as in congestive heart failure.
- **Anemic hypoxia** is due to anemia and the resulting inability of the blood to carry adequate oxygen.
- **Histotoxic hypoxia** occurs when a metabolic poison such as cyanide prevents the tissues from using the oxygen delivered to them.

Hypoxia is often marked by **cyanosis,** blueness of the skin. Whatever the cause, its primary danger is the necrosis of oxygen-starved tissues. This is especially critical in organs with the highest metabolic demands, such as the brain, heart, and kidneys.

An oxygen excess is also dangerous. It is safe to breathe 100% oxygen at 1 atm for a few hours, but **oxygen toxicity** rapidly develops when pure oxygen is breathed at 2.5 atm or greater. Excess oxygen generates hydrogen peroxide and free radicals that destroy enzymes and damage nervous tissue; thus, it can lead to seizures, coma, and death. This is why scuba divers breathe a mixture of oxygen and nitrogen rather than pure compressed oxygen (see Deeper Insight 22.5). Hyperbaric oxygen was formerly used to treat premature infants for respiratory distress syndrome, but it caused retinal deterioration and blinded many infants before the practice was discontinued.

22.4b Chronic Obstructive Pulmonary Diseases

Chronic obstructive pulmonary diseases (COPDs) are defined by a long-term obstruction of airflow and substantial reduction of pulmonary ventilation. The major COPDs are *chronic bronchitis* and *emphysema*. COPDs are leading causes of adult mortality in the United States. They are almost always caused by cigarette smoking, but occasionally result from air pollution, occupational exposure to airborne irritants, or a hereditary defect. Most COPD patients exhibit mixed chronic bronchitis and emphysema, but one form or the other often predominates.

Chronic bronchitis is severe, persistent inflammation of the lower respiratory tract. Goblet cells of the bronchial mucosa enlarge and secrete excess mucus, while at the same time, the cilia are immobilized and unable to discharge it. Thick, stagnant mucus accumulates in the lungs and furnishes a growth medium for bacteria. Furthermore, tobacco smoke incapacitates the alveolar

TABLE 22.5	Some Disorders of the Respiratory System
Acute rhinitis	The common cold. Caused by many types of viruses that infect the upper respiratory tract. Symptoms include congestion, increased nasal secretion, sneezing, and dry cough. Transmitted especially by contact of contaminated hands with mucous membranes; not transmitted orally.
Adult respiratory distress syndrome	Acute lung inflammation and alveolar injury stemming from trauma, infection, burns, aspiration of vomit, inhalation of noxious gases, drug overdoses, and other causes. Alveolar injury is accompanied by severe pulmonary edema and hemorrhaging, followed by fibrosis that progressively destroys lung tissue. Fatal in about 40% of cases under age 60 and in 60% of cases over age 65.
Pneumonia	A lower respiratory infection caused by any of several viruses, fungi, or protozoans, but most often the bacterium *Streptococcus pneumoniae.* Causes filling of alveoli with fluid and dead leukocytes and thickening of the respiratory membrane, which interferes with gas exchange and causes hypoxemia. Especially dangerous to infants, the elderly, and people with compromised immune systems, such as AIDS and leukemia patients.
Sleep apnea	Cessation of breathing for 10 seconds or longer during sleep; sometimes occurs hundreds of times per night, often accompanied by restlessness and alternating with snoring. Can result from altered function of CNS respiratory centers, airway obstruction, or both. Over time, may lead to daytime drowsiness, hypoxemia, polycythemia, pulmonary hypertension, congestive heart failure, and cardiac arrhythmia. Most common in obese people and men.
Tuberculosis (TB)	Pulmonary infection with the bacterium *Mycobacterium tuberculosis,* which invades the lungs by way of air, blood, or lymph. Stimulates the lung to form fibrous nodules called tubercles around the bacteria. Progressive fibrosis compromises the elastic recoil and ventilation of the lungs and causes pulmonary hemorrhaging as it invades blood vessels. Especially common among impoverished and homeless people and becoming increasingly common among people with AIDS.

You can find other respiratory system disorders described in the following places:
Cystic fibrosis in Deeper Insight 3.2; *pulmonary hypertension* and *pulmonary edema* in section 19.5d; *cor pulmonale* in sections 19.6d and 22.4b; *asthma* in Deeper Insight 21.3; *Ondine's curse* in Deeper Insight 22.2; *pneumothorax* and *atelectasis* in section 22.2c; *apnea, dyspnea, orthopnea, hyperpnea, tachypnea, hyper-* and *hypoventilation, Kussmaul respiration,* and *respiratory arrest* in table 22.3; *carbon monoxide poisoning* in Deeper Insight 22.4; *hypoxia, COPDs (emphysema* and *chronic bronchitis),* and *lung cancer* in section 22.4; *decompression sickness* in Deeper Insight 22.5; *respiratory acidosis* and *alkalosis* in section 24.3d; and *infant respiratory distress syndrome* in section 29.3b.

macrophages and reduces one's defense against respiratory infection. Smokers with chronic bronchitis develop a chronic cough and bring up a thick mixture of mucus and cellular debris called **sputum** (SPEW-tum). Since blood flowing through congested areas of the lung cannot load a normal amount of oxygen, the ventilation–perfusion ratio is reduced and such patients commonly exhibit hypoxemia and cyanosis.

In **emphysema**[31] (EM-fih-SEE-muh), alveolar walls break down and alveoli converge into fewer and larger spaces (see fig. 22.21c). Thus, there is much less respiratory membrane available for gas exchange. In severe cases, the lungs are flabby and cavitated with spaces as big as grapes or even ping-pong balls. The severity of the disease may not be fully appreciated by looking only at histological specimens, since such large spaces are not seen on microscope slides. The lungs also become fibrotic and less elastic. The air passages open adequately during inspiration, but they tend to collapse and obstruct the outflow of air. Air becomes trapped in the lungs, and over a period of time a person becomes barrel-chested. The overly stretched thoracic muscles contract weakly, which further contributes to the difficulty of expiration. Since proportionate amounts of alveolar wall and capillaries are both destroyed, the ventilation–perfusion ratio of the lung is relatively normal, and

persons with emphysema don't necessarily show the cyanosis that typifies chronic bronchitis. People with emphysema can become exhausted and emaciated because they expend three to four times the normal amount of energy just to breathe. Even slight physical exertion, such as walking across a room, can cause severe shortness of breath.

▶▶▶**APPLY WHAT YOU KNOW**

Explain how the length–tension relationship of skeletal muscle (see fig. 11.12 and associated text) accounts for the weakness of the respiratory muscles in emphysema.

COPD tends to reduce vital capacity and causes hypoxemia, hypercapnia, and respiratory acidosis. Hypoxemia stimulates the kidneys to secrete erythropoietin, which leads to accelerated erythrocyte production and polycythemia (see fig. 18.8). As the blood thickens and lung tissue deteriorates, the right ventricle has to work harder to force blood through the lungs. Like any heavily used muscle, it enlarges and may eventually fail. Such ventricular hypertrophy and failure resulting from obstructed pulmonary circulation is called **cor pulmonale.**[32]

---

[31]*emphys* = inflamed

[32]*cor* = heart; *pulmo* = lung

22.4c Smoking and Lung Cancer

Lung cancer (**fig. 22.27**) accounts for more deaths than any other form of cancer. The most important cause of lung cancer is cigarette smoking, distantly followed by air pollution. Cigarette smoke contains at least 60 carcinogenic compounds. Lung cancer commonly follows or accompanies COPD.

There are three forms of lung cancer, the most common of which is **squamous-cell carcinoma.** In its early stage, basal cells of the bronchial epithelium multiply and the ciliated pseudostratified epithelium transforms into the stratified squamous type. As the dividing epithelial cells invade the underlying tissues of the bronchial wall, the bronchus develops bleeding lesions. Dense masses of keratin and malignant squamous cells appear in the lung parenchyma and replace functional respiratory tissue.

A second form of lung cancer, nearly as common, is **adenocarcinoma,**[33] which originates in the mucous glands of the lamina propria. The least common (10% to 20% of lung malignancies) but most dangerous form is **small-cell (oat-cell) carcinoma,** named for clusters of cells that resemble oat grains. This originates in the main bronchi but invades the mediastinum and metastasizes quickly to other organs.

Over 90% of lung tumors originate in the mucous membranes of the large bronchi. As a tumor invades the bronchial wall and grows around it, it compresses the airway and may cause atelectasis (collapse) of more distal parts of the lung. Growth of the tumor produces a cough, but coughing is such an everyday occurrence among smokers it seldom causes much alarm. Often, the first sign of serious trouble is coughing up blood. Lung cancer metastasizes so rapidly that it has usually spread to other organs by the time it's diagnosed. Common sites of metastasis are the pericardium, heart, bones, liver, lymph nodes, and brain. The chance of recovery is poor relative to other cancers, but is improving with advances in treatment. About 18% of patients survive for 5 years after diagnosis.

The popular use of recreational marijuana and its legalization in some states has sparked attention to it as a risk factor for lung cancer. Marijuana smokers inhale more deeply and hold it longer than cigarette smokers do, and they smoke the marijuana "joint" down to its last nub, loaded with tar and other carcinogens. Studies to date have been too limited to establish a significant correlation between marijuana use and lung cancer. Ongoing investigations aim to improve study methods and survey older people with a long history of marijuana use. The growing popularity of electronic cigarettes ("vaping") is also cause for concern. It has been associated with a serious lung disease called *popcorn lung,* but the composition of vaping liquids has undergone changes and the jury is still out on the seriousness of this public health risk.

[33]*adeno* = gland; *carcino* = cancer; *oma* = tumor

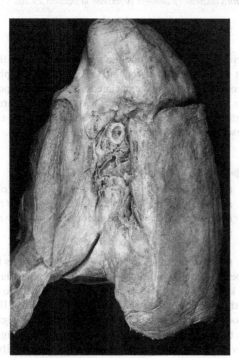 

(a) Healthy lung, mediastinal surface   **(b) Smoker's lung with carcinoma**

Tumors

FIGURE 22.27 Effects of Smoking. (a) Photograph of a healthy lung, mediastinal surface. (b) Photograph of a smoker's lung with carcinoma.

a: Dennis Strete/McGraw-Hill Education; **b:** Biophoto Associates/Science Source

BEFORE YOU GO ON
Answer the following questions to test your understanding of the preceding section.

23. Describe the four classes of hypoxia.

24. Name and compare the two COPDs and describe some pathological effects that they have in common.

25. In what lung tissue does lung cancer originate? How does it kill?

DEEPER INSIGHT 22.5

CLINICAL APPLICATION

Diving Physiology and Decompression Sickness

Because of the popularity of scuba diving, many people know something about the scientific aspects of breathing under high pressure. But diving is by no means a new fascination. As early as the fifth century BCE, Aristotle described divers using snorkels and taking containers of air underwater in order to stay down longer. Some Renaissance artists depicted divers many meters deep breathing from tubes to the water surface. In reality, this would be physically impossible. For one thing, such tubes would have so much dead space that fresh air from the surface wouldn't reach the diver. The short snorkels used today are about the maximum length that will work for surface breathing. Another reason snorkels can't be used at greater depths is that water pressure increases by 1 atm for every 10 m of depth, and even at 1 m the pressure is so great that a diver can't expand the chest muscles without help. This is one reason why scuba divers use pressurized air tanks. The tanks create a positive intrapulmonary pressure and enable the diver to inhale with only slight assistance from the thoracic muscles. Scuba tanks also have regulators that adjust the outflow pressure to the diver's depth and the opposing pressure of the surrounding water.

But breathing pressurized (hyperbaric) gas presents its own problems. Divers can't use pure oxygen because of the problem of oxygen toxicity. Instead, they use compressed air—a mixture of 21% oxygen and 79% nitrogen. On land, nitrogen presents no physiological problems; it dissolves poorly in blood and it is physiologically inert. But under hyperbaric conditions, larger amounts of nitrogen dissolve in the blood. (Which of the gas laws in table 22.1 applies here?) Even more dissolves in adipose tissue and the myelin of the brain, since nitrogen is more soluble in lipids. In the brain, it causes *nitrogen narcosis*, or what scuba inventor Jacques Cousteau (1910–1997) termed "rapture of the deep." A diver can become dizzy, euphoric, and dangerously disoriented; for every 15 to 20 m of depth, the effect is said to be equivalent to that of one martini on an empty stomach.

Strong currents, equipment failure, and other hazards sometimes make scuba divers panic, hold their breath, and quickly swim to the surface (a *breath-hold ascent*). Ambient (surrounding) pressure falls rapidly as a diver ascends, and the air in the lungs expands just as rapidly. (Which gas law is demonstrated here?) It is imperative that an ascending diver keep his or her airway open to exhale the expanding gas; otherwise it's likely to cause *pulmonary barotrauma*—ruptured alveoli. Then, when the diver takes a breath of air at the surface, alveolar air goes directly into the bloodstream and causes air embolism (see Deeper Insight 20.3).

After passing through the heart, the emboli enter the cerebral circulation because the diver is head-up and air bubbles rise in liquid. The resulting cerebral embolism can cause motor and sensory dysfunction, seizures, unconsciousness, and drowning.

Barotrauma can be fatal even at the depths of a backyard swimming pool. In one case, children trapped air in a bucket 1 m underwater and then swam under the bucket to breathe from the air space. Because the bucket was under water, the air in it was compressed. One child filled his lungs under the bucket, did a "mere" 1 m breath-hold ascent, and his alveoli ruptured. He died in the hospital, partly because the case was mistaken for drowning and not treated for what it really was. This would not have happened to a person who inhaled at the surface, did a breath-hold dive, and then resurfaced—nor is barotrauma a problem for those who do breath-hold dives to several meters. (Why? What is the difference?)

Even when not holding the breath, but letting the expanding air escape from the mouth, a diver must ascend slowly and carefully to allow for decompression of the nitrogen that has dissolved in the tissues. *Decompression tables* prescribe safe rates of ascent based on the depth and the length of time a diver has been down. When pressure drops, nitrogen dissolved in the tissues can go either of two places—it can diffuse into the alveoli and be exhaled, or it can form bubbles like the CO_2 in a bottle of soda when the cap is removed. The diver's objective is to ascend slowly, allowing for the former and preventing the latter. If a diver ascends too rapidly, nitrogen "boils" from the tissues—especially in the 3 m just below the surface, where the relative pressure change is greatest. A diver may double over in pain from bubbles in the joints, bones, and muscles—a disease called the *bends* or *decompression sickness (DCS)*. Nitrogen bubbles in the pulmonary capillaries cause *chokes*—substernal pain, coughing, and dyspnea. DCS is sometimes accompanied by mood changes, seizures, numbness, and itching. These symptoms usually occur within an hour of surfacing, but they are sometimes delayed for up to 36 hours. DCS is treated by putting the individual in a hyperbaric chamber to be recompressed and then *slowly* decompressed.

DCS is also called *caisson disease*. A caisson is a watertight underwater chamber filled with pressurized air. Caissons are used in underwater construction work on bridges, tunnels, ships' hulls, and so forth. Caisson disease was first reported in the late 1800s among workmen building the foundations of the Brooklyn Bridge.

CONNECTIVE ISSUES

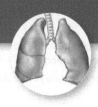

Effects of the RESPIRATORY SYSTEM on Other Organ Systems

ALL SYSTEMS
Delivers oxygen to the tissues and removes their carbon dioxide; maintains proper acid–base balance in the tissues

INTEGUMENTARY SYSTEM
Respiratory disorders can cause such skin discolorations as the cyanosis of hypoxemia or the cherry-red color of carbon monoxide poisoning.

SKELETAL SYSTEM
Any respiratory disorder that causes hypoxemia stimulates accelerated erythropoiesis in the red bone marrow.

MUSCULAR SYSTEM
Acid–base imbalances of respiratory origin can affect neuromuscular function.

NERVOUS SYSTEM
Respiration affects the pH of the cerebrospinal fluid, which in turn affects neural function with effects ranging from hyperexcitability to depressed excitability and coma.

ENDOCRINE SYSTEM
Lungs produce angiotensin-converting enzyme (ACE), which converts angiotensin I to the hormone angiotensin II; hypoxemia stimulates secretion of erythropoietin.

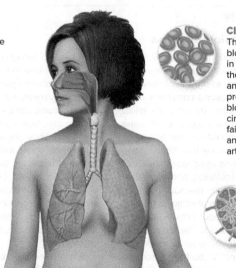

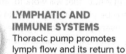

CIRCULATORY SYSTEM
Thoracic pump aids venous return of blood; proplatelets break up into platelets in the lungs; angiotensin II, produced in the lungs, stimulates vasoconstriction and helps regulate blood volume and pressure; respiration strongly influences blood pH; obstruction of pulmonary circulation can lead to right-sided heart failure; lungs filter blood clots and emboli and prevent them from obstructing vital arteries elsewhere.

LYMPHATIC AND IMMUNE SYSTEMS
Thoracic pump promotes lymph flow and its return to the bloodstream.

URINARY SYSTEM
Valsalva maneuver aids in urination; urinary and respiratory systems collaborate in acid–base balance and compensate for each other's deficiencies in maintaining normal pH; hypoxemia stimulates kidneys to secrete erythropoietin.

DIGESTIVE SYSTEM
Valsalva maneuver aids in defecation.

REPRODUCTIVE SYSTEM
Valsalva maneuver aids in childbirth.

STUDY GUIDE

▶ Assess Your Learning Outcomes

To test your knowledge, discuss the following topics with a study partner or in writing, ideally from memory.

22.1 Anatomy of the Respiratory System

1. Two meanings of the word *respiration*
2. Functions of the respiratory system
3. The distinction between the respiratory and conducting divisions of this system, and constituents of each division
4. The distinction between the upper and lower respiratory tract and the dividing line between them
5. The extent of the nasal cavity, names of its anterior and posterior openings, and names of the two chambers separated by the nasal septum, and histology of its mucosa
6. Names and functions of the scroll-like folds that arise from each lateral wall of the nasal cavity
7. Anatomy and functions of the pharynx, larynx, and trachea
8. Gross anatomy of the lungs; how the right and left lungs differ; and the structures that enter or leave through the hilum
9. Divisions of the bronchial tree from main bronchus to segmental bronchi, and histological changes along the way
10. How bronchioles differ from bronchi; two types of bronchioles; and how the two differ in histology and function
11. Alveolar ducts and alveoli; cell types of the alveoli and their functions; the relationship of pulmonary blood vessels to the alveoli; and the structure of the respiratory membrane in relation to its function
12. The parietal and visceral pleurae, pleural cavity, and pleural fluid

22.2 Pulmonary Ventilation

1. The two phases of the respiratory cycle
2. Actions of the respiratory muscles; the prime mover and synergists of respiration
3. Locations and functions of the brainstem respiratory centers; their connections with each other and with other levels of the CNS; and routes of CNS output to the respiratory muscles
4. Locations and roles of the central and peripheral chemoreceptors, stretch receptors, and irritant receptors in modulating the respiratory rhythm

5. The neural pathway for voluntary control of respiration
6. The mathematical relationship of airflow, pressure, and resistance
7. Actions of the sternum and rib cage during the respiratory cycle
8. Why the pressures driving respiratory airflow are measured in cm H_2O rather than mm Hg like other pressures considered in this and previous chapters
9. How and why intrapulmonary pressure changes relative to atmospheric pressure during inspiration; how Boyle's and Charles's laws relate to pulmonary ventilation
10. The role of elastic recoil of the thorax in expiration; how and why intrapulmonary pressure changes relative to atmospheric pressure in expiration
11. How pulmonary ventilation is affected by bronchodilation, bronchoconstriction, pulmonary compliance, and alveolar surfactant
12. A typical adult tidal volume; how much of this ventilates the alveoli and how much remains in the anatomical dead space; and how to calculate alveolar ventilation rate
13. Use of the spirometer to measure pulmonary ventilation; the meanings and typical values of the four respiratory volumes and four capacities
14. How to determine forced expiratory volume, minute respiratory volume, and maximum voluntary ventilation
15. The difference between restrictive and obstructive disorders of respiration, their respective effects on certain respiratory volumes and capacities, and examples of each
16. Definitions of *eupnea, dyspnea, hyperpnea, hyperventilation, hypoventilation, Kussmaul respiration, orthopnea, respiratory arrest,* and *tachypnea*

22.3 Gas Exchange and Transport

1. Composition of the atmosphere and average partial pressures of its constituent gases at sea level; the application of Dalton's law to partial pressures and total atmospheric pressure
2. Differences between the composition of atmospheric air and alveolar air, and reasons for the differences

3. Why gas exchange depends on the ability of the gases to dissolve in water; the application of Henry's law to the air–water interface in the alveoli
4. Four variables that determine the rate of O_2 loading and CO_2 unloading by blood passing through the alveolar capillaries
5. How ventilation–perfusion coupling matches pulmonary airflow to blood flow for optimal gas exchange
6. The two modes of O_2 transport in the blood and the relative amounts of O_2 transported by each; where O_2 binds to the hemoglobin molecule; how much O_2 a hemoglobin molecule can carry; and what hemoglobin is called when O_2 is bound to it
7. Interpretation of the oxyhemoglobin dissociation curve, including the reason for its shape and how it can be used to show the amount of O_2 unloading as hemoglobin passes through a typical systemic tissue
8. Three modes of CO_2 transport in the blood and the relative amounts of CO_2 transported by each; where CO_2 binds to hemoglobin; and what hemoglobin is called when CO_2 is bound to it
9. How carbonic anhydrase (CAH) and the chloride shift aid in the loading of CO_2 from the tissue fluids; the reaction catalyzed by CAH
10. How the loading of CO_2 in systemic tissues influences the unloading of O_2; the meaning of the *utilization coefficient* and a typical resting value
11. How the loading of O_2 in the lungs influences the unloading of CO_2
12. Four mechanisms that adjust the amount of O_2 unloaded by hemoglobin to the needs of individual tissues
13. How the Haldane effect modifies CO_2 loading in relation to the metabolic rates of individual tissues
14. Three factors that stimulate the central and peripheral chemoreceptors, and their relative influences on breathing

STUDY GUIDE

15. The normal pH range of the blood; terms for deviations above and below this range; terms for the CO_2 imbalances that cause these pH deviations; and how the body homeostatically regulates blood pH
16. The mechanism by which exercise increases respiration

22.4 Respiratory Disorders

1. The definition of *hypoxia;* its four varieties and the cause of each; and the consequences of uncorrected hypoxia
2. The mechanism and effects of oxygen toxicity

3. The names, most common cause, and pathology of the two chronic obstructive pulmonary diseases (COPDs)
4. The most common cause of lung cancer, and the names and pathological differences between the three forms of lung cancer

▶ Testing Your Recall

Answers in Appendix A

1. The nasal cavity is divided by the nasal septum into right and left
   a. nares.
   b. vestibules.
   c. fossae.
   d. choanae.
   e. conchae.

2. The intrinsic laryngeal muscles regulate speech by rotating
   a. the extrinsic laryngeal muscles.
   b. the corniculate cartilages.
   c. the arytenoid cartilages.
   d. the hyoid bone.
   e. the vocal cords.

3. The largest air passages that engage in gas exchange with the blood are
   a. the respiratory bronchioles.
   b. the terminal bronchioles.
   c. the primary bronchi.
   d. the alveolar ducts.
   e. the alveoli.

4. Respiratory arrest would most likely result from a tumor of the
   a. pons.
   b. midbrain.
   c. thalamus.
   d. cerebellum.
   e. medulla oblongata.

5. Which of these values is normally highest?
   a. tidal volume
   b. inspiratory reserve volume
   c. expiratory reserve volume
   d. residual volume
   e. vital capacity

6. The _____ protects the lungs from injury by excessive inspiration.
   a. pleura
   b. rib cage
   c. inflation reflex
   d. Haldane effect
   e. Bohr effect

7. According to _____, the warming of air as it is inhaled helps to inflate the lungs.
   a. Boyle's law
   b. Charles's law
   c. Dalton's law
   d. the Bohr effect
   e. the Haldane effect

8. Poor blood circulation causes _____ hypoxia.
   a. ischemic
   b. histotoxic
   c. hemolytic
   d. anemic
   e. hypoxemic

9. Most of the CO_2 that diffuses from the blood into an alveolus comes from
   a. dissolved gas.
   b. carbaminohemoglobin.
   c. carboxyhemoglobin.
   d. carbonic acid.
   e. expired air.

10. The duration of an inspiration is set by
    a. the pneumotaxic center.
    b. the phrenic nerves.
    c. the vagus nerves.
    d. the I neurons.
    e. the E neurons.

11. The superior opening into the larynx is guarded by a tissue flap called the _____.

12. Within each lung, the airway forms a branching complex called the _____.

13. The great alveolar cells secrete a phospholipid–protein mixture called _____.

14. Intrapulmonary pressure must be lower than _____ pressure for inspiration to occur.

15. _____ disorders reduce the speed of airflow through the airway.

16. Some inhaled air does not participate in gas exchange because it fills the _____ of the respiratory tract.

17. Inspiration depends on the ease of pulmonary inflation, called _____, whereas expiration depends on _____, which causes pulmonary recoil.

18. Inspiration is caused by the firing of I neurons in the _____ of the medulla oblongata.

19. The matching of airflow to blood flow in any region of the lung is called _____.

20. A blood pH > 7.45 is called _____ and can be caused by a CO_2 deficiency called _____.

STUDY GUIDE

▶ Building Your Medical Vocabulary

Answers in Appendix A

State a meaning of each word element, and give a medical term from this chapter that uses it or a slight variation of it.

1. atel-

2. capni-

3. carcino-

4. corni-

5. eu-

6. -meter

7. naso-

8. -pnea

9. spiro-

10. thyro-

▶ What's Wrong with These Statements?

Answers in Appendix A

Briefly explain why each of the following statements is false, or reword it to make it true.

1. The phrenic nerves fire during inspiration only.

2. There is one segmental bronchus for each lobe of the lung.

3. The most abundant cells in the lung are the squamous alveolar cells.

4. If you increase the volume of a given quantity of gas, its pressure increases.

5. Atelectasis is always preceded by pneumothorax.

6. The greatest effect of accelerated breathing is to increase the oxygen content of the blood.

7. Oxygen is the only gas we inhale from the atmosphere, since we can't use the nitrogen or other gases in it.

8. Most of the air one inhales never makes it to the alveoli.

9. The lower the P_{CO_2} of the blood is, the lower its pH is.

10. Most of the CO_2 transported by the blood is in the form of dissolved gas.

▶ Testing Your Comprehension

1. Discuss how the different functions of the conducting division and respiratory division relate to differences in their histology.

2. State whether hyperventilation would raise or lower each of the following—the blood P_{O_2}, P_{CO_2}, and pH—and explain why. Do the same for emphysema.

3. Some competitive swimmers hyperventilate before a race, thinking they can "load up extra oxygen" and hold their breaths longer underwater. While they can indeed hold their breaths longer, it is not for the reason they think. Furthermore, some have lost consciousness and drowned because of this practice. What is wrong with this thinking, and what accounts for the loss of consciousness?

4. Consider a man in good health with a 650 mL tidal volume and a respiratory rate of 11 breaths per minute. Report his minute respiratory volume in liters per minute. Assuming his anatomical dead space is 185 mL, calculate his alveolar ventilation rate in liters per minute.

5. An 83-year-old woman is admitted to the hospital, where a critical care nurse attempts to insert a nasoenteric tube ("stomach tube") for feeding. The patient begins to exhibit dyspnea, and a chest X-ray reveals air in the right pleural cavity and a collapsed right lung. The patient dies 5 days later from respiratory complications. Name the conditions revealed by the X-ray and explain how they could have resulted from the nurse's procedure.

CHAPTER

13

THE SPINAL CORD, SPINAL NERVES, AND SOMATIC REFLEXES

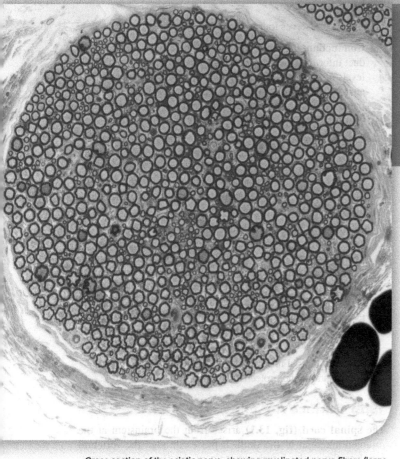

Cross section of the sciatic nerve, showing myelinated nerve fibers (large pale circles) and small unmyelinated fibers scattered among them
Science Photo Library/Alamy Stock Photo

Anatomy & Physiology
Revealed 4.0

Module 7: Nervous System

Every year in the United States, thousands of people become paralyzed by spinal cord injuries, with devastating effects on their quality of life. The treatment of such injuries is one of the most lively areas of medical research today. Therapists in this specialty must know spinal cord anatomy and function to understand their patients' functional deficits and prospects for improvement and to plan a regimen of treatment. Such knowledge is necessary, as well, for understanding paralysis resulting from strokes and other brain injuries. The spinal cord is the "information highway" that connects the brain with the lower body; it contains the neural routes that explain why a lesion to a specific part of the brain results in a functional loss in a specific locality in the lower body.

In this chapter, we will study not only the spinal cord but also the spinal nerves that arise from it with ladderlike regularity at intervals along its length. Thus, we will examine components of both the central and peripheral nervous systems, but these are so closely related, structurally and functionally, that it is appropriate to consider them together. Similarly, the brain and cranial nerves will be considered together in the following chapter. Chapters 13 and 14 therefore elevate our study of the nervous system from the cellular level (chapter 12) to the organ and system levels.

13.1   The Spinal Cord

Expected Learning Outcomes

When you have completed this section, you should be able to

a. state the three principal functions of the spinal cord;

b. describe its gross and microscopic structure; and

c. trace the pathways followed by nerve signals traveling up and down the spinal cord.

13.1a Functions

The spinal cord serves four principal functions:

1. **Conduction.** It contains bundles of nerve fibers that conduct information up and down the cord, connecting different levels of the trunk with each other and with the brain. This enables sensory information to reach the brain, motor commands to reach the effectors, and input received at one level of the cord to affect output from another level.

2. **Neural integration.** Pools of spinal neurons receive input from multiple sources, integrate the information, and execute an appropriate output. For example, the spinal cord can integrate the stretch sensation from a full bladder with cerebral input concerning the appropriate time and place to urinate and execute control of the bladder accordingly.

3. **Locomotion.** Walking involves repetitive, coordinated contractions of several muscle groups in the limbs. Motor neurons in the brain initiate walking and determine its speed, distance, and direction, but the simple repetitive muscle contractions that put one foot in front of another, over and over, are coordinated by groups of neurons called **central pattern generators** in the cord. These neural circuits produce the sequence of outputs to the extensor and flexor muscles that cause alternating movements of the lower limbs.

4. **Reflexes.** Spinal reflexes play vital roles in posture, motor coordination, and protective responses to pain or injury.

13.1b Surface Anatomy

The **spinal cord (fig. 13.1)** arises from the brainstem at the foramen magnum of the skull. It passes through the vertebral canal as far as the inferior margin of the first lumbar vertebra (L1) or slightly beyond. In adults, it averages about 45 cm long and 1.8 cm thick (about as thick as one's little finger). Early in fetal development, the cord extends for the full length of the vertebral column. However, the vertebral column grows faster than the spinal cord, so the cord extends only to L3 by the time of birth and to L1 in an adult. Thus, it occupies only the upper two-thirds of the vertebral canal; the lower one-third is described shortly.

The cord gives rise to 31 pairs of *spinal nerves*. Although the spinal cord is not visibly segmented, the part supplied by each pair of nerves is called a *segment*. The cord exhibits longitudinal grooves on its anterior and posterior sides—the *anterior median fissure* and *posterior median sulcus*, respectively (**fig. 13.2**).

The spinal cord is divided into **cervical, thoracic, lumbar, and sacral regions.** It may seem odd that it has a sacral region when the cord itself ends well above the sacrum. These regions, however, are named for the level of the vertebral column from which the spinal nerves emerge, not for the vertebrae that contain the cord itself.

In two areas, the cord is a little thicker than elsewhere. In the inferior cervical region, a **cervical enlargement** gives rise to nerves of the upper limbs. In the lumbosacral region, there is a similar **lumbosacral enlargement** that issues nerves to the pelvic

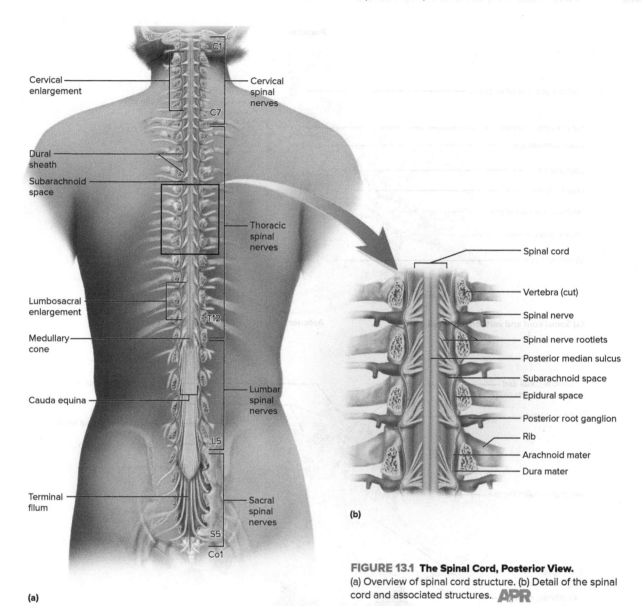

FIGURE 13.1 The Spinal Cord, Posterior View.
(a) Overview of spinal cord structure. (b) Detail of the spinal cord and associated structures. **APR**

region and lower limbs. Inferior to the lumbosacral enlargement, the cord tapers to a point called the **medullary cone.** Arising from the lumbosacral enlargement and medullary cone is a bundle of nerve roots that occupy the vertebral canal from L2 to S5. This bundle, named the **cauda equina**[1] (CAW-duh ee-KWY-nah) for its resemblance to a horse's tail, innervates the pelvic organs and lower limbs.

▶▶▶**APPLY WHAT YOU KNOW**

Spinal cord injuries commonly result from fractures of vertebrae C5 to C6, but never from fractures of L3 to L5. Explain both observations.

13.1c Meninges of the Spinal Cord

The spinal cord and brain are enclosed in three fibrous membranes called **meninges**[2] (meh-NIN-jeez)—singular, *meninx* (MEN-inks) (fig. 13.2). These membranes separate the soft tissue of the central nervous system from the bones of the vertebrae and skull. From superficial to deep, they are the dura mater, arachnoid mater, and pia mater.

The **dura mater**[3] (DOO-ruh MAH-tur) forms a loose-fitting sleeve called the **dural sheath** around the spinal cord. It is a tough membrane about as thick as a rubber kitchen glove, composed of multiple layers of dense irregular connective tissue. The space between the sheath and vertebral bones, called the **epidural space,** is occupied by

---

[1]*cauda* = tail; *equin* = horse

[2]*menin* = membrane

[3]*dura* = tough; *mater* = mother, womb

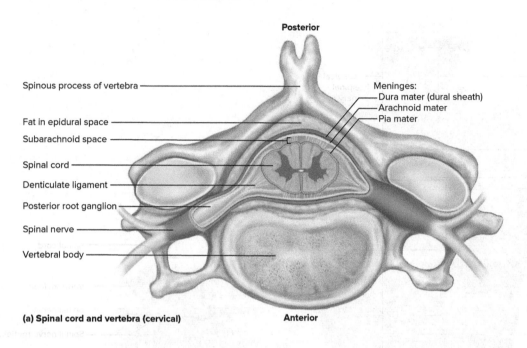

Posterior

Spinous process of vertebra

Fat in epidural space
Subarachnoid space

Spinal cord
Denticulate ligament
Posterior root ganglion
Spinal nerve
Vertebral body

Meninges:
Dura mater (dural sheath)
Arachnoid mater
Pia mater

(a) Spinal cord and vertebra (cervical)

Anterior

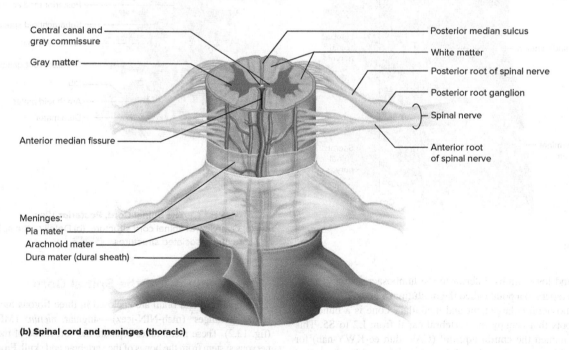

Central canal and
gray commissure
Gray matter

Posterior median sulcus
White matter
Posterior root of spinal nerve
Posterior root ganglion
Spinal nerve

Anterior median fissure

Anterior root
of spinal nerve

Meninges:
Pia mater
Arachnoid mater
Dura mater (dural sheath)

(b) Spinal cord and meninges (thoracic)

FIGURE 13.2 Cross-Sectional Anatomy of the Spinal Cord. (a) Relationship to the vertebra, meninges, and spinal nerves. (b) Detail of the spinal cord, meninges, and spinal nerve roots. See figure 13.3 for details of the gray and white matter.

blood vessels, adipose tissue, and loose connective tissue. Anesthetics can be introduced to this space to block pain signals during childbirth or surgery; this procedure is called *epidural anesthesia.*

The **arachnoid**[4] **mater** (ah-RACK-noyd) consists of the *arachnoid membrane*—five or six layers of squamous to cuboidal

cells adhering to the inside of the dura—and a looser array of cells and collagenous and elastic fibers spanning the gap between the arachnoid membrane and the pia mater. This gap, the **subarachnoid space,** is filled with **cerebrospinal fluid (CSF)** (see section 14.2b). Inferior to the medullary cone, the subarachnoid space is called the **lumbar cistern** and is occupied by the cauda equina and CSF. When a sample of CSF is needed for clinical purposes, it is

[4]*arachn* = spider, spider web; *oid* = resembling

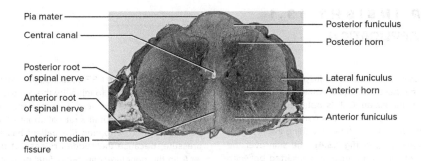

Pia mater

Central canal

Posterior root
of spinal nerve

Anterior root
of spinal nerve

Anterior median
fissure

Posterior funiculus

Posterior horn

Lateral funiculus

Anterior horn

Anterior funiculus

FIGURE 13.3 **Cross Section of the Spinal Cord (Lumbar Region).**

Jose Luis Calvo/Shutterstock

taken from the lumbar cistern by a procedure called a **spinal tap** or **lumbar puncture** (see Deeper Insight 13.1).

The **pia**[5] **mater** (PEE-uh) is a delicate, transparent membrane composed of one or two layers of squamous to cuboidal cells and delicate collagenous and elastic fibers. It closely follows the contours of the spinal cord. It continues beyond the medullary cone as a fibrous strand, the **terminal filum,** within the lumbar cistern. At the level of vertebra S2, it exits the lower end of the cistern and fuses with the dura mater, and the two form a **coccygeal ligament** that anchors the cord and meninges to vertebra Co1. At regular intervals along the cord, extensions of the pia called **denticulate**[6] **ligaments** extend through the arachnoid to the dura, anchoring the cord and limiting side-to-side movements.

13.1d Cross-Sectional Anatomy

Figure 13.2a shows the relationship of the spinal cord to a vertebra and spinal nerve, and **figure 13.3** shows the cord itself in more detail. The spinal cord, like the brain, consists of two kinds of nervous tissue called gray and white matter. **Gray matter** has a relatively dull color because it contains little myelin. It contains the somas, dendrites, and proximal parts of the axons of neurons. It is the site of synaptic contact between neurons, and therefore the site of all neural integration in the spinal cord. **White matter,** by contrast, has a bright, pearly white appearance due to an abundance of myelin. It is composed of bundles of axons, called **tracts,** that carry signals from one level of the CNS to another. Both gray and white matter also have an abundance of glial cells. Nervous tissue is often histologically stained with silver compounds, which give the gray matter a brown or golden color and white matter a lighter tan to amber color on slides that you may study.

Gray Matter

The spinal cord has a central core of gray matter that looks somewhat butterfly- or H-shaped in cross sections. The core consists mainly of two **posterior (dorsal) horns,** which extend toward the posterolateral

surfaces of the cord, and two thicker **anterior (ventral) horns,** which extend toward the anterolateral surfaces. The right and left sides of the gray matter are connected by a median bridge called the **gray commissure.** In the middle of the commissure is the **central canal,** which is collapsed in most areas of the adult spinal cord, but in some places (and in young children) remains open, lined with ependymal cells, and filled with CSF.

The posterior horn receives sensory nerve fibers from the spinal nerves, which usually synapse with networks of interneurons in the horn. The anterior horn contains the large neurosomas of motor neurons whose axons lead out to the skeletal muscles. The interneurons and motor neurons are especially abundant in the cervical and lumbosacral enlargements and are quite conspicuous in histological sections from these levels. The high density of neurons in these regions is related to motor control and sensation in the upper and lower limbs.

An additional **lateral horn** is visible on each side of the gray matter from segments T2 through L1 of the cord. It contains neurons of the sympathetic nervous system, which send their axons out of the cord by way of the anterior root along with the somatic efferent fibers.

White Matter

The white matter of the spinal cord surrounds the gray matter. It consists of bundles of axons that course up and down the cord and provide avenues of communication between different levels of the CNS. These bundles are arranged in three pairs called **funiculi**[7] (few-NIC-you-lie)—a **posterior (dorsal), lateral,** and **anterior (ventral) funiculus** on each side. Each column consists of subdivisions called **tracts** or **fasciculi**[8] (fah-SIC-you-lye).

13.1e Spinal Tracts

Knowledge of the locations and functions of the spinal tracts is essential in diagnosing and managing spinal cord injuries. **Ascending tracts** carry sensory information up the

---

[5]*pia* = through mistranslation, now construed as tender, thin, or soft
[6]*denti* = tooth; *cul* = little; *ate* = resembling

[7]*funicul* = little rope, cord
[8]*fascicul* = little bundle

DEEPER INSIGHT 13.1

CLINICAL APPLICATION

Spinal Tap

Several neurological diseases are diagnosed in part by examining cerebrospinal fluid (CSF) for bacteria, blood, white blood cells, or abnormalities of chemical composition. CSF is obtained by a procedure called a *spinal tap*, or *lumbar puncture*. The patient leans forward or lies on one side with the spine flexed, thus spreading the vertebral laminae and spinous processes apart **(fig. 13.4)**. The skin over the lumbar vertebrae is anesthetized, and a needle is inserted between the spinous processes of L3 and L4 (sometimes L4 and L5). This is the

safest place to obtain CSF because the spinal cord doesn't extend this far and isn't exposed to injury by the needle. At a depth of 4 to 6 cm, the needle punctures the dura mater and enters the lumbar cistern. CSF normally drips out at a rate of about 1 drop per second. A lumbar puncture is not performed if a patient has signs of high intracranial pressure, because the sudden release of pressure (causing CSF to jet from the puncture) can cause fatal herniation of the brainstem and cerebellum into the vertebral canal.

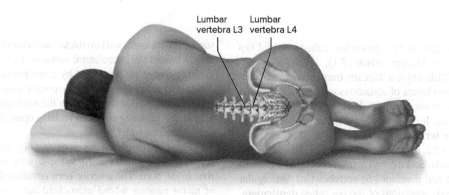

Lumbar vertebra L3   Lumbar vertebra L4

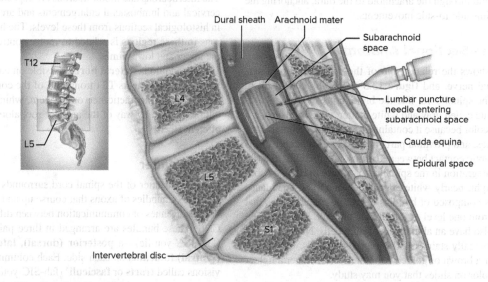

T12

L4

L5

Dural sheath   Arachnoid mater

Subarachnoid space

Lumbar puncture needle entering subarachnoid space

Cauda equina

Epidural space

L5

S1

Intervertebral disc

FIGURE 13.4 Spinal Tap (Lumbar Puncture).

cord, and **descending tracts** conduct motor impulses down **(fig. 13.5)**. All nerve fibers in a given tract have a similar origin, destination, and function. Many of these fibers have their origin or destination in a region called the *brainstem*. Described more fully in section 14.3 (see fig. 14.1), this is a vertical stalk

that supports the large *cerebellum* at the rear of the head and, even larger, two *cerebral hemispheres* that dominate the brain. In the following discussion, you will find references to brainstem and other regions where spinal tracts begin and end. Spinal cord anatomy will grow in meaning as you study the brain.

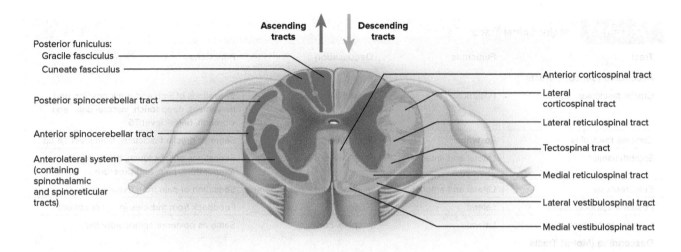

FIGURE 13.5 Tracts of the Spinal Cord. All of the illustrated tracts occur on both sides of the cord, but only the ascending sensory tracts are shown on the left (red), and only the descending motor tracts on the right (green).

❓ *If you were told that this cross section is either at level T4 or T10, how could you determine which is correct?*

Several of these tracts undergo **decussation**[9] (DEE-cuh-SAY-shun) as they pass up or down the brainstem and spinal cord—meaning that they cross over from the left side of the body to the right, or vice versa. As a result, the left side of the brain receives sensory information from the right side of the body and sends motor commands to that side, while the right side of the brain senses and controls the left side of the body. Therefore, a stroke that damages motor centers of the right side of the brain can cause paralysis of the left limbs and vice versa.

When the origin and destination of a tract are on opposite sides of the body, we say they are **contralateral**[10] to each other. When a tract doesn't decussate, its origin and destination are on the same side of the body and we say they are **ipsilateral.**[11]

The major spinal tracts are summarized in **table 13.1** and the following text. Bear in mind that each tract is repeated on the right and left sides of the spinal cord.

Ascending Tracts

Ascending tracts carry sensory signals up the spinal cord. Sensory signals typically travel across three neurons from their origin in the receptors to their destination in the brain: a **first-order neuron** that detects a stimulus and transmits a signal to the spinal cord or brainstem; a **second-order neuron** that continues as far as a "gateway" called the *thalamus* at the upper end of the brainstem; and a **third-order neuron** that carries the signal the rest of the way to the cerebral cortex. The axons of these neurons are called the *first-* through *third-order nerve fibers* (**fig. 13.6**).

The major ascending tracts are as follows. The names of most of them consist of the prefix *spino-* followed by a root denoting the destination of its fibers in the brain, although this naming system does not apply to the first two.

- The posterior funiculus consists of the **cuneate**[12] **fasciculus** (CUE-nee-ate) and **gracile**[13] **fasciculus** (GRAS-el) from level T6 to the brain, and only the gracile fasciculus from T7 down (fig. 13.6a). The gracile fasciculus carries sensory signals from the lower trunk and lower limbs, and the cuneate fasciculus from the chest and upper limbs. These signals include the senses of vibration, visceral pain, deep touch, and especially proprioception from the lower limbs and lower trunk. **Proprioception**[14] is one's nonvisual sense of the position and movements of the body and its parts, coming from sensory nerve endings in the muscles, tendons, and joints. The brain uses this information to adjust muscle tone and actions to maintain equilibrium (balance), posture, and coordination. The first-order nerve fibers of these fasciculi end in the medulla oblongata of the brainstem, but the second-order fibers decussate there to the other side of the brain. Thus, the right brain receives signals from the left side of the body and vice versa.

- The **spinothalamic tract** (SPY-no-tha-LAM-ic) (fig. 13.6b) and some smaller tracts form the *anterolateral system,* which passes up the anterior and lateral funiculi of the spinal cord. The spinothalamic tract carries signals for pain, temperature, pressure, tickle, itch, and light touch. Light touch is the

[9]*decuss* = to cross, form an X
[10]*contra* = opposite; *later* = side
[11]*ipsi* = the same; *later* = side
[12]*cune* = wedge
[13]*gracil* = thin, slender
[14]*proprio* = one's own; *ception* = sensation

TABLE 13.1	Major Spinal Tracts		
Tract	Funiculus	Decussation	Functions
Ascending (Sensory) Tracts			
Gracile fasciculus	Posterior	In medulla	Sensations of limb and trunk position and movement, deep touch, visceral pain, and vibration, below level T6
Cuneate fasciculus	Posterior	In medulla	Same as gracile fasciculus, from level T6 up
Spinothalamic	Lateral and anterior	In spinal cord	Sensations of light touch, tickle, itch, temperature, pain, and pressure
Spinoreticular	Lateral and anterior	In spinal cord (some fibers)	Sensation of pain from tissue injury
Posterior spinocerebellar	Lateral	None	Feedback from muscles (proprioception)
Anterior spinocerebellar	Lateral	In spinal cord	Same as posterior spinocerebellar
Descending (Motor) Tracts			
Lateral corticospinal	Lateral	In medulla	Fine control of limbs
Anterior corticospinal	Anterior	In spinal cord	Fine control of limbs
Tectospinal	Anterior	In midbrain	Reflexive head turning in response to visual and auditory stimuli
Lateral reticulospinal	Lateral	None	Balance and posture; regulation of awareness of pain
Medial reticulospinal	Anterior	None	Same as lateral reticulospinal
Lateral vestibulospinal	Anterior	None	Balance and posture
Medial vestibulospinal	Anterior	In medulla (some fibers)	Control of head position

sensation produced, for example, by stroking hairless skin with a feather or cotton wisp, without indenting the skin. In this pathway, first-order neurons end in the posterior horn of the spinal cord near the point of entry. Here they synapse with second-order neurons, which decussate and form the contralateral ascending spinothalamic tract. These fibers lead all the way to the thalamus. Therefore, here again, each hemisphere of the brain receives sensory input from the opposite side of the body.

- The **spinoreticular tract** carries pain signals up the anterolateral system. First-order pain fibers enter the posterior horn and immediately synapse with second-order neurons. These decussate to the opposite anterolateral system, ascend the cord, and end in a loosely organized core of gray matter called the *reticular*[15] *formation* in the medulla oblongata and pons. Pain pathways are further discussed in chapter 16.

- The **posterior** and **anterior spinocerebellar tracts** (SPY-no-SERR-eh-BEL-ur) travel through the lateral funiculus and carry proprioceptive signals from the limbs and trunk to the cerebellum at the rear of the brain. Their first-order neurons originate in muscles and tendons and end in the posterior horn of the spinal cord. Second-order neurons send their fibers up the spinocerebellar tracts and end in the cerebellum. Both tracts provide the cerebellum with feedback needed to coordinate muscle action.

Descending Tracts

Descending tracts carry motor signals down the brainstem and spinal cord. A descending motor pathway typically involves two neurons called the upper and lower motor neurons. The **upper motor neuron** begins with a neurosoma in the cerebral cortex or brainstem and has an axon that terminates on a **lower motor neuron** in the brainstem or spinal cord. The axon of the lower motor neuron then leads the rest of the way to the muscle or other target organ. The names of most descending tracts consist of a word root denoting the point of origin in the brain, followed by the suffix -*spinal*. The major descending tracts are described here.

- The **lateral** and **anterior corticospinal tracts** (COR-tih-co-SPY-nul) **(fig. 13.7)** carry motor signals from the cerebral cortex for precise, finely coordinated limb movements. The fibers of this system form ridges called *pyramids* on the anterior surface of the medulla oblongata, so these tracts were once called *pyramidal tracts*. Their fibers decussate either in the lower medulla or lower in the spinal cord, so each cerebral hemisphere controls muscles on the contralateral side of the body. The anterior tract gets smaller as it descends and gives off nerve fibers, and usually disappears by the midthoracic level.

- The **tectospinal**[16] **tract** (TEC-toe-SPY-nul) begins in the roof of the midbrain and descends the contralateral spinal

---

[15]*reticul* = little network

[16]*tectum* = roof (of the midbrain)

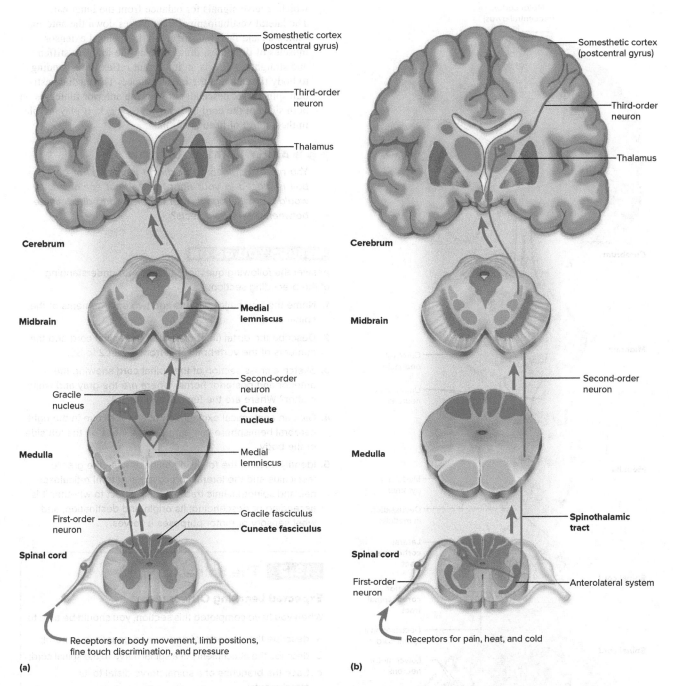

FIGURE 13.6 Some Ascending Pathways of the CNS. The spinal cord, medulla, and midbrain are shown in cross section and the cerebrum and thalamus (top) in frontal section. Nerve signals enter the spinal cord at the bottom of the figure and carry somatosensory information up to the cerebral cortex. (a) The cuneate fasciculus. (b) The spinothalamic tract.

cord only as far as the neck. It is involved in reflex turning of the head, especially in response to sights and sounds.

- The **lateral** and **medial reticulospinal tracts** (reh-TIC-you-lo-SPY-nul) originate in the reticular formation of the brainstem. They control muscles of the upper and lower

limbs, especially to maintain posture and balance. They also contain *descending analgesic pathways* that regulate the transmission of pain signals to the brain.

- The **lateral** and **medial vestibulospinal tracts** (vess-TIB-you-lo-SPY-nul) begin in the brainstem *vestibular nuclei,*

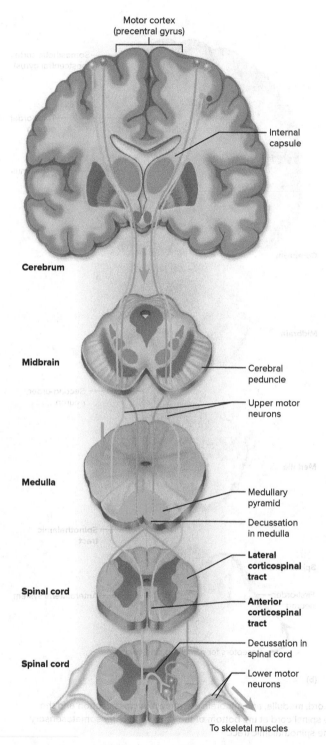

FIGURE 13.7 Two Descending Pathways of the CNS. The lateral and anterior corticospinal tracts, which carry signals for voluntary muscle contraction. Nerve signals originate in the cerebral cortex at the top of the figure and carry motor commands down the spinal cord.

which receive signals for balance from the inner ear. The lateral vestibulospinal tract passes down the anterior funiculus and facilitates neurons that control extensor muscles of the limbs, thus inducing the limbs to stiffen and straighten. This is an important reflex in responding to body tilt and keeping one's balance. The medial vestibulospinal tract descends through the anterior funiculus on both sides of the cord and ends in the neck. It plays a role in the control of head position.

▶▶▶**APPLY WHAT YOU KNOW**

You are blindfolded and either a tennis ball or an iron ball is placed in your right hand. What spinal tract(s) would carry the signals that enable you to discriminate between these two objects?

BEFORE YOU GO ON

Answer the following questions to test your understanding of the preceding section:

1. Name the four major regions and two enlargements of the spinal cord.

2. Describe the distal (inferior) end of the spinal cord and the contents of the vertebral canal from level L2 to S5.

3. Sketch a cross section of the spinal cord showing the anterior and posterior horns. Where are the gray and white matter? Where are the funiculi and tracts?

4. Give an anatomical explanation of why a stroke in the right cerebral hemisphere can paralyze the limbs on the left side of the body.

5. Identify each of the following spinal tracts—the gracile fasciculus and the lateral corticospinal, lateral reticulospinal, and spinothalamic tracts—with respect to whether it is ascending or descending; its origin and destination; and what sensory or motor purposes it serves.

13.2   The Spinal Nerves

Expected Learning Outcomes

When you have completed this section, you should be able to

a. describe the anatomy of nerves and ganglia in general;

b. describe the attachments of a spinal nerve to the spinal cord;

c. trace the branches of a spinal nerve distal to its attachments;

d. name the five plexuses of spinal nerves and describe their general anatomy;

e. name some major nerves that arise from each plexus and identify what they innervate; and

f. explain the relationship of dermatomes to the spinal nerves.

DEEPER INSIGHT 13.2

CLINICAL APPLICATION

Poliomyelitis and Amyotrophic Lateral Sclerosis

Poliomyelitis[17] and amyotrophic lateral sclerosis[18] (ALS) are two diseases that involve destruction of motor neurons. In both diseases, the skeletal muscles atrophy from lack of innervation.

Poliomyelitis is caused by the poliovirus, which destroys motor neurons in the brainstem and anterior horn of the spinal cord. Signs of polio include muscle pain, weakness, and loss of some reflexes, followed by paralysis, muscular atrophy, and sometimes respiratory arrest. The virus spreads by fecal contamination of water. Historically, polio afflicted many children who contracted the virus from swimming in contaminated pools. For a time, the polio vaccine nearly eliminated new cases, but the disease has lately begun to reemerge among children in some parts of the world because of antivaccination politics.

ALS is also known as Lou Gehrig[19] disease after the baseball player who had to retire from the sport because of it. It is marked not only by the degeneration of motor neurons and atrophy of the muscles, but also sclerosis (scarring) of the lateral regions of the spinal cord—hence its name. Most cases occur when astrocytes fail to reabsorb the neurotransmitter glutamate from the tissue fluid, allowing it to accumulate to a neurotoxic level. The early signs of ALS include muscular weakness and difficulty in speaking, swallowing, and using the hands. Sensory and intellectual functions remain unaffected, as evidenced by the accomplishments of astrophysicist and best-selling author Stephen Hawking **(fig. 13.8),** who was stricken with ALS in college. Despite near-total paralysis, he had a slowly progressing form of the disease, remained intellectually undiminished, and communicated with the aid of a speech synthesizer and computer. Tragically, many people are quick to assume that those who have lost most of their ability to communicate their ideas and feelings have few ideas and feelings to communicate. To a victim, this may be more unbearable than the loss of motor function itself.

FIGURE 13.8 Stephen Hawking (1942–2018). "When I was first diagnosed with ALS, I was given two years to live. Now 45 years later, I am doing pretty well" (CNN interview, 2010).

Geoff Robinson Photography/REX/Shutterstock

13.2a General Anatomy of Nerves and Ganglia

The spinal cord communicates with the rest of the body by way of the spinal nerves. Before we discuss those specific nerves, however, it is necessary to be familiar with the structure of nerves and ganglia in general.

A **nerve** is a cordlike organ composed of numerous nerve fibers (axons) bound together by connective tissue **(fig. 13.9).** If we compare a *nerve fiber* to a wire carrying an electrical current in one direction, a *nerve* would be comparable to an electrical cable composed of hundreds of wires carrying currents in opposite directions. A nerve contains anywhere from a few nerve fibers to (in the optic nerve) a million. Nerves usually have a pearly white color and resemble frayed string as they divide into smaller and smaller branches. As we move away from the spinal nerves proper, the smaller branches are called **peripheral nerves,** and their disorders are collectively called *peripheral neuropathy.*

Nerve fibers of the peripheral nervous system are ensheathed in Schwann cells, which form a neurilemma and often a myelin sheath around the axon (see section 12.3b). External to the neurilemma, each fiber is surrounded by a basal lamina and then a thin sleeve of loose connective tissue called the **endoneurium.** In most nerves, the fibers are gathered in bundles called **fascicles,** each wrapped in a sheath called the **perineurium.** The perineurium is composed of up to 20 layers of overlapping, squamous, epithelium-like cells. Several fascicles are then bundled together and wrapped in an outer **epineurium** to compose the nerve as a whole. The epineurium consists of dense irregular connective tissue and protects the nerve from stretching and injury. Nerves have a high metabolic rate and need a plentiful blood supply, which is furnished by blood vessels that penetrate these connective tissue coverings.

▶▶▶**APPLY WHAT YOU KNOW**

How does the structure of a nerve compare to that of a skeletal muscle? Which of the descriptive terms for nerves have similar counterparts in muscle histology?

---

[17]*polio* = gray matter; *myel* = spinal cord; *itis* = inflammation
[18]*a* = without; *myo* = muscle; *troph* = nourishment; *sclerosis* = hardening
[19]Lou Gehrig (1903–41), New York Yankees baseball player

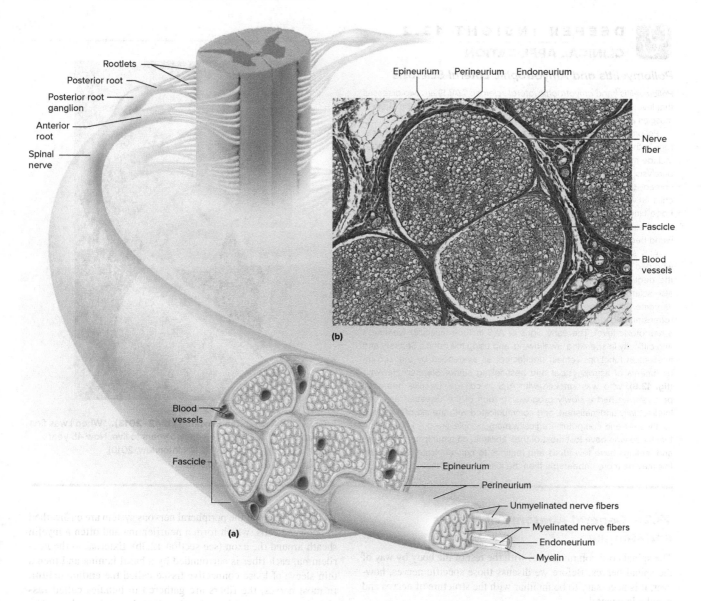

FIGURE 13.9 Anatomy of a Nerve. (a) A spinal nerve and its association with the spinal cord. (b) Cross section of a nerve. Individual nerve fibers show as tiny red dots, each surrounded by a light ring of myelin.

b: PASIEKA/Science Photo Library/Getty Images

As we saw in section 12.1, peripheral nerve fibers are of two kinds: sensory (afferent) fibers carrying signals from sensory receptors to the CNS, and motor (efferent) fibers carrying signals from the CNS to muscles and glands. Both types can be classified as *somatic* or *visceral* and as *general* or *special* depending on the organs they innervate (**table 13.2).**

Purely **sensory nerves,** composed only of afferent fibers, are rare; they include nerves for smell and vision. **Motor nerves** carry only efferent fibers. Most nerves, however, are **mixed nerves,** which consist of both afferent and efferent fibers and therefore conduct signals in two directions. However, any one fiber in the nerve conducts signals in one direction only. Many nerves commonly described as motor are actually mixed because they carry sensory signals of proprioception from the muscle back to the CNS.

If a nerve resembles a thread, a **ganglion**[20] resembles a knot in the thread. A ganglion is a cluster of neurosomas outside the CNS. It is enveloped in an epineurium continuous with that of the nerve. Among the neurosomas are bundles of nerve fibers leading into and out of the ganglion. **Figure 13.10** shows a type of ganglion associated with the spinal nerves.

[20]*gangli* = knot

TABLE 13.2	The Classification of Nerve Fibers
Class	**Description**
Afferent fibers	Carry sensory signals from receptors to the CNS
Efferent fibers	Carry motor signals from the CNS to effectors
Somatic fibers	Innervate skin, skeletal muscles, bones, and joints
Visceral fibers	Innervate blood vessels, glands, and viscera
General fibers	Innervate widespread organs such as muscles, skin, glands, viscera, and blood vessels
Special fibers	Innervate more localized organs in the head, including the eyes, ears, olfactory and taste receptors, and muscles of chewing, swallowing, and facial expression

13.2b Spinal Nerves

There are 31 pairs of **spinal nerves:** 8 cervical (C1–C8), 12 thoracic (T1–T12), 5 lumbar (L1–L5), 5 sacral (S1–S5), and 1 coccygeal (Co1) **(fig. 13.11).** The first cervical nerve emerges between the skull and atlas, and the others emerge through intervertebral foramina, including the anterior and posterior foramina of the sacrum and the sacral hiatus. Thus, spinal nerves C1 through C7 emerge superior to the correspondingly numbered vertebrae (nerve C5 above vertebra C5, for example); nerve C8 emerges inferior to vertebra C7; and below this, all the remaining nerves emerge inferior to the correspondingly numbered vertebrae (nerve L3 inferior to vertebra L3, for example).

Proximal Branches

Each spinal nerve arises from two points of attachment to the spinal cord. In each segment of the cord, six to eight nerve **rootlets** emerge from the anterior surface and converge to form the **anterior (ventral) root** of the spinal nerve. Another six to eight rootlets emerge from the posterior surface and converge to form the **posterior (dorsal) root (figs. 13.12, 13.13).** A short distance away from the spinal cord, the posterior root swells into a **posterior (dorsal) root ganglion,** which contains the neurosomas of sensory neurons (fig. 13.10). There is no corresponding ganglion on the anterior root because the neurosomas are in the anterior horns of the spinal cord.

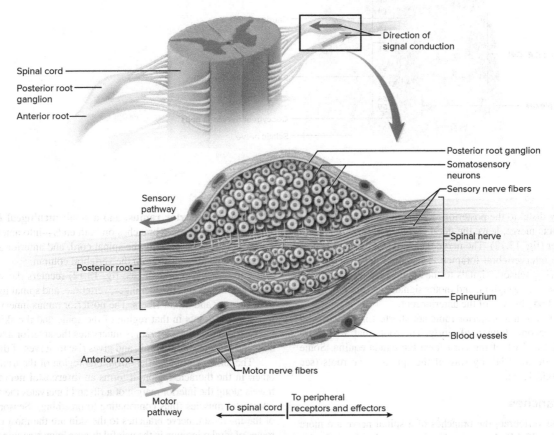

FIGURE 13.10 Anatomy of a Ganglion (Longitudinal Section). The posterior root ganglion contains the neurosomas of unipolar sensory neurons conducting signals from peripheral sense organs toward the spinal cord. Below this is the anterior root of the spinal nerve, which conducts motor signals away from the spinal cord, toward peripheral effectors. (The anterior root is not part of the ganglion.)

❓ *Where are the neurosomas of the neurons that give rise to the motor nerve fibers seen here?*

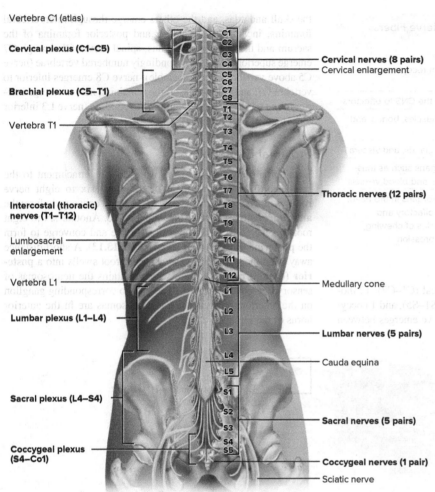

Vertebra C1 (atlas)

Cervical plexus (C1–C5)

Brachial plexus (C5–T1)

Vertebra T1

Intercostal (thoracic) nerves (T1–T12)

Lumbosacral enlargement

Vertebra L1

Lumbar plexus (L1–L4)

Sacral plexus (L4–S4)

Coccygeal plexus (S4–Co1)

C1 C2 C3 C4 C5 C6 C7 C8
T1 T2 T3 T4 T5 T6 T7 T8 T9 T10 T11 T12
L1 L2 L3 L4 L5
S1 S2 S3 S4 S5

Cervical nerves (8 pairs)
Cervical enlargement

Thoracic nerves (12 pairs)

Medullary cone

Lumbar nerves (5 pairs)

Cauda equina

Sacral nerves (5 pairs)

Coccygeal nerves (1 pair)

Sciatic nerve

FIGURE 13.11 The Spinal Nerve Roots and Plexuses, Posterior View.

Slightly distal to the posterior root ganglion, the anterior and posterior roots merge, leave the dural sheath, and form the spinal nerve proper (fig. 13.12). The nerve then exits the vertebral canal through the intervertebral foramen. The spinal nerve is a mixed nerve, carrying sensory signals to the spinal cord by way of the posterior root and ganglion, and motor signals out to more distant parts of the body by way of the anterior root.

The anterior and posterior roots are shortest in the cervical region and become longer inferiorly. The roots that arise from segments L2 to Co1 of the cord form the cauda equina. Some viruses invade the CNS by way of the spinal nerve roots (see Deeper Insight 13.3).

Distal Branches

Distal to the vertebrae, the branches of a spinal nerve are more complex **(fig. 13.14).** Immediately after emerging from the intervertebral foramen, the nerve divides into an **anterior ramus**[21]

---

[21]*ramus* = branch

(RAY-mus), **posterior ramus,** and a small **meningeal branch.** Thus, each spinal nerve branches on both ends—into anterior and posterior *roots* approaching the spinal cord, and anterior and posterior *rami* leading away from the vertebral column.

The meningeal branch (see fig. 13.12) reenters the vertebral canal and innervates the meninges, vertebrae, and spinal ligaments with sensory and motor fibers. The posterior ramus innervates the muscles and joints in that region of the spine and the skin of the back. The larger anterior ramus innervates the anterior and lateral skin and muscles of the trunk, and gives rise to nerves of the limbs.

The anterior ramus differs from one region of the trunk to another. In the thoracic region, it forms an **intercostal nerve,** which travels along the inferior margin of a rib and innervates the skin and intercostal muscles (thus contributing to breathing). Sensory fibers of the intercostal nerve branches to the skin are the most common routes of viral migration in the painful disease known as shingles (see Deeper Insight 13.3). Motor fibers of the intercostal nerves innervate the internal oblique, external oblique, and transverse abdominal muscles. All other anterior rami form the *nerve plexuses,* described next.

FIGURE 13.12 Branches of a Spinal Nerve in Relation to the Spinal Cord and Vertebra (Cross Section). **APR**

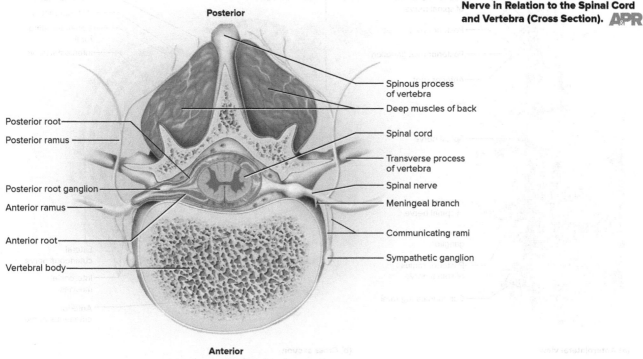

Posterior

Spinous process of vertebra

Deep muscles of back

Posterior root

Posterior ramus

Spinal cord

Transverse process of vertebra

Posterior root ganglion

Spinal nerve

Anterior ramus

Meningeal branch

Anterior root

Communicating rami

Vertebral body

Sympathetic ganglion

Anterior

FIGURE 13.13 The Point of Entry of Two Spinal Nerves into the Spinal Cord. Posterior (dorsal) view with vertebrae cut away. Note that each posterior root divides into several rootlets that enter the spinal cord. A segment of the spinal cord is the portion receiving all the rootlets of one spinal nerve.

Courtesy of Dr. Robert A. Chase, M.D.

❓ *In the labeled rootlets of spinal nerve C5, are the nerve fibers afferent or efferent? How do you know?*

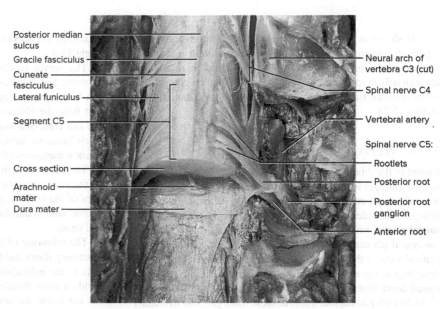

Posterior median sulcus

Gracile fasciculus

Cuneate fasciculus

Lateral funiculus

Segment C5

Cross section

Arachnoid mater

Dura mater

Neural arch of vertebra C3 (cut)

Spinal nerve C4

Vertebral artery

Spinal nerve C5:

Rootlets

Posterior root

Posterior root ganglion

Anterior root

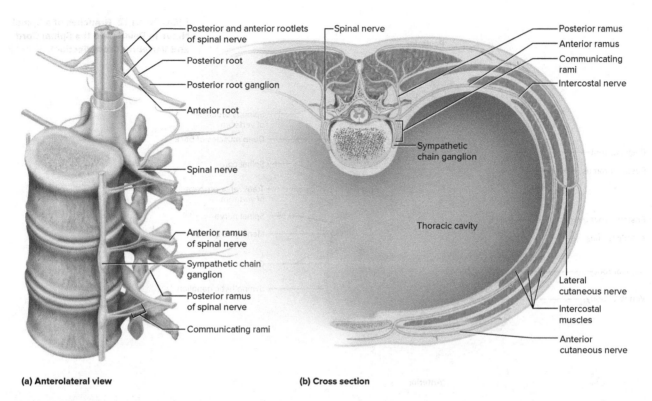

(a) Anterolateral view

(b) Cross section

FIGURE 13.14 Rami of the Spinal Nerves. (a) Anterolateral view of the spinal nerves and their subdivisions in relation to the spinal cord and vertebrae. (b) Cross section of the thorax showing innervation of muscles and skin of the chest and back. This section is cut through the intercostal muscles between two ribs.

As shown in figure 13.14, the anterior ramus also gives off a pair of *communicating rami,* which connect with a string of *sympathetic chain ganglia* alongside the vertebral column. These are seen only in spinal nerves T1 through L2. They are components of the sympathetic nervous system and are discussed more fully in section 15.2a.

13.2c Nerve Plexuses

Except in the thoracic region, the anterior rami branch and anastomose (merge) repeatedly to form five webs called nerve plexuses: the small **cervical plexus** in the neck, the **brachial plexus** near the shoulder, the **lumbar plexus** of the lower back, the **sacral plexus** immediately inferior to this, and finally, the tiny **coccygeal plexus** adjacent to the lower sacrum and coccyx. A general view of these plexuses is shown in figure 13.11; they are described in the next four tables, beginning with table 13.3. The spinal nerve roots that give rise to each plexus are indicated in violet in each illustration. Some of these roots give rise to smaller branches called *trunks, anterior divisions, posterior divisions,* and *cords,* which are color-coded and explained in the individual figures. Two of the nerves arising from these plexuses, the *radial*

and *sciatic,* are sites of unique nerve injuries described in Deeper Insight 13.4.

The nerves tabulated here have somatosensory and motor functions. *Somatosensory* means that they carry sensory signals from bones, joints, muscles, and the skin, in contrast to sensory input from the viscera or from special sense organs such as the eyes and ears. Somatosensory signals are for touch, heat, cold, stretch, pressure, pain, and other sensations. One of the most important somatosensory roles of these nerves is proprioception.

The motor function of these nerves is primarily to stimulate the contraction of skeletal muscles. They also innervate the bones of the corresponding regions, and carry autonomic fibers to some viscera and blood vessels, thus adjusting blood flow to local needs.

The following tables identify the areas of skin innervated by the sensory fibers and the muscle groups innervated by the motor fibers of the individual nerves. The muscle tables in chapter 10 provide a more detailed breakdown of the muscles supplied by each nerve and the actions they perform. You may assume that for each muscle, these nerves also carry sensory fibers from its proprioceptors. Throughout these tables, *nerve* is abbreviated *n.* and *nerves* as *nn.*

The Cervical Plexus

The cervical plexus on each side of the neck (**fig. 13.15**) receives fibers from the anterior rami of nerves C1 to C5 and gives rise to the nerves listed in **table 13.3**, in order from superior to inferior. The most important of these are the *phrenic*[22] *nerves* (FREN-ic), which travel

down each side of the mediastinum, innervate the diaphragm, and play an indispensable role in breathing (see fig. 15.3). In addition to the major nerves listed in table 13.3, the cervical plexus gives off several motor branches that innervate the geniohyoid, thyrohyoid, scalene, levator scapulae, trapezius, and sternocleidomastoid muscles.

[22]*phren* = diaphragm

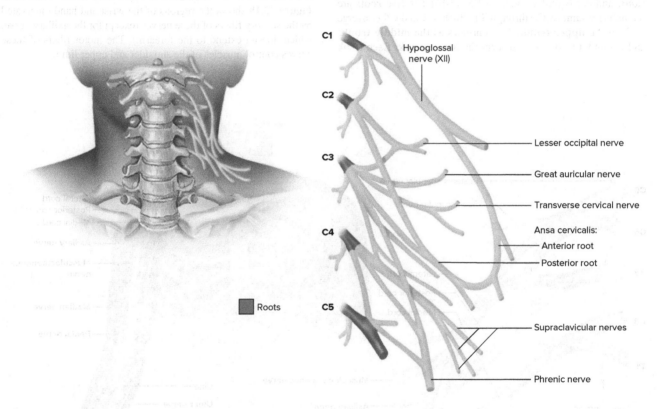

FIGURE 13.15 The Cervical Plexus. APR

? *Predict the consequences of a surgical accident in which a phrenic nerve is severed.*

TABLE 13.3	The Cervical Plexus		
Nerve	**Composition**	**Cutaneous and Other Sensory Innervation**	**Muscular Innervation (Motor and Proprioceptive)**
Lesser occipital n.	Somatosensory	Upper third of medial surface of external ear, skin posterior to ear, posterolateral neck	None
Great auricular n.	Somatosensory	Most of the external ear, mastoid region, region from parotid salivary gland (see fig. 10.7) to slightly inferior to angle of mandible	None
Transverse cervical n.	Somatosensory	Anterior and lateral neck, underside of chin	None
Ansa cervicalis	Motor	None	Omohyoid, sternohyoid, and sternothyroid muscles (see table 10.2)
Supraclavicular nn.	Somatosensory	Lower anterior and lateral neck, shoulder, anterior chest	None
Phrenic n.	Mixed	Diaphragm, pleura, and pericardium	Diaphragm (see table 10.4)

The Brachial Plexus

The **brachial plexus (figs. 13.16, 13.17)** is formed predominantly by the anterior rami of nerves C5 to T1 (C4 and T2 make small contributions). It passes over the first rib into the axilla and innervates the upper limb and some muscles of the neck and shoulder. This plexus is well known for its conspicuous M or W shape seen in cadaver dissections.

The subdivisions of this plexus are called *roots, trunks, divisions,* and *cords* (color-coded in fig. 13.16).The five **roots** are the anterior rami of C5 through T1. Roots C5 and C6 converge to form the **upper trunk;** C7 continues as the **middle trunk;** and C8 and T1 converge to form the **lower trunk.** Each trunk divides into an **anterior** and **posterior division.** As the body is dissected from the anterior side of the shoulder inward, the anterior divisions are found in front of the posterior ones. Finally, the six divisions merge to form three large fiber bundles—the **lateral, posterior,** and **medial cords.** From these cords arise the five major nerves listed in **table 13.4** in the order of figure 13.16 from superior to inferior.

Among other functions, these nerves carry sensory signals from the skin of the shoulder and upper limb to the spinal cord. **Figure 13.18** shows the regions of the wrist and hand innervated by the sensory fibers of these nerves (except for the axillary nerve, which doesn't extend to the forearm). The motor fibers of these nerves control muscles of the shoulder and upper limb.

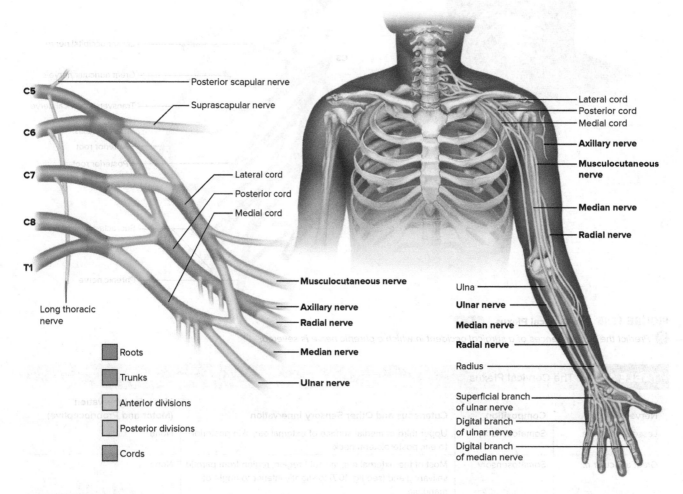

FIGURE 13.16 The Brachial Plexus. The labeled nerves innervate muscles tabulated in chapter 10, and those in boldface are further detailed in this table. **APR**

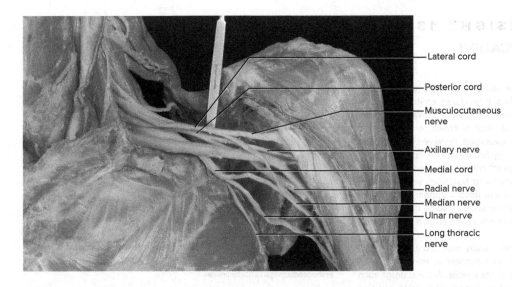

FIGURE 13.17 Brachial Plexus of the Cadaver. Anterior view of the left shoulder. Most of the other structures resembling nerves in this photograph are blood vessels.

Christine Eckel/McGraw-Hill Education

TABLE 13.4	The Brachial Plexus			
Nerve	Composition	Cord of Origin	Cutaneous and Joint Innervation (Sensory)	Muscular Innervation (Motor and Proprioceptive)
Musculocutaneous n.	Mixed	Lateral	Skin of anterolateral forearm; elbow joint	Brachialis, biceps brachii, and coracobrachialis muscles (see tables 10.9, 10.10)
Axillary n.	Mixed	Posterior	Skin of lateral shoulder and arm; shoulder joint	Deltoid and teres minor muscles (see table 10.9)
Radial n.	Mixed	Posterior	Skin of posterior arm; posterior and lateral forearm and wrist; joints of elbow, wrist, and hand	Mainly extensor muscles of posterior arm and forearm (see tables 10.10, 10.11)
Median n.	Mixed	Lateral and medial	Skin of lateral two-thirds of hand; tips of digits I–IV; joints of hand	Mainly forearm flexors; thenar group and lumbricals I–II of hand (see tables 10.10–10.12)
Ulnar n.	Mixed	Medial	Skin of palmar and medial hand and digits III–V; joints of elbow and hand	Some forearm flexors; adductor pollicis; hypothenar group; interosseous muscles; lumbricals III–IV (see tables 10.11, 10.12)

■ Radial n.   ■ Ulnar n.

□ Median n.   ■ Musculocutaneous n.

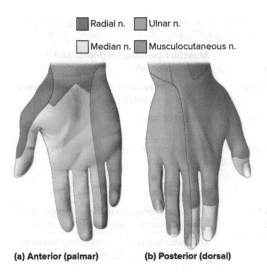

(a) Anterior (palmar)   **(b) Posterior (dorsal)**

FIGURE 13.18 Cutaneous Innervation of the Hand by Nerves from the Brachial Plexus. (a) Anterior (palmar) view. (b) Posterior (dorsal) view.

DEEPER INSIGHT 13.3

CLINICAL APPLICATION

Shingles

Chickenpox *(varicella)*, a common disease of early childhood, is caused by the *varicella-zoster*[23] virus. It produces an itchy rash that usually clears up without complications. The virus, however, remains for life in the posterior root ganglia, kept in check by the immune system. If the immune system is compromised, however, the virus can travel along the sensory nerve fibers by *fast axonal transport* (see section 12.2d) and cause *shingles (herpes*[24] *zoster)*. The signs of shingles are a painful trail of skin discoloration and fluid-filled vesicles along the path of the nerve **(fig. 13.19)**. These usually appear in the chest and waist, often on just one side of the body. In some cases, lesions appear on one side of the face, especially in and around the eye, and occasionally in the mouth.

There is no cure, and the vesicles usually heal spontaneously in 1 to 3 weeks. In the meantime, aspirin and steroidal ointments can help to relieve the pain and inflammation of the lesions. Antiviral drugs such as acyclovir can shorten the course of an episode of shingles, but only if taken within the first 2 to 3 days of outbreak. Even after the lesions disappear, however, some people suffer intense pain along the course of the nerve *(postherpetic neuralgia, PHN)*, lasting for months or even years. PHN is difficult to treat, but pain relievers and antidepressants

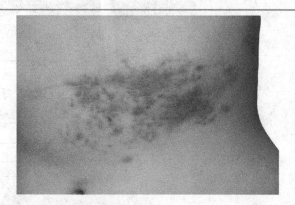

FIGURE 13.19 Shingles Lesion Tracking the Course of a Sensory Nerve.
Franciscodiazpagador/Getty Images

are of some help. Shingles is particularly common after the age of 50. Childhood vaccination against varicella reduces the risk of shingles later in life. Adult vaccination is recommended in the United States for healthy persons over age 60.

---

[23]*varicella* = little spot; *zoster* = girdle
[24]*herpes* = creeping

The Lumbar Plexus

The **lumbar plexus (fig. 13.20)** is formed from the anterior rami of nerves L1 to L4 and some fibers from T12. With only five roots and two divisions, it is less complex than the brachial plexus. It gives rise to six major nerves, listed in **table 13.5** in anatomically descending order.

The sensory fibers of these nerves carry signals from the hip and knee joints and from skin of the genitalia, lower abdominal and gluteal regions, and the thigh, leg, and foot. The motor fibers control muscles of the hip, thigh, and scrotum.

TABLE 13.5	The Lumbar Plexus		
Nerve	Composition	Cutaneous and Joint Innervation (Sensory)	Muscular Innervation (Motor and Proprioceptive)
Iliohypogastric n.	Mixed	Skin of lower anterior abdominal and posterolateral gluteal regions	Internal and external oblique and transverse abdominal muscles (see table 10.5)
Ilioinguinal n.	Mixed	Skin of upper medial thigh; male scrotum and root of penis; female labia majora	Internal oblique
Genitofemoral n.	Mixed	Skin of middle anterior thigh; male scrotum; female labia majora	Male cremaster muscle (see fig. 27.7)
Lateral femoral cutaneous n.	Somatosensory	Skin of anterior and upper lateral thigh	None
Femoral n.	Mixed	Skin of anterior, medial, and lateral thigh and knee; skin of medial leg and foot; hip and knee joints	Iliacus, pectineus, quadriceps femoris, and sartorius muscles (see tables 10.13, 10.14)
Obturator n.	Mixed	Skin of medial thigh; hip and knee joints	Obturator externus; medial (adductor) thigh muscles (see table 10.13)

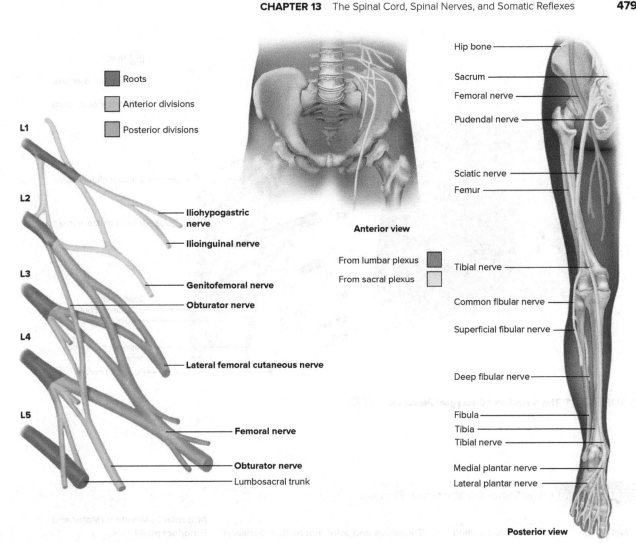

Roots
Anterior divisions
Posterior divisions

L1

L2
Iliohypogastric nerve
Ilioinguinal nerve

L3
Genitofemoral nerve
Obturator nerve

L4
Lateral femoral cutaneous nerve

L5
Femoral nerve
Obturator nerve
Lumbosacral trunk

Anterior view

From lumbar plexus
From sacral plexus

Hip bone
Sacrum
Femoral nerve
Pudendal nerve
Sciatic nerve
Femur
Tibial nerve
Common fibular nerve
Superficial fibular nerve
Deep fibular nerve
Fibula
Tibia
Tibial nerve
Medial plantar nerve
Lateral plantar nerve

Posterior view

FIGURE 13.20 The Lumbar Plexus. APR

The Sacral and Coccygeal Plexuses

The **sacral plexus** is formed from the anterior rami of nerves L4, L5, and S1 through S4. It has six roots and anterior and posterior divisions. Since it is connected to the lumbar plexus by fibers that run through the *lumbosacral trunk,* the two plexuses are sometimes referred to collectively as the *lumbosacral plexus.* The **coccygeal plexus** is a tiny plexus formed from the anterior rami of S4, S5, and Co1 (**fig. 13.21; table 13.6**).

The *tibial* and *common fibular nerves* travel together through a connective tissue sheath; they are referred to collectively as the **sciatic nerve** (sy-AT-ic), a common focus of injury and pain (see Deeper Insight 13.4). The sciatic nerve passes through the greater sciatic notch of the hip bone, extends for the length of the thigh, and ends at the popliteal fossa (back of the knee). Here, the tibial and common fibular nerves diverge and follow their separate paths into the leg. The tibial nerve descends through the leg and then gives rise to the *medial* and *plantar nerves* of the foot. The common fibular nerve divides into *deep* and *superficial fibular nerves.*

The sensory fibers of these nerves carry signals from joints of the hip, knee, and foot; from the gluteal and perineal regions and the genitals; and from skin from the gluteal region to the foot. The motor fibers control muscles of the gluteal and perineal regions, thigh, leg, and foot.

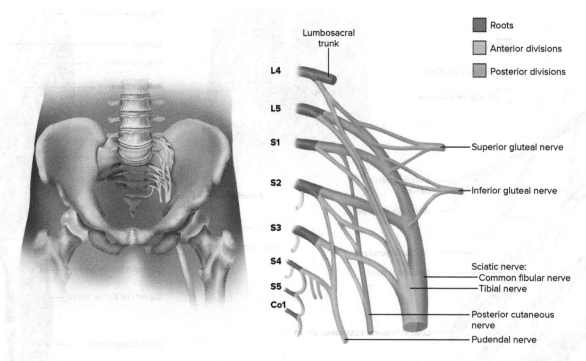

FIGURE 13.21 The Sacral and Coccygeal Plexuses. APR

TABLE 13.6	The Sacral and Coccygeal Plexuses		
Nerve	**Composition**	**Cutaneous and Joint Innervation (Sensory)**	**Muscular Innervation (Motor and Proprioceptive)**
Superior gluteal n.	Mixed	Hip joint	Gluteus minimus, gluteus medius, and tensor fasciae latae muscles (see table 10.13)
Inferior gluteal n.	Mixed	None	Gluteus maximus muscle (see table 10.13)
Posterior cutaneous n.	Somatosensory	Skin of gluteal region, perineum, posterior and medial thigh, popliteal fossa, and upper posterior leg	None
Tibial n.	Mixed	Skin of posterior leg; plantar skin; knee and foot joints	Hamstring muscles; posterior muscles of leg (see tables 10.14, 10.15); most intrinsic foot muscles (via plantar nerves) (see table 10.16)
Fibular (peroneal) nn. (common, deep, and superficial)	Mixed	Skin of anterior distal third of leg, dorsum of foot, and toes I–II; knee joint	Biceps femoris muscle; anterior and lateral muscles of leg; extensor digitorum brevis muscle of foot (see tables 10.14–10.16)
Pudendal n.	Mixed	Skin of penis and scrotum of male; clitoris, labia majora and minora, and lower vagina of female	Muscles of perineum (see table 10.7)

DEEPER INSIGHT 13.4

CLINICAL APPLICATION

Nerve Injuries

The radial and sciatic nerves are especially vulnerable to injury. The radial nerve, which passes through the axilla, may be compressed against the humerus by improperly adjusted crutches, causing *crutch paralysis*. A similar injury often resulted from the now-discredited practice of correcting a dislocated shoulder by putting a foot in a person's armpit and pulling on the arm. One consequence of radial nerve injury is *wrist drop*—the fingers, hand, and wrist are chronically flexed because the extensor muscles supplied by the radial nerve are paralyzed and cannot oppose the flexors.

Because of its position and length, the sciatic nerve of the hip and thigh is the most vulnerable nerve in the body. Trauma to this nerve produces *sciatica*, a sharp pain that travels from the gluteal region along the posterior side of the thigh and leg as far as the ankle. Ninety percent of cases result from a herniated intervertebral disc or osteoarthritis of the lower spine, but sciatica can also be caused by pressure from a pregnant uterus, dislocation of the hip, injections in the wrong area of the buttock, or sitting for a long time on the edge of a hard chair. Men sometimes suffer sciatica because of the habit of sitting on a wallet carried in the hip pocket.

13.2d Cutaneous Innervation and Dermatomes

Each spinal nerve except C1 receives sensory input from a specific area of skin called a **dermatome**.[25] A *dermatome map* (**fig. 13.22**) is a diagram of the cutaneous regions innervated by each spinal nerve. Such a map is oversimplified, however, because the dermatomes overlap at their edges by as much as 50%. Therefore, severance of one sensory nerve root does not entirely deaden sensation from a dermatome. It is necessary to sever or anesthetize three sequential spinal nerves to produce a total loss of sensation from one dermatome. Spinal nerve damage is assessed by testing the dermatomes with pinpricks and noting areas in which the patient has no sensation.

BEFORE YOU GO ON

Answer the following questions to test your understanding of the preceding section:

6. What is meant by the *anterior and posterior roots* of a spinal nerve? Which of these is sensory and which is motor?

7. Where are the neurosomas of the posterior root located? Where are the neurosomas of the anterior root?

8. List the five plexuses of spinal nerves and state where each one is located.

9. Identify which plexus gives rise to each of the following nerves: axillary, ilioinguinal, obturator, phrenic, pudendal, radial, and sciatic.

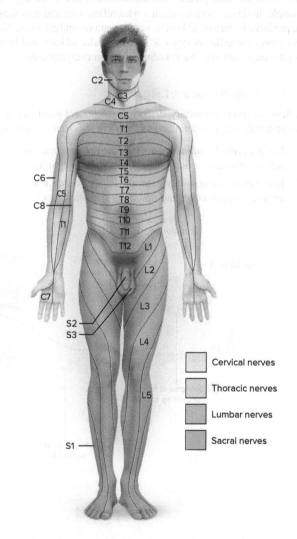

FIGURE 13.22 A Dermatome Map of the Anterior Aspect of the Body. Each zone of the skin is innervated by sensory branches of the spinal nerves indicated by the labels. Nerve C1 does not innervate the skin.

---

[25]*derma* = skin; *tome* = segment, part

13.3 Somatic Reflexes

Expected Learning Outcomes

When you have completed this section, you should be able to

a. define *reflex* and explain how reflexes differ from other motor actions;

b. describe the general components of a typical reflex arc; and

c. explain how the basic types of somatic reflexes function.

Most of us have had our reflexes tested with a little rubber hammer; a tap below the knee produces an uncontrollable jerk of the leg, for example. In this section, we discuss what reflexes are and how they are produced by an assembly of receptors, neurons, and effectors. We also survey the different types of neuromuscular reflexes and how they are important in motor coordination of our everyday tasks.

13.3a The Nature of Reflexes

Reflexes are quick, involuntary, stereotyped reactions of glands or muscles to stimulation. This definition sums up four important properties:

1. Reflexes *require stimulation*—they are not spontaneous actions like muscle tics but responses to sensory input.

2. Reflexes are *quick*—they generally involve only a few interneurons, or none, and minimum synaptic delay.

3. Reflexes are *involuntary*—they occur without intent, often without our awareness, and they are difficult to suppress. Given an adequate stimulus, the response is essentially automatic. You may become conscious of the stimulus that evoked a reflex, and this awareness may enable you to correct or avoid a potentially dangerous situation, but awareness is not a part of the reflex itself. It may come after the reflex action has been completed, and somatic reflexes can occur even if the spinal cord has been severed so that no stimuli reach the brain.

4. Reflexes are *stereotyped*—they occur in essentially the same way every time; the response is very predictable, unlike the variability of voluntary movement.

Reflexes include glandular secretion and contractions of all three types of muscle. The reflexes of skeletal muscle are called **somatic reflexes**, since they involve the somatic nervous system. Chapter 15 concerns the *visceral reflexes* of organs such as the heart and intestines. Somatic reflexes have traditionally been called *spinal reflexes*, but this is a misleading expression for two reasons: (1) Spinal reflexes are not exclusively somatic; visceral reflexes also involve the spinal cord. (2) Some somatic reflexes are mediated more by the brain than by the spinal cord.

A somatic reflex employs a **reflex arc,** in which signals travel along the following pathway **(fig. 13.23):**

1. *somatic receptors* in the skin, muscles, and tendons;

2. *afferent nerve fibers,* which carry information from these receptors to the posterior horn of the spinal cord or to the brainstem;

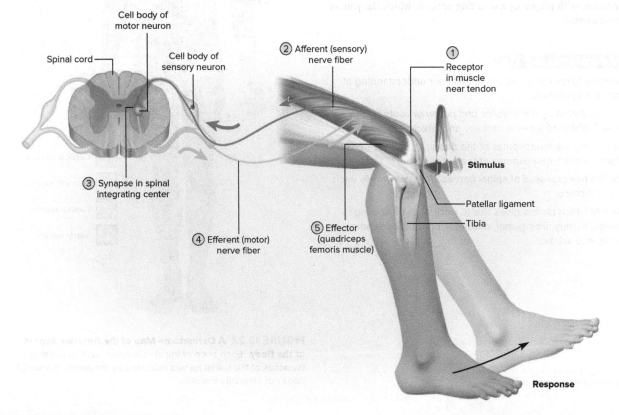

FIGURE 13.23 A Representative Reflex Arc.

3. an *integrating center,* a point of synaptic contact between neurons in the gray matter of the cord or brainstem;

4. *efferent nerve fibers,* which carry motor impulses to the muscles; and

5. *effectors,* the muscles that carry out the response.

In most reflex arcs, the integrating center includes one or more interneurons. Synaptic events in the integrating center determine whether the efferent neurons issue signals to the muscles. The more interneurons there are, the more complex the information processing can be, but with more synapses, there is a longer delay between input and output.

13.3b The Muscle Spindle

Many somatic reflexes involve stretch receptors called **muscle spindles** embedded in the muscles. These are among the

body's **proprioceptors,** sense organs specialized to monitor the position and movement of body parts. The function of muscle spindles is to inform the brain of muscle length and body movements. This enables the brain to send motor commands back to the muscles that control muscle tone, posture, coordinated movement, and corrective reflexes (for example, to keep one's balance). Spindles are especially abundant in muscles that require fine control. Hand and foot muscles have 100 or more spindles per gram of muscle, whereas there are relatively few in large muscles with coarse movements, and none at all in the middle-ear muscles.

A muscle spindle is a bundle of usually seven or eight small, modified muscle fibers enclosed in an elongated fibrous capsule about 5 to 10 mm long (**fig. 13.24**). Spindles are especially concentrated at the ends of a muscle, near its tendons. The modified muscle fibers within the spindle are called

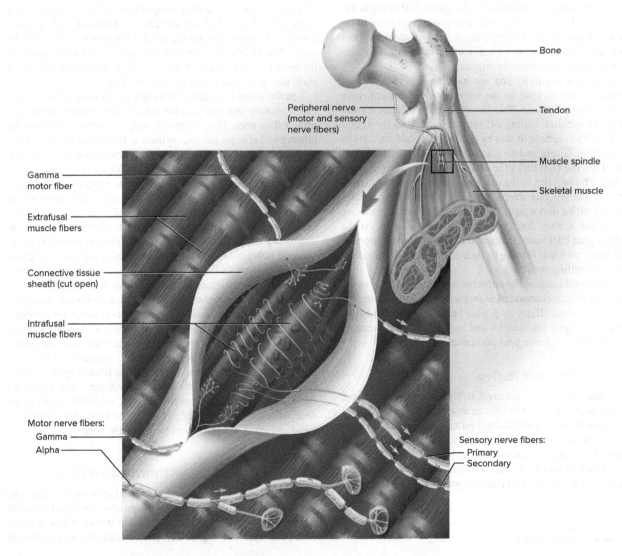

FIGURE 13.24 **A Muscle Spindle and Its Innervation.**

intrafusal[26] **fibers,** whereas those that make up the rest of the muscle and do its work are called **extrafusal fibers.**

Each end of an intrafusal fiber has a few sarcomeres. A **gamma motor neuron** of the spinal cord innervates each end and stimulates its contraction. This maintains tension and sensitivity of the intrafusal fiber, preventing it from going slack like an unstretched rubber band when a muscle shortens. Spinal motor neurons that supply the extrafusal muscle fibers are called **alpha motor neurons.** Up to now, we have studied only that type and the neuromuscular junctions they form with muscle, but nearly one-third of all spinal motor neurons are the gamma type—evidence of the great importance of muscle spindles.

The long midportion of an intrafusal fiber lacks sarcomeres and cannot contract, but is supplied by two types of sensory nerve fibers: *primary afferent fibers* that monitor muscle length and how rapidly it changes, which are therefore very responsive to sudden body movements; and *secondary afferent fibers* that monitor length only, not rate of change. Both of these sensory fiber types enter the posterior horn of the spinal cord, synapse on the alpha motor neurons and regulate their firing, and also send branches up the spinal cord to the brain. Through these fibers, the brain constantly but subconsciously monitors the length and tension of nearly every skeletal muscle throughout the body. This input is vital to the maintenance of posture, fine control of movements, and corrective reflexes.

Suppose, for example, you are standing on the deck of a boat that is gently rocking on the waves. At one moment, your body begins to tip forward. This stretches your calf muscles and their muscle spindles, setting off sensory signals to the spinal cord. The CNS responds to this by tensing your calf muscles to keep you from falling and to restore or maintain your upright posture. Then the boat rocks the other way and you begin to tip to the rear. The spindles in the calf muscles are now compressed and their signaling rate drops. Such input from the spindles inhibits the alpha motor neurons of the calf muscles, relaxing those muscles so they don't pull you farther backward. At the same time, your backward tilt stretches spindles in your anterior leg and thigh muscles, leading to their contraction and preventing you from falling over backward.

You can well imagine the importance of these reflexes to the coordination of such common movements as walking and dancing. In more subtle ways, all day long, your brain monitors input from the spindles of opposing muscles and makes fine adjustments in muscle tension to maintain your posture and coordination.

13.3c The Stretch Reflex

When a muscle is suddenly stretched, it "fights back"—it contracts, increases tone, and feels stiffer than an unstretched muscle. This response, called the **stretch (myotatic**[27]**) reflex,** helps to maintain equilibrium and posture, as we just saw in the rocking boat example. To take another case, if your head starts to tip forward, it stretches muscles at the back of your neck. This stimulates their muscle spindles, which send signals to the cerebellum by way of the brainstem. The

cerebellum integrates this information and relays it to the cerebral cortex, and the cortex sends signals back, via the brainstem, to the muscles. The muscles contract and raise your head.

Stretch reflexes often feed back not to a single muscle but to a set of synergists and antagonists. Since the contraction of a muscle on one side of a joint stretches the antagonist on the other side, the flexion of a joint creates a stretch reflex in the extensors, and extension creates a stretch reflex in the flexors. (Think of the way your biceps brachii is stretched when you extend your elbow, for example.) Consequently, stretch reflexes are valuable in stabilizing joints by balancing the tension of the extensors and flexors. They also dampen (smooth out) muscle action. Without stretch reflexes, a person's movements tend to be jerky. Stretch reflexes are especially important in coordinating vigorous and precise movements such as dance.

A stretch reflex is mediated primarily by the brain and is not, therefore, strictly a spinal reflex, but a weak component of it is spinal and occurs even if the spinal cord is severed from the brain. The spinal component can be more pronounced if a muscle is stretched very suddenly. This occurs in the reflexive contraction of a muscle when its tendon is tapped, as in the familiar *patellar* (knee-jerk) *reflex.* Tapping the patellar ligament with a reflex hammer abruptly stretches the quadriceps femoris muscle of the thigh **(fig. 13.25).** This stimulates numerous muscle spindles in the quadriceps and sends an intense volley of signals to the spinal cord, mainly by way of primary afferent fibers.

In the spinal cord, these fibers synapse directly with the alpha motor neurons that return to the muscle, thus forming **monosynaptic reflex arcs.** That is, there is only one synapse between the afferent and efferent neuron, so there is little synaptic delay and a very prompt response. The alpha motor neurons excite the quadriceps, making it contract and creating the knee jerk.

There are many other tendon reflexes. A tap on the calcaneal tendon causes plantar flexion of the foot, a tap on the triceps brachii tendon causes extension of the elbow, and a tap on the masseter causes clenching of the jaw. Testing somatic reflexes is valuable in diagnosing many diseases that cause exaggeration, inhibition, or absence of reflexes—for example, neurosyphilis and other infectious diseases, diabetes mellitus, multiple sclerosis, alcoholism, hormone and electrolyte imbalances, and lesions of the nervous system.

Stretch reflexes and other muscle contractions often depend on **reciprocal inhibition,** a reflex that prevents muscles from working against each other by inhibiting antagonists. In the knee jerk, for example, the quadriceps wouldn't produce much joint movement if its antagonists, the hamstring muscles, contracted at the same time. But reciprocal inhibition prevents that from happening. Some branches of the sensory fibers from the quadriceps muscle spindles stimulate spinal interneurons that, in turn, *inhibit* the alpha motor neurons of the hamstrings (fig. 13.25). The hamstrings remain relaxed and allow the quadriceps to extend the knee.

13.3d The Flexor (Withdrawal) Reflex

A **flexor reflex** is the quick contraction of flexor muscles resulting in the withdrawal of a limb from an injurious stimulus. For example, suppose you are wading in a lake and step on a broken bottle with your right foot **(fig. 13.26).** Even before you are consciously

---

[26]*intra* = within; *fus* = spindle
[27]*myo* = muscle; *tat* (from *tasis*) = stretch

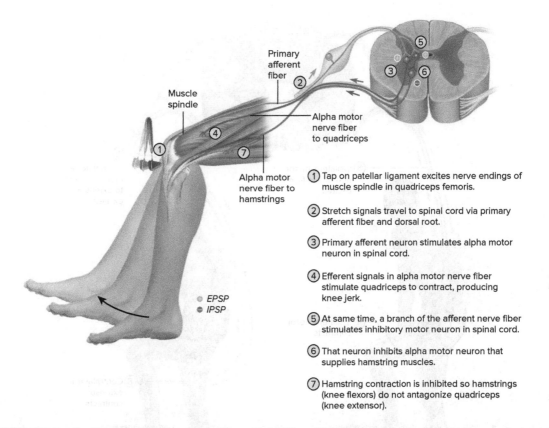

1. Tap on patellar ligament excites nerve endings of muscle spindle in quadriceps femoris.

2. Stretch signals travel to spinal cord via primary afferent fiber and dorsal root.

3. Primary afferent neuron stimulates alpha motor neuron in spinal cord.

4. Efferent signals in alpha motor nerve fiber stimulate quadriceps to contract, producing knee jerk.

5. At same time, a branch of the afferent nerve fiber stimulates inhibitory motor neuron in spinal cord.

6. That neuron inhibits alpha motor neuron that supplies hamstring muscles.

7. Hamstring contraction is inhibited so hamstrings (knee flexors) do not antagonize quadriceps (knee extensor).

FIGURE 13.25 The Patellar Tendon Reflex Arc and Reciprocal Inhibition of the Antagonistic Muscle. Plus signs indicate excitation of a postsynaptic cell (EPSP), and the minus sign indicates inhibition (IPSP). The tendon reflex occurs in the quadriceps femoris muscle, while the hamstring muscles exhibit reciprocal inhibition so they don't contract and oppose the quadriceps.

Why is no IPSP shown at point 7 if the contraction of this muscle is being inhibited?

aware of the pain, you quickly pull your foot away before the glass penetrates any deeper. This action involves contraction of the flexors and relaxation of the extensors in that limb; the latter is another case of reciprocal inhibition.

The protective function of this reflex requires more than a quick jerk like a tendon reflex, so it involves more complex neural pathways. Sustained contraction of the flexors is produced by a parallel after-discharge circuit in the spinal cord (see fig. 12.32). This circuit is part of a **polysynaptic reflex arc**—a pathway in which signals travel over many synapses on their way back to the muscle. Some signals follow routes with only a few synapses and return to the flexor muscles quickly. Others follow routes with more synapses, and therefore more delay, so they reach the flexor muscles a little later. Consequently, the flexor muscles receive prolonged output from the spinal cord and not just one sudden stimulus as in a stretch reflex. By the time these efferent signals begin to die out, you will probably be consciously aware of the pain and begin taking voluntary action to prevent further harm.

13.3e The Crossed Extension Reflex

In the preceding situation, if *all* you did was to quickly lift the injured leg from the lake bottom, you would fall over. To prevent this and maintain your balance, other reflexes shift your center of gravity over the leg that is still planted on the ground. The **crossed extension reflex** is the contraction of extensor muscles in the limb opposite from the one that is withdrawn (fig. 13.26). It extends and stiffens that limb and enables you to keep your balance. To produce this reflex, branches of the afferent nerve fibers cross from the stimulated side of the body to the contralateral side of the spinal cord. There, they synapse with interneurons, which, in turn, excite or inhibit alpha motor neurons to the muscles of the contralateral limb.

In the ipsilateral leg (the side that was hurt), you would contract your flexors and relax your extensors to lift the leg from the ground. On the contralateral side, you would relax your flexors and contract the extensors to stiffen that leg, since it must suddenly support your entire body. At the same time, signals travel up the spinal cord and cause contraction of contralateral muscles of the hip and abdomen, such as your internal and external obliques, to shift your center of gravity over the extended leg. To a large extent, the coordination of all these muscles and maintenance of equilibrium are mediated by the cerebellum and cerebral cortex.

The flexor reflex employs an **ipsilateral reflex arc**—one in which the sensory input and motor output are on the same side of the spinal cord. The crossed extension reflex employs a **contralateral reflex arc,** in which the input and output are on opposite sides. An

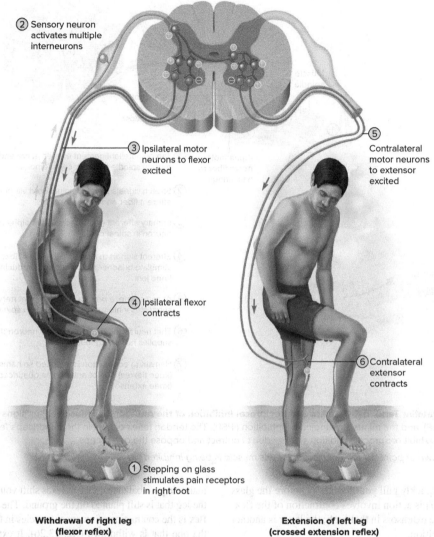

② Sensory neuron activates multiple interneurons

③ Ipsilateral motor neurons to flexor excited

⑤ Contralateral motor neurons to extensor excited

④ Ipsilateral flexor contracts

⑥ Contralateral extensor contracts

① Stepping on glass stimulates pain receptors in right foot

Withdrawal of right leg (flexor reflex)

Extension of left leg (crossed extension reflex)

FIGURE 13.26 The Flexor and Crossed Extension Reflexes. A pain stimulus triggers a withdrawal reflex, which results in contraction of flexor muscles of the injured limb. At the same time, a crossed extension reflex results in contraction of extensor muscles of the opposite limb. The latter reflex aids in balance when the injured limb is raised. Note that for each limb, while the agonist contracts, the alpha motor neuron to its antagonist is inhibited, as indicated by the red minus signs in the spinal cord. **APR**

❓ *Would you expect this reflex arc to show more synaptic delay, or less, than the ones in figure 13.25? Why?*

intersegmental reflex arc is one in which the input and output occur at different levels (segments) of the spinal cord—for example, when pain to the foot causes contractions of abdominal and hip muscles higher up the body. Note that all of these reflex arcs can function simultaneously to produce a coordinated protective response to pain.

▶▶▶**APPLY WHAT YOU KNOW**

In section 12.6d, you read of serial and parallel processing. Which of these do you think best describes the stretch reflex, flexor reflex, and crossed extension reflex? Explain.

13.3f The Tendon Reflex

Tendon organs are proprioceptors located in a tendon near its junction with a muscle **(fig. 13.27)**. A tendon organ is about 0.5 mm long. It consists of an encapsulated bundle of small, loose collagen fibers and one or more nerve fibers that penetrate the capsule and end in flattened leaflike processes between the collagen fibers. As long as the tendon is slack, its collagen fibers are slightly spread and put little pressure on the nerve endings. When muscle contraction pulls on the tendon, the collagen fibers come together like the two sides of a stretched rubber band and squeeze the nerve endings

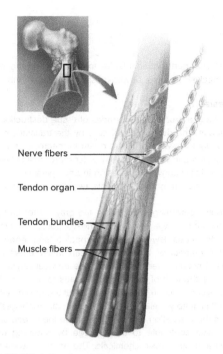

FIGURE 13.27 A Tendon Organ.

Nerve fibers

Tendon organ

Tendon bundles

Muscle fibers

between them. The nerve fiber sends signals to the spinal cord that provide the CNS with feedback on the degree of muscle tension at the joint.

The **tendon reflex** is a response to excessive tension on the tendon. It inhibits alpha motor neurons to the muscle so the muscle doesn't contract as strongly. This moderates muscle contraction before it tears a tendon or pulls it loose from the muscle or bone. Nevertheless, strong muscles and quick movements sometimes damage a tendon before the reflex can occur, causing such athletic injuries as a ruptured calcaneal tendon.

The tendon reflex also functions when some parts of a muscle contract more than others. It inhibits the muscle fibers connected with overstimulated tendon organs so their contraction is more comparable to the contraction of the rest of the muscle. This spreads the workload more evenly over the entire muscle, which is beneficial in such actions as maintaining a steady grip on a tool.

Table 13.7 and Deeper Insight 13.5 describe some injuries and other disorders of the spinal cord and spinal nerves.

BEFORE YOU GO ON

Answer the following questions to test your understanding of the preceding section:

10. Name five structural components of a typical somatic reflex arc. Which of these is absent from a monosynaptic arc?

11. State the function of each of the following in a muscle spindle: intrafusal fibers, gamma motor neurons, and primary afferent fibers.

12. Explain how nerve fibers in a tendon sense the degree of tension in a muscle.

13. Why must the withdrawal reflex, but not the stretch reflex, involve a polysynaptic reflex arc?

14. Explain why the crossed extension reflex must accompany a withdrawal reflex of the leg.

TABLE 13.7	Some Disorders of the Spinal Cord and Spinal Nerves
Guillain–Barré syndrome	An acute demyelinating nerve disorder often triggered by viral infection, resulting in muscle weakness, elevated heart rate, unstable blood pressure, shortness of breath, and sometimes death from respiratory paralysis
Neuralgia	General term for nerve pain, often caused by pressure on spinal nerves from herniated intervertebral discs
Paresthesia	Abnormal sensations of prickling, burning, numbness, or tingling in the absence of actual stimulation; a symptom of peripheral nerve disorders
Peripheral neuropathy	Any loss of sensory or motor function due to nerve injury; also called *nerve palsy*
Rabies (hydrophobia)	A disease usually contracted from animal bites, involving viral infection that spreads via somatic motor nerve fibers to the CNS and then autonomic nerve fibers; leads to seizures, coma, and death; invariably fatal if not treated before CNS symptoms appear
Spinal meningitis	Inflammation of the spinal meninges due to viral, bacterial, or other infection

You can find other spinal cord and peripheral nerve disorders described in the following places:

Carpal tunnel syndrome in Deeper Insight 10.5; *multiple sclerosis* and *Tay–Sachs disease* in Deeper Insight 12.2; *polio* and *amyotrophic lateral sclerosis* in Deeper Insight 13.2; *shingles* in Deeper Insight 13.3; *crutch paralysis* and *sciatica* in Deeper Insight 13.4; spinal cord trauma and the forms of paralysis in Deeper Insight 13.5; *leprosy* and *diabetic neuropathy* in section 16.2d, and the latter also in section 17.7e.

DEEPER INSIGHT 13.5

CLINICAL APPLICATION

Spinal Cord Trauma

In the United States, 10,000 to 12,000 people are newly paralyzed each year by spinal cord trauma, usually as a result of vertebral fractures. The greatest incidence is among males from 16 to 30 years old, because of their high-risk behaviors. Fifty-five percent of their injuries are from automobile and motorcycle accidents, 18% from sports, and 15% from gunshot and stab wounds. Elderly people are also at above-average risk because of falls, and in times of war, battlefield injuries account for many cases.

Effects of Injury

Complete *transection* (severance) of the spinal cord causes immediate loss of motor control at and below the level of the injury. Transection superior to segment C4 presents a threat of respiratory failure. Victims also lose sensation from the level of injury and below, although some patients temporarily feel burning pain within one or two dermatomes of the level of the lesion.

In the early stage, victims exhibit a syndrome called *spinal shock*. Muscles below the level of injury exhibit flaccid paralysis (inability to contract) and an absence of reflexes because of the lack of stimulation from higher levels of the CNS. For 8 days to 8 weeks after the accident, the patient typically lacks bladder and bowel reflexes and thus retains urine and feces. Lacking sympathetic stimulation to the blood vessels, a patient may exhibit *neurogenic shock* in which the vessels dilate and blood pressure drops dangerously low. Fever may occur because the hypothalamus cannot induce sweating to cool the body. Spinal shock can last from a few days to several weeks (usually 7 to 20 days).

As spinal shock subsides, somatic reflexes begin to reappear, at first in the toes and progressing to the feet and legs. Autonomic reflexes also reappear. Contrary to the earlier urinary and fecal retention, a patient now has the opposite problem, incontinence, as the rectum and bladder empty reflexively in response to stretch. Both the somatic and autonomic nervous systems typically exhibit exaggerated reflexes, a state called *hyperreflexia* or the *mass reflex reaction*. Stimuli such as a full bladder or cutaneous touch can trigger an extreme cardiovascular reaction. The systolic blood pressure, normally about 120 mm Hg, jumps to as high as 300 mm Hg. This causes intense headaches and sometimes a stroke. Pressure receptors in the major arteries sense this rise in blood pressure and activate a reflex that slows the heart, sometimes to a rate as low as 30 or 40 beats/minute (*bradycardia*), compared with a normal rate of 70 to 80. The patient may also experience profuse sweating and blurred vision.

Men at first lose the capacity for erection and ejaculation. They may recover these functions later and become capable of ejaculating and fathering children, but without sexual sensation. In females, menstruation may become irregular or cease.

The most serious permanent effect of spinal cord trauma is paralysis. The flaccid paralysis of spinal shock later changes to spastic paralysis as spinal reflexes are regained but lack inhibitory control from the brain. Spastic paralysis typically starts with chronic flexion of the hips and knees (flexor spasms) and progresses to a state in which the limbs become straight and rigid (extensor spasms). Three forms of muscle paralysis are *paraplegia*, a paralysis of both lower limbs resulting from spinal cord lesions at levels T1 to L1; *quadriplegia*, the paralysis of all four limbs resulting from lesions above level C5; and *hemiplegia*, paralysis of one side of the body, usually resulting not from spinal cord injuries but from a stroke or other brain lesion. Spinal cord lesions from C5 to C7 can produce a state of partial quadriplegia—total paralysis of the lower limbs and partial paralysis (*paresis*, or weakness) of the upper limbs.

Pathogenesis

Spinal cord trauma produces two stages of tissue destruction. The first is instantaneous—the destruction of cells by the traumatic event itself. The second stage, a wave of tissue death by necrosis and apoptosis, begins in minutes and lasts for days. It is far more destructive than the initial injury, typically converting a lesion in one spinal cord segment to a lesion that spans four or five segments, two above and two below the original site.

Microscopic hemorrhages appear in the gray matter and pia mater within minutes and grow larger over the next 2 hours. The white matter becomes edematous (swollen). Hemorrhaging and edema spread to adjacent segments of the cord and can fatally affect respiration or brainstem function when it occurs in the cervical region. *Ischemia* (iss-KEE-me-uh), the lack of blood, quickly leads to necrosis. The white matter regains circulation in about 24 hours, but the gray matter remains ischemic. Inflammatory cells (leukocytes and macrophages) infiltrate the lesion as the circulation recovers, and while they clean up necrotic tissue, they also contribute to the damage by releasing destructive free radicals and other toxic chemicals. The necrosis worsens, and is accompanied by another form of cell death, apoptosis. Apoptosis of the spinal oligodendrocytes, the myelinating glial cells of the CNS, results in demyelination of spinal nerve fibers, followed by death of the neurons.

In as little as 4 hours, this second wave of destruction, called *posttraumatic infarction*, consumes about 40% of the cross-sectional area of the spinal cord; within 24 hours, it destroys 70%. As many as five segments of the cord become transformed into a fluid-filled cavity, which is replaced with collagenous scar tissue over the next 3 to 4 weeks. This scar is one of the obstacles to the regeneration of lost nerve fibers.

Treatment

The first priority in treating a spinal injury patient is to immobilize the spine to prevent further trauma. Respiratory or other life support may also be required. Methylprednisolone, a steroid, dramatically improves recovery. Given within 3 hours of the trauma, it reduces injury to cell membranes and inhibits inflammation and apoptosis.

After these immediate requirements are met, reduction (repair) of the fracture is important. If a CT or MRI scan indicates spinal cord compression by the vertebral canal, a *decompression laminectomy* may be performed, in which vertebral laminae are removed from the affected region. CT and MRI have helped a great deal in recent decades for assessing vertebral and spinal cord damage, guiding surgical treatment, and improving recovery. Physical therapy is important for maintaining muscle and joint function as well as promoting the patient's psychological recovery.

Treatment strategies for spinal cord injuries are a vibrant field of contemporary medical research. Some current interests are the use of antioxidants to reduce free radical damage, and the implantation of pluripotent stem cells, which has produced significant (but not perfect) recovery from spinal cord lesions in rats. Public hopes have often been raised by promising studies reported in the scientific literature and news media, only to be dashed by the inability of other laboratories to repeat and confirm the results.

STUDY GUIDE

▶ Assess Your Learning Outcomes

To test your knowledge, discuss the following topics with a study partner or in writing, ideally from memory.

13.1 The Spinal Cord

1. Functions of the spinal cord
2. Skeletal landmarks that mark the extent of the adult spinal cord, and what occupies the vertebral canal inferior to the spinal cord
3. The four regions of the spinal cord and the basis for their names
4. What defines one segment of the cord
5. Two enlargements of the cord and why the cord is wider at these points
6. Names and structures of the three spinal meninges, in order from superficial to deep, and the relationships of the epidural and subarachnoid spaces to the meninges
7. The two types of ligaments that arise from the pia mater; where they are found and what purpose they serve
8. Organization of spinal gray and white matter as seen in cross sections of the cord; how gray and white matter differ in composition; and why they are called *gray* and *white matter*
9. The position of the posterior and anterior horns of the gray matter; where lateral horns are also found, and the functions of all three
10. The anatomical basis for dividing white matter into three funiculi on each side of the cord, and for dividing each funiculus into tracts
11. Names and functions of the ascending tracts of the spinal cord
12. The meanings of *first-* through *third-order* neurons in an ascending tract

13. Names and functions of the descending tracts
14. The locations and distinctions between upper and lower motor neurons in the descending tracts
15. Decussation and its implications for cerebral function in relation to sensation and motor control of the lower body, and for the effects of a stroke
16. What it means to say that the origin and destination of a tract, or any two body parts, are ipsilateral or contralateral

13.2 The Spinal Nerves

1. Structure of a nerve, especially the relationship of the endoneurium, perineurium, and epineurium to nerve fibers and fascicles
2. The basis for classifying nerve fibers as afferent or efferent, somatic or visceral, and special or general
3. The basis for classifying entire nerves as sensory, motor, or mixed
4. The definition and structure of a *ganglion*
5. The number of spinal nerves and their relationship to the spinal cord and intervertebral foramina
6. Anatomy of the posterior and anterior roots of a spinal nerve; the rootlets; and the posterior root ganglion
7. Anatomy of the anterior ramus, posterior ramus, and meningeal branch of a spinal nerve
8. What arises from the anterior ramus in the thoracic region as opposed to all other regions of the spinal cord
9. General structure of a spinal nerve plexus and the names and locations of the five plexuses

10. Distinctions between the roots, trunks, anterior and posterior divisions, and cords of a spinal nerve plexus; which of these five features occur in each of the five plexuses
11. Nerves that arise from each plexus and the body regions or structures to which each nerve provides sensory innervation, motor innervation, or both
12. Dermatomes and why they are relevant to the clinical diagnosis of nerve disorders

13.3 Somatic Reflexes

1. Four defining criteria of a reflex; how somatic reflexes differ from other types; and the flaw in calling somatic reflexes spinal reflexes
2. The pathway and constituents of a somatic reflex arc
3. The role of proprioceptors in somatic reflexes
4. Structure and function of muscle spindles
5. Stretch reflexes; one or more examples; the purpose they serve in everyday function; the mechanism of a stretch reflex; and an anatomical reason why stretch reflexes are often quicker than other types of somatic reflexes
6. Reciprocal inhibition and why it is important that it often accompany a stretch reflex
7. Flexor reflexes; a common purpose that they serve; and why it is beneficial for flexor reflexes to employ polysynaptic reflex arcs
8. Crossed extension reflexes and why it is important for this type of reflex to accompany a withdrawal reflex
9. The structure, location, and function of a tendon organ

STUDY GUIDE

▶ Testing Your Recall

Answers in Appendix A

1. Below L2, the vertebral canal is occupied by a bundle of spinal nerve roots called
   a. the terminal filum.
   b. the descending tracts.
   c. the gracile fasciculus.
   d. the medullary cone.
   e. the cauda equina.

2. The brachial plexus gives rise to all of the following nerves *except*
   a. the axillary nerve.
   b. the radial nerve.
   c. the obturator nerve.
   d. the median nerve.
   e. the ulnar nerve.

3. Nerve fibers that adjust the tension in a muscle spindle are called
   a. intrafusal fibers.
   b. extrafusal fibers.
   c. alpha motor neurons.
   d. gamma motor neurons.
   e. primary afferent fibers.

4. A stretch reflex requires the action of _____ to prevent an antagonistic muscle from interfering with the agonist.
   a. gamma motor neurons
   b. a withdrawal reflex
   c. a crossed extension reflex
   d. reciprocal inhibition
   e. a contralateral reflex

5. A patient has a gunshot wound that caused a bone fragment to nick the spinal cord. The patient now feels no pain or temperature sensations from that level of the body down. Most likely, the _____ was damaged.
   a. gracile fasciculus
   b. medial lemniscus

   c. tectospinal tract
   d. lateral corticospinal tract
   e. spinothalamic tract

6. Which of these is *not* a region of the spinal cord?
   a. cervical
   b. thoracic
   c. pelvic
   d. lumbar
   e. sacral

7. In the spinal cord, the somas of the lower motor neurons are found in
   a. the cauda equina.
   b. the posterior horns.
   c. the anterior horns.
   d. the posterior root ganglia.
   e. the fasciculi.

8. The outermost connective tissue wrapping of a nerve is called the
   a. epineurium.
   b. perineurium.
   c. endoneurium.
   d. arachnoid mater.
   e. dura mater.

9. The intercostal nerves between the ribs arise from which spinal nerve plexus?
   a. cervical
   b. brachial
   c. lumbar
   d. sacral
   e. none of them

10. All somatic reflexes share all of the following properties *except*
    a. they are quick.
    b. they are monosynaptic.

    c. they require stimulation.
    d. they are involuntary.
    e. they are stereotyped.

11. Outside the CNS, the somas of neurons are clustered in swellings called _____.

12. Distal to the intervertebral foramen, a spinal nerve branches into an anterior and posterior _____.

13. The cerebellum receives feedback from the muscles and joints by way of the _____ tracts of the spinal cord.

14. In the _____ reflex, contraction of flexor muscles in one limb is accompanied by the contraction of extensor muscles in the contralateral limb.

15. Modified muscle fibers serving primarily to detect stretch are called _____.

16. The _____ nerves arise from the cervical plexus and innervate the diaphragm.

17. The crossing of a nerve fiber or tract from the right side of the CNS to the left, or vice versa, is called _____.

18. The nonvisual awareness of the body's position and movements is called _____.

19. The _____ ganglion contains the somas of neurons that carry sensory signals to the spinal cord.

20. The sciatic nerve is a composite of two nerves, the _____ and _____.

▶ Building Your Medical Vocabulary

Answers in Appendix A

State a meaning of each word element, and give a medical term from this chapter that uses it or a slight variation of it.

1. arachno-

2. caudo-

3. contra-

4. cune-

5. ipsi-

6. phreno-

7. pia

8. proprio-

9. ram-

10. tecto-

STUDY GUIDE

▶ What's Wrong with These Statements?

Answers in Appendix A

Briefly explain why each of the following statements is false, or reword it to make it true.

1. The gracile fasciculus is a descending spinal tract.

2. The adult spinal cord terminates in the sacral canal.

3. Each spinal nerve rootlet is connected to its own segment of the spinal cord.

4. Some spinal nerves are sensory and others are motor.

5. The dura mater adheres tightly to the bone of the vertebral canal.

6. The anterior and posterior horns of the spinal cord are composed of white matter.

7. The corticospinal tracts carry sensory signals from the spinal cord to the cerebral cortex.

8. The dermatomes are nonoverlapping regions of skin innervated by different spinal nerves.

9. Somatic reflexes are those that do not involve the brain.

10. Ipsilateral reflex arcs are monosynaptic whereas contralateral arcs are polysynaptic.

▶ Testing Your Comprehension

1. Jillian is thrown from a horse. She strikes the ground with her chin, causing severe hyperextension of the neck. Emergency medical technicians properly immobilize her neck and transport her to a hospital, but she dies 5 minutes after arrival. An autopsy shows multiple fractures of vertebrae C1, C6, and C7 and extensive damage to the spinal cord. Explain why she died rather than being left quadriplegic.

2. Wallace is the victim of a hunting accident. A bullet grazed his vertebral column, and bone fragments severed the left half of his spinal cord at segments T8 through T10. Since the accident, Wallace has had a condition called *dissociated sensory loss,* in which he feels no sensations of deep touch or limb position on the *left* side of his body below the injury, and no sensations of pain or heat from the *right* side. Explain what spinal tract(s) the injury has affected and why these sensory losses are on opposite sides of the body.

3. Anthony gets into a fight between rival gangs. As an attacker comes at him with a knife, he turns to flee, but stumbles. The attacker stabs him on the medial side of the right gluteal fold and Anthony collapses. He loses all use of his right limb, being unable to extend his hip, flex his knee, or move his foot. He never fully recovers these lost functions. Explain what nerve injury Anthony has most likely suffered.

4. Stand with your right shoulder, hip, and foot firmly against a wall. Raise your left foot from the floor without losing contact with the wall at any point. What happens? Why? What principle of this chapter does this demonstrate?

5. When a patient needs a tendon graft, surgeons sometimes use the tendon of the palmaris longus, a relatively dispensable muscle of the forearm. The median nerve lies nearby and looks very similar to this tendon. There have been cases in which a surgeon mistakenly removed a section of this nerve instead of the tendon. What effects do you think such a mistake would have on the patient?

Units 3 & 4

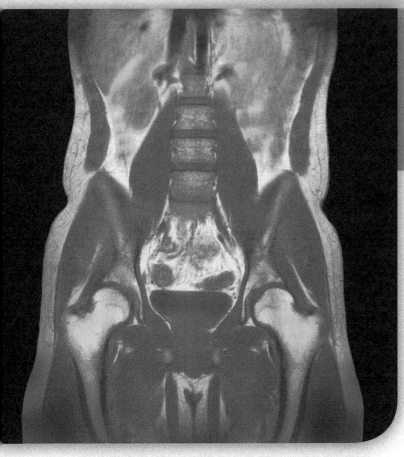

CHAPTER 10

THE MUSCULAR SYSTEM

Colorized MRI scan showing muscles of the lumbar, pelvic, and upper femoral regions

Simon Fraser/Science Source

Anatomy & Physiology Revealed 4.0

Module 6: Muscular System

BRUSHING UP

- Understanding of the skeletal muscles depends on a thorough knowledge of skeletal anatomy (chapter 8), including not just the bones but also their surface features (table 8.2), many of which are muscle attachments.

- This chapter describes the movements produced by muscles, called their *actions*, using the terminology of joint movements in section 9.2c.

Muscles constitute nearly half of the body's weight and occupy a place of central interest in several fields of health care and fitness. Physical and occupational therapists must be well acquainted with the muscular system to plan and carry out rehabilitation programs. Athletes and trainers, dancers and acrobats, and amateur fitness enthusiasts follow programs of resistance training to strengthen individual muscle groups through movement regimens based on knowledge of muscle, bone, and joint anatomy. Nurses employ their knowledge of the muscular system to give intramuscular injections correctly and to safely and effectively move patients who are physically incapacitated. Gerontological nurses are keenly aware of how deeply a person's muscular condition affects the quality of life in old age. The muscular system is highly important to biomedical disciplines even beyond the scope of the movement sciences. For example, it is the primary source of body heat in the moving individual, and loss of muscle mass can be a contributing factor in diabetes mellitus.

The muscular system is closely related to what we have covered in the preceding chapters. After this, we will examine the mechanisms of muscle contraction at the cellular and molecular levels in chapter 11, and chapter 12 will shed light on the relationship of the muscles to the nerves that control them.

10.1   Structural and Functional Organization of Muscles

Expected Learning Outcomes

When you have completed this section, you should be able to

a. describe the various functions of muscular tissue;

b. describe the connective tissue components of a muscle and their relationship to the internal organization of a muscle and compartmentalization of muscle groups;

c. relate muscle fascicles to the shapes and relative strengths of muscles;

d. name the types of muscle–bone attachments and explain the shortcoming of calling their attachments *origins* and *insertions*;

e. distinguish between intrinsic and extrinsic muscles;

f. describe the ways muscles work in groups to aid, oppose, and moderate each other's actions;

g. describe in general terms the nerve and blood supply to skeletal muscles; and

h. explain how the Latin names of muscles aid in visualizing and remembering them.

The word ***muscle***[1] means "little mouse," and apparently was coined by one of the ancient Greek authorities who thought that skeletal muscles rippling under the skin resembled scurrying mice. As we saw in chapter 5, however, there are three kinds of muscle—skeletal, cardiac, and smooth. Despite their differences, all muscle is specialized for one fundamental purpose: to convert the chemical energy of ATP into the mechanical energy of motion. Muscle cells exert force on other tissues and organs, either to produce desirable movements or to prevent undesirable ones.

10.1a The Functions of Muscles

Collectively, the three types of muscle serve the following functions:

- **Movement.** Muscles enable us to move from place to place and to move individual body parts; they move body contents in the course of breathing, blood circulation, feeding and digestion, defecation, urination, and childbirth; and they serve various roles in communication—speech, writing, facial expressions, and other body language.

- **Stability.** Muscles maintain posture by preventing unwanted movements. Some are called *antigravity muscles* because, at least part of the time, they resist the pull of gravity and prevent us from falling or slumping over. Many muscles also stabilize the joints by maintaining tension on tendons and bones.

- **Control of body openings and passages.** Muscles encircling the mouth serve not only for speech but also for food intake and retention of food while chewing. In the eyelid and pupil, they regulate the admission of light to the eye. Internal muscular rings control the movement of food, bile, blood, and other materials within the body. Muscles encircling the urethra and anus control the elimination of waste. (Some of these muscles are called *sphincters,* but not all; this is clarified later.)

- **Heat production (thermogenesis).** The skeletal muscles produce 20% to 30% of the body's heat at rest and up to 85% during exercise. This body heat is vital to the functioning of enzymes and therefore to all metabolism.

- **Glycemic control.** This means the regulation of blood glucose concentration within its normal range. The skeletal muscles absorb, store, and use a large share of one's glucose and play a highly significant role in stabilizing its blood concentration. In old age, in obesity, and when muscles become deconditioned and weakened, people suffer an increased risk of type 2 diabetes mellitus because of the decline in this glucose-buffering function.

The rest of this chapter concerns only the skeletal muscles. The term **muscular system** refers only to these, not the other two types of muscle. The study of skeletal muscles is called **myology.**[2]

---

[1]*mus* = mouse; *cle* = little
[2]*myo* = muscle; *logy* = study of

There are about 600 muscles in the human muscular system, but fortunately you aren't expected to learn 600 names! Many have repetitious names, such as the right and left muscles of the same name and muscle series between ribs and vertebrae. This chapter describes fewer than one-third of the muscles.

10.1b Muscle Connective Tissues, Fascicles, and Compartments

A skeletal muscle consists of more than muscular tissue. It also includes connective tissue, nerves, and blood vessels. The connective tissue components, from the smallest to largest and from deep to superficial, are as follows (**fig. 10.1**):

- **Endomysium**[3] (EN-doe-MIZ-ee-um). This is a thin sleeve of loose connective tissue that surrounds each muscle fiber. It creates room for blood capillaries and nerve fibers to reach every muscle fiber, ensuring that no muscle cell is without stimulation and nourishment. The endomysium also provides the extracellular chemical environment for the muscle fiber and its associated nerve ending. Excitation of a muscle fiber is based on the exchange of calcium, sodium, and potassium ions between the endomysial tissue fluid and the nerve and muscle fibers.

---

[3]*endo* = within; *mys* = muscle

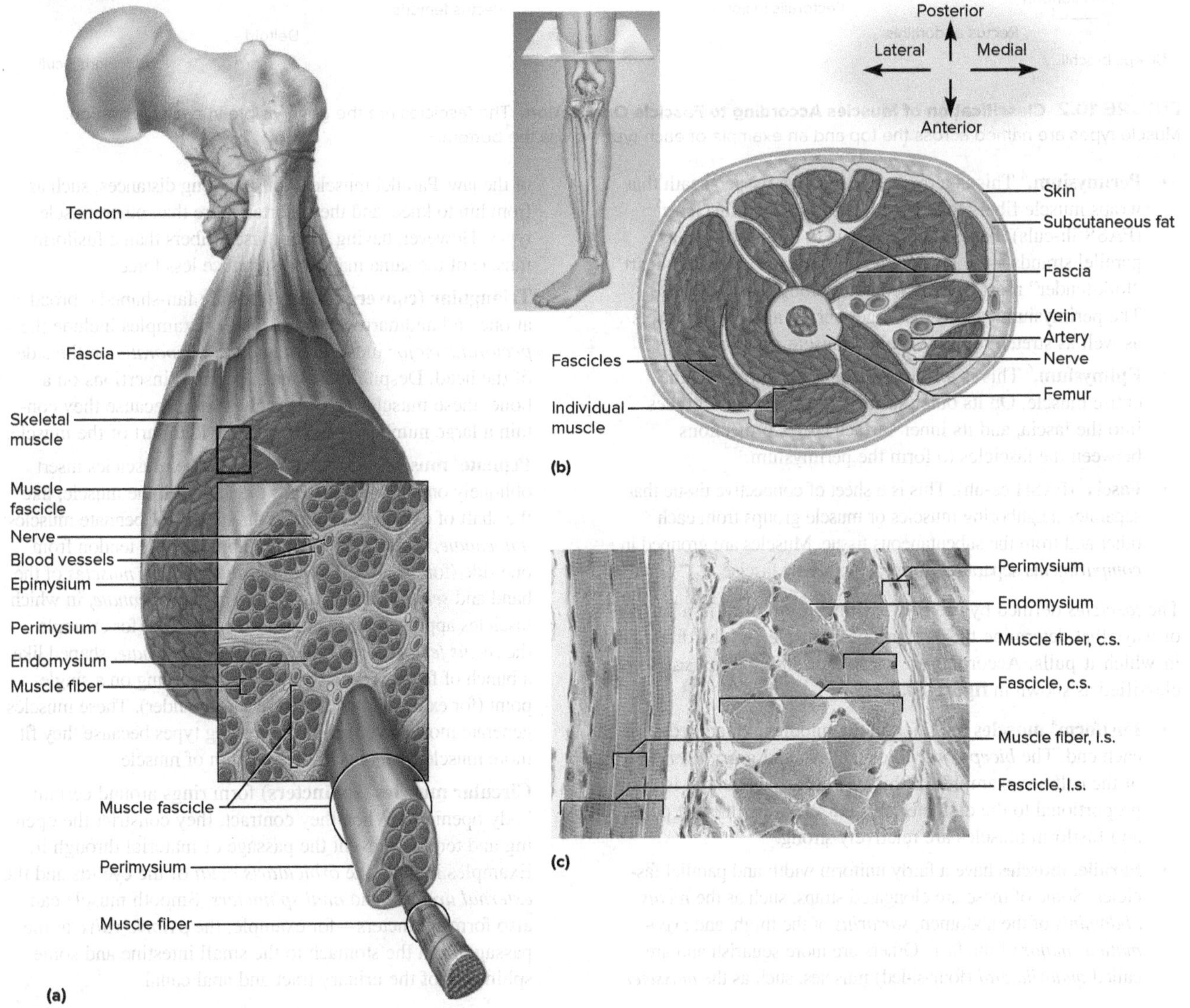

FIGURE 10.1 Connective Tissues of a Muscle. (a) The muscle–bone attachment and subdivisions of a skeletal muscle. (b) A cross section of the thigh showing the relationship of neighboring muscles to fasciae and bone. (c) Muscle fascicles in the tongue. Vertical fascicles passing between the superior and inferior surfaces of the tongue are seen alternating with cross-sectioned horizontal fascicles that pass from the rear to the tip of the tongue. A fibrous perimysium can be seen between the fascicles, and endomysium can be seen between the muscle fibers within each fascicle. (c.s. = cross section; l.s. = longitudinal section)

c: Victor Eroschenko

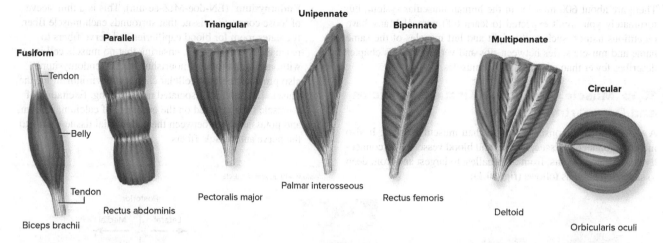

FIGURE 10.2 Classification of Muscles According to Fascicle Orientation. The fascicles are the grain visible in each illustration. Muscle types are named across the top and an example of each type across the bottom.

- **Perimysium.**[4] This is a thicker connective tissue sheath that wraps muscle fibers together in bundles called **fascicles**[5] (FASS-ih-culs). Fascicles are visible to the naked eye as parallel strands—the grain in a cut of meat; if you pull apart "fork-tender" roast beef, it separates along these fascicles. The perimysium carries the larger nerves and blood vessels as well as stretch receptors called muscle spindles.

- **Epimysium.**[6] This is a fibrous sheath that surrounds the entire muscle. On its outer surface, the epimysium grades into the fascia, and its inner surface issues projections between the fascicles to form the perimysium.

- **Fascia**[7] (FASH-ee-uh). This is a sheet of connective tissue that separates neighboring muscles or muscle groups from each other and from the subcutaneous tissue. Muscles are grouped in *compartments* separated from each other by fasciae.

The *fascicles* defined by the perimysium are oriented in a variety of ways that determine the strength of a muscle and the direction in which it pulls. According to fascicle orientation, muscles are classified as shown in **figure 10.2.**

- **Fusiform**[8] **muscles** are thick in the middle and tapered at each end. The *biceps brachii* of the arm and *gastrocnemius* of the calf are examples of this type. Muscle strength is proportional to the diameter of a muscle at its thickest point, and fusiform muscles are relatively strong.

- **Parallel muscles** have a fairly uniform width and parallel fascicles. Some of these are elongated straps, such as the *rectus abdominis* of the abdomen, *sartorius* of the thigh, and *zygomaticus major* of the face. Others are more squarish and are called *quadrilateral* (four-sided) muscles, such as the *masseter*

of the jaw. Parallel muscles can span long distances, such as from hip to knee, and they shorten more than other muscle types. However, having fewer muscle fibers than a fusiform muscle of the same mass, they produce less force.

- **Triangular (convergent) muscles** are fan-shaped—broad at one end and narrower at the other. Examples include the *pectoralis major* in the chest and the *temporalis* on the side of the head. Despite their small localized insertions on a bone, these muscles are relatively strong because they contain a large number of fibers in the wider part of the muscle.

- **Pennate**[9] **muscles** are feather-shaped. Their fascicles insert obliquely on a tendon that runs the length of the muscle, like the shaft of a feather. There are three types of pennate muscles: *unipennate,* in which all fascicles approach the tendon from one side (for example, the *palmar interosseous muscles* of the hand and *semimembranosus* of the thigh); *bipennate,* in which fascicles approach the tendon from both sides (for example, the *rectus femoris* of the thigh); and *multipennate,* shaped like a bunch of feathers with their quills converging on a single point (for example, the *deltoid* of the shoulder). These muscles generate more force than the preceding types because they fit more muscle fibers into a given length of muscle.

- **Circular muscles (sphincters)** form rings around certain body openings. When they contract, they constrict the opening and tend to prevent the passage of material through it. Examples include the *orbicularis oculi* of the eyelids and the *external urethral* and *anal sphincters.* Smooth muscle can also form sphincters—for example, the *pyloric valve* at the passage from the stomach to the small intestine and some sphincters of the urinary tract and anal canal.

The fasciae are not components of the muscles themselves, but package groups of functionally related muscles into **muscle compartments (fig. 10.3)** and stand between the muscles and the overlying

[4]*peri* = around; *mys* = muscle
[5]*fasc* = bundle; *icle* = little
[6]*epi* = upon, above; *mys* = muscle
[7]*fascia* = band
[8]*fusi* = spindle; *form* = shape

[9]*penna* = feather; *ate* = characterized by

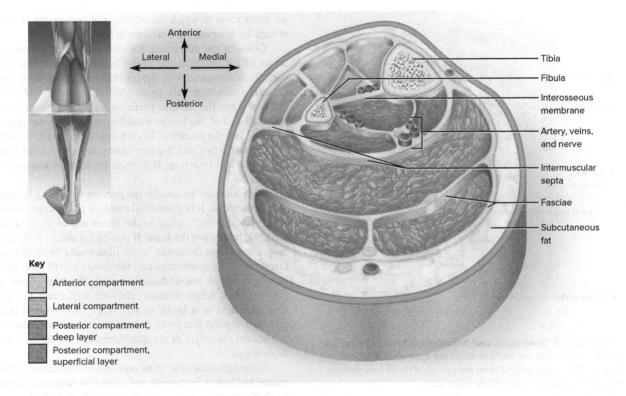

Key
- Anterior compartment
- Lateral compartment
- Posterior compartment, deep layer
- Posterior compartment, superficial layer

(labels on figure) Anterior · Lateral · Medial · Posterior · Tibia · Fibula · Interosseous membrane · Artery, veins, and nerve · Intermuscular septa · Fasciae · Subcutaneous fat

FIGURE 10.3 Muscle Compartments. A cross section of the left leg slightly above midcalf, oriented the same way as the reader's left leg.

hypodermis and skin. A compartment also contains the nerves and blood vessels that supply the muscle group. Such compartmentalization occurs in the thoracic and abdominal walls, pelvic floor, and limbs. Some of these fasciae are particularly thick and are called **intermuscular septa.** The tight binding of muscles by these fasciae contributes to a clinical problem described in Deeper Insight 10.1.

DEEPER INSIGHT 10.1

CLINICAL APPLICATION

Compartment Syndrome

Muscle compartments are very snugly contained in their fasciae. If a blood vessel in a compartment is damaged by overuse or contusion (a bruising injury), blood and tissue fluid accumulate in the compartment. The inelastic fascia prevents the compartment from expanding to relieve the pressure. Mounting pressure on the muscles, nerves, and blood vessels triggers a sequence of degenerative events called *compartment syndrome.* Blood flow to the compartment is obstructed by pressure on its arteries. If *ischemia* (poor blood flow) persists for more than 2 to 4 hours, nerves begin to die, and after 6 hours, so does muscle tissue. Nerves can regenerate after the pressure is relieved, but muscle necrosis is irreversible. The breakdown of muscle releases myoglobin into the blood. *Myoglobinuria,* the presence of myoglobin in the urine, gives the urine a dark color and is one of the key signs of compartment syndrome and some other degenerative muscle disorders. Compartment syndrome is treated by immobilizing and resting the limb and, if necessary, making an incision *(fasciotomy)* to relieve the pressure.

10.1c Muscle Attachments

Connective tissue components of a muscle emerge from it as collagenous fibers that continue into its tendon or other bone attachment, then into the periosteum and matrix of the bone, creating very strong structural continuity from muscle to bone. Some muscles insert not on bones but on the fascia or tendon of another muscle or on collagen fibers of the dermis. The distal tendon of the biceps brachii, for example, inserts partly on the fascia of the forearm. Many muscles of the face insert in the skin of the lips, eyelids, and other areas, enabling them to produce expressions such as a smile.

Direct and Indirect Attachments

Muscles have two forms of attachment to bones—direct and indirect. In a **direct (fleshy) attachment,** such as in the *brachialis* and the lateral head of the *triceps brachii* in **figure 10.4,** there is so little separation between muscle and bone that to the naked eye, the red muscular tissue seems to emerge directly from the bone. At a microscopic level, however, the muscle fibers stop slightly short of the bone and the gap between muscle and bone is spanned by collagen fibers.

In an **indirect attachment,** the muscle ends visibly short of its bony destination, and the gap is bridged by a fibrous cord or band called a **tendon.** See, for example, the two ends of the biceps brachii in figure 10.4 and the photographs of tendons in figures 10.32b and 10.37. You can easily palpate tendons and feel their texture just above your heel (your *calcaneal* or *Achilles tendon*) and on the anterior side of your wrist (tendons of the *palmaris longus* and *flexor carpi radialis* muscles).

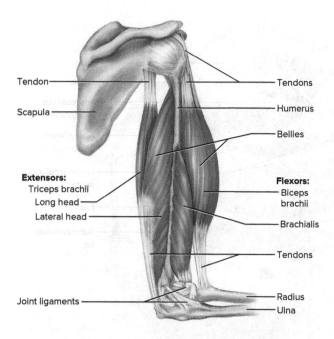

Tendon

Scapula

Extensors:
 Triceps brachii
 Long head
 Lateral head

Joint ligaments

Tendons

Humerus

Bellies

Flexors:
 Biceps
 brachii

Brachialis

Tendons

Radius
Ulna

FIGURE 10.4 Synergistic and Antagonistic Muscle Pairs. The biceps brachii and brachialis muscles are synergists in elbow flexion. The triceps brachii is an antagonist of those two muscles and is the prime mover in elbow extension.

? *Which of these muscles have direct attachments to the bones, and which have indirect attachments?*

In some cases, the tendon is a broad sheet called an **aponeurosis**[10] (AP-oh-new-RO-sis). This term originally referred to the tendon located beneath the scalp (hence the word root *neuro-*), but now it also refers to similar tendons associated with certain abdominal, lumbar, hand, and foot muscles. For example, the palmaris longus tendon passes through the wrist and then expands into a fanlike *palmar aponeurosis* beneath the skin of the palm (see fig. 10.29a).

In some places, groups of tendons from separate muscles pass under a band of connective tissue called a **retinaculum.**[11] One of these covers each surface of the wrist like a bracelet, for example. The tendons of several forearm muscles pass under them on their way to the hand (see figs. 5.13, 10.29a).

Moving and Stationary Attachments

Since most muscles span at least one joint and attach to a different bone at each end, their contraction moves one bone relative to the other. Traditionally, the attachment at the stationary end has been called the **origin** of the muscle and the attachment at the moving end has been called the **insertion.** *Gray's Anatomy* and other current authorities, however, have largely abandoned the *origin* and *insertion* terms because they are imperfect and sometimes misleading. There

[10]*apo* = upon, above; *neuro* = nervous system, brain
[11]*retinac* = retainer, bracelet; *cul* = little

are many cases in which the moving and nonmoving ends of the muscle are reversed when different actions are performed.

Consider the difference, for example, in the relative movements of the humerus and ulna when flexing the elbow to lift barbells as compared with flexing the elbow to perform chin-ups or scale a climbing wall. In weight lifting, the arm is relatively stationary and the forearm performs most of the motion, so the proximal end of the biceps would be considered the origin and its distal end the insertion. In chin-ups, by contrast, the forearm is more stationary and the arm moves more to lift the body, so the origin and insertion, if defined by relative motion, would be reversed.

Also consider the *quadriceps femoris* muscle on the anterior side of the thigh. It is a powerful extensor of the knee, connected at its proximal end mainly to the femur and at its distal end to the tibia, just below the knee. If you kick a soccer ball, the tibia moves more than the femur, so the tibia would be considered the insertion of the quadriceps and the femur would be considered its origin. But as you sit down in a chair, the femur moves more than the tibia, which remains relatively stationary. The quadriceps then acts as a brake so you don't sit down too abruptly and hard. By the foregoing definitions, the tibia would now be considered the origin of the quadriceps and the femur would be its insertion.

Some authorities therefore now speak of proximal and distal, medial and lateral, or superior and inferior muscle attachments, but no single system of naming applies throughout the body.

Even though *origin–insertion* terminology is becoming obsolete, it may still appear in some courses, board examinations, and other places. Therefore, for each muscle in tables 10.1 through 10.16, there are two bullet points (•) in the "Skeletal Attachments" column. The first bullet point denotes what has traditionally been called that muscle's origin, and the second one its insertion, enabling you to study the anatomy that way if your course so requires. These are aptly called skeletal attachments in the tables, because that applies to *nearly* all of them. Notwithstanding the table headers, though, be aware that a few of these muscles attach not to bone but to dermis, fasciae, or other soft connective tissues.

10.1d Functional Groups of Muscles

Consider the human hand. It requires subtle, finely controlled movement for such tasks as handwriting and keyboarding, but also powerful movements for such actions as climbing and tightly grasping tools. Muscles big enough to provide such power would be too bulky to fit within the hand itself, so they lie in the forearm and connect to the metacarpal bones and phalanges through long slender tendons that pass through the wrist. The more subtle movements are controlled by small muscles located entirely within the hand. Any muscle contained entirely within a region of interest is called an **intrinsic muscle.** A muscle that acts upon a designated organ or region such as the hand, but arises from another region such as the forearm, is called an **extrinsic muscle.** The intrinsic–extrinsic distinction applies not only to the hand but also to the muscles of the tongue, larynx, back, foot, and other regions. You will find several muscles classified this way in the tables in this chapter.

The effect produced by a muscle, whether it is to produce or prevent a movement, is called its **action.** Skeletal muscles seldom act independently; instead, they function in groups whose combined actions produce the coordinated control of a joint. Muscles can be classified into four categories according to their actions, but it must be stressed that a particular muscle can act in a certain way during one joint action and in a different way during other actions of the same joint. Furthermore, the action of a given muscle depends on what other muscles are doing. For example, the *gastrocnemius* of the posterior calf usually flexes the knee, but if the *quadriceps* of the anterior thigh prevents knee flexion, the gastrocnemius flexes the ankle, causing plantar flexion. The following categories of muscle action are exemplified by muscles that act on the elbow (fig. 10.4):

1. The **prime mover (agonist)** is the muscle that produces most of the force during a particular joint action. In flexing the elbow, for example, the prime mover is the brachialis.

2. A **synergist**[12] (SIN-ur-jist) is a muscle that aids the prime mover. Two or more synergists acting on a joint can produce more power than a single larger muscle. The biceps brachii, for example, overlies the brachialis and works with it as a synergist to flex the elbow. The actions of a prime mover and its synergist aren't necessarily identical and redundant. If the prime mover worked alone at a joint, it could cause rotation or other undesirable movements of a bone. A synergist may stabilize a joint and restrict these movements, or modify the direction of a movement so that the action of the prime mover is more coordinated and specific.

3. An **antagonist**[13] is a muscle that opposes the prime mover. In some cases, it relaxes to give the prime mover almost complete control over an action. More often, however, the antagonist maintains some tension on a joint and thus limits the speed or range of the prime mover, preventing excessive movement, joint injury, or inappropriate actions. If you extend your arm to reach out and pick up a cup of tea, for example, your triceps brachii serves as the prime mover of elbow extension, and your brachialis acts as an antagonist to slow the extension and stop it at the appropriate point. If you extend your arm rapidly to throw a dart, however, the brachialis must be quite relaxed. The brachialis and triceps represent an **antagonistic pair** of muscles that act on opposite sides of a joint. We need antagonistic pairs at a joint because a muscle can only pull, not push—for example, a single muscle cannot flex *and* extend the elbow. Which member of the pair acts as the prime mover depends on the motion under consideration. In flexion of the elbow, the brachialis is the prime mover and the triceps is the antagonist; when the elbow is extended, their roles are reversed.

4. A **fixator** is a muscle that prevents a bone from moving. To *fix* a bone means to hold it steady, allowing another muscle attached to it to pull on something else. For example, consider again the flexion of the elbow by the biceps brachii. The biceps originates on the scapula, crosses both the shoulder and elbow joints, and inserts on the radius and forearm fascia. The scapula is loosely attached to the axial skeleton, so when the biceps contracts, it seems that it would pull the scapula

laterally. However, there are fixator muscles (the *rhomboids*) that attach the scapula to the vertebral column (see fig. 10.18). They contract at the same time as the biceps, holding the scapula firmly in place and ensuring that the force generated by the biceps moves the radius rather than the scapula.

10.1e Innervation and Blood Supply

A skeletal muscle cannot contract unless it is stimulated by a nerve fiber. If its nerve is severed, the muscle is paralyzed. The nerve that supplies a given muscle is called its **innervation.** Knowing the innervation to each muscle enables clinicians to diagnose nerve, spinal cord, and brainstem injuries from their effects on muscle function, and to set realistic goals for rehabilitation. The innervations described in this chapter will be more meaningful after you have studied the peripheral nervous system (chapters 13 and 14), but a brief orientation will be helpful here. The muscles are innervated by nerve branches that arise from these two groups:

- **Spinal nerves** arise from the spinal cord, emerge through the intervertebral foramina, and supply branches to muscles below the neck. Spinal nerves are identified by letters and numbers that refer to the adjacent vertebrae—for example, T6 for the sixth thoracic nerve and S2 for the second sacral nerve. Immediately after emerging from an intervertebral foramen, each spinal nerve branches into a *posterior* and *anterior ramus.* You will note references to nerve numbers and rami in many of the muscle tables. The term *plexus* in some of the tables refers to weblike networks of spinal nerves adjacent to the vertebral column. All of the spinal nerves named here are illustrated, and most are also discussed, in chapter 13 (see the four tables starting at table 13.3).

- **Cranial nerves** arise from the base of the brain, emerge through the skull foramina, and innervate muscles of the head and neck. Cranial nerves are identified by roman numerals (CN I to CN XII) and by names given in table 14.1, although not all 12 of them innervate skeletal muscles.

The muscular system has a very heavy demand for energy, obtained from ATP, and thus it receives a generous flow of blood delivering oxygen and organic nutrients. Even at rest, it receives about one-quarter of all the blood pumped by the heart, or about 1.24 L/min. During exercise, its share may rise as high as three-quarters of the cardiac output, or about 11.6 L/min. Blood capillaries branch extensively through the endomysium to reach every muscle fiber, sometimes so intimately associated with the muscle fibers that the fibers have surface indentations to accommodate them. The capillaries of skeletal muscle undulate or coil when the muscle is contracted, allowing them enough slack to stretch out straight, without breaking, when the muscle lengthens. Chapter 20 describes some special physiological properties of muscle circulation and names the major arteries that supply the skeletal muscle groups.

10.1f Muscle Names and Learning Strategy

Figures 10.5 and **10.6** show an overview of the major superficial muscles. Learning the names of these and other muscles may seem a forbidding task at first, especially when some of them have such

---

[12]*syn* = together; *erg* = work
[13]*ant* = against; *agonist* = actor, competitor

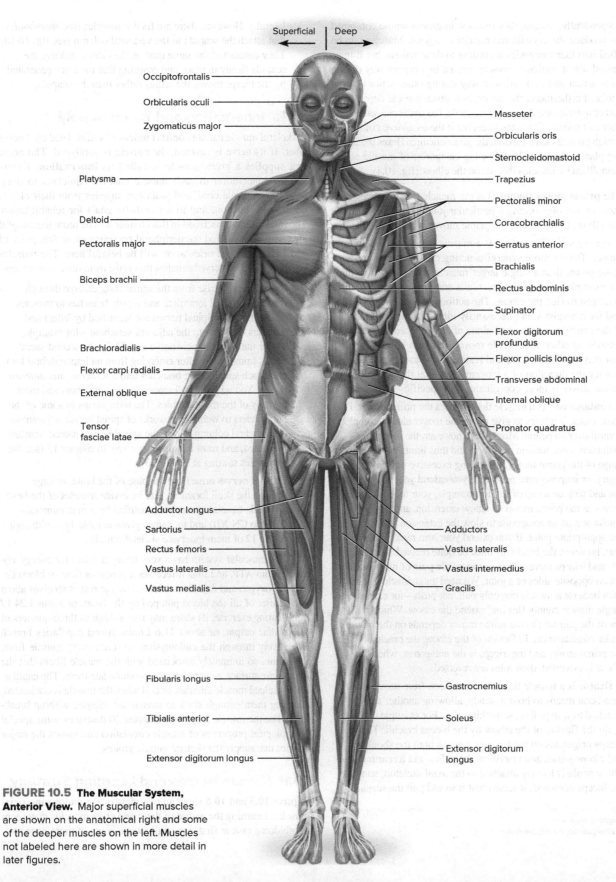

Superficial | Deep

Occipitofrontalis

Orbicularis oculi

Zygomaticus major

Platysma

Deltoid

Pectoralis major

Biceps brachii

Brachioradialis

Flexor carpi radialis

External oblique

Tensor
fasciae latae

Adductor longus

Sartorius

Rectus femoris

Vastus lateralis

Vastus medialis

Fibularis longus

Tibialis anterior

Extensor digitorum longus

Masseter

Orbicularis oris

Sternocleidomastoid

Trapezius

Pectoralis minor

Coracobrachialis

Serratus anterior

Brachialis

Rectus abdominis

Supinator

Flexor digitorum
profundus

Flexor pollicis longus

Transverse abdominal

Internal oblique

Pronator quadratus

Adductors

Vastus lateralis

Vastus intermedius

Gracilis

Gastrocnemius

Soleus

Extensor digitorum
longus

**FIGURE 10.5 The Muscular System,
Anterior View.** Major superficial muscles
are shown on the anatomical right and some
of the deeper muscles on the left. Muscles
not labeled here are shown in more detail in
later figures.

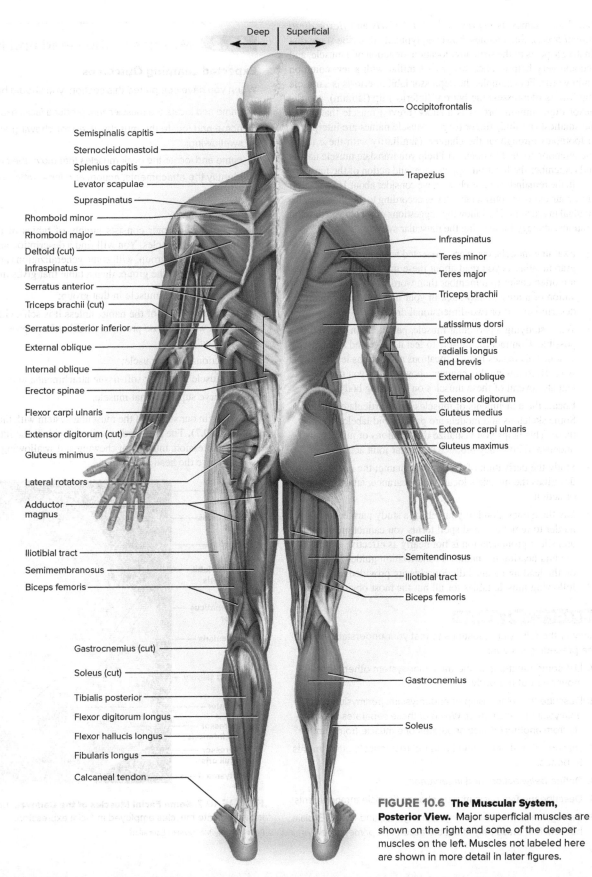

Deep | Superficial

Occipitofrontalis

Semispinalis capitis
Sternocleidomastoid
Splenius capitis
Levator scapulae
Supraspinatus
Rhomboid minor
Rhomboid major
Deltoid (cut)
Infraspinatus
Serratus anterior
Triceps brachii (cut)
Serratus posterior inferior
External oblique
Internal oblique
Erector spinae
Flexor carpi ulnaris
Extensor digitorum (cut)
Gluteus minimus
Lateral rotators
Adductor magnus
Iliotibial tract
Semimembranosus
Biceps femoris

Gastrocnemius (cut)
Soleus (cut)
Tibialis posterior
Flexor digitorum longus
Flexor hallucis longus
Fibularis longus
Calcaneal tendon

Trapezius

Infraspinatus
Teres minor
Teres major
Triceps brachii

Latissimus dorsi
Extensor carpi radialis longus and brevis
External oblique
Extensor digitorum
Gluteus medius
Extensor carpi ulnaris
Gluteus maximus

Gracilis
Semitendinosus
Iliotibial tract
Biceps femoris

Gastrocnemius

Soleus

FIGURE 10.6 The Muscular System, Posterior View. Major superficial muscles are shown on the right and some of the deeper muscles on the left. Muscles not labeled here are shown in more detail in later figures.

long Latin names as *depressor labii inferioris* and *flexor digiti minimi brevis*. Such names, however, typically describe some distinctive aspects of the structure, location, or action of a muscle, and become very helpful once we grow familiar with a few common Latin words. For example, the depressor labii inferioris is a muscle that lowers (depresses) the bottom (inferior) lip (labium), and the flexor digiti minimi brevis is a short (brevis) muscle that flexes the smallest (minimi) finger (digit). Muscle names are interpreted in footnotes throughout the chapter. Familiarity with these terms and attention to the footnotes will help you translate muscle names and remember the location, appearance, and action of the muscles.

In the remainder of this chapter, we consider about 160 muscles; most courses cover considerably fewer according to the choices of individual instructors. The following suggestions may help you develop a rational strategy for learning the muscular system:

- Examine models, cadavers, dissected animals, or a photographic atlas as you read about these muscles. Visual images are often easier to remember than words, and direct observation of a muscle may stick in your memory better than descriptive text or two-dimensional drawings.

- When studying a particular muscle, palpate it on yourself if possible. Contract the muscle to feel it bulge and sense its action. This makes muscle locations and actions less abstract. Atlas B, following this chapter, shows where you can see and palpate several of these muscles on the living body.

- Locate the attachments of muscles on an articulated skeleton. Some skeletons and models are painted and labeled to show these. This helps you visualize the locations of muscles and understand how they produce particular joint actions.

- Study the derivation of each muscle name; the name usually describes the muscle's location, appearance, attachments, or action.

- Say the names aloud to yourself or a study partner. It is harder to remember and spell terms you cannot pronounce, and silent pronunciation is not nearly as effective as speaking and hearing the names. Pronunciation guides based on the leading medical dictionaries are provided in the following muscle tables for all but the most obvious cases.

BEFORE YOU GO ON

Answer the following questions to test your understanding of the preceding section:

1. List some functions of the muscular system other than movement of the body.

2. Describe the relationship of endomysium, perimysium, and epimysium to each other. Which of these separates one fascicle from another? Which separates one muscle from another?

3. Distinguish between direct and indirect muscle attachments to bones.

4. Define *belly*, *action*, and *innervation*.

5. Describe the five basic muscle shapes (fascicle arrangements).

6. Distinguish between a synergist, antagonist, and fixator. Explain how each of these may affect the action of a prime mover.

10.2 Muscles of the Head and Neck

Expected Learning Outcomes

When you have completed this section, you should be able to

a. name and locate the muscles that produce facial expressions;

b. name and locate the muscles used for chewing and swallowing;

c. name and locate the neck muscles that move the head; and

d. identify the attachments, action, and innervation of these muscles.

The rest of this chapter consists largely of tables of the body's principal skeletal muscles. You will find a description and illustrations of each muscle group, with some generalizations and special-interest points about the group, then a table that gives the details:

- the name of each muscle in that group;

- the pronunciation of the name, unless it is self-evident or repeats words whose pronunciation has been provided in a recent entry;

- the actions of the muscle;

- the muscle's bony or soft-tissue attachments; and

- the nerve supply to that muscle.

We begin our survey of the muscular system with the head and neck (**fig. 10.7**). The first three sections divide these into muscles of facial expression, muscles of chewing and swallowing, and muscles that move the head as a whole.

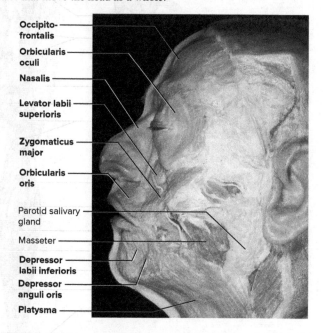

Occipito-frontalis
Orbicularis oculi
Nasalis
Levator labii superioris
Zygomaticus major
Orbicularis oris
Parotid salivary gland
Masseter
Depressor labii inferioris
Depressor anguli oris
Platysma

FIGURE 10.7 Some Facial Muscles of the Cadaver. Boldface labels indicate muscles employed in facial expression.

Rebecca Gray/McGraw-Hill Education

10.2a Muscles of Facial Expression

Humans have much more expressive faces than other mammals because of a complex array of muscles that insert in the dermis and subcutaneous tissues. These muscles tense the skin and produce such expressions as a pleasant smile, a flirtatious wink, a puzzled frown, or a threatening scowl **(fig. 10.8).** They add subtle shades of meaning to our spoken words. Facial muscles also contribute directly to speech, chewing, and other oral functions. All but one of them are innervated by the facial nerve (cranial nerve VII). This nerve is especially vulnerable to injury from lacerations and skull fractures, which can paralyze the muscles and cause parts of the face to sag. The only muscle not innervated by CN VII is the levator palpebrae superioris of the upper eyelid, innervated by the oculomotor nerve (CN III). **Table 10.1** groups these muscles into the following regions: the scalp; orbital and nasal regions (eye and nose); the oral region (encircling the mouth); and mental and buccal regions (chin and cheeks).

The Scalp

The **occipitofrontalis muscle** overlies the dome of the cranium. It is divided into a *frontal belly* in the forehead and *occipital belly* at the rear of the head **(fig. 10.9),** named for the underlying cranial bones. They are connected to each other by a broad aponeurosis, the **galea aponeurotica**[14] (GAY-lee-uh AP-oh-new-ROT-ih-cuh).

The Orbital and Nasal Regions

The **orbicularis oculi** is a sphincter of the eyelid that encircles and closes the eye. Deep to it, in the eyelid and orbit, is the **levator palpebrae superioris,** which opens the eye. Other muscles in this group move the eyelids and skin of the forehead and dilate the nostrils. Muscles within the orbit that move the eyeball itself are discussed in relation to vision in chapter 16.

---

[14]*galea* = helmet; *apo* = above; *neuro* = nervous system, brain

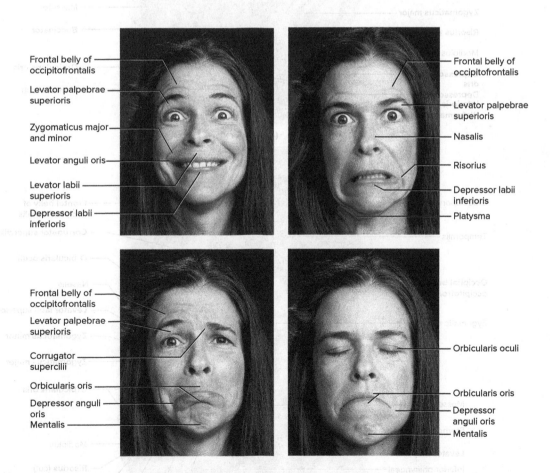

FIGURE 10.8 Expressions Produced by Several of the Facial Muscles. The ordinary actions of these muscles are usually more subtle than these demonstrations.

Joe DeGrandis/McGraw-Hill Education

? *Name an antagonist of each of these muscles: the depressor anguli oris, orbicularis oculi, and levator labii superioris.*

FIGURE 10.9 Muscles of Facial Expression.
(a) Anterior view. (b) Lateral view. Boldface
labels indicate muscles employed in facial
expression. **APR**

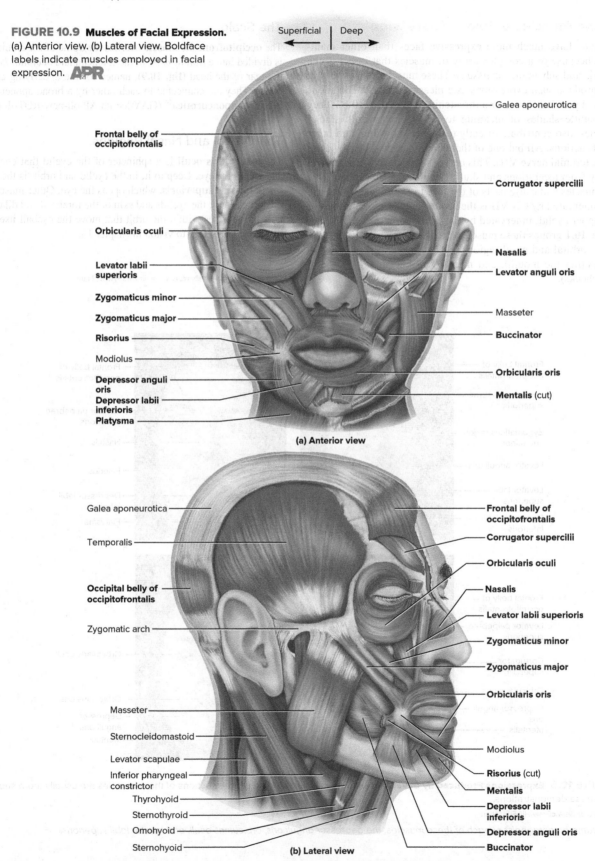

Superficial ← | → Deep

(a) Anterior view

Galea aponeurotica

Frontal belly of occipitofrontalis

Corrugator supercilii

Orbicularis oculi

Nasalis

Levator anguli oris

Levator labii superioris

Zygomaticus minor

Zygomaticus major

Masseter

Risorius

Buccinator

Modiolus

Orbicularis oris

Depressor anguli oris

Mentalis (cut)

Depressor labii inferioris

Platysma

(b) Lateral view

Galea aponeurotica

Frontal belly of occipitofrontalis

Temporalis

Corrugator supercilii

Orbicularis oculi

Occipital belly of occipitofrontalis

Nasalis

Levator labii superioris

Zygomatic arch

Zygomaticus minor

Zygomaticus major

Masseter

Orbicularis oris

Sternocleidomastoid

Modiolus

Levator scapulae

Risorius (cut)

Inferior pharyngeal constrictor

Mentalis

Thyrohyoid

Depressor labii inferioris

Sternothyroid

Omohyoid

Depressor anguli oris

Sternohyoid

Buccinator

The Oral Region

The mouth is the most expressive part of the face, and lip movements are necessary for intelligible speech; thus, it's not surprising that the muscles here are especially diverse. The **orbicularis oris** is a complex of muscles in the lips that encircles the mouth; until recently it was misinterpreted as a sphincter, or circular muscle, but it is actually composed of four independent quadrants that interlace and give only an appearance of circularity. Other muscles in this region approach the lips from all directions and thus draw the lips or angles (corners) of the mouth upward, laterally, and downward. Some of these arise from a complex cord called the **modiolus**[15] just lateral to each angle of the lips (fig. 10.9b). Named for the hub of a cartwheel, the modiolus is a point of convergence of several muscles of the lower face. You can palpate it by inserting one finger just inside the corner of your lips and pinching the corner between the finger and thumb, feeling for a thick knot of tissue.

The Mental and Buccal Regions

Adjacent to the oral orifice are the *mental region* (chin) and *buccal region* (cheek). In addition to muscles already discussed that act on the lower lip, the mental region has a pair of small **mentalis muscles** extending from the upper margin of the mandible to the skin of the chin. In some people, they are especially thick and have a visible dimple between them called the mental cleft (see fig. 4.17). The **buccinator** is the muscle of the cheek. It has multiple functions in chewing, sucking, and blowing. If the cheeks are inflated with air, compression of the buccinators blows it out. Sucking is achieved by contracting the buccinators to draw the cheeks inward, then relaxing them. This action is especially important in nursing infants. To feel this action, hold your fingertips lightly against your cheeks as you make a kissing noise. You will notice relaxation of the buccinators at the moment air is sharply drawn in through the pursed lips. The **platysma** is a thin superficial muscle of the upper chest and lower face. It is relatively unimportant, but when men shave they tend to tense the platysma to make the concavity between the jaw and neck shallower and the skin tauter.

TABLE 10.1	Muscles of Facial Expression		
Name	**Action**	**Skeletal Attachments**	**Innervation**
The Scalp			
Occipitofrontalis, frontal belly (oc-SIP-ih-toe-frun-TAY-lis)	Elevates eyebrows in glancing upward and expressions of surprise or fright; draws scalp forward and wrinkles skin of forehead	• Galea aponeurotica • Subcutaneous tissue of eyebrows	Facial nerve
Occipitofrontalis, occipital belly	Retracts scalp; fixes galea aponeurotica so frontal belly can act on eyebrows	• Superior nuchal line and temporal bone • Galea aponeurotica	Facial nerve
The Orbital and Nasal Regions			
Orbicularis oculi[16] (or-BIC-you-LERR-is OC-you-lye)	Sphincter of the eyelids; closes eye in blinking, squinting, and sleep; aids in flow of tears across eye	• Lacrimal bone; adjacent regions of frontal bone and maxilla; medial angle of eyelids • Upper and lower eyelids; skin around margin of orbit	Facial nerve
Levator palpebrae superioris[17] (leh-VAY-tur pal-PEE-bree soo-PEER-ee-OR-is)	Elevates upper eyelid; opens eye	• Lesser wing of sphenoid in posterior wall of orbit • Upper eyelid	Oculomotor nerve
Corrugator supercilii[18] (COR-oo-GAY-tur SOO-per-SIL-ee-eye)	Draws eyebrows medially and downward in frowning and concentration; reduces glare of bright sunlight	• Medial end of supraorbital margin • Skin of eyebrow	Facial nerve
Nasalis[19] (nay-ZAY-lis)	Widens nostrils; narrows internal air passage between vestibule and nasal cavity	• Maxilla just lateral to nose • Bridge and alar cartilages of nose	Facial nerve
The Oral Region			
Orbicularis oris[20] (or-BIC-you-LERR-is OR-is)	Encircles mouth, closes lips, protrudes lips as in kissing; uniquely developed in humans for speech	• Modiolus of mouth • Submucosa and dermis of lips	Facial nerve

(continued)

[15]*modiolus* = hub
[16]*orb* = circle; *ocul* = eye
[17]*levator* = that which raises; *palpebr* = eyelid; *superior* = upper

[18]*corrug* = wrinkle; *supercilii* = of the eyebrow
[19]*nas* = of the nose
[20]*orb* = circle; *oris* = of the mouth

TABLE 10.1	Muscles of Facial Expression (continued)		
Name	**Action**	**Skeletal Attachments**	**Innervation**
The Oral Region *(continued)*			
Levator labii superioris[21] (leh-VAY-tur LAY-bee-eye soo-PEER-ee-OR-is)	Elevates and everts upper lip in sad, sneering, or serious expressions	• Zygomatic bone and maxilla near inferior margin of orbit • Muscles of upper lip	Facial nerve
Levator anguli oris[22] (leh-VAY-tur ANG-you-lye OR-is)	Elevates angle of mouth as in smiling	• Maxilla just below infraorbital foramen • Muscles at angle of mouth	Facial nerve
Zygomaticus[23] major (ZY-go-MAT-ih-cus)	Draws angle of mouth upward and laterally in laughing	• Zygomatic bone • Superolateral angle of mouth	Facial nerve
Zygomaticus minor	Elevates upper lip, exposes upper teeth in smiling or sneering	• Zygomatic bone • Muscles of upper lip	Facial nerve
Risorius[24] (rih-SOR-ee-us)	Draws angle of mouth laterally in expressions of laughing, horror, or disdain	• Zygomatic arch; fascia near ear • Modiolus	Facial nerve
Depressor anguli oris[25]	Draws angle of mouth laterally and downward in opening mouth or sad expressions	• Inferior margin of mandibular body • Modiolus	Facial nerve
Depressor labii inferioris[26]	Draws lower lip downward and laterally in chewing and expressions of melancholy or doubt	• Mandible near mental protuberance • Skin and mucosa of lower lip	Facial nerve
The Mental and Buccal Regions			
Mentalis (men-TAY-lis)	Elevates and protrudes lower lip in drinking, pouting, and expressions of doubt or disdain; elevates and wrinkles skin of chin	• Mandible near inferior incisors • Skin of chin at mental protuberance	Facial nerve
Buccinator[27] (BUC-sin-AY-tur)	Compresses cheek against teeth and gums; directs food between molars; retracts cheek from teeth when mouth is closing to prevent biting cheek; expels air and liquid from the mouth	• Alveolar processes on lateral surfaces of mandible and maxilla • Orbicularis oris; submucosa of cheek and lips	Facial nerve
Platysma[28] (plah-TIZ-muh)	Draws lower lip and angle of mouth downward in expressions of horror or surprise; may aid in opening mouth widely; tenses skin of the chin and neck	• Fascia of deltoid and pectoralis major • Mandible; skin and subcutaneous tissue of lower face	Facial nerve

10.2b Muscles of Chewing and Swallowing

The muscles in this section are concerned primarily with the manipulation of food, including tongue movements, chewing, and swallowing.

Muscles of the Tongue

The tongue is a very agile organ. It pushes food between the molars for chewing and later forces it into the pharynx for swallowing. It is also, of course, crucial to articulate speech. Both intrinsic and extrinsic muscles are responsible for its complex movements. The *intrinsic muscles* consist of a variable number of vertical fascicles that extend from the superior to the inferior side of the tongue, transverse fascicles that extend from left to right, and longitudinal fascicles than extend from front to rear (see figs. 10.1c, 25.5b).

Table 10.2 describes the *extrinsic muscles* that connect the tongue to other structures in the head (**fig. 10.10**).

Muscles of Chewing

Four pairs of muscles produce the biting and cutting movements of the mandible: the **temporalis, masseter,** and two pairs of **pterygoid muscles (fig. 10.11).** Their actions include depression of the mandible for opening the mouth to receive food, elevation for biting off a piece of food or crushing it between the teeth; protraction so the incisors meet in cutting off a piece of food; retraction to draw the lower incisors behind the upper ones and make the rear teeth (premolars and molars) meet; and lateral and medial excursion, the side-to-side movements that grind food between the rear teeth (see fig. 9.20).

---

[21]*levat* = to raise; *labi* = lip; *superior* = upper
[22]*angul* = angle, corner; *oris* = of the mouth
[23]*zygo* = join, unite (refers to zygomatic bone)
[24]*risor* = laughter

[25]*depress* = to lower; *angul* = angle, corner; *oris* = of the mouth
[26]*labi* = lip; *inferior* = lower
[27]*buccinator* = trumpeter
[28]*platy* = flat

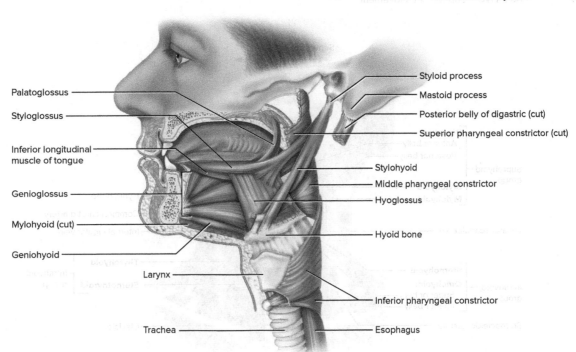

FIGURE 10.10 Muscles of the Tongue and Pharynx.

Palatoglossus

Styloglossus

Inferior longitudinal muscle of tongue

Genioglossus

Mylohyoid (cut)

Geniohyoid

Larynx

Trachea

Styloid process

Mastoid process

Posterior belly of digastric (cut)

Superior pharyngeal constrictor (cut)

Stylohyoid

Middle pharyngeal constrictor

Hyoglossus

Hyoid bone

Inferior pharyngeal constrictor

Esophagus

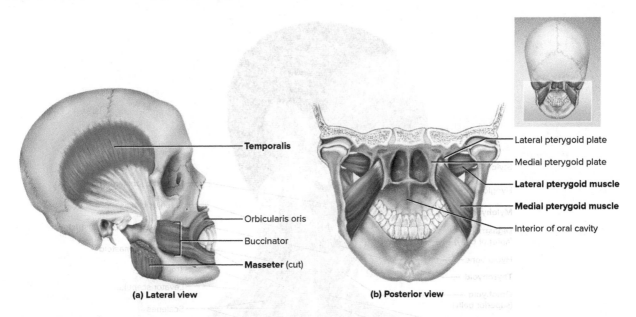

Temporalis

Orbicularis oris

Buccinator

Masseter (cut)

Lateral pterygoid plate

Medial pterygoid plate

Lateral pterygoid muscle

Medial pterygoid muscle

Interior of oral cavity

(a) Lateral view

(b) Posterior view

FIGURE 10.11 Muscles of Chewing. Boldface labels indicate muscles that act on the mandible in its chewing movements. (a) Right lateral view. In order to expose the insertion of the temporalis muscle on the mandible, part of the zygomatic arch and masseter muscle are removed. (b) View of the pterygoid muscles looking into the oral cavity from behind the skull.

Suprahyoid Muscles

The hyoid bone, you will recall, is a slender U-shaped bone beneath the chin (see fig. 8.16). Eight pairs of *hyoid muscles* associated with this bone aid in chewing, swallowing, and speaking **(fig. 10.12).** Four of them, the *suprahyoid group,* are superior to the hyoid bone—the **digastric, geniohyoid, mylohyoid,** and **stylohyoid.** The digastric is an unusual muscle named for its two bellies. Its *posterior belly* arises from the *mastoid notch* of the cranium and slopes downward and forward. The *anterior belly* arises from a trench called the *digastric fossa* on the inner surface of the mandibular body. It slopes downward and backward. The two bellies meet at a constriction, the *intermediate tendon.* This

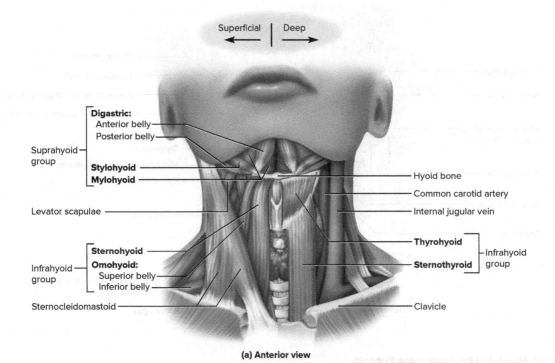

Superficial | Deep

Digastric:
Anterior belly
Posterior belly

Suprahyoid group

Stylohyoid
Mylohyoid

Hyoid bone
Common carotid artery

Levator scapulae

Internal jugular vein

Sternohyoid
Omohyoid:
Superior belly
Inferior belly

Thyrohyoid

Sternothyroid

Infrahyoid group

Infrahyoid group

Sternocleidomastoid

Clavicle

(a) Anterior view

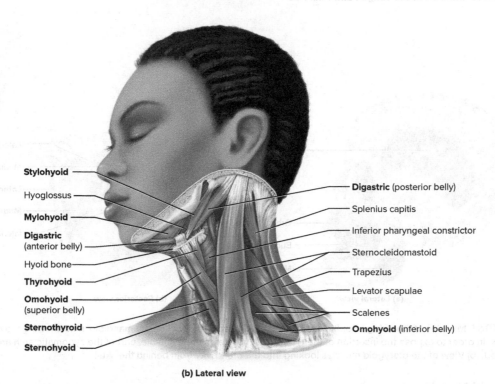

Stylohyoid

Hyoglossus

Mylohyoid

Digastric
(anterior belly)

Hyoid bone

Thyrohyoid

Omohyoid
(superior belly)

Sternothyroid

Sternohyoid

Digastric (posterior belly)

Splenius capitis

Inferior pharyngeal constrictor

Sternocleidomastoid

Trapezius

Levator scapulae

Scalenes

Omohyoid (inferior belly)

(b) Lateral view

FIGURE 10.12 Muscles of the Neck. (a) Anterior view. (b) Lateral view. Boldface labels indicate muscles of the suprahyoid and infrahyoid groups. Another muscle of the suprahyoid group, the geniohyoid, lies deep to the mylohyoid and can be seen in figure 10.10. **APR**

tendon passes through a connective tissue loop, the *fascial sling*, attached to the hyoid bone. Therefore, when the two bellies of the digastric contract, they elevate the hyoid; but if the hyoid is fixed from below, the digastric aids in wide opening of the mouth. The lateral pterygoids are more important in mouth opening, however, with the digastrics coming into play only in extreme opening, as in yawning or taking a large bite from an apple.

Infrahyoid Muscles

The *infrahyoid muscles* are inferior to the hyoid bone. By fixing the hyoid from below, they enable the suprahyoid muscles to open the mouth. The **omohyoid** is unusual in that it arises from

the shoulder, passes under the sternocleidomastoid muscle, then ascends to the hyoid bone. Like the digastric, it has two bellies—superior and inferior. The **thyrohyoid,** named for the hyoid bone and the large shield-shaped thyroid cartilage of the larynx, helps prevent choking. It elevates the larynx during swallowing so its superior opening is sealed by a flap of tissue, the epiglottis. You can feel this effect by holding a fingertip on your "Adam's apple" (anterior prominence of the thyroid cartilage) and feeling it bob up as you swallow.

The infrahyoid muscles are also regarded as extrinsic muscles of the larynx, since they act on it from outside. The intrinsic muscles of the larynx are described in relation to breathing and speech in chapter 22. The *ansa cervicalis*[29] in table 10.2 is a loop

TABLE 10.2	Muscles of Chewing and Swallowing		
Name	**Action**	**Skeletal Attachments**	**Innervation**
Extrinsic Muscles of the Tongue			
Genioglossus[30] (JEE-nee-oh-GLOSS-us)	Unilateral action draws tongue to one side; bilateral action depresses midline of tongue or protrudes tongue	• Superior mental spine on posterior surface of mental protuberance • Inferior surface of tongue from root to apex	Hypoglossal nerve
Hyoglossus[31] (HI-oh-GLOSS-us)	Depresses tongue	• Body and greater horn of hyoid bone • Lateral and inferior surfaces of tongue	Hypoglossal nerve
Styloglossus[32] (STY-lo-GLOSS-us)	Draws tongue upward and posteriorly	• Styloid process of temporal bone and ligament from styloid process to mandible • Superolateral surface of tongue	Hypoglossal nerve
Palatoglossus[33] (PAL-a-toe-GLOSS-us)	Elevates root of tongue and closes oral cavity off from pharynx; forms palatoglossal arch at rear of oral cavity	• Soft palate • Lateral surface of tongue	Accessory and vagus nerves
Muscles of Chewing			
Temporalis[34] (TEM-po-RAY-liss)	Elevation, retraction, and lateral and medial excursion of the mandible	• Temporal lines and temporal fossa of cranium • Coronoid process and anterior border of mandibular ramus	Trigeminal nerve
Masseter[35] (ma-SEE-tur)	Elevation of the mandible, with smaller roles in protraction, retraction, and lateral and medial excursion	• Zygomatic arch • Lateral surface of mandibular ramus and angle	Trigeminal nerve
Medial pterygoid[36] (TERR-ih-goyd)	Elevation, protraction, and lateral and medial excursion of the mandible	• Medial surface of lateral pterygoid plate; palatine bone; lateral surface of maxilla near molar teeth • Medial surface of mandibular ramus and angle	Trigeminal nerve
Lateral pterygoid	Depression (in wide opening of the mouth), protraction, and lateral and medial excursion of the mandible	• Lateral surfaces of lateral pterygoid plate; greater wing of sphenoid • Neck of mandible (just below condyle); articular disc and capsule of temporomandibular joint	Trigeminal nerve

(continued)

---

[29]*ansa* = handle; *cervic* = neck; *alis* = of, belonging to
[30]*genio* = chin; *gloss* = tongue
[31]*hyo* = hyoid bone; *gloss* = tongue
[32]*stylo* = styloid process; *gloss* = tongue

[33]*palato* = palate; *gloss* = tongue
[34]*temporalis* = of the temporal region of the head
[35]*masset* = chew
[36]*pteryg* = wing; *oid* = resembling (refers to pterygoid plate of sphenoid bone)

TABLE 10.2	Muscles of Chewing and Swallowing (continued)		
Name	**Action**	**Skeletal Attachments**	**Innervation**
Suprahyoid Muscles			
Digastric[37]	Depresses mandible when hyoid is fixed; opens mouth widely, as when ingesting food or yawning; elevates hyoid when mandible is fixed	• Mastoid notch of temporal bone; digastric fossa of mandible • Hyoid bone via fascial sling	Posterior belly: facial nerve Anterior belly: trigeminal nerve
Geniohyoid[38] (JEE-nee-oh-HY-oyd)	Depresses mandible when hyoid is fixed; elevates and protracts hyoid when mandible is fixed	• Inferior mental spine of mandible • Hyoid bone	Spinal nerve C1 via hypoglossal nerve
Mylohyoid[39]	Spans mandible from side to side and forms floor of mouth; elevates floor of mouth in initial stage of swallowing	• Mylohyoid line near inferior margin • Hyoid bone	Trigeminal nerve
Stylohyoid	Elevates and retracts hyoid, elongating floor of mouth; roles in speech, chewing, and swallowing are not yet clearly understood	• Styloid process of temporal bone • Hyoid bone	Facial nerve
Infrahyoid Muscles			
Omohyoid[40]	Depresses hyoid after it has been elevated	• Superior border of scapula • Hyoid bone	Ansa cervicalis
Sternohyoid[41]	Depresses hyoid after it has been elevated	• Manubrium of sternum; medial end of clavicle • Hyoid bone	Ansa cervicalis
Thyrohyoid[42]	Depresses hyoid; with hyoid fixed, elevates larynx as in singing high notes	• Thyroid cartilage of larynx • Hyoid bone	Spinal nerve C1 via hypoglossal nerve
Sternothyroid	Depresses larynx after it has been elevated in swallowing and vocalization; aids in singing low notes	• Manubrium of sternum; costal cartilage • Thyroid cartilage of larynx	Ansa cervicalis
Pharyngeal Muscles			
Superior, middle, and inferior pharyngeal constrictors	During swallowing, contract in order from *superior* to *middle* to *inferior con-strictor* to drive food into esophagus	• Medial pterygoid plate; mandible; hyoid; stylohyoid ligament; cartilages of larynx • Posteromedial seam of pharynx; basilar part of occipital bone	Glossopharyngeal and vagus nerves

of nerve on the side of the neck that innervates three of the infrahyoid muscles; it is formed by certain nerve fibers from cervical nerves 1 to 3 (see fig. 13.15).

Pharyngeal Muscles

Three pairs of **pharyngeal constrictors** encircle the pharynx on its posterior and lateral sides, forming a muscular funnel (see fig. 10.10). In swallowing, they push food from the pharynx into the esophagus.

10.2c Muscles Acting on the Head and Neck

Muscles that move the head arise from the vertebral column, thoracic cage, and pectoral girdle and end on the cranial bones **(table 10.3).** Their actions include flexion (tipping the head forward), extension (holding the head erect), hyperextension (as in looking upward), lateral flexion (tilting the head to one side), and rotation (turning the head to look left or right). Flexion, extension, and hyperextension involve simultaneous action of the right and left muscles of a pair; the other actions require the muscle

---

[37]*di* = two; *gastr* = bellies
[38]*genio* = chin
[39]*mylo* = mill, molar tooth

[40]*omo* = shoulder
[41]*sterno* = chest, sternum
[42]*thyro* = shield, thyroid cartilage

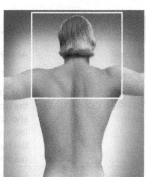

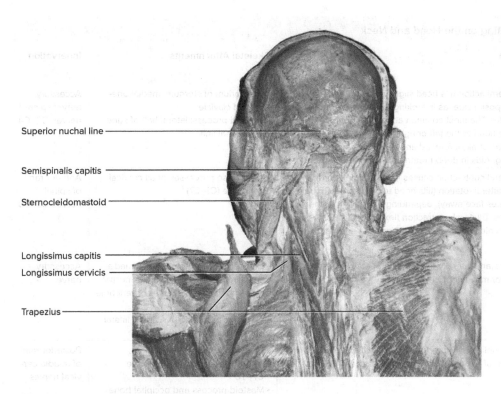

Superior nuchal line

Semispinalis capitis

Sternocleidomastoid

Longissimus capitis
Longissimus cervicis

Trapezius

FIGURE 10.13 **Muscles of the Shoulder and Nuchal Regions of the Cadaver.**

Rebecca Gray/Don Kincaid/McGraw-Hill Education

on one side to contract more strongly than its mate. Many head actions result from a combination of these movements—for example, looking up over the shoulder involves a combination of rotation and hyperextension.

Depending on its skeletal attachments, a muscle may cause a *contralateral* movement of the head (toward the opposite side, as when contraction of a muscle on the left turns the face toward the right) or an *ipsilateral* movement (toward the same side as the muscle, as when contraction of a muscle on the left tilts the head to the left).

Flexors of the Neck

The prime mover of neck flexion is the **sternocleidomastoid,** a thick muscular cord that extends from the upper chest (sternum and clavicle) to the mastoid process behind the ear (fig. 10.12). This is most easily seen when the head is rotated to one side and slightly extended. To visualize the action of a single sternocleidomastoid, place the index finger of your left hand on your left mastoid process and the index finger of your right hand on your suprasternal notch. Now contract your left sternocleidomastoid to bring your two fingertips as close together as possible. You will see that this tilts your face upward and to the right.

The three **scalenes**[43] on the side of the neck are named for their staircase-like arrangement. Their actions are similar so they are considered collectively in the table.

Extensors of the Neck

The extensors are located mainly in the nuchal region (back of the neck; **fig. 10.13**) and therefore tend to hold the head erect or draw it back. The **trapezius** is the largest and most superficial of these. It extends from the nuchal region over the shoulders and halfway down the back. It is named for the fact that the right and left trapezii together form a diamond or trapezoidal shape (see fig. 10.6). The *splenius* is a deeper, elongated muscle with **splenius capitis** and **splenius cervicis** regions in the head and neck, respectively. It is nicknamed the "bandage muscle" because of the way it wraps around still deeper neck muscles. One of those deeper muscles is the *semispinalis,* another elongated muscle with head, neck, and thoracic regions. Only the **semispinalis capitis** and **cervicis** are tabulated here; the *semispinalis thoracis* doesn't act on the neck, but is included in table 10.6.

▶▶▶ APPLY WHAT YOU KNOW

Of the muscles you have studied so far, name three that you would consider intrinsic muscles of the head and three that you would classify as extrinsic. Explain your reason for each.

---

[43]*scal* = staircase

TABLE 10.3	Muscles Acting on the Head and Neck		
Name	**Action**	**Skeletal Attachments**	**Innervation**
Flexors of the Neck			
Sternocleidomastoid[44] (STIR-no-CLY-do-MAST-oyd)	Unilateral action tilts head slightly upward and toward the opposite side, as in looking over one's contralateral shoulder. The most common action is probably rotating the head to the left or right. Bilateral action draws the head straight forward and down, as when eating or reading. Aids in deep breathing when head is fixed.	• Manubrium of sternum; medial one-third of clavicle • Mastoid process; lateral half of superior nuchal line	Accessory nerve; spinal nerves C2–C4
Anterior, middle, and posterior scalenes (SCAY-leens)	Unilateral contraction causes ipsilateral flexion or contralateral rotation (tilts head toward same shoulder, or rotates face away), depending on action of other muscles. Bilateral contraction flexes neck. If spine is fixed, scalenes elevate ribs 1–2 and aid in breathing.	• Transverse processes of all cervical vertebrae (C1–C7) • Ribs 1–2	Anterior rami of spinal nerves C3–C8
Extensors of the Neck			
Trapezius[45] (tra-PEE-zee-us)	Extends and laterally flexes neck. See also roles in scapular movement in table 10.8.	• External occipital protuberance; medial one-third of superior nuchal line; nuchal ligament; spinous processes of vertebrae C7–T12 • Acromion and spine of scapula; lateral one-third of clavicle	Accessory nerve
Splenius capitis[46] and splenius cervicis[47] (SPLEE-nee-us CAP-ih-tiss, SIR-vih-sis)	Acting unilaterally, produce ipsilateral flexion and slight rotation of head; extend head when acting bilaterally	• Inferior half of nuchal ligament; spinous processes of vertebrae C7–T6 • Mastoid process and occipital bone just inferior to superior nuchal line; cervical vertebrae C1–C2 or C3	Posterior rami of middle cervical nerves
Semispinalis capitis and semispinalis cervicis (SEM-ee-spy-NAY-lis)	Extend and contralaterally rotate head	• Articular processes of vertebrae C4–C7; transverse processes of T1–T6 • Occipital bone between nuchal lines; spinous processes of vertebrae C2–C5	Posterior rami of cervical and thoracic nerves

---

BEFORE YOU GO ON

Answer the following questions to test your understanding of the preceding section:

7. Name two muscles that elevate the upper lip and two that depress the lower lip.

8. Name the four paired muscles of mastication and state where they insert on the mandible.

9. Distinguish between the functions of the suprahyoid and infrahyoid muscles.

10. List the muscles of neck extension and flexion.

10.3 Muscles of the Trunk

Expected Learning Outcomes

When you have completed this section, you should be able to

a. name and locate the muscles of respiration and explain how they affect airflow and abdominal pressure;

b. name and locate the muscles of the abdominal wall, back, and pelvic floor; and

c. identify the skeletal attachments, action, and innervation of these muscles.

In this section, we will examine muscles of the trunk of the body in four functional groups concerned with respiration, support of the abdominal wall, movement of the vertebral column, and support of the pelvic floor. In the illustrations, you will note some major muscles that are not discussed in the associated tables—for example, the pectoralis major and serratus anterior. Although they are *located* in the trunk, they *act upon* the limbs and limb girdles, and are further discussed in sections 10.4 and 10.5.

---

[44]*sterno* = chest, sternum; *cleido* = hammer, clavicle; *masto* = breastlike, mastoid process

[45]*trapez* = table, trapezoid

[46]*splenius* = bandage; *capitis* = of the head

[47]*cervicis* = of the neck

10.3a Muscles of Respiration

We breathe primarily by means of muscles that enclose the thoracic cavity—the diaphragm, external intercostal, internal intercostal, and innermost intercostal muscles (**fig. 10.14, table 10.4**).

The **diaphragm** is a muscular dome between the thoracic and abdominal cavities, bulging upward against the base of the lungs. It has openings for passage of the esophagus, major blood and lymphatic vessels, and nerves between the two cavities. Its fibers converge from the margins toward a fibrous **central tendon.** When the diaphragm contracts, it flattens slightly and enlarges the thoracic cavity, causing air intake (inspiration); when it relaxes, it rises and shrinks the thoracic cavity, expelling air (expiration).

Three layers of muscle lie between the ribs: the external, internal, and innermost intercostal muscles. The 11 pairs of **external intercostal muscles** constitute the most superficial layer. They extend from the rib tubercle posteriorly almost to the beginning of the costal cartilage anteriorly. Each one slopes downward and anteriorly from one rib to the next inferior one.

The 11 pairs of **internal intercostal muscles** lie deep to the external intercostals and extend from the margin of the sternum to the angles of the ribs. They are thickest in the region between the costal cartilages and grow thinner in the region where they overlap the internal intercostals. Their fibers slope downward and posteriorly from each rib to the one below, at nearly right angles to the external intercostals. Each is divided into an *intercartilaginous part* between the costal cartilages and an *interosseous part* between the bony part of the ribs. The two parts differ in their respiratory roles.

The **innermost intercostal muscles** vary in number, as they are sometimes absent from the upper thoracic cage. Their fibers run in the same direction as the internal intercostals, and they are presumed to serve the same function. The internal and innermost intercostals are separated by a fascia that allows passage for intercostal nerves and blood vessels (see fig. 13.14b).

The primary function of the intercostal muscles is to stiffen the thoracic cage during respiration so it doesn't cave inward when the diaphragm descends. However, they also contribute to enlargement and contraction of the thoracic cage and thus add to the air volume that ventilates the lungs.

Many other muscles of the chest and abdomen contribute significantly to breathing: the sternocleidomastoid and scalenes of the neck; pectoralis major and serratus anterior of the chest; latissimus dorsi of the lower back; internal and external obliques and transverse abdominal muscle; and even some of the anal muscles. The respiratory actions of all these muscles are described in section 22.2a.

▶▶▶**APPLY WHAT YOU KNOW**

A young thoracic surgery resident performing an operation for esophageal cancer accidentally severs the patient's left phrenic nerve. Predict the effect of this accident on the patient's respiration.

▶▶▶**APPLY WHAT YOU KNOW**

Carl and Carla are enjoying a platter of barbecued ribs. What muscles are they eating? What is the tough fibrous membrane between the meat and the bone?

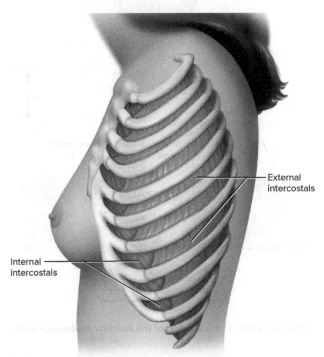

(a) Lateral view of intercostal muscles

- External intercostals
- Internal intercostals

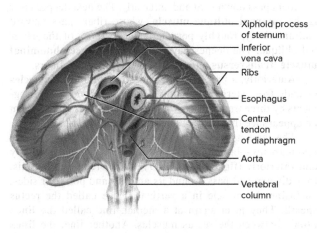

- Xiphoid process of sternum
- Inferior vena cava
- Ribs
- Esophagus
- Central tendon of diaphragm
- Aorta
- Vertebral column

(b) Inferior view of diaphragm

FIGURE 10.14 Muscles of Respiration. (a) Lateral view of the intercostal muscles. (b) Inferior view of the diaphragm.

TABLE 10.4	Muscles of Respiration		
Name	**Action**	**Skeletal Attachments**	**Innervation**
Diaphragm[48] (DY-ah-fram)	Prime mover of inspiration (responsible for about two-thirds of air intake); contracts in preparation for sneezing, coughing, crying, laughing, and weight lifting; contraction compresses abdominal viscera and aids in childbirth and expulsion of urine and feces.	• Xiphoid process of sternum; ribs and costal cartilages 7–12; lumbar vertebrae • Central tendon of diaphragm	Phrenic nerves
External intercostals[49] (IN-tur-COSS-tulz)	When scalenes fix rib 1, external intercostals elevate and protract ribs 2–12, expanding the thoracic cavity and creating a partial vacuum causing inflow of air; exercise a braking action during expiration so that expiration is not overly abrupt.	• Inferior margins of ribs 1–11 • Superior margin of next lower rib	Intercostal nerves
Internal intercostals	In inspiration, the intercartilaginous part aids in elevating the ribs and expanding the thoracic cavity; in expiration, the interosseous part depresses and retracts the ribs, compressing the thoracic cavity and expelling air; the latter occurs only in forceful expiration, not in relaxed breathing.	• Superior margins and costal cartilages of ribs 2–12; margin of sternum • Inferior margin of next higher rib	Intercostal nerves
Innermost intercostals	Presumed to have the same action as the internal intercostals	• Superomedial surface of ribs 2–12; may be absent from upper ribs • Medial edge of costal groove of next higher rib	Intercostal nerves

10.3b Muscles of the Abdominal Wall

Unlike the thoracic cavity, the abdominal cavity has little skeletal support. It is enclosed, however, in layers of broad flat muscles whose fibers run in different directions, strengthening the abdominal wall on the same principle as the alternating layers of wood fibers in plywood (**table 10.5**).

Three layers of muscle enclose the lumbar region and extend about halfway across the anterior abdomen (**fig. 10.15**). The most superficial layer is the **external oblique muscle.** Its fibers pass downward and anteriorly. The next deeper layer is the **internal oblique muscle,** whose fibers pass upward and anteriorly, roughly perpendicular to those of the external oblique. The deepest layer is the **transverse abdominal muscle (transversus abdominis),** with horizontal fibers.

Anteriorly, a pair of vertical **rectus abdominis muscles** extends from sternum to pubis. These are divided into segments by three transverse *tendinous intersections,* giving them an appearance that body builders nickname the "six pack."

The tendons of the oblique and transverse muscles are *aponeuroses*—broad fibrous sheets that continue medially and inferiorly (**figs. 10.16, 10.17**). At the rectus abdominis, they diverge and pass around its anterior and posterior sides, enclosing the muscle in a vertical sleeve called the rectus sheath. They meet again at a median line called the **linea alba**[50] between the rectus muscles. Another line, the **linea semilunaris,**[51] marks the lateral boundary where the rectus sheath meets the aponeurosis. The aponeurosis of the external

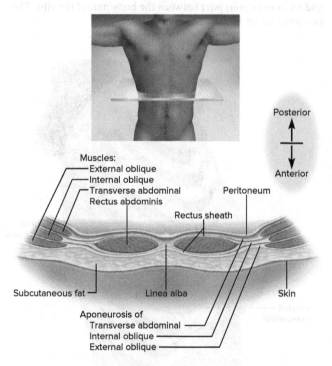

FIGURE 10.15 Cross Section of the Anterior Abdominal Wall.

Labels in figure:
Posterior
Anterior
Muscles:
External oblique
Internal oblique
Transverse abdominal
Rectus abdominis
Peritoneum
Rectus sheath
Subcutaneous fat
Linea alba
Skin
Aponeurosis of
Transverse abdominal
Internal oblique
External oblique

---

[48]*dia* = across; *phragm* = partition
[49]*inter* = between; *costa* = rib

[50]*linea* = line; *alba* = white
[51]*linea* = line; *semilunar* = half-moon

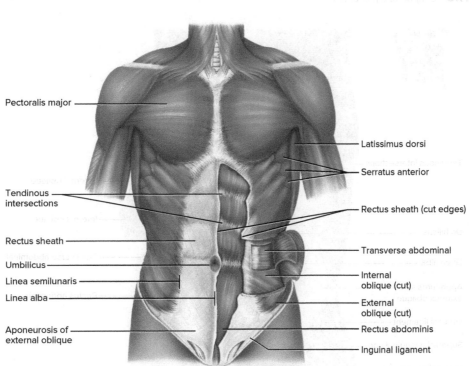

Pectoralis major

Latissimus dorsi

Serratus anterior

Tendinous
intersections

Rectus sheath (cut edges)

Rectus sheath

Transverse abdominal

Umbilicus

Internal
oblique (cut)

Linea semilunaris

Linea alba

External
oblique (cut)

Aponeurosis of
external oblique

Rectus abdominis

Inguinal ligament

(a) Superficial

Subclavius

Pectoralis minor (cut)

Pectoralis minor

Internal intercostals

Serratus anterior

External intercostals

Rectus abdominis (cut)

Rectus sheath

External
oblique (cut)

Internal oblique

Internal
oblique (cut)

Posterior wall of rectus sheath
(rectus abdominis removed)

Inguinal ligament

Transverse abdominal (cut)

(b) Deep

FIGURE 10.16 Thoracic and Abdominal Muscles. (a) Superficial muscles. The left rectus sheath is cut away to expose the rectus abdominis muscle. (b) Deep muscles. On the anatomical right, the external oblique has been removed to expose the internal oblique and the pectoralis major has been removed to expose the pectoralis minor. On the anatomical left, the internal oblique has been cut to expose the transverse abdominal and the middle of the rectus abdominis has been cut out to expose the posterior rectus sheath. **APR**

❓ *Name at least three muscles that lie deep to the pectoralis major.*

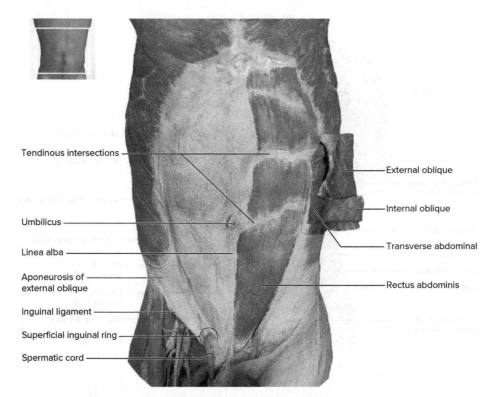

FIGURE 10.17 Thoracic and Abdominal Muscles of the Cadaver. The rectus sheath has been removed on the anatomical left to expose the left rectus abdominis muscle. Inset shows area of dissection.

Christine Eckel/McGraw-Hill Education

TABLE 10.5	Muscles of the Abdominal Wall		
Name	**Action**	**Skeletal Attachments**	**Innervation**
External oblique	Supports abdominal viscera against pull of gravity; stabilizes vertebral column during heavy lifting; maintains posture; compresses abdominal organs, thus aiding in deep breathing, loud vocalizations such as singing and public speaking, and in expulsion of abdominopelvic contents during childbirth, urination, defecation, and vomiting; unilateral contraction causes contralateral rotation of the spine, as in twisting at the waist.	• Ribs 5–12 • Anterior half of iliac crest; symphysis and superior margin of pubis	Anterior rami of spinal nerves T7–T12
Internal oblique	Same as external oblique except that unilateral contraction causes ipsilateral rotation of waist	• Inguinal ligament; iliac crest; thoracolumbar fascia • Ribs 10–12; costal cartilages 7–10; pubis	Anterior rami of spinal nerves T7–L1
Transverse abdominal	Compresses abdominal contents, with same effects as external oblique, but does not contribute to movements of vertebral column	• Inguinal ligament; iliac crest; thoracolumbar fascia; costal cartilages 7–12 • Linea alba; pubis; aponeurosis of internal oblique	Anterior rami of spinal nerves T7–L1
Rectus[52] abdominis (REC-tus ab-DOM-ih-nis)	Flexes waist, as in bending forward or doing sit-ups; stabilizes pelvic region during walking; and compresses abdominal viscera	• Pubic symphysis and superior margin of pubis • Xiphoid process; costal cartilages 5–7	Anterior rami of spinal nerves T6–T12

[52]*rectus* = straight

oblique also forms a cordlike **inguinal ligament** at its inferior margin. This extends obliquely from the anterior superior spine of the ilium to the pubis. The linea alba, linea semilunaris, and inguinal ligament are externally visible on a person with good muscle definition (see atlas B, fig. B.8). Weak points in the abdominal wall can be sites of inguinal and umbilical hernias (see Deeper Insight 10.3).

▶▶▶**APPLY WHAT YOU KNOW**

Alice works out at a fitness center three times a week doing weight lifting and abdominal crunches. Martha prefers to sit on the sofa eating potato chips and watching

TV. Both become pregnant. Other things being equal, give one reason related to table 10.5 why Alice may have an easier time with her childbirth than Martha will.

10.3c Muscles of the Back

Muscles of the back (**table 10.6**) primarily extend, rotate, and laterally flex the vertebral column. The most prominent superficial back muscles are the *latissimus dorsi* and *trapezius* (**fig. 10.18**), but they are concerned with upper limb movements and covered in tables 10.8 and 10.9. Deep to these are the **serratus posterior superior** and **inferior** (figs. 10.18, **10.19**). They extend from the

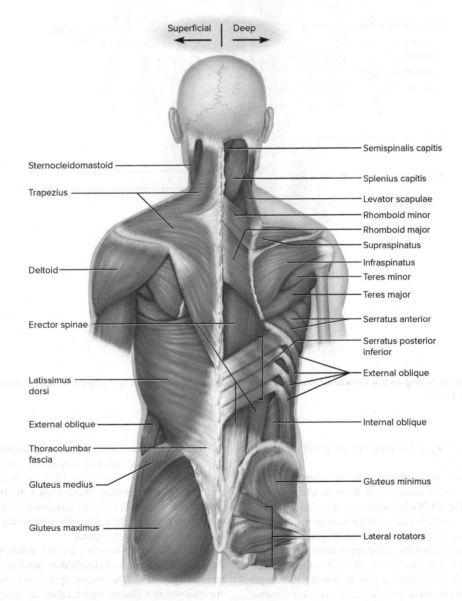

Superficial | Deep

Sternocleidomastoid

Trapezius

Deltoid

Erector spinae

Latissimus dorsi

External oblique

Thoracolumbar fascia

Gluteus medius

Gluteus maximus

Semispinalis capitis

Splenius capitis

Levator scapulae

Rhomboid minor

Rhomboid major

Supraspinatus

Infraspinatus

Teres minor

Teres major

Serratus anterior

Serratus posterior inferior

External oblique

Internal oblique

Gluteus minimus

Lateral rotators

FIGURE 10.18 Neck, Back, and Gluteal Muscles. The most superficial muscles are shown on the left and the next deeper layer on the right. **A&PR**

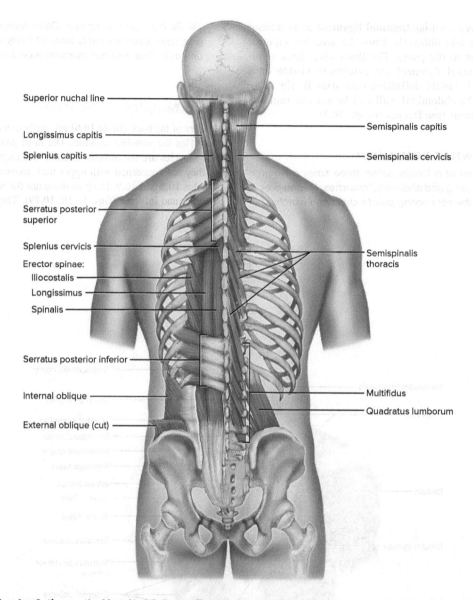

FIGURE 10.19 Muscles Acting on the Vertebral Column. These are deeper than the muscles in figure 10.18, and those on the right are deeper than those on the left.

Labels (left side):
- Superior nuchal line
- Longissimus capitis
- Splenius capitis
- Serratus posterior superior
- Splenius cervicis
- Erector spinae:
  - Iliocostalis
  - Longissimus
  - Spinalis
- Serratus posterior inferior
- Internal oblique
- External oblique (cut)

Labels (right side):
- Semispinalis capitis
- Semispinalis cervicis
- Semispinalis thoracis
- Multifidus
- Quadratus lumborum

vertebrae to the ribs. They aid in deep breathing and are further discussed in chapter 22.

Deep to these is a prominent muscle, the **erector spinae,** which runs vertically for the entire length of the back from the cranium to the sacrum **(fig. 10.20).** It is a thick muscle, easily palpated on each side of the vertebral column in the lumbar region. (Pork chops and T-bone steaks are cut from the erector spinae muscles of animals.) As it ascends, it divides in the upper lumbar region into three parallel columns. The most lateral of these is the **iliocostalis,** which from inferior to superior is divided into the *iliocostalis lumborum, iliocostalis thoracis,* and *iliocostalis cervicis* (lumbar, thoracic, and cervical regions).

The next column medially is the **longissimus,** divided from inferior to superior into the *longissimus thoracis, longissimus cervicis,* and *longissimus capitis* (thoracic, cervical, and cephalic regions). The most medial column is the **spinalis,** divided into *spinalis thoracis, spinalis cervicis,* and *spinalis capitis.* The functions of all three columns are sufficiently similar that we will treat them collectively as the erector spinae.

The major deep muscles are the **semispinalis thoracis** in the thoracic region and **quadratus lumborum** in the lumbar region (fig. 10.19). The erector spinae and quadratus lumborum are enclosed in a fibrous sheath called the **thoracolumbar fascia** (fig. 10.18), which is the origin of some of the abdominal and

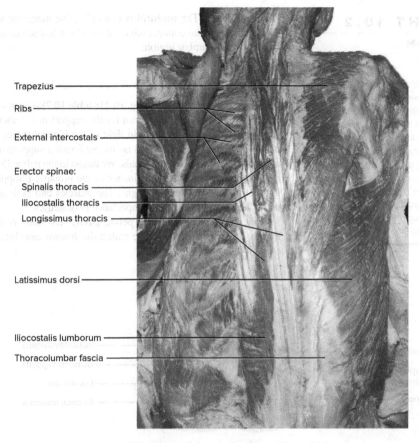

Trapezius

Ribs

External intercostals

Erector spinae:

Spinalis thoracis

Iliocostalis thoracis

Longissimus thoracis

Latissimus dorsi

Iliocostalis lumborum

Thoracolumbar fascia

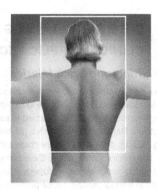

FIGURE 10.20 Deep Back Muscles of the Cadaver.

Rebecca Gray/Don Kincaid/McGraw-Hill Education

TABLE 10.6	Muscles of the Back		
Name	**Action**	**Skeletal Attachments**	**Innervation**
Erector spinae (eh-REC-tur SPY-nee)	Aids in sitting and standing erect; straightens back after one bends at waist, and is employed in arching the back; unilateral contraction flexes waist laterally; the longissimus capitis also produces ipsilateral rotation of the head.	• Nuchal ligament; ribs 3–12; thoracic and lumbar vertebrae; median and lateral sacral crests; thoracolumbar fascia • Mastoid process; cervical and thoracic vertebrae; all ribs	Posterior rami of cervical to lumbar spinal nerves
Semispinalis thoracis (SEM-ee-spy-NAY-liss tho-RA-sis)	Extension and contralateral rotation of vertebral column	• Vertebrae T6–T10 • Vertebrae C6–T4	Posterior rami of cervical and thoracic spinal nerves
Quadratus lumborum[53] (quad-RAY-tus lum-BORE-um)	Unilateral contraction causes ipsilateral flexion of lumbar spine; bilateral contraction extends lumbar spine. Aids respiration by fixing rib 12 and stabilizing attachments of diaphragm.	• Iliac crest; iliolumbar ligament • Rib 12; vertebrae L1–L4	Anterior rami of spinal nerves T12–L4
Multifidus[54] (mul-TIFF-ih-dus)	Stabilizes adjacent vertebrae, maintains posture, controls vertebral movement when erector spinae acts on spine	• Vertebrae C4–L5; posterior superior iliac spine; sacrum; aponeurosis of erector spinae • Laminae and spinous processes of vertebrae superior to origins	Posterior rami of cervical to lumbar spinal nerves

[53]*quadrat* = four-sided; *lumborum* = of the lumbar region   [54]*multi* = many; *fid* = branched, sectioned

DEEPER INSIGHT 10.2

CLINICAL APPLICATION

Heavy Lifting and Back Injuries

When you are fully bent over forward, as in touching your toes, the erector spinae is fully stretched. Because of the *length–tension relationship* explained in section 11.4e, muscles that are stretched to such extremes cannot contract very effectively. Standing up from such a position is therefore initiated by the hamstring muscles on the back of the thigh and the gluteus maximus of the buttocks. The erector spinae joins in the action when it is partially contracted.

Standing too suddenly or improperly lifting a heavy weight, however, can strain the erector spinae, cause painful muscle spasms, tear tendons and ligaments of the lower back, and rupture intervertebral discs. The lumbar muscles are adapted for maintaining posture, not for lifting. This is why it is important, in heavy lifting, to crouch and use the powerful extensor muscles of the thighs and buttocks to lift the load.

lumbar muscles. The **multifidus** is a collective name for a series of tiny muscles that connect adjacent vertebrae to each other from the cervical to lumbar region.

10.3d Muscles of the Pelvic Floor

The floor of the pelvic cavity (**fig. 10.21; table 10.7**) is a strong multilayered muscular sheet important for the support of the abdominal and pelvic viscera—especially in light of the bipedal stance of humans, since the abdominal wall no longer forms a supportive floor as it does in quadrupedal mammals. Weakness in the pelvic floor can result in urinary or fecal incontinence or the prolapse (dropping) of internal organs between the thighs. The muscles and skeletal landmarks here are also of special importance in obstetrics.

Viewed from within the pelvic cavity, its floor is formed mainly by an extensive muscle called the *levator ani*. Inferior to

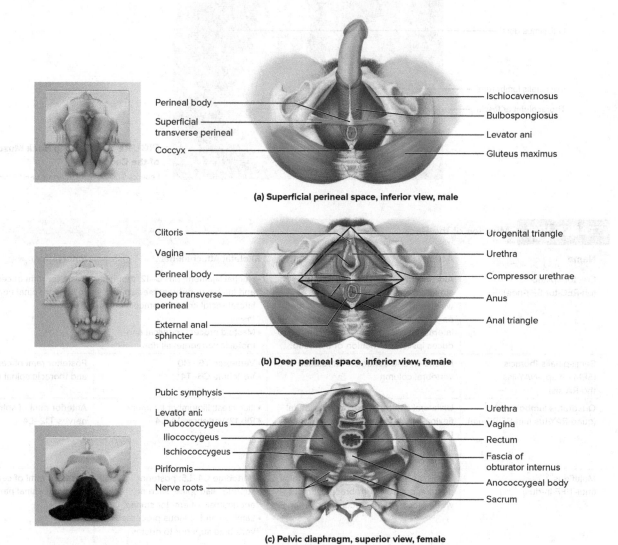

(a) Superficial perineal space, inferior view, male

Perineal body
Superficial transverse perineal
Coccyx

Ischiocavernosus
Bulbospongiosus
Levator ani
Gluteus maximus

(b) Deep perineal space, inferior view, female

Clitoris
Vagina
Perineal body
Deep transverse perineal
External anal sphincter

Urogenital triangle
Urethra
Compressor urethrae
Anus
Anal triangle

(c) Pelvic diaphragm, superior view, female

Pubic symphysis
Levator ani:
 Pubococcygeus
 Iliococcygeus
 Ischiococcygeus
Piriformis
Nerve roots

Urethra
Vagina
Rectum
Fascia of obturator internus
Anococcygeal body
Sacrum

FIGURE 10.21 Muscles of the Pelvic Floor. (a) The superficial perineal space, male, viewed from below (the inferior aspect). (b) The deep perineal space, female, viewed from the same perspective. Other than the vaginal canal, the sexes are nearly identical at this level, including the urogenital and anal triangles. The root of the penis does not extend to this level. (c) The pelvic diaphragm, female, viewed from above (from within the pelvic cavity).

TABLE 10.7	Muscles of the Pelvic Floor		
Name	Action	Skeletal Attachments	Innervation
Superficial Perineal Space			
Ischiocavernosus[55] (ISS-kee-oh-CAV-er-NO-sus)	Maintains erection of the penis or clitoris by compressing deep structures of the organ and forcing blood forward into its body	• Ramus and tuberosity of ischium • Ensheaths internal structures of penis and clitoris	Pudendal nerve
Bulbospongiosus[56] (BUL-bo-SPUN-jee-OH-sus)	Expels residual urine from urethra after bladder has emptied. Aids in erection of penis or clitoris. In male, spasmodic contractions expel semen during ejaculation. In female, contractions constrict vaginal orifice and expel secretions of greater vestibular glands.	• Perineal body and median raphe • Male: ensheaths root of penis Female: pubic symphysis	Pudendal nerve
Deep Perineal Space			
Deep transverse perineal	Anchors perineal body, which supports other pelvic muscles; supports vaginal and urethral canals	• Ischiopubic rami • Perineal body	Pudendal nerve
Compressor urethrae (yu-REE-three)	Aids in urine retention; found in females only	• Ischiopubic rami • Right and left compressor urethrae meet each other inferior to external urethral sphincter	Pudendal nerve; spinal nerves S2–S4; pelvic splanchnic nerve
Anal Triangle			
External anal sphincter	Retains feces in rectum until voluntarily voided	• Coccyx, perineal body • Encircles anal canal and orifice	Pudendal nerve; spinal nerves S2–S4; pelvic splanchnic nerve
Pelvic Diaphragm			
Levator ani[57] (leh-VAY-tur AY-nye)	Compresses anal canal and reinforces external anal and urethral sphincters; supports uterus and other pelvic viscera; aids in falling away of the feces; vertical movements affect pressure differences between abdominal and thoracic cavities and thus aid in deep breathing.	• Inner surface of lesser pelvis from pubis through margin of obturator internus to spine of ischium • Coccyx via anococcygeal body; walls of urethra, vagina, and anal canal	Pudendal nerve; spinal nerves S2–S3

this is the **perineum** (PERR-ih-NEE-um), a diamond-shaped area between the thighs bordered by four bony landmarks: the pubic symphysis anteriorly, the coccyx posteriorly, and the ischial tuberosities laterally. The pelvic floor and perineum are penetrated by the anal canal, urethra, and vagina. The anterior half of the perineum is the **urogenital triangle** and the posterior half is the **anal triangle.**

The urogenital triangle is divided into two muscle compartments separated by a strong fibrous **perineal membrane.** The muscle compartment between this membrane and the skin is called *superficial perineal space,* and the compartment between the perineal membrane and levator ani is the *deep perineal space.* We will examine these structures beginning inferiorly, just beneath the skin, and progressing superiorly to the pelvic floor.

The Superficial Perineal Space

The **superficial perineal space** (fig. 10.21a) contains three pairs of muscles: the *ischiocavernosus, bulbospongiosus,* and *superficial transverse perineal muscle.* In females, this space also contains the clitoris; various glands and erectile tissues of the genitalia (see fig. 28.8); and adipose tissue, which extends into and fattens the mons pubis and labia majora. In males, it contains the root of the penis.

The **ischiocavernosus** muscles converge like a V from the ischial tuberosities toward the penis or clitoris. In males, the **bulbospongiosus (bulbocavernosus)** muscles form a sheath around the root of the penis, and in females they enclose the vagina like a pair of parentheses. *Cavernosus* in these names refers to the spongy, cavernous structure of tissues in the penis and clitoris.

The **superficial transverse perineal muscles** extend from the ischial tuberosities to a strong median fibromuscular anchorage, the **perineal body,** and a median seam called the **perineal raphe** (RAY-fee) that extends anteriorly from the perineal body. These muscles may help to anchor the perineal body, but they are weakly developed and not always present, therefore not included in table 10.7. The other two muscle pairs of this layer serve primarily sexual functions.

[55]*ischio* = ischium of hip bone; *cavernosus* = corpus cavernosum of the penis or clitoris
[56]*bulbo* = bulb of the penis; *spongiosus* = corpus spongiosum of the penis

[57]*levator* = that which elevates; *ani* = of the anus

DEEPER INSIGHT 10.3

CLINICAL APPLICATION

Hernias

A hernia is any condition in which the viscera protrude through a weak point in the muscular wall of the abdominopelvic cavity. The most common type to require treatment is an *inguinal hernia* (fig. 10.22). In the male fetus, each testis descends from the pelvic cavity into the scrotum by way of a passage called the *inguinal canal* through the muscles of the groin. A long pouch of peritoneum descends with the testis, but usually disappears by birth. Hernias occur in infants and children when this pouch persists, allowing a loop of intestine to enter it and appear near or in the scrotum *(indirect hernia)*. Adult hernias may appear similar but are often due to a weakening of the inguinal canal *(direct hernia)*. This can result from repetitive stress such as lifting weights. When the diaphragm and abdominal muscles contract, pressure in the abdominal cavity can soar to 1,500 pounds per square inch—more than 100 times the normal pressure and quite sufficient to produce an inguinal hernia, or "rupture." Inguinal hernias in women occur through the pelvic floor and other nearby sites.

Two other sites of hernia are the diaphragm and navel. A *hiatal hernia* is a condition in which part of the stomach protrudes through the diaphragm into the thoracic cavity. This is most common in overweight people over 40. It may cause heartburn due to the regurgitation of stomach acid into the esophagus, but most cases go undetected. In an *umbilical hernia,* abdominal viscera protrude through the navel.

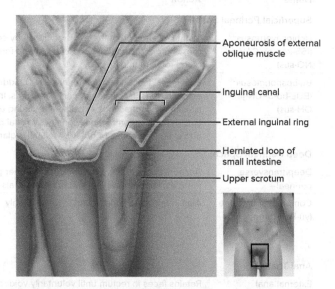

FIGURE 10.22 Inguinal Hernia. A loop of small intestine has protruded through the inguinal canal into a space beneath the skin.

The Deep Perineal Space

The **deep perineal space** (fig. 10.21b) contains a pair of **deep transverse perineal muscles** and, in females only, the **compressor urethrae muscles.** The deep transverse perineal muscles anchor the perineal body on the median plane; the perineal body, in turn, anchors other pelvic muscles. The female external urethral sphincter, long thought to be part of the deep perineal space, is now regarded as part of the urethra itself and not part of the pelvic floor musculature.

The Anal Triangle

The **anal triangle** contains the **external anal sphincter** and **anococcygeal ligament** (fig. 10.21b). The external anal sphincter is a tubular muscle surrounding the lower anal canal. The anococcygeal ligament is the median insertion of the levator ani muscles, and the ligament, in turn, inserts on the coccyx. It is therefore a major anchorage for the structures that compose the pelvic floor.

The Pelvic Diaphragm

The **pelvic diaphragm** (fig. 10.21c) is deep to the foregoing structures (uppermost in the pelvic floor) and is composed mainly of the right and left **levator ani** muscles. (The piriformis, also illustrated, is primarily a lower limb muscle.) The levator ani spans most of the pelvic outlet and forms the floor of the lesser (true) pelvis. It is divided into three portions that are sometimes regarded as separate muscles—the *ischiococcygeus* (or *coccygeus*), *iliococcygeus,* and *pubococcygeus*. The left and right levator ani muscles converge on the anococcygeal ligament, through which they are indirectly anchored to the coccyx.

BEFORE YOU GO ON

Answer the following questions to test your understanding of the preceding section:

11. Which muscles are used more often, the external intercostals or internal intercostals? Explain.

12. Explain how pulmonary ventilation affects abdominal pressure and vice versa.

13. Name a major superficial muscle and two major deep muscles of the back.

14. Define *perineum, urogenital triangle,* and *anal triangle.*

15. Name one muscle in the superficial perineal space, one in the urogenital diaphragm, and one in the pelvic diaphragm. State the function of each.

10.4 Muscles Acting on the Shoulder and Upper Limb

Expected Learning Outcomes

When you have completed this section, you should be able to

a. name and locate the muscles that act on the pectoral girdle, shoulder, elbow, wrist, and hand;

b. relate the actions of these muscles to the joint movements described in chapter 9; and

c. describe the skeletal attachments, action, and innervation of these muscles.

The upper and lower limbs have numerous muscles that serve primarily for movement of the body and manipulation of objects. These muscles are organized into distinct compartments separated from each other by the interosseous membranes of the forearm and leg (see figs. 8.34, 8.40) and by intermuscular septa. In the ensuing tables, you will find muscles of the upper limb divided into anterior and posterior compartments, and those of

the lower limb divided into anterior, posterior, medial, and lateral compartments. In most limb regions, the muscle groups are further subdivided by thinner fasciae into superficial and deep layers.

The upper limb is used for a broad range of both powerful and subtle actions, ranging from climbing, grasping, and throwing to writing, playing musical instruments, and manipulating small objects. It therefore has an especially complex array of muscles, but the muscles fall into logical groups that make their functional relationships and names easier to understand. The next five tables group these into muscles that act on the scapula, those that act on the humerus and shoulder joint, those that act on the forearm and elbow joint, extrinsic (forearm) muscles that act on the wrist and hand, and intrinsic (hand) muscles that act on the fingers.

10.4a Muscles Acting on the Shoulder

Muscles that act on the pectoral girdle (**table 10.8**) extend from the axial skeleton to the clavicle and scapula. The scapula is only loosely attached to the thoracic cage and is capable of considerable movement (**fig. 10.23**)—rotation (as in raising and lowering the apex of the shoulder), elevation and depression (as in shrugging and lowering the shoulders), and

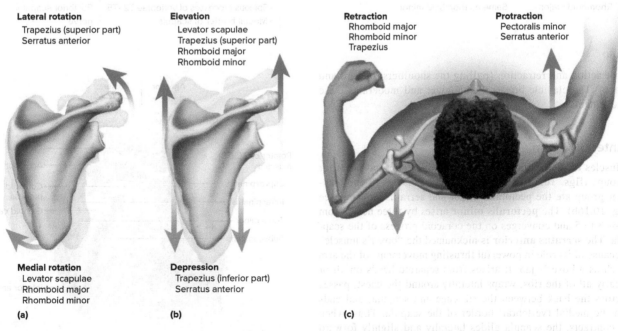

Lateral rotation
Trapezius (superior part)
Serratus anterior

Elevation
Levator scapulae
Trapezius (superior part)
Rhomboid major
Rhomboid minor

Retraction
Rhomboid major
Rhomboid minor
Trapezius

Protraction
Pectoralis minor
Serratus anterior

Medial rotation
Levator scapulae
Rhomboid major
Rhomboid minor

(a)

Depression
Trapezius (inferior part)
Serratus anterior

(b)

(c)

FIGURE 10.23 Actions of Some Thoracic Muscles on the Scapula. (a) Lateral and medial rotation. (b) Elevation and depression. (c) Retraction and protraction. Note that an individual muscle can contribute to multiple actions, depending on which fibers contract and what synergists act with it.

TABLE 10.8	Muscles Acting on the Shoulder		
Name	Action	Skeletal Attachments	Innervation
Anterior Group			
Pectoralis minor (PECK-toe-RAY-liss)	With serratus anterior, draws scapula laterally and forward around chest wall; with other muscles, rotates scapula and depresses apex of shoulder, as in reaching down to pick up a suitcase	• Ribs 3–5 and overlying fascia • Coracoid process of scapula	Medial and lateral pectoral nerves
Serratus[58] anterior (serr-AY-tus)	With pectoralis minor, draws scapula laterally and forward around chest wall; protracts scapula, and is the prime mover in all forward-reaching and pushing actions; aids in rotating scapula to elevate apex of shoulder; fixes scapula during abduction of arm	• All or nearly all ribs • Medial border of scapula	Long thoracic nerve
Posterior Group			
Trapezius (tra-PEE-zee-us)	Stabilizes scapula and shoulder during arm movements; elevates and depresses apex of shoulder; acts with other muscles to rotate and retract scapula (see also roles in head and neck movements in table 10.3)	• External occipital protuberance; medial one-third of superior nuchal line; nuchal ligament; spinous processes of vertebrae C7–T12 • Acromion and spine of scapula; lateral one-third of clavicle	Accessory nerve
Levator scapulae (leh-VAY-tur SCAP-you-lee)	Elevates scapula if cervical vertebrae are fixed; flexes neck laterally if scapula is fixed; retracts scapula and braces shoulder; rotates scapula and depresses apex of shoulder	• Transverse processes of vertebrae C1–C4 • Superior angle to medial border of scapula	Spinal nerves C3–C4, and C5 via posterior scapular nerve
Rhomboid minor (ROM-boyd)	Retracts scapula and braces shoulder; fixes scapula during arm movements	• Spinous processes of vertebrae C7–T1; nuchal ligament • Medial border of scapula	Posterior scapular nerve
Rhomboid major	Same as rhomboid minor	• Spinous processes of vertebrae T2–T5 • Medial border of scapula	Posterior scapular nerve

protraction and retraction (pulling the shoulders forward and back). The clavicle braces the shoulder and moderates these movements.

Anterior Group

Muscles of the pectoral girdle fall into anterior and posterior groups (**figs. 10.24, 10.25**). The major muscles of the anterior group are the pectoralis minor and serratus anterior (see fig. 10.16b). The **pectoralis minor** arises by three heads from ribs 3 to 5 and converges on the coracoid process of the scapula. The **serratus anterior** is nicknamed the "boxer's muscle" because of its role in powerful thrusting movements of the arm such as a boxer's jab. It arises from separate heads on all or nearly all of the ribs, wraps laterally around the chest, passes across the back between the rib cage and scapula, and ends on the medial (vertebral) border of the scapula. Thus, when it contracts, the scapula glides laterally and slightly forward around the ribs.

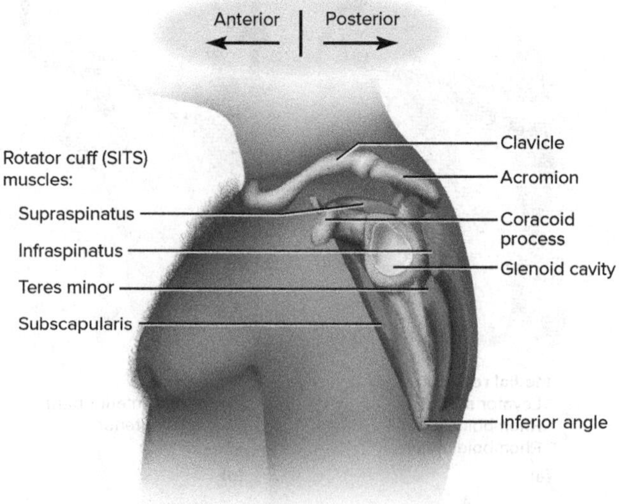

FIGURE 10.24   Rotator Cuff Muscles in Relation to the Scapula (Lateral View). For posterior and anterior views of these muscles, see figure 10.25, b and d.

---
[58]*serrate* = scalloped, zigzag

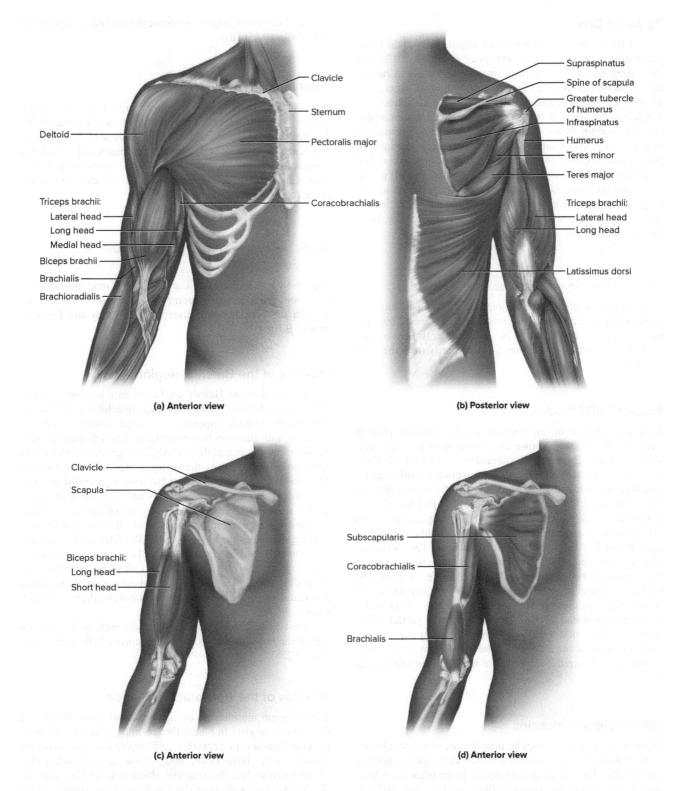

(a) Anterior view

(b) Posterior view

(c) Anterior view

(d) Anterior view

FIGURE 10.25 Pectoral and Brachial Muscles. (a) Superficial muscles, anterior view. (b) Superficial muscles, posterior view. (c) The biceps brachii, the superficial flexor of the elbow. (d) The brachialis, the deep flexor of the elbow, and the coracobrachialis and subscapularis, which act on the humerus. **APR**

Posterior Group

The posterior muscles that act on the scapula include the large, superficial **trapezius,** already discussed (see table 10.3), and three deep muscles: the **levator scapulae, rhomboid minor, and rhomboid major.** The action of the trapezius depends on whether its superior, middle, or inferior fibers contract and whether it acts alone or with other muscles. The levator scapulae and superior fibers of the trapezius rotate the scapula in opposite directions if either of them acts alone. If both act together, their opposite rotational effects balance each other and they elevate the scapula and shoulder, as when you lift a suitcase from the floor. Depression of the scapula occurs mainly by gravitational pull, but the trapezius and serratus anterior can depress it more rapidly and forcefully, as in swimming, hammering, and rowing.

10.4b Muscles Acting on the Arm

Nine muscles cross the shoulder joint and insert on the humerus **(table 10.9).** Seven of them are considered *scapular muscles* because they arise from the scapula, and the other two are considered *axial muscles* because they arise primarily from the axial skeleton.

Rotator Cuff Muscles

Tendons from four of the scapular muscles form the **rotator cuff** (fig. 10.24), well known as a common site of musculoskeletal injury. These are nicknamed the "SITS muscles" for the first letters of their names—**supraspinatus, infraspinatus, teres minor,** and **subscapularis.** The first three of these lie on the posterior side of the scapula (fig. 10.25b). The supraspinatus and infraspinatus occupy the supraspinous and infraspinous fossae, above and below the scapular spine. The teres minor lies inferior to the infraspinatus. The subscapularis occupies the subscapular fossa on the anterior surface of the scapula, between the scapula and ribs (fig. 10.25d). The tendons of these muscles merge with the joint capsule of the shoulder as they cross it en route to the humerus. They insert on the proximal end of the humerus, forming a partial sleeve around it. The rotator cuff reinforces the joint capsule and holds the head of the humerus in the glenoid cavity. It is easily damaged by strenuous actions of the shoulder (see Deeper Insight 10.4).

Other Scapular Muscles

Of the remaining three scapular muscles, the most conspicuous is the **deltoid,** the thick triangular muscle that caps the shoulder (fig. 10.25a). Intramuscular drug injections are often given here. Its anterior, lateral, and posterior fibers act like three different

muscles. The **teres major** and **coracobrachialis** complete this group (fig. 10.25b, d).

Axial Muscles

The two axial muscles, both prominent, are the pectoralis major anteriorly and latissimus dorsi posteriorly (fig. 10.25a, b; **fig. 10.26**). The **pectoralis major** is the thick, fleshy muscle of the mammary region and the **latissimus dorsi** is a broad muscle of the back that extends from the waist to the axilla. These muscles bear the primary responsibility for attaching the arm to the trunk and are the prime movers of the shoulder joint.

10.4c Muscles Acting on the Elbow and Forearm

The elbow and forearm are capable of four motions—flexion, extension, pronation, and supination—carried out by muscles in both the brachium and antebrachium (arm and forearm) **(table 10.10).**

Muscles of the Brachial Region

The principal elbow flexors are in the anterior compartment of the arm—the **brachialis** and **biceps brachii** (fig. 10.25c, d). The biceps brachii appears as a large anterior bulge on the arm and commands considerable interest among body builders, but the brachialis underlying it generates about 50% more power and is thus the prime mover of elbow flexion. The biceps is not only a flexor but also a powerful forearm supinator. It is named for its two heads: a *short head* whose tendon arises from the coracoid process of the scapula, and a *long head* whose tendon arises from the superior margin of the glenoid cavity, loops over the shoulder, and braces the humerus against the glenoid cavity. The two heads converge close to the elbow on a single distal tendon that terminates on the radius and on the fascia of the medial side of the upper forearm. Note that *biceps* is the singular term; there is no such word as *bicep.*

The **triceps brachii** is a three-headed muscle on the posterior side of the humerus, and is the prime mover of elbow extension (fig. 10.25b).

Muscles of the Antebrachial Region

Most forearm muscles act on the wrist and hand, but two of them are synergists in elbow flexion and extension and three of them function in pronation and supination. The **brachioradialis** is the large fleshy mass of the lateral (radial) side of the forearm just distal to the elbow (fig. 10.25a; also see fig. 10.29a). It extends from the distal end of the humerus to the

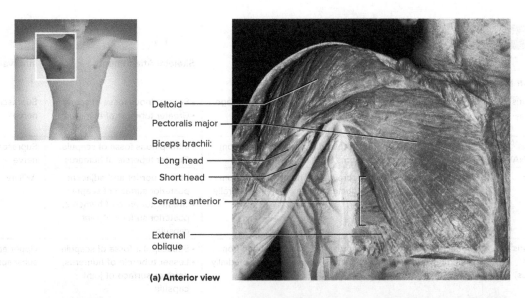

Deltoid

Pectoralis major

Biceps brachii:

Long head

Short head

Serratus anterior

External
oblique

(a) Anterior view

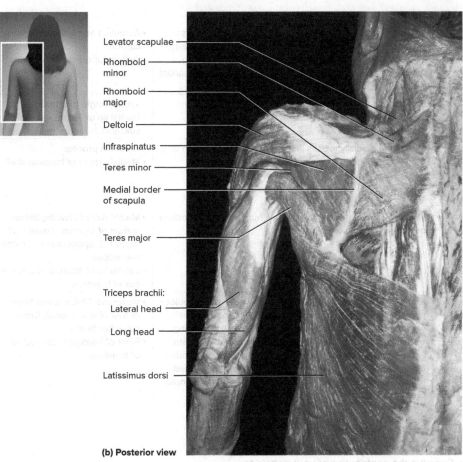

Levator scapulae

Rhomboid
minor

Rhomboid
major

Deltoid

Infraspinatus

Teres minor

Medial border
of scapula

Teres major

Triceps brachii:

Lateral head

Long head

Latissimus dorsi

(b) Posterior view

FIGURE 10.26 Pectoral, Brachial, and Upper Back Muscles of the Cadaver. (a) Anterior view. (b) Posterior view.

a–b: Rebecca Gray/McGraw-Hill Education

TABLE 10.9	Muscles Acting on the Arm		
Name	**Action**	**Skeletal Attachments**	**Innervation**
Rotator Cuff Muscles			
Supraspinatus[59] (SOO-pra-spy-NAY-tus)	Aids deltoid in abduction of arm; resists downward slippage of humeral head when arm is relaxed or when carrying weight	• Supraspinous fossa of scapula • Greater tubercle of humerus	Suprascapular nerve
Infraspinatus[60] (IN-fra-spy-NAY-tus)	Modulates action of deltoid, preventing humeral head from sliding upward; rotates humerus laterally	• Infraspinous fossa of scapula • Greater tubercle of humerus	Suprascapular nerve
Teres minor (TERR-eez)	Modulates action of deltoid, preventing humeral head from sliding upward as arm is abducted; rotates humerus laterally	• Lateral border and adjacent posterior surface of scapula • Greater tubercle of humerus; posterior surface of joint capsule	Axillary nerve
Subscapularis[61] (SUB-SCAP-you-LERR-iss)	Modulates action of deltoid, preventing humeral head from sliding upward as arm is abducted; rotates humerus medially	• Subscapular fossa of scapula • Lesser tubercle of humerus; anterior surface of joint capsule	Upper and lower subscapular nerves
Other Scapular Muscles			
Deltoid	Anterior fibers flex and medially rotate arm; lateral fibers abduct arm; posterior fibers extend and laterally rotate arm; involved in arm swinging during such actions as walking or bowling, and in adjustment of hand height for various manual tasks	• Acromion and spine of scapula; clavicle • Deltoid tuberosity of humerus	Axillary nerve
Teres major (TERR-eez)	Extends and medially rotates humerus; contributes to arm swinging	• Inferior angle of scapula • Medial lip of intertubercular sulcus of humerus	Lower subscapular nerve
Coracobrachialis (COR-uh-co-BRAY-kee-AY-lis)	Flexes and medially rotates arm; resists deviation of arm from frontal plane during abduction	• Coracoid process • Medial aspect of humeral shaft	Musculocutaneous nerve
Axial Muscles			
Pectoralis major (PECK-toe-RAY-liss)	Flexes, adducts, and medially rotates humerus, as in climbing or hugging; aids in deep inspiration	• Medial half of clavicle; lateral margin of sternum; costal cartilages 1–7; aponeurosis of external oblique • Lateral lip of intertubercular sulcus of humerus	Medial and lateral pectoral nerves
Latissimus dorsi[62] (la-TISS-ih-mus DOR-sye)	Adducts and medially rotates humerus; extends the shoulder joint as in pulling on the oars of a rowboat; produces backward swing of arm in such actions as walking and bowling; with hands grasping overhead objects, pulls body forward and upward, as in climbing; aids in deep inspiration, sudden expiration such as sneezing and coughing, and prolonged forceful expiration as in singing or blowing a sustained note on a wind instrument	• Vertebrae T7–L5; lower three or four ribs; iliac crest; thoracolumbar fascia • Floor of intertubercular sulcus of humerus	Thoracodorsal nerve

▶▶▶**APPLY WHAT YOU KNOW**

Perform an action as if lifting a cup to your mouth to take a sip of tea. Describe the contribution of your deltoid to this action, using the terminology of joint movement in section 9.2c.

---

[59]*supra* = above; *spin* = spine of scapula
[60]*infra* = below, under; *spin* = spine of scapula

[61]*sub* = below, under
[62]*latissimus* = broadest; *dorsi* = of the back

DEEPER INSIGHT 10.4

CLINICAL APPLICATION

Rotator Cuff Injury

Rotator cuff injury is a tear in the tendon of any of the SITS (rotator cuff) muscles, most often the supraspinatus. Such injuries are caused by strenuous circumduction of the arm, shoulder dislocation, hard falls or blows to the shoulder, or repetitive use of the arm in a position above the horizontal. They are common among baseball pitchers and third basemen, bowlers, swimmers, and weight lifters, and in racquet sports. Recurrent inflammation of a SITS tendon can cause a tendon to degenerate and then to rupture in response to moderate stress. Injury causes pain and makes the shoulder joint unstable and subject to dislocation.

distal end of the radius. With the latter attachment so far from the fulcrum of the elbow, it does not generate as much force as the brachialis and biceps; it is effective mainly when those muscles have already partially flexed the elbow. The **anconeus** is a weak synergist of elbow extension on the posterior side of the elbow (see fig. 10.30).

Pronation and supination are important forearm movements for such purposes as eating, manipulating and inspecting objects in the hands, and generating force in twisting movements of the hand (see fig. 9.18). The prime mover of pronation is the **pronator quadratus** near the wrist; the **pronator teres** near the elbow is a synergist. Supination is usually achieved by the **supinator** of the upper forearm, with the biceps brachii aiding when additional speed or power is required **(fig. 10.27)**.

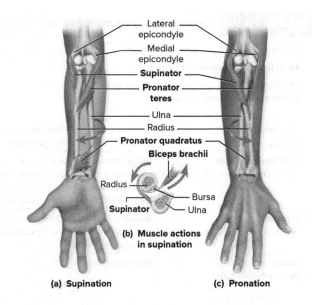

FIGURE 10.27 Actions of the Rotator Muscles on the Forearm. (a) Supination. (b) Cross section just distal to the elbow, showing the synergistic action of the biceps brachii and supinator. (c) Pronation.

What do the names of the pronator teres and pronator quadratus muscles indicate about their shapes?

10.4d Muscles Acting on the Wrist and Hand

The hand is acted upon by extrinsic muscles in the forearm **(table 10.11)** and intrinsic muscles in the hand itself. The bellies of the extrinsic muscles, along with the brachioradialis,

TABLE 10.10	Muscles Acting on the Elbow and Forearm		
Name	**Action**	**Skeletal Attachments**	**Innervation**
Muscles of the Brachial Region			
Brachialis (BRAY-kee-AY-lis)	Prime mover of elbow flexion	• Anterior surface of distal half of humerus • Coronoid process and tuberosity of ulna	Musculocutaneous nerve; radial nerve
Biceps brachii (BY-seps BRAY-kee-eye)	Rapid or forceful supination of forearm; synergist in elbow flexion; slight shoulder flexion; tendon of long head stabilizes shoulder by holding humeral head against glenoid cavity	• Long head: superior margin of glenoid cavity Short head: coracoid process • Tuberosity of radius; fascia of forearm	Musculocutaneous nerve
Triceps brachii (TRI-seps BRAY-kee-eye)	Extends elbow; long head extends and adducts humerus	• Long head: inferior margin of glenoid cavity and joint capsule Lateral head: posterior surface of proximal end of humerus Medial head: posterior surface of entire humeral shaft • Olecranon; fascia of forearm	Radial nerve

(continued)

TABLE 10.10	Muscles Acting on the Elbow and Forearm (continued)		
Name	Action	Skeletal Attachments	Innervation
Muscles of the Antebrachial Region			
Brachioradialis (BRAY-kee-oh-RAY-dee-AY-lis)	Flexes elbow	• Lateral supracondylar ridge of humerus • Lateral surface of radius near styloid process	Radial nerve
Anconeus[63] (an-CO-nee-us)	Extends elbow; may help to control ulnar movement during pronation	• Lateral epicondyle of humerus • Olecranon and posterior surface of ulna	Radial nerve
Pronator quadratus (PRO-nay-tur quad-RAY-tus)	Prime mover of forearm pronation; also resists separation of radius and ulna when force is applied to forearm through wrist, as in doing push-ups	• Anterior surface of distal ulna • Anterior surface of distal radius	Median nerve
Pronator teres (PRO-nay-tur TERR-eez)	Assists pronator quadratus in pronation, but only in rapid or forceful action; weakly flexes elbow	• Humeral shaft near medial epicondyle; coronoid process of ulna • Lateral surface of radial shaft	Median nerve
Supinator (SOO-pih-NAY-tur)	Supinates forearm	• Lateral epicondyle of humerus; supinator crest and fossa of ulna just distal to radial notch; anular and radial collateral ligaments of elbow • Proximal one-third of radius	Radial nerve

form the fleshy roundness of the upper forearm; their tendons extend into the wrist and hand. Their actions are mainly flexion and extension of the wrist and digits, but also include radial and ulnar flexion, finger abduction and adduction, and thumb opposition. These muscles are numerous and complex, but their names often describe their location, appearance, and function.

Many of them act on the **metacarpophalangeal joints** between the metacarpal bones of the hand and the proximal phalanges of the fingers, and the **interphalangeal joints** between the proximal and middle or the middle and distal phalanges of the fingers (or between the proximal and distal phalanges in the thumb, which has no middle phalanx). The metacarpophalangeal joints form the knuckles at the bases of the fingers, and the interphalangeal joints form the second and third knuckles. Some tendons cross multiple joints before inserting on a middle or distal phalanx, and can flex or extend all the joints they cross.

Fasciae divide the forearm muscles into anterior and posterior compartments and each compartment into superficial and deep layers (**fig. 10.28**). The muscles in these four groups are described in the following sections.

The Anterior (Flexor) Compartment, Superficial Layer

Most muscles of the anterior compartment are wrist and finger flexors that arise from a common tendon on the humerus (**fig. 10.29**). The two prominent tendons you can palpate at the wrist belong to the **palmaris longus** on the medial side and the

flexor carpi radialis on the lateral side (see fig. B.19a). The latter is an important landmark for finding the radial artery, where the pulse is usually taken. The palmaris longus is absent on one or both sides (most commonly the left) in about 14% of people. To see if you have one, flex your wrist and touch the tips of your thumb and little finger together. If present, the palmaris longus tendon will stand up prominently on the wrist.

Most tendons of these flexor muscles pass under a fibrous, braceletlike ligament called the **flexor retinaculum** on the anterior side of the wrist (see fig. 5.13); the palmaris longus tendon, unlike the rest, passes over it. The retinaculum prevents the tendons from standing up like taut bowstrings when the flexors contract. The **carpal tunnel** is a tight space between the flexor retinaculum and carpal bones. The flexor tendons passing through the tunnel are enclosed in tendon sheaths that enable them to slide back and forth quite easily, although continual repetitive motion of these tendons can cause the painful inflammation known as *carpal tunnel syndrome* (see Deeper Insight 10.5).

The Anterior (Flexor) Compartment, Deep Layer

Two anterior flexors constitute the deep layer—the **flexor digitorum profundus,** which flexes fingers II–V, and the **flexor pollicis longus,** which flexes only the thumb (fig. 10.29c). The latter is one of several muscles serving exclusively for thumb movements, attesting to the supreme importance of the thumb for hand function.

The Posterior (Extensor) Compartment, Superficial Layer

Superficial muscles of the posterior compartment are mostly wrist and finger extensors, and share a single tendon arising from the humerus (**fig. 10.30a**). The first of these, the **extensor digitorum,**

---

[63]*anconeus* = elbow

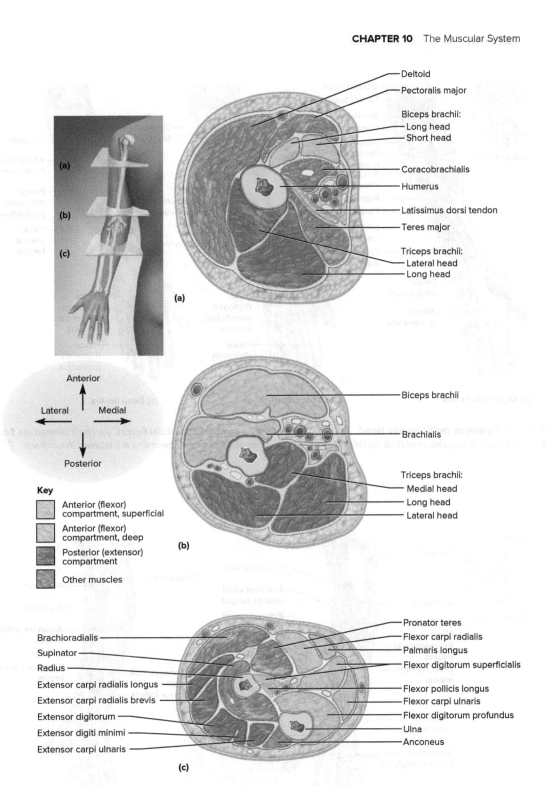

FIGURE 10.28 Serial Cross Sections Through the Upper Limb. Each section is taken at the correspondingly lettered level in the figure at the left and is pictured with the posterior muscle compartment facing the bottom of the page, as if viewing a person's right limb extended toward you with the palm up. (a) Superior arm at axilla. (b) Inferior arm. (c) Superior forearm.

❓ *Why are the extensor pollicis longus and extensor indicis not seen in part (c)?*

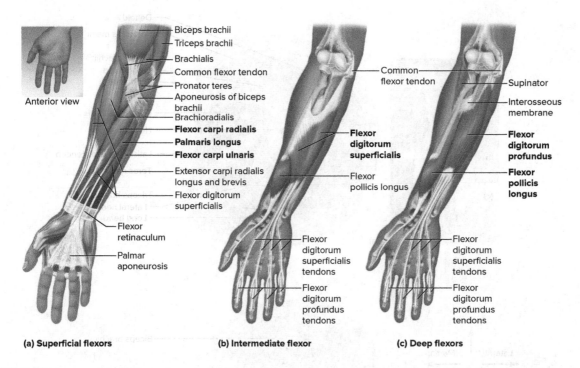

(a) Superficial flexors

(b) Intermediate flexor

(c) Deep flexors

FIGURE 10.29 Flexors of the Wrist and Hand. Anterior views of the forearm. (a) Superficial flexors. (b) The intermediate flexor digitorum superficialis, deep to the muscles in part (a). (c) Deep flexors. Flexor muscles of each compartment are labeled in boldface. **APR**

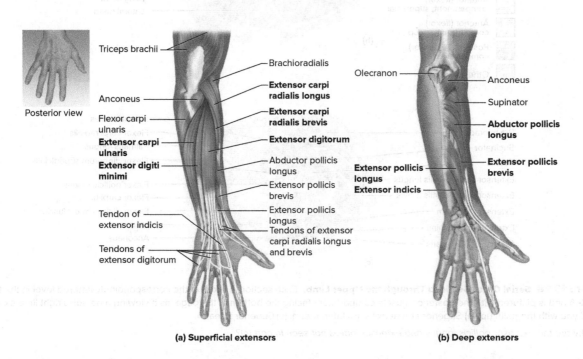

(a) Superficial extensors

(b) Deep extensors

FIGURE 10.30 Extensors of the Wrist and Hand. Posterior views of the forearm. Extensor muscles of each compartment are labeled in boldface. (a) Superficial extensors. (b) Deep extensors. **APR**

has four distal tendons that can easily be seen and palpated on the back of the hand when the fingers are strongly extended (see fig. B.19b). It serves digits II through V, and the other muscles in this group each serve a single digit. These superficial extensors are tabulated as follows and in the table from lateral to medial.

The Posterior (Extensor) Compartment, Deep Layer

The deep muscles that follow serve only the thumb and index finger **(fig. 10.30b).** By strongly abducting and extending the thumb into a hitchhiker's position, you may see a deep

dorsolateral pit at the base of the thumb, with a taut tendon on each side of it (see fig. B.19b). This depression is called the *anatomical snuffbox* because it was once fashionable to place a pinch of snuff here and inhale it. It is bordered laterally by the tendons of the **abductor pollicis longus** and **extensor pollicis brevis,** and medially by the tendon of the **extensor pollicis longus.** Dedication of so many muscles to the thumb alone (to which *pollicis* refers) attests to the supreme importance of the thumb for so much of the hand's functionality; try to imagine how much less you could do with your hands without the thumbs and these muscles.

TABLE 10.11	Muscles Acting on the Wrist and Hand		
Name	**Action**	**Skeletal Attachments**	**Innervation**
The Anterior (Flexor) Compartment, Superficial Layer			
Flexor carpi radialis[64] (FLEX-ur CAR-pye RAY-dee-AY-lis)	Flexes wrist anteriorly; aids in radial flexion of wrist	• Medial epicondyle of humerus • Base of metacarpals II–III	Median nerve
Flexor carpi ulnaris[65] (ul-NAY-ris)	Flexes wrist anteriorly; aids in ulnar flexion of wrist	• Medial epicondyle of humerus; medial margin of olecranon; posterior surface of ulna • Metacarpal V; pisiform; hamate	Ulnar nerve
Flexor digitorum superficialis[66] (DIDJ-ih-TOE-rum SOO-per-FISH-ee-AY-lis)	Flexes wrist, metacarpophalangeal, and interphalangeal joints depending on action of other muscles	• Medial epicondyle of humerus; ulnar collateral ligament; coronoid process; superior half of radius • Middle phalanges II–V	Median nerve
Palmaris longus (pal-MERR-iss)	Anchors skin and fascia of palmar region; resists shearing forces when stress is applied to skin by such actions as climbing and tool use. Weakly developed and sometimes absent.	• Medial epicondyle of humerus • Flexor retinaculum, palmar aponeurosis	Median nerve
Anterior (Flexor) Compartment, Deep Layer			
Flexor digitorum profundus[67]	Flexes wrist, metacarpophalangeal, and interphalangeal joints; sole flexor of the distal interphalangeal joints	• Proximal three-quarters of ulna; coronoid process; interosseous membrane • Distal phalanges II–V	Median nerve; ulnar nerve
Flexor pollicis[68] longus (PAHL-ih-sis)	Flexes phalanges of thumb	• Radius; interosseous membrane • Distal phalanx I	Median nerve

(continued)

---

[64]*carpi* = of the wrist; *radialis* = of the radius
[65]*ulnaris* = of the ulna
[66]*digitorum* = of the digits; *superficialis* = shallow, near the surface

[67]*profundus* = deep
[68]*pollicis* = of the thumb

TABLE 10.11	Muscles Acting on the Wrist and Hand (continued)		
Name	**Action**	**Skeletal Attachments**	**Innervation**
Posterior (Extensor) Compartment, Superficial Layer			
Extensor carpi radialis longus	Extends wrist; aids in radial flexion of wrist	• Lateral supracondylar ridge of humerus • Base of metacarpal II	Radial nerve
Extensor carpi radialis brevis (BREV-iss)	Extends wrist; aids in radial flexion of wrist	• Lateral epicondyle of humerus • Base of metacarpal III	Radial nerve
Extensor digitorum	Extends wrist, metacarpophalangeal, and interphalangeal joints; tends to spread digits apart when extending metacarpophalangeal joints	• Lateral epicondyle of humerus • Dorsal surfaces of phalanges II–V	Radial nerve
Extensor digiti minimi[69] (DIDJ-ih-ty MIN-ih-my)	Extends wrist and all joints of little finger	• Lateral epicondyle of humerus • Proximal phalanx V	Radial nerve
Extensor carpi ulnaris	Extends and fixes wrist when fist is clenched or hand grips an object; aids in ulnar flexion of wrist	• Lateral epicondyle of humerus; posterior surface of ulnar shaft • Base of metacarpal V	Radial nerve
Posterior (Extensor) Compartment, Deep Layer			
Abductor pollicis longus	Abducts thumb in frontal (palmar) plane (radial abduction); extends thumb at carpometacarpal joint	• Posterior surfaces of radius and ulna; interosseous membrane • Trapezium; base of metacarpal I	Radial nerve
Extensor pollicis brevis	Extends metacarpal I and proximal phalanx of thumb	• Shaft of radius; interosseous membrane • Proximal phalanx I	Radial nerve
Extensor pollicis longus	Extends distal phalanx I; aids in extending proximal phalanx I and metacarpal I; adducts and laterally rotates thumb	• Posterior surface of ulna; interosseous membrane • Distal phalanx I	Radial nerve
Extensor indicis (IN-dih-sis)	Extends wrist and index finger	• Posterior surface of ulna; interosseous membrane • Middle and distal phalanges of index finger	Radial nerve

10.4e Intrinsic Muscles of the Hand

The intrinsic muscles of the hand **(table 10.12)** assist the flexors and extensors in the forearm and make finger movements more precise. They are divided into three groups: the *thenar group* at the base of the thumb, the *hypothenar group* at the base of the little finger, and the *midpalmar group* between these **(fig. 10.32)**.

The Thenar Group

The **thenar group** of muscles forms the thick fleshy mass *(thenar eminence)* at the base of the thumb, and the **adductor pollicis** forms the web between the thumb and palm. All are concerned with thumb movements. The adductor pollicis has an

oblique head that extends from the capitate bone of the wrist to the ulnar side of the base of the thumb, and a transverse head that extends from metacarpal III to the same termination as the oblique head.

The Hypothenar Group

The **hypothenar group** forms the fleshy mass *(hypothenar eminence)* at the base of the little finger. All of these muscles are concerned with movement of that digit.

The Midpalmar Group

The **midpalmar group** occupies the hollow of the palm. It has 11 small muscles divided into three groups—four **dorsal interosseous,** three **palmar interosseous,** and four **lumbrical muscles.**

---

[69]*digit* = finger; *minim* = smallest

DEEPER INSIGHT 10.5

CLINICAL APPLICATION

Carpal Tunnel Syndrome

Prolonged, repetitive motions of the wrist and fingers can cause tissues in the carpal tunnel to become inflamed, swollen, or fibrotic. Since the carpal tunnel cannot expand, swelling puts pressure on the median nerve of the wrist, which passes through the carpal tunnel with the flexor tendons **(fig. 10.31)**. This pressure causes tingling and muscular weakness in the palm and medial side of the hand and pain that may radiate

to the arm and shoulder. This condition, called *carpal tunnel syndrome*, is common among keyboard operators, pianists, meat cutters, and others who spend long hours making repetitive wrist motions. Carpal tunnel syndrome is treated with aspirin and other anti-inflammatory drugs, immobilization of the wrist, and sometimes dividing the flexor retinaculum with a longitudinal incision to relieve pressure on the nerve.

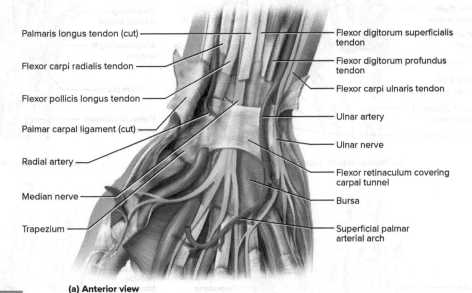

Palmaris longus tendon (cut)
Flexor carpi radialis tendon
Flexor pollicis longus tendon
Palmar carpal ligament (cut)
Radial artery
Median nerve
Trapezium

Flexor digitorum superficialis tendon
Flexor digitorum profundus tendon
Flexor carpi ulnaris tendon
Ulnar artery
Ulnar nerve
Flexor retinaculum covering carpal tunnel
Bursa
Superficial palmar arterial arch

(a) Anterior view

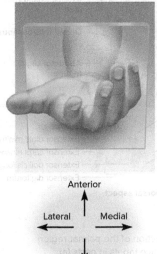

Anterior

Lateral   Medial

Posterior

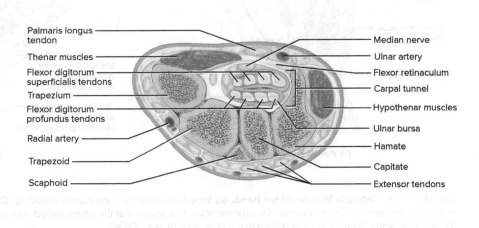

Palmaris longus tendon
Thenar muscles
Flexor digitorum superficialis tendons
Trapezium
Flexor digitorum profundus tendons
Radial artery
Trapezoid
Scaphoid

Median nerve
Ulnar artery
Flexor retinaculum
Carpal tunnel
Hypothenar muscles
Ulnar bursa
Hamate
Capitate
Extensor tendons

(b) Cross section

FIGURE 10.31 The Carpal Tunnel. (a) Dissection of the wrist (anterior view) showing the tendons, nerve, and bursae that pass under the flexor retinaculum. **APR** (b) Cross section of the wrist, viewed as if from the distal end of a person's right forearm extended toward you with the palm up. Note how the flexor tendons and median nerve are confined in the tight space between the carpal bones and flexor retinaculum. That tight packing and repetitive sliding of the flexor tendons through the tunnel contribute to carpal tunnel syndrome.

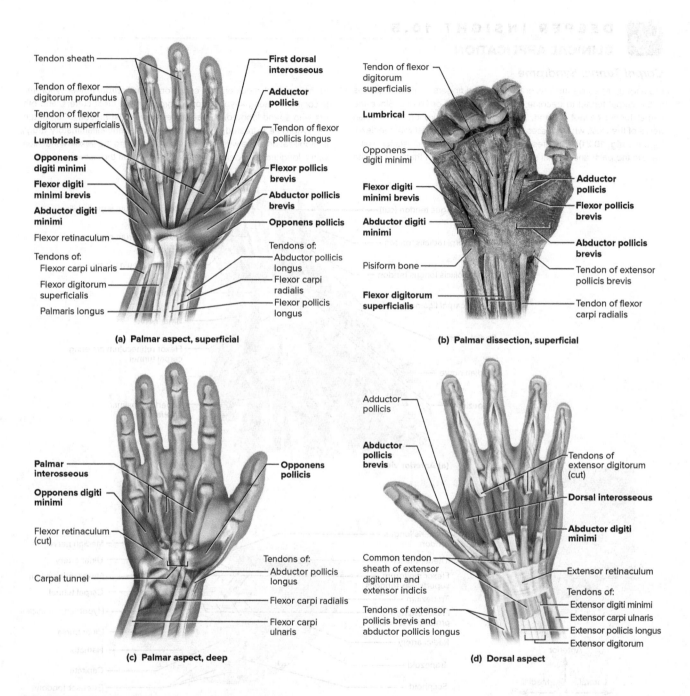

FIGURE 10.32 Intrinsic Muscles of the Hand. (a) Superficial muscles of the palmar aspect. (b) Dissection of the palmar region of the cadaver hand. (c) Deep muscles of the palmar aspect. (d) Muscles of the dorsal aspect. The boldface labels in parts (a), (c), and (d) indicate the muscles that belong to the respective layers. **APR**

b: Rebecca Gray/Don Kincaid/McGraw-Hill Education

TABLE 10.12	Intrinsic Muscles of the Hand		
Name	**Action**	**Skeletal Attachments**	**Innervation**
Thenar Group			
Adductor pollicis	Draws thumb toward palm as in gripping a tool	• Capitate; bases of metacarpals II–III; anterior ligaments of wrist; tendon sheath of flexor carpi radialis • Medial surface of proximal phalanx I	Ulnar nerve
Abductor pollicis brevis	Abducts thumb in sagittal plane	• Mainly flexor retinaculum; also scaphoid, trapezium, and abductor pollicis longus tendon • Lateral surface of proximal phalanx I	Median nerve
Flexor pollicis brevis	Flexes metacarpophalangeal joint of thumb	• Trapezium; trapezoid; capitate; anterior ligaments of wrist; flexor retinaculum • Proximal phalanx I	Median nerve; ulnar nerve
Opponens pollicis (op-PO-nenz)	Flexes metacarpal I to oppose thumb to fingertips	• Trapezium; flexor retinaculum • Metacarpal I	Median nerve
Hypothenar Group			
Abductor digiti minimi	Abducts little finger, as in spreading fingers apart	• Pisiform; tendon of flexor carpi ulnaris • Medial surface of proximal phalanx V	Ulnar nerve
Flexor digiti minimi brevis	Flexes little finger at metacarpophalangeal joint	• Hamulus of hamate bone; flexor retinaculum • Medial surface of proximal phalanx V	Ulnar nerve
Opponens digiti minimi	Flexes metacarpal V at carpometacarpal joint when little finger is moved into opposition with tip of thumb; deepens palm of hand	• Hamulus of hamate bone; flexor retinaculum • Medial surface of metacarpal V	Ulnar nerve
Midpalmar Group			
Four dorsal interosseous[70] muscles (IN-tur-OSS-ee-us)	Abduct fingers; strongly flex metacarpophalangeal joints but extend interphalangeal joints, depending on action of other muscles; important in grip strength	• Each with two heads arising from facing surfaces of adjacent metacarpals • Proximal phalanges II–IV	Ulnar nerve
Three palmar interosseous muscles	Adduct fingers; other actions same as for dorsal interosseous muscles	• Metacarpals I, II, IV, V • Proximal phalanges II, IV, V	Ulnar nerve
Four lumbrical[71] muscles (LUM-brih-cul)	Extend interphalangeal joints; contribute to ability to pinch objects between fleshy pulp of thumb and finger, instead of these digits meeting by the edges of their nails	• Tendons of flexor digitorum profundus • Proximal phalanges II–V	Median nerve; ulnar nerve

BEFORE YOU GO ON

Answer the following questions to test your understanding of the preceding section:

16. Name a muscle that inserts on the scapula and plays a significant role in each of the following actions:

   a. pushing a stalled car,

   b. paddling a canoe,

   c. squaring the shoulders in military attention,

   d. lifting the shoulder to carry a heavy box on it, and

   e. lowering the shoulder to lift a suitcase.

17. Describe three contrasting actions of the deltoid muscle.

18. Name the four rotator cuff muscles and describe the scapular surfaces against which they lie.

19. Name the prime movers of elbow flexion and extension.

20. Identify three functions of the biceps brachii.

21. Name three extrinsic muscles and two intrinsic muscles that flex the phalanges.

---

[70]*inter* = between; *osse* = bones
[71]*lumbrical* = resembling an earthworm

10.5   Muscles Acting on the Hip and Lower Limb

Expected Learning Outcomes

When you have completed this section, you should be able to

a. name and locate the muscles that act on the hip, knee, ankle, and toe joints;

b. relate the actions of these muscles to the joint movements described in chapter 9; and

c. describe the skeletal attachments, action, and innervation of these muscles.

The largest muscles are found in the lower limb. Unlike those of the upper limb, they are adapted less for precision than for the strength needed to stand, maintain balance, walk, and run. Several of them cross and act upon two or more joints, such as the hip and knee. To avoid confusion in this discussion, remember that in the anatomical sense the word *leg* refers only to that part of the limb between the knee and ankle. The *foot* includes the tarsal region, metatarsal region, and toes. The next four tables group the muscles of the lower limb into those that act on the thigh and hip joint, those that act on the leg and knee joint, extrinsic (leg) muscles that act on the foot and ankle joint, and intrinsic (foot) muscles that act on the arches and toes.

10.5a   Muscles Acting on the Hip and Thigh

The hip joint and thigh are acted on by muscles arising from both the pelvic girdle and the femur (**table 10.13**).

Anterior Muscles of the Hip

Most muscles that act on the femur originate on the hip bone. The two principal anterior muscles are the **iliacus,** which fills most of the broad iliac fossa of the pelvis, and the **psoas major,** a thick rounded muscle that arises mainly from the lumbar vertebrae (**fig. 10.33**). Collectively, they are called the **iliopsoas** and share a common tendon to the femur.

Lateral and Posterior Muscles of the Hip

On the lateral and posterior sides of the hip are the **tensor fasciae latae** and three gluteal muscles. The **fascia lata** is a fibrous sheath that encircles the thigh like a subcutaneous stocking and tightly binds its muscles. On the lateral surface, it combines with the tendons of the gluteus maximus and tensor fasciae latae to form the **iliotibial tract,** which extends from

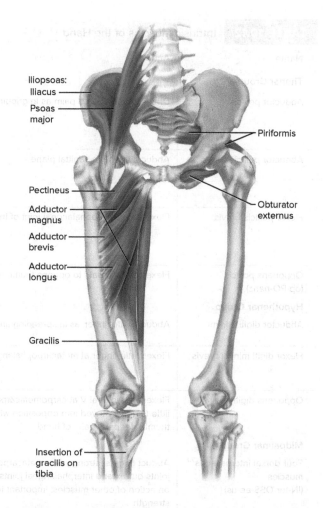

FIGURE 10.33   Muscles That Act on the Hip and Femur (Anterior View). APR

Labels: Iliopsoas: Iliacus; Psoas major; Pectineus; Adductor magnus; Adductor brevis; Adductor longus; Gracilis; Insertion of gracilis on tibia; Piriformis; Obturator externus

the iliac crest to the lateral condyle of the tibia (see fig. 10.34; table 10.14). The tensor fasciae latae tautens the iliotibial tract and braces the knee, especially when the opposite foot is lifted.

The gluteal muscles are the **gluteus maximus, gluteus medius,** and **gluteus minimus (fig. 10.34).** The gluteus maximus is the largest of these and forms most of the lean mass of the buttock. It is an extensor of the hip joint that produces the backswing of the leg in walking and provides most of the lift when you climb stairs. It generates its maximum force when the thigh is flexed at a 45° angle to the trunk. This is the advantage in starting a foot race from a crouched position. The gluteus medius is deep and lateral to the gluteus maximus. Its name refers to its size, not its position. The gluteus minimus is the smallest and deepest of the three.

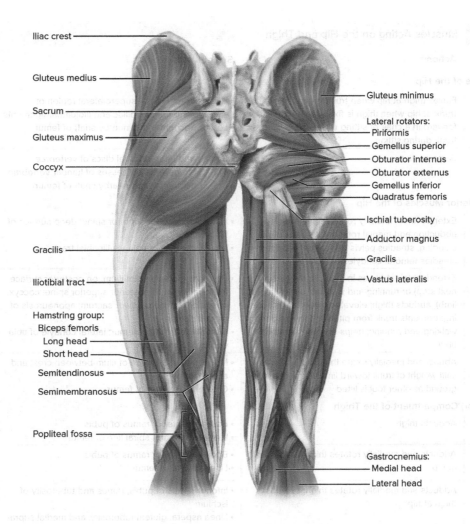

FIGURE 10.34 Posterior Gluteal and Thigh Muscles. The left side shows the superficial muscles. On the right, the gluteus medius and maximus are removed to show the deeper gluteus minimus, lateral rotator group, and hamstring origins. The oblique white tendinous band across the semitendinosus is not always present. **APR**

? *Describe two everyday movements of the body that employ the power of the gluteus maximus.*

Medial (Adductor) Compartment of the Thigh

Fasciae divide the thigh into three compartments: the anterior (extensor) compartment, posterior (flexor) compartment, and medial (adductor) compartment (see fig. 10.41). Muscles of the anterior and posterior compartments function mainly as extensors and flexors of the knee, respectively, and are treated in table 10.14. The five muscles of the medial compartment act primarily as adductors of the thigh (see fig. 10.33), but some of them cross both the hip and knee joints and have additional actions as follows.

Lateral Rotators

Inferior to the gluteus minimus and deep to the other two gluteal muscles are six muscles called the **lateral rotators,** named for their action on the femur (fig. 10.34). Their action is most clearly visualized when you cross your legs to rest an ankle on your knee, causing your femur to rotate and the knee to point laterally. Thus, they oppose medial rotation by the gluteus medius and minimus. Most of them also abduct or adduct the femur. The abductors are important in walking because when one lifts a foot from the ground, they shift the body weight to the other leg and prevent falling.

TABLE 10.13	Muscles Acting on the Hip and Thigh		
Name	**Action**	**Skeletal Attachments**	**Innervation**
Anterior Muscles of the Hip			
Iliacus[72] (ih-LY-uh-cus)	Flexes thigh at hip when trunk is fixed; flexes trunk at hip when thigh is fixed, as in bending forward in a chair or sitting up in bed; balances trunk during sitting	• Iliac crest and fossa; superolateral region of sacrum; anterior sacroiliac and iliolumbar ligaments • Lesser trochanter and nearby shaft of femur	Femoral nerve
Psoas[73] major (SO-ass)	Same as iliacus	• Bodies and intervertebral discs of vertebrae T12–L5; transverse processes of lumbar vertebrae • Lesser trochanter and nearby shaft of femur	Anterior rami of lumbar spinal nerves
Lateral and Posterior Muscles of the Hip			
Tensor fasciae latae[74] (TEN-sur FASH-ee-ee LAY-tee)	Extends knee, laterally rotates tibia, aids in abduction and medial rotation of femur; during standing, steadies pelvis on femoral head and steadies femoral condyles on tibia	• Iliac crest; anterior superior spine; deep surface of fascia lata • Lateral condyle of tibia via iliotibial tract	Superior gluteal nerve
Gluteus maximus[75]	Extends thigh at hip as in stair climbing (rising to next step) or running and walking (backswing of limb); abducts thigh; elevates trunk after stooping; prevents trunk from pitching forward during walking and running; helps stabilize femur on tibia	• Posterior gluteal line of ilium, on posterior surface from iliac crest to posterior superior spine; coccyx; posterior surface of lower sacrum; aponeurosis of erector spinae • Gluteal tuberosity of femur; lateral condyle of tibia via iliotibial tract	Inferior gluteal nerve
Gluteus medius and gluteus minimus	Abduct and medially rotate thigh; during walking, shift weight of trunk toward limb with foot on the ground as other foot is lifted	• Most of lateral surface of ilium between crest and acetabulum • Greater trochanter of femur	Superior gluteal nerve
Medial (Adductor) Compartment of the Thigh			
Adductor brevis	Adducts thigh	• Body and inferior ramus of pubis • Linea aspera and spiral line of femur	Obturator nerve
Adductor longus	Adducts and medially rotates thigh; flexes thigh at hip	• Body and inferior ramus of pubis • Linea aspera of femur	Obturator nerve
Adductor magnus	Adducts and medially rotates thigh; extends thigh at hip	• Inferior ramus of pubis; ramus and tuberosity of ischium • Linea aspera, gluteal tuberosity, and medial supracondylar line of femur	Obturator nerve; tibial nerve
Gracilis[76] (GRASS-ih-lis)	Flexes and medially rotates tibia at knee	• Body and inferior ramus of pubis; ramus of ischium • Medial surface of tibia just below condyle	Obturator nerve
Pectineus[77] (pec-TIN-ee-us)	Flexes and adducts thigh	• Superior ramus of pubis • Spiral line of femur	Femoral nerve
Lateral Rotators			
Gemellus[78] superior (jeh-MEL-us)	Laterally rotates extended thigh; abducts flexed thigh; sometimes absent	• Ischial spine • Greater trochanter of femur	Nerve to obturator internus
Gemellus inferior	Same actions as gemellus superior	• Ischial tuberosity • Greater trochanter of femur	Nerve to quadratus femoris
Obturator[79] externus (OB-too-RAY-tur)	Not well understood; thought to laterally rotate thigh in climbing	• External surface of obturator membrane; rami of pubis and ischium • Femur between head and greater trochanter	Obturator nerve

[72]*ili* = loin, flank
[73]*psoa* = loin
[74]*fasc* = band; *lat* = broad
[75]*glut* = buttock; *maxim* = largest

[76]*gracil* = slender
[77]*pectin* = comb
[78]*gemellus* = twin
[79]*obtur* = to close, stop up

TABLE 10.13	Muscles Acting on the Hip and Thigh (continued)		
Name	Action	Skeletal Attachments	Innervation
Lateral Rotators (continued)			
Obturator internus	Not well understood; thought to laterally rotate extended thigh and abduct flexed thigh	• Ramus of ischium; inferior ramus of pubis; antero-medial surface of lesser pelvis • Greater trochanter of femur	Nerve to obturator internus
Piriformis[80] (PIR-ih-FOR-mis)	Laterally rotates extended thigh; abducts flexed thigh	• Anterior surface of sacrum; gluteal surface of ilium; capsule of sacroiliac joint • Greater trochanter of femur	Spinal nerves L5–S2
Quadratus femoris[81] (quad-RAY-tus FEM-oh-ris)	Laterally rotates thigh	• Ischial tuberosity • Intertrochanteric crest of femur	Nerve to quadratus femoris

10.5b Muscles Acting on the Knee and Leg

The following muscles (**table 10.14**) form most of the mass of the thigh and produce their most obvious actions on the knee joint. Some of them, however, cross both the hip and knee joints and produce actions at both, moving the femur, tibia, and fibula.

Anterior (Extensor) Compartment of the Thigh

The anterior compartment of the thigh contains the large **quadriceps femoris,** the prime mover of knee extension and the most powerful muscle of the body (**figs. 10.35, 10.36**). As the name *quadriceps* implies, it has four heads: the **rectus femoris, vastus lateralis, vastus medialis,** and **vastus intermedius.** All four converge on a single **quadriceps (patellar) tendon,** which extends to the patella, then continues as the **patellar ligament** and inserts on the tibial tuberosity. (Remember that a tendon usually extends from muscle to bone, and a ligament from bone to bone.) The patellar ligament is struck with a rubber reflex hammer to test the knee-jerk reflex. The quadriceps extends the knee when you stand up, take a step, or kick a ball. One head, the rectus femoris, contributes to running by acting with the iliopsoas to flex the hip in each airborne phase of the leg's cycle of motion. The rectus femoris also flexes the hip in such actions as high kicks, stair climbing, or simply drawing the leg forward during a stride.

Crossing the quadriceps from the lateral side of the hip to the medial side of the knee is the narrow, straplike **sartorius,** the longest muscle of the body. It flexes the hip and knee joints and laterally rotates the thigh, as in crossing the legs. It is colloquially called the "tailor's muscle" after the cross-legged posture of a tailor supporting his work on the raised knee.

Posterior (Flexor) Compartment of the Thigh

The posterior compartment contains three muscles colloquially known as the **hamstring muscles;** from lateral to medial, they

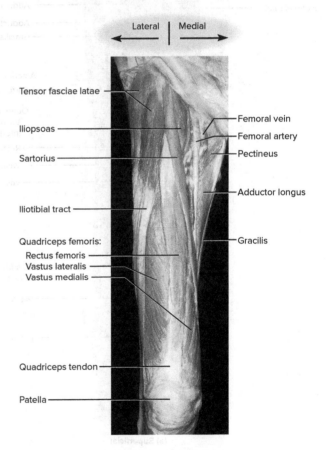

FIGURE 10.35 Superficial Anterior Thigh Muscles of the Cadaver. Right thigh.

Rebecca Gray/McGraw-Hill Education

are the **biceps femoris, semitendinosus,** and **semimembranosus** (see fig. 10.34). The pit at the back of the knee, known anatomically as the **popliteal fossa,** is colloquially called the *ham.* The tendons of these muscles can be felt as prominent cords on both sides of the fossa—the biceps tendon on the lateral side and the

---

[80]*piri* = pear; *form* = shaped
[81]*quadrat* = four-sided; *femoris* = of the thigh or femur

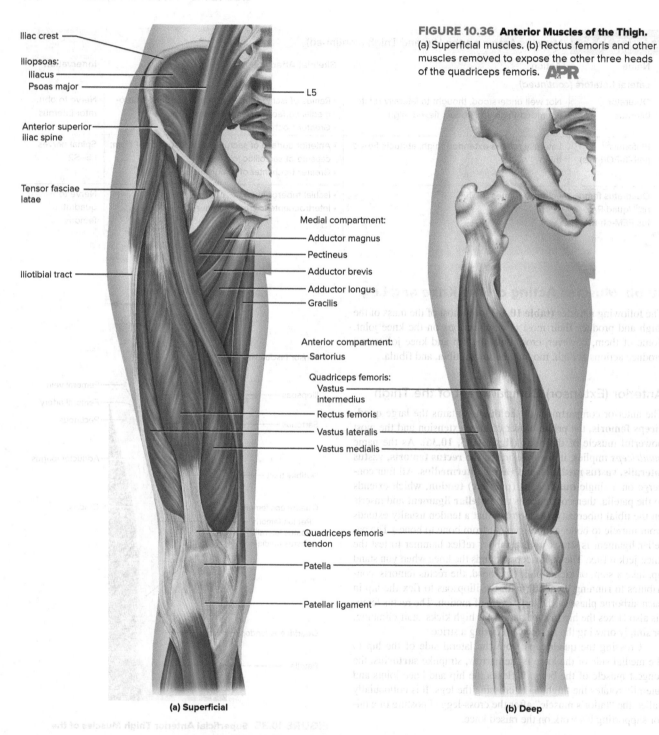

Iliac crest

Iliopsoas:
  Iliacus
  Psoas major

L5

Anterior superior
iliac spine

Tensor fasciae
latae

Iliotibial tract

Medial compartment:
— Adductor magnus
— Pectineus
— Adductor brevis
— Adductor longus
— Gracilis

Anterior compartment:
— Sartorius

Quadriceps femoris:
  Vastus
  intermedius
— Rectus femoris
— Vastus lateralis
— Vastus medialis

Quadriceps femoris
tendon

Patella

Patellar ligament

(a) Superficial

(b) Deep

FIGURE 10.36 Anterior Muscles of the Thigh.
(a) Superficial muscles. (b) Rectus femoris and other
muscles removed to expose the other three heads
of the quadriceps femoris. **APR**

semimembranosus and semitendinosus tendons on the medial side.
When wolves attack large prey, they instinctively attempt to sever
the hamstring tendons, because this renders the prey helpless.
The hamstrings flex the knee, and aided by the gluteus maximus,
they extend the hip during walking and running. The semitendinosus is named for its unusually long tendon. This muscle also
is usually bisected by a transverse or oblique tendinous band.

The semimembranosus is named for the flat shape of its superior
attachment.

Posterior Compartment of the Leg

Most muscles in the posterior compartment of the leg act on the
ankle and foot and are reviewed in table 10.15, but the **popliteus**
acts on the knee (see figs. 10.39, 10.40).

TABLE 10.14	Muscles Acting on the Knee and Leg		
Name	**Action**	**Skeletal Attachments**	**Innervation**
Anterior (Extensor) Compartment of the Thigh			
Quadriceps femoris (QUAD-rih-seps FEM-oh-ris)	Extends the knee, in addition to the actions of individual heads noted subsequently	• Varies; see individual heads • Patella; tibial tuberosity; lateral and medial condyles of tibia	Femoral nerve
Rectus femoris	Extends knee; flexes thigh at hip; flexes trunk on hip if thigh is fixed	• Ilium at anterior inferior spine and superior margin of acetabulum; capsule of hip joint • See quadriceps femoris	Femoral nerve
Vastus[82] lateralis	Extends knee; retains patella in groove on femur during knee movements	• Femur at greater trochanter and intertrochanteric line, gluteal tuberosity, and linea aspera • See quadriceps femoris	Femoral nerve
Vastus medialis	Same as vastus lateralis	• Femur at intertrochanteric line, spiral line, linea aspera, and medial supracondylar line • See quadriceps femoris	Femoral nerve
Vastus intermedius	Extends knee	• Anterior and lateral surfaces of femoral shaft • See quadriceps femoris	Femoral nerve
Sartorius[83]	Aids in knee and hip flexion, as in sitting or climbing; abducts and laterally rotates thigh	• On and near anterior superior spine of ilium • Medial surface of proximal end of tibia	Femoral nerve
Posterior (Flexor) Compartment of the Thigh			
Biceps femoris	Flexes knee; extends hip; elevates trunk from stooping posture; laterally rotates tibia on femur when knee is flexed; laterally rotates femur when hip is extended; counteracts forward bending at hips	• Long head: ischial tuberosity Short head: linea aspera and lateral supracondylar line of femur • Head of fibula	Tibial nerve; common fibular nerve
Semitendinosus[84] (SEM-ee-TEN-din-OH-sus)	Flexes knee; medially rotates tibia on femur when knee is flexed; medially rotates femur when hip is extended; counteracts forward bending at hips	• Ischial tuberosity • Medial surface of upper tibia	Tibial nerve
Semimembranosus[85] (SEM-ee-MEM-bran-OH-sus)	Same as semitendinosus	• Ischial tuberosity • Medial condyle and nearby margin of tibia; intercondylar line and lateral condyle of femur; ligament of popliteal region	Tibial nerve
Posterior Compartment of the Leg			
Popliteus[86] (pop-LIT-ee-us)	Rotates tibia medially on femur if femur is fixed (as in sitting down), or rotates femur laterally on tibia if tibia is fixed (as in standing up); unlocks knee to allow flexion; may prevent forward dislocation of femur during crouching	• Lateral condyle of femur; lateral meniscus and joint capsule • Posterior surface of upper tibia	Tibial nerve

[82]*vastus* = large, extensive
[83]*sartor* = tailor
[84]*semi* = half; *tendinosus* = tendinous

[85]*semi* = half; *membranosus* = membranous
[86]*poplit* = ham (pit) of the knee

10.5c Muscles Acting on the Ankle and Foot

The fleshy mass of the leg is formed by a group of crural muscles (**table 10.15**), which act on the foot (**fig. 10.37**). These muscles are tightly bound by fasciae that compress them and aid in the return of blood from the legs. The fasciae separate the crural muscles into anterior, lateral, and posterior compartments (see fig. 10.41b).

Anterior (Extensor) Compartment of the Leg

Muscles of the anterior compartment dorsiflex the ankle and prevent the toes from scuffing the ground during walking. From lateral to medial, these muscles are the **fibularis tertius, extensor digitorum longus** (extensor of toes II–V), **extensor hallucis longus** (extensor of the great toe), and **tibialis anterior** (**fig. 10.38**). Their tendons are held tightly against the ankle and kept from bowing by two **extensor retinacula** similar to the one at the wrist.

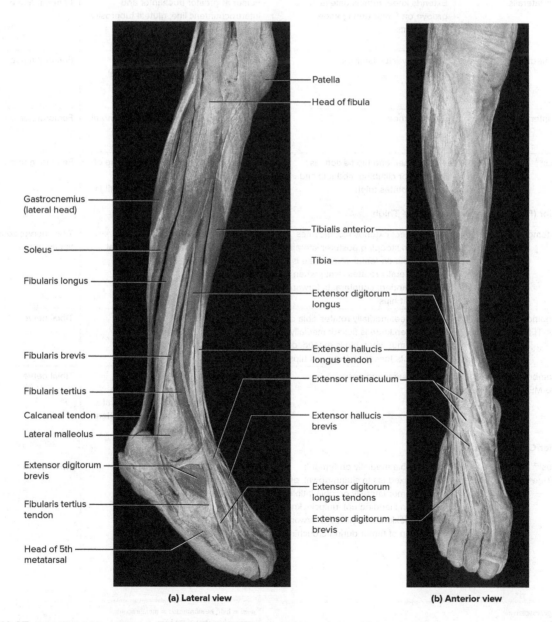

(a) Lateral view   (b) Anterior view

FIGURE 10.37 Superficial Crural Muscles of the Cadaver. Right leg. (a) Lateral view. (b) Anterior view.

a, b: Christine Eckel/McGraw-Hill Education

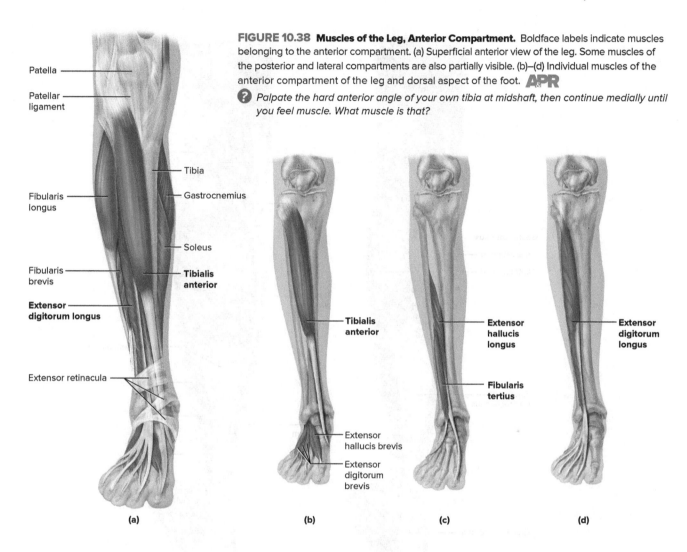

FIGURE 10.38 Muscles of the Leg, Anterior Compartment. Boldface labels indicate muscles belonging to the anterior compartment. (a) Superficial anterior view of the leg. Some muscles of the posterior and lateral compartments are also partially visible. (b)–(d) Individual muscles of the anterior compartment of the leg and dorsal aspect of the foot. **APR**

❓ *Palpate the hard anterior angle of your own tibia at midshaft, then continue medially until you feel muscle. What muscle is that?*

Inflammation of these tendons is one of the causes of *shinsplints* (see Deeper Insight 10.6).

Posterior (Flexor) Compartment of the Leg, Superficial Group

The posterior compartment has superficial and deep muscle groups (**fig. 10.39**). The three muscles of the superficial group are plantar flexors: the **gastrocnemius, soleus,** and **plantaris.** The first two of these, collectively known as the **triceps surae,**[87] insert on the calcaneus by way of the **calcaneal (Achilles) tendon.** This is the strongest tendon of the body but is nevertheless a common site of sports injuries resulting from sudden stress (see Deeper Insight 10.7). The *plantaris,* a weak synergist of the triceps surae, is a relatively unimportant muscle and is absent from many people; it is not tabulated here. Surgeons often use the plantaris tendon for tendon grafts needed in other parts of the body.

DEEPER INSIGHT 10.6

CLINICAL APPLICATION

Shinsplints

Shinsplints is a general term embracing several kinds of injury with pain in the crural region: tendinitis of the tibialis posterior muscle, inflammation of the tibial periosteum, and anterior compartment syndrome. Shinsplints can result from unaccustomed jogging, walking on snowshoes, or any vigorous activity of the legs after a period of relative inactivity.

Posterior (Flexor) Compartment of the Leg, Deep Group

There are four muscles in the deep group (**fig. 10.40**). The **flexor digitorum longus, flexor hallucis longus,** and **tibialis posterior** are plantar flexors. The fourth muscle, the *popliteus,* is described in table 10.14 because it acts on the knee rather than on the foot.

---

[87]*tri* = three; *ceps* = heads; *surae* = of the calf

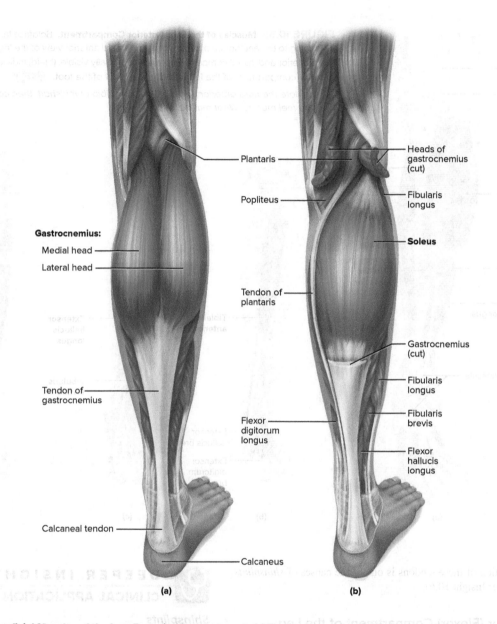

FIGURE 10.39 Superficial Muscles of the Leg, Posterior Compartment. (a) The gastrocnemius. (b) The soleus, deep to the gastrocnemius and sharing the calcaneal tendon with it. **APR**

 DEEPER INSIGHT 10.7

CLINICAL APPLICATION

Calcaneal Tendon Rupture

Calcaneal tendon rupture is a common injury experienced in amateur, strenuous sports such as basketball and tennis. When pushing off strongly from the ground as in a basketball jump shot, the tendon may rupture with a loud pop, described by some as sounding like a gunshot. The rupture causes pain just above the heel and inability to stand or walk on the affected leg. Two visible signs of a ruptured tendon are a large knot, the contracted triceps surae, in the upper calf; and abnormal

dorsiflexion of the foot, caused by the action of the tibialis anterior suddenly unfettered by the opposing action of the triceps. Calcaneal tendon rupture is most common in overweight men, 30 to 40 years old, who are not in great physical condition but partake in an unaccustomed game such as pickup basketball or backyard football. A ruptured tendon can often heal on its own with rest and proper care, but may require surgical repair, especially in young physically active people not inclined to rest it for months.

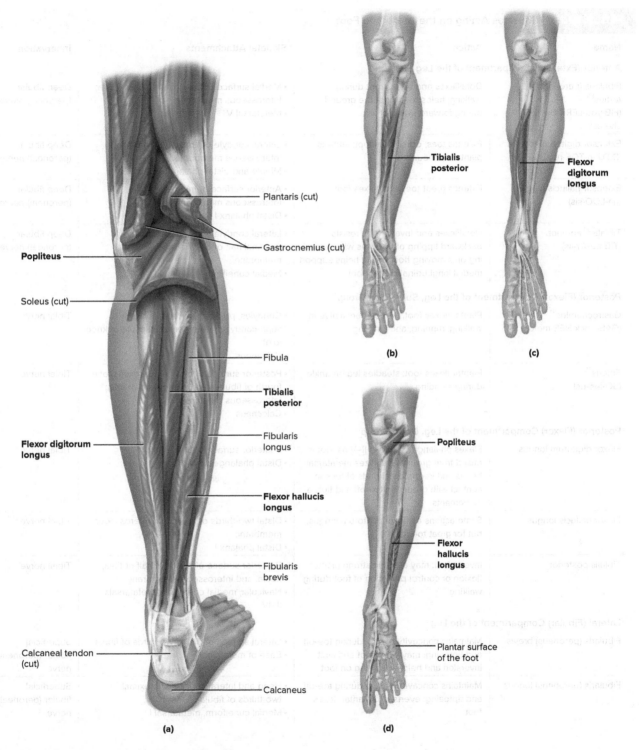

FIGURE 10.40 Deep Muscles of the Leg, Posterior and Lateral Compartments. (a) Muscles deep to the soleus. (b)–(d) Exposure of some individual deep muscles with the foot plantar flexed (sole facing viewer). APR

TABLE 10.15	Muscles Acting on the Ankle and Foot		
Name	**Action**	**Skeletal Attachments**	**Innervation**
Anterior (Extensor) Compartment of the Leg			
Fibularis (peroneus[88]) tertius[89] (FIB-you-LERR-iss TUR-she-us)	Dorsiflexes and everts foot during walking; helps toes clear the ground during forward swing of leg	• Medial surface of lower one-third of fibula; interosseous membrane • Metatarsal V	Deep fibular (peroneal) nerve
Extensor digitorum longus (DIDJ-ih-TOE-rum)	Extends toes; dorsiflexes foot; tautens plantar aponeurosis	• Lateral condyle of tibia; shaft of fibula; interosseous membrane • Middle and distal phalanges II–V	Deep fibular (peroneal) nerve
Extensor hallucis longus (ha-LOO-sis)	Extends great toe; dorsiflexes foot	• Anterior surface of middle of fibula, interosseous membrane • Distal phalanx I	Deep fibular (peroneal) nerve
Tibialis[90] anterior (TIB-ee-AY-lis)	Dorsiflexes and inverts foot; resists backward tipping of body (as when standing on a moving boat deck); helps support medial longitudinal arch of foot	• Lateral condyle and lateral margin of proximal half of tibia; interosseous membrane • Medial cuneiform, metatarsal I	Deep fibular (peroneal) nerve
Posterior (Flexor) Compartment of the Leg, Superficial Group			
Gastrocnemius[91] (GAS-trock-NEE-me-us)	Plantar flexes foot, flexes knee; active in walking, running, and jumping	• Condyles, popliteal surface, and lateral supracondylar line of femur; capsule of knee joint • Calcaneus	Tibial nerve
Soleus[92] (SO-lee-us)	Plantar flexes foot; steadies leg on ankle during standing	• Posterior surface of head and proximal one-fourth of fibula; middle one-third of tibia; interosseous membrane • Calcaneus	Tibial nerve
Posterior (Flexor) Compartment of the Leg, Deep Group			
Flexor digitorum longus	Flexes phalanges of digits II–V as foot is raised from ground; stabilizes metatarsal heads and keeps distal pads of toes in contact with ground in toe-off and tiptoe movements	• Posterior surface of tibial shaft • Distal phalanges II–V	Tibial nerve
Flexor hallucis longus	Same actions as flexor digitorum longus, but for great toe (digit I)	• Distal two-thirds of fibula and interosseous membrane • Distal phalanx I	Tibial nerve
Tibialis posterior	Inverts foot; may assist in strong plantar flexion or control pronation of foot during walking	• Posterior surface of proximal half of tibia, fibula, and interosseous membrane • Navicular, medial cuneiform, metatarsals II–IV	Tibial nerve
Lateral (Fibular) Compartment of the Leg			
Fibularis (peroneus) brevis	Maintains concavity of sole during toe-off and tiptoeing; may evert foot and limit inversion and help steady leg on foot	• Lateral surface of distal two-thirds of fibula • Base of metatarsal V	Superficial fibular (peroneal) nerve
Fibularis (peroneus) longus	Maintains concavity of sole during toe-off and tiptoeing; everts and plantar flexes foot	• Head and lateral surface of proximal two-thirds of fibula • Medial cuneiform, metatarsal I	Superficial fibular (peroneal) nerve

[88]*perone* = pinlike (fibula)
[89]*fibularis* = of the fibula; *tert* = third
[90]*tibialis* = of the tibia

[91]*gastro* = belly; *cnem* = leg
[92]Named for its resemblance to a flatfish (sole)

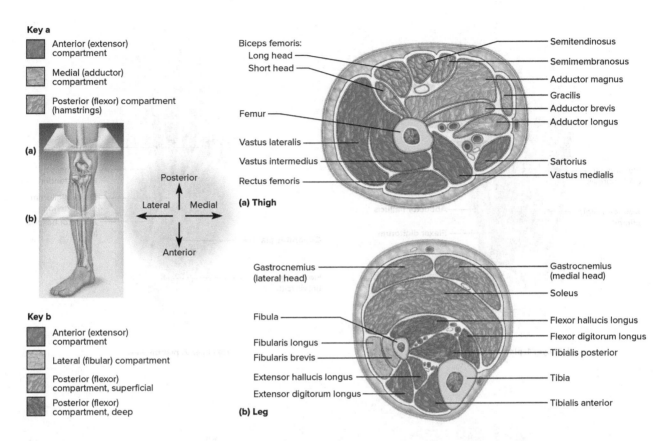

Key a

Anterior (extensor) compartment

Medial (adductor) compartment

Posterior (flexor) compartment (hamstrings)

(a)

(b)

Posterior

Lateral — Medial

Anterior

Key b

Anterior (extensor) compartment

Lateral (fibular) compartment

Posterior (flexor) compartment, superficial

Posterior (flexor) compartment, deep

Biceps femoris:
Long head
Short head

Femur

Vastus lateralis

Vastus intermedius

Rectus femoris

(a) Thigh

Semitendinosus

Semimembranosus

Adductor magnus

Gracilis

Adductor brevis

Adductor longus

Sartorius

Vastus medialis

Gastrocnemius (lateral head)

Fibula

Fibularis longus

Fibularis brevis

Extensor hallucis longus

Extensor digitorum longus

(b) Leg

Gastrocnemius (medial head)

Soleus

Flexor hallucis longus

Flexor digitorum longus

Tibialis posterior

Tibia

Tibialis anterior

FIGURE 10.41 Serial Cross Sections Through the Lower Limb. Cross sections of the femur (a) and leg (b) are taken at the correspondingly lettered levels in the figure at the left.

Lateral (Fibular) Compartment of the Leg

The lateral compartment includes the **fibularis brevis** and **fibularis longus** (see figs. 10.37a, 10.38a; **fig. 10.41**). They plantar flex and evert the foot. Plantar flexion is important not only in standing on tiptoes but in providing lift and forward thrust each time you take a step.

▶▶▶ **APPLY WHAT YOU KNOW**

Suppose you tilt your foot upward to trim or paint your toenails. Identify as many muscles as you know that can contribute to this action.

▶▶▶ **APPLY WHAT YOU KNOW**

Suppose you are playing Frisbee and your Frisbee lands on the roof of your house. You have to climb a ladder to get it. Identify as many muscles as you can that would aid you in ascending from one rung of the ladder to the next.

10.5d Intrinsic Muscles of the Foot

The intrinsic muscles of the foot (**table 10.16**) help to support the arches and act on the toes in ways that aid locomotion. Several of them are similar in name and location to the intrinsic muscles of the hand.

Dorsal (Superior) Aspect of the Foot

Only one of the intrinsic muscles, the **extensor digitorum brevis**, is on the dorsal (superior) side of the foot. The medial slip of this muscle, serving the great toe, is sometimes called the *extensor hallucis brevis.*

Ventral Layer 1 (Most Superficial)

All remaining intrinsic muscles are on the ventral (inferior) aspect of the foot or between the metatarsal bones. They are grouped in four layers (**fig. 10.42**). Dissecting into the foot from the plantar surface, one first encounters a tough fibrous sheet, the **plantar aponeurosis,** between the skin and muscles. It diverges like a fan from the calcaneus to the bases of all the toes, and is a common site of painful inflammation (see Deeper Insight 10.8). Several ventral muscles arise from this aponeurosis. The ventral muscles include the stout **flexor digitorum brevis** on the midline of the foot, with four tendons that supply all digits except the great toe. It is flanked by the **abductor digiti minimi** laterally and the **abductor hallucis** medially.

Ventral Layer 2

The next deeper layer consists of the thick **quadratus plantae (flexor accessorius)** in the middle of the foot and the four **lumbrical muscles** located between the metatarsals.

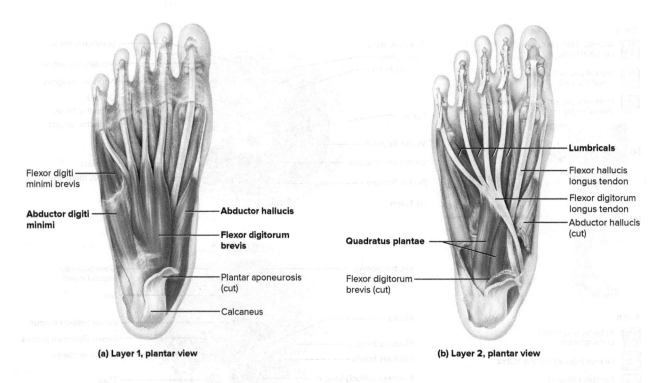

(a) Layer 1, plantar view

Flexor digiti minimi brevis

Abductor digiti minimi

Abductor hallucis

Flexor digitorum brevis

Plantar aponeurosis (cut)

Calcaneus

(b) Layer 2, plantar view

Lumbricals

Flexor hallucis longus tendon

Flexor digitorum longus tendon

Abductor hallucis (cut)

Quadratus plantae

Flexor digitorum brevis (cut)

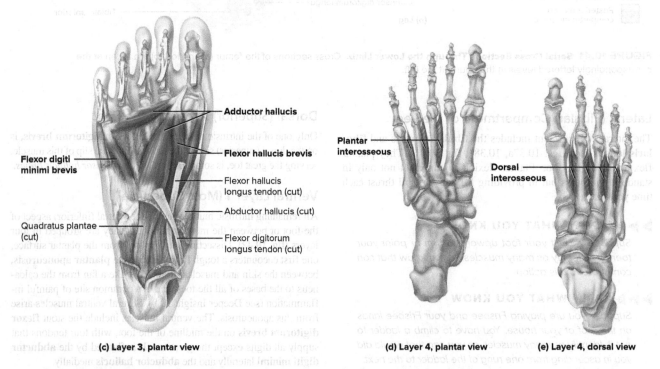

(c) Layer 3, plantar view

Adductor hallucis

Flexor hallucis brevis

Flexor digiti minimi brevis

Flexor hallucis longus tendon (cut)

Abductor hallucis (cut)

Quadratus plantae (cut)

Flexor digitorum longus tendon (cut)

(d) Layer 4, plantar view

(e) Layer 4, dorsal view

Plantar interosseous

Dorsal interosseous

FIGURE 10.42 **Intrinsic Muscles of the Foot.** (a)–(d) First through fourth layers, respectively, in ventral (plantar) views. (e) Fourth layer, dorsal view. The muscles belonging to each layer are shown in color and with boldface labels. **APR**

DEEPER INSIGHT 10.8

CLINICAL APPLICATION

Plantar Fasciitis

Plantar fasciitis (FASH-ee-EYE-tis) is inflammation of the plantar apo-neurosis, typically felt as a recurring pain in the heel and medial aspect of the foot. The pain is often most severe when one begins to walk after prolonged sitting or when rising from bed. It usually subsides in 5 to 10 minutes, but occurs again after the next period of rest. Dorsiflexion of the foot often intensifies the pain. Plantar fasciitis typically results from excessive or unaccustomed running and high-impact aerobics, especially in persons who don't wear properly supportive athletic footwear.

TABLE 10.16	Intrinsic Muscles of the Foot		
Name	**Action**	**Skeletal Attachments**	**Innervation**
Dorsal (Superior) Aspect of Foot			
Extensor digitorum brevis	Extends proximal phalanx I and all phalanges of digits II–IV	• Calcaneus; inferior extensor retinaculum of ankle • Proximal phalanx I, tendons of extensor digitorum longus to middle and distal phalanges II–IV	Deep fibular (peroneal) nerve
Ventral Layer 1 (Most Superficial)			
Flexor digitorum brevis	Flexes digits II–IV; supports arches of foot	• Calcaneus; plantar aponeurosis • Middle phalanges II–V	Medial plantar nerve
Abductor digiti minimi[93]	Abducts and flexes little toe; supports arches of foot	• Calcaneus; plantar aponeurosis • Proximal phalanx V	Lateral plantar nerve
Abductor hallucis	Abducts great toe; supports arches of foot	• Calcaneus; plantar aponeurosis; flexor retinaculum • Proximal phalanx I	Medial plantar nerve
Ventral Layer 2			
Quadratus plantae[94] (quad-RAY-tus PLAN-tee)	Same as flexor digitorum longus (table 10.15); flexion of digits II–V and associated locomotor functions	• Two heads on the medial and lateral sides of calcaneus • Distal phalanges II–V via flexor digitorum longus tendons	Lateral plantar nerve
Four lumbrical muscles (LUM-brih-cul)	Flex toes II–V	• Tendon of flexor digitorum longus • Proximal phalanges II–V	Lateral and medial plantar nerves
Ventral Layer 3			
Flexor digiti minimi brevis	Flexes little toe	• Metatarsal V, sheath of fibularis longus • Proximal phalanx V	Lateral plantar nerve
Flexor hallucis brevis	Flexes great toe	• Cuboid; lateral cuneiform; tibialis posterior tendon • Proximal phalanx I	Medial plantar nerve
Adductor hallucis	Adducts great toe	• Metatarsals II–IV; fibularis longus tendon; ligaments at bases of digits III–V • Proximal phalanx I	Lateral plantar nerve
Ventral Layer 4 (Deepest)			
Four dorsal interosseous muscles	Abduct toes II–IV	• Each with two heads arising from facing surfaces of two adjacent metatarsals • Proximal phalanges II–IV	Lateral plantar nerve
Three plantar interosseous muscles	Adduct toes III–V	• Medial aspect of metatarsals III–V • Proximal phalanges III–V	Lateral plantar nerve

[93]*digit* = toe; *minim* = smallest

[94]*quadrat* = four-sided; *plantae* = of the plantar region

Ventral Layer 3

The muscles of this layer serve only the great and little toes. They are the **flexor digiti minimi brevis, flexor hallucis brevis,** and **adductor hallucis.** The adductor hallucis has an oblique head that extends diagonally from the midplantar region to the base of the great toe, and a transverse head that passes across the bases of digits II–IV and meets the long head at the base of the great toe.

Ventral Layer 4 (Deepest)

This layer consists only of the small interosseous muscles located between the metatarsal bones—four dorsal and three plantar. Each **dorsal interosseous muscle** is bipennate and originates on two adjacent metatarsals. The **plantar interosseous muscles** are unipennate and originate on only one metatarsal each.

▶▶▶**APPLY WHAT YOU KNOW**

Not everyone has the same muscles. From the information provided in this chapter, identify at least three muscles that are lacking in some people.

BEFORE YOU GO ON

Answer the following questions to test your understanding of the preceding section:

22. In the middle of a stride, you have one foot on the ground and you are about to swing the other leg forward. What muscles produce the movements of that leg?

23. Name the muscles that cross both the hip and knee joints and produce actions at both.

24. List the major actions of the muscles of the anterior, medial, and posterior compartments of the thigh.

25. Describe the roles of plantar flexion and dorsiflexion in walking. What muscles produce these actions?

DEEPER INSIGHT 10.9

CLINICAL APPLICATION

Common Athletic Injuries

Although the muscular system is subject to fewer diseases than most organ systems, it is particularly vulnerable to injuries resulting from sudden and intense stress placed on muscles and tendons. Each year, thousands of athletes from the high-school to professional level sustain some type of injury to their muscles, as do the increasing numbers of people who have taken up running and other forms of physical conditioning. Overzealous exertion without proper conditioning and warm-up is frequently the cause. This chapter has already described several examples: compartment syndrome, rotator cuff injury, shinsplints, calcaneal tendon rupture, and plantar fasciitis. A few more are described here.

Baseball finger—tears in the extensor tendons of the fingers resulting from the impact of a baseball with the extended fingertip.

Blocker's arm—abnormal calcification in the lateral margin of the forearm as a result of repeated impact with opposing players.

Charley horse—any painful tear, stiffness, and blood clotting in a muscle. A charley horse of the quadriceps femoris is often caused by football tackles.

Pitcher's arm—inflammation at the proximal attachment of the flexor carpi muscles resulting from hard wrist flexion in releasing a baseball.

Pulled groin—strain in the adductor muscles of the thigh; common in gymnasts and dancers who perform splits and high kicks.

Pulled hamstrings—strained hamstring muscles or a partial tear in their tendons, often with a hematoma (blood clot) in the fascia lata. This condition is frequently caused by repetitive kicking (as in football and soccer) or long, hard running.

Tennis elbow—inflammation at the proximal attachment of the extensor carpi muscles on the lateral epicondyle of the humerus. It occurs when these muscles are repeatedly tensed during backhand strokes and then strained by sudden impact with the tennis ball. Any activity that requires rotary movements of the forearm and a firm grip of the hand (for example, using a screwdriver) can cause the symptoms of tennis elbow.

Most athletic injuries can be prevented by proper conditioning. A person who suddenly takes up vigorous exercise may not have sufficient muscle and bone mass to withstand the stresses such exercise entails. These must be developed gradually. Stretching exercises keep ligaments and joint capsules supple and therefore reduce injuries. Warm-up exercises promote more efficient and less injurious musculoskeletal function in several ways. Most of all, moderation is important, as most injuries simply result from overuse of the muscles. "No pain, no gain" is a risky misconception.

Muscular injuries can be treated initially with "RICE": rest, ice, compression, and elevation. Rest prevents further injury and allows repair processes to occur; ice reduces swelling; compression with an elastic bandage helps to prevent fluid accumulation and swelling; and elevation of an injured limb promotes drainage of blood from the affected area and limits further swelling. If these measures are not enough, anti-inflammatory drugs may be employed, including corticosteroids as well as aspirin and other nonsteroidal agents. Serious injuries, such as compartment syndrome, require emergency attention by a physician.

STUDY GUIDE

▶ Assess Your Learning Outcomes

To test your knowledge, discuss the following topics with a study partner or in writing, ideally from memory.

10.1 Structural and Functional Organization of Muscles

1. Which muscles are included in the muscular system and which ones are not; the name of the science that specializes in the muscular system
2. Functions of the muscular system
3. The relationship of muscle structure to the endomysium, perimysium, and epimysium; what constitutes a fascicle of skeletal muscle and how it relates to these connective tissues; and the relationship of a fascia to a muscle
4. Classification of muscles according to the orientation of their fascicles
5. Muscle compartments, interosseous membranes, and intermuscular septa
6. Direct, indirect, moving, and stationary muscle attachments
7. The flaw in *origin–insertion* terminology of muscle attachments
8. The action of a muscle; how it relates to the classification of muscles as *prime movers, synergists, antagonists,* or *fixators;* why these terms are not fixed for a given muscle but differ from one joint movement to another, and examples to illustrate this point
9. Intrinsic versus extrinsic muscles, with examples
10. The nerve and blood supplies to muscles
11. Features to which the Latin names of muscles commonly refer, with examples

10.2 Muscles of the Head and Neck

Know the locations, actions, skeletal attachments, and innervations of the named muscles in each of the following groups, and be able to recognize them on laboratory specimens or models to the extent required in your course.

1. The occipitofrontalis muscle of the scalp, eyebrows, and forehead (table 10.1)
2. The orbicularis oculi, levator palpebrae superioris, and corrugator supercilii muscles, which move the eyelid and other tissues around the eye (table 10.1)
3. The nasalis muscle, which flares and compresses the nostrils (table 10.1)
4. The orbicularis oris, levator labii superioris, levator anguli oris, zygomaticus major

and minor, risorius, depressor anguli oris, depressor labii inferioris, and mentalis muscles, which act on the lips (table 10.1)
5. The buccinator muscles of the cheeks (table 10.1)
6. The platysma, which acts upon the mandible and the skin of the neck (table 10.1)
7. The intrinsic muscles of the tongue in general, and specific extrinsic muscles: the genioglossus, hyoglossus, styloglossus, and palatoglossus muscles (table 10.2)
8. The temporalis, masseter, medial pterygoid, and lateral pterygoid muscles of biting and chewing (table 10.2)
9. The suprahyoid group: the digastric, geniohyoid, mylohyoid, and stylohyoid muscles (table 10.2)
10. The infrahyoid group: the omohyoid, sternohyoid, thyrohyoid, and sternothyroid muscles (table 10.2)
11. The superior, middle, and inferior pharyngeal constrictor muscles of the throat (table 10.2)
12. The sternocleidomastoid and three scalene muscles, which flex the neck, and the trapezius, splenius capitis, and semispinalis capitis muscles, which extend it (table 10.3)

10.3 Muscles of the Trunk

For the following muscles, know the same information as for section 10.2.

1. The diaphragm and the external intercostal, internal intercostal, and innermost intercostal muscles of respiration (table 10.4)
2. The external oblique, internal oblique, transverse abdominal, and rectus abdominis muscles of the anterior and lateral abdominal wall (table 10.5)
3. The superficial erector spinae muscle (and its subdivisions) and the deep semispinalis thoracis, quadratus lumborum, and multifidus muscles of the back (table 10.6)
4. The perineum, its two triangles, and their skeletal landmarks (table 10.7)
5. The ischiocavernosus and bulbospongiosus muscles of the superficial perineal space of the pelvic floor (table 10.7)
6. The deep transverse perineal muscle, and in females, the compressor urethrae of the deep perineal space of the pelvic floor, and the external anal sphincter of the anal triangle (table 10.7)

7. The levator ani muscle of the pelvic diaphragm, the deepest compartment of the pelvic floor (table 10.7)

10.4 Muscles Acting on the Shoulder and Upper Limb

For the following muscles, know the same information as for section 10.2.

1. The pectoralis minor, serratus anterior, trapezius, levator scapulae, rhomboid major, and rhomboid minor muscles of scapular movement (table 10.8)
2. Muscles that act on the humerus, including the pectoralis major, latissimus dorsi, deltoid, teres major, coracobrachialis, and four rotator cuff (SITS) muscles—the supraspinatus, infraspinatus, teres minor, and subscapularis (table 10.9)
3. The brachialis, biceps brachii, triceps brachii, brachioradialis, anconeus, pronator quadratus, pronator teres, and supinator muscles of forearm movement (table 10.10)
4. The relationship of the flexor retinaculum, extensor retinaculum, and carpal tunnel to the tendons of the forearm muscles
5. The palmaris longus, flexor carpi radialis, flexor carpi ulnaris, and flexor digitorum superficialis muscles of the superficial anterior compartment of the forearm, and the flexor digitorum profundus and flexor pollicis longus muscles of the deep anterior compartment (table 10.11)
6. The extensor carpi radialis longus, extensor carpi radialis brevis, extensor digitorum, extensor digiti minimi, and extensor carpi ulnaris muscles of the superficial posterior compartment (table 10.11)
7. The abductor pollicis longus, extensor pollicis brevis, extensor pollicis longus, and extensor indicis muscles of the deep posterior compartment (table 10.11)
8. The thenar group of intrinsic hand muscles: adductor pollicis, abductor pollicis brevis, flexor pollicis brevis, and opponens pollicis (table 10.12)
9. The hypothenar group of intrinsic hand muscles: abductor digiti minimi, flexor digiti minimi brevis, and opponens digiti minimi (table 10.12)
10. The midpalmar group of intrinsic hand muscles: four dorsal interosseous muscles, three palmar interosseous muscles, and four lumbrical muscles (table 10.12)

STUDY GUIDE

10.5 Muscles Acting on the Hip and Lower Limb

For the following muscles, know the same information as for section 10.2.

1. The iliopsoas muscle of the hip, and its two subdivisions, the iliacus and psoas major (table 10.13)
2. The tensor fasciae latae, gluteus maximus, gluteus medius, and gluteus minimus muscles of the hip and buttock, and the relationship of the first two to the fascia lata and iliotibial tract (table 10.13)
3. The lateral rotators: gemellus superior, gemellus inferior, obturator externus, obturator internus, piriformis, and quadratus femoris muscles (table 10.13)
4. The compartments of the thigh muscles: anterior (extensor), medial (adductor), and posterior (flexor) compartments
5. Muscles of the medial compartment of the thigh: adductor brevis, adductor longus,

adductor magnus, gracilis, and pectineus (table 10.13)

6. Muscles of the anterior compartment of the thigh: sartorius and quadriceps femoris, and the four heads of the quadriceps (table 10.14)
7. The hamstring muscles of the posterior compartment of the thigh: biceps femoris, semitendinosus, and semimembranosus (table 10.14)
8. The compartments of the leg muscles: anterior, posterior, and lateral (table 10.15)
9. Muscles of the anterior compartment of the leg: fibularis tertius, extensor digitorum longus, extensor hallucis longus, and tibialis anterior muscles of the anterior compartment (table 10.15)
10. Muscles of the superficial posterior compartment of the leg: popliteus and triceps surae (gastrocnemius and soleus), and the relationship of the triceps surae to the calcaneal tendon and calcaneus (table 10.15)

11. Muscles of the deep posterior compartment of the leg: flexor digitorum longus, flexor hallucis longus, and tibialis posterior muscles of the deep posterior compartment
12. Muscles of the lateral compartment of the leg: fibularis brevis and fibularis longus (table 10.15)
13. The extensor digitorum brevis of the dorsal aspect of the foot (table 10.16)
14. The four muscle compartments (layers) of the ventral aspect of the foot, and the muscles in each: the flexor digitorum brevis, abductor digiti minimi, and abductor hallucis (layer 1); the quadratus plantae and four lumbrical muscles (layer 2); the flexor digiti minimi brevis, flexor hallucis brevis, and adductor hallucis (layer 3); and the four dorsal interosseous muscles and three plantar interosseous muscles (layer 4) (table 10.16)

▶ Testing Your Recall

Answers in Appendix A

1. Which of the following muscles does *not* contribute to the rotator cuff?
   a. teres minor
   b. teres major
   c. subscapularis
   d. infraspinatus
   e. supraspinatus

2. Make a fist, then straighten your fingers. The muscles that performed the latter action have tendons that pass through
   a. the flexor retinaculum.
   b. the extensor retinaculum.
   c. the carpal tunnel.
   d. the rotator cuff.
   e. the plantar region of the wrist.

3. Which of these is *not* a suprahyoid muscle?
   a. genioglossus
   b. geniohyoid
   c. stylohyoid
   d. mylohyoid
   e. digastric

4. Which of these muscles is an extensor of the neck?
   a. external oblique
   b. sternocleidomastoid
   c. splenius capitis
   d. iliocostalis
   e. latissimus dorsi

5. Which of these muscles of the pelvic floor is the deepest?
   a. superficial transverse perineal
   b. bulbospongiosus
   c. ischiocavernosus
   d. deep transverse perineal
   e. levator ani

6. Which of these actions is *not* performed by the trapezius?
   a. extension of the neck
   b. depression of the scapula
   c. elevation of the scapula
   d. rotation of the scapula
   e. adduction of the humerus

7. Both the hands and feet are acted upon by a muscle or muscles called
   a. the extensor digitorum.
   b. the abductor digiti minimi.
   c. the flexor digitorum profundus.
   d. the abductor hallucis.
   e. the flexor digitorum longus.

8. Which of the following muscles does *not* extend the hip joint?
   a. quadriceps femoris
   b. gluteus maximus
   c. biceps femoris
   d. semitendinosus
   e. semimembranosus

9. Both the gastrocnemius and _____ muscles insert on the heel by way of the calcaneal tendon.
   a. semimembranosus
   b. tibialis posterior
   c. tibialis anterior
   d. soleus
   e. plantaris

10. Which of the following muscles raises the upper lip?
    a. levator palpebrae superioris
    b. orbicularis oris
    c. zygomaticus minor
    d. masseter
    e. mentalis

11. What muscle is the prime mover in sucking through a soda straw or spitting out a mouthful of liquid?

12. A bundle of muscle fibers surrounded by perimysium is called a/an _____.

13. The _____ is the muscle that generates the most force in a given joint movement.

14. The three large muscles on the posterior side of the thigh are commonly known as the _____ muscles.

STUDY GUIDE

15. Connective tissue bands called _____ prevent flexor tendons of the forearm and leg from rising like bowstrings.

16. The anterior half of the perineum is a region called the _____.

17. The abdominal aponeuroses converge on a median fibrous band on the abdomen called the _____.

18. A muscle that works with another to produce the same or similar movement is called a/an _____.

19. A muscle somewhat like a feather, with fibers obliquely approaching its tendon from both sides, is called a/an _____ muscle.

20. A circular muscle that closes a body opening is called a/an _____.

▶ Building Your Medical Vocabulary   *Answers in Appendix A*

State a meaning of each word element, and give a medical term from this chapter that uses it or a slight variation of it.

1. capito-

2. ergo-

3. fasc-

4. labio-

5. lumbo-

6. mus-

7. mys-

8. omo-

9. penn-

10. tert-

▶ What's Wrong with These Statements?   *Answers in Appendix A*

Briefly explain why each of the following statements is false, or reword it to make it true.

1. Each skeletal muscle fiber is enclosed in a perimysium that separates it from adjacent fibers.

2. The orbicularis oris is a sphincter.

3. The biceps brachii is a bipennate muscle.

4. A synergist is a muscle whose action is opposite that of an agonist.

5. Each skeletal muscle is innervated by at least one spinal nerve.

6. One must contract the internal intercostal muscles in order to exhale.

7. In climbing stairs, the hamstrings provide much of the thrust that lifts the body to each higher step.

8. Severing the large trigeminal nerve would paralyze more facial muscles than severing the facial nerve.

9. The following intrinsic hand muscles are listed in order from strongest to weakest: abductor digiti minimi, adductor pollicis, dorsal interosseous.

10. The tibialis anterior and tibialis posterior are synergists.

▶ Testing Your Comprehension

1. Radical mastectomy, once a common treatment for breast cancer, involved removal of the pectoralis major along with the breast. What functional impairments would result from this? What synergists could a physical therapist train a patient to use to recover some lost function?

2. Removal of cancerous lymph nodes from the neck sometimes requires removal of the sternocleidomastoid on that side. How would this affect a patient's range of head movement?

3. Bicycles are designed so the rider leans forward at about a 45° angle rather than sitting upright. Aside from issues of wind resistance, explain the advantage of this in terms of musculoskeletal anatomy of the hip region.

4. Women who wear high heels most of the time may suffer painful "high heel syndrome" when they go barefoot or wear flat shoes. What muscle(s) and tendon(s) are involved? Explain.

5. A student moving out of a dormitory crouches, in correct fashion, to lift a heavy box of books. What prime movers are involved as he straightens his legs to lift the box?

ATLAS

B

ATLAS

REGIONAL AND SURFACE ANATOMY

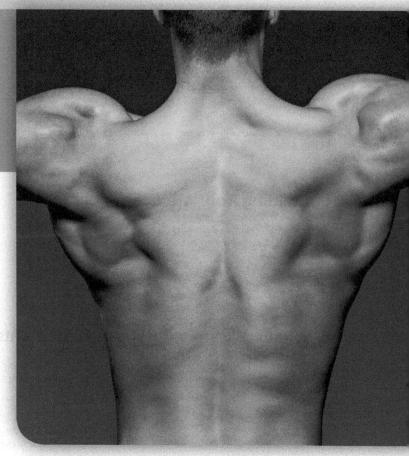

How many muscles can you identify from their surface appearance?
Y Photo Studio/Shutterstock

Anatomy & Physiology Revealed® 4.0

Module 6: Muscular System

B.1   Regional Anatomy

On the whole, this book takes a systems approach to anatomy, examining the structure and function of each organ system, one at a time, regardless of which body regions it may traverse. Physicians and surgeons, however, think and act in terms of regional anatomy. If a patient presents with pain in the lower right quadrant (see atlas A, fig. A.4a), the source may be the appendix, an ovary, or an inguinal muscle, among other possibilities. The question is to think not of an entire organ system (the esophagus is probably irrelevant to that quadrant), but of what organs are present in that region and what possibilities must be considered as the cause of the pain. This atlas presents several views of the body region by region so that you can see some of the spatial relationships that exist among the organ systems considered in their separate chapters.

B.2   The Importance of Surface Anatomy

In the study of human anatomy, it is easy to become so preoccupied with internal structure that we forget the importance of what we can see and feel externally. Yet external anatomy and appearance are major concerns in giving a physical examination and in many aspects of patient care. A knowledge of the body's surface landmarks is essential to one's competence in physical therapy, cardiopulmonary resuscitation, surgery, making X-rays and electrocardiograms, giving injections, drawing blood, listening to heart and respiratory sounds, measuring the pulse and blood pressure, and finding pressure points to stop arterial bleeding, among other procedures. A misguided attempt to perform some of these procedures while disregarding or misunderstanding external anatomy can be very harmful and even fatal to a patient.

Having just studied skeletal and muscular anatomy in the preceding chapters, this is an opportune time for you to study the body surface. Much of what we see there reflects the underlying structure of the superficial bones and muscles. A broad photographic overview of surface anatomy is given in atlas A (see fig. A.3), where it is necessary for providing a vocabulary for reference in subsequent chapters. This atlas shows this surface anatomy in closer detail so you can relate it to the musculoskeletal anatomy of the three preceding chapters.

B.3   Learning Strategy

To make the most profitable use of this atlas, refer back to earlier chapters as you study these illustrations. Relate drawings of the clavicle in figure 8.31 to the photograph in figure B.1, for example. Study the shape of the scapula in figure 8.32 and see how much of it you can trace on the photographs in figure B.9. See if you can relate the tendons visible on the hand (see fig. B.19) to the muscles of the forearm illustrated in figures 10.29 and 10.30, and the external markings of the pelvic girdle (see fig. B.15) to bone structure in section 8.5a.

For learning surface anatomy, there is a resource available to you that is far more valuable than any laboratory model or textbook illustration—your own body. For the best understanding of human structure, compare the art and photographs in this book with your body or with structures visible on a study partner. In addition to bones and muscles, you can palpate a number of superficial arteries, veins, tendons, ligaments, and cartilages, among other structures. By palpating regions such as the shoulder, elbow, or ankle, you can develop a mental image of the subsurface structures better than the image you can obtain by looking at two-dimensional textbook images. And the more you can study with other people, the more you will appreciate the variations in human structure and be able to apply your knowledge to your future patients or clients, who will not look quite like any textbook diagram or photograph you have ever seen. Through comparisons of art, photography, and the living body, you will get a much deeper understanding of the body than if you were to study this atlas in isolation from the earlier chapters.

At the end of this atlas, you can test your knowledge of externally visible muscle anatomy. The two photographs in figure B.25 have 30 numbered muscles and a list of 26 names, some of which are shown more than once in the photographs and some of which are not shown at all. Identify the muscles to your best ability without looking back at the previous illustrations, and then check your answers in appendix A.

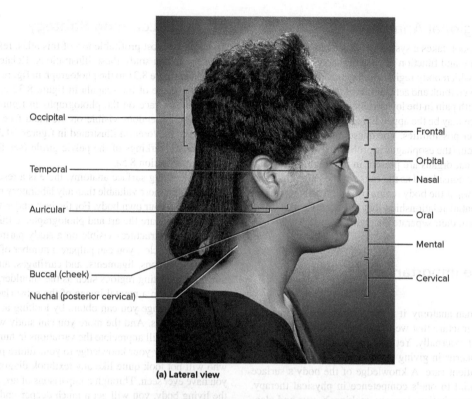

Occipital

Frontal

Temporal

Orbital

Nasal

Auricular

Oral

Mental

Cervical

Buccal (cheek)

Nuchal (posterior cervical)

(a) Lateral view

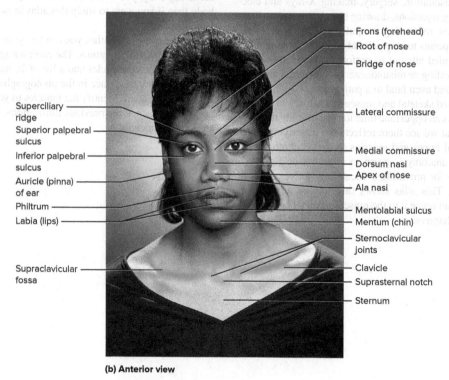

Frons (forehead)

Root of nose

Bridge of nose

Superciliary ridge

Superior palpebral sulcus

Lateral commissure

Inferior palpebral sulcus

Medial commissure

Auricle (pinna) of ear

Dorsum nasi

Apex of nose

Philtrum

Ala nasi

Labia (lips)

Mentolabial sulcus

Mentum (chin)

Sternoclavicular joints

Supraclavicular fossa

Clavicle

Suprasternal notch

Sternum

(b) Anterior view

FIGURE B.1 The Head and Neck. (a) Anatomical regions of the head. (b) Features of the facial region and upper thorax.

a–b: Joe DeGrandis/McGraw-Hill Education

❓ *What muscle underlies the region of the philtrum? What muscle forms the slope of the shoulder?*

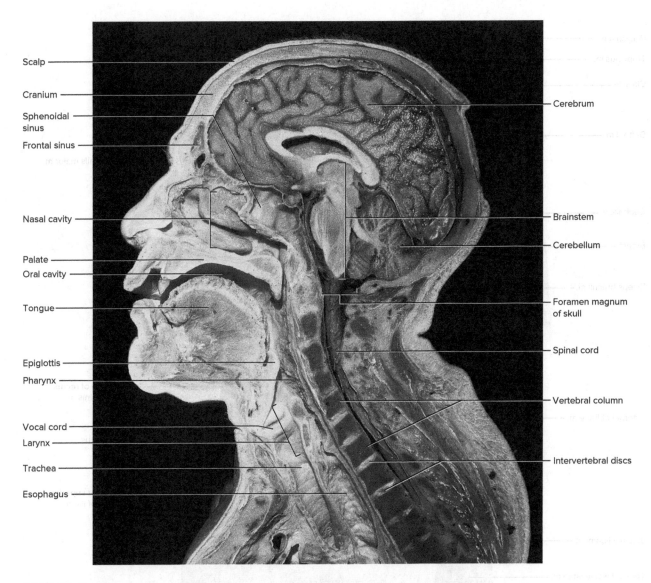

Scalp

Cranium

Sphenoidal sinus

Frontal sinus

Nasal cavity

Palate

Oral cavity

Tongue

Epiglottis

Pharynx

Vocal cord

Larynx

Trachea

Esophagus

Cerebrum

Brainstem

Cerebellum

Foramen magnum of skull

Spinal cord

Vertebral column

Intervertebral discs

FIGURE B.2 Median Section of the Head. Shows contents of the cranial, nasal, and oral cavities.
Rebecca Gray/McGraw-Hill Education

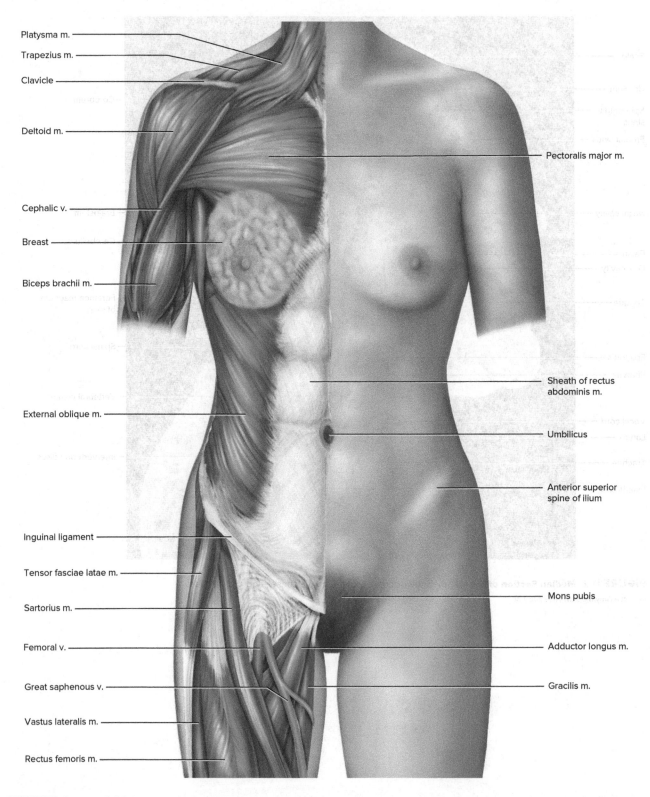

FIGURE B.3 **Superficial Anatomy of the Trunk (Female).** Surface anatomy is shown on the anatomical left, and structures immediately deep to the skin on the right.

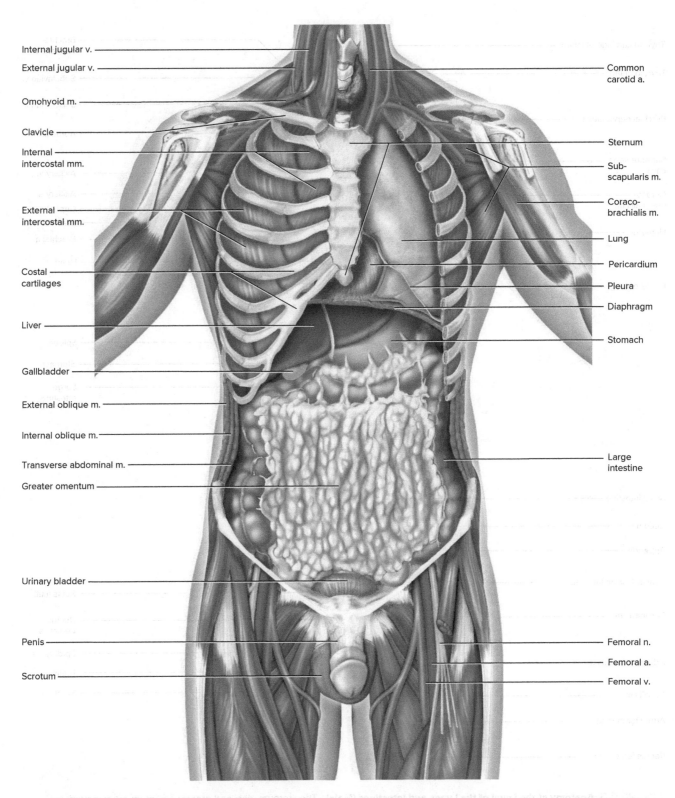

Internal jugular v.

External jugular v.

Omohyoid m.

Clavicle

Internal
intercostal mm.

External
intercostal mm.

Costal
cartilages

Liver

Gallbladder

External oblique m.

Internal oblique m.

Transverse abdominal m.

Greater omentum

Urinary bladder

Penis

Scrotum

Common
carotid a.

Sternum

Sub-
scapularis m.

Coraco-
brachialis m.

Lung

Pericardium

Pleura

Diaphragm

Stomach

Large
intestine

Femoral n.

Femoral a.

Femoral v.

FIGURE B.4 Anatomy at the Level of the Rib Cage and Greater Omentum (Male). The anterior body wall is removed, and the ribs, intercostal muscles, and pleura are removed from the anatomical left.

368 **PART TWO** Support and Movement

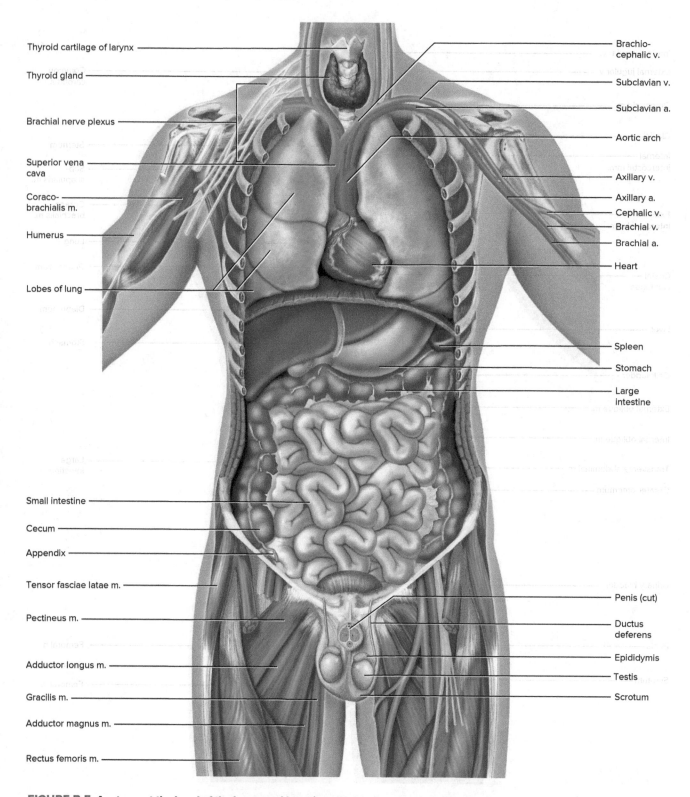

Thyroid cartilage of larynx

Thyroid gland

Brachial nerve plexus

Superior vena cava

Coraco-brachialis m.

Humerus

Lobes of lung

Small intestine

Cecum

Appendix

Tensor fasciae latae m.

Pectineus m.

Adductor longus m.

Gracilis m.

Adductor magnus m.

Rectus femoris m.

Brachio-cephalic v.

Subclavian v.

Subclavian a.

Aortic arch

Axillary v.

Axillary a.

Cephalic v.

Brachial v.

Brachial a.

Heart

Spleen

Stomach

Large intestine

Penis (cut)

Ductus deferens

Epididymis

Testis

Scrotum

FIGURE B.5 Anatomy at the Level of the Lungs and Intestines (Male). The sternum, ribs, and greater omentum are removed.

❓ *Name several viscera that are protected by the rib cage.*

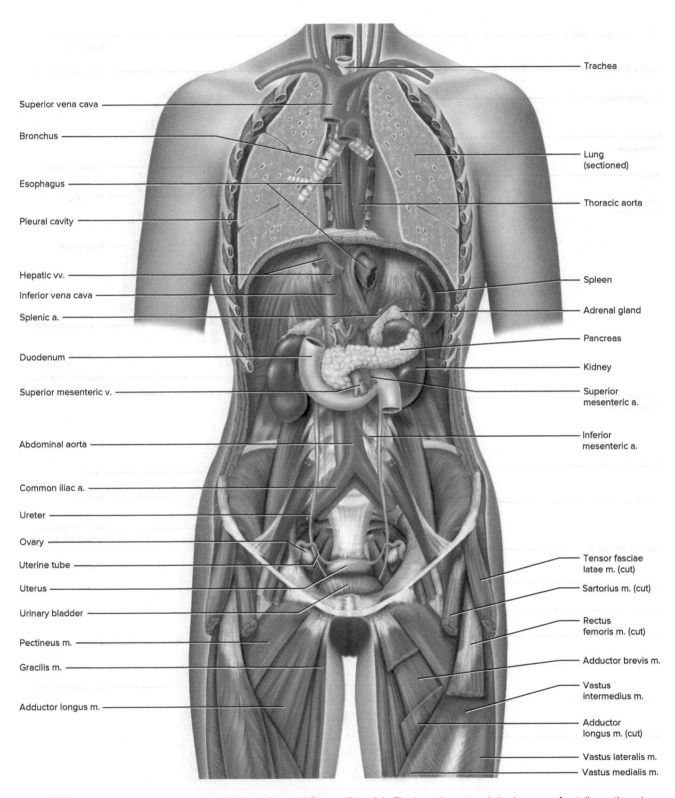

Trachea

Superior vena cava

Bronchus

Lung (sectioned)

Esophagus

Thoracic aorta

Pleural cavity

Hepatic vv.

Spleen

Inferior vena cava

Adrenal gland

Splenic a.

Pancreas

Duodenum

Kidney

Superior mesenteric v.

Superior mesenteric a.

Abdominal aorta

Inferior mesenteric a.

Common iliac a.

Ureter

Ovary

Uterine tube

Tensor fasciae latae m. (cut)

Uterus

Sartorius m. (cut)

Urinary bladder

Rectus femoris m. (cut)

Pectineus m.

Adductor brevis m.

Gracilis m.

Vastus intermedius m.

Adductor longus m.

Adductor longus m. (cut)

Vastus lateralis m.

Vastus medialis m.

FIGURE B.6 Anatomy at the Level of the Retroperitoneal Viscera (Female). The heart is removed, the lungs are frontally sectioned, and the viscera of the peritoneal cavity and the peritoneum itself are removed.

370   **PART TWO**   Support and Movement

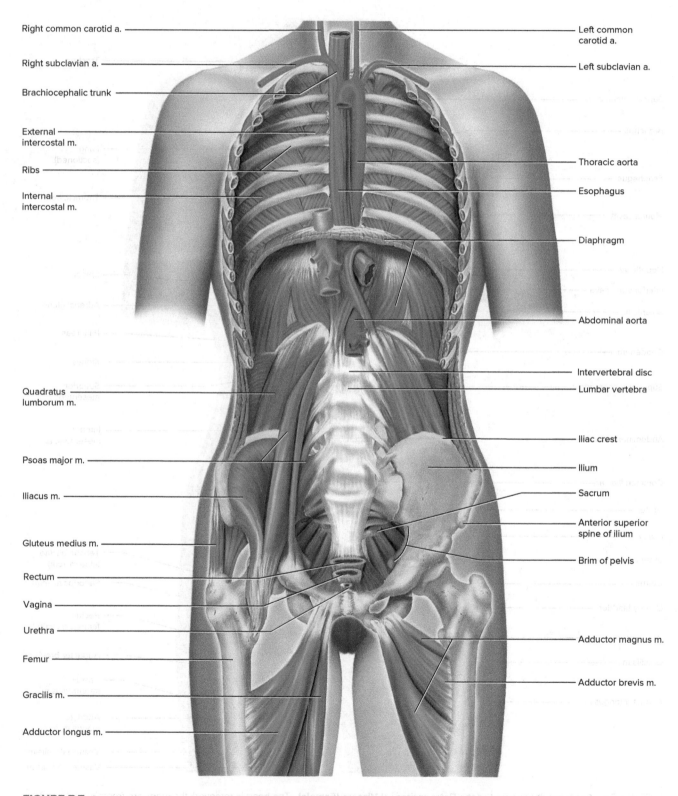

Right common carotid a.

Right subclavian a.

Brachiocephalic trunk

External intercostal m.

Ribs

Internal intercostal m.

Quadratus lumborum m.

Psoas major m.

Iliacus m.

Gluteus medius m.

Rectum

Vagina

Urethra

Femur

Gracilis m.

Adductor longus m.

Left common carotid a.

Left subclavian a.

Thoracic aorta

Esophagus

Diaphragm

Abdominal aorta

Intervertebral disc

Lumbar vertebra

Iliac crest

Ilium

Sacrum

Anterior superior spine of ilium

Brim of pelvis

Adductor magnus m.

Adductor brevis m.

FIGURE B.7 Anatomy at the Level of the Posterior Body Wall (Female). The lungs and retroperitoneal viscera are removed.

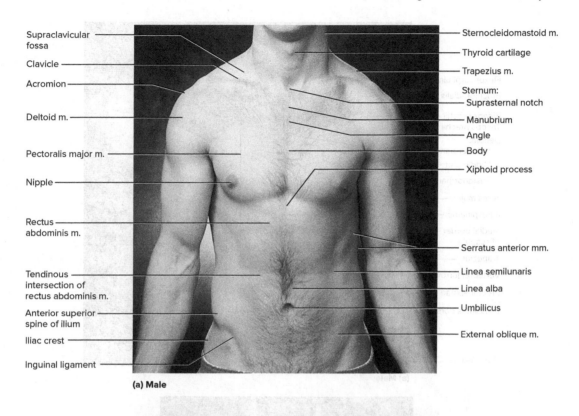

(a) Male

Supraclavicular fossa
Clavicle
Acromion
Deltoid m.
Pectoralis major m.
Nipple
Rectus abdominis m.
Tendinous intersection of rectus abdominis m.
Anterior superior spine of ilium
Iliac crest
Inguinal ligament

Sternocleidomastoid m.
Thyroid cartilage
Trapezius m.
Sternum:
Suprasternal notch
Manubrium
Angle
Body
Xiphoid process
Serratus anterior mm.
Linea semilunaris
Linea alba
Umbilicus
External oblique m.

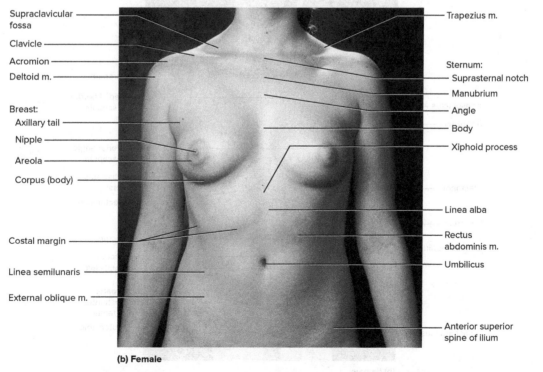

(b) Female

Supraclavicular fossa
Clavicle
Acromion
Deltoid m.
Breast:
Axillary tail
Nipple
Areola
Corpus (body)
Costal margin
Linea semilunaris
External oblique m.

Trapezius m.
Sternum:
Suprasternal notch
Manubrium
Angle
Body
Xiphoid process
Linea alba
Rectus abdominis m.
Umbilicus
Anterior superior spine of ilium

FIGURE B.8 The Thorax and Abdomen (Anterior View). (a) Male. (b) Female. All of the features labeled are common to both sexes, though some are labeled only on the photograph that shows them best.

a–b: Joe DeGrandis/McGraw-Hill Education

 The V-shaped tendons on each side of the suprasternal notch in part (a) belong to what muscles?

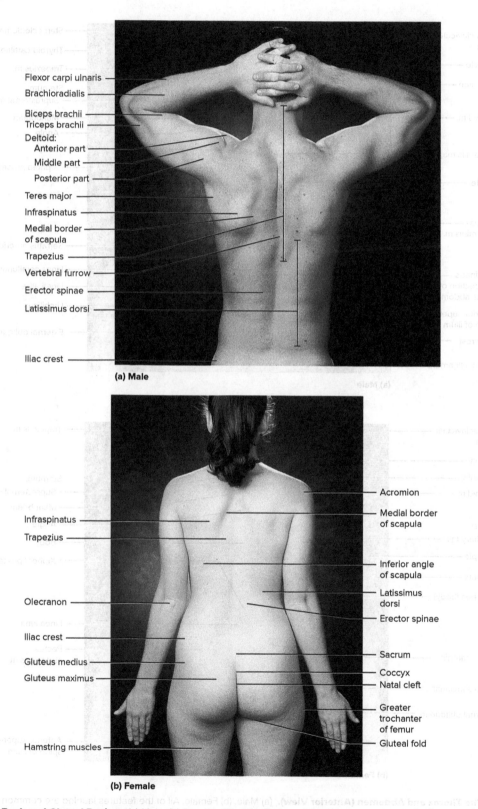

FIGURE B.9 The Back and Gluteal Region. (a) Male. (b) Female. All of the features labeled are common to both sexes, though some are labeled only on the photograph that shows them best.

a–b: Joe DeGrandis/McGraw-Hill Education

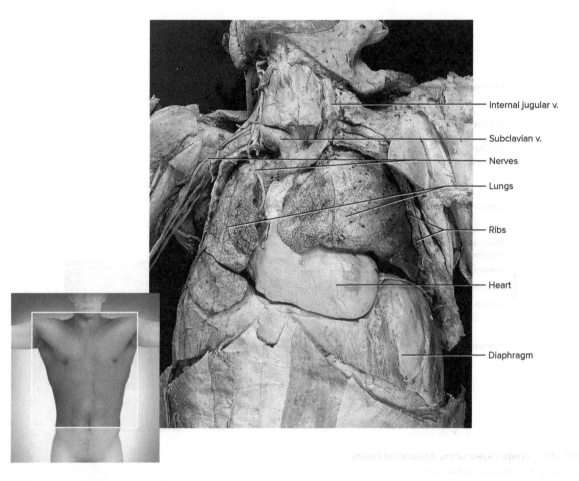

FIGURE B.10 Frontal View of the Thoracic Cavity.

Rebecca Gray/McGraw-Hill Education

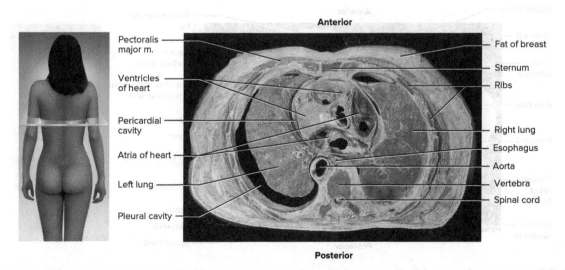

FIGURE B.11 Transverse Section of the Thorax. Section taken at the level shown by the inset and oriented the same as the reader's body.

Rebecca Gray/Don Kincaid/McGraw-Hill Education

In this section, which term best describes the position of the aorta relative to the heart: posterior, lateral, inferior, or proximal?

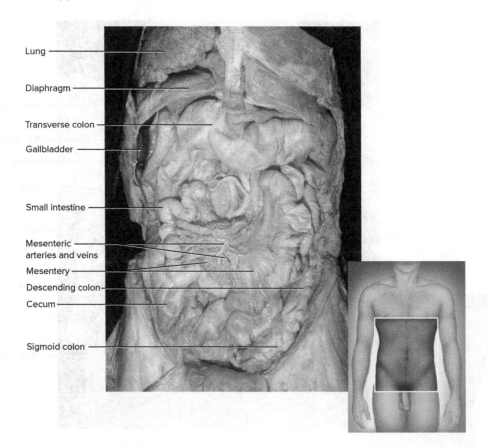

FIGURE B.12 **Frontal View of the Abdominal Cavity.**

Rebecca Gray/Don Kincaid/McGraw-Hill Education

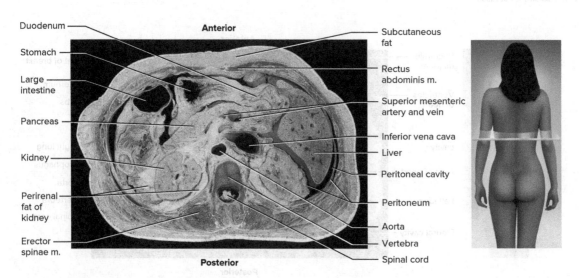

FIGURE B.13 **Transverse Section of the Abdomen.** Section taken at the level shown by the inset and oriented the same as the reader's body.

Rebecca Gray/Don Kincaid/McGraw-Hill Education

❓ *What tissue in this photograph is immediately superficial to the rectus abdominis muscle?*

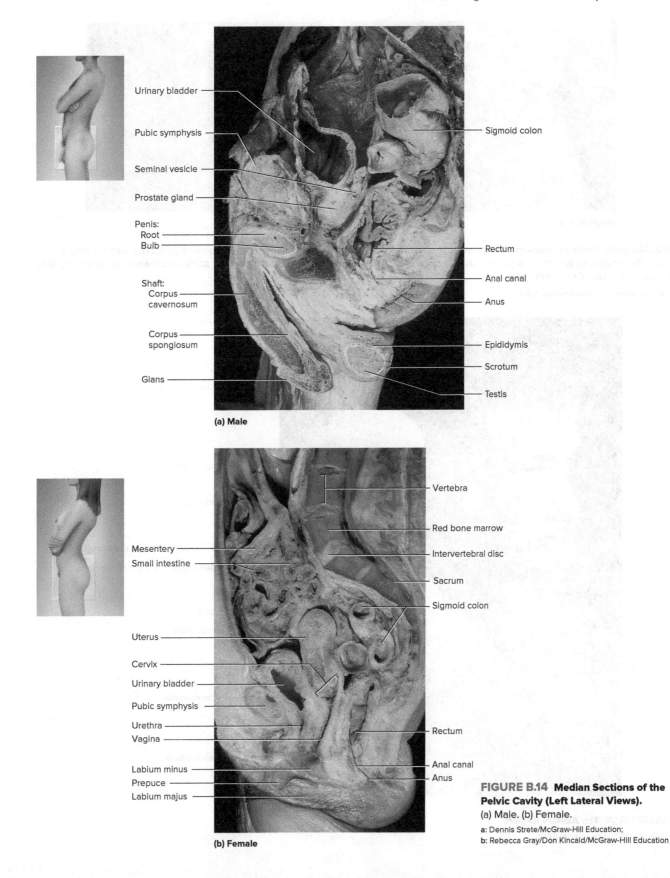

(a) Male

(b) Female

FIGURE B.14 Median Sections of the Pelvic Cavity (Left Lateral Views).
(a) Male. (b) Female.

a: Dennis Strete/McGraw-Hill Education;
b: Rebecca Gray/Don Kincaid/McGraw-Hill Education

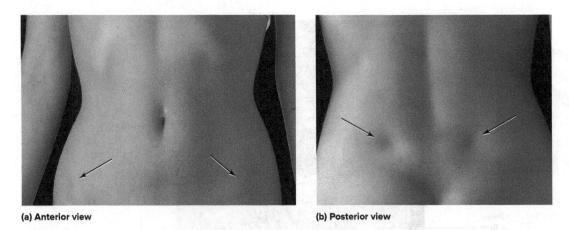

(a) Anterior view

(b) Posterior view

FIGURE B.15 Pelvic Landmarks. (a) The anterior superior spines of the ilium are marked by anterolateral protuberances (arrows) at about the location where the front pockets usually open on a pair of pants. (b) The posterior superior spines are marked in some people by dimples in the sacral region (arrows).

a–b: Joe DeGrandis/McGraw-Hill Education

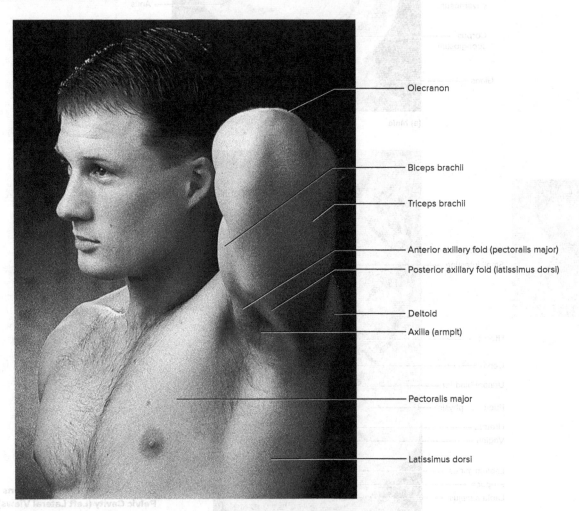

— Olecranon

— Biceps brachii

— Triceps brachii

— Anterior axillary fold (pectoralis major)
— Posterior axillary fold (latissimus dorsi)

— Deltoid
— Axilla (armpit)

— Pectoralis major

— Latissimus dorsi

FIGURE B.16 The Axillary Region.
Joe DeGrandis/McGraw-Hill Education

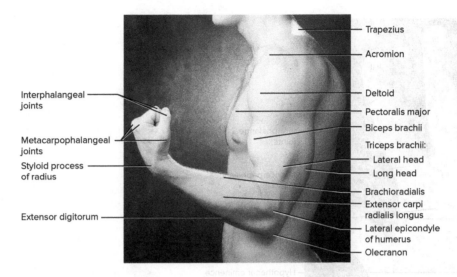

FIGURE B.17 The Upper Limb (Left Lateral View).

Joe DeGrandis/McGraw-Hill Education

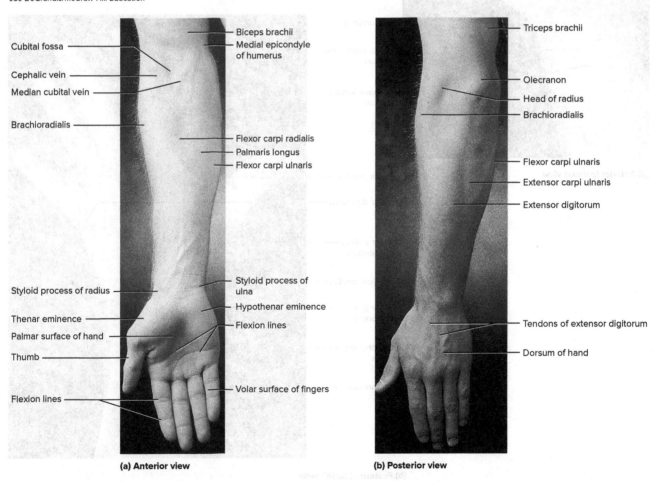

(a) Anterior view

(b) Posterior view

FIGURE B.18 The Antebrachium (Forearm). (a) Anterior view. (b) Posterior view.

a–b: Joe DeGrandis/McGraw-Hill Education

❓ *Only two tendons of the extensor digitorum are labeled, but how many tendons does this muscle have in all?*

378   **PART TWO**   Support and Movement

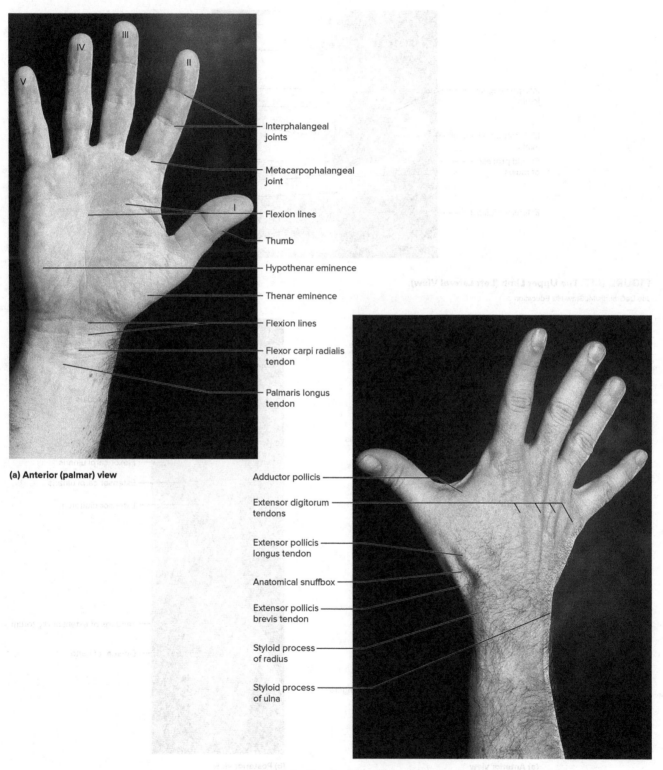

(a) Anterior (palmar) view

Interphalangeal joints

Metacarpophalangeal joint

Flexion lines

Thumb

Hypothenar eminence

Thenar eminence

Flexion lines

Flexor carpi radialis tendon

Palmaris longus tendon

Adductor pollicis

Extensor digitorum tendons

Extensor pollicis longus tendon

Anatomical snuffbox

Extensor pollicis brevis tendon

Styloid process of radius

Styloid process of ulna

(b) Posterior (dorsal) view

FIGURE B.19   **The Wrist and Hand.** (a) Anterior (palmar) view. (b) Posterior (dorsal) view.

a–b: Joe DeGrandis/McGraw-Hill Education

? *Mark the spot on one or both photographs where a saddle joint can be found.*

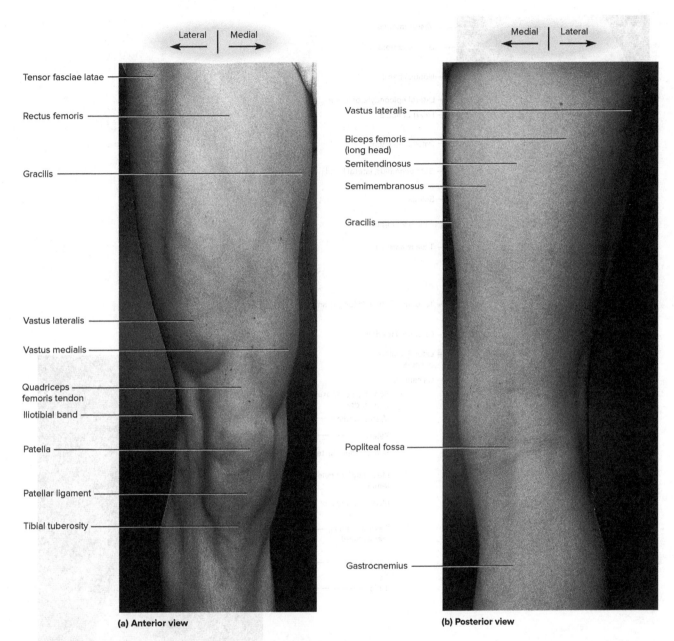

Lateral | Medial

Tensor fasciae latae

Rectus femoris

Gracilis

Vastus lateralis

Vastus medialis

Quadriceps femoris tendon

Iliotibial band

Patella

Patellar ligament

Tibial tuberosity

(a) Anterior view

Medial | Lateral

Vastus lateralis

Biceps femoris (long head)

Semitendinosus

Semimembranosus

Gracilis

Popliteal fossa

Gastrocnemius

(b) Posterior view

FIGURE B.20 The Thigh and Knee. (a) Anterior view. (b) Posterior view. Locations of posterior thigh muscles are indicated, but the boundaries of the individual muscles are rarely visible on a living person.

a–b: Joe DeGrandis/McGraw-Hill Education

❓ *Mark the spot on part (a) where the vastus intermedius would be found.*

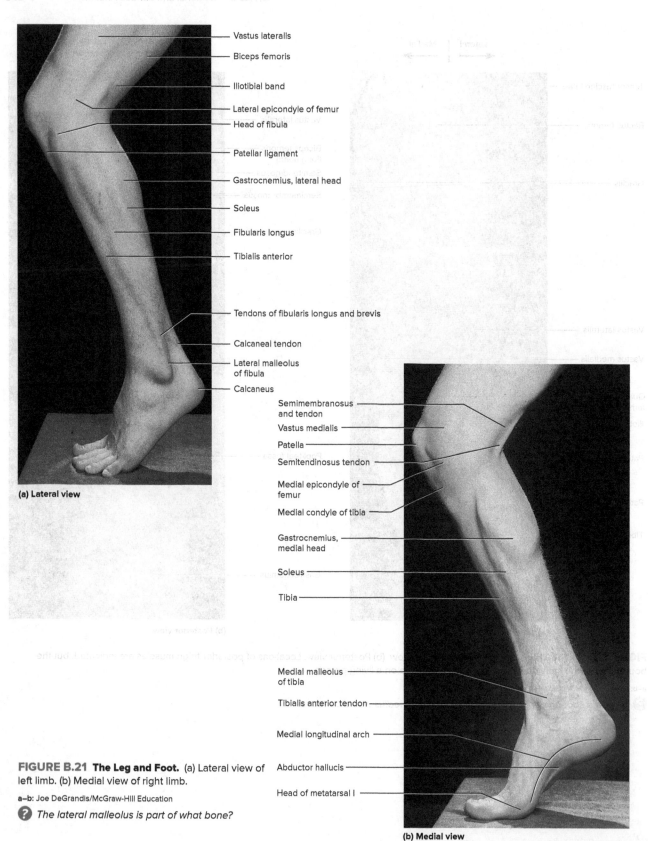

(a) Lateral view

- Vastus lateralis
- Biceps femoris
- Iliotibial band
- Lateral epicondyle of femur
- Head of fibula
- Patellar ligament
- Gastrocnemius, lateral head
- Soleus
- Fibularis longus
- Tibialis anterior
- Tendons of fibularis longus and brevis
- Calcaneal tendon
- Lateral malleolus of fibula
- Calcaneus

- Semimembranosus and tendon
- Vastus medialis
- Patella
- Semitendinosus tendon
- Medial epicondyle of femur
- Medial condyle of tibia
- Gastrocnemius, medial head
- Soleus
- Tibia
- Medial malleolus of tibia
- Tibialis anterior tendon
- Medial longitudinal arch
- Abductor hallucis
- Head of metatarsal I

(b) Medial view

FIGURE B.21 The Leg and Foot. (a) Lateral view of left limb. (b) Medial view of right limb.

a–b: Joe DeGrandis/McGraw-Hill Education

❓ *The lateral malleolus is part of what bone?*

Medial | Lateral

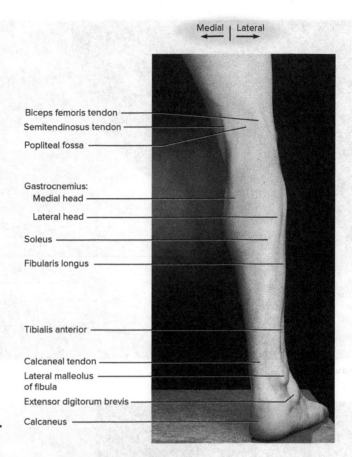

- Biceps femoris tendon
- Semitendinosus tendon
- Popliteal fossa

Gastrocnemius:
- Medial head
- Lateral head
- Soleus
- Fibularis longus

- Tibialis anterior

- Calcaneal tendon
- Lateral malleolus of fibula
- Extensor digitorum brevis
- Calcaneus

FIGURE B.22 The Leg and Foot, Posterior View.

Joe DeGrandis/McGraw-Hill Education

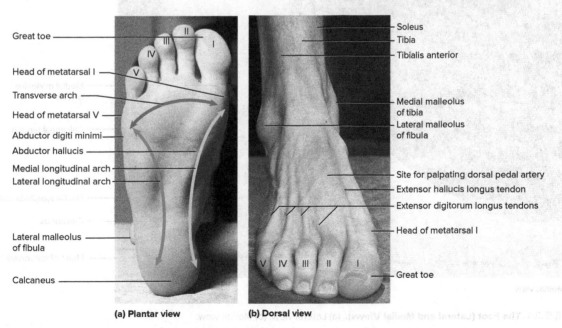

- Great toe
- Head of metatarsal I
- Transverse arch
- Head of metatarsal V
- Abductor digiti minimi
- Abductor hallucis
- Medial longitudinal arch
- Lateral longitudinal arch
- Lateral malleolus of fibula
- Calcaneus

- Soleus
- Tibia
- Tibialis anterior
- Medial malleolus of tibia
- Lateral malleolus of fibula
- Site for palpating dorsal pedal artery
- Extensor hallucis longus tendon
- Extensor digitorum longus tendons
- Head of metatarsal I
- Great toe

(a) Plantar view   **(b) Dorsal view**

FIGURE B.23 The Foot (Plantar and Dorsal Views). (a) Plantar view. (b) Dorsal view. Compare the arches in part (a) to the skeletal anatomy in figure 8.43.

a–b: Joe DeGrandis/McGraw-Hill Education

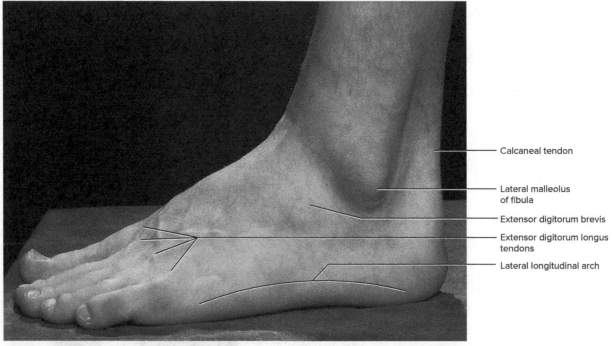

(a) Lateral view

Calcaneal tendon

Lateral malleolus
of fibula

Extensor digitorum brevis

Extensor digitorum longus
tendons

Lateral longitudinal arch

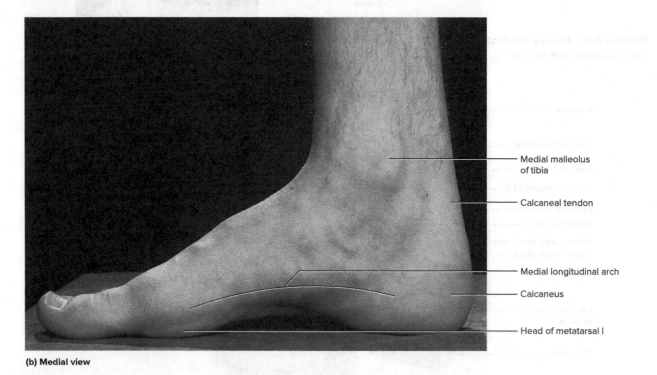

(b) Medial view

Medial malleolus
of tibia

Calcaneal tendon

Medial longitudinal arch

Calcaneus

Head of metatarsal I

FIGURE B.24 The Foot (Lateral and Medial Views). (a) Lateral view. (b) Medial view.

a–b: Joe DeGrandis/McGraw-Hill Education

❓ *Indicate the position of middle phalanx I on each photograph.*

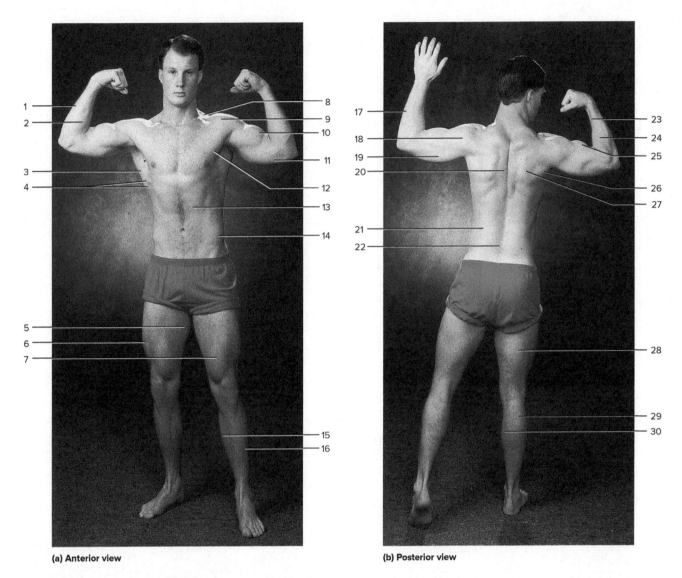

(a) Anterior view

(b) Posterior view

FIGURE B.25 Test of Muscle Recognition. To test your knowledge of muscle anatomy, match the 30 labeled muscles on these photographs to the following alphabetical list of muscles. Answer as many as possible without referring back to the previous illustrations. Some of these names will be used more than once since the same muscle may be shown from different perspectives, and some of these names will not be used at all. The answers are in appendix A.

a–b: Joe DeGrandis/McGraw-Hill Education

Throughout these illustrations, the following abbreviations apply: a. = artery; m. = muscle; n. = nerve; v. = vein. Double letters such as mm. or vv. represent the plurals.

a. biceps brachii

b. brachioradialis

c. deltoid

d. erector spinae

e. external oblique

f. flexor carpi ulnaris

g. gastrocnemius

h. gracilis

i. hamstrings

j. infraspinatus

k. latissimus dorsi

l. pectineus

m. pectoralis major

n. rectus abdominis

o. rectus femoris

p. serratus anterior

q. soleus

r. splenius capitis

s. sternocleidomastoid

t. subscapularis

u. teres major

v. tibialis anterior

w. trapezius

x. triceps brachii

y. vastus lateralis

z. vastus medialis

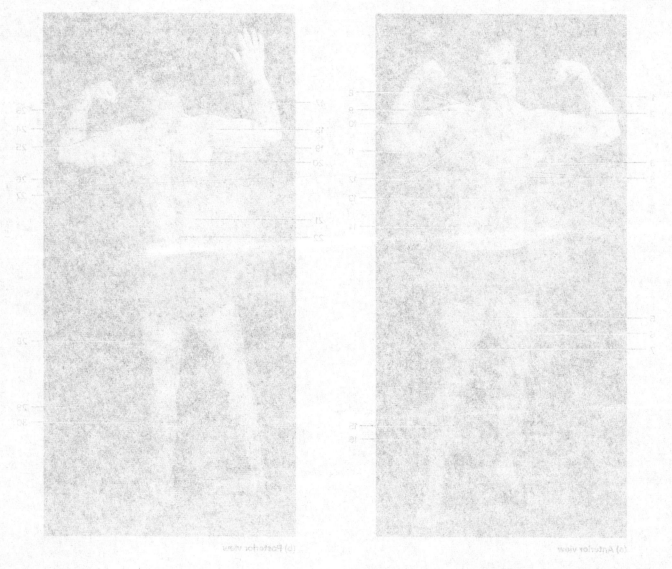

(a) Anterior view (b) Posterior view

GLOSSARY

A

abdominal cavity The body cavity between the diaphragm and pelvic brim. fig. A.5

abduction (ab-DUC-shun) Movement of a body part away from the median plane, as in raising an arm away from the side of the body. fig. 9.13

absorption 1. Process in which a chemical passes through a membrane or tissue surface and becomes incorporated into a body fluid or tissue. 2. Any process in which one substance passes into another and becomes a part of it. *Compare* adsorption.

acetylcholine (ACh) (ASS-eh-till-CO-leen) A neurotransmitter released by somatic motor fibers, parasympathetic fibers, and some other neurons, composed of choline and an acetyl group. fig. 12.22

acetylcholinesterase (AChE) (ASS-eh-till-CO-lin-ESS-ter-ase) An enzyme that hydrolyzes acetylcholine, thus halting signal transmission at a cholinergic synapse.

acid A proton (H^+) donor; a chemical that releases protons into solution.

acidosis An acid–base imbalance in which the blood pH is lower than 7.35.

acinus (ASS-ih-nus) A sac of secretory cells at the inner end of a gland duct. fig. 5.30

actin A filamentous intracellular protein that provides cytoskeletal support and interacts with other proteins, especially myosin, to cause cellular movement; important in muscle contraction and membrane actions such as phagocytosis, ameboid movement, and cytokinesis. fig. 11.3

action The movement produced by contraction of a particular muscle, or its role in preventing an unwanted movement; the function of a muscle.

action potential A rapid voltage change in which a plasma membrane briefly reverses electrical polarity; has a self-propagating effect that produces a traveling wave of excitation in nerve and muscle cells.

active site The region of a protein that binds to a ligand, such as the substrate-binding site of an enzyme or the hormone-binding site of a receptor.

active transport Transport of particles through a selectively permeable membrane, up their concentration gradient, with the aid of a carrier that consumes ATP.

acute Pertaining to a disease with abrupt onset, intense symptoms, and short duration. *Compare* chronic.

adaptation 1. An evolutionary process leading to the establishment of species characteristics that favor survival and reproduction. 2. Any characteristic of anatomy, physiology, or behavior that promotes survival and reproduction. 3. A sensory process in which a receptor adjusts its sensitivity or response to the prevailing level of stimulation, such as dark adaptation of the eye.

adaptive immunity A system of pathogen-specific defenses, developed upon initial exposure to an antigen and entailing cellular memory and accelerated responses to the pathogen on later reexposure, thereby preventing or minimizing disease. Includes various T and B lymphocytes, plasma cells, and antibodies. *Compare* innate immunity.

adduction (ad-DUC-shun) Movement of a body part toward the median plane, such as bringing the feet together from a spread-legged position. fig. 9.13

adenosine triphosphate (ATP) (ah-DEN-oh-seen tri-FOSS-fate) A molecule composed of adenine, ribose, and three phosphate groups that functions as a universal energy-transfer molecule; yields adenosine diphosphate (ADP) and an inorganic phosphate group (Pi) upon hydrolysis. fig. 2.29a

adenylate cyclase (ah-DEN-ih-late SY-clase) An enzyme of the plasma membrane that makes cyclic adenosine monophosphate (cAMP) by removing two phosphate groups from ATP; important in the activation of the cAMP second-messenger system.

adipocyte (AD-ih-po-site) A fat cell.

adipose tissue A connective tissue composed predominantly of adipocytes; fat.

adrenergic (AD-ren-UR-jic) Pertaining to norepinephrine (NE) and epinephrine, as in adrenergic nerve fibers that secrete NE, adrenergic receptors that bind it, and adrenergic effects on a target organ.

adrenocorticotropic hormone (ACTH) A hormone secreted by the anterior pituitary gland that stimulates the adrenal cortex to secrete cortisol and other glucocorticoids; one of the stress hormones.

adsorption The binding of one substance to the surface of another without becoming a part of the latter. *Compare* absorption.

aerobic exercise (air-OH-bic) Exercise in which oxygen is used to produce ATP; endurance exercise.

aerobic respiration Oxidation of organic compounds in a reaction series that requires oxygen and produces ATP.

afferent (AFF-ur-ent) Carrying toward, as in a blood vessel that carries blood toward a tissue or a nerve fiber that conducts signals toward the central nervous system.

agglutination (ah-GLUE-tih-NAY-shun) Clumping of cells by antibodies.

albumin (al-BYU-min) A class of small proteins constituting about 60% of the protein fraction of the blood plasma; plays roles in blood viscosity, colloid osmotic pressure, and solute transport.

aldosterone (AL-doe-steh-RONE, al-DOSS-teh-rone) A steroid hormone secreted by the adrenal cortex that acts on the kidneys to promote sodium retention and potassium excretion.

alkalosis An acid–base imbalance in which the blood pH is higher than 7.45.

allele (ah-LEEL) Any of the alternative forms that one gene can take, such as dominant and recessive alleles.

alveolus (AL-vee-OH-lus) 1. A microscopic air sac of the lung. 2. A gland acinus. 3. A tooth socket. 4. Any small anatomical space.

amino acid A small organic molecule with an amino group and a carboxyl group; amino acids are the monomers of which proteins are composed, and function also as neurotransmitters and in other roles.

amnion A transparent sac that encloses the fetus and amniotic fluid.

amphipathic (AM-fih-PATH-ic) Pertaining to a molecule that has both hydrophilic and hydrophobic regions, such as phospholipids, bile acids, and some proteins.

ampulla (am-PULL-uh) A wide or saclike portion of a tubular organ such as a semicircular duct or uterine tube.

anabolism (ah-NAB-oh-lizm) Any metabolic reactions that consume energy and construct more complex molecules with higher free energy from less complex molecules with lower free energy; for example, the synthesis of proteins from amino acids. *Compare* catabolism.

anaerobic fermentation (AN-err-OH-bic) A reduction reaction independent of oxygen that converts pyruvate to lactate and enables glycolysis to continue under anaerobic conditions.

anastomosis (ah-NASS-tih-MO-sis) An anatomical convergence, the opposite of a branch; a point where two blood vessels merge and combine their bloodstreams or where two nerves or ducts converge. fig. 20.10

anatomical position A reference posture that allows for standardized anatomical terminology. A subject in anatomical position is standing with the feet flat on the floor, arms down to the sides, and the palms and eyes directed forward. fig. A.1

androgen (AN-dro-jen) Testosterone or a related steroid hormone. Stimulates bodily changes at puberty in both sexes, adult libido in both sexes, development of male anatomy in the fetus and adolescent, and spermatogenesis.

aneurysm (AN-you-rizm) A weak, bulging point in the wall of a heart chamber or blood vessel that presents a threat of hemorrhage.

angiogenesis (AN-jee-oh-GEN-eh-sis) The growth of new blood vessels.

angiotensin II (AN-jee-oh-TEN-sin) A hormone produced from angiotensinogen (a plasma protein) by the kidneys and lungs; raises blood pressure by stimulating vasoconstriction and stimulating the adrenal cortex to secrete aldosterone.

anion (AN-eye-on) An ion with more electrons than protons and consequently a net negative charge.

antagonist 1. A muscle that opposes the agonist at a joint. **2.** Any agent, such as a hormone or drug, that opposes another.

antagonistic effect 1. An effect in which two hormones, neurotransmitters, or divisions of the nervous system oppose each other and produce opposite effects on a target cell or organ. **2.** An effect in which a drug blocks or otherwise opposes the action of one of the body's own signaling mechanisms.

antebrachium (AN-teh-BRAY-kee-um) The region from elbow to wrist; the forearm.

anterior Pertaining to the front (facial-abdominal aspect) of the body; ventral.

anterior root The branch of a spinal nerve that emerges from the anterior side of the spinal cord and carries efferent (motor) nerve fibers; often called *ventral root*. fig. 13.2b

antibody A protein of the gamma globulin class that reacts with an antigen and aids in protecting the body from its harmful effects; found in the blood plasma, in other body fluids, and on the surfaces of certain leukocytes and their derivatives.

antidiuretic hormone (ADH) (AN-tee-DYE-you-RET-ic) A hormone released by the posterior lobe of the pituitary gland in response to low blood pressure; promotes water retention by the kidneys. Also known as *arginine vasopressin.*

antigen (AN-tih-jen) Any large molecule capable of binding to an antibody or immune cells and

triggering an immune response; usually a protein, glycoprotein, or glycolipid.

antigen-presenting cell (APC) A cell that phagocytizes an antigen and displays fragments of it on its surface for recognition by other cells of the immune system; chiefly macrophages and B lymphocytes.

antiport A cotransport protein that moves two or more solutes in opposite directions through a cellular membrane, such as the Na$^+$–K$^+$ pump.

apical surface The uppermost surface of an epithelial cell, usually exposed to the lumen of an organ. fig. 3.4

apocrine Pertaining to certain sweat glands with large lumens and relatively thick, aromatic secretions and to similar glands such as the mammary gland; named for a mistaken belief that they form secretions by pinching off bits of apical cytoplasm.

apoptosis (AP-op-TOE-sis) Programmed cell death; the normal death of cells that have completed their function. *Compare* necrosis.

appendicular (AP-en-DIC-you-lur) Pertaining to the limbs and their supporting skeletal girdles. fig. 8.1

areolar tissue (AIR-ee-OH-lur) A fibrous connective tissue with loosely organized, widely spaced fibers and cells and an abundance of fluid-filled space; found under nearly every epithelium, among other places. fig. 5.14

arrector A smooth muscle associated with each hair follicle that serves to erect the hair. fig. 6.7

arteriole (ar-TEER-ee-ole) A small artery that empties into a metarteriole or capillary.

arteriosclerosis (ar-TEER-ee-o-sclair-O-sis) Stiffening of the arteries correlated with age or disease processes, caused primarily by cumulative free radical damage and tissue deterioration. *Compare* atherosclerosis.

articular cartilage A thin layer of hyaline cartilage covering the articular surface of a bone at a synovial joint, serving to reduce friction and ease joint movement. fig. 9.5

articulation A skeletal joint; any point at which two bones meet; may or may not be movable.

aspect A particular view of the body or one of its structures, or a part that faces in a particular direction, such as the anterior aspect.

atherosclerosis (ATH-ur-oh-skleh-ROE-sis) A degenerative disease of the blood vessels characterized by the presence of lipid deposits; often leading to calcification of the vessel wall and obstruction of coronary, cerebral, or other vital arteries. *Compare* arteriosclerosis.

atrioventricular (AV) node (AY-tree-oh-ven-TRIC-you-lur) A group of autorhythmic cells in the interatrial septum of the heart that relays excitation from the atria to the ventricles.

atrioventricular (AV) valves The mitral (left) and tricuspid (right) valves between the atria

and ventricles of the heart; the left AV valve was formerly known as the *bicuspid valve*.

atrophy (AT-ro-fee) Shrinkage of a tissue due to age, disuse, or disease.

autoantibody An antibody that fails to distinguish the body's own molecules from foreign molecules and thus attacks host tissues, causing autoimmune diseases.

autoimmune disease Any disease in which antibodies fail to distinguish between foreign and self-antigens and attack the body's own tissues; for example, systemic lupus erythematosus and rheumatic fever.

autolysis (aw-TOLL-ih-sis) Digestion of cells by their own internal enzymes.

autonomic nervous system (ANS) (AW-toe-NOM-ic) A motor division of the nervous system that innervates glands, smooth muscle, and cardiac muscle; consists of sympathetic and parasympathetic divisions and functions largely without voluntary control. *Compare* somatic nervous system.

autoregulation The ability of a tissue to adjust its own blood supply through vasomotion or angiogenesis.

autosome (AW-toe-some) Any chromosome except the sex chromosomes. Genes on the autosomes are inherited without regard to the sex of the individual.

avascular Devoid of blood vessels, as in epithelia and cartilage.

axial (AC-see-ul) Pertaining to the head, neck, and trunk; the part of the body excluding the appendicular portion. fig. 8.1

axillary (ACK-sih-LERR-ee) Pertaining to the armpit.

axon terminal The swollen tip at the distal end of an axon; the site of synaptic vesicles and neurotransmitter release. fig. 12.21

axoneme The central core of a cilium or flagellum, composed of microtubules; these are arranged in a circular array of nine microtubule pairs, and in flagella and mobile cilia, another microtubule pair at the center of the circle.

B

baroreceptor (BER-oh-re-SEP-tur) A cardiovascular pressure sensor that triggers autonomic reflexes in response to fluctuations in blood pressure; baroreceptors are located in the heart, aortic arch, and carotid sinuses.

basal surface The lowermost surface of an epithelial cell, attached to either a basement membrane or an underlying epithelial cell. fig. 3.4

base 1. A chemical that binds protons from solution; a proton acceptor. **2.** Any of the purines or pyrimidines of a nucleic acid (adenine, thymine, guanine, cytosine, or uracil) serving in part to code for protein structure. **3.** The broadest part of a tapered organ such as the uterus or heart or the inferior aspect of an organ such as the brain.

basement membrane A thin layer of glycoproteins, collagen, and glycosaminoglycans beneath the deepest cells of an epithelium, serving to bind the epithelium to the underlying tissue. fig. 5.33

basophil (BAY-so-fill) A granulocyte with coarse cytoplasmic granules that produces heparin, histamine, and other chemicals involved in inflammation. table 18.6

belly The thick part of a skeletal muscle between its origin and insertion. fig. 10.4

bicarbonate buffer system An equilibrium mixture of carbonic acid, bicarbonate ions, and hydrogen ions ($H_2CO_3 \rightleftharpoons HCO_3^- + H^+$) that stabilizes the pH of the body fluids.

bicarbonate ion An anion, HCO_3^-, that functions as a base in the buffering of body fluids.

biogenic amines A class of chemical messengers with neurotransmitter and hormonal functions, synthesized from amino acids and retaining an amino group; also called *monoamines*. Examples include epinephrine and thyroxine.

bipedalism The habit of walking on two legs; a defining characteristic of the family Hominidae that underlies many skeletal and other characteristics of humans.

blood–brain barrier (BBB) A barrier between the bloodstream and nervous tissue of the CNS that is impermeable to many blood solutes and thus prevents them from affecting the brain tissue; formed by the tight junctions between capillary endothelial cells, the basement membrane of the endothelium, and the perivascular feet of astrocytes.

B lymphocyte A lymphocyte that functions as an antigen-presenting cell and, in humoral immunity, differentiates into an antibody-producing plasma cell; also called a *B cell*.

body 1. The entire organism. **2.** Part of a cell, such as a neuron, containing the nucleus and most other organelles. **3.** The largest or principal part of an organ such as the stomach or uterus; also called the *corpus*.

brachial (BRAY-kee-ul) Pertaining to the arm proper, the region from shoulder to elbow.

bradykinin (BRAD-ee-KY-nin) An oligopeptide produced in inflammation that stimulates vasodilation, increases capillary permeability, and stimulates pain receptors.

brainstem The stalklike lower portion of the brain, composed of the medulla oblongata, pons, and midbrain. fig. 14.8

bronchiole (BRON-kee-ole) A pulmonary air passage that is usually 1 mm or less in diameter and lacks cartilage but has relatively abundant smooth muscle, elastic tissue, and a simple cuboidal, usually ciliated epithelium.

bronchus (BRONK-us) A relatively large pulmonary air passage with supportive cartilage in the wall; any passage beginning with the main bronchus at the fork in the trachea and ending with segmental bronchi, from which air continues into the bronchioles.

brush border A fringe of microvilli on the apical surface of an epithelial cell, serving to enhance surface area and promote absorption. fig. 5.6

bursa A sac filled with synovial fluid at a synovial joint, serving to facilitate muscle or joint action. fig. 9.6

C

calcification The hardening of a tissue due to the deposition of calcium salts.

calorie The amount of thermal energy that will raise the temperature of 1 g of water by 1°C. Also called a *small calorie* to distinguish it from a dietary Calorie (capital *C*), or kilocalorie.

Calorie *See* kilocalorie.

canaliculus (CAN-uh-LIC-you-lus) A microscopic canal, as in osseous tissue. fig. 7.4

capillary (CAP-ih-LERR-ee) The narrowest type of vessel in the cardiovascular and lymphatic systems; engages in fluid exchanges with surrounding tissues.

capillary exchange The process of fluid transfer between the bloodstream and tissue fluid through the walls of the blood capillaries.

capsule The fibrous covering of a structure such as the spleen or a synovial joint.

carbohydrate A hydrophilic organic compound composed of carbon and a 2:1 ratio of hydrogen to oxygen; includes sugars, starches, glycogen, and cellulose.

carbonic anhydrase An enzyme found in erythrocytes and kidney tubule cells that catalyzes the decomposition of carbonic acid into carbon dioxide and water or the reverse reaction ($H_2CO_3 \rightleftharpoons CO_2 + H_2O$).

carcinogen (car-SIN-oh-jen) An agent capable of causing cancer, including certain chemicals, viruses, and ionizing radiation.

cardiac output *(CO)* The amount of blood pumped by each ventricle of the heart in 1 minute.

cardiomyocyte A cardiac muscle cell.

cardiovascular system An organ system consisting of the heart and blood vessels, serving for the transport of blood. *Compare* circulatory system.

carpal Pertaining to the wrist (carpus).

carrier 1. A protein in a cellular membrane that performs carrier-mediated transport. **2.** A person who is heterozygous for a recessive allele and does not exhibit the associated phenotype, but may transmit this allele to his or her children; for example, a carrier for sickle-cell disease.

carrier-mediated transport Any process of transporting materials through a cellular membrane that involves reversible binding to a transport protein.

catabolism (ca-TAB-oh-lizm) Any metabolic reactions that release energy and break relatively complex molecules with high free energy into less complex molecules with lower free energy; for example, digestion and glycolysis. *Compare* anabolism.

catecholamine (CAT-eh-COAL-uh-meen) A subclass of biogenic amines that includes epinephrine, norepinephrine, and dopamine. fig. 12.22

cation (CAT-eye-on) An ion with more protons than electrons and consequently a net positive charge.

caudal (CAW-dul) **1.** Pertaining to a tail or narrow tail-like part of an organ. **2.** Pertaining to the inferior part of the trunk of the body, where the tail of other animals arises. *Compare* cranial. **3.** Relatively distant from the forehead, especially in reference to structures of the brain and spinal cord; for example, the medulla oblongata is caudal to the pons. *Compare* rostral.

celiac (SEEL-ee-ac) Pertaining to the abdomen.

central nervous system (CNS) The brain and spinal cord.

centriole (SEN-tree-ole) An organelle composed of a short cylinder of nine triplets of microtubules, usually paired with another centriole perpendicular to it; origin of the mitotic spindle; identical to the basal body of a cilium or flagellum. fig. 3.33

cephalic (seh-FAL-ic) Pertaining to the head.

cerebellum (SER-eh-BELL-um) A large portion of the brain posterior to the brainstem and inferior to the cerebrum, responsible for equilibrium, motor coordination, and memory of learned motor skills. fig. 14.11

cerebrospinal fluid (CSF) (SERR-eh-bro-SPY-nul, seh-REE-bro-SPY-nul) A liquid that fills the ventricles of the brain, the central canal of the spinal cord, and the space between the CNS and dura mater.

cerebrum (seh-REE-brum, SERR-eh-brum) The largest and most superior part of the brain, divided into two convoluted cerebral hemispheres separated by a deep longitudinal fissure.

cervical (SUR-vih-cul) Pertaining to the neck or a narrow part (cervix) of certain organs.

cervix (SUR-vix) **1.** The neck. **2.** A narrow or necklike part of an organ such as the uterus and gallbladder. fig. 28.3

channel protein A transmembrane protein that has a pore through it for the passage of materials between the cytoplasm and extracellular fluid. fig. 3.7

chemical bond A force that attracts one atom to another, such as their opposite charges or the sharing of electrons.

chemical synapse A meeting of a nerve fiber and another cell with which the neuron communicates by releasing neurotransmitters. fig. 12.21

chemoreceptor An organ or cell specialized to detect chemicals, as in the carotid bodies and taste buds.

chief cells The majority type of cell in an organ or tissue such as the parathyroid glands or gastric glands.

cholecystokinin (CCK) (CO-leh-SIS-toe-KY-nin) A polypeptide employed as a hormone and neurotransmitter, secreted by some brain neurons and cells of the digestive tract. fig. 12.22

cholesterol (co-LESS-tur-ol) A steroid that functions as part of the plasma membrane and as a precursor for all other steroids in the body.

cholinergic (CO-lin-UR-jic) Pertaining to acetylcholine (ACh), as in cholinergic nerve fibers that secrete ACh, cholinergic receptors that bind it, or cholinergic effects on a target organ.

chondrocyte (CON-dro-site) A cartilage cell; a former chondroblast that has become enclosed in a lacuna in the cartilage matrix. figs. 5.19 to 5.21

chorion (CO-ree-on) An embryonic membrane external to the amnion; forms part of the placenta and has diverse functions including fetal nutrition, waste removal, and hormone secretion. fig. 29.7f

chromatin (CRO-muh-tin) Filamentous material in the interphase nucleus, composed of DNA and associated proteins.

chromosome A complex of DNA and protein carrying the genetic material of a cell's nucleus. Normally there are 46 chromosomes in the nucleus of each cell except germ cells. fig. 4.5

chronic 1. Long-lasting. **2.** Pertaining to a disease that progresses slowly and has a long duration. *Compare* acute.

chronic bronchitis A chronic obstructive pulmonary disease characterized by damaged and immobilized respiratory cilia, excessive mucus secretion, infection of the lower respiratory tract, and bronchial inflammation; caused especially by cigarette smoking. *See also* chronic obstructive pulmonary disease.

chronic obstructive pulmonary disease (COPD) Certain lung diseases (chronic bronchitis and emphysema) that result in long-term obstruction of airflow and substantially reduced pulmonary ventilation; one of the leading causes of death in old age.

cilium (SILL-ee-um) A hairlike process, with an axoneme, projecting from the apical surface of an epithelial cell; often motile and serving to propel matter across the surface of an epithelium, but sometimes nonmotile and serving sensory roles. fig. 3.10

circulatory shock A state of cardiac output inadequate to meet the metabolic needs of the body.

circulatory system An organ system consisting of the heart, blood vessels, and blood. *Compare* cardiovascular system.

circumduction A joint movement in which one end of an appendage remains relatively stationary and the other end is moved in a circle. fig. 9.16

cirrhosis (sih-RO-sis) A degenerative liver disease characterized by replacement of functional parenchyma with fibrous and adipose tissue; causes include alcohol, other poisons, and viral and bacterial inflammation.

cistern (SIS-turn) A fluid-filled space or sac, such as the cisterna chyli of the lymphatic system and cisterns of the endoplasmic reticulum and Golgi complex. fig. 3.28

climacteric A period in the lives of men and women, usually in the early 50s, marked by changes in the level of reproductive hormones; a variety of somatic and psychological effects; and, in women, cessation of ovulation and menstruation (menopause).

clone A population of cells that are mitotically descended from the same parent cell and are identical to each other genetically or in other respects, such as a B- or T-cell clone.

coagulation (co-AG-you-LAY-shun) The clotting of blood, lymph, tissue fluid, or semen.

coenzyme (co-EN-zime) A small organic molecule, usually derived from a vitamin, that is needed to make an enzyme catalytically active; acts by accepting electrons from an enzymatic reaction and transferring them to a different reaction chain.

cofactor A nonprotein such as a metal ion or coenzyme needed for an enzyme to function.

cohesion The clinging of identical molecules such as water to each other.

collagen (COLL-uh-jen) The most abundant protein in the body, forming the fibers of many connective tissues in places such as the dermis, tendons, and bones.

colloid An aqueous mixture of particles that are too large to pass through most selectively permeable membranes but small enough to remain evenly dispersed through the solvent by the thermal motion of solvent particles; for example, the proteins in blood plasma.

colloid osmotic pressure *(COP)* A portion of the osmotic pressure of a body fluid that is due to its protein. *Compare* oncotic pressure.

column *See* funiculus.

columnar A cellular shape that is significantly taller than it is wide. fig. 5.6

commissure (COM-ih-shur) **1.** A bundle of nerve fibers that crosses from one side of the brain or spinal cord to the other. fig. 14.2 **2.** A corner or angle at which the eyelids, lips, or genital labia meet; in the eye, also called the *canthus*. fig. 16.23

complement 1. To complete or enhance the structure or function of something else, as in the coordinated action of two hormones. **2.** A system of plasma proteins involved in defense against pathogens.

computerized tomography (CT) A method of medical imaging that uses X-rays and a computer to create an image of a thin section of the body; also called a *CT scan*.

concentration gradient A difference in chemical concentration from one point to another, as on two sides of a plasma membrane.

conception The fertilization of an egg, producing a zygote.

conceptus All products of conception, ranging from a fertilized egg to the full-term fetus with its embryonic membranes, placenta, and umbilical cord. *Compare* embryo, fetus, preembryo.

condyle (CON-dile) A rounded knob on a bone serving to smooth the movement of a joint. fig. 8.2

conformation The three-dimensional structure of a protein that results from interaction among its amino acid side groups, its interactions with water, and the formation of disulfide bonds.

congenital Present at birth; for example, an anatomical defect, a syphilis infection, or a hereditary disease.

conjugated A state in which one organic compound is bound to another compound of a different class, such as a protein conjugated with a carbohydrate to form a glycoprotein.

connective tissue A tissue usually composed of more extracellular than cellular volume and usually with a substantial amount of extracellular fiber; forms supportive frameworks and capsules for organs, binds structures together, holds them in place, stores energy (as in adipose tissue), or transports materials (as in blood).

contractility 1. The ability to shorten. **2.** The amount of force that a contracting muscle fiber generates for a given stimulus; may be increased by epinephrine, for example, while stimulus strength remains constant. **3.** The amount of force that a contracting heart chamber generates for a given preload.

contralateral On opposite sides of the body, as in reflex arcs in which the stimulus comes from one side of the body and a response is given by muscles on the other side. *Compare* ipsilateral.

cooperative effect Effect in which two hormones, or both divisions of the autonomic nervous system, work together to produce a single overall result.

corona A halo- or crownlike structure, as in the corona radiata of the brain and ovaries, coronary circulation of the heart, and coronal suture of the skull.

corona radiata 1. An array of nerve tracts in the brain that arise mainly from the thalamus and fan out to different regions of the cerebral cortex. **2.** The first layer of cuboidal cells immediately external to the zona pellucida around an egg cell.

coronal plane *See* frontal plane.

coronary circulation A system of blood vessels that serve the wall of the heart. fig. 19.10

corpus 1. Body or mass, such as the corpus callosum and corpus luteum. **2.** The main part of an organ such as the stomach or uterus, as opposed to such regions as the head, tail, or cervix.

corrosion cast *See* vascular corrosion cast.

cortex The outer layer of some organs such as the adrenal glands, kidneys, cerebrum, lymph nodes, ovaries, and hairs; usually covers or encloses tissue called the *medulla*.

corticosteroid (COR-tih-co-STERR-oyd) Any steroid hormone secreted by the adrenal cortex, such as aldosterone, cortisol, and sex steroids.

costal (COSS-tul) Pertaining to the ribs.

cotransport A form of carrier-mediated transport in which a membrane protein transports two solutes simultaneously or within the same cycle of action by either facilitated diffusion or active transport; for example, the sodium–glucose transporter and the Na^+–K^+ pump.

countercurrent A situation in which two fluids flow side by side in opposite directions, as in the countercurrent multiplier of the kidney and the countercurrent heat exchanger of the scrotum.

cranial (CRAY-nee-ul) **1.** Pertaining to the cranium of the skull. **2.** In a position relatively close to the head or a direction toward the head. *Compare* caudal.

cranial nerve Any of 12 pairs of nerves connected to the base of the brain and passing through foramina of the cranium.

crista (plural, *cristae*) An anatomical crest, such as the crista galli of the ethmoid bone or the crista of a mitochondrion.

cross section A cut perpendicular to the long axis of the body or an organ.

crural (CROO-rul) Pertaining to the leg proper or to the crus (leg) of a organ.

crus (pronounced cruss; plural, *crura*) **1.** A leglike extension of an organ such as the penis or clitoris. figs. 27.10b, 28.8 **2.** The leg proper (crural region, from knee to ankle) of the lower limb.

cuboidal (cue-BOY-dul) A cellular shape that is roughly like a cube or in which the height and width are about equal; typically looks squarish in tissue sections. fig. 5.5

current A moving stream of charged particles such as ions or electrons.

cusp 1. One of the flaps of a valve of the heart, veins, and lymphatic vessels. **2.** A conical projection on the occlusal surface of a premolar or molar tooth.

cutaneous (cue-TAY-nee-us) Pertaining to the skin.

cyanosis (SY-uh-NO-sis) A bluish color of the skin and mucous membranes due to ischemia or hypoxemia.

cyclic adenosine monophosphate (cAMP) A cyclic molecule produced from ATP by the enzymatic removal of two phosphate groups; serves as a second messenger in many hormone and neurotransmitter actions. fig. 2.29b

cytolysis (sy-TOL-ih-sis) The rupture and destruction of a cell by such agents as complement proteins and hypotonic solutions.

cytoplasm The contents of a cell between its plasma membrane and its nuclear envelope, consisting of cytosol, organelles, inclusions, and the cytoskeleton.

cytoskeleton A system of protein microfilaments, intermediate filaments, and microtubules in a cell, serving in physical support, cellular movement, and the routing of molecules and organelles to their destinations within the cell. fig. 3.24

cytosol A clear, featureless, gelatinous colloid in which the organelles and other internal structures of a cell are embedded.

cytotoxic T cell A T lymphocyte that directly attacks and destroys infected body cells, cancerous cells, and the cells of transplanted tissues.

D

daughter cells Cells that arise from a parent cell by mitosis or meiosis.

deamination (dee-AM-ih-NAY-shun) Removal of an amino group from an organic molecule; a step in the catabolism of amino acids.

decomposition reaction A chemical reaction in which a larger molecule is broken down into smaller ones. *Compare* synthesis reaction.

decussation (DEE-cuh-SAY-shun) The crossing of nerve fibers from the right side of the central nervous system to the left or vice versa, especially in the spinal cord, medulla oblongata, and optic chiasma.

deep Relatively far from the body surface; opposite of *superficial*. For example, most bones are deep to the skeletal muscles.

degranulation Exocytosis and disappearance of cytoplasmic granules, especially in platelets and granulocytes.

denaturation A change in the three-dimensional conformation of a protein that destroys its enzymatic or other functional properties, usually caused by extremes of temperature or pH.

dendrite Extension of a neuron that receives information from other cells or from environmental stimuli and conducts signals to the soma. Dendrites are usually shorter, more branched, and more numerous than the axon and are incapable of producing action potentials. fig. 12.4

dendritic cell An antigen-presenting cell of the epidermis and mucous membranes. fig. 6.3

denervation atrophy The shrinkage of skeletal muscle that occurs when the motor neuron dies or is severed from the muscle.

dense connective tissue A connective tissue with a high density of fiber, relatively little ground substance, and scanty cells; seen in tendons and the dermis, for example.

depolarization A shift in the electrical potential across a plasma membrane to a value less negative than the resting membrane potential; associated with excitation of a nerve or muscle cell. *Compare* hyperpolarization.

dermal papilla A bump or ridge of dermis that extends upward to interdigitate with the epidermis and create a wavy boundary that resists stress and slippage of the epidermis.

dermis The deeper of the two layers of the skin, underlying the epidermis and composed of fibrous connective tissue.

desmosome (DEZ-mo-some) A patchlike intercellular junction that mechanically links two cells together. fig. 5.28

diabetes (DY-uh-BEE-teez) Any disease characterized by chronic polyuria of metabolic origin; diabetes mellitus unless otherwise specified.

diabetes insipidus (in-SIP-ih-dus) A form of diabetes that results from hyposecretion of antidiuretic hormone; unlike other forms, it is not characterized by hyperglycemia or glycosuria.

diabetes mellitus (DM) (mel-EYE-tus) A form of diabetes that results from hyposecretion of insulin or from a deficient target-cell response to it; signs include hyperglycemia and glycosuria.

diaphysis (dy-AF-ih-sis) The shaft of a long bone. fig. 7.1

diarthrosis (DY-ar-THRO-sis) *See* synovial joint.

diastole (dy-ASS-toe-lee) A period in which a heart chamber relaxes and fills with blood; especially ventricular relaxation.

diastolic pressure (DY-ah-STAHL-ic) The minimum arterial blood pressure measured during the interval between heartbeats

diencephalon (DY-en-SEFF-uh-lon) A portion of the brain between the midbrain and corpus callosum; composed of the thalamus, epithalamus, and hypothalamus. fig. 14.12

differentiation Development of a relatively unspecialized cell or tissue into one with a more specific structure and function.

diffusion Spontaneous net movement of particles from a place of high concentration to a place of low concentration (down a concentration gradient).

diploid (2n) In humans, having 46 chromosomes in 23 homologous pairs, with one member of each chromosome pair coming from each parent.

disaccharide (dy-SAC-uh-ride) A carbohydrate composed of two simple sugars (monosaccharides) joined by a glycosidic bond; for example, lactose, sucrose, and maltose. fig. 2.16

disseminated intravascular coagulation (DIC) Widespread clotting of the blood within unbroken vessels, leading to hemorrhaging, congestion of the vessels with clotted blood, and ischemia and necrosis of organs.

distal Relatively distant from a point of origin or attachment; for example, the wrist is distal to the elbow. *Compare* proximal.

disulfide bond A covalent bond that links two cysteine residues through their sulfur atoms, serving to join one peptide chain to another or to hold a single chain in its three-dimensional conformation.

diuretic (DY-you-RET-ic) A chemical that increases urine output.

dominant 1. Pertaining to a genetic allele that is phenotypically expressed in the presence of any other allele. **2.** Pertaining to a trait that results from a dominant allele.

dopamine (DOE-puh-meen) An inhibitory catecholamine neurotransmitter of the central nervous system, especially of the basal nuclei, where it acts to suppress unwanted motor activity. fig. 12.22

dorsal Toward the back (spinal) side of the body; in humans, usually synonymous with *posterior*.

dorsal root *See* posterior root.

dorsiflexion (DOR-sih-FLEC-shun) A movement of the ankle that reduces the joint angle and raises the toes. fig. 9.22

duodenum (DEW-oh-DEE-num, dew-ODD-eh-num) The first portion of the small intestine extending for about 25 cm from the pyloric valve of the stomach to a sharp bend called the *duodenojejunal flexure*; receives chyme

from the stomach and secretions from the liver and pancreas. fig. 25.25

dynein (DINE-een) A motor protein involved in the beating of cilia and flagella and in the movement of molecules and organelles within cells, as in retrograde transport in a nerve fiber.

E

eccrine (ECK-rin) Pertaining to gland cells that release their product by exocytosis; also called *merocrine*.

ectoderm The outermost of the three primary germ layers of an embryo; gives rise to the epidermis and nervous system.

ectopic (ec-TOP-ic) In an abnormal location; for example, ectopic pregnancy and ectopic pacemakers of the heart.

edema (eh-DEE-muh) Abnormal accumulation of tissue fluid resulting in swelling of the tissue.

effector A molecule, cell, or organ that carries out a response to a stimulus.

efferent (EFF-ur-ent) Carrying away or out, as in a blood vessel that carries blood away from a tissue or a nerve fiber that conducts signals away from the central nervous system.

elastic fiber A connective tissue fiber, composed of the protein elastin, that stretches under tension and returns to its original length when released; responsible for the resilience of organs such as the skin and lungs.

elasticity The tendency of a stretched structure to return to its original dimensions when tension is released.

electrical synapse A gap junction that enables one cell to stimulate another directly, without the intermediary action of a neurotransmitter; such synapses connect the cells of cardiac muscle and single-unit smooth muscle.

electrolyte A salt that ionizes in water and produces a solution that conducts electricity; loosely speaking, any ion that results from the dissociation of such salts, such as sodium, potassium, calcium, chloride, and bicarbonate ions.

elevation A joint movement that raises a body part, as in hunching the shoulders or closing the mouth.

embolism (EM-bo-lizm) The obstruction of a blood vessel by an embolus.

embolus (EM-bo-lus) Any abnormal traveling object in the bloodstream, such as agglutinated bacteria or blood cells, a blood clot, or an air bubble.

embryo A developing individual from the sixteenth day of gestation when the three primary germ layers have formed, through the end of the eighth week when all of the organ systems are present. *Compare* conceptus, fetus, preembryo.

emphysema (EM-fih-SEE-muh) A degenerative lung disease characterized by a breakdown of alveoli and diminishing surface area available for gas exchange; occurs with aging of the lungs but is greatly accelerated by smoking or air pollution.

endocrine gland (EN-doe-crin) A ductless gland that secretes hormones into the bloodstream; for example, the thyroid and adrenal glands. *Compare* exocrine gland.

endocytosis (EN-doe-sy-TOE-sis) Any process in which a cell forms vesicles from its plasma membrane and takes in large particles, molecules, or droplets of extracellular fluid; for example, phagocytosis and pinocytosis.

endoderm The innermost of the three primary germ layers of an embryo; gives rise to the mucosae of the digestive and respiratory tracts and to their associated glands.

endogenous (en-DODJ-eh-nus) Originating internally, such as the endogenous cholesterol synthesized in the body in contrast to the exogenous cholesterol coming from the diet. *Compare* exogenous.

endometrium (EN-doe-MEE-tree-um) The mucosa of the uterus; the site of implantation and source of menstrual discharge.

endoplasmic reticulum (ER) (EN-doe-PLAZ-mic reh-TIC-you-lum) An extensive system of interconnected cytoplasmic tubules or channels; classified as rough ER or smooth ER depending on the presence or absence of ribosomes on its membrane. fig. 3.28

endothelium (EN-doe-THEEL-ee-um) A simple squamous epithelium that lines the lumens of the blood vessels, heart, and lymphatic vessels.

enteric (en-TERR-ic) Pertaining to the small intestine, as in enteric hormones and enteric nervous system.

eosinophil (EE-oh-SIN-oh-fill) A granulocyte with a large, often bilobed nucleus and coarse cytoplasmic granules that stain with eosin; phagocytizes antigen–antibody complexes, allergens, and inflammatory chemicals and secretes enzymes that combat parasitic infections. table 18.6

epidermis A stratified squamous epithelium that constitutes the superficial layer of the skin, overlying the dermis. fig. 6.3

epinephrine (EP-ih-NEFF-rin) A catecholamine that functions as a neurotransmitter in the sympathetic nervous system and as a hormone secreted by the adrenal medulla; also called *adrenaline*. fig. 12.22

epiphysial plate (EP-ih-FIZ-ee-ul) A plate of hyaline cartilage between the epiphysis and diaphysis of a long bone in a child or adolescent, serving as a growth zone for bone elongation. figs. 7.9, 7.11

epiphysis (eh-PIF-ih-sis) **1.** The head of a long bone. fig. 7.1 **2.** The pineal gland (epiphysis cerebri).

epithelium A type of tissue consisting of one or more layers of closely adhering cells with little intercellular material and no blood vessels; forms the coverings and linings of many organs and the parenchyma of the glands. Also known as *epithelial tissue*.

erectile tissue A tissue that functions by swelling with blood, as in the penis and clitoris and inferior concha of the nasal cavity.

erythrocyte (eh-RITH-ro-site) A red blood cell.

erythropoiesis (eh-RITH-ro-poy-EE-sis) The production of erythrocytes.

erythropoietin (eh-RITH-ro-POY-eh-tin) A hormone that is secreted by the kidneys and liver in response to hypoxemia and stimulates erythropoiesis.

estrogens (ESS-tro-jenz) A family of steroid hormones known especially for producing female secondary sex characteristics and regulating various aspects of the menstrual cycle and pregnancy; major forms are estradiol, estriol, and estrone.

evolution A change in the relative frequencies of alleles in a population over a period of time; the mechanism that produces adaptations in human form and function. *See also* adaptation.

excitability The ability of a cell to respond to a stimulus, especially the ability of nerve and muscle cells to produce membrane voltage changes in response to stimuli.

excitation–contraction coupling Events that link the synaptic stimulation of a muscle cell to the onset of contraction.

excitatory postsynaptic potential (EPSP) A partial depolarization of a postsynaptic neuron or muscle cell in response to a neurotransmitter, making it more likely to reach threshold and produce an action potential.

excretion The process of eliminating metabolic waste products from a cell or from the body. *Compare* secretion.

exocrine gland (EC-so-crin) A gland that secretes its products into another organ or onto the body surface, usually by way of a duct; for example, salivary and gastric glands. *Compare* endocrine gland.

exocytosis (EC-so-sy-TOE-sis) A process in which a vesicle in the cytoplasm of a cell fuses with the plasma membrane and releases its contents from the cell; used in the elimination of cellular wastes, in the release of gland products and neurotransmitters, and for the replacement of membrane removed by endocytosis.

exogenous (ec-SODJ-eh-nus) Originating externally, such as exogenous (dietary) cholesterol; extrinsic. *Compare* endogenous.

expiration 1. Exhaling. **2.** Dying.

extension Movement of a joint that increases the angle between articulating bones (straightens the joint). fig. 9.12 *Compare* flexion.

extracellular fluid (ECF) Any body fluid that is not contained in the cells; for example, blood, lymph, and tissue fluid.

extrinsic (ec-STRIN-sic) **1.** Originating externally, such as extrinsic blood-clotting factors; exogenous. **2.** Not fully contained within a specified organ or region but acting on it, such as the extrinsic muscles of the hand and eye. *Compare* intrinsic.

F

facilitated diffusion The process of transporting a chemical through a cellular membrane, down its concentration gradient, with the aid of a carrier that does not consume ATP; enables substances to diffuse through the membrane that would do so poorly, or not at all, without a carrier.

facilitation Making a process more likely to occur, such as the firing of a neuron, or making it occur more easily or rapidly, as in facilitated diffusion.

fascia (FASH-ee-uh) A layer of connective tissue between the muscles or separating the muscles from the skin. fig. 10.1

fascicle (FASS-ih-cul) A bundle of muscle or nerve fibers ensheathed in connective tissue; multiple fascicles bound together constitute a muscle or nerve as a whole. figs. 10.1, 13.9

fat 1. A triglyceride molecule. **2.** Adipose tissue.

fatty acid An organic molecule composed of a chain of an even number of carbon atoms with a carboxyl group at one end and a methyl group at the other; one of the structural subunits of triglycerides and phospholipids.

fenestrated (FEN-eh-stray-ted) Perforated with holes or slits, as in fenestrated blood capillaries and the elastic sheets of large arteries. fig. 20.5

fetus In human development, an individual from the beginning of the ninth week when all of the organ systems are present, through the time of birth. *Compare* conceptus, embryo, preembryo.

fibrin (FY-brin) A sticky fibrous protein formed from fibrinogen in blood, tissue fluid, and lymph; forms the matrix of a blood clot.

fibroblast A connective tissue cell that produces collagen fibers and ground substance; the only type of cell in tendons and ligaments.

fibrosis Replacement of damaged tissue with fibrous scar tissue rather than by the original tissue type; scarring. *Compare* regeneration.

fibrous connective tissue Any connective tissue with a preponderance of fiber, such as areolar, reticular, dense regular, and dense irregular connective tissues.

filtration A process in which hydrostatic pressure forces a fluid through a selectively permeable membrane (especially a capillary wall).

fire To produce an action potential, as in nerve and muscle cells.

fix 1. To hold a structure in place; for example, by fixator muscles that prevent unwanted joint movements. **2.** To preserve a tissue by means of a fixative such as formalin.

flexion A joint movement that, in most cases, decreases the angle between two bones. fig. 9.12 *Compare* extension.

fluid balance A state in which average daily water gains (by intake and synthesis) equal water losses, and water is properly distributed among the body's fluid compartments. *Also called* water balance.

fluid compartment Any of the major categories of fluid in the body, separated by selectively permeable membranes and differing from each other in chemical composition. Primary examples are the intracellular fluid, tissue fluid, blood, and lymph.

follicle (FOLL-ih-cul) **1.** A small space, such as a hair follicle, thyroid follicle, or ovarian follicle. **2.** An aggregation of lymphocytes in a lymphatic organ or mucous membrane.

follicle-stimulating hormone (FSH) A hormone secreted by the anterior pituitary gland that stimulates development of the ovarian follicles and egg cells in females and sperm production in males.

foramen (fo-RAY-men) (plural, *foramina*) A hole through a bone or other organ, in many cases providing passage for blood vessels and nerves.

formed element An erythrocyte, leukocyte, or platelet; any cellular component of blood or lymph as opposed to the extracellular fluid component.

fossa (FOSS-uh) A depression in an organ or tissue, such as the fossa ovalis of the heart, cranial fossa of the skull, or olecranon fossa of the elbow.

fovea (FO-vee-uh) A small pit, such as the fovea capitis of the femur or fovea centralis of the retina.

free energy The potential energy in a chemical that is available to do work.

free radical A particle derived from an atom or molecule, having an unpaired electron that makes it highly reactive and destructive to cells; produced by intrinsic processes such as aerobic respiration and by extrinsic agents such as chemicals and ionizing radiation.

frenulum (FREN-you-lum) A fold of tissue that attaches a movable structure to a relatively immovable one, such as the lip to the gum or the tongue to the floor of the mouth. fig. 25.4

frontal plane An anatomical plane that passes through the body or an organ from right to left and superior to inferior, dividing the body or organ into anterior and posterior portions; also called a *coronal plane*. fig. A.1

fundus The base, the broadest part, or the part farthest from the opening of certain viscera such as the stomach and uterus.

funiculus (few-NICK-you-lus) A bundle of nerve fibers in the spinal cord, arranged in three pairs constituting the spinal white matter; subdivided into tracts (fasciculi). fig. 13.3

fusiform (FEW-zih-form) Shaped like the spindle of a spinning wheel; elongated, thick in the middle, and tapered at both ends, such as the shape of a smooth muscle cell or a muscle spindle.

G

gamete (GAM-eet) An egg or sperm cell.

gametogenesis (geh-ME-to-JEN-eh-sis) The production of eggs or sperm.

ganglion (GANG-glee-un) A cluster of nerve cell bodies in the peripheral nervous system, often resembling a knot in a string.

gangrene Tissue necrosis resulting from ischemia.

gap junction A junction between two cells consisting of a pore surrounded by a ring of proteins in the plasma membrane of each cell; allows solutes to diffuse from the cytoplasm of one cell to the next; functions include cell-to-cell nutrient transfer in the developing embryo and electrical communication between cells of cardiac and smooth muscle. *See also* electrical synapse. fig. 5.28

gastric Pertaining to the stomach.

gate A protein channel in a cellular membrane that can open or close in response to chemical, electrical, or mechanical stimuli, thus controlling when substances are allowed to pass through the membrane. May occur in the plasma membrane as well as the membranes of cytoplasmic organelles.

gene An information-containing segment of DNA that codes for the production of a molecule of RNA, which in most cases goes on to play a role in the synthesis of one or more proteins.

gene locus The site on a chromosome where a given gene is located.

genome (JEE-nome) All the genes of one individual, estimated at about 20,000 genes in humans.

genotype (JEE-no-type) The pair of alleles possessed by an individual at one gene locus on a pair of homologous chromosomes; strongly influences the individual's phenotype for a given trait.

germ cell A gamete (sperm or egg) or any precursor cell destined to become a gamete, such as a primary oocyte or spermatogonium.

germ layer Any of the first three tissue layers of an embryo: ectoderm, mesoderm, or endoderm.

gestation (jess-TAY-shun) Pregnancy.

globulin (GLOB-you-lin) A globular protein such as an enzyme, antibody, or albumin; especially a family of proteins in the blood plasma that includes albumin, antibodies, fibrinogen, and prothrombin.

glomerular capsule (glo-MERR-you-lur) A double-walled capsule around each glomerulus of the kidney; receives glomerular filtrate and empties into the proximal convoluted tubule. fig. 23.7

glomerulus (glo-MERR-you-lus) **1.** A spheroidal mass of blood capillaries in the kidney that filters plasma and produces glomerular filtrate, which is further processed to form the urine. fig. 23.7 **2.** A spheroidal mass of nerve endings in the olfactory bulb where olfactory neurons from the nose synapse with mitral and dendritic cells of the bulb. fig. 16.7

glucagon (GLUE-ca-gon) A hormone secreted by alpha cells of the pancreatic islets in response to hypoglycemia; promotes glycogenolysis and other effects that raise blood glucose concentration.

glucocorticoid (GLUE-co-COR-tih-coyd) Any hormone of the adrenal cortex that affects carbohydrate, fat, and protein metabolism; chiefly cortisol and corticosterone.

gluconeogenesis (GLUE-co-NEE-oh-JEN-eh-sis) The synthesis of glucose from noncarbohydrates such as fats and amino acids.

glucose A monosaccharide ($C_6H_{12}O_6$) also known as blood sugar; glycogen, starch, cellulose, and maltose are made entirely of glucose, and glucose constitutes half of a sucrose or lactose molecule. The isomer involved in human physiology is also called *dextrose*.

glucose-sparing effect An effect of fats or other energy substrates in which they are used as fuel by most cells, so that those cells do not consume glucose; this makes more glucose available to cells such as neurons that cannot use alternative energy substrates.

glycocalyx (GLY-co-CAY-licks) A layer of carbohydrate molecules covalently bonded to the phospholipids and proteins of a plasma membrane; forms a surface coat on all human cells.

glycogen (GLY-co-jen) A glucose polymer synthesized by liver, muscle, uterine, and vaginal cells that serves as an energy-storage polysaccharide.

glycogenesis (GLY-co-JEN-eh-sis) The synthesis of glycogen.

glycogenolysis (GLY-co-jeh-NOLL-ih-sis) The hydrolysis of glycogen, releasing glucose.

glycolipid (GLY-co-LIP-id) A phospholipid molecule with a carbohydrate covalently

bonded to it, found in the plasma membranes of cells.

glycolysis (gly-COLL-ih-sis) A series of anaerobic oxidation reactions that break a glucose molecule into two molecules of pyruvate and produce a small amount of ATP.

glycoprotein (GLY-co-PRO-teen) A protein molecule with a smaller carbohydrate covalently bonded to it; found in mucus and the glycocalyx of cells, for example.

glycosaminoglycan (GAG) (GLY-co-seh-ME-no-GLY-can) A polysaccharide composed of modified sugars with amino groups; the major component of a proteoglycan. GAGs are largely responsible for the viscous consistency of tissue gel and the stiffness of cartilage.

glycosuria (GLY-co-SOOR-ee-uh) The presence of glucose in the urine, typically indicative of a kidney disease, diabetes mellitus, or other endocrine disorder.

goblet cell A mucus-secreting gland cell, shaped somewhat like a wineglass, found in the epithelia of many mucous membranes. fig. 5.33a

Golgi complex (GOAL-jee) An organelle composed of several parallel cisterns, somewhat like a stack of saucers, that modifies and packages newly synthesized proteins and synthesizes carbohydrates. fig. 3.29

Golgi vesicle A membrane-bounded vesicle pinched from the Golgi complex, containing its chemical product; may be retained in the cell as a lysosome or become a secretory vesicle that releases the product by exocytosis.

gonad The ovary or testis.

gonadotropin (go-NAD-oh-TRO-pin) A pituitary hormone that stimulates the gonads; specifically FSH and LH.

G protein A protein of the plasma membrane that is activated by a membrane receptor and, in turn, opens an ion channel or activates an intracellular physiological response; important in linking ligand–receptor binding to second-messenger systems.

gradient A difference or change in any variable, such as pressure or chemical concentration, from one point in space to another; provides a basis for molecular movements such as gas exchange, osmosis, and facilitated diffusion, and for bulk movements such as the flow of blood, air, and heat.

gray matter A zone or layer of tissue in the central nervous system where the neuron cell bodies, dendrites, and synapses are found; forms the cerebral cortex and basal nuclei; cerebellar cortex and deep nuclei; nuclei of the brainstem; and core of the spinal cord. fig. 14.6c

gross anatomy Bodily structure that can be observed without magnification.

growth factor A chemical messenger that stimulates mitosis and differentiation of target cells that have receptors for it; important in such processes as fetal development, tissue maintenance and repair, and hematopoiesis; sometimes a contributing factor in cancer.

growth hormone (GH) A hormone of the anterior pituitary gland with multiple effects on many tissues, generally promoting tissue growth.

gustation (gus-TAY-shun) The sense of taste.

gyrus (JY-rus) A wrinkle or fold in the cortex of the cerebrum or cerebellum.

H

hair cell Sensory cell of the cochlea, semi-circular ducts, utricle, and saccule, with a fringe of surface microvilli that respond to the relative motion of a gelatinous membrane at their tips; responsible for the senses of hearing, body position, and motion.

hair follicle An epidermal pit that contains a hair and extends into the dermis or hypodermis.

half-life (T$_{1/2}$) 1. The time required for one-half of a quantity of a radioactive element to decay to a stable isotope *(physical half-life)* or to be cleared from the body through a combination of radioactive decay and physiological excretion *(biological half-life)*. **2.** The time required for one-half of a quantity of hormone to be cleared from the bloodstream.

haploid (n) In humans, having 23 unpaired chromosomes instead of the usual 46 chromosomes in homologous pairs; in any organism or cell, having half the normal diploid number of chromosomes for that species.

helper T cell A type of lymphocyte that performs a central coordinating role in humoral and cellular immunity; target of the human immunodeficiency virus (HIV).

hematocrit (he-MAT-oh-crit) The percentage of blood volume that is composed of erythrocytes; also called *packed cell volume.*

hematoma (HE-muh-TOE-muh) A mass of clotted blood in the tissues; forms a bruise when visible through the skin.

hematopoiesis (he-MAT-o-poy-EE-sis) Production of any of the formed elements of blood.

hematopoietic stem cell (HSC) A cell of the red bone marrow that can give rise, through a series of intermediate cells, to erythrocytes, platelets, various kinds of macrophages, and any type of leukocyte.

heme (pronounced "heem") The nonprotein, iron-containing prosthetic group of hemoglobin or myoglobin; oxygen binds to its iron atom. fig. 18.5

hemoglobin (HE-mo-GLO-bin) The red gas transport pigment of an erythrocyte.

heparin (HEP-uh-rin) A polysaccharide secreted by basophils and mast cells that inhibits blood clotting.

hepatic (heh-PAT-ic) Pertaining to the liver.

hepatic portal system A network of blood vessels that connect capillaries of the intestines to capillaries (sinusoids) of the liver, thus delivering newly absorbed nutrients directly to the liver.

heterozygous (HET-er-oh-ZY-gus) Having nonidentical alleles at the same gene locus of two homologous chromosomes.

high-density lipoprotein (HDL) A lipoprotein of the blood plasma that is about 50% lipid and 50% protein; functions to transport phospholipids and cholesterol from other organs to the liver for disposal. A high proportion of HDL to low-density lipoprotein (LDL) is desirable for cardiovascular health.

hilum (HY-lum) A point on the surface of an organ where blood vessels, lymphatic vessels, or nerves enter and leave, usually marked by a depression and slit; the midpoint of the concave surface of any organ that is roughly bean-shaped, such as the lymph nodes, kidneys, and lungs. Also called the *hilus.* fig. 22.9b

histamine An amino acid derivative secreted by basophils, mast cells, and some neurons; functions as a paracrine secretion and neurotransmitter to stimulate effects such as gastric secretion, bronchoconstriction, and vasodilation. fig. 12.22

histology 1. The microscopic structure of tissues and organs. **2.** The study of such structure.

homeostasis (HO-me-oh-STAY-sis) The tendency of a living body to maintain relatively stable internal conditions in spite of greater changes in its external environment.

homologous (ho-MOLL-uh-gus) **1.** Having the same embryonic or evolutionary origin but not necessarily the same function, such as the scrotum and labia majora. **2.** Pertaining to two chromosomes with identical structures and gene loci but not necessarily identical alleles; each member of the pair is inherited from a different parent.

homozygous (HO-mo-ZY-gus) Having identical alleles at the same gene locus of two homologous chromosomes.

hormone A chemical messenger that is secreted by an endocrine gland or isolated gland cell, travels in the bloodstream, and triggers a physiological response in distant cells with receptors for it.

host cell Any cell belonging to the human body, as opposed to foreign cells introduced to it by such causes as infections and tissue transplants.

human chorionic gonadotropin (HCG) A hormone of pregnancy secreted by the chorion that stimulates continued growth of the corpus luteum and secretion of its hormones. HCG in urine is the basis for pregnancy testing.

human immunodeficiency virus (HIV) A virus that infects human helper T cells and other cells, suppresses immunity, and causes AIDS.

hyaline cartilage (HY-uh-lin) A form of cartilage with a relatively clear matrix and fine collagen fibers but no conspicuous elastic fibers or coarse collagen bundles as in other types of cartilage.

hyaluronic acid (HI-ul-yur-ON-ic) A glycosaminoglycan that is particularly abundant in connective tissues, where it becomes hydrated and forms the tissue gel.

hydrogen bond A weak attraction between a slightly positive hydrogen atom on one molecule and a slightly negative oxygen or nitrogen atom on another molecule, or between such atoms on different parts of the same molecule; responsible for the cohesion of water and the coiling of protein and DNA molecules, for example.

hydrolysis (hy-DROL-ih-sis) A chemical reaction that breaks a covalent bond in a molecule by adding an —OH group to one side of the bond and —H to the other side, thus consuming a water molecule.

hydrophilic (HY-dro-FILL-ic) Pertaining to molecules that attract water or dissolve in it because of their polar nature.

hydrophobic (HY-dro-FOE-bic) Pertaining to molecules that do not attract water or dissolve in it because of their nonpolar nature; such molecules tend to dissolve in lipids and other nonpolar solvents.

hydrostatic pressure The physical force exerted against a surface by a liquid such as blood or tissue fluid, as opposed to osmotic and atmospheric pressures.

hypercalcemia (HY-per-cal-SEE-me-uh) An excess of calcium ions in the blood.

hypercapnia (HY-pur-CAP-nee-uh) An excess of carbon dioxide in the blood.

hyperextension A joint movement that increases the angle between two bones beyond 180°. fig. 9.12

hyperglycemia (HY-pur-gly-SEE-me-uh) An excess of glucose in the blood.

hyperkalemia (HY-pur-ka-LEE-me-uh) An excess of potassium ions in the blood.

hypernatremia (HY-pur-na-TREE-me-uh) An excess of sodium ions in the blood.

hyperplasia (HY-pur-PLAY-zhuh) The growth of a tissue through cellular multiplication, not cellular enlargement. *Compare* hypertrophy.

hyperpolarization A shift in the electrical potential across a plasma membrane to a value more negative than the resting membrane potential, tending to inhibit a nerve or muscle cell. *Compare* depolarization.

hypersecretion Excessive secretion of a hormone or other gland product; can lead to endocrine disorders such as Addison disease or gigantism, for example.

hypertension Excessively high blood pressure; criteria vary but it is often considered to be a condition in which systolic pressure exceeds 140 mm Hg or diastolic pressure exceeds 90 mm Hg at rest.

hypertonic Having a higher osmotic pressure than human cells or some other reference solution and tending to cause osmotic shrinkage of cells.

hypertrophy (hy-PUR-truh-fee) The growth of a tissue through cellular enlargement, not cellular multiplication; for example, the growth of muscle under the influence of exercise. *Compare* hyperplasia.

hypocalcemia (HY-po-cal-SEE-me-uh) A deficiency of calcium ions in the blood.

hypocapnia (HY-po-CAP-nee-uh) A deficiency of carbon dioxide in the blood.

hypodermis (HY-po-DUR-miss) A layer of connective tissue deep to the skin; also called *superficial fascia, subcutaneous tissue,* or when it is predominantly adipose, *subcutaneous fat.*

hypoglycemia (HY-po-gly-SEE-me-uh) A deficiency of glucose in the blood.

hypokalemia (HY-po-ka-LEE-me-uh) A deficiency of potassium ions in the blood.

hyponatremia (HY-po-na-TREE-me-uh) A deficiency of sodium ions in the blood.

hyposecretion Inadequate secretion of a hormone or other gland product; can lead to endocrine disorders such as diabetes mellitus or pituitary dwarfism, for example.

hypothalamic thermostat A nucleus in the hypothalamus that monitors body temperature and sends afferent signals to hypothalamic heat-promoting or heat-losing centers to maintain thermal homeostasis.

hypothalamus (HY-po-THAL-uh-muss) The inferior portion of the diencephalon of the brain, forming the walls and floor of the third ventricle and giving rise to the posterior pituitary gland; controls many fundamental physiological functions such as appetite, thirst, and body temperature and exerts many of its effects through the endocrine and autonomic nervous systems. fig. 14.12b

hypothesis An informed conjecture that is capable of being tested and potentially falsified by experimentation or data collection. *See also* theory.

hypotonic Having a lower osmotic pressure than human cells or some other reference solution and tending to cause osmotic swelling and lysis of cells.

hypoxemia (HY-pock-SEE-me-uh) A deficiency of oxygen in the bloodstream.

hypoxia (hy-POCK-see-uh) A deficiency of oxygen in any tissue.

I

immune system A system of diverse defenses against disease, including leukocytes and other immune cells, defensive chemicals such as antibodies, physiological processes such as fever and inflammation, and physical barriers to infection such as the skin and mucous membranes; not an organ system in itself but an inclusive term for defensive components of multiple organ systems. *See also* adaptive immunity; innate immunity.

immunity The ability to ward off a specific infection or disease by means of any of the body's innate or adaptive immune mechanisms.

immunoglobulin (IM-you-no-GLOB-you-lin) *See* antibody.

implantation The attachment of a conceptus to the endometrium of the uterus.

inclusion Any visible object in the cytoplasm of a cell other than an organelle or cytoskeletal element; usually a foreign body or a stored cell product, such as a virus, dust particle, lipid droplet, glycogen granule, or pigment.

infarction (in-FARK-shun) **1.** The sudden death of tissue from a lack of blood perfusion. **2.** An area of necrotic tissue produced by this process; also called an *infarct.*

inferior Lower than another structure or point of reference from the perspective of anatomical position; for example, the stomach is inferior to the diaphragm.

inflammation A complex of tissue responses to trauma or infection serving to ward off a pathogen and promote tissue repair; recognized by the cardinal signs of redness, heat, swelling, and pain.

inguinal (IN-gwih-nul) Pertaining to the groin.

inhibitory postsynaptic potential (IPSP) Hyperpolarization of a postsynaptic neuron in response to a neurotransmitter, making it less likely to reach threshold and fire.

innate immunity Nonspecific defenses against infection or disease that are present and functional from birth, work equally against multiple disease agents, do not require prior exposure, and do not possess immune memory. Includes epithelial barriers, natural killer cells, other leukocytes, macrophages, antimicrobial proteins, and the processes of inflammation and fever. *See also* adaptive immunity.

innervation (IN-ur-VAY-shun) The nerve supply to an organ.

insertion Traditionally, the attachment of a skeletal muscle to a bone or other structure that moves when the muscle contracts. This term is now being abandoned by authorities in human anatomy. *Compare* origin.

inspiration 1. Inhaling. **2.** The stimulus that resulted in this book.

integral protein A protein of the plasma membrane that penetrates into or all the way through the phospholipid bilayer. fig. 3.6

integration A process in which a neuron receives input from multiple sources and their combined effects determine its output; the cellular basis of information processing by the nervous system.

intercalated disc (in-TUR-ka-LAY-ted) A complex of fascia adherens, gap junctions, and desmosomes that join two cardiac muscle cells end to end, microscopically visible as a dark line that helps to histologically distinguish this muscle type; functions as a mechanical and electrical link between cells. fig. 19.11

intercellular Between cells.

intercostal (IN-tur-COSS-tul) Between the ribs, as in the intercostal muscles, arteries, veins, and nerves.

interdigitate (IN-tur-DIDJ-ih-tate) To fit together like the fingers of two folded hands; for example, at the dermal–epidermal boundary, intercalated discs of the heart, and foot processes of the podocytes in the kidney. fig. 23.10b

interleukin (IN-tur-LOO-kin) A hormonelike chemical messenger from one leukocyte to another, serving as a means of communication and coordination during immune responses.

interneuron (IN-tur-NEW-ron) A neuron that is contained entirely in the central nervous system and, in the path of signal conduction, lies anywhere between an afferent pathway and an efferent pathway.

interosseous membrane (IN-tur-OSS-ee-us) A fibrous membrane that connects the radius to the ulna and the tibia to the fibula along most of the shaft of each bone. fig. 8.34

interphase That part of the cell cycle between one mitotic phase and the next, from the end of cytokinesis to the beginning of the next prophase.

interstitial (IN-tur-STISH-ul) **1.** Pertaining to the extracellular spaces in a tissue. **2.** Located between other structures, as in the interstitial cells of the testis and interstitial (extracellular) fluid of the tissues.

intervertebral disc A cartilaginous pad between the bodies of two adjacent vertebrae.

intracellular Within a cell.

intracellular fluid (ICF) The fluid contained in the cells; one of the body's major fluid compartments.

intravenous (I.V.) 1. Present or occurring within a vein, such as an intravenous blood clot. **2.** Introduced directly into a vein, such as an intravenous injection or I.V. drip.

intrinsic (in-TRIN-sic) **1.** Arising from within, such as intrinsic blood-clotting factors; endogenous. **2.** Fully contained within a specified organ or region, such as the intrinsic muscles of the hand and eye. *Compare* extrinsic.

involuntary Not under conscious control, including tissues such as smooth and cardiac muscle and events such as reflexes.

involution (IN-vo-LOO-shun) Shrinkage of a tissue or organ by autolysis, such as involution of the thymus after childhood and of the uterus after pregnancy.

ion A chemical particle with unequal numbers of electrons or protons and consequently a net negative or positive charge; it may have a single atomic nucleus as in a sodium ion or a few atoms as in a bicarbonate ion, or it may be a large molecule such as a protein.

ionic bond The force that binds a cation to an anion.

ionizing radiation High-energy electromagnetic rays that eject electrons from atoms or molecules and convert them to ions, frequently causing cellular damage; for example, X-rays and gamma rays.

ipsilateral (IP-sih-LAT-ur-ul) On the same side of the body, as in reflex arcs in which a muscular response occurs on the same side of the body as the stimulus. *Compare* contralateral.

ischemia (iss-KEE-me-uh) Insufficient blood flow to a tissue, typically resulting in metabolite accumulation and sometimes tissue death.

isometric Pertaining to a form of muscle contraction in which internal tension increases but the muscle does not change length or move a resisting object.

isotonic 1. Having the same osmotic pressure as human cells or some other reference solution. **2.** Pertaining to a form of muscle contraction in which a muscle changes length but maintains a constant amount of tension.

J

jaundice (JAWN-diss) A yellowish color of the skin, corneas, mucous membranes, and body fluids due to an excessive concentration of bilirubin; usually indicative of a liver disease, obstructed bile secretion, or hemolytic disease.

K

ketone (KEE-tone) Any organic compound with a carbonyl (C=O) group covalently bonded to a two-carbon backbone.

ketone bodies Certain ketones (acetone, acetoacetic acid, and β-hydroxybutyric acid) produced by the incomplete oxidation of fats, especially when fats are being rapidly catabolized. *See also* ketosis.

ketonuria (KEE-toe-NEW-ree-uh) The abnormal presence of ketones in the urine; a sign of diabetes mellitus but also occurring in other conditions that entail rapid fat oxidation.

ketosis (kee-TOE-sis) An abnormally high concentration of ketone bodies in the blood, occurring in pregnancy, starvation, diabetes mellitus, and other conditions; tends to cause acidosis and to depress the nervous system.

kilocalorie The amount of heat energy needed to raise the temperature of 1 kg of water by 1°C; 1,000 calories. Also called a *Calorie* or *large calorie*. *See also* calorie.

kinase Any enzyme that adds an inorganic phosphate (P_i) group to another organic molecule. Also called a *phosphokinase*.

L

labium (LAY-bee-um) A lip, such as those of the mouth and the labia majora and minora of the vulva.

lactate A small organic acid produced as an end product of the anaerobic fermentation of pyruvate; called *lactic acid* in its nonionized form.

lacuna (la-CUE-nuh) (plural, *lacunae*) A small cavity or depression in a tissue such as bone or cartilage; called a *cavernous space* in erectile tissues of the penis and clitoris.

lamella (la-MELL-uh) A little plate, such as a lamella of bone. fig. 7.4

lamina (LAM-ih-nuh) A thin layer, such as the lamina of a vertebra or the lamina propria of a mucous membrane. fig. 8.22

lamina propria (LAM-ih-nuh PRO-pree-uh) A thin layer of areolar tissue immediately deep to the epithelium of a mucous membrane. fig. 5.33a

larynx (LAIR-inks) A cartilaginous chamber in the neck containing the vocal cords; colloquially called the voicebox.

latent period The interval between a stimulus and response, especially in the action of nerve and muscle cells.

lateral Away from the midline of an organ or median plane of the body; toward the side. *Compare* medial.

law A verbal or mathematical description of a predictable natural phenomenon or of the relationship between variables; for example, Boyle's law of gases and the law of complementary base pairing in DNA.

lesion A circumscribed zone of tissue injury, such as a skin abrasion or myocardial infarction.

leukocyte (LOO-co-site) A white blood cell.

leukotriene (LOO-co-TRY-een) An eicosanoid that promotes allergic and inflammatory responses such as vasodilation and neutrophil chemotaxis; secreted by basophils, mast cells, and damaged tissues.

libido (lih-BEE-do) Sex drive; psychological motivation to engage in sex.

ligament A collagenous band or cord that binds one organ to another, especially one bone to another, and serves to hold organs in place; for example, the cruciate ligaments of the knee, broad ligament of the uterus, and falciform ligament of the liver.

ligand (LIG-and, LY-gand) A chemical that binds reversibly to a receptor site on a protein, such as a neurotransmitter that binds to a membrane receptor or a substrate that binds to an enzyme.

ligand-gated channel A channel protein in a plasma membrane that opens or closes when another chemical (ligand) binds to it, enabling the ligand to determine when substances can enter or leave the cell.

light microscope (LM) A microscope that produces images with visible light.

linea (LIN-ee-uh) An anatomical line, such as the linea alba of the abdomen or linea aspera of the femur.

lingual (LING-gwul) Pertaining to the tongue, as in lingual papillae.

lipase (LY-pace) An enzyme that hydrolyzes a triglyceride into fatty acids and glycerol.

lipid A hydrophobic organic compound composed mainly of carbon and a high ratio of hydrogen to oxygen; includes fatty acids, fats, phospholipids, steroids, and prostaglandins.

lipoprotein (LIP-oh-PRO-teen) A protein-coated lipid droplet in the blood plasma or lymph, serving as a means of lipid transport; for example, chylomicrons and high- and low-density lipoproteins.

load 1. To pick up a gas for transport in the bloodstream. **2.** The resistance acted upon by a muscle.

lobule (LOB-yool) A small subdivision of an organ or of a lobe of an organ, especially of a gland.

locus The site on a chromosome where a given gene is located.

long bone A bone such as the femur or humerus that is markedly longer than wide and that generally serves as a lever.

longitudinal Oriented along the longest dimension of the body or of an organ.

loose connective tissue *See* areolar tissue.

low-density lipoprotein (LDL) A lipoprotein of the blood plasma that is about 80% lipid (mainly cholesterol) and 20% protein; functions to transport cholesterol to target cells. A high proportion of LDL to high-density lipoprotein (HDL) is a risk factor for cardiovascular disease.

lumbar Pertaining to the lower back and sides, between the thoracic cage and pelvis.

lumen (LOO-men) The internal space of a hollow organ such as a blood vessel or the esophagus, or a space surrounded by secretory cells as in a gland acinus.

luteinizing hormone (LH) (LOO-tee-in-ize-ing) A hormone secreted by the anterior pituitary gland that stimulates ovulation in females and testosterone secretion production in males.

lymph The fluid contained in lymphatic vessels and lymph nodes, produced by the absorption of tissue fluid.

lymphatic system (lim-FAT-ic) An organ system consisting of lymphatic vessels, lymph nodes, the tonsils, spleen, and thymus; functions include tissue fluid recovery and immunity.

lymph node A small organ found along the course of a lymphatic vessel that filters the lymph and contains lymphocytes and macrophages, which respond to antigens in the lymph. fig. 21.11

lymphocyte (LIM-fo-site) A relatively small agranulocyte with numerous types and roles in innate, humoral, and cellular immunity. table 18.6

lysosome (LY-so-some) A membrane-bounded organelle containing a mixture of enzymes with a variety of intracellular and extracellular roles in digesting foreign matter, pathogens, and expired organelles.

lysozyme (LY-so-zime) An enzyme found in tears, milk, saliva, mucus, and other body fluids that destroys bacteria by digesting their cell walls. Also called *muramidase*.

M

macromolecule Any molecule of large size and high molecular weight, such as a protein, nucleic acid, polysaccharide, or triglyceride.

macrophage (MAC-ro-faje) Any cell of the body, other than a leukocyte, that is specialized for phagocytosis; usually derived from a blood monocyte and often functioning as an antigen-presenting cell.

macula (MAC-you-luh) A patch or spot, such as the macula lutea of the retina and macula sacculi of the inner ear.

malignant (muh-LIG-nent) Pertaining to a cell or tumor that is cancerous; capable of metastasis.

mast cell A connective tissue cell, similar to a basophil, that secretes histamine, heparin, and other chemicals involved in inflammation; often concentrated along the course of blood capillaries.

matrix 1. The extracellular material of a tissue. **2.** The fluid within a mitochondrion containing enzymes of the citric acid cycle. **3.** The substance or framework within which other structures are embedded, such as the fibrous matrix of a blood clot. **4.** A mass of epidermal cells from which a hair root or nail root develops.

mechanoreceptor A sensory nerve ending or organ specialized to detect mechanical stimuli such as touch, pressure, stretch, or vibration.

medial Toward the midline of an organ or median plane of the body. *Compare* lateral.

median plane The sagittal plane that divides the body or an organ into equal right and left halves; also called *midsagittal plane*. fig. A.1

mediastinum (MEE-dee-ah-STY-num) The thick median partition of the thoracic cavity that separates one pleural cavity from the other and contains the heart, great blood vessels, esophagus, trachea, and thymus. fig. A.5

medulla (meh-DULE-uh, meh-DULL-uh) Tissue deep to the cortex of certain two-layered organs such as the lymph nodes, adrenal glands, hairs, and kidneys.

medulla oblongata (meh-DULL-uh OB-long-GAH-ta) The most caudal part of the brainstem, immediately superior to the foramen magnum of the skull, connecting the spinal cord to the rest of the brain. figs. 14.2, 14.8

meiosis (my-OH-sis) A form of cell division in which a diploid cell divides twice and produces four haploid daughter cells; occurs only in gametogenesis.

melanocyte A cell of the stratum basale of the epidermis that synthesizes melanin and transfers it to the keratinocytes.

meninges (meh-NIN-jeez) (singular, *meninx*) Three fibrous membranes between the central nervous system and surrounding bone: the dura mater, arachnoid mater, and pia mater. fig. 14.5

merocrine (MERR-oh-crin) *See* eccrine.

mesenchyme (MES-en-kime) A gelatinous embryonic connective tissue derived from the mesoderm; differentiates into all permanent connective tissues and cardiac and smooth muscle.

mesentery (MESS-en-tare-ee) A serous membrane that binds the intestines together and suspends them from the abdominal wall; the visceral continuation of the peritoneum. fig. 25.3

mesoderm (MES-oh-durm) The middle layer of the three primary germ layers of an embryo; gives rise to muscle and connective tissue.

metabolism (meh-TAB-oh-lizm) Chemical reactions within a living organism.

metabolite (meh-TAB-oh-lite) Any chemical produced by metabolism.

metaplasia Transformation of one mature tissue type into another; for example, a change from pseudostratified to stratified squamous epithelium in an overventilated nasal cavity.

metastasis (meh-TASS-tuh-sis) The spread of cancer cells from the original tumor to a new location, where they seed the development of a new tumor.

microtubule An intracellular cylinder composed of the protein tubulin, forming centrioles, the axonemes of cilia and flagella, and part of the cytoskeleton.

microvillus An outgrowth of the plasma membrane that increases the surface area of a cell and functions in absorption and some sensory processes; distinguished from cilia and flagella by its smaller size and lack of an axoneme.

milliequivalent One-thousandth of an equivalent, which is the amount of an electrolyte that would neutralize 1 mole of H^+ or OH^-. Electrolyte concentrations are commonly expressed in milliequivalents per liter (mEq/L).

mitochondrion (MY-toe-CON-dree-un) An organelle specialized to synthesize ATP, enclosed in a double unit membrane with infoldings of the inner membrane called cristae.

mitosis (my-TOE-sis) A form of cell division in which a cell divides once and produces two genetically identical daughter cells; sometimes used to refer only to the division of the genetic material or nucleus and not to include cytokinesis, the subsequent division of the cytoplasm.

moiety (MOY-eh-tee) A chemically distinct subunit of a macromolecule, such as the heme and globin moieties of hemoglobin or the lipid and carbohydrate moieties of a glycolipid.

molarity A measure of chemical concentration expressed as moles of solute per liter of solution.

mole The mass of a chemical equal to its molecular weight in grams, containing 6.023×10^{23} molecules.

monocyte (MON-oh-site) An agranulocyte specialized to migrate into the tissues and transform into a macrophage. table 18.6

monomer (MON-oh-mur) **1.** One of the identical or similar subunits of a larger molecule in the dimer to polymer range; for example, the glucose monomers of starch, the amino acids of a protein, or the nucleotides of DNA. **2.** One subunit of an antibody molecule, composed of four polypeptides.

monosaccharide (MON-oh-SAC-uh-ride) A simple sugar, or sugar monomer; chiefly glucose, fructose, and galactose.

motor neuron A neuron that transmits signals from the central nervous system to any effector (muscle or gland cell); its axon is an efferent nerve fiber.

motor protein Any protein that produces movements of a cell or its components owing to its ability to undergo quick repetitive changes in conformation and to bind reversibly to other molecules; for example, myosin, dynein, and kinesin.

motor unit One motor neuron and all the skeletal muscle fibers innervated by it.

mucosa (mew-CO-suh) A tissue layer that forms the inner lining of an anatomical tract that is open to the exterior (the respiratory, digestive, urinary, and reproductive tracts). Composed of epithelium, connective tissue (lamina propria), and often smooth muscle (muscularis mucosae). fig. 5.33a

mucous membrane See *mucosa.*

multipotent Pertaining to a stem cell that has the potential to develop into two or more types of fully differentiated, functional cells, but not into an unlimited variety of cell types.

muscle fiber One skeletal muscle cell; a myofiber.

muscle tone A state of continual, partial contraction of resting skeletal or smooth muscle.

muscular system An organ system composed of the skeletal muscles, specialized mainly for maintaining postural support and producing movements of the bones.

muscularis externa The external muscular wall of certain viscera such as the esophagus and small intestine. fig. 25.2

muscularis mucosae (MUSK-you-LERR-iss mew-CO-see) A layer of smooth muscle immediately deep to the lamina propria of a mucosa. fig. 5.33a

mutagen (MEW-tuh-jen) Any agent that causes a mutation, including viruses, chemicals, and ionizing radiation.

mutation Any change in the structure of a chromosome or a DNA molecule, often resulting in a change of organismal structure or function.

myelin (MY-eh-lin) A lipid sheath around a nerve fiber, formed from closely spaced spiral layers of the plasma membrane of a Schwann cell or oligodendrocyte. fig. 12.8

myelin sheath gap A short unmyelinated segment between Schwann cells of a myelinated nerve fiber; site of action potential generation during saltatory conduction; also called *node of Ranvier.* fig. 12.4

myocardium (MY-oh-CAR-dee-um) The middle, muscular layer of the heart.

myoepithelial cell An epithelial cell that has become specialized to contract like a muscle cell; important in dilation of the pupil and ejection of secretions from gland acini.

myofilament A protein microfilament responsible for the contraction of a muscle cell, composed mainly of myosin or actin. fig. 11.2

myoglobin (MY-oh-GLO-bin) A red oxygen-storage pigment of muscle; supplements hemoglobin in providing oxygen for aerobic muscle metabolism.

myosin A motor protein that constitutes the thick myofilaments of muscle and has globular, mobile heads of ATPase that bind to actin molecules; also serves contractile functions in other cell types. fig. 11.3

N

necrosis (neh-CRO-sis) Pathological tissue death due to such causes as infection, trauma, or hypoxia. *Compare* apoptosis.

negative feedback A self-corrective mechanism that underlies most homeostasis, in which a bodily change is detected and responses are activated that reverse the change and restore stability and preserve normal body function.

negative feedback inhibition A mechanism for limiting the secretion of a pituitary tropic hormone. The tropic hormone stimulates another endocrine gland to secrete its own hormone, and that hormone inhibits further release of the tropic hormone.

neonate (NEE-oh-nate) A newborn infant up to 4 weeks old.

neoplasia (NEE-oh-PLAY-zhuh) Abnormal growth of new tissue, such as a tumor, with no useful function.

nephron (NEF-ron) One of approximately 1 million blood-filtering, urine-producing units in each kidney; consists of a glomerulus, glomerular capsule, proximal convoluted tubule, nephron loop, and distal convoluted tubule. fig. 23.8

nerve A cordlike organ of the peripheral nervous system composed of multiple nerve fibers ensheathed in connective tissue.

nerve fiber The axon of a single neuron.

nerve impulse A wave of self-propagating action potentials traveling along a nerve fiber.

nervous tissue A tissue composed of neurons and neuroglia.

net filtration pressure A net force favoring filtration of fluid from a capillary or venule when all the hydrostatic and osmotic pressures of the blood and tissue fluids are taken into account.

neural pool A group of interconnected neurons of the central nervous system that perform a single collective function; for example, the vasomotor center of the brainstem and speech centers of the cerebral cortex.

neural tube A dorsal hollow tube in the embryo that develops into the central nervous system. fig. 14.3

neuroglia (noo-ROG-lee-uh) All cells of nervous tissue except neurons; cells that perform various supportive and protective roles for the neurons.

neuromuscular junction A synapse between a nerve fiber and a muscle fiber; also called a *motor end plate.* fig. 11.7

neuron (NOOR-on) A nerve cell; an electrically excitable cell specialized for producing and conducting action potentials and secreting chemicals that stimulate adjacent cells.

neuropeptide A peptide secreted by a neuron, often serving to modify the action of a neurotransmitter; for example, endorphins, enkephalin, and cholecystokinin. fig. 12.22

neurotransmitter A chemical released at the distal end of an axon that stimulates an adjacent cell; for example, acetylcholine, norepinephrine, or serotonin.

neutrophil (NEW-tro-fill) A granulocyte, usually with a multilobed nucleus, that serves especially to destroy bacteria by means of phagocytosis, intracellular digestion, and secretion of bactericidal chemicals. table 18.6

nitrogenous base (ny-TRODJ-eh-nus) An organic molecule with a single or double carbon–nitrogen ring that forms one of the building blocks of ATP, other nucleotides, and nucleic acids; the basis of the genetic code. fig. 4.1

nitrogenous waste Any nitrogen-containing substance produced as a metabolic waste and excreted in the urine; chiefly ammonia, urea, uric acid, and creatinine.

nociceptor (NO-sih-SEP-tur) A nerve ending specialized to detect tissue damage and produce a sensation of pain; pain receptor.

norepinephrine (NE) (nor-EP-ih-NEF-rin) A catecholamine that functions as a neurotransmitter and adrenal hormone, especially in the sympathetic nervous system. fig. 12.22

nuclear envelope A pair of membranes enclosing the nucleus of a cell, with prominent pores allowing traffic of molecules between the nucleoplasm and cytoplasm. fig. 3.27

nucleic acid (new-CLAY-ic) An acidic polymer of nucleotides found or produced in the nucleus, functioning in heredity and protein synthesis; of two types, DNA and RNA.

nucleotide (NEW-clee-oh-tide) An organic molecule composed of a nitrogenous base, a monosaccharide, and a phosphate group; the monomer of a nucleic acid.

nucleus (NEW-clee-us) **1.** A cell organelle containing DNA and surrounded by a double membrane. **2.** A mass of neurons (gray matter) surrounded by white matter of the brain, including the basal nuclei and brainstem nuclei. **3.** The positively charged core of an atom, consisting of protons and neutrons. **4.** A central structure, such as the nucleus pulposus of an intervertebral disc.

nurse cell A supporting cell in the seminiferous tubules of the testes, acting to enfold and protect developing germ cells and promote the production of sperm; also called *Sertoli cell; sustentacular cell.*

O

olfaction (ole-FAC-shun) The sense of smell.

oncotic pressure (on-COT-ic) The difference between the colloid osmotic pressure of the blood and that of the tissue fluid, usually favoring fluid absorption by the blood capillaries. *Compare* colloid osmotic pressure.

oocyte (OH-oh-site) In the development of an egg cell, any haploid stage between meiosis I and fertilization.

oogenesis (OH-oh-JEN-eh-sis) The production of a fertilizable egg cell through a series of mitotic and meiotic cell divisions; female gametogenesis.

opposition A movement of the thumb in which it approaches or touches any fingertip of the same hand.

orbit The eye socket of the skull.

organ Any anatomical structure that is composed of at least two different tissue types, has recognizable structural boundaries, and has a discrete function different from the structures around it. Many organs are microscopic and many organs contain smaller organs, such as the skin containing numerous microscopic sense organs.

organelle Any structure within a cell that carries out one of its metabolic roles, such as mitochondria, centrioles, endoplasmic reticulum, and the nucleus; an intracellular structure other than the cytoskeleton and inclusions.

origin Traditionally, the relatively stationary attachment of a skeletal muscle to a bone or other structure. This term is now being abandoned by authorities in human anatomy. *Compare* insertion.

osmolality (OZ-mo-LAL-ih-tee) The molar concentration of dissolved particles in 1 kg of water.

osmolarity (OZ-mo-LERR-ih-tee) The molar concentration of dissolved particles in 1 L of solution.

osmoreceptor (OZ-mo-re-SEP-tur) A neuron of the hypothalamus that responds to changes in the osmolarity of the extracellular fluid.

osmosis (oz-MO-sis) The net flow of water through a selectively permeable membrane, resulting from either a chemical concentration difference or a mechanical force across the membrane.

osmotic pressure The amount of pressure that would have to be applied to one side of a selectively permeable membrane to stop osmosis; proportional to the concentration of nonpermeating solutes on that side and therefore serving as an indicator of solute concentration.

osseous (OSS-ee-us) Pertaining to bone.

ossification (OSS-ih-fih-CAY-shun) Bone formation.

osteoblast Bone-forming cell that arises from an osteogenic cell, deposits bone matrix, and eventually becomes an osteocyte.

osteoclast Macrophage of the bone surface that dissolves the matrix and returns minerals to the extracellular fluid.

osteocyte A mature bone cell formed when an osteoblast becomes surrounded by its own matrix and entrapped in a lacuna.

osteon A structural unit of compact bone consisting of a central canal surrounded by concentric cylindrical lamellae of matrix. fig. 7.4

osteoporosis (OSS-tee-oh-pore-OH-sis) A degenerative bone disease characterized by a loss of bone mass, increasing susceptibility to spontaneous fractures, and sometimes deformity of the vertebral column; causes include aging, estrogen hyposecretion, and insufficient resistance exercise.

ovulation (OV-you-LAY-shun) The release of a mature oocyte by the bursting of an ovarian follicle.

ovum Any stage of the female gamete from primary oocyte until fertilization; a primary or secondary oocyte; an egg.

oxidation A chemical reaction in which one or more electrons are removed from a molecule, lowering its free energy content; opposite of reduction and always linked to a reduction reaction.

P

pancreatic islet (PAN-cree-AT-ic EYE-let) A small cluster of endocrine cells in the pancreas that secretes insulin, glucagon, somatostatin, and other intercellular messengers; also called *islet of Langerhans.* fig. 17.12

papilla (pa-PILL-uh) A conical or nipplelike structure, such as a lingual papilla of the tongue or the papilla of a hair bulb.

papillary (PAP-ih-lerr-ee) **1.** Pertaining to or shaped like a nipple, such as the papillary muscles of the heart. **2.** Having papillae, such as the papillary layer of the dermis.

paracrine (PAIR-uh-crin) **1.** A chemical messenger similar to a hormone whose effects are restricted to the immediate vicinity of the cells that secrete it; sometimes called a *local hormone.* **2.** Pertaining to such a secretion, as opposed to *endocrine.*

parasympathetic nervous system (PERR-uh-SIM-pa-THET-ic) A division of the autonomic nervous system that issues efferent fibers through the cranial and sacral nerves and exerts cholinergic effects on its target organs.

parathyroid hormone (PTH) A hormone secreted by the parathyroid glands that raises blood calcium concentration by stimulating bone resorption by osteoclasts, promoting intestinal absorption of calcium, and inhibiting urinary excretion of calcium.

parenchyma (pa-REN-kih-muh) The tissue that performs the main physiological functions of an organ, especially a gland, as opposed to the tissues (stroma) that mainly provide structural support.

parietal (pa-RY-eh-tul) **1.** Pertaining to a wall, as in the parietal cells of the stomach and parietal bone of the skull. **2.** Pertaining to the outer or more superficial layer of a two-layered membrane such as the pleura, pericardium, or glomerular capsule. *Compare* visceral. fig. A.6

pathogen Any disease-causing microorganism.

pedicle (PED-ih-cul) A small footlike process, as in the vertebrae and renal podocytes; also called a *pedicel.*

pelvic cavity The space enclosed by the true (lesser) pelvis, containing the urinary bladder, rectum, and internal reproductive organs.

pelvis A basinlike structure such as the pelvic girdle of the skeleton or the urine-collecting space near the hilum of the kidney. figs. 8.36, 23.4

peptide Any chain of two or more amino acids. *See also* polypeptide, protein.

peptide bond A group of four covalently bonded atoms (a —C=O group bonded to an —NH group) that links two amino acids in a protein or other peptide. fig. 2.23b

perfusion The amount of blood supplied to a given mass of tissue in a given period of time (such as mL/g/min.).

perichondrium (PERR-ih-CON-dree-um) A layer of fibrous connective tissue covering the surface of hyaline or elastic cartilage.

perineum (PERR-ih-NEE-um) The region between the thighs bordered by the coccyx, pubic symphysis, and ischial tuberosities; contains the orifices of the urinary, reproductive, and digestive systems. figs. 27.6, 28.8

periosteum (PERR-ee-OSS-tee-um) A layer of fibrous connective tissue covering the surface of a bone. fig. 7.1

peripheral nervous system (PNS) A subdivision of the nervous system composed of all nerves and ganglia; all of the nervous system except the central nervous system.

peripheral protein A protein of the plasma membrane that clings to its intracellular or extracellular surface but does not penetrate into the phospholipid bilayer.

peristalsis (PERR-ih-STAL-sis) A wave of constriction traveling along a tubular organ such as the esophagus or ureter, serving to propel its contents.

peritoneum (PERR-ih-toe-NEE-um) A serous membrane that lines the peritoneal cavity of the abdomen and covers the mesenteries and viscera.

perivascular (PERR-ih-VASS-cue-lur) Pertaining to the region surrounding a blood vessel.

phagocytosis (FAG-oh-sy-TOE-sis) A form of endocytosis in which a cell surrounds a foreign particle with pseudopods and engulfs it, enclosing it in a cytoplasmic vesicle called a *phagosome*.

phalanx (FAY-lanks) (plural, *phalanges*) Any of the bones in the fingers or toes; there are two in the thumb and great toe and three in each of the other digits.

pharynx (FAIR-inks, FAR-inks) A muscular passage in the throat at which the respiratory and digestive tracts cross.

phospholipid An amphipathic molecule composed of two fatty acids and a phosphate-containing group bonded to the three carbons of a glycerol molecule; composes most of the molecules of the plasma membrane and other cellular membranes.

phosphorylation Addition of an inorganic phosphate (P_i) group to an organic molecule.

piloerector *See* arrector.

pinocytosis (PIN-oh-sy-TOE-sis) A form of endocytosis in which the plasma membrane sinks inward and imbibes droplets of extracellular fluid.

plantar (PLAN-tur) Pertaining to the sole of the foot.

plaque A small scale or plate of matter, such as dental plaque, the fatty plaques of atherosclerosis, and the amyloid plaques of Alzheimer disease.

plasma The noncellular portion of the blood; its liquid matrix, usually constituting slightly over one-half of its volume.

plasma membrane The membrane that encloses a cell and controls the traffic of molecules in and out of the cell. fig. 3.5

platelet A formed element of the blood derived from a megakaryocyte, known especially for its role in stopping bleeding, but with additional roles in dissolving blood clots, stimulating inflammation, promoting tissue growth and blood vessel maintenance, and destroying bacteria.

pleura (PLOOR-uh) A double-walled serous membrane that encloses each lung.

plexus A network of blood vessels, lymphatic vessels, or nerves, such as a choroid plexus of the brain or brachial plexus of nerves.

pluripotent Pertaining to a stem cell of the inner cell mass of a blastocyst that is capable of developing into any type of embryonic cell, but not into cells of the accessory organs of pregnancy.

polymer A molecule that consists of a long chain of identical or similar subunits, such as protein, DNA, and starch.

polypeptide Any chain of more than 10 or 15 amino acids. *See also* protein.

polysaccharide (POL-ee-SAC-uh-ride) A polymer of simple sugars; for example, glycogen, starch, and cellulose. fig. 2.17

polyuria (POL-ee-YOU-ree-uh) Excessive output of urine.

popliteal (pop-LIT-ee-ul) Pertaining to the posterior aspect of the knee.

positron emission tomography (PET) A method of producing a computerized image of the physiological state of a tissue using injected radioisotopes that emit positrons.

posterior Near or pertaining to the back or spinal side of the body; dorsal.

posterior root The branch of a spinal nerve that enters the posterior side of the spinal cord and carries afferent (sensory) nerve fibers; often called *dorsal root*. fig. 13.2b

postganglionic (POST-gang-glee-ON-ic) Pertaining to a neuron that conducts signals from a ganglion to a more distal target organ.

postsynaptic (POST-sih-NAP-tic) Pertaining to a neuron or other cell that receives signals from the presynaptic neuron at a synapse. fig. 12.19

potential A difference in electrical charge from one point to another, especially on opposite sides of a plasma membrane; usually measured in millivolts.

preembryo A developing individual from the time of fertilization to the time, at 16 days, when the three primary germ layers have formed. *Compare* conceptus, embryo, fetus.

preganglionic (PRE-gang-glee-ON-ic) Pertaining to a neuron that conducts signals from the central nervous system to a ganglion.

presynaptic (PRE-sih-NAP-tic) Pertaining to a neuron that conducts signals to a synapse. fig. 12.19

primary germ layers The ectoderm, mesoderm, and endoderm; the three tissue layers of an early embryo from which all later tissues and organs arise.

prime mover The muscle that produces the most force in a given joint action; agonist.

programmed cell death *See* apoptosis.

prolactin (PRL) A hormone secreted by the anterior pituitary gland that stimulates the mammary glands to secrete milk.

pronation (pro-NAY-shun) A rotational movement of the forearm that turns the palm downward or posteriorly. fig. 9.18

proprioception (PRO-pree-oh-SEP-shun) The nonvisual perception, usually subconscious, of the position and movements of the body, resulting from input from proprioceptors and the vestibular apparatus of the inner ear.

proprioceptor (PRO-pree-oh-SEP-tur) A sensory receptor of the muscles, tendons, and joint capsules that detects muscle contractions and joint movements.

prostaglandin (PROSS-ta-GLAN-din) An eicosanoid with a five-sided carbon ring in the middle of a hydrocarbon chain, playing a variety of roles in inflammation, neurotransmission, vasomotion, reproduction, and metabolism. fig. 2.21

prostate (PROSS-tate) A male reproductive gland that encircles the urethra immediately inferior to the bladder and contributes to the semen. (Avoid the mispronunciation "prostrate.") fig. 27.10

protein A large polypeptide; while criteria for a protein are somewhat subjective and variable, polypeptides over 50 amino acids long are generally classified as proteins.

proteoglycan (PRO-tee-oh-GLY-can) A large molecule composed of a bristlelike arrangement of glycosaminoglycans surrounding a protein core in a shape resembling a bottle brush. Binds cells to extracellular materials and gives the tissue fluid a gelatinous consistency.

proximal Relatively near a point of origin or attachment; for example, the shoulder is proximal to the elbow. *Compare* distal.

pseudopod (SOO-doe-pod) A temporary cytoplasmic extension of a cell used for locomotion (ameboid movement) and phagocytosis.

pseudostratified columnar epithelium A type of epithelium with tall columnar cells reaching the free surface and shorter basal cells that do not reach the surface, but with all cells resting on the basement membrane; creates a false appearance of stratification. fig. 5.7

pulmonary circuit A route of blood flow that supplies blood to the pulmonary alveoli for gas exchange and then returns it to the heart; all blood vessels between the right ventricle and the left atrium of the heart.

pyrogen (PY-ro-jen) A fever-producing agent.

R

ramus (RAY-mus) An anatomical branch, as in a nerve or in the pubis.

receptor 1. A cell or organ specialized to detect a stimulus, such as a taste cell or the eye. 2. A protein molecule that binds and responds to a chemical such as a hormone, neurotransmitter, or odor molecule.

receptor-mediated endocytosis A process in which certain molecules in the extracellular fluid bind to receptors in the plasma membrane, these receptors gather together, the membrane sinks inward at that point, and the molecules are incorporated into vesicles in the cytoplasm. fig. 3.21

receptor potential A variable, local change in membrane voltage produced by a stimulus acting on a receptor cell; generates an action potential if it reaches threshold.

recessive 1. Pertaining to a genetic allele that is not phenotypically expressed in the presence of a dominant allele. **2.** Pertaining to a trait that results from a recessive allele.

reduction 1. A chemical reaction in which one or more electrons are added to a molecule, raising its free energy content; opposite of *oxidation* and always linked to an oxidation reaction. **2.** Treatment of a fracture by restoring the broken parts of a bone to their proper alignment.

reflex A stereotyped, automatic, involuntary response to a stimulus; includes somatic reflexes, in which the effectors are skeletal muscles, and visceral (autonomic) reflexes, in which the effectors are usually visceral muscle, cardiac muscle, or glands.

reflex arc A simple neural pathway that mediates a reflex; involves a receptor, an afferent nerve fiber, often one or more interneurons, an efferent nerve fiber, and an effector.

refractory period 1. A period of time after a nerve or muscle cell has responded to a stimulus in which it cannot be reexcited by a threshold stimulus. **2.** A period of time after male orgasm when it is not possible to reattain erection or ejaculation.

regeneration Replacement of damaged tissue with new tissue of the original type. *Compare* fibrosis.

renin (REE-nin) An enzyme secreted by the kidneys in response to hypotension; converts the plasma protein angiotensinogen to angiotensin I, leading indirectly to a rise in blood pressure.

repolarization Reattainment of the resting membrane potential after a nerve or muscle cell has depolarized.

residue Any one of the amino acids in a protein or other peptide.

resistance 1. A force that opposes the flow of a fluid such as air or blood. **2.** A force, or load, that opposes the action of a muscle or lever.

resting membrane potential (RMP) A stable voltage across the plasma membrane of an unstimulated nerve or muscle cell.

reticular cell (reh-TIC-you-lur) A delicate, branching phagocytic cell found in the reticular connective tissue of the lymphatic organs.

reticular fiber A fine, branching collagen fiber coated with glycoprotein, found in the stroma of lymphatic organs and some other tissues and organs.

reticular tissue A connective tissue composed of reticular cells and reticular fibers, found in bone marrow, lymphatic organs, and in lesser amounts elsewhere.

ribosome A granule found free in the cytoplasm or attached to the rough endoplasmic reticulum or nuclear envelope composed of ribosomal RNA and enzymes; specialized to read the nucleotide sequence of messenger RNA and assemble a corresponding sequence of amino acids to make a protein.

risk factor Any environmental factor or characteristic of an individual that increases one's chance of developing a particular disease; includes such intrinsic factors as age, sex, and race and such extrinsic factors as diet, smoking, and occupation.

rostral Relatively close to the forehead, especially in reference to structures of the brain and spinal cord; for example, the frontal lobe is rostral to the parietal lobe. *Compare* caudal.

ruga (ROO-ga) (plural *rugae,* ROO-jee) **1.** An internal fold or wrinkle in the mucosa of a hollow organ such as the stomach and urinary bladder; typically present when the organ is empty and relaxed but not when the organ is full and stretched. **2.** Tissue ridges in such locations as the hard palate and vagina. fig. 25.12

S

saccule (SAC-yule) A saclike receptor in the inner ear with a vertical patch of hair cells, the macula sacculi; senses the orientation of the head and responds to vertical acceleration, as when riding in an elevator or standing up. fig. 16.20

sagittal plane (SADJ-ih-tul) Any plane that extends from anterior to posterior and cephalic to caudal and that divides the body into right and left portions. *Compare* median plane.

sarcomere (SAR-co-meer) In skeletal and cardiac muscle, the portion of a myofibril from one Z disc to the next, constituting one contractile unit. fig. 11.5

sarcoplasmic reticulum (SR) The smooth endoplasmic reticulum of a muscle cell, serving as a calcium reservoir. fig. 11.2

scanning electron microscope (SEM) A microscope that uses an electron beam in

place of light to form high-resolution, three-dimensional images of the surfaces of objects; capable of much higher magnifications than a light microscope.

sclerosis (scleh-RO-sis) Hardening or stiffening of a tissue, as in multiple sclerosis of the central nervous system or atherosclerosis of the blood vessels.

sebum (SEE-bum) An oily secretion of the sebaceous glands that keeps the skin and hair pliable.

secondary active transport A mechanism in which solutes are moved through a plasma membrane by a carrier that does not itself use ATP but depends on a concentration gradient established by an active transport pump elsewhere in the cell.

second messenger A chemical that is produced within a cell (such as cAMP) or that enters a cell (such as calcium ions) in response to the binding of a messenger to a membrane receptor, and that triggers a metabolic reaction in the cell.

secretion 1. A chemical released by a cell to serve a physiological function, such as a hormone or digestive enzyme. **2.** The process of releasing such a chemical, often by exocytosis. *Compare* excretion.

selectively permeable membrane A membrane that allows some substances to pass through while excluding others; for example, the plasma membrane and dialysis membranes.

semicircular ducts Three ring-shaped, fluid-filled tubes of the inner ear that detect angular accelerations of the head; each is enclosed in a bony passage called the semicircular canal. fig. 16.21

semilunar valve A valve that consists of crescent-shaped cusps, including the aortic and pulmonary valves of the heart and valves of the veins and lymphatic vessels. fig. 19.8

semipermeable membrane *See* selectively permeable membrane.

senescence (seh-NESS-ense) Degenerative changes that occur with age.

sensation Conscious perception of a stimulus; pain, taste, and color, for example, are not stimuli but sensations resulting from stimuli.

sensory nerve fiber An axon that conducts information from a receptor to the central nervous system; an afferent nerve fiber.

serosa (seer-OH-sa) A thin epithelial membrane composed of a simple squamous epithelium overlying a thin layer of areolar tissue; covers the external surfaces of viscera such as the lungs, stomach, and intestines, and forms membranes such as the peritoneum, pleura, and pericardium, or a portion of such membranes. Also called *serous membrane.*

serous fluid (SEER-us) A watery, low-protein fluid similar to blood serum, formed as a filtrate of the blood or tissue fluid or as a secretion of serous gland cells; moistens the serous membranes.

serous membrane A membrane such as the peritoneum, pleura, or pericardium that lines a body cavity or covers the external surfaces of the viscera; composed of a simple squamous mesothelium and a thin layer of areolar connective tissue. Also called *serosa*. fig. 5.33b

sex chromosomes The X and Y chromosomes, which determine the sex of an individual.

shock 1. Circulatory shock, a state of cardiac output that is insufficient to meet the body's physiological needs, with consequences ranging from fainting to death. **2.** Insulin shock, a state of severe hypoglycemia caused by administration of insulin. **3.** Spinal shock, a state of depressed or lost reflex activity inferior to a point of spinal cord injury. **4.** Electrical shock, the effect of a current of electricity passing through the body, often causing muscular spasm and cardiac arrhythmia or arrest.

sign An objective manifestation of illness that any observer can see, such as cyanosis or edema. *Compare* symptom.

simple epithelium An epithelium in which all cells rest directly on the basement membrane; includes simple squamous, cuboidal, and columnar types, and pseudostratified columnar. fig. 5.3

sinuatrial node The pacemaker of the heart; a patch of autorhythmic cells in the right atrium that initiates each heartbeat.

sinus 1. An air-filled space in the cranium. **2.** A modified, relatively dilated vein that lacks smooth muscle and is incapable of vasomotion, such as the dural sinuses of the cerebral circulation and coronary sinus of the heart. **3.** A small fluid-filled space in an organ such as the spleen and lymph nodes. **4.** Pertaining to the sinuatrial node of the heart, as in *sinus rhythm*.

sodium–glucose transporter (SGLT) A symport that simultaneously transports Na^+ and glucose into a cell.

sodium–potassium (Na^+–K^+) pump An active transport mechanism in the plasma membrane that uses energy from ATP to expel three sodium ions from the cell and import two potassium ions into the cell for each cycle of the pump; used to drive secondary active transport processes, regulate cell volume, maintain an electrical charge gradient across the plasma membrane, and generate body heat.

somatic 1. Pertaining to the body as a whole. **2.** Pertaining to the skin, bones, and skeletal muscles as opposed to the viscera. **3.** Pertaining to cells other than germ cells.

somatic nervous system A division of the nervous system that includes efferent fibers mainly from the skin, muscles, and skeleton and afferent fibers to the skeletal muscles. *Compare* autonomic nervous system.

somatosensory 1. Pertaining to widely distributed *general senses* in the skin, muscles, tendons, joint capsules, and viscera, as opposed to the *special senses* found in the head only; also called *somesthetic*. **2.** Pertaining to the cerebral cortex of the postcentral gyrus, which receives input from such receptors.

somite One segment in a linear series of mesodermal masses that form on each side of the neural tube and give rise to trunk muscles, vertebrae, and dermis. fig. 29.7

spermatogenesis (SPUR-ma-toe-JEN-eh-sis) The production of sperm cells through a series of mitotic and meiotic cell divisions; male gametogenesis.

spermatozoon (spur-MAT-oh-ZO-on) A sperm cell.

sphincter (SFINK-tur) A ring of muscle that opens or closes an opening or passageway; found, for example, in the eyelids, around the urinary orifice, and at the beginning of a blood capillary.

spinal nerve Any of the 31 pairs of nerves that arise from the spinal cord and pass through the intervertebral foramina or through the gap between the spine and cranium.

spindle 1. An elongated structure that is thick in the middle and tapered at the ends (fusiform). **2.** A football-shaped complex of microtubules that guide the movement of chromosomes in mitosis and meiosis. fig. 4.15 **3.** A stretch receptor in the skeletal muscles. fig. 13.24

spine 1. The vertebral column. **2.** A pointed process or sharp ridge on a bone, such as the styloid process of the cranium and spine of the scapula.

splanchnic (SPLANK-nic) Pertaining to the digestive tract.

squamous (SKWAY-mus) **1.** Thin and flat. **2.** A cellular shape that is flat or scaly; pertains especially to a class of epithelial cells. figs. 5.4, 5.12

stem cell Any undifferentiated cell that can divide and differentiate into more functionally specific cell types such as blood cells and germ cells.

stenosis (steh-NO-sis) The narrowing of a passageway such as a heart valve or uterine tube; a permanent, pathological constriction as opposed to physiological constriction of a passageway.

steroid (STERR-oyd, STEER-oyd) A lipid molecule that consists of four interconnected carbon rings; cholesterol and several of its derivatives.

stimulus A chemical or physical agent in a cell's surroundings that is capable of creating a physiological response in the cell; especially agents detected by sensory cells, such as chemicals, light, and pressure.

strain The extent to which a body, such as a bone, is deformed when subjected to stress. *Compare* stress.

stratified epithelium A type of epithelium in which some cells rest on top of others instead of on the basement membrane; includes stratified squamous, cuboidal, and columnar types, and urothelium. fig. 5.3

stress 1. A mechanical force applied to any part of the body; important in stimulating bone growth, for example. *Compare* strain. **2.** A condition in which any environmental influence disturbs the homeostatic equilibrium of the body and stimulates a physiological response, especially involving the increased secretion of certain adrenal hormones.

stroke volume The volume of blood ejected by one ventricle of the heart in one contraction.

stroma The connective tissue framework of a gland, lymphatic organ, or certain other viscera, as opposed to the tissue (parenchyma) that performs the physiological functions of the organ.

subcutaneous (SUB-cue-TAY-nee-us) Beneath the skin.

substrate 1. A chemical that is acted upon and changed by an enzyme. **2.** A chemical used as a source of energy, such as glucose and fatty acids.

substrate specificity The ability of an enzyme to bind only one substrate or a limited range of related substrates.

sulcus (SUL-cuss) A groove in the surface of an organ, as in the cerebrum or heart.

summation 1. A phenomenon in which multiple stimuli combine their effects on a cell to produce a response; seen especially in nerve and muscle cells. **2.** A phenomenon in which multiple muscle twitches occur so closely together that a muscle fiber cannot fully relax between twitches but develops more tension than a single twitch produces. fig. 11.15

superficial Relatively close to the surface; opposite of deep. For example, the ribs are superficial to the lungs.

superior Higher than another structure or point of reference from the perspective of anatomical position; for example, the lungs are superior to the diaphragm.

supination (SOO-pih-NAY-shun) A rotational movement of the forearm that turns the palm so that it faces upward or forward. fig. 9.18

surfactant (sur-FAC-tent) A chemical that reduces the surface tension of water and enables it to penetrate other substances more effectively. Examples include pulmonary surfactant and bile acids.

sympathetic nervous system A division of the autonomic nervous system that issues efferent fibers through the thoracic and lumbar nerves and usually exerts adrenergic effects on its target organs; includes a chain of paravertebral ganglia adjacent to the vertebral column, and the adrenal medulla.

symphysis (SIM-fih-sis) A joint in which two bones are held together by fibrocartilage; for example, between bodies of the vertebrae and between the right and left pubic bones.

symport A cotransport protein that moves two solutes simultaneously through a plasma membrane in the same direction, such as the sodium–glucose transporter.

symptom A subjective manifestation of illness that only the ill person can sense, such as dizziness or nausea. *Compare* sign.

synapse (SIN-aps) **1.** A junction at the end of an axon where it stimulates another cell. **2.** A gap junction between two cardiac or smooth muscle cells at which one cell electrically stimulates the other; called an *electrical synapse*.

synaptic cleft (sih-NAP-tic) A narrow space between an axon terminal and the membrane of the postsynaptic cell, across which a neurotransmitter diffuses. fig. 12.21

synaptic vesicle A spheroidal organelle in an axon terminal containing neurotransmitter. fig. 12.21

syndrome A suite of related signs and symptoms stemming from a specific pathological cause.

synergist (SIN-ur-jist) A muscle that works with the prime mover (agonist) to contribute to the same overall action at a joint.

synergistic effect An effect in which two agents working together (such as two hormones) exert an effect that is greater than the sum of their separate effects. For example, neither follicle-stimulating hormone nor testosterone alone stimulates significant sperm production, but the two of them together stimulate production of vast numbers of sperm.

synovial fluid A lubricating fluid similar to egg white in consistency, found in the synovial joint cavities and bursae.

synovial joint A point where two bones are separated by a narrow, encapsulated space filled with lubricating synovial fluid; most such joints are relatively mobile. Also called *diarthrosis*.

synthesis reaction A chemical reaction in which relatively small molecules are combined to form a larger one. *Compare* decomposition reaction.

systemic (sis-TEM-ic) Widespread or pertaining to the body as a whole, as in the systemic circulation.

systemic circuit All blood vessels that convey blood from the left ventricle to all organs of the body and back to the right atrium of the heart; all of the cardiovascular system except the heart and pulmonary circuit.

systole (SIS-toe-lee) The contraction of any heart chamber; ventricular contraction unless otherwise specified.

systolic pressure (sis-TOLL-ic) The peak arterial blood pressure measured during ventricular systole.

T

target cell A cell acted upon by a nerve fiber, hormone, or other chemical messenger.

tarsal Pertaining to the ankle (tarsus).

T cell A type of lymphocyte involved in innate immunity, humoral immunity, and cellular immunity; occurs in several forms including helper, cytotoxic, and suppressor T cells and natural killer cells.

tendon A collagenous band or cord associated with a muscle, usually attaching it to a bone and transferring muscular tension to it.

tetanus 1. A state of sustained muscle contraction produced by temporal summation as a normal part of contraction; also called *tetany*. **2.** Spastic muscle paralysis produced by the toxin of the bacterium *Clostridium tetani* or other causes.

thalamus (THAL-uh-muss) The largest part of the diencephalon, located immediately inferior to the corpus callosum and bulging into each lateral ventricle; a point of synaptic relay of nearly all signals passing from lower levels of the CNS to the cerebrum. figs. 14.8, 14.12a

theory An explanatory statement, or set of statements, that concisely summarizes the state of knowledge on a phenomenon and provides direction for further study; for example, the fluid-mosaic theory of the plasma membrane and the sliding filament theory of muscle contraction. *See also* hypothesis.

thermogenesis The production of heat, for example, by shivering or by the action of thyroid hormones.

thermoreceptor A neuron specialized to respond to heat or cold, found in the skin and mucous membranes, for example.

thermoregulation Homeostatic regulation of the body temperature within a narrow range by adjustments of heat-promoting and heat-losing mechanisms.

thorax A region of the trunk between the neck and the diaphragm; the chest.

threshold 1. The minimum voltage to which the plasma membrane of a nerve or muscle cell must be depolarized before it produces an action potential. **2.** The minimum combination

of stimulus intensity and duration needed to generate an afferent signal from a sensory receptor.

thrombosis (throm-BO-sis) The formation or presence of a thrombus.

thrombus A clot that forms in a blood vessel or heart chamber; may break free and travel in the bloodstream as a thromboembolus. *Compare* embolus.

thyroid hormone Either of two similar hormones, thyroxine and triiodothyronine, synthesized from iodine and tyrosine.

thyroid-stimulating hormone (TSH) A hormone of the anterior pituitary gland that stimulates the thyroid gland; also called *thyrotropin*.

thyroxine (thy-ROCK-seen) The thyroid hormone secreted in greatest quantity, with four iodine atoms; also called *tetraiodothyronine*. fig. 17.17

tight junction A region in which adjacent cells are bound together by fusion of the outer phospholipid layer of their plasma membranes; forms a zone that encircles each cell near its apical pole and reduces or prevents flow of material between cells. fig. 5.28

tissue An aggregation of cells and extracellular materials, usually forming part of an organ and serving some discrete aspect of that organ's function; all tissues belong to one of the four primary classes—epithelial, connective, muscular, and nervous tissue.

totipotent Pertaining to a stem cell of the early preembryo, prior to development of a blastocyst, that has the potential to develop into any type of embryonic, extraembryonic, or adult cell.

trabecula (tra-BEC-you-la) A thin plate or layer of tissue, such as the calcified trabeculae of spongy bone or the fibrous trabeculae that subdivide a gland. fig. 7.4

trachea (TRAY-kee-uh) A cartilage-supported tube from the inferior end of the larynx to the origin of the main bronchi; conveys air to and from the lungs; colloquially called the *windpipe*.

translation The process in which a ribosome reads an mRNA molecule and synthesizes the protein specified by its genetic code.

transmembrane protein An integral protein that extends through a plasma membrane and contacts both the extracellular and intracellular fluid. fig. 3.6

transmission electron microscope (TEM) A microscope that uses an electron beam in place of light to form high-resolution, two-dimensional images of ultrathin slices of cells or tissues; capable of extremely high magnification.

triglyceride (try-GLISS-ur-ide) A lipid composed of three fatty acids joined to a glycerol; also called a *triacylglycerol* or *neutral fat*. fig. 2.18

trunk 1. That part of the body excluding the head, neck, and appendages. **2.** A major blood vessel, lymphatic vessel, or nerve that gives rise to smaller branches; for example, the pulmonary trunk and spinal nerve trunks.

T tubule Transverse tubule; a tubular extension of the plasma membrane of a muscle cell that conducts action potentials into the sarcoplasm and excites the sarcoplasmic reticulum. fig. 11.2

tunic (TOO-nic) A layer that encircles or encloses an organ, such as the tunics of a blood vessel or eyeball.

tympanic membrane The eardrum.

U

ultrastructure Fine details of tissue and cell structure, as far down as the molecular level, revealed by the electron microscope.

ultraviolet radiation Invisible, ionizing, electromagnetic radiation with shorter wavelength and higher energy than violet light; causes skin cancer and photoaging of the skin but is required in moderate amounts for the synthesis of vitamin D.

unipotent Pertaining to a stem cell that has the potential to develop into only one type of fully differentiated, functional cell, such as an epidermal stem cell that can become only a keratinocyte.

unmyelinated (un-MY-eh-lih-NAY-ted) Lacking a myelin sheath. fig. 12.9

urea (you-REE-uh) A nitrogenous waste produced from two ammonia molecules and carbon dioxide; the most abundant nitrogenous waste in the blood and urine. fig. 23.2

urothelium A type of stratified epithelium that lines much of the urinary tract, characterized by domed *umbrella cells* at the surface, protecting underlying cells from the acidity and hypertonicity of urine. Also called *transitional epithelium*. fig. 5.11

uterine tube A duct that extends from the ovary to the uterus and conveys an egg or conceptus to the uterus; also called *fallopian tube* or *oviduct*.

utricle (YOU-tri-cul) A saclike receptor in the inner ear with a nearly horizontal patch of hair cells, the macula utriculi; senses the orientation of the head and responds to horizontal acceleration, as when accelerating or decelerating in a car. fig. 16.20

V

van der Waals force A weak attraction between two atoms occurring when a brief fluctuation in the electron cloud density of one atom induces polarization of an adjacent atom; important in association of lipids with each other, protein folding, and protein–ligand binding.

varicose vein A vein that has become permanently distended and convoluted due to a loss of competence of the venous valves; especially common in the lower limb, esophagus, and anal canal (where they are called hemorrhoids).

vas (vass) (plural, *vasa*) A vessel or duct.

vascular Pertaining to blood vessels.

vascular corrosion cast A technique for visualizing the blood vessels of organs and tissues, especially the microvasculature, by flushing blood from the vessels, injecting a resin and letting it solidify, then digesting the actual tissue away with a corrosive agent, leaving only the resin cast; this is then viewed with a scanning electron microscope. figs. 20.1b, 23.10a

vasoconstriction (VAY-zo-con-STRIC-shun) The narrowing of a blood vessel due to muscular contraction of its tunica media.

vasodilation (VAY-zo-dy-LAY-shun) The widening of a blood vessel due to relaxation of the muscle of its tunica media and the outward pressure of the blood exerted against the wall.

vasomotion Collective term for vasoconstriction and vasodilation; any change in the diameter of a blood vessel.

vasomotor center A nucleus in the medulla oblongata that transmits signals to the blood vessels and regulates vessel diameter.

ventral Pertaining to the front of the body, the regions of the chest and abdomen; anterior.

ventral root *See* anterior root.

ventricle (VEN-trih-cul) A fluid-filled chamber of the brain or heart.

venule (VEN-yule) The smallest type of vein, receiving drainage from capillaries.

vertebra (VUR-teh-bra) One of the bones of the vertebral column.

vertebral column (VUR-teh-brul) A posterior series of usually 33 vertebrae; encloses the spinal cord, supports the skull and thoracic cage, and provides attachment for the limbs and postural muscles. Also called *spine* or *spinal column*.

vesicle A fluid-filled tissue sac or an organelle such as a synaptic or secretory vesicle.

vesicular transport The movement of particles or fluid droplets through the plasma membrane by the process of endocytosis or exocytosis.

viscera (VISS-er-uh) (singular, *viscus*) The organs contained in the body cavities, such as the brain, heart, lungs, stomach, intestines, and kidneys.

visceral (VISS-er-ul) **1.** Pertaining to the viscera. **2.** The inner or deeper layer of a two-layered membrane such as the pleura, pericardium, or glomerular capsule. *Compare* parietal. fig. A.6

visceral muscle Unitary smooth muscle found in the walls of blood vessels and the digestive, respiratory, urinary, and reproductive tracts.

viscosity The resistance of a fluid to flow; the thickness or stickiness of a fluid.

voluntary muscle Muscle that is usually under conscious control; skeletal muscle.

vulva The female external genitalia; the mons, labia majora, and all superficial structures between the labia majora.

W

water balance An equilibrium between fluid intake and output or between the amounts of fluid contained in the body's different fluid compartments.

white matter White myelinated nervous tissue deep to the cortex of the cerebrum and cerebellum and superficial to the gray matter of the spinal cord. fig. 14.6

X

X chromosome The larger of the two sex chromosomes; males have one X chromosome and females have two in each somatic cell.

X-ray 1. A high-energy, penetrating electromagnetic ray with wavelengths in the range of 0.1 to 10 nm; used in diagnosis and therapy. **2.** A photograph made with X-rays; radiograph.

Y

Y chromosome Smaller of the two sex chromosomes, found only in males and having little if any genetic function except development of the testis.

yolk sac An embryonic membrane that encloses the yolk in vertebrates that lay eggs and serves in humans as the origin of the first blood and germ cells.

Z

zygomatic arch An arch of bone anterior to the ear, formed by the zygomatic processes of the temporal, frontal, and zygomatic bones; origin of the masseter muscle.

zygote A single-celled, fertilized egg.

APPENDIX A

ANSWER KEYS

This appendix provides answers to questions in the figure legends and the end-of-chapter questions in the "Testing Your Recall," "Building Your Medical Vocabulary," and "What's Wrong with These Statements?" sections. Answers to "Apply What You Know" and "Testing Your Comprehension" questions are available to instructors on the text Connect site at www.mcgrawhillconnect.com.

CHAPTER 1

Figure Legend Questions

1.7 Vasodilation allows more blood to flow close to the body surface and to lose heat through the skin; thus, it cools the body.

1.9 Yes; one could say that pregnancy activates a series of events leading to childbirth, the termination of the pregnancy. Thus, it has the qualities of a negative feedback loop.

1.11 MRI is better than X-rays for visualizing nervous tissue, since X-rays do not penetrate bone very well. It also shows better contrast than X-rays in visualization of other soft tissues. X-rays are better than PET scans for visualizing bones, teeth, and other hard or dense tissues, as PET scans have relatively low resolution and do not serve well to visualize tissues with little regional variation in metabolic rate.

Testing Your Recall

1. a	8. c	15. homeostasis
2. e	9. d	16. set point
3. d	10. b	17. negative feedback
4. a	11. dissection	18. organ
5. c	12. gradient	19. stereoscopic
6. c	13. deduction	20. prehensile,
7. a	14. psychosomatic	opposable

Building Your Medical Vocabulary (Answers may vary; these are acceptable examples.)

1. listen—auscultation	6. nature—physiology
2. apart—dissection	7. cut—dissection
3. the same—homeostasis	8. to stay—homeostasis
4. change—metabolism	9. solid—stereoscopic
5. touch—palpation	10. to cut—tomography

What's Wrong with These Statements?

1. Auscultation means listening to body sounds, not inspecting the body by touch.
2. MRI does not involve ionizing radiation and has no known risk to a fetus.
3. Positive feedback is beneficial in limited cases, but more often it causes rapid departure from the homeostatic set point and may cause illness or death.
4. Each cell has many organelles, so organelles far outnumber cells.
5. Matter will move spontaneously down a gradient without the need for application of external energy.
6. Leeuwenhoek was a textile merchant who built microscopes to examine fabric.

7. A scientific theory is founded on a large body of evidence and summarizes what is already known.
8. Both the treatment and control groups consist of volunteer patients.
9. Evolutionary biologists do not believe humans evolved from monkeys, but that humans and apes evolved from the same ancestor.
10. Negative feedback is a self-corrective process with a beneficial effect on the body.

ATLAS A

Figure Legend Questions

A.4 Right lower quadrant (RLQ)

A.8 No, it is inferior to the peritoneal cavity, since the peritoneum passes over its superior surface.

Testing Your Recall

1. d	8. d	15. contralateral
2. c	9. b	16. meninges
3. e	10. d	17. retroperitoneal
4. d	11. mesenteries	18. medial
5. d	12. parietal	19. inferior
6. a	13. mediastinum	20. cubital, popliteal
7. a	14. nuchal	

Building Your Medical Vocabulary (Answers may vary; these are acceptable examples.)

1. before—antebrachium	6. within—intraperitoneal
2. neck—cervical	7. wall—parietal
3. above—epigastric	8. around—peritoneum
4. below—hypochondriac	9. behind—retroperitoneal
5. groin—inguinal	10. arrow—sagittal

What's Wrong with These Statements?

1. A sagittal section could only pass between the lungs or through one lung, not through both of them.
2. A frontal section passes from left to right and could include both eyes.
3. The knee is proximal to the ankle (tarsal region).
4. The diaphragm is inferior to the lungs.
5. The esophagus is superior to the stomach.
6. The liver extends from the hypochondriac to the epigastric region, superior to the lumbar region.
7. The heart is enfolded by the pericardial cavity but not contained within it.
8. The kidneys are retroperitoneal.
9. The peritoneum lines the outside of the stomach and intestines.
10. The sigmoid colon is in the lower left quadrant.

CHAPTER 2

Figure Legend Questions

2.8 Because water molecules are attracted to each other, it requires more thermal energy for any one of them to break free and evaporate.

2.12 Decomposition

2.26 No, the amount of energy released is the same with or without an enzyme.

Testing Your Recall

1. a	9. b	16. -ose, -ase
2. c	10. d	17. phospholipids
3. a	11. cation	18. cyclic adenosine
4. c	12. free radicals	monophosphate
5. a	13. catalyst, enzymes	19. anaerobic
6. e	14. anabolism	fermentation
7. b	15. dehydration	20. substrate
8. c	synthesis	

Building Your Medical Vocabulary (Answers may vary; these are acceptable examples.)

1. not—atom	6. water—hydrolysis
2. oxygen—aerobic	7. part—polymer
3. both—amphipathic	8. one—monomer
4. heat—calorie	9. few—oligosaccharide
5. glue—colloid	10. loving—hydrophilic

What's Wrong with These Statements?

1. The monomers of a polysaccharide are monosaccharides (simple sugars).
2. ATP is not an energy-storage molecule. Most of our reserve energy is stored in fat.
3. Such molecules are called isomers, not isotopes.
4. Catabolism produces products with less energy than the reactants.
5. Peptide bonds join amino acids together, not sugars.
6. A saturated fat is one to which no more hydrogen can be added.
7. Enzymes, like all catalysts, are not consumed by the reactions they catalyze.
8. Above a certain temperature, enzymes denature and cease working.
9. These solutes have different molecular weights, so 2% solutions would not contain the same number of molecules per unit volume.
10. A solution with pH 8 has one-tenth the hydrogen ion concentration of one with pH 7.

CHAPTER 3

Figure Legend Questions

3.8 Adenylate cyclase is a transmembrane protein. The G protein is peripheral.
3.19 The Na^+–K^+ pump requires ATP, whereas osmosis does not. ATP is quickly depleted after a cell dies.
3.22 Transcytosis is a combination of endocytosis and exocytosis.
3.27 Large molecules such as enzymes and RNA must pass through the nuclear pores, but pores in the plasma membrane must be small enough to prevent such large molecules from escaping the cell.
3.33 A centriole is composed of a cylinder of nine groups of microtubules, but in a centriole, there are three microtubules in each group and in an axoneme there are only two. Also, an axoneme usually has a central pair of microtubules, whereas a centriole does not.

Testing Your Recall

1. e	9. d	16. exocytosis
2. b	10. b	17. Ribosomes,
3. d	11. micrometers	proteasomes
4. b	12. second messenger	18. smooth ER,
5. e	13. Voltage-gated	peroxisomes
6. e	14. hydrostatic	19. ligand-gated
7. a	pressure	channel
8. c	15. hypertonic	20. cistern

Building Your Medical Vocabulary (Answers may vary; these are acceptable examples.)

1. opposite—antiport	6. easy—facilitated
2. color—chromatin	7. spindle—fusiform
3. together—cotransport	8. study of—cytology
4. cell—cytoplasm	9. process—pinocytosis
5. into, within—endocytosis	10. eat—phagocytosis

What's Wrong with These Statements?

1. Osmosis does not require ATP, so it can continue even after cell death.
2. Some cells have two or more nuclei and some cells have none.
3. Second messengers activate enzymes in the cell; they are not transport proteins.
4. Peroxisomes are produced by the endoplasmic reticulum, not by the Golgi complex.
5. A channel could not move material from the outside of a cell to the inside unless it extended all the way across the membrane; it must be a transmembrane protein.
6. The plasma membrane consists primarily of phospholipid molecules.
7. The brush border is composed of microvilli.
8. Cells in hypertonic saline will lose water and shrivel.
9. Osmosis is not a carrier-mediated process and therefore not subject to a transport maximum.
10. Many ribosomes lie free in the cytosol, not attached to the ER or nucleus.

CHAPTER 4

Figure Legend Questions

4.1 The helix would bulge where two purines were paired and would be constricted where two pyrimidines were paired.
4.8 The ribosome would have no way of holding the partially completed peptide in place while adding the next amino acid.

Testing Your Recall

1. a	8. d	14. polyribosome
2. e	9. d	15. RNA polymerase
3. c	10. a	16. genome
4. c	11. cytokinesis	17. 46, 92, 92
5. e	12. cyclin-dependent	18. ribosome
6. b	kinases	19. growth factors
7. a	13. genetic code	20. autosomes

Building Your Medical Vocabulary (Answers may vary; these are acceptable examples.)

1. different—allele	6. nucleus—karyotype
2. finger—polydactyly	7. next in a series—metaphase
3. double—diploid	8. shape—polymorphism
4. half—haploid	9. change—mutation
5. different—heterozygous	10. many—polydactyly

What's Wrong with These Statements?

1. There are no ribosomes on the Golgi complex; they are on the rough ER.
2. There are no genes for steroids, carbohydrates, or phospholipids, but only for proteins.
3. RNA is half the weight of a DNA of the same length because it has only one nucleotide strand, whereas DNA has two.
4. Each amino acid is represented by a triplet, a sequence of three bases, not one base pair.
5. A single gene can code for multiple proteins.

6. This law describes the pairing of bases between the two strands of DNA, not between mRNA and tRNA.
7. Only about 2% of the human DNA codes for proteins.
8. Mutations can be harmful, beneficial, or neutral.
9. Males have only one X chromosome, but have two sex chromosomes (the X and Y).
10. Several RNA polymerase molecules at once can transcribe a gene.

CHAPTER 5

Figure Legend Questions

5.2 They are longitudinal sections. In a cross section, both the egg white and yolk would look circular. In an oblique section, the white would look elliptical but the yolk would still look circular.
5.12 The epithelia of the tongue, oral cavity, esophagus, and anal canal would look similar to this.
5.28 Gap junctions
5.30 Exocytosis
5.31 The sketch would look like one of the purple sacs in the middle figure, budding directly from the epithelial surface with no duct.
5.32 Holocrine glands, because entire cells break down to become the secretion, and these must be continually replaced.

Testing Your Recall

1. a	9. b	17. basement
2. b	10. b	membrane
3. c	11. necrosis	18. matrix (extracel-
4. e	12. mesothelium	lular material)
5. c	13. lacunae	19. multipotent
6. a	14. fibers	20. simple
7. b	15. collagen	
8. e	16. skeletal muscle	

Building Your Medical Vocabulary (Answers may vary; these are acceptable examples.)

1. away—apoptosis	6. whole—holocrine
2. cartilage—chondrocyte	7. glassy—hyaline
3. outer—ectoderm	8. dead—necrosis
4. producing—collagen	9. formed—neoplasia
5. tissue—histology	10. scale—squamous

What's Wrong with These Statements?

1. The esophageal epithelium is nonkeratinized.
2. All of them contact the basement membrane.
3. There are a few cases of skeletal muscles not attached to bones.
4. Glandular secretions are produced by cells of the parenchyma; the stroma is nonsecretory supportive connective tissue.
5. Adipose tissue is an exception; cells constitute most of its volume.
6. Adipocytes are also found in areolar tissue, either singly or in small clusters.
7. Tight junctions serve mainly to restrict the passage of material between cells.
8. Neoplasia is abnormal tissue growth, such as tumors; development of mature tissue types from nonspecialized tissues is called differentiation.
9. Excitability is characteristic of all living cells, but most highly developed in nerve and muscle cells.
10. Perichondrium is lacking from fibrocartilage and from hyaline articular cartilage.

CHAPTER 6

Figure Legend Questions

6.5 Keratinocytes
6.8 Cuticle
6.11 Asymmetry (A), irregular border (B), and color (C). The photo does not provide enough information to judge the diameter of the lesion (D).

Testing Your Recall

1. d	8. a	14. cyanosis
2. c	9. a	15. dermal papillae
3. d	10. d	16. earwax
4. b	11. Insensible	17. sebaceous glands
5. a	perspiration	18. anagen
6. e	12. arrector muscle	19. dermal papilla
7. c	13. debridement	20. third-degree

Building Your Medical Vocabulary (Answers may vary; these are acceptable examples.)

1. substance—melanin	6. injure—lesion
2. white—albinism	7. black—melanoma
3. skin—dermatology	8. tumor—carcinoma
4. through—diaphoresis	9. nail—eponychium
5. same—homograft	10. hair—piloerector

What's Wrong with These Statements?

1. Basal cell carcinoma is the most common form of skin cancer.
2. The number of melanocytes is about the same in all skin colors; dark skin results from the accumulation of melanin in keratinocytes.
3. Keratin is the protein of the epidermis; the dermis is composed mainly of collagen.
4. Vitamin D synthesis begins in the keratinocytes.
5. Epidermal cell multiplication occurs in the stratum basale.
6. Cells of the cortex are also dead; the only living hair cells are in and near the hair bulb.
7. The hypodermis is not considered to be a layer of the skin.
8. Different races have about the same density of melanocytes but different amounts of melanin.
9. A genetic lack of melanin causes albinism, not pallor. Pallor is a temporary, nonhereditary paleness of the skin.
10. Apocrine sweat glands develop at puberty.

CHAPTER 7

Figure Legend Questions

7.1 The wider epiphyses provide surface area for muscle attachment and bone articulation, while the narrowness of the diaphysis minimizes weight.
7.6 Places where bone comes close to the skin, such as the sternum and hips
7.7 Temporal bone, parietal bone, and several others
7.9 Humerus, radius, ulna, femur, tibia, fibula
7.10 An infant's joints are still cartilaginous.
7.12 The zones of cell proliferation and cell hypertrophy

Testing Your Recall

1. e	8. e	15. hypocalcemia
2. a	9. b	16. Osteoblasts
3. d	10. d	17. calcitriol
4. c	11. hydroxyapatite	18. osteoporosis
5. d	12. canaliculi	19. metaphysis
6. a	13. appositional	20. osteomalacia
7. d	14. solubility product	

A-4   **APPENDIX A**   Answer Keys

Building Your Medical Vocabulary (Answers may vary; these are acceptable examples.)

1. calcium—hypocalcemia
2. destroy—osteoclast
3. softening—osteomalacia
4. marrow—osteomyelitis
5. straight—orthopedics
6. bone—osseous
7. bone—osteocyte
8. growth—diaphysis
9. dart—spicule
10. place—ectopic

What's Wrong with These Statements?

1 Flat cranial bones have a middle layer of spongy bone called the diploe.
2. Cartilage is removed and replaced by bone, not calcified and transformed into bone.
3. The most common bone disease is osteoporosis, not fractures.
4. Bones elongate at the epiphysial plate, not the articular cartilage.
5. Osteoclasts develop from stem cells in the bone marrow, not from osteoblasts.
6. Osteoblasts give rise only to osteocytes and are therefore unipotent.
7. Hydroxyapatite is the major mineral of bone; the major protein is collagen.
8. Osteons have blood vessels in their central canals, not in the canaliculi.
9. The major effect of vitamin D is bone resorption, though it also promotes deposition.
10. Parathyroid hormone indirectly promotes bone resorption, not deposition.

CHAPTER 8

Figure Legend Questions

8.10 Any five of these: the occipital, parietal, sphenoid, zygomatic, and palatine bones, and the mandible and maxilla
8.12 Any five of these: the frontal, lacrimal, and sphenoid bones, and the vomer, maxilla, and inferior concha
8.25 Rupture of this ligament allows the atlas to slip anteriorly and the dens of the axis to tear into the spinal cord.
8.35 The adult hand lacks epiphysial plates, the growth zones of a child's long bones.
8.41 The three cuneiforms and the cuboid bone of the tarsus are arranged in a row similar to the distal carpal bones (trapezium, trapezoid, capitate, and hamate), with the trapezium corresponding to the median cuneiform (proximal to digit I in each case). In the proximal row, the navicular bone of the tarsus is somewhat similar to the scaphoid of the carpus, being proximal to digit I and articulating with three bones of the distal row, but the calcaneus and talus are very different, being adapted to their load-bearing role.

Testing Your Recall

1. b
2. e
3. a
4. d
5. a
6. e
7. c
8. b
9. e
10. b
11. fontanelles
12. temporal
13. sutures
14. sphenoid
15. anulus fibrosus
16. dens
17. auricular
18. styloid
19. foramina
20. medial longitudinal

Building Your Medical Vocabulary (Answers may vary; these are acceptable examples.)

1. rib—intercostal
2. helmet—cranium
3. tough—dura mater
4. tongue—hypoglossa
5. little—ossicle
6. breast—mastoid

7. foot—bipedal
8. wing—pterygoid
9. above—supraorbital
10. ankle—metatarsal

What's Wrong with These Statements?

1. It passes out the jugular foramen.
2. Each hand and foot has 14 phalanges.
3. The female pelvis is wider and shallower than the male's.
4. The carpal bones are in the base of the hand, not the narrow wrist region.
5. Muscles of the infraspinous fossa are easily palpated on the back, inferior to the scapular spine.
6. You would be resting your elbow on the olecranon.
7. The lumbar vertebrae have transverse processes but no transverse costal facets.
8. The most frequently broken bone is the clavicle.
9. *Arm* refers to the region containing only the humerus; *leg* refers to the region containing the tibia and fibula.
10. These extra bones in the cranium are called sutural bones, not sesamoid bones.

CHAPTER 9

Figure Legend Questions

9.2 The gomphosis, because a tooth is not a bone
9.4 The pubic symphysis consists of the cartilaginous interpubic disc and the adjacent parts of the two pubic bones.
9.5 Interphalangeal joints are not subjected to a great deal of compression.
9.7 $MA = 1.0$. Shifting the fulcrum to the left would increase the MA of this lever, while the lever would remain first class.
9.19 The atlas (C1)

Testing Your Recall

1. c
2. b
3. a
4. e
5. c
6. c
7. a
8. d
9. b
10. d
11. synovial fluid
12. bursa
13. pivot
14. Kinesiology
15. gomphosis
16. serrate
17. extension
18. range of motion
19. articular disc
20. talus

Building Your Medical Vocabulary (Answers may vary; these are acceptable examples.)

1. away—abduction
2. joint—arthritis
3. characterized by—cruciate
4. letter X—cruciate
5. leg—talocrural
6. to lead—adduction
7. movement—kinesiology
8. moon—meniscus
9. to lay back—supination
10. to pull—protraction

What's Wrong with These Statements?

1. Osteoarthritis occurs in almost everyone after a certain age; rheumatoid arthritis is less common.
2. A kinesiologist studies joint movements; a rheumatologist treats arthritis.
3. Synovial joints are diarthroses and amphiarthroses, but never synarthroses.
4. There is no meniscus in the elbow.
5. This action involves hyperextension of the shoulder.
6. The cruciate ligaments are in the knee.
7. The round ligament is somewhat slack and probably does not secure the femoral head.
8. The knuckles are diarthroses.

9. Synovial fluid is secreted by the synovial membrane of the joint capsule and fills the bursae.
10. A tooth is not a bone.

CHAPTER 10

Figure Legend Questions

10.4   The brachialis and lateral head of the triceps brachii have direct attachments; the biceps brachii and long head of the triceps brachii have indirect attachments.
10.8   The zygomaticus major, levator palpebrae superioris, and orbicularis oris
10.16   Pectoralis minor, serratus anterior, and all three layers of the upper intercostal muscles
10.27   *Teres* refers to the round or cordlike shape of the first muscle, and *quadratus* refers to the four-sided shape of the second.
10.28   Part (c) represents a cross section cut too high on the forearm to include these muscles.
10.34   Climbing stairs, walking, running, or riding a bicycle
10.38   The soleus

Testing Your Recall

1. b	9. d	16. urogenital
2. b	10. c	triangle
3. a	11. buccinator	17. linea alba
4. c	12. fascicle	18. synergist
5. e	13. prime mover	19. bipennate
6. e	(agonist)	20. sphincter
7. b	14. hamstring	
8. a	15. flexor retinacula	

Building Your Medical Vocabulary (Answers may vary; these are acceptable examples.)

1. head—splenius capitis
2. work—synergist
3. bundle—fascicle
4. lip—levator labii superioris
5. lower back—quadratus lumborum
6. mouse—muscle
7. muscle—perimysium
8. shoulder—omohyoid
9. feather—bipennate
10. third—peroneus tertius

What's Wrong with These Statements?

1. The connective tissue that encloses individual muscle fibers is endomysium.
2. The orbicularis was once thought to be a sphincter but is no longer interpreted as such.
3. The biceps brachii is fusiform.
4. A synergist aids an agonist in its function; it does not oppose the agonist.
5. Many skeletal muscles are innervated by cranial nerves (those in the head and neck).
6. Normally, no muscular effort is needed to exhale.
7. The hamstrings flex the knee and therefore would not aid in lifting the body to the next step.
8. The facial nerve innervates 16 of the facial muscles tabulated in this chapter. The trigeminal innervates 6 tabulated muscles, but they are muscles of chewing and swallowing, not facial expression.
9. The adductor pollicis is by far the strongest of the three listed muscles (important in the strength of the hand grip), but is not listed first.
10. They are on opposite sides of the tibia and act as antagonists.

ATLAS B

Figure Legend Questions

B.1   Orbicularis oris; trapezius
B.5   The lungs, heart, liver, stomach, gallbladder, and spleen, among others
B.8   Sternocleidomastoids
B.11   Posterior
B.13   Fat (adipose tissue)
B.18   Five: one tendon proximally (at the humerus) and four distally (in the hand)
B.19   The mark would belong close to where the leader for the styloid process of the radius ends in figure B.19b.
B.20   The mark would belong close to where the leader for the rectus femoris ends; the vastus intermedius is deep to this.
B.21   The fibula
B.24   There is no such bone; digit I (the great toe) has only a proximal and distal phalanx.
B.25   Answers to the muscle test are as follows:

1. f	11. x	21. k
2. b	12. m	22. d
3. k	13. n	23. f
4. p	14. e	24. b
5. h	15. g	25. a
6. y	16. v	26. u
7. z	17. f	27. j
8. w	18. c	28. i
9. c	19. x	29. g
10. a	20. w	30. q

CHAPTER 11

Figure Legend Questions

11.1   The striations distinguish it from smooth muscle; the multiple nuclei adjacent to the plasma membrane and the parallel fibers distinguish it from both cardiac and smooth muscle.
11.2   The electrical excitation spreading down the T tubule must excite the opening of calcium gates in the terminal cisterns.
11.13   ATP is needed to pump Ca^{2+} back into the sarcoplasmic reticulum by active transport and to induce each myosin head to release actin so the sarcomere can relax.
11.16   The gluteus maximus and quadriceps femoris
11.17   The muscle tension curve would drop gradually while the muscle length curve would rise.

Testing Your Recall

1. a	8. c	15. acetylcholine
2. c	9. e	16. myoglobin
3. b	10. b	17. Z discs
4. d	11. threshold	18. varicosities
5. c	12. oxidative	19. muscle tone
6. c	13. terminal cisterns	20. Isometric
7. e	14. myosin	contraction

Building Your Medical Vocabulary (Answers may vary; these are acceptable examples.)

1. weak—myasthenia
2. self—autorhythmic
3. abnormal—dystrophy
4. same—isometric
5. length—isometric
6. muscle—myocyte
7. flesh—sarcolemma
8. time—temporal
9. tension—isotonic
10. growth—dystrophy

What's Wrong with These Statements?

1. A motor neuron may supply 1,000 or more muscle fibers; a motor unit consists of one motor neuron and all the muscle fibers it innervates.
2. Somatic motor neurons do not innervate cardiac muscle.
3. Fast glycolytic fibers fatigue relatively quickly.
4. Thin myofilaments extend well into the A bands, where they overlap with thick myofilaments.
5. Thin and thick myofilaments do not shorten, but glide over each other.
6. Thick and thin myofilaments are present but not arranged in a way that produces striations.
7. Under natural conditions, a muscle seldom or never attains complete tetanus.
8. Even excitation would be impossible without ATP, because ATP drives the active transport (Na^+–K^+) pumps that maintain membrane potential and excitability.
9. A muscle produces most of its ATP during this time by anaerobic fermentation, which generates lactate; it does not consume lactate.
10. Autorhythmicity is limited to unitary smooth muscle.

CHAPTER 12

Figure Legend Questions

12.9 Its conduction speed is relatively slow, but it has a small diameter and contributes relatively little bulk to the nervous tissue.
12.25 One EPSP is a voltage change of only 0.5 mV or so. A change of about 15 mV is required to reach threshold and make a neuron fire.
12.30 The CNS interprets a stimulus as more intense if it receives signals from high-threshold sensory neurons than if it receives signals only from low-threshold neurons.
12.32 A reverberating circuit, because a neuron early in the circuit is continually restimulated

Testing Your Recall

1. e	9. d	16. myelin sheath
2. c	10. b	gaps
3. d	11. afferent	17. axon hillock, ini-
4. a	12. conductivity	tial segment
5. c	13. absolute refrac-	18. norepinephrine
6. e	tory period	19. facilitated zone
7. d	14. dendrites	20. Neuromodulators
8. a	15. oligodendrocytes	

Building Your Medical Vocabulary (Answers may vary; these are acceptable examples.)

1. forward—anterograde	6. knot—ganglion
2. to touch—synapse	7. to walk—retrograde
3. star—astrocyte	8. nerve—neuroglia
4. tree—dendrite	9. hard—sclerosis
5. carry—afferent	10. body—somatic

What's Wrong with These Statements?

1. A neuron never has more than one axon.
2. Oligodendrocytes of the brain perform the same function as Schwann cells of the PNS.
3. The extracellular concentration of Na^+ is greater than its intracellular concentration.
4. Only a small fraction of the neuron's Na^+ and K^+ exchange places across the plasma membrane.

5. The threshold stays the same but an EPSP brings the membrane potential closer to the threshold.
6. The absolute refractory period sets an upper limit on firing frequency.
7. The effect of a neurotransmitter varies from place to place depending on the type of receptor present.
8. The signals travel rapidly through the internodal segments and slow down at each myelin sheath gap.
9. Learning involves modification of the synapses of existing neurons, not an increase in the neuron population.
10. Neurons cannot undergo mitosis to replace those that are lost, although limited replacement occurs through multiplication and differentiation of stem cells.

CHAPTER 13

Figure Legend Questions

13.5 If it were T10, there would be no cuneate fasciculus; that exists only from T6 up.
13.10 They are in the anterior horn of the spinal cord.
13.13 They are afferent, because they arise from the posterior root of the spinal nerve.
13.15 Severing one phrenic nerve paralyzes the diaphragm on the ipsilateral side; severing both of them paralyzes the entire diaphragm and causes respiratory arrest.
13.25 Motor neurons are capable only of exciting skeletal muscle (endplate potentials are always excitatory). To inhibit muscle contraction, it is necessary to inhibit the motor neuron at the CNS level (point 6).
13.26 They would show more synaptic delay, because there are more synapses in the pathway.

Testing Your Recall

1. e	8. a	15. intrafusal fibers
2. c	9. e	16. phrenic
3. d	10. b	17. decussation
4. d	11. ganglia	18. proprioception
5. e	12. ramus	19. posterior root
6. c	13. spinocerebellar	20. tibial, common
7. c	14. crossed extension	fibular

Building Your Medical Vocabulary (Answers may vary; these are acceptable examples.)

1. spider—arachnoid	6. diaphragm—phrenic
2. tail—cauda equina	7. tender—pia mater
3. opposite—contralateral	8. oneself—proprioception
4. wedge—cuneate	9. branch—ramus
5. same—ipsilateral	10. roof—tectospinal

What's Wrong with These Statements?

1. The gracile fasciculus is an ascending (sensory) tract.
2. It terminates in the upper lumbar region of the vertebral column.
3. Each segment of the spinal cord has several rootlets.
4. All spinal nerves are mixed nerves; none are purely sensory or motor.
5. The dura is separated from the bone by a fat-filled epidural space.
6. The horns of the spinal cord are gray matter.
7. Corticospinal tracts are descending (motor) tracts, not sensory.
8. Dermatomes overlap each other by as much as 50%.
9. Some somatic reflexes are mediated primarily through the brainstem and cerebellum.
10. Many ipsilateral reflex arcs are also polysynaptic.

CHAPTER 14

Figure Legend Questions

14.9   Signals in the cuneate fasciculus ascend to the cuneate nucleus in part (c), and signals in the gracile fasciculus ascend to the nearby gracile nucleus. Both of them decussate together to the contralateral medial lemniscus in parts (b) and (a) and travel this route to the thalamus.

14.10   The reticular formation is labeled on all three parts of the figure.

14.14   Commissural tracts also cross through the anterior and posterior commissures shown in figure 14.2.

14.15   Dendrites; the axons project downward into the white matter.

14.22   Regions with numerous small muscles

Testing Your Recall

1. c	8. d	14. vagus nerve
2. a	9. e	15. choroid plexus
3. e	10. e	16. precentral
4. a	11. corpus callosum	17. frontal
5. b	12. ventricles,	18. association areas
6. c	cerebrospinal	19. categorical
7. a	13. arbor vitae	20. Broca area

Building Your Medical Vocabulary (Answers may vary; these are acceptable examples.)

1. pain—neuralgia
2. head—hydrocephalus
3. brain—cerebrospinal
4. body—corpus callosum
5. brain—encephalitis
6. record of—electroencephalogram
7. island—insula
8. eye—oculomotor
9. pulley—trochlea
10. little—peduncle

What's Wrong with These Statements?

1. The optic nerve is purely sensory. Eye movements are controlled by the oculomotor, trochlear, and abducens nerves.
2. The cerebral hemispheres do not develop from neural crest tissue.
3. The midbrain is rostral to the pons.
4. The Broca and Wernicke areas are ipsilateral, both in the left hemisphere in most people.
5. The choroid plexuses produce only 30% of the CSF.
6. Hearing is a temporal lobe function; vision resides in the occipital lobe.
7. Respiration is controlled by nuclei in the pons and medulla oblongata.
8. The trigeminal nerve carries sensory signals from the largest area of the face.
9. The vagus nerve (cranial nerve X) innervates organs of the thoracic and abdominopelvic cavities.
10. The cerebellum contains more than half of all brain neurons.

CHAPTER 15

Figure Legend Questions

15.4   No; inhaling and exhaling are controlled by the somatic motor system and skeletal muscles.

15.5   The neurosoma of the somatic efferent neuron is in the anterior horn and the neurosoma of the sympathetic preganglionic neuron is in the lateral horn.

15.7   The vagus nerve

15.9   The pupils dilate because fear increases sympathetic output, which induces dilation.

Testing Your Recall

1. b	3. e	5. a
2. c	4. e	6. e

7. d	12. Dual innervation	17. sympathetic
8. d	13. Autonomic tone	18. preganglionic,
9. a	14. vagus	postganglionic
10. c	15. enteric	19. cAMP
11. adrenergic	16. norepinephrine	20. vasomotor tone

Building Your Medical Vocabulary (Answers may vary; these are acceptable examples.)

1. pressure—baroreflex
2. dissolve—sympatholytic
3. wall—intramural
4. rule—autonomic
5. ear—otic
6. feeling—parasympathetic
7. kidney—adrenal
8. internal organs—splanchnic
9. together—sympathetic
10. internal organs—visceral

What's Wrong with These Statements?

1. Both systems are always simultaneously active.
2. Cutaneous blood vessels receive only sympathetic fibers.
3. In biofeedback and other circumstances, limited voluntary control of the ANS is possible.
4. The sympathetic division inhibits digestion.
5. The sympathetic division has a few cholinergic postganglionic fibers, although most are adrenergic.
6. Waste elimination can occur by autonomic spinal reflexes without necessarily involving the brain.
7. All parasympathetic fibers are cholinergic.
8. The sympathetic division has more neural divergence and therefore more widespread, less organ-specific, effects than the parasympathetic division.
9. The hypoglossal nerve carries no parasympathetic fibers.
10. They have antagonistic effects on the iris.

CHAPTER 16

Figure Legend Questions

16.1   Yes; two touches are felt separately if they straddle the boundary between two separate receptive fields.

16.9   The lower margin of the violet zone ("all sound") would be higher in that frequency range.

16.15   They are the outer hair cells, which function to "tune the cochlea" and improve discrimination between sounds of different pitches.

16.16   It would oppose the inward movement of the tympanic membrane and, thus, reduce the amount of vibration transferred to the inner ear.

16.24   This would prevent tears from draining into the lacrimal canals, resulting in more watery eyes.

16.25   Cranial nerve III, because it controls more eye movements than IV or VI.

16.30   It is the right eye. The optic disc is always medial to the fovea, so this has to be a view of the observer's left and the subject's right.

16.42   Approximately 68:20:0, and yellow

16.45   It would cause blindness in the left half of the visual field. It would not affect the visual reflexes.

Testing Your Recall

1. a	8. c	15. outer hair cells
2. c	9. c	16. stapes
3. b	10. b	17. inferior colliculi
4. a	11. fovea centralis	18. basal cells
5. e	12. ganglion	19. olfactory bulb
6. e	13. photopsin	20. referred pain
7. d	14. otoliths	

Building Your Medical Vocabulary (Answers may vary; these are acceptable examples.)

1. two—binaural
2. cross over—hemidecussation
3. half—hemidecussation
4. tears—lacrimal
5. stone—otolithic
6. spot—macula sacculi
7. pain—nociceptor
8. dark—scotopic
9. infection—asepsis
10. hair—peritrichial

What's Wrong with These Statements?

1. These fibers end in the medulla oblongata.
2. They are perceived in the right hemisphere because of decussation.
3. Because of hemidecussation, each hemisphere receives signals from both eyes.
4. Chemoreceptors that monitor blood chemistry, for example, are interoceptors.
5. The posterior chamber, the space between iris and lens, is filled with aqueous humor.
6. Descending analgesic fibers block signals that have reached the dorsal horn of the spinal cord.
7. Cranial nerve VIII carries both auditory and equilibrium signals.
8. The tympanic cavity is filled with air.
9. Rods release glutamate in the dark and stop when they are illuminated.
10. The trochlear and abducens nerves control the superior oblique and lateral rectus, respectively.

CHAPTER 17

Figure Legend Questions

17.1 Heart, liver, stomach, small intestine, placenta (any three)
17.4 The posterior pituitary (neurohypophysis)
17.19 Steroids enter the target cell; they do not bind to membrane receptors or activate second messengers.
17.24 Such a drug would block leukotriene synthesis and thus inhibit allergic and inflammatory responses.

Testing Your Recall

1. b	9. a	16.	interstitial endocrine
2. d	10. e		crine
3. a	11. adenohypophysis	17.	negative feedback
4. c	12. tyrosine		inhibition
5. c	13. acromegaly	18.	hypophysial por-
6. c	14. cortisol		tal system
7. d	15. glucocorticoids	19.	permissive
8. c		20.	Up-regulation

Building Your Medical Vocabulary (Answers may vary; these are acceptable examples.)

1. gland—adenohypophysis
2. bile—cholecystokinin
3. flow through—diabetes
4. twenty—eicosanoid
5. yellow—luteinizing
6. resembling—thyroid
7. full of—glomerulosa
8. favoring—progesterone
9. turn—gonadotropin
10. urine—glycosuria

What's Wrong with These Statements?

1. Gonadotropin secretion would rise because of a lack of negative feedback inhibition from the testes.
2. Glycoproteins cannot enter the target cell; they bind to surface receptors of the plasma membrane.
3. Thyroglobulin can be synthesized, but it cannot be iodinated, so no thyroid hormone is produced.
4. Tumors can cause hypersecretion but can also destroy endocrine cells and lead to hyposecretion.

5. Hormones are also secreted by the heart, liver, kidneys, and other organs not generally regarded as glands.
6. Most cases of diabetes mellitus are caused by insensitivity to insulin, not a lack of insulin.
7. The pineal gland and thymus undergo involution with age; they are larger in children than they are later in life.
8. Without iodine, there is no thyroid hormone (TH); without TH, there can be no negative feedback inhibition.
9. The tissue at the center is the adrenal medulla.
10. There are also two testes, two ovaries, and four parathyroid glands.

CHAPTER 18

Figure Legend Questions

18.1 (Answering this requires labeling the illustration.)
18.4 The sunken center represents the former location of the nucleus.
18.5 Hemoglobin consists of a noncovalent association of four protein chains. The prosthetic group is the heme moiety of each of the four chains.
18.18 *Myelo-* refers to the bone marrow, where these cells develop.
18.19 Although numerous, these WBCs are immature and incapable of performing their defensive roles.
18.21 A platelet plug lacks the fibrin mesh that a blood clot has.
18.22 It would affect only the intrinsic mechanism.
18.23 In both blood clotting and hormonal signal amplification, the product of one reaction step is an enzyme that catalyzes the production of many more molecules of the next product. Thus, there is a geometric increase in the number of product molecules at each step and ultimately, a large final result from a small beginning.
18.25 The older theory of leeching was that many disorders are caused by "bad blood," which could be removed painlessly by medicinal leeches. The modern practice is to take advantage of the anticoagulants in the leech saliva to promote blood flow to a tissue or to dissolve and remove clots that have already formed.

Testing Your Recall

1. b	9. d	16.	hemostasis
2. c	10. c	17.	Sickle-cell
3. c	11. hematopoiesis		disease
4. a	12. hematocrit (packed	18.	polycythemia
5. b	cell volume)	19.	vitamin B$_{12}$
6. d	13. thromboplastin	20.	erythropoietin
7. d	14. agglutinogens		
8. c	15. hemophilia		

Building Your Medical Vocabulary (Answers may vary; these are acceptable examples.)

1. without—anemia
2. producing—erythroblast
3. red—erythrocyte
4. aggregate—agglutination
5. blood—hemostasis
6. white—leukocyte
7. deficiency—leukopenia
8. vein—phlebotomy
9. formation—hemopoiesis
10. clot—thrombosis

What's Wrong with These Statements?

1. Most of the volume is usually plasma.
2. Hyperproteinemia causes retention of more water in the circulatory system and raises blood pressure.
3. Oxygen deficiency is the result of anemia, not its cause.
4. Clotting (coagulation) is one mechanism of hemostasis, but hemostasis includes other mechanisms (vascular spasm and platelet plug), so it is not synonymous with the other two terms.
5. He can be the father if he is heterozygous for type A ($I^A i$), the mother is heterzygous for type B ($I^B i$), and both are heterzygous for

Rh type *(Dd)*. The baby could then inherit *ii* and *dd,* and have phenotype O–.

6. The most abundant WBCs are neutrophils.
7. Blood clotting requires Ca^{2+} at several steps.
8. Even platelets arise ultimately from hematopoietic stem cells.
9. The heme is excreted; the globin is broken down into amino acids that can be reused.
10. In leukemia, there is an excess of WBCs. A WBC deficiency is leukopenia.

CHAPTER 19

Figure Legend Questions

19.1   Both; they receive pulmonary arteries from the pulmonary circuit and bronchial arteries from the systemic circuit.
19.2   To the left
19.7   The trabeculae carneae
19.12 The right atrium
19.14 It ensures that wave summation and tetanus will not occur, thus ensuring relaxation and refilling of the heart chambers.
19.19 They prevent prolapse of the AV valves during ventricular systole.
19.20 This is the point at which the aortic valve opens and blood is ejected into the aorta, raising its blood pressure.

Testing Your Recall

1. d	9. a	16. T wave
2. b	10. c	17. vagus
3. d	11. systole, diastole	18. myocardial
4. a	12. systemic	infarction
5. a	13. atrioventricular	19. endocardium
6. d	(coronary) sulcus	20. cardiac output
7. d	14. Na⁺	
8. c	15. gap junctions	

Building Your Medical Vocabulary (Answers may vary; these are acceptable examples.)

1. entryway—atrium	6. nipple—papillary
2. slow—bradycardia	7. semi—semilunar
3. heart—cardiology	8. fast—tachycardia
4. crown—coronary	9. vessel—vasomotor
5. moon—semilunar	10. belly—ventricle

What's Wrong with These Statements?

1. The coronary circulation is part of the systemic circuit; the other division is the pulmonary circuit.
2. There are no valves at the openings of the venae cavae.
3. The first two-thirds of ventricular filling occurs before the atria contract. The atria add only about 31% of the blood that fills the ventricles.
4. The vagus nerves affect heart rate but not contraction strength.
5. High CO_2 and low pH accelerate the heart rate.
6. The first heart sound occurs at the time of the QRS complex.
7. The heart has its own internal pacemaker and would continue beating; the nerves only alter the heart rate.
8. That would result from clamping the pulmonary veins, not the pulmonary arteries.
9. Cardiomyocytes do have a stable resting potential when they are at rest.
10. The ECG is a composite record of the electrical activity of the entire myocardium, not a record from a single myocyte. It looks much different from an action potential.

CHAPTER 20

Figure Legend Questions

20.2   Veins are subjected to less pressure than arteries and have less need of elasticity.
20.5   Endocrine glands, kidneys, the small intestine, and choroid plexuses of the brain
20.8   Veins have less muscular and elastic tissue, so they expand more easily than arteries.
20.10 Arterial anastomoses: the arterial circle of the brain, the celiac circulation, encircling the heads of the humerus and femur, and the arterial arches of the hand and foot. Venous anastomoses: the jugular veins, the azygos system, the mesenteric veins, and venous networks of the hand and foot. Portal systems: the hepatic portal system and (outside of this chapter) the hypophysial portal system. Answers may vary.
20.20 Nothing would happen if he lifted his finger from point O because the valve at that point would prevent blood from flowing downward and filling the vein. If he lifted his finger from point H, blood would flow upward, fill the vein, and the vein between O and H would stand out.
20.27 Aorta → left common carotid a. → external carotid a. → superficial temporal a.
20.36 The ovaries and testes begin their embryonic development near the kidneys. The gonadal veins elongate as the gonads descend to the pelvic cavity and scrotum.
20.39 Joint movements may temporarily compress an artery. Anastomoses allow for continued blood flow through alternative routes to more distal regions.
20.40 The cephalic, basilic, and median cubital vv.

Testing Your Recall

1. c	9. e	16. transcytosis
2. b	10. d	17. sympathetic
3. a	11. systolic, diastolic	18. baroreceptors
4. e	12. continuous	19. cerebral arterial
5. b	capillaries	circle
6. c	13. Anaphylactic	20. basilic, cephalic
7. e	14. thoracic pump	
8. a	15. oncotic pressure	

Building Your Medical Vocabulary (Answers may vary; these are acceptable examples.)

1. vessel—angiogenesis	6. belonging to—vasa vasorum
2. arm—brachiocephalic	7. standing—saphenous
3. abdomen—celiac	8. below—subclavian
4. window—fenestrations	9. chest—thoracoacromial
5. neck—jugular	10. bladder—vesical

What's Wrong with These Statements?

1. Blood can bypass capillaries by flowing through an arteriovenous anastomosis.
2. Blood drains from the brain by way of the internal jugular veins.
3. The longest blood vessel is the great saphenous vein.
4. Some veins have valves, but arteries do not.
5. By the formula $F \propto r^4$, the flow increases in proportion to the fourth power of radius, or 16-fold.
6. The femoral triangle is bordered by the inguinal ligament, sartorius muscle, and adductor longus muscle.
7. The lungs also receive blood from the bronchial arteries of the systemic circuit.
8. Most capillaries reabsorb only a portion (typically about 85%) of the fluid they filter; the rest is absorbed by the lymphatic system.

9. An aneurysm is a weak, bulging vessel that *may* rupture.
10. The response to falling blood pressure is a corrective vasoconstriction.

CHAPTER 21

Figure Legend Questions

21.2 There are much larger gaps between the endothelial cells of lymphatic capillaries than between those of blood capillaries.
21.3 There would be no consistent one-way flow of lymph. Lymph and tissue fluid would accumulate, especially in the lower regions of the body.
21.4 (1) Prevention of excess tissue fluid accumulation and (2) monitoring the tissue fluids for pathogens
21.5 Lymph flows from the breast to the axillary lymph nodes. Therefore, metastatic cancer cells tend to lodge first in those nodes.
21.13 Erythrocytes in the red pulp; lymphocytes and macrophages in the white pulp
21.15 Both of these produce a ring of proteins in the target-cell plasma membrane, opening a hole in the membrane through which the cell contents escape.
21.23 All three defenses depend on the action of helper T cells, which are destroyed by HIV.
21.26 The ER is the site of antibody synthesis.

Testing Your Recall

1. b	9. a	16. pyrogen
2. c	10. c	17. interleukins
3. a	11. pathogen	18. antigen-binding
4. a	12. lysozyme	site, epitope
5. d	13. Lymphadenitis	19. clonal deletion
6. b	14. diapedesis (emi-	20. autoimmune
7. e	gration)	
8. d	15. opsonization	

Building Your Medical Vocabulary (Answers may vary; these are acceptable examples.)

1. apart—anaphylactic
2. secrete—paracrine
3. outside—extravasated
4. arising—endogenous
5. freedom—immunology
6. set in motion—cytokine
7. water—lymphatic
8. enlargement—splenomegaly
9. disease—lymphadenopathy
10. fire—pyrogen

What's Wrong with These Statements?

1. Lysozyme is a bacteria-killing enzyme.
2. The principal birthplace of lymphocytes is the red bone marrow; T lymphocytes migrate from there to the thymus.
3. Interferons promote inflammation.
4. Helper T cells are also necessary to humoral and innate immunity.
5. Negative selection serves to eliminate or deactivate self-reactive T cells (not unresponsive ones), thus preventing immune attack on one's own tissues.
6. The thymus and spleen do not receive or filter any incoming lymph; only lymph nodes do this.
7. Only antibodies of the IgG and IgM classes employ complement fixation.
8. One can be HIV-positive without having AIDS. AIDS is defined by a low helper T cell count ($< 200/\mu L$), not by the presence of the virus.
9. Anergy is a loss of lymphocyte activity, whereas autoimmune diseases result from misdirected activity.
10. Plasma cells are antibody-synthesizing cells of the connective tissues that develop from B cells; they are not found in the blood plasma.

CHAPTER 22

Figure Legend Questions

22.3 The line would cross the figure just slightly above the trachea label.
22.4 Epiglottic, corniculate, and arytenoid
22.7 The right main bronchus is slightly wider and more vertical than the left, making it easier for aspirated objects to fall into the right.
22.8 To secrete mucus
22.17 Any airflow through the nose would not be registered by the spirometer, and the spirometer could not give a correct reading of pulmonary ventilation.
22.19 P_{O_2} drops from 104 to 95 mm Hg on its way out of the lungs because of some mixing with systemic blood. It drops farther to 40 mm Hg when the blood gives up O_2 to respiring tissues, and remains at this level until the blood is reoxygenated back in the lungs. P_{CO_2} is 40 mm Hg leaving the lungs and rises to 46 mm Hg when CO_2 is picked up from respiring tissues. It remains at that level until the blood returns to the lungs and unloads CO_2.
22.23 About 40%
22.25 In the alveoli, CO_2 leaves the blood, O_2 enters, and all the chemical reactions are the reverse of those in figure 22.23. The blood bicarbonate concentration will be reduced following alveolar gas exchange because bicarbonate is taken up by the chloride shift antiport and converted to CO_2 and water.
22.26 A higher temperature suggests a relatively high metabolic rate and, thus, an elevated need for oxygen. Comparison of these curves shows that for a given P_{O_2}, hemoglobin gives up more oxygen at warmer temperatures.

Testing Your Recall

1. c	10. a	17. compliance,
2. c	11. epiglottis	elasticity
3. a	12. bronchial tree	18. ventral respiratory
4. e	13. pulmonary	group
5. e	surfactant	19. ventilation–
6. c	14. atmospheric	perfusion coupling
7. b	15. Obstructive	20. alkalosis,
8. a	16. anatomical dead	hypocapnia
9. d	space	

Building Your Medical Vocabulary (Answers may vary; these are acceptable examples.)

1. imperfect—atelectasis
2. smoke—hypercapnia
3. cancer—carcinoma
4. horn—corniculate
5. true—eupnea
6. measuring device—spirometer
7. nose—nasofacial
8. breathing—dyspnea
9. breath—spirometry
10. shield—thyroid

What's Wrong with These Statements?

1. They also fire during expiration (although at a lower rate) to exert a braking action on the diaphragm.
2. The two lungs have a total of 18 segmental bronchi but only 5 lobes.
3. The most abundant cells are alveolar macrophages.
4. When volume increases, pressure decreases.
5. Atelectasis can have other causes such as airway obstruction.
6. The greatest effect is to lower the CO_2 level; accelerated breathing has little effect on blood O_2.
7. We inhale all the gases of the atmosphere, whether the body uses them or not; there is no way to separate one gas from another as we inhale.

8. In an average 500 mL tidal volume, 350 mL reaches the alveoli.
9. The lower the P_{CO_2}, the higher the pH.
10. Most blood CO_2 is transported as bicarbonate ions.

CHAPTER 23

Figure Legend Questions

23.2   Ammonia is produced by the deamination of amino acids; urea is synthesized from ammonia and carbon dioxide; uric acid is produced from nucleic acids; and creatinine is produced from creatine phosphate.

23.3   It would be in the dark space at the top of the figure, where the spleen, colon, and small intestine are shown.

23.10 The afferent arteriole is larger. The relatively large inlet to the glomerulus and its small outlet result in high blood pressure in the glomerulus. This is the force that drives glomerular filtration.

23.16 It lowers the urine pH; the more Na^+ that is reabsorbed, the more H^+ is secreted into the tubular fluid. This is seen at the Na^+–H^+ antiport along the right margin of the figure.

23.23 The relatively short female urethra is less of an obstacle for bacteria traveling from the perineum to the urinary bladder.

Testing Your Recall

1. a	9. c	16. transport
2. d	10. a	maximum
3. b	11. micturition	17. Antidiuretic
4. c	12. Renal autoregula-	hormone
5. b	tion	18. internal urethral
6. b	13. trigone	19. protein
7. d	14. macula densa	20. arcuate
8. e	15. podocytes	

Building Your Medical Vocabulary (Answers may vary; these are acceptable examples.)

1. nitrogen—azotemia	6. kidney—nephron
2. bladder—cystitis	7. foot—podocyte
3. ball—glomerulus	8. sagging—nephroptosis
4. next to—juxtaglomerular	9. pus—pyelonephritis
5. middle—mesangial	10. straight—vasa recta

What's Wrong with These Statements?

1. Calcium and sodium reabsorption by the PCT are influenced by parathyroid hormone and angiotensin II.
2. Urine contains more urea and chloride than sodium.
3. There is one renal corpuscle per nephron and many nephrons drain into each collecting duct, so renal corpuscles substantially outnumber collecting ducts.
4. "Tight" junctions of the renal tubule are quite leaky, and a substantial amount of tubular fluid passes through them to be reabsorbed by the paracellular route.
5. Diabetes insipidus shows no glucose in the urine.
6. Dilation of the efferent arteriole reduces resistance and thus lowers the glomerular blood pressure and filtration rate.
7. Angiotensin II stimulates aldosterone secretion and Na^+ reabsorption, thus reducing urine output.
8. Urine can be as dilute as 50 mOsm/L.
9. Normally there is abundant sodium but no glucose in the urine.
10. Micturition is caused by contraction of the detrusor.

CHAPTER 24

Figure Legend Questions

24.1   The tissue fluid compartment
24.8   Ingestion of water

24.10 It would decrease along with the pH.
24.13 Reverse both arrows to point to the left.

Testing Your Recall

1. c	9. d	16. hyperkalemia
2. a	10. b	17. hyponatremia
3. a	11. Na^+	18. respiratory
4. a	12. K^+ and Mg^{2+}	acidosis
5. d	13. metabolic water	19. limiting pH
6. c	14. cutaneous transpi-	20. osmolarity
7. e	ration	
8. b	15. fluid sequestration	

Building Your Medical Vocabulary (Answers may vary; these are acceptable examples.)

1. food—hyperalimentation	6. next to—parenteral
2. blood—hypoxemia	7. isolate—sequestration
3. intestine—parenteral	8. breathing—transpiration
4. potassium—hyperkalemia	9. across—transpiration
5. sodium—hyponatremia	10. volume—hypovolemia

What's Wrong with These Statements?

1. This is an effect of hypokalemia, not hyperkalemia.
2. Aldosterone has only a small influence on blood pressure.
3. Such injuries elevate the ECF potassium level.
4. Phosphate concentration is less critical than that of other electrolytes and can safely vary over a relatively broad range.
5. PTH promotes calcium absorption but phosphate excretion.
6. Protein buffers more acid than bicarbonate or phosphates do.
7. Increased sodium reabsorption increases urinary H^+ excretion and lowers the urine pH.
8. Alkalosis tends to cause a reduction of respiratory rate and pulmonary ventilation so the ECF pH will rise again.
9. More water than salt is lost in true dehydration, so the body fluids become hypertonic.
10. Oral wetting and cooling have only a short-term effect on thirst.

CHAPTER 25

Figure Legend Questions

25.6   The first and second premolars and third molar
25.7   The enamel is a secretion, not a tissue; all the rest are living tissues.
25.11 Blockage of the mouth by the root of the tongue and blockage of the nose by the soft palate
25.12 The muscularis externa of the esophagus has two layers of muscle, with skeletal muscle in the upper to middle regions and smooth muscle in the middle to lower regions. In the stomach, it has three layers of muscle, all of which are smooth muscle.
25.14 It exchanges H^+ for K^+ (H^+–K^+ ATPase is an active transport pump).
25.20 The hepatic artery and the hepatic portal vein
25.32 Lipids do not enter the hepatic portal system that leads directly to the liver. Dietary fats are absorbed into the lacteals of the small intestine, then would have to travel the following route, at a minimum, to reach the liver: intestinal trunk → thoracic duct → left subclavian vein → heart → aorta → celiac trunk → common hepatic artery → hepatic artery proper → hepatic arteries → liver.
25.33 The internal anal sphincter is composed of smooth muscle and therefore controlled by the autonomic nervous system. The external anal sphincter is composed of skeletal muscle and therefore controlled by the somatic nervous system.

Testing Your Recall

1. b	8. a	15. vagus
2. d	9. a	16. gastrin
3. c	10. a	17. sinusoids
4. e	11. occlusal	18. dipeptidase
5. a	12. amylase, lipase	19. bile acids
6. c	13. parotid	20. iron
7. a	14. enteric	

Building Your Medical Vocabulary (Answers may vary; these are acceptable examples.)

1. cavity—antrum	6. liver—hepatocyte
2. juice—chylomicron	7. dry—jejunum
3. little—micelle	8. gateway—portal
4. vomiting—emetic	9. gateway—pyloric
5. bridle—frenulum	10. S-shaped—sigmoid

What's Wrong with These Statements?

1. Fat digestion begins in the stomach.
2. Most of the tooth is dentin.
3. Hepatocytes secrete bile into the bile canaliculi.
4. The ileal papilla regulates the passage of residue from the ileum of the small intestine into the cecum of the large intestine.
5. The lacteals take up chylomicrons, not micelles.
6. Hepcidin inhibits iron absorption and prevents iron overload.
7. The small intestine absorbs not only glucose but also fructose and galactose.
8. Most of the water is absorbed by the small intestine.
9. Secretin stimulates the liver and pancreas to secrete bicarbonate and inhibits gastric secretion.
10. Water, glucose, and other nutrients pass between cells, through the tight junctions.

CHAPTER 26

Figure Legend Questions

26.4 A high HDL:LDL ratio indicates that excess cholesterol is being transported to the liver for removal from the body. A high LDL:HDL ratio indicates a high rate of cholesterol deposition in the walls of the arteries.

26.7 NADH and $FADH_2$

26.11 Acidosis, ketoacidosis, or metabolic acidosis

26.12 Amino acids → keto acids → pyruvate → glucose

Testing Your Recall

1. a	8. a	15. liver
2. c	9. d	16. insulin
3. b	10. d	17. core temperature
4. e	11. incomplete	18. arcuate
5. b	12. glycogenolysis	19. cytochromes
6. e	13. gluconeogenesis	20. ATP synthase,
7. c	14. urea	ATP

Building Your Medical Vocabulary (Answers may vary; these are acceptable examples.)

1. bag—ascites	6. like—ascites
2. bad—cachexia	7. thin—leptin
3. color—cytochrome	8. splitting—glycolysis
4. producing—lipogenesis	9. new—gluconeogenesis
5. sugar—hypoglycemia	10. push—chemiosmotic

What's Wrong with These Statements?

1. Leptin suppresses the appetite.
2. A nutrient is a dietary substance that is absorbed into the tissues and becomes part of the body; water meets this criterion and is considered a nutrient.
3. Fat has more than twice as many calories per gram as carbohydrate does.
4. Most of the cholesterol is endogenous, not dietary.
5. Excessive protein intake generates excess nitrogenous waste and can cause renal damage.
6. Excessive ketone production is an effect of high-fat diets.
7. The membrane reactions produce up to 28 ATP per glucose, whereas glycolysis and the matrix reactions produce only 4 ATP.
8. Gluconeogenesis is a postabsorptive phenomenon.
9. Brown fat does not generate ATP.
10. At 21°C, the body loses about 60% of its heat by radiation.

CHAPTER 27

Figure Legend Questions

27.1 Both disorders result from defects in hormone receptors rather than from a lack of the respective hormone.

27.5 The word *vagina* means "sheath." The tunica vaginalis partially ensheathes the testis.

27.10 An enlarged prostate compresses the urethra and interferes with emptying of the bladder.

27.11 A tunica albuginea would allow excessive pressure to build in the corpus spongiosum, compressing the urethra and interfering with ejaculation.

27.13 The crossing-over in prophase I results in a mixture of maternal and paternal genes in each chromosome.

27.14 The next cell stage in meiosis, the secondary spermatocyte, is genetically different from the other cells of the body and would be subject to immune attack if not isolated from the antibodies in the blood.

Testing Your Recall

1. a	9. d	15. tunica albuginea
2. a	10. d	16. seminal vesicles
3. a	11. mesonephric	17. nurse
4. c	12. zinc	18. secondary
5. a	13. pampiniform	spermatocyte
6. d	plexus	19. deep
7. e	14. secondary	20. acrosome
8. c	spermatocytes	

Building Your Medical Vocabulary (Answers may vary; these are acceptable examples.)

1. hidden—cryptorchidism	6. reduction—meiosis
2. twins—epididymis	7. testis—cryptorchidism
3. out—ejaculation	8. network—rete testis
4. union—gamete	9. body—acrosome
5. condition—cryptorchidism	10. sheath—tunica vaginalis

What's Wrong with These Statements?

1. Testosterone is secreted by the interstitial endocrine cells.
2. The sperm DNA is contained in the nucleus in the sperm head.
3. Meiosis II is completed before spermiogenesis, which is the conversion of the four spermatids to mature sperm.
4. Only the testes are primary sex organs; the penis is a secondary sex organ.

5. Female fetal development results from a low testosterone level, not from estrogen.
6. The seminal vesicles contribute about 60% of the semen.
7. The pampiniform plexus prevents the testes from overheating.
8. Sperm have no testosterone receptors; testosterone binds to androgen-binding protein in the seminiferous tubules.
9. There is no such phenomenon as male menopause, and sperm production normally continues throughout old age.
10. Erection is the result of parasympathetic stimulation of the blood vessels of the erectile tissues.

CHAPTER 28

Figure Legend Questions

28.4   To move the egg or conceptus toward the uterus
28.8   Paraurethral glands
28.9   They cause milk to flow from the acinus into the ducts of the mammary gland.
28.10   This results in a clearer image since the X-rays do not have to penetrate such a thick mass of tissue.
28.18   The rising ratio of estradiol to progesterone makes the uterus more irritable.

Testing Your Recall

1. a	8. b	15. corona radiata
2. d	9. c	16. antrum
3. c	10. c	17. climacteric
4. a	11. follicle	18. conceptus
5. e	12. endometrium	19. infundibulum,
6. b	13. menarche	fimbriae
7. b	14. corpus luteum	20. lochia

Building Your Medical Vocabulary (Answers may vary; these are acceptable examples.)

1. beginning—menarche	6. milk—lactation
2. of—gravidarum	7. to tie—tubal ligation
3. mound—cumulus	8. uterus—endometrium
4. pregnancy—progesterone	9. egg—oogenesis
5. uterus—hysterectomy	10. first—primipara

What's Wrong with These Statements?

1. Only the ovum and cumulus oophorus cells enter the uterine tube, not the whole follicle.
2. HCG is secreted by the placenta.
3. Meiosis II is not completed until after ovulation, and only if the egg is fertilized.
4. Such girls often have lower than average body fat and delayed menarche because of this.
5. Many eggs and follicles undergo atresia during childhood, so their number is greatly reduced by the age of puberty.
6. Prolactin is secreted during pregnancy but does not induce lactation then.
7. Colostrum is lower in fat than milk is.
8. Up to two dozen follicles mature to the secondary follicle stage in each cycle, but usually only one of them ovulates.

9. Progesterone inhibits uterine contractions.
10. Only the superficial (functional) layer is shed.

CHAPTER 29

Figure Legend Questions

29.2   An unfertilized egg dies long before it reaches the uterus.
29.8   About 8 weeks
29.13   XXY (Klinefelter syndrome) and YO (a zygote that would not survive)
29.15   Female, as seen from the two X chromosomes at the lower right

Testing Your Recall

1. b	8. a	15. chorionic villi
2. b	9. d	16. acrosome
3. c	10. d	17. collagen
4. c	11. teratogens	18. Down syndrome
5. a	12. nondisjunction	(trisomy-21)
6. e	13. life span	19. foramen ovale
7. c	14. life expectancy	20. embryo

Building Your Medical Vocabulary (Answers may vary; these are acceptable examples.)

1. with—congenital	6. double—aneuploidy
2. falling off—decidual	7. aging—senescence
3. old age—progeria	8. together—syncytiotrophoblast
4. mulberry—morula	9. end—telomere
5. flat cake—placenta	10. monster—teratogen

What's Wrong with These Statements?

1. The ability to fertilize an egg increases in the first 10 hours as sperm become capacitated.
2. Fertilization occurs in the uterine tube.
3. Several early-arriving sperm clear a path for the one that fertilizes the egg.
4. Early cell divisions occur while the conceptus is still in the uterine tube, about 2 days before arrival in the uterus.
5. The individual is considered an embryo then; it is not a fetus until all of the major organs have formed.
6. As they develop, the chorionic villi become thinner and more permeable.
7. The kidneys exhibit one of the greatest degrees of senescence, shrinking 60% to 80% by age 90.
8. The foramen ovale is a shunt in the heart by which blood bypasses the lungs; the shunt that bypasses the liver is the ductus venosus.
9. Blood in the umbilical vein is returning from the placenta, where it has picked up oxygen and thus has a high P_{O_2}.
10. Telomerase is a telomere-repairing enzyme that prolongs cell life, as in stem cells and cancer cells.

APPENDIX D

Table D.2 Question

Asn-Ile-Tyr-Val-Arg-Asp

Credits

Online Supplements

Online Supplements

Anatomy & Physiology REVEALED®

Anatomy and Physiology Revealed

Anatomy & Physiology Revealed is the ultimate online interactive cadaver dissection experience. This state-of-the-art program uses cadaver photos combined with a layering technique that allows the student to peel away layers of the human body to reveal structures beneath the surface, and see the relationships of structures at different depths. *Anatomy & Physiology Revealed* also offers animations, histologic and radiologic imaging, audio pronunciations, and comprehensive quizzing. It can be used as part of any one or two semester undergraduate anatomy & physiology or human anatomy course; *Anatomy & Physiology Revealed* is available stand-alone, or can be combined with any McGraw-Hill book.

GETTING STARTED:

Go to www.aprevealed.com
- Click the screen that says "Version 3.2 with customization"
- Click "Student Access"
- Click "Register as a student"
- Enter the Access code printed in your book and an Email address, then click Submit

Where does my Access Code appear?

> Your access code will appear at the back of your book. Refer to the Table-of-Contents for an exact page number.

Need Help?
Contact us online: www.mcgrawhillconnect.com/support
Give us a call: 1-800-331-5094